CATALOGUE

OF THE

LINONIAN AND BROTHERS'

LIBRARY,

YALE COLLEGE.

New Haven:

TUTTLE, MOREHOUSE & TAYLOR, PRINTERS.

1873.

THE last printed catalogue of the Linonian Library, in 1860, gives a total of 11300 volumes, and the last Brothers' Library Catalogue, in 1851, 11652 volumes. In 1871, when by a vote of the two Societies, the care of their Libraries was transferred to the College Library Committee, the number had increased to about 13500 each. In the consolidation of the two Libraries, and the rearrangement for the present Catalogue, many useless duplicates and many worn-out and valueless books have been thrown out, and other volumes more appropriate in character to the College Library have been transferred; so that the present number of volumes is 17000.

Books are generally entered under the name of the *author*, and also under subjects. *Novels* appear under the *first word* of the title (except an article or preposition), as well as under the author.

In consulting the catalogue it should be remembered that when *more than one copy* of a work is in the Library, only one copy is referred to under the title or subject, but all the different copies will be found *under the author's name.*

CATALOGUE.

A.

Abbot, The. Scott. Edinb., 1870. 8°. 1882
Abbotsford, Visit to. Irving. Philad., 1835. 12°. 4246
Abbott, E. A. Shakespearian Grammar. 3d ed. Lond., 1871. 16°. 1477
and **Seeley, J. R.** English Lessons for English People. Bost., 1872. 16°. 62
Abbott, Jacob. Corner-Stone. Bost., 1834. 12°. 9994
Hist. of Cleopatra. N. Y. [1851.] 16°. 7497
Hoaryhead. Bost., 1838. 12°. 2725
Summer in Scotland. N. Y., 1848. 12°. 16742
The Teacher. Bost., 1834. 12°. 17039
Way to do Good. Bost., 1836. 12°. 9995
Young Christian. N. Y., 1834. 12°. 9993
Abbott, John S. C. Empire of Austria. N. Y., 1859. 12°. . . 5812
Russia. N. Y., 1860. 12°. . . 6443
Hist. of the Civil War. N. Y., 1863–66. 2 v. 8°. 6275
Italy. N. Y. [1860.] 12°. 4688
Josephine. N. Y. [1851.] 16°. 5450
Napoleon I. N. Y., 1855–56. 2 v. 8°. 5712
Napoleon III. (2 copies.) Bost., 1868–69. 8°. . . 5714
Romance of Spanish Hist. N. Y., 1869. 12°. 6405
Abdallah, Death of. [B. Allen.] N. Y., 1814. 12°. 14924
A'Becket, Thomas. See BECKET.
A'Beckett, G. A. Comic Blackstone. Lond. 16°. 4274
Hist. of England. Lond., 1865. 8°. . 4262
of Rome. Lond. 8°. . . . 4314
Abeel, D. Residence in China, etc. N. Y., 1834. 12°. . . . 16477
Abelard, P., and Héloïse, Hist. of. Berington. Philad., 1819. 8°. . 16407
Abercrombie, J. Essays. N. Y., 1845. 12°. 9805
Inquiries concerning Intellectual Powers. N. Y., 1841. 12°. . 11041
Philosophy of Moral Feelings. N. Y., 1840. 12°. . . . 11278
Abipones of Paraguay, Account of. Dobrizhoffer. Lond., 1822. 3 v. 8°. 5828
Abolition. See SLAVERY.
About, E. F. V. The Fellah. Lond., 1870. 8°. 2395
Germaine. Bost., 1860. 12°. 2597
Man with the Broken Ear. N. Y., 1867. 12°. 2394
The Roman Question. Bost., 1859. 12°. 4689

Abraham, Lectures on Hist. of. Blunt. Philad., 1839. 12°. . . . 17353

Abraham, C. J. Unity of History. Eton, 1845. 8°. 4087

Abraham Page, Esq. A Novel. [Holt.] Philad., 1868. 12°. . . 15643

Abrantes, Duchesse d'. See Mme. JUNOT.

Abruzzi, Excursions in the. Craven. Lond., 1838. 2 v. 8°. . . 16715

Abyssinia, Hist., etc., of. Russell. N. Y., 1840. 12°. . . . 11281

Journal in, 1830–32. Gobat. N. Y., 1850. 12°. . . . 8251

Life in, 1847–50. Parkyns. N. Y., 1854. 2 v. 12°. . . 7978

Abyssinia. See, also, EGYPT; DONGOLA.

Academician, The. Ed. Picket. N. Y., 1820. v. 1. 8°. . . . 14079

Acoustics. See SOUND.

Across the Continent. Bowles. Springf'ld, 1865. 12°. . . . 8414

Acting; Actors. See DRAMA; THEATER.

Actress of Padua. [R. P. Smith.] Philad., 1836. 2 v. 12°. . . 15644

Acts of the Apostles, Notes on. Barnes. N. Y., 1841. 12°. . . 9860

Ad Fidem. Burr. Bost., 1871. 12°. 9990

Adam, A. Summary of Geography and History. 3d ed. Lond., 1802. 8°. 16322

Adam Bede. M. J. Lewes. N. Y., 1871. 12°. 2529

Adam Blair. [Lockhart.] Bost., 1822. 12°. 15359

Adams, Mrs. A. Letters. Bost., 1840. 16°. 7217

Adams, Miss A. Journal and Correspondence. N. Y., 1841. 12°. . 7220

Adams, C. J. and H. Chapters of Erie and other Essays. Bost., 1871. 12°. 8643

Adams, F. C. Justice in the By-Ways. N. Y., 1856. 12°. . . . 15727

Adams, Hannah. Compendium of Religious Sects. Bost., 1784. 8°. 16465

Hist. of New England. Dedham, 1799. 8°. 5848

Adams, H. G. Cyclopædia of Female Biography. Lond., 1869. 16°. 6675

[**Adams, Rev. John.**] Hist. of Spain. Lond., 1793. 3 v. 8°. . . 16156

Adams, Pres't John. Defence of Constitutions of U. S. 3d ed. Philad., 1799. 3 v. 8°. 6138

Letters to his Wife. Bost., 1841. 2 v. 16°. 7218

Messages, etc. (Statesman's Manual, v. 1.) N. Y., 1854. 8°. . 6200

Works, ed. C. F. Adams. Bost., 1850–56. 10 v. 8°. . . 9688

CONTENTS.—1, Life, by editor. 2, Diary, 1755–77; Notes of Debates in Congress, 1775–76; Autobiography for 1775–76. 3, Autobiography for 1775–77; Diary, 1778–96; Essays and Controversial Papers of the Revolution. 4, Novanglus; Works on Government. 4–6, Defence of the Constitutions. 6, Discourses on Davila; Letters, etc. 7–9, Official Letters, Messages, etc. 9, 10, General Correspondence: Index.

Lecture on. Theodore Parker. Bost., 1870. 12°. . . . 7409

and Cunningham, W. Correspondence. Bost., 1823. 8°. . 7344

Adams, John Q. Lectures on Rhetoric and Oratory. Cambr., 1810. 2 v. 8°. 17527

Messages, etc. (Statesman's Manual, v. 1.) N. Y., 1854. 8°. . 6200

Poems. Auburn, 1854. 16°. 719

Life of. Seward. Auburn, 1849. 12°. 7325

Adams, John S. Town and Country. Bost., 1855. 12°. . . . 14594

Adams, M. New Biographical Dictionary. Lond. v. 1. 8°. . . 16399

Adams, S., Life of. Wells. Bost., 1865. 3 v. 8°. 7444

Adams, W. H. D. Lighthouses and Lightships. N. Y., 1870. 12°. . 10132

The Queen of the Adriatic. Lond., 1869. 8°. 8213

Adamson, J. Memoirs of Camoens. Lond., 1820. 2 v. 8°. . . 7695
Addington, J. F. Poetical Quotations. Philad., 1829. 4 v. 12°. . 4320
Addison, C. G. Damascus and Palmyra. Lond., 1838. 2 v. 8°. . 8099
Knights Templars. 2d ed. Lond., 1842. 8°. 4617
Addison, J. Cato. (Brit. Drama, v. 1.) Lond., 1804. 8°. . . . 1629
Criticism on Paradise Lost. Ed. Arber. Lond., 1868. 16°. . 3887
Miscellaneous Works. Lond., 1830. 4 v. 12°. 3991

CONTENTS.—1, Poems; Essay on Georgics; Discourse on Ancient and Modern Learning. 2, Dramas; Whig Examiner; Lover. 3, Evidences of Religion; Dialogues on Medals; State of the War; Trial of Count Tariff. 4, Remarks on Italy.

Poetical Works. Ed. Bell. Lond., 1807. 24°. 270
Poetical Works. With Life, by Sanford. Philad., 1819. 24°. . 10
The same. Ed. Johnson. Dubl., 1804. 8°. 15098
Works. N. Y., 1855. 3 v. 8°. 3791

CONTENTS.—1, 2, The Spectator. 3, Tatler; Guardian; Freeholder; Whig-Examiner; Lover; Dialogues on Medals Remarks on Italy; State of the War; Evidences; Poems; Dramas, etc.

Works. Ed. G. W. Greene. N. Y., 1856. 6 v. 12°. . . 3995

CONTENTS.—1, Poems; Dramas. 2, Dialogues on Medals; Remarks on Italy; Essay on Georgics; Discourse on Ancient and Modern Learning; of the Christian Religion; Letters; Political Writings. 3, Freeholder; Plebeian; Old Whig; Lover. 4, Tatler; Guardian. 5, 6, Spectator.

Works, except the Spectator. N. Y., 1811. v. 1–5. 12°. . 3816

CONTENTS.—1, 2, Tattler. 2, Guardian. 3, Freeholder; Whig Examiner; Lover. 4, Dialogues on Medals; Remarks on Italy. 5, Present State of the War; Evidences; Poems.

Life of. Aikin. Lond., 1843. 2 v. 12°. 6993
See, also, The SPECTATOR.
Addisoniana. Lond. [1804.] 2 v. 16°. 3808
Adela Cathcart. MacDonald. Bost. 12°. 2584
Adeline Mowbray. Opie. Bost., 1827. 12°. 14439
Adirondacks, Adventures in the. Murray. Bost., 1869. 16°. . . 8226
Admirals, British, Lives of. Southey. Lond., 1833–40. 5 v. 16°. . 5171
Adolphus, J. Memoirs of Bannister. Lond., 1839. 2 v. 8°. . . 7996
Memoirs of the French Revolution. Lond., 1799. 2 v. 8°. . 5563
The same. 16248
[**Adolphus, J. L.**] Letters to Heber on the Waverley Novels. Bost., 1822. 12°. 15227
Adshead, J. Prisons and Prisoners. Lond., 1845. 8°. . . . 17097
Adultery, Essay on. Polwhele. Lond., 1823. 12°. 17006
Advent; a Mystery. Coxe. N. Y., 1837. 12°. 801
Adventurer, The. Ed. Hawkesworth. Lond., 1823. 3 v. 12° . 3128
Essays illustrating the. Drake. Lond., 1809–10. 2 v. 8°. . 3236
Adventures of Harry Franco. [Briggs.] N. Y., 1839. 2 v. 12°. . 15646
of Verdant Green. [Bradley.] N. Y., 1870. 12°. . . . 9250
of a Younger Son. [Trelawny.] N. Y., 1832. 2 v. 12°. . 15360
Aeronauts. See AIR; BALLOONS.
Æschylus. Agamemnon and Choephoræ, tr. Potter. Philad., 1823. 24°. 245
Prometheus Bound, transl. by E. B. Browning. N. Y., 1851. 16°. 1150
Tragedies, transl. by Plumptre. Lond., 1868. 2 v. 8°. . . 873
transl. by Potter. N. Y., 1839. 12°. . . . 4520
The same. N. Y., 1834. 12°. . . . 4541
for English Readers. Copleston. Philad., 1871. 12°. . . 77
Æsop. Fables, ed. Croxall. N. Y., 1861. 12°. 1924

Æsop Junior in America. N. Y., 1834. 12°. 15652
Æsthetic Letters and Essays. Schiller. Bost., 1845. 16°. . . . 8847
Æsthetic Works. F. v. Schlegel. Lond., 1849. 8°. 431
Æsthetics. See, also, BEAUTY, TASTE.
Afghanistan, Journal of Disasters in, 1841–42. Sale. Lond., 1843. 12°. 7975
Memoir of. Harlan. Philad., 1842. 12°. . . . .
Afghans, Rohilla, Hist. of the. Hamilton. Lond., 1787. 8°. . . 16052
Africa and the American Flag. Foote. N. Y., 1854. 12°. . . . 8572
Discovery in. Murray, etc. N. Y., 1840. 12°. 11016
Hist. of Discoveries and Travels in. Murray. Edinb., 1818. 2 v. 8°. 8088
Popular Description of. Conder. Lond. 3 v. 12°. . . . 7848
Researches on Nations of. Heeren. Oxf'd., 1832. 2 v. 8°. . 4117
Central, Journey to, 1851–52. Bayard Taylor. N. Y., 1867. 12°. 8281
Travels in, 1780–85. Le Vaillant. Dubl., 1790. 8°. . 16523
Travels in, 1795–97. Park. Philad., 1800. 8°. . . 16526
Equatorial, Explorations in, 1856–59. DuChaillu. Lond., 1861. 8°. 8090
Northern and Central, Travels in, 1822–24. Denham & Clapperton. Bost., 1826. 8°. 16530
Southern, Five Years in, 1843–48. Cumming. N. Y., 1851. 2 v. 12°. 7980
Hist. of Brit. Colonies in. Martin. Lond., 1843. 16°.. 7898
Missionary Labors in. Moffat. N. Y., 1843. 12°. . 16521
Missionary Travels in. Livingstone. N. Y., 1868. 8°. 8124
Residence in, 1820–25. Pringle. Lond., 1840. 8°. . 8101
Travels in, 1797–98. Barrow. N. Y., 1802. 8°. . . 16534
Wanderings in. Steedman. Lond., 1835. 2 v. 8°. . . 16527
South-Western, Explorations in, 1850–54. Andersson. N. Y., 1857. 8°. 8091
Western, Condition of. East. Lond., 1844. 12°. 16472
Exc. in, 1834–35. Alexander. Lond., 1840. 2 v. 8°. 8114
Hist. of Brit. Settlements in. Martin. Lond., 1837. 16°. 7905
African Cruiser, Journal of an. [Bridge.] N. Y., 1845. 12°. . . 16291
Slaver, Twenty Years of an. Canot. N. Y., 1866. 12°. . . 8573
Africa. See, also, the NILE, EGYPT, etc.
After Dark; a Novel. Collins. N. Y. 8°. 2298
Agassiz, E. C. and A. Seaside Studies in Nat. Hist; Radiates. Bost., 1865. 8°. 9002
Agassiz, L. Geological Sketches. (2 copies.) Bost., 1866–70. 12°. 8955
Methods of Study in Natural Hist. Bost., 1864. 12°. . . . 8835
Structure of Animal Life. N. Y., 1866. 8°. 9099
and Eliz. C. Journey in Brazil. (2 copies.) Bost., 1868. 8°. 8461
and Gould, A. A. Principles of Zoology. Pt. I. (2 copies.) Bost., 1848. 12°. 8890
Agatha's Husband. Craik. N. Y., 1871. 12°. 2485
Agnes de Mansfeldt. Grattan. Philad., 1836. 2 v. 12°. . . . 15362
Agnes of Sorrento. Stowe. Bost., 1862. 12°. 2962
Agriculture on the Rhine. Banfield. Lond., 1846. 12°. . . . 8795
Agrippa, H. Cornelius, Life of. Morley. Lond., 1856. 2 v. 8°. . 7766

Aguesseau, H. F. d', Memoir of. Butler. Lond., 1830. 8°. . . . 7682
Aguilar, G. Days of Bruce. N. Y., 1857. 2 v. 12°. 2525
Home Influence. N. Y., 1850. 12°. 2418
Home Scenes. N. Y., 1853. 12°. 2527
Mother's Recompense. (2 copies.) N. Y., 1856–68. 12°. . 2516
Vale of Cedars. (3 copies.) N. Y., 1851–68. 12°. 2520
Woman's Friendship. (2 copies.) N. Y., 1851–57. 12°. . . 2518
Women of Israel. N. Y., 1851. 2 v. 12°. 2523
Ahasuerus; a Poem. [Tyler.] N. Y., 1842. 12°. 15039
Aids to Faith. Ed. W. Thomson. N. Y., 1862. 12°. 9955
Aikin, J. Annals of Reign of Geo. III. Lond., 1816. 2 v. 8°. . 5322
Essays on Song-Writing, with Songs. Ed. Evans. (2 copies.)
Lond., 1810. 8°. 1210
Letters on English Poetry. Bost., 1806. 12°. 60
from a Father to his Son. Lond., 1838. 16°. 9133
Lives of Selden and Usher. Lond., 1812. 8°. 7116
Select Works of Brit. Poets. (2 copies.) Philad., 1831–39. 8°. 1304
Memoir and Miscellanies of. L. Aikin. Philad., 1824. 8°. . 7170
Aikin, L. Court of Chas. I. Philad., 1833. 2 v. 8°. 5302
of Elizabeth. Philad., 1823. 8°. 5295
of James I. Bost., 1822. 2 v. 8°. 5300
Life of Addison. Lond., 1843. 2 v. 12°. 6993
Ainslie, H. The Pilgrim and the Shrine. Lond., 1871. 8°. . . 9814
Ainsworth, W. F. Researches in Assyria, etc. Lond., 1838. 8°. . 8048
Ainsworth, W. H. The Tower of London. Lond. 8°. . . . 2661
Air, The. Mudie. Lond. 1835. 12°. 14632
Queen of the. Ruskin. N. Y., 1869. 12°. 9047
Travels in the. Ed. by Glaisher. Lond., 1871. 8°. . . . 9093
See, also, BALLOON.
Aird, T. The Old Bachelor in the Old Scottish Village. Edinb.,
1845. 16°. 15531
Othuriel; and other Poems. Edinb., 1840. 8°. . . . 15076
Akenside, M. Poetical Works. Ed. Bell. Lond., 1807. 24°. . . 539
Select Poems. Ed. Walsh. Philad., 1822. 24°. 22
The same. Ed. Johnson. Dubl., 1804. 8°. . . . 15101
Alain Family, The. Karr. Lond., 1853. 8°. 2646
Alaska, Travel and Adventure in. Whymper. N. Y., 1869. 12°. . 8399
Albergati-Capacelli, F. Pleasures of Beneficence. (Ital. Novelists, 4.)
Lond., 1836. 12°. 1902
Alberoni, J., Life of. James. Lond., 1837. 16°. 5769
Albert, Prince. Speeches and Addresses. Lond., 1862. 8°. . . 5337
Early Years of. Queen Victoria. N. Y., 1868. 12°. . . 5336
Albert N'yanza, The. Baker. Lond., 1866. 8°. 8118
Albigenses, Crusades against the. Sismondi. Lond., 1826. 8°. . 6343
See, also, WALDENSES.
Alchymists, The. Mackay. Lond., 1869. 8°. 8525
Alcibiades, a Tragedy. Otway. (Works, v. 1.) Lond., 1812. 8°. . 1475
Alciphron; or the Minute Philosopher. Berkeley. Lond., 1837. 8°. . 8759
Alcock, R. Three Years in Japan. N. Y., 1863. 2 v. 12°. . . 7952

Alcott, L. M. Hospital Sketches. Bost., 1863. 12°. 6106
Little Men. Bost., 1871. 16°. 2743
Little Women. (2 copies.) Bost., 1869. 2 v. 16°. 2737
Old-Fashioned Girl. (2 copies.) Bost., 1870. 16°. 2741
Alcott, W. A. Confessions of a School Master. Andover, 1839. 12°. 17041
House I live in. 2d ed. Bost., 1837. 12°. 9126
Moral Reformer. Bost., 1835. v. 1. 12°. 16966
The Sabbath School as it should be. N. Y., 1841. 12°. . . 17361
Vegetable Diet. Bost., 1838. 12°. 9170
Young Man's Guide. Bost., 1835. 12°. 9138
The same. Bost., 1837. 12°. 9172
Young Wife. Bost., 1837. 12°. 17010
Alcuin, Life of. Lorenz. Lond., 1837. 16°. 7507
Alderbrook. [Mrs. Judson.] Bost., 1850. 2 v. 12° 15650
Alec Forbes. MacDonald. Lond. 8°. 2582
Alexander the Great, Life of. Williams. N. Y., 1841. 12°. . . 11006
Alexander, James E. Exc. in W. Africa. 2d ed. Lond., 1840. 2 v. 8°. 8114
Travels from India to England. Lond., 1827. 4°. 16032
through Russia and the Crimea. Lond., 1830. 2 v. 8°. 16487
Alexander, Joseph A. The Psalms. N. Y., 1851. 3 v. 12°. . . 9875
Alexander, Wm. (Earl of Stirling.) Select Poems, with Life. Ed. Sanford. Philad., 1819. 24°. 2
Alexander, Wm., M.D. Hist. of Women. Lond., 1782. 2 v. 8°. . 17007
Alexandra, Empress of Russia, Mem. of. Grimm. Edinb., 1870. 2 v. 8°. 6444
Alfieri, V. Autobiography, ed. Lester. N. Y., 1845. 12°. . , . 7748
Alford, H. Abbot of Muchelnaye, Sonnets, etc. Lond., 1841. 12°. . 599
How to study the N. T. Lond., 1865–70. 3 v. 16°. . . . 9838
Plea for the Queen's English. Lond., 1866. 16°. . . . 57
Alfred the Great. T. Hughes. Lond. 8°. 5134
(An historical Play.) Knowles. (Works, v. 1.) Lond., 1841. 12°. 1432
Life of. Asser. Lond., 1848. 8°. 499
The same. Dunham. Lond., 1840. 16°. 5774
The same; with version of Orosius. Pauli. Lond., 1857. 8°. 402
Alfred Hagart's Household. A. Smith. Bost., 1865. 12°. . . . 2449
Alger, W. R. Hist. of Doctrine of a Future Life. N. Y., 1869. 8°. . 10022
Friendships of Women. Bost., 1870. 16°. 9209
Poetry of the East. Bost., 1856. 12°. 875
Solitudes of Nature and Man. (2 copies.) Bost., 1867. 16°. . 3567
Algeria, A Whirl through. Browne. N. Y., 1866. 12°. . . . 8315
Algerine Captive, The. [Tyler.] Hartf'd, 1816. 12° 15653
Algic Researches. Schoolcraft. N. Y., 1839. 2 v. 12°. . . . 5755
Algiers, with Notices of Barbary. Lord. Lond., 1835. 2 v. 12°. . 7976
The French in, 1836–41. Lamping and de France. N. Y., 1845. 12°. 8369
Sketches of. Shaler. Bost., 1826. 8°. 16524
Alhambra, The. Irving. Philad., 1872. 12°. 4364
Ali Pacha, of Jannina, Life of. Lond., 1823. 8°. 16413
Alice; or, the Mysteries. Bulwer. N. Y., 1838. 2 v. 12°. . . 2072
Alison, Rev. A. Essay on Taste. Bost., 1812. 8°. 17067

Alison, Sir A. Hist. of Europe, 1789–1815. (2 copies.) Edinb., 1839–42. 10 v. 8°. 4636
The same, 1815–52. N. Y., 1855–60. 4 v. 8°. . . 4804
Lives of Castlereagh and Stewart. Edinb., 1861. 3 v. 8°. . 6790
Miscellaneous Essays. Philad., 1845. 8°. 3462
The same. N. Y., 1860. 8°. 3461
All the Year Round. New Series. Lond., 1868–72. 8 v. 8°. . . 12404
Allan, G. Life of Sir W. Scott. (2 copies.) Philad., 1835. 8°. . 7174
Allen, B. Death of Abdallah. N. Y., 1814. 12°. 12924
Urania. N. Y., 1814. 24°. 12925
Allen, D. O. India, Ancient and Modern. Bost., 1856. 8°. . . 6559
Allen, Ethan. Narrative. Bost., 1845. 12°. 7494
Life of. Sparks. (Amer. Biogr., 1.) Bost., 1834. 16°. . . 7250
Memoir of. Moore. Plattsburgh. 1834. 12°. . . . 7495
Allen, P. Hist. of Amer. Revolution. Balt., 1822. 2 v. 8°. . . 6156
Exped. of Lewis and Clarke. Philad., 1814. 2 v. 8°. 16867
The same. (Abridged.) N. Y., 1842. 2 v. 12°. . 11756
Allen, W. Book of Christian Sonnets. Northampton, 1860. 12°. . 15046
Wunnissoo; a Poem. Bost., 1856. 12°. 14969
Allen, Z. Practical Tourist. Prov., 1832. 2 v. 12°. 16766
Allen Prescott. [Mrs. Sedgwick.] N. Y., 1834. 2 v. 12°. . . 15654
Allston, W. Lectures on Art, and Poems. N. Y., 1850. 12°. . . 8885
Monaldi. Bost., 1841. 12°. 15744
Sylphs of the Seasons, with other Poems. Bost., 1813. 12°. . 14970
Almack's. A Novel. N. Y., 1827. 2 v. 12°. 15364
Almack's revisited. [White.] N. Y., 1828. 2 v. 12°. . . . 15366
Almanac, Tribune. 1838–68. N. Y. 2 v. 12°. 6103
[**Almon, J.**] Anecdotes of Pitt. Lond., 1792. 4 v. 8°. . . . 6795
Biogr. Anecdotes of Eminent Persons. Lond., 1797. 3 v. 8°. 16372
Almost a Heroine. [Sheppard.] Bost., 1860. 12°. 2512
Alone to the Alone. Cobbe. Lond., 1871. 8°. 9967
Alonzo and Melissa. Jackson. Hartf'd. 1853. 16°. 15656
Alps, Glaciers of the. Tyndall. Bost., 1861. 8°. 8957
The High, without Guides. Girdlestone. Lond., 1870. 8°. . 8383
Hours of Exercise in the. Tyndall. N. Y., 1872. 12°. . . 8382
Scrambles amongst the, 1860–69. Whymper. Lond., 1871. 8°. 8380
Sketches of the. Headley. N. Y., 1846. 12°. 16574
Vacation Rambles in the, 1841–43. Talfourd. Lond., 1845. 12°. 8381
Alroy, Tale of. Disraeli. Lond., 1833. 3 v. 12°. 2124
[**Altop, R.,** and Dwight, Th.] The Echo. N. Y., 1807. 8°. . . 814
Altanesi, G. F. Novels. (Roscoe, Ital. Novelists, 4.) Lond., 1836. 12°. 1902
Alson Locke. Kingsley. N. Y., 1861. 12°. 2562
Alves, R. Hist. of Literature. Edinb., 1794. 8°. 209
Amadis of Gaul. Trans. by Southey. Lond., 1872. 3 v. 16° . . 2007
Amaranth, The. Philad., 1842. 12°. 14881
Amazon R., Voyages up the, 1846. Edwards. N. Y., 1847. 12°. . 17140
Amazonian Republic, The. Savage. N. Y., 1842. 12°. . . . 17091
Amber Witch, The. Meinhold. N. Y., 1845. 12°. 3044
Amelia. Fielding. Lond., 1871. 2 v. 8°. 1983

America and the Amer. People. v. Raumer. N. Y., 1846. 8°. . 6172
and her Commentators. Tuckerman. N. Y., 1864. 12°. . . 6183
and England. A Comparison. N. Y., 1834. 8°. . . . 5860
and Europe. Gurowski. N. Y., 1857. 12°. 6101
before Europe. Gasparin. N. Y., 1862. 12°. 8560
Account of European Settlements in. Burke. Bost., 1835. 8°. 5946
Annals of, to 1826. Holmes. Cambr., 1829. 2 v. 8°. . . 5966
Democracy in. De Tocqueville. N. Y., 1845. 2 v. 8°. . 6134
historical and descriptive. Buckingham. Lond., [1841.] 3 v. 8°. 5857
Hist. of [Disc. and Conq. of]. Robertson. Lond., 1792. 3 v. 8°. 16138
Myths of. Brinton. N. Y., 1868. 8°. 1925
Realities and Resources of. Wyse. Lond., 1846. 3 v. 8°. . 5892
The Spanish Conquest in. Helps. N. Y., 1856–68. 4 v. 12°. 5820
Survey of Polit. Situation of. [A. H. Everett.] Philad., 1827. 8°. 16126
Travels in, 1791–92. Chateaubriand. Lond., 1828. 2 v. 8°. . 16898
British, Hist., *etc.*, of. Murray. Edinb., 1839. 3 v. 16°. . 5716
Central, Inc. of Trav. in, 1839–40. Stephens. N. Y., 1841. 2 v. 8°. 8454
Travels in, 1850. Froebel. Lond., 1859. 8°. . . 8437
Travels in. Morelet. N. Y., 1871. 12°. . . . 8431
Voyages in, 1816. Roberts. Edinb., 1827. 12°. . 4479
New. Dixon. Philad., 1867. 12°. 8427
North, Anti-Slavery Mission to, 1863. Massie. Lond., 1864. 8°. 8555
Description of. Conder. Lond. 2 v. in 1. 12°. . . 7857
Diary in. Marryatt. Philad., 1839. 2 v. 12°. . . 16800
The same. 2d series. Philad., 1840. 12°. . . 16803
France and Eng. in. Parkman. Bost., 1865–69. 3 v. 12°. 6131

CONTENTS.—1, Pioneers of France in the New World. 2, The Jesuits in the 17th century. 3, Discovery of the Great West.

Hist. of Disc. and Trav. in. Murray. Lond., 1829. 2 v. 8°. 16782
Dispute with, 1754–74. J. Adams. (Works, v. 4.) Bost., 1851. 8°. 9691
European Settlements in. Raynal. Lond., 1776. 5 v. 8°. 16149
Impressions of, 1833–35. Power. Philad., 1836. 2 v. 12°. 16796
Journey through, 1819–21. Hodgson. N. Y., 1823. 8°. 16781
Men and Manners in. Hamilton. Edinb., 1843. 16°. . 8222
New Tracks in, 1867–68. Bell. Lond., 1869. 2 v. 8°. 8422
Rambler in, 1832–33. Latrobe. N. Y., 1835. 2 v. 12°. 16804
Residence in Deserts of. Domenech. Lond., 1860. 2 v. 8°. 8497
Rule and Misrule of the English in. Haliburton. N. Y., 1851. 12°. 6025
Society in. Martineau. N. Y., 1837. 2 v. 12°. . . 5998
Stranger in. Lieber. Philad., 1835. 8°. . . . 16780
Three Years (1828–31) in. Stuart. N. Y., 1833. 2 v. 12°. 16790
Travels in, 1776–81. [Anburey.] Lond., 1791. 2 v. 8°. 16784
in 1827–28. B. Hall. Philad., 1829. 2 v. 12°. 16786
in 1841–42. Lyell. N. Y., 1845. 2 v. in 1. 12°. 8410
in 1834–36. Murray. N. Y., 1839. 2 v. 12°. . 16788
1825–26. Duke of Saxe-Weimar. Philad., 1828. 8°. 16924

America, North, Travels in, 1861. A. Trollope. N. Y., 1862. 12°. . 8413
South, Letters on the United Prov. of. Pazos. N. Y., 1819. 8°. 17138
Life and Nature under the Tropics of. Myers. N. Y., 1871. 12°. 8433
Voyage to, 1817–18. Brackenridge. Balt., 1819. 2 v. 8°. 17127
1735. Juan and Ulloa. Lond., 1772. 2 v. 8°. 17125
Wild Scenes in. Paez. N. Y., 1862. 12°. 8434
Spanish, Outline of Revolution in. N. Y., 1817. 12°. . . 5735
American Adventure by Land and Sea. N. Y. [1841.] 2 v. 12°. . 11775
Antiquities. Bradford. N. Y., 1843. 8°. 5954
Artist Life. Tuckerman. N. Y., 1867. 8°. 8126
Biblical Repository. See BIBLICAL.
Biography. Belknap. N. Y., 1846. 3 v. 12°. 11762
Library of. Sparks. Bost., 1834–48. 25 v. 16°. 7250
For Contents, see SPARKS.
Colleges and the Amer. Public. Porter. N. H., 1870. 12°. . 9254
Criminal Trials. Chandler. Bost., 1844. v. 2. 12°. . . . 9226
Eclectic. See ECLECTIC.
Eloquence. Ed. Moore. N. Y., 1857. 2 v. 8°. 9432
Specimens of. Middletown, 1837. 12°. . . 9291
Facts. Putnam. Lond., 1845. 12°. 6184
Female Poets. Griswold. Philad., 1849. 8°. 924
Journal of Science. N. H., 1818–45. 49 v. 8°. 17545
Index (v. 50). N. H., 1846. 8°.
The same. 2d Series. N. H., 1846–70. 50 v. 8°. . . 17594
The same. 3d Series. N. H., 1871–72. v. 1–4. 8°. . 17644
Law, Commentaries on. Kent. N. Y., 1840. 4 v. 8°. . . 9356
Library of Useful Knowledge. Bost., 1831–32. 5 v. 12°. . 8824
Life, Traits of. Hale. Philad., 1835. 12°. 15805
Literary Magazine, ed. Sprague. Albany & Hartf'd. 1847–49. 5 v. in 3. 8°. 13254
Literati, The. Poe. N. Y., 1857. 12°. 1378
Literature and Manners. Chasles. N. Y., 1852. 12°. . . 124
Cyclopædia of. Duyckinck. N. Y., 1866. 2 v. 8°. 234
Views and Reviews in. [Simms.] N. Y., 1845. 12°. 3587
Lounger, The. [Ingraham.] Philad., 1839. 12°. . . . 15657
Military Biography. 1825. 12°. 16434
Monthly Magazine. N. Y., 1817–18. v. 1–4. 8°. . . . 13558
The same. Ed. N. P. Willis. Bost., 1829. v. 1. 8°. . 13113
The same. New Series. N. Y., 1836. v. 1, 2. 8°. . 13114
Museum. Ed. Carey. 1787–98. Philad. v. 1–9, 11–13. 8°. 14758
Naval Battles. Bost., 1837. 12°. 16120
Officers, Lives of. J. F. Cooper. Philad., 1846. 2 v. 12°. 7275
For Contents, see COOPER.
Newspaper Literature, Specimens of. Buckingham. Bost., 1850. 2 v. 12°. 125
Note Books. Hawthorne. Bost., 1868. 2 v. 8°. 8388
Notes. Dickens. N. Y., 1865. 2 v. 16°. 2164
Orator, The. Ed. Munn. Worc., 1855. 12°. 9292

American Oratory, Selections from. (2 copies.) Philad., 1836–40. 8°. 9430
Painters, Sketches of. Tuckerman. N. Y., 1847. 12°. . . 7917
Poetry, Selections of, N. Y., 1794. 12°. 14966
Specimens of. Kettell. Bost., 1829. 3 v. 12°. , . 678
Poets. Keese. N. Y., 1841–42. 2 v. 12°. 684
and Poetry. Griswold. Philad., 1855. 8°. . . . 238
Golden Leaves from. Hows. N. Y., 1865. 12°. . 687
Selections from. Bryant. N. Y., 1841. 12°. . . 11586
Politics, Issues of. Skinner. Philad., 1872. 12°. . . . 10205
Prose Writers. Griswold. Philad., 1855. 8°. . . . 236
Pulpit, Annals of the. Sprague. N. Y., 1857–69. 9 v. 8°. . 7730
Quarterly Observer. (2 copies.) Bost., 1833–34. 3 v. 8°. . 13880
Review. Philad., 1827–37. 22 v. 8°. . . . 13213
The same. v. 3–7, 9–20. 13235
Rejected Addresses. [Bigelow.] N. Y. [1855.] 12°. . . 686
Review. Ed. R. Walsh. (2 copies.) Philad., 1811–12. v. 1–4. 8°. 14038
Revolution. See UNITED STATES HISTORY.
Society. Towle. Lond., 1870. 2 v. 8°. 8386
Speeches, Select. Carpenter. Philad., 1815. 2 v. 8°. . . 9428
Theatre, Hist. of. Dunlap. N. Y., 1832. 8°. 1616
Theatrical Management. Sol. Smith. N. Y., 1868. 8°. . . 1617
Whig Review. N. Y., 1845–52. 16 v. 8°. 12561
The same. v. 3–10, 12–16. 12723
Women, Noble Deeds of. Clement. Buffalo, 1851. 12°. . 9208
Year Book. Camp. Hartf'd, 1869. 8°. 6145
Americanisms. Schele de Vere. N. Y., 1872. 12°. 182
Dict. of. Bartlett. 3d ed. Bost., 1860. 8°. 212
American's Guide, The; the Constitutions, etc. Philad., 1832. 12°. . 6032
Own Book, The; the Constitution, etc. N. Y. 12°. . . 6033
Americans, in moral, social, and political relations. Grund. Bost., 1837. 12°. 6019
of Recent Times, Famous. Parton. Bost., 1869. 12°. . . 7410
Domestic Manners of. Mrs. Trollope. N. Y., 1832. 8°. . 8440
Notions of the. J. F. Cooper. N. Y., 1859. 12°. . . . 2805
Ames, F. Works, with Life. Bost., 1809. 8°. 9644
The same. [2d ed.] Bost., 1854. 2 v. 8°. . . . 9698
Among the Pines. [Gilmore.] N. Y., 1862. 12°. 2929
Amoor, Russians on the. Ravenstein. Lond., 1861. 8°. . . . 8013
Travels in the Regions of the. Atkinson. Lond., 1860. 8°. . 8136
Amusements. See GAMES; SPORTS.
Amyas Leigh. Kingsley. Lond., 1871. 8°. 2566
Anacharsis, Travels of. Barthélemy. Lond., 1798. 8°. . . . 15953
Anacreon. Odes, transl. by Bourne. N. Y., 1837. 12°. . . . 4540
by T. Moore. Philad., 1804. 8°. . . . 14775
in Dublin. 2d ed. Lond., 1814. 12°. 14866
Analectic Magazine. Philad., 1814–20. 16 v. 8°. 14235
Anastasius. [Hope.] N. Y., 1832. 2 v. 12°. 15157
Anatomy, Wonders of. Le Pileur. N. Y., 1870. 12°. . . . 10131
of Melancholy. Burton. N. Y., 1870. 3 v. 12°. . . . 3941

Anburey, T. Travels in America. Lond., 1791. 2 v. 8°. . . . 16784
Ancient Régime, The. James. N. Y., 1841. 2 v. 12°. . . . 15213
Andersen, H. C. The Improvisatore. N. Y., 1869. 8°. 2602
O. T. A Danish Romance. (2 copies.) N. Y., 1870. 8°. . 2606
Only a Fiddler. (2 copies.) N. Y., 1870. 8°. 2608
Only a Fiddler! and O. T. N. Y., 1845. 8°. 2652
A Poet's Bazaar. N. Y., 1871. 8°. 2614
In Spain and Portugal. (2 copies.) N. Y., 1870. 8°. . . 2604
Stories and Tales. (2 copies.) N. Y., 1871. 8°. . . . 2612
Story of My Life. (2 copies.) N. Y., 1871. 8°. . . . 2610
Two Baronesses. N. Y., 1869. 8°. 2603
Anderson, Adam. Hist. of Commerce. Dubl., 1790. 6 v. 8°. . 4067
Anderson, Æneas. Narrative of Embassy to China. N. Y., 1795. 12°. 16480
Anderson, F. Zenaida. Philad., 1858. 12°. 15820
Anderson, James. The Bee. Edinb., 1791–93. 18 v. 8°. . . 13041
Anderson, John. Course of Creation. Cincinn., 1851. 12°. . . 16946
Anderson, R. Foreign Missions. N. Y., 1869. 8°. 6289
The Hawaiian Islands. Bost., 1864. 12°. 8330
Andersson, C. J. Lake Ngami. N. Y., 1857. 8°. 8091
Andes and the Amazon, The. Orton. N. Y., 1870. 8432
Andre, J. Life of. Sargent. Bost., 1861. 12°. 7307
Andrews, A. Hist. of British Journalism. Lond., 1859. 2 v. 8°. . . 5273
Andrews, J. R. Life of Cromwell. Lond., 1870. 8°. . . . 5311
Andrews, S. J. Life of our Lord. N. Y., 1862. 8°. 9907
Andryane, A. Memoirs of a Prisoner of State. Lond., 1840. 2 v. 12°. 7683
Anecdotes of Churches and Sects. Lond., 1825. 3 v. 16°. . . 13184
of Distinguished Persons. Seward. Lond., 1795–97. 5 v. 16°. 13202
Encyclopædia of. Oxberry. Lond., 1821. 3 v. 12°. . . 4331
for the Family. N. Y. 16°. 15830
Book of 1000. Byrn. Bost., 1859. 12° 4319
Common-Place Book of. N. Y., 1830. 16°. 15831
Cyclopædia of. Arvine. Bost., 1856. 8°. 4432
Moral and Religious, Cyclopædia of. Arvine. N. Y. [1848.] 8°. 4341
Religious, Moral, and Entertaining. Buck. N. Y., 1831. 8°. 15826
Angelo, Michael. See M. A. BUONARROTI.
Angels, On. Tonna. N. Y., 1842. 12°. 15170
Angler, Complete. Walton and Cotton. N. Y., 1848. 2 v. in 1. 12°. 3920
Anglo-Saxon and Early Eng., Hand-Book of. Corson. N. Y., 1871. 12°. 94
Chronicle. Ed. Giles. Lond., 1847. 8°. 497
Home, The. Thrupp. Lond., 1862. 8°. 5264
Anglo-Saxons, Hist. of the. Turner. Paris., 1840. 3 v. 8°. . . 5075
Animal Kingdom, The. Cuvier. N. Y., 1831. 4 v. 8°. . . . 16954
Life, Structure of. Agassiz. N. Y., 1866. 8°. . . . 9049
Magnetism. See MAGNETISM; MESMERISM.
Mechanism and Physiology. Griscom. N. Y., 1840. 12°. . 11409
Animals under Domest., Variation of. Darwin. N. Y. [1868]. 2 v. 12°. 8930
in Menageries. Swainson. Lond., 1838. 16°. . . . 6053
Geography and Classification of. Swainson. Lond., 1835. 16°. 6056
Habits and Instincts of. Swainson. Lond., 1840. 16°. . . 6054

Animals, Hist., Habits, etc., of. Kirby. Philad., 1837. 8°. . . 16984
Instinct in. Chadbourne. N. Y., 1872. 12°. 8946
Intelligence of. Menault. N. Y., 1869. 12°. 10119
Animated Nature, Hist. of. Goldsmith. Philad., 1823–25. 5 v. 8°. 16925
See, also, BIRDS; FISHES; NATURAL HISTORY; QUADRUPEDS, etc.
Annals of the Parish. Galt. Philad., 1821. 12°. 2365
of a Quiet Neighborhood. MacDonald. N. Y., 1867. 12°. . 2578
Anne of Austria, Memoirs of. De Motteville. Lond., 1726. 5 v. 12°. 14627
Anne of Geierstein. Scott. Bost., 1845. 12°. 1837
Anne Grey. [Lister.] N. Y., 1835. 12°. 15111
Anne Severin. Craven. N. Y., 1869. 12°. 2391
Annihilation Theory, Refutation of the. Bartlett. Bost. [1866.] 12°. 10000
Annual Review, The. Ed. A. Aikin. Lond., 1802–04. v. 1–3. 8°. 14536
Scrap-Book. Lond., 1838. 16°. 15828
Anquetil, L. P. Memoirs of Court of Lewis XIV. Edinb., 1791. 2 v. 8° 16199
Anson, G. Voyage round the World. Edinb., 1776. 2 v. 12°. . . 16317
The same. (Mavor, v. 4.) Lond., 1796. 12° . . 13847
Life of. Barrow. Lond., 1839. 8°. 6850
Anspach, Eliz., Margavine of, Memoirs of, by herself. Lond., 1826. 2 v. 8°. 16355
Ansted, D. T. The Ancient World. Philad., 1847. 12°. . . . 8983
Anster Fair. [Tennant.] Bost., 1815. 12°. 14893
Antelope, Shipwreck of the. [Constable's Misc., v. 4.] Edinb., 1827. 12°. 4466
Antenor, Travels of. Lantier. Lond., 1799. 3 v. 8°. . . . 16513
Anthon, C. E. Pilgrimage to Treves. N. Y., 1845. 12°. . . . 16704
Antidote to Miseries of Human Life. [Carp.] N. H., 1809. 12°. . 15368
Sequel to. [Carp.] N. Y., 1810. 12°. . 15369
Anti-Jacobin, or Weekly Examiner. [Ed. W. Gifford.] 4th ed. Lond., 1799. 2 v. 8°. 11300
Review and Magazine. Lond., 1798–1800. v. 1–5. 8°. . . 11302
Antiquary. Scott. Edinb., 1870. 8°. 1863
Antiquities, American. Bradford. N. Y., 1843. 8°. 5954
British. Brand. Lond., 1848–49. 3 v. 8°. 504
Christian. Coleman. Andover, 1841. 8°. 10014
Northern. Mallet. Lond., 1859. 8°. 507
Popular. Chambers. Edinb., 1863–64. 2 v. 8°. . . . 4437
Roman. Fuss. Oxf'd, 1840. 8°. 4751
Anti-Slavery Conflict, Recollections of our. May. Bost., 1869. 12°. 8545
Measures in Congress, 1861–64. H. Wilson. Bost., 1864. 12°. 8579
Mission to America, 1863. Massie. Lond., 1864. 8°. . . 8555
Papers. Thoreau. Bost., 1866. 8°. 3556
Society, Inquiry into Character of the. Jay. N. Y., 1835. 12°. 8549
See, also, SLAVERY.
Antommarchi, F. Derniers momens de Napoléon. Paris, 1825. 2 v. 8°. 5632
Antonia. G. Sand. Bost., 1870. 16°. 2350
Antoninus, M. Aurelius. Meditations, transl. by Graves. Bath, 1792. 8°. 4231
Thoughts, transl. by Long. Bost., 1864. 12°. 4232
Apician Anecdotes. N. Y., 1836. 12°. 16963
Apocryphal N. T., The. N. Y. 8°. 10003

Apostles, Hist. of the. Renan. N. Y., 1866. 12°. 9895

Lives of the. [Bacon.] N. H. [1835.] 8°. 16463

Cave. Oxf'd, 1840. 8°. 10009

Apparitions, Hist. of. DeFoe. Oxf'd, 1840. 16°. 3878

See, also, DEMONOLOGY; GHOSTS; MAGIC.

Appletons' Cyclopædia of Biography. (2 copies.) N. Y., 1856. 8°. . 6909

Journal. N. Y., 1869–72. v. 2–8. 4°. 14392

New American Cyclopædia. N. Y., 1864. 16 v. 8°. . .

Annual Cyclopædia, for 1861–71. N. Y., 1864–72. 11 v. 8°. .

Aquarelles. Samuel Sombre. *(Pseud.)* N. Y., 1858. 12°. . . . 15035

Arabia, Hist., etc., of. Crichton. N. Y., 1834. 2 v. 12°. . . . 11286

Popular Description of. Conder. Lond. 12°. 7843

Travels through, 1761–63. Niebuhr. Edinb., 1792. 2 v. 8°. . 8246

Petræa, Impressions of Travel in, 1830. Dumas. N. Y., 1839. 12°. 7973

See, also, EXODUS; SINAI.

Arabian Nights' Entertainments. (2 copies.) N. Y., 1831. 8°. . . 1674

The same, transl. by Lane. Lond., 1840–41. 3 v. 8°. . 1671

The same. 2d ed. Lond., 1847. 3 v. 8°. 2002

Tales from the. Hanley. N. Y., 1869. 16°. 1907

Arabs under the Caliphs, Hist. of the. De Marigny. Lond., 1758. 4 v. 8°. 16055

in Spain, The. Lond., 1840. 2 v. 12°. 6399

Hist. of [710–1493]. Conde. Lond., 1854. 3 v. 8°. . . . 424

See, also, SARACENS; SPAIN.

Ararat, Journey to. Parrot. N. Y., 1846. 16°. 16278

Aratra Pentelici. Ruskin. N. Y., 1872. 12°. 9048

Araucanians, The. E. R. Smith. N. Y., 1855. 12°. 17131

Arber, E. English Reprints. Lond., 1868–71. 14 v. 16°. . . . 3885

CONTENTS.—1, Milton's Areopagitica; Latimer's Sermon on the Ploughers; Gosson's Schoole of Abuse. 2, Sidney's Apologie for Poetrie; Webbe's Travailes; Selden's Table-Talk. 3, Ascham's Toxophilus; Addison on 'Paradise Lost.' 4, Lyly's Euphues. 5, Villiers' Rehearsal; Gascoigne's Steele Glas, etc.; Earle's Micro-Cosmographie. 6, Latimer's Seven Sermons; More's Utopia. 7, Puttenham's Arte of Engl. Poesie; 8, Howell's Instructions for Travell; Udall's Roister Doister; Revelation to Monk of Evesham; James I., Essayes in Poesie, and Counterblast to Tobacco. 9, Naunton's Fragmenta Regalia; Watson's Poems; 10, Habington's Castara; Ascham's Scholemaster. 11, Tottel's Miscellany, by Surrey, Wyatt, Grimald, etc. 12, Lever's Sermons; Webbe's Discourse of Poetrie. 13, Bacon's Essays. 14, Roy and Barlow's Rede me and be nott Wrothe, etc.; Raleigh, Markham, and van Linschoten's Last Fight of the Revenge; Googe's Eglogs, etc.

Arblay. See D'ARBLAY.

Arc. See JOAN OF ARC.

Arcadia, The. Sidney. Lond., 1867. 8°. 3940

Archæology. See ANTIQUITIES.

Archer, Maj. Tours in Upper India and the Himalayas. Philad., 1833. 8°. 15356

Architects, Lives of. Vasari. Lond., 1850–52. 5 v. 8°. . . . 474

Architecture, Gothic. F. v. Schlegel. Lond., 1849. 8°. . . . 431

Hist. of. Memes. Bost., 1831. 12°. 8858

Lectures on. Ruskin. N. Y., 1859. 12°. 9034

Rural. Downing. N. Y., 1844. 8°. 9084

Seven Lamps of. Ruskin. N. Y., 1849. 12°. 9031

Wonders of. Lefèbre. N. Y., 1870. 12°. 10121

See, also, ART.

Arctic Adventure, Hist of. Sargent. Bost., 1857. 12°. . . . 8294
Expedition in Search of Franklin, The U. S. (1850–51.) Kane. Philad., 1856. 8°. 8106
Explorations; Second Expedition in Search of Franklin, 1853–55. Kane. Philad., 1857. 2 v. 8°. 8107
Journal, Leaves from an, 1850–51. Osborn. N. Y., 1852. 12°. 8295
Land Expedition, Narrative of the, 1833–35. Back. Lond., 1836. 8°. 8105
Researches, 1860–62. Hall. N. Y., 1865. 8°. 8113
Voyage, Journal of Parry's, 1818. [Fisher.] Lond., 1819. 8°. 8051
Letters written during Parry's, 1819–20. (Voyages, v. 5.) Lond., 1821. 8°. 8055
Narrative of Second, 1829–33. Ross. Philad., 1835. 8°. 8104
Voyages, 1818–39. Abridged by Barrow. N. Y., 1846. 16°. . 7906
See, also, POLAR Regions.
Arcturus. N. Y., 1841–42. v. 3. 8°. 12768
Argenson, M. P. d'. Essays. Worc., 1797. 12°. 15251
Argentine Republic, 24 Years in the. King. N. Y., 1846. 12°. . 5736
Argosy, The. Lond., 1866–67. 4 v. 8°. 14388
Argyll, Duke of. Reign of Law. 5th ed. Lond., 1868. 16°. . . 8839
Ariosto, L. Orlando Furioso: transl. by Hoole. Philad., 1816. 6 v. 12°. 567
The same. Lond., 1783. 5 v. 8°. 901
The same: transl. by Rose. Lond., 1823–31. 8 v. 8°. . 893
Stories. (Hunt's Ital. Poets.) N. Y., 1846. 12°. 887
Aristocracy. Brougham. (Polit. Philos., v. 2.) Lond., 1844. 8°. . 8681
Aristophanes. Wasps, tr. by Mitchell. Ed. Walsh. Philad., 1822. 24°. 36
Aristotle. Ethics and Politics, tr. by Gillies. 3d ed. Lond., 1813. 2 v. 8°. 8705
Arithmetic, Comic. [Forrester.] Lond., 1843. 12°. 4278
Treatise on. Lardner. Lond., 1836. 16°. 6048
Arkansas Territory, Journal of Travels in, 1819. Nuttall. Philad., 1821. 8°. 16866
Armadale. Collins. N. Y., 1866. 8°. 2301
Armata. 2d ed. N. Y., 1817. 12°. 15370
Arminius, J., Life of. Bangs. N. Y., 1843. 12°. 7514
Armstrong, John, M.D. Art of Preserving Health. Walpole, 1808. 12°. 14807
Poetical Works. Ed. Bell. Lond., 1807. 24°. 543
Select Poems. Ed. Walsh. Philad., 1822. 24°. 25
Armstrong, Gen. **John.** Life of Montgomery. (Sparks, v. 1.) Bost., 1834. 16°. 7250
of Wayne. (Sparks, v. 4.) Bost., 1835. 16°. 7253
Notices of the War of 1812. (3 copies.) N. Y., 1840. 2 v. 12°. 6081
Army. See MILITARY; also, names of Countries.
Arnault, V., etc. Memoirs of Napoleon. Bost. 1839. 2 v. 12°. . 5444
Arne. Björnson. Bost., 1869. 16°. 2615
Arnold, B., Life of. Sparks. (Amer. Biogr., 3.) Bost., 1835. 16°. 7252
Arnold, G. Poems grave and gay. Bost., 1867. 16°. 777
Arnold, H. P. European Mosaic. Bost., 1864. 16°. 8205
The Great Exhibition, etc. N. Y., 1868. 16°. 8206

Arnold, J. L. Poems. Prov., 1797. 12°. 14968
Arnold, M. Culture and Anarchy. Lond., 1869. 8°. 3736
Essays in Criticism. (2 copies.) Bost., 1865. 12°. . . . 3734
New Poems. Bost., 1867. 16°. 1193
• Poems. Bost., 1856. 16°. 1192
St. Paul and Protestantism. Lond., 1870. 8°. 9910
Arnold, S. J. Shipwreck. (Oxberry's Plays, v. 7.) Bost., 1822. 24°. 1351
Arnold, T. Christian Life; and Sermons at Rugby. (2 copies.) 2d ed. Lond., 1843. 8°. 10050
Hist. of the later Roman Commonwealth. (2 copies.) N. Y., 1846. 8°. 4748
Hist. of Rome. 2d. ed. Lond., 1840–45. 3 v. 8°. . . . 4743
The same. N. Y., 1846. 2 v. 8°. 4746
Lectures on Modern History. (2 copies.) 2d ed. Lond., 1843. 8°. 4718
The same, ed. H. Reed. (2 copies). N. Y., 1845. 12°. 4567
Miscellaneous Works. N. Y., 1845. 8°. 3426
Sermons at Rugby. (2 copies.) N. Y., 1846. 16°. . . . 9823
Life and Correspondence of. Stanley. Lond., 1844. 2 v. 8°. 7130
Arnold, W. D. Oakfield. Bost., 1855. 12°. 15528
Arrivabene, C. Italy under Victor Emmanuel. Lond., 1862. 2 v. 8°. 4777
[**Arrom, C. Bohl de.**] La Gaviota. N. Y., 1864. 12°. . . . 2601
Art, a Dramatic Tale. Reade. Bost., 1855. 12°. 2096
Art Criticism, Elements of. Samson. Philad., 1867. 12°. . . 9057
Criticisms on. Hazlitt. Lond., 1843–44. 2 v. 16°. . . 8856
Education. W. Smith. Bost., 1872. 8°. 9054
in England. Waagen. Lond., 1838. 3 v. 12°. . . . 9068
Essays on. Goethe. N. Y., 1862. 16°. 8846
The same. Palgrave. N. Y., 1867. 16°. 8859
in Europe. Wallace. Philad., 1857. 12°. 8886
European, Wonders of. Viardot. N. Y., 1871. 12°. . . 10124
Fine: Hist., Theory, Practice, etc. of. Wyatt. Lond., 1870. 8°. 9076
in Greece. Taine. N. Y., 1871. 12°. 8850
Handbook to the Galleries of, in and near London. Jameson. Lond., 1842. 2 v. 12°. 8874
Hist. of, in the Schools of Italy. Fuseli. (Works. v. 3.) Lond., 1831. 8°. 9053
The Ideal in. Taine. N. Y., 1869. 12°. 8848
Italian, Wonders of. Viardot. N. Y., 1870. 12°. . . . 10122
Lectures on. Allston. N. Y., 1850. 12°. 8885
The same. Ruskin. Oxf'd, 1870. 8°. 8884
Memoirs and Essays on. Jameson. N. Y., 1846. 12°. . . 3954
Monuments of. Lübke, etc. N. Y. 8°. and 2 v. of plates. 4°.
in the Netherlands. Taine. N. Y., 1871. 12°. . . . 8849
Political Economy of. Ruskin. N. Y., 1860. 12°. . . . 9041
Rhymes on. Shee. Philad., 1815. 12°. 14845
Sacred and Legendary. Jameson. Bost., 1865. 2 v. 16°. . 8854
Studies. Jarves. N. Y., 1861. 8°. 9067
Thoughts. Jarves. N. Y., 1869. 12°. 8888
Thoughts about. Hamerton. Bost., 1871. 16°. . . . 8858

Artevelde, Philip van; a dramatic romance. Taylor. Cambr., 1835.
2 v. 16°. 1001
Art-Idea, The. Jarves. N. Y., 1864. 16°. 8861
Art-Journal, The. Lond., 1852–60. 8 v. 4°. . . . . . .
Artist's Tour in England. Passavant. Lond., 1836. 2 v. 12°. . . 17121
Arthur, King, Story of. Cox and Jones. (Popular Romances.)
Lond., 1871. 8°. 2010
and his Knights. Bulfinch. Bost., 1861. 12°. 1910
Book of. Malory. Lond., 1868. 12°. . . 1912
Arthur, T. S. Illustrated Temperance Tales. Philad., 1850. 8°. . 15305
Sketches of Life and Character. Philad., 1850. 12°. . . 15304
Arthur, Wm. Etymological Dict. of Names. N. Y., 1860. 12°. . 102
Arthur, Wm. Italy in Transition, 1860. 2d ed. Lond., 1860. 8°. . 4593
Arthur Arundel. [Horace Smith.] N. Y., 1844. 8°. 2328
Arthur Clenning. [Flint.] Philad., 1828. 2 v. 12°. 15659
Arthur Mervyn. C. B. Brown. Bost., 1827. 2 v. 12°. 15297
Arts and Artists, The. Elmes. Lond., 1825. 3 v. 16°. 8851
Ancient, Hist. of. Rollin. Lond., 1768. 3 v. 8°. 15898
Dictionary of. Ure. N. Y., 1847. 8°. . . . . . .
Domestic and Mechanic, Science applied to the. Potter. Bost.,
1841. 12°. 17002
of the Greeks and Romans. Fosbrooke. Lond., 1833–35. 2 v. 16°. 4869
The Fine. (From Encycl. Britannica.) Hazlitt. Edinb., 1838. 12°. 8876
Contributions to Literature of. Eastlake. Lond.,
1870. 2 v. 8°. 9074
Discourses on. Reynolds. Lond., 1852. 2 v. 8°. . 482
Imitation in. Quatremère de Quincy. Lond., 1837. 8°. 9071
Origin, etc., of, in Gt. Britain and Ireland. Taylor.
Lond., 1841. 2 v. 12°. 8872
Outline Hist. of. Lossing. N. Y., 1840. 12°. . . 11427
The Useful. Bigelow. Bost., 1840. 2 v. 12°. 17003
Cyclopædia of. Tomlinson. Lond., 1854. 2 v. 8°.
See, also, ARCHITECTURE; MANUFACTURES; PAINTING.
Arundel. Vincent. Lond., 1840. 3 v. 8°. 15371
Arvine, K. Cyclopædia of Anecdotes. 3d ed. Bost., 1856. 8°. . 4432
Moral and Relig. Anec. N. Y. [1848.] 8°. . 4341
Arwed Gyllenstierna. Van der Velde. Bost., 1837. 12°. . . . 3029
Aryan Nations, Mythology of. Cox. Lond., 1870. 2 v. 8°. . . 4103
Ascham, R. The Scholemaster. Ed. Arber. Lond., 1870. 16°. . 3894
Toxophilus. Ed. Arber. Lond., 1868. 16°. 3887
Asgard, Heroes of. Keary. Lond., 1871. 12°. 1700
[**Ash, E.**] The Speculator. Dubl., 1791. 12°. 13037
Ashango-Land, Journey to. 1863–64. Du Chaillu. N. Y., 1867. 8°. 8122
Asia, Hist. of Discoveries and Travels in. Murray. Edinb., 1820.
3 v. 8°. 8060
Central, Travels in, 1863. Vámbéry. N. Y., 1865. 8°. . . 8141
Asia-Minor, Travels in, 1864. Van Lennep. N. Y., 1870. 2 v. 12°. 8244
See, also, SYRIA.

Asiatic Nations, Ancient, Researches on. Heeren. Oxf'd., 1833. 3 v. 8°. 4114
Aslauga's Knight. La Motte Fouqué. Tr. Carlyle. Bost., 1841. 12°. 3107
Asmodeus at large. Bulwer. Philad., 1833. 12°. 2147
Aspendale. Preston. Bost., 1871. 16°. 2744
Assent, Grammar of. Newman. N. Y., 1870. 12°. 9599
Asser. Annals of Alfred. Ed. Giles. Lond., 1848. 8°. . . . 499
Assyria, Hist., etc., of. Fraser. N. Y., 1845. 12°. 11759
Researches in. Ainsworth. Lond., 1838. 8°. 8048
Assyrian Monarchy, The. Rawlinson. (v. 1, 2.) N. Y., 1871. 8°. . 4063
Astoria. Irving. N. Y., 1850. 12°. 8403
Astronomer, Practical. Dick. N. Y., 1846. 16°. 16974
Astronomy of the Bible. Mitchel. N. Y., 1863. 12°. . . . 8915
Discourses on the Christian Revelation in connexion with. Chalmers. (Works, v. 1.) Bridgep't., 1829. 8°. . . 9633
Letters on. Olmsted. Bost., 1841. 12°. 16971
Parish. [Burr.] Bost., 1870. 12°. 8917
Planetary and Stellar, Worlds of. Mitchel. N. Y., 1863. 12°. 8912
Popular. Mitchel. N. Y., 1860. 12°. 8913
with reference to Natural Theology. Whewell. Philad., 1836. 8°. 16983
Solar System of. Hind. N. Y., 1852. 12°. 8845
Treatise on. Herschel. Lond., 1839. 16°. 6045
Atala. Chateaubriand. Lond., 1825. 24°. 2346
Athanasion. [Coxe.] N. Y., 1842. 12°. 803
Atheism, Polit., Lectures on. L. Beecher (Works, 1). Bost., 1852. 12°. 12753
Sermons on Folly of. Bentley (v. 3). Lond., 1838. 8°. . . 17229
Atheists, Voltaire and Rousseau against the. Ed. Akerly. N. Y., 1845. 12°. 9979
Athelwold; a Tragedy. W. Smith. Lond., 1842. 8°. . . . 845
Athenæum, The. N. H., 1814. v. 1. 8°. 17475
Athenaid, The. Lond., 1787. 3 v. 12°. 14867
Atheneum, The. Bost., 1817–25. 16 v. 8°. 14578
Athens, Public Economy of. Boeckh, tr. by Lewis. Lond., 1842. 8°. 4430
Atkinson, T. W. Upper and Lower Amoor. Lond., 1860. 8°. . . 8136
Atlantic Club Book, The. N. Y., 1834. 2 v. 12°. 14879
Monthly. Bost., 1857–70. 26 v. 8°. 13429
The same. v. 1–30. 13455
Telegraph, Hist. of the. H. M. Field. N. Y., 1866. 12°. . 8900
Atlas, Family. Johnson. N. Y., 1866. 4°. . . . .
General. Colton. N. Y., 1868. 4°. . . . .
Atmospheric System, The. Butler. Hartf'd., 1870. 12°. . . . 8919
Atonement, The; a Story. Hook. N. Y., 1839. 12°. . . . 2594
Attila. A Romance. James. N. Y., 1837. 2 v. 12°. . . . 15211
Atwater, C. Tour to Prairie du Chien. Columbus, 1831. 12°. . 16818
Aubigne, J. H. Merle d'. See MERLE.
Aubigne, T. A. d', Life of. [S. Scott.] Lond., 1772. 8°. . . . 7646
Audubon, J. J., Life of. By his Widow. N. Y., 1869. 12°. . . 7311
Auerbach, B. Black Forest Village Stories. (2 copies.) N. Y., 1869. 12°. 3024
Country House on the Rhine. Lond., 1870. 3 v. 8°. . . 3026
Edelweiss. (2 copies.) Bost., 1869. 12°. 2710

Auerbach, B. On the Heights. (2 copies.) Bost., 1868–69. 16°. . 2712
Auf der Höhe. 6 te. Aufl. Stuttg., 1868. 2 Bde. in 1. 16°. . 9758
Schwarzwälder Dorfgeschichten. Stuttg., 1861–62. 6 Bde. in 3. 16°. . 9461
Augustine, St. Confessions. N. Y., 1844. 12°. . 9945
Aumale, H. E. P. L., Duc d'. Hist. of the Princes de Condé. Lond., 1872. 2 v. 8°. . 5657
Aurelius Antoninus. See ANTONINUS.
Aurora Floyd. Braddon. N. Y., 1863. 8°. . 2311
Austen, Jane. Northanger Abbey. (2 copies.) Philad., 1833. 2 v. 12°. 2473
Novels. Philad., 1838. 2 v. in 1. 8°. . 2662
Persuasion. N. Y., 1832. 2 v. 12°. . 2477
Pride and Prejudice; Northanger Abbey. Bost., 1863. 12°. . 2479
Memoir of. Austen-Leigh. Lond., 1870. 8°. . 7068
Austin, James T. Life of Gerry. Bost., 1828–29. 2 v. 8°. . 7365
Austin, S. Characteristics of Goethe. (2 copies.) Lond., 1833. 3 v. 12°. 7829
The same. Philad., 1841. 2 v. 12°. . 7835
Fragments from German Prose Writers. (2 copies.) Lond., 1841. 12°. . 3950
The same. N. Y., 1841. 16°. . 114
Austin, W. Letters from London. Bost., 1804. 8°. . 16750
Austin, Elliot. H. Kingsley. Bost., 1863. 12°. . 2575
Australasia, Hist. of. Martin. Lond., 1839. 16°. . 7897
Australia, Expeditions in, 1831–36. Mitchell. Lond., 1839. 2 v. 8°. 8085
Felix, Impressions of, 1839–44. Howitt. Lond., 1845. 16°. . 7985
Southern, Expeditions in, 1828–31. Sturt. Lond., 1834. 2 v. 8°. 8083
Austria as it is. Lond., 1828. 8°. . 16611
in 1848–49. Stiles. N. Y., 1852. 2 v. 8°. . 5930
and the Austrians. Lond., 1837. 2 v. 8°. . 5813
Empire of. J. S. C. Abbott. N. Y., 1859. 12°. . 5812
Hist. of House of (1218–1792). Coxe. 3d ed. Lond., 1847. 3 v. 8°. 413
Travels in, 1834–36, etc. Turnbull. Lond., 1840. 2 v. 8°. . 16659
Authors, Calamities and Quarrels of. I. Disraeli. N. Y., 1841. 12°. 3391
See, also, LITERATURE.
Autobiographers, Half-Hours with. Knight. Lond., 1867. 8°. . 3769
Autobiography. Lond., 1826–31. v. 1–32. 12°. . 6639

CONTENTS.—1, Cibber. 2, Hume; Lilly; Voltaire. 3, 4, Marmontel. 5, R. Drury. 6, Whitefield; J. Ferguson. 7, Mrs. M. Robinson; Mrs. Charke. 8, Lord Herbert of Cherbury; Eugene of Savoy. 9, 10, Kotzebue. 11, Creichton; W. Gifford; Ellwood. 12, Holberg. 13, J. H. Vaux. 14, 15, Gibbon. 16, 17, Cellini. 18, J. Lackington. 19, T. W. Tone. 20, 21, Margravine of Bareith. 22, G. B. Doddington. 23, 24, Goldoni. 25–28, Vidocq. 29–32, Mme. Du Barri.

Autocrat of the Breakfast Table. Holmes. Bost., 1860. 12°. . 3606
Ava, Embassy to, 1795. Symes. Edinb., 1827. 2 v. 12°. . 4470
Avesta, Studies on the. Whitney. N. Y., 1872. 12°. . 136
Axel and Anna. Bremer. Lond., 1853. 8°. . 471
Aytoun, W. E. Lays of Scottish Cavaliers, etc. (2 copies.) N. Y., 1866. 12°. . 1097
Life of Richard I. Lond., 1840. 16°. . 5128
Azarian. H. P. Spofford. Bost., 1864. 8°. . 3011
Azeglio, M. d'. Ettore Fieramosca, or the Challenge of Barletta. N. Y., 1845. 12°. . 15171

B.

Babbage, C. Ninth Bridgewater Treatise. A Fragment. Lond., 1837. 8°. 16989
Babo, J. M. Otto of Wittlesbach; Dagobert. Transl. by Thompson. (German Theatre, v. 4.) Lond., 1811. 12°. 1359
Babylonia, Researches in. Ainsworth. Lond., 1838. 8°. . . . 8048
Babylonian Monarchy, The. Rawlinson. N. Y., 1871. 8°. . . 4064
Bacchus: an Essay on Intemperance. Grindrod. N. Y., 1840. 12°. 16967
Bachelor of the Albany. [Savage.] N. Y., 1848. 12°. . . . 15374
of Salamanca. Le Sage. Philad., 1854. 2 v. 12°. . . . 1691
Bachelors, The. Knapp. N. Y., 1836. 12°. 15662
Back, G. Narrative of Arctic Expedition. Lond., 1836. 8°. . . 8105
Bacon, David F. Lives of the Apostles. N. H. [1835.] 8°. . . 16463
[**Bacon, Delia.**] Bride of Fort Edward. N. Y., 1839. 12°. . . 15666
Tales of the Puritans. (2 copies.) N. H., 1831. 12°. . . 15799
Bacon, F. Essays. Lond., 1801. 16°. 3523
The same. Philad., 1818. 2 v. 24°. 3524
The same. Bost., 1820. 16°. 3843
The same. N. Y., 1845. 12°. 11772
The same. 12285
The same. Bost., 1868. 16°. 3155
The same. Ed. B. Montagu. Lond., 1836. 16°. . . 3154
The same. Ed. by Whately. N. Y., 1857. 8°. . . 3394
The same. Revised ed. Bost., 1861. 8°. . . 3395
The same. Ed. Arber. Lond., 1871. 16°. . . . 3897
Works. Lond., 1824. 10 v. 8°. 9678
The same. 9621
The same. Lond., 1838. 2 v. 8°. 9738
Life of. Campbell (Ld. Chancellors, v. 2). Lond., 1845. 8°. . 6867
Novum Organon of, Account of. [Hoppus.] Lond., 1829. 8°. 16468
Personal History of. Dixon. Bost., 1861. 12°. . . . 6755
Bacon, J. Life of Francis I. 2d ed. Lond., 1830. 2 v. 8°. . . 5651
Bacon, L. Historical Discourses at N. Haven. N. H., 1839. 8°. . 5897
Slavery discussed in Occasional Essays. N. Y., 1846. 12°. . 8570
Bacon, N., Memoir of. Ware. Bost., 1844. 16°. 7262
Bacon, W. T. Poems. N. H., 1839. 8°. 15047
The same. Bost., 1837. 12°. 14971
Bagehot, W. Physics and Politics. N. Y., 1873. 12°. . . . 10183
Bagg, J. H. Magnetism. Detroit, 1845. 12°. 8527
[**Bagg, L. H.**] Four Years at Yale. (2 copies.) N. H., 1871. 8°. . 9275
Bailey, P. J. The Angel World, etc. Bost., 1850. 16°. . . . 832
Festus. N. Y. 16°. 981
The Mystic, etc. Bost., 1856. 16°. 831
[**Bailey, S.**] Essays on Formation, etc., of Opinions. Philad., 1831. 12°. 3165
Baillie, J. Complete Poetical Works. Philad., 1832. 8°. . . . 1655
Plays. Lond., 1821. 3 v. 8°. 1592

Baillie, R. Letters and Journals, 1637–62. Ed. Laing. Edinb., 1841–42. 3 v. 8°. 7213
Bainbridge, W., Life of. Cooper (Naval Biogr., v. 1). Philad., 1846. 12°. 7275
The same. Harris. Philad., 1837. 8°. 7458
Baines, E. Hist. of the French Revolution. Philad., 1835. 2 v. and 1 v. maps. 8°. 5671
Baird, H. M. Modern Greece. N. Y., 1856. 12°. 8323
Baird, R. Protestantism in Italy. Bost., 1847. 12°. 17263
Visit to Northern Europe. N. Y., 1841. 2 v. 12°. 16597
Baker, H. The Universe. 2d ed. Lond. 8°. 14806
Baker, S. W. The Albert N'yanza. (2 copies.) Lond., 1866. 8°. . 8118
Eight Years' Wanderings in Ceylon. Philad., 1869. 12°. . 7909
Nile Tributaries of Abyssinia. Lond., 1868. 8°. . . . 8120
The same. Hartf'd., 1868. 8°. 8121
Baker, W. M. The New Timothy. N. Y., 1870. 12°. . . . 2852
Bakewell, R. Introd. to Geology. Ed. Silliman. N. H., 1839. 8°. 9008
Balboa, V. N. de, Life of. Bost., 1840. 12°. 7511
Baldwin, E. Annals of Yale College. N. H., 1831. 8°. . . . 9322
Baldwin, J. D. Pre-Historic Nations. N. Y., 1869. 12°. . . . 15936
Baldwin, T. Airopaidia; a Balloon Excursion. Chester, 1786. 8°. 16944
Bale, J. God's Promises. (Old Plays, v. 1.) Lond., 1825. 8°. . 1508
Balearic Islands, Hist. of. [Dameto and Mut.] Lond., 1719. 8°. . 16163
Ball, A. M. W. Claim to the Authorship of "Rock Me to Sleep." N. Y., 1867. 8°. 15048
Ball, C., Life of. Fisher. N. Y., 1837. 12°. 8569
Ballads, Ancient, Imitations of. Sir W. Scott. (Poems, v. 6.) Bost., 1871. 16°. 1076
Ancient Spanish. Lockhart. N. Y., 1842. 8°. 913
English and Scottish. Child. Bost., 1857–59. 8 v. 16°. . 1038
Old. Evans. Lond., 1810. 4 v. 16°. 1089
Pictorial Book of. J. S. Moore. Lond., 1847–48. 2 v. 8°. . 1205
relating to Robin Hood. Ritson. [Lond., 1845.] 8°. . . 948
Scottish. Chambers. Edinb., 1829. 12°. 955
See, also, MINSTRELSY; POETRY; SONGS.
Ballard, G. Memoirs of Learned Ladies of Grt. Brit. Oxf'd., 1752. 4°. 16030
Balloon Ascents. Marion. N. Y., 1870. 12°. 10116
Excursion, Narrative of. Baldwin. Chester, 1786. 8°. . . 16944
See, also, AIR.
Ballston Springs. Poems. N. Y., 1806. 12°. 14965
Balmes, J. L. Protestantism and Catholicity compared. Balt., 1851. 8°. 6492
Baltic, Letters from the Shores of the. 2d ed. Lond., 1842. 2 v. 12°. 16613
Balwhidder, Micah. Annals of the Parish. [Galt.] Philad., 1821. 12°. 2365
Bancroft, A. Life of Washington. Bost., 1826. 2 v. 12°. . . 7490
Bancroft, G. Hist. of the U. S. (2 copies.) Bost., 1841–66. 9 v. 8°. 6203
The same. v. 2, 3. 6221
Literary and Historical Miscellanies. (2 copies.) N. Y., 1855. 8°. 3473
Bandello, M. Novels. (Ital. Novelists, v. 3.) Lond., 1836. 12°. . 1901
Bandinel, J. Trade in Slaves from Africa. Lond., 1842. 8°. . . 8753

Banditti, Lives of. MacFarlane. Philad., 1839. 2 v. 12°. . . . 6705
See, also, BRIGANDS.
Banfield, T. C. Agriculture on the Rhine. Lond., 1846. 12°. . . 8795
Bangs, N. Life of Arminius. N. Y., 1843. 12°. 7514
[**Banim, J.**] The Croppy. Philad., 1839. 2 v. 12°. 15408
The Mayor of Wind-Gap. N. Y., 1835. 12°. 15505
The Smuggler. N. Y., 1832. 2 v. 12°. 15159
Banker's Wife, The. Gore. N. Y., 1843. 8°. 2313
Banking in America, Hist. of. Gilbart. Lond., 1837. 8°. . . . 8649
Treatise on. Raguet. Philad., 1839. 8°. 8755
Bankrupt Stories. [Briggs.] N. Y., 1844. 8°. 15078
Banks, W. English Master. Lond., 1823. 8°. 17528
Banks, Hist. of. Goddard. N. Y., 1831. 8°. 8650
Theory of. Tucker. Bost., 1839. 12°. 8648
Bannister, J., Memoirs of. Adolphus. Lond., 1839. 2 v. 8°. . . 7996
Bannockburn; a Novel. Porter. Philad., 1822. 2 v. 12°. . . 15192
Banvard, J. Life of Webster. Bost., 1853. 16°. 7541
Baptist Pulpit, Annals of the American. Sprague. N. Y., 1860. 8°. 7735
Barbacovi, F. V. Literary Hist. of Italy. Edinb., 1835. 12°. . . 112
Barbary States, Hist., etc., of the. Russell. N. Y., 1835. 12°. . 11290
See, also, ALGIERS.
Barbauld, A. L. Works. N. Y., 1826. 2 v. 12°. 13672
Barber, John W. Hist. Collections of Mass. Worc., 1841. 8°. . 5937
Hist. of N. E., N. Y., and N. J. Worc., 1841. 8°. . . . 5936
Interesting Events in U. S. History. N. H., 1829. 12°. . . 16050
and Howe, H. Hist. Collections of N. J. N. Y., 1844. 8°. . 5938
Barber, Jos. Crumbs from the Round Table. N. Y., 1866. 12°. . 3579
Bareith, F. S. W., Margravine of, Memoirs of. By herself. Lond., 1827. 2 v. 12°. 6658
Bargagli, S. A Novel. (Ital. Novelists, v. 4.) Lond., 1836. 12°. . 1902
Barham, R. H. Ingoldsby Legends. Philad., 1844. 12°. . . . 4255
My Cousin Nicholas; Rubber of Life. Lond., 1841. 3 v. 12°. 15519
Baring-Gould, S. Curious Myths of Middle Ages. 2 Series in 1. New ed. Lond., 1869. 16°. 1915
The same. 2d Series. Lond., 1868. 8°. 1916
In Exitu Israel. N. Y., 1870. 8°. 2442
Legends of Patriarchs and Prophets. N. Y., 1872. 8°. . . 1914
Origin and Development of Religious Belief. N. Y., 1870. 2 v. 12°. 9959
Barker, Lady F. N. Spring Comedies. Lond., 1871. 8°. . . . 2515
Station Life in N. Zealand. Lond., 1870. 8°. 7988
[**Barker, M. H.**] The Warlock. Philad., 1836. 2 v. 12°. . . 15633
Barlow, Joel. Vision of Columbus. Hartf'd., 1787. 8°. . . . 14926
The same. 2d ed. Hartf'd., 1787. 12°. 688
Barlow, J. Physiology and Intellectual Philosophy; Man's Power over himself to control Insanity. (Small Books, v. 1.) Philad., 1847. 12°. 8496
Barnabee's Journal. [Braithwait.] Lond., 1818. 12°. . . . 14810
Barnaby Rudge. Dickens. N. Y., 1871. 16°. 2173

[**Barnard, C. F.**] The Soprano. Bost. [1869.] 12°. 3012
Barnes, A. Inquiry into Scriptural Views of Slavery. Philad., 1846. 12°. 8577
Lectures on Evidences of Christianity. N. Y., 1868. 12°. . 9998
Notes on Isaiah. Bost., 1840. 3 v. 8°. 10016
The same. 3d ed. N. Y., 1851. 2 v. 12°. . . . 9856
Notes on Job. 5th ed. (2 copies.) N. Y., 1847. 2 v. 12°. . 9852
Notes on the N. T. N. Y., 1836–52. 8 v. 12°. 9858
CONTENTS.—1, 2, Gospels. 3, Acts. 4, Romans. 5, I Corinthians. 6, II Corinthians, Galatians. 7, Hebrews. 8, Revelation.
The same. Gospels to Hebrews. 9866
The same. Romans; I Corinthians. 9873
Practical Sermons. Philad., 1841. 12°. 17360
Sermons on Revivals. N. Y., 1841. 12°. 17271
Barnes, R. Writings. Lond. 12°. 9482
Barnett, F., Memoirs of. By himself. Bost., 1823. 2 v. 12°. . . 16384
Barney, J., Biogr. Memoir of. Bost., 1832. 8°. 7418
Barnum, H. L. The Spy Unmasked. N. Y., 1828. 8°. . . . 6124
Barnum, P. T. Humbugs of the World. N. Y., 1865. 12°. . . 17104
Life of. By himself. N. Y., 1855. 12°. . . . . . .
Barnum, S. W. Comprehensive Dict. of the Bible. N. Y., 1869. 12°. 10058
Baron, J. Life of Jenner. Lond., 1838. 2 v. 8°. 7160
Barr, W. Journal of March to Câbul, etc. Lond., 1844. 12°. . . 7939
Barren Honour. [Lawrence.] N. Y. 8°. 2311
Barrera, Mme. de. Memoirs of Rachel. N. Y., 1858. 12°. . . 7965
Barrett, E. G. Poems. N. Y., 1866. 12°. 14972
Barrett, Walter. Old Merchants of N. Y. [Scoville.] N. Y., 1863. 2 v. 12°. 7415
Barrington, D. Possibility of approaching the N. Pole. N. Y., 1818. 8°. 16593
Barrington, G. Voyage to New South Wales. N. Y. 8°. . . . 16288
Barrington, J. Personal Sketches of his Times. Philad., 1827. 2 v. in 1. 8°. 16341
Rise and Fall of the Irish Nation. N. Y., 1860. 12°. . . 5253
Barrow, I. Works, ed. Hughes. Lond., 1830. 5 v. 12°. . . 12756
Barrow, Sir John. Life of Lord Anson. Lond., 1839. 8°. . . 6850
Life of Earl Howe. Lond., 1838. 8°. 6849
Memoir of Peter the Great. N. Y., 1841. 12°. 11285
The same. N. Y., 1834. 12°. 12115
Pitcairn's Island, and Mutiny of the Bounty. N. Y., 1840. 12°. 11033
Travels in China. Philad., 1805. 8°. 16520
in S. Africa. N. Y., 1802. 8°. 16534
Voyages in Arctic Regions. N. Y., 1846. 16°. . . . 7906
Barrow, John, Jr. Tour round Ireland. Lond., 1836. 12°. . . 8307
Visit to Iceland. Lond., 1835. 12°. 8292
Barruel, A. Hist. of Jacobinism. N. Y., 1799. 4 v. 8°. . . . 16201
of the Clergy during the French Revol. Dubl., 1795. 12°. 16220
Barry, J., etc. Lectures on Painting. (2 copies.) Lond., 1848. 8°. . 8881
Barry, L. Ram-Alley. (Old Plays, v. 5.) Lond., 1825. 8°. . . 1512

Barry Lyndon. Thackeray. Lond., 1872. 8°. 2192
Barthelemy, J. J. Travels of Anacharsis. Lond., 1798. 8°. . . 15953
Bartholomew, Massacre of St. White. N. Y., 1868. 12°. . . . 6327
Bartlett, D. W. What I saw in London. Auburn, 1852. 12°. . . 16759
Bartlett, J. Familiar Quotations. (2 copies.) 5th ed. Bost., 1868–69. 16°. 4348
Bartlett, J. R. Dict. of Americanisms. 3d ed. Bost., 1860. 8°. . 212
Narrative of Explor. in Texas, etc. N. Y., 1854. 2 v. in 1. 8°. 8087
Bartlett, S. C. Life and Death Eternal. Bost. [1866.] 12°. . . 10000
Bartlett, W. H. Pictures from Sicily. Lond., 1869. 8°. . . . 8352
Barton, B. Poems. Philad., 1821. 12°. 819
Barton, W., Life of. Williams. Prov., 1839. 12°. 16430
Bascom, J. Science, Philosophy and Religion. N. Y.,' 1871. 12°. . 8512
Bashan, Giant Cities of. Porter. N. Y., 1866. 12°. 8256
Basil Barrington and his Friends. Lond., 1830. 3 v. 8°. . . . 15375
Baskerville, A. Poetry of Germany. 3d ed. (2 copies.) Philad., 1856. 8°. 857
Bass Rock, Geology of the. Miller. N. Y., 1851. 12°. . . . 8829
Bassompierre, F. de. Embassy to England. Lond., 1819. 8°. . . 5073
Bastile, Hist. of the. Davenport. Lond., 1839. 16°. 5512
Bates, W. Spiritual Perfection unfolded. Lond., 1834. 16°. . . 9487
Bathing, Hist. of. Mahomed. Lond., 1843. 12°. 9230
Bathurst, Lord H., Observations on Speech of. N. Y., 1818. 12°. 16222
Battle of the Books. Swift. (Works, v. 3.) N. Y., 1812. 12°. . . 3849
Battles of the World, Decisive. Creasy. N. Y., 1863. 12°. . . 4572
Baur, W. Religious Life in Germany. Lond., 1870. 2 v. 8°. . . 6323
Bausset, L. F. de. Life of Fenelon. Lond., 1810. 2 v. 8°. . . 7672
Bausset, L. F. J. de. Memoirs of Court of Napoleon. Philad., 1828. 8°. 5590
Bautain, L. E. M. Art of Extempore Speaking. (2 copies.) N. Y., 1859–67. 12°. 9294
Baviad, The. Gifford. N. Y., 1800. 12°. 14823
Baxter, G. R. W. Humour and Pathos. Lond., 1842. 12°. . . 4264
Baxter, R. Call to the Unconverted. N. Y. 12°. 9807
Dying Thoughts. Ed. Stebbing. Lond., 1834. 16°. . . 9489
Jesuit Juggling. N. Y., 1835. 12°. 9580
The Reformed Pastor. Ed. Park. Andover, 1845. 12°. . . 9913
Bay Path, The. Holland. N. Y., 1862. 12°. 2918
Bayley, F. W. N. New Tale of a Tub. N. Y., 1854. 12°. . . 15049
Bayley, J. Hist. of Tower of London. (2 copies.) Lond., 1830. 8°. 5116
Bayne, P. The Christian Life, Bost., 1860. 12°. 9975
Essays on Biography and Criticism. Bost., 1860. 2 v. 12°. . 3729
Life of H. Miller. Bost., 1871. 2 v. 12°. 7101
Testimony of Christ to Christianity. Bost., 1862. 16°. . . 9901
Bazar Book of Decorum. (2 copies.) N. Y., 1870. 16°. . . . 9131
Beach, S. B. Escalala. Utica, 1824. 12°. 14973
Beale, T. Nat. Hist. of the Sperm Whale; Sketch of a Whaling Voyage. Lond., 1839. 12°. 16330
Beard, J. R. Schools. Lond., 1842. 12°. 9107

Beatrice. Sinclair. N. Y. 12°. 15378

Beattie, J. Essays on Poetry, Music, etc. 3d ed. Lond., 1779. 8°. 214

The Minstrel; with other Poems. N. Y., 1802. 16°. . . 14808

Poetical Works. Philad., 1842. 8°. 945

Select Poems. Ed. Walsh. Philad., 1822. 24°. 26

Works. Philad., 1809. 10 v. 12°. 12287

Life, etc., of. Forbes. N. Y., 1807. 8°. 16354

Beattie, W. Life of Campbell. (2 copies.) N. Y., 1850. 2 v. 12°. 7038

Beaumarchais, P. A. C. de, and his Times. De Loménie. N. Y., 1857. 12°. 7623

Beaumont, F., and Fletcher, J. Selected Works. Ed. L. Hunt. Lond., 1855. 8°. 449

Works. Lond., 1711. v. 1, 3–7. 8°. 1426

Works, ed Darley. Lond., 1840. 2 v. 8°. 1625

Works, ed. Dyce. Lond., 1843–46. 11 v. 8°. 1497

CONTENTS.—1, Memoir; Woman-Hater; Thierry and Theodoret; Philaster; Maid's Tragedy. 2, Faithful Shepherdess; Kt. of Burning Pestle; King and No King; Cupid's Revenge; Masque; Four Plays in One. 3, Scornful Lady; Coxcomb; Captain; Honest Man's Fortune; French Lawyer. 4, Wit at several Weapons; Wit without Money; Faithful Friends; Widow; Custom of the Country. 5, Bonduca; Kt. of Malta; Valentinian; Laws of Candy; Q. of Corinth. 6, Loyal Subject; Mad Lover; False One; Double Marriage; Humorous Lieutenant. 7, Women Pleased; Woman's Prize; Chances; M. Thomas; Island Princess. 8, Pilgrim; Wild-Goose-Chase; Prophetess; Sea-Voyage; Spanish Curate. 9, Beggars' Bush; Love's Cure; Maid in the Mill; Wife for a Month; Rule a Wife and Have a Wife. 10, Fair Maid of the Inn; Noble Gentleman; Elder Brother; Nice Valour; Bloody Brother, or Rollo, D. of Normandy. 11, Lover's Progress; Night-Walker; Love's Pilgrimage; Two Noble Kinsmen; Poems; Index.

Beaumont, G. de. Ireland. Lond., 1839. 2 v. 12°. 5419

Beautiful, Origin of Ideas of the. Burke. Bost., 1839. 8°. . . . 9649

See, also, ÆSTHETICS; TASTE.

Beauty and the Beast. Bayard Taylor. N. Y., 1872. 12°. . . 2941

Beazley, S. Is he Jealous? (Oxberry's Plays, v. 8.) Bost., 1822. 24°. 1352

Becker, W. A. Charicles, tr. by Metcalfe. Lond., 1845. 12°. . . 4326

Gallus, tr. by Metcalfe. Lond., 1844. 12°. 4324

The same. 3d ed. N. Y., 1866. 8°. 4325

Becket, Thomas a; a Drama. Darley. Lond., 1840. 8°. 844

Life of. Campbell (Ld. Chancellors, v. 1). Lond., 1845. 8°. . 6866

Beckford, W. Excursion to Monasteries of Alcobaca, etc. Philad., 1835. 12°. 8317

Hist. of Vathek. N. Y., 1869. 12°. 10078

Italy, Spain and Portugal. Philad., 1834. 2 v. 12°. . . . 8217

Beckman, J. Hist. of Inventions. Lond., 1817. 4 v. 8°. . . 15854

The same. (2 copies.) Lond., 1846. 2 v. 8°. . . . 354

Beckwourth, J. P., Life and Adventures of. N. Y., 1856. 12°. . 7407

Becon, T. Writings. Lond. 12°. 9481

Bede, Cuthbert. *(Pseudonym.)* See E. BRADLEY.

Bede, Venerable. Eccl. Hist. of England. (2 copies.) Lond., 1847. 8°. 497

Bedell, W., Life of. Burnet. Lond. 24°. 6677

Bedford Row Conspiracy. Thackeray. (Works, v. 9.) Lond., 1872. 8°. 2197

Bee, The; or, Literary Weekly Intelligencer. Anderson. Edinb., 1791–93. 18 v. 8°. 13041

Beecher, C. E. Essay on Slavery. Philad., 1837. 12°. . . . 8470

Beecher, H. W. Eyes and Ears. Bost., 1863. 12°. 3592

Freedom and War. Bost., 1863. 12°. 3593

Beecher, H. W. Lecture Room Talks. N. Y., 1870. 12°. . . . 9879
Lectures to Young Men. Salem, 1846. 12°. 9179
The same. Revised ed. (2 copies.) Bost., 1866–68. 12°. 9180
Life of Jesus. N. Y., 1871. v. 1. 8°. 6539
Life Thoughts. (2 copies.) Bost., 1858. 12°. 3588
Norwood. (2 copies.) N. Y., 1868. 12°. 2943
Sermons. N. Y., 1869. 2 v. 8°. 10053
Sermons ("Plymouth Pulpit"). N. Y., 1869. 2 v. 8°. . . 10055
Star Papers. (2 copies.) N. Y., 1855. 12°. 3590
Yale Lectures on Preaching. (2 copies.) N. Y., 1872. 12°. . 9919
Beecher, L. Autobiography, Correspondence, etc. (2 copies.) N. Y., 1864–65. 2 v. 12°. 7634
Lectures on Scepticism. (2 copies.) Cincinn., 1835. 12°. . 9811
Plea for the West. Cincinn., 1835. 12°. 17303
Works. Bost., 1852–53. 3 v. 12°. 12753
Beecher, T. K. Our Seven Churches. N. Y., 1870. 16°. . . . 9833
Beechey, H. W. Life and Works of Reynolds. Lond., 1835. 2 v. 16°. 8879
Bees, Natural Hist. of. Huber. Lond., 1841. 12°. 8893
Beethoven, L. v. Letters. N. Y., 1868. 2 v. in 1. 16°. . . . 7880
Life of. Moscheles. Lond., 1841. 2 v. 12°. 7961
Beets, N. Life of van der Palm. N. Y., 1865. 8°. 7770
Behemoth; a Legend. [Mathews.] N. Y., 1839. 12°. . . . 15663
Belcher, Lady. Mutineers of the Bounty. N. Y., 1871. 12°. . . 8324
Belden, L. W. Account of a Somnambulist. Springf'ld., 1834. 12°. 8483
Belford Regis. Mitford. Philad. 8°. 2675
Belgian Traveller, in Holland, France and Switzerland. Middletown, 1807. 8°. 16658
Belgiojoso, C. T. de. Oriental Harems and Scenery. N. Y., 1862. 12°. 8252
Belgium. Tennent. Lond., 1841. 2 v. 12°. 16654
in 1833. Mrs. Trollope. Philad., 1834. 8°. 16656
Belgravia. Lond., 1870–72. v. 10–14, 17. 8°. 17757
Belinaye, H. Sources of Health and Disease. Bost., 1833. 12°. . 9169
Belinda. Edgeworth. (Works, v. 3.) Bost., 1824. 8°. . . . 15337
Belisarius. A Tale. Marmontel. Lond., 1794. 12°. . . . 2355
Belisarius, Life of. Lord Mahon. Philad., 1832. 12°. . . . 7576
Belknap, J. Amer. Biography, ed. Hubbard. N. Y., 1846. 3 v. 12°. 11762
The same. N. Y., 1844. 3 v. 12°. 12278
Hist. of N. Hampshire. Bost., 1792. 3 v. 8°. 16133
The same. 2d ed. Bost., 1813. 3 v. 8°. 5861
Bell, Acton. *(Pseudonym.)* See A. BRONTË.
Bell, Chas. The Hand, as evincing Design. Philad., 1836. 8°. . 16983
Letters. Lond., 1870. 8°. 7105
Bell, Currer. *(Pseudonym.)* See C. BRONTË.
Bell, Ellis. *(Pseudonym.)* See E. BRONTË.
Bell, H. G. Birmese War, etc. Edinb., 1827. 12°. 4471
Life of Mary, Queen of Scots. Edinb., 1828. 2 v. 12°. . . 4486
The same. N. Y., 1831–44. 2 v. 12°. 11023
The same. N. Y., 1837. 2 v. 12°. 11949
The same. N. Y., 1833. 2 v. 12°. 11951

Bell, James S. Residence in Circassia. Lond., 1840. 2 v. 8°. . . 8040

Bell, John. (Born 1691.) Travels to Asia. Edinb., 1788. 2 v. 8°. . 16509

Bell, John. Poets of Great Britain. [Bagster's ed.] Lond., 1807. 62 double vols. 24°. (10 v. wanting.) 246

CONTENTS.—V. ii-v, vii, Chaucer. viii-xi, Spenser. xii, Denham. xiii, Waller. xiv, xv, Milton. xvii, Butler, Dillon (Earl of Roscommon). xviii, xix, Cowley. xix, Wilmot (Earl of Rochester). xx-xxiv, Dryden. xxv, W. King. xxvi, xxvii, Prior. xxvii, Granville (Lord Lansdowne). xxxi, Addison. xxxii, xxxiii, Rowe. xxxiv, xxxv, Watts. xxxv, J. Philips, E. Smith. xxxvi Parnell. xxxvii, Garth, Fenton. xxxviii, Somerville. xl-xliii, xliv, Pope. xliv, A. Philips. xlv, xlvi, Gay. xlvi, Tickell. xlvii, Broome, Pitt, Green. xlviii, xlix, Young. l, Savage. li, J. Thomson. lii, Dyer, G. West, Lyttelton. liii, Hammond, Collins, E. Moore. liv, Shenstone. lv, Mallet, Gray, R. West. lvi, Akenside. lvii, lviii, Churchill. lviii, Jenyns. lix, Falconer, J. Cunningham. lx, Armstrong, Goldsmith, Johnson.

Bell, R. Hist. of Russia. (2 copies.) Lond., 1836–38. 3 v. 16°. . 5480

Life of Canning. N. Y., 1846. 16°. 6695

Lives of English Poets. (2 copies.) Lond.. 1839. 2 v. 16°. . 5777

CONTENTS.—1, Drayton; Cowley; Waller; Milton; Butler. 2, Dryden; Minor Poets; Prior; Pope; Young; Akenside.

Bell, W. A. New Tracks in N. A. Lond., 1869. 2 v. 8°. . . 8422

Bellows, H. W. The Old World in its New Face. N. Y., 1869. 2 v. 12°. 8273

Beloe, W. The Sexagenarian. 2d ed. Lond., 1818. 2 v. 8°. . . 3487

Belsham, W. Memoirs of Geo. I, II, and III. Dubl., 1796. 3 v. 8°. 5282

Belton Estate, The. A. Trollope. N. Y., 1866. 8°. 2290

Beltz, G. F. Memorials of Order of the Garter. Lond., 1841. 8°. . 5114

Ben Brace. Chamier. Philad., 1836. 2 v. 12°. 15379

Bench and the Bar, The. [Grant.] Philad., 1837. 2 v. 12°. . . 6605

[**Benedict, F. L.**] Miss Van Kortland. N. Y., 1870. 8°. . . 2688

Benevolence, Philosophy of. Church. N. Y., 1836. 12°. . . . 17356

Systematic, Essays on. N. Y., 12°. 9803

Benger, E. O. Memoirs of A. Boleyn. Philad., 1822. 8°. . . 5239

Benjamin, S. G. W. The Turk and the Greek. N. Y., 1867. 16°. . 8198

Bennet, J. H. Winter and Spring on Mediterranean Shores. 4th ed. N. Y., 1870. 8°. 8375

Bentham, J., Select Extracts from. Ed. Burton. Philad., 1844. 12°. 9589

Works. Edinb., 1838–43. 11 v. in 22 pts. 8°. 9700

CONTENTS.—1, Principles of Morals and Legislation; on the Promulgation of Laws; Specimen of a Penal Code; Influence of Time and Place in Legislation; Table of Springs of Action; Fragments on Government. 2, Principles of the Civil Code; Principles of Penal Law. 3, The Hard-Labour Bill; Panopticon, etc.; Plea for the Constitution; Draught of Code for a Judicial Establishment in France. 4, Organization of Judicial Establishments; Emancipate your Colonies; on Houses of Peers and Senates; Papers on Codification. 5, Scotch Reform; Plan of a Judicatory; Art of Packing Juries; Swear not at all; Truth *vs.* Ashurst; The King against Edmonds, etc.; the King against Wolseley; Official Aptitude maximized. 6, The last, continued; on Humphreys' Real Property Code; Plan of a General Register of Real Property; Justice and Codification Petitions; Ld. Brougham displayed. 7, Principles of Judicial Procedure; Rationale of Reward; Principles of a Constitutional Code; Liberty of the Press, etc. 8, Political Tactics; Book of Fallacies; Anarchical Fallacies; Principles of International Law; Junctiana Proposal; Protest against Law Taxes; Supply without Burden; Tax with Monopoly. 9, Defence of Usury; Manual of Polit. Economy; Restrictive Commercial System; Circulating Annuities; View of a Complete Code of Laws; Pannomial Fragments; Nomography; Logical Arrangements. 10, Equity Dispatch Court Proposal,—and Bill; Plan of Parliamentary Reform; Radical Reform Bill; Radicalism not dangerous. 11–14, Rationale of Judicial Evidence. 15, Chrestomathia; Ontology; Logic; Language. 16, The last, continued; Universal Grammar; Poor Laws and Pauper Management; Tracts on Spanish and Portuguese Affairs; Letters to Toreno on the Spanish Penal Code; Reformation in Tripoli. 17, 18, The Constitutional Code. 19–21, Memoirs by Bowring. 21, 22, Index. 22, Introd. to Study of Bentham, by J. H. Burton.

Bentley, R. Works, ed. Dyce. Lond., 1836–38. 3 v. 8°. . . 17227

Essay on. De Quincey. (Works, v. 7.) Edinb., 1858. 8°. . 3280

Life of. H. Coleridge (Worthies). Lond., 1836. 8°. . . 6904

Bentley's Miscellany. Lond., 1837–44. v. 1–3, 5–10, 13–16. 8°. . 14212

The same. N. Y. v. 8, 9. 14225

Benton, T. H. Examination of the Dred Scott case. N. Y., 1858. 8°. 8679
Thirty Years' View. (2 copies.) N. Y., 1854–56. 2 v. 8°. . 6244
Benyowsky, M. A. de. Memoirs and Travels. Dubl., 1790. 2 v. 8°. 16294
Beranger, P. J. de. Lyrical Poems, transl. by Young. N. Y., 1850. 12°. 919
Songs. Philad., 1844. 12°. 918
Berber, The. Mayo. N. Y., 1850. 12°. 15664
Berg, J. F. Lectures on Romanism. Philad., 1840. 12°. . . 9605
Berger, E. *(Pseudonym.)* See E. S. SHEPPARD.
Berington, J. Hist. of Abeillard and Heloisa. Lond., 1815. 4°. . 16036
The same. Philad., 1819. 8°. 16407
Hist. of Henry II, Richard I, and John. Dubl., 1790. 2 v. 8°. 5255
Lit. Hist. of Middle Ages. (2 copies.) Lond., 1846. 8°. . . 321
Berkeley, G. Works. Lond., 1837. 8°. 8759
The same. Lond., 1820. 3 v. 8°. 8760
Berkeley, H. Memoirs of Mme. D'Arblay. N. Y., 1844. 2 v. in 1. 12°. 6987
Berlin and Sans-Souci. A Novel. [Mundt.] N. Y., 1869. 8°. . 3079
Bermingham, J. Memoir of Father Mathew. N. Y., 1841. 12°. . 16336
Bernadotte, C. J., Memoirs of. Philippart. Bost., 1815. 8°. . . 16172
Bernard of Cluny. O Mother Dear Jerusalem, ed. Prime. N. Y., 1865. 12°. 292
Bernard, F., and Whiteing, R. Wonderful Escapes. N. Y., 1871. 12°. 10129
Bernays, L. J. Goethe's Faust, pt. 2, with other Poems. Lond., 1839. 8°. 1300
Berni, F. Orlando Innamorato, transl. by Rose. Lond., 1823. 8°. 892
Bernier, F. Travels in the Mogul Empire. Lond., 1826. 2 v. 8°. 16541
Berri, Duchess of, in La Vendée. Dermoncourt. Lond., 1833. 8°. 5666
Berry, M. Journals and Correspondence. 2d ed. Lond., 1866. 3 v. 8°. 7065
Bertha and Lily. E. O. Smith. N. Y., 1854. 12°. 15665
Berthre de Bournisseaux, P. V. J. Hist. of the Vendée War. Paris, 1802. 8°. 16251
Bertrams, The. A. Trollope. N. Y., 1859. 12°. 2107
Bertrand de Moleville, A. F. Memoirs of last year of reign of Louis XVI. Lond., 1797. 3 v. 8°. 16183
Bethune, G. W. British Female Poets. Philad., 1848. 8°. . . 946
Lays of Love and Faith, etc. Philad. [1847.] 8°. . . . 15050
Memoir of. Van Nest. N. Y., 1867. 12°. 7643
Bethune, J. E. D. Lives. (Libr. of U. K.) Lond., 1833. 8°. . . 6751
Specimens of Swedish and German Poetry. Lond., 1848. 8°. 921
Betrothed, The. Scott. Edinb., 1871. 8°. 1888
Betterton, T. Hist. of the English Stage. Bost., 1814. 8°. . . 1610
Beveridge, W. Private Thoughts on Religion. Ed. Stebbing. Lond., 1834. 2 v. 16°. 9492
Beyond the Breakers. Owen. Philad., 1870. 8°. 2693
Beza, T. Life of Calvin. (2 copies.) Philad., 1836. 12°. . . 7667
Biber, E. Life of Pestalozzi. Philad., 1833. 8°. 15356
Bible, Apology for the. Watson. N. Y., 1835. 8°. 17269
Astronomy of the. Mitchel. N. Y., 1863. 12°. 8915
Bards of the. Gilfillan. N. Y., 1851. 12°. 9886
Biography. Sears. N. Y., 1842. 8°. 17511

Bible, Commentary on the. Clarke. N. Y., 1840. v. 1, 3–5. 8°. . 17325
Comprehensive Dict. of the. Smith and Barnum. N. Y., 1869. 8°. 10058
Concordance to the. Cruden. Lond., 1867. 8°. 9836
Cottage; with Notes by Williams and Patton. Hartf'd., 1834. 2 v. 8°. 17315
Evidences of the. Burr. Bost., 1871. 12°. 9990
Exposition of the. Henry. N. Y., 1831. 6 v. 8°. 17309
Historical Geography of the. Coleman. Philad., 1850. 12°. 9884
Hist. of the. Gleig. N. Y., 1841. 2 v. 12°. 11012
Hist. of the. Sears. N. Y., 1845. 8°. 10011
Legends of Patriarchs and Prophets of the. Baring-Gould. N. Y., 1872. 8°. 1914
Night Scenes in the. March. Philad., 1869. 8°. 10012
Notes on the. Pres. Edwards. (Works, v. 9.) N. Y., 1830. 8°. 17184
The same. T. Scott. Bost., 1830. 6 v. 8°. 17330
Obligations of the World to the. Spring. N. Y., 1854. 12°. 17166
Opinions of Eminent Men on the. Lond., 1839. 12°. . . 9887
in our Public Schools, Right of the. Cheever. N. Y., 1854. 12°. 9146
and the School Fund, The. Clark. Bost., 1870. 16°. . . 9147
Smaller Dict. of the. W. Smith. Bost., 1866. 8°. . . . 9881
in Spain, The. Borrow. Philad., 1843. 8°. 2308
Old Testament, History of the. W. Smith. N. Y., 1866. 12°. 9837
Notes on Genesis, Exodus, Leviticus, Joshua, Judges. Bush. N. Y., 1841–44. 7 v. 12°. 9845
Speaker's Commentary. Lond., 1871. v. 1 in 2 pts. 8°. 10267

CONTENTS.—Pt. 1, Genesis, Exodus. 2, Leviticus-Deuteronomy.

Notes on Isaiah. Barnes. Bost., 1840. 3 v. 8°. . . 10016
New Testament, transl. by Tyndale, 1526, ed. Dabney. Andover, 1837. 12°. 9890
Hist. of Books of the. Stowe. Hartf'd., 1867. 8°. . 10020
How to study the. Alford. Lond., 1865–70. 3 v. 16°. 9838
Notes on the. Barnes. N. Y., 1836–52. 8 v. 12°. . 9858
Revision of English Version of. Lightfoot, Trench, and Ellicott. Ed. Schaff. N. Y., 1873. 8°. 10263
Synonyms of the. Trench. N. Y., 1855. 12°. . . 9891
Gospels, Origin of the. Tischendorf. Bost. [1867.] 16°. 9802
Studies in the. Trench. N. Y., 1867. 8°. . 10008
Paraphase and Notes on Romans, Corinthians, Galatians, Ephesians. Locke. Lond., 1801. 8°. . . . 9597
Lectures on Romans. Chalmers. N. Y., 1843. 8°. . 10010
Sermons on Corinthians. Robertson. Bost., 1860. 12°. 9927
Commentary on I Peter. Leighton. Edinb., 1840. 8°. . 10068
See, also, GOSPELS; PALESTINE; SCRIPTURE.

Biblical Archaeology. Jahn. N. Y., 1832. 8°. 10015
Legends of Mussulmans. Weil. N. Y., 1846. 12°. . . 9548
Repository. Andover and N. Y., 1831–50. 30 v. in 3 series. 8°. 12776
The same. 1st series, v. 1–7, 11, 12; 2d series, v. 1–9, 11, 12. 3d series, 6 v. 12821
Index, v. 1–24. (2 copies.)

Biblical Studies. Plumptre. Lond., 1870. 8°. 9889
Bibliotheca Sacra. Andover, 1844–72. 29 v. 8°. 12851
The same. v. 9–26. 12803
Index, v. 1–13.
Bickerstaff, I. Dr. Last; Love in a Village; Maid of the Mill; Padlock; Sultan. (Brit. Drama, v. 5.) Lond., 1804. 8°. 1633
Hypocrite; Maid of the Mill; Lionel and Clarissa; Love in a Village. (Oxberry's Plays, v. 2.) Bost., 1822. 24°. 1347
Love in a Village; Lionel and Clarissa; Maid of the Mill. (Brit. Theatre, v. 27.) Lond. 12°. 1345
The Padlock; Maid of the Mill; Hypocrite. N. Y. 8°. 1669
Bickersteth, E. H. Two Brothers, etc. N. Y., 1871. 12°. 822
Yesterday, To-day, and Forever. 2d ed. N. Y., 1869. 12°. 823
Bigelow, Jacob. Eolopoesis. American Rejected Addresses. N. Y. [1855.] 12°. 686
The Useful Arts. Bost., 1840. 2 v. 12°. 17003
Bigelow, John. Jamaica in 1850. N. Y., 1851. 12°. 8547
Memoir of Frémont. N. Y., 1856. 12°. 7397
Bigland, J. Letters on History. Philad., 1806. 8°. 15878
Sketch of Hist. of Europe. Lond., 1810. 2 v. 8°. 15915
Biglow Papers. [Lowell.] Cambr., 1848–67. 2 v. 16°. 729
Bingham, H. 21 Years in the Sandwich Islands. 3d ed. Hartf'd., 1849. 8°. 8082
Biographical Anecdotes of Eminent Persons. [Almon.] Lond., 1797. 3 v. 8°. 16372
Dictionary. Blake. Bost., 1848. 8°. 6908
of Scotsmen. Chambers. Glasgow, 1835. 4 v. 8°. 6862
Essays. Tuckerman. Bost., 1857. 8°. 3475
Memoirs of Celebrated Characters. Lamartine. N. Y., 1854–56. 3 v. 12°. 6725
For Contents, see LAMARTINE.
Sketches. Knapp. Bost., 1821. 8°. 7471
The same. H. Martineau, N. Y., 1869, 12°. 6748
of American Artists. Tuckerman. N. Y., 1867. 8°. 8126
of living characters of France. [de Loménie.] Philad., 1841. 12°. 7612
Biography, American. Belknap. N. Y., 1846. 3 v. 12°. 11762
Library of. Sparks. Bost., 1834–48. 25 v. 16°. 7250
For contents, see SPARKS.
Military. 1825. 12°. 16434
Naval. Cooper. Philad., 1846. 2 v. 12°. 7275
of Famous Americans of Recent Times. Parton. Bost., 1869. 12°. 7410
Appleton's Cyclopædia of. N. Y., 1856. 8°. 6909
Bible. Sears. N. Y., 1842. 8°. 17511
British Naval. Charnock. Lond., 1794–98. 6 v. 8°. 6897
of Brit. Painters and Sculptors. Cunningham. N. Y., 1839–40. 5 v. 12°. 11017
of the British Stage. N. Y., 1824. 12°. 7895

Biography of Celebrated Women. Ed. G. P. R. James. Philad., 1839. 2 v. 12°. 6701
Cottage Cyclopedia of. Pierce. Hartf'd., 1867. 8°. . .
of Distinguished Men of Modern Times. N. Y., 1840. 2 v. 12°. 11598
Eccentric. Bost., 1825. 12°. 6608
The same. Lond., 1826. 12°. 6703
of Eminent Christians. Frost. Hartf'd., 1860. 8°. . . 16400
of Eminent Englishmen [to 1688]. Cunningham. Glasg., 1836. 3 v. in 6. 8°. 6886
of Eminent Persons. (Libr. of Useful Knowledge.) Lond., 1833. 8°. 6751

CONTENTS.—Galileo, Kepler, Sir I. Newton, Mahomet, Wolsey, Sir E. Coke, Lord Somers, Caxton, Admiral Blake, Adam Smith, C. Niebuhr, Wren, Michael Angelo.

of Eminent Women of the Age. Hartf'd., 1868. 8°. . . 6905
of English Poets. Cary. Lond., 1846. 16°. 6599
The same. Johnson. Lond., 1831. 16°. . . . 6598
Exemplary and Instructive. Chambers. Edinb., 1836. 16°. . 6680
Female. Hays. Lond., 1803. 6 v. 12°. 14426
The same. Knapp. Philad., 1836. 12°. 16303
Cyclopædia of. Adams. Lond., 1869. 16°. . . . 6675
of Female Sovereigns. Jameson. N. Y., 1845–48. 2 v. 12°. 12095
of French Writers. Mrs. Shelley, etc. Philad., 1840. 2 v. 12°. 7615
of Georgian Era in Grt. Brit. Lond., 1832–34. 4 v. 8°. . . 6721
of Great Commanders. James. Philad., 1835. 2 v. 12°. . 6699
of Great Men, Lectures on. Myers. Lond., 1856. 8°. . . 6711
of Illustrious Men, New. (From Encyl. Brit.) Bost., 1857. 12°. 6715
Imaginative. Brydges. Lond., 1834. 2 v. 12°. . . . 3406
Indian. Thatcher. N. Y., 1840. 2 v. 12°. 11049
of Italian Poets. Stebbing. Lond., 1831. 3 v. 12°. . . 7775
of literary and scientific men of Italy. Mrs. Shelley, etc. Philad., 1841. 2 v. 12°. 7773
of Learned British Ladies. Ballard. Oxf'd., 1752. 4°. . . 16030
of Pious Women. Burder. Philad. [1836.] 8°. . . . 16361
of the Players. Galt. Bost., 1831. v. 1. 12°. . . . 16402
Popular. Peter Parley. N. Y., 1854. 12°. 6604
of Public Characters of 1800–1801. Lond., 1801. 8°. . . 16359
Romance of; Women Loved by Poets. Jameson. Lond., 1837. 2 v. 8°. 6709
Romantic, of Age of Eliz. Taylor. Philad., 1842. 2 v. 12°. 6746
of Scottish Poets. Lond., 1822. 3 v. in 4. 24°. . . . 6609
of Scottish Writers. Irving. Edinb., 1839. 2 v. in 1. 12°. . 6714
of Self-taught Men. Edwards, etc. Bost., 1846–47. 2 v. 12°. 6672
of Travellers. St. John. N. Y., 1841. 3 v. 12°. . . . 12097
Universal. Lempriere, ed. Lord. N. Y., 1825. 2 v. 8°. . 16315
Hand-Book of. Godwin. N. Y., 1852. 12°. . 6716
chronologically arranged [to 1600]. Platts. Lond., 1825–26. 5 v. 8°. 6892
of Wonderful Characters. Wilson. N. Y., 1834. 8°. . . 6906

Biology, Principles of. H. Spencer. N. Y., 1866–67. 2 v. 12°. . 8599

Bird, R. M. Adventures of Robin Day. Philad., 1839. 2 v. 12°. 15648
Calavar. Philad., 1835. 2 v. 12°. 15670
The Hawks of Hawk-Hollow. Philad., 1835. 2 v. 12°. . 15714
The Infidel. 2d ed. Philad., 1835. 2 v. 12°. 15724
Sheppard Lee. N. Y., 1836. 2 v. 12°. 15775
Birds, Architecture, Domestic Habits, and Faculties of. [Rennie.] Lond., 1831-35. 3 v. 12°. 8821
Natural Hist. of. [Rennie.] N. Y., 1840. 12°. . . . 11422
Nat. Hist. and Classification of. Swainson. Lond., 1836-37. 2 v. 16°. 6058
Popular Account of the Orders of. Figuier. Lond. [1869.] 8°. 8997
Water, of U. S. and Canada. Nuttall. Bost., 1834. 12°. . 8892
Births, Deaths, and Marriages. Hook. Philad., 1839. 2 v. 12°. . 15381
Bisaccioni, M. Novels. (Ital. Novelists, v. 4.) Lond., 1836. 12°. . 1902
Bishop, S. Poetical Works. Lond., 1796. 2 v. 4°. 15084
Bismarck, K. W. F. v., Life of. Hesekiel. N. Y., 1870. 8°. . . 7758
Bisset, R. Hist. of Reign of Geo. III. Balt., 1810. 4 v. 8°. . . 16105
Life of Burke. 2d ed. Lond., 1800. 2 v. 8°. 16342
Bits of Travel. [H. Hunt.] Bost., 1872. 12°. 8167
Bjornson, B. Arne. (2 copies.) Bost., 1869. 16°. 2615
The Happy Boy. (2 copies.) Bost., 1870. 16°. . . . 2617
Love and Life in Norway. Lond. 16°. 2715
The Railroad and Churchyard, etc. Bost., 1870. 16°. . . 2619
Black Dwarf, The. Scott. Edinb., 1870. 8°. 1870
Black-Forest Village Stories. Auerbach. N. Y., 1869. 12°. . . 3024
Black Watch, The. Picken. Philad., 1835. 2 v. 12°. . . . 15384
Blackgown Papers. Mariotti. Lond., 1846. v. 2. 12°. . . . 15383
Blacklock, T. Select Poems. Ed. Walsh. Philad., 1822. 24°. . 29
Blackmore, R. Creation. Philad., 1806. 12°. 14809
The same. With Life, by Sanford. Philad., 1819. 24°. 11
Blackstone, W. Commentaries on the Laws of England. Lond., 1783. v. 2-4. 8°. 9328
The same. N. Y., 1845. v. 2. 8°. 9331
The same. Ed. Sharswood. N. Y., 1872. 2 v. 8°. . 9395
Blackstone, The Comic. á Beckett. Lond. 16°. 4274
Blackwood's Magazine. Edinb. & N. Y., 1817-72. v. 1-4, 6-30, 32-112. 11620
The same. v. 1-18, 21, 24-26, 28, 33-91, 93-106. . . 11957
Blair, H., Account of Life of, etc., of. Hill. Philad., 1808. 8°. . 16352
Rhetoric and Belles-Lettres. Dubl., 1789. 2 v. 8°. . . 17524
The same. N. Y., 1815. 8°. 17526
Blair, R. The Grave. Bost., 1808. 16°. 820
Select Poems. Ed. Walsh. Philad., 1819. 24°. . . . 15
Blake, J. L. Biographical Dict. 8th ed. Bost., 1848. 8°. . . 6908
Blake, R., Life of. (Libr. of Useful Knowl.) Lond., 1833. 8°. , 6751
Blakeman, R. Essay on Credulity and Superstition. N. H., 1849. 12°. 8613
Blakiston, T. W. 5 Months on the Yang-Tsze. Lond., 1862. 8°. . 8008
Blanc, L. History of 1830-40; or, France under Louis Philippe. (2 copies.) Philad., 1848. 2 v. 8°. 5575
Blanchard, A. Book of Martyrs. Buffalo, 1852. 8°. 16401

Blanchard, L. Life and Remains of L. E. L. Philad., 1841. 2 v. 12°. 15239
Sketches from Life. (2 copies.) N. Y., 1846. 2 v. in 1. 12°. 3959
Blaquiere, E. Letters from Greece. Lond., 1828. 8°. . . . 16027
Bleak House. Dickens. N. Y., 1871. 16°. 2179
Bleecker, A. E. Posthumous Works. N. Y., 1793. 12°. . . . 15273
Bleek, W. H. I. Reynard the Fox in S. Africa; Hottentot Fables. Lond., 1864. 8°. 1891
Blennerhassett, H., Life of. Safford. Cincinn., 1853. 12°. . . 7357
Blessington, Lady. See M. GARDINER.
Blindness. Kitto. Lond., 1845. 12°. 8487
Blindpits. A Story of Scottish Life. N. Y., 1869. 12°. . . . 15386
Blithedale Romance. Hawthorne. Bost., 1862. 16°. . . . 2889
Blockade of Phalsburg. Erckmann-Chatrain. N. Y., 1871. 12°. . 2363
Bloomfield, R. Poems & Remains. Lond., 1822–27. 5 v. in 4. 12°. 1008
Blucher, G. L. v., Life and Campaigns of. Gneisenau and Marston. Lond., 1815. 8°. 7759
Blunt, H. Lectures on Abraham and Jacob. Philad., 1839. 12°. . 17353
on Hist. of St. Paul. Philad., 1839. 12°. . . 9909
Blunt, J. J. Essays. Lond., 1860. 8°. 3430
Sketch of the Reformation in England. Philad., 1837. 12°. . 6312
Boaden, J. Memoirs of Kemble. Philad., 1825. 8°. . . . 7998
Mrs. Siddons. Lond., 1827. 2 v. 8°. . 7969
The same. Philad., 1827. 8°. . . 7971
Boardman, H. A. The Bible in the Counting-House. Philad., 1859. 12°. 17305
The Bible in the Family. Philad., 1859. 12°. 17306
The Great Question. Philad. [1855]. 12°. . , , . 17346
Boardman, W. E. He that overcometh. Bost. [1869.] 12°. . . 17342
Boat Races, Oxford and Cambridge, 1829–69. Macmichael. Cambr., 1870. 16°. 9116
Boccaccio, G. The Decameron. Lond. (Bohn's ed.) 8°. . . . 473
Selected Novels. (Ital. Novelists, v. 1.) Lond., 1836. 12°. . 1899
Boeckh, A. Public Economy of Athens, ed. Lewis. 2d ed. Lond., 1842. 8°. 4430
Boelte, A. Mme. de Staël: a Novel. N. Y., 1869. 12°. . . . 3023
Boiardo, M. M. Orlando innamorato, transl. by Rose. Lond., 1823. 8°. 892
Stories. (Hunt's Ital. Poets.) N. Y., 1846. 12°. . . . 887
Boissy, T. G., Marquise de. Recollections of Byron. (2 copies.) N. Y., 1869. 12°. 7096
Boker, G. H. Poems of the War. Bost., 1864. 8°. 773
Bokhara, Mission to, 1843–45. Wolff. N. Y., 1845. 8°. . . . 8049
Boleyn, A., a dramatic poem. Milman. (Works, v. 3.) Lond., 1839. 16°. 997
Life of. Strickland. Philad., 1851. 8°. 5229
Memoirs of. Benger. Philad., 1822. 8°. 5239
Bolingbroke, Lord. See H. ST. JOHN.
Bolivar, S., Memoirs of. Ducoudray-Holstein. Bost., 1829. 8°. . 7699
Bombet, L. A. C. Lives of Haydn and Mozart, etc. Bost., 1839. 16°. 7881
Bonaparte Family, Hist. of the. [Lester.] N. Y., 1852. 8°. . . 5600
Bonaparte, Louis. On the Gov't of Holland. Lond., 1820. 3 v. 8°. 5877
Bonaparte, Louis Napoleon. See NAPOLEON III.

Bonaparte, Lucien. Charlemagne ; an Epic. Philad., 1815. 2 v. 16°. 13829
Memoirs of himself. Pt. 1. N. Y., 1836. 12°. 5507
Bonaparte, Napoleon. See NAPOLEON I.
Boniface, J. X. Picciola. N. Y., 1861. 12°. 2596
Bonneau, A. Life of Mme. de Miramion. Lond., 1870. 8°. . . . 7676
Bonneville, B. L. E. Adventures. See W. IRVING.
Bonnycastle, R. H. The Canadas in 1841. Lond., 1841. 2 v. 12°. . 16771
Bonstetten, C. V. de. The Man of the North and of the South. N. Y., 1864. 12°. 8552
Book of Common Prayer, Illustration of. Wheatley. Lond., 1849. 8°. 496
Book-Hunter. Burton. Ed. R. G. White. N. Y., 1863. 12°. . . 142
Book without a Name, The. Morgan. N. Y., 1841. 2 v. 12°. . 15387
Book of Snobs. Thackeray. (Works, v. 9.) Lond., 1872. 8°. . . 2197
Books and Reading. Porter. N. Y., 1871. 12°. 122
Ancient, Hist. of transmission of. I. Taylor. Lond., 1827. 8°. 244
See, also, READING.
Boone, D., Adventures of ; a Poem. Bryan. Harrisburg, 1813. 12°. 14928
Life of. Peck. (Sparks, v. 23.) Bost., 1847. 16°. . . . 7272
Booth, D. Art of Brewing. (Libr. of U. K.) Lond. [1835.] 8°, . 16468
Principles of English Composition. Lond., 1831. 12°. . . 9187
Boothby, H. Letters to Dr. Johnson. Lond., 1805. 16°. . . . 6925
Border Wars of Amer. Revolution. Stone. N. Y., 1845. 2 v. 12°. 12282
Borneo, Expedition to, 1843. Keppel. N. Y., 1846. 16°. . . . 8195
Borrow, G. Bible in Spain. Philad., 1843. 8°. 2308
Lavengro. (3 copies.) N. Y., 1851. 12°. 2157
The Romany Rye ; Sequel to Lavengro. N. Y., 1859. 8°. . 2316
The Zincali ; or, Gypsies of Spain. Lond., 1841. 2 v. 12°. . 17115
Boscana, G. Chinigchinich. N. Y., 1846. 12°. 16888
Bossuet, J. B. Hist. of France. Edinb., 1762. 4 v. 12°. . . 5523
Universal History. Dubl., 1785. 8°. 15934
Boston Bard, Poems of the. [Coffin.] Prov., 1826. 8°. . . . 15052
Book, The. Ed. Thatcher. Bost., 1836–37. 2 v. 12°. . . 15065
Lectures, 1870. Christianity and Scepticism. (2 copies.) Bost., 1870. 12°. 9996
Miscellany. Ed. Hale. Bost., 1842. v. 1. 8°. 14519
Tea-Party, Retrospect of the. N. Y., 1834. 12°. . . . 6013
Trip to, in 1838. [Wines.] Bost., 1838. 12°. 16846
Boswell, J. Account of Corsica. Glasg., 1768. 8°. 16718
Life of Johnson. (2 copies.) Bost., 1824. 5 v. 12°. . . 6926
The same. Dubl., 1792. 3 v. 8°. 7119
The same. Lond., 1840. 16°. 6936
The same. Ed. Croker. N. Y., 1837. 2 v. 8°. . . 7209
The same. v. 2. N. Y., 1840. 8°. 7211
Tour to the Hebrides. Philad., 1810. 8°. 8354
Botanic Garden, The ; a Poem. Darwin. Dubl., 1790–93. 2 v. 8°. 14791
Botanical Harmony. St. Pierre. Worc., 1797. 8°. 16976
Text-Book. Gray. N. Y., 1850. 12°. 8986
Botany, Physiological and Descriptive. Henslow. Lond., 1836. 16°. 6064
of Northern U. S., Manual of. Gray. N. Y., 1869. 8°. . . 8985

Both Sides of the Sea, On. [Charles.] N. Y., 1868. 12°. . . . 2469
Botta, A. C. L. Hand-Book of Universal Literature. Bost., 1863. 12°. 137
Rhode Island Book. Prov., 1841. 12°. 15004
Botta, C. Hist. of Italy under Napoleon. Lond., 1828. 2 v. 8°. . 4775
War of Independence. N. H., 1842. 2 v. 8°. . 6119
The same. Philad., 1820–21. 3 v. 8°. . 6121
Botta, V. Dante. N. Y., 1865. 12°. 7751
Bottari, G. A Novel. (Ital. Novelists, v. 4.) Lond., 1836. 12°. . 1902
Bounty, Mutineers of the. Lady Belcher. N. Y., 1871. 12°. . . 8324
Mutiny of the. [Barrow.] N. Y., 1840. 12°. 11033
Bourdaloue, L., in the Court of Louis XIV. Bungener. Bost., 1853. 12°. 9968
Bourgoing, J. F. de. Travels in Spain. Lond., 1789. 3 v. 8°. . 16665
Bourne, G. Picture of Slavery. Middletown, 1834. 12°. . . . 8468
Bourne, V. Poetical Works. Oxf'd., 1826. 8°. 818
Bourrienne, F. de. Memoirs of Napoleon. Philad., 1832. 8°. . 5631
Bouterwek, F. Hist. of Spanish Literature. Lond., 1847. 8°. . 323
Bowditch, N., Memoir of. By his Son. Bost., 1841. 12°. , . 7552
Bowdler, E. Poems and Essays. N. Y., 1811. 12°. 14776
Bowen, F. American Polit. Economy. N. Y., 1870. 8°. . . . 8640
Life of B. Lincoln. Bost., 1847. 16°. 7272
Otis. Bost., 1844. 16°. 7261
Sir W. Phips. Bost., 1837. 16°. 7256
Steuben. Bost., 1838. 16°. 7258
Bowen, H. L. Memoir of T. Burges. Prov., 1835. 8°. . . . 7362
Bower, A. Life of Luther. Philad., 1824. 8°. 6429
The same. 6512
Bower of Spring, The. Philad., 1817. 12°. 14906
Bowles, C. See C. B. SOUTHEY.
Bowles, S. Across the Continent. (2 copies.) Springf'ld., 1865. 12°. 8414
Our New West. Hartf'd., 1869. 8°. 8416
The Switzerland of America. Springf'ld., 1869. 12°. . . 8169
Bowles, W. L. Scenes of Days departed ; with Poems. Lond., 1837. 16°. 1179
Bowman, S. M., and Irwin, R. B. Sherman and his Campaigns. N. Y., 1865. 8°. 7402
Bowring, J. Ancient Poetry and Romances of Spain. (2 copies.) Lond., 1824. 8°. 915
Memoirs of Bentham. Edinb., 1842. 3 v. 8°. . . . 9718
Specimens of Russian Poets. Lond., 1821–23. 2 v. 12°. . 288
Boyd, A. K. H. Autumn Holidays. (2 copies.) Bost., 1865. 8°. . 3685
Counsel and Comfort. (2 copies.) Bost., 1864. 8°. . . 3683
Every-Day Philosopher. (2 copies.) Bost., 1863. 8°. . . 3681
Graver Thoughts of a Country Parson. (2 copies.) Bost., 1863–65. 2 v. 8°. 3677
Leisure Hours in Town. (2 copies.) Bost., 1862. 8°. . . 3675
Recreations of a Country Parson. (2 copies.) Bost., 1861. 2 v. 8°. 3671
Boydell, J. Illustrations of Shakspeare. N. Y., 1852. fol. . .
Boyhood of Extraordinary Men. Russell. Lond., 1853. 12°. . . 6754
Boyle, R. Treatise on Veneration, Things above Reason, and Style of the Scriptures. Ed. Rogers. Lond., 1835. 16°. . . . 9500

Boyse, S. Deity, a Poem. Lond., 1752. 8°. 14806

The same. Ed. Walsh. Philad., 1822. 24°. 25

Boz. See C. DICKENS.

Brace, C. L. Hungary in 1851. N, Y., 1852. 12°. 8316

The New West. N. Y., 1869. 12°. 8426

The Norse-Folk. N. Y., 1857. 12°. 8303

Races of the Old World. N. Y., 1863. 12°. 8965

Bracebridge Hall. Irving. N. Y., 1850. 12°. 4361

Brackenridge, Henry M. Hist. of the late War. Philad., 1836. 12°. 6002

Voyage to S. America. Balt., 1819. 2 v. 8°. 17127

Brackenridge, Hugh H. Modern Chivalry. Philad., 1804. 2 v. 12°. 15742

Brackett, A. G. Hist. of U. S. Cavalry. N. Y., 1865. 12°. . . 6102

Braddon, M. E. Aurora Floyd. N. Y., 1863. 8°. 2311

Dead-Sea Fruit. N. Y., 1868. 8°. 2674

Lady Audley's Secret. N. Y. 8°. 2673

Bradford, Alden. Hist. of Mass., 1775–89. Bost., 1825. 8°. . . 5849

Bradford, Alex. W. Am. Antiquities, etc. N. Y., 1843. 8°. . . 5954

Bradford, J. Writings. Lond. 12°. 9476

Bradford, W. J. A. Notes on the Northwest. N. Y., 1846. 12°. . 16863

[**Bradley, E.**] Adventures of Verdant Green. (2 copies.) N. Y. 1860–70. 12°. 9249

Nearer and Dearer. N. Y., 1864. 12°. 2431

Brahe, T., Life of. Brewster. N. Y., 1841. 12°. 11605

Brain, Functions of the. Gall. Bost., 1835. 6 v. 12°. . . . 12761

and Mind. Laycock. N. Y., 1869. 2 v. 8°. 8581

Brainard, J. G. C. Literary Remains. Hartf'd. [1832]. 12°. . . 14975

Occasional Pieces of Poetry. N. Y., 1825. 12°. . . . 14974

Poems, with Memoir. Hartf'd., 1846. 12°. 806

Brainerd, D., Life of. Peabody. Bost., 1837. 16°. 7257

Memoirs and Journal of. Edwards, ed. Dwight. N. H., 1822. 8°. 7632

[**Braithwait, R.**] Barnabee's Journal, ed. Haslewood. Lond., 1818. 12°. 14810

Brambletye House. H. Smith. N. Y., 1835. 12°. 15111

Brand, B. [Lady Dacre.] Tales of Peerage and Peasantry. N. Y., 1835. 2 v. 12°. 15598

Brand, J. Popular Antiquities of Grt. Brit. Lond., 1810. 8°. . . 16117

The same. Ed. Ellis. Lond., 1841–42. 3 v. 8°. . . 5138

The same. (Bohn's ed.) Lond., 1848–49. 3 v. 8°. . 504

Brande, W. T. Dict. of Science, Literature, and Art. (2 copies.) N. Y., 1848. 8°. . . . .

Brandenburg, Memoirs of House of. [Frederick II.] Lond., 1751. 12°. 16456

Brant, J., Life of. Stone. N. Y., 1838. 2 v. 8°. 5952

Brassey, T. Work and Wages. N. Y., 1872. 8°. 8628

Brave Lady, A. [Craik.] N. Y., 1870. 8°. 2682

Bravo, The. Cooper. Philad., 1831. 2 v. 12°. 2771

Brawnville Papers. Tyler. Bost., 1869. 12°. 3566

Bray, A. E. The Protestant. N. Y., 1829. 2 v. 12°. . . . 15557

Traditions of Devonshire. Lond., 1838. 3 v. 12°. . . 5266

Trials of the Heart. Philad., 1839. 2 v. 12°. . . . 15614

Brazil and the Brazilians. Kidder and Fletcher. Philad., 1857. 8°. 8460

Brazil, Description of. Conder. Lond., 1825. 2 v. 12°. . . . 7860
Geology and Phys. Geogr. of. Hartt. Bost., 1870. 8°. . . 9013
Journey in, 1865. Agassiz. Bost., 1868. 8°. 8461
Notices of, in 1828–29. Walsh. Bost., 1831. 2 v. 12°. . . 17134
Travels in, 1815–17. Prince Maximilian. Lond., 1820. 8°. . 8053
Travels in, 1817–20. Spix and Martius. Lond., 1824. 2 v. 8°. 8435
Breckenridge, J. Discussion with Hughes. Philad., 1836. 8°. . 9606
Breitmann, Hans. Ballads. [By C. G. Leland.] Philad., 1869. 12°. 4293
Bremer, F. A Diary; and Strife and Peace. N. Y., 1844. 8°. . 2652
Four Sisters. Philad. 12°. 15136
H—— Family; Tralinnan; Axel and Anna. N. Y., 1844. 8°. 2654
The same. N. Y., 1867. 8°. 2657
Hertha. N. Y., 1856. 12°. 2623
The Home. N. Y., 1843. 8°. 2656
The same. N. Y., 1844. 8°. 2653
The same. N. Y. 8°. 2657
The Midnight Sun. N. Y. 8°. 2655
The Neighbours. N. Y., 1844. 8°. 2654
The same. N. Y., 1850. 12°. 2622
President's Daughters. Bost., 1843. 12°. 2621
The same. N. Y., 1843. 2 pts. in 1. 8°. 2653
Strife and Peace. Lond., 1844. 16°. . , ... 2714
Works, tr. by Howitt. (Bohn's ed.) Lond., 1852–53. 4 v. 8°. 468

CONTENTS.—i, The Neighbours; Hopes; the Twins; the Solitary; the Comforter; Letter about Suppers; Tralinnan. ii, The President's Daughters; Nina. iii, The Home; Strife and Peace. iv, A Diary; the H—— Family; Axel and Anna.

Life, Letters, etc., of. C. Bremer. N. Y., 1868. 8°. . . 7586
Bremner, R. Excursions in Russia. Lond., 1839. 2 v. 8°. . . 8296
Brenton, E. P. Naval. Hist. of Grt. Brit. Lond., 1837. 2 v. 8°. . 5338
Brevio, G. Novels. (Ital. Novelists, v. 2.) Lond., 1836. 12°. . 1900
Brewer, A. Lingua. (Old Plays, v. 5.) Lond., 1825. 8°. . . 1512
Brewer, G. Hours of Leisure. Lond., 1806. 12°. 15176
Brewer, J. Patmos and the Seven Churches. Bridgep't., 1851. 8°. . 6450
Residence at Constantinople. N. H., 1830. 12°. 16636
Brewing, Art of. [Booth.] Lond. [1835.] 8°. 16468
Brewster, A. H. M. Compensation. Philad., 1860. 12°. . . . 2982
St. Martin's Summer. Bost., 1866. 8°. 8211
Brewster, D. Letters on Natural Magic. N. Y. [1840.] 12°. . . 11270
The same. N. Y., 1832. 12°. 12106
Life of Newton. N. Y., 1840. 12°. 11028
The same. N. Y., 1833. 12°. 11955
Martyrs of Science. N. Y., 1841. 12°. 11605
The same. 12272
Treatise on Optics. Lond., 1838. 16°. 6050
Bride of Fort Edward. [D. Bacon.] N. Y., 1839. 12°. . . . 15666
Lammermoor. Scott. Edinb., 1870. 8°. 1875
[**Bridge, H.**] Journal of an African Cruiser. N. Y., 1845. 12°. . 16291
Bridgewater Treatises. Philad. and Lond., 1836–37. 7 v. 8°. . . 16982

CONTENTS.—1, Chalmers, Adaptation of Nature to the Moral and Intellectual Constitution of Man; Prout, Chemistry, Meteorology, and Digestion. 2, Kidd, Adaptation of Nature to Physical Condition of Man; Whewell, Astronomy and General Physics; Bell, The Hand. 3, Kirby, Habits, etc., of Animals. 4, 5, Roget, Animal and Vegetable Physiology. 6, 7, Buckland, Geology and Mineralogy.

Brierre de Boismont, A. J. F. Hist. of Dreams, etc. Philad., 1855. 8°. 8763
Briffault, F. T. The Prisoner of Ham. Lond., 1846. 12°. . . . 5640
Brigands, Italian. Moens. N. Y., 1866. 12°. 8347
See, also, BANDITTI.
[**Briggs, C. F.**] Adventures of Harry Franco. N. Y., 1839. 2 v. 12°. 15646
Bankrupt Stories. N. Y., 1844. 8°. 15078
Briggs, G. N., Memoir of. Richards. Bost., 1856. 12°. . . . 7339
Brigham, A. Influence of Mental Cultivation on Health. Bost., 1833. 12°. 9171
Religion on Health. Bost., 1835. 12°. . . 17351
Bright, J. Speeches on the American Question. (2 copies.) Bost., 1865. 12°. 6111
on Questions of Public Policy. Lond., 1868. 2 v. 8°. 9351
Bright, Miss. [*Lyndon.*] Margaret. N. Y., 1868. 12°. . . . 15739
Brightwell, D. B. Concordance to Tennyson. Lond., 1869. 8°. . 1241
Brindley, C. Stable Talk and Table Talk. Philad., 1845. 12°. . 10163
Brinton, D. G. Myths of the New World. (2 copies.) N. Y., 1868. 8°. 1925
Brisbane, A. Social Destiny of Man. Philad., 1840. 12°. . . 17087
Brissot de Warville, J. P., and **Claviere, E.** Commerce of America with Europe. N. Y., 1795. 12°. 16045
Bristed, C. A. Five Years in an English University. N. Y., 1852. 2 v. 12°. 9237
The same. v. 2. 9239
The same. 3d ed. N. Y., 1873. 12°. 10240
Interference Theory of Gov't. N. Y., 1867. 12°. . . . 8539
The same. 2d ed. N. Y., 1868. 12°. 8540
Bristed, J. Resources of the Brit. Empire. N. Y., 1811. 8°. . . 16115
of the U. S. N. Y., 1818. 8°. 5846
Britain, Ancient, under the Romans. F. Thackeray. Lond., 1843. 2 v. 8°. 5069
Hist. of Celt, Roman, and Saxon. T. Wright. Lond., 1861. 8°. 5272
British Admirals, Lives of; with Naval Hist. to 1816. Campbell. Lond., 1817. 8 v. 8°. 6878
Lives of. Southey. Lond., 1833–40. 2 v. 16°. . 5171
Antiquities. Brand. Lond., 1848–49. 3 v. 8°. . . . 504
Cicero, The; a Selection of Speeches. Browne. Philad., 1810. 3 v. 8°. 9415
Colonies, Description of. Martin. Lond., 1836–44. 10 v. 16°. 7896
For Contents, see MARTIN.
Commerce, Hist. of. Craik. Lond., 1844. 3 v. 12°. . . 8783
Constitution, The. Brougham. Lond., 1861. 16°. . . . 4854
Costume, Hist. of. Planché. Lond., 1846. 12°. . . . 4814
Drama, The; a Collection. Lond., 1824. 2 v. 8°. . . . 1660
The same. Philad., 1833. 2 v. 8°. 1662
Drama, The. [Ed. W. Scott.?] Lond., 1804. 5 v. 8°. . . 1629
For Contents, see DRAMA.
Eloquence, Common-place Book of. (2 copies.) Lond., 1827. 24°. 9149
Select. Goodrich. N. Y., 1861. 8°. . . . 9426
Essayists. Ed. J. Ferguson. Lond., 1823. 40 v. 12°. . . 3109

CONTENTS.—1-4, Tatler. 5-12, Spectator. 13-15, Guardian. 16-18, Rambler. 19, Idler. 20-22, Adventurer. 23-25, World. 26-27, Connoisseur. 28-29, Mirror. 30, 31, Lounger. 32-34, Observer. 35-37, Knox's Essays. 38-40, Knox's Winter Evenings.

The same (wanting v. 6). 3149

British Female Poets. Bethune. Philad., 1848. 8°. 946
and Foreign Review. Lond., 1835–44. v. 1–16. 8°. . . . 11440
Military Commanders, Lives of. Gleig. Lond., 1831–32. 3 v. 16°. 5771
For Contents, see GLEIG.
Novelists. Masson. Bost., 1859. 12°. 51
Orators of the Age. Francis. N. Y., 1847. 16°. 6697
Painters and Sculptors, Lives of. Cunningham. N. Y., 1839–40. 5 v. 12°. 11017
Plutarch, The. 3d ed. Lond., 1791. 8 v. 12°. 14006
Plutarch, The Modern. Taylor. N. Y., 1846. 16°. 6678
Poets. Ed. J. Bell. Lond., 1807. 52 v. 24°. 246
For Contents, see BELL.
Golden Leaves from. Hows. N. Y., 1865. 12°. . 1099
Homes and Haunts of. Howitt. N. Y., 1847. 2 v. 12°. 6600
Lives and Works of. S. Johnson. Dubl., 1804. 8 v. 8°. 15095
For Contents, see JOHNSON.
Selections from. Halleck. N. Y., 1840. 2 v. 12°. . 11587
Select Works of, Chaucer to Jonson. Ed. Southey. Lond., 1831. 8°. 1302
Select Works of, Jonson to Beattie. Aikin. Philad., 1839. 8°. 1304
Select Works of, Falconer to Scott. Ed. Frost. Philad., 1838. 8°. 1306
The same. Southey to Croly. Ed. Frost. Philad., 1843. 8°. 1308
Works of. Sanford & Walsh. Philad., 1819–23. 50 v. 24°. 1
For Contents, see E. SANFORD.
Portraits. Lodge. Lond., 1849–50. 8 v. 8°. 515
Prose Writers. Bost., 1820. 8 v. 16°. 3839

CONTENTS.—1, H. Walpole, Reminiscences and Walpoliana. 2, Burns, Letters. 3, Goldsmith, Essays and the Bee. 4, T. Gray, Letters. 5, Bacon and Clarendon, Essays. 6, Lady Russell, Letters. 7, Cowley and Shenstone, Essays. 8, S. Johnson, Sermons.

Reformers, Writings of the. Lond. 8 v. 12°. 9476

CONTENTS.—1, Bradford. 2, Latimer. 3, Ridley; Philpot. 4, Hooper. 5, Knox. 6, Becon. 7, Tindal; Frith; Barnes. 8, Cranmer; Rogers; Saunders; Taylor; Careless.

Senate, Eloquence of the, 1625–1802. Ed. Hazlitt. Brooklyn, 1810. 2 v. 8°. 9423
Spy, Letters of the. Wirt. N. Y., 1832. 12°. 6074
Stage, Biogr. of the. N. Y., 1824. 12°. 7895
Statesmen, Lives of. Forster, etc. Lond., 1831–39. 7 v. 16°. 5759
For Contents, see FORSTER.
of time of Geo. III. See BROUGHAM.
Theatre. See THEATRE.
Tourists, The. Mavor. Lond., 1798. 5 v. 12°. 8181
Worthies, Cabinet Portrait Gallery of. Lond., 1845–46. 8 v. 12°. 6615
See, also, ENGLAND; GREAT BRITAIN.

Brittany, Ramble into, 1869. Musgrave. Lond., 1870. 2 v. 8°. . 8371
Broad Stone of Honour. Digby. Lond., 1844. 12°. 4620
Brocklesby, J. Elements of Meteorology. N. Y., 1849. 12°. . . 8894
[**Brockway, T.**] The Gospel Tragedy. Worc., 1795. 12°. . . 14976

Brockwell, C. Hist. of Portugal. Lond., 1726. 8°. 16165
[**Bronte, A.**] Tenant of Wildfell Hall. N. Y., 1857. 12°. . . . 2557
Bronte, C. Jane Eyre. (4 copies.) N. Y., 1869–72. 12°. . . 2546
The Professor. (2 copies.) N. Y., 1861–68. 12°. . . . 2555
Shirley. Lond., 1870. 16°. 2550
The same. (2 copies.) N. Y., 1856–60. 12°. . . . 2551
Villette. (2 copies.) N. Y., 1856. 12°. 2553
Life of. Gaskell. N. Y., 1857. 2 v. 12°. 6985
[**Bronte, E.**] Wuthering Heights. N. Y., 1857. 12°. . . . 2419
[**Brooke, F. M.**] History of Emily Montague. Lond. 4 v. 12°. . 15422
Brooke, H. Brookiana. Lond., 1804. 2 v. 16°. 3810
Fool of Quality. Lond., 1777. 5 v. 12°. 1701
The same. Ed. C. Kingsley. Lond., 1859. 2 v. 8°. . 2011
Gustavus Vasa. (Brit. Drama, v. 1, pt. 2.) Lond., 1804. 8°. . 1630
Brooke, S. A. Life of Robertson. (2 copies.) Bost., 1865. 2 v. 12°. 7603
Brooke, T. H. Hist. of St. Helena. Lond., 1808. 8°. . . . 16168
Brooke and Brooke Farm. Martineau. Bost., 1832. 12°. . . . 14610
Brooks, C. S. The Gordian Knot. N. Y., 1868. 8°. 2308
Brooks, J. G. and **M. E.** Rivals of Este and other Poems. N. Y., 1829. 12°. 14977
Brooks, Maria. Zóphiël. Bost., 1834. 16°. 720
Brooks, N. C. Literary Amaranth. Philad., 1840. 12°. . . . 15274
Scriptural Anthology. Balt. [1836.] 12°. 14927
Broome, R. The Jovial Crew. (Old Plays, v. 10.) Lond., 1826. 8°. 1517
Broome, W. Poetical Works. Ed. Bell. Lond., 1807. 24°. . . 530
The same. Ed. Johnson. Dubl., 1804. 8°. . . . 15099
Brothers in Unity. See YALE COLLEGE.
Brougham, H. The British Constitution. 2d ed. Lond., 1861. 16°. 4854
Crit. and Miscellaneous Writings. (2 copies.) Philad., 1841. 2 v. 12°. 3202
Dialogues on Instinct. Lond., 1844. 12°. 8488
Discourse of Natural Theology. Philad., 1835. 12°. . . 16981
Discourse on the Objects, etc., of Science. N. Y. [1840.] 12°. 11779
Hist. Sketches of Statesmen of the Time of Geo. III. 1st Series. Philad., 1840. 2 v. 12°. 6733
The same. 1st and 2d Series. Philad., 1839. 4 v. 12°. 6735
The same. 3d Series. New ed. Lond., 1845. 2 v. 12°. 6613
Letters and Speeches. Philad., 1840. 2 v. 12°. . . . 9271
Lives of Men of Letters and Science of Time of Geo. III. Philad., 1845–46. 2 v. 12°. 6739
Opinions of, as exhibited in his writings. Paris, 1841. 8°. . 9341
Political Philosophy. Lond., 1844. 3 v. 8°. 8680
Sketches of Public Characters, Discourses, etc. Philad., 1839. 2 v. 12°. 6741
Speeches on Questions relating to Public Interests; with Dissertation on Eloquence of the Ancients. Edinb., 1838. 4 v. 8°. 9337
Life and Times of. By himself. N. Y., 1871–72. 3 v. 12°. . 6772
Brown, C. B. Edgar Huntly. Philad., 1799. 3 v. 12°. . . . 15293

Brown, C. B. Novels. Bost., 1827. 7 v. 12°. 15296

CONTENTS.—1, Wieland. 2, 3, Arthur Mervyn. 4, Ormond. 5, Jane Talbot. 6, Clara Howard. 7, Edgar Huntly.

Wieland. N. Y., 1798. 12°. 15292
Life of. Prescott. Bost., 1834. 16°. 7250

Brown, Captain John., Public Life of. Redpath. Bost., 1860. 12°. . 7393
See, also, HARPER'S FERRY.

Brown, John (of Cambr., Engl.). Gleanings from Life's Harvest. N. Y., 1859. 12°. 16358

Brown, John, M.D. Horæ Subsecivæ. Edinb., 1859–61. 2 v. 8°. 3687
Spare Hours. (2 copies.) Bost., 1866. 2 v. 8°. 3689

Brown, John W. Life of L. da Vinci. Lond., 1828. 8°. 7919

Brown, Samuel G. Life of Choate. (2 copies.) 2d ed. Bost., 1870. 12°. 7333
Works of Choate, with Memoir. (2 copies.) Bost., 1862. 2 v. 8°. 9668

Brown, Solyman. Dental Hygeia. N. Y., 1838. 12°. 14979
Dentologia. N. Y., 1840. 8°. 15051
Essay on Amer. Poetry, with Miscellaneous Pieces. N. H., 1818. 12°. 14978

Brown, Thos. Inquiry into Cause and Effect. Andover, 1822. 8°. 8728
Lectures on Philosophy of the Mind. Hallowell, 1829. 2 v. 8°. 17061

Brown, Thos. N. Life of Hugh Miller. N. Y., 1860. 12°. . . . 6978

[**Browne, C. F.**] Artemus Ward; his Travels. N. Y., 1865. 12°. . 4291

Browne, Dunn, in Foreign Parts. [Fiske.] Bost., 1857. 12°. . . 16568

Browne, J. Ross. American Family in Germany. N. Y., 1866. 8°. 8315
Etchings of a Whaling Cruise, etc. N. Y., 1846. 8°. . . . 8080
Yusef; a Crusade in the East. N. Y., 1855. 12°. 8238

Browne, M. Chaucer's England. Lond., 1869. 2 v. 16°. . . . 215

Browne, Sir T. Christian Morals. Lond., 1756. 12°. 17288
Miscellaneous Works. [Ed. Young.] Cambr., 1831. 12°. . 3906
Religio Medici, Christian Morals, Urn-Burial, etc. Bost., 1862. 8°. 3902
Works, ed. Wilkin. Lond., 1835–36. 4 v. 8°. 3986

CONTENTS.—1, Life; Letters; Journals. 2, Religio Medici. 2, 3, Pseudodoxia Epidemica (Vulgar Errors). 3, Garden of Cyrus; Hydriotaphia (Urn-Burial), etc. 4, Repertorium, or Antiquities of Norwich; Letter to a Friend; Christian Morals; Miscellanies.

The same. v. 1. Lond., 1836. 8°. 3990

Browne, Thos. The British Cicero. Philad., 1810. 3 v. 8°. . . 9415

[**Brownell, H. H.**] Lyrics of a Day. N. Y., 1864. 12°. 772

Browning, E. B. Aurora Leigh. (2 copies.) N. Y., 1857. 16°. . 1151
Drama of Exile: and other Poems. N. Y., 1845. 2 v. 12°. . 1148
Essays on the Poets. (2 copies.) N. Y., 1863. 16°. 39
Last Poems. With Memorial, by Tilton. (2 copies.) N. Y., 1862. 16°. 1153
Poems. N. Y., 1858. 2 v. 12°. 1146
Prometheus Bound, Casa Guidi Windows, etc. N. Y., 1851. 16°. 1150

Browning, R. Balaustion's Adventure. Bost., 1871. 16°. . . . 1143
Bells and Pomegranates. Lond., 1841–46. 8 pts. in 1. 8°. . 1259
Dramatis Personæ. Bost., 1864. 16°. 1138
Fifine at the Fair, etc. Bost., 1872. 16°. 1145
Men and Women. Bost., 1869. 16°. 1134

Browning, R. Paracelsus. Lond., 1835. 16°. 1135
Poems. Bost., 1850. 2 v. 16°. 1132
Prince Hohenstiel-Schwangau. Lond., 1871. 16°. 1144
The Ring and the Book. (2 copies.) Bost., 1869. 2 v. 16°. . 1139
Sordello. Lond., 1840. 16°. 1136
Sordello, Strafford, Christmas-Eve, and Easter-Day. Bost., 1864. 16°. 1137
Browning, W. S. Hist. of the Huguenots in the 16th Century. Lond., 1829. 2 v. 8°. 6485
The same. 1598–1838. (2 copies.) Paris, 1839. 8°. 6487
Brownlee, W. C. Letters on the Rom. Cath. Controversy. (2 copies.) N. Y., 1834. 8°. 9607
Brownlow, W. G. Rise and Decline of Secession. Philad., 1862. 12°. 6108
Brownson, O. A. The American Republic. N. Y., 1866. 8°. . . 6177
Charles Elwood. Bost., 1840. 16°. 15676
Quarterly Review. Bost., 1844–46. 3 v. 8°. 14251
The same. New Series. Bost., 1849–50. v. 3, 4. 8°. . 14256
Bruce, James, Life of. Head. N. Y., 1841. 12°. 11603
The same. St. John. N. Y., 1841. 12°. 11043
Travels to Source of the Nile. Dubl., 1790–91. 6 v. 8°. . 8092
The same. (Mavor, v. 14.) Lond., 1797. 12°. . . 13857
Bruce, James, (Earl of Elgin,) Mission of, to China, etc. Oliphant. Edinb., 1859. 2 v. 8°. 8006
Bruce, M. Select Poems. Ed. Walsh. Philad., 1822. 24°. . . 31
Bruce, P. H., Memoirs of. By himself. Dubl., 1783. 8°. . . . 16375
Bruce, Days of; a Story. Aguilar. N. Y., 1857. 2 v. 12°. . . 2525
[**Bruen, M.**] Journal of a Tour in Italy. N. Y., 1824. 8°. . . 16736
Brummell, G., Life of. Jesse. Philad., 1844. 8°. 6826
Brunel, I. K., Life of. By his Son. Lond., 1870. 8°. 7159
Brunton, M. Emmeline, etc. With Memoir. N. Y., 1819. 12°. . 15426
Brutus. Foreign Conspiracy against U. S. [Morse.] N. Y., 1835. 12°. 17278
Bryan, D. Mountain Muse. Harrisonburg, 1813. 12°. . . . 14928
Bryant, E. What I saw in California. N. Y., 1848. 12°. . . . 16889
Bryant, J. D. Redemption. Philad., 1859. 12°. 17543
Bryant, W. C. The Fountain and other Poems. N. Y., 1842. 12°. . 693
Letters from the East. N. Y., 1869. 12°. 8239
of a Traveller. 2d ed. N. Y., 1850. 12°. . . . 8320
Poems. N. Y., 1832. 12°. 689
The same. Bost., 1834. 12°. 690
The same. 4th ed. Philad., 1848. 8°. 927
The same. N. Y., 1857. 2 v. 12°. 691
Selections from American Poets. N. Y., 1841. 12°. . . . 11586
Thirty Poems. (2 copies.) N. Y., 1864. 12°. 694
etc. The Talisman. N. Y., 1833. 3 v. 12°. 4132
Brydges, Sir E. Autobiography. Lond., 1834. 2 v. 8°. . . . 7136
Imaginative Biography. Lond., 1834. 2 v. 12°. . . . 3406
Brydone, P. Tour through Sicily and Malta. Edinb., 1791. 2 v. 12°. 16731
Bubbles from the Brunnen of Nassau. [Head.] N. Y., 1845. 12°. . 8366

Buccaneers, The. N. Y., 1827. 2 v. 12°. 15667
of America, Hist. of the. N. Y., 1826. 3 v. 12°. . . . 6009
The same. 13842
Buchanan, G. Hist. of Scotland. Continued by Watkins. Lond. 2 v. 8°. 5406
Buchanan, Jas. Sketches of the Indians. N. Y., 1824. 2 v. in 1. 12°. 5749
[**Buchanan, Pres't. Jas.**] Mr. Buchanan's Administration. N. Y., 1866. 8°. 6192
Life of. Horton. N. Y., 1856. 12°. 7332
Buck, Rev. Chas. Anecdotes. N. Y., 1831. 2 v. in 1. 8°. . . 15826
The same. N. Y., 1841. 12°. 15827
Bucke, Chas. Beauties and Sublimities of Nature. Lond., 1837. 3 v. 8°. 16990
The same. Ed. Page. N. Y., 1842. 12°. 11747
Book of Human Character. Lond., 1837. 2 v. 16°. . . 4329
of Table-Talk. Lond., 1836. 2 v. 16°. 4327
Ruins of Ancient Cities. N. Y., 1841. 2 v. 12°. 11609
Buckingham, Duke of. See G. VILLIERS.
Buckingham, J. S. America. Lond. [1841.] 3 v. 8°. . . . 5857
The same. N. Y., 1841. 2 v. 8°. 16843
Notes on Lectures of. Hildreth. N. Y., 1838. 12°. . . . 16279
Buckingham, Joseph T. Specimens of Newspaper Literature. Bost., 1850. 2 v. 12°. 125
Buckland, W. Geology and Mineralogy. Philad., 1837. 2 v. 8°. . 16987
Buckle, H. T. Essays, with Biogr. Sketch. N. Y., 1863. 12°. . . 3219
Hist. of Civilization in England. (2 copies.) N. Y., 1858–66. 2 v. 8°. 5065
Buddhist Nihilism, with transl. of Buddha's "Path of Virtue." N. Y., 1872. 8°. 3733
Budget of the Bubble Family. Lady Bulwer-Lytton. N. Y., 1840. 2 v. 12°. 15389
Büchner, L. Man in the Past, Present, and Future. Lond., 1872. 8°. 8993
Buenos Ayres, Five Years (1820–25) in. Lond., 1825. 8°. . . . 17132
See, also, BRAZIL.
Büsching, J. G. G. Popular Traditions. (German Novelists, v. 2.) Lond., 1826. 12°. 1896
Buffum, E. G. Sights and Sensations in France, Germany, etc. N. Y., 1869. 12°. 8272
Buffon, G. L. L. de, etc. Natural Hist. Ed. J. Wright. Lond., 1831. 4 v. 8°. 8801
Bulfinch, T. Age of Chivalry. Bost., 1861. 12°. 1910
Fable. Bost., 1863. 12°. 1909
Legends of Charlemagne. Bost., 1864. 12°. 1911
Bull, L. C. A Child's Poems. Hartf'd., 1872. 12°. 14929
Bulla. *(Pseudonym.)* Beauties of Brother Bullus. N. Y., 1812. 12°. 15658
Bulls, Irish, Essay on. Edgeworth. (Works, v. 2.) Bost., 1824. 8°. 15336
Bulwer-Lytton, E. L. Alice. (2 copies.) N. Y., 1838. 2 v. 12°. . 2072
Asmodeus at large. Philad., 1833. 12°. 2147
Caxtoniana: a Series of Essays. N. Y., 1864. 12°. . . . 3216
The Caxtons. N. Y., 1860. 12°. 2133
The same. Philad., 1860. 2 v. 12°. 2134

Bulwer-Lytton, E. L. Chairolas. Philad., 1836. 12°. 2149
Crit. and Misc. Writings. (2 copies.) Philad., 1841. 2 v. 12°. 3212
Devereux. (2 copies.) N. Y., 1829. 2 v. 12°. 2052
The same. N. Y., 1829. 2 v. in 1. 12°. 2056
The Disowned. Philad., 1868. 12°. 2038
Dramas and Poems. Bost., 1863. 16°. 976
Dramatic Works. Leipz., 1860. 2 v. in 1. 16°. . . . 1446
Duchess de la Valliere: a Play. (2 copies.) N. Y., 1836. 12°. 1443
England and the English. N. Y., 1833. 2 v. 12°. 3209
The same. 4828
Ernest Maltravers. N. Y., 1837. 2 v. 12°. 2069
The same. 2 v. in 1. 12°. 2071
Eugene Aram. (2 copies.) N. Y., 1832. 2 v. 12°. . . . 2059
Falkland. N. Y., 1830. 12°. 2050
The same. N. Y., 1835. 12°. 2150
Godolphin. N. Y., 1840. 2 v. 12°. 2153
Harold. Lond., 1853. 8°. 2152
The same. Philad., 1871. 16°. 2037
Last of the Barons. Philad., 1861. 2 v. 12°. 2081
The same. Philad., 1867. 2 v. in 1. 12°. 2083
Last Days of Pompeii. Lond., 1854. 12°. 2064
The same. (2 copies.) N. Y., 1835. 2 v. in 1. 12°. . 2065
Leila; Calderon, the Courtier; Pilgrims of the Rhine. Philad., 1868. 12°. 2036
Lost Tales of Miletus. (2 copies.) N. Y., 1866. 12°. . . 837
Lucretia. Lond., 1853. 8°. 2144
Miscellaneous Prose Works. N. Y., 1868. 2 v. 12°. . . 3217
My Novel. N. Y. 8°. 2315
The same. (2 copies.) N. Y., 1860. 2 v. 12°. . . 2136
The same. N. Y. 8°. [Imperfect.] 2309
The New Timon. Philad., 1847. 12°. 836
Night and Morning. N. Y., 1841. 2 v. in 1. 12°. . . . 2151
The Oxonians. N. Y., 1830. 2 v. 12°. 2145
Paul Clifford. N. Y., 1830. 2 v. 12°. 2057
The same. Philad., 1868. 12°. 2035
Pelham. Lond. 12°. 2051
The same. Leipz., 1842. 16°. 2034
Pilgrims of the Rhine. N. Y., 1834. 12°. 2063
The Rebel, and other Tales, etc. N. Y., 1835. 12°. . . . 3211
Rienzi. N. Y., 1836. 2 v. in 1. 12°. 2078
The same. 2148
The same. Philad., 1836. 2 v. 12°. 2079
Siamese Twins, with other Poems. N. Y., 1831. 12°. . . 835
Strange Story. Bost., 1862. 12°. 2143
Strange Story; the Haunted and the Haunters. Philad., 1868. 12°. 2084
The Student. N. Y., 1836. 2 v. in 1. 12°. 2068
The same, v. 2. N. Y., 1832. 12°. 2067
What will he do with it? Philad., 1860. 3 v. 12°. . . . 2140
The same. (2 copies.) Philad., 1871–72. 2 v. 16°. . 2039

Bnlwer-Lytton, E. L. Zanoni. N. Y., 1842. 2 v. 12°. 2076

Bulwer-Lytton, Robert. (Owen Meredith.) Lucile. (2 copies.) Bost., 1866. 16°. 1180

New Poems. Bost., 1868. 2 v. 16°. 1182

Ring of Amasis. N. Y., 1863. 12°. 2154

Serbski Pesme; National Songs of Servia. Lond., 1861. 16°. 1184

Bulwer-Lytton, Lady Rosina. Budget of the Bubble Family. N. Y., 1840. 2 v. 12°. 15389

Cheveley. N. Y., 1839. 2 v. 12°. 15396

Bulwer, H. L. E. France, social, literary, political. N. Y., 1834. 2 v. 12°. 5527

The same. Lond., 1834. 2 v. 12°. 5451

Life of Palmerston. Philad., 1871. 2 v. 12°. 6775

Bungener, L. F. The Preacher and the King. Bost., 1853. 12°. . 9968

The Priest and the Huguenot. Bost., 1856. 2 v. 12°. . . 2647

Bunn, A. The Stage. Philad., 1840. 2 v. 12°. 1614

Bunsen, C. C. J. Life of Niebuhr. N. Y., 1852. 12°. . . . 7762

Memoir of. By his Widow. Lond., 1868. 2 v. 8°. . . . 7756

Bunyan, J. Holy War. Ed. Burder. Hartf'd., 1850. 12°. . . 9948

Jerusalem Sinner Saved, etc. N. Y., 1846. 16°. . . . 9545

Pilgrim's Progress. Ed. T. Scott. Hartf'd., 1833. 12°. . . 9813

The same. Northampton, 1826. 8°. 17267

Lectures on, and on Pilgrim's Progress. Cheever. N. Y., 1845. 8°. 10037

Life and Times of. Philip. N. Y., 1839. 12°. 7597

Buonarotti, Michael Angelo, und Raphael. Grimm. Bost. 12°. . 9614

considered as a Poet. Taylor. Lond., 1840. 12°. . . . 7506

Life of. (Libr. of Useful Knowl.) Lond., 1833. 8°. . . . 6751

The same. Duppa. Lond., 1846. 8°. 345

The same. Grimm. Bost., 1866. 2 v. 12°. . . . 7957

The same. Harford. Lond., 1858. 2 v. 8°. . . . 7989

Burder, H. F. Mental Discipline; Hints to Theol. Students. N. Y., 1830. 12°. 17035

Burder, S. Memoirs of Pious Women. Philad. [1836.] 8°. . . 16361

[Burdett, C. D.] English Fashionables abroad. Bost., 1828. 2 v. 12°. 15427

Burges, T., Memoir of. Bowen. Prov., 1835. 8°. 7362

Burghley, W. Cecil, *Lord,* Life of. Lond., 1831. 16°. . . . 5759

Burgoyne, J. Dramatic and Poetical Works. Lond., 1808. 2 v. 12°. 1450

Burke, E. Correspondence, 1744–97. Lond., 1844. 4 v. 8°. . . 7197

European Settlements in America. Lond., 1757. 2 v. 8°. . 16129

The same. (2 copies.) Bost., 1835. 8°. 5946

Works. Bost. & N. Y., 1806–13. 6 v. 8°. 9740

The same. N. Y., 1837. 3 v. 8°. 9560

The same. Bost., 1839. 9 v. 8°. 9649

CONTENTS.—1, Vindication of Natural Society; on the Sublime and Beautiful; Observations on "The Present State of the Nation"; Cause of the Present Discontents; Speech on Amer. Taxation. 2, Speeches at Bristol and on E. India Bill, and on Nabob of Arcot's Debts. 3, Speech on the Army Estimates; Reflections on the Revolution in France; Appeal to the Old Whigs; Letters on the Irish Catholics. 4, On French Affairs; on the Conduct of the Minority; Preface to Brissot's Address; Thoughts on Scarcity; Letters on a Regicide Peace; etc. 5, Letter on a Regicide Peace; Miscellaneous Letters on Irish and American Affairs: Tracts on the Popery Laws; Fragments and Notes of Speeches in Parliament; Hints on the Drama; English History. 6, Reports on Indian Affairs; Articles of Charge against Hastings. 7, 8, Speeches on Impeachment of Hastings. 9, European Settlements in America; Correspondence with Dr. Laurence.

Burke, E. Beauties of. Lond. 16°. 3527
a historical study. Morley. Lond., 1867. 8°. 6811
Life of. Bisset. Lond., 1800. 2 v. 8°. 16342
The same. P. Burke. Lond., 1853. 8°. 6812
Memoir of. Prior. Lond., 1839. 8°. 6809
Burke, J. W. Life of R. Emmett. Charleston, 1852. 12°. . . 6682
Burkhard, J. G. Philosophy of Nat. Hist. N. Y., 1804. 12°. . . 16937
Burlamaqui, J. J. Nat. and Politic Law. Philad., 1830. 2 v in 1. 8°. 8635
Burmah, Popular Description of. Conder. Lond. 12°. . . . 7843
Burman Empire, Journal of Resid. in, 1796–97. Cox. Lond., 1821. 8°. 11506
Burmese War, Narrative of the, 1824–26. Snodgrass. Lond., 1827. 8°. 6504
Burnes, A. Cabool. Philad., 1843. 8°. 8050
Burnap, G. W. Life of L. Calvert. Bost., 1846. 16°. . . . 7268
Burnet, G. Hist. of my own Time. Edinb., 1753. 6 v. 12°. . . 4817
The same. Lond., 1818. 4 v. 8°. 5352
the Reformation of the Church of England. (2 copies.) Lond., 1825. 3 v. in 6. 12°. . 6357
Lives of Hale, Bedell, and Rochester. Lond. 24°. . . . 6677
Burney, C., Memoirs of. D'Arblay. Philad., 1833. 8°. . . . 7139
Burney, F. See F. D'ARBLAY.
Burns, R. Correspondence with Clarinda. N. Y. [1843.] 12°. . . 7043
Letters. Bost., 1820. 16°. 3840
Poems. 2d ed. Edinb., 1793. 2 v. 8°. 1236
Poetical Works. Leipz., 1845. 16°. 959
The same. Ed. Walsh. Philad., 1822. 2 v. 24°. . . 32
Tam O'Shanter. (Illustrated.) N. Y., 1868. 4°. . . . .
Works. Philad., 1801. 4 v. 12°. 14777
Works, with Life, by Currie. Philad., 1837. 8°. . . . 1281
Works, with Life, by Cunningham. Bost., 1834–35. 4 v. 12°. 584
The same. Lond., 1840. 8°. 1279
The same. Bost., 1852. 8°. 1280
Genius and Character of. J. Wilson. N. Y., 1861. 12°. . . 7044
Life of. Lockhart. N. Y., 1831. 12°. 6951
Life and Land of. Cunningham. N. Y., 1841. 12°. . . 7042
Burr, A. Private Journal, 1808–12. N. Y., 1838. 2 v. 8°. . . 7352
Arguments on Trial of. Wirt. Richmond, 1808. 12°. . . 7487
Life and Times of. Parton. N. Y., 1858. 12°. . . . 7356
Memoirs of. Davis. N. Y., 1836. 2 v. 8°. 7354
Reports of Trials of. Philad., 1808. 2 v. 8°. 7358
[**Burr, E. F.**] Ad Fidem ; Evidences of the Bible. Bost., 1871. 12°. 9990
Ecce Cœlum. (2 copies.) Bost., 1870. 12°. 8917
Pater Mundi. Bost., 1870. v. 1. 12°. 9989
Burroughs, S., Memoirs of. By himself. Albany, 1811. 12°. . . 7573
Burton, E. Description of Rome. 2d ed. Lond., 1828. 2 v. 12°. . 16725
Burton, J. H. Book-Hunter. Ed. White. (2 copies.) N. Y., 1863. 12°. 142
Hist. of Scotland, 1689–1748. Lond., 1853. 2 v. 8°. . . 5408
Life and Correspondence of Hume. Edinb., 1846. 2 v. 8°. . 7128
Lives of Lord Lovat and D. Forbes. Lond., 1847. 8°. . . 6762
Burton, Richard F. City of the Saints. Lond., 1861. 8°. . . 8417

Burton, Richard F. Vikram and the Vampire. Lond., 1870. 8°. . 1923
Burton, Robert. Anatomy of Melancholy. N. Y., 1870. 3 v. 8°. . 3941
The same. Lond., 1826. 2 v. 8°. 3806
[**Bury, Lady C.**] Diary of Times of Geo. IV. Philad., 1838–39. 4 v. 12°. 5217
Bush, A. F. Memoirs of Queens of France. Lond., 1843. 2 v. 8°. 5432
Bush, G. Life of Mohammed. N. Y., 1841. 12°. 11010
The same. (2 copies.) N. Y., 1830. 12°. 11937
Notes on the O. T. N. Y., 1841–44. 7 v. 12°. . . . 9845
CONTENTS.—1, 2, Genesis. 3, 4, Exodus. 5, Leviticus. 6, Joshua. 7, Judges.
Bush, R. J. Reindeer, Dogs, and Snow-Shoes. N. Y., 1871. 8°. . 8299
Bushnell, H. Character of Jesus. N. Y., 1861. 16°. . . . 9804
Christ and his Salvation. N. Y., 1864. 12°. 9941
Christ in Theology. Hartf'd., 1851. 12°. 9939
Christian Nurture. N. Y., 1861. 12°. 9940
God in Christ. Hartf'd., 1849. 12°. 9935
Moral Uses of Dark Things. (2 copies.) N. Y., 1868–69. 12°. 9943
Nature and the Supernatural. 4th ed. (2 copies.) N. Y., 1859. 8°. 10023
Oration at Y. C., 1865. N. H., 1866. 8°. 9280
Sermons on Living Subjects. N. Y., 1872. 12°. . . . 9938
for the New Life. (2 copies.) N. Y., 1859. 12°. . 9936
The Vicarious Sacrifice. N. Y., 1866. 8°. 10025
Woman Suffrage. (2 copies.) N. Y., 1869. 12°. . . . 9211
Work and Play. N. Y., 1864. 12°. 9942
Busby, T. Hist. of Music. Lond., 1819. 2 v. 8°. 9078
Busk, M. M. Hist. of Spain and Portugal. (2 copies.) Lond., 1833. 8°. 16154
Bussey, G. M., and Gaspey, T. Pictorial Hist. of France. Lond., 1843. 2 v. 8°. 5704
Butler, B. F., (of N. Y.) Life and Opinions of. Mackenzie. Bost., 1845. 8°. 7433
Butler, Gen. B. F., in New Orleans. Parton. N. Y., 1864. 12°. . 7403
Butler, C. Life of Erasmus. Lond., 1825. 8°. 7686
Fénelon. Philad., 1811. 12°. 7557
Grotius. Lond., 1826. 8°. 7685
Memoir of d'Aguesseau, and Account of Roman and Canon Law. Lond., 1830. 8°. 7682
Reminiscences. Bost., 1827. 12°. 7046
Butler, Frances K. See F. A. KEMBLE.
Butler, Fred'k. Hist. of U. S. Hartf'd., 1821. 3 v. 8°. . . . 5843
Sketches of Universal Hist. Hartf'd., 1819. 12°. . . . 15924
Butler, James. American Bravery. Carlisle, 1816. 12°. . . . 16051
Butler, Joseph. Analogy of Religion. Ed. Croly. Lond., 1834. 16°. 9490
The same. Ed. Barnes. (2 copies.) N. Y., 1833. 12°. . 9949
The same. N. Y., 1857. 12°. 9951
Sermons. Ed. Cattermole. Lond., 1836. 16°. . . . 9509
Works. Lond., 1834. 8°. 10069
Works. Lond., 1836. 12°. 9546
Lectures on the Analogy of. Chalmers. N. Y., 1850. 12°. . 9530
Butler, S. Poetical Works, [with Life by Mitford.] Lond., 1835. 2 v. 16°. 1027
The same. Ed. Johnson. Dubl., 1804. 8°. 15096
The same. With Life, by Sanford. Philad., 1819. 2 v. 24°. 6

Butler, S. Satires. Ed. Bell. Lond., 1807. 24°. 259
and his Works. Ramsay. Lond., 1846. 12°. 6954
Butler, T. B. The Atmospheric System. Hartf'd., 1870. 12°. . . 8919
Buxton, T. F. The African Slave Trade. N. Y., 1840. 12°. . . 8554
Memoirs of. By his Son. Philad., 1849. 12°. 6771
Byrn, M. L. Repository of Wit and Humor. Bost., 1859. 12°. . 4319
Byron, Lady A., vindicated. Stowe. Bost., 1870. 12°. . . . 6988
Byron, Lord G. G. N. Correspondence with Dallas. Philad., 1825. 12°. 6944
The Island. N. Y., 1823. 12°. 14811
Lara. N. Y., 1814. 12°. 14812
Works. Philad., 1846. 8°. 1283
The same. Bost., 1852. 8°. 1282
The same. Philad., 1824. v. 1–5, 7, 8. 24°. 552

CONTENTS.—1, Childe Harold. 2, Corsair; Lara; Bride of Abydos; Parisina; Beppo; Engl. Bards and Scotch Reviewers; Manfred. 3, Marino Faliero; Mazeppa; Prisoner of Chillon; Prophecy of Dante; Ode to Napoleon; Vision of Judgment; Morgante Maggiore; etc. 4, Cain; Sardanapalus; Deformed Transformed; Hebrew Melodies. 5, Two Foscari; Werner; The Giaour. 7, 8, Don Juan.

The same, with Life, by Lake. Philad., 1834. 8 v. 16°. 559

CONTENTS.—1, Life; Hours of Idleness; Engl. Bards and Scotch Reviewers. 2, Childe Harold. 3, Giaour; Bride of Abydos; Corsair; Lara; Curse of Minerva; Siege of Corinth; Parisina; Prisoner of Chillon; Beppo; Mazeppa. 4, Manfred; Marino Faliero; Sardanapalus. 5, Two Foscari; Cain; Werner. 6, Deformed Transformed; Heaven and Earth; Prophecy of Dante; Island; Vision of Judgment; Morgante Maggiore; Hebrew Melodies; etc. 7, Miscellaneous. 7; 8, Don Juan.

The same, with Life, by Moore. Lond., 1832–33. v. 1–7, 9–15. 16°. 306

CONTENTS.—1-6, Life and Letters. 6, Miscellaneous Prose Pieces. 7, Hours of Idleness; Engl. Bards and Scotch Reviewers; Occasional Pieces. 9, Hints from Horace; Curse of Minerva; The Waltz; The Giaour; Bride of Abydos; The Corsair; Occasional Pieces. 10, Ode to Napoleon; Lara; Hebrew Melodies; Siege of Corinth; Domestic and Occasional Pieces; Prisoner of Chillon; The Dream. 11, Manfred; Lament of Tasso; Beppo; Mazeppa; Ode on Venice; Morgante Maggiore; Prophecy of Dante; Occasional Pieces. 12, Francesca of Rimini; The Blues; Marino Faliero; Vision of Judgment; Occasional Pieces. 13, Heaven and Earth; Sardanapalus; The Two Foscari; The Deformed Transformed. 14, Cain; Werner; Age of Bronze; The Island; etc. 15, Testimonies of Authors concerning Don Juan; Byron's Observations; Don Juan, Cantos 1-3.

and his Contemporaries. L. Hunt. Lond., 1828. 2 v. 8°. . 7187
Beauties of. Philad., 1826. 12°. 14813
Biography of, with Critical Essay on. Elze. Lond., 1872. 8°. 7094
Conversations with. Lady Blessington. Philad., 1838. 8°. . 2669
on Religion. Kennedy. Philad., 1833. 12°. 6942
Life of. Galt. N. Y., 1841. 12°. 11009
Life, Letters and Journals of. Moore. Lond., 1844. 8°, . 7186
Recollections of. Dallas. Philad., 1825. 8°. 7190
The same. Guiccioli. N. Y., 1869. 12°. 7095

C.

Caballero, Fernan. *(Pseudonym.)* La Gaviota. [de Arrom.] N. Y., 1864. 12°. 2601
Cabinet of Curiosities. Goodrich. Hartf'd., 1822, 2 v. 12°. . . 16939
Cyclopædia, The. Lardner. Lond. 171 v. 16°. . . . 4855
Minister, The. Gore. N. Y., 1839. 2 v. 12°. . . . 15391
Portrait Gallery of Brit. Worthies. Lond., 1845–46. 8 v. 12°. 6615
of Romantic Tales, The. N. Y., 1836. 12°. 14871
Cabot, S., Life of. Hayward. Bost., 1838. 16°. 7258

Cabul, Military Operations at, 1841–42. Eyre. Philad., 1843. 8°. . 8050
Residence in, 1836–38. Burnes. Philad., 1843. 8°. . . 8050
Cademosto, M. Novel. (Ital. Novelists, v. 2.) Lond., 1836. 8°. . 1900
Cæsar, C. J. Works, tr. by Duncan. N. Y., 1840. 2 v. 12°. . . 4513
Abstract of. Trollope. Philad., 1870. 16°. 74
Hist. of. Napoléon III. N. Y., 1865–66. 2 v. 8°. . . . 4779
Cæsars, The [Twelve]. De Quincey. (Selec., v. 10). Edinb., 1858. 8°. 3283
Lives of. Rogers. Lond., 1811. 5 v. 8°. . . 16001
Caged Lion, The. Yonge. Lond., 1870. 8°. 2504
Cailliaud, F. Travels in Oasis of Thebes. Lond., 1822. 8°. . . 8057
Calavar. [Bird.] Philad., 1835. 2 v. 12°. 15670
Calderon de la Barca, F. E. Life in Mexico. Bost., 1843. 2 v. 12°. 16905
Calderon de la Barca, P., Life and Genius of; with Specimens.
Trench. N. Y., 1856. 12°. 7697
Calderon, the Courtier. A Tale. Bulwer. Philad., 1868. 12°. . 2036
Caldwell, D., Sketch of. Caruthers. Greensborough, 1842. 8°. . 16416
Caldwell, J. S. Results of Reading. Lond., 1843. 8°. . . . 4335
Caldwell, M. Manual of Elocution. 3d ed. Philad., 1846. 12°. . 9301
Caledonian Muse. Ritson. Lond., 1785. 16°. 1096
Calendar of the Church, Analysis of. Martyndale. Lond. 12°. . 4622
Calhoun, J. C. Disquisition on Gov't., etc. Charleston, 1851. 8°. . 6171
Life of, to 1843. (2 copies.) N. Y., 1843. 8°. 7431
Life of. Jenkins. Auburn. [1850.] 12°. 7330
California; a book for travellers and settlers. Nordhoff. N. Y., 1873. 8°. 10241
in 1867–68. Brace. N. Y., 1869. 12°. 8426
Hist. of. Greenhow. Bost., 1845. 8°. 5993
Life in, 1829–45. [Robinson.] N. Y., 1846. 12°. . . . 16888
Life in, 1849–50. Bayard Taylor. N. Y., 1867. 12°. . . 8280
Resources of. Hittel. S. Francisco, 1863. 12°. . . . 8402
Travels in, 1841. Farnham. N. Y., 1844. 12°. 16887
What I saw in, 1846–47. Bryant. N. Y., 1848. 12°. . . 16889
Caliphs and Sultans. Hanley. N. Y., 1869. 16°. 1907
Callcott, J. W. Musical Grammar. Bost., 1833. 12°. . . . 17117
Callcott, M. Hist. of Spain. (2 copies.) Lond., 1828. 2 v. 12°. . 6401
Calverley, C. S. Fly Leaves, etc. N. Y., 1872. 16°. 4248
Calvert, G. H. The Gentleman. (2 copies.) Bost., 1863. 8°. . . 9175
Goethe; his Life and Works. Bost., 1872. 16°. . . . 7837
Scenes and Thoughts in Europe. N. Y., 1846. 12°. . . . 16291
The same. Bost., 1863. 2 v. 16°. 8201
Calvert, L., Life of. Burnap. Bost., 1846. 16°. 7268
Calvin, J. Institutes of the Christian Religion, ed. Allen. Lond.,
1838. 2 v. 8°. 10034
Life of. Beza. Philad., 1836. 12°. 7667
Memoirs of. Waterman. Hartf'd., 1813. 8°. 7666
Calvinism, Address on. Froude. N. Y., 1871. 12°. 9961
Cambaceres, J. J. R. de, Evenings with. Langon. Lond., 1837. 2 v. 8°. 5601
Cambridge Univ., England, Conversations at. Lond., 1836. 16°. . 9115
Essays. 1855, 1857, 1858. Lond. 3 v. 8°. 3439
Five Years in. Bristed. N. Y., 1873. 12°. 10240

Cambridge Univ., Hist. of. Fuller. Lond., 1840. 8°. 9286
Lectures on. W. Everett. Cambr., 1865. 12°. 9240
Letters from. Lond., 1828. 16°. 9236
and Oxford Boat Races, 1829–69. Macmichael. Cambr., 1870. 16°. 9116
See, also, ENGLISH UNIVERSITIES.
Camel Hunt, The. Fabens. Cambr., 1851. 12°. 16872
Camilla. D'Arblay. Bost., 1797. 3 v. 12°. 2397
Camoens, L. de. The Lusiad. Transl. by Mickle. 3d. ed. Dubl., 1791. 2 v. 8°. 911
Memoirs of. Adamson. Lond., 1820. 2 v. 8°. 7695
Camp, D. N. Amer. Year-Book for 1869. Hartf'd., 1869. 8°. . . 6145
Camp, G. S. Democracy. N. Y., 1841. 12°. 11613
Camp, H. W., Biogr. of. Trumbull. Bost., 1865. 12°. 7280
Camp Meeting, The; a Poem. W. Holmes. Bost., 1842. 12°. . . 14936
Camp of Refuge, The. [Macfarlane.] Lond., 1844. 2 v. 12°. . . 2380
Campan, J. L. H. G. Memoirs of Marie Antoinette. Philad., 1823. 8°. 5630
Campaner Thal, The. Richter. Bost., 1864. 8°. 3056
Camperdown. Philad., 1836. 12°. 15672
Campbell, A. Voyage round the World. N. Y., 1819. 12°. . . 16301
Campbell, C. Traveller's Guide through Belgium, Holland, and Germany. Lond., 1815. 12°. 16610
Campbell, Donald. Narrative of Adventures. N. Y., 1798. 12°. . 16274
Campbell, Duncan, Life of. De Foe. Oxf'd., 1841. 12°. . . . 3884
Campbell, Geo. Lectures on Pulpit Eloquence, ed. Park. Andover, 1845. 12°. 9913
Lectures on Theology and Eloquence. Bost., 1832. 8°. . . 10038
Philosophy of Rhetoric. Edinb., 1816. 2 v. 8°. . . . 17519
Campbell, Geo. J. D., Duke of Argyll. Reign of Law. 5th ed. Lond., 1868. 16°. 8839
Campbell, John. Lives of Brit. Admirals, &c. Lond., 1817. 8 v. 8°. 6878
Campbell, Lord John. Lives of Atrocious Judges, ed. Hildreth. N. Y., 1856. 12°. 6759
Lives of Chief Justices. Philad., 1851. 2 v. 8°. 6873
of Lord Chancellors and Keepers. Lond. and Philad., 1845–48. v. 1–7. 8°. 6866

CONTENTS.—1, to 1547. 2, 1547–1645. 3, 1642–88. 4, 1688–1737. 5, 1737–92. 6, 1792–1807. 7, 1801–27.

Campbell, John W. Hist. of Va. Philad., 1813. 12°. 6005
Campbell, T. Essay on English Poetry. Bost., 1819. 12°. . . 55
Letters from the South. Philad., 1836. 12°. 16470
Life of Petrarch. Philad., 1841. 8°. 7753
The same. 2d ed. Lond., 1843. 2 v. 8°. 7754
Poetical Works. Philad., 1827. 24°. 962
The same. Philad., 1830. 8°. 944
The same. 947
The same. N. Y., 1850. 12°. 963
The same, with Life, by Hill. Bost., 1857. 16°. . . 972
Theodric; and other Poems. N. Y., 1825. 12°. . . . 14814
Life and Letters of. Beattie. N. Y., 1850. 2 v. 12°. . . 7038
Campbell, Wm. British India. Lond., 1839. 8°. 16498

Carleton, W. Traits and Stories of Irish Peasantry. Lond., 1836. 5 v. 16°. 2017
Carleton, Memoirs of Captain. DeFoe. Oxf'd., 1840. 16°. . . . 3876
Carleton. [C. C. Coffin.] Our New Way round the World. Bost., 1869. 8°. 8059
Carlos, Don; a Drama. Schiller. Lond., 1847. 8°. 437
a Tragedy. Otway. (Works, v. 1.) Lond., 1812. 8°. . . 1475
Carlton, R. The New Purchase. N. Y., 1843. 2 v. 12°. 15753
Carlyle, A. Autobiography. Bost., 1861. 12°. 7135
Carlyle, T. Chartism. Bost., 1840. 12°. 3366
Critical and Miscellaneous Essays. Bost., 1855. 8°. . . . 3467
The same. (2 copies.) Bost., 1838–39. 4 v. 12°. . . 3355
The French Revolution. (2 copies.) N. Y., 1856–60. 2 v. 12°. 5566
The same. Bost., 1838. 2 v. 12°. 5570
German Romance. Bost., 1841. 2 v. 12°. 3107
Heroes and Hero-Worship. (2 copies.) N. Y., 1859–61. 12°. . 3363
Hist. of Frederick the Great. N. Y., 1859–66. 6 v. 12°. . 5791
The same. v. 1, 2, 4–6. 5797
Latter-Day Pamphlets. N. Y., 1850. 12°. 3370
Life of Schiller. (2 copies.) Lond., 1825. 12°. 7838
The same. Ed. Follen. Bost., 1833. 12°. 7840
of Sterling. Bost., 1852. 12°. 6999
Past and Present. Bost., 1843. 12°. 3365
The same. N. Y., 1843. 12°. 2115
The same; and Chartism. N. Y., 1848. 8°. 3368
The same; and Sartor Resartus. N. Y., 1859. 12°. . 3369
Sartor Resartus. N. Y., 1844. 12°. 3367
Collected Works. Lond., 1869–72. 31 v. 8°. 4020

CONTENTS.—1, Sartor Resartus. 2-4, French Revolution. 5, Life of Schiller. 6-11, Miscellaneous Essays. 12, Heroes and Hero-Worship. 13, Past and Present. 14-18, Cromwell's Letters and Speeches. 19, Latter-Day Pamphlets. 20, Life of Sterling. 21-30, Hist. of Frederick the Great. 31, Index.

Works. Lond., 1871–72. 18 v. 16°. 3922

CONTENTS.—1, Sartor Resartus. 2-4, French Revolution. 5, Life of Sterling. 6-10, Cromwell's Letters and Speeches. 11, Heroes, etc. 12-18, Essays.

Carmichael, A. Memoir of Spurzheim. Bost., 1833. 12°. . . . 8532
Carmichael, Mrs. Manners in the W. I. Philad., 1833. 8°. . . 15537
Carmina Collegensia. Waite. Bost. [1868.] 8°. 9091
[**Carne, J.**] Stratton Hill. N. Y., 1829. 2 v. 12°. 15589
Tales of the West. N. Y., 1828. 2 v. 12°. 15600
Carolinas, Campaign of 1781 in the. Lee. Philad., 1824. 8°. . . 6117
Caroline, Queen, Speeches in Defence of. Brougham. Edinb., 1838. 8°. 9337
[**Carp. H.**] Antidote to Miseries of Human Life. N. H., 1809. 12°. 15368
Sequel to the above. N. Y., 1810. 12°. 15639
Cœlebs Deceived. Philad., 1817. 12°. 15400
Carpenter, F. B. Six Months at the White House. N. Y., 1866. 8°. 7542
Carpenter, S. C. Memoirs of Jefferson. N. Y., 1809. 2 v. 8°. . 7349
Select American Speeches. Philad., 1815. 2 v. 8°. . . . 9428
Carpenter, W. W. Travels in Mexico. N. Y., 1851. 12°. . . . 16908
Carr, J. Caledonian Sketches. Philad., 1809. 8°. 16739
A Northern Summer. Philad., 1805. 8°. 16602

Carr, J. Stranger in France. Hartf'd., 1804. 12°. 16703
Stranger in Ireland. N. Y., 1807. 12°. 16770
Carrel, N. A. Hist. of Counter-Revolution in England. (2 copies.) Lond., 1846. 8°. 338
Carrick, J. D. Life of Wallace. Lond., 1840. 8°. 6840
The same. 3d ed. Lond. 8°. 6841
Cartaphilus, Chronicles of. Hoffman. Lond., 1853. 2 v. 8°. . . 10059
Carter, E. Letters to Mrs. Montagu. Lond., 1817. 3 v. 8°. . . 7070
Memoirs of. Pennington. Bost., 1809. 8°. 16371
Carter, N. H. Letters from Europe. N. Y., 1827. 2 v. 8°. . . 16535
Carter, R. A Summer Cruise. Bost., 1864. 8°. 16808
Cartwright, W. The Ordinary. (Old Plays, v. 10.) Lond., 1826. 8°. 1517
Caruthers, E. W. Sketch of D. Caldwell. Greensborough, 1842. 8°. 16416
Carver, J. *(Pseudonym.)* Sketches of N. England. N. Y., 1842. 12°. 15780
Cary, A. Pictures of Country Life. N. Y., 1866. 12°. . . . 2987
Cary, H. F. Lives of Engl. Poets. Lond., 1846. 16°. . . . 6599
Memoir of. By his Son. Lond., 1847. 2 v. 12°. . . . 7091
Cary, P. Poems and Parodies. Bost., 1854. 12°. 813
Casimir Maremma. Helps. Bost., 1870. 16°. 2377
[**Cass, L.**] France, its King, Court, and Gov't.; and Three Hours at St. Cloud. 2d ed. N. Y., 1841. 12°. 16700
Castellan, A. L. Letters on Italy. Lond., 1820. 8°. 8053
[**Castera, J. H.**] Life of Catherine II., transl. by Dakins. Lond., 1799. 2 v. 8°. 16178
Castilian, The. De Trueba y Cosio. N. Y., 1829. 2 v. 12°. . . 15140
Castilian Days. Hay. Bost., 1871. 8°. 8210
Castle Dangerous. Scott. Bost., 1845. 12°. 1845
of Otranto. Walpole. Philad., 1840. 12°. 2458
Rackrent. Edgeworth. Bost., 1824. 8°. 15336
Richmond. Trollope. N. Y., 1860. 12°. 2110
Castlereagh, Lord (R. Stewart), Life of. Alison. Edinb., 1861. 3 v. 8°. 6790
Castles in the Air. Barry Gray. N. Y., 1871. 8°. 2928
Castriot, G. *(Scanderbeg)*, Life of. Moore. N. Y., 1850. 12°. . . 7583
Catacombs of Rome, The. Kip. N. Y., 1854. 12°. . . . . , 6308
Church in the. Maitland. Lond., 1846. 8°. . 6451
Catherine II. of Russia, Life of. [Castéra.] Transl. by Dakins. Lond., 1799. 2 v. 8°. , ... , . 16178
The same. Tooke. Lond., 1800. 3 v. 8°. 6439
Memoirs of, by herself. (?) N. Y., 1859. 12°. 6442
Catherine; a Story. Thackeray. Lond., 1872. 8°. 2199
Catherine's Lovers. Erckmann-Chatrain. Bost., 1871. 16°. . . . 2360
Catholic Church. See ROMAN Catholic.
World. N. Y., 1865–72. v. 1–11, 13–15. 8°. 14272
Catlin, G. Letters and Notes on the N. A. Indians. 3d ed. N. Y., 1844. 2 v. 8°. 5948
Notes in Europe. Lond., 1848. 2 v. 8°. 8304
Cattermole, R. The Great Civil War. Lond., 1857. 8°. . . . . .
Caucasus, Letters from the, 1811–12. Lond., 1823. 8°. 16519
Tour to the, 1847–48. Ditson. N. Y., 1850. 12°. 16489

Caucasus, Travels in, 1837. Wilbraham. Lond., 1839. 8°. . . . 8039
Western, Travels in the, 1836. Spencer. Lond., 1838. 2 v. 8°. 8044
See, also, CIRCASSIA.
Caudle, Mrs. Curtain Lectures. [Jerrold.] N. Y., 1867. 12°. . 4253
Caulaincourt, A. A. L. de. Napoleon and his Times. Philad., 1838. 2 v. 12°. 5503
Recollections. Lond., 1838. 2 v. 12°. 5501
Caulkins, F. M. Hist. of Norwich. N., 1845. 12°. 6113
Cause and Effect, Relation of. T. Brown. Andover, 1822. 8°. . . 8728
Caustic, Christopher. *(Pseudonym.)* See T. G. FESSENDEN.
Cave, W. Lives of the Apostles, etc. Ed. Stebbing. Lond., 1834. 2 v. 16°. 9485
The same. Ed. Cary. Oxf'd., 1840. 8°. . . , . 10009
of the Fathers. Ed. Cary. Oxf'd., 1840. 3 v. 8°. 9970
Primitive Christianity. Ed. Trollope. Lond., 1834–35. 2 v. 16°. 9494
Cavendish, G. Life of Wolsey. Ed. Singer. Lond., 1827. 8°. . 6813
Cavendish, T., Life of. N. Y. 1840. 12°. 11032
Cavour, C. B. di, Reminiscences of. De la Rive. Lond., 1862. 8°. . 7788
Cawthorne, J. Select Poems. Ed. Sanford. Philad., 1819. 24°. . 18
The same. Ed. Johnson. Dubl., 1804. 8°. 15101
Caxton, W., Biogr. of. Knight. Lond., 1844. 12°. 6914
Life of. (Libr. of Useful Knowl.) Lond., 1833. 8°. . . . 6751
Caxtons, The. Bulwer. N. Y., 1860. 12°. . . . , . . 2133
Cazin, A. Phenomena and Laws of Heat. N. Y., 1869. 12°. . . 10111
Cecil, R. (Earl of Salisbury), Life of. Courtenay. Lond., 1838. 16°. 5763
Cecil, W. (Lord Burghley), Life of. Lond., 1831. 16°. . . . 5759
Cecil Dreeme. Winthrop. Bost., 1861. 12°. 2856
Cecilia. D'Arblay. Bost., 1803. 3 v. 12°. 2400
Celestial Scenery. Dick. N. Y., 1841. 12°. 11408
Cellini, B., Life of. By himself. Tr. by Nugent. Philad., 1812. 2 v. 12°. 7876
The same. Lond., 1828. 2 v. 12°. 6654
The same. Tr. by Roscoe. (Bohn's ed.) (2 copies.) Lond., 1847–50. 8°. 427
Celnart, E. F. Book of Politeness. Bost., 1833. 12°. . . . 17051
Celt, Roman, and Saxon, Hist. of. Wright. Lond., 1861. 8°. . . 5272
Celtic Antiquities. Pezron. Lond., 1809. 16°. 15931
Religion and Learning, Hist. of. Toland. Lond. [1814.] 8°. . 16073
Celuta. Chateaubriand. Lond., 1832. 3 v. 16°. 2387
Centlivre, S. Bold Stroke for a Wife; The Wonder. (Brit. Drama, v. 2, pt. 2.) Lond., 1804. 8°. 1632
Bold Stroke for a Wife; Busy Body; Wonder. (Brit. Theatre, v. 18.) Lond. 12°. 1342
Busy Body. (Brit. Drama, v. 2, pt. 1.) Lond., 1804. 8°. . . 1631
Central America. See AMERICA.
Cerceau, J. A. Du. Life of Rienzi. Philad., 1836. 12°. . . . 7750
Cervantes-Saavedra, M. de. Don Quixote. N. Y., 1855. 12°. . 1624
The same, transl. by Jarvis. Lond., 1837–39. 3 v. 8°. . 1619
The same. Philad., 1852. 2 v. 8°. 1622
The same, ed. by Clark, illust. by Doré. Lond. 4°. .

Ceylon, Eight Years' Wanderings in, 1845–52. Baker. Philad., 1869. 12°. 7909
Hist. etc., of. Martin. Lond., 1837. 16°. 7905
Travels in. Haafner. Lond., 1821. 8°. 8055
Chadbourne, P. A. Instinct. N. Y., 1872. 12°. 8946
Chadwick, W. Life of DeFoe. Lond., 1859. 8°. 7082
Chainbearer, The. Cooper. N. Y., 1856. 12°. 2822
Chairolas. Bulwer. Philad., 1836. 12°. 2149
Chaldæa, Researches in. Ainsworth. Lond., 1838. 8°. 8048
Chaldæan Monarchy, The. Rawlinson. N. Y., 1871. 8°. . . . 4063
Chalmers, T. Adaptation of Nature to Man. Philad., 1836. 8°. . 16982
Astronomical Discourses. 3d ed. Glasg., 1817. 8°. . . 16972
Lectures on Romans. N. Y., 1843. 8°. 10010
Miscellanies. N. Y., 1847. 8°. 3427
Political Economy. N. Y., 1832. 12°. 8543
Posthumous Works. N. Y., 1848–50. 9 v. 12°. 9522

Contents.—1–3, Daily Scripture Readings. 4, 5, Sabbath Scripture Readings. 6, Sermons. 7, 8, Institutes of Theology. 9, Lectures on Butler's Analogy and Paley's Evidences; Notes on Hill's Lectures in Divinity; Addresses at New College, Edinburgh.

Select Correspondence. N. Y., 1855. 12°. 7602
Sermons. N. Y., 1848. 2 v. 8°. 17507
Works. Philad., 1833. 8°. 9632
The same. Bridgeport, 1829. 3 v. 8°. 9633
Works. N. Y., 1840–41. 6 v. 12°. 9516

Contents.—1, 2, Natural Theology. 3, 4, Evidences of the Christian Revelation. 5, Moral and Mental Philosophy. 6, Commercial Discourses.

Memoir of. Wayland. Bost., 1864. 16°. 7566
Chambers, R. Biogr. Dict. of Eminent Scotsmen. Glasg., 1835. 4 v. 8°. 6862
Book of Days. Edinb., 1863–64. 2 v. 8°. 4437
Cyclopædia of English Literature. Edinb., 1844. 2 v. 8°. . 222
The same. Bost., 1847. 2 v. 8°. 224
Hist. of Rebellions in Scotland, 1638–60. Edinb., 1828. 2 v. 12°. 4493
The same, 1689 and 1715. Edinb., 1829. 12°. . . 4504
The same, 1745–46. Edinb., 1827. 2 v. 12°. . . . 4477
The same. 7th ed. Edinb., 1869. 8°. 5278
Popular Rhymes of Scotland. Edinb., 1870. 8°. 1095
Scottish Ballads. Edinb., 1829. 12°. 955
Songs. Edinb., 1829. 2 v. 12°. 956
Traditions of Edinburgh. Edinb., 1869. 8°. 5154
Popular Rhymes of Scotland. Edinb., 1870. 8°. 1095
Memoir of, with Autobiogr. W. Chambers. N. Y., 1872. 8°. . 7099
Chambers, W. and **R.** Exemplary Biography. Edinb., 1836. 16°. . 6680
Miscellany. Bost. 10 v. 12°. 9156
Papers for the People. Philad., 1851. 6 v. 8°. 3665
Pocket Miscellany. Bost., 1852. v. 1. 12°. 9166
Chamier, F. Ben Brace. Philad., 1836. 2 v. 12°. 15379
Jack Adams. Philad., 1839. 2 v. 12°. 15466
Walsingham. Philad., 1838. 2 v. in 1. 12°. 15630
Chamisso, A. v. Peter Schlemihl's Wundersame Geschichte. Hamb. 12°. 9615

Champion, The. [Fielding, etc.] 2d ed. London, 1743. 2 v. 12°. . 13035
Champions of Freedom. Woodworth. N. Y., 1816. 12°. . . . 15675
Chandler, P. W. American Criminal Trials. Bost., 1844. v. 2. 12° . 9226
Channing, E. T. Lectures [on Rhetoric and Oratory.] Bost., 1856. 12°. 9306
Life of W. Ellery. (Sparks, v. 6.) Bost., 1836. 16°. . . 7255
Channing, Rev. W. E. The Perfect Life. Bost., 1873. 12°. . . 10264
Slavery. (2 copies.) Bost., 1835. 16°. 8550
Works. Bost., 1841. 6 v. 12°. 9568

CONTENTS.—1, Remarks on Milton; on Napoleon; on Fenelon; Moral Argument against Calvinism; National Literature; Associations; The Union; Education. 2, Slavery, etc.; Annexation of Texas; Catholicism; Creeds; Temperance; Self-Culture. 3, 4, Discourses. 5, Remarks on the Slavery Question; Lecture on War; Lectures on the Elevation of Laborers; Discourse on Dr. Follen; Ordination Charges: Miscellanies. 6, Emancipation; Discourse on Dr. Tuckerman; The Present Age; The Church; Duty of the Free States; Address at Lenox.

The same. v. 1–5. 9574
Memoir of. W. H. Channing. 2d ed. Bost., 1848. 3 v. 12°. 7607
Channing, W. E. Poems. Bost., 1843. 16°. 721
Channing, W. H. Memoir of J. H. Perkins. Bost., 1851. 12°. . 3637
Chaplet of Pearls. Yonge. N. Y., 1869. 8°. 2665
Chapman, G. All Fools; Eastward Hoe. (Old Plays, v. 4.) Lond., 1825. 8°. 1511
Widow's Tears. (Old Plays, v. 6.) Lond., 1825. 8°. . . 1513
Chapman, N. Select Speeches. Philad., 1808. 5 v. 8°. . . . 9418
Chapone, H. Letters on Improvement of the Mind. Bost., 1834. 12°. 9182
Chapsal, C. P. Leçons et modèles de littérature française. N. Y., 1845. 12°. 9620
Character. Smiles. N. Y., 1872. 12°. 3703
and Characteristic Men. Whipple. Bost., 1866. 12°. . . 3544
Human, Book of. Bucke. Lond., 1837. 2 v. 16°. . . . 4329
National, Essay on. Chenevix. Lond., 1832. 2 v. 8°. . . 8670
Charcoal Sketches. Neal. Philad., 1838. 12°. 2868
Chardin, J. Travels. (Mavor, v. 11.) Lond., 1797. 12°. . . . 13854
Charicles; Private Life of the Greeks. Becker. Lond., 1845. 12°. 4326
Charity, The Romance of. De Liefde. Lond., 1867. 8°. . . . 8542
Charke, C., Life of. By herself. Lond., 1829. 12°. 6645
Charlemagne, Hist. of. James. N. Y., 1841. 12°. 11280
Legends of. Bulfinch. Bost., 1864. 12°. 1911
Charles I. of England. Eikon Basilike [by Gauden]. Lond., 1824. 12°. 4906
a Tragedy. Mitford. Philad. 8°. 2675
Life of. Harris. Lond., 1814. 8°. 5305
Memoirs of Court of. Aikin. Philad., 1833. 2 v. 8°. . . 5302
The same. Jesse. Philad., 1840. 12°. 5212
Charles II, Preservation of; also, Letters. By himself. Lond., 1766. 8°. 5151
Beauties of Court of. Jameson. Philad., 1834. 8°. . . 6907
Life of. Harris. Lond., 1814. 2 v. 8°. 5306
Memoirs of Court of. Jesse. Philad., 1840. 2 v. 12°. . . 5213
Personal Hist. of. [Bohn.] Lond., 1846. 8°. 4836
Charles V. of Germany. Autobiography. (1516–48.) Lond., 1862. 8°. 6408
Cloister Life of. Stirling. Lond., 1853. 8°. 6409
Hist. of Reign of. Robertson, ed. Prescott. Phil., 1872. 3 v. 8°. 10335
Charles XII. of Sweden, Hist. of. Voltaire. Otsego, 1811. 12°. . 5818

Charles XIV., Memoirs of. Philippart. Balt., 1815. 8°. . . . 16172
Charles the Bold (of Burgundy), Hist. of. Kirk. Philad., 1864. 2 v. 8°. 5653
[**Charles, E.**] On both Sides of the Sea. N. Y., 1868. 12°. . . 2469
Chronicles of Schönberg-Cotta Family. Lond., 1868. 8°. . 2463
The same. N. Y., 1864. 12°. 2464
The same. N. Y., 1865. 16°. 2424
Diary of Kitty Trevelyan. Lond., 1866. 8°. 2465
The same. N. Y., 1864. 8°. 2466
The Draytons and Davenants. (2 copies.) N. Y., 1866. 12°. . 2467
The Early Dawn; Christian Life in England in the Olden Time. N. Y., 1864. 12°. 2472
Mary, the Handmaid of the Lord. N. Y., 1865. 12°. . . 9842
Winifred Bertram. (2 copies.) N. Y., 1866. 12°. . . . 2470
Charles Auchester. [Sheppard.] N. Y., 1862. 8°. 2666
Charles Elwood. Brownson. Bost., 1840. 16°. 15676
Charles Lever; a Tale. Gresley. N. Y., 1843. 12°. 15395
Charles O'Malley. Lever. Dubl., 1841. 8°. 2318
Charmed Sea, The. Martineau. Bost., 1833. 12°. 14620
Charnock, J. Naval Biography. Lond., 1794–98. 6 v. 8°. . . 6897
Chartism. Carlyle. Lond., 1869. 8°. 4029
Chase, L. B. Hist. of the Polk Administration. N. Y., 1850. 8°. . 6272
Chase, M. M., Life and Writings of. Bost., 1855. 12°. . . . 14980
Chase, T. Hellas. Cambr., 1863. 16°. 8208
Chasles, V. E. P. Anglo-Amer. Literature and Manners. N. Y., 1852. 12°. 124
Chastity, Lecture on. Graham. Bost., 1847. 12°. 17024
Chateaubriand, F. A. de. Atala. Lond., 1825. 24°. 2346
Celuta; or, the Natchez. 2d ed. Lond., 1832. 3 v. 16°. . 2387
Congress of Verona. Lond., 1838. 2 v. 8°. 4656
The Martyrs. N. Y., 1812. 3 v. 12°. 15133
Recollections of Italy, England, America, etc. Philad., 1816. 8°. 16286
Sketches of English Literature. Lond., 1837. 2 v. 8°. . . 226
Travels in America and Italy. Lond., 1828. 2 v. 8°. . . 16898
in Greece, Palestine, Egypt, etc. Philad., 1816. 8°. . 16724
Châteauvieux de Lullin, J. F. Travels in Italy. Lond., 1819. 8°. . 8051
Chatfield, C. Teutonic Antiquities. Lond., 1828. 8°. . . . 4675
Chatham, Earl of. See W. Pitt.
Chatham and Mary Kay. Martineau. Hartf'd., 1845. 12°. . . 14624
Chatterton, T. Poetical Works, with Life and select Prose Works. (2 copies.) Cambr., 1842. 2 v. 16°. 661
Poetical Works, ed. Skeat and Bell. Lond., 1871. 2 v. 8°. . 665
Select Poems. Ed. Walsh. Philad., 1822. 24°. . . . 23
Works, with Life by Gregory. Lond., 1803. 3 v. 8°. . . 1244
Biogr. of. Wilson. Lond., 1869. 8°. 6998
Life of. Davis. Lond. 16°. 6939
The same. Dix. Lond., 1851. 16°. 6956
Chaucer, G. Canterbury Tales, ed. T. Wright. Lond. 8°. . . 1261
Canterbury Tales, Selections from. Ed. Saunders. Lond., 1845. v. 1. 24°. 951

Chaucer, G. Legende of Goode Women, ed. Corson. Philad., 1864. 12°. 1023
Poems, modernized. Lond., 1841. 16°. 1016
Poetical Works. ' Ed. Bell. Lond., 1807. 14 v. in 7. (v. 1, 6, wanting.) 24°. 246
The same, with Tyrwhitt's Essay, etc. Lond., 1847. 8°. 1260
The same, with Life by H. Nicolas. Lond., 1845. 6 v. 16°. 1017

CONTENTS.—1, Memoir; Essay on Language and Versification of Chaucer by Tyrwhitt; Introd. to Canterbury Tales. 2, 3, Canterbury Tales. 4, Romaunt of the Rose; Troilus and Creseide. 5, The Last Concluded; Legend of Good Women, Goodly Ballade; Booke of the Dutchesse; Assembly of Foules. 6, Miscellaneous.

The Prologue, the Knightes Tale, the Nonne Prestes Tale. Ed. Morris. 2d ed. Oxf'd., 1869. 16°. 1015
Select Poems, with Life. Ed. Sanford. Philad., 1819. 24°. . 1
Chapters on. Hippisley. Lond., 1837. 12°. 163
The same. Morley. (v. 2, pt. 1.) Lond., 1867. 8°. . . . 160
Pictures of English Life from. Saunders. Lond., 1845. 24°. . 44
Chaucer's England. M. Browne. Lond., 1869. 2 v. 16°. . . 215
Cheetham, J. Life of T. Paine. Lond., 1817. 8°. 7419
Cheever, G. B. Amer. Common-Place Book of Prose. Bost., 1832. 12°. 4347
Bible in our Schools. N. Y., 1854. 12°. 9146
Lectures on Pilgrim's Progress. 3d ed. N. Y., 1845. 8°. . 10027
The Pilgrim in Shadow of Mont Blanc. N. Y., 1846. 12°. . 16554
Punishment by Death. N. Y., 1842. 12°. 17080
The same. N. Y., 1849. 12°. 17079
Studies in Poetry. Bost., 1830. 12°. 293
Cheever, H. T. Life in the Sandwich Islands. N. Y., 1851. 12°. . 8329
Chelsea Hospital, and its Traditions. [Gleig.] Lond., 1838. 3 v. 12°. 16067
Chemical Manufactures of Grt. Brit. Dodd. Lond., 1844. 16°. . 8787
Chemistry of Common Life. Johnston. N. Y., 1863. 2 v. 12°. . 8948
and Digestion. Prout. Philad., 1836. 8°. 16988
Treatise on. Donovan. Lond., 1837. 16°. 6041
Chenevix, R. Essay on National Character, Lond., 1832. 2 v. 8°. 8670
Chenier, L. S. de. State of Morocco. Lond., 1788. 2 v. 8°. . . 16532
Cherbuliez, V. Joseph Noirel's Revenge. (2 copies.) N. Y., 1872. 12°. 2392
Cherry, A. Soldier's Daughter. (Oxberry's Plays, v. 4.) Bost., 1822. 24°. 1348
Chess-Games, Morphy's. N. Y., 1860. 12°. 10175
Player's Companion. Staunton. Lond., 1849. 8°. . . . 10173
Chester, J. L. Greenwood Cemetery and other Poems. N. Y., 1843. 12°. 14981
Chesterfield, Earl of. See P. D. STANHOPE.
Chevalier, M. Society, etc., in the U. S. Bost., 1839. 8°. . . 6191
Cheveley. Lady Bulwer-Lytton. N. Y., 1839. 2 v. 12°. . . 15396
Chicago and the Great Conflagration. Colbert and Chamberlin. Cincinn., 1872. 12°. 6092
Chief Justices of England, Lives of. Campbell. Philad., 1851. 2 v. 8°. 6873
U. S., Lives of. Flanders. Philad., 1855. 8°. . 7473
Child, F. J. English and Scottish Ballads. Bost., 1857–59. 8 v. 16°. 1038
Child, L. M. Autumnal Leaves. N. Y., 1857. 12°. 15661
Biogr. of Mme. de Staël and of Lady Russell. Edinb., 1836. 16°. 6633
Hist. of Condition of Women. Bost., 1835. 2 v. 12°. . . 9193

Child, L. M. Hobomok. Bost., 1824. 12°. 15717
I. T. Hopper; a true Life. Bost., 1854. 12°. 7610
Letters from N. Y. N. Y., 1844–45. 2 v. 12°. 16851
Memoirs of Mme. de Staël, and of Mme. Roland. N. Y., 1854. 16°. 7659
The Oasis. Bost., 1834. 12°. 8466
Philothea. Bost., 1836. 12°. 15762
The Rebels. Bost., 1825. 12°. 15765
A Romance of the Republic. Bost., 1867. 12°. 3013
Chili, Journal on Coast of, 1820–22. Hall. Lond., 1840. 8°. . . 8101
Tour among the Araucanians of. E. R. Smith. N. Y., 1855. 12°. 17131
Travels in, 1819–25. Miers. Lond., 1826. 2 v. 8°. . . 8463
China and the Chinese. Nevius. N. Y. 1869. 12°. 7948
and the English. N. Y., 1835. 12°. 16476
Commercial Intercourse with. Lond., 1842. 12°. 7866
Elgin's Mission to, 1857–59. Oliphant. Edinb., 1859. 2 v. 8°. 8006
Embassy to, 1792. Staunton. Dubl., 1798. 2 v. 8°. . . 16474
Hist., etc., of. Gutzlaff. N. Y., 1834. 2 v. 12°. . . . 6475
Journal in, 1829–33. Abeel. N. Y., 1834. 12°. . . . 16477
Journal of Embassy to, 1816–17. Ellis. Lond., 1840. 8°. . 8101
The last year [1841–42] in. Philad., 1843. 8°. 8050
Memoirs of Residence in, 1706–19. Ripa. N. Y., 1846. 12°. . 8365
The Middle Kingdom; A Survey of. Williams. N. Y., 1849. 2 v. 12°. 6471
Narrative of Embassy to, 1792–94. Anderson. N. Y., 1795. 12°. 16480
Sketches of. Wood. Philad., 1830. 12°. 16479
State and Prospects of. Medhurst. Lond., 1838. 8°. . . 8004
Travels in, 1803. Barrow. Philad., 1805. 8°. 16520
The same, 1844–46. Huc. Lond., 1856. 8°. . . . 7945
Visit to, 1853. Bayard Taylor. N. Y., 1855. 12°. . . . 8283
Visit to Consular Cities of, 1844–46. G. Smith. N. Y., 1847. 12°. 7944
Voyage to, 1816. Hall. Lond., 1840. 8°. 8101
Voyages along Coast of, 1831–32. Gutzlaff. N. Y., 1833. 12°. 16478
North, Journeys in, 1865–69. Williamson. Lond., 1870. 2 v. 8°. 7950
Chinese as they are, The. Lay. Lond., 1841. 8°. 8005
Description of the. Davis. Lond., 1844. 4 v. 12°. . . 8154
Dissertations on the. De Pauw. Lond., 1795. 2 v. 8°. . . 16169
Social Life of the. Doolittle. N. Y., 1865. 2 v. 12°. . . 7942
Empire, Journey through the, 1846–52. Huc. N. Y., 1857. 2 v. 12°. 7946
View of the. Winterbotham. Lond., 1795. 8°. . 16473
Expedition, Six Months with the, 1840. Jocelyn. Lond., 1841. 16°. 7941
Chittenden, L. E. Debates, etc., of Conference Convention in 1861. N. Y., 1864. 8°. 6250
Chivalry, Age of. Bulfinch. Bost., 1861. 12°. 1910
Hist. of. James. N. Y., 1840. 12°. 11022
The same. Mills. Philad., 1825. 8°. 4737
Letters on. [Hurd.] Lond., 1762. 8°. 15932
True Sense and Practice of. Digby. Lond., 1844. 12°. . . 4620
Ancient, Memoirs of. La Curne de Ste. Palaye. Lond., 1784. 8°. 4619
See, also, KNIGHTS.

Choate, R. Works, with Memoir. (2 copies.) Bost., 1862. 2 v. 8°. 9668
Life of. Brown. 2d ed. Bost., 1870. 12°. 7333
Chorley, H. F. Memorials of Mrs. Hemans. N. Y., 1836. 2 v. in 1. 12°. 16379
Sketches of a Sea-Port Town. Philad., 1836. 2 v. 12°. . . . 15584
Choules, J. O. and T. Smith. Hist. of Missions. Bost., 1837. 2 v. 4°. 6596
Chris and Otho. J. P. Smith. N. Y., 1870. 12°. 15677
Christ of the Gospels, The. Schaff and Roussel. N. Y., 1869. 16°. 9896
of History, The. Young. N. Y., 1860. 12°. 9899
the Life and Light of Men. Young. Lond., 1866. 8°. . . 9900
and his Salvation. Bushnell. N. Y., 1864. 12°. . . . 9941
in Theology. Bushnell. Hartf'd., 1851. 12°. 9939
God in. Bushnell. Hartf'd., 1849. 12°. 9935
Imitation of. Thomas à Kempis. Bost., 1861. 12°. . . . 9947
Kingdom of, delineated. Whately. N. Y., 1842. 12°. . . 9953
Testimony of, to Christianity. Bayne. Bost., 1862. 8°. . . 9901
Vicarious Sacrifice of. Bushnell. N. Y., 1866. 8°. . . . 10025
Witness of History to. Farrar. Lond., 1871. 8°. . . . 9906
See, also, JESUS.
Christian, The Young. Abbott. N. Y., 1834. 12°. 9993
Ballads. [Coxe.] N. Y., 1840. 12°. 802
Character, Formation of. Ware. Cambr., 1831. 12°. . . 9808
Church. See ECCLESIASTICAL History.
Denominations, Book of the. Lond., 1837. 16°. . . . 6352
Doctrine and Practice in 2d Century. Philad., 1846. 12°. . 8497
Treatise on. Milton. (Works, v. 4, 5.) Lond., 1868–70. 2 v. 8°. 457
Life, The. Bayne. Bost., 1860. 12°. 9975
in Early and Middle Ages. Neander. Lond., 1852. 8°. 487
Endeavors after the. Martineau. Bost., 1858. 12°. . 9974
Nurture. Bushnell. N. Y., 1861. 12°. 9940
Philosophy. Knox. Lond., 1835. 16°. 9501
Professor, The. James. N. Y., 1838. 12°. 17349
Religion, Evidences, Doctrines, and Duties of. Gregory. Lond., 1851. 8°. 486
Institutes of the. Calvin. Lond., 1838. 2 v. 8°. . 10034
Truth of the. Grotius. Lond., 1825. 12°. . . 9810
Sects in 19th Century. Philad., 1846. 12°. 8498
Spectator, Monthly. N. H., 1819–28. 10 v. 8°. . . . 12940
Quarterly. (2 copies.) N. H., 1829–38. 10 v. 8°. . 12950
Christianity and Positivism. M'Cosh. N. Y., 1871. 12°. . . . 9999
and Scepticism. Boston Lectures, 1870. Bost. 12°. . . 9996
Ancient, and the Oxford Tracts. Taylor. Philad., 1840. 12°. 9541
Apology for. Watson. N. Y., 1835. 8°. 17269
Evidences of. Barnes. N. Y., 1868. 12°. 9998
The same. Chalmers. N. Y., 1840–41. 2 v. 12°. . 9518
The same. Gurney. Bost., 1833. 12°. 17292
The same. Paley. Philad., 1831. 8°. 9631
The same, abridged by Wrangham. Edinb., 1828. 12°. . 4488
Latin, Hist. of, to 1854. Milman. N. Y., 1860–61. 8 v. 8°. . 6391

Christianity, Meditations on Essence of. Guizot. N. Y., 1865. 12°. 9982
Origins of. Renan. N. Y., 1866–69. 3 v. 12°. 9893
CONTENTS.—1, Life of Jesus. 2, The Apostles. 3, St. Paul.
Primitive. Cave. Lond., 1834–35. 2 v. 16°. 9494
Reasonableness of. Locke. (Works, v. 7.) Lond., 1801. 8°. . 9596
Spiritual. I. Taylor. N. Y., 1841. 12°. 9542
Supernatural Origin of. Fisher. N. Y., 1866. 8°. . . . 10026
Women of. Kavanagh. N. Y., 1852. 12°. 7568
See, also, ECCLESIASTICAL History.
Christian's Defensive Dictionary. Sleigh. Philad., 1837. 12°. . . 17304
Christian's Mistake. A Novel. Craik. N. Y., 1866. 12°. . . 2486
Christians, Eminent, Lives of. Frost. Hartf'd., 1850. 8°. . . 16400
Professing, Lectures to. Finney. N. Y., 1837. 12°. . . 17352
Christie, R. Military Operations in the Canadas. Quebec, 1818. 12°. 5720
Christie, W. D. Life of Earl of Shaftesbury. Lond., 1871. 2 v. 8°. 6624
Christie Johnstone. Reade. Bost., 1871. 16°. 2094
Christmas, Book of. Hervey. N. Y., 1845. 12°. 3899
Stories. Dickens. N. Y., 1871. 16°. 2174
Christopher Kenrick. Hatton. N. Y., 1869. 12°. 2432
Christus. Longfellow. Bost., 1872. 3 v. 12°. 715
Chronicles of the Canongate. Scott. Bost., 1834–45. 4 v. in 2. 12°. 1833
Clovernook. Jerrold. Lond., 1846. 16°. 4251
Schönberg-Cotta Family. Charles. Lond., 1868. 8°. 2463
Chronology of History, The. Nicolas. Lond., 1838. 16°. . . . 4855
Haydn's Dict. of, with Amer. Supplement. N. Y., 1867. 8°. . 4066
The World's Progress of. Putnam. N. Y., 1851. 12°. . . 4605
Chrysostom, Life of. Neander. Lond., 1845. 8°. 7700
Chubbuck, E. See Mrs. E. C. JUDSON.
Chunder, B. Travels of a Hindoo. Lond., 1869. 2 v. 8°. . . 8018
Church, P. Philosophy of Benevolence. N. Y., 1836. 12°. . . 17356
Church, T. Hist. of the Indian War, 1675–76, and of French and Indian Wars, 1689–1704. Ed. Drake. Hartf'd. [1845.] 8°. 5957
The same. Exeter, 1834. 12°. 5748
Church, Antiquities of the. Coleman. Andover, 1841. 8°. . . 10014
in the Catacombs, The. Maitland. Lond., 1846. 8°. . . 6451
Doctrine, Bible Truth. Sadler. N. Y., 1869. 12°. . . . 9821
Government, Reason of. Milton. Lond., 1848. 8°. . . . 455
History. See ECCLESIASTICAL History.
Music, Our. Willis. N. Y., 1856. 12°. 8866
and State. Coleridge. (Works, 6.) N. Y., 1871. 12°. . . 4018
The same. Gladstone. Lond., 1841. 2 v. 8°. . . 8693
Early English. Churton. N. Y., 1852. 16°. 6311
Eastern, Hist. of [to 1860]. Stanley. N. Y., 1870. 8°. . . 6418
of England, Essays on. Stanley. Lond., 1870. 8°. . . . 3436
Jewish. See JEWISH.
Lectures on the. Hyacinthe. N. Y., 1870. 12°. . . . 9984
Churches, Lectures on Reunion of. Döllinger. N. Y., 1872. 12°. . 10266
Our Seven. Beecher. N. Y., 1870. 16°. 9833
See, also, CHRISTIANITY.

Churchill, C. Poems. Lond., 1763. 4°. 15086
The same. 3d ed. Lond., 1766. 2 v. 8°. 1242
The same. Ed. Bell. Lond., 1807. 3 v. in 2. 24°. . 540
The same. Ed. Johnson. Dubl., 1804. 8°. 15102
Select Poems. Ed. Walsh. Philad., 1822. 24°. 21
Churchill, J. (Duke of Marlborough,) Life of. Gleig. Lond., 1831–32. 2 v. 16°. 5771
Memoirs of. Coxe. Lond., 1847–48. 3 v. 8°. 369
Churchill, S. (Duchess of Marlborough.) Correspondence, etc. 2d ed. Lond., 1838. 2 v. 8°. 7164
Churchyards, Chapters on. C. Southey. N. Y., 1842. 12°. . . 3746
Churton, E. The Early English Church. N. Y., 1842. 16°. . . 6311
Cibber, C. Dramatic Works. Lond., 1777. 5 v. 12°. 1454
She Would and She Would Not; Love makes a Man; Careless Husband. (Brit. Theatre, v. 17.) Lond. 12°. . . . 1341
Apology for Life of. By himself. Lond., 1750. 8°. 7991
The same. Lond., 1826. 12°. 6639
Cicero, M. T. Letters to Friends, transl. by Melmoth. Dubl., 1753. 3 v. 12°. 13995
The same. Lond., 1803. v. 2, 3. 8°. 15859
Orations, Offices, Cato, and Lælius, translated. N. Y., 1840–45. 3 v. 12°. 4515
Tusculan Questions, transl. by Otis. Bost., 1839. 12°. . . 4623
Works, translated. Lond., 1804–08. 11 v. 8°. 4624
CONTENTS.—1-3, Letters. 4-6, Epistles to Atticus. 7, 8, Orations. 9, 10, De Oratore. 11, De Senectute and De Amicitia.
Life of. Forsyth. N. Y., 1866. 2 v. 8°. 7744
The same. Middleton. Lond., 1837. 8°. 7743
Cid, Chronicle of the. Ed. Southey. (2 copies.) Lowell, 1846. 8°. . 1676
Romance of the, Analysis of. N. Y., 1842. 8°. 913
Translations from. Dennis. Lond., 1845. 24°. 284
Cinq-Mars; an Historical Romance. De Vigny. Lond., 1847. 8°. . 472
Circassia, Residence in, 1837–39. Bell. Lond., 1840. 2 v. 8°. . 8040
Tour to, 1847–48. Ditson. N. Y., 1850. 12°. 16489
Travels in, 1836. Spencer. Lond., 1839. 2 v. 8°. . . . 8042
See, also, CAUCASUS.
Circumnavigation of the Globe, Hist. of. N. Y., 1840. 12°. . . . 11407
See, also, VOYAGES.
Cities and Principal Towns of the World, The. Lond., 1830. v. 1. 16°. 5789
CONTENTS.—Grt. Britain; Netherlands; France; Spain.
Moral Influence of. Todd. Northampton, 1841. 12°. . . 17290
Ancient, Ruins of. Bucke. N. Y., 1841. 2 v. 12°. . . 11609
City of the Saints, The. Burton. Lond., 1861. 8°. 8417
Civil Liberty and Self-Government. Lieber. Philad., 1859. 8°. . 8686
Civilization, Hist. of. Guizot. Lond., 1846. 3 v. 8°. 326
Origin of. Lubbock. N. Y., 1870. 12°. 4073
in England, Hist. of. Buckle. N. Y., 1859–66. 2 v. 8°. . 5065
Clara; or, Slave Life in Europe. Hackländer. N. Y., 1856. 12°. . 15130
Clara Howard. C. B. Brown. Bost., 1827. 12°. 15301

Clarence. Sedgwick. Lond., 1830. 3 v. 12°. 15310
Clarendon, Lord. See E. HYDE.
Clarissa Harlowe. Richardson. Lond., 1811. 8 v. 16°. 1931
Clark, John A. Glimpses of the Old World. Philad., 1840. 2 v. 12°. 16576
Clark, L. G. Knick-knacks. (2 copies.) N. Y., 1853. 12°. . . . 4299
Clark, N. G. Elements of the English Language. N. Y., 1863. 16°. 63
Clark, R. W. The Bible and the School Fund. (2 copies.) Bost., 1870. 16°. 9147
Clark, V. Rhyming Geography. Hartf'd., 1819. 12°. 14982
Clark, W. G. Literary Remains. N. Y., 1844. 8°. 3660
The same. 15079
Clarke, Adam. Commentary on the Bible. N. Y., 1840. v. 1, 3–5. 8°. 17325
Life of. N. Y., 1833. 12°. 16338
Clarke, A. B. Travels in Mexico and California. Bost., 1852. 12°. 16896
[**Clarke, C.**] Three Courses and a Dessert. (2 copies.) Lond., 1850–67. 8°. 523
Clarke, Chas. C. Wonders of the World. N. H., 1821. 12°. . . . 16941
Clarke, E. A. Tales and Sketches. Lond., 1838. 8°. 15348
Clarke, Edward D. Travels. Lond., 1816–24. 11 v. 8°. . . . 8020
CONTENTS.—1, 2, Russia, Tahtary, Turkey. 3-8, Greece, Egypt, Holy Land. 9-11, Scandinavia.
Life and Remains of. Otter. N. Y., 1827. 8°. 7151
Clarke, F. J., and **Dunlap, W.** Life of Wellington. N. Y., 1814. 8°. 16353
Clarke, James F. Eleven Weeks in Europe. Bost., 1852. 12°. . 16579
Ten Great Religions. Bost., 1871. 8°. 10265
Clarke, John. Letters to a Student. Bost., 1796. 12°. 17023
Clarke, M. C. Concordance to Shakspere. N. Y., 1846. 8°. . . . 1657
The same. Bost. 8°. 1658
The Iron Cousin. N. Y., 1862. 12°. 15463
Portia, and other Stories of Shakespeare's Heroines. N. Y., 1868. 12°. 1493
Shakespeare Proverbs. Lond., 1848. 16°. 1366
Clarke, S. R. Vestigia Anglicana. Lond., 1826. 2 v. 8°. . . . 5102
Clarkson, T. Hist. of Abolition of Slave Trade. (2 copies.) Lond., 1808. 2 v. 8°. 8672
Classical Studies. Sears, Edwards, and Felton. Bost., 1843. 12°. . 9259
Study, Method of. Taylor. Bost., 1861. 12°. 9273
Value of, illustrated. Taylor. Andover, 1870. 12°. . 9263
Claverings, The. A. Trollope. N. Y., 1866. 8°. 2291
Clavers, Mary. *(Pseudonym.)* See C. M. KIRKLAND.
Clavigero, F. S. Hist. of Mexico. Philad., 1804. 3 v. 8°. . . . 5974
Claxton, T., Memoir of. By himself. Bost., 1839. 12°. 6941
Clay, C. M. Writings. N. Y., 1848. 8°. 17163
Clay, H. Speeches. Philad., 1827. 8°. 9434
Biogr. of. Prentice. Hartf'd., 1831. 12°. 7327
Life of. Sargent and Greeley. Auburn, 1852. 12°. 7326
and Speeches of. (2 copies.) N. Y., 1843. 2 v. 8°. . 9437
The same, ed. by D. Mallory. N. Y., 1844. 2 v. 8°. 9435
and Times of. Colton. N. Y., 1846. 2 v. 8°. . . . 7429
[**Clemens, S. L.**] Innocents Abroad. (2 copies.) Hartf'd., 1869. 8°. 4285

[**Clemens, S. L.**] Mark Twain's Autobiography. N. Y., 1871. 12°. . 4287
Roughing it. Hartf'd., 1872. 8°. 4288
Clement, J. Noble Deeds of American Women. Buffalo, 1851. 12°. 9208
Clement Falconer. Balt., 1838. 2 v. 12°. 15678
Cleopatra, Hist. of. Abbott. N. Y. [1851.] 16°. 7497
Clergy, Book about the. Jeaffreson. Lond., 1870. 2 v. 8°. . . 6456
Clerical Manners and Habits, Letters on. Miller. N. Y., 1827. 12°. 9828
Cleveland, C. D. Compendium of English Literature [to 1800]. Philad., 1847. 12°. . . . . , 139
Concordance to Poet. Works of Milton. Lond., 1867. 16°. . 1203
English Literature of 19th century. Philad., 1865. 12°. . . 140
Cleveland, H. R. Life of Hudson. Bost., 1839. 16°. . . . 7259
The same. Bost., 1839. 12°. 16314
Clever Woman of the Family. Yonge. N. Y., 1865. 8°. . . . 2664
Cliffton, W. Poems. N. Y., 1800. 12°. 14930
Climate, Influence of. De Bonstetten. N. Y., 1864. 12°. . . . 8552
Clinton, D. Letters on Nat. Hist., etc., of N. Y. N. Y., 1822. 12°. . 16847
Speeches and Messages, as Governor. Albany, 1825. 8°. . 17538
Life of. Renwick. N. Y., 1841. 12°. 11600
Tribute to Memory of. [Staats.] Albany, 1828. 12°. . . 7551
[**Clive, C.**] Paul Ferroll. N. Y., 1856. 12°. 11534
Clive, Lord R., Life of. Gleig. Lond., 1832. 16°. 5773
Cloister and the Hearth. Reade. N. Y., 1868. 8°. 2279
Cloney, T. Personal Narrative of Transactions in 1798. Dubl., 1832. 8°. 5244
Cloquet, J. Private Life of Lafayette. N. Y., 1836. 2 v. 12°. . . 7624
Cloudesley. Godwin. N. Y., 1830. 2 v. 12°. 15398
Clouds and Sunshine. Reade. Bost., 1855. 12°. . , . . 2096
Clough, A. H. Poems, with Memoir by Norton. Bost., 1862. 16°. . 980
Poems and Prose Remains. Lond., 1869. 2 v. 16°. . . 846
Club-Book, The. N. Y., 1831. 2 v. 12°. 14638
Cobb, J. Wife of 2 Husbands; Ramah Droog. (Mod. Theatre, v. 6.) Lond., 1811. 12°. 1332
Cobbe, F. P. Alone to the Alone: Prayers for Theists. Lond., 1871. 8°. 9967
Broken Lights. 2d ed. Lond., 1865. 8°. 9965
Darwinism in Morals, and other Essays. Lond., 1872. 8°. . 10028
Dawning Lights. Lond., 1868. 8°. 9966
Hours of Work and Play. Lond., 1867. 8°. 3984
Italics. Lond., 1864. 12°. 8348
Studies of Ethical and Social Subjects. Lond., 1865. 8°. . 3985
Cobbe, T. Hist. of Norman Kings of England. Lond., 1869. 8°. . 5285
Cobbett, W. Advice to Young Men, etc. N. Y., 1831. 12°. . . 17025
Bloody Buoy. By Peter Porcupine. 2d ed. Philad., 1796. 12°. 16223
Grammar of the English Language. N. Y., 1846. 12°. . . 90
Hist. of the Reformation in England and Ireland. N. Y., 1832–34. 2 v. 12°. 6369
Legacy to Parsons. N. Y., 1844. 12°. 17283
Paper against Gold. Lond., 1815. 2 v. 8°. 8655
The same. N. Y., 1834. 12°. 8465
Porcupine's Works. Lond., 1801. 12 v. 8°. 17210

Cobbett, W. Thirteen Sermons. N. Y., 1846. 12°. 17282
Life of. Philad., 1835. 12°. 6692
Sketch of. Thorold Rogers. Lond., 1869. 8°. 6731
Cobden, R. Political Writings. Lond., 1867. 2 v. 8°. . . . 9587
Biography of. McGilchrist. N. Y., 1865. 16°. . . . 6688
Cochin, A. Results of Emancipation. (2 copies.) Bost., 1863. 12°. 8562
of Slavery. (2 copies.) Bost., 1863. 12°. . . 8564
Cochin-China, Embassy to, 1832. Roberts. N. Y., 1837. 8°. . . 16499
Cochrane, G. Wanderings in Greece. Lond., 1837. 2 v. 8°. . . 8321
Cochrane, J. D. Journey through Russia, etc. Edinb., 1829. 2 v. 12°. 4498
Cochrane, Lord T., Trial, etc., of. N. Y., 1814. 12°. 9152
Cockburn, G. Diary of Voyage to St. Helena. Bost., 1833. 12°. . 5438
Cockburn, H. T. Life of Lord Jeffrey. Philad., 1852. 2 v. 12°. . 7014
Codman, J. Visit to England. Bost., 1836. 12°. 16760
Cœlebs deceived. [Carp.] Philad., 1817. 12°. 15400
in search of a Wife. More. N. Y., 1809. 2 v. 12°. . . 2403
Coffey, C. Devil to pay. (Brit. Drama, v. 5.) Lond., 1804. 8°. . 1663
Coffin, C. C. Our New Way round the World. Bost., 1869. 8°. . 8059
[**Coffin, Robert B.**] Castles in the Air, etc. N. Y., 1871. 8°. . . 2928
Matrimonial Infelicities. (2 copies.) N. Y., 1865–66. 12°. . 2925
My Married Life at Hillside. (2 copies.) N. Y., 1865. 12°. . 2923
Out of Town. N. Y., 1866. 8°. 2927
[**Coffin, Robert S.**] Poems of the Boston Bard. Prov., 1826. 8°. . 15052
Coghlan, M., Memoirs of. By herself. N. Y., 1795. 12°. . . 16433
Cogswell, W. Letters to Young Men. Bost., 1837. 12°. . . . 17036
Cohen, M. M. Florida and the Campaigns. (2 copies.) Charleston, 1836. 12°. 5732
Coit, T. W. Puritanism. N. Y., 1845. 12°. 6332
Coke, Sir E., Life of. (Libr. of Useful Knowl.) Lond., 1833. 8°. . 6751
Life of. Campbell (Chief Justices, v. 1.) Philad., 1851. 8°. . 6873
Coke, E. T. A Subaltern's Furlough. N. Y., 1833. 2 v. 12°. . 16794
Colbert E. and Chamberlin, E. Chicago and the Great Conflagration. Cincinn., 1872. 12°. 6092
Colbert, J. B., Life of. G. P. R. James. Philad., 1837. 2 v. 12°. . 7613
Colden, C. D. Life of Fulton. N. Y., 1817. 8°. 16423
[**Cole, M.**] Rutledge. N. Y., 1860. 12°. 2985
St. Philip's. N. Y., 1865. 12°. 2986
Cole, S. W. The Muse. Cornish, 1827. 12°. 14967
Coleman, L. Antiquities of the Christian Church. Andover, 1841. 8°. 10014
Historical Geography of the Bible. Philad., 1849. 12°. . . 9883
The same. New ed. Philad., 1850. 12°. 9884
Coleridge, Hartley. Worthies of Yorkshire and Lancashire. Leeds, 1836. 8°. 6904
Coleridge, Henry N. Introd. to Greek Poets. (2 copies.) Philad., 1831. 12°. 41
Coleridge, J. T. Memoir of Keble. 2d ed. Oxf'd., 1869. 2 v. 8°. 7003
Coleridge, Samuel T. Aids to Reflection, ed. Marsh. Burlington, 1829. 8°. 8729
The same, ed. McVickar. N. Y., 1841. 12°. . . . 8603

Coleridge, Samuel T. Biographia Literaria. N. Y., 1834. 8°. . . . 4005
The same. New ed. N. Y., 1847. v. 1. 12°. . . . 3983
Church and State; Lay Sermons. Lond., 1839. 16°. . . 8538
Confessions of an Inquiring Spirit. Bost., 1841. 16°. . . 9834
The Friend. Burlington, 1831. 8°. 3425
Idea of Life. Philad., 1848. 12°. 16948
Letters, Conversations, etc. (2 copies.) N. Y., 1836. 12°. . 3980
Literary Remains. Lond., 1836–39. 4 v. 8°. 4006

CONTENTS.—1, Fall of Robespierre; Poems; Lectures; Notes and Fragments; Omniana. 2, Notes on Shakespeare, Jonson, Beaumont and Fletcher, Prometheus, etc. 3, Notes on Hooker, Field, Donne, Jer. Taylor, etc. 4, Notes on Luther, Baxter, Leighton, Sherlock, Waterland, etc.

The same. v. 1, 3, 4. 4010
Poetical Works. Lond., 1829. 3 v. 16°. 848
The same. Lond., 1840. 3 v. 16°. 967
Poetical and Dramatic Works. Bost., 1864. 24°. . . . 975
Specimens of Table Talk. N. Y., 1835. 2 v. in 1. 12°. . . 3982
Statesman's Manual. Burlington, 1832. 12°. 8629
Works, ed. Shedd. N. Y., 1868–71. 7 v. 12°. 4013

CONTENTS.—1, Introd. Essay; Aids to Reflection; Statesman's Manual. 2, The Friend. 3, Biographia Literaria. 4, Notes and Lectures on Shakspeare and other Dramatists, etc. 5, Literary Remains. 6, Church and State; Lay Sermon; Table Talk. 7, Poems; Dramas.

Life of. Gillman. Lond., 1838. 2 v. 8°. 7182
Reminiscences of. Cottle. N. Y., 1847. 12°. 7097
[**Coleridge, Sara H.**] Phantasmion. N. Y., 1839. 2 v. 12°. . . 15544
Colin Clink. Hooton. Philad., 1840–41. 2 v. 12°. 15401
College, Letters to Sons in. Miller. Philad., 1843. 12°. . . . 17031
Courant, The. N. H., 1867–70. v. 3–7. (2 copies of v. 3–5.) 4°.
Words and Customs. Hall. Cambr., 1856. 12°. 9258
Colleges, American. Porter. N. H., 1870. 12°. 9254
Songs of. Waite. Bost. [1868.] 8°. . . . 9091
Collegiate Addresses. Maxcy. Lond. 16°. 9128
System in U. S., Thoughts on. Wayland. Bost., 1842. 16°. . 9183
See, also, EDUCATION; UNIVERSITIES.
Collier, J. P. Annals of the Stage. (2 copies.) Lond., 1831. 3 v. 16°. 1556
Notes to Shakespeare. (2 copies.) N. Y., 1853. 12°. . . . 1554
Poetical Decameron. Lond., 1820. 2 v. 16°. 128
Reasons for new ed. of Shakespeare. Lond., 1842. 8°. . . 1553
Collins, L. Hist. Sketches of Ky. Cincinn., 1850. 8°. 5891
Collins, Wm. Poetical Works. Philad., 1842. 8°. 945
The same. Bost., 1854. 16°. 970
The same. Ed. Bell. Lond., 1857. 24°. 536
The same. Ed. Johnson. Dubl., 1804. 8°. 15101
The same. Ed. Walsh. Philad., 1819. 24°. 17
Collins, Wm. L. Ancient Classics for English Readers. (2 copies.)
Philad., 1870–71. 8 v. 16°. 71

CONTENTS.—1, Homer's Iliad. 2, Homer's Odyssey. 3, Herodotus. 4, Cæsar. 5, Virgil. 6, Horace. 7, Æschylus. 8, Xenophon.

Collins, Wm. Wilkie. Armadale. (2 copies.) N. Y., 1866. 8°. . 2301
After Dark. N. Y. 8°. 2298
Hide and Seek. N. Y. 8°. 2297
Man and Wife. (2 copies.) N. Y., 1870. 8°. 2304
The Moonstone. N. Y., 1869. 8°. 2303

Collins, Wm. Wilkie. No Name. N. Y., 1863. 8°. 2299
Poor Miss Finch. N. Y., 1872. 8°. . . . . , 2306
Woman in White. N. Y., 1871. 8°. 2300
Colman, Geo. Clandestine Marriage; English Merchant; Jealous Wife. (Brit. Drama.) Lond., 1804. 8°. 1632
Deuce is in him. (Brit. Drama.) Lond., 1804. 8°. . . . 1633
English Merchant. (Mod. Theatre, v. 9.) Lond., 1811. 12°. . 1335
Jealous Wife. (Oxberry's Plays, v. 11.) Bost., 1822. 24°. . 1355
and **Thornton, B.** The Connoisseur. Lond., 1823. 2 v. 12°. 3134
Colman, Geo., Jr. Poetical Works. Philad., 1834. 12°. . . . 14781
Who Wants a Guinea? (Mod. Theatre, v. 3.) Lond., 1811. 12°. 1329
Colman, H. European Life and Manners. Bost., 1850. 2 v. 12°. . 16562
Colombia, Popular Description of. Conder. Lond. 12°. . . 7859
Recollections of Service in. Lond., 1828. 2 v. 8°. . . . 17129
Visit to, 1822–23. Duane. Philad., 1826. 8°. 17133
Colombo, M. Novel. (Ital. Novelists, v. 4.) Lond., 1836. 12°. . 1902
Colonies, Emancipate your. Bentham. (Works, v. 4.) Edinb., 1838. 8°. 9703
European. Howison. Lond., 1834. 2 v. 8°. 4711
Colonization and Christianity. Howitt. Lond., 1838. 12°. . . 15886
Society, Inquiry into Character of the. Jay. N. Y., 1835. 12°. 8549
Colorado, the Switzerland of America. Bowles. Springf'ld., 1869. 12°. 8169
Colors, Theory of. Goethe, tr. by Eastlake. Lond., 1840. 8°. . . 9072
Colton, C. Four Years in Grt. Brit. N. Y., 1835. 2 v. 12°. . . 16755
Life of Clay. 2d ed. N. Y., 1846. 2 v. 8°. 7429
Colton, Geo. H. Tecumseh. N. Y., 1842. 12°. 14983
Colton, G. W. General Atlas. N. Y., 1868. 4°. . . . . .
Colton, W. The Sea and the Sailor, etc. N. Y., 1851. 12°. . . 15269
Ship and Shore. N. Y., 1835. 12°. 16648
Visit to Constantinople and Athens. N. Y., 1856. 12°. . . 16635
Columba, St., Life of. Dunham. Lond., 1840. 16°. 5774
Columbia R., Adventures on the, 1811–17. Cox. N. Y., 1832. 8°. . 16862
Columbian Muse, The. N. Y., 1794. 12°. 14966
Columbus, C. Narrative of First Voyage to America. Bost., 1827. 8°. 7783
Life of. Helps. Lond., 1869. 16°. 7822
and Voyages of. Irving. N. Y., 1850–51. 3 v. 12°. . 7816
Voyages of Companions of. Irving. Philad., 1831. 8°. . 7815
Combe, A. Principles of Physiology. N. Y., 1840. 12°. . . . 9125
The same. N. Y., 1841. 12°. 11289
The same. N. Y., 1835. 12°. 12116
Combe, G. Constitution of Man. (2 copies.) Bost., 1833. 12°. . 8533
The same. Hartf'd., 1842. 8°. 3472
Moral Philosophy. N. Y., 1844. 12°. 8495
Notes on the U. S. Philad., 1841. 2 v. 12°. 16826
Physiology of Digestion. N. Y., 1836. 12°. 9124
System of Phrenology. Bost., 1834. 8°. 8780
Combe, W. Tour of Dr. Syntax. Philad., 1829. 12°. 984
Comic Almanack, Cruikshank's. Lond. 2 v. 8°. 4260
Arithmetic. [Forrester.] Lond., 1843. 12°. 4278

Comic Blackstone. A'Beckett. Lond. 16.° 4274
English Grammar, The. Lond., 1840. 12°. 4275
Hist. of England. A'Beckett. Lond., 1865. 8°. . . . 4262
of Rome. A'Beckett. Lond. 8°. 4314
of U. S. Sherwood. Bost., 1870. 12°. 4311
Writers, English, Lectures on. Hazlitt. Lond., 1819. 8°. . 68
Literature. See, also, CARICATURE; DRAMA; THEATER.
Comines, P. de. Memoirs. Lond., 1823. 2 v. 8°. 5532
Coming out. Porter. N. Y., 1828. 2 v. 12°. 15179
Coming Race, The. N. Y., 1871. 12°. 9202
Commander of Malta. Sue. N. Y., 1860. 8°. 2311
Commerce, Hist. of. Anderson. Dubl., 1790. 6 v. 8°. . . . 4067
British, Hist. of. Craik. Lond., 1844. 3 v. 12°. . . . 8783
U. S., Statistics of. Pitkin. N. H., 1835. 8°. 5854
Commercial Affairs, Application of Christianity to. Chalmers. N. Y., 1840. 12°. 9521
Common Prayer Book, Illustration of. Wheatly. Lond., 1849. 8°. . 496
Commune of Paris, Hist. of the. Vésinier. Lond., 1872. 8°. . . 5554
Communion, Terms of. R. Hall. (Works, v. 1.) N. Y., 1833. 8°. . 10070
Comnenus, Isaac; a Play. Taylor. Lond., 1845. 24°. , . . 983
Companions of my Solitude. Helps. Bost., 1852. 16°. . . . 3695
Compensation. Brewster. Philad., 1860. 12°. 2982
Composition, Letters on. Gregory. Philad., 1809. 12°. . . . 17028
Principles of. Booth. Lond., 1831. 12°. 9187
Student's Guide to. Banks. Lond., 1823. 8°. 17528
See, also, ENGLISH.
Comstock, John L. Hist. of the Greek Revolution. N. Y., 1828. 12°. 4559
Comstock, Joseph. Tongue of Time. N. Y., 1838. 12°. . . . 16999
Comte, A., Positive Philosophy of. J. S. Mill. Bost., 1871. 12°. . 8590
Concord and Merrimack Rivers, A Week on. [1839.] Thoreau. Bost., 1863. 12°. 3557
Concordance to the Bible. Cruden. Lond., 1867. 8°. . . . 9836
Poems of Milton. Cleveland. Lond., 1867. 16°. . 1203
Shakspeare. Clarke. Bost. 8°. 1658
Tennyson. Brightwell. Lond., 1869. 8°. . . 1241
Conde, J. A. Hist. of Arabs in Spain. Lond., 1854. 3 v. 8°. . 424
Condé, L., Prince de, Life of. Lord Mahon. N. Y., 1845. 12°. . 7619
Condé, Princes de, Hist. of the. Duc d'Aumale. Lond., 1872. 2 v. 8°. 5657
Condensed Novels. Bret Harte. Bost., 1871. 8°. 2916
Conder, J. Italy. Lond., 1834. 3 v. 12°. 8178
Modern Traveller. Lond., 1825–39. 21 v. 12°. . . . 7841
Condorcet, M. J. A. N. C. de. Hist. of Progress of the Mind. Philad., 1796. 12°. 8499
Confessional, Hist. of the. Hopkins. N. Y., 1850. 12°. . . . 9609
Confessions of an Elderly Gentleman and Lady. Lady Blessington. Philad., 1838. 8°. 2668
of an Inquirer. Jarves. Bost., 1857. 12°. 15680
of a Poet. Philad., 1835. 2 v. 12°. 15681
Confidence-Man, The. Melville. N. Y., 1857. 12°. 15683

Confirmation, Discourse on. Jer. Taylor. (Works, 3.) Lond., 1836. 8°. 10064

Confucius. Morals, ed. Gowan. N. Y., 1835. 12°. 9531

Congregational Pulpit, Annals of the American. Sprague. N. Y., 1857. 2 v. 8°. 7730

Congregationalism, Hist. of, to 1616. Punchard. Salem, 1841. 12°. 6310

Congress of Nations, Prize Essays on a. Bost., 1840. 8°. 8701

Congress of the U. S. See U. S.

Congreve, W. Double Dealer; Way of the World; Love for Love. (Brit. Drama.) Lond., 1804. 8°. 1631

Dramatic Works. Ed. Hunt. Lond., 1849. 8°. . . . 10300

Mourning Bride. (Brit. Drama.) Lond., 1804. 8°. . . . 1629

Select Poems. With Life, by Sanford. Philad., 1819. 24° . 10

The same. Ed. Johnson. Dubl., 1804. 8°. . . . 15098

Coningsby. Disraeli. N. Y., 1845. 8°. 2344

Conn., Hist. of, to 1764. Trumbull. N. H., 1818. 2 v. 8°. . . 5962

to 1776. [Peters.] N. H., 1829. 12°. . . . 6006

to 1841. Dwight. N. Y., 1842. 12°. 11608

during the Revolution. Hinman. Hartf'd., 1842. 8°. . . 6295

during the War, 1861–65. Croffut and Morris. N. Y., 1868. 8°. 6261

Hist. of 27th Regiment. Sheldon. N. H., 1866. 8°. . 6110

Poets of. Everest. Hartf'd., 1843. 8°. 926

Report on Geology of. Percival. N. H., 1842. 8°. . . . 9102

Connoisseur, The. Colman and Thornton. Lond., 1823. 2 v. 12°. . 3134

Conolly, A. Journey to India. 2d ed. Lond., 1838. 2 v. 8°. . 8037

Conscience, Liberty of. See TOLERATION.

The Rule of. Jer. Taylor. (Works, 3.) Lond., 1836. 8°. . 10064

Conspiracies in Europe, Hist. of. Lawson. Edinb., 1829. 2 v. 12°. 4505

Constable's Miscellany. Edinb., 1826–9. 45 v. 12°. 4463

CONTENTS.—1–3, Voyages; B. Hall. 4, Adventures of British Seamen; Murray. 5, La Rochejaquelein; Memoirs. 6, 7, Converts from Infidelity; Crichton. 8, 9, Embassy to Ava; Symes. 10, Table Talk. 11, Perils and Captivity. 12, Phenomena of Nature; Bell. 13, 14, Account of the Tonga Islands; W. Mariner. 15, 16, Hist. of the Rebellion in 1745, 1746; R. Chambers. 17, Voyages and Excursions in Central America; Roberts. 18, 19, Thirty Years' War; Schiller. 20, 21, Illustrations of the History of Great Britain; R. Thomson. 22, Register of Politics and Literature in Europe and America, 1827. 23, Life of Burns; Lockhart. 24, 25, Life of Mary, Queen of Scots; Bell. 26, Evidences of Christianity; F. Wrangham. 27, 28, Memorials of the Peninsular War. 29, 30, Tour in Germany; J. Russell. 31, 32, Hist. of Rebellions in Scotland, 1638–1660; R. Chambers. 33–35, Hist. of Revolutions in Europe; C. W. Koch. 36, 37, Pedestrian Journey through Russia, etc.; J. D. Cochrane. 38, Journey through Norway, Sweden, and Denmark; H. D. Inglis. 39, Hist. of Sculpture, Painting, and Architecture; Memes. 40, 41, Hist. of the Ottoman Empire; E. Upham. 42, History of Rebellions in Scotland, 1689 and 1715; R. Chambers. 43, 44, History of Remarkable Conspiracies; J. P. Lawson. 62, Hist. of Conquest of Peru; Trueba y Cosio.

Constance. Mancur. Philad. 8°. 2313

Constant-Rebecque, H. B. de. Philosophical Miscellanies, tr. by Ripley. Bost., 1838. 12°. 8585

Constantinople, the City of the Sultan. Pardoe. Philad., 1837. 2 v. 12°. 16639

Promenades round. Pertusier. Lond., 1820. 8°. . . . 8054

Residence at, 1820–34. Walsh. Lond., 1838. 2 v. 8°. . . 8446

Residence at, 1827. Brewer. N. H., 1830. 12°. . . . 16636

Visit to. Colton. N. Y., 1836. 12°. 16635

Constitution. See ENGLAND, U. S., etc.

Contarini Fleming. Disraeli. N. Y., 1832. 2 v. 12°. . . . 2046

Contemporary Review. Lond., 1866–72. v. 1–20. 8°. . . . 12231

Continental Monthly. N. Y., 1862–64. 6 v. 8°. 13332

Contrast. Roche. N. Y., 1828. 2 v. 12°. 15403

Conversation, Book of. Charleston, 1837. 12°. 17021
Conway, Derwent. *(Pseudonym.)* See H. D. INGLIS.
Conybeare, W. J., and **Howson, J. S.** Life and Epistles of S. Paul. N. Y., 1866. 2 v. 8°. 6566
Cook, James. Narrative of Voyages. N. Y., 1824. 2 v. 16°. . . 8192
Voyages. Lond., 1796. 2 v. 12°. 13849
Life of. Coleridge (Worthies.) Leeds, 1836. 8°. . . . 6904
Cook, John. Green's Tu quoque. (Old Plays, v. 7.) Lond., 1825. 8°. 1514
Cooke, Geo. F., Memoirs of. Dunlap. N. Y., 1813. 2 v. 12°. . 7893
Cooke, Geo. W. Hist. of Party. Lond., 1836–37. 3 v. 8°. . . 4991
Life of Shaftesbury. Lond., 1836. 2 v. 8°. 6823
Cooke, P. Divine Law of Beneficence. N. Y. 12°. 9803
Cooke, Wm. Memoirs of Foote. N. Y., 1806. 2 v. 12°. . . . 7928
Cookery, Crumbs of, from the Round Table. Barber. N. Y., 1866. 12°. 3579
Cooley, J. E. The American in Egypt. N. Y., 1842. 8°. . . . 8068
Cooley, W. D. Hist. of Discovery. Lond., 1830–31. 3 v. 16°. . 5786
Coolie, Rights and Wrongs of the. [Jenkins.] N. Y., 1871. 12°. . 6470
Cooper, A. A., 1st Earl of Shaftesbury, Life of. Campbell (Ld. Chancellors, 3.) Lond., 1845. 8°. 6868
The same. Christie. Lond., 1871. 2 v. 8°. 6624
The same. Cooke. Lond., 1836. 2 v. 8°. 6823
Cooper, A. A., 3d Earl of Shaftesbury. Characteristicks. 2d ed. Lond., 1714–15. 3 v. 8°. 15840
Cooper, James Fenimore. The Bravo. (3 copies.) Philad., 1831–33. 2 v. 12°. 2771
The Chainbearer. (2 copies.) N. Y., 1856. 12°. 2822
The Crater. (2 copies.) N. Y., 1855. 12°. 2826
The Deerslayer. (2 copies.) N. Y., 1857–59. 12°. . . . 2815
The same. N. Y., 1872. 12°. 2840
Gleanings in England. Philad., 1837. 2 v. 12°. . . . 16761
France. Philad., 1837. 2 v. 12°. . . . 16556
The Headsman. (3 copies.) Philad., 1833–36. 2 v. 12°. . 2779
The Heidenmauer. Philad., 1836. 2 v. 12°. 2777
The same. Philad., 1832. 2 v. 12°. 2835
Hist. of U. S. Navy. (2 copies.) Philad., 1839. 2 v. 8°. . 6146
Home as Found. Philad., 1838. 2 v. 12°. 2787
The same. Philad., 1838. 2 v. in 1. 12°. . . . 2789
Homeward Bound. Philad., 1838. 2 v. 12°. 2785
The same. (2 copies.) Philad., 1838–42. 2 v. in 1. 12°. 2810
The same. N. Y., 1865. 12°. 2812
Jack Tier. N. Y., 1848. 2 v. in 1. 12°. 2832
The same. N. Y., 1856. 12°. 15468
Last of the Mohicans. N. Y., 1856. 12°. 2802
The same. (2 copies.) N. Y., 1873. 12°. . . . 2842
Lionel Lincoln. Philad., 1836. 2 v. 12°. 2753
Lives of Naval Officers. Philad., 1846. 2 v. 8°. . . . 7275

CONTENTS.—1, Bainbridge; Somers; Howe; Shubrick; Preble. 2, J. P. Jones; Woolsey; Perry; Dale.

Mercedes of Castile. Philad., 1840. 2 v. in 1. 12°. . . . 2794

Cooper, James Fenimore. Miles Wallingford. N. Y., 1856. 12°. . 2820
The Monikins. Philad., 1841. 2 v. in 1. 12°. 2809
The same. Philad., 1835. 2 v. 12°. 2833
Ned Myers. (2 copies.) N. Y., 1854–57. 12°. . . . 2818
The Oak-Openings. N. Y., 1857. 12°. 2828
The Pathfinder. (2 copies.) N. Y., 1851–56. 12°. . . . 2813
The same. N. Y., 1873. 12°. 2841
The Pilot. (2 copies.) Philad., 1833–36. 2 v. 12°. . . . 2749
The same. Philad., 1841. 2 v. in 1. 12°. . . . 2800
The same. N. Y., 1856. 12°. 2801
The Pioneers. N. Y., 1870. 12°. 2792
The Prairie. (2 copies.) Philad., 1827–36. 2 v. 12°. . . 2757
The same. Philad., 1841. 2 v. in 1. 12°. . . . 2803
Precaution. N. Y., 1820. 2 v. 12°. 2745
The same. Philad., 1839. 2 v. in 1. 12°. . . . 2798
The same. N. Y., 1855. 12°. 2799
The Red Rover. Philad., 1836. 2 v. 12°. 2755
The same. N. Y., 1872. 12°. 2839
The Redskins. (2 copies.) N. Y., 1855–56. 12°. . . . 2824
Satanstoe. N. Y., 1845. 12°. 2795
The same. N. Y., 1855. 12°. 2821
The Sea Lions. N. Y., 1849. 2 v. in 1. 12°. 2793
The same. N. Y., 1855. 12°. 2829
Sketches of Switzerland. Philad., 1836. 2 v. 12°. . . . 16683
The Spy. Philad., 1836. 2 v. 12°. 2747
The same. (2 copies.) N. Y., 1872. 12°. . . . 2837
See, also, H. L. BARNUM. (The Spy Unmasked.)
The Travelling Bachelor; or, Notions of the Americans. (2 copies.) N. Y., 1859. 12°. 2805
The same. Philad., 1836. 2 v. 12°. 16812
The same. Philad., 1841. 2 v. in 1. 12°. . . . 2804
The Two Admirals. (2 copies.) N. Y., 1849–51. 12°. . . 2796
The Water-Witch. (4 copies.) Philad., 1831–36. 2 v. 12°. . 2763
The same. Philad., 1841. 2 v. in 1. 12°. . . . 2808
Ways of the Hour. (2 copies.) N. Y., 1850–55. 12°. . . 2830
Wept of Wish-Ton-Wish. Philad., 1831. 2 v. 12°. . . 2761
The same. Philad., 1841. 2 v. in 1. 12°. . . . 2807
Wing-and-Wing. Philad., 1842. 2 v. 12°. 2790
The same. N. Y., 1867. 12°. 2817

Cooper, John G. Select Poems. Ed. Walsh. Philad., 1822. 24°. . 22
Cooper, S. F. Rural Hours. N. Y., 1850. 12°. 16977
Coppée, H. Grant and his Campaigns. N. Y., 1866. 8°. . . . 7401
Corals and Coral Islands. Dana. N. Y., 1872. 8°. 9101
Corbet, R. Select Poems, with Life. Ed. Sanford. Philad., 1819. 24°. 2
Corinne; or, Italy. De Staël-Holstein. N. Y., 1844. 8°. . . . 2626
Corinthians, Notes on Epistles to. Barnes. N. Y., 1841. 2 v. 12°. 9862
Cormenin, L. M. de la H. de. Orators of France. N. Y., 1849. 12°. 7611
Corn-Laws, Hist. of the. Platt. Lond., 1842. 12°. 8479
Cornaro, L. Writings on Health. Abridged. Andover, 1824. 12°. 16964

Corneille, P., and his Times. Guizot. N. Y., 1852. 12°. 7650
Corner-Stone, The. Abbott. Bost., 1834. 12°. 9994
Cornhill Magazine. Lond., 1867–72. v. 16–25. 8°. 17666
Cornwall, Barry. *(Pseudonym.)* See B. W. PROCTER.
Cornwall, S. P. The Finland Family. N. Y., 1853. 16°. . . . 2736
Cornwallis, C. F. Brief View of Greek Philosophy. Philad., 1846. 12°. 8497
Philosophical Theories and Experience. Philad., 1847. 12°. . 8496
Correlation and Conservation of Forces. Grove, Mayer, etc. N. Y., 1869. 12°. 8895
Correspondence, Epistolary, Gems of. Wilmott. Lond., 1846. 12°. 7045
See, also, LETTERS.
Corse de Leon. James. Lond., 1841. 3 v. 8°. 15224
Corsica, Account of. Boswell. Glasg., 1768. 8°. 16718
Corson, H. Hand-Book of Anglo-Saxon and Early English. N. Y., 1871. 12°. 94
Cortes, H. Despatches, written during the Conquest. Ed. Folsom. (2 copies.) N. Y., 1843. 12°. 7693
Hist. Notice of. Sands. N. Y., 1835. 8°. 15354
Life of. Bost., 1840. 12°. 7511
The same. Helps. N. Y., 1871. 16°. 7692
The same. De Trueba y Cosio. Edinb., 1829. 12°. . 7510
Cosmos. Humboldt. Lond. and N. Y., 1849–68. 5 v. 12°. . . 8960
Costello, L. S. Early Poetry of France. Lond., 1835. 8°. . . 917
Tour to and from Venice. Lond., 1846. 8°. 8449
Costume, British, Hist of. Planché. Lond., 1846. 12°. 4814
Cottage Tales of Magic, etc. Philad., 1852. 12°. 8482
Cottin, S. R. Elizabeth. Philad., 1811. 12°. 2358
The same. N. Y., 1853. 12°. 2359
Cottle, J. Reminiscences of Coleridge and Southey. (2 copies.) N. Y., 1847–48. 12°. 7097
Cotton, N. Select Poems. Ed. Walsh. Philad., 1822. 24°. . . 29
Cotton Kingdom, The. Olmsted. N. Y., 1861. 2 v. 12°. . . 6093
Count of Monte-Cristo. Dumas. Lond. 8°. 2628
Robert of Paris. Scott. Bost., 1839. 12° 1839
Counterparts. [Sheppard.] Bost., 1859. 8°. 2667
Countess, The; and other Tales. Philad., 1836. 2 v. 12°. . . 14872
Gisela. [John.] Philad., 1869. 12°. 3039
Ida, The. [Fay.] N. Y., 1840. 12°. 15684
Country House on the Rhine. Auerbach. Lond., 1870. 3 v. 8°. . 3026
Living and Thinking. Gail Hamilton. Bost., 1863. 8°. . . 3647
Parson. See A. K. H. BOYD.
Sketch Book. January Searle. [Philips.] Lond., 1851. 12°. 8186
Year-Book. Howitt. N. Y., 1850. 12°. 16978
Court, Book of the. Thoms. Lond., 1844. 8°. 5265
Courtenay, T. P. Commentaries on Shakspeare. Lond., 1840. 2 v. 12°. 1545
Lives of Cecil and Danby. Lond., 1838. 16°. 5763
Memoirs of Temple. Lond., 1836. 2 v. 8°. 6832

Courtney, J. Manners, Arts, and Politics. Lond., 1794. 8°. . . 14806
Cousin, V. Course of Hist. of Modern Philosophy. N. Y., 1857. 2 v. 8°. 8717
Elements of Psychology. (2 copies.) Hartf'd., 1834. 8°. . 8588
Introd. to Hist. of Philosophy. (2 copies.) Bost., 1832. 8°. . 8715
Lectures on the True, the Beautiful, the Good. N. Y., 1866. 8°. 8734
Philosophical Miscellanies, tr. by Ripley. Bost., 1838. 12°. . 8584
Cousin Marshall. Martineau. Bost., 1833. 12°. 14614
Covenanters, Traditions of the. Simpson. Edinb. 16°. . . . 4813
Coventry, G. Enquiry regarding Junius. Lond., 1825. 8°. . . 6857
Cowell, J. Thirty Years among the Players. N. Y., 1845. 8°. . 1670
Cowley, A. Essays, in Prose and Verse. Bost., 1820. 16°. . . 3845
Poems, ed. Johnson. Dubl., 1804. 8°. 15096
Poetical Works. Ed. Bell. Lond., 1807. 2 v. 24°. . . 260
Select Poems, with Life. Ed. Sanford. Philad., 1819. 24°. . 3
Cowley, H. Belle's Stratagem. (Oxberry's Plays.) Bost., 1822. 24°. 1348
Which is the Man? (Mod. Theatre, v. 10.) Lond., 1811. 12°. 1336
Cowper, W. Poems. Amherst, 1808. 3 v. 12°. 14815
Bost., 1833. 3 v. 12°. 14782
Bost., 1826. 3 v. 12°. 13831
Poems, with Life by Johnson. Bost., 1841. 3 v. 12°. . . 604
Poet. Works, ed. Benham. Lond., 1870. 16°. 1111
Select Poems. Ed. Walsh. Philad., 1822. 2 v. 24°. . . 30
The Task. Bost., 1842. 12°. 607
The Task, and other Poems. Philad., 1849. 8°. . . . 1238
Works. Philad., 1831. 8°. 1253
Ed. Grimshawe. (2 copies.) N. Y., 1849. 8°. . . 938
With Life, by Hayley. Ed. Grimshawe. Lond., 1835. 8 v. 16°. 624

CONTENTS.—1-5, Life and Letters. 6-8, Poems.

With Life, by Southey. Lond., 1835–37. 15 v. 16°. . 609

CONTENTS.—1-3, Life. 3-7, 15, Letters. 8, Early Poems; Olney Hymns; Anti-Thelyphthora; Poems publ. 1782. 9, Translations from Mme. Guion; The Task, etc. 10, Posthumous Poems; Miscellaneous Translations. 11, 12, Iliad. 13, 14, Odyssey. 15, Papers in the Connoisseur; Commentary on Paradise Lost.

Life of. Taylor. Philad., 1833. 12°. 7109
Life and Posthumous Writings of. Hayley. Bost., 1803. 2 v. 12°. 16381
Cox, F. A. Life of Melancthon. 2d ed. Lond., 1817. 8°. . . 7665
Cox, G. V. Recollections of Oxford. Lond., 1868. 8°. . . . 9246
Cox, G. W. Mythology of Aryan Nations. Lond., 1870. 2 v. 8°. . 4103
and **Jones, E. H.** Romances of the Middle Ages. Lond., 1871. 8°. 2010
Cox, H. Residence in the Burmhan Empire. Lond., 1821. 8°. . 16506
Cox, R. Adventures on the Columbia R., etc. N. Y., 1832. 8°. . 16862
Cox, S. S. Search for Winter Sunbeams. N. Y., 1870. 8°. . . 8277
Cox's Diary. Thackeray. (Works, v. 8.) Lond., 1872. 8°. . . 2196
Coxe, A. C. Advent, a Mystery. N. Y., 1837. 12°. 801
Athanasion; also, Miscellaneous Poems. N. Y., 1842. 12°. . 803
Christian Ballads. N. Y., 1840. 12°. 802
St. Jonathan, the Lay of a Scald. N. Y., 1838. 12°. . . . 804

Coxe, W. Hist. of House of Austria. 3d ed. (Bohn's.) (2 copies.) Lond., 1847. 3 v. 8°. 413
Memoirs of Duke of Marlborough. (Bohn's ed.) (2 copies.) Lond., 1847–48. 3 v. 8°. 369
of Walpole. Lond., 1800. 3 v. 8°. 6827
Travels in Poland, Russia, etc. 5th ed. Lond., 1802. 5 v. 8°. 16605
in Switzerland. Basil, 1802. 3 v. 8°. 16685
Crabb, G. English Synonymes. N. Y., 1839. 8°. 173
Crabbe, G. The Borough. Philad., 1810. 12°. 14786
Poems. N. Y., 1808. 12°. 14785
Poetical Works. Philad., 1839. 8°. 1247
The same: with Letters and Life. Lond., 1834–35. 8 v. 16°. 653

CONTENTS.—I, Life. II, The Library; The Village; The Newspaper; Parish Register, etc.; Juvenile Poems. III, IV, The Borough; Occasional Pieces. IV, V, Tales; Occasional Pieces. VI, VII, Tales of the Hall. VIII, Posthumous Tales; Index.

Posthumous Poems. Philad., 1835. 12°. 14788
Tales. N. Y., 1813. 2 v. 12°. 14818
Tales of the Hall. Lond., 1819. . 2 v. 8°. 1248
Life of. By his Son. Cambr., 1834. 12°. 6981
with Letters and Journals. Philad., 1835. 12°. . . . 14787
Crafts, W. Sullivan's Island, and other Poems. Charleston, 1820. 8°. 15053
Craftsman, The. D'Anvers. Lond., 1731. v. 1–7. 12°. 12025
Craik, D. M., (Miss Mulock.) Agatha's Husband. N. Y., 1871. 12°. 2485
A Brave Lady. (2 copies.) N. Y., 1870. 8°. 2682
Christian's Mistake. (2 copies.) N. Y., 1865–66. 12°. . . . 2486
Fair France. N. Y., 1871. 12°. 8374
Hannah. N. Y., 1872. 12°. 2494
Head of the Family. N. Y., 1864. 8°. 2680
John Halifax. (3 copies.) N. Y., 1860–72. 12°. 2480
A Life for a Life. (2 copies.) N. Y., 1859–69. 12°. . . . 2492
Mistress and Maid. N. Y., 1867. 8°. 2310
The same. (2 copies.) N. Y., 1863. 8°. 2679
A Noble Life. (2 copies.) N. Y., 1866–68. 12°. 2483
The Ogilvies. N. Y., 1864. 8°. 2680
Olive. N. Y., 1864. 8°. 2679
Poems. Bost., 1864. 16°. 1169
The same. New ed. Bost., 1868. 16°. 1170
Two Marriages. (2 copies.) N. Y., 1867. 12°. 2490
Unkind Word, and other Stories. (2 copies.) N. Y., 1870. 12°. 2488
The Woman's Kingdom. N. Y., 1868. 8°. 2681
Craik, G. L. Compendious Hist. of Eng. Lit. N. Y., 1863. 2 v. 8°. 195
English *Causes célèbres.* (2 copies.) Lond., 1844. 16°. . . . 9154
Hist. of British Commerce. Lond., 1844. 3 v. 12°. . . . 8783
Pursuit of Knowledge under Difficulties. N. Y., 1840. 2 v. 12°. 11418
The same. Bost., 1830. v. 1. 12°. 8807
The same. v. 2. Bost., 1831. 12°. 8812
The same. New ed. Lond., 1845. 3 v. 12°. . . . 9104
Sketches of Literature and Learning in Eng. Lond., 1844–45. 6 v. 24°. 45
Spenser and his Poetry. Lond., 1845. 3 v. 12°. . , . 285

Craik, G. L., and **MacFarlane, C.** Pictorial Hist. of England, [to 1688.] Lond., 1841. 4 v. 8°. 5104
The same, during reign of Geo. III. Lond., 1841–44. v. 1, 3, 4. 8°. 5108
Cramp, J. M. Text Book of Popery. N. Y., 1831. 12°. . . . 9610
Cranmer, T. Writings. Lond. 12°. 9483
Life of. (Cabinet Cyclopædia.) Lond., 1831. 16°. . . . 5759
The same. LeBas. N. Y., 1833. 3 v. 12°. . . . 7518
and Times of. [Lee.] Bost., 1841. 16°. 7556
Crater, The. Cooper. N. Y., 1855. 12°. 2826
Craven, Mrs. A. Anne Séverin. N. Y., 1869. 12°. 2391
A Sister's Story. N. Y., 1868. 8°. 2644
Craven, K. Excursions in the Abruzzi, etc. Lond., 1838. 2 v. 8°. 16715
Crawford, C. The Christian. Philad., 1802. 8°. 14789
Crayon, Geoffrey. *(Pseudonym.)* See W. IRVING.
Creasy, E. S. Decisive Battles of the World. (2 copies.) N. Y., 1851–63. 12°. 4571
Rise, etc., of the English Constitution. 3d ed. N. Y., 1856. 12°. 4852
Creation, The Course of. Anderson. Cincinn., 1851. 12°. . . 16946
Sketches of. Winchell. N. Y., 1870. 12°. 8958
Vestiges of Nat. Hist. of, with Sequel. N. Y., 1846. 12°. . 8927
Credo. [Townsend.] Bost., 1869. 16°. 9830
Credulity, Essay on. Blakeman. N. H., 1849. 12°. 8613
Creichton, J., Memoirs of. By himself. Lond., 1830. 12°. . . 6649
Crete, Notes on. Lord Strangford. (v. 2.) Lond., 1869. 8°. . . 3711
Travels in, 1817. Sieber. (Voyages, v. 8.) Lond., 1823. 8°. 8058
Crevier, J. B. L. Hist. of Roman Emperors. Lond., 1755–61. v. 2–10. 8°. 15937
Crichton, A. Converts from Infidelity. Edinb., 1827. 2 v. 12°. . 4468
Hist. of Arabia. N. Y., 1834. 2 v. 12°. 11286
and **Wheaton, H.** Scandinavia. N. Y., 1841. 2 v. 12°. . 11611
The same. N. Y., 1843. 2 v. 12°. 12274
Crimea, Invasion of the. Kinglake. N. Y., 1863–68. 2 v. 12°. . 4613
Travels through the, 1829. Alexander. Lond., 1830. 2 v. 8°. 16487
Criminal Law, Principles of. Philad., 1846. 12°. 8498
See, also, PRISONS ; TRIALS.
Critic in Parliament and in Public, The. Lond., 1841. 12°. . . 5275
Criticism, Elements of. Kames. N. Y., 1855. 12°. 9298
Essays in. Arnold. Bost., 1865. 12°. . . . . . , 3734
Critick of Pure Reason. Kant. Lond., 1838. 8°. 8732
Crock of Gold, The. Tupper. N. Y., 1846. 12°. 15619
Crockett, D. Exploits, etc., in Texas. (2 copies.) Philad., 1836. 12°. 16439
Narrative of Life of. By himself. Philad., 1834. 12°. . . 16438
Sketches and Eccentricities of. (2 copies.) N. Y., 1833. 12°. . 16436
Crockford's; or, Life in the West. N. Y., 1828. 2 v. 12°. . . 15406
Croffut, W. A., and **Morris, J. M.** Hist. of Conn. during the War. N. Y., 1868. 8°. 6261
Crofton Boys, The. Martineau. N. Y., 1867. 12°. 14621
Croker, T. C. Popular Songs of Ireland. Lond., 1839. 12°. . . 1204

Croly, G. Hist. Sketches, Speeches and Characters. Lond., 1842. 8°. 4602
Life of Geo. IV. N. Y., 1840. 12°. 11015
The same. N. Y., 1831. 12°. 11941
Marston. Philad., 1845. 8°. 2325
Poetical Works. Lond., 1830. 2 v. 8°. 854
Salathiel. N. Y., 1833. 2 v. in 1. 12°. 2089
The same. N. Y., 1850. 8°. 2326
Tales of the Great St. Bernard. N. Y., 1829. 2 v. 12°. . . 15592
Cromwell; a Novel. [Herbert.] N. Y., 1838. 2 v. 12°. . . . 15685
Cromwell, O. Letters and Speeches, ed. Carlyle. (2 copies.) N. Y., 1845–56. 2 v. 12°. 5221
The same. Lond., 1870. 5 v. 8°. 4033
The same. Lond., 1871–72. 5 v. 16°. 3927
The Protector. Merle D'Aubigné. N. Y., 1857. 12°. . . 5312
Hist. of. Guizot. Philad., 1854. 2 v. 12°. 5226
Lecture on. Goldwin Smith. N. Y., 1867. 12°. 6749
Life of, to 1649. Andrews. Lond., 1870. 8°. 5311
Life of. Forster. Lond., 1838–39. 2 v. 16°. 5764
The same. Gleig. Lond., 1831. 16°. 5771
The same. Harris. Lond., 1814. 8°. 5306
The same. [Kimber.] Lond., 1724. 8°. 5225
The same. Russell. N. Y., 1844. 2 v. 12°. 11282
The same. Southey. N. Y., 1845. 12°. 5135
Memoirs of. Lamartine. N. Y., 1854. 12°. 6726
of Court of. Jesse. Philad., 1840. 12°. 5213
Cromwell, R., Hist of. Guizot. Lond., 1856. 2 v. 8°. . . . 5023
Croppy, The. [Banim.] Philad., 1839. 2 v. 12°. 15408
Crosby, E., Memoirs of; the Spy unmasked. Barnum. N. Y., 1828. 8°. 6124
Crosby, H. Jesus; His Life and Work. N. Y., 1871. 8°. . . . 6593
Crowe, C. Night-Side of Nature. N. Y., 1850. 12°. 8615
Crowe, E. E. Hist. of France. Philad., 1832. 3 v. 12°. . . . 6067
The same. Lond., 1836–37. 3 v. (2 copies of v. 1, 3.) 16°. 5186
The same. Enlarged ed. Lond., 1858–68. 5 v. 8°. . 5643
Lives of Eminent Foreign Statesmen. Lond., 1833. 16°. . 5766
For Contents, see G. P. R. James.
Crowfield, Christopher. *(Pseudonym.)* See H. B. Stowe.
Crown of Wild Olive, The. Ruskin. N. Y., 1866. 12°. 9042
Crowquill, Alfred. *(Pseudonym.)* See A. H. Forrester.
Cruden, A. Concordance to the Bible, ed. Carey. Lond., 1867. 8°. 9836
Cruikshank, G. Comic Almanack, 1835–53. Lond. 2 v. 8°. . . 4260
Three Courses and a Dessert. (Bohn's ed.) Lond., 1867. 8°. 524
at Home; and the Odd Volume. Lond., 1845. 4 v. in 2. 16°. 4258
Cruise of the Betsey. Miller. Bost., 1862. 12°. 8980
Crusaders, The. Keightley. Lond., 1834. 2 v. 16°. 4585
Crusades, Chronicles of the. Bohn's ed. (2 copies.) Lond., 1848. 8°. 512
Hist. of the. Mills. Philad., 1824. 8°. 4738
The same. Procter. Edinb., 1854. 8°. 4621
Crusius, L. Lives of Roman Poets. 3d ed. Lond., 1753. 2 v. 12°. 7771
Crust and the Cake, The. Garrett. N. Y. 8°. 2436

Cryptogram, The. De Mille. N. Y., 1871. 8°. 2690
Cuba and Back, Voyage to, 1859. Dana. Bost., 1860. 12°. . . . 8225
and the Cubans. [Kimball.] N. Y., 1850. 12°. 16917
Notes on. Wuderman. Bost., 1844. 12°. 16918
See, also, WEST INDIES.
Cudjo's Cave. Trowbridge. Bost., 1864. 12°. 2954
Culture and Anarchy. Arnold. Lond., 1869. 8°. 3736
and Religion. Shairp. N. Y., 1871. 16°. 9819
Conversations on. Helps. Bost., 1871. 16°. 3700
Primitive. Tylor. Lond., 1871. 2 v. 8°. 4075
Cumberland, R. Brothers; Choleric Man; W. Indian. (Brit. Drama, v. 2, pt. 2.) Lond., 1804. 8°. 1632
Calvary. Burlington, 1795. 12°. 14820
The same. Morris-Town, 1815. 8°. 15077
False Impressions; Mysterious Husband; Box-Lobby Challenge; Natural Son; Carmelite; Impostors. (Mod. Theatre, v. 5, 6.) Lond., 1811. 12°. 1331
Retrospection. Bost., 1812. 12°. 14790
West Indian; She Would and She Would Not; Wheel of Fortune. (Oxberry's Plays, v. 6.) Bost., 1822. 24°. . . . 1350
Wheel of Fortune; West Indian; Jew; Brothers; First Love. (Brit. Theatre, v. 16, 23.) Lond. 12°. 1340
Memoirs of. By himself. N. Y., 1806. 8°. 7124
Cumming, G. Wild Men and Wild Beasts. N. Y., 1872. 12°. . . 10178
Cumming, J. Last Warning Cry. N. Y., 1867. 12°. 17350
Cumming, R. G. Five Years in S. Africa. N. Y., 1851. 2 v. 12°. . 7980
Cummings, A. Memoir of Payson. Bost., 1830. 12°. 16420
Cummins, M. S. Haunted Hearts. Bost., 1864. 12°. 15713
Cunningham, A. Life and Land of Burns. N. Y., 1841. 12°. . . 7042
of Scott. Bost., 1832. 12°. 6923
of Wilkie. Lond., 1843. 3 v. 8°. 7999
Lives of Painters and Sculptors. N. Y., 1839–40. 5 v. 12°. . 11017
The same. N. Y., 1831–34. 5 v. 12°. 11942
Lord Rolden. N. Y., 1836. 2 v. in 1. 12°. 15496
Paul Jones. Philad., 1827. 3 v. 12°. 15535
Cunningham, G. G. Lives of Eminent Englishmen. Glasg., 1836. 3 v. in 6. 8°. 6886
Cunningham, John. Poetical Works. Ed. Bell. Lond., 1807. 24°. 542
Select Poems. Ed. Walsh. Philad., 1822. 24°. 26
Cunningham, John W. De Rance. N. Y., 1816. 24°. 14821
The Velvet Cushion. Lond., 1815. 12°. 15627
Cunningham, W. and **Adams, J.** Correspondence. Bost., 1823. 8°. 7344
Curran, J. P. Speeches. N. Y., 1809. 2 v. 8°. 9349
Life of. By his son. N. Y., 1820. 8°. 6803
Recollections of. Phillips. N. Y., 1818. 8°. 6804
Currency. See BANKING.
[**Curtis, A. W.**] The Spirit of '76, etc. Bost., 1868. 16°. 9213
Curtis, Geo. T. Hist. of the Constitution. (2 copies.) N. Y., 1854–63. 2 v. 8°. 6223

Curtis, Geo. T. Life of Webster. 2d ed. N. Y., 1870. 2 v. 8°. . 7427
Curtis, Geo. W. The Howadji in Syria. (2 copies.) N. Y., 1852. 12°. 8236
Lotus-Eating. (2 copies.) N. Y., 1856. 12°. 3585
Nile Notes of a Howadji. (2 copies.) N. Y., 1851–52. 12°. . 8234
The Potiphar Papers. (2 copies.) N. Y., 1856–69. 12°. . . 2871
Prue and I. N. Y., 1857. 12°. 2870
Trumps. (2 copies.) N. Y., 1861. 12°. 2873
Curtius, E. Hist. of Greece. (2 copies.) N. Y., 1871–72. 3 v. 12°. 4396
Curzon, R. Monasteries in the Levant. N. Y., 1849. 12°. . . 8254
Cushing, C. Reminiscences of Spain. Bost., 1833. 2 v. 12°. . . 6410
The same. 16669
Review of the Revolution in France. Newburyport, 1833. 2 v. 12°. 5453
Cushing, L. S. Law and Practice of Legislative Assemblies. Bost., 1866. 8°. 8727
Manual of Parliamentary Practice. Bost., 1857. 16°. . . 8475
Custis, G. W. P. Recollections of Washington. N. Y., 1860. 8°. . 7486
Cuvier, G. L. C. F. The Animal Kingdom. N. Y., 1831. 4 v. 8°. 16954
and Zoology. Lond., 1844. 12°. 8798
Memoirs of. Mrs. Lee. N. Y., 1833. 12°. 7629
Cyclopædia. See DICTIONARY; ENCYCLOPÆDIA.
Cynick, The. Philad., 1812. 12°. 15325
Cyril Thornton. [Hamilton.] N. Y., 1827–32. 2 v. 12°. . . . 15149
Cyrilla. Tautphoeus. N. Y. 8°. 2311

D.

Dacre, Lady. See B. BRAND.
Dahlmann, F. E. Hist. of the Engl. Revolution. Lond., 1844. 8°. . 5012
Dairy, The. Lond., 1843. 12°. 16952
Daisy, The. S. Warner. Philad., 1868. 12°. 3002
Daisy Chain, The. Yonge. N. Y., 1871. 2 v. 12°. 2501
Dakota Land. Hankins. N. Y., 1869. 12°. 8429
Dale, R., Life of. Cooper. (Naval Biogr.) Phil., 1846. 12°. . . 7276
Dale, T. Widow of Nain, and other Poems. Lond., 1842. 16°. . 1202
Dallas, E. S. The Gay Science. Lond., 1866. 2 v. 8°. . . . 9055
Dallas, R. C. Recollections of Byron. Philad., 1825. 8°. . . 7190
Dallas Galbraith. Davis. Philad., 1868. 8°. 2696
Dalzel, A. Lectures on the Ancient Greeks. Edinb., 1821. 2 v. 8°. 15868
Damascus and Palmyra, in 1835. Addison. Lond., 1838. 2 v. 8°. . 8099
Dameto, J., and **Mut, V.** Hist. of the Balearic Islands. Tr. by Campbell. Lond., 1719. 8°. 16163
Dampier, W., Life of. N. Y., 1840. 12°. 11032
Dana, C. A. Household Book of Poetry. Revised ed. N. Y., 1867. 8°. 1311
Dana, J. D. Coral Reefs and Islands. N. Y., 1853. 8°. . . . 9100
Corals and Coral Islands. N. Y., 1872. 8°. 9101
Manual of Geology. (2 copies.) Philad., 1863. 8°. . . . 9011
of Mineralogy. N. H., 1848. 12°. 8920
The same. 3d ed. N. H., 1851. 12°. . . 8921

Dana, M. S. B. The Parted Family, etc. N. Y., 1842. 12°. . . . 14984
Dana, R. H. The Idle Man. N. Y., 1821. 8°. 15303
Poems and Prose Writings. Bost., 1833. 12°. 13187
The same. (2 copies.) N. Y., 1850. 2 v. 12°. . . . 3661
Dana, R. H. (Jr.) To Cuba and back. Bost., 1860. 12°. 8225
Two Years before the Mast. N. Y., 1846. 12°. 11430
The same. N. Y., 1840. 12°. 12125
The same. Bost., 1869. 12°. 8199
Danby, Earl of, T. Osborne, Life of. Courtenay. Lond., 1838. 16°. 5763
Danforth, J. N. Memoir of W. C. Walton. Hartf'd., 1837. 12°. . 16422
Daniel, Gabriel. Hist. of France. Lond., 1726. 5 v. 8°. . . . 16236
Daniel, George. England in the Olden Time. Lond., 1842. v. 2. 12°. 4263
Dante Alighieri. Abstract of his Vision, by L. Hunt. N. Y., 1846. 12°. 887
Divina Commedia. Transl. by H. Boyd. Lond., 1802. v. 2, 3. 8°. 890
The same, transl. by Longfellow. Bost., 1867. 3 v. 8°. 1324
The Inferno. Prose transl. by Carlyle. 2d ed. Lond., 1867. 8°. 882
The Vision, transl. by Cary. N. Y., 1845. 12°. 878
The same. N. Y., 1861. 12°. 879
The same. v. 2, 3. Lond., 1831. 16°. 880
The same, illustrated by Doré. Lond., 1868. 2 v. fol.
The Vita Nuova, transl. by Martin. Lond., 1862. 8°. . . . 3948
Compositions from. Flaxman. Lond., 1807. 4°. . . . .
Life of. Stebbing. Lond., 1831. 12°. 7775
as Philosopher, Patriot, and Poet: with Analysis of the Divina Commedia. Botta. N. Y., 1865. 12°. 7751
A Shadow of. M. F. Rossetti. Bost., 1872. 8°. 877
Danube, Voyage down the. Quin. N. Y., 1836. 12°. . . . 16619
D'Anvers, C. The Craftsman. Lond., 1731. v. 1–7. 12°. . . 12025
D'Arblay, F. Camilla. Bost., 1797. 3 v. 12°. 2397
Cecilia. Bost., 1803. 3 v. 12°. 2400
Diary and Letters. Philad., 1842. 2 v. 8°. 7063
Evelina. N. Y., 1832. 2 v. in 1. 12°. . . . . . , 2511
Memoirs of Dr. Burney. (2 copies.) Philad., 1833. 8°. . . 7139
Memoirs of. Berkeley. N. Y., 1844. 2 v. in 1. 12°. . . 6987
Darby, W. Tour to Detroit. N. Y., 1819. 8°. 16825
Dard, C. A. Shipwreck of the Medusa. Edinb., 1827. 12°. . . 4473
Dark Night's Work, A. Gaskell. N. Y., 1863. 8°. 2311
Darley, F. O. C. Illustrations of Rip Van Winkle. N. Y., 1848. 4°.
Sketches abroad with Pen and Pencil. N. Y., 1868. 8°. . . 8376
Darley, G. Sylvia. Lond., 1827. 16°. 843
Thomas à Becket. Lond., 1840. 8°. 844
Darnley. G. P. R. James. N. Y., 1830. 2 v. 12°. 15219
Darwin, C. The Descent of Man. (3 copies.) N. Y., 1871. 2 v. 12°. 8932
Expression of Emotions. N. Y., 1873. 12°. 8938
Journal of Voyage of the Beagle. (2 copies.) N. Y., 1846. 2 v. 16°. 8831
Origin of Species. 2d ed. N. Y., 1860. 12°. 8928
The same. 5th ed. N. Y., 1871. 12°. 8929
Variation of Animals and Plants under Domestication. N. Y. [1868.] 2 v. 12°. 8930

Darwin, C. Facts and Arguments for. Müller. Lond., 1869. 8°. . 8945
Darwin, E. The Botanic Garden. Dubl., 1790–93. 2 v. 8°. . . 14791
Memoirs of. Seward. Philad., 1804. 8°. 7147
Darwinism in Morals. Cobbe. Lond., 1872. 8°. 10028
Dates. See CHRONOLOGY.
D'Aubigné, J. H. Merle. See MERLE.
Daughter of an Empress, The. [Mundt.] N. Y., 1867. 8°. . . 3089
Daughters of England. Ellis. N. Y., 1843. 12°. 9200
Davenant, W. The Wits. (Old Plays, v. 8.) Lond., 1825. 8°. . 1515
Davenport, C. A. Gifts of Genius. N. Y. [1859.] 12°. . . . 14882
Davenport, Richard A. Hist. of the Bastile. (2 copies.) Lond., 1839. 16°. 5512
Narratives of Peril and Suffering. Lond., 1840. 2 v. 16°. . 8164
Perilous Adventures. N. Y., 1846. 12°. 11761
Davenport, Robert. City Night-Cap. (Old Plays, v. 11.) Lond., 1827. 8°. 1518
David Copperfield. Dickens. N. Y., 1871. 16°. 2178
David Elginbrod. MacDonald. Bost. 12°. 2583
Davidson, L. M. Amir Khan, and other Poems. N. Y., 1829. 12°. . 769
Memoir of. Sedgwick. Bost., 1837. 16°. 7256
Davidson, Mrs. M. M., Selections from Writings of. Philad., 1843. 12°. 771
Davidson, Miss M. M., Biography and Poems of. Irving. 2d ed. Philad., 1841. 12°. 770
Davie, W. R., Life of. Hubbard. Bost., 1848. 16°. 7274
Davies, Life of Mrs. Christian. DeFoe. Oxf'd., 1840. 16°. . . 3876
Davies, J. Select Poems, with Life. Ed. Sanford. Philad., 1819. 24°. 2
Davies, T. Dramatic Miscellanies. New ed. Lond., 1785. 3 v. 16°. 1494
Memoirs of Garrick. Bost., 1818. 2 v. 12°. 7891
Davila, E. C. Hist. of Civil Wars in France. Lond., 1758. 2 v. 4°. 5706
Discourses on. J. Adams. (Works, v. 6.) Bost., 1851. 8°. . 9693
Davis, E. The Half Century. Bost., 1851. 12°. 4606
Davis, John. Life of Chatterton. Lond. 16°. 6939
Davis, John F. The Chinese. Lond., 1840. 8°. 7913
The same. N. Y., 1840. 2 v. 12°. 11405
The same. New ed. (with Supplement.) Lond., 1844–45. 4 v. 12°. 8154
The same. v. 4. (Supplement.) (Sketches of China.) Lond., 1845. 12°. 7914
Davis, M. L. Memoirs of Burr. N. Y., 1836. 2 v. 8°. 7354
[**Davis, P. S.**] The Young Parson. (2 copies.) N. Y., 1866. 12°. . 2853
Davis, R. H. Dallas Galbraith. Philad., 1868. 8°. 2696
Waiting for the Verdict. N. Y., 1868. 8°. 2695
[**Davis, S. M.**] Life of Sidney. Bost., 1859. 16°. 6992
Davy, H. Consolations in Travel. Philad., 1830. 12°. 7867
Fragmentary Remains, with Life, by J. Davy. Lond., 1858. 8°. 7150
Life of. J. A. Paris. Lond., 1831. 2 v. 8°. 7148
Dawes, R. Geraldine, and other Poems. N. Y., 1839. 12°. . . 14985
Dawning Lights. Cobbe. Lond., 1868. 8°. 9966
Day, Henry N. Elements of Rhetoric. 4th ed. N. Y., 1854. 12°. . 9305
Introd. to English Literature. N. Y., 1869. 16°. . . . 138

[**Day, Horace.**] The Opium Habit. N. Y., 1868. 12°. 9233
Day, M. Literary Remains. N. H., 1834. 12°. 15054
Day, S. Hist. Collections of Pa. Philad. [1843.] 8°. . . . 5939
Days, The Book of. Chambers. Edinb., 1863–64. 2 v. 8°. . . 4437
Days of Bruce. Aguilar. N. Y., 1857. 2 v. 12°. 2525
[**Deacon, W. F.**] Warreniana. Bost., 1824. 12°. 14793
Dead-Sea Fruit. A Novel. Braddon. N. Y., 1868. 8°. . . . 2674
Deaf and Dumb, The. Mann. Bost., 1836. 12°. 17075
Deafness. Kitto. Lond., 1845. 12°. 8486
Death's Doings. Bost., 1828. 2 v. 8°. 4282
Debit and Credit. A Novel. Freytag. N. Y., 1863. 12°. . . 3042
Decameron, The. Boccaccio, tr. by Kelly. Lond. 8°. . . . 473
Decatur, S., Life of. Mackenzie. Bost., 1846. 16°. 7270
The same. Waldo. Hartf'd., 1821. 12°. . . . 16426
Decision, The. [Kennedy.] N. Y., 1829. 12°. 15410
Declaration of Independence, Lives of Signers of. Goodrich. Hartf'd. [1848.] 12°. 16403
The same. Sanderson. Philad., 1823–27. 9 v. 8°. . 7462
Decorum, Bazar Book of. N. Y., 1870. 16°. 9131
Deep, Wonders of the. Schele de Vere. N. Y., 1869. 12°. . . 16949
Deerslayer, The. Cooper. N. Y., 1872. 12°. 2840
De Foe, D. Hist. of the Great Plague. Lond., 1832. 16°. . . 4844
Hist. of Plague; and Religious Courtship. N. Y., 1857. 12°. 4228
Hist. of the Plague; the Storm; True-born Englishman. Lond., 1855. 8°. 4227
Novels. Edinb., 1810. v. 2–12. 16°. 4160

CONTENTS.—2, 3, Robinson Crusoe. 4, 5, Memoirs of a Cavalier. 6, 7, Life of Col. Jack. 8, 9, Adventures of Capt. Singleton. 10, 11, New Voyage round the World. 12, Hist. of the Plague.

Novels and Miscellaneous Works. Oxf'd., 1840–41. v. 1–3, 6–8, 12–19. 16°. 3871

CONTENTS.—1, 2, Robinson Crusoe. 3, Life of Capt. Singleton. 6, Memoirs of a Cavalier. 7, New Voyage round the World. 8, Memoirs of Capt. Carleton; Life of Mrs. Davies. 12, System of Magic. 13, Hist. of Apparitions. 14, Religious Courtship. 15, 16, Family Instructor. 17, 18, English Tradesman. 19, Life of Duncan Campbell; Dumb Philosopher; Everybody's Business is Nobody's Business.

Robinson Crusoe, ed. Clark. Cambr., 1866. 16°. . . . 1706
Life and Times of. Chadwick. Lond., 1859. 8°. . . . 7082
Life and Writings of. Lee. Lond., 1869. 3 v. 8°. . . . 7083
De Forest, J. W. Hist. of Indians of Conn. Hartf'd., 1851. 12°. . 5847
Miss Ravenel's Conversion. N. Y., 1867. 12°. . . . 2942
Overland. N. Y. [1871.] 8°. 2697
Degerando, J. M. Self-Education. Bost., 1830. 8°. 17052
Deism, Gospel its own Witness against. Fuller. Lond., 1852. 8°. . 495
[**DeKay, J. E.**] Sketches of Turkey. N. Y., 1833. 8°. . . . 16632
Dekker, T. Honest Whore. (Old Plays, v. 3.) Lond., 1825. 8°. . 1510
Delano, A. Narrative of Voyages. Bost., 1818. 8°. 16282
Delany, M. G. Autobiography and Correspondence. Lond., 1861–62. 6 v. 8°. 7057
De Lisle. [Grey.] N. Y., 1828. 2 v. 12°. 15411
De Lolme, J. L. Constitution of England. Dubl., 1785. 8°. . . 5001
The same. (Bohn's ed.) Lond., 1853. 8°. . . . 484

Delusions, Popular, Memoirs of. Mackay. Lond., 1869. 8°. . . . 8525
See, also, APPARITIONS; MAGIC; SUPERSTITION; etc.
Demerara. A Tale. Martineau. Bost., 1832. 12°. 14611
De Mille, J. The Cryptogram. (2 copies.) N. Y., 1871. 8°. . . 2690
The Dodge Club. N. Y., 1870. 8°. 2689
Deming, H. C. Life of Grant. Hartf'd., 1868. 8°. 7400
Democratic Review. Wash. and N. Y., 1837–52. v. 1–21, 23–31. 8°. 13059
The same. v. 1–5, 9–21, 23–25, 27–31. 13089
Democracy. Brougham. (Polit. Philos., v. 3.) Lond., 1844. 8°. . 8682
in America. De Tocqueville, ed. Bowen. Bost., 1863. 2 v. 12°. 6185
Treatise on. Camp. N. Y., 1841. 12°. 11613
The same. Partridge. Philad., 1866. 8°. 8695
Demonology, Letters on. Sir W. Scott. N. Y., 1839. 12°. . . 11011
See, also, APPARITIONS; GHOSTS; MAGIC; NECROMANCERS; PLANCHETTE.
De Morgan, A. Essay on Probabilities. Lond., 1838. 16°. . . 6043
Demosthenes. Orations, tr. by Leland. N. Y., 1840. v. 1. 12°. . 4511
Dendy, W. C. Phenomena of Dreams. Lond., 1832. 12°. . . 8481
Philosophy of Mystery. (2 copies.) N. Y., 1845–47. 12°. . 8518
Denham, D., and **Clapperton, H.** Travels in Africa. Bost., 1826. 8°. 16530
Denham, J. Poetical Works. Ed. Bell. Lond., 1807. 24°. . . 255
The same, ed. Johnson. Dubl., 1804. 8°. . . . 15096
Works, with Life. Ed. Sanford. Philad., 1819. 24°. . . 3
Denis Duval. Thackeray. Lond., 1872. 8°. 2199
Denmark, etc., Hist. of [to 1814]. Dunham. Lond., 1839–40. 3 v. 16°. 5468
Dennis, G. The Cid. Lond., 1845. 24°. 284
Denominations. See SECTS.
Denon, D. V. Travels in Egypt. N. Y., 1803. 2 v. 8°. . . . 16483
Dent, A. Ruin of Rome. Lond., 1828. 8°. 17261
Depping, G., and **Russell, C.** Wonders of Strength and Skill. N. Y., 1871. 12°. 10130
De Profundis. Gilbert. Lond., 1866. 8°. 15413
De Quincey, T. Autobiographic Sketches. (2 copies.) Bost., 1855–56. 16°. 3319
Beauties. Bost., 1862. 12°. 3332
Biographical Essays. Bost., 1850. 16°. 3313
CONTENTS.—**Shakspeare; Pope; Lamb; Goethe; Schiller.**
The Cæsars. Bost., 1851. 16°. 3314
Confessions of an English Opium Eater. Bost., 1841. 16°. . 3180
The same, and Suspiria de Profundis. Bost., 1856. 16°. 3312
Essays on Philosophical Writers, etc. Bost., 1854. 2 v. 16°. . 3326
on the Poets, etc. Bost., 1855. 16°. 3325
Historical and Critical Essays. Bost., 1856. 2 v. 16°. . . 3323
Klosterheim. Bost., 1855. 8°. 2559
Letters to a Young Man. Philad., 1843. 12°. 3164
The same. (2 copies.) Bost., 1856–58. 16°. . . . 3330
Literary Reminiscences. Bost., 1851. 2 v. 16°. . . . 3315
The same. New ed. Bost., 1859. 2 v. 16°. . . . 3317
Logic of Polit. Economy. Edinb., 1844. 8°. 8624

De Quincey, T. Narrative and Misc. Papers. Bost., 1854. 2 v. 16°. 3321
Selections from his Writings. Edinb., 1856–60. 14 v. 8°. . 3274
Theological Essays, etc. Bost., 1854. 2 v. 16°. 3328
[**Derby, G. H.**] Phenixiana. (2 copies.) N. Y., 1856–67. 12°. . 4295
Squibob Papers. N. Y., 1865. 12°. 4297
Dermoncourt, Gen. The Duchess of Berri in La Vendée. 3d ed. Lond., 1833. 8°. 5666
De Rohan. Sue. N. Y., 1845. 8°. 2324
Derrick and Drill. [Morris.] N. Y., 1865. 12°. 17000
De Saumarez, Lord J., Memoirs of. Ross. Lond., 1838. 2 v. 8°. . 16386
Despotism, Spiritual. Taylor. N. Y., 1835. 12°. 9538
Desultory Man, The. James. N. Y., 1836. 2 v. 12°. 15209
DeVere, A. Song of Faith, etc. Lond., 1842. 16°. 598
De Vere. [Ward.] N. Y., 1831. 2 v. 12°. 15155
Devereux. Bulwer-Lytton. N. Y., 1829. 2 v. 12°. 2052
Devil. See Apparitions; Demonology; etc.
Devonshire, Traditions of. Bray. Lond., 1838. 3 v. 12°. . . 5266
Devrient, E. Recollections of Mendelssohn. Lond., 1869. 8°. . 7922
Dewar, D. Observations on Ireland. Lond., 1812. 8°. . . . 16746
De Wette, W. M. L. Theodore; or, the Skeptic's Conversion. Bost., 1841. 2 v. 12°. 17264
Dewey, O. The Old World and New. N. Y., 1836. 2 v. 12°. . 16564
Dial, The. Bost., 1843–44. v. 4. 8°. 12767
Dialogues of the Dead. [Lyttelton.] Lond., 1768. 8°. 15241
Diary of Besieged Resident in Paris. N. Y., 1871. 8°. . . . 5642
of a Désennuyée. Gore. Philad., 1836. 12°. 15415
of an Ennuyée. Jameson. Philad., 1826. 12°. 16722
of Kitty Trevelyan. [Charles.] Lond., 1866. 8°. 2465
of a late Physician. Warren. Edinb., 1871. 8°. 2447
Diaz del Castillo, B. Hist. of Conquest of Mexico. Salem, 1803. 2 v. 8°. 5972
Dibble, S. Hist. of Sandwich Islands' Mission. N. Y., 1839. 12°. . 6416
Dibdin, C. Deserter; Quaker. (Oxberry's Plays.) Bost., 1823. 24°. 1353
Songs. 2d ed. Lond., 1841. 16°. 677
Dibdin, T. Reminiscences. N. Y., 1828. 2 v. in 1. 8°. 7993
School for Prejudice. (Mod. Theatre, v. 4.) Lond., 1811. 12°. 1330
Dick, J. Lectures on Theology. N. Y., 1846. 2 v. 8°. . . . 17512
Dick, T. Celestial Scenery. N. Y., 1841. 12°. 11408
Improvement of Society. N. Y., 1840. 12°. 11279
Philosophy of Religion. Brookfield, 1830. 12°. 17363
Practical Astronomer. (2 copies.) N. Y., 1846. 16°. . . 16974
Sidereal Heavens, etc. N. Y., 1840. 12°. 11423
Dickens, C. Barnaby Rudge. N. Y., 1871. 16°. 2173
The same. N. Y., 1872. 16°. 10212
The same. (4 copies.) Philad. 8°. 2253
Bleak House. (2 copies.) N. Y., 1871–72. 16°. 2179
The same. N. Y., 1873. 16°. 10218
Christmas Stories. N. Y., 1871. 16°. 2174
The same. N. Y., 1873. 16°. 10220
The same. Philad. 8°. 2263

Dickens, C. David Copperfield. Lond., 1864. 12°. 2208
The same. (2 copies.) Philad. 12°. 2209
The same. (2 copies.) N. Y., 1869–71. 16°. 2177
The same. N. Y., 1872. 16°. 10216
The same. Philad. 8°. 2262
Dombey and Son. N. Y., 1871. 16°. 2176
The same. N. Y., 1872. 16°. 10214
The same. (3 copies.) Philad. 8°. 2259
Great Expectations. N. Y., 1871. 16°. 2171
The same. N. Y., 1872. 16°. 10215
The same. (3 copies.) Philad. 8°. 2272
Hard Times. N. Y., 1854. 12°. 2211
The same. (2 copies.) N. Y., 1868–71. 16°. . . . 2181
The same. N. Y., 1872. 16°. 10217
The same. N. Y., 1854. 8°. 2264
Lamplighter's Story; Hunted Down, etc. Philad. 8°. . . 2265
Little Dorrit. N. Y., 1871. 16°. 2183
The same. N. Y., 1873. 16°. 10219
The same. Philad. 8°. 2266
Martin Chuzzlewit. Bost., 1869. 2 v. 8°. 2204
The same. N. Y., 1871. 16°. 2175
The same. N. Y., 1873. 16°. 10213
The same. (2 copies.) Philad. 8°. 2257
Mystery of Edwin Drood. N. Y., 1871. 16°. 2186
The same. N. Y., 1873. 16°. 10224
The same. (2 copies.) Bost., 1870. 8°. 2277
New Stories. (2 copies.) Philad. 8°. 2275
Nicholas Nickleby. (2 copies.) N. Y., 1867–71. 16°. . . 2169
The same. N. Y., 1872. 16°. 10210
The same. (2 copies.) Philad. 8°. 2246
Old Curiosity Shop, and Reprinted Pieces. N. Y., 1871. 16°. . 2172
The same. N. Y., 1872. 16°. 10211
The same. (3 copies.) Philad. 8°. 2250
Oliver Twist. Bost., 1868. 8°. 2206
The same. N. Y., 1871. 16°. 2171
The same. N. Y., 1872. 16°. 10215
The same. (2 copies.) Philad. 8°. 2248
Our Mutual Friend. N. Y., 1868. 16°. 2184
The same. N. Y., 1872. 16°. 10221
The same. (2 copies.) N. Y., 1865. 8° 2269
The same. Philad. [1865.] 8°. 2271
Pic Nic Papers. Philad., 1841. 2 v. 12°. 2166
The same. 2201
Pickwick Papers. N. Y., 1872. 16°. 2168
The same. N. Y., 1873. 16°. 10222
The same. (2 copies.) Philad. 8°. 2244
The same. Philad. 12°. 2203
Pictures from Italy. N. Y., 1846. 12°. 8368
and American Notes. Bost., 1867. 8°. . 2207

Dickens, C. Pictures from Italy, and American Notes. N. Y., 1865. 2 v. 16°. 2164
The same. N. Y., 1871. 16°. 2174
The same. N. Y., 1873. 16°. 10220
Sketches by Boz. N. Y., 1871. 2 v. 16°. 2172
The same. N. Y., 1872. 2 v. 16°. 10211
The same. (3 copies.) Philad., 1839. 8°. 2241
Tale of Two Cities. (2 copies.) N. Y., 1868–71. 16°. . . 2181
The same. N. Y., 1872. 16°. 10217
The same. (2 copies.) Philad. [1859.] 8°. . . . 2267
The Tuggs at Ramsgate, and other Sketches. Philad., 1837. 12°. 2187
Uncommercial Traveller; Master Humphrey's Clock; New Christmas Stories; General Index of Characters in his Novels. N. Y., 1871. 16°. 2185
The same. N. Y., 1873. 16°. 10223
Works. Philad. v. 1, 2, 4–6. 8°. 2236

CONTENTS.—1, Pickwick Papers; Old Curiosity Shop. 2, Oliver Twist; Sketches by Boz; Barnaby Rudge. 4, David Copperfield; Dombey & Son; Christmas Stories; Pictures from Italy. 5, New Stories (Seven Poor Travelers, New Christmas Stories, Hard Times, etc.); Bleak House. 6, Little Dorrit.

Life of. Forster. Philad., 1872. 2 v. 12°. 7020
Mackenzie. Philad., 1870. 12°. 7019
Pen Photographs of Readings of. Field. Bost., 1871. 16°. . 2188
Story of Life of. [Taylor.] Lond. [1870.] 8°. 7018
Yesterdays with. Fields. Bost., 1872. 8°. 3612
Dictionary. Pierce and Wheeler. Bost., 1872. 12°. . . 2212

Dickinson, A. E. What Answer? (2 copies.) Bost., 1868. 12°. . 2983

Dickinson, B. Prize Letters to Students. N. Y., 1831. 12°. . . 17022

Dickson, W. Japan. Edinb., 1869. 8°. 6505

Dictionary of Arts, Manufactures, and Mines. Ure. N. Y., 1847. 8°.
American, of the English Language. Webster, Goodrich and Porter. Springf'ld., 1869. 4°. . . . .
See, also, ENCYCLOPÆDIA.

Diderot, D., and **Grimm, F. M. de.** Select Correspondence, 1753–69. Lond., 1814. 2 v. 8°. 7648

Didier, F. J. Letters from France, etc. N. Y., 1821. 8°. . . . 16694

Diet, Vegetable. Alcott. Bost., 1838. 12°. 9170

Digby, G. Elvira. (Old Plays, v. 12.) Lond., 1827. 8°. . . . 1519

Digby, Sir K., Memoirs of. By himself. Lond., 1827. 8°. . . . 6816

Digby, K. H. The Broad Stone of Honour. Lond., 1844. 12°. . 4620

Digestion, Physiology of. Combe. N. Y., 1836. 12°. 9124
See, also, CHEMISTRY; FOOD.

Dilke, C. W. Greater Britain. Philad., 1869. 12°. 8438

Dillon, A. A Winter in Iceland and Lapland. Lond., 1840. 2 v. 8°. 8290

Dillon, W. (Earl of Roscommon.) Poetical Works. Ed. Bell. Lond. 1807. 24°. 259
The same, ed. Johnson. Dubl., 1804. 8°. 15096
Select Poems. With Life, by Sanford. Philad., 1819. 24°. . 7

Diplomatists of Europe, The [in 19th century]. Capefigue. Lond., 1845. 16°. 6676

Dircks, H. Life of Marquis of Worcester. Lond., 1865. 8°. . . 7152
Discovery, Maritime and Inland, Hist. of. Cooley. Lond., 1830–31.
3 v. 16°. 5786
See, also, GEOGRAPHY ; INVENTIONS ; TRAVELS ; VOYAGES.
Disgrace to the Family, The. Jerrold. Lond., 1848. 8°. . . . 2453
Disowned, the. Bulwer. Philad., 1868. 12°. 2038
Disraeli, B. Coningsby. N. Y., 1845. 8°. 2344
Contarini Fleming. (2 copies.) N. Y., 1832. 2 v. 12°. . . 2046
Henrietta Temple. Philad., 1837. 2 v. 12°. 2127
Lothair. (2 copies.) N. Y., 1870. 12°. 2131
Novels. Philad., 1840. 8°. 2343
CONTENTS.—Vivian Grey; Young Duke; Contarini Fleming; Tale of Alroy; Rise of Iskander; Henrietta Temple; Venetia.
Sybil. N. Y. Philad., 1845. 8°. 2345
Venetia. Philad., 1837. 2 v. 12°. 2129
Voyage of Captain Popanilla. (2 copies.) Philad., 1828. 12°. 2155
Wondrous Tale of Alroy, and Rise of Iskander. Lond., 1833.
3 v. 12°. 2124
The Young Duke. N. Y., 1831. 2 v. 12°. 15153
Disraeli, I. Amenities of Literature. (2 copies.) Lond., 1841. 3 v. 8°. 3412
The same. N. Y., 1845. 2 v. 12° 3389
Curiosities of Literature. 1st series. 7th ed. (2 copies.)
Lond., 1823. 5 v. 8°. 3375
The same. 2d series. Lond., 1824. 3 v. 8°. . . . 3409
The same. 2d series. Bost., 1834. 2 v. 12°. . . 3385
The same. 2d series. Bost., 1834. (2 copies of v. 1.) 12°. 3387
The same. 2 series in 1 v. N. Y. 8°. 3408
The Literary Character. 3d ed. Lond., 1822. 2 v. 8°. . . 3373
The same. 5th ed. Lond., 1839. 16°. 3187
Miscellanies of Literature. N. Y., 1841. 3 v. 12°. . . . 3391
CONTENTS.—1, Miscellanies; Calamities of Authors. 2, Quarrels of Authors. 3, The Literary Character; Character of James I.
Narrative Poems. Philad., 1803. 12°. 14794
Quarrels of Authors. (2 copies.) N. Y., 1814. 2 v. 12°. . 3183
Ditson, G. L. Circassia; a Tour to the Caucasus. N. Y., 1850. 12°. 16489
Divorce and Divorce Legislation. Woolsey. N. Y., 1869. 12°. . 8642
Doctrine, etc., of. Milton. Lond., 1848. 8°. 456
Dix, J. Life of Chatterton. Lond., 1851. 16°. 6956
Dixon, W. H. Free Russia. N. Y., 1870. 12°. 8298
Her Majesty's Tower. N. Y. and Philad., 1869. 2 v. 12°. . 5148
New America. (2 copies.) Philad., 1867. 12°. 8427
Personal Hist. of Lord Bacon. (2 copies.) Bost., 1861. 12°. . 6755
William Penn. Philad., 1851. 12°. 7313
Dobrizhoffer, M. The Abipones. Lond., 1822. 3 v. 8°. . . . 5828
Dobson, S. Life of Petrarch. Philad., 1809. 2 v. 12°. 7508
The same. Philad., 1817. 8°. 7752
Doctor, The, &c. Southey. N. Y., 1836. 12°. 3272
Antonio. Ruffini. N. Y., 1862. 12°. 2446
Austin's Guests. Gilbert. Lond., 1867. 8°. 15414
Goethe's Courtship. Müller. Lond., 1866. 16°. 3046

Doctor Howell's Family. Goodwin. Bost., 1869. 12°. 2989
Johns. Mitchell. N. Y., 1866. 2 v. 8°. 2909
Thorne. A. Trollope. N. Y. 12°. 2109
Doctors, Book about. Jeaffreson. N. Y., 1862. 12°. . . . 8988
Dodd, G. Manufactures of Grt. Brit. Lond., 1844–46. 6 v. 12°. . 8786
CONTENTS.—1, Textile. 2, Chemical. 3, Metals. 4-6, Miscellaneous.
Dodd, W. Beauties of Shakspeare. Philad., 1830. 24°. 1378
Doddridge, P. Works. Lond., 1803–04. 5 v. 8°. 17201
[**Dodge, M. A.**] *(Gail Hamilton.)* Battle of the Books. Cambr., 1870. 8°. 3645
Country Living and Thinking. Bost., 1863. 8°. . . . 3647
Gala-Days. Bost., 1864. 8°. 3648
A New Atmosphere. (2 copies.) Bost., 1865. 8°. . . . 3650
Skirmishes and Sketches. (2 copies.) Bost., 1865. 8°. . . 3652
Stumbling-Blocks. Bost., 1864. 8°. 3649
Summer Rest. Bost., 1866. 8°. 3654
Woman's Worth and Worthlessness. N. Y., 1872. 12°. . . 9216
Wrongs. (2 copies.) Bost., 1868. 16°. . . . 9214
Dodge Club, The. De Mille. N. Y., 1870. 8°. 2689
Dodington, G. B. Diary. Lond., 1828. 12°. 6660
The same. Lond., 1823. 8°. 7143
Dodsley, R. Collection of Old Plays. [Ed. Collier.] Lond., 1825–27. 12 v. 8°. 1508
The same. v. 1, 2, 4–12, ... 1520
For Contents, see PLAYS.
Collection of Poems. Lond., 1770. v. 2–6. 12°. . . . 14019
King and Miller of Mansfield; Sir John Cockle at Court. (Brit. Drama, v. 5.) Lond., 1804. 8°. 1633
Select Poems. Ed. Walsh. Philad., 1822. 24°. . . . 20
Döllinger, J. J. I. v. Lectures on Reunion. N. Y., 1872. 12°. . . 10266
Dollars and Cents. Warner. N. Y., 1852. 2 v. 12°. . . . 3007
Dombey and Son. Dickens. N. Y., 1871. 16°. 2176
Domenech, E. Residence in Deserts of N. America. Lond., 1860. 2 v. 8°. 8497
Domestic Economy. Donovan. Lond., 1830–37. 2 v. 16°. . . 6035
Happiness portrayed. N. Y., 1835. 12°. 17009
Manners and Sentiments in England, in Middle Ages. Wright. Lond., 1862. 8°. 5263
Donaldson, P. Life of Wallace. Hartf'd., 1830. 12°. . . . 16444
Dongola, Expedition to, 1820. English. Bost., 1823. 8°. . . . 16529
Doni, A. F. Novels. (Ital. Novelists, v. 3.) Lond., 1836. 12°. . 1901
Donne, J. Poetical Works. Bost., 1871. 16°. 1034
Select Poems, with Life. Ed. Sanford. Philad., 1819. 24°. . 2
Life of. Walton. [Lond., 1845.] 8°. 948
Donovan, M. Domestic Economy. Lond., 1830–37. 2 v. 16°. . 6035
Treatise on Chemistry. Lond., 1837. 16°. 6041
Don Quixote. Cervantes. Lond., 1837–39. 3 v. 8°. . . . 1619
Rambles in the Footsteps of. Inglis. Philad., 1840. 12°. . 16680
Doolittle, J. Social Life of the Chinese. N. Y., 1865. 2 v. 12°. . 7942

Dora. Kavanagh. N. Y., 1868. 8°. 2685
Doran, J. Annals of the English Stage. N. Y., 1865. 2 v. 12°. . 1612
Knights and their days. Lond., 1856. 8°. 5141
The same. N. Y., 1856. 12°. 5142
Monarchs retired from business. N. Y., 1857. 2 v. 12°. . 6752
Doré, G. Illustrations of Dante. Lond., 1868. 2 v. fol. . .
—— of Don Quixote. Lond. 4°. . . . . .
Legend of the Wandering Jew. 12 Designs. Lond. fol. .
Doré. By a Stroller in Europe. N. Y., 1857. 12°. 8276
Dorset, Earl of. See SACKVILLE.
Douglas, J. Advancement of Society in Knowledge and Religion. Hartf'd., 1830. 12°. 17345
Douglas, S. A. Treatise on Constitutional and Party Questions. N. Y., 1866. 8°. 6173
and **Lincoln, A.** Political Debates. Columbus, 1860. 8°. . . 9388
Douglass, F. My Bondage and Freedom. Auburn, 1855. 12°. . 8577
Life of. By himself. Bost., 1847. 12°. 8576
Dove in the Eagle's Nest. Yonge. N. Y., 1866. 12°. . . . 2503
Dover, *Lord.* See G. J. W. A. ELLIS.
Dowling, J. Hist. of Romanism. 3d ed. N. Y., 1845. 8°. . . 9672
Down-Easters, The. Neal. N. Y., 1833. 2 v. 12°. 15689
Downes, J. The Mountain Decameron. Lond., 1836. 3 v. 12°. . 15513
Downing, A. J. Landscape Gardening and Rural Architecture. 2d ed. N. Y., 1844. 8°. 9084
Downing, Major Jack. *(Pseudonym.)* See SEBA SMITH.
Doyle, R. Manners and Customs of ye Englyshe. Lond. 2 v. 4°.
Drake, B. Life of Tecumseh, etc. Cincinn., 1841. 12°. . . . 5751
Drake, Sir F., Life of. N. Y., 1840. 12°. 11032
Voyages of. Lond., 1774. 8°. 16306
Drake, J. R. Culprit Fay, etc. (2 copies.) N. Y., 1836. 8°. . . 929
Drake, L. Heroes of England. Lond., 1843. 16°. 6674
Drake, N. Essays illustrative of the Rambler, Adventurer, and Idler. Lond., 1809–10. 2 v. 8°. 3236
—— of the Tatler, Spectator, and Guardian. Lond., 1805. 3 v. 8°. 3233
Literary Hours. Lond., 1804. 3 v. 8°. 3418
Memorials of Shakspeare. Lond., 1828. 8°. 1585
Mornings in Spring. Lond., 1828. 2 v. 8°. 296
Noontide Leisure; with a Tale of the Days of Shakspeare. Lond., 1824. 2 v. 16°. 1488
Shakspeare and his Times. (2 copies.) Paris, 1838. 8°. . . 1583
Drama, Defence of the. N. Y., 1826. 16°. 1395
British. [Ed. W. Scott.] Lond., 1804. 3 v. in 5. 8°. . . 1629

CONTENTS.—1, *Tragedies.* Pt. 1, Maid's Tragedy, Philaster, False One, Bonduca, by Beaumont and Fletcher; Bondman, Fatal Dowry, Massinger; Rival Queens, Lee; All for Love, Dryden; Orphan, Venice Preserved, Otway; Mourning Bride, Congreve; Tamerlane, Fair Penitent, Jane Shore, Lady J. Gray, Rowe; Cato, Addison; Distressed Mother, Philips; Siege of Damascus, Hughes; Revenge, Young; George Barnwell, Lillo. Pt. 2, Zara, by Hill; Fatal Curiosity, Arden of Feversham, Lillo; Gustavus Vasa, Brooke; Mahomet, Miller; Tancred and Sigismunda, Thomson; Irene, Johnson; Roman Father, Creusa, Whitehead; Brothers, Young; Gamester, Moore; Boadicea, Glover; Barbarossa, Brown; Douglas, Home; Isabella, Southern; Orphan of China, Zenobia, Grecian Daughter, Murphy; Countess of Salisbury, Hartson; Earl of Warwick, Matilda, Francklin. 2, *Comedies.* Pt. 1, Every Man in his Humour, Alchymist, by Jonson; New Way to Pay Old Debts, D. of Florence, Massinger; Rule a Wife and Have a Wife, Beaumont and Fletcher;

Plain Dealer, Wycherley; Double Dealer, Way of the World, Love for Love, Congreve; Provoked Wife, Vanbrugh; Love makes a Man, She would and She would not, Careless Husband, Double Gallant, Cibber; Constant Couple, Inconstant, Recruiting Officer, Beaux' Stratagem, Farquhar; Busy Body, Centlivre. Pt. 2, Wonder, Bold Stroke for a Wife, by Centlivre; Drummer, Addison; Conscious Lovers, Steele; Provoked Husband, Vanbrugh and Cibber; Suspicious Husband, Hoadly; Way to keep him, All in the Wrong, Murphy; Jealous Wife, Clandestine Marriage, English Merchant, Colman; School for Lovers, Whitehead; Brothers, W. Indian, Choleric Man, Cumberland; She Stoops to Conquer, Goldsmith; School for Wives, Kelly; Rivals, Sheridan. 3, *Operas* and *Farces*. Cheats of Scapin, by Otway; Country House, Vanbrugh; Contrivances, Chrononhotonthologos, Honest Yorkshireman, Carey; Devil to pay, Coffey; Beggar's Opera, Gay; Intriguing Chambermaid, Mock Doctor, Fielding; King and the Miller of Mansfield, Sir John Cockle at Court, Dodsley; Lying Valet, Miss in her Teens, Male-Coquette, Guardian, Neck or Nothing, Peep behind the Curtain, Irish Widow, Bon Ton, Garrick; Taste, Englishman in Paris, Knights, Englishman from Paris, Author, Minor, Liar, Orators, Mayor of Garratt, Patron, Commissary, Devil on Two Sticks, Lame Lover, Maid of Bath, Foote; Apprentice, Upholsterer, Old Maid, Citizen, 3 Weeks after Marriage, Murphy; Deuce is in him, Colman; Love in a Village, Maid of the Mill, Padlock, Dr. Last in his Chariot, Sultan, Bickerstaff; High Life Below Stairs [Townley]; Midas.

Drama, The British. Philad., 1833. 2 v. 8°. 1662

CONTENTS.—1, Fatal Curiosity, Lillo; Guardian, Lying Valet, Garrick; Grecian Daughter, Murphy; Man of the World, Macklin; Apprentice, Murphy; J. Shore, Rowe; Ways and Means, Colman; Devil to Pay, Coffey; Fair Penitent, Rowe; Bold Stroke for a Wife, Centlivre; Midas, O'Hara; Douglas, Home; Inconstant, Farquhar; Mayor of Garratt, Foote; Barbarossa, Brown; Recruiting Sergeant, Bickerstaff; Hero and Leander, Jackman; Isabella, Southern; Quaker, C. Dibdin; Rosina, Brooke; Venice Preserved, Otway; The Wonder, Centlivre; 3 Weeks after Marriage, Murphy; Cato, Addison; Fortune's Frolic, Allingham; Padlock, Bickerstaff; Revenge, Young; Rivals, Sheridan; Deuce is in him, Colman; Gustavus Vasa, H. Brooke; She Stoops to Conquer, Goldsmith; Bon Ton, Garrick; Orphan, Otway; New Way to Pay Old Debts, Massinger; Doctor and Apothecary, Cobb; Gamester, Moore; Suspicious Husband, Hoadly; Tom Thumb, O'Hara; Percy, H. More; Belle's Stratagem, Crowley; Critic, Sheridan; Oroonoko, Southern; Country Girl, Irish Widow, Garrick; Arden of Feversham, Lillo; Jealous Wife, Colman; Beggar's Opera, Gay; G. Barnwell, Lillo; Hypocrite, Bickerstaff; Mock Doctor, Fielding; Mourning Bride, Congreve; Clandestine Marriage, Garrick and Colman; Liar, Foote; Tancred and Sigismunda, Thomson; Beaux' Stratagem, Farquhar. 2, Lionel and Clarissa, Bickerstaff; Zara, Hill; W. Indian, Cumberland; High Life below Stairs, Townley; Tamerlane, Rowe; He would be a Soldier, Pilon; Miss in her Teens, Garrick; Distressed Mother, Philips; Tender Husband, Steele; Who's the Dupe, Cowley; Pizarro, Kotzebue; Every man in his Humour, Jonson; Love in a Village, Bickerstaff; All the World's a Stage, Jackman; Alex. the Great, Lee; Way to keep him, Murphy; Duenna, Sheridan; Ximena, Cibber; Rule a Wife and Have a Wife, Beaumont and Fletcher; Love a la Mode, Macklin; Roman Father, from Whitehead; Love for Love, Congreve; The Chances, from Beaumont and Fletcher; Intriguing Chambermaid, Fielding; All for Love, Dryden; City Wives' Confederacy, Vanburgh; Lame Lover, Foote; Earl of Essex, H. Jones; Brothers, Cumberland; Careless Husband, Cibber; Comus, Milton; Orphan of China, Murphy; Provoked Husband, Vanburgh and Cibber; Inkle and Yarico, Colman; Mahomet, Miller; Drummer, Addison; Recruiting Officer, Farquhar; First Floor, Cobb; Siege of Damascus, Hughes; Provoked Wife, Vanbrugh; Alzira, Hill; School for Scandal, Sheridan.

Engl., Hist. of, to Shakspeare. Hudson. (Shakspeare, v. 11.) Bost., 1859. 12°. 1388

Musical, Memoirs of the. Hogarth. Lond., 1838. 2 v. 8°. . 9080

Dramatic Art and Literature. A. v. Schlegel. Lond., 1846. 8°. . 429

Literature of Age of Eliz. Hazlitt. Lond., 1840. 16°. . . 69

Miscellanies. Davies. Lond., 1785. 3 v. 16°. 1494

Poetry, English, Hist of. Collier. Lond., 1831. 3 v. 16°. . 1556

Poets, Brit. and Amer., Golden Leaves from. Hows. N. Y., 1865. 12°. 1403

British, Lives of. Dunham, Bell, etc. Lond., 1837–40. 3 v. 16°. 5774

For contents, see DUNHAM.

English, Specimens of. Lamb. N. Y., 1845. 12°. . 1426

See, also, PLAYS; THEATERS.

Draper, J. W. Hist. of American Civil War. N. Y., 1868–70. 3 v. 8°. 6252

Hist. of Intellectual Development of Europe. N. Y., 1863. 8°. 4753

Drawing, Elements of. Ruskin. N. Y., 1867. 12°. 9032

See, also, ART.

Draytons and Davenants. [Charles.] N. Y., 1866. 12°. 2467

Dreams, Hist. of. Brierre de Boismont. Philad., 1855. 8°. . . 8763

Literature of. Seafield. Lond., 1865. 2 v. 8°. . . . 8528

Phenomena of. Dendy. Lond., 1832. 12°. 8481

of a Quiet Man. Fay. N. Y., 1832. 2 v. 12°. . . . 3569

See, also, APPARITIONS; SLEEP.

Dreamthorp. A. Smith. Bost., 1864. 8°. 3747
Dred. Mrs. Stowe. Bost., 1856. 2 v. 12°. 2959
Dress. See COSTUME.
Drew, S., Life of. By his son. N. Y., 1835. 12°. 16369
Dring, T. Recollections of the Jersey Prison-Ship. Ed. Greene. Prov., 1829. 12°. 16121
Droz, F. X. J. Art of being happy. Ed. Flint. Bost., 1832. 12°. . 17032
Druids. See CELTIC.
Drummond, W. Poems. (2 copies.) Lond., 1790. 16°. 952
Drunkenness, Anatomy of. Macnish. Hartf'd., 1842. 8°. . . 3472
See, also, INTEMPERANCE; TEMPERANCE.
Drury, A. H. Eastbury. N. Y., 1856. 12°. 15418
Drury, R., Adventures of. By himself. Lond., 1831. 12°. . . 6643
Dryden, J. Critical and Miscellaneous Prose Works. With Life, by Malone. Lond., 1800. 3 v. in 4. 8°. 3772
Dramatic Works. (2 copies). Lond., 1725. 6 v. 12°. . . 1405
Poetical Works. Ed. Bell. Lond., 1807. 5 v. 24°. . . 262
The same, with Memoir, by Christie. Lond., 1870. 16°. 1110
The same. With Life, by Sanford. Philad., 1819. 2 v. 24°. 8
The same, ed. Johnson. Dubl., 1804. 8°. . . . 15097
Works, with Life, by Mitford. N. Y., 1836. 2 v. 12°. . . 1108
Life of. W. Scott. Bost., 1829. 12°. 3188
Duane, W. Visit to Colombia. Philad., 1826. 8°. 17133
Du Barri, M. J. G. de V., Memoir of. By herself. Lond., 1830–31. 4 v. 12°. 6667
Dublin University Magazine. Dubl., 1841–72. v. 18–22, 79. 8°. . 17691
Dubois, J. A. Manners and Customs of India. Philad., 1818. 2 v. 8°. 16504
Ducas, T. Travels in Italy. Lond., 1822. 2 v. 8°. 16733
DuCerceau, J. A. Life and Times of Rienzi. Philad., 1836. 12°. . 7750
DuChaillu, P. B. Explorations in Equatorial Africa. Lond., 1861. 8°. 8090
Journey to Ashango-Land. (2 copies.) N. Y., 1867. 8°. . 8122
Ducoudray-Holstein, H. L. V. Memoirs of Bolivar. Bost., 1829. 8°. 7699
of Lafayette. N. Y., 1824. 12°. 7593
Du Deffand, M. de V. C. Correspondence. Lond., 1810. 2 v. 8°. 7655
Dudevant A. L. A. D. (*George Sand.*) Antonia. Bost., 1870. 16°. . 2350
Mauprat. Bost., 1870. 16°. 2349
Miller of Angibault. Bost., 1871. 16°. 2352
M. Sylvestre. Bost., 1870. 16°. 2351
Duelling, Hist of. Millingen. Lond., 1841. 2 v. 8°. . . . 15148
Romance of. Steinmetz. Lond., 1868. 2 v. 8°. . . . 15146
Dürer, A., Life, Journal, and Works of. Heaton. Lond., 1870. 8°. . 8125
Life and Works of. Scott. Lond., 1869. 8°. 7956
Married Life of. Schefer. N. Y., 1862. 16°. 7878
Du Fresnoy, C. A. Art of Painting; transl. by Mason, with Reynolds' notes. Lond., 1811. 8°. 17239
Du Hausset, *Mme.*, Memoirs of. By herself. N. Y., 1827. 12°. . 7654
Duke, R. Poems, ed. Johnson. Dubl., 1804. 8°. 15097
Duke Christian. J. Porter. Bost., 1824. 2 v. 12°. 15182

Dumas, A. Count of Monte-Cristo. Lond. 8°. 2628

The same, with Edmond 'Dantes. Philad. 3 v. in 1. 8°. 2629

Impressions of Travel, in Egypt and Arabia. N. Y., 1839. 12°. 7973

Marguerite of Valois. N. Y., 1846. 8°. 2630

Memoirs of a Physician; Queen's Necklace; Six Years Later. Philad. 8°. 2627

Pascal Bruno. Philad., 1839. 12°. 2594

Progress of Democracy; Gaul and France. N. Y., 1841. 12°. 5421

Dumas, M. Memoirs of my own Time. Philad., 1839. 2 v. 12°. . 16207

Dumont, P. E. L. Recollections of Mirabeau. Lond., 1835. 8°. . 7721

Dumont, P. J. Narrative of Slavery in Africa. Lond., 1819. 8°. . 8052

Dunallan. [Kennedy.] Bost., 1827. 2 v. 12°. 15416

Duncan, H. Philosophy of the Seasons. Bost., 1839. 4 v. 12°. . 16995

Duncan, John M. Travels in U. S. and Canada. N. H., 1823. 2 v. 12°. 16792

Duncan, Jonathan. The Dukes of Normandy. Lond., 1839. 12°. . 5422

Dunham, I. Memoir of B. Swift. Bost., 1842. 12°. 7526

Dunham, S. A. Hist. of Denmark, Sweden, and Norway. (2 copies.) Lond., 1839–40. 3 v. 16°. 5468

of Europe during the Middle Ages. (2 copies.) Lond., 1833–34. 4 v. 16°. 4874

of the Germanic Empire. (2 copies.) Lond., 1834–35. 3 v. 16°. 5462

of Poland. (2 copies.) Lond., 1836. 16°. . 5478

of Spain and Portugal. Lond., 1832–33. 5 v. 16°. 5456

The same. 5191

and others. Lives of Literary and Scientific Men of Grt. Brit. Lond., 1837–40. 3 v. 16°. 5774

CONTENTS.—1, St. Columba; Alfred the Great; Chaucer; Heywood; Spenser. 2, Shakespear; Jonson; Massinger; etc. 3, Shirley; Davenant: Otway; Lee; Behn; Shadwell; Wycherly; Vanbrugh; Congreve; Farquhar; Cibber; Centlivre; Murphy; Cumberland; Cowley.

Dunlap, ——. Thirty Years ago: Memoirs of a Water-Drinker. N. Y., 1836. 2 v. 12°. 15802

Dunlap, W. Hist. of the American Theatre. N. Y., 1832. 8°. . . 1616

Memoirs of G. F. Cooke. N. Y., 1813. 2 v. 12°. . . . 7893

Narrative of Events following Bonaparte's Russian Campaign. Hartf'd., 1814. 12°. 16189

Dunlop, J. Hist. of Fiction. 2d ed. Edinb., 1816. 3 v. 8°. . . 144

of Roman Literature. Phil. and Lond., 1827. 3 v. 8°. 198

The same. v. 1, 2. [to B. C. 31.] Philad., 1827. 8°. 201

Memoirs of Spain, 1621–1700. (2 copies.) Edinb., 1834. 2 v. 8°. 6520

Dunn, H. Guatimala. N. Y., 1828. 8°. 16901

Du Paty, C. M. J. B. M. Sentimental Letters on Italy. Lond., 1789. 2 v. 12°. 16723

Dupin, C. Excursions to British Posts. Lond., 1819. 8°. . . 8051

Tour through Naval and Military Establishments of Grt. Brit. Lond., 1822. 8°. 8057

Duplessis, G. Wonders of Engraving. N. Y., 1871. 12°. . . . 10125

Duppa, R. Life of Michael Angelo. Lond., 1846. 8°. . . . 345

Durbin, J. P. Observations in the East. N. Y., 1845. 2 v. 12°. . 16494

in Europe. N. Y., 1844. 2 v. 12°. . 16558

E.

East, D. J. Western Africa. Lond., 1844. 12°. 16472
East, Ancient History of the. Lenormant and Chevallier. Lond., 1869–70. 2 v. 8°. 4057
Diary in the, 1869. Russell. Lond., 1869. 8°. 8075
Letters from the, 1852–53. Bryant. N. Y., 1869. 12°. . . . 8239
Poetry of the. Alger. Bost., 1856. 12°. 875
Sketches of Travel in the. Spencer. N. Y., 1850. 8°. . . . 8069
See, also, the LEVANT; ORIENTAL; and names of countries.
East India Co., Hist. of Possessions of the. Martin. Lond., 1837. 2 v. 16°. 7903
East Indies, Hist. of English Transactions in. Cambr., 1776. 12°. . 16072
of European Settlements in. Raynal. Lond., 1776. 2 v. 8°. 16149
See, also, INDIA.
Eastburn, J. W., and **Sands, R. C.** Yamoyden. N. Y., 1820. 12°. . 14987
Eastbury. Drury. N. Y., 1856. 12°. 15418
Easter, Sermons for. Ed. Stebbing. Lond., 1835. 16°. 9498
Eastern Church. See CHURCH.
Life, present and past. Martineau. Philad., 1848. 8°. . . . 8098
Travel, Romance of. MacFarlane. Lond., 1846. 12°. . . . 8150
Eastlake, C. L. Contributions to Literature of the Fine Arts. With Memoir. Lond., 1870. 2 v. 8°. 9074
Eastman, F. S. Hist. of N. Y. State. N. Y., 1828. 12°. 6012
Eaton, C. A. W. Rome in the 19th Century. N. Y., 1827. 2 v. 12°. 16728
The same. 5th ed. (Bohn.) Lond., 1852. v. 1. 8°. . . . 527
Eaton, W., Life of. Felton. Bost., 1838. 16°. 7258
The same. [Prentiss.] Brookfield, 1813. 8°. 16396
Eberhard, P. Popular Traditions. Lond., 1826. 12°. 1896
Ebers, G. Daughter of an Egyptian King. Philad., 1871. 12°. . . 3041
Ecce Cœlum. [Burr.] Bost., 1870. 12°. 8917
Deus. [Parker.] Bost., 1867. 16°. 9905
Femina. White. Bost., 1870. 16°. 9210
Homo. [Seeley.] Bost., 1867. 16°. 9902
On. Gladstone. Lond., 1868. 16°. 9843
Ecclesiastical Hist., Apostolic. Neander. Edinb., 1842. 2 v. 16°. . 6339
Era of. De Pressensé. N. Y., 1870. 12°. 6307
Commentaries on, A. D. 1–200. Mosheim. Lond., 1813. 2 v. 8°. 6591
to 380. W. C. Taylor. Lond., 1844. 16°. . . 6333
to 412. Milman. Lond., 1840. 3 v. 8°. . . 6568
to 1073. Neander, transl. by Torrey. Bost., 1848. 3 v. 8°. 6563
to 1492. Stebbing. Lond., 1833–34. 2 v. 16°. 5488
to the Reformation. Waddington. Lond., 1833. 8°. 16467
to 1530. Milner. Bost., 1822. 5 v. 12°. . . 6334
to 1700. Jones. Philad., 1832. 8°. 16466
Institutes of, to 1750. Mosheim, tr. Murdock. N. H., 1832. 3 v. 8°. 6585
to 1790. Gregory. Lond., 1790. 2 v. 12°. . 14636
to 1839. Palmer. N. Y., 1841. 12°. . . 16461

Ecclesiastical Hist., Studies in ; Rise of the Temporal Power ; Benefit of Clergy ; Excommunication. Lea. Philad., 1839. 12°. 6314
Polity. Hooker. Lond., 1830. 3 v. 8°. 8688
See, also, CHRISTIANITY ; CHURCH.
Echard, L. Hist. of the Revolution in 1688. Lond., 1725. 8°. . . 16065
Echo, The. [Alsop and Dwight.] N. Y., 1807. 8°. 814
Eckardt, J. Modern Russia. Lond., 1870. 8°. 6448
Eckermann, J. P. Conversations with Goethe. Bost., 1839. 12°. . 7828
Eclectic, The American. (2 copies.) N. Y., 1841–42. 4 v. 8°. . 13741
The Eclectic Museum, v. 1–3, is a continuation (as v. 5–7).
Magazine, The. N. Y., 1844–64. v. 1–9, 11–63 ; and New Series. N. Y., 1865–72. 16 v. 8°. 13562
The same. v. 1–33, and N. S., v. 1–8. 13752
Museum, The. N. Y., 1843. 3 v. 8°. 13749
Review, The. Lond., 1805–10. 6 v. in 11. 8°. 14377
Edda of Sæmund. Transl. by Cottle. Bristol, 1797. 8°. . . . 920
Songs from the. Ed. Morris. Lond., 1870. 8°. 1922
See, also, SCANDINAVIAN Mythology.
Eddy, Z. Immanuel ; or the Life of Jesus. (2 copies.) Springf'ld., 1870. 8°. 6541
Edelweiss. Auerbach. Bost., 1869. 12°. 2710
Edgar, S. Variations of Popery. 2d ed. Lond., 1838. 8°. . . 6491
Edgar Huntly. C. B. Brown. Bost., 1827. 12°. 15302
Edgewood, My Farm of. Mitchell. N. Y., 1863. 12°. . . . 8922
Wet Days at. Mitchell. N. Y., 1865. 12°. 8924
Edgeworth, M. Tales and Novels. N. Y., 1834–35. 20 v. in 10. 12°. 13662
Works. Bost., 1823–26. 13 v. 8°. 15335
Edgeworth, R. L. and **M.** Essay on Irish Bulls. N. Y., 1803. 12°. 17050
Edinburgh, Traditions of. Chambers. Edinb., 1869. 8°. . . . 5154
Annual Register, for 1808–15. Edinb., 1810–17. 8 v. in 13. 8°. 11731
Monthly Review. Edinb., 1819–21. v. 1–5. 8°. . . . 13116
Review. Edinb. and N. Y., 1802–72. v. 1–22, 24–38, 40–83, 86–130, 133–136. 8°. 11051
The same. v. 1–17, 19–90, 93–122, 125–132. 11154
Index to v. 1–20. (2 copies.) Also, Index to v. 21–50. .
Selections from. Ed. Cross. Lond., 1833. v. 1, 4. 8°. 11293
The same. Paris, 1835. v. 1, 2, 4–6. 8°. . . . 11295
Weekly Magazine. Edinb., 1771–72. v. 14, 15 (in 1). 8°. . 12745
Edmond Dantes. Dumas. Philad. 8°. 2629
Education, Dialogues concerning. Fordyce. Lond., 1745. 8°. . 17043
Discussions on. Sir W. Hamilton. N. Y., 1861. 8°. . . 8769
Doctrine of. Richter. Bost., 1863. 8°. 3067
Essays on. Milton, Locke, etc. Lond., 1761. 8°. . . . 17046
Hints on. Home. Dubl., 1782. 12°. 17015
Hist. of. Schmidt. N. Y., 1844. 12°. 11758
Home. I. Taylor. N. Y., 1838. 12°. 9307
intellectual, moral, and physical. H. Spencer. N. Y., 1866. 12° 8595
Liberal. Knox. Lond., 1785. 2 v. 12°. 9108

Education, Liberal, Essays on a. Ed. Farrar. Lond., 1868. 8°. 9289
Physical. Maclaren. Oxf'd., 1869. 16°. 9118
Practical. Edgeworth. (Works, v. 1.) Bost., 1823. 8°. 15335
Importance of. Everett. Bost., 1840. 12°. 9266
Speeches connected with. Brougham. Edinb., 1838. 8°. 9339
See, also, COLLEGES; STUDENTS; UNIVERSITIES.
Edward. (A Novel.) Moore. (Works, v. 6.) Edinb., 1820. 8°. 17322
Edward I, Chronicle of. Peele. (Works, v. 1.) Lond., 1829. 8°. 1463
Edward II, a Tragedy. Marlowe. Lond., 1870. 8°. 1572
Edward III. of England, Life of. Longman. Lond., 1869. 2 v. 8°. 5286
The same. Williams. Lond., 1843. 12°. 5133
Edward the Black Prince, Hist. of. James. Lond., 1839. 2 v. 8°. 5131
Life of. Williams. Lond., 1843. 12°. 5133
Edward, D. B. Hist of Texas. Cincinn., 1836. 12°. 5994
Edwards, Bela B. Biography of Self-taught Men. Bost., 1832. 12°. 6696
The same, enlarged. Bost., 1846–47. 2 v. 12°. 6672
Slavery in Ancient Greece. Edinb., 1835. 16°. 9137
and others. Classical Studies. Bost., 1843. 12°. 9257
and **Park, E. A.** Selections from German Literature. (2 copies.) Andover, 1839. 8°. 10061
Edwards, Bryan. Hist. of Brit. Colonies in the W. I. Dubl., 1793. 2 v. 8°. 5832
Edwards, E. Life of Ralegh. Lond., 1868. 2 v. 8°. 6814
Edwards, J. Freedom of the Will. Lond., 1775. 8°. 17063
Memoirs of Brainerd. Ed. Dwight. N. H., 1822. 8°. 7632
Works, with Memoir by Dwight. N. Y., 1829–30. 10 v. 8°. 17176
Life of. Dwight. N. Y., 1830. 8°. 7709
The same. Miller. Bost., 1837. 16°. 7257
Edwards, R. Damon and Pithias. (Old Plays, v. 1.) Lond., 1825. 8°. 1508
Edwards, S. Hist. of the Opera. Lond., 1862. 2 v. 12°. 8863
Edwards, T. The World's Laconics. N. Y., 1856. 12°. 4338
Edwards, W. H. Voyage up the Amazon. N. Y., 1847. 12°. 17140
Edwin Brothertoft. Winthrop. Bost., 1862. 12°. 2858
Edwin Drood. Dickens. N. Y., 1871. 16°. 2186
Edwin the Fair; a drama. Taylor. Lond., 1845. 24°. 983
Egan, P. Life in London. Lond., 1823. 8°. 16713
Egede, H. Description of Greenland. Lond., 1818. 8°. 16595
Eggleston, E. The End of the World. N. Y. [1872.] 12°. 10298
Egypt 3300 years ago. De La Noye. N. Y., 1870. 12°. 10128
American in, 1839–40. Cooley. N. Y., 1842. 8°. 8068
Englishwoman in, 1842–46. Poole. Lond., 1844–46. 3 v. 12°. 8151
Hist. of, to A. D. 640. Sharpe. Lond., 1846. 8°. 4446
of Brit. Exped. to, 1801. Wilson. Philad., 1803. 8°. 5281
Impressions of Travel in, 1830. Dumas. N. Y., 1839. 12°. 7973
Incidents of Travel in, 1836. [Stephens.] N. Y., 1837. 2 v. 12°. 16490
Journal of Visit to, 1869. Grey. N. Y., 1870. 12°. 8253
Letters on. Savary. Dubl., 1787. 2 v. 8°. 16485
Monuments of. Hawks. N. Y., 1850. 8°. 4456
past and present. Thompson. Bost., 1854. 12°. 7972

Egypt, Sketches of Travel in, 1848–49. Spencer. N. Y., 1850. 8°. . 8069
Travels in, 1777–78. Sonnini. Lond., 1799. 3 v. 8°. . . 16516
1783–85. Volney. Dubl., 1788. 8°. . . . 16481
1798. Denon. N. Y., 1803. 2 v. 8°. . . . 16483
1817–18. Forbin. Lond., 1819. 8°. . . . 8052
1818–19. Montulé. Lond., 1821. 8°. . . . 8055
1821. Scholz. Lond., 1822. 8°. 8058
1827–28. Webster. Lond., 1830. 2 v. 8°. . . 8065
1840. Olin. N. Y., 1843. 2 v. 12°. . . . 16492
View of Ancient and Modern. Russell. N. Y., 1831. 12°. . 11025
and Nubia, Boat Life in. Prime. N. Y., 1857. 12°. . . 8233
Travels in, 1817. Irby and Mangles. Lond., 1844. 16°. 8197
1825–27. Madden. Lond., 1829. 8°. . 8067
and Abyssinia, Description of. Conder. Lond. 2 v. in 1. 12°. 7847
the Soudan, and Central Africa, 1845–61. Petherick. Edinb., 1861. 8°. 8071
Egyptians, Dissertations on the. De Pauw. Lond., 1795. 2 v. 8°. 16169
Ancient, Manners and Customs of. Wilkinson. Lond., 1837. 3 v. 8°. 4447
The same. 2d series. Lond., 1841. 2 v. and 1 v. pl. 8°. 4453
Modern, Manners and Customs of. Lane. Lond., 1842. 2 v. 8°. 8063
See, also, NILE.
Eichendorff, J. v. Aus dem Leben eines Taugenichts. Bost., 1866. 12°. 9615
Memoirs of a Good-for-Nothing. N. Y., 1866. 12°. . . 2709
Eikon Basilike. Lond., 1824. 12°. 4906
Eisdell, J. S. Treatise on Industry of Nations. Lond., 1839. 2 v. 8°. 8661
Elder, W. Biogr. of Dr. Kane. Philad., 1858. 8°. 7475
Elder Sister, The. James. N. Y., 1855. 12°. 15419
Eldon, *Lord* (J. Scott), Life of. Campbell. Lond., 1847. 8°. . 6872
Eldorado; Life in California and Mexico, 1849–50. Taylor. N. Y., 1867. 12°. 8280
Electricity, Notes of Lectures on. Tyndall. N. Y., 1871. 12°. . 8907
Papers on. Franklin. (Works, v. 5.) Bost., 1837. 8°. . . 9752
Elegant Extracts in Poetry. Lond., 1801. 2 v. 8°. 15836
The same. [Revised ed.] Lond., 1816. 2 v. 8°. . 15838
in Prose. 2d ed. Lond. [1784.] 12°. . . . 13357
in Prose. Bost., 1826. 6 v. 12°. 13358
in Verse. Bost., 1826. 6 v. 12°. 13364
Elephant, The. [Ogilby.] Lond., 1844. 12°. 8792
Elgin, Earl of. See J. BRUCE.
Elia. See C. LAMB.
Eliot, George. See M. J. LEWES.
Eliot, Sir John, Life of. Forster. Lond., 1836. 16°. 5760
Eliot, Rev. John, Life of. Francis. Bost., 1836. 16°. . . . 7254
Eliot, S. The Liberty of Rome. N. Y., 1849. 2 v. 8°. 16028
Elizabeth, Queen, and Mary Q. of Scotts. v. Raumer. Lond., 1836. 12°. 5210
and her Times. Original Letters, ed. Wright. Lond., 1838. 2 v. 8°. 5293

Elizabeth, Queen, Life of. Strickland. Philad., 1847. 8°. . . . 5230
Memoirs of Court of. Aikin. Philad., 1823. 8°. 5295
and Isabella, Review of Prescott's Comparison of. Bost., 1841. 12.° 16164
Elizabeth, Charlotte. See C. E. TONNA.
Elizabeth; or, the Exiles of Siberia. Cottin. N. Y., 1853. 12°. . 2359
Elizabeth de Bruce. [Johnstone.] N. Y., 1827. 2 v. 12°. . . 15420
Elkswatawa. N. Y., 1836. 2 v. 12°. 15687
Ella of Garveloch. Martineau. Bost., 1832. 12°. 14612
Ellery, W., Life of. Channing. Bost., 1836. 16°. 7255
Ellet, E. F. Poems. Philad., 1835. 12°. 14988
Women of the Revolution. N. Y., 1848–50. 3 v. 12°. . . 7300
Ellicott, C. J. Considerations on Revision of N. T. N. Y., 1873. 8°. 10263
Lectures on Life of Christ. Bost., 1862. 12° 6420
Elliot, J. Debates on Adoption of Constitution. Wash., 1828. v. 2–4. 8°. 6126
[**Elliot, S. H.**] The Parish-Side. N. Y., 1854. 12°. 15756
Elliott, C. B. Letters from North of Europe. Philad., 1833. 12°. . 16575
Elliott, C. W. New England History. N. Y., 1857. 2 v. 8°. . . 6175
Remarkable Characters of the Holy Land. Hartf'd., 1867. 8°. 10013
Wind and Whirlwind. (2 copies.) N. Y., 1868. 12°. . . 15817
Elliott, E. Poems. Lond., 1833–34. 2 v. 12°. 1006
Poetical Works. (2 copies.) Edinb., 1840. 8°. 940
Elliott, G. D. Journal during the French Revolution. Lond., 1859. 8°. 5711
Ellis, G. Early English Metrical Romances. (Bohn's ed.) Lond., 1848. 8°. 501
Specimens of Early English Poets. 4th ed. Lond., 1811. 3 v. 16°. 1080
The same. 5th ed. Lond., 1845. 3 v. 16°. 1083
Ellis, G. E. Life of Anne Hutchinson. Bost., 1845. 16°. . . . 7265
of J. Mason. Bost., 1844. 16°. 7262
of Penn. Bost., 1847. 16°. 7271
Ellis, G. J. W. A. (*Lord* Dover.) Life of Frederic II. N. Y., 1839. 2 v. 12°. 11045
The same. N. Y., 1832. 2 v. 12°. 12100
Ellis, H. Journal of Embassy to China. Lond., 1840. 8°. . . . 8101
Ellis, S. S. Daughters of England. N. Y., 1843. 12°. 9200
Hearts and Homes. N. Y., 1850. 8°. 2671
Home. N. Y., 1836. 2 v. in 1. 12°. 15457
Irish Girl: and other Poems. N. Y., 1844. 12°. 1231
Minister's Family. N. Y., 1844. 12°. 15509
Mothers of England. N. Y., 1844. 12°. 9201
Pictures of Private Life. Philad., 1833–34. 2 v. 12°. . . 15548
Poetry of Life. Philad., 1835. 2 v. 12°. 15242
Pretension. Philad., 1837. 2 v. 12°. 15555
Temper and Temperament. N. Y., 1846. 12°. 2426
Wives of England. N. Y., 1843. 12°. 9199
Women of England. N. Y., 1839. 12°. 9197
The same. N. Y., 1843. 12°. 9198

Ellis, S. S. Works. N. Y., 1843–44. 3 v. 8°. 15349

CONTENTS.—1, Women of England; Wives of England; Daughters of England. 2, Pictures of Private Life; Voice from the Vintage. 3, Mothers of England; Poetry of Life.

Ellis, W. Hist. of Madagascar. Lond. [1838.] 2 v. 8°. . . . 6494
Ellsworth, H. W. Valley of the Upper Wabash. N. Y., 1838. 12°. 16877
Ellwood, T., Life of. By himself. Lond., 1829. 12°. 6649
Elmes, J. The Arts and Artists. Lond., 1825. 3 v. 16°. . . . 8851
Classic Quotations. N. Y., 1863. 16°. 4337
Elocution, Cultivation of the Voice in. Russell. Bost., 1851. 12°. . 9303
Essay on. Dwyer. N. Y., 1828. 12°. 17530
Exercises in. Russell. Bost., 1841. 12°. 9302
Lectures on. Sheridan. Lond., 1798. 8°. 17523
Manual of. Caldwell. Philad., 1846. 12°. 9301
Philosophy of the Voice in. Rush. Philad., 1833. 8°. . . 17540
See, also, ORATORY; RHETORIC.
Eloisa. Rousseau. Lond., 1810. 3 v. 8°. 15146
Eloquence, American. Ed. Moore. N. Y., 1857. 2 v. 8°. . . 9432
Specimens of. Middletown, 1837. 12°. . 9291
of the Ancients. Brougham. Philad., 1839. 12°. . . . 6742
British, Common-place Book of. Lond., 1827. 24°. . . . 9149
Select. Goodrich. N. Y., 1861. 8°. 9425
of the British Senate, 1625–1802. Ed. Hazlitt. Brooklyn, 1810.
2 v. 8°. 9423
Dialogues on. Fénelon. Andover, 1845. 12°. 9913
Irish, Specimens of. Phillips. N. Y., 1820. 8°. . . . 9427
Lectures on. Porter. Andover, 1836. 8°. 17521
Patriotic (U. S.) Ed. Mrs. Kirkland. N. Y., 1866. 12°. . . 9325
Principles of. Maury. N. Y., 1848. 12°. 11926
Pulpit, Lectures on. Campbell. Bost., 1832. 8°. . . . 10038
of the XIX. century. Fish. N. Y., 1857. 8°. . . 10057
of the U. S. Williston. Middletown, 1827. 5 v. 8°. . . 9332
See, also, ORATORY; SPEECHES.
Elphinstone, M. Hist. of India [to 1761.] Lond., 1841. 2 v. 8°. . 6500
Elsie Venner. Holmes. Bost., 1861. 2 v. 16°. 2720
Elze, K. Lord Byron. Lond., 1872. 8°. 7094
Emancipation. See SLAVERY.
[**Embury, E. C. M.**] Guido, and other Poems. N. Y., 1828. 12°. . 14989
Emerson, J., Life of. R. Emerson. Bost., 1834. 12°. . . . 16419
Emerson, R. W. The Conduct of Life. (2 copies.) Bost., 1861. 12°. 3633
English Traits. (2 copies.) Bost., 1856–57. 12°. . . . 3627
Essays. 1st Series. (2 copies.) Bost., 1850–63. 12°. . . 3619
2d Series. (2 copies.) Bost., 1844–45. 12°. . . 3621
2d Series. 2d ed. (2 copies.) Bost., 1850–55. 12°. . 3623
May-Day, etc. Bost., 1867. 16°. 810
Miscellanies: Nature, Addresses, and Lectures. (2 copies.)
Bost., 1856–60. 12°. 3625
Poems. (2 copies.) Bost., 1847–50. 16°. 808
Representative Men. (4 copies.) Bost., 1849–68. 12°. . . 3629
Society and Solitude. (2 copies.) Bost., 1870. 12°. . . . 3635

Emily Montague. [Brooke.] Lond. 4 v. 12°. 15422
Emma. Austen. Philad., 1838. 8°. 2662
Emmet, R., Life of. Burke. Charleston, 1852. 12°. 6682
Emmet, T. A., Memoir of. Haines. N. Y., 1829. 12°. 6681
Emmons, N. Works. Bost., 1842. 6 v. 8°. 17186
Emmons, R. The Fredoniad. 2d ed. Philad., 1830. 4 v. 12°. . 15071
Emotions, Expression of. Darwin. N. Y., 1873. 12°. . . . 8938
Emptor, Caveat. *(Pseudonym.)* See G. STEPHEN.
Encyclopædia Americana. Lieber. Philad., 1830–33. 13 v. 8°.
Appleton's New American. N. Y., 1864. 16 v. 8°.
Annual Supplement, 1861–71. N. Y., 1864–72. 11 v. 8°. . . . .
British, of Arts and Sciences. Nicholson. Philad., 1819–21. 12 v. 8°. . . . .
Family. Goodrich. Hartf'd., 1849. 12°. . . . . . .
Iconographic. Heck. N. Y., 1851. 4 v. 8°. and 2 v. 4°. .
of Political Knowledge, etc. [Long.] Lond., 1848–49. 4 v. 8°. 350
of Science, Literature and Art. Brande. N. Y., 1848. 8°. .
See, also, DICTIONARIES.
End of the World, The. Eggleston. N. Y. [1872.] 12°. . . . 10298
Enfield, W. Hist. of Philosophy. Lond., 1837. 8°. 8719
Scientific Recreations. Lond., 1825. 12°. 16943
Engel, M. E. Novels. (German Novelists, v. 4.) Lond., 1826. 12°. 1898
England in 1835. v. Raumer. Philad., 1836. 8°. 5334
Abbeys, Castles, etc., of. Timbs. Lond. 2 v. 8°. . . . 5136
and America. A Comparison. N. Y., 1834. 8°. 5860
The American in, 1834. [Mackenzie.] N. Y., 1835. 2 v. 12°. 16757
Biogr. of Reform Ministers of. Jones. Lond., 1832. 8°. . 5330
Book of the Court of. Thoms. Lond., 1844. 8°. 5265
Christian Leaders of, in 18th century. Ryle. Lond., 1869. 8°. 6607
Comic Hist. of. A'Beckett. Lond., 1865. 8°. 4262
Commentaries on Laws of. Blackstone. N. Y., 1872. 2 v. 8°. 9395
Constitution of. Brougham. Lond., 1861. 16°. 4854
De Lolme. Lond., 1853. 8°. 484
Book of. Stephens. Glasgow, 1835. 8°. . . 5000
Growth of. Freeman. Lond., 1872. 8°. . . 5011
Hist. of. Russell. Lond., 1823. 8°. . . . 4988
Lectures on. Sullivan. Dubl., 1790. 8°. . . 4949
Manual of. Rowland. Lond., 1859. 12°. . . 4853
Rise and Progress of. Creasy. N. Y., 1856. 12°. 4852
The same. (Anglo-Saxon period.) Palgrave. Lond., 1832. 2 v. 4°. 5111
Constitutional Hist. of, 1485–1760. Hallam. Bost., 1861. 3 v. 8°. 4907
The same, 1760–1860. May. Bost., 1862–63. 2 v. 8°. . 4912
Illustrations of, to 1300. Stubbs. Oxf'd., 1870. 8°. 4851
Dialogue of the Common Law of. Hobbes. Lond., 1840. 8°. 9677
Domestic Manners and Sentiments in, in Middle Ages. Wright. Lond., 1862. 8°. 5263
Eccl. Hist. of [to A. D. 731]. Bede. Lond., 1847. 8°. . . 497

England, Embassy to, 1626. Bassompierre. Lond., 1819. 8°. . . 5073
1840. Guizot. Lond., 1862. 8°. . . . 5259
and the English. Bulwer. N. Y., 1833. 2 v. 12°. . . . 4828
Fame and Glory of, vindicated. N. Y., 1842. 12°. . . . 4832
Foreigner's Opinion of. Göde. Bost., 1822. 8°. . . . 16749
German Artist's Tour in. Passavant. Lond., 1836. 2 v. 12°. 17121
Gleanings in. [Cooper.] Philad., 1837. 2 v. 12°. . . . 16761
Hist. of (under the Romans). Thackeray. Lond., 1843. 2 v. 8°. 5069
in 6 early chronicles. Ed. Giles. Lond., 1848. 8°. . 499
of (to A. D. 1066). Milton. (Works, v. 5.) Lond., 1868. 8°. 458
The same. Temple. (Works, v. 3.) Lond., 1814. 8°. . 17199
of the Four Conquests of (to 1087). St. John. Lond., 1862. 2 v. 8°. 4994
Abridgement of, to 1216. Burke. (v. 5.) Bost., 1839. 8°. 9653
of, to 1485. Clarke. Lond., 1826. 2 v. 8°. 5102
to 1547, as illustrated by Shakspeare. Reed. Philad., 1857. 16°. 1478
to 1603. Turner. Lond., 1839. 12 v. 8°. 5078
to 1671. Lingard. Lond. and Philad., 1823–30. 12 v. 8°. 4950
to 1688. Hume. Bost., 1849–50. 6 v. 12°. . . 4892
Pictorial, to 1688. Craik, etc. Lond., 1841. 4 v. 8°. . 5104
to 1730, Remarks on. Bolingbroke. Lond., 1809. 8°. 17223
[to 1760.] Mackintosh, Wallace and Bell. Lond., 1830–40. 10 v. 16°. 4882
to 1760. Rapin and Tindal. Lond., 1757–62. 21 v. 8°. 16074
to 1821. Hume, Smollett, and Miller. Philad., 1836–37. 4 v. 8°. 5389
to 1835. Hume, Smollett, and Hughes. Paris, 1835–36. v. 2–15. 8°. 5365
to 1839. Keightley. N. Y., 1840. 5 v. 12°. . . 11589
to 1858. "The Student's Hume." N. Y., 1862. 12°. . 4904
to 1858. White. Lond., 1864. 16°. 4849
to 1867. Knight. Lond. 8 v. 8°. 5049
447–1235. Roger of Wendover. Lond., 1849. 2 v. 8°. 510
449–1142. Wm. of Malmesbury. Lond., 1847. 8°. . 508
Norman Conquest of. Freeman. Oxf'd., 1869–71. 4 v. 8°. 5006
The same. Thierry. Lond., 1847. 2 v. 8°. . . 332
Norman Kings of. (1066–1154.) Cobbe. Lond., 1869. 8°. 5285
Henry II, Richard I, and John. (1154–1216). Berington. Dubl., 1790. 2 v. 8°. 5255
1326–99. Froissart. Lond., 1839. 2 v. 8°. . . . 5696
1527–88. Froude. N. Y., 1865–70. 12 v. 8°. . . 4924
Political, 1528–1660. v. Raumer. Lond., 1837. 2 v. 8°. 4996
Reformation in (1527–59). Blunt. Philad., 1837. 12°. . 6312
The same. Burnet. Lond., 1825. 6 v. 12°. . . 6357
The same. Cobbett. N. Y., 1832–34. 2 v. 12°. . 6369
1547–57, in original letters. Ed. Tytler. Lond., 1839. 2 v. 8°. 5291
1603–60. Mrs. C. Macaulay. Lond., 1769–72. 5 v. 8°. 16095

England, Hist. of Rebellion, etc., in (1625–60). Clarendon. Bost., 1827. 6 v. 8°. 5340
The same. Cattermole. Lond., 1857. 8°. .
The same. Guizot. Lond., 1846. 8°. . . 337
Rebellion, Causes of. Hobbes. Lond., 1840. 8°. 9677
Commonwealth of. Godwin. Lond., 1824–27. v. 1–3. 8°. 5360
R. Cromwell and the Restoration in. Guizot. Lond., 1856. 2 v. 8°. 5023
Counter-Revolution in (1658–89). Carrel. Lond., 1846. 8°. 338
1685–1702. Macaulay. N. Y., 1849–71. 5 v. 8°. 5025
Revolution in, 1688. Dahlmann. Lond., 1844. 8°. 5012
The same. Echard. Lond., 1725. 8°. . . 16065
The same. Mackintosh. Philad., 1835. 8°. . 5013
1701–13. Stanhope. Lond., 1870. 8°. . . . 5040
[1709–13.] J. Swift. (Works, v. 7.) N. Y., 1812. 12°. 4177
1713–83. Stanhope. Leipz., 1853–54. 7 v. 16°. . 4837
1760–1801. Bisset. Balt., 1810. 4 v. 8°. . . 16105
1760–1820. Jones. Lond., 1825. 3 v. 8°. . . 4985
Pictorial, 1760–1820. Lond., 1841–44. v. 1, 3, 4. 8°. 5108
1800–1854. Martineau. Bost., 1864–66. 4 v. 8°. 4916
1826–36. Fonblanque. Lond., 1837. 3 v. 8°. . 4823
of Civilization in. Buckle. N. Y., 1859–66. 2 v. 8°. 5065
of Party in, 1666–1832. Cooke. Lond., 1836–37. 3 v. 8°. 4991
of Representative Gov't. in, to 1485. Guizot. Lond., 1852. 8°. 362
Letters from. By Espriella. [Southey.] Lond., 1808. 3 v. 12°. 8173
Letters on. A. de Stael-Holstein. Lond., 1830. 8°. . . 16748
Lives of Queens of. Strickland. Philad., 1851–52. 12 v. in 6. 8°. 5228
For Contents, see STRICKLAND.
Lives of Tudor Princesses of. Strickland. Lond., 1868. 8°. . 5208
Naval Hist. of. See NAVAL.
Notes on, 1861–71. Taine. N. Y., 1872. 8°. 5158
Old. Hoppin. N. Y., 1872. 16°. 8362
Sketch of. [Paulding.] N. Y., 1822. 2 v. in 1. 12°. . 15286
and its People. Hugh Miller. Bost., 1856. 12°. 8355
Religious Life in. Esquiros. Lond., 1867. 8°. 6325
Romance of Hist. of. Neele. Philad., 1828. 2 v. 12°. . . 15563
Rural Life of. Howitt. Lond., 1840. 8°. 5260
Social Condition and Education of. Kay. N. Y., 1864. 12°. . 5271
Stories of the Heroes of. Drake. Lond., 1843. 16°. . . 6674
Works of Art and Artists in. Waagen. Lond., 1838. 3 v. 8°. 9068
English, G. B. Narrative of Exped. to Dongola. Bost., 1823. 8°. . 16529
English Antiquities, Popular. Brand. Lond., 1841–42. 3 v. 8°. . 504
causes célèbres. Craik. Lond., 1844. 16°. 9154
Church, The Early. Churton. N. Y., 1842. 16°. 6311
Composition. See COMPOSITION.

English, The Dean's. [Criticism on Alford.] Moon. 4th ed. [Lond., 1865.] 16°. 58
Fashionables abroad. [Burdett.] Bost., 1828. 2 v. 12°. . 15427
Good; or, Errors in Language. Gould. N. Y., 1867. 12°. . 107
Gov't., Essay on hist. of the. Russell. Lond., 1823. 8°. . 4988
Historical View of, to 1688. Millar. Lond., 1803. 4 v. 8°. 5356
Grammar. See GRAMMAR.
Home, Our. Oxf'd., 1861. 12°. 5271
Ladies in XVII. century, Home Life of. Lond., 1860. 16°. . 9127
Language. See LANGUAGE.
Lessons for English People. Abbott and Seeley. Bost., 1872. 16°. 62
Literature, Amenities of. Disraeli. Lond., 1841. 3 v. 8°. . 3412
Compendium of, to 1800. Cleveland. Philad., 1847. 12°. 139
Curiosities of. Disraeli. N. Y. 8°. . . . 3408
Cyclopædia of. Chambers. Edinb., 1844. 2 v. 8°. 222
Early, Chapters on. Hippisley. Lond., 1837. 12°. 163
Handbook of. Corson. N. Y., 1871. 12°. . 94
Hist. of. Craik. N. Y., 1863. 2 v. 8°. 195
The same. Gray. Oxf'd., 1835. 8°. . . 180
The same. Spalding. N. Y., 1853. 12°. . 15069
The same. Taine. N. Y., 1871. 2 v. 8°. . 189
Introd. to. Day. N. Y., 1869. 16°. 138
and Learning. Craik. Lond., 1844–45. 6 v. 24°. . 45
Lectures on. Reed. Philad., 1863. 12°. . . . 66
and Literary Men. Mills. N. Y., 1856. 2 v. 8°. . 228
of the 19th century. Cleveland. Philad., 1865. 12°. 140
Outlines of. Shaw. Philad., 1864. 12°. . . . 141
Sketches of. De Chateaubriand. Lond., 1837. 2 v. 8°. 226
of Age of Elizabeth. Whipple. Bost., 1869. 8°. . 70
Metrical Romances. Ellis. Lond., 1848. 8°. 501
Note-Books, 1853–57. Hawthorne. Bost., 1870. 2 v. 12°. . 8358
Plea for the Queen's. Alford. Lond., 1866. 16°. . . . 57
Poetry. See POETRY.
Sketches; Our Old Home. Hawthorne. Bost., 1863. 8°. . 8357
Traits. Emerson. Bost., 1856. 12°. 3627
Writers. Morley. Lond., 1866–67. 2 v. in 3. 8°. . . . 158
See, also, ANGLO-SAXON; BRITISH; GREAT BRITAIN; and names of Sovereigns.
Englishman's Sketch-Book. N. Y., 1828. 12°. 16848
Engraving, Wonders of. Duplessis. N. Y., 1871. 12°. . . . 10125
Ennis, J. Origin of the Stars. N. Y., 1867. 12°. 16973
Ensenore. A Poem. [Myers.] N. Y., 1840. 8°. 15061
Enthusiasm, Natural Hist. of. Taylor. Bost., 1830. 12°. . . 9534
Eolopoesis. Amer. Rejected Addresses. [Bigelow.] N. Y. [1855.] 12°. 686
Eothen. [Kinglake.] N. Y., 1850. 12°. 7974
Epaminondas, Life of. Séran de la Tour. Lond., 1787. 2 v. 8°. . 16018
Epictetus. Morals, transl. by Stanhope. Lond., 1700. 8°. . . 4229
Epicurean, The; a Tale. T. Moore. N. Y., 1862. 12°. . . . 2461

Episcopacy, Sacred Order and Offices of. Jer. Taylor. Lond., 1836. 8°. 10063
Episcopalian Pulpit, Annals of American. Sprague. N. Y., 1859. 8°. 7734
Episodes in an Obscure Life. N. Y., 1871. 8°. 2433
Erasmus, D., Life of. Butler. Lond., 1825. 8°. 7686
The same. Jortin. Lond., 1808. 3 v. 8°. 7687
The same. Milman. Lond., 1870. 8°. 3435
Erckmann, E., and **Chatrain, A.** Blockade of Phalsburg. N. Y., 1871. 12°. 2363
Forest House, and Catherine's Lovers. Bost., 1871. 16°. . 2360
Invasion of France in 1814. N. Y., 1871. 12°. 2362
Madame Thérèse; or, the Volunteers of '92. N. Y., 1869. 12°. 2361
A Miller's Story of the War; or, the Plébiscite. N. Y., 1872. 12°. 2364
Outbreak of the French Revolution. Lond., 1871. 3 v. 8°. . 2598
Eric, or, Little by Little. Farrar. N. Y., 1866. 12°. 2427
Erie, Chapters of. Adams. Bost., 1871. 12°. 8643
Erizzo, S. Novels. (Ital. Novelists, 3.) Lond., 1836. 12°. . . 1901
Ernest Maltravers. Bulwer. N. Y., 1837. 2 v. 12°. 2069
Errata. [J. Neal.] N. Y., 1823. 2 v. 12°. 15691
Errors, Popular. Timbs. Lond., 1841. 16°. 16980
Erskine, T., Life of. Campbell. Lond., 1847. 8°. 6871
Escapes, Wonderful. Bernard. N. Y., 1871. 12°. 10129
Eskimos, Life among the, 1860–62. Hall. N. Y., 1865. 8°. . . 8113
Espriella, M. A. *(Pseudonym.)* See R. SOUTHEY.
Esquiros, A. Religious Life in England. Lond., 1867. 8°. . . 6325
Essayists, British. Ed. Ferguson. Lond., 1823. 40 v. 12°. . . 3109
For Contents, see BRITISH.
Essays and Reviews. 2d ed., ed. by Hedge. Bost., 1861. 12°. . 9954
Reply to. Ed. Thomson. N. Y., 1862. 12°. . 9955
on Social Subjects, from the Saturday Review. Bost., 1865. 8°. 3704
written in Intervals of Business. Helps. Bost., 1871. 16°. . 3698
Essenes, The. De Quincey. Bost., 1856. 16°. 3323
Estelle Russell. N. Y., 1870. 8°. 2327
Estlack, R. Ethick Diversions. N. Y., 1807. 12°. 15045
Ethel. James. N. Y., 1855. 12°. 15429
Ethelwerd, F. Chronicle. Ed. Giles. Lond., 1848. 8°. 499
Ethics of the Dust. Ruskin. N. Y., 1866. 12°. 9043
Ethics. See PHILOSOPHY.
Ethiopia, Highlands of. Harris. N. Y. [1845.] 8°. 16525
Ethnology. See MAN; RACE.
Eton, W. Survey of Turkish Empire. Lond., 1799. 8°. . . . 16061
Eton, Recollections of. Lond., 1870. 8°. 9248
Etonian, The. 3d ed. Lond., 1823. 3 v. 12°. 12297
Etruria, Hist. of, to the Foundation of Rome. Gray. Lond., 1843. 12°. 4728
Tour to Sepulchres of, 1839. Gray. Lond., 1841. 12°. . . 8870
Eudoxia, Hist. of. Kortz. Hudson, 1816. 12°. 16180
Eugene Aram. Bulwer. N. Y., 1832. 2 v. 12°. 2059
Eugene of Savoy, Prince, Memoirs of. By himself. Lond., 1830. 12°. 6646
The same. Lond., 1811. 8°. 7645
Eugene of Savoy, Prince. A Novel. [Mundt.] N. Y., 1869. 8°. . 3068

Eulenspiegel, or Howleglass ; transl. by Roscoe. Lond., 1826. 12°. . 1895
Euler, L. Letters on Nat. Philosophy. N. Y., 1840. 2 v. 12°. . 11275
Euphues. Lyly. Ed. Arber. Lond., 1868. 16°. 3888
Euripides. Bacchæ and Iphigenia in Aulis, tr. by Potter. Ed. Walsh.
Philad., 1823. 24°. 245
Tragedies, transl. by Potter. N. Y., 1834–41. 3 v. 12°. . 4522
The same. N. Y., 1834–35. 3 v. 12°. 4543
Europe in 1821. De Pradt. Lond., 1822. 2 v. 8°. 15884
in 1827. [Constable's Misc., v. 22.] Edinb., 1828. 12°. . . 4484
in 1840. Menzel. Edinb., 1841. 8°. 4635
after Congress of Aix-la-Chapelle, 1818. De Pradt. Philad.,
1820. 8°. 15921
before and after the French Revolution. Gentz. Lond., 1804. 8°. 15919
The Continent of, in 1835. Hoppus. Lond., 1836. 2 v. 12°. . 16587
Fresh Gleanings from. Ik. Marvel. N. Y.,
1856. 12°. 8270
Diplomatists of [in 19th century]. Capefigue. Lond., 1845. 16°. 6676
Eastern, and the Emperor Nicholas. Lond., 1846. 3 v. 12°. . 16175
Eleven Weeks in, 1849. Clarke. Bost., 1852. 12°. . . 16579
Familiar Letters from, 1853–54. Felton. Bost., 1865. 8°. . 8275
Glimpses of, in 1838. Clark. Philad., 1840. 2 v. 12°. . 16576
Hist of, Ancient. Russell. Lond., 1793. 2 v. 8°. . . 15904
Progress of Society in, to 1500. Robertson. Philad.,
1871. 8°. 10335
Introduction to (to 1743). Puffendorf. Lond., 1764.
2 v. 8°. 15912
during Middle Ages. Dunham. Lond., 1833–34.
4 v. 16°. 4874
The same. Hallam. N. Y., 1862. 3 v. 8°. . 4669
Student's Manual of. (340–1840.) Taylor. Lond.,
1841. 12°. 4564
Revolutions of, 400–1400. Taylor. Lond., 1843. 2 v. 8°. 4088
The same, 406–1848. Koch, etc. Hartf'd., 1849. 8°. 15858
philosophically illustrated, 476–1789. Miller. Lond.,
1848–49. 4 v. 8°. 358
Modern, to 1783. Smyth. Lond., 1854. 2 v. 8°. . 363
to 1815. Russell. Philad., 1822. 6 v. 8°. . 15906
to 1857. Dyer. Lond., 1861–64. 4 v. 8°. . 4720
Lectures on. v. Schlegel. Lond., 1847. 8°. 433
Conspiracies in, 1437–1678. Lawson. Edinb., 1829.
2 v. 12°. 4505
Political System of, 1492–1830. Heeren. Oxf'd., 1834.
2 v. 8°. 4716
XVI. and XVII. centuries in. v. Raumer. Lond.,
1835. 2 v. 12°. 4607
1665–81. Temple. (Works, v. 1, 2.) Lond., 1814. 8°. 17197
18th century in. Schlosser. Lond., 1843–45. 6 v. 8°. 4798
from Peace of Utrecht. [1710–23.] J. Russell. Lond.,
1826. 2 v. 8°. 4600

Europe, Hist. of, 1713–18. Gibson. Lond., 1725. 8°. . . . 15914
1740–78. Frederic II. (Works, 1–4.) Lond., 1789. 8°. 17244
1783–1810. Bigland. Lond., 1810. 2 v. 8°. . . 15915
1789–1815. Alison. Edinb., 1839–42. 10 v. 8°. . 4636
1815–52. Alison. N. Y., 1855–60. 4 v. 8°. . . 4804
of Civilization in. Guizot. Lond., 1846. 3 v. 8°. . 326
of Intellectual Development of. Draper. N. Y., 1863. 8°. 4753
of Repres. Gov't. in. Guizot. Lond., 1852. 8°. . . 362
Impressions of, in 1867–68. Bellows. N. Y., 1869. 2 v. 12°. 8273
Letters from, 1867. Forney. Philad. 12°. 16575
Literature of, 1400–1700. Hallam. Lond., 1837–39. 4 v. 8°. 150
during Middle Ages. Berington. Lond., 1846. 8°. 321
of South of. Sismondi. Lond., 1850. 2 v. 8°. 346
Notes in, 1839–47. Catlin. Lond., 1848. 2 v. 8°. . . . 8304
past and present. Ungewitter. N. Y., 1850. 12°. . . . 8266
Poets and Poetry of. Longfellow. Philad., 1847. 8°. . . 218
Polit. Survey of. Zimmermann. Dubl., 1788. 8°. . . . 15917
Present Situation of. [A. H. Everett.] Bost., 1822. 8°. . . 15922
Rambles in, in 1836. Hall. N. Y., 1839. 2 v. 12°. . . 16571
in 1839. Gibson. Philad., 1841. 12°. . . . 16573
Saunterings in. Warner. Bost., 1872. 12°. 8166
Scenes and Thoughts in. [1840–41.] Calvert. Bost., 1863. 2 v. 16°. 8201
State of Polite Learning in. Goldsmith. (Works, 1.) Lond., 1837. 8°. 3778
Tales and Souvenirs of a Residence in. Philad., 1842. 12°. . 16555
Tour in, 1825–27. Carter. N. Y., 1827. 2 v. 8°. . . . 16535
Tourist in. N. Y., 1838. 12°. 16578
View of Society in. Stuart. Edinb., 1792. 8°. . . . 15918
Visit to, in 1851. Silliman. N. Y., 1856. 2 v. 12°. . . 8263
A Year in, 1818–19. Griscom. N. Y., 1823. 2 v. 8°. . . 16538

European Capitals, Sketches of. Ware. Bost., 1851. 12°. . . 8267
Colonies. Howison. Lond., 1834. 2 v. 8°. 4711
Life and Manners. Colman. Bost., 1850. 2 v. 12°. . . 16562
Morals, Hist. of, from Augustus to Charlemagne. Lecky. N. Y., 1869. 2 v. 8°. 4709
Mosaic. Arnold. Bost., 1864. 16°. 8205
Travel, Bits of. [Hunt.] Bost., 1872. 12°. 8167
Reminiscences of, 1866–67. Peabody. N. Y., 1868. 16°. 8209
1834–41. Mott. N. Y., 1842. 8°. 16621
1835–36. Fisk. N. Y., 1838. 8°. 16537

Eusebius Pamphilus. Eccl. History, tr. Cruse. Philad., 1840. 8°. . 6449

Eustace, J. C. Classical Tour through Italy. 8th ed. Lond., 1841. 3 v. 12°. 8333

Eustaphiève, A. Demetrius. Bost., 1818. 12°. 14795
Resources of Russia. 2d ed. Bost., 1813. 12°. . . . 16174

Evans, A. J. See Mrs. A. J. Wilson.

Evans, G. W. D. Classic and Connoisseur in Italy and Sicily. Lond., 1835. 3 v. 8°. 9060

Evans, J. Parnassian Garland. Philad., 1814. 12°. 14905
Evans, N. Poems, etc. Philad., 1772. 8°. 15055
Evans, T. Old Ballads. New ed. Lond., 1810. 4 v. 16°. . . 1089
[**Evarts, J.**] Condition of the Amer. Indians. Bost., 1829. 8°. . 5895
Evelina. D'Arblay. N. Y., 1832. 12°. 2511
Evelyn, J. Life of Mrs. Godolphin. N. Y., 1847. 12°. . . . 7050
Memoirs of; Diary and Letters. Lond., 1827. 5 v. 8°. . . 7023
Everest, C. W. Poets of Connecticut. Hartf'd., 1843. 8°. . . 926
Everett, A. H. America. (2 copies.) Philad., 1827. 8°. . . 16126
Crit. and Misc. Essays. Bost., 1845–46. 2 v. 12°. . . . 3576
Europe. Bost., 1822. 8°. 15922
Life of P. Henry. Bost., 1844. 16°. 7260
of J. Warren. Bost., 1839. 16°. 7259
The same. 16314
Everett, E. Importance of Practical Education, etc. (2 copies.) Bost., 1840. 12°. 9266
Life of Stark. Bost., 1834. 16°. 7250
The same. Bost., 1839. 12°. 16313
of Washington. N. Y., 1860. 12°. 7293
Mount Vernon Papers. N. Y., 1860. 12°. 3578
Orations and Speeches. Bost., 1859–68. 4 v. 8°. . . . 9378
The same. v. 1–3. 9382
Everett, W. On the Cam. Cambr., 1865. 12°. 9240
Evesham, Monk of, Revelation to. Ed. Arber. Lond., 1869. 16°. . 3892
Evidence, Judicial, Rationale of. Bentham. (Works, pts. 11–14.) Edinb., 1839–40. 4 v. 8°. 9710
Evidences, Christian. See CHRISTIANITY; SCRIPTURE.
Ewald, H. F. Waldemar Krone's Youth. Philad., 1868. 12°. . . 3040
Examiner, The. Swift. (Works, v. 5.) N. Y., 1812. 12°. . . . 3851
Exercises, Physical, Manual of. Wood. N. Y., 1867. 12°. . . 9268
Exitu Israel, In. Baring-Gould. N. Y., 1870. 8°. 2442
Exmouth, Viscount. See E. PELLEW.
Exodus, Desert of the. Palmer. Cambr., 1871. 2 v. 8°. . . . 8046
Notes on. Bush. N. Y., 1841. 2 v. 12°. 9847
See, also, ARABIA; SINAI.
Extemporary Preaching. Zincke. N. Y., 1867. 12°. 9915
Speaking, Art of. Bautain. N. Y., 1867. 12°. 9294
Extracts, Elegant. See ELEGANT.
Eyes, Hints on Use of the. Reynolds. Edinb., 1835. 16°. . . 9137
Eyre, V. Military Operations at Cabul. Philad., 1843. 8°. . . 8050

F.

Fabens, J. W. The Camel Hunt. Cambr., 1851. 12°. 16872
Faber, G. S. Difficulties of Infidelity. Philad., 1829. 12°. . . 9912
of Romanism. Philad., 1840. 12°. . . 9550
Faber, T. Internal State of France. Philad., 1812. 12°. . . . 16188

Fable, Age of. Bulfinch. Bost., 1863. 12°. 1909
for Critics. [Lowell.] N. Y., 1848. 12°. 727
Fables. Æsop, ed. Croxall. N. Y., 1861. 12°. 1924
La Fontaine. Transl. by Wright. Bost., 1843. 2 v. 12°. . 985
Hottentot. Bleek. Lond., 1864. 8°. 1891
Russian. Krilof. Lond., 1869. 8°. 2624
Fabliaux, French. Ed. Legrand. Transl. by Way. Lond., 1815. 3 v. 16°. 302
Factory System of Great Brit. Ure. Lond., 1835. 12°. . . . 17001
Fair Harvard. [Washburne.] N. Y., 1869. 12°. 9264
Fairfax, Lord T. Life of. H. Coleridge. Leeds, 1836. 8°. . . 6904
The same. Markham. Lond., 1870. 8°. . . . 6821
Fairfield, S. L. Last Night of Pompeii, etc. N. Y., 1832. 8°. . . 15056
Poems. N. Y., 1823. 12°. 14931
The same. Philad., 1841. 8°. 15057
Fairy Mythology. Keightley. Lond., 1860. 16°. 1892
Tales and Romances. Hamilton. Lond., 1849. 8°. . . 452
Falconer, W. Poetical Works. Ed. Bell. Lond., 1807. 24°. . . 542
The same. Ed. Johnson. Dubl., 1804. 8°. . . . 15102
The Shipwreck. Philad., 1830. 12°. 14822
The same. Ed. Walsh. Philad., 1822. 24°. . . . 21
Faliero, Marino; a Tragedy. Byron. (Works, v. 12.) Lond., 1832. 16°. 316
Falk, J. Goethe pourtrayed. Tr. Austin. (v. 1, 2.) Lond., 1833. 12°. 7829
[**Falkenskjold, S. O.**] Hist. of Struensee and Brandt, tr. by Latrobe. Lond., 1789. 12°. 5819
Falkland. [Bulwer-Lytton.] N. Y., 1835. 12°. 2150
Falkner. Mrs. Shelley. N. Y., 1837. 12°. 15430
Fallacies, Book of. Bentham. (Works, pt. 8.) Edinb., 1839. 8°. . 9707
Falloux, F. A. P. de. Life of Mme. Swetchine. Bost., 1868. 16°. . 7558
False Favourite Disgrac'd. [d'Ouvilly.] Lond., 1657. 12°. . . 13354
Family, Lectures on the. Hyacinthe. N. Y., 1870. 12°. . . . 9984
Instructor, The. De Foe. Oxf'd., 1841. 2 v. 16°. . . . 3880
Fanaticism. Taylor. N. Y., 1834. 12°. 9536
Fanning, E. Voyages to the South Seas, etc. N. Y., 1838. 12°. . 16319
round the World. N. Y., 1833. 8°. . . 8076
Fanshawe, Lady A., Memoirs of. By herself. Lond., 1830. 12°. . 6781
Fanshawe. [Willis.] Bost., 1828. 12°. 15326
Far West, The. [Flagg.] N. Y., 1838. 2 v. 12°. 16857
Faraday, M., as a Discoverer. Tyndall. N. Y., 1868. 12°. . . 7158
Life and Letters of. Bence Jones. Philad., 1870. 2 v. 8°. . 7156
Farjeon, B. L. Joshua Marvel. Bost., 1871. 8°. 2335
Farmer, R. Essay on Learning of Shakespeare. 2d ed. Cambr., 1767. 16°. 1483
Farnham, E. W. Life in Prairie Land. N. Y., 1847. 16°. . . . 16865
Farnham, T. J. Travels in the Californias, etc. N. Y., 1844. 12°. . 16887
Farquhar, G. Beaux' Stratagem; Recruiting Officer; Inconstant. (Oxberry's Plays, v. 5.) Bost., 1822. 24°. 1349
Constant Couple; Inconstant; Recruiting Officer; Beaux' Stratagem. (Brit. Drama, v. 2, pt. 1.) Lond., 1804. 8°. 1631
Dramatic Works. Ed. L. Hunt. Lond., 1849. 8°. 10300

Farrar, A. S. Critical Hist. of Free Thought. N. Y., 1866. 12°. . 6322
Farrar, E. Recollections of 70 Years. (2 copies.) Bost., 1866. 12°. 6990
Farrar, F. W. Eric. N. Y., 1866. 12°. 2427
Julian Home. N. Y., 1866. 12°. 2428
St. Winifred's. (2 copies.) N. Y., 1867. 12°. 2429
Witness of History to Christ. Lond., 1871. 8°. 9906
and others. Essays on a Liberal Education. 2d ed. Lond., 1868. 8°. 9289
Farrar, T. Manual of the Constitution. Bost., 1867. 8°. 6181
Farreno, E. Carlotina; a Night with the Jesuits. N. Y., 1853. 12°. 17258
Fashion and Famine. Stephens. N. Y., 1854. 12°. 15693
Fashionable World displayed, The. Owen. N. Y., 1806. 12°. . 17048
Fast of St. Magdalen, The. A. M. Porter. Bost., 1819. 2 v. 12°. . 15194
Fatalla Sayeghir. Residence among the Arabs. Philad., 1840. 12°. 16471
Father Clement. [Kennedy.] N. Y., 1829. 12°. 15410
and Daughter. Opie. Bost., 1827. 12°. 14446
Father's Letters to his Son. Aikin. Lond., 1838. 16°. 9133
Fathers of the Church, Lives of. Cave. Oxf'd., 1840. 3 v. 8°. . 9970
and Sons. A Novel. Turgeneff. N. Y., 1867. 12°. . . . 2716
Fauriel, C. C. Hist. of Provençal Poetry. Tr. by Adler. N. Y., 1860. 8°. 241
Faustus, Doctor, Hist. of. [Widmann.] Tr. by Roscoe. Lond., 1826. 12°. 1895
Life of, etc. Lond., 1840. 16°. 2699
See, also, GOETHE; MARLOWE.
Fawcett, H. Manual of Polit. Economy. 3d ed. Cambr., 1869. 12°. 10206
and **M. G. Fawcett.** Essays and Lectures. Lond., 1872. 8°. 8636
Fay, T. S. The Countess Ida. N. Y., 1840. 2 v. in 1. 12°. . . 15684
Dreams and Reveries of a Quiet Man; the Little Genius; etc. N. Y., 1832. 2 v. 12°. 3569
Sydney Clifton. N. Y., 1839. 2 v. 12°. 15790
Featherstonhaugh, G. W. Excursion through the Slave States. N. Y., 1844. 8°. 9734
Feats on the Fiord. Martineau. Lond. 16°. 14622
Federalist, The. See A. HAMILTON.
Félice, G. de. Hist. of Protestants of France. N. Y., 1851. 8°. . 6484
Felix Holt. [Lewes.] N. Y., 1866. 8°. 2676
Fell, J. Life of Hammond. Lond. 24°. 6677
Fellah, The. About. Lond., 1870. 8°. 2395
Felltham, O. Resolves. [Ed. Young.] Cambr., 1832. 12°. . . 3907
The same. 3913
The same. Lond., 1840. 16°. 3918
Felton, C. C. Familiar Letters from Europe. Bost., 1865. 8°. . . 8275
Greece, Ancient and Modern. (2 copies.) Bost., 1867. 2 v. 8°. 4421
Life of W. Eaton. Bost., 1838. 16°. 7258
and others. Classical Studies. Bost., 1843. 12°. . . . 9259
Felton, H. Dissertation on Reading the Classics, etc. Lond., 1753. 12°. 91
Felton, J. B. The Horse-Shoe. Cambr., 1849. 12°. 14990
Female Biography. Hays. Lond., 1803. 6 v. 12°. 14426
Knapp. Philad., 1836. 12°. 16310
Mentor, The. Philad., 1802. 2 v. in 1. 12°. 17014

Female Quixotism. [Tenney.] Bost., 1825. 2 v. 12°. 15694
Sovereigns, Memoirs of. Jameson. N. Y., 1845–48. 2 v. 12°. 11037
See, also, WOMEN.
Fénelon, F. de S. de La M. Adventures of Telemachus. Lond. 8°. 1996
Dialogues on Eloquence. Bost., 1832. 8°. 10038
The same, ed. Park. Andover, 1845. 12°. 9913
Lives of Ancient Philosophers. N. Y., 1842. 12°. 11615
Selections from, with Memoir by Follen. 4th ed. Bost., 1841. 12°. 9980
The same. Bost., 1829. 12°. 17298
Treatise on Education of Daughters. Bost., 1820. 12°. . . 17059
Life of. Bausset. Lond., 1810. 2 v. 8°. 7672
Life of. Butler. Philad., 1811. 12°. 7557
Remarks on. Channing. (Works, v. 1.) Bost., 1841. 12°. . 9568
Fennell, J. H. Nat. Hist. of Quadrupeds. Lond., 1843. 8°. . . 9004
Fenton, E. Poetical Works. Ed. Bell. Lond., 1807. 24°. . . 276
Select Poems. With Life, by Sanford. Philad., 1819. 24°. . 10
The same. Ed. Johnson. Dubl., 1804. 8°. 15098
Ferdinand and Isabella, Hist. of. Prescott. Philad., 1871. 3 v. 8°. 10332
Ferdinand Count Fathom. Smollett. N. Y., 1860. 12°. . . . 1956
Fergus, H. Hist. of the U. S. Lond., 1837–38. 2 v. 16°. . . 5486
Ferguson, A. Essay on Hist. of Civil Society. Philad., 1819. 8°. . 17085
Hist. of the Roman Republic. Lond., 1829. 8°. 15988
The same. Dubl., 1783. 3 v. 8°. 15985
The same, abridged. N. Y. [1836.] 12°. 11928
Ferguson, J., Life of. By himself. Lond., 1830. 12°. . . . 6644
Fergusson, J. Rude Stone Monuments. Lond., 1872. 8°. . . 9096
Ferishtah, M. C. Hist. of Hindostan, transl. by Dow. 3d ed. Dubl., 1792. 3 v. 8°. 16448
Fern Leaves. [Parton.] Auburn, 1854. 12°. 3659
Ferrex and Porrex. Sackville. (Old Plays, v. 1.) Lond., 1825. 8°. 1508
Ferrier, S. Marriage. N. Y., 1847. 8°. 2672
Ferris, J. A. Financial Economy of U. S. S. Francisco, 1867. 12°. 8630
[**Fessenden, T. G.**] Democracy unveiled. 3d ed. N. Y., 1806. 2 v. 12°. 14992
Original Poems. Philad., 1806. 12°. 14991
Terrible Tractoration. 2d ed. Lond., 1803. 12°. 14932
The same. Philad., 1806. 8°. 15058
Festivals, Games, and Amusements. H. Smith. N. Y., 1868. 12°. . 11027
Feuerbach, P. J. A. v. Account of Casper Hauser. Bost., 1832. 12°. 7528
Remarkable Criminal Trials. N. Y., 1846. 16°. . 9153
Fibbleton, G. *(Pseudonym.)* See A. GREENE.
Fichte, J. G. Science of Knowledge. Philad., 1868. 12°. . . 8583
Memoir of. W. Smith. Bost., 1846. 12°. 7795
Fiction, Dict. of Noted Names of. Wheeler. Bost., 1868. 12°. . 301
Hist. of. Dunlop. Edinb., 1816. 3 v. 8°. 144
Fictions, Popular. Keightley. Lond., 1834. 12°. 1698
See, also, NOVELS; ROMANCE.
Fidler, I. Observations in U. S. and Canada. N. Y., 1833. 12°. . 16798
Field, H. M. Hist. of Atlantic Telegraph. (2 copies.) N. Y., 1866. 12°. 8900
The Irish Confederates, and Rebellion of '98. N. Y., 1851. 12°. 5243

Field, K. Pen Photographs of Dickens. Bost., 1871. 16°. . . . 2188
Field, S. Miscellaneous Poetry and Prose. Greenfield, 1818. 12°. 14933
Field, T. W. The Minstrel Pilgrim. N. Y., 1848. 12°. 14994
Field of the Forty Footsteps, The. J. Porter. N. Y., 1828. 12°. . 15181
Sports of U. S. Frank Forrester. N. Y., 1849. v. 1. 8°. . 10207
Fielding, H. Miscellaneous Works. N. Y., 1861. 4 v. (2 copies of v. 3.) 12°. 1971

CONTENTS.—1, 2, Tom Jones. 3, Amelia. 4, Joseph Andrews; Jonathan Wild.

The same, v. 4. 10301
Select Works. Philad., 1832. 2 v. 8°. 1987

CONTENTS.—1, Tom Jones. 2, Joseph Andrews; Amelia; Jonathan Wild.

Works. N. Y., 1813–16. v. 1–5, 7, 8, 10–14. 12°. 4215

CONTENTS.—1–5, Life; Plays. 7, 8, Tom Jones. 10, 11, Amelia. 12, Jonathan Wild; Causes of the increase of Robbers. 13, Journey from this World to the Next; Voyage to Lisbon; the True Patriot. 14, Covent-Garden Journal; Essays; &c.

Works. Ed. Browne. Lond., 1871–72. 11 v. 8°. 1976

CONTENTS.—1–4, Dramas; 4, Jonathan Wild; Journey from this World to the Next. 5, Joseph Andrews; Prefaces to David Simple. 6, 7, Tom Jones. 8, Miscellaneous; Amelia. 9, Amelia, concluded; Essays. 10, Covent-Garden Journal; Essay on Nothing; Voyage to Lisbon; etc. 11, Miscellanies; Poems.

Fielding; or, Society. Ward. Philad., 1838. 12°. 15431
Fields, J. T. Yesterdays with Authors. Bost., 1872. 8°. . . . 3612
Fiesco: a tragedy. Schiller. Lond., 1849. 8°. 438
Fifteen Years. Talvi. N. Y., 1871. 12°. 15696
Figuier, L. Insect World. Lond., 1868. 8°. 8999
Mammalia. Lond., 1870. 8°. 8996
Ocean World. Lond. [1869.] 8°. 8998
Primitive Man. Lond., 1870. 8°. 8994
Reptiles and Birds. Lond. [1869.] 8°. 8997
Vegetable World. Lond., 1869. 8°. 9000
World before the Deluge. Lond. [1866.] 8°. 8995
Fillmore, M. Messages, etc. (Statesman's Manual, v. 3.) N. Y., 1854. 8°. 6202
Finance, Essays on. P. Webster. Philad., 1791. 8°. 17095
Finances of the U. S. Gallatin. N. Y., 1796. 8°. 6240
Financial Economy of U. S. Ferris. S. Francisco, 1867. 12°. . 8630
Finati, G., Life of. By himself. Lond., 1830. 2 v. 16°. . . 7502
Findley, W. Hist. of Insurrection in Pa. Philad., 1796. 8°. . . 6091
Fine Arts. See ARTS; ARCHITECTURE; MUSIC; PAINTING.
Finland Family, The. Cornwall. N. Y., 1853. 16°. 2736
Finlayson, G. Mission to Siam and Huc. Lond., 1826. 8°. . . 16482
Finn, J. Sephardim. Lond., 1841. 12°. 6300
Finney, C. G. Lectures to Professing Christians. N. Y., 1837. 12°. 17352
on Revivals. N. Y., 1835. 12° . . . 17300
Fior d'Aliza. Lamartine. N. Y., 1868. 16°. 2347
Fiorentino, G. Novels. (Ital. Novelists, v. 1.) Lond., 1836. 12°. . 1899
Firenzuola, A. Novels. (Ital. Novelists, v. 2.) Lond., 1836. 12°. . 1900
First of the Knickerbockers. N. Y., 1848. 12°. 15697
Fish, F. W. Poems. N. H., 1855. 12°. 14934
Fish, H. C. Pulpit Eloquence of XIX. Century. N. Y., 1857. 8°. . 10057
[Fisher, A.] Journal of Arctic Voyage. Lond., 1819. 8°. . . 8051

Fisher, G. P. Essays on Supernatural Origin of Christianity. (2 copies.) N. Y., 1866. 8°. 10026
Life of Silliman. (2 copies.) N. Y., 1866. 2 v. 12°. . . . 7372
The Reformation. (2 copies.) N. Y., 1873. 8°. 10260
Fisher, J. Fuimus Troes. (Old Plays, v. 7.) Lond., 1825. 8°. . 1514
Fishes, Nat. Hist. and Classification of. Swainson. Lond., 1838–39. 2 v. 16°. 6060
Fishing. See ANGLER.
Fisk, W. Travels on the Continent. 3d ed. N. Y., 1838. 8°. . 16537
Fiske, J. Myths and Myth-Makers. Bost., 1873. 8°. 10262
[**Fiske, S.**] Dunn Browne's Experiences in Foreign Parts. Bost., 1857. 12°. 16568
Fitch, E. T. Sermons. N. H., 1871. 8°. 10052
Fitch, J., Life of. Whittlesey. Bost., 1845. 16°. 7265
Fitzboodle Papers. Thackeray. (Works, v. 9.) Lond., 1872. 8°. . 2197
Fitzgerald, *Lord* **E.,** Life of. Moore. N. Y., 1831. 2 v. 12°. . . 6684
Fitzosborne. *(Pseudonym.)* See W. MELMOTH.
Flagg, E. The Far West. N. Y., 1838. 2 v. 12°. 16857
Flammarion, C. Travels in the Air. Lond., 1871. 8°. 9093
Wonders of the Heavens. N. Y., 1871. 12°. . . . . , 10114
Flanders, H. Lives of the Chief Justices. Philad., 1855. 8°. . . 7473
Flavel, J. Fountain of Life. N. Y. 12°. 17347
Flaxman, J. Compositions from Dante. Lond., 1807. 4°.
from the Iliad. Lond., 1805. 4°. . .
Fleetwood. Godwin. N. Y., 1805. 2 v. 12°. 2015
Fletcher, James. Hist. of Poland. N. Y., 1840. 12°. 11026
The same. N. Y., 1831. 12°. 11953
Fletcher, John. See F. BEAUMONT.
Fletcher, M. J. Three Histories. Bost., 1831. 12°. 15604
[**Fleury, J. A. B.**] Adventures of an Actor. Ed. Hook. Lond., 1842. 2 v. 12°. 1608
Flint, T. Arthur Clenning. Philad., 1828. 2 v. 12°. 15659
Recollections of 10 years in Mississippi Valley. Bost., 1826. 8°. 16861
Flood, H., Sketch of. Lecky. N. Y., 1872. 12°. 6743
Floral Biography. Charlotte Elizabeth. N. Y., 1840. 12°. . . 15168
Florence, Hist. of [to 1492]. Machiavelli. Lond., 1847. 8°. . . 389
to 1531. Trollope. Lond., 1865. 4 v. 8°. . 4676
Florentine Republic, Hist. of the. Da Ponte. N. Y., 1833. 2 v. 12°. 4587
See, also, TUSCANY.
Florian, J. P. C. de. Hist. of the Moors of Spain. N. Y. [1840.] 12°. 11777
The same. N. Y., 1841. 12°. 16160
Florida and the Campaigns. Cohen. Charleston, 1836. 12°. . . 5732
Conquest of, by De Soto. T. Irving. Philad., 1835. 2 v. 12°. 5728
Exiles of. Giddings. Columbus, 1858. 12°. 16891
War, The. Sprague. N. Y., 1848. 8°. 5955
Floridas, Observations on the. Vignoles. N. Y., 1823. 8°. . . 16919
Flower, Fruit and Thorn Pieces. Richter. Bost., 1845. 2 v. 8°. . 3054
Garden, The. Charlotte Elizabeth. N. Y., 1840. 12°. . . 15169
Fly Leaves, etc. Calverley. N. Y., 1872. 16°. 4248

Flying Mail, The. Goldschmidt. Bost., 1870. 12°. 2619
Follen, C. T. C. Works. Bost., 1841. v. 1–3, 5. 12°. 12746
Follen, M. Sketches of Married Life. Bost., 1839. 12°. . . . 15779
[**Folsom, G.**] Mexico in 1842. N. Y., 1842. 12°. 16911
Fonblanque, A. England under 7 Administrations. Lond., 1837. 3 v. 8°. 4823
Fontenelle, B. Le B. de. Northern Worthies; Lives of Peter the Great and Catherine. Lond., 1728. 12°. . . . 16182
Fonvielle, W. de. Thunder and Lightning. (2 copies.) N. Y., 1869. 12°. 10112
Travels in the Air. Lond., 1871. 8°. 9093
Food, Human. Donovan. Lond., 1837. 16°. 6036
Useful Arts employed in Production of. Lond., 1844. 12°. . 8800
Vegetable Substances used for. Bost., 1832. 12°. . 8819
Fool of Quality, The. Brooke. Lond., 1859. 2 v. 8°. 2011
Foote, A. H. Africa and the American Flag. N. Y., 1854. 12°. . 8572
Foote, H. S. Texas and the Texans. Philad., 1841. 2 v. 12°. . 5995
The same. 16884
Foote, S. Farces. (Brit. Drama, v. 5.) Lond., 1804. 8°. . . . 1633
Works. Lond., 1830. 3 v. 12°. 1399
Memoirs of. Cooke. N. Y., 1806. 2 v. 12°. 7928
Footprints: or, Fugitive Poems. [Passmore.] Philad., 1843. 12°. . 15016
Foot-Prints of the Creator, The. Miller. Bost., 1850. 12°. . . 8974
Forbes, C. S. Campaign of Garibaldi in the Sicilies. Edinb., 1861. 8°. 4690
Forbes, D., Life of. Burton. Lond., 1847. 8°. 6762
Forbes, W. Life and Writings of Beattie. N. Y., 1807. 8°. . . 16354
Forbin, L. N. P. A. de. Travels in Egypt. Lond., 1819. 8°. . . 8052
in the Levant. Lond., 1819. 8°. . 8051
Force of Truth. Scott. N. Y., 1825. 12°. 17289
Forces, Correlation and Conservation of. Grove, etc. N. Y., 1869. 12°. 8895
Ford, J. Dramatic Works. N. Y., 1831. 2 v. 12°. 1689
The same, ed. H. Coleridge. Lond., 1840. 8°. . . 1627
Ford, R. The Spaniards and their Country. N. Y., 1847. 12°. . 8364
Ford, S. R. Grace Truman. N. Y., 1857. 12°. 15707
Fordyce, D. Dialogues concerning Education. 2d ed. Lond., 1745. 8°. 17043
Fordyce, J. Addresses to Young Men. Lond., 1789. 2 v. 16° . 17054
Foreign Quarterly Review. Lond. and N. Y., 1827–46. v. 1–3, 5–37. 8°. 12682
The same. v. 11, 12, 14–23, 26–30, 32–36. 12709
Review. Lond., 1828–30. 5 v. 8°. 11435
Forest, The; a Story. Huntington. N. Y., 1852. 12°. . . . 15698
of Arden, The. Gresley. N. Y., 1843. 12°. 15432
Days. G. P. R. James. N. Y. 8°. 2323
House, The. Erckmann-Chatrain. Bost., 1871. 16°. . . 2360
Life and Trees. Springer. N. Y., 1851. 12°. 16820
Forester, Fanny. *(Pseudonym.)* See E. C. JUDSON.
Forester, Frank. *(Pseudonym.)* See H. W. HERBERT.
Foresters, The. J. Wilson. Bost., 1845. 12°. 15433
Forget me not. Lond., 1826. 12°. 13840
Forney, J. W. Letters from Europe. Philad. [1867.] 12°. . . 16575
[**Forrester, A. H.**] Comic Figures of Arithmetic. Lond., 1843. 12°. 4278
Fors Clavigera. Ruskin. N. Y., 1871–72. 2 v. 12°. . . . 8632

Forster, Johann R. Hist. of Northern Voyages. Dubl., 1786. 8°. . 16594
Forster, John. Landor. A Biography. Bost., 1869. 8°. . . . 7093
Life of Dickens. Philad., 1872. v. 1, 2. 12°. 7020
of Goldsmith. New ed. Lond., 1855. 8°. . . . 6997
Statesmen of the Commonwealth. N. Y., 1846. 8°. . . 6903
and others. Lives of Eminent British Statesmen. Lond., 1831–39. 7 v. 16°. 5759

CONTENTS.—1, Sir T. More (by J. Mackintosh); Wolsey; Cranmer; Lord Burleigh. 2, Eliot; Strafford. 3, Pym; Hampden. 4, Vane; Marten. 5, Robert Cecil; Earl of Danby. (By T. P. Courtenay.) 6, 7, Cromwell.

Forsyth, J. Antiquities, etc., in Italy. 4th ed. Lond., 1835. 16°. . 8216
Forsyth, W. Life of Cicero. (2 copies.) N. Y., 1865–66. 2 v. 8°. 7744
Novels and Novelists of 18th century. N. Y., 1871. 12°. . 231
Fortini, P. Novel. (Ital. Novelists, v. 2.) Lond., 1836. 12°. . . 1900
Fortnightly Review. Lond., 1865–72. v. 1–18. 8°. 12195
Fortunes of Nigel. Scott. Bost., 1845. 12°. 1809
Fosbrooke, T. D. Arts, etc., of Greeks and Romans. (2 copies.) Lond., 1833–35. 2 v. 16°. 4869
Foscari, a Tragedy. Mitford. Philad. 8°. 2675
The Two; A Tragedy. Byron. [Works, v. 14.] Lond., 1833. 16°. 318
Foster, James. The Married State. N. Y., 1845. 12°. 11016
Foster, John. Contributions to Eclectic Review. Lond., 1844. 2 v. 8°. 3459
Essay on Popular Ignorance. Bost., 1821. 12°. 17049
Essays. Hartf'd., 1842. 8°. 3472
Lectures at Broadmead Chapel. Lond., 1844. 8°. 17506
The same. (Bohn's ed.) Lond., 1853. 2 v. 8°. . . 491
Life and Correspondence of. Ryland. Lond., 1852. 2 v. 8°. 489
The same. N. Y., 1846. 2 v. 12°. 7680
Foster-Brother, The. Hunt. N. Y., 1846. 8°. 2686
Fouché, J., Memoirs of. By himself. Bost., 1825. 8°. 7716
The same. 5634
Foul Play. Reade. Bost., 1869. 16°. 2098
Fouqué. See LAMOTHE FOUQUÉ.
Four Sisters, The. Bremer. Philad. 12°. 15136
Fourteen to Fourscore, From. Jewett. N. Y., 1871. 12°. . . 15699
Fowler, O. S., etc. Phrenology proved and illustrated. N. Y., 1837. 12°. 8531
Fowler, W. C. English Grammar. N. Y., 1851. 8°. 166
The same. Revised. N. Y., 1865. 8°. 167
Fox, C. J. Hist. of reign of James II. (2 copies.) Philad., 1808. 8°. 5257
The same. (2 copies.) Lond., 1846. 8°. 338
Characters of. [Parr.] Lond., 1809. 2 v. 8°. 6793
Memoirs of latter years of. Trotter. Philad., 1812. 8°. . . 16346
Memorials and Correspondence of. Russell. Philad., 1853. 2 v. 12°. 6629
Recollections of. Walpole. Lond., 1806. 12°. 6628
Fox, G., Life of. Janney. Philad., 1853. 8°. 6825
Fox, J. Book of Martyrs. Philad., 1830. 2 v. in 1. 4°. . . . 17329
Framley Parsonage. A Trollope. N. Y., 1862. 12°. 2108
France, A. de. See C. LAMPING.

France in 1816. Lady Morgan. Philad., 1817. 8°. 8448
in 1829–30. Lady Morgan. N. Y., 1830. 2 v. 12°. . . . 16692
and England in America. Parkman. Bost., 1865–69. 3 v. 12°. 6131
and Germany, Campaign in, 1813–14. Philippart. Lond., 1814. 2 v. 8°. 16186
and Germany, Narrative of War in, 1813–14. Londonderry. Philad., 1831. 12°. 16191
Constitutional Monarchy in. Renan. Bost., 1871. 16°. . . 5573
Early Poetry of. Costello. Lond., 1835. 8°. 917
Fair; Impressions of a Traveller, 1867. Mrs. Craik. N. Y., 1871. 12°. 8374
Gallery of Portraits of National Assembly of. [Luchet, etc.] Dubl., 1790. 2 v. in 1. 12°. 5508
Hist. of, to 1453. Michelet. Lond., 1844–46. 2 v. 8°. . . 5648
to 1529. Smedley. Lond., 1836. 8°. 16210
to 1574. Bossuet. Edinb., 1762. 4 v. 12°. . . . 5523
to 1715. Daniel. Lond., 1726. 5 v. 8°. . . . 16236
Lectures on, to 1715. Stephen. N. Y., 1852. 8°. . 5710
to 1793. Ranken. Lond., 1801–22. 9 v. 8°. . . 16227
Pictorial, to 1793. Bussey and Gaspey. Lond., 1843. 2 v. 8°. 5704
to 1814. Crowe. Lond., 1836–37. 3 v. 16°. . . 5186
to 1852. Crowe. Lond., 1858–68. 5 v. 8°. . . 5643
to 1852, Student's. (3 copies.) N. Y., 1862–72. 12° . 5529
1326–99. Froissart. Lond., 1839. 2 v. 8°. . . 5698
1400–1516. Monstrelet. Lond., 1840. 2 v. 8°. . . 5700
1464–98. De Comines. Lond., 1823. 2 v. 8°. . . 5532
Civil Wars in, 1547–98. Davila. Lond., 1758. 2 v. 4°. 5706
1574–1610. Wraxall. Lond., 1814. 6 v. 8°. . . 16241
1773–1826. Dumas. Philad., 1839. 2 v. 12°. . . 16207
Revolution of 1789 in, etc. Lond., 1817–26. 4 v. 8°. 5690

CONTENTS.—1, 2, Reign of Terror. 3, Sufferings of the Royal Family. 4, Hist. of France, 1792–1815.

The same. Baines. Philad., 1835. 3 v. 8°. . 5671
The same. Carlyle. Lond., 1870. 3 v. 8°. . 4021
The same. (1789–1814.) Mignet. Lond., 1856. 8°. 377
The same. v. Sybel. Lond., 1867–69. 4 v. 8°. 5667
The same. Thiers. Philad., 1840. 3 v. 8°. . 5674
Revolution of '89, Biogr. Memoirs of. Adolphus. Lond., 1799. 2 v. 8°. 5563
Causes and Progress of. Moore. Edinb., 1820. 8°. 17320
Clergy during. Barruel. Dubl., 1795. 12°. . 16220
Considerations on. De Staël. N. Y., 1818. 2 v. 8°. 5686
Defence of. Mackintosh. Philad., 1847. 8°. . 3470
Girondists of. Lamartine. N. Y., 1868. 3 v. 12°. 5560
Jacobinism in. Barruel. N. Y., 1799. 4 v. 8°. 16201
Journal during. Mrs. Elliott. Lond., 1859. 8°. . 5711
The same. J. Moore. Edinb., 1820. 8°. . . 17319
Lectures on. W. Smyth. Lond., 1855. 2 v. 8°. 380

Francis of Assisi, Hist. of. Oliphant. Lond. 8°. 7669

Francis of Sales. Introd. to a Devout Life. Balt., 1816. 12°. . . 17295

Francis, C. Life of Eliot. (Sparks, v. 5.) Bost., 1836. 16°. . . 7254

of S. Rale. (Sparks, v. 17.) Bost., 1845. 16°. . 7266

Francis, G. H. Orators of the Age. (2 copies.) N. Y., 1847. 16°. . 6697

Francis, P., Memoirs of. Parkes and Merivale. Lond., 1867. 2 v. 8°. 6852

Francklin, T. Earl of Warwick; Matilda. (Brit. Drama.) Lond., 1804. 8°. 1630

Franco, Harry. *(Pseudonym.)* See C. F. BRIGGS.

Frank Mildmay. Marryat. N. Y., 1835. 12°. 15522

Frankenstein. Mrs. Shelley. Philad., 1833. 2 v. 12°. 2406

Franklin, B. Autobiography, ed. Bigelow. Philad., 1869. 12°. . 7316

Autobiography and Essays. Easton, 1810. 12°. 7550

The same. Bost., 1825. 12°. 7512

Essays and Letters. N. Y., 1821. 2 v. 12°. 3533

Essays and Life. N. Y., 1825. 12°. 3535

Familiar Letters, *etc.* Bost., 1833. 12°. 7317

Memoirs, Essays, *etc.* N. Y., 1840. 2 v. 12°. 11416

The same. 12120

Works. Lond., 1806. 3 v. 8°. 17152

The same. Philad., 1809–18. 5 v. 8°. 17155

Works, ed. Sparks. Bost., 1836–40. 10 v. 8°. 9748

CONTENTS.—1, Autobiography; continued by the editor. 2, Essays on Moral subjects; Bagatelles; Essays on Commerce, Polit. Economy, etc. 3, Hist. of Pa. 3, 4, Essays and Tracts, Historical and Political, before the Revolution. 5, Political Papers during and after the Revolution; Letters and Papers on Electricity. 6, Letters and Papers on Philosophical Subjects. 7, Letters, 1725–72. 8, Letters, 1772–81. 9, Letters, 1781–83; Journal of Negotiation of Treaty of Peace. 10, Letters, 1783–90; Index.

Anecdotes of. [Almon, v. 2.] Lond., 1797. 8°. 16372

Lecture on. Theodore Parker. Bost., 1870. 12°. . . . 7409

Life and Times of. Parton. N. Y., 1864. 2 v. 12°. . . 7314

Life and Writings of. Ed. Duane. Philad., 1834. 2 v. 8°. . 9746

Franklin, James. Present state of Hayti. Lond., 1828. 8°. . . 16912

Franklin, *Sir* **John.** Journeys to the Polar Sea. Lond., 1829. 4 v. 12°. 7868

Narrative of 2d Polar Expedition. Philad., 1828. 8°. . . 8103

Fraser, J. B. The Kuzzilbash. N. Y., 1828. 2 v. 12°. . . . 15481

Mesopotamia and Assyria. N. Y., 1845. 12°. 11759

Persia. N. Y., 1841. 12°. 11288

The Persian Adventurer. Philad., 1831. 2 v. 12°. . . 15542

Fraser, S. (Lord Lovat), Life of. Burton. Lond., 1847. 8°. . . 6762

Fraser's Magazine. Lond., 1830–69. 79 v. 8°. 12300

The same. New series. Lond., 1870–72. 6 v. 8°. . 12380

Freaks of Cupid. Philad. 8°. 2312

Frederic II. (the Great), of Prussia. Memoirs of House of Brandenburg. Lond., 1751. 12°. 16456

Posthumous Works. Lond., 1789. 13 v. 8°. 17244

and his Court. A Romance. [Mundt.] N. Y., 1868. 12°. . 3099

and his Family. A Novel. [Mundt.] N. Y., 1867. 8°. . 3080

and his Times. v. Raumer. Lond., 1837. 12°. 5802

Court and Times of. Ed. T. Campbell. 2d ed. Lond., 1844. 2 v. 12°. 5803

Frederic II. Hist. of. Carlyle. Lond., 1870–71. 10 v. 8°. . . . 4040
The same. Ségur. Lond., 1801. 3 v. 8°. 5880
Life of. Lord Dover. N. Y., 1839. 2 v. 12°. . . . 11045
Life and Character of. Zimmermann. Dubl., 1792. 12°. . 16453
Reign of. Gillies. Dubl., 1789. 8°. 16452
Frederic III, Memoirs of. Towers. Dubl., 1789. 2 v. 8°. . . 16454
Fredet, P. Ancient History. 2d ed. Balt., 1851. 12°. 4054
Modern History. Balt., 1850. 12°. 4570
Fredoniad, The. Emmons. Philad., 1830. 4 v. 12°. . . . 15071
Free Institutions, Nature and Tendency of. Grimke. Cincinn., 1848. 8°. 8697
Man's Companion. Hartf'd., 1827. 8°. 17092
Masonry exposed. N. Y., 1828. 8°. 17110
Letters on. Stone. N. Y., 1832. 8°. . . . 17111
Masons, Proofs of Conspiracy by. Robison. N. Y., 1798. 8°. 17108
Thought, Hist. of. Farrar. N. Y., 1866. 12°. 6322
Freedom and Bondage, Jurisprudence of. Hurd. N. Y., 1856. 8°. 9282
of the Press. See LIBERTY.
of the Will, Inquiry into the. Edwards. N. Y., 1829. 8°. . 17177
Freeholder, The. (Addison's Works, v. 3.) N. Y., 1856. 12°. . 3997
Freeman, E. A. Growth of the English Constitution. Lond., 1872. 8°. 5011
Historical Essays. Lond., 1871. 8°. 4658
Hist. of the Norman Conquest. Oxf'd., 1869–71. 4 v. 8°. . 5006
of the Saracens. Oxf'd., 1870. 16°. 6341
Outlines of History. N. Y., 1872. 12°. 4561
Frémont, J. C., Life of. Upham. Bost., 1856. 12°. 7398
Memoir of. Bigelow. N. Y., 1856. 12°. 7397
French Fabliaux, ed. Legrand. Tr. by Way. Lond., 1815. 3 v. 16°. 302
Note-Books, Passages from (1858–59). Hawthorne. Bost., 1872. 2 v. 12°. 8203
Revolutionary Plutarch. [Stewarton.] Lond., 1805. 3 v. 12°. 5509
Stage, Picture of. [Fleury.] Ed. Hook. Lond., 1842. 2 v. 12°. 1608
Sticks, A Faggot of; or, Paris in '51. Head. N. Y., 1852. 12°. 8373
Wines and Politics. Martineau. Lond., 1833. 12°. . . 14619
Freneau, P. Poems. 2d ed. Monmouth, 1795. 8°. 935
Freytag, G. Debit and Credit. (2 copies.) N. Y., 1863. 12°. . 3042
Pictures of German Life. Lond., 1862. 2 v. 8°. . . . 5806
Soll und Haben. 13te. Aufl. Leipz., 1867. 2 Bde. in 1. . 9759
Die verlorene Handschrift. 4te. Aufl. Leipz., 1865. 3 Th. 16°. 9616
Friedländer, H. Views in Italy. Lond., 1821. 8°. 8055
Friend, The: a Series of Essays. Coleridge. (Works, 2.) N. Y., 1868. 12°. 4014
Friends in Council. Helps. 2d Series. N. Y., 1863. 2 v. 16°. . 3696
Friendship, Essay on. Cicero. Lond., 1807. 8°. 4634
Friendships of Women. Alger. Bost., 1870. 16°. 9209
Fright, The. Pickering. Philad., 1840. 2 v. 12°. 15434
Frith, J. Writings. Lond. 12°. 9482
Frithiof's Saga. Tegner. Transl. by Strong. Lond., 1833. 8°. . 922
Froebel, J. 7 Years' Travel in Central Amer., etc. Lond., 1859. 8°. 8437

Froissart, J. Chronicles, tr. by Johnes. (2 copies.) Lond., 1839. 2 v. 8°. 5696
Stories from. Lond., 1832. 3 v. 8°. 5423
Frost, J. Book of the Indians. Hartf'd., 1852. 12°. 5746
of the Navy. N. Y., 1843. 12°. 16119
Lives of Eminent Christians. Hartf'd., 1850. 8°. . . . 16400
Pictorial Life of Jackson. Hartf'd., 1847. 8°. 7425
Select Works of Brit. Poets, Falconer to Scott. (2 copies.)
Philad., 1838. 8°. 1306
The same, Southey to Croly. Philad., 1843. 8°. . . 1308
Froude, J. A. Calvinism. (2 copies.) N. Y., 1871. 12°. . . 9961
The English in Ireland. (2 copies.) N. Y., 1873. v. 1. 12°. . 10233
Hist. of England. (2 copies.) N. Y., 1865–70. 12 v. 8°. . 4924
The same, v. 1. 4948
Short Studies on Great Subjects. N. Y., 1868–71. 2 series. 12°. 3726
The same. 1st series. 3728
Fruits, Description of. Bost., 1830. 12°. 8806
Fry, C. The Listener. Philad., 1837. 2 v. 12°. 15172
Fudge Doings. Mitchell. N. Y., 1855. 2 v. 12°. 2907
Family in Paris, The. [Moore.] N. Y., 1818. 12°. . . 14837
Fuller, A. Works; with Memoir. (Bohn's ed.) Lond., 1852. 8°. . 495
Fuller, Margaret, Memoirs of. Bost., 1857. 2 v. 12°. . . . 7391
Fuller, T. Good Thoughts in Bad Times, etc. Bost., 1863. 8°. . 3903
Hist. of Univ. of Cambridge, and of Waltham Abbey. With the
Appeal of Injured Innocence. Ed. Nichols. Lond.,
1840. 8°. 9286
Holy and Profane States. [Abridged.] Camb., 1831. 12°. . 3904
The same. . . . , ... 3911
Fullerton, G. A Stormy Life. N. Y., 1868. 8°. 2684
Too Strange not to be True. Leipzig, 1864. 2 v. in 1. 16°. . 2408
Fulton, R., Life of. Colden. N. Y., 1817. 8°. 16423
The same. Renwick. Bost., 1839. 16°. . . . 7259
Furness, W. H. The Veil partly Lifted. Bost., 1864. 8°. . . 9815
Fuseli, H. Lectures on Painting. (2 copies.) Lond., 1848. 8°. . 8881
Life and Writings of. Knowles. Lond., 1831. 3 v. 8°. . 9051
Fuss, J. D. Roman Antiquities. Oxf'd., 1840. 8°. 4751
Future Life, Doctrine of a. Hudson. Bost., 1858. 12°. . . . 9911
Hist. of. Alger. N. Y., 1869. 8°. . . . 10022
Physical Theory of. Taylor. N. Y., 1836. 12°. . . 9540
Punishment, Lectures on. Tyler. Middletown, 1829. 12°. . 17299

G.

Gaël, The Scotish. Logan. Hartf'd., 1846. 8°. 5410
Gain of a Loss, The. N. Y., 1869. 12°. 2454
Gajani, G. The Roman Exile. Bost., 1856. 12°. 4691
Galatians, Notes on Epistle to. Barnes. N. Y., 1841. 12°. . . 9863
Galaxy, The. N. Y., 1868–69. v. 5–8. 8°. 13886
The same. N. Y., 1868–72. v. 6–10, 12–14. . . . 13890

Galileo, G., Life of. [Bethune.] Lond., 1833. 8°. 6751
The same. Brewster. N. Y., 1841. 12°. 11605
Private Life of. Lond., 1870. 8°. 7778
Gall, F. J. Works. Bost., 1835. 6 v. 12°. 12761
Gallatin, A. Sketch of Finances of U. S. N. Y., 1796. 8°. . . 6240
Gallus; Roman Scenes in Time of Augustus. Becker. N. Y., 1866. 8°. 4325
Galt, J. Annals of the Parish. Philad., 1821. 12°. 2365
Autobiography. Philad., 1833. 2 v. 12°. 6979
The same. Philad., 1833. 8°. 15358
Flowers of Literature. Lond., 1803. 12°. 15834
Last of the Lairds. N. Y., 1827. 12°. 15235
Lawrie Todd. N. Y., 1830. 2 v. 12°. 15237
Life of Byron. N. Y., 1841. 12°. 11009
The same. N. Y., 1830. 12°. 11936
of West. Lond., 1820. 8°. 7966
of Wolsey. 3d ed. (2 copies.) Lond., 1846. 8°. . . 340
Lives of the Players. Bost., 1831. v. 1. 12°. 16402
The Provost. N. Y., 1822. 12°. 15232
Sir Andrew Wylie. N. Y., 1822. 2 v. 12°. 15233
Stanley Buxton. Philad., 1833. 2 v. 12°. 15228
The Steam-Boat. N. Y., 1823. 12°. 15230
The Stolen Child. Philad., 1833. 12°. 15231
Galton, F. Hereditary Genius. N. Y., 1870. 8°. 8992
Vacation Tourists, 1860–61. Cambr., 1861–62. 2 v. 8°. . . 8378
Gambling, Exposure of Arts of. Green. Philad., 1847. 12°. . . 10171
unmasked. Green. Philad., 1847. 12°. 10172
Game of Life, The. Ritchie. Philad., 1833. 8°. 15356
Games, Amusements, etc. H. Smith. N. Y., 1868. 12°. . . . 11027
Hand-book of. Lond. (Bohn), 1850. 8°. 10176
See, also, CHESS ; SPORTS.
Gaming, Victims of. Bost., 1838. 12°. 10170
Gammell, W. Life of S. Ward. Bost., 1846. 16°. 7268
of R. Williams. Bost., 1845. 16°. . . . 7263
Gammer Gurton's Needle. (Old Plays, v. 2.) Lond., 1825. 8°. . 1509
Gardening, Landscape. Downing. N. Y., 1844. 8°. 9084
for Ladies. Loudon. N. Y., 1843. 12°. 16979
Gardiner, J., Life of. Doddridge. (Works, v. 1.) Lond., 1804. 8°. 17201
Gardiner, M. *(Lady Blessington.)* Desultory Thoughts. N. Y., 1839. 16°. 4159
The Governess. Philad., 1839. 2 v. 12°. 15453
The Idler in France. Philad., 1841. 2 v. 12°. 16707
in Italy. Paris, 1839. 8°. 8336
Works. Philad., 1838. 2 v. 8°. 2668
Life and Correspondence of. Madden. N. Y., 1856. 2 v. 12°. 7076
Gardiner, W. Music and Friends. Lond., 1838. 2 v. 8°. . . 9082
Gardner, A. K. Old Wine in New Bottles. N. Y., 1848. 12°. . . 16705
Garibaldi, G., Life of. By himself. Ed. by Dwight. N. Y., 1861. 12°. 7785
The Rule of the Monk. N. Y., 1870. 8°. 2651
Campaign of, in the Sicilies. Forbes. Edinb., 1861. 8°. . . 4690

Garland, H. A. Life of Randolph. N. Y., 1851. 2 v. 12°. . . . 7309
Garrett, Edward. *(Pseudonym.)* See I. F. MAYO.
Garrick, D. Dramatic Works. Lond., 1798. 3 v. 12°. 1396
Farces. (Brit. Drama, v. 5.) Lond., 1804. 8°. 1633
Life of. Murphy. Lond., 1801. 2 v. 8°. 7967
Memoirs of. Davies. Bost., 1818. 2 v. 12°. 7891
Garstangs, The. T. A. Trollope. Leipz., 1870. 2 v. 16°. . . 2375
Garter, Memorials of Order of the. Beltz. Lond., 1841. 8°. . . 5114
Garth, S. Poetical Works. Ed. Bell. Lond., 1807. 24°. . . . 276
The same, ed. Johnson. Dubl., 1804. 8°. . . . 15098
Select Poems. With Life, by Sanford. Philad., 1819. 24°. . 10
Gascoigne, G. The Steele Glas; etc. Ed. Arber. Lond., 1868. 16°. 3889
Select Poems, with Life. Ed. Sanford. Philad., 1819. 24°. . 1
Gaskell, E. C. A Dark Night's Work. N. Y., 1863. 8°. . . . 2311
Life of C. Brontë. N. Y., 1857. 2 v. 12°. 6985
Wives and Daughters. N. Y., 1866. 8°. 2663
Gasparin, A. de. America before Europe. (2 copies.) N. Y., 1862. 12°. 8560
Uprising of a Great People. (2 copies.) N. Y., 1861. 12°. . 8558
Gaston de Blondeville. Radcliffe. Philad., 1826. 2 v. 12°. . . 15436
Gates, T. R. Life and Writings. Philad., 1818. 12°. . . . 13681
Gates Ajar, The. Phelps. Bost., 1869. 12°. 2972
[**Gauden, J.**] Eikon Basilike. Lond., 1824. 12°. 4906
Gaussen, S. R. L. Canon of the Scriptures. Bost. [1862.] 12°. . 9885
Theopneusty; Inspiration of the Scriptures. N. Y., 1842. 12°. 9981
The same. N. Y., 1845. 12°. 9800
Gaviota, La. Caballero. N. Y., 1864. 12°. 2601
Gay, J. Beggar's Opera. (Brit. Drama, v. 5.) Lond., 1804. 8°. . 1633
The same. (Oxberry's Plays, v. 12.) Bost., 1822. 24°. . 1356
Poems. Glasg., 1751. 2 v. 16°. 675
Poetical Works. Ed. Bell. Lond., 1807. 2 v. 24°. . . 528
The same. Ed. Johnson. Dubl., 1804. 8°. . . . 15101
The same. With Life, by Sanford. Philad., 1819. 24°. . 12
Gay Science, The. Dallas. Lond., 1866. 2 v. 8°. 9055
Gayarré, C. A. Louisiana. N. Y., 1851. 8°. 5992
Philip II. of Spain. N. Y., 1866. 8°. 6584
Gayworthys, The. Whitney. Bost. [1865.] 12°. 2967
Gazetteers. See GEOGRAPHY.
Gebel Teir. [Tudor.] Bost., 1829. 12°. 15700
Geijer, E. G. Hist. of the Swedes. (2 copies.) Lond., 1845. 8°. . 5924
Genesis, Notes on. See BIBLE.
Geneva and France, Letters from, 1803–06. Bost., 1819. 2 v. 8°. . 16688
Genius, Hereditary. Galton. N. Y., 1870. 8°. 8992
Illustrations of. Giles. Bost., 1854. 8°. 3551
Infirmities of. Madden. Philad., 1833. 2 v. 12°. . . 3181
Genlis, S. F. de, Memoirs of. By herself. N. Y., 1825. 2 v. 8°. . 7652
New Moral Tales. N. Y., 1825. 12°. 2589
Gentleman, The. Calvert. Bost., 1863. 8°, ... 9175
Character of. Lieber. Philad., 1864. 12°. 9129
of the Old School. A Tale. James. N. Y., 1839. 2 v. 12°. . 15215

Gentleman's Magazine, Curious Articles from the. Lond., 1814. 4 v. 8°. 14227
Gentz, F. Europe before and after the French Revolution. Lond., 1804. 8°. 15919
Geoffrey of Monmouth. British History. Ed. Giles. Lond., 1848. 8°. 499
Geoffrey de Vinsauf. Chronicle. Lond., 1848. 8°. 512
Geoffrey the Knight. A Tale. Lond., 1869. 8°. 1913
Geographical Dictionary. McCulloch. N. Y., 1847–48. 2 v. 8°. . 8143
Discovery, Hist. of. Cooley. Lond., 1830–31. 3 v. 16°. . 5786
Studies. Ritter. Bost., 1863. 12°. 8970
Geography, Encyclopædia of. Murray. Philad., 1849. 3 v. 8°. . 8145
Physical. Somerville. Philad., 1848. 12°. 8969
as modified by Human Action. Marsh. N. Y., 1867. 8°. 8966
of the Sea. Maury. N. Y., 1857. 8°. 9103
See, also, ATLAS; EARTH; TRAVELS; VOYAGES.
Geological Sketches. Agassiz. Bost., 1870. 12°. 8956
Geology, Elementary. Hitchcock. N. Y., 1856. 12°. 8981
Elements of. Lee. N. Y., 1846. 12°. 11778
Foot-Prints of the Creator in. Miller. Bost., 1850. 12°. . 8974
Introduction to. Bakewell. N. H., 1839. 8°. 9008
Man in Genesis and in. Thompson. N. Y., 1870. 12°. . 8959
Manual of. Dana. Philad., 1863. 8°. 9011
and Natural Religion. Hitchcock. Edinb., 1835. 16°. . . 9137
and Natural Theology. Buckland. Philad., 1837. 2 v. 8°. . 16987
Popular. H. Miller. Bost., 1865. 12°. 8978
Principles of. Lyell. Philad., 1837. 2 v. 8°. 9009
The old Red Sandstone in. Miller. Bost., 1851. 12°. . . 8972
Religion of. Hitchcock. Bost., 1851. 12°. 8840
and Revelation. Molloy. N. Y., 1870. 12°. 8982
Treatise on. Phillips. Lond., 1837–39. 2 v. 16°. . . . 6051
of the Bass Rock. Miller. N. Y., 1851. 12°. 8829
of Brazil. Hartt. Bost., 1870. 8°. 9013
of Conn., Report on. Percival. N. H., 1842. 8°. . . . 9102
George I, II, III, and **IV,** of Grt. Brit., Caricature Hist. of. Wright. Lond. 8°. 4281
Lectures on. Thackeray. Lond., 1872. 8°. 2198
Memoirs of Era of. Lond., 1832–34. 4 v. 8°. . . . 6721
George I, II, and **III,** of England, Memoirs of. Belsham. Dubl., 1796. 3 v. 8°. 5282
George II, Hist. Sketches of Reign of. Oliphant. Bost. 8°. . . 5393
Memoirs of Reign of [1727–42]. Hervey. Philad., 1848. 2 v. 12°. 5215
George III, Annals of Reign of. 1760–1815. Aikin. Lond., 1816. 2 v. 8°. 5322
Memoirs of Reign of [1760–71]. Walpole. Philad., 1845. 2 v. 8°. 5320
[1772–89.] Wraxall. Philad., 1836–37. 2 v. 8°. . 5324
George IV, Diary of Times of (1810–30). [Bury.] Philad., 1838–39. 4 v. 12°. 5217
Life and Times of. Croly. N. Y., 1840. 12°. 11015
George a Greene, the Pinner of Wakefield. (Old Plays.) Lond., 1825. 8°. 1510

Georgia, Journal on Plantation in, 1838–39. Kemble. N. Y., 1863. 12°. 8408
Scenes. [Longstreet.] N. Y., 1843. 12°. 15701
Gérando, J. M. de. Self-Education. Bost., 1830. 8°. . . . 17052
[**Gerbier d'Ouvilly, G.**] The False Favourite disgraced. Lond., 1657. 12°. 13354
Germaine. E. About. Bost., 1860. 12°. 2597
German Dictionary. Kunst. Harrisburg, 1847. 12°. . . . 9619
Experiences. Howitt. Lond., 1844. 16°. 8220
Life in XVth, XVIth, and XVIIth Centuries, Pictures of. Freytag. Lond., 1862. 2 v. 8°. 5806
and Manners. Mayhew. Lond., 1864. 2 v. 8°. . . 8313
Literature. Menzel. Transl. by Gordon. Oxf'd., 1840. 4 v. 16°. 115
Selections from. Edwards and Park. Andover, 1839. 8°. 10061
Studies in. Bancroft. (Miscellanies.) N. Y., 1855. 8°. 3473
Modern. Heine. Bost., 1836. 16°. . . . 43
Novelists, transl. by Roscoe. Lond., 1826. 4 v. 12°. . . 1895
For Contents, see ROSCOE.
Poetry, Transl. by Baskerville. Philad., 1856. 8°. . . . 857
Historic Survey of. W. Taylor. Lond., 1830. 3 v. 8°. 206
Popular Tales. Grimm. Bost., 1862. 2 v. 12°. . . . 1917
Prose Writers. [Translated] by Hedge. N. Y., 1856. 8°. . 243
Fragments from. Austin. Lond., 1841. 12°. . . 3950
Romance, Specimens of. Carlyle. Bost., 1841. 2 v. 12°. . 3107
Theatre, The. Transl. by Thompson. Lond., 1811. v. 2–6. 12°. 1357
For Contents, see THEATRE.
Universities, View of. Robinson. Edinb., 1835. 16°. . . 9137
Theology, and Religion. Schaff. Philad., 1857. 12°. 9252
University Education. Perry. Lond., 1845. 12°. . . . 9251
Germanic Empire, Hist. of the [to 1792]. Dunham. Lond., 1834–35. 3 v. 16°. 5462
Empire, Hist. of Polit. Constitution of. Pütter. Lond., 1790. 3 v. 8°. 16457
Germany. Hawkins. Lond., 1838. 8°. 5883
Mme. de Staël. Lond., 1814. 3 v. 8°. 8307
in 1831. Strang. N. Y., 1836. 12°. 16653
American Family in. Browne. N. Y., 1866. 8°. . . . 8315
Hist. of (to 1814). Kohlrausch. N. Y., 1845. 8°. . . . 5874
(to 1842). Menzel. Lond., 1848–49. 3 v. 8°. . . 404
of Thirty Years' War in (1618–48). Schiller. Lond., 1846. 8°. 435
Notes during Ramble in, 1825. [Sherer.] Bost., 1827. 12°. . 8191
Religious Life in, during the Wars of Independence. Baur. Lond., 1870. 2 v. 8°. 6323
and the Revolution [1813–19]. v. Görres. Lond., 1820. 8°. . 5876
Rural and Domestic Life of. Howitt. Philad., 1843. 8°. . 8050
Student-Life of. Howitt. Philad., 1842. 8°. 8310
Tour in, 1820–22. J. Russell. Edinb., 1828. 2 v. 12°. . . 16649
Travels through, 1780. v. Riesbeck. Dubl., 1787. 2 v. 8°. . 16651

Gerry, E., Life of. Austin. Bost., 1828–29. 2 v. 8°. 7365
Gervinus, G. G. Shakespeare Commentaries. Lond., 1863. 2 v. 8°. 1580
Gessner, S. Death of Abel; Idylls; First Navigator. Lond., 1825. 24°. 2346
Works. Liverpool, 1802. 3 v. in 1. 16°. . . . 13207
Gesta Romanorum, Select Tales from the. N. Y., 1845. 12°. . . 1908
The same. 3956
Ghosts and Ghost-Seers. Crowe. N. Y., 1850. 12°. . . . 8615
See, also, APPARITIONS; DEMONOLOGY; MAGIC.
Giafar al Barmeki. N. Y., 1836. 2 v. 12°. 15702
Gibbon, E. Essay on Study of Literature. Dubl., 1788. 12°. . . 89
Hist. of Decline and Fall of the Roman Empire. Dubl., 1781–88. 12 v. 8°. 16006
The same. Dubl., 1789. 6 v. 8°. 4769
The same. N. Y., 1826. 6 v. 8°. 4784
The same. N. Y., 1835. 4 v. 8°. 4790
The same. Ed. Milman. N. Y., 1841. 4 v. 8°. . . 4794
The same. (2 copies.) Bost. and N. Y., 1850–64. 6 v. 12°. 4754
The same. Abridged by W. Smith. (2 copies.) N. Y., 1857–60. 12°. 4766
Memoirs of. By himself. Lond., 1827–30. 2 v. 12°. . . 6652
The same. Lond., 1829–30. 2 v. 12°. 6947
Miscellaneous Works. Dublin, 1796. 3 v. 8°. . . . 3785
The same. (2 copies.) Lond., 1837. 8°. . . . 3770
Life and Correspondence of. Milman. Lond., 1839. 8°. . 7123
Gibbs, G. Memoirs of Administrations of Washington and Adams. From O. Wolcott's Papers. N. Y., 1846. 2 v. 8°. . 6248
Gibraltar, Hist. of. Martin. Lond., 1837. 16°. 7902
Gibson, Walter M. The Prison of Weltevreden; and E. Indian Archipelago. N. Y., 1855. 12°. 16296
Gibson, Wm. Hist. of Europe, 1713–1718. Lond., 1725. 8°. . . 15914
Gibson, Wm. (M. D.) Rambles in Europe. Philad., 1841. 12°. . 16573
Giddings, J. R. Exiles of Florida. Columbus, 1858. 12°. . . 16891
Giffard, E. Visit to the Ionian Islands, etc. Lond., 1837. 12°. . 16647
Gifford, W. The Baviad and Mæviad. N. Y., 1800. 12°. . . 14823
Memoir of. By himself. Lond., 1831. 12°. 6649
Gil Blas. Le Sage. Lond. 8°. 1997
Gilbart, J. W. Hist. of Banking in America. Lond., 1837. 8°. . 8649
Gilbert, W. De Profundis. 2d ed. Lond., 1866. 8°. . . . 15413
Doctor Austin's Guests. Lond., 1867. 8°. 15414
Struggle in Ferrara. Philad., 1871. 8°. 2692
Gildas. Works. Ed. Giles. Lond., 1848. 8°. 499
Giles, H. Christian Thought on Life. 2d ed. Bost., 1851. 8°. . 3547
Human Life in Shakespeare. (2 copies,) Bost., 1868. 16°. . 1480
Illustrations of Genius. Bost., 1854. 8°. 3551
Lectures and Essays. Bost., 1851. 2 v. 8°. 3548
The same. vol. I. 3550
Giles, W. B. Political Miscellanies. 1829. 8°. 16128
Gilfillan, G. Bards of the Bible. N. Y., 1851. 12°. 9886
Life of Scott. Edinb., 1870. 16°. 6975

Gillett, E. H. Life of Huss. Bost., 1863. 2 v. 8°. 6509
Gillies, J. Hist. Collections of the Success of the Gospel. Ed. Bonar. Lond., 1845. 8°. 6595
Hist. of Ancient Greece. Dubl., 1786. 3 v. 8°. 15949
of the World. Philad., 1809. 3 v. 8°. 15892
Memoirs of Whitefield. Lond., 1772. 8°. 16363
Memoirs and Writings of Whitefield. Middletown, 1838. 8°. 10048
View of Reign of Frederick II. Dubl., 1789. 8°. 16452
Gillman, J. Life of Coleridge. Lond., 1838. 2 v. 8°. 7182
Gilly, W. S. Excursion to Piemont, and Researches among the Vaudois. Lond., 1824. 4°. 16035
Memoir of Neff. Philad., 1832. 12°. 7572
The same. Bost., 1832. 12°. 7520
Valdenses, Valdo, and Vigilantius. Edinb., 1841. 12°. . . 6342
Gilman, C. H. Love's Progress. N. Y., 1840. 12°. 15738
Poetry of Travelling in U. S. · N. Y., 1838. 12°. 16835
Recollections of a Housekeeper. N. Y., 1836. 12°. . . 15766
of a Southern Matron. N. Y., 1838. 12°. . . 15767
Tales and Ballads. Bost., 1839. 12°. 15794
[**Gilmore, J. R.**] Among the Pines. (2 copies.) N. Y., 1862. 12°. 2929
My Southern Friends. (3 copies.) N. Y., 1863. 12°. . . 2931
Gilpin, J. Lives of Wiclif, Cobham, Huss, etc. N. Y., 1814. 12°. . 16376
Ginx's Baby. [Jenkins.] N. Y., 1871. 12°. 8541
Giovanni Sbogarro. N. Y., 1820. 2 v. in 1. 12°. 15139
Gipsy. See GYPSY.
Giraldi-Cintio, G. B. Novels. (Ital. Novelists, v. 2.) Lond., 1836. 12°. 1900
Girard, S., Biogr. of. Simpson. Philad., 1832. 12°. 16428
Girdlestone, A. G. The High Alps without Guides. Lond., 1870. 8°. 8383
Girondists, Hist. of the. Lamartine. N. Y., 1868. 3 v. 12°. . . 5560
Gisborne, T. Enquiry into the Duties of Men. Lond., 1797. 2 v. 8°. 17083
Glaciers of the Alps. Tyndall. Bost., 1861. 8°. 8957
Gladstone, T. H. Englishman in Kansas. N. Y., 1857. 12°. . . 16855
Gladstone, W. E. "Ecce Homo." (2 copies.) Lond., 1868. 8°. . 9843
Juventus Mundi. Lond., 1869. 8°. 4235
State and Church. 4th ed. Lond., 1841. 2 v. 8°. . . . 8693
Glaisher, J. Travels in the Air. Lond., 1871. 8°. 9093
Glass and Porcelain, Manufacture of. Porter. Lond., 1832. 16°. . 6040
Glass-making, Wonders of. Sauzay. N. Y., 1870. 12°. . . . 10126
Glaucus; or, Wonders of the Shore. Kingsley. Bost., 1855. 16°. . 8836
Gleig, G. R. The Brit. Army at Washington and N. Orleans. 4th ed. Lond., 1836. 12°. 6003
Chelsea Hospital, and its Traditions. Lond., 1838. 3 v. 12°. 16067
Essays. Lond., 1858. 2 v. 8°. 3428
Hist. of the Bible. N. Y., 1841. 2 v. 12°. 11012
Lives of Brit. Military Commanders. Lond., 1831–32. 3 v. 16°. 5771

CONTENTS.—1, Manny; De Vere; Cromwell. 1, 2, Duke of Marlborough. 2, Earl of Peterborough; Wolfe. 3, Clive; Cornwallis; Abercromby; Moore.

Memoirs of Hastings. Lond., 1841. 3 v. 8°. 6805
The Subaltern. N. Y., 1825. 12°. 2085
The Subaltern in America. Philad., 1833. 12°. 6004

Glenarvon. [Lady C. Lamb.] Philad., 1816. 2 v. 12°. 15441
Gliddon, J. R. See J. C. Nott.
Glide, Wreck of the. Oliver. N. Y., 1848. 12°. 16298
Glover, R. The Athenaid. Lond., 1787. 3 v. 12°. 14867
Boadicea. (Brit. Drama.) Lond., 1804. 8°. 1630
Select Poems. Ed. Walsh. Philad., 1822. 24°. 27
Gneisenau, A. N. v., and **Marston, J. E.** Life of Blücher. Lond., 1815. 8°. 7759
Gobat, S. Journal in Abyssinia. N. Y., 1850. 12°. 8251
God in Christ. Bushnell. Hartf'd., 1849. 12°. 9935
Goddard, J. Search for the *Gral.* Lond. 16°. 2422
Goddard, T. H. Hist. of Banks. N. Y., 1831. 8°. 8650
Godolphin, Gregory. *(Pseudonym.)* The Unique. Bost., 1844. 12°. 17285
Godolphin, M., Life of. Evelyn. N. Y., 1847. 12°. 7050
Godolphin, a Novel. Bulwer. N. Y., 1840. 2 v. 12°. 2153
Godwin, M. W., Memoirs of. [W. Godwin.] Philad., 1804. 12°. 6938
Godwin, P. Hand-Book of Universal Biography. N. Y., 1852. 12°. 6716
Political Essays. (2 copies.) N. Y., 1856. 12°. 3560
Godwin, W. Cloudesley. N. Y., 1830. 2 v. 12°. 15398
Fleetwood. N. Y., 1805. 2 v. 12°. 2015
Hist. of the Commonwealth. Lond., 1824–27. v. 1–3. 8°. 5360
Lives of Necromancers. (2 copies.) N. Y., 1835. 12°. 6707
Mandeville. Philad., 1818. 2 v. 12°. 15501
St. Leon. Alexandria, 1801. 2 v. 12°. 1707
Transfusion. N. Y., 1836. 12°. 15112
[**Godwine, A.**] The Refugee. N. Y., 1825. 2 v. 12°. 15769
Goede, C. A. G. A Foreigner's Opinion of England. Bost., 1822. 8°. 16749
Görres, J. J. v. Germany and the Revolution. Lond., 1820. 8°. 5876
Goethe, J. W. v. Autobiography; Letters from Switzl'd. and Italy. (2 copies.) Lond., 1848–49. 2 v. 8°. 444
Correspondence with a Child. Lowell, 1841. 2 v. 12°. 7805
with Schiller. N. Y., 1845. v. 1. 12°. 7827
Elective Affinities. N. Y., 1872. 12°. 2704
Essays on Art. Tr. by Ward. N. Y., 1862. 16°. 8846
Faust, transl. by Brooks. 7th ed. Bost., 1868. 16°. 10304
The same, transl. by Hayward. Bost., 1872. 16°. 10305
The same, transl. by B. Taylor. Bost., 1871. 2 v. 8°. 1298
The same, pt. 2. Transl. by Bernays. Lond., 1839. 8°. 1300
Faustus; Bride of Corinth; First Walpurgis Night. Transl. by Anster. Lond., 1835. 16°. 1435
Goetz of Berlichingen, transl. by Scott. N. Y., 1814. 24°. 1362
Hermann and Dorothea, transl. by Frothingham. Bost., 1870. 16°. 862
Memoirs of. By himself. Lond., 1824. 2 v. 8°. 7823
The same. (2 copies.) N. Y., 1824. 8°. 7825
Novels and Tales. Lond. (Bohn's ed.), 1871. 8°. 448
Poems and Ballads, transl. by Aytoun & Martin. N. Y., 1871. 12°. 863
Reynard the Fox, tr. by Arnold. Lond., 1860. 8°. 1301

Goethe, J. W. v. Sämmtliche Werke. Stuttg. und Tüb., 1840. 40 Bde. in 20. 16°. 9441
The same. Bde. 1-4, 6-40. 9760
Select Minor Poems, transl. by Dwight. (2 copies.) Bost., 1839. 12°. 859
Sorrows of Werter. Ithaca. 12°. 2700
Stella. (German Theatre, v. 6.) Lond., 1811. 12°. . . . 1361
Theory of Colours. Tr. by Eastlake. Lond., 1840. 8°. . . 9072
Wilhelm Meister's Apprenticeship. Transl. by Carlyle. Bost., 1828. 3 v. 12°. 2701
The same. Philad., 1840. 3 v. 12°. 3047
The same. Bost., 1865. 2 v. 8°. 3050
The same. Lond., 1871. 2 v. 8°. 4051
Characteristics of. Ed. Mrs. Austin. Lond., 1833. 3 v. 12°. 7829
Conversations with. Eckermann. Bost., 1839. 12°. . . 7828
Essay on Life and Works of. Calvert. Bost., 1872. 16°. . 7837
Female Characters of, from Kaulbach's Drawings. N. Y. fol.
and his Influence. Hutton. (Essays, v. 2.) Lond., 1871. 8°. 3709
and Schiller. A Romance. [Mundt.] N. Y., 1868. 8°. . 3086
Goethe's Courtship, Dr. A Tale. Müller. Lond., 1866. 16°. . . 3046
Goguet, A. Y. Origin of Laws, Arts, etc. Edinb., 1775. 3 v. 8°. . 15895
Gold Elsie. John. Philad., 1868. 12°. 3038
and Name. Schwartz. Bost., 1871. 8°. 3096
Golden Christmas, The. Simms. Charleston, 1852. 12°. . . . 15704
Dagon. [Palmer.] N. Y., 1856. 12°. 7910
Lion of Granpere. A. Trollope. N. Y., 1872. 8°. . . . 2296
Goldoni, C., Memoirs of. By himself. Lond., 1828. 2 v. 12°. . . 6661
Goldschmidt, —. The Flying Mail. Bost., 1870. 16°. . . . 2619
Goldsmith, J. Geogr. View of the World. Ed. Percival. N. Y., 1826. 12°. 16265
Manners, etc., of Nations. N. H., 1822. 2 v. 12°. . . . 16266
Goldsmith, O. Essays; and The Bee. Bost., 1820. 16°. . . . 3841
Goodnatured Man; She Stoops to Conquer. (Brit. Theatre, v. 16.) Lond. 12°. 1340
Grecian Hist., ed. Grimshaw. Philad., 1833. 12°. . . . 15870
Hist. of the Earth, and Animated Nature. (2 copies.) Philad., 1823–25. 5 v. 8°. 16925
Miscellaneous Works. Balt., 1809. 5 v. 12°. 4195

CONTENTS.—1, Life; Vicar of Wakefield. 2, Citizen of the World. 3, The same, concluded; The Bee. 4, Present State of Polite Learning; Essays; Life of T. Parnell; Life of Lord Bolingbroke. 5, Prefaces; Poems; Plays.

The same. Ed. Irving. (2 copies.) Philad., 1830–34. 8°. 3782
The same. Ed. Prior. Lond., 1837. 4 v. 8°. . . 3778

CONTENTS.—1, The Bee; Essays; Present State of Polite Learning in Europe; Prefaces and Introductions. 2, Letters of a Citizen of the World; Natural History. 3, Vicar of Wakefield; Biographies; Miscellaneous Criticism. 4, Poems; Dramas; Criticism of Poetry and Belles-Lettres.

The same. N. Y., 1850. 4 v. 12°. 4001
Poetical Works. Ed. Bell. Lond., 1807. 24°. 543
The same, with Life by Macaulay. Bost., 1862. 16°. . 1054
Roman Hist., abridged. Hartf'd. 12°. 15948

Goldsmith, O. Select Poems. Ed. Walsh. Philad., 1822. 24°. . 24
Select Works, in French and Eng. (2 copies.) N. Y., 1815. 12°. 13200
She Stoops to Conquer. (Brit. Drama.) Lond., 1804. 8°. . 1632
The same. Philad., 1833. 8°. 1662
The same. (Oxberry's Plays, v. 1.) Bost., 1822. 24°. . 1346
Vicar of Wakefield. N. Y., 1845. 12°. 3899
The same. Lond., 1838. 16°. 2384
Works. Lond., 1867. 16°. 3921
Works. Edinb., 1836. v. 3, 4. 12°. 13198

CONTENTS.—3, Citizen of the World. 4, State of Polite Learning; The Bee; Lives of Parnell and Bolingbroke, etc.

Biogr. of. Irving. N. Y., 1860. 12°. 6995
Life of. Prior. Lond., 1837. 2 v. 8°. 3776
Life and Times of. Forster. Lond., 1855. 8°. 6997
Gondi, J. F. P. de (Cardinal de Retz), Life of. James. Philad., 1837. 12°. 7613
Memoirs of. By himself. Philad., 1817. 3 v. 8°. . . . 7713
See, also, JOLY's Memoirs.
Good, J. Poems. Sherborne. 8°. 14806
Good Words. Lond., 1866–67. v. 7, 8. 8°. 14534
Goodman, G. Court of James I, ed. Brewer. Lond., 1839. 2 v. 8°. 5298
Goodrich, Chas. A. Family Encyclopædia. Hartf'd, 1849. 12°. .
Tourist, in Amer. Cities. Hartt'd., 1848. 8°. 16897
Great Events in Hist. of America. Hartf'd., 1851. 8°. . . 16146
Hist. of the U. S. Hartf'd., 1824. 12°. 16047
Lives of the Signers. Hartf'd. [1848.] 12°. 16403
Pictorial View of Religions. Hartf'd., 1851. 12°. . . . 6298
Universal Traveller. Hartf'd., 1850. 12°. 16259
Goodrich, Chauncey A. Select British Eloquence. (2 copies.) N. Y., 1861. 8°. 9425
Goodrich, S. G. Cabinet of Curiosities. Hartf'd., 1822. 2 v. 12°. . 16939
History of All Nations. N. Y., 1857. 2 v. 8°. 4122
The Outcast, and other Poems. Bost., 1836. 12°. . . . 14995
Pictorial Hist. of England. Philad., 1846. 12°. . . . 16064
Popular Biography. N. Y., 1854. 12°. 6604
Recollections of a Lifetime. (2 copies.) N. Y., 1856. 2 v. 12°. 7367
Sketches from a Student's Window. Bost., 1841. 12°. . . 15068
Goodwin, H. B. Dr. Howell's Family. Bost., 1869. 12°. . . . 2989
Madge. N. Y., 1863. 12°. 2988
Goodyear, C., Life of. Peirce. N. Y. [1866.] 16°. 7278
Googe, B. Eglogs, Sonettes, etc. Ed. Arber. Lond., 1871. 16°. . 3898
Gordian Knot, The. Brooks. N. Y., 1868. 8°. 2308
Gordon, C. *(Vieux Moustache.)* Two Lives in One. N. Y., 1870. 16°. 2922
Gordon, J. Hist. of Ireland. Lond., 1806. 2 v. 8°. 5412
Gordon, M. Memoir of J. Wilson. N. Y., 1863. 8°. . . . 7086
Gordon, T. F. Hist. of Penns., to 1776. Philad., 1829. 8°. . . 5840
Gore, C. G. F. Banker's Wife. N. Y., 1843. 8°. 2313
The Cabinet Minister. N. Y., 1839. 2 v. 12°. 15391
Diary of a Désennuyée. Philad., 1836. 12°. 15415
Polish Tales. Lond., 1833. 3 v. 12°. 15550

Gore, C. G. F. Preferment. N. Y., 1840. 2 v. 12°. 15553
Sketch-Book of Fashion. N. Y., 1833. 2 v. 12°. 15581
Soldier of Lyons. Philad. 8°. 2313
Gorton, S., Life of. Mackie. Bost., 1845. 16°. 7264
Goslington Shadow. N. Y., 1825. 2 v. 12°. 15705
Gospel Tragedy, The. [Brockway.] Worc., 1795. 12°. . . . 14976
Gospels. See BIBLE.
Gosson, S. School of Abuse, etc. Ed. Arber. Lond., 1868. 16°. . 3885
Gothic Architecture. See ARCHITECTURE.
Gotthelf, J. Wealth and Welfare. Lond., 1867. 8°. 2452
Gotthold's Emblems. Scriver. Bost. [1859.] 12°. 3106
Gottschalck, C. F. Popular Traditions. (German Novelists, v. 2.) Lond., 1826. 12°. . , ... 1896
Gough, J. B. Autobiography. (2 copies.) Springf'ld., 1869–70. 8°. 7434
Goulburn, E. M. The Idle Word. N. Y., 1866. 12°. . . . 9817
Thoughts on Personal Religion. N. Y., 1866. 12°. . . 9816
Gould, E. S. Good English. (2 copies.) N. Y., 1867. 12°. . . 107
Gould, H. F. Poems. Bost., 1839. 2 v. 12°. 14996
Gould, S. Baring. See BARING.
Gourbillon, J. A. de. Travels in Sicily. Lond., 1820. 8°. . . 8054
Gourgaud, G. Memoirs of Hist. of France. See NAPOLÉON I.
Governess, The. Lady Blessington. Philad., 1839. 2 v. 12°. . 15453
Government, Discourses on. A. Sidney. N. Y., 1805. 3 v. 8°. . 17199
Disquisition on. Calhoun. Charleston, 1851. 8°. . . . 6171
Essay on origin and nature of. Temple. Lond., 1814. 8°. . 17197
Interference Theory of. Bristed. N. Y., 1868. 12°. . . 8540
Principles of. See BENTHAM.
Thoughts on. Helps. Bost., 1872. 8°. 8620
Two Treatises of. Locke. (Works, v. 5.) Lond., 1801. 8°. . 9594
Representative, Considerations on. J. S. Mill. N. Y., 1867. 12°. 8618
See, also, POLITICS.
Gower, J. Select Poems, with Life. Ed. Sanford. Philad., 1819. 24°. 1
Gozzi, C. Novels. (Ital. Novelists, v. 4.) Lond., 1836. 12°. . . 1902
Grace Truman. Ford. N. Y., 1857. 12°. 15707
Graham, James, *(Earl of Montrose,)* Life and Times of. Napier. Edinb., 1840. 8°. 6760
Graham, James. Life of Gen. Morgan. N. Y., 1859. 12°. . . 7306
Graham, S. Lecture to Young Men on Chastity. Bost., 1847. 12°. 17024
Graham, W. Travels through Portugal and Spain. Lond., 1820. 8°. 8053
Graham, W. S. Remains. Philad., 1849. 12°. 14998
Grahame, *Rev.* **James.** Birds of Scotland, with other Poems. Bost., 1807. 12°. 14824
The Sabbath: a Poem. N. Y., 1805. 12°. 14796
Grahame, James. Hist. of the U. S. (2 copies.) Lond., 1833. 2 v. 8°. 5940
Grainger, J. Select Poems. Ed. Walsh. Philad., 1822. 24°. . 21
Grammar of Assent. Newman. N. Y., 1870. 12°. 9599
English. Cobbett. N. Y., 1846. 12°. 90
The same. Fowler. N. Y., 1865. 8°. 167
The same. Ben Johnson. Lond., 1842. 8°. 1607

Grammar, English, Comic. Lond., 1840. 12°. 4275
Diversions of Purley in. Horne Tooke. Lond., 1829. 2 v. 8°. 210
Principles of. Philad., 1847. 12°. 8498
Shakespearian. Abbott. Lond., 1871. 16°. . . 1477
See, also, ENGLISH; LANGUAGE; PHILOLOGY.
Grammont, P. de, Memoirs of. Hamilton. Lond., 1846. 8°. . . 320
Granada, Chronicle of Conquest of. Irving. N. Y., 1868. 12°. . 6407
Granby. [Lister.] N. Y., 1826. 2 v. 12°. 15455
Granger, J. Letters and Miscellanies. Lond., 1805. 8°. . . . 16347
Grant, A. The Highlanders, and other Poems. Edinb., 1803. 8°. . 15075
Memoirs of an American Lady. N. Y., 1846. 12°. . . . 16398
The same. Bost., 1809. 12°. 16397
Memoir and Correspondence of. By her son. Lond., 1844. 3 v. 8°. 7078
Grant, J. Bench and Bar. Philad., 1839. 2 v. 12°. 6605
The Great Metropolis. N. Y., 1837. 2 v. 12°. 5144
Metropolitan Pulpit. N. Y., 1839. 12°. 9914
Paris and its People. Lond., 1844. 2 v. 12°. 16701
Random Recollections of House of Commons. Phil., 1836. 12°. 4845
of House of Lords. Philad., 1836. 12°. 4846
Sketches of London. Philad., 1839. 2 v. 12°. 5146
Grant, U. S., and his Campaigns. Coppée. N. Y., 1866. 8°. . . 7401
The same. Larke. N. Y., 1864. 12°. 7399
Life of. Deming. Hartf'd., 1868. 8°. 7400
Granucci, N. Novel. (Ital. Novelists, v. 3.) Lond., 1836. 12°. . 1901
Granville, G. (*Lord* Lansdowne.) Poetical Works. Ed. Bell. Lond., 1807. 24°. 269
Select Poems. With Life, by Sanford. Philad., 1819. 24°. . 13
The same. Ed. Johnson. Dubl., 1804. 8°. . . . 15099
Grattan, H. Speeches. Dubl., 1811. 8°. 9347
The same. N. Y., 1813. 8°. 9348
Memoirs of. By his Son. Lond., 1839–46. 5 v. 8°. . . 6784
Sketch of. Lecky. N. Y., 1872. 12°. 6743
Grattan, T. C. Agnes de Mansfeldt. Philad., 1836. 2 v. 12°. . 15362
Heiress of Bruges. N. Y., 1831. 2 v. 12°. 15446
Highways and Byways. Bost., 1840. 3 v. 12°. . . . 15450
Hist. of the Netherlands. (2 copies.) Lond., 1833–38. 16°. . 5474
The same. Philad., 1831. 12°. 6070
Jacqueline of Holland. N. Y., 1831. 2 v. 12°. . . . 15469
Traits of Travel. N. Y., 1829. 2 v. 12°. 15609
Gravenhurst. W. Smith. Edinb., 1862. 8°. 9964
Graves, *Mrs.* **A. J.** Woman in America. N. Y., 1844. 12°. . . 11767
The same. N. Y., 1843. 12°. 12281
Gray, A. Botanical Text-Book. 3d ed. N. Y., 1850. 12°. . . 8986
Manual of Botany of Northern U. S. Cambr., 1848. 12°. . 8984
The same. 5th ed. N. Y., 1869. 8°. 8985
Gray, Barry. *(Pseudonym.)* See R. B. COFFIN.
Gray, D. Poems, with Memoirs. (2 copies.) Bost., 1864. 16°. . 1197

Gray, *Mrs.* **H.** Hist. of Etruria. Lond., 1843. v. 1. 12°. . . . 4728
Tour to the Sepulchres of Etruria. 2d ed. Lond., 1841. 12°. 8870
Gray, T. Letters. Bost., 1820. 16°. 3842
Letters and Poems. Philad., 1842. 8°. 945
Poetical Works. Ed. Bell. Lond., 1807. 24°. . . . 538
The same [with Memoir by Mitford]. Lond., 1853. 16°. 1029
The same, ed Johnson. Dubl., 1804. 8°. . . . 15101
Select Poems. Ed. Walsh. Philad., 1822. 24°. . . . 23
Works [with Life by Mitford]. Lond, 1836. 4 v. 16°. . . 1030
Gray, W. Hist. Sketch of Engl. Prose Literature. Oxf'd., 1835. 8°. 180
Gray's Inn Journal. Murphy. Lond., 1756. 2 v. 12°. . . . 13031
Grazzini, A. F. Novels. (Ital. Novelists, v. 2.) Lond., 1836. 8°. . 1900
Great Britain in 1833. d'Haussez. Philad., 1833. 12°. . . . 5333
Appeal from Judgments of. Walsh. Philad., 1819. 8°. . . 5991
Continental Interests of. Heeren. Oxf'd., 1836. 8°. . . 4713
Four Years in, 1831–35. Colton. N. Y., 1835. 2 v. 12°. . 16755
Hist. of, to 1547. Henry. Lond., 1788–95. 12 v. 8°. . . 4973
[1660–1713]. Burnet. Edinb., 1753. 6 v. 12°. . 4817
Illustrations of. Thomson. Edinb., 1828. 2 v. 12°. . 4482
Journal of Tour and Residence in, 1810–11. N. Y., 1815. 2 v. 8°. 16751
of Travels in, 1805–06. Silliman. Bost., 1812. 2 v. 12°. 8261
Resources of. Bristed. N. Y., 1811. 8°. 16115
Sketches of Society in, 1832. Stewart. Philad., 1834. 2 v. 12°. 16753
Statistical Account of. McCulloch. Lond., 1837. 2 v. 8°. . 4989
See, also, BRITISH ; ENGLAND.
Great Expectations. Dickens. N. Y., 1871. 16°. 2171
Great Hoggarty Diamond. Thackeray. Lond., 1872. 8°. . . 2196
Greater Britain. Travel in English-speaking Countries. Dilke.
Philad., 1869. 12°. 8438
Grecian Wreath of Victory. N. Y., 1824. 12°. 4558
Greece, Antiquities of. Potter. N. Y., 1825. 8°. 15867
Art in. Taine. N. Y., 1871. 12°. 8850
Hist. of, to B. C. 404. Curtius. N. Y., 1871–72. 3 v. 12°. . 4396
to B. C. 337. Gillies. Dubl., 1786. 3 v. 8°. . . 15949
The same. Mitford. Lond., 1820. 10 v. 8°. . . 15954
to B. C. 300. Grote. N. Y., 1857. 12 v. 12°. . . 4384
to B. C. 147. [Malkin.] Lond., 1829. 8°. . . 16022
to B. C. 146. Robertson. Edinb., 1821. 8°. . . 16026
The same. Thirlwall. Lond., 1835–44. 8 v. 16°. . 4426
Literature of. Müller. v. 1. Lond., 1840. 8°. . . 197
Monuments and Scenery of. Chase. Cambr., 1863. 16°. . 8208
Political Antiquities of. Hermann. Oxf'd., 1836. 8°. . . 4431
Politics of. Heeren. Oxf'd., 1824. 8°. 4406
Politics and Literature of. Dalzel. Edinb., 1821. 2 v. 8°. . 15868
Slavery in. Edwards. Edinb., 1835. 16°. 9137
Travels of Anacharsis in. Barthélemy. Lond., 1798. 8°. . 15953
Ancient and Modern. Felton. Bost., 1867. 2 v. 8°. . . 4421
Modern, in 1823–4. Stanhope. Philad., 1825. 8°. . . . 16020
in 1827–28. Miller. N. Y., 1828. 12°. . . . 15952

Greece of the Greeks. Perdicaris. N. Y., 1845. 2 v. 12°. . . 16645
and the Greeks, Notes on, 1866–68. Strangford. Lond., 1869. 8°. 3710
Modern, Hist. of. Bost., 1827. 8°. 16021
Revolution in, 1820–27. Comstock. N. Y., 1828. 12°. 4559
The same. Howe. N. Y., 1828. 12°. 4560
Modern, Hist. of, Literary. Negris. Edinb., 1835. 16°. . . 9137
Incidents of Travel in, 1835. [Stephens.] N. Y., 1841. 2 v. 12°. 16637
Journal in, 1858. Senior. Lond., 1859. 8°. 8243
Journey through, 1821. Müller. Lond., 1822. 8°. . . . 8058
Letters on. Savary. Dubl., 1788. 8°. 16628
Letters from, 1826–27. Blaquiere. Lond., 1828. 8°. . . 16027
Popular Description of. Conder. Lond. 2 v. in 1. 12°. . 7851
Tour through, 1818–19. Laurent. Lond., 1822. 8. . . . 16641
Modern, Travels in. Baird. N. Y., 1856. 12°. . . . 8323
The same. Clarke. Lond., 1818. 3 v. 8°. . . . 8025
The same. 1805–16. Pouqueville. (Voyages, v. 4, 7.) Lond., 1820–22. 8°. 8054
The same. 1834. Temple. Lond., 1836. 2 v. 12°. . 16625
The same. 1858. Bayard Taylor. N. Y., 1859. 12°. . 8285
Visit to, 1827–28. Post. N. Y., 1830. 8°. 16627
Wanderings in, 1828–36. Cochrane. Lond., 1837. 2 v. 8°. . 8321

Greek Church. See CHURCH.
Etymology. Peile. Lond., 1872. 16°. 93
Mythology. Cox. Lond., 1870. 2 v. 8°. 4103
The same. Keightley. Lond., 1838. 8°. . . . 4425
Philosophy, Brief View of. [Cornwallis.] Philad., 1846. 12°. 8497
Poets, Introd. to. H. N. Coleridge. Philad., 1831. 12°. . . 41
Specimens of. Peter. Philad., 1847. 8°. . . . 239
Christian, Essays on. E. B. Browning. N. Y., 1863. 16°. 39

Greeks, Arts, Manners, etc., of the. Fosbrooke. Lond., 1833–35. 2 v. 16°. 4869
Dissertations on the. Pauw. Lond., 1793. 2 v. 8°. . . 15871
Private Life of the Ancient. Becker. Lond., 1845. 12°. . 4326

Greeley, H. The American Conflict. (2 copies.) Hartf'd., 1864–66. 2 v. 8°. 6257
Hints towards Reforms. N. Y., 1850. 12°. 8622
Recollections of a Busy Life. (2 copies.) N. Y., 1868. 8°. . 7438

Green, J. H. Exposure of Gambling. Philad., 1847. 12°. . . 10171
Gambling unmasked. Philad., 1847. 12°. 10172

Green, M. Poetical Works. Ed. Bell. Lond., 1807. 24°. . . 530
The same. With Life, by Sanford. Philad., 1819. 24°. 13

Green, T. J. Journal of Texan Exped. N. Y., 1845. 8°. . . . 16902

Green Book, The. O'Callaghan. Philad., 1842. 12°. . . . 5254

Greenbank, T. K. Periodical Library. Philad., 1833. 3 v. 8°. . 15356

[**Greene, A.**] Perils of Pearl Street. N. Y., 1834. 12°. . . . 15761
Travels in America. By G. Fibbleton. N. Y., 1833. 12°. . 16799

Greene, G. W. Hist. View of the Revolution. (2 copies.) Bost., 1865. 12°. 6099

Greene, G. W. Life of N. Greene. Bost., 1846. 16°. 7269
Greene, Gen. Nath'l., Life of. G. W. Greene. Bost., 1846. 16°. . 7269
The same. Simms. N. Y., 1859. 12°. 7303
Greene, Nath'l. Tales from the German. Bost., 1837. 2 v. 12°. . 3029
Greene, R. Dramatic Works. Ed. Dyce. Lond., 1831. 2 v. 8°. . 1466
Greenhow, R. Hist. of Oregon, California, etc. 2d ed. Bost., 1845. 8°. 5993
Greenland, Description of. Egede. Lond., 1818. 8°. . . . 16595
Hist. and Description of. [Russell.] N. Y., 1841. 12°. . . 11606
See, also, ARCTIC; POLE.
Greenough, H., Memorial of. Tuckerman. N. Y., 1853. 12°. . . 7938
Greenwell, D. Essays. Lond., 1866. 16°. 9547
Greenwood, Grace. *(Pseudonym.)* See S. J. LIPPINCOTT.
Greenwood, J. The Seven Curses of London. Bost., 1869. 12°. . 8617
Gregg, J. Commerce of the Prairies. N. Y., 1844. 2 v. 12°. . . 16878
Grégoire, H. Enquiry concerning Negroes. Brooklyn, 1810. 8°. . 17113
Gregory, G. Hist. of the Christian Church. Lond., 1790. 2 v. 12°. 14636
Letters on Literature, Taste, and Composition. Philad., 1809. 12°. 17028
Gregory, J., Life of. Smellie. Edinb., 1800. 8°. 7138
Gregory, O. Evidences, etc., of the Christian Religion. Lond., 1851. 8°. 486
Grenville, G. N. T. (*Lord* Nugent.) Lands, Classical and Sacred. Lond., 1846. 2 v. 12°. 8162
Memorials of Hampden. (2 copies.) 2d ed. Lond., 1832. 2 v. 8°. 6842
Gresham, Sir T., Life of. Lond., 1845. 12°. 6623
Gresley, W. Charles Lever. N. Y., 1843. 12°. 15395
Forest of Arden. N. Y., 1843. 12°. 15432
Siege of Lichfield. Lond., 1841. 12°. 15580
Grettir the Strong, Story of. Ed. Morris. Lond., 1869. 8°. . . 1921
[**Grey,** *Mrs.*] De Lisle. N. Y., 1828. 2 v. 12°. 15411
Trials of Life. N. Y., 1829. 2 v. 12°. 15616
Grey, Lady J., Life of. Strickland. Lond., 1868. 8°. . . . 5208
and her times. Howard. Lond., 1822. 8°. . . 5209
Romance of. Miller. Philad., 1840. 2 v. 12°. . . . 15483
Grey, T. Journal of Visit to Egypt, etc. N. Y., 1870. 12°. . . 8253
Greylock, Godfrey. *(Pseudonym.)* See J. E. A. SMITH.
Greyslaer. Hoffman. N. Y., 1840. 2 v. 12°. 15708
Griffin, E. D. Sermons. N. Y., 1839. 2 v. 8°. 17504
Memoir of. Sprague. N. Y., 1839. 8°. 7740
Griffin, G. The Rivals; Tracy's Ambition. N. Y., 1830. 2 v. 12°. 15561
Tales of My Neighborhood. Philad., 1836. 2 v. 12°. . . 15596
Griffith Gaunt. Reade. Bost., 1866. 8°. 2282
Grimald, N. Poems, ed. Arber. Lond., 1870. 16°. 3895
Grimaldi, J., Memoirs of. Ed. by "Boz." Lond., 1838. 2 v. 12°. . 7925
Grimké, F. Nature and Tendency of Free Institutions. Cincinn., 1848. 8°. 8697
Grimm, A. T. v. Alexandra, Empress of Russia. Edinb., 1870. 2 v. 8°. 6444
Grimm, H. Life of M. Angelo. (2 copies.) Bost., 1865–66. 2 v. 12°. 7957
Die Venus von Milo; Rafael und Michael Angelo. Bost. 12°. 9614

Grimm, F. M. de, and **Diderot, D.** Correspondence, 1753–69. Lond., 1814. 2 v. 8°. 7648
Grimm, J. L. C. and **W. C.** German Popular Tales. Bost., 1862. 2 v. 12°. 1917
Popular Traditions. (German Novelists, v. 2.) Lond., 1826. 12°. 1896
Grimshaw, W. Hist. of the U. S. Philad., 1830. 12°. 16049
Grimshawe, T. S. Memoir of L. Richmond, abridged. N. Y., 1829. 12°. 7563
Grindrod, R. B. Bacchus: an Essay on Intemperance. (2 copies.) N. Y., 1840. 12°. 16967
Gringo, Harry. *(Pseudonym.)* See H. A. Wise.
Griscom, John. A Year in Europe. N. Y., 1823. 2 v. 8°. . . 16538
Griscom, John H. Animal Mechanism and Physiology. N. Y., 1840. 12°. 11409
Griswold, R. W. Curiosities of American Literature. N. Y. 8°. . 3408
Female Poets of America. Philad., 1849. 8°. 924
Poets and Poetry of America. Philad., 1842. 8°. 923
The same. Philad., 1855. 8°. 238
Prose Writers of America. (2 copies.) Philad., 1847. 8°. . 236
Grosvenor, W. M. Does Protection protect? N. Y., 1871. 8°. . 8669
Grote, G. Hist. of Greece. N. Y., 1857. 12 v. 12°. 4384
The same. v. 1–8. Lond., 1846–50. 8°. 4409
The same. v. 1–4. 2d ed. Lond., 1849. 8°. . . . 4417
Plato and the Companions of Sokrates. 2d ed. Lond., 1867. 3 v. 8°. 4443
Grote, H. Collected Papers. Lond., 1862. 8°. 3438
Grotius, H. Truth of the Christian Religion. Lond., 1825. 12°. . 9810
Life of. Butler. Lond., 1826. 8°. 7685
Grout, L. Zulu-Land. Philad. [1864.] 12°. 7982
Grove, W. R., etc. Correlation and Conservation of Forces. (2 copies.) N. Y., 1865–69. 12°. 8895
Grund, F. J. The Americans. Bost., 1837. 12°. 6019
Guardian, The. Steele, etc. Philad., 1831. 8°. 3398
The same. Ed. Ferguson. Lond., 1823. 3 v. 12°. . 3121
Addison's Contributions to. See Addison.
Essays illustrative of. Drake. Lond., 1805. 3 v. 8°. . . 3233
Guardian Angel, The. Holmes. Bost., 1871. 12°. 2900
Guatemala in 1827–28. Dunn. N. Y., 1828. 8°. 16901
Journey to, 1838. Montgomery. N. Y., 1839. 8°. . . . 16900
See, also, Mexico.
Gubernatis, A. de. Zoological Mythology. Lond., 1872. 2 v. 8°. . 10341
Guérin, E. de. Journal. Lond., 1866. 16°. 7662
Letters. N. Y., 1868. 16°. 7663
Guérin, M. de. Journal. N. Y., 1867. 12°. 7664
Guest, E. Hist. of English Rhythms. (2 copies.) Lond., 1838. 2 v. 8°. 174
Guettée, R. F. The Papacy. N. Y., 1867. 12°. 9579
Guiana, Voyages to. Raleigh. (Hist., v. 6.) Edinb., 1820. 8°. . 4077
Guiccioli, *Countess.* Recollections of Byron. (2 copies.) N. Y., 1869. 12°. 7095
Guild, C. Over the Ocean. Bost., 1871. 12°. 8377

Guillemin, A. The Sun. N. Y., 1870. 12°. 10115
Wonders of the Moon. N. Y., 1873. 12°. 10150
Guizot, E. Young Student. (2 copies.) N. Y., 1844–45. 12°. . . 2353
Guizot, F. P. G. Corneille and his Times. N. Y., 1852. 12°. . . 7650
Embassy to Court of St. James in 1840. Lond., 1862. 8°. . 5259
Essay on Washington. Bost., 1840. 16° 7492
The same. N. Y., 1863. 16°. 7493
Hist. of Civilization in Europe. Oxf'd., 1837. 8°. . . . 4659
The same [with 2 courses of Lectures, on Hist. of Civ. in France]. N. Y., 1861. 4 v. 12°. 4660
The same. (Bogue's ed.) 2 copies. Lond., 1846. 3 v. 8°. 326
of O. Cromwell. Philad., 1854. 2 v. 12°. . . . 5226
of R. Cromwell and the Restoration. Lond., 1856. 2 v. 8°. 5023
of the English Revolution. Transl. by Coutier. (4 copies.) Oxf'd., 1838. 2 v. 8°. 5015
The same. Transl. by Hazlitt. Lond., 1846. 8°. . . 337
of Representative Gov't. Lond., 1852. 8°. . . . 362
Last Days of Reign of Louis Philippe. Lond., 1867. 8°. . 5583
Meditations on Christianity. N. Y., 1865. 12°. . . . 9982
Memoirs of Monk. Lond., 1838. 8°. 6822
of my own Time. Lond., 1858–61. 4 v. 8°. . . 5579
Gulistan, or Rose Garden. Sadi. Tr. Gladwin. Bost., 1865. 12°. . 876
Gulliver's Travels. Swift. Philad., 1869. 12°. 1970
Gurney, J. J. Hints on the Evidence of Christianity. Bost., 1833. 12°. 17292
Gurowski, A. G. de. America and Europe. N. Y., 1857. 12°. . 6101
Russia as it is. N. Y., 1854. 12°. . . . , . . . 6447
Gustavus Adolphus II, King of Sweden, Life of. Harte. Lond., 1807. 2 v. 8°. 5928
Guthrie, W. Hist. of Scotland. Lond., 1767–68. 10 v. 8°. . . 5394
Gutzlaff, C. Journal along Coast of China. N. Y., 1833. 12°. . 16478
Sketch of Chinese Hist., etc. N. Y., 1834. 2 v. 12°. . . 6475
Guy, W. A. Public Health. Lond., 1870. 8°. 9168
Guy Livingstone. [Lawrence.] N. Y., 1871. 12°. 2462
Guy Mannering. Scott. Edinb., 1871. 8°. 1860
Guy Rivers. Simms. N. Y., 1834. 2 v. 12°. 15710
Guyon, J. M. B. de la Mothe. Method of Prayer. Balt., 1812. 12°. 17294
Life of. Upham. N. Y., 1847. 2 v. 12°. 7674
Guyot, A. Earth and Man. 2d ed. Bost., 1850. 12°. . . . 8967
The same. 3d ed. Bost., 1851. 12°. 8968
Gymnastics, The New. Lewis. Bost., 1862. 12°. 9228
for Youth. Salzmann. Philad., 1803. 8°. 17058
Gypsies of the Danes' Dike; a Story. Phillips. Bost., 1864. 12°. . 2851
Hist. of the. Simson. N. Y., 1866. 12°. 17114
of Spain, The. Borrow. Lond., 1841. 2 v. 12°. . . . 17115
Gypsy, The; a Tale. G. P. R. James. N. Y., 1864. 2 v. in 1. 12°. 2163

H.

H—— Family, The. Bremer. Lond., 1852. 8°. 471
Habermeister, The. Schmid. N. Y., 1869. 16°. 2706
Habington, W. Castara. Ed. Arber. Lond., 1870. 16°. . . . 3894
The Queen of Arragon. (Old Plays, v. 9.) Lond., 1825. 8°. . 1516
Habit and Discipline, Thoughts on. Lond., 1844. 16°. . . . 8510
Habits of Good Society. (2 copies.) N. Y., 1863–65. 12°. . . 9269
Hackett, H. B. Illustrations of Scripture. Bost., 1860. 12°. . . 9888
Hackett, J. H. Notes on Shakespeare, etc. (2 copies.) N. Y., 1863. 12°. 1547
Hackländer, F. W. Clara; or, Slave Life in Europe. N. Y., 1856. 12°. 15130
Haffner, J. Travels in Ceylon. Lond., 1821. 8°. 8055
Hahn-Hahn, I. Adventures and Travels. 2d ed. Lond. 3 v. 12°. 8248
Haines, C. G. Memoir of Emmet. N. Y., 1829. 12°. . . . 6681
Hajji Baba in England. [Morier.] N. Y., 1828. 2 v. 12°. . . 15443
Halcyon Luminary. N. Y., 1812. v. 1. 8°. 14080
Hale, E. E. His Level Best, etc. Bost., 1873. 16°. 10303
If, Yes, and Perhaps. (2 copies.) Bost., 1868. 16°. . . 2945
Ingham Papers. Bost., 1869. 16°. 2947
Sybaris and Other Homes. Bost., 1869. 16°. 2948
Ten times One are Ten. (2 copies.) Bost., 1871. 16°. . . 2732
Hale, Sir M. Advice to his grandchildren. Bost., 1817. 12°. . . 17033
Life of. Burnet. Lond. 24°. 6677
Campbell. (Chief Justices, v. 1.) Philad., 1851. 8°. 6873
Hale, Salma. Hist. of the U. S. N. Y., 1827. 12°. 16048
The same. N. Y., 1841. 2 v. 12°. 11594
Hale, Sarah J. Traits of Amer. Life. Philad., 1835. 12°. . . . 15805
Halen, J. van. Narrative of Imprisonment, and Journey. N. Y., 1828. 8°. 16405
Half-Hours with the Best Authors. Knight. Lond., 1865–67. 2 v. 8°. 3764
with Letter-Writers and Autobiographers. Knight. Lond., 1867. 8°. 3769
Haliburton, T. C. The Bubbles of Canada. Philad., 1839. 12°. . 16118
Hist. of Nova-Scotia. Halifax. [1829.] 2 v. 8°. 5888
Rule and Misrule of the English in America. (3 copies.) N. Y., 1851. 12°. 6025
Sayings and Doings of Sam. Slick. (2 copies.) Philad., 1837–38. 12°. 4305
The same. 2d series. Philad., 1839. 12°. 4307
Halifax, *Earl of.* See C. MONTAGU.
Hall, A. M. (Mrs. S. C.) Lights and Shadows of Irish Life. Philad., 1838. 2 v. 12°. 15487
Midsummer Eve. N. Y., 1848. 8°. 2312
Sketches of Irish Character. N. Y., 1829. 12°. . . . 15583
Uncle Horace. Philad., 1838. 2 v. 12°. 15623
Hall, Basil. Fragments of Voyages and Travels. Philad., 1831. 2 v. 12°. 16253
Journal on the Coast of America. Lond., 1840. 8°. . . . 8101
The same. Philad., 1824. 2 v. 12°. 17144
Patchwork. Philad., 1841. 2 v. 12°. 15850

Hall, Basil. Skimmings. Philad., 1836. 12°. 16612
Travels in N. Amer. Philad., 1829. 2 v. 12°. 16786
Voyage to Java, etc. Lond., 1840. 8°. 8101
Voyages. Edinb., 1826. 3 v. 12°. 4463
Hall, Benj. H. College Words and Customs. Cambr., 1851. 12°. . 9257
The same. Revised ed. Cambr., 1856. 12°. 9258
Hall, C. F. Arctic Researches, etc. N. Y., 1865. 8°. . . . 8113
Hall, E. The Puritans. 2d ed. N. Y., 1846. 8°. 6458
Hall, F. W. Rambles in Europe. N. Y., 1839. 2 v. 12°. . . 16571
Hall, James. The Harpe's Head. Philad., 1833. 12°. . . . 15712
Legends of the West. 2d ed. Philad., 1833. 12°. . . . 15729
Memoir of Harrison. Philad., 1836. 12°. 7279
of Posey. (Sparks, v. 19.) Bost., 1846. 16°. . . 7268
Notes on the Western States. Philad., 1838. 12°. . . . 16880
Sketches of the West. Philad., 1835. 2 v. 12°. . . . 6079
The Wilderness and the War Path. N. Y., 1846. 12°. . . 15816
Hall, Joseph. Satires, and other Poems. Lond., 1838. 8°. . . 1250
Select Poems, with Life. Ed. Sanford. Philad., 1819. 24°. . 2
Treatises, devotional and practical. Ed. Cattermole. Lond., 1834. 16°. 9488
Hall, N. From Liverpool to St. Louis. (2 copies.) Lond., 1870. 16°. 8223
Sermons. N. Y., 1868. 12°. 9932
Hall, R. Miscellaneous Works, with Memoir. (2 copies.) Lond., 1846. 8°. 493
Polemical Miscellanies, etc.; Freedom of the Press. Bost., 1827. 12°. 17088
Works. (2 copies.) N. Y., 1832–38. 3 v. 8°. 10070
Hall, Samuel C. and **A. M.** Ireland. Lond., 1841–43. 3 v. 8°. . 8441
Hall, Samuel R. Lectures on School-Keeping. Bost., 1830. 12°. . 17040
Hallam, A. H. Remains. Bost., 1863. 8°. 3952
Hallam, H. Constitutional Hist. of England. Paris, 1827. 4 v. 8°. 5002
The same. (2 copies.) Bost., 1861. 3 v. 8°. 4907
Europe during the Middle Ages. Philad., 1821. 4 v. 8°. . 4664
Supplemental Notes to. Lond., 1848. 8°. . . . 4668
The same. [New ed.] 2 copies. N. Y., 1862. 3 v. 8°. . . 4669
Introd. to Literature of Europe, 1400–1700. [1st ed.] Lond., 1837–39. 4 v. 8°. 150
The same. Paris, 1837–39. 4 v. 8°. . . . 154
Hallberg, *Baron* **von.** Journey through N. Germany, etc. Lond., 1821. 8°. 8055
Halleck, F. G. Alnwick Castle, etc. N. Y., 1836. 8°. . . . 933
Fanny. N. Y., 1819. 8°. 16779
Fanny, with other Poems. N. Y., 1839. 12°. 799
Poetical Works. N. Y., 1847. 8°. 931
The same. 3d ed. N. Y., 1850. 8°. 932
Selections from British Poets. N. Y., 1840. 2 v. 12°. . . 11587
Young America: a Poem. N. Y., 1865. 16°. 800
Life and Letters of. Wilson. N. Y., 1869. 12°. . . . 7386

Halliwell, J. O. Dict. of Archaic and Provincial Words. 3d ed. Lond., 1855. 2 v. 8°. 171
of Old English Plays. Lond., 1860. 8°. . 1635
Introd. to Midsummer Night's Dream. Lond., 1840. 8°. . . 1587
Hallock, *Mrs.* **G.** A Mother's Love. N. Y., 1867. 12°. . . . 17047
Hallock, W. A. Memoir of H. Page. N. Y. 12°. 7523
Hallucinations, Hist. of. Brierre de Boismont. Philad., 1855. 8°. . 8763
Halsted, C. A. Richard III. Philad., 1844. 8°. 5288
Halyburton, T., Memoirs of. By himself. Princeton, 1833. 12°. . 16368
Hamerton, P. G. Thoughts about Art. Revised ed. Bost., 1871. 16°. 8858
Hamilton, Alex. Official Papers, etc. N. Y., 1842. v. 1. 8°. . . 17102
Works, except the Federalist; ed. J. C. Hamilton. N. Y., 1851. 7 v. 8°. 9661

CONTENTS.—1, Letters, to 1789. 2, Other Writings, to 1789. 3, Official Papers, 1790-95. 4, Cabinet Papers, 1789-94. 5, Cabinet Papers, 1794-95; Military Papers, etc.; Letters, 1789-95. 6, Letters, 1795-1804; Miscellaneous Political Papers. 7, Political Essays; Law Papers; Index.

Life of. J. C. Hamilton. N. Y., 1834. v. 1. 8°. 7461
The same. N. Y., 1840–41. 2 v. 8°. 7459
Life of. Renwick. N. Y., 1841. 12°. 11604
and others. The Federalist. N. Y., 1802. 2 v. 8°. . . 6089
The same, ed. Dawson. N. Y., 1863. 8°. . . . 6198
The same, ed. J. C. Hamilton. Philad., 1864. 8°. . . 6199
Hamilton, Anthony. Fairy Tales and Romances. (2 copies.) Lond., 1849. 8°. 452
Memoirs of Court of Chas. II., by Count Grammont. Lond., 1846. 8°. 320
The same. 4836
The same. Philad., 1836. 8°. 5310
Hamilton, C. Hist. of the Rohilla Afgans. Lond., 1787. 8°. . . 16052
Hamilton, E. Popular Essays. Bost., 1817. 2 v. 12°. . . . 13845
Hamilton, Gail. *(Pseudonym.)* See M. A. DODGE.
Hamilton, J. A. Reminiscences. N. Y., 1869. 8°. 7426
Hamilton, T. Annals of Peninsular Campaigns. Philad., 1831. 3 v. 12°. 6412
Cyril Thornton. N. Y., 1827–32. 2 v. 12°. 15149
Men and Manners in America. Edinb., 1843. 16°. . . . 8222
The same. Philad., 1833. 2 v. 12°. 16806
Hamilton, *Sir* **W.** Discussions on Philosophy, etc. N. Y., 1861. 8°. 8769
Lectures on Logic. Bost., 1860. 8°. 8742
Metaphysics. (2 copies.) Bost., 1860. 8°. . . . 8740
Hamlets, The. Martineau. Bost., 1836. 12°. 14625
Hammer and Anvil. A Novel. Spielhagen. N. Y., 1870. 12°. . 3022
Hammond, H., Life of. Fell. Lond. 24°. 6677
Hammond, Jabez D. Hist. of Political Parties in N. Y. Albany, 1842. 2 v. 8°. 5900
Hammond, James. Poetical Works. Ed. Bell. Lond., 1807. 24°. 536
The same, with Life, by Sanford. Philad., 1819. 24°. . 13
The same, ed. Johnson. Dubl., 1804. 8°. . . . 15099
Hampden, J., Life of. Forster. Lond., 1837. 16°. 5761
Memorials of. Nugent. Lond., 1832. 2 v. 8°. . . . 6842

Hampden in the 19th Century. Lond., 1834. 2 v. 8°. 3481
Hancock, T. Principles of Peace. Philad., 1829. 12°. . . . 8473
Hand, The, as evincing Design. Bell. Philad., 1836. 8°. . . 16983
Handy Andy. Lover. Lond. 8°. 2659
Hankin, C. C. Life of Mrs. Schimmel Penninck. Lond., 1858. 2 v. 8°. 7051
Hankins, C. Dakota Land. 2d ed. N. Y., 1869. 12°. . . . 8429
Hanley, S. Caliphs and Sultans. N. Y., 1869. 16°. . . . 1907
Hannah, J. Courtly Poets from Raleigh to Montrose. Lond., 1870. 16°. 1005
Hannah. [*Mrs.* Craik.] N. Y., 1872. 12°. 2494
Hannah Thurston. Bayard Taylor. N. Y., 1864. 12°. . . . 2934
Hans of Iceland. Hugo. N. Y., 1862. 8°. 2635
Happy, Art of being. Droz. Bost., 1832. 12°. 17032
Harbaugh, H. Poems. Philad., 1860. 16°. 775
Hardenberg, F. v. Henry of Ofterdingen. Cambr., 1842. 12°. . 3014
Harding, R. B. See Mrs. R. H. DAVIS.
Hardinge, G. Miscellaneous Works. Lond., 1818. 3 v. 8°. . . 17206
Hard Times. Dickens. N. Y., 1871. 16°. 2181
Hardwicke, *Lord* (P. Yorke), Life of. Campbell. Philad., 1848. 8°. 6870
Hare, A. J. C. Walks in Rome. Lond., 1871. 2 v. 8°. 8349
Harford, J. S. Life of M. Angelo. 2d ed. Lond., 1858. 2 v. 8°. . 7989
Harlan, J. Memoir of India and Avghanistaun. Philad., 1842. 12°. 6417
Harland, Marion. *(Pseudonym.)* See M. V. TERHUNE.
Harold. Bulwer-Lytton. Lond., 1853. 8°. 2152
Haroon Er-Rashid and Zobéidéh. Lond., 1840. 12°. 15479
Harper, R. G. *and* **Walsh, R.** Correspondence, etc., respecting Russia. Philad., 1813. 8°. 16173
Harper's Classical Library. N. Y. 31 v. 12°. 4510
Family Library. N. Y. 182 v. 12°. 11000
Ferry, Echoes of. Redpath. Bost., 1860. 12°. . . . 8575
New Monthly Magazine. N. Y., 1850–72. 45 v. 8°. . . 13121
The same. v. 1–36, 38–42. 13291
Index, v. 1–40. 2 copies.
Harpe's Head, The. J. Hall. Philad., 1833. 12°. 15712
Harrington; a Tale. Edgeworth. (Works, v. 8.) Bost., 1825. 8°. . 15342
Harris, James (1st Earl of Malmesbury). Letters of himself, his Family, and Friends. Lond., 1870. 2 v. 8°. . . 6830
Harris, John. The Pre-Adamite Earth. Bost., 1850. 12°. . . 16947
Harris, S. Zaccheus; or, the Scriptural Plan of Benevolence. N. Y., 12°. 9803
Harris, T. Life of Bainbridge. Philad., 1837. 8°. 7458
Harris, Wm. Lives of James I, etc. Lond., 1814. 5 v. 8°. . . 5304
CONTENTS.—1, Hugh Peters; James I. 2, Chas. I. 3, Cromwell. 4, 5, Chas. II.
The same. v. 2. 5309
Harris, Wm. C. Highlands of Ethiopia. N. Y. [1845.] 8°. . . 16525
Harrison, W. H., Memoir of. Hall. Philad., 1836. 12°. . . 7279
Sketch of. Todd & Drake. Cincinn., 1847. 16°. . . . 7496
Harsha, D. A. Eminent Orators and Statesmen. N. Y., 1855. 8°. . 6875
Hart, A. M. Hist. of Discov. of Mississippi Valley. St. Louis, 1852. 12°. 16876

Hart, J. S. Essay on Spenser. N. Y., 1847. 8°. 1275
Harte, F. Bret. Condensed Novels. Bost., 1871. 8°. 2916
East and West Poems. Bost., 1871. 12°. 764
Luck of Roaring Camp, etc. Bost., 1871. 8°. . , . . 2915
Mrs. Skaggs's Husbands, etc. Bost., 1873. 12°. . . . 10302
Poems. Bost., 1871. 12°. 765
Harte, W. Life of Gustavus Adolphus. 2d ed. Lond., 1767. 2 v. 8°. 5926
The same. 3d ed. Lond., 1807. 2 v. 8°. 5928
Select Poems. Ed. Walsh. Philad., 1822. 24°. 23
Hartford Convention, Hist. of. Dwight. N. Y., 1833. 8°. . . 6143
Letters in Defence of. Otis. Bost., 1824. 8°. 6141
Hartson, H. Countess of Salisbury. (Brit. Drama.) Lond., 1804. 8°. 1630
Hartt, C. F. Geol. and Phys. Geogr. of Brazil. Bost., 1870. 8°. . 9013
Hartwig, G. The Polar World. N. Y., 1869. 8°. 8102
Harvard, Fair; a Story. [Washburne.] N. Y., 1869. 12°. . . 9264
University, Hist. of. Quincy. Cambr., 1840. 2 v. 8°. . . 9398
Lyceum. Cambr., 1810–11. 8°. 17472
Magazine. (2 copies.) Cambr., 1855–60. v. 1–6. 8°. . . 17462
[**Harvey, C.**] The Synagogue. Lond., 1838. 16°. 1024
Haskins, J. Poetical Works. Hartf'd., 1848. 12°. 14797
Haskins, R. W. Hist. of Phrenology. Buffalo, 1839. 12°. . . 8609
Hastings, —. A Winter in the W. I. and Florida. N. Y., 1839. 12°. 16915
Hastings, W., Impeachment of. (Burke's Works, v. 6–8.) Bost., 1839. 8°. 9654
Memoirs of. Gleig. Lond., 1841. 3 v. 8°. 6805
Trial of. Lond., 1796. 8°. 6808
Hatfield, E. F. Universalism. (2 copies.) N. Y., 1841. 12°. . . 17343
Hatton, J. Christopher Kenrick. N. Y., 1869. 12°. 2432
Haunted Hearts. Cummins. Bost., 1864. 12°. 15713
Hauser, C., Account of. Feuerbach. Bost., 1832. 12°. . . . 7528
Haussez, C. d'. Great Britain in 1833. Philad., 1833. 12°. . . 5333
Havelock, H., Life of. Headley. N. Y., 1861. 12°. 6782
Haverhill; or, Memoirs of an Officer in Wolfe's Army. Jones. N. Y., 1831. 2 v. 12°. 15720
Hawaiian Islands, Hist. of. Jarves. Bost., 1843. 8°. 6506
Life in. Cheever. N. Y., 1851. 12°. 8329
Past and Present of. Hunt. San Francisco, 1853. 16° . . 16303
Progress and Condition of. Anderson. Bost., 1864. 12°. . 8330
Residence in, 1823–25. Stewart. Bost., 1839. 12°. . . . 16321
21 years in. Bingham. Hartf'd, 1849. 8°. 8082
Mission, Hist. of. Dibble. N. Y., 1839. 12°. 6416
Haweis, H. R. Music and Morals. N. Y., 1872. 12°. . . . 8865
Hawes, J. Lectures to Young Men. 3d ed. Hartf'd., 1829. 12°. . 9173
Travels in the East. Hartf'd., 1847. 12°. 16277
Life of. Lawrence. Hartf'd., 1871. 8°. 7712
Hawkesworth, J. The Adventurer. Lond., 1823. 3 v. 12°. . . 3128
Hawkins, B. Germany. Lond., 1838. 8°. 5883
Hawkins, *Sir* **John.** Hist of Music, ed. Busby. Lond., 1819. 2 v. 8°. 9078
Life of Johnson. Dubl., 1787. 8°. 7122
Hawkins, John H. W., Life of. By his son. Bost., 1859. 12°. . 16424

Hawks, F. L. Monuments of Egypt. 2d ed. N. Y., 1850. 8°. . 4456
Narrative of Perry's Expedition. N. Y., 1857. 8°. 8135
Hawks of Hawk Hollow, The. Bird. Philad., 1835. 2 v. 12°. . 15714
Hawley, Z. Journal of Tour. N. H., 1822. 12°. 16890
Hawthorne, N. Blithedale Romance. (2 copies.) Bost., 1852–62. 16°. 2889
House of Seven Gables. (2 copies.) Bost., 1851–60. 16°. . 2887
Marble Faun. (3 copies.) Bost., 1860–69. 2 v. 16°. . . 2892
Mosses from an Old Manse. N. Y., 1846. 12°. . . . 2879
The same. Bost., 1860. 2 v. 16°. 2880
The same. vol. 1. Bost., 1865. 16°. 2882
Our Old Home. Bost., 1863. 8°. 8357
Passages from American Note-Books. (2 copies.) Bost., 1868. 2 v. 8°. 8388
English Note-Books. Bost., 1870. 2 v. 12°. . 8358
French and Italian Note-Books. Bost., 1872. 2 v. 12°. 8203
Scarlet Letter. (4 copies.) Bost., 1850–66. 16°. . . . 2883
Septimius Felton. (2 copies.) Bost., 1872. 16°. . . . 2898
The Snow-Image, and other twice-told Tales. Bost., 1852. 12°. 2722
The same. Bost., 1857. 12°. 2891
Twice-Told Tales. (2 copies.) Bost., 1842–45. 2 v. 16°. . 2875
Hawthorne, S. Notes in England and Italy. (2 copies.) N. Y., 1869. 12°. 8360
Hay, J. Castilian Days. Bost., 1871. 8°. 8210
Haydn, F. J., Life of. Bombet. Bost., 1839. 16°. 7881
Haydn and other Poems. N. Y., 1870. 16°. 812
Haydn's Dictionary of Dates. Vincent. N. Y., 1867. 8°. . . 4066
Haydon, B. R. Autobiogr. and Journals. Ed. Taylor. Lond., 1853. 3 v. 8°. 7934
Painting. (2 copies.) Edinb., 1838. 12°. 8876
Hayes, I. I. Open Polar Sea. N. Y., 1867. 8°. 8111
Hayley, W. Life of Cowper. Bost., 1803. 2 v. 12°. . . . 16381
The same. Ed. Grimshawe. Lond., 1835. 5 v. 16°. . 624
Life of Milton. Dubl., 1797. 8°. 7110
Triumphs of Temper. Newburyport. 12°. 14798
Hays, M. Female Biography. Lond., 1803. 6 v. 12°. . . . 14426
Hayti. See SAINT DOMINGO.
Hayward, C. Life of S. Cabot. (Sparks, v. 9.) Bost., 1838. 16°. . 7258
The same. Bost., 1837. 12°. 16314
Hazen, E. Popular Technology. N. Y., 1842. 2 v. 12°. . . 11751
Hazlitt, W. Characters of Shakspeare's Plays. Bost., 1818. 12°. . 1485
Conversations of Northcote. Lond., 1830. 12°. . . . 3421
Criticisms on Art. Lond., 1843–44. 2 v. 16°. . . . 8856
Eloquence of Brit. Senate. Brooklyn, 1810. 2 v. 8°. . . 9423
The Fine Arts. (2 copies.) Edinb., 1838. 12°. . . . 8876
Lectures on Dramatic Literature of Age of Eliz. Lond., 1840. 16°. 69
on English Comic Writers. Lond., 1819. 8°. . . 162
The same. 3d ed. Lond., 1841. 16°. . . . 68

Hazlitt, W. Lectures on English Poets. 3d ed. Lond., 1841. 16°. 67
The same. N. Y., 1849. 12°. 127
Life of Napoleon. (2 copies.) N. Y., 1847–49. 3 v. 12°. . 5492
Literary Remains. (3 copies.) N. Y., 1836. 8°. . . . 3454
Notes of Journey through France and Italy. Philad., 1833. 8°. 15356
Plain Speaker. Lond., 1826. 2 v. 8°. 3457
Round Table. 3d ed. Lond., 1841. 16°. 3177
Sketches and Essays. Lond., 1839. 16°. 3176
Spirit of the Age. 2d ed. Lond., 1825. 12°. 3422
The same. N. Y., 1849. 12°. 3225
Table-Talk. Lond., 1846–57. 2 v. 16°. 3178
The same. N. Y., 1847. 2 pts. in 1. 12°. . . . 3222
The same. 2d series. (2 copies.) N. Y., 1846. 2 pts. in 1. 12°. 3223
View of the English Stage. Lond., 1818. 8°. 1611
Hazlitt, W. C. English Proverbs. Lond., 1869. 8°. . . . 4439
[**Head,** *Miss.*] Rybrent de Cruce. N. Y., 1829. 2 v. 12°. . . 15571
Head, F. B. Bubbles from the Brunnen of Nassau. (2 copies.) N. Y., 1845. 12°. 8366
A Faggot of French Sticks. N. Y., 1852. 12°. 8373
Life of Bruce. N. Y., 1841. 12°. 11603
A Narrative [of Affairs in Canada]. Lond., 1839. 8°. . . 5856
Rough Notes in Journeys across the Pampas. Lond., 1826. 12°. 17136
Head of the Family, The. [Mrs. Craik.] N. Y., 1864. 8°. . . 2680
Headley, J. T. The Alps and Rhine; and Letters from Italy. N. Y., 1846. 12°. 16574
Life of Havelock. N. Y., 1861. 12°. 6782
Napoleon and his Marshals. (2 copies.) N. Y., 1846–47. 2 v. 12°. 5434
Sacred Mountains. N. Y., 1851. 12°. 17301
Scenes and Characters. N. Y., 1851. 12°. . . . 17302
Washington and his Generals. (2 copies.) N. Y., 1847. 2 v. 12°. 7294
Headlong Hall. Peacock. N. Y., 1845. 12°. 3956
Heads, Lecture on. Stevens. Lond., 1795. 12°. . . . . .
Heads of the People. Philad., 1841. 8°. 15352
Headsman, The. Cooper. Philad., 1836. 2 v. 12°. 2781
Health, Code of. Sinclair. Lond., 1844. 8°. 8987
and Disease in Communities. Belinaye. Bost., 1833. 12°. . 9169
Economy of. Johnson. N. Y., 1837. 12°. 9123
Effects of the Trades, etc., on. Thackrah. Philad., 1831. 12°. 16965
Herald of. N. Y., 1867–70. v. 43, 44, 49, 50 (in 2 v.) 8°. . . 17488
Influence of Mental Habits on. Brigham. Bost., 1833. 12°. . 9171
of Religion on. Brigham. Bost., 1835. 12°. . . 17351
Philosophy of. S. Smith. Lond., 1838. 2 v. 12°. . . . 9119
Public. Guy. Lond., 1870. 8°. 9168
Heard, F. F. Curiosities of Law Reporters. Bost., 1871. 16°. . 4346
Heard, I. V. D. Hist. of Sioux War. N. Y., 1864. 12°. . . . 5745
Heart of the Continent, The. Ludlow. N. Y., 1870. 8°. . . . 8418
of Mid-Lothian. Scott. Edinb., 1870. 8°. 1872
Heartsease. Yonge. N. Y., 1871. 2 v. 12°. 2499

Heat as a Mode of Motion. Tyndall. N. Y., 1868. 12°. 8902
Phenomena and Laws of. Cazin. N. Y., 1869. 12°. . . . 10111
Treatise on. Lardner. Lond., 1833. 16°. 6047
Heaton, M. M. Life of A. Dürer. Lond., 1870. 8°. 8125
Heavens, The. Mudie. Lond., 1835. 12°. 14634
Wonders of. Flammarion. N. Y., 1871. 12°. 10114
Heber, R. Journeys through India, etc. Philad., 1828. 2 v. 8°. . 8016
Life of Jer. Taylor. Lond., 1824. 2 v. 16°. 7559
Palestine and other Poems. Philad., 1828. 12°. . . . 14825
Poetical Works. Philad., 1839. 8°. 1247
Life of. By his Widow. N. Y., 1830. 2 v. 8°. 7705
Hebrew Poetry, Spirit of. Taylor. N. Y., 1862. 12°. 9544
Hebrews, Notes on Epistle to the. Barnes. N. Y., 1844. 12°. . 9864
Hebrides, Cruise of the Betsey in the. Miller. Bost., 1862. 12°. . 8980
Journey to the, 1773. Boswell. Philad., 1810. 8°. 8354
The same. Johnson. (Works, v. 4.) Dubl., 1793. 8°. 3751
Voyage to the. Necker de Saussure. Lond., 1822. 8°. . . 8058
Heck, J. G. Iconographic Encyclopædia. N. Y., 1851. 4 v. 8°.
and 2 v. 4°. . . . .
Hedge, F. H. Prose Writers of Germany. Philad., 1849. 8°. . . 242
The same. N. Y., 1856. 8°. 243
Hedged in. Phelps. Bost., 1870. 12°. 2977
Heeren, A. L. H. Historical Researches on Asiatic Nations. Oxf'd.,
1833. 3 v. 8°. 4114
on Nations of Africa. Oxf'd.,
1832. 2 v. 8°. 4117
Historical Treatises; on the Reformation; Political Theories;
Continental Interests of Grt. Brit. Oxf'd., 1836. 8°. . 4713
Hist. of Polit. System of Europe. Oxf'd., 1834. 2 v. 8°. . 4716
The same. Northampton, 1829. 2 v. 8°. 4714
of States of Antiquity. Northampton, 1828. 8°. . . 4112
Manual of Ancient History. Oxf'd., 1833. 8°. 4113
Reflections on Politics of Ancient Greece. Bost., 1824. 8°. . 4406
Heidenmauer, The. Cooper. Philad., 1836. 2 v. 12°. 2777
Heine, H. Book of Songs, transl. by Leland. (2 copies.) Philad.,
1864. 16°. 868
Letters on Modern Literature in Germany. Bost., 1836. 16°. 43
Reisebilder. Philad., 1865. 12°. 9613
Heir of Redclyffe. Yonge. N. Y., 1871. 2 v. 12°. 2495
of Wast Wayland. Howitt. N. Y., 1851. 12°. . . . 15445
Heiress of Bruges. Grattan. N. Y., 1831. 2 v. 12°. . . . 15446
He knew he was right. Trollope. N. Y., 1869. 8°. 2293
Hellas, Monuments and Scenery of. Chase. Cambr., 1863. 16°. . 8208
Hellborn, K. v. Life of Schubert. Lond., 1869. 2 v. 8°. . . 7920
Héloïse, Hist. of. Berington. Philad., 1819. 8°. 16407
Helon's Pilgrimage to Jerusalem. Strauss. Bost., 1835. 12°. . . 6306
Helper, H. R. Impending Crisis of the South. N. Y., 1857. 12°. . 8574
Helps, A. Brevia. Bost., 1871. 16°. 3699
Casimir Maremma. Bost., 1870. 16°. 2377

Helps, A. Companions of my Solitude. Bost., 1852. 16°. . . 3695
Conversations on War and Culture. (2 copies.) Bost., 1871. 16°. 3700
Essays written in Intervals of Business. Lond., 1843. 16°. . 3693
The same. And Essay on Organization. Bost., 1871. 16°. 3698
Friends in Council. 2d Series. Bost., and N. Y., 1860–63. 2 v. 16°. 3696
Fruits of Leisure: or, Essays written in Intervals of Business. N. Y., 1851. 12°. 3694
Life of Columbus. Lond., 1869. 16°. 7822
of Cortes. N. Y., 1871. 16°. 7692
of Pizarro. Lond., 1869. 16°. 7691
Realmah. (2 copies.) Bost., 1869. 16°. 2450
Spanish Conquest in America. N. Y., 1856–68. 4 v. 12°. . 5820
Thoughts on Government. Bost., 1872. 8°. 8620
Helvetic Union. See SWITZERLAND.[1]
Hemans, C. J. Hist. of Mediæval Christianity and Sacred Art in Italy. Lond., 1869. 8°. 6309
Hemans, F. D. Poems. Bost., 1827. 2 v. 8°. 1255
Poetical Works. Philad., 1836. 8°. 15087
Records of Woman: with other Poems. N. Y., 1828. 12°. . 14826
Works, with Memoir, by her sister. Philad., 1840. 7 v. 12°. 668
Memorials of. Chorley. N. Y., 1836. 12°. 16379
Henderson, E. Iceland. 2d ed. Edinb., 1819. 8°. 8293
Journal in Iceland; abridged. Bost., 1831. 12°. 16599
Henderson, J. Observations on New South Wales, etc. Calcutta, 1832. 8°. 16287
Henningsen, C. F. Campaign with Zumalacarregui. Philad., 1836. 12°. 16161
Henrietta Temple. Disraeli. Philad., 1837. 2 v. 12°. . . . 2127
Henry I., of England, Hist. of. Cobbe. Lond., 1869. 8°. . . 5285
Henry II., Hist. of. Lyttelton. Lond., 1769–73. 6 v. 8°. . . 16109
Henry VII., Hist. of England under. Bacon. (Works, v. 1.) Lond., 1838. 8°. 9738
Henry VIII., Memoirs of Court of. Thomson. Lond., 1826. 2 v. 8°. 5289
and his Court; a Novel. [Mundt.] N. Y., 1868. 12°. . 3102
Henry IV., of France, Life of. James. N. Y., 1850. v. 1. 12°. . 5537
Memoirs of, and of his Court. [Ireland.] Lond., 1824. 2 v. 8°. 5538
Henry, J. J. Campaign against Quebec, 1775. Lancaster, 1812. 12°. 5721
Henry, M. Exposition of the Bible. N. Y., 1831. 6 v. 8°. . . 17309
Henry, P., Life of. A. H. Everett. Bost., 1844. 16°. . . . 7260
Sketches of Life of. Wirt. Ithaca, 1850. 8°. 7342
Henry, R. Hist. of Grt. Brit. Lond., 1788–95. 12 v. 8°. . . 4973
Henry Esmond. Thackeray. Lond., 1872. 8°. 2192
Henry of Guise: a Novel. James. N. Y., 1839. 2 v. 12°. . . 15205
Henry Milner. Sherwood. (Works, v. 1, 15.) N. Y., 1837. 12°. . 15113
Henry of Ofterdingen; a Romance. v. Hardenberg. Cambr., 1842. 12°. 3014
Henry Powers *(Banker)*. Kimball. N. Y., 1868. 12°. . . . 15716

Henslow, J. S. Descriptive and Physiological Botany. Lond., 1836. 16°. 6064
[**Hentz, N. M.**] The Valley of Shenandoah. N. Y., 1824. 2 v. 12°. 15808
Herald of Health. N. Y., 1867–70. v. 43, 44, 49, 50 (in 2 v.) 8°. . 17488
Herbert, C. Italy and Italian Literature. Lond., 1835. 12°. . . 111
Herbert, *Lord* **E.,** Life of. By himself. Lond., 1830. 12°. . . . 6646
Herbert, G. The Country Parson, ed. Park. Andover, 1845. 12°. . 9913
The Temple. Sacred Poems. Lond., 1838. 16°. . . . 1024
Writings, with Life. Lowell, 1834. 16°. 1025
Life of. Walton. [Lond. 1845.] 8°. 948
[**Herbert, H. W.**] Cromwell. N. Y., 1838. 2 v. 12°. . . . 15685
Field Sports of U. S. N. Y., 1849. v. 1. 8°. 10207
Manual for Young Sportsmen. N. Y., 1857. 12°. . . . 10160
Sporting Scenes and Characters. Philad. [1857.] 2 v. 12°. . 10161
CONTENTS.—1, My Shooting Box. 2, Warwick Woodlands.
Herbert Lacy. [Lister.] Philad., 1828. 2 v. 12°. 15448
Hereditary Genius. Galton. N. Y., 1870. 8°. 8992
Hereward the Wake. C. Kingsley. Lond., 1867. 8°. . . . 2570
Hermann, C. F. Polit. Antiquities of Greece. Oxf'd., 1836. 8°. . 4431
Hermann Agha. Palgrave. N. Y., 1872. 16°. 2371
Hermit in the Country, The. N. Y., 1820. 2 v. 12°. 15249
London, The. Philad., 1820. 2 v. 12°. 15247
Hermits, Lives of the. Kingsley. Philad., 1868. 8°. . . . 6315
Herodotus. History, transl. by Beloe. N. Y., 1836–41. 3 v. 12°. . 4536
The same. N. Y., 1836–44. 3 v. 12°. 4552
The same. Lond., 1821. v. 1–3. 8°. 16023
The same. Lond., 1791. v. 1, 2, 4. 8°. 15875
transl. by Cary. (2 copies.) Lond., 1850. 8°. 4233
Abstract of. Swayne. Philad., 1870. 16°. 73
Geography of. Niebuhr. Oxf'd., 1830. 8°. 4442
Heroes and Hero-Worship. Carlyle. Lond., 1870. 8°. . . . 4031
Herrick, R. Hesperides. Bost., 1856. 2 v. 16°. 1036
Herschel, J. F. W. Discourse on Study of Nat. Philosophy. Lond., 1835. 16°. 6042
Familiar Lectures on Scientific Subjects. Lond., 1869. 8°. . 8898
Treatise on Astronomy. Lond., 1839. 16°. 6045
Hertha. Bremer. N. Y., 1856. 12°. 2623
Hertz, H. King René's Daughter. N. Y., 1867. 12°. . . . 14883
Hervey, James. Meditations. N. Y., 1824. 2 v. in 1. 12°. . . 17296
Hervey, *Lord* **John.** Memoirs of Reign of Geo. II. Philad., 1848. 2 v. 12°. 5215
Hervey, T. K. The Book of Christmas. N. Y., 1845. 12°. . . 3899
Herzen, A. My Exile. Lond., 1855. 2 v. 12°. 7584
Hesekiel, J. G. L. Life of Bismarck. N. Y., 1870. 8°. . . . 7758
Hesiod. Works and Days, transl. by Chapman. Ed. Hooper. Lond., 1858. 16°. 993
Hesperus. Richter. Bost., 1865. 2 v. 8°. 3059
Hess, J. G. Life of Zwingle. Lond., 1812. 8°. 7555
The same. 7630

Hetherington, W. M. Hist. of Westminster Assembly. N. Y., 1843. 12°. 6313
Hetty. H. Kingsley. N. Y., 1869. 8°. 2330
Hewitt, M. E. Songs of Our Land and Other Poems. Bost., 1846. 12°. 14999
Hey, W., Life of. Pearson. Lond., 1827. 2 v. 8°. 7569
Heyse, P. Anfang und Ende; Die Einsamen. Bost. 12°. . . 9615
Heywood, J. The Four P's. (Old Plays, v. 1.) Lond., 1825. 8°. . 1508
Life of. Dunham. Lond., 1840. 16°. 5774
Heywood, T. Plays. See DODSLEY's Old Plays, v. 6, 7.
Hiatt, J. M. Voter's Text-Book. (2 copies.) Indianapolis, 1868. 12°. 6017
Hibernicus. *(Pseudonym.)* See D. CLINTON.
Hickey, W. Constitution of the U. S., etc. (3 copies.) 2d ed. Philad., 1847. 12°. 6028
The same. 6th ed. Philad., 1853. 12°. 6031
Hide and Seek. Collins. N. Y. 8°. 2297
Hieover, Harry. *(Pseudonym.)* See C. BRINDLEY.
Hiestand, H. Travels. N. Y., 1837. 12°. 16584
Higgins, W. M. The Earth. N. Y., 1840. 12°. 11403
Higginson, T. W. Out-Door Papers. Bost., 1863. 8°. 3559
High Life below Stairs. Townley. N. Y. 8°. 1669
Highland Widow, The. W. Scott. Edinb., 1871. 8°. 1888
Highlanders. See SCOTLAND.
Highways and Byways. Grattan. Bost., 1840. 3 v. 12°. . . 15450
Hildreth, R. Hist. of the U. S. N. Y., 1849–52. 2 Series in 6 v. 8°. 6228
The same. [Revised ed. of 2d Series.] N. Y., 1849–60. 6 v. 8°. 6234
Lives of Atrocious Judges, from Lord Campbell. N. Y., 1856. 12°. 6759
Hill, A. Zara. (Brit. Drama, v. 1, pt. 2.) Lond., 1804. 8°. . . 1630
Hill, Geo. Ruins of Athens; and other Poems. Bost., 1839. 8°. . 15059
[**Hill, Geo. C.**] Homespun. By Thomas Lackland. N. Y., 1867. 12°. 3564
Hill, J. Life of Dr. Blair. Philad., 1808. 8°. 16352
Hill, R., Life of. Sidney. N. Y., 1834. 12°. 16337
Hillard, G. S. Life of McClellan. Philad., 1864. 12°. . . . 7281
of Capt. J. Smith. Bost., 1834. 16°. . . . 7251
The same. Bost., 1839. 12°. 16313
Six Months in Italy. Bost., 1860. 12°. 8341
Hillhouse, J. A. Dramas, Discourses, etc. Bost., 1839. 2 v. 16°. . 796
Hadad. N. Y., 1825. 8°. 798
Percy's Masque. N. Y., 1820. 12°. 795
Hills of the Shatemuc. Warner. N. Y., 1857. 12°. 3004
Hind, J. R. The Solar System. N. Y., 1852. 12°. 8845
Hindostan. See INDIA.
Hinman, R. R. Conn. during the Revolution. Hartf'd., 1842. 8°. . 6295
Hinton, J. H. Hist. and Topography of the U. S. Bost., 1850–51. 2 v. 4°. 6289
The same. Lond., 1830. 3 v. 4°. 6286
Hints to my Countrymen. N. Y., 1826. 12°. 15276
Hippisley, J. H. Chapters on Early Eng. Lit. Lond., 1837. 12°. . 163
Historical Causes and Effects, 476–1517. Sullivan. Bost., 1838. 12°. 4569

Historical Parallels. [Malkin, etc.] Lond., 1846. 3 v. 12°. . . . 4555
Proof, Process of. I. Taylor. Lond., 1828. 8°. . . .
History, Dark Scenes of. James. N. Y., 1850. 12°. 4573
Great Events in. Lieber. Bost., 1840. 12°. 15930
Lectures on Study of. Goldwin Smith. N. Y., 1866. 12°. . 4581
Letters on Study and Use of. Bolingbroke. (Works, v. 3, 4.) Lond., 1809. 8°. 3796
philosophically illustrated (A. D. 476–1789). Miller. Lond., 1848–49. 4 v. 8°. 358
Philosophy of. v. Schlegel. Lond., 1835. 2 v. 8°. 4100
The same. Shedd. Andover, 1856. 12°. . . . 4584
Sketches of. Lord Kames. Edinb., 1813. 3 v. 8°. . . . 4097
of Society, Natural. Taylor. N. Y., 1841. 2 v. 12°. . . 4562
Unity of. Abraham. Eton, 1845. 8°. 4087
Use and Study of. McCullagh. Dubl., 1842. 8°. . . . 4090
Ancient. Fredet. Balt., 1851. 12°. 4054
The same. Raleigh. Edinb., 1820. 6 v. 8°. . . 4077
The same. Rollin. N. Y., 1834. 2 v. 8°. . . . 4124
The same. P. Smith. N. Y., 1870–72. 3 v. 8°. . . 4119
The same. Tylor. 2d ed. Lond., 1870. 8°. . . 4074
Lectures on. Niebuhr. Philad., 1852. 3 v. 12°. . 4059
Manual of. Heeren. Oxf'd., 1833. 8°. 4113
The same. Rawlinson. Oxf'd., 1869. 8°. . . . 4062
Outline of. [Ellis.] Libr. of Useful Knowl., v. 12. Lond., 1831. 8°. 16468
of the East. Lenormant and Chevallier. Lond., 1869–70. 2 v. 8°. 4057
of the Minor Kingdoms. Lond., 1845. 8°. . . . 4096
Modern, 18 Christian Centuries of. White. N. Y., 1863. 12°. 4566
A. D. 1–1850. Fredet. Balt., 1850. 12°. . . . 4570
Student's Manual of, 340–1840. Taylor. Lond., 1841. 12°. 4564
(1453–1789.) Michelet. N. Y., 1843. 12°. . . 11771
1520–1815. Lord. Philad., 1862. 12°. . . . 4565
of the 18th Century. Miller. N. Y., 1803. 2 v. 8°. 15902
The same. Schlosser. Lond., 1843–45. 6 v. 8°. . . 4798
1800–1850. Davis. Bost., 1851. 12°. . . . 4606
of Our Own Times. Lond., 1843–45. 2 v. 12°. . 4611
Lectures on. Arnold. Lond., 1843. 8°. . . . 4718
The same. W. Smyth. Cambr., 1841. 2 v. 8°. . . 4808
Universal, to 800. Bossuet. Dubl., 1785. 8°. 15934
to 1783. v. Müller. Lond., 1818. 3 v. 8°. . . 4107
to 1801. Mavor. N. Y., 1803–05. 25 v. 12°. . 13497
to 1820. Tytler. N. Y., 1840. 6 v. 12°. . . 11410
[to 1840.] v. Rotteck. Philad., 1840–41. 4 v. 8°. 4083
to 1857. Goodrich. N. Y., 1857. 2 v. 8°. . . 4122
Essay on. Voltaire. Edinb., 1777. 4 v. 12°. . 14014
The Fifteen Decisive Battles of. Creasy. N. Y., 1863. 12°. . 4571
Outlines of [to 1815]. Keightley. Lond., 1830. 16°. . . 4856

History, Universal, Outlines of, to 1872. Freeman. N. Y., 1872. 12°. 4561
System of. Whitaker. Lond., 1821. 4 v. 4°. . 16038
Hitchcock, D. Poetical Dictionary. Part 1. Lenox, 1808. 12°. . 14935
Hitchcock, E. Connection of Geology and Natural Religion. Edinb., 1835. 16°. 9137
Dyspepsy forestalled and resisted. Amh., 1830. 12°. . . 16969
Elementary Geology. 30th ed. N. Y., 1856. 12°. . . . 8981
Hist. of a Zoological Temperance Convention. Northampton, 1850. 16°. 9121
Life of Mary Lyon. Northampton, 1851. 12°. 16417
Religion of Geology. Bost., 1851. 12°. 8840
Religious Lectures on the Seasons. Bost., 1861. 12°. . . 16994
Truth illustrated from Science. Bost., 1857. 12°. . 17354
Sketch of Scenery of Mass. Northampton, 1842. 4°. . .
Hitherto. Whitney. Bost. 12°. 2969
Hittel, J. S. Resources of California. S. Francisco, 1863. 12°. . 8402
Hoadly, B. Suspicious Husband. (Brit. Drama.) Lond., 1804. 8°. 1632
Hoaryhead. Abbott. Bost., 1838. 12°. 2725
Hobart, N. Life of Swedenborg. Bost., 1845. 12°. 7562
Hobbes, T. English Works, ed. Molesworth. Lond., 1839–41. v. 1, 3–6. 8°. . . . . . , ... 9673

CONTENTS.—1, Elements of Philosophy, concerning Body. 3, Leviathan. 4, Discourses on Human Nature, on the Elements of Law, and on Liberty and Necessity; Answers to Bramhall and Davenant; Heresy; on the Reputation, etc., of T. Hobbes. 5, Questions concerning Liberty, Necessity, and Chance, debated by Bramhall. 6, Dialogue of the Common Law of England; Behemoth; Rhetoric; Sophistry.

Hobomok. Child. Bost., 1824. 12°. 15717
Hochelaga. [Warburton.] N. Y., 1846. 12°. 8370
Hodgson, A. Journey through N. America. N. Y., 1823. 8°. . . 16781
Hofer, Andreas. A Novel. [Mundt.] N. Y., 1868. 8°. . . . 3088
Hoffman, C. F. Administration of Leisler. (Sparks, v. 13.) Bost., 1844. 16°. 7262
Greyslaer. N. Y., 1840. 2 v. 12°. 15708
A Winter in the West. 2d ed. N. Y., 1835. 2 v. 12°. . . 16859
Hoffman, D. Chronicles of Cartaphilus. Lond., 1853. 2 v. 8°. . 10059
Course of Legal Study. 2d ed. Balt., 1836. 2 v. 8°. . . 9354
Thoughts, by A. Grumbler. Balt., 1841. 12°. 15275
Hoffmann, E. T. W. The Golden Pot, transl. by Carlyle. Bost., 1841. 12°. 3108
Hofland, B. Tales of the Manor. N. Y., 1822. 2 v. 12°. . . 15594
Hogarth, G. Memoirs of the Musical Drama. Lond., 1838. 2 v. 8°. 9080
Musical History, Biography and Criticism. N. Y., 1845. 8°. . 9077
Hogarth, W. Works, in a Series of Engravings, with Descriptions. Lond., 1833. 2 v. 4°. . . . .
Hogg, Jabez. The Microscope. 7th ed. Lond., 1869. 8°. . . 8899
Hogg, James. Familiar Anecdotes of Scott. (2 copies.) N. Y., 1834. 12°. 6921
Poet. Works, with Autobiogr. Glasg., 1838–40. 5 v. 12°. . 573
The Queen's Wake. Bost., 1815. 16°. 14827
Songs. N. Y., 1832. 12°. 608
Tales and Sketches. Glasg., 1836–37. 6 v. 12°. 578

Hogg, T. J. Life of Shelley. Lond., 1858. 2 v. 8°. 7001
Hohensteins, The. Spielhagen. N. Y., 1870. 12°. 3021
Holberg, L., Memoirs of. By himself. Lond., 1830. 12°. . . 6650
Holcombe, J. P. Literature in Letters. (2 copies.) N. Y., 1866. 8°. 7162
Holcroft, T. Duplicity; School for Arrogance; Seduction. (Mod. Theatre, v. 4.) Lond., 1811. 12°. 1330
Holland, H. Essays. Lond., 1862. 8°. 9001
Recollections of past Life. N. Y., 1872. 12°. 7106
Holland, John. On Manufactures in Metal. Lond., 1831–34. 3 v. 16°. 6037
Holland, Josiah G. The Bay Path. (2 copies.) N. Y., 1862. 12°. 2918
Bitter-Sweet: a Poem. (2 copies.) N. Y., 1862. 12°. . . 760
Gold-Foil, hammered from Proverbs. N. Y., 1863. 12°. . 3642
Kathrina: a Poem. (2 copies.) N. Y., 1867–69. 12°. . . 762
Lessons in Life. (2 copies.) N. Y., 1862. 12°. . . . 3643
Letters to the Joneses. N. Y., 1863. 12°. 3646
to Young People. (2 copies.) N. Y., 1862–63. 12°. . 3640
Life of Lincoln. Springfield, 1866. 8°. 7405
Miss Gilbert's Career. (2 copies.) N. Y., 1860–62. 12°. . 2920
Plain Talks on Familiar Subjects. N. Y., 1866. 12°. . . 3645
Holland, *Lady* **S.** Memoir of Sydney Smith. (2 copies.) N. Y., 1855–56. 2 v. 12°. 7010
Holland, W. M. Life of Van Buren. (3 copies.) Hartf'd., 1835. 12°. 7322
Holland, The Gov't. of. L. Bonaparte. Lond., 1820. 3 v. 8°. . 5877
See, also, DUTCH; NETHERLANDS.
Hollister, G. H. Mount Hope. (2 copies.) N. Y., 1851. 12°. . 15749
Holman, J. G. Votary of Wealth. (Mod. Theatre.) Lond., 1811. 12°. 1329
Holmes, A. American Annals. Cambr., 1805. 2 v. 8°. . . . 16141
The same. 2d ed. Cambr., 1829. 2 v. 8°. . . . 16143
The same. (2 copies.) 5966
Life of Stiles. Bost., 1798. 8°. 9274
Holmes, E. Life of Mozart. N. Y., 1845. 16°. 7882
Holmes, O. W. Astræa. Bost., 1850. 12°. 748
Autocrat of the Breakfast-Table. Bost., 1860. 12°. . . 3606
Border Lines of Knowledge in Medical Science. Bost., 1862. 12°. 8947
Currents and Counter-Currents in Medical Science, etc. Bost., 1861. 12°. 3605
Elsie Venner. Bost., 1861. 2 v. 16°. 2720
The Guardian Angel. Bost., 1871. 12°. 2900
Mechanism in Thought and Morals. Bost., 1871. 16°. . . 10107
Poems. Bost., 1861. 16°. 746
The same. New ed. Bost., 1864. 16°. 747
Poet at the Breakfast-Table. Bost., 1872. 12°. . . . 3609
Professor at the Breakfast-Table. (2 copies.) Bost., 1860–68. 12°. 3607
Soundings from the Atlantic. (2 copies.) Bost., 1864. 12°. . 3610
Holmes, W. The Camp Meeting. Bost., 1842. 12°. 14936
[**Holt, J. S.**] Abraham Page, Esq. Philad., 1868. 12°. . . . 15643
[**Holthaus, P. D.**] Wanderings of a Tailor. Lond., 1844. 16°. . 8194
Holy War, The. Bunyan. Hartf'd., 1850. 12°. 9948

Home, D. D. Incidents in my Life. 2d Series. N. Y., 1872. 12°. 8524
Home, H. (*Lord* Kames.) Elements of Criticism. Edin., 1769. 2 v. 8°. 17533
The same. Ed. Boyd. N. Y., 1855. 12°. 9298
Loose Hints on Education. Dubl., 1782. 12°. 17015
Sketches of Hist. of Man. Glasg., 1802. 4 v. 16°. . . 8500
The same. Edinb., 1813. 3 v. 8°. 4097
Life of. Smellie. Edinb., 1800. 8°. 7138
Home, J. Douglas: a Tragedy. N. Y. 8°. 1669
The same. (Brit. Drama.) Lond., 1804. 8°. 1630
The same. (Brit. Drama.) Philad., 1833. 8°. . . . 1662
Works. Edinb., 1822. 3 v. 8°. 17514
Home. A story. Mrs. Ellis. N. Y., 1836. 2 v. in 1. 12°. . . 15457
The; a Tale. F. Bremer. N. Y., 1843. 8°. 2656
Education. Taylor. N. Y., 1838. 12°. 9307
as Found. Cooper. Philad., 1838. 2 v. in 1. 12°. . . 2789
Influence. Aguilar. N. Y., '1850. 12°. 2418
Life of English Ladies in XVII. century. Lond., 1860. 12°. . 9127
and Social Philosophy. N. Y., 1852. 2 v. 12°. . . . 3353
Homer, Iliad, transl. by Cowper. N. Y., 1850. 8°. 1319
The same. Philad., 1838. 2 v. 24°. 988
transl. by Earl of Derby. N. Y., 1865. 2 v. 8°. 871
transl. by Pope. Ed. Bell. Lond., 1807. 2 v. 24°. 279
The same. Ed. Walsh. Philad., 1822. 2 v. 24°. 34
Abstract of. Collins. Philad., 1870. 16°. 71
Flaxman's Illustrations of. Lond., 1805. 4°. . .
Iliad and Odyssey, transl. by Cowper. Lond., 1837. 4 v. 16°. 619
The same. Lond., 1854–55. 2 v. 8°. 466
The same, transl. by Bryant. Bost., and N. Y., 1870–72. 4 v. 8°. 1320
Odyssey, transl. by Pope. Philad., 1822. 24°. 987
Abstract of. Collins. Philad., 1870. 16°. 72
Works, transl. by Chapman, ed. Hooper. Lond., 1857–58. v. 1, 2, 4, 5. 16°. 990
CONTENTS.—v. 1, 2, Iliad. 4, Odyssey. 5, Hymns, etc.
and the Homeridæ. De Quincey. (Works, v. 6.) Edinb., 1857. 8°. 3279
Introduction to. H. N. Coleridge. Philad., 1831. 12°. . . 41
On Translating. M. Arnold. Bost., 1865. 12°. 3734
Homes Abroad. Martineau. Bost., 1833. 12°. 14617
without Hands. Wood. N. Y., 1866. 8°. 9605
Homespun; or, five and twenty years ago. [Hill.] N. Y., 1867. 8°. 3564
Homeward Bound. Cooper. N. Y., 1865. 12°. 2812
Homilist, The. Editor's Series. Lond., 1870–71. 4 v. 8°. . . 12888
Homœopathy, Lectures on. O. W. Holmes. Bost., 1861. 12°. . 3605
Hone, W. Table-Book. Lond., 1827–28. v. 1, 2, in 1. 8°. . . 4342
Year Book. Lond., 1838. 8°. 4343
Honeywood, St. J. Poems, etc. N. Y., 1801. 12°. 14937

Honor O'Hara. A. M. Porter. N. Y., 1827. 2 v. 12°. 15196
Hood, E. P. Milton : the Patriot and Poet. Lond., 1852. 12°. . 6953
Hood, Robin, Poems, etc., relative to. Ritson. [Lond., 1845.] 8°. . 948
Hood, T. Hood's Own. Selected Papers. N. Y., 1852. 12°. . . 4268
Poetical Works. Bost., 1859–66. 5 v. 16°. 1061
Tylney Hall. N. Y., 1835. 12°. 15110
Up the Rhine. N. Y., 1852. 2 v. 12°. 4269
The same. Lond., 1869. 8°. 4271
Whims and Oddities. (2 copies.) N. Y., 1861–67. 12°. . . 4272
Works. N. Y., 1861. 6 v. 8°. 3961

CONTENTS.—1-3, Poems. 4, Whims and Oddities; National Tales; Humorous Tales. 5, Up the Rhine; Romances and Extravaganzas. 6, Our Family; Comic Miscellany; Autobiogr.

Memorials of. By his children. Bost., 1861. 2 v. 8°. . . 6983
[**Hook, J.**] Pen Owen. N. Y., 1822. 2 v. 12°. 15538
Percy Mallory. Philad., 1824. 2 v. 12°. 15540
Hook, T. E. Adventures of an Actor. Lond., 1842. 2 v. 12°. . 1608
The Atonement. Philad., 1839. 12°. 2594
Births, Deaths and Marriages. Philad., 1839. 2 v. 12°. . . 15381
The Humorist. Philad., 1837. 12°. 4256
Hooke, N. Roman Hist. Lond. 3 v. 8°. 15998
Hooker, R. Eccl. Polity and other Works. Ed. Hanbury. Lond., 1830. 3 v. 8°. 8688
Works. Oxf'd., 1843. 2 v. 8°. 8691
Life of. Walton. [Lond., 1845.] 8°. 948
Hooker, W. Hist. of Medical Delusions. N. Y., 1850. 12°. . . 16970
Hooper, J. Writings. Lond. 12°. 9479
Hooper, L. Poetical Remains. N. Y., 1842. 12°. 15000
Hooton, C. Colin Clink. Philad., 1840–41. 2 v. 12°. . . . 15401
[**Hope, T.**] Anastasius. N. Y., 1832. 2 v. 12°. 15157
Hope Leslie. Sedgwick. N. Y., 1827. 2 v. 12°. 15314
Hopkins, J. H. Hist. of the Confessional. N. Y., 1850. 12°. . . 9609
Hopkins, M. Law of Love and Love as a Law. N. Y., 1869. 12°. 8607
Moral Science. Bost., 1865. 12°. 8606
Hopkins, Rev. Sam'l., Reminiscences of. Patten. N. Y., 1843. 12°. 7521
Hopkins, Sam'l. The Puritans. Bost., 1860–61. 3 v. 8°. . . 5314
Hopkinson, F. Miscellaneous Essays, etc. Philad., 1792. 3 v. 8°. 12750
Hopper, I. T., Life of. Child. Bost., 1854. 12°. 7610
Hoppin, J. M. Notes of a Theol. Student. N. Y., 1854. 12°. . . 16331
Old England. 4th ed. N. Y., 1872. 16°. 8362
Hoppus, J. Account of Bacon's Novum Organon. Lond. [1829.] 8°. 16468
The Continent in 1835. Lond., 1836. 2 v. 12°. . . . 16587
Horace. Works, transl. by Francis. N. Y., 1835–44. 2 v. 12°. . 4525
The same. N. Y., 1835–40. 2 v. 12°. 4546
for English Readers. Martin. Philad., 1871. 16°. 76
Horace in London. [H. and J. Smith.] Lond., 1815. 12°. . . 14887
Hordynski, J. Hist. of the Polish Revolution. Bost., 1833. 8°. . 16167
Horne, G. Commentary on Psalms. With Memoir by W. Jones. Lond., 1836. 3 v. 16°. 9510
Horne, R. H. New Spirit of the Age. (2 copies.) N. Y., 1844. 16°. 3423

Horne, T. H. A Protestant Memorial. N. Y., 1844. 12°. . . . 17279
Horne Tooke, J. See TOOKE.
Horner, F., Memoirs of. Edinb., 1849. 16°. 6691
Horner, S. A Century of Despotism in Naples and Sicily. Edinb., 1860. 16°. 4592
Horry, P., and **Weems, M. L.** Life of Marion. Philad., 1839. 12°. . 16395
Horse, The. Youatt. Lond., 1842. 12°. 16951
Adventures in search of a. [Stephens.] Philad., 1836. 12°. . 10169
Art of taming. Rarey. Lond., 1862. 16°. 10168
Hist. of the. Martin. Lond., 1845. 12°. 8782
See, also, STABLE ; SPORTS.
Horse Shoe Robinson. Kennedy. Philad., 1836. 2 v. 12°. . . 15718
Hortense, Queen. A Novel. [Mundt.] N. Y., 1870. 8°. . . . 3076
Horton, R. G. Life of Buchanan. N. Y., 1856. 12°. . . . 7332
Hosack, J. Mary Queen of Scots and her Accusers. 2d ed. Edinb., 1870–73. 2 v. 8°. 5240
Hospital Sketches. Alcott. Bost., 1863. 12°. 6106
Hot Corn. Robinson. N. Y., 1854. 12°. 15722
Hottentot Fables and Tales. Bleek. Lond., 1864. 8°. . . . 1891
Hours at Home. N. Y., 1865–70. 11 v. 8°. 13397
The same. v. 4, 5, 7. 13408
House of Commons, Random Recollections of. Grant. Philad., 1836. 12°. 4845
of Lords, Random Recollections of. Grant. Philad., 1836. 12°. 4846
I live in, The. Alcott. Bost., 1837. 12°. 9126
on the Moor, The. [Oliphant.] N. Y., 1861. 12°. . . . 2514
of the Seven Gables, The. Hawthorne. Bost., 1860. 16°. . 2888
Housekeeper, Recollections of a. [Gilman.] N. Y., 1836. 12°. . 15766
Household Words. Ed. Dickens. Lond. and N. Y., 1850–59. v. 1–4, 15, 16, 18. 8°. 17497
The same. v. 1. 17496
Chapters reprinted from : or, Home and Social Philosophy. N. Y., 1862. 2 v. 12°. 3353
Housman, R. F. Collection of English Sonnets. (2 copies.) Lond. [1835.] 12°. 1093
Houssaye, A. Philosophers and Actresses. N. Y., 1852. 2 v. 12°. 3737
Houston, S., Life of. N. Y., 1855. 12°. 7328
Houstoun, *Mrs.* Texas and the Gulf of Mexico. Philad., 1845. 12°. 16881
Howard, E. Jack Ashore. Philad., 1840. 2 v. 12°. . . . 2437
Outward Bound. Philad., 1838. 2 v. 12°. 2439
Howard, G. Lady Jane Grey, and her Times. Lond., 1822. 8°. . 5209
Howard, H. (*Earl of Surrey.*) Poems. Ed. Arber. Lond., 1870. 16°. 3895
Poet. Works, with Memoir. Bost., 1854. 16° 1052
Select Poems, with Life. Ed. Sanford. Philad., 1819. 24°. . 1
Howe, H. Hist. Collections of the Great West. Cincinn., 1851. 8°. 16145
Howe, John. Theological Treatises. With Memoir by T. Taylor. Lond., 1835. 16°. 9502
Works, with Memoirs by Calamy. N. Y., 1838. 2 v. 8°. . 10065
Howe, Julia W. From the Oak to the Olive. Bost., 1868. 16°. . 8207

Howe, R., Life of. Barrow. Lond., 1838. 8°. 6849
Howe, S. G. Hist. of the Greek Revolution. 2d ed. N. Y., 1828. 12°. 4560
Howell, J. Instructions for Forreine Travell, ed Arber. Lond., 1869. 16°. 3892
Howells, W. D. Italian Journeys. Bost., 1872. 12°. . . . 10238
Their Wedding Journey. Bost., 1872. 12°. 2952
Venetian Life. 2d ed. N. Y., 1867. 8°. 8212
Howison, J. European Colonies. Lond., 1834. 2 v. 8°. . . 4711
Howison, R. R. Hist. of Va. Philad., 1846–48. 2 v. 8°. . . 5898
Howitt, M. Ballads and other Poems. N. Y., 1847. 12°. . . 1168
The same. N. Y., 1848. 12°. 1167
Birds and Flowers, etc. Bost., 1839. 16°. 14799
Heir of Wast-Wayland. N. Y., 1851. 12°. 15445
Strive and Thrive. Bost., 1840. 12°. 15591
Wood Leighton. N. Y., 1847. 8°. 2313
The same. Philad., 1837. 3 v. 12°. 15635
Howitt, R. Impressions of Australia. Lond., 1845. 16°. . . 7985
Howitt, W. Book of the Seasons. 6th ed. Lond., 1840. 16°. . 8797
Colonization and Christianity. Lond., 1858. 12°. . . . 15886
Country Year Book. N. Y., 1850. 12°. 16978
German Experiences. 2d ed. Lond., 1844. 16°. . . . 8220
Homes of British Poets. (2 copies.) N. Y., 1847. 2 v. 12°. . 6600
Land, Labor and Gold; or, Two Years in Victoria. Bost., 1855. 2 v. 12°. 7986
Popular Hist. of Priestcraft. 7th ed. Lond., 1845. 16°. . . 6331
Rural and Domestic Life of Germany. Philad., 1843. 8°. . 8050
The same. 8310
Rural Life of England. (2 copies.) Lond., 1840. 8°. . . 5260
Student-Life of Germany. Philad., 1842. 8°. 9397
Traditions of Ancient Times. Lond., 1839. 2 v. 12°. . . 1893
Visits to Remarkable Places. 2d ed. Lond., 1840. 8°. . . 8353
Woodburn Grange. Philad. 12°. 15638
Howleglass. Transl. by Roscoe. (German Novelists.) Lond., 1826. 12°. 1895
Hows, J. W. S. Golden Leaves from Amer. Poets. N. Y., 1865. 12°. 687
from Brit. Poets. N. Y., 1865. 12°. 1099
from Dramatic Poets. N. Y., 1865. 12°. 1403
Hoyt, J. G. Miscellaneous Writings. Bost., 1863. 12°. . . . 3656
Hubbard, F. M. Life of W. R. Davie. (Sparks, v. 25.) Bost., 1848. 16°. 7274
Huber, F. Nat. Hist. of Bees. Lond., 1841. 12°. 8893
Huber, V. A. The English Universities. Ed. Newman. Lond., 1843. 2 v. in 3. 8°. 9283
Huc, E. R. Journey through the Chinese Empire. N. Y., 1857. 2 v. 12°. 7946
Recollections of Journey through Tartary, Thibet, and China. Condensed transl. by Mrs. Sinnott. N. Y., 1852. 2 v. 16°. 7915
Travels in Tartary, Thibet, and China. Tr. by Hazlitt. 3d ed. Lond., 1856. 8°. 7945
Hudson, C. F. Doctrine of a Future Life. 2d ed. Bost., 1858. 12°. 9911
Hudson, F. Journalism in the U. S. N. Y., 1873. 8°. . . . 10209
Hudson, Henry, Life of. Cleveland. Bost., 1839. 16°. . . . 7259

Hudson, Henry N. Lectures on Shakspeare. (2 copies.) N. Y., 1848. 2 v. 12°. 1549
Shakespeare: his Life, Art, and Characters. Bost., 1872. 2 v. 12°. 1490
Hudson River, Legends and Poetry of the. N. Y., 1868. 12°. . . 8228
Letters about the. [Hunt.] N. Y., 1836. 12°. . . . 16849
Hudson's Bay, Voyage to, 1812. McKeevor. Lond., 1819. 8°. . 8052
Hughes, *Mrs.* Memoir of Mrs. Hemans. Philad, 1839. 12°. . . 6940
Hughes, John. Select Poems. With Life, by Sanford. Philad., 1819. 24°. 10
The same. Ed. Johnson. Dubl., 1804. 8°. . . . 15098
Siege of Damascus. (Brit. Drama, v. 1.) Lond., 1804. 8°. . 1629
Hughes, *Abp.* **John.** Discussion with Breckenridge. Philad., 1836. 8°. 9606
Hughes, Thos. Alfred the Great. Lond. 8°. 5134
Scouring of the White Horse. Bost., 1859. 12°. . . . 2444
Tom Brown at Oxford. Lond., 1870. 8°. 9245
The same. Bost., 1870. 2 v. 8°. 9243
Tom Brown's School Days at Rugby. (2 copies.) Bost., 1864–70. 8°. 9241
Hughes, Thos. S. Hist. of England, 1760–1835. Paris, 1836. 5 v. 8°. 5374
Hugo, V. M. The Destroyer of the Second Republic, Napoleon the Little. N. Y., 1870. 12°. 5547
Hans of Iceland. N. Y., 1862. 8°. 2635
L'Homme qui rit. N. Y., 1869. 8°. 9735
The Man who laughs. (2 copies.) N. Y., 1869. 8°. . . 2642
Les Misérables, transl. by C. E. Wilbour. (3 copies.) N. Y., 1862–63. 8°. 2636
The Rhine. N. Y., 1845. 12°. 8365
William Shakespeare. Lond., 1864. 8°. 1582
Slave-King. Lond., 1833. 16°. 2390
Toilers of the Sea. (2 copies.) N. Y., 1866. 8°. . . . 2640
Les Travailleurs de la Mer. Brux., 1866. 8°. 2639
Life of. By his Wife. (2 copies.) N. Y., 1863–64. 8°. . . 7728
Huguenot, The: a Tale. James. N. Y., 1839. 2 v. 12°. . . . 15217
Galley-Slave, The. Marteilhe. N. Y., 1867. 12°. . . . 6355
and Priest. Bungener. Bost., 1856. 2 v. 12°. . . . 2647
Huguenots in England and Ireland, The. Smiles. Lond., 1867. 8°. 6430
in France and America, The. [Mrs. Lee.] Cambr., 1843. 2 v. 12°. 6353
Hist. of, in the 16th Century. Browning. Lond., 1829. 2 v. 8°. 6485
1598–1838. Browning. Paris, 1839. 8°. . . . 6487
See, also, FRANCE.
Hull, T. Henry II. (Mod. Theatre, v. 9.) Lond., 1811. 12°. . . 1335
Hull, W. Defence of himself. Bost., 1814. 12°. 6024
Humboldt, A. v. Cosmos. Lond. and N. Y., 1849–68. 5 v. 12°. . 8960
Letters to Varnhagen. N. Y., 1860. 12°. 7764
Views of Nature. (2 copies.) Lond., 1850. 8°. . . . 8841
Travels and Researches of. Macgillivray. Lond., 1852. 8°. . 8439
Humbugs of N. Y. Reese. N. Y., 1838. 12°. 17103
of the World, The. Barnum. N. Y., 1865. 12°. . . . 17104
Hume, D. Hist. of England. (2 copies.) Bost., 1849–50. 6 v. 12°. 4892
The same, abridged and continued to 1858. (2 copies.) ("The Student's Hume.") N. Y., 1862–63. 12°. . . . 4904

Hume, D. Hist. of England. Continued by Smollett. Lond., 1825. v. 3, 5–13. 8°. 5379
The same, continued by Smollett and Hughes. Paris, 1835–36. v. 2–15. 8°. 5365
The same, continued by Smollett and Miller. Philad., 1836–37. 4 v. 8°. 5389
Philosophical Essays. (2 copies.) Georgetown, 1817. 2 v. 8°. 3399
Works. Edinb., 1826. 4 v. 8°. . . . 8735

CONTENTS.—1, Life. 1, 2, Treatise of Human Nature. 2, Dialogues on Natural Religion. 3, Essays. 4, Inquiry concerning the Understanding; Inquiry concerning Morals; Nat. Hist. of Religion; Additional Essays.

Life of. By himself. Lond., 1829. 12°. 6640
Life of. Smellie. Edinb., 1800. 8°. 7138
Life and Correspondence of. Burton. Edinb., 1846. 2 v. 8°. 7128
Humor and Pathos. Baxter. Lond., 1842. 12°. 4264
Humorist, The. Hook. Philad., 1837. 12°. 4256
Humorists, English, of 18th century. Thackeray. Lond., 1872. 8°. 2198
Humphrey, H. Great Brit., France, and Belgium. N. Y., 1838. 2 v. 12°. 16549
Letters to a Son in the Ministry. Amh., 1842. 12°. 9917
The same. N. Y., 1845. 12°. 17034
Miscellaneous Discourses, etc. Amh., 1834. 12°. 17359
Humphreys, D. Life of Putnam. N. Y., 1815. 12°. 16431
The same. N. Y., 1835. 12°. 16432
The same. Bost., 1818. 12°. 7538
Miscellaneous Works. (2 copies.) N. Y., 1790–1804. 8°. . 14595
Humphry Clinker. Smollett. N. Y., 1860. 12°. 1965
Hungary in 1835. Paget. Lond., 1839. 2 v. 8°. 16617
in 1851. Brace. N. Y., 1852. 12°. 8316
and Kossuth. Tefft. Philad., 1852. 12°. 5815
Revolution in, 1849. Pragay. N. Y., 1850. 12°. 5816
and its Revolutions [to 1853; with Memoir of Kossuth.] Lond., 1854. 8°. 422
Hunt, C. H. Life of E. Livingston. N. Y., 1864. 8°. 7457
Hunt, F. Letters about the Hudson R. N. Y., 1836. 12°. . . 16849
Hunt, H. Bits of Travel. Bost., 1872. 12°. 8167
Hunt, L. Autobiography. Lond., 1870. 8°. 7047
Book for a Corner. N. Y., 1852. 12°. 3228
Byron and Contemporaries, etc. 2d ed. Lond., 1828. 2 v. 8°. 7187
The same. Philad., 1828. 8°. 7189
Correspondence. Lond., 1862. 2 v. 8°. 7048
A Day by the Fire, etc. Bost., 1870. 16°. 3171
Imagination and Fancy. (2 copies.) N. Y., 1845. 12°. . . 1234
The Indicator and Companion. (2 copies.) N. Y., 1845. 2 v. in 1. 12°. 3226
Men, Women, and Books. (2 copies.) N. Y., 1847. 2 v. 12°. 3229
Poetical Works. (2 copies.) Lond., 1832. 8°. 1257
Rimini and other Poems. Bost., 1844. 16°. 1220
The Seer. Bost., 1865. 2 v. 16°. 3168
The same. v. 1. 3170

Hunt, L. Stories from Italian Poets. (2 copies.) N. Y., 1846. 3 pts. in 1. 12°. 887
Wit and Humor. N. Y., 1847. 12°. 1234
and **Lee, S, A.** Book of the Sonnet. Bost., 1867. 2 v. 16°. . 294
Hunt, R. The Poetry of Science. Bost., 1850. 12°. 16993
Hunt, Thornton. The Foster-Brother. N. Y., 1846. 8°. . . . 2686
Hunt, Timothy D. Past and Present of the Sandwich Isl. S. Francisco, 1853. 16°. 16303
Hunter, T. Reflections on Letters of Lord Chesterfield. Lond., 1777. 8°. 17044
Hunter, W. P. Expedition to Syria. Lond., 1842. 2 v. 12°. . . 5160
Hunting Grounds, Adventures on. Meunier. N. Y., 1869. 12°. . 10120
Huntington, S. S. H., *Countess of,* Life and Times of. Lond., 1844. 2 v. 8°. 7678
Huntington, F. D. Christian Believing and Living. Bost., 1860. 12°. 9976
Home and College. Bost., 1860. 16°. 9185
Huntington, G. The Shadowy Land, and other Poems. N. Y., 1861. 8°. 15060
Huntington, J. V. The Forest. N. Y., 1852. 12°. 15698
Huntley, L. See *Mrs.* L. H. SIGOURNEY.
Hunt's Merchants' Magazine. N. Y., 1839–59. v. 1–5, 8–13, 20–40. 8°. 13525
Hurd, J. C. Jurisprudence of Freedom and Bondage. N. Y., 1856. 8°. 9282
Hurd, R. Letters on Chivalry and Romance; Dialogues on Travel. Lond., 1762. 8°. 15932
Moral and Polit. Dialogues, etc. 3d ed. Lond., 1765. 3 v. 16°. 15844
Hurdis, J. Lectures on Poetry. Bishopstone, 1797. 4°. . . . 15083
Hurst, J. F. Hist. of Rationalism. N. Y., 1865. 8°. . . . 6519
Huskisson, W. Select Speeches. Ed. Walsh. Philad., 1837. 8°. . 9367
Speeches, with Memoir. Lond., 1831. 3 v. 8°. . . . 9364
Huss, J., Life and Times of. Gillett. Bost., 1863. 2 v. 8°. . . 6509
Husson, ——. Report on Magnetical Experiments. Bost., 1836. 12°. 8526
Hutchinson, Anne, Life of. Ellis. Bost., 1845. 16°. . . . 7265
Hutchinson, J., Memoirs of. By his Widow. Lond., 1808. 4°. . 6911
The same. (Bohn's ed.) 2 copies. Lond., 1846. 8°. . 367
Hutchinson, T. Hist. of Mass., 1628–1750. 3d ed. Bost., 1795. 2 v. 8°. 5836
Hutton, C. Oakwood Hall. Philad., 1819. 2 v. 12°. . . . 15529
Hutton, R. H. Essays. Lond., 1871. 2 v. 8°. 3708
Huyshe, G. L. The Red River Expedition. Lond., 1871. 8°. . . 8396
Huxley, T. H. Lay Sermons, Addresses, and Reviews. N. Y., 1871. 12°. 8941
Man's Place in Nature. N. Y., 1863. 12°. 8939
More Criticisms on Darwin, and Administrative Nihilism. N. Y., 1872. 12°. 8942
Origin of Species. N. Y., 1863. 12°. 8940
Hyacinthe, *Père.* See C. LOYSON.
Hyde, E., *Lord* Clarendon. Essays. Bost., 1820. 16°. . . . 3843
The same. Lond., 1815. 2 v. 12°. 3530
Hist. of the Rebellion. (2 copies.) Bost., 1827. 6 v. 8°. . 5340
Life of. Campbell. (Ld. Chancellors, v. 3.) Lond., 1845. 8°. 6868
The same. Lister. Lond., 1837–38. 3 v. 8°. . . 6846

Hyder Ali, Life of. Robson. Lond., 1786. 8°. 16414
Hydrostatics, Treatise on. Lardner. Lond., 1836. 16°. . . . 6044
Hymns, National. White. N. Y., 1861. 8°. 925
Hypatia. C. Kingsley. Bost., 1859. 12°. 2564
Hyperion. Longfellow. Bost., 1853. 16°. 2723

I.

I says, says I. A Novel. Bost., 1812. 12°. 15459
Ianthe. *(Pseudonym.)* See Mrs. EMBURY.
Icebergs with a Painter, After. Noble. N. Y., 1862. 12°. . . 8112
Iceland, Hist. and Description of. [Russell.] N. Y., 1841. 12°. . 11606
Journey to, 1845. Pfeiffer. N. Y., 1852. 12°. 8200
Letters on, 1772. von Troil. Lond., 1780. 8°. 16596
Residence in, 1814–15. Henderson. Edinb., 1819. 8°. . . 8293
Visit to, 1834. Barrow. Lond., 1835. 12°. 8292
A Winter in, 1834–35. Dillon. Lond., 1840. 8°. . . . 8290
See, also, EDDA ; SCANDINAVIA.
Icon Basilike. [Gauden.] Lond., 1824. 12°. 4906
Ida May. [Pike.] Bost., 1855. 12°. 15723
Idle Man, The. [Dana.] N. Y., 1821. 8°. 15303
Word, The. Goulburn. N. Y., 1866. 12°. 9817
Idler, The. Ed. Ferguson. Lond., 1823. 12°. 3127
Essays illustrating. Drake. Lond., 1809–10. 2 v. 8°. . . 3236
If, Yes, and Perhaps. Hale. Bost., 1868. 16°. 2945
Iffland, A. W. Conscience. (German Theatre, v. 5.) Lond., 1811. 12°. 1360
Ihne, W. Hist. of Rome. Lond., 1871. 2 v. 8°. 4729
Iliad, The. See HOMER.
of the East ; Selections from the Ramayana. Lond., 1870. 8°. 1906
Illicini, B. Novel. (Ital. Novelists, v. 2.) Lond., 1836. 12°. . . 1900
Imagination and Fancy ; Selections from English Poets. Hunt. N. Y., 1845. 12°. 1234
Imitation of Christ, The. Thomas à Kempis. Bost., 1861. 12°. . 9947
in the Fine Arts, Essays on. Quatremère de Quincy. Lond., 1837. 8°. 9071
Imitations of Celebrated Authors. H. and J. Smith. Lond., 1844. 8°. 3258
Imlay, G. Description of Western N. America. Lond., 1792. 8°. . 16814
Immola, and the Two Milanese : Tragedies. 1835. 12°. . . . 1448
Immortality of the Soul, Discourses on. Richter. Bost., 1864. 8°. 3056
Impending Crisis of the South. Helper. N. Y., 1857. 12°. . . 8574
Improvisatore, The. Andersen. N. Y., 1869. 8°. 2602
Inchbald, E. British Theatre. Lond. v. 11–13, 16–19, 23, 27. 12°. 1337
For Contents, see THEATRE.
Modern Theatre ; a Collection. Lond., 1811. v. 2–10. 12°. . 1328
For Contents, see THEATRE.
The Mourning Ring. N. Y., 1821. 12°. 15516
Inchiquin. *(Pseudonym.)* See C. J. INGERSOLL.
Incognito, The. De Trueba y Cosio. N. Y., 1831. 2 v. 12°. . . 15142

India, Considerations on Polit. State of. Tytler. Lond., 1815. 2 v. 8°. 16446
Hist. of [to 1761]. Elphinstone. Lond., 1841. 2 v. 8°. . . 6500
977–1669. Ferishtah. Dubl., 1792. 3 v. 8°. . . 16448
Hist., etc., of. Rickards. Lond., 1829–32. 2 v. 8°. . . 6502
of Burmese War in, 1824–26. Snodgrass. Lond., 1827. 8°. 6504
Journeys through, 1824–26. Heber. Philad., 1828. 2 v. 8°. 8016
Letters from, 1828–31. Jacquemont. Lond., 1835. 2 v. 16°. 7911
Manners and Customs of. Dubois. Philad., 1818. 2 v. 8°. 16504
A Memoir of. Harlan. Philad., 1842. 12°. 6417
Origin of Burmese War in, 1851–52. Cobden. Lond., 1867. 8°. 9588
Popular Description of. Conder. Lond. 4 v. in 2. 12°. . 7841
Scenes and Characteristics of. Roberts. Philad., 1836. 2 v. 12°. 16502
Travels of a Hindoo in, 1845–66. Chunder. Lond., 1869. 2 v. 8°. 8018
Visit to, 1853. Bayard Taylor. N. Y., 1855. 12°. 8283
Ancient, Disquisition concerning. Robertson. Dubl., 1791. 8°. 16451
and Modern. Allen. Bost., 1856. 8°. 6559
British, and the Decline of Hindooism. Campbell. Lond., 1839. 8°. 16498
Hist of. Martin. Lond., 1835. 8°. 16116
[to 1805.] Mill. Lond., 1826. 6 v. 8°. . . 6464
and Description of. Murray, etc. N. Y., 1840. 3 v. 12°. 11267
Lectures on. Thompson. Pawtucket, 1840. 12°. . 16500
See, also, East Indies.

Indian Archipelago. See Malay Archipelago.
Biography of N. A. Thatcher. N. Y., 1840. 2 v. 12°. . . 12104
Sketches, among the Pawnees. Irving. Philad., 1835. 2 v. 12°. 5752
Wars of U. S. Moore. Philad., 1840. 12°. 5747
1675–1704, Hist. of. Church. Hartf'd. [1845.] 8°. . 5957

Indians of N. Amer., Book of. Frost. Hartf'd., 1852. 12°. . . 5746
Essays, on Condition of. [Evarts.] Bost., 1829. 8°. . . . 5895
Notes on Manners, etc., of. Catlin. N. Y., 1844. 2 v. 8°. . 5948
Researches respecting. Schoolcraft. N. Y., 1839. 2 v. 12°. 5755
into Origin and Hist. of. Bradford. N. Y., 1843. 8°. 5954
Sketches of. Buchanan. N. Y., 1824. 2 v. in 1. 12°. . . 5749
Speeches on Removal of. Bost., 1830. 12°. 5754
Travels among. McKenney. N. Y., 1846. 2 v. in 1. 8°. . 5950
of Conn., Hist. of. De Forest. Hartf'd., 1851. 12°. . . 5847

Indicator, The. L. Hunt. N. Y., 1845. 12°. 3226

Industry of Nations, Treatise on. Eisdell. Lond., 1839. 2 v. 8°. 8661

Infidel, The: a Romance. [Bird.] Philad., 1835. 2 v. 12°. . . 15724

Infidelity, Cause and Cure of. Nelson. N. Y. 12°. . . . 9880
Counsels to Young Men on. Morison. N. Y. 12°. . . 17018
Difficulties of. Faber. Philad., 1829. 12°. 9912
Lives of Converts from. Crichton. Edinb., 1827. 2 v. 12°. . 4468
Sermons on. Thomson. Windsor, 1833. 12°. 17270

Ingelow, J. Monitions of the Unseen, and Poems of Love and Childhood. (2 copies.) Bost., 1871. 16°. . . . 1175

Ingelow, J. Off the Skelligs. Bost., 1872. 16°. 10297
Poems. Bost., 1863. 16°. 1173
The same. New ed. Bost., 1869. 16°. 1174
Studies for Stories. Bost., 1865. 16°. 2421
Ingersoll, C. J. Hist. of War of 1812. Philad., 1845. v. 1. 8°. . 5990
Inchiquin's Letters. N. Y., 1810. 8°. 6227
Remarks on a Review of. [Dwight.] Bost., 1815. 8°. 16810
Ingham Papers, The. Hale. Bost., 1869. 16°. 2947
Inglis, H. D. Journey through Norway, etc. Edinb., 1829. 12°. . 4500
Rambles in Footsteps of Don Quixote. Philad., 1840. 12°. . 16680
Spain in 1830. Lond., 1831. 2 v. 8°. 8450
Ingoldsby Legends. Barham. Philad., 1844. 12°. 4255
[**Ingraham, J. H.**] The American Lounger. Philad., 1839. 12°. . 15657
Initials, The. Tautphoeus. Philad. 12°. 2505
Innisfoyle Abbey. Moriarty. Lond., 1840. 3 v. 12°. . . . 15460
Innocents Abroad, The. Mark Twain. Hartf'd., 1869. 8°. . . 4285
Inquisition Unmasked, The. Puigblanch. Lond., 1816. 2 v. 8°. . 6426
of Spain, Hist. of. Llorente. Lond., 1826. 8°. . . . 6425
Insanity, Man's power to control. Barlow. Philad., 1847. 12°. . 8496
Shakspeare's Delineations of. Kellogg. N. Y., 1866. 16°. . 1482
Insect Architecture, Ravages, etc. Rennie. Lond., 1845. 2 v. 12°. 8793
Miscellanies. [Rennie and Westwood.] Bost., 1832. 12°. . 8816
Transformations. [Rennie and Westwood.] Bost., 1831. 12°. 8810
World, The. Figuier. Lond., 1868. 8°. 8999
Insects, Nat. Hist. of. [Rennie and Westwood.] N. Y., 1840. 2 v. 12°. 11007
See, also, ZOOLOGY.
Inspiration of the Scriptures. Gaussen. N. Y., 1842. 12°. . . 9981
Instinct in Animals and Men. Chadbourne. N. Y., 1872. 12°. . 8946
Dialogues on. Brougham. Lond., 1844. 12°. 8488
Insurance, Probabilities in. De Morgan. Lond., 1838. 16°. . . 6043
Intellectual Qualities, Transmission of. N. Y., 1843. 12°. . . 8530
Powers, Inquiries concerning the. Abercrombie. N. Y., 1841. 12°. 11041
Intemperance, Essay on. Grindrod. N. Y., 1840. 12°. . . . 16967
Lectures on. L. Beecher. (Works, v. 1.) Bost., 1852. 12°. . 12753
Plea for. Reese. N. Y., 1841. 12°. 9122
See, also, DRUNKENNESS; TEMPERANCE.
Interest. See USURY.
Intermarriage. Walker. N. Y., 1839. 12°. 16959
International Law, Elements of. Wheaton, ed. Dana. Bost., 1866. 8°. 8704
Introd. to. Woolsey. N. Y., 1864. 8°. . . 8702
Principles of. Bentham. (Works, pt. 8.) Edinb., 1839. 8°. 9707
Inventions, Hist. of. Beckmann. Lond., 1846. 2 v. 8°. . . . 354
The same. Williams. Lond., 1820. 2 v. 8°. . . 4105
Ionian Islands, Hist., etc., of. Martin. Lond., 1837. 16°. . . . 7902
Visit to, 1836. Giffard. Lond., 1837. 12°. . . 16647
Irby, C. L., and **Mangles, J.** Travels in Egypt, etc. Lond., 1844. 16°. 8197

Ireland. A Tale. Martineau. Bost., 1833. 12°. 14616
Biogr. Dict. of Worthies of. Ryan. Lond., 1821. 2 v. 8°. . 6876
The English in, in 18th century. Froude. N. Y., 1873. v. 1. 12°. 10233
Hist. of [to 1545]. T. Moore. Lond., 1837-40. 3 v. 16°. . 5176
[to 1700]. Mac Geoghegan. N. Y. 8°. 5411
to 1801. Gordon. Lond., 1806. 2 v. 8°. . . . 5412
to 1803. Taylor. N. Y., 1841. 2 v. 12°. . . . 12107
Journals, Essays, etc., relating to. Senior. Lond., 1868. 2 v. 8°. 5245
Legends of Wars in. Joyce. Bost., 1870. 16°. . . . 2366
Scenery, Character, etc., of. Hall. Lond., 1841-43. 3 v. 8°. . 8441
social, polit., and religious. Beaumont. Lond., 1839. 2 v. 12°. 5419
Songs of. Croker. Lond., 1839. 12°. 1204
State of, to 1652. Clarendon. (Hist., v. 6.) Bost., 1827. 8°. . 5345
State of, to 1801. Plowden. Philad., 1805-06. 5 v. 8°. . . 5414
Tour in, 1805. Carr. N. Y., 1807. 12°. 16770
Tour round, in 1835. Barrow. Lond., 1836. 12°. . . . 8307
Travels in, 1843. Kohl. N. Y., 1844. 8°. 1670
Views of. O'Driscol. Lond., 1823. 2 v. 8°. 16744
[**Ireland, W. H.**] Memoirs of Henry the Great. Lond., 1824. 2 v. 8°. 5538
of Jeanne d'Arc. Lond., 1824. 2 v. 8°. . 5534
Irish Bar, Sketches of the. Shiel. N. Y., 1858. 2 v. 12°. . . 6744
Bulls, Essay on. Edgeworth. (Works, v. 2.) Bost., 1824. 8°. . 15336
character, etc., Observations on. Dewar. Lond., 1812. 8°. . 16746
Sketches of. Mrs. Hall. N. Y., 1829. 12°. . . 15583
Confederates, The, and the Rebellion of '98. Field. N. Y., 1851. 12°. 5243
Eloquence, Specimens of. Phillips. N. Y., 1820. 8°. . . 9427
Life, Lights and Shadows of. Mrs. Hall. Philad., 1838. 2 v. 12°. 15487
Realities of. Trench. Lond., 1869. 8°. 5252
Nation, Rise and Fall of. Barrington. N. Y., 1860. 12°. . . 5253
Peasantry, Traits and Stories of. Carleton. Lond., 1836. 5 v. 16°. 2017
Rebellion of 1798, Narrative of. Cloney. Dubl., 1832. 8°. . 5244
The same. Jones. Cambr. 12°. 5242
Sketch Book of 1842. Thackeray. Lond., 1872. 8°. . . . 2195
Irishmen, The United. Madden. [1st Series.] Philad., 1842. 2 v. 12°. 5247
The same. 3d Series. Dubl., 1846. 3 v. 12°. . . 5249
Proceedings of Dublin Society of. Philad., 1795. 12°. . . 16063
Iron and Steel Manufactures. Holland. (v. 1, 2.) Lond., 1831-33. 2 v. 16°. 6037
Iron Cousin, The. M. C. Clarke. N. Y., 1862. 12°. 15463
Irvine, W. Letters on Sicily. Lond., 1813. 8°. 16714
Irving, D. Lives of Scotish Writers. Edinb., 1839. 2 v. in 1. 12°. . 6714
Irving, E. Orations, for the Oracles of God, for Judgment to come, and for Missionaries. N. Y., 1825. 8°. 9969
Life of. Oliphant. N. Y., 1862. 8°. 7739
Irving, J. T. Indian Sketches. Philad., 1835. 2 v. 12°. . . . 5752
Irving, T. Conquest of Florida. (2 copies.) Philad., 1835. 2 v. 12°. 5728
Irving, W. Adventures of Capt. Bonneville in Rocky Mts., etc. Philad., 1837. 2 v. 12°. 8404
The same. (2 copies.) N. Y., 1850-51. 12°. . . . 8406

Irving, W. The Alhambra. N. Y., 1863. 12°. 4363
The same. Philad., 1872. 12°. 4364
Astoria. N. Y., 1850. 12°. 8403
The same. Philad., 1836. 2 v. 8°. 8424
Biogr. of M. M. Davidson. 2d ed. Philad., 1841. 12°. . . 770
Bracebridge Hall. (2 copies.) N. Y., 1850. 12°. 4361
Conquest of Granada. (2 copies.) N. Y., 1860–68. 12°. . . 6406
Crayon Miscellany. N. Y., 1850. 12°. 4367
The same. Philad., 1835. 3 v. 12°. 4243

CONTENTS.—1, Tour on the Prairies. 2, Abbotsford and Newstead Abbey. 3, Legends of the Conquest of Spain.

The same. v. 2, 3. 4246
Goldsmith: a Biography. (2 copies.) N. Y., 1851–60. 12°. . 6995
Knickerbocker's Hist. of N. Y. N. Y., 1824. 2 v. 12°. . 4239
The same. Philad., 1834. 2 v. 12°. 4237
The same. Philad., 1835. 2 v. in 1. 12°. 4356
The same. Revised ed. N. Y., 1850. 12°. . . . 4357
Letters of Jonathan Oldstyle. N. Y., 1824. 8°. 16779
Life and Voyages of Columbus. (2 copies.) N. Y., 1828. 3 v. 8°. 7807
The same. N. Y., 1831. 2 v. 8°. 7813
The same. (2 copies.) N. Y., 1850–51. 3 v. 12°. . 7816
The same, abridged. N. Y., 1829. 12°. 7554
The same. Bost., 1839. 12°. 7587
Life and Select Writings of Goldsmith. N. Y., 1840. 2 v. 12°. 11596
Life of Washington. (2 copies.) N. Y., 1856–59. 5 v. 12°. . 7283
Mahomet and his Successors. (2 copies.) N. Y., 1859–60. 2 v. 12°. 7577
The same. N. Y., 1850–68. 2 v. 12° and 16°. . . 7581
Sketch Book of Geoffrey Crayon. Philad., 1834. 2 v. 12°. . 4241
The same. (2 copies.) N. Y., 1851–53. 12°. . . . 4358
The same. Philad., 1871. 12°. 4360
Spanish Papers and Miscellanies. (2 copies.) N. Y., 1866. 2 v. 12°. 4368
Voyages of Companions of Columbus. Philad., 1831. 8°. . 7815
Wolfert's Roost, etc. (2 copies.) N. Y., 1855–61. 12°. . . 4365
Life and Letters of. P. M. Irving. (2 copies.) N. Y., 1864. 4 v. 12°. 7376

Isabel. *(Pseudonym.)* See W. G. SIMMS.

Isabella and Elizabeth, Review of Prescott's comparison of. Bost., 1841. 12°. 16164
See, also, FERDINAND.

Isaiah, Notes on. Barnes. N. Y., 1851. 2 v. 12°. 9856

Israel, Land of. Keith. N. Y., 1844. 12°. 16275

Israel Potter. Melville. N. Y., 1855. 12°. 15726

Italian Art, Wonders of. Viardot. N. Y., 1870. 12°. . . . 10122
Brigands. Moens. N. Y., 1866. 12°. 8347
Journeys, 1864–65. Howells. Bost., 1872. 12°. . . . 10238
Life and Legends. Ritchie. N. Y., 1870. 12°. . . . 8342
Note-Books, Passage from (1858–59). Hawthorne. Bost., 1872. 2 v. 12°. 8203
Novelists, transl. by Roscoe. Lond., 1836. 4 v. 12°. . . 1899
For Contents, see ROSCOE.
Poets, see POETS.

Italy, Travels in, in 16th Century. Ducas. Lond., 1822. 2 v. 8°. 16733
[1786-87]. Goethe. Lond., 1849. 8°. 445
1803. Chateaubriand. Lond., 1828. 8°. . . . 16899
1812-13. Lullin de Châteauvieux. Lond., 1819. 8°. 8051
View of Society and Manners in, 177-. J. Moore. (Works, v. 2.) Edinb., 1820. 8°. 17318
Views in, 1815-16. Friedländer. Lond., 1821. 8°. . . . 8055
under Victor Emmanuel. Arrivabene. Lond., 1862. 2 v. 8°. . 4777
Visit to, 1841-42. Mrs. Trollope. Lond., 1842. 2 v. 8°. . 8339
Ancient, Mythology of. Keightley. Lond., 1838. 8°. . . 4425
Ivanhoe. Scott. Edinb., 1871. 8°. 1877
Ives, C. Chips from the Workshop. N. H., 1843. 12°. . . . 15001
Ivimey, J. Milton. N. Y., 1833. 12°. 6952

J.

Jack, Colonel, Life of. De Foe. Edinb., 1810. 2 v. 16°. . . . 4164
Jack Adams. Chamier. Philad., 1839. 2 v. 12°. 15466
Jack Ashore. Howard. Philad., 1840. 2 v. 12°. 2437
Jack Tier. Cooper. N. Y., 1848. 12°. 2832
Jackson, A. Messages. Concord, 1837. 12°. 6023
Messages, etc. (Statesman's Manual.) N. Y., 1854. 8°. . 6201
Life of. Parton. N. Y., 1861. 3 v. 12°. 7318
The same, condensed. N. Y., 1863. 12°. . . . 7321
Memoirs of. Waldo. Hartf'd., 1819. 12°. 16394
Pictorial Life of. Frost. Hartf'd., 1847. 8°. 7425
Jackson, D. Alonzo and Melissa. Hartf'd., 1853. 16°. . . . 15656
Jackson, J. R. What to Observe. Lond., 1841. 12°. . . . 8952
Jackson, T. Curiosities of the Pulpit. N. Y. [1868.] 16°. . . 9831
Jacksonism, Review of. N. Y., 1835. 12°. 6016
Jacob, Lectures on Hist. of. Blunt. Philad., 1869. 12°. . . . 17353
Jacob Faithful. Marryatt. N. Y., 1835. 12°. 15110
Jacobinism, Hist of. Barruel. N. Y., 1799. 4 v. 8°. . . . 16201
See, also, FRANCE.
Jacqueline of Holland. Grattan. N. Y., 1831. 2 v. 12°. . . . 15469
Jacquemont, V. Letters from India. 2d ed. Lond., 1835. 2 v. 16°. 7911
Jacquerie, The. James. N. Y., 1842. 12°. 15204
Jahn, J. Biblical Archæology, ed. Upham. 3d ed. N. Y., 1832. 8°. 10015
Jamaica in 1850. Bigelow. N. Y., 1851. 12°. 8547
Past and Present of. Phillippo. Philad., 1843. 8°. . . 16921
Tour through, 1823. Williams. Lond., 1827. 8°. . . . 16920
See, also, WEST INDIES.
James I, of England. Essayes, in Poesie; Counterblaste to Tobacco. Ed. Arber. Lond., 1869. 16°. 3892
Character of. I. Disraeli. (Misc., v. 3.) N. Y., 1841. 12°. . 3393
Court of. Goodman. Lond., 1839. 2 v. 8°. 5298
Memoirs of. Aikin. Bost., 1822. 2 v. 8°. . . 5300
The same. Jesse. Philad., 1840. 12°. . 5211

James I., Life of. Harris. Lond., 1814. 8°. 5304
James II., Hist. of part of reign of. Fox. Lond., 1846. 8°. . . . 338
Memoirs of Court of. Jesse. Philad., 1840. 12°. 5214
James, G. P. R. The Ancient Régime. N. Y., 1841. 2 v. 12°. . 15213
Attila. N. Y., 1837. 2 v. 12°. 15211
Blanche of Navarre, a Play. N. Y., 1839. 12°. 1449
Corse de Leon. Lond., 1841. 3 v. 8°. 15224
Dark Scenes of History. N. Y., 1850. 12°. 4573
Darnley. N. Y., 1830. 2 v. 12°. 15219
The Desultory Man. N. Y., 1836. 2 v. 12°. 15209
Forest Days. N. Y. 8°. 2323
Gentleman of the Old School. N. Y., 1839. 2 v. 12°. . . 15215
The Gipsy. N. Y., 1836. 2 v. in 1. 12°. 2088
The same. 15223
The same. N. Y., 1864. 12°. 2163
Henry of Guise. N. Y., 1839. 2 v. 12°. 15205
Hist. of Charlemagne. N. Y., 1841. 12°. 11280
The same. N. Y., 1833. 12°. 12110
The same. N. Y., 1837. 12°. 12111
of Chivalry. N. Y., 1840. 12°. 11022
The same. (2 copies.) N. Y., 1831. 12°. 11947
of Edward the Black Prince. 2d ed. Lond., 1839. 2 v. 16°. 5131
of Richard Cœur-de-Lion. N. Y., 1842. 2 v. 12°. . . 5129
The same. (Bohn's ed.) Lond., 1854. 2 v. 8°. . . 365
The Huguenot. N. Y., 1839. 2 v. 12°. 15217
The Jacquerie. N. Y., 1842. 2 v. 12°. 15202
The same. 2 v. in 1. 15204
The King's Highway. (2 copies.) N. Y., 1840. 2 v. 12°. . 15198
Life of Henry IV. of France. N. Y., 1850. v. 1. 12°. . . 5537
of John Marston Hall. N. Y., 1834. 2 v. 12°. . . 15151
of Louis XIV. (Bohn's ed.) Lond., 1851. 2 v. 8°. . 375
Lives of de Retz, Colbert, de Witt, and de Louvois. Philad., 1837. 2 v. 12°. 7613
Margaret Graham. N. Y., 1847. 8°. 2313
Mary of Burgundy. N. Y., 1833. 2 v. 12°. 2086
Memoirs of Great Commanders. Philad., 1835. 2 v. 12°. . 6699
Old Oak Chest. N. Y., 1850. 8°. 2309
One in a Thousand. N. Y., 1836. 2 v. in 1. 12°. . . . 15221
Richelieu. N. Y., 1833. 2 v. 12°. 2044
The same. N. Y., 1835. 2 v. 12°. 2160
The same. N. Y., 1860. 2 v. in 1. 12°. 2162
The Robber. N. Y., 1838. 2 v. 12°. 15207
Rose d'Albert. N. Y. 8°. 2312
Russell. N. Y., 1847. 8°. 2322
String of Pearls. N. Y., 1833. 12°. 15222
A Whim, and its Consequences. N. Y., 1848. 8°. . . . 2324
and others. Lives of Eminent Foreign Statesmen. Lond., 1833–38, 5 v. 16°. 5766

CONTENTS.—1, (by E. E. Crowe) Amboise; Ximenes; Leo X.; Cardinal Granvelle, and Maurice of Saxony; Barneveldt; Sully; Duke of Lerma; Duke of Ossuno; Lorenzo de' Medici. 2,

Richelieu; Oxenstiern; Olivarez; Mazarin. 3, de Retz; Colbert; John de Witt; Marquis de Louvois. 4, de Haro; Cardinal Dubois; Alberoni; Duke of Ripperda. 5, Fleury; Zinzendorf; Marquis of Pombal; Count of Florida Blanca; Duke of Choiseul; Necker.

James H. Substance and Shadow. 2d ed. Bost., 1866. 8°. . . . 9985
James, J. A. The Anxious Enquirer. N. Y., 1834. 12°. 17293
The Christian Professor. N. Y., 1838. 12°. 17349
Young Man from Home. N. Y. 12°. 17056
Young Man's Friend. (2 copies.) N. Y., 1852. 12°. . . . 9144
James, J. Travels in Sicily, Italy and France. Albany, 1820. 12°. . 16730
James, M. Elder Sister. N. Y., 1855. 12°. 15419
Ethel. N. Y., 1855. 12°. 15429
James, W. Military Occurrences of the late War. (2 copies.) Lond., 1818. 2 v. 8°. 5868
Naval Occurrences of the late War. Lond., 1817. 8°. . . . 5872
Jameson, A. Beauties of Court of Chas. II. Philad., 1834. 8°. . 6907
Characteristics of [Shakspeare's] Women. N. Y., 1833. 12°. . 1486
The same. Bost., 1866. 16°. 1487
Diary of an Ennuyée. Philad., 1826. 12°. 16722
Handbook to Public Galleries. Lond., 1842. 2 v. 12°. . . 8874
Memoirs and Essays. N. Y., 1846. 12°. 3954
The same. 8368
of Female Sovereigns. N. Y., 1845–48. 2 v. 12°. . 11037
The same. N. Y., 1832. 2 v. 12°. 12095
Romance of Biography; or, Women loved by Poets. 3d ed. Lond., 1837. 2 v. 8°. 6709
The same. 16311
Sacred and Legendary Art. Bost., 1865. 2 v. 16°. . . . 8854
Visits and Sketches at home and abroad, with Tales, and Diary of an Ennuyée. N. Y., 1834. 2 v. 12°. 8318
Winter Studies and Summer Rambles in Canada. N. Y., 1839. 2 v. 12°. 16773
Jamieson, A. Grammar of Rhetoric. N. H., 1821. 12°. . . . 17531
Jamieson, R. Eastern Manners and the Gospels. Edinb., 1837. 12°. 9841
Jane Bouverie. Sinclair. N. Y., 1851. 12°. 15471
Jane Eyre. Brontë. N. Y., 1872. 12°. 2549
Jane Lomax. [Horace Smith.] Philad., 1838. 2 v. 12°. . . . 15472
Jane Talbot. C. B. Brown. Bost., 1827. 12°. 15300
Janin, J. G. The American in Paris. N. Y., 1844. 8°. . . . 16699
Janney, S. M. Life of G. Fox. Philad., 1853. 8°. 6825
Janus. The Pope and the Council. (2 copies.) Bost., 1870. 16°. . 9514
Japan, Elgin's Mission to, 1857–59. Oliphant. Edinb., 1859. 2 v. 8°. 8006
Hist., etc., of. Dickson. Edinb., 1869. 8°. 6505
Narrative of Perry's Exped. to, 1852–54. Hawks. N. Y., 1857. 8°. 8135
in our day. Ed. Bayard Taylor. N. Y., 1872. 12°. 10177
Our Life in (1866–67). Jephson and Elmhirst. Lond., 1869. 8°. 8011
Ten Weeks in (1860). G. Smith. Lond., 1861. 8°. 8012
Three Years in, 1859–62. Alcock. N. Y., 1863. 2 v. 12°. . 7952
Visit to, 1853. Bayard Taylor. N. Y., 1855. 12°. 8283

Japan, Voyage to, 1775–76. Thunberg. (Travels, v. 3, 4.) Lond., 1795. 8°. 16263
Old, Tales of. Mitford. Lond., 1871. 2 v. 8°. 2005
Japanese in America, The. Lanman. N. Y., 1872. 12°. 7955
Manners and Customs of the. Lond., 1841. 12°. 7954
The same. N. Y., 1841. 12°. 11607
Japhet in Search of a Father. Marryat. Philad., 1835. 2 v. 12°. . 2090
[**Jardine, D.**] Criminal Trials. Bost., 1832. v. 1. 12°. 8820
Jarves, J. J. The Art-Idea. N. Y., 1864. 16°. 8861
Art Studies. N. Y., 1861. 8°. 9067
Art Thoughts. (2 copies.) N. Y., 1869. 12°. 8888
Hist. of Sandwich Islands. Bost., 1843. 8°. 6506
Why and What am I? Confessions of an Inquirer. Bost., 1857. 12°. 15680
Java, Hist. of (to 1811). Raffles. Lond., 1830. 2 v. 8°. 6496
Illustrations to the same. Lond., 1844. 4°. . . . . .
Voyage to, 1816. Hall. Lond., 1840. 8°. 8101
Jay, J., Life of. Flanders. Philad., 1855. 8°. 7473
W. Jay. N. Y., 1833. 2 v. 8°. 7363
Renwick. N. Y., 1841. 12°. 11604
Jay, W. Inquiry into Colonization and Anti-Slavery Societies. 3d ed. N. Y., 1835. 12°. 8549
Life of John Jay. N. Y., 1833. 2 v. 8°. 7363
Jeaffreson, J. C. Annals of Oxford. Lond., 1871. 2 v. 8°. . . . 9287
Book about the Clergy. 2d ed. Lond., 1870. 2 v. 8°. . . 6456
about Doctors. N. Y., 1862. 12°. 8988
about Lawyers. 2d ed. Lond., 1867. 2 v. 8°. . . 9218
Not Dead Yet. N. Y., 1864. 8°. 2332
Jeanne d'Arc. See JOAN of Arc.
Jefferson, T. Manual of Parliamentary Practice. Philad., 1840. 12°. 8474
Messages, etc. (Statesman's Manual, v. 1.) N. Y., 1854. 8°. 6200
Notes on Virginia. Bost., 1829. 12°. 5743
Character of, from his Writings. Dwight. Bost., 1839. 12°. 7224
Domestic Life of. Randolph. N. Y., 1871. 12°. 7351
Lecture on. Theodore Parker. Bost., 1870. 12°. 7409
Life of. Randall. N. Y., 1858. 3 v. 8°. 7440
Rayner. Bost., 1834. 12°. 7223
Tucker. Philad., 1837. 2 v. 8°. 7345
Memoir, Correspondence, and Miscellanies, ed. Randolph. 2d ed. (2 copies.) Bost., 1830. 4 v. 8°. 9636
Memoirs of. [Carpenter.] N. Y., 1809. 2 v. 8°. 7349
Private Life of. Pierson. N. Y., 1862. 8°. 7443
Jeffrey, F. Contributions to the Edinb. Review. N. Y., 1864. 4 v. in 1. 8°. 3463
The same. Lond., 1844. v. 2–4. 8°. 3464
Life of. Cockburn. Philad., 1852. 2 v. 12°. 7014
Jeffreys, *Judge* **G.,** Life of. Campbell. (Ld. Chancellors, v. 3.) Lond., 1845. 8°. 6868

Jeffreys, *Judge* **G.** Memoirs of. Woolrych. Lond., 1829. 8°. . 6757
Jenkin, C. Madame de Beaupré. N. Y., 1869. 12°. 2423
Jenkins, E. The Coolie. N. Y., 1871. 12°. 6470
Ginx's Baby. N. Y., 1871. 12°. 8541
Jenkins, J. S. Life of Calhoun. Auburn. [1850.] 12°. . . . 7330
of Polk. Auburn. [1850.] 12°. 7331
of S. Wright. Auburn, 1850. 12°. . . . 7329
Jenkinson, R. B. (*Earl of* Liverpool), Public Life of. Lond., 1827. 8°. 6783
Jenner, E., Life of. Baron. Lond., 1838. 2 v. 8°. 7160
Jenyns, S. Poetical Works. Ed. Bell. Lond., 1807. 24°. . . 541
Select Poems. Ed. Walsh. Philad., 1822. 24°. . . . 26
Works. Dubl., 1790. 2 v. 8°. 13252
Jephson, R. Law of Lombardy; Braganza. (Mod. Theatre.) Lond., 1811. 12°. 1332
Jephson, R. M., *and* **Elmhirst, E. P.** Our Life in Japan. Lond., 1869. 8°. 8011
Jericho, Going to. Swift. N. Y., 1868. 12°. 8240
Jerningham, E. Poems. Lond., 1767. 12°. 14828
Jeronimo; Part 1. (Old Plays, v. 3.) Lond., 1825. 8°. . . . 1510
Jerrold, D. Chronicles of Clovernook. Lond., 1846. 16°. . . 4251
Hist. of St. Giles and St. James. N. Y., 1845. 8°. . . . 2321
Men of Character. N. Y. 12°. 4254
Mrs. Caudle's Curtain Lectures. N. Y., 1867. 16°. . . . 4253
Punch's Complete Letter Writer. Lond., 1845. 16°. . . 4250
Specimens of Wit of. Bost., 1858. 16°. 4252
Jerrold, W. B. The Disgrace to the Family. Lond., 1848. 8°. . 2453
Jersey Prison-Ship, Recollections of the. Dring. Prov., 1829. 12°. 16121
Jesse, J. H. Court of England under the Stuarts, etc. Lond., 1840. 2 v. 8°. 5296
The same (with continuation). Philad., 1840. 4 v. 12°. 5211
Jesse, W. Life of Brummell. Philad., 1844. 8°. 6826
Jest Book. Lemon. Cambr., 1865. 16°. 4276
Jesuit Juggling. Baxter. N. Y., 1835. 12°. 9580
Missions in N. America, Early. Kip. N. Y., 1847. 12°. . 6098
Hist. of the. Poynder. Lond., 1816. 2 v. 8°. . . . 6423
The same. Steinmetz. Philad., 1848. 2 v. 8°. . . 6421
A Night with the. Farrenc. N. Y., 1853. 12°. . . . 17258
in N. America, in the 17th century, The. Parkman. Bost., 1868. 12°. . . . . , ... 6132
Provincial Letters exposing the. Pascal. N. Y., 1828. 12°. . 9586
at Rome, Mornings among the. Seymour. N. Y., 1849. 12°. 9582
Travels of the. Lockman. Lond., 1762. 2 v. 8°. . . . 16324
A Year among the English. Steinmetz. N. Y., 1846. 12°. . 17274
See, also, LOYOLA; ROMAN CATHOLIC.
Jesus Christ, Character of. Bushnell. N. Y., 1861. 16°. . . . 9804
Life of. Andrews. N. Y., 1862. 8°. 9907
The same. Beecher. N. Y., 1871. v. 1. 8°. . . 6539
The same. Eddy. Springf'ld., 1870. 8°. . . . 6541
The same. Ellicott. Bost., 1862. 12°. 6420

Jesus Christ, Life of. Neander. N. Y., 1848. 8°. 6537
The same. Renan. N. Y., 1869. 12°. 9894
The same. Jer. Taylor. Lond., 1835. 3 v. 16°. . . 9504
and Doctrine of. (Ecce Deus.) [Parker.] Bost., 1867. 16°. 9905
and Work of. Crosby. N. Y., 1871. 8°. 6593
The same. (Ecce Homo.) [Seeley.] Bost., 1866. 16°. 9902
Modern Representatives of Life of. Uhlhorn. Bost., 1868. 16°. 9898
See, also, CHRIST.
Jew, The. A Novel. Spindler. N. Y. 8°. 2312
Jewett, I. A. Passages in Foreign Travel. Bost., 1838. 2 v. 12°. . 16560
Jewett, Mrs. S. W. From Fourteen to Fourscore. N. Y., 1871. 12°. 15699
Jewish Church, Hist. of the. Stanley. N. Y., 1866–67. 2 v. 8°. . 6533
Jews, Antiquities of the. Josephus. Philad., 1841. 2 v. 8°. . . 4407
Hist. of the. Ed. by Berk. Bost., 1844. 12°. 6301
The same. Enlarged ed. Bost., 1847. 12°. . . . 6302
The same. Milman. N. Y., 1864. 3 v. 8°. . . . 6303
in Spain and Portugal. Finn. Lond., 1841. 12°. 6300
Jewsbury, M. J. Three Histories. Bost., 1831. 12°. . . . 15604
Joan of Arc. De Quincey. (Miscellanies, v. 3.) Edinb., 1858. 8°. 3276
[a Novel.] Serle. Lond., 1841. 3 v. 12°. 15474
[a Poem.] Southey. Lond., 1838. 16°. 633
The Maid of Orleans: a Drama. Schiller. Lond., 1847. 8°. . 438
Life of. Parr. Lond., 1866. 2 v. in 1. 16°. 5536
Memoirs of. [Ireland.] Lond., 1824. 2 v. 8°. 5534
The same. Ed. G. P. R. James. Philad., 1839. 12°. . 6701
Trial of. (Celebrated Trials, v. 1.) Lond., 1825. 8°. . . . 9220
Joanna of Naples. A Tale. Park. Bost., 1838. 12°. 2731
Job, Notes on. Barnes. N. Y., 1847. 2 v. 12°. 9852
Jobsiad, The. Kortum. Philad., 1863. 12°. 870
Jocelin. Life of St. Patrick. Philad., 1823. 12°. 16339
Jocelyn, *Lord.* Six Months with the Chinese Expedition. 4th ed. Lond., 1841. 16°. 7941
John, *St.*, Pupils of. Yonge. Lond. [1868.] 8°. 6316
See, also, BIBLE.
[**John, E.**] Countess Gisela. Philad., 1869. 12°. 3039
Gold Elsie. Philad., 1868. 12°. 3038
The Old Mam'selle's Secret. Philad., 1868. 12°. 3037
John Brent. Winthrop. Bost., 1862. 12°. 2857
John Bull and Brother Jonathan. Paulding. N. Y., 1835. 12°. . 15285
John of Gaunt, Adventures of. J. White. Dubl., 1790. 2 v. 12°. . 15477
John Godfrey's Fortunes. Bayard Taylor. N. Y., 1864. 12°. . . 2936
John Halifax, Gentleman. Mrs. Craik. N. Y., 1872. 12°. . . 2482
John Marston Hall. G. P. R. James. N. Y., 1834. 2 v. 12°. . . 15151
Johnson, A. J. Illustrated Family Atlas. N. Y., 1866. 4°. . .
Johnson, C. Hist. of the Pirates. Norwich, 1814. 12°. . . . 16323
Johnson, G. W. Memoirs of Selden. Lond., 1835. 8°. 7212
Johnson, J. Economy of Health. N. Y., 1837. 12°. 9123
Johnson, Richard M. Biography of. N. Y., 1833. 12°. . . . 16435
Johnson, R. Introd. to Study of Hist. Lond., 1772. 12°. . . . 15923

Johnson, S. History of Rasselas. Lond., 1838. 16°. 2385
The Idler. Lond., 1823. 16°. 3127
Irene. (Brit. Drama.) Lond., 1804. 8°. 1630
Lives of the Poets. Lond., 1831. 16°. 6598
Lives and Works of Brit. Poets. Dubl., 1804. 8 v. 8°. . . 15095

CONTENTS.—1, Lives. 2, Cowley, Denham, Milton, Butler, Rochester, Roscommon, Otway, Waller, Pomfret, C. Sackville, Stepney, J. Philips, Walsh. 3, Dryden, E. Smith, Duke, King, Sprat, Montagu. 4, Garth, Rowe, Addison, Hughes, Sheffield, Prior, Congreve, Fenton. 5, Granville, Yalden, Tickell, Hammond, Somerville, Savage, Swift, Broome, Parnell. 6, Pope. 7, E. Moore, Cawthorne, Collins, Dyer, Shenstone, Mallet, Akenside, Gray, Lyttleton, Gay. 8. Churchill, Falconer, Lloyd, Young, Thomson.

Poetical Works. Lond., 1789. 16°. 14829
The same. Ed. Bell. Lond., 1807. 24°. 543
The Rambler. Lond., 1823. 3 v. 12°. 3124
Select Poems. Ed. Walsh. Philad., 1822. 24°. 25
Sermons. Bost., 1820. 16°. 3846
Table-Talk. Lond., 1798. 8°. 3759
Works. Dubl., 1793. 6 v. 8°. 3748

CONTENTS.—Essay on his Life and Genius, by Murphy; Poems; Philological Tracts; Political and Miscellaneous Essays. 2, Greek Comedy, etc.; Observations on Macbeth; Papers from the Adventurer; Rasselas. 2, 3, The Rambler. 4, The Idler; Essays; Political Tracts; Journey to Western Islands of Scotland. 5, 6, Lives of English Poets. 6, Lives of Eminent Persons; Letters; Prayers.

The same. v. 1, 3–6. 3754
The same. Lond., 1816. v. 1, 2, 4–11. 12° . . . 3828

CONTENTS.—1, Life; Poems. 2, Philological Tracts; Political Essays. 4–6, The Rambler. 7, The Idler. 8, Miscellaneous Essays; Journey to the Hebrides; etc. 9–11, The Lives of the English Poets. 12, Lives of Eminent Persons; Letters; Prayers.

Life of. Boswell, ed. Croker. N. Y., 1837. 2 v. 8°. . . 7209
The same. Hawkins. Dubl., 1787. 8°. . . . 7122
to his 11th year. By himself. Lond., 1805. 16°. . . 6925
Life and Select Writings of. Ed. Page. N. Y., 1844. 2 v. 12°. 11433
The same. N. Y., 1841. 2 v. 12°. 12126
Literary Life of. Drake. Lond., 1809. 8°. 3236
Tour to the Hebrides with. Boswell. Philad., 1810. 8°. . 8354
Johnsoniana. Ed. Croker. Philad., 1842. 12°. 3760
The same. 6924
Johnston, J. F. Chemistry of Common Life. N. Y., 1863. 2 v. 12°. 8948
Johnstone, Mrs. Elizabeth de Bruce. N. Y., 1827. 2 v. 12°. . . 15420
Joinville, J. *de*. Memoirs of Louis IX. (2 copies.) Lond., 1848. 8°. 512
Joly, G. and **C.** Memoirs. Lond., 1775. 3 v. 12°. 7498
Jomini, H. *de*. Hist. of Campaign of Waterloo. N. Y., 1860. 12°. . 5572
Jonathan Wild. Fielding (v. 4). Lond., 1871. 8°. 1979
Jones, B. Life of Faraday. Philad., 1870. 2 v. 8°. 7156
Jones, G. Sketches of Naval Life. N. H., 1829. 2 v. 12°. . . 16272
Jones, James A. Haverhill. N. Y., 1831. 2 v. 12°. . . . 15720
Jones, J. Narrative of the Irish Rebellion. Camb. 12°. . . . 5242
Jones, John. Attempts in Verse. Ed. Southey. Lond., 1831. 16°. 305
Jones, John Paul, Life of. Cooper. (Naval Biog.) Philad., 1846. 12°. 7276
The same. Mackenzie. N. Y., 1846. 2 v. 16°. . . 7536
The same. Sherburne. Wash., 1825. 8°. . . . 7360
and Correspondence of. N. Y., 1830. 8°. 7361
Memoirs of, from his Journals. Lond., 1843. 2 v. in 1. 12°. . 7535
Jones, L. Memoir of Mrs. Taylor. N. Y., 1847. 12°. . . . 7525

Jones, P. My Uncle Hobson and I. N. Y., 1845. 12°. 15751
Jones, Samuel. Treatise on Right of Suffrage. Bost., 1842. 12°. . 8537
[**Jones, Stephen.**] Hist. of Poland. Dubl., 1795. 8°. 16054
Jones, *Sir* **Wm.** Poetical Works, with Life. Lond., 1810. 2 v. 12°. 14830
Select Poems. Ed. Walsh. Philad., 1822. 24°. 29
Memoirs of. Teignmouth. Philad., 1805. 8°. 7146
[**Jones, Rev. Wm.**] Observations in Journey to Paris. Lond., 1777. 2 v. 16°. 8188
Jones, Wm. Hist. of England, under Geo. III. Lond., 1825. 3 v. 8°. 4985
Jones, *Rev.* **Wm.** Hist. of the Christian Church. Philad., 1832. 8°. 16466
Jones, Wm. Biogr. Sketches of Reform Ministers. Lond., 1832. 8°. 5330
The same, in 2 v. 5331
Jonson, B. Works. Lond., 1716. 6 v. 12°. 1420
The same, with Memoir by B. Cornwall. Lond., 1842. 8°. 1607
Jortin, J. Life of Erasmus. Lond., 1808. 3 v. 8°. 7687
Joseph II., and his Court. A Novel. [Mundt.] N. Y., 1867. 8°. . 3084
Joseph Andrews. Fielding. (v. 5.) Lond., 1871. 8°. 1980
Joseph and his Friend. A Story. B. Taylor. N. Y., 1870. 12°. . 2939
Joseph Noirel's Revenge. Cherbuliez. N. Y., 1872. 12°. . . . 2392
Joséphine, Empress. Correspondence with Napoléon. N. Y., 1856. 12°. 5447
Historical Sketch of. N. Y., 1867. 8°. . . . . . .
Hist. of. Abbott. N. Y. [1851.] 16°. 5450
Memoirs of. Le Normand. Philad., 1848. 2 v. 12.° . . 5448
The same. Memes. N. Y., 1834. 12°. 11030
Josephus. Works, transl. by L'Estrange. Philad. and N. Y., 1773–75. 4 v. 8°. 15964
transl. by Whiston. N. Y., 1824. 6 v. 12°. . 15968
The same. Philad., 1841. 2 v. 8°. . . . 4407
Joshua, Notes on. Bush. N. Y., 1844. 12°. 9850
Joshua Marvel. Farjeon. Bost., 1871. 8°. 2335
Jouffroy, T. S. T. Introd. to Ethics, tr. by Channing. Bost., 1840. 2 v. 12°. 8586
Philosophical Miscellanies, tr. by Ripley. Bost., 1838. 2 v. 12°. 8584
Journalism, British, Hist. of. Andrews. Lond., 1859. 2 v. 8°. . 5273
in the U. S., 1690–1872. Hudson. N. Y., 1873. 8°. . . 10209
See, also, NEWSPAPERS.
Joyce, R. D. Legends of Wars in Ireland. Bost., 1870. 16°. . . 2366
Juan, G., and **Ulloa, A. de.** Voyage to S. America. Lond., 1772. 2 v. 8°. 17125
Judæa capta. Charlotte Elizabeth. N. Y., 1845. 12°. . . . 14916
Judah's Lion. Charlotte Elizabeth. N. Y., 1843. 12°. . . . 15166
Judd, S. Margaret. Bost., 1845. 12°. 2953
Philo. Bost., 1850. 12°. 15002
Judges, Notes on. Bush. N. Y., 1844. 12°. 9851
Judges, Atrocious, Lives of. Campbell, ed. Hildreth. N. Y., 1856. 12°. 6759
See, also, CHIEF JUSTICES.
Judicial Establishments, *etc.* See BENTHAM'S Works.
Judiciary, Debates in U. S. Senate on the. Philad., 1802. 8°. . . 9353
Judson, Adoniram, Memoir of. Wayland. Bost., 1853. 2 v. 12° . 7638

Judson, Amos M. The Wanderer and other Poems. Philad., 1859. 12°. 15003
Judson, Ann H., Memoir of. Knowles. Bost., 1829. 12°. . . . 16421
Judson, E. C. Alderbrook. Bost., 1850. 2 v. 12°. 15650
Judson, S. B., Memoir of. E. C. Judson. N. Y., 1849. 12°. . . . 7524
Jukes, J. B. Excursions in Newfoundland. Lond., 1842. 2 v. 12°. 16777
Julia de Roubigné. Mackenzie. N. Y., 1837. 12°. 1992
Julian: or, Scenes in Judea. Ware. N. Y., 1841. 2 v. 12°. . . . 2864
Julian Home. Farrar. N. Y., 1866. 12°. 2428
Junius, Letters of. N. Y., 1821. 2 v. 12°. 6635
The same. Bost., 1826. 2 v. 12°. 6637
The same. With additional Letters. Philad., 1836. 2 v. 8°. 6854
The same. Ed. by Wade. Lond. (Bohn), 1855–68. 2 v. 8°. 464
Posthumous Works. With Sketch of Horne Tooke. N. Y., 1829. 8°. 6859
Enquiry regarding the Author of. Coventry. Lond., 1825. 8°. 6857
Essay on. Waterhouse. Bost., 1831. 8°. 6858
Identity of with [Sir P. Francis]. Taylor. N. Y., 1818. 8°. . 6856
Junkin, G. Political Fallacies. N. Y., 1863. 12°. 6105
Junot, L. P. Memoirs of Napoleon. N. Y., 1860. 2 v. 8°. . . . 5543
Juries, Art of Packing. Bentham. (Works, pt. 5.) Edinb., 1838. 8°. 9704
Juvenal. Satires, transl. by Badham. N. Y., 1837. 12°. . . . 4539
Juventus Mundi. Gladstone. Lond., 1869. 8°. 4235

K.

Kalevala, Selections from the. Transl. by Porter. N. Y., 1868. 16°. 290
Kaloolah. Mayo. N. Y., 1849. 12°. 7984
Kames, *Lord.* See H. HOME.
Kamtschatka, Travels in, 1787–88. De Lesseps. Lond., 1790. 2 v. 8°. 16507
Kane, E. K. Arctic Explorations ; the Second Expedition in search of Franklin. (2 copies.) Philad., 1857. 2 v. 8°. . . 8107
U. S. Expedition in Search of Franklin. Philad., 1856. 8°. . 8106
Biogr. of. Elder. Philad., 1858. 8°. 7475
Kansas, The Englishman in, 1856. Gladstone. N. Y., 1857. 12°. . 16855
Life of. Robinson. Bost., 1857. 12°. 16856
Kant, I. Critick of Pure Reason. Lond., 1838. 8°. 8732
The Metaphysic of Ethics. Tr. by Semple. Edinb., 1836. 8°. 8733
Metaphysical Works, ed. Richardson. (2 copies.) Lond., 1836. 8°. 8730
Last Days of. De Quincey. (Miscellanies, v. 3.) Edinb., 1858. 8°. 3276
Life of. Stapfer. Edinb., 1836. 16°. 6633
Karr, A. The Alain Family. Lond., 1853. 8°. 2646
Kater, H. and **Lardner, D.** Treatise on Mechanics. Bost., 1831. 12°. 8825
The same. Lond., 1837. 16°. 6046
Kaulbach, W. Drawings of Female Characters of Goethe. N. Y. fol.
Kavanagh, J. Dora. N. Y., 1868. 8°. 2685
Women of Christianity. N. Y., 1852. 12°. 7568
Kay, J. Social Condition and Education of the English. N. Y., 1864. 12°. 5276

Kean, E., Life of. [Procter.] N. Y., 1835. 12°. 7927
Keary, A. and **E.** Heroes of Asgard. [2d ed.] Lond., 1871. 12°. . 1700
Keate, G. Sketches from Nature. 3d ed. Lond., 1782. 2 v. 12°. . 15245
Keats, J. Poetical Works, with Life. Bost., 1859. 16°. 1056
Life, Letters, etc., of. Milnes. N. Y., 1848. 12°. 7000
Keble, J. The Christian Year. [Ed. Doane.] Philad., 1834. 12°. . 1177
Miscellaneous Poems. N. Y., 1869. 16°. 1178
Memoir of. Coleridge. Oxf'd., 1869. 2 v. 8°. 7003
Keeler, R. Vagabond Adventures. Bost., 1870. 12°. 16258
Keese, J. Poets of America. N. Y., 1841–42. 2 v. 12°. 684
Keightley, T. The Crusaders. Lond., 1834. 2 v. 16°. 4585
Fairy Mythology. Lond., 1833. vol. 2. 16°. 1692
The same. Revised ed. Lond., 1860. (2 v. in 1.) 16°. 1892
Hist. of England. N. Y., 1840. 5 v. 12°. 11589
The same. 12267
The same. Ed. J. T. Smith. Bost., 1840. 2 v. 8°. . 5363
The same. Bost., 1840. 2 v. 12°. 4826
of the Roman Empire. Bost., 1841. 8°. 4750
Mythology of Greece and Italy. 2d ed. Lond., 1838. 8°. . 4425
Outlines of History. Lond., 1830. 16°. 4856
Tales and Popular Fictions. Lond., 1834. 12°. 1698
Keith, A. Land of Israel. N. Y., 1844. 12°. 16275
Signs of the Times. N. Y., 1832. 2 v. 12°. 17340
Kellogg, A. O. Shakspeare's Delineations of Insanity, etc. N. Y., 1866. 16°. 1482
Kellogg, E. Labor and other Capital. N. Y., 1849. 8°. 8623
Kelly, H. School for Wives. Lond., 1811. 12°. 1335
Kelly, M. Reminiscences. N. Y., 1826. 8°. 7995
Kelly, W. K. Hist. of Russia. (Bohn's ed.) Lond., 1854–55. 2 v. 8°. 420
Syria and the Holy Land. Lond., 1844. 8°. 8070
Kemble, C. Point of Honour. (Brit. Theatre, v. 27.) Lond. 12°. . 1345
Kemble-Butler, F. A. Journal [in the U. S.] Philad., 1835. 2 v. in 1. 12°. 16834
Journal on a Georgian Plantation. N. Y., 1863. 12°. . . 8408
Star of Seville. N. Y., 1837. 12°. 1442
The same. 1444
A Year of Consolation. N. Y., 1847. 2 v. in 1. 12°. . . 16548
Kemble, J. P. Memoirs of. Boaden. Philad., 1825. 8°. 7998
Kempis, Thomas à. See THOMAS.
Kendall, E. A. Travels in U. S. N. Y., 1809. 3 v. 12°. 16815
Kendall, G. W. Narrative of Texan Santa Fe Exped. N. Y., 1844. 2 v. 12°. 16903
Kenilworth. Scott. Edinb., 1870. 8°. 1883
Kenilworth Castle, Pageants at, 1575. Laneham. Philad., 1822. 12°. 4816
Kennan, G. Tent-Life in Siberia. N. Y., 1870. 12°. 8257
Kennedy, G. The Decision; Profession is not Principle; Father Clement. N. Y., 1829. 12°. 15410
Dunallan. Bost., 1827. 2 v. 12°. 15416
Kennedy, James. Conversations with Byron. (2 copies.) Philad., 1833. 12°. 6942

Kennedy, John P. Annals of Quodlibet. Philad., 1840. 12°. . . 4292
Horse Shoe Robinson. Philad., 1836. 2 v. 12°. . . . 15718
Memoirs of Wirt. Philad., 1850. 2 v. 8°. 7420
Rob of the Bowl. Philad., 1838. 2 v. 12°. 15771
Swallow Barn. Philad., 1832. 2 v. 12°. 15788
Kent, J. Commentaries on Amer. Law. 3d ed. N. Y., 1836. 4 v. 8°. 9356
The same. 4th ed. N. Y., 1840. 4 v. 8°. . . . 9360
Course of Reading. N. Y., 1840. 12°. 298
The same. Ed. King. N. Y., 1853. 12°. . . . 299
Kentucky, Hist. Sketches of. Collins. Cincinn., 1850. 8°. . . 5891
Kepler, J., Life of. [Bethune.] Lond., 1833. 8°. 6751
The same. Brewster. N. Y., 1841. 12°. . . . 11605
Keppel, G. Journey from India. 2d ed. Lond., 1827. 2 v. 8°. . 8035
Keppel, H. Expedition to Borneo. N. Y., 1846. 16°. . . . 8195
Kerr, Orpheus C. *(Pseudonym.)* See R. H. NEWELL.
Kett, H. Flowers of Wit. Hartf'd., 1825. 12°. 4284
Kettell, S. Specimens of Amer. Poetry. (2 copies.) Bost., 1829. 3 v. 12°. 678
Key, F. S. Poems. N. Y., 1857. 12°. 14938
Khalif Haroon Er-Rashid and Princess Zobéidéh. Lond., 1840. 12°. 15479
Kidd, J. Adaptation of Nature to Man. Philad., 1836. 8°. . . 16983
Kidder, D. P., and **Fletcher, J. C.** Brazil and the Brazilians. Philad., 1857. 8°. 8460
Killegrew, T. The Parson's Wedding. (Old Plays, v. 11.) Lond., 1827. 8°. 1518
Kimball, R. B. Cuba and the Cubans. N. Y., 1850. 12°. . . . 16917
Henry Powers, (Banker.) N. Y., 1868. 12°. 15716
Romance of Student Life Abroad. N. Y., 1862. 12°. . . 15784
Saint Leger. N. Y., 1862. 12°. 15773
In the Tropics. N. Y., 1863. 12°. 16895
Undercurrents. N. Y., 1862. 12°. 15806
[**Kimber, I.**] Life of Cromwell. Lond., 1724. 8°. 5225
King, C. Mountaineering in the Sierra Nevada. Bost., 1872. 8°. . 8401
King, J. A. 24 years in the Argentine Republic. N. Y., 1846. 12°. . 5736
King, *(Lord)* **P.** Life of Locke. Lond., 1830. 2 v. 8°. . . . 7126
King, T. Starr. Patriotism, and other Papers. Bost., 1864. 12°. . 3594
The White Hills. N. Y., 1870. 8°. 8392
King, Wm. (born 1663.) Poetical Works. Ed. Bell. Lond., 1807. 24°. 267
The same. Ed. Johnson. Dubl., 1804. 8°. . . . 15097
King, Wm., LL.D. (born 1685.) Anecdotes of his Times. Bost., 1819. 12°. 16377
Kinglake, A. W. Eōthen. N. Y., 1850. 12°. 8255
The same. N. Y., 1846. 12°. 8369
The same. Auburn, 1845. 12°. 7974
Invasion of the Crimea. (2 copies.) N. Y., 1863–68. 2 v. 12°. 4613
King's Highway, The. James. N. Y., 1840. 2 v. 12°. . . . 15198
King's Own. Marryat. N. Y., 1837. 12°. 2111
Kingsford, Jane. *(Pseudonym.)* [C. F. Barnard.] The Soprano. Bost. 12°. 3012
Kingsley, C. Alton Locke. (3 copies.) N. Y., 1850–61. 12°. . . 2560

Kingsley, C. Andromeda, and other Poems. Bost., 1858. 16°. . 1191
Glaucus. (2 copies.) Bost., 1855. 16°. 8836
Hereward. (2 copies.) Bost., 1866. 12°. 2571
The same. Lond., 1867. 8°. 2570
The Hermits. Philad., 1868. 8°. 6315
Hypatia. (2 copies.) Bost., 1859–64. 12°. 2564
The same. Leipzig, 1866. 2 v. 16°. 2373
At Last: Christmas in the W. I. Lond., 1871. 8°. . . . 8430
New Miscellanies. Bost., 1860. 12°. 3763
Poems. (2 copies.) Bost., 1856. 16°. 1189
Sir Walter Raleigh, etc. (2 copies.) Bost., 1859. 12°. . . 3761
Two Years Ago. Bost., 1857. 12°. 2569
Westward Ho! or, Sir Amyas Leigh. (2 copies.) Bost., 1857. 12°. 2567
The same. Lond., 1871. 8°. , ... 2566
Yeast. N. Y., 1864. 12°. 2563
Kingsley, H. Austin Elliot. Bost., 1863. 12°. 2575
Hetty. N. Y., 1869. 8°. 2330
The same. 2310
Leighton Court. (2 copies.) Bost., 1866. 12°. . . . 2576
Ravenshoe. (2 copies.) Bost., 1862–66. 12°. 2573
Stretton. (2 copies.) N. Y., 1869. 8°. 2329
Tales of Old Travel. Lond., 1869. 8°. 7940
Kingsley, J. L. Hist. Discourse at New Haven. N. H., 1838. 8°. . 5896
Life of Stiles. (Sparks, v. 16.) Bost., 1845. 16°. . . . 7265
Kingston, W. H. G. Lusitanian Sketches. Lond., 1845. 2 v. 12°. . 8452
Kip, W. I. Catacombs of Rome. N. Y., 1854. 12°. 6308
Christmas Holydays in Rome. N. Y., 1846. 12°. . . . 8351
Early Jesuit Missions to N. America. N. Y., 1847. 12°. . 6098
The same. N. Y., 1848. 12°. 17260
Kirby, W. Hist., Habits, etc., of Animals. Philad., 1837. 8°. . . 16984
Kirk, E. N. Sermons. N. Y., 1841. 12°. 17358
Kirk, J. F. Hist. of Charles the Bold. (2 copies.) Philad., 1864. 2 v. 8°. 5653
Kirke, Edmund. *(Pseudonym.)* See J. R. GILMORE.
Kirkland, C. M. Holidays abroad. N. Y., 1849. 2 v. 12°. . . 16566
A New Home. Who'll Follow? N. Y., 1839. 12°. . . 15752
Patriotic Eloquence. N. Y., 1866. 12°. 9325
Western Clearings. N. Y., 1846. 12°. 15812
Kirkland, S., Life of. Lothrop. (Sparks, v. 25.) Bost., 1848. 16°. . 7274
Kitchi-Gami. Kohl. Lond., 1860. 8°. 8421
Kitto, J. The Lost Senses. Lond., 1845. 2 v. 12°. 8486
Scripture Lands. (Bohn's ed.) Lond., 1850. 8°. 526
Klopstock, F. G. Odes, transl. by Nind. Lond., 1848. 16°. . . 291
and **M.,** Memoirs of. 2d ed. Bath, 1809. 8°. 7796
Klosterheim. De Quincey. Bost., 1855. 8°. 2559
Knapp, G. C. Lectures on Christian Theology. N. Y., 1831. 2 v. 8°. 10076
[**Knapp, J. L.**] Journal of a Naturalist. Philad., 1831. 12°. . . 8830
Knapp, S. L. Advice in Pursuits of Literature. N. Y., 1832. 12°. . 59
The same. 64
The Bachelors, and other Tales. N. Y., 1836. 12°. . . . 15662

Knapp, S. L. Biogr. Sketches. Bost., 1821. 8°. 7471
Female Biography. Philad., 1836. 12°. 16303
Memoir of Webster. Bost., 1831. 12°. 7308
Sketches of Public Characters. N. Y., 1830. 12°. . . . 16443
Tales of the Garden of Kosciusko. N. Y., 1834. 12°. . . 15797
Knickerbocker, The. N. Y., 1833–62. 59 v. 8°. 14457
The same. v. 2–5, 7, 8, 10–25, 27–30, 32, 35, 36, 38–41, 43–45, 47–66. 14640
Knickerbocker, Diedrich. *(Pseudonym.)* See W. IRVING.
Knight, C. W. Caxton: a Biography. Lond., 1844. 12°. . . . 6914
Half-Hours with the Best Authors. Lond., 1865–67. 2 v. 8°. 3764
The same. N. Y., 1848–49. v. 2–4. 8°. 3766
Half-Hours with Letter-Writers and Autobiographers. Lond., 1867. 8°. 3769
Hist. of England. (2 copies.) Lond. 8 v. 8°. 5049
London. Lond., 1841–44. 6 v. 8°. 5118
The same. 6 v. in 3. 8°. 5124
Penny Magazine. Lond., 1846–47. 2 v. in 1. 8°. 14597
Pictorial Hist. of England. See G. L. CRAIK.
A Volume of Varieties. Lond., 1844. 12°. 2379
[**Knight, Henry C.**] Letters from the South and West. By A. Singleton. Bost., 1824. 8°. 16779
Poems. 2d ed. Bost., 1821. 2 v. 12°. 14939
Knight, Henry G. Eastern Sketches. Lond., 1819. 16°. . . . 14800
Knight, R. P. Inquiry into Principles of Taste. Lond., 1808. 8°. . 17066
Knight, T. Honest Thieves. (Oxberry's Plays, v. 6.) Bost., 1822. 24°. 1350
Knight, W. Oriental Outlines. Lond., 1839. 16°. 8196
Knighton, *Sir* **W.,** Memoirs of. Lady Knighton. Philad., 1838. 8°. 6836
Knights and their Days. Doran. Lond., 1856. 8°. 5141
of Malta, Achievements of the. Sutherland. Philad., 1846. 12°. 4618
Templars, The. Addison. Lond., 1842. 8°. 4617
See, also, CHIVALRY; GARTER.
Knorring, A. v. The Peasant and his Landlord. N. Y., 1848. 12°. . 2658
Knowledge, Human, Treatise concerning the Principles of. Berkeley. Lond., 1837. 8°. 8759
Science of. Fichte. Philad., 1868. 12°. 8583
Knowles, James D. Memoir of Mrs. Judson. Bost., 1829. 12°. . 16421
Memoir of R. Williams. (2 copies.) Bost., 1834. 12°. . . 7548
Knowles, James S. Dramatic Works. Lond., 1841–43. 3 v. 12°. , 1432
The Love Chase. N. Y., 1838. 12°. 1441
The Magdalen, and other Tales. N. Y., 1835. 12°. . . . 15110
Select Dramatic Works. Balt., 1835. 12°. 1364
Select Works. Bost., 1833. 2 v. in 1. 16°. 1392
The same. Bost., 1836. v. 1. 12°. 1393
The Wife. Philad., 1833. 12°. 13356
Woman's Wit. N. Y., 1838. 12°. 1449
Knowles, John. Life of Fuseli. Lond., 1831. 3 v. 8°. . . . 9051
Knox, J. Hist. of Reformation in Scotland. Ed. McGavin. Glasg., 1832. 8°. 6478

Knox, J. Writings. Lond. 12°. 9480
Life of. McCrie. Edinb., 1839. 8°. 7702
Knox, V. Christian Philosophy. Ed. Stebbing. Lond., 1835. 16°. 9501
Essays. Ed. Ferguson. Lond., 1823. 3 v. 12° 3143
Liberal Education. 7th ed. Lond., 1785. 2 v. 12°. . . 9108
Winter Evenings. Ed. Ferguson. Lond., 1823. 3 v. 12°. . 3146
Koch, C. W. Hist. of Revolutions in Europe. Hartf'd., 1849. 8°. . 15858
The same. Edinb., 1828. 3 v. 12°. 4495
Kock, C. P. de. The Modern Cymon. Philad., 1833. 2 v. 12°. . 15137
Körner, C. T., Life of. By his Father. Lond., 1827. 2 v. 8°. . . 7797
Kohl, J. G. Ireland. N. Y., 1844. 8°. 1670
Kitchi-Gami. Lond., 1860. 8°. 8421
Russia and the Russians in 1842. Philad., 1843. 8°. . . 16615
Kohlrausch, F. Hist. of Germany. Lond., 1844. 8°. . . . 5874
The same. N. Y., 1845. 8°. 5875
Koningsmarke. Paulding. N. Y., 1838. 2 v. 12°. 15283
Koran, The. Transl. by Sale. Lond., 1825. 2 v. 8°. . . . 10032
Kortum, C. A. The Jobsiad, transl. by Brooks. Philad., 1863. 12°. 870
Kortz, J. Hist. of Eudoxia. Hudson, 1816. 12°. 16180
Kosciusko, Tales of the Garden of. Knapp. N. Y., 1834. 12°. . 15797
Kossuth, L. See HUNGARY.
Kotzebue, A. F. F. v. 7 Plays, transl. by Thompson. (German Theatre, v. 2–5.) Lond., 1811. 12°. 1357
Life of. By himself. Lond., 1830. 2 v. 12°. 6647
Kotzebue, O. v. Voyage of Discovery. Lond., 1821. 8°. . . 8056
Krasinski, V. Hist. of the Reformation in Poland. Lond., 1838–40. 2 v. 8°. 6454
Krilof, I. A., and his Fables. Ralston. Lond., 1869. 8°. . . . 2624
Kugler, F. T. Handbook of Painting: Italian Schools. Ed. Eastlake. Lond., 1869. 2 v. 8°. 9058
Kunst, P. J. English and German Dictionary. Harrisburg, 1847. 12°. 9619
Kuzzilbash, The. [Fraser.] N. Y., 1828. 2 v. 12°. 15481
Kyd, T. Cornelia, and the Spanish Tragedy. (Old Plays, v. 2, 3.) Lond., 1825. 8°. 1509

L.

L. E. L. See L. E. LANDON.
Labaume, E. Narrative of Campaign in Russia. Philad., 1815. 8°. 16190
Labor and other Capital. Kellogg. N. Y., 1849. 8°. . . . 8623
Essays on. Lieber. N. Y., 1841. 12°. 11748
See, also, WORK.
Laboulaye, E. Paris in America. N. Y., 1863. 12°. . . . 2649
Labrador, Summer Voyage to, 1859. Noble. N. Y., 1862. 12°. . 8112
Lackington, J., Memoirs of. By himself. Lond., 1830. 12°. . . 6656
Lackland, Thomas. *(Pseudonym.)* See G. C. HILL.
Laconics. Philad., 1829. 3 v. 12°. 13370
La Curne de Ste. Palaye, J. B. Memoirs of Chivalry. Lond., 1784. 8°. 4619

Ladd, J. B. Literary Remains. N. Y., 1832. 12°. 15007
Lady Audley's Secret. Braddon. N. Y. 8°. 2673
Lady of the Manor, The. Sherwood. N. Y., 1837. 4 v. 12°. . 15121
Lady Willoughby's Diary. [Rathbone.] N. Y., 1845. 12°. . . 2558
Lafayette, G. de M. de, Journey of, in America, 1824–25. Levasseur. Philad., 1829. 2 v. 12°. 16831
Memoirs of. Bost., 1824. 12°. 7594
The same. Hartf'd., 1825. 12°. 7592
The same. Ducoudray-Holstein. N. Y., 1824. 12°. . 7593
The same. Sarrans. Lond., 1832. 2 v. 8°. . . . 7724
Memoirs, Correspondence and MSS. of. N. Y., 1837. 2 v. 8°. 7726
Private Life of. Cloquet. N. Y., 1836. 2 v. 12°. . . . 7624
La Fontaine, J. de. Fables, tr. by Wright. Bost., 1843. 2 v. 12°. . 985
The same. Bost., 1841. v. 1. 8°. 1327
Laing, S. Notes of a Traveller in Europe. Philad., 1846. 8°. . . 16622
Residence in Norway. 2d ed. Lond., 1837. 8°. . . . 8301
Tour in Sweden. Lond., 1839. 8°. 8302
Lamartine, M. L. A. P. de. Fior d'Aliza. N. Y., 1868. 16°. . . 2347
Hist. of the Girondists. (2 copies.) N. Y., 1848–68. 3 v. 12°. 5557
The same. (Bohn's ed.) Lond., 1848–49. 3 v. 8°. . 382
Hist. of the Restoration. (Bohn's ed.) Lond., 1854. 4 v. 8°. 385
Memoirs of celebrated characters. (2 copies.) N. Y., 1854–56. 3 v. 12°. 6725

CONTENTS.—1, Nelson; Heloise; Columbus; Palissy; Roostam; Cicero. 2, Socrates; Jacquard; Joan of Arc; Cromwell; Homer; Gutenberg; Fenelon. 3, Tell; Mme. de Sevigne; Milton; Antar; Bossuet.

Pilgrimage to the Holy Land. Philad., 1835. 2 v. 12°. . . 8229
Lamb, Lady Caroline. Glenarvon. Philad., 1816. 2 v. 12°. . . 15441
Lamb, Charles. Eliana. Bost., 1864. 8°. 3979
Essays of Elia. Philad., 1828. 2 v. 12°. 3528
Last Essays of Elia. (Period. Libr., i.) Philad., 1833. 8°. . 15356
Letters, with Life by Talfourd. Lond., 1837. 2 v. 12°. . . 3970
The same, with Poems. N. Y., 1838. 12°. . . . 3972
Poetical Works. Lond., 1836. 16°. 632
The same. Philad., 1830. 8°. 947
The same. . . . . , ... 944
Prose Works. Lond., 1836. 3 v. 12°. 3967
Specimens of Engl. Dramatic Poets. Lond., 1813. 16°. . . 1402
The same. N. Y., 1845. 2 pts. in 1. 12°. 1436
Works. N. Y., 1871. 5 v. 12°. 3974

CONTENTS.—1, 2, Life, Letters, and Final Memorials, by Talfourd. 3, Elia. 4, Rosamond Gray; Essays; Letters, from the Reflector; Mr. H——; Poems. 5, Eliana; Uncollected Essays; Pawnbroker's Daughter; Adventures of Ulysses; Tales; Poems; Letters.

Final Memorials of. Talfourd. N. Y., 1849. 12°. . . . 3973
Memoir of. Barry Cornwall. Bost., 1866. 16°. . . . 6959
Lamballe, M. T. L. de. Secret Memoirs of the Royal Family. (2 copies.) Philad., 1826. 8°. 5694
Lambert, E. R. Hist. of Colony of N. Haven. N. H., 1838. 12°. . 5727
Lambeth and the Vatican. Lond., 1825. 3 v. 16°. 13184
Lamon, W. H. Life of Lincoln. Bost., 1872. 8°. 7406

Lamothe-Langon, E. L. de. Evenings with Prince Cambacérès. Lond., 1837. 2 v. 8°. 5601
Memoirs of Court of Louis XVIII. Lond., 1830. 2 v. 8°. . 5638
La Motte Fouqué, F. de. Aslauga's Knight, transl. by Carlyle. Bost., 1841. 12°. 3107
Popular Traditions. (German Novelists, v. 2.) Lond., 1826. 12°. 1896
Thiodolf the Icelander. Philad., 1863. 12°. 3019
Thiodolf the Icelander. And Aslauga's Knight. (2 copies.) N. Y., 1845–48. 12°. 3017
Undine. N. Y., 1857. 12°. 2705
The same, with Sintram. (2 copies.) N. Y., 1862. 8°. . 3015
The same. N. Y., 1845. 12°. 3044
Lampadius, W. A. Life of Mendelssohn. (2 copies.) N. Y., 1865. 16°. 7885
Lamping, C. and **France, A. de.** The French in Algiers. N. Y., 1845. 12°. 8369
Lancashire, Popular Traditions of. Roby. Lond., 1343. v. 2, 3. 12°. 5269
Worthies of. H. Coleridge. Lond., 1836. 8°. 6904
Land we Love, The. Charlotte, N. C., 1866–69. v. 1–6. 8°. . . 12934
Lander, R. and **J.** Journal of Niger Expedition. N. Y., 1841. 2 v. 12°. 11039
Lando, O. Novels. (Roscoe's Ital. Novelists, v. 3.) Lond., 1836. 12°. 1901
Landon, L. E. (Mrs. Maclean.) The Golden Violet: and other Poems. Philad., 1827. 12°. 14832
Poetical Works. Philad., 1838. 8°. 943
The Troubadour; Catalogue of Pictures, etc. Philad., 1825. 12°. 14803
Works. Philad., 1838. 2 v. in 1. 8°. 3784
Life and Remains of. Blanchard. Philad., 1841. 2 v. 12°. . 15239
Landor, E. W. Adventures in North of Europe. Lond., 1836. 2 v. 12°. 16600
Landor, W. S. Exam. of Shakspeare before Sir T. Lucy, etc. Lond., 1834. 16°. 1492
Gebir, Count Julian, and other Poems. Lond., 1831. 8°. . 1222
Imaginary Conversations. 2 Series. Lond., 1826–29. 5 v. 8°. 3442
The same. 1st Series. Lond., 1826–28. 3 v. 8°. . . 3447
Pericles and Aspasia. (2 copies.) Philad., 1839. 2 v. 8°. . 3450
Biogr. of. Forster. Bost., 1869. 8°. 7093
Landscape Gardening. Downing. N. Y., 1844. 8°. 9084
Lane, B. I. Mysteries of Tobacco. N. Y., 1846. 12°. . . . 9231
Responses on the Use of Tobacco. N. Y., 1846. 12°. . . 9232
Lane, E. W. Modern Egyptians. Lond., 1836–37. 2 v. 12°. . . 8171
The same. 3d ed. Lond., 1842. 2 v. 8°. 8063
The same. Lond., 1846. 3 v. 12°. 8158
Laneham, R. Letter describing Pageants at Kenilworth. Philad., 1822. 12°. 4816
Lanfrey, P. Hist. of Napoléon I. Lond., 1871–72. 2 v. 8°. . . 5586
Langbein, A. F. E. Novels. (German Nov., v. 4.) Lond., 1826. 12°. 1898
Langdon, Mary. *(Pseudonym.)* See M. H. PIKE.
Langhorne, J. Fables of Flora. N. Y., 1804. 12°. 14833
Select Poems. Ed. Walsh. Philad., 1822. 24°. 24
Langon, L. See LAMOTHE-LANGON.
Langsdorff, G. v. Voyages. Carlisle, 1817. 8°. 16300

Language. By a Heteroscian. Prov., 1836. 12°. 15006
Essay on. Bentham. (Works, pts. 15, 16.) Edinb., 1841. 8°. 9714
Science of. Max Müller. N. Y., 1862–65. 2 v. 12°. . . 130
and the Study of Language. Whitney. N. Y., 1867. 12°. . 134
Theory of. Beattie. (Works, v. 2.) Philad., 1809. 12°. . . 12288
English, Dissertations on. Webster. Bost., 1789. 8°. . . 230
Elements of. Clark. N. Y., 1863. 16°. . . . 63
Hand-Book of. Latham. N. Y., 1852. 12°. . . 92
Lectures on. Marsh. N. Y., 1863. 8°. . . . 169
Origin and Hist. of. Marsh. N. Y., 1862. 8°. . . 170
past and present. Trench. N. Y., 1871. 12°. . . 106
Studies in. Schele de Vere. N. Y., 1867. 12°. . . 99
Synonymes of. Crabb. N. Y., 1839. 8°. . . . 173
Selection of. [Whately.] Bost., 1832. 12°. 101
Words of, Dict. of Archaic and Provincial. Halliwell. Lond., 1855. 2 v. 8°. 171
Rambles among. Swinton. N. Y., 1859. 12°. 95
Select Glossary of. Trench. N. Y., 1859. 12°. 103
Study of. Trench. N. Y., 1856. 12°. . 104
Thesaurus of. Roget. Bost., 1856. 12°. . 96
and their Uses. White. N. Y., 1870. 12°. 97
See, also, ENGLISH ; GRAMMAR ; PHILOLOGY.
Lanman, C. The Japanese in America. N. Y., 1872. 12°. . . 7955
Private Life of Webster. N. Y., 1852. 12°. 7221
Lanman, J. H. Hist. of Michigan. N. Y., 1841. 12°. . . . 11614
The same. N. Y., 1843. 12°. 12276
The same. N. Y., 1839. 8°. 5890
La Noye, F. de. Egypt 3300 years ago. N. Y., 1870. 12°. . . 10128
The Sublime in Nature. N. Y., 1871. 12°. 10117
Lansdowne, *Viscount.* See GRANVILLE.
Lantièr, E. F. Travels of Antenor. Lond., 1799. 3 v. 8°. . . 16513
Lanzi, L. Hist. of Painting in Italy. Lond., 1828. 6 v. 8°. , . 9085
The same. (Bohn's ed.) Lond., 1847. 3 v. 8°. . . 479
Lapland, A Winter in, 1836. Dillon. Lond., 1840. 8°. . . . 8291
La Plata, Travels in, 1819–25. Miers. Lond., 1826. 2 v. 8°. . . 8463
See, also, ARGENTINE Republic.
[**La Rame, L. de.**] Tricotrin. Philad., 1869. 12°. 15618
Lardner, D. The Cabinet Cyclopædia. Lond. 171 v. 16°. . . 4855
The Steam Engine. 7th ed. Lond., 1840. 8°. 17005
Treatise on Arithmetic. Lond., 1836. 16°. 6048
on Heat. Lond., 1833. 16°. 6047
on Hydrostatics and Pneumatics. Bost., 1832. 12°. 8827
The same. Lond., 1836. 16°. 6044
on Mechanics. Lond., 1837. 16°. 6046
Larke, J. K. Grant and his Campaigns. N. Y., 1864. 12°. . . 7399
La Rive, G. de. Reminiscences of Cavour. Lond., 1862. 8°. . . 7788
La Rochefoucauld, F. de. Moral Reflections, Sentences and Maxims. N. Y., 1853. 12°. 4334

La Rochefoucauld-Liancourt, F. A. F. de. Travels through U. S., etc. Lond., 1799. 2 v. 4°. 16033
La Rochejaquelein, Marquise de, Memoirs of. By herself. Edinb., 1827. 12°. 4467
La Salle, R. C. de, Life of. Sparks. Bost., 1844. 16°. 7260
Las Cases, M. J. E. D. Journal of Napoleon at St. Helena. Lond., 1823. 8 v. 8°. 16212
Last of the Barons. Bulwer. Philad., 1861. 2 v. 12°. 2081
Last Chronicle of Barset. Trollope. N. Y., 1867. 8°. 2288
Last Days of Pompeii. Bulwer. Lond., 1854. 12°. 2064
Last of the Lairds. Galt. N. Y., 1827. 12°. 15235
Last of the Mohicans. Cooper. N. Y., 1873. 12°. 2842
Last of the Plantagenets. N. Y., 1829. 2 v. 12°. 15485
Latham, R. G. Hand-Book of the English Language. N. Y., 1852. 12°. 92
Man and his Migrations. N. Y., 1852. 12°. 17107
Lathy, T. P. Memoirs of Court of Louis XIV. Lond., 1819. 3 v. 8°. 5635
Latimer, H. Select Sermons. Ed. A. Young. Cambr., 1832. 12°. . 3910
and Letters. Lond., 12°. 9477
Sermon on the Ploughers. Ed. Arber. Lond., 1868. 16°. . 3885
Seven Sermons before Edw. VI. Ed. Arber. Lond., 1869. 16°. 3890
Latin Christianity, Hist. of, to 1454. Milman. N. Y., 1860–61. 8 v. 8°. 6391
Etymology. Peile. 2d ed. Lond., 1872. 16°. 93
See, also, ITALY; ROME.
Latrobe, C. J. The Rambler in Mexico. N. Y., 1836. 12°. . . 16909
in N. Amer. N. Y., 1835. 2 v. 12°. . 16804
Laud, W. Autobiography. Oxf'd., 1839. 16°. 6671
Life and Times of. Lawson. Lond., 1829. 2 v. 8°. . . 6819
Sketch of. Thorold Rogers. Lond., 1870. 8°. . . . 6732
Laughter, Essay on. Beattie. Lond., 1779. 8°. 214
Laurent, Paul M. Hist. of Napoleon. N. Y., 1842. 2 v. 8°. . . 5603
Laurent, Peter E. Classical Tour through Greece, etc. Lond., 1822. 8°. 16641
La Valliere, Duchess de; a Play. Bulwer. N. Y., 1836. 12°. . 1443
Lavengro. Borrow. N. Y., 1851. 12°. 2157
Law, J., Memoir of. Thiers. N. Y., 1859. 12°. 6634
Law, Elements of. Hobbes (v. 4). Lond., 1840. 8°. 9675
of Love and Love as a Law, The. Hopkins. N. Y., 1869. 12°. 8607
Principles of, etc. See BENTHAM'S Works.
Reform. Brougham. (Speeches, v. 2.) Edinb., 1838. 8°. . 9338
Reign of. Duke of Argyll. Lond., 1868. 16°. 8839
Reporters, Curiosities of the. Heard. Bost., 1871. 16°. . 4346
Studies, Popular Introd. to. Warren. Lond., 1835. 8°. . 9217
Tracts. Lord Bacon. (Works, v. 1.) Lond., 1838. 8°. . . 9738
American, Commentaries on. Kent. N. Y., 1840. 4 v. 8°. . 9356
Ancient. Maine. N. Y., 1864. 8°. 8687
Criminal, Principles of. Philad., 1846. 12°. 8498
English, Commentaries on. Blackstone, ed. Sharswood. N. Y., 1872. 2 v. 8°. 9395
Common, Dialogue of the. Hobbes. Lond., 1840. 8°. 9677

Law, Natural and Politic, Principles of. Burlamaqui. Philad., 1830. 8°. 8635
Roman and Canon. Butler. Lond., 1830. 8°. 7682
See, also, INTERNATIONAL Law ; LEGAL ; TRIALS.
Lawrence, A. Diary and Correspondence. Bost., 1856. 8°. . . . 7644
Lawrence, E. A. Life of J. Hawes. Hartf'd., 1871. 8°. 7712
Systematic Beneficence. N. Y. 12°. 9803
[**Lawrence, G. A.**] Barren Honour. N. Y. 8°. 2311
Guy Livingstone. N. Y., 1871. 12°. 2462
Maurice Dering. N. Y., 1865. 8°. 2331
Lawrence, H. London in the Olden Time. Lond., 1827. v. 2. 8°. 15495
Lawrence, J. Biography of. N. Brunswick, 1813. 16°. 7489
Lawrie Todd. Galt. N. Y., 1830. 2 v. 12°. 15237
Laws, Spirit of. Montesquieu. Lond., 1766. 2 v. 8°. 14771
Lawson, J. P. Hist. of European Conspiracies. Edinb., 1829. 2 v. 12°. 4505
Life of Abp. Laud. Lond., 1829. 2 v. 8°. 6819
Lawyers, Book about. Jeaffreson. Lond., 1867. 2 v. 8°. . . . 9218
Lay, G. T. The Chinese as they are. Lond., 1841. 8°. 8005
Lay of the Scottish Fiddle. [Paulding.] N. Y., 1813. 24°. . . 14947
Layard, A. H. Nineveh and its Remains. (2 copies.) N. Y., 1849. 2 v. 8°. 8137
The same. N. Y., 1849. 2 v. 12°. 8014
Laycock, T. Mind and Brain. 2d ed. N. Y., 1869. 2 v. 8°. . 8581
Lea, H. C. Studies in Church Hist. Philad., 1869. 12°. 6314
Superstition and Force. 2d ed. Philad., 1870. 12°. . . . 3657
Leaves from Margaret Smith's Journal. Whittier. Bost., 1849. 16°. 2950
Le Bas, C. W. Life of Cranmer. N. Y., 1833. 2 v. 12°. . . . 7518
of Wiclif. (2 copies.) N. Y., 1832. 12°. . 7516
Lecky, W. E. H. Hist. of European Morals. N. Y., 1869. 2 v. 8°. 4709
of Rationalism in Europe. N. Y., 1866. 2 v. 8°. 6320
Leaders of Public Opinion in Ireland. N. Y., 1872. 12°. . 6743
Ledyard, J., Life of. Sparks. Bost., 1847. 16°. 7273
Lee, A., Life of. R. H. Lee. Bost., 1829. 2 v. 8°. 7453
Lee, Chas., Life of. Sparks. Bost., 1846. 16°. 7267
Life and Memoirs of. N. Y., 1813. 12°. 7553
Memoirs, Letters, etc., of. [Langworthy.] Dubl., 1792. 8°. . 7450
Lee, Chas. A. Elements of Geology. N. Y. [1846.] 12°. 11778
Lee, E. B. Life of Jean Paul. (2 copies.) Bost., 1842. 2 v. 16°. . 7799
The same. 3d ed. (2 copies.) Bost., 1864. 8°. . . 7803
[**Lee, Hannah F.**] Hist. Sketches of old Painters. Bost., 1841. 12°. 8878
Huguenots in France and America. Cambr., 1843. 2 v. 12°. 6353
Life of Cranmer. Bost., 1841. 16°. 7556
and Times of Luther. Bost., 1841. 16°. 6347
Three Experiments of Living, etc. Bost., 1837. 12°. . . 15804
The World before you. Philad., 1844. 12°. 15819
Lee, Harriet. Canterbury Tales. N. Y., 1857. 2 v. 12°. 15393
Lee, Henry. Campaign of '81 in the Carolinas. Philad., 1824. 8°. . 6117
Lee, N. Alex. the Great. (Oxberry's Plays.) Bost., 1822. 24°. . 1351
Rival Queens. (Brit. Drama.) Lond., 1804. 8°. 1629

Lee, R. H., Memoir of. By his Grandson. Philad., 1825. 2 v. 8°. . 7451
Lee, Sarah. Memoirs of Cuvier. N. Y., 1833. 12°. 7629
Lee, Sophia. Chapter of Accidents. (Mod. Theater, v. 9.) Lond., 1811. 12°. 1335
Lee, W. Defoe's Life and Writings. Lond., 1869. 3 v. 8°. . . 7083
Leech, H. H. Letters of a Sentimental Idler. N. Y., 1869. 12°. . 16280
Lefanu, A. Memoirs of Mrs. Sheridan. Lond., 1824. 8°. . . 7081
Lefèbre. Wonders of Architecture. N. Y., 1870. 12°. . . . 10121
Legal Study, Course of. Hoffman. Balt., 1836. 2 v. 8°. . . . 9354
and Political Hermeneutics. Lieber. Bost., 1839. 12°. . . 8621
Legaré, H. S. Writings. Charleston, 1845–46. 2 v. 8°. . . . 17192
Legend of Montrose, The. Scott. Edinb., 1870. 8°. 1870
Legendary, The. Ed. Willis. Bost., 1828. 2 v. 12°. 14877
Legends of Patriarchs and Prophets. Baring-Gould. N. Y., 1872. 8°. 1914
Legge, A. O. Temporal Power of the Papacy. Lond., 1870. 8°. . 6326
Leggett, W. Political Writings. N. Y., 1840. 2 v. 12°. . . . 17194
Legislative Assemblies, Law and Practice of. Cushing. Bost., 1866. 8°. 8727
Legrand d'Aussy, P. J. B. Fabliaux, transl. by Way. Lond., 1815. 3 v. 16°. 302
Leigh, P. Mr. Pips, hys Diary. Lond. 2 v. 4°. . . . . .
Leighton, J. Paris under the Commune. Lond., 1871. 8°. . . 5553
Leighton, R. Expositions on the Creed, Lord's Prayer, etc. Lond., 1835. 16°. 9496
Works, with Life by Aikman. (2 copies.) Edinb., 1835–40. 8°. 10067
Leighton Court. H. Kingsley. Bost., 1866. 12°. 2576
Leila. Bulwer-Lytton. Philad., 1868. 12°. 2036
Leipoldt, W. Memoir of Rauschenbusch. Lond., 1843. 16°. . . 7532
Leisler, J., Administration of. Hoffman. Bost., 1844. 16°. . . 7262
Leisure Hours. Bost., 1835. 12°. 14870
Leland, C. G. Hans Breitmann's Ballads. Philad., 1869. 12°. . 4293
Sunshine in Thought. N. Y., 1862. 12°. 3565
Leland, H. P. Americans in Rome. N. Y., 1863. 12°. . . . 16721
Leland, T. Hist. of Philip of Macedon. Lond., 1820. 2 v. 8°. . 4428
Lemaistre, J. G. Travels through France, etc. Lond., 1806. 3 v. 8°. 16543
Lemon, M. The Jest Book. (2 copies.) Cambr., 1865. 16°. . . 4276
Lempriere, J. Universal Biography. Ed. by E. Lord. N. Y., 1825. 2 v. 8°. 16315
Lempriere, W. Tour to Morocco. 2d ed. Lond., 1793. 8°. . . 16531
Lennox, C. R. Shakspeare Illustrated, ed. Noah. Philad., 1809. v. 1. 8°. 1591
Le Normand, M. A. Memoirs of Josephine. Philad., 1848. 2 v. 12°. 5448
Lenormant, F., and **Chevallier, E.** Ancient Hist. of the East. Lond., 1869–70. 2 v. 8°. 4057
Lent, Sermons for. Ed. Cattermole. Lond., 1835. 16°. . . . 9497
Leo X., Life of. Roscoe. Lond., 1846. 2 v. 8°. 396
Leonora. Edgeworth. (Works, v. 2.) Bost., 1824. 8°. . . . 15336
Leonowens, A. H. English Governess at the Siamese Court. Bost., 1870. 12°. 8010
Le Pileur, A. Wonders of the Human Body. N. Y., 1870. 12°. . 10131

Les Misérables, transl. by Wilbour. Hugo. N. Y., 1863. 8°. . . 2636
Lesage, A. R. Bachelor of Salamanca. Philad., 1854. 2 v. 12°. . 1691
Gil Blas. (2 copies.) Lond. and N. Y., 1863. 8°. . . . 1997
The same. N. Y., 1824. 3 v. 8°. 1999
Leslie, C. R. Autobiogr. Recollections, ed. Taylor. Bost., 1860. 8°. 7937
Leslie, E. Mr. and Mrs. Woodbridge. Prov., 1841. 12°. . . . 14923
Pencil Sketches. Philad., 1833–37. 3 v. 12°. 15758
Leslie Linkfield. Roch., 1826. 2 v. 12°. 15730
Lesseps, J. B. B. de. Travels in Kamtschatka. Lond., 1790. 2 v. 8°. 16507
Lessing, G. E. Emilia Galotti. (German Theatre, v. 6.) Lond., 1811. 12°. 1361
Life and Works of. Stahr. Bost., 1866. 2 v. 12°. . . 7791
Lester, C. E. Condition and Fate of England. N. Y., 1843. 2 v. 12°. 4833
Glory and Shame of England. N. Y., 1841–42. 2 v. 12°. . 4830
The Napoleon Dynasty; Hist. of the Bonaparte Family. N. Y., 1852. 8°. 5600
and **Foster, A.** Life of Americus Vespucius. N. H., 1852. 8°. 7782
Letters, Familiar, on Public Characters. [Sullivan.] Bost., 1834. 12°. 7277
Literature in. Holcombe. N. Y., 1866. 8°. 7162
Letter-Writers, Half-Hours with the best. Knight. Lond., 1867. 8°. 3769
Letter-Writing, Young Man's Book of. Philad., 1835. 12°. . . 17026
See, also, CORRESPONDENCE.
Le Vaillant, F. Travels in Interior of Africa. Dubl., 1790. 8°. . 16523
Levana; or, the Doctrine of Education. Richter. Bost., 1863. 8°. . 3067
Levant, Tour in the, 1812–15. Turner. Lond., 1820. 3 v. 8°. . . 16629
Travels in the, 1817–18. Forbin. Lond., 1819. 8°. . . . 8051
Visit to Monasteries in the, 1833. Curzon. N. Y., 1849. 12°. 8254
Levasseur, A. Lafayette in America. Philad., 1829. 2 v. 12°. . 16831
Le Vassor, M. Hist. of Reign of Lewis XIII. Lond., 1700. 8°. . 16198
Lever, C. J. Charles O'Malley. Dubl., 1841. 2 v. in 1. 8°. . . 2318
Confessions of Harry Lorrequer. Lond. 8°. 2660
Maurice Tiernay, the Soldier of Fortune. N. Y., 1863. 8°. . 2319
The Nevilles of Garretstown. N. Y., 1846. 8°. . . . 2317
The O'Donoghue. N. Y., 1847. 8°. 2317
Tony Butler. N. Y., 1865. 8°. 2320
Lever, T. Sermons, ed. Arber. Lond., 1870. 16°. 3896
Leviathan. Hobbes. (Works, v. 3.) Lond., 1839. 8°. . . . 9674
Leviticus, Notes on. Bush. N. Y., 1843. 12°. 9849
Lewes, G. H. Biogr. Hist. of Philosophy. Lond., 1846. v. 3, 4. 12°. 8489
The same. [2d ed.] N. Y., 1859. 8°. 8723
The same. 4th ed. Lond., 1871. 2 v. 8°. . . . 8724
Physiology of Common Life. N. Y., 1860. 2 v. 12°. . . 8950
Sea-Side Studies. Edinb., 1858. 8°. 9003
[**Lewes, M. J.**] *(George Eliot.)* Adam Bede. (4 copies.) N. Y., 1868–71. 12°. 2529
Felix Holt, the Radical. N. Y., 1866. 12°. 2539
The same. (2 copies.) N. Y., 1866. 8°. 2676
Middlemarch. (3 copies.) N. Y., 1872–73. 2 v. 12°. . . 2540
Mill on the Floss. (2 copies.) N. Y., 1872. 12°. . . . 2533

[Lewes, M. J.] Romola. (2 copies.) N. Y., 1872. 12°. 2537
The same. N. Y., 1863. 8°. 2678
Scenes of Clerical Life; Silas Marner. N. Y., 1871. 12°. . 2528
Silas Marner. (2 copies.) N. Y., 1861. 12°. 2535
The Spanish Gypsy, a Poem. (2 copies.) Bost., 1868. 16°. . 1171
Lewis, D. The New Gymnastics. Bost., 1862. 12°. 9228
Weak Lungs. Bost., 1864. 12°. 9229
Lewis, Matthew G. Rugantino. (Oxberry's Plays, v. 11.) Bost., 1822. 24°. 1355
Life, Correspondence, etc., of. Lond., 1839. 2 v. 8°. . . . 7089
Lewis, Meriwether, and **Clarke, W.,** Hist. of Exped. of. Allen. Philad., 1814. 2 v. 8°. 16867
Travels of. Philad., 1809. 12°. 16869
Liberty, On. J. S. Mill. Bost., 1863. 16°. 3714
and Necessity. Hobbes. (Works, v. 4, 5.) Lond., 1840–41. 8°. 9675
of the Press. R. Hall. Lond., 1846. 8°. 493
and of Discussion. Bentham. (Works, pt. 7.) Edinb., 1838. 8°. 9706
of Printing. Milton. Lond., 1848. 8°. 455
of Rome, etc., Hist of. Eliot. N. Y., 1849. 2 v. 8°. . . 16028
See, also, TOLERATION.
Library of Entertaining Knowledge. Bost., 1830–32. 16 v. 12°. . 8805

CONTENTS.—1, The Menageries; Quadrupeds. 2, Vegetable Substances; Trees, Fruits. 3, Pursuit of Knowledge under Difficulties, v. 1. 4, Insect Architecture. 5, The New Zealanders. 6, Insect Transformations. 7, The Menageries; Elephant. 8, Pursuit of Knowledge under Difficulties, v. 2. 9, Architecture of Birds. 10, Paris and its Historical Scenes, v. 1. 11, Historical Parallels. 12, Insect Miscellanies. 13, Pompeii. 14, Paris and its Historical Scenes, v. 2. 15, Vegetable Substances; Food. 16, Criminal Trials.

of Useful Knowledge, American. Bost., 1831–32. 5 v. 12°. . 8824
Libyan Desert, Adventures in the, 1847. St. John. N. Y., 1850. 12°. 16522
License Law, Reports to Mass. Legislature on the. Bost., 1867. 8°. 9323
Lichfield, Siege of. Gresley. Lond., 1841. 12°. 15580
Lichtensteins, The. van der Velde. (Tales, v. 2.) Bost., 1837. 12°. 3030
Liddell, H. G. Hist. of Rome. N. Y., 1860. 12°. 4725
Lieber, F. Character of the Gentleman. (2 copies.) 3d ed. Philad., 1864. 12°. 9129
Civil Liberty and Self Government. Philad., 1859. 8°. . . 8686
Essays on Property and Labour. N. Y., 1841. 12°. . . . 11748
The same. 12277
Great Events by Great Historians. Bost., 1840. 12°. . . 15930
Legal and Political Hermeneutics. Bost., 1839. 12°. . . 8621
Manual of Political Ethics. Bost., 1838–39. 2 v. 8°. . . 8683
The same. Lond., 1839. v. 1. 8°. 8685
Reminiscences of Niebuhr. Philad., 1835. 12°. . . . 7763
The Stranger in America. Philad., 1835. 8°. 16780
and others. Encyclopædia Americana. Philad., 1830–33. 13 v. 8°.
Liefde, J. de. The Romance of Charity. Lond., 1867. 8°. . . 8542
Life as it is. Leslie, etc. Prov., 1841. 12°. 14923
below: in 7 Poems. N. Y., 1868. 16°. 811
Christian Thought on. Giles. Bost., 1851. 8°. 3547
here and there. Willis. N. Y., 1850. 12°. 15331

Life, Idea of. Coleridge. Philad., 1848. 12°. 16948
on the Lakes. N. Y., 1836. 2 v. 12°. 16853
for a Life, A. Mrs. Craik. N. Y., 1869. 12°. 2493
The Transmission of. Napheys. Philad., 1871. 12°. . . . 9167
View of. Petrarch. Lond., 1791. 8°. 3949
in the Wilds. Martineau. Bost., 1833. 12°. 14608
Liffith Lank. Webb. N. Y., 1866. 12°. 4301
Lifting the Veil. N. Y., 1870. 16°. 2728
Light of Nature pursued. Tucker. Lond., 1807. 8°. 17082
See, also, OPTICS.
Lightfoot, J. B. Revision of the English N.T. 2d ed. N. Y., 1873. 8°. 10263
Lighthouses and Lightships. Adams. N. Y., 1870. 12°. . . . 10132
and Smeaton. Lond., 1844. 12°. 8799
Lights and Shadows of Domestic Life, etc. Bost., 1850. 16°. . . 15732
of Irish Life. Hall. Philad., 1838. 2 v. 12°. . 15487
of Scottish Life. Wilson. Philad. 16°. . . 2023
Ligne, C. J. de. Letters and Reflections. Philad., 1809. 12°. . . 15843
Lillo, G. Dramatic Works, ed. Davies. 2d ed. Lond., 1810. 2 v. in 1. 12°. 1363
Lilly, J. Alexander and Campaspe. (Old Plays, v. 2.) Lond., 1825. 8°. 1509
Dramatic Works, ed. Fairholt. Lond., 1858. 2 v. 16°. . . 1390
Euphues; the Anatomy of Wit; Euphues and his England. Ed. Arber. Lond., 1868. 16°. 3888
Lilly, W. Hist. of my Life and Times. Lond., 1829. 12°. . . 6640
Lincoln, A. The President's Words. Bost., 1865. 16°. . . . 7513
Life of. Holland. Springf'ld., 1866. 8°. 7405
to 1861. Lamon. Bost., 1872. 8°. 7406
Six Months at the White House with. Carpenter. N. Y., 1866. 8°. 7542
and **Douglas, S. A.** Political Debates. Columbus, 1860. 8°. 9388
Lincoln, B., Life of. Bowen. Bost., 1847. 16°. 7272
Lingard, J. Hist. of England. Lond. and Philad., 1823–30. 12 v. 8°. 4950
The same. Philad., 1827–30. 12 v. in 11. 8°. . . . 4962
Linonian Society. See YALE College.
Lionel Lincoln. Cooper. Philad., 1836. 2 v. 12°. 2753
Lionel Wakefield. [Massey.] Philad., 1837. 2 v. 12°. . . . 15490
[**Lippincott, S. J.**] Records of Five Years. Bost., 1867. 8°. . . 3558
Lippincott's Magazine. Philad., 1868–72. 9 v. 8°. 13373
Listener, The. Fry. Philad., 1837. 2 v. 12°. 15172
Lister, T. H. Anne Grey. N. Y., 1835. 12°. 15111
Granby. N. Y., 1826. 2 v. 12°. 15455
Herbert Lacy. Philad., 1828. 2 v. 12°. 15448
Life of Clarendon. Lond., 1837–38. 3 v. 8°. 6846
Literary Character, The. I. Disraeli. Lond., 1839. 16°. . . . 3187
Gem, The. Bost., 1827. 12°. 13841
Portfolio. Philad., 1830. v. 1. 4°. 14412
and Theological Review. N. Y., 1834–38. v. 1–5. 8°. . . 12771
Literature, Amenities of. Disraeli. Lond., 1841. 3 v. 8°. . . 3412

Literature, Characteristics of. Tuckerman. Philad., 1849. 12°. . 3571
Curiosities of. Disraeli. N. Y. 8°. 3408
Essay on Study of. Gibbon. Dubl., 1788. 12°. 89
Flowers of. Galt. Lond., 1803. 12°. 15834
Hist. of. F. von Schlegel. Philad., 1818. 2 v. 8°. . . 147
to the 15th century. Tannehill. Nashville, 1827. 8°. 15070
Sketches of. Alves. Edinb., 1794. 8°. 209
Miscellanies of. I. Disraeli. N. Y., 1841. 3 v. 12°. . . 3391
Pursuits of. [Mathias.] Lond., 1798. 8°. 15088
Advice in. Knapp. N. Y., 1832. 12°. 59
National, Importance and Means of a. Channing. Edinb., 1835. 16°. 9137
Universal, Hand-Book of. Botta. Bost., 1863. 12°. . . . 137
See, also, BOOKS; POETRY.
Also, AMERICAN, ENGLISH, GERMAN, etc.

Littell's Living Age. Bost., 1844–72. v. 1–14, 16–103, 105–107, 109–114. 8°. 13924

Little Dinner at Timmins's. Thackeray. (Works, v. 9.) Lond., 1872. 8°. 2197
Dorrit. Dickens. N. Y., 1871. 16°. 2266
Gentleman, The. N. H., 1831. 12°. 15733
Henry and his Bearer. Sherwood. (Works, v. 3.) N. Y., 1836. 12°. 15115
Men. Alcott. Bost., 1871. 16°. 2743
Savage, The. Marryat. N. Y., 1849. 8°. 2122
Women. Alcott. Bost., 1869. 2 v. 16°. 2737

Liturgy, Apology for Forms of. Jer. Taylor. Lond., 1836. 8°. . 10063

Live and Let Live. Sedgwick. N. Y., 1837. 12°. 15316

Liverpool, *Earl of*, Public Life of. Lond., 1827. 8°. 6783

Liverpool to St. Louis, From. N. Hall. Lond., 1870. 16°. . . 8223

Living Beings, Lectures on Physical Phenomena of. Matteucci. Philad., 1848. 12°. 16961
and the Dead, The. [Neale.] N. Y., 1827. 12°. . . . 15492

Livingston, E., Life of. Hunt. N. Y., 1864. 8°. 7457

Livingston, W., Memoir of. Sedgwick. N. Y., 1833. 8°. . . 7456

Livingstone, D. Travels in S. Africa. N. Y., 1858. 8°. 8124
How I found. Stanley. N. Y., 1872. 8°. 10239

Livy. Hist. of Rome, transl. by Baker. N. Y., 1823. 6 v. 8°. . 15989
The same. N. Y., 1841–63. 5 v. 12°. 4531

Liza. Turgénieff. N. Y., 1872. 12°. 10079

Llorente, J. A. Hist. of the Inquisition of Spain. Lond., 1826. 8°. 6425

Lloyd, R. Poems. Ed. Johnson. Dubl., 1804. 8°. 15102

Lobeira, V. Amadis of Gaul, tr. by Southey. Lond., 1872. 3 v. 16°. 2007

[**Locke, D. R.**] (P. Nasby.) Ekkoes from Kentucky. Bost., 1868. 12°. 4290
"Swingin Round the Cirkle." Bost., 1867. 12°. 4289

Locke, J., Beauties of. Lond. 16°. 3526
Conduct of the Understanding. N. Y., 1845. 12°. 11772
The same. 12285
The same. Chiswick, 1829. 12°. 8492

Locke, J. Essay concerning Human Understanding. Lond., 1753. 2 v. 8°. 9590

The same. N. Y., 1824. 2 v. 8°. 8757

Reasonableness of Christianity, etc. Ed. St. John. Lond., 1836. 16°. 9507

Two Treatises of Government. Lond., 1772. 8°. 17198

Works. 10th ed. Lond., 1801. v. 3–8. 8°. 9592

CONTENTS.—3, Letters; Constitution of Carolina; Vine and Silk Culture; Hist. of Navigation; Catalogue of Voyages. 4, Answers to Remarks on Essay of Human Understanding. 5, Of lowering of Interest, and raising the Value of Money; of Government. 6, Letters on Toleration. 7, Reasonableness of Christianity. 8, Paraphrase and Notes on Paul's Epistles.

Life, Correspondence, etc., of. King. Lond., 1830. 2 v. 8°. 7126

Locke Amsden. Thompson. Bost., 1856. 12°. 15734

Lockhart, J. G. Ancient Spanish Ballads. (2 copies.) N. Y., 1842. 8°. 913

Hist. of Napoleon. N. Y., 1840. 2 v. 12°. 11003

The same. N. Y., 1830. 2 v. 12°. 11932

Life of Burns. Edinb., 1828. 12°. 4485

The same. N. Y., 1831. 12°. 6951

Memoirs of Scott. (2 copies.) Bost. and Philad., 1837–38. 7 v. 12°. 6961

Passages in Life of Adam Blair. Bost., 1822. 12°. 15359

Valerius. Bost., 1821. 2 v. 12°. 15625

and others. Peter's Letters to his Kinsfolk. (2 copies.) N. Y., 1820. 8°. 3396

Lockman, J. Entertaining Instructor. Lond., 1765. 12°. 15829

Travels of the Jesuits. 2d ed. Lond., 1762. 2 v. 8°. 16324

Lockwood, J. D., Memoir of. By his father. N. Y., 1845. 12°. 7527

Lodge, E. British Portraits. (Bohn's ed.) Lond., 1849–50. 8 v. 8°. 515

Lodge, T. Wounds of Civil War. Lond., 1825. 8°. 1515

Lodoli, C. Novels. (Ital. Novelists, v. 4.) Lond., 1836. 12°. 1902

Logan, J. The Scottish Gaël. Hartf'd., 1846. 8°. 5410

Logan, O. Before the Footlights and Behind the Scenes. Philad., 1870. 8°. 1618

Logan. [J. Neal.] Philad., 1822. 2 v. 12°. 15735

Logic. Kant. Lond., 1819. 8°. 8730

Essay on. Bentham. (Works, pt. 15.) Edinb., 1841. 8°. 9714

Lectures on. Hamilton. Bost., 1860. 8°. 8742

System of. J. S. Mill. N. Y., 1864. 8°. 8743

Loménie, L. de. Beaumarchais and his Times. N. Y., 1857. 12°. 7623

Sketches of living characters of France. Philad., 1841. 12°. 7612

London Art-Galleries, Handbook to the. Jameson. Lond., 1842. 2 v. 12°. 8874

Bridge, Chronicles of. [Thomson.] Lond., 1839. 16°. 5143

Daily News, War Correspondence of, 1870–71. Lond., 1871. 2 v. 8°. 5551

the Great Metropolis. [Grant.] N. Y., 1837. 2 v. 12°. 5144

Life in. Egan. Lond., 1823. 8°. 16713

Nights' Entertainments. Ritchie. Philad., 1833. 2 v. 12°. 15493

in the Olden Time; tales. Lawrence. Lond., 1827. 8°. 15495

pictorially illustrated. Knight. Lond., 1841–44. 6 v. in 3. 8°. 5118

London, Pulpit of. [Grant.] N. Y., 1839. 12°. 9914
The Seven Curses of. Greenwood. Bost., 1869. 12°. . . 8617
Sketches of. Grant. Philad., 1839. 2 v. 12°. 5146
Society. Lond., 1868–71. v. 13, 14, 16–19. 8°. . . . 17798
Stage, The; a Collection of Tragedies, etc. Lond. [1830.] 4 v. 8°. 1664
The same. v. 4. 1668
Times, Essays from the. N. Y., 1852. 2 v. 12°. . . . 3166
Tower of; a Romance. Ainsworth. Lond. 8°. . . . 2661
Her Majesty's. Dixon. N. Y. and Philad., 1869. 2 v. 12°. 5148
Hist. of. Bayley. Lond., 1830. 8°. 5116
What I saw in. Bartlett. Auburn, 1852. 12°. . . . 16759
Londonderry, *Marquis of.* See C. W. Vane.
Long, G. Civil Wars of Rome. Lond., 1844–46. 3 v. 12°. . . 4594
Decline of the Roman Republic. Lond., 1864–72. 4 v. 8°. . 4732
Grammar Schools. Lond., 1842. 12°. 9107
Standard Library Cyclopædia. Lond., 1848–49. 4 v. 8°. . 350
Long Look Ahead, A. Roe. N. Y., 1856. 12°. 15737
Longevity, Code of. Sinclair. Lond., 1844. 8°. 8987
Longfellow, H. W. Christus, a Mystery. Bost., 1872. 3 v. 12°. . 715
Contents.—1, Divine Tragedy. 2, Golden Legend. 3, New England Tragedies.
Courtship of Miles Standish, etc. (2 copies.) Bost., 1859. 16°. 708
The Divine Tragedy. Bost., 1871. 16°. 713
Evangeline. (2 copies.) 6th ed. Bost., 1848. 16°. . . . 701
Hyperion. N. Y., 1839. 2 v. 12°. 2905
The same. Bost., 1853. 16°. 2723
New England Tragedies. (2 copies.) Bost., 1868. 16°. . . 711
Outre-Mer. N. Y., 1835. 2 v. 12°. 2901
The same. (2 copies.) Bost., 1850. 16°. 2903
Poems. Bost., 1856. 2 v. 16°. 703
The same. v. 2. Bost., 1852. 16°. 705
The same. Bost., 1857. 2 v. 16°. 588
Poets and Poetry of Europe. (2 copies.) Philad., 1845–47. 8°. 217
Song of Hiawatha. (2 copies.) Bost., 1856. 16°. . . . 706
Tales of a Wayside Inn. Bost., 1863. 12°. 710
Three Books of Song. Bost., 1872. 16°. 714
Voices of the Night. (2 copies.) Cambr., 1839–40. 16°. . . 699
Longman, W. Life of Edward III. Lond., 1869. 2 v. 8°. . . 5286
[**Longstreet, A. B.**] Georgia Scenes. 2d ed. N. Y., 1843. 12°. . 15701
Looker-On, The. Ed. Roberts. Philad., 1796. 4 v. in 2. 12°. . . 13033
Lord, J. Modern History. Philad., 1862. 12°. 4565
The Old Roman World. N. Y., 1867. 8°. 4752
Lord, P. B. Algiers and Barbary. Lond., 1835. 2 v. 12°. . . 7976
Lord Chancellors and Keepers of England, Lives of. Campbell. Lond. and Philad., 1845–48. v. 1–7. 8°. 6866
Lord Nial, etc. N. Y., 1834. 12°. 15009
Lord Roldan. Cunningham. N. Y., 1836. 12°. 15496
Lorenz, F. Life of Alcuin. Lond., 1837. 16°. 7507

Lorgnette, The. [D. G. Mitchell.] N. Y., 1854. 2 v. 12°. . . . 3603
Loring, F. W. The Boston Dip, and other Verses. Bost., 1871. 16°. 807
Lorrequer, Harry. *(Pseudonym.)* See C. LEVER.
Lossing, B. J. Outline Hist. of the Fine Arts. N. Y., 1840. 12°. . 11427
Pictorial Field-Book of the Revolution. (2 copies.) N. Y.,
1855–59. 2 v. 8°. 6291
Hist. of the Civil War. Philad., 1866–68. 3 v. 8°. . 6269
Lothair. Disraeli. N. Y., 1870. 12°. 2131
Lothrop, S. K. Life of Kirkland. Bost., 1848. 16°. 7274
Lotus-Eating. Curtis. N. Y., 1856. 12°. 3585
Loudon, J. W. Gardening for Ladies. N. Y., 1843. 12°. . . . 16979
Louis IX., of France, Memoirs of. De Joinville. (Bohn's ed.) Lond.,
1848. 8°. 512
Louis XIII., Hist. of Reign of. Levasseur. Lond., 1700. 8°. . . 16198
Louis XIV., Age of. Voltaire. Lond., 1779–81. 3 v. 8°. . . . 5540
and his Court. Pardoe. N. Y., 1847–48. 2 v. 12°. . . 5428
Life and Times of. G. P. R. James. Lond., 1851. 2 v. 8°. . 375
Memoirs of Court of. Anquetil. Edinb., 1791. 2 v. 8°. . 16199
The same. [Lathy.] Lond., 1819. 3 v. 8°. . . . 5635
Louis XVI. Correspondence, ed. H. M. Williams. Lond., 1803. 3 v. 8°. 5624
Memoirs of Reign of. Soulavie. Lond., 1802. 6 v. 8°. . 16192
Memoirs of last year of reign of. Bertrand de Moleville.
Lond., 1797. 3 v. 8°. 16183
Louis XVIII., Memoirs of Court of. De Lamothe-Langon. Lond.,
1830. 2 v. 8°. 5638
Louis Philippe, France under, 1830–40. Blanc. Philad., 1848. 2 v. 8°. 5575
Last Days of Reign of (1840–48). Guizot. Lond.,
1867. 8°. 5583
Life and Times of. Wright. Lond. 8°. 5584
Louisa of Prussia and her Times. A Novel. [Mundt.] N. Y., 1867. 8°. 3085
Louisiana, Colonial Hist. and Romance of. Gayarré. N. Y., 1851. 8°. 5992
Lounger, The. Ed. Ferguson. Lond., 1823. 2 v. 12°. . . . 3138
L'Ouverture, T., Biography and Autobiography of. Bost., 1863. 12°. 7698
Louvois, F. M. le T. de, Life of. James. Philad., 1837. 12°. . . 7614
Lovat, *Lord* **(S. Fraser),** Life of. Burton. Lond., 1847. 8°. . . 6762
Love, Anecdotes of. Lola Montez. N. Y. [1858.] 12°. . . . 15824
Love me little, love me long. Reade. N. Y., 1859. 12°. . . . 2102
Lovejoy, E. P., Memoir of. By his Brothers. N. Y., 1838. 12°. . 8546
Lovejoy, J. C. Memoir of Torrey. Bost., 1847. 12°. . . . 8566
Lovel the Widower. Thackeray. Lond., 1872. 8°. 2199
Lover, S. Handy Andy. Lond. 8°. 2659
The same. N. Y. 8°. 2310
Songs and Ballads. 3d ed. N. Y., 1847. 12°. . . . 1233
Love's Progress. Gilman. N. Y., 1840. 12°. 15738
Lovibond, E. Select Poems. Ed. Walsh. Philad., 1822. 24°. . 31
Lovzinski, *Baron* **de.,** Hist of. By himself. Hartf'd., 1800. 24°. . 7533
Low, S. Poems. N. Y., 1800. 2 v. in 1. 12°. 15008
Lowell, J. R. Biglow Papers. Camb., 1848–67. 2 v. 16°. . . 729
Among my Books. (2 copies.) Bost., 1870. 12°. . . . 3616

Lowell, J. R. The Cathedral. (2 copies.) Bost., 1870. 12°. . . . 732
Conversations on Old Poets. Cambr., 1845. 16°. 53
Fable for Critics. (2 copies.) N. Y., 1848. 12°. 727
Fireside Travels. (2 copies.) Bost., 1864. 8°. 3614
My Study Windows. Bost., 1871. 8°. 3618
Poems. 2d ed. Camb., 1844. 16°. 722
The same. [Revised ed.] 2 copies. Bost., 1849. 2 v. 16°. 723
Under the Willows, and other Poems. Bost., 1869. 12°. . 731
Lowell, R. New Priest in Conception Bay. Bost., 1864. 2 v. in 1. 8°. 2914
Lowell Offering, Selection from the. Lond., 1845. 12°. 2727
Lowth, R. Life of William Wykeham. Lond., 1758. 8°. . . 16340
Loyola, I., and the Early Jesuits. Rose. Lond., 1870. 8°. . . 7671
and Jesuitism. I. Taylor. N. Y., 1851. 12°. 7670
See, also, JESUITS.
Loyson, C. (Père Hyacinthe.) Discourses. N. Y., 1869. 12°. . 9983
The Family and the Church. N. Y., 1870. 12°. 9984
Lubbock, J. W. Origin of Civilization, etc. N. Y., 1870. 12°. . 4073
Pre-Historic Times. N. Y., 1872. 8°. 8991
and Bethune, J. E. D. On Probability. Lond. [1835.] 8°. . 16468
Lucan. Pharsalia, tr. by Rowe. Ed. Bell. Lond., 1807. 2 v. 24°. 271
[**Luchet, J. P. L., etc.**] Gallery of Portraits of the Nat. Assembly. Dubl., 1790. 2 v. in 1. 12°. 5508
Luck of Barry Lyndon. Thackeray. Lond., 1872. 8°. 2192
of Roaring Camp. Bret Harte. Bost., 1871. 8°. 2915
Lucretia. Bulwer. Lond., 1853. 8°. 2144
Ludlow, F. H. The Heart of the Continent. N. Y., 1870. 8°. . . 8418
Lübke, W., etc. Monuments of Art. N. Y. 8°. and 2 v. of plates. 4°.
Luke, St. See BIBLE.
Lullin de Châteauvieux, J. F. Travels in Italy. Lond., 1819. 8°. 8051
Lungs, Weak, and how to make them strong. Lewis. Bost., 1864. 12°. 9229
Lusitanian Sketches, 1843. Kingston. Lond., 1845. 2 v. 12°. . 8452
Luther, M. Select Treatises, in German. Ed. Sears. Andover, 1846. 12°. 9611
Table Talk. Ed. Hazlitt. (2 copies.) Lond., 1848. 8°. . . 343
and the Lutheran Reformation. Scott. N. Y., 1833. 2 v. 12°. 6349
and his Times. Riddle. Lond., 1837. 16°. 6346
Life of. Bower. Philad., 1824. 8°. 6429
The same, by himself. Michelet. Lond., 1846. 8°. . 342
The same. Meurer. N. Y., 1848. 8°. 6511
The same. Sears. Philad. [1850.] 8°. 6571
The same. Tischer. Hudson, 1818. 12°. 6348
Life and Times of. [Lee.] Bost., 1841. 16°. 6347
Lutheran Pulpit, Annals of the American. Sprague. N. Y., 1869. 8°. 7738
Lyell, C. Antiquity of Man. (2 copies.) Philad., 1863. 8°. . . 8989
Principles of Geology. From 5th ed. Philad., 1837. 2 v. 8°. 9009
Second Visit to the U. S. N. Y., 1850. 2 v. 12°. 8411
Travels in N. A. N. Y., 1845. 2 v. in 1. 12°. 8410
Lying, Illustrations of. Opie. Bost., 1827. 12°. 14447
Lyly. See LILLY.

[**Lyman, S. P.**] Life and Memorials of Webster. N. Y., 1853. 2 v. 16°. 7539
Lyman, T. Diplomacy of the U. S. Bost., 1826. 8°. 6160
The same. 2d ed. Bost., 1828. 2 v. 8°. 6161
Polit. State of Italy. Bost., 1820. 8°. 15997
Lynch, A. C. See Mrs. BOTTA.
Lyndon. *(Pseudonym.)* See Miss BRIGHT.
Lyon, G. F. Journal in Mexico. Lond., 1828. 2 v. in 1. 8° . . . 16910
on Parry's Voyage. Bost., 1824. 12°. . . . 16592
Lyon, M., Life of. N. Y. [1858.] 12°. 16418
The same. Hitchcock. Northampton, 1851. 12°. . 16417
Lyttelton, G. *(Lord).* Dialogues of the Dead. 5th ed. Lond., 1768. 8°. 15241
Hist. of Henry II. Lond., 1769–73. 6 v. 8°. 16109
Letters. 8th ed. Lond., 1793. 2 v. 16°. 15847
Poetical Works. Ed. Bell. Lond., 1807. 24°. 535
The same. Ed. Johnson. Dubl., 1804. 8°. 15101
Select Poems. Ed. Walsh. Philad., 1822. 24°. 25
Lyttelton, *Lord* **T.** Letters. Philad., 1821. 24°. 15849

M.

Mabinogion. Bulfinch. (Age of Chivalry.) Bost., 1861. 12°. . . . 1910
Macaulay, C. Hist. of England. Lond., 1769–72. 5 v. 8°. . . 16095
Macaulay, T. B. Biographical and Historical Sketches. (2 copies.) N. Y., 1857. 12°. 3243
Essays, critical and miscellaneous. (2 copies.) N. Y., 1867–68. 8°. 3468
The same. Philad. and N. Y., 1841–60. 5 v. 12°. . 3238
The same. v. 2–4. 3245
The same. v. 2, 3. 3248
The same. N. Y.. 1871. 6 v. 12°. 3252
Essays and Poems. (2 copies.) N. Y., 1860. 12°. 3250
Hist. of England. (3 copies.) N. Y., 1849–71. 5 v. 8° and 12°. 5025
Speeches. N. Y., 1853. 2 v. 12°. 9345
and others. New Biographies. (From Encycl. Brit.) Bost., 1857. 12°. 6715
McCarthy, D. The Siege of Florence. Philad., 1841. 2 v. 12°. . 15575
McCarty, W. Songs, etc., on National Subjects. Philad., 1842. 3 v. 12°. 592
McClellan, G. B., Life and Campaigns of. Hillard. Philad., 1864. 12°. 7281
MacColl, M. Ober-Ammergau Passion Play. 4th ed. Lond., 1871. 16°. 1453
McCosh, J. Christianity and Positivism. N. Y., 1871. 12°. . . 9999
M'Crie, T. Hist. of the Reformation in Italy. Edinb., 1827. 8°. . 6452
in Spain. Edinb., 1829. 8°. . 6453
Life of Knox. N. Y., 1813. 8°. 7701
The same. 6th ed. Edinb., 1839. 8°. 7702
McCullagh, W. T. Use and Study of History. (2 copies.) Dubl., 1842. 8°. 4090

McCulloch, J. R. Statistical Account of Brit. Empire. Lond., 1837. 2 v. 8°. 4989
Universal Gazetteer, ed. Haskel. N. Y., 1847–48. 2 v. 8°. . 8143
MacDonald, G. Adela Cathcart. Bost. 12°. 2584
Alec Forbes. Lond. 8°. 2582
Annals of a Quiet Neighborhood. N. Y., 1867. 12°. . . 2578
David Elginbrod. Bost. 12°. 2583
Robert Falconer. Bost. 12°. 2581
Seaboard Parish. Lond., 1869. 8°. 2579
Vicar's Daughter. Bost., 1872. 12°. 2580
Wilfrid Cumbermede. N. Y., 1872. 12°. 2585
Within and Without. [A Poem.] N. Y., 1872. 16°. . . 1196
MacFarlane, C. Camp of Refuge. Lond., 1844. 2 v. 12°. . . 2380
The Dutch in the Medway. Lond., 1845. 12°. . . . 2382
Legend of Reading Abbey. Lond., 1845. 12°. . . . 2383
Lives of Banditti and Robbers. Philad., 1833. 12°. . . 6704
The same. Philad., 1839. 2 v. 12°. 6705
Romance of Eastern Travel. Lond., 1846. v. 1. 12°. . . 8150
Macfie, M. Vancouver Island and Brit. Columbia. Lond., 1865. 8°. 8395
McGee, T. D. Poems. N. Y., 1869. 8°. 821
MacGeoghegan, J. Hist. of Ireland. N. Y. 8°. 5411
McGilchrist, J. Richard Cobden. N. Y., 1865. 16°. . . . 6688
Macgillivray, W. Travels of Humboldt. Lond., 1852. 8°. . . 8439
The same. N. Y., 1840. 12°. 11274
The same. N. Y., 1833. 12°. 12109
Macgregor, J. A Thousand Miles in the Rob Roy Canoe. Bost., 1871. 16°. 8221
McGuire, E. C. Religious Opinions of Washington. (2 copies.) N. Y., 1836. 12°. 16389
McHarg, C. K. Life of Talleyrand. N. Y., 1857. 12°. . . . 7626
McHenry, J. Pleasures of Friendship and other Poems. Philad., 1836. 12°. 14834
Machiavelli, N. Hist. of Florence ; the Prince ; etc. (2 copies.) Lond., 1847. 8°. 389
Story of Belphagor. (Ital. Novelists, v. 2.) Lond., 1836. 8°. 1900
Machin, L. The Dumb Knight. (Old Plays, v. 4.) Lond., 1825. 8°. 1511
Mackay, C. Collected Songs. Lond., 1859. 16°. 1012
Memoirs of Popular Delusions. Lond., 1869. 8°. 8525
Voices from the Mountains, etc. [Poems.] Bost., 1853. 16°. . 830
McKeevor, T. Voyage to Hudson's Bay. Lond., 1819. 8°. . . 8052
McKenney, T. L. Memoirs ; with Travels among the Indians. N. Y., 1846. 2 v. in 1. 8°. 5950
Tour to the Lakes. Balt., 1827. 8°. 16823
Mackenzie, A. S. The American in England. N. Y., 1835. 2 v. 12°. 16757
Life of Decatur. (Sparks, v. 21.) Bost., 1846. 16°. . . . 7270
Life of Paul Jones. N. Y., 1846. 2 v. 16°. 7536
Life of Perry. N. Y., 1840. 2 v. 12°. 11601
Spain Revisited. N. Y., 1836. 2 v. 12°. 16678
A Year in Spain. 3d ed. N. Y., 1836. 3 v. 12°. . . . 16675

Mackenzie, C. Notes on Haiti. Lond., 1830. 2 v. 12°. . . . 16913
Mackenzie, H. Man of the World. Philad., 1799. 12°. . . . 15500
Miscellaneous Works. N. Y., 1837. 12°. 1992
Works. Glasg., 1818. 3 v. 12°. 13992

CONTENTS.—1, Man of Feeling, etc. 2, Man of the World. 3, Julia de Roubigne.

Mackenzie, R. S. Life of Dickens. Philad., 1870. 12°. . . . 7019
Mackenzie, W. L. Lives of Butler and Hoyt, etc. Bost., 1845. 8°. 7433
Mackie, J. M. From Cape Cod to Dixie. N. Y., 1864. 12°. . . 8409
Life of Gorton. (Sparks, v. 15.) Bost., 1845. 16°. . . . 7264
of Tai-Ping-Wang. N. Y., 1857. 12°. 6477
Mackintosh, *Sir* **J.** Dissertation on Progress of Ethical Philosophy. 2d ed. Philad., 1834. 8°. 8721
The same. Ed. by Wetherell. Edinb., 1837. 8°. . . 8722
Hist. of the Revolution in 1688. (2 copies.) Philad., 1835. 8°. 5013
Life of Sir T. More. Lond., 1831. 16°. 5759
Miscellaneous Works. Philad., 1847. 8°. 3470
The same. Lond., 1846. 3 v. 8°. 9658
Vindiciæ Gallicæ. Defence of the French Revolution. 4th ed. Lond., 1792. 8°. 5565
Memoirs of. R. J. Mackintosh. 2d ed. Lond., 1836. 2 v. 8°. 6834
and others. Hist. of England. Lond., 1830–40. 10 v. 16°. . 4882
The same. v. 1–9. 5162
Maclaren, A. A System of Physical Education. Oxf'd., 1869. 16°. 9118
Maclear, G. F. Apostles of Mediæval Europe. Lond., 1869. 8°. . 6317
McLellan, H. Journal in Scotland, etc. Bost., 1834. 12°. . . 16743
McLellan, J. Mount Auburn, and other Poems. Bost., 1843. 12°. . 14941
Macleod, N. Eastward. (2 copies.) Lond., 1866. 8°. . . . 8073
Macmichael, W. F. Oxford and Cambridge Boat Races. Cambr., 1870. 16°. 9116
Macmillan's Magazine. Lond., 1859–72. v. 1–8, 16–26. 8°. . . 12155
McMurtrie, H. Scientific Lexicon. Philad., 1847. 12°. . . . 16936
Macnally, L. Fashionable Levities. (Mod. Theatre, v. 10.) Lond., 1811. 12°. 1336
Macneill, H. Select Poems. Ed. Walsh. Philad., 1822. 24°. . . 33
Macnish, R. Anatomy of Drunkenness. N. Y., 1835. 12°. . . 9324
Philosophy of Sleep. (2 copies.) N. Y., 1834. 12°. . . 17076
Philosophy of Sleep; Anatomy of Drunkenness. Hartford, 1842. 8°. 3472
Tales, Essays, and Sketches. With Life, by Moir. 2d ed. Lond., 1844. 2 v. 16°. 2367
Macready, W. The Bank Note. (Mod. Theatre, v. 9.) Lond., 1811. 12°. 1335
Madagascar and its People. Sibree. Lond. [1870.] 8°. . . . 7983
Hist. of. Ellis. Lond. [1838.] 2 v. 8°. 6494
Madame de Beaupré. Jenkin. N. Y., 1869. 12°. 2423
Madame Thérèse. Erckmann-Chatrain. N. Y., 1869. 12°. . . 2361
Madden, R. R. Infirmities of Genius. Philad., 1833. 2 v. 12°. . 3181
Life of Countess of Blessington. N. Y., 1856. 2 v. 12°. . 7076
The Mussulman. Philad., 1830. 2 v. 12°. 15517
Travels in Turkey, Egypt, etc. Lond., 1829. 2 v in 1. 8°. . 8067

Madden, R. R. Twelvemonth in the W. I. Lond., 1835. v. 1. 12°. 16916
The United Irishmen. [1st Series.] Philad., 1842. 2 v. 12°. 5247
The same. 3d Series. Dubl., 1846. 3 v. 12°. . . 5249
Madeline. Opie. Bost., 1827. 12°. 14438
Madge. Goodwin. N. Y., 1863. 12°. 2988
Madison, J. Messages, etc. (Statesman's Manual, v. 1.) N. Y., 1854. 8°. 6200
Papers. (2 copies.) Wash., 1840. 3 v. 8°. 6163

CONTENTS.—1, Debates in 1776; Debates in Congress, 1782-83; Letters, 1780-83. 2, Debates in Congress, 1787; Letters, 1787-88. 2, 3, Debates in Federal Convention, 1787.

Life and Times of. Rives. Bost., 1859–68. 3 v. 8°. . . 7447
Madrid in 1835. N. Y., 1836. 2 v. in 1. 8°. 16661
Magalotti, L. Sigismond and Claudia. (Ital. Novelists, v. 4.) Lond., 1836. 12°. 1902
Magellan, Voyage to Strait of. Lond., 1819. 8°. 8052
Magic, Narratives of. Wright. N. Y., 1852. 12°. 8614
Philosophy of. Salverte. N. Y., 1847. 2 v. 12°. . . . 8520
System of. De Foe. Oxf'd., 1840. 16°. 3877
Natural, Letters on. Brewster. N. Y. [1840.] 12°. . . 11270
See, also, APPARITIONS; DEMONOLOGY; NECROMANCERS.
Magie, D. Spring-Time of Life. N. Y., 1853. 12°. 17053
Maginn, W. Shakespeare Papers. Ed. Mackenzie. N. Y., 1856. 12°. 1484
Maglathlin, H. B. The National Speaker. Bost., 1851. 12°. . . 9304
Magnetical Experiments, Report on. Husson. Bost., 1836. 12°. . 8526
Magnetism, or the Doctrine of Equilibrium. Bagg. Detroit, 1845. 12°. 8527
See, also, MESMERISM.
Magoon, E. L. Living Orators in America. N. Y., 1849. 12°. . 7412
Orators of the Revolution. N. Y., 1848. 12°. 7411
Mahomed, H. The Bath. Lond., 1843. 12°. 9230
Mahomet. See MOHAMMED.
Mahon, *Lord.* See P. H. STANHOPE.
Mahoney, S. I. Six Years in Monasteries of Italy. Bost., 1845. 12°. 9583
Maine, H. S. Ancient Law. N. Y., 1864. 8°. 8687
Village Communities in East and West. Lond., 1871. 8°. . 4102
Maine Woods. Thoreau. Bost., 1864. 8°. 10226
Mainstone's Housekeeper. Meteyard. Bost., 1864. 12°. . . . 15497
Maintenon, F. d'Aubigné, *Mme.* **de,** Memoirs of. Philad., 1839. 12°. 6702
Maistre, X. de. Journey round My Room. N. Y., 1871. 16°. . 3198
Maitland, C. Church in the Catacombs. Lond., 1846. 8°. . . 6451
Maitland, F. L. Narrative of Surrender, etc., of Bonaparte. Bost., 1826. 12°. 16221
Malacology. Swainson. Lond., 1840. 16°. 6062
Malay Archipelago, The. Wallace. N. Y., 1869. 8°. . . . 8032
Voyages in, 1832–34. Earl. Lond., 1836. 8°. . 8031
Malcolm, J. Sketches of Persia. Lond., 1828. 2 v. 8°. . . . 8231
Malcom, H. Travels in S. E. Asia. Bost., 1839. 2 v. 12°. . . 16511
Malespini, C. Novels. (Ital. Novelists, v. 3.) Lond., 1836. 12°. . 1901
Malibran, M. F., Memoirs and Letters of. De Merlin. Philad., 1840. 2 v. 12°. 7923

[**Malkin, F.**] Hist. of Greece. Lond., 1829. 8°. 16022
[**Malkin, J. H.**, *etc.*] Historical Parallels. Lond., 1846. 3 v. 12°. . 4555
The same. v. 1. Bost., 1831. 12°. 8815
Mallet, D. Poetical Works. Ed. Bell. Lond., 1807. 24°. . . . 538
Select Poems. Ed. Walsh. Philad., 1822. 24°. . . . 20
The same. Ed. Johnson. Dubl., 1804. 8°. 15101
Mallet, P. H. Northern Antiquities. (Bohn's ed.) Lond., 1859. 8°. 507
Mallet du Pan, J. Hist. of Destruction of the Helvetic Union.
Bost., 1799. 12°. 16162
Malmesbury, Earl of. (J. Harris.) Letters. Lond., 1870. 2 v. 8°. 6830
Malmesbury, William of. Chronicle. (2 copies.) Lond., 1847. 8°. 508
Malone, E. Life of Dryden. Lond., 1800. 8°. 3772
Malory, T. Morte d'Arthur. Lond., 1868. 12°. 1912
Malta, Achievements of Knights of. Sutherland. Philad., 1846. 12°. 4618
Hist. of. Martin. (Colonial Libr., v. 7.) Lond., 1837. 16°. . 7902
Malthus, T. R. Essay on Population. Wash., 1809. 2 v. 8°. . . 8657
The same. 6th ed. Lond., 1826. 2 v. 8°. . . . 8659
Principles of Polit. Economy. Bost., 1821. 8°. . . . 8634
Mammalia, Orders and Habits of. Figuier. Lond., 1870. 8°. . . 8996
Man, Adaptation of Nature to moral and intellectual constitution of.
Chalmers. Philad., 1836. 8°. 16982
to Physical Condition of. Kidd. Philad.,
1836. 8°. 16983
Antiquity of. Lyell. Philad., 1863. 8°. 8989
with the Broken Ear, The. About. N. Y., 1867. 12°. . . 2394
Constitution of. Combe. Hartf'd., 1842. 8°. 3472
Descent of. Darwin. N. Y., 1871. 2 v. 12°. 8932
of Feeling. Mackenzie. N. Y., 1837. 12°. 1992
in Genesis and in Geology. Thompson. N. Y., 1870. 12°. . 8959
and his Migrations. Latham. N. Y., 1852. 12°. . . . 17107
and his Motives. Moore. N. Y., 1848. 16°. 8517
and Nature. Marsh. N. Y., 1867. 8°. 8966
in the Past, Present, and Future. Büchner. Lond., 1872. 8°. 8993
Physical Structure of. Mudie. Bost., 1838. 12°. . . . 9117
Place of, in Nature, Evidence as to. Huxley. N. Y., 1863. 12°. 8939
Primitive. Figuier. Lond., 1870. 8°. 8994
Condition of. Lubbock. N. Y., 1870. 12°. . . 4073
Culture of. Tylor. Lond., 1871. 2 v. 8°. . . 4075
about Town, The. Webbe. Lond., 1838. 2 v. 12°. . . 15498
who laughs, The. Hugo. N. Y., 1869. 8°. 2642
and Wife. W. Collins. N. Y., 1870. 8°. 2304
of the World. Mackenzie. N. Y., 1837. 12°. 1992
See, also, RACE.
Manchester Strike, A. Martineau. Bost., 1833. 12°. . . . 14614
Mancur, J. H. Constance. Philad. 8°. 2313
Mandeville, Sir J. Voiage and Travaile. Ed. Halliwell. Lond.,
1839. 8°. 8034
Mandeville. Godwin. Philad., 1818. 2 v. 12°. 15501
Mankind, Types of. Nott and Gliddon. Philad., 1855. 8°. . . 9094

Mann, E. J. The Deaf and Dumb. Bost., 1836. 12°. . . . 17075
Mann, H. Slavery: Letters and Speeches. Bost., 1853. 12°. . . 8578
Thoughts for a Young Man. Bost., 1850. 16°. 9114
Life of. By his Wife. Bost., 1865. 8°. 7371
Manni, D. M. Ginevra. (Ital. Novelists, v. 4.) Lond., 1836. 12°. . 1902
[**Manning, A.**] Maiden and Married Life of Mary Powell. N. Y. 16°. 2420
Mansfield, E. D. Life of Gen. Scott. N. Y., 1848. 12°. . . . 7394
Political Grammar of U. S. Cincinn., 1836. 12°. . . . 6020
Mansfield, *Earl of.* See W. MURRAY.
Mansfield Park. Austen. Philad., 1838. 8°. 2662
Mansie Wauch. [Moir.] N. Y., 1828. 12°. 15236
Manufactures, Cyclopædia of. Tomlinson. Lond., 1854. 2 v. 8°.
Philosophy of. Ure. Lond., 1835. 12°. 17001
British. Dodd. Lond., 1844–46. 6 v. 12°. 8786
of the Greeks and Romans. Fosbrooke. Lond., 1833–35. 2 v. 16°. 4869
See, also, ARTS.
Manzoni, A. I Promessi Sposi. Wash., 1834. 8°. 2650
[**Marana, J. P.**] Letters by a Turkish Spy. Lond., 1753–54. 8 v. 12°. 13682
Marble Faun, The. Hawthorne. Bost., 1860. 2 v. 16°. . . . 2892
March, D. Night Scenes in the Bible. Philad., 1869. 8°. . . 10012
Yankee Land. Hartf'd., 1840. 12°. 15010
Marcy, R. B. Army Life on the Border. N. Y., 1866. 12°. . . 6129
Margaret: a Story. Lyndon. N. Y., 1868. 12°. 15739
a Tale. Judd. Bost., 1845. 12°. 2953
of Anjou, Life of. Strickland. Philad., 1847. 8°. . . . 5234
Memoirs of. Ed. G. P. R. James. Philad., 1839. 12°. . . 6701
Graham. G. P. R. James. N. Y., 1847. 8°. 2313
Lyndsay. [Wilson.] N. Y., 1823. 12°. 2460
Ravenscroft. St. John. Philad., 1836. 2 v. 12°. . . . 15503
Marguerite of Valois; a Romance. Dumas. N. Y., 1846. 8°. . 2630
Maria del Occidente. See M. BROOKS.
Marie Antoinette, Memoirs of. Campan. Philad., 1823. 8°. . . 5630
The same. Weber. Lond., 1805–25. 3 v. 8°. . . 5627
and her Son. A Novel. [Mundt.] N. Y., 1867. 8°. . . 3072
Marigny, A. de. Hist. of the Arabians. Lond., 1758. 4 v. 8°. . 16055
Mariner, W. The Tonga Islands, ed. Martin. 3d ed. Edinb., 1827. 2 v. 12°. 4475
Mariner's Chronicle, The. N. H., 1835. 12°. 16255
Marion, *Gen.* **Francis,** Life of. Horry and Weems. Philad., 1839. 12°. 16395
The same. Simms. N. Y., 1845. 12°. 7305
Marion, F. Wonderful Balloon Ascents. N. Y., 1870. 12°. . . 10116
Wonders of Optics. (2 copies.) N. Y., 1870. 12°. . . . 10109
of Vegetation. N. Y., 1872. 12°. 10148
Mariotti, L. The Blackgown Papers. Lond., 1846. v. 2. 12°. . 15383
Italy. Lond., 1841. 2 v. 12°. 4686
Mark, St. See BIBLE.
Markham, C. R. Life of Lord Fairfax. Lond., 1870. 8°. . . 6821
Markham, G. Tragedy of Sir R. Grenville. Ed. Arber. Lond., 1871. 16°. 3898

Marlborough, *Duke of*, and *Duchess*. See CHURCHILL.
Marlitt, E. *(Pseudonym.)* See E. JOHN.
Marlowe, C. Works, ed. Dyce. New ed. Lond., 1870. 8°. . . 1572
The same. [Ed. Robinson.] Lond., 1826. v. 1, 2. 16°. 1473
Marmion, S. The Antiquary. (Old Plays, v. 10.) Lond., 1826. 8°. 1517
Marmontel, J. F. Belisarius. Lond., 1794. 12°. 2355
Memoirs of. By himself. Philad., 1807. 2 v. 12°. . . 7590
The same. Lond., 1826–30. 2 v. 12°. 6641
Moral Tales. Lond., 1800. 2 v. 12°. 15131
Maroncelli, P. See S. PELLICO.
Marot, C., and other Studies. Morley. Lond., 1871. 2 v. 8°. . . 3740
Marquette, J., Life of. Sparks. Bost., 1839. 16°. 7259
Marriage. A Novel. Ferrier. N. Y., 1847. 8°. 2672
Married State, Duties of the. Foster. N. Y., 1845. 12°. . . . 17016
Marryat, F. Diary in America. Philad., 1839. 2 v. 12°. . . 16800
The same. N. Y., 1839. 12°. 16802
The same. 2d series. Philad., 1840. 12°. . . . 16803
Jacob Faithful. N. Y., 1835. 12°. 15110
The same. (2 copies.) Philad., 1834. 3 v. 12°. . . 2116
Japhet, in search of a Father. Philad., 1835. 2 v. 12°. . . 2090
The same. 2 v. in 1. 12°. 2092
The King's Own. N. Y., 1836. 12°. 15480
The same. N. Y., 1837. 12°. 2111
The Little Savage. (2 copies.) N. Y., 1849. 12°. . . . 2122
The Naval Officer; or, Frank Mildmay. N. Y., 1835. 12°. . 15522
Pacha of Many Tales; the Three Cutters. N. Y., 1836. 12°. . 15112
The Phantom Ship. Philad., 1839. 12°. 15546
The Pirate, and the Three Cutters. (2 copies.) Philad., 1836. 2 v. in 1. 12°. 2112
Snarleyyow. Philad., 1837. 2 v. in 1. 12°. 2115
Stories of the Sea. (Pirate, and Three Cutters.) N. Y., 1836. 12°. 2114
Marsh, G. P. Lectures on the English Language. 3d ed. N. Y., 1860. 8°. 168
The same. 4th ed. N. Y., 1863. 8°. 169
Man and Nature. N. Y., 1864. 8°. 9092
The same. N. Y., 1867. 8°. 8966
Origin and Hist. of the English Language. N. Y., 1862. 8°. . 170
Marsh, J. Epitome of Eccl. Hist. N. Y., 1828. 12°. . . . 16462
Temperance Recollections. An Autobiography. N. Y., 1866. 12°. 16425
Marsh-Caldwell, A. The Reformation in France. Lond., 1847. 2 v. 8°. 6431
Tales of the Woods and Fields. N. Y., 1836. 12°. . . . 15603
Marshall, C., Passages from the Remembrancer of. Philad., 1839. 12°.
Marshall, E. C. Hist. of U. S. Naval Academy. N. Y., 1862. 12°. 6034
Marshall, J. Life of Washington. Philad., 1804–07. 5 v. 8°. . 7476
The same. Philad., 1833. 2 v. and Atlas. 8°. . . 7481
Writings on the Federal Constitution. (2 copies.) Bost., 1839. 8°. 6283

Marston, John. The Malcontent. (Old Plays, v. 4.) Lond., 1825. 8°. 1511
Works. Lond., 1856. 3 v. 16°. 1417
Marston, John W. Gerald ; and other Poems. Lond., 1842. 12°. . 14847
Marston, P. B. Song-Tide, and other Poems. Bost., 1871. 12°. . 1194
Marston. [Croly.] Philad., 1845. 8°. 2325
Marteilhe, J. The Huguenot Galley-Slave. (2 copies.) N. Y., 1867. 12°. 6355
Marten, H., Life of. Forster. Lond., 1838. 16°. 5762
Martin, A. Natural History. N. Y., 1861–62. 2 v. 12°. 8953
Martin, J. Account of the Tonga Islands. 3d ed. Edinb., 1827. 2 v. 12°. 4475
Martin, R. M. British Colonial Library. Lond., 1836–44. 10 v. 16°. 7896

CONTENTS.—1, The Canadas. 2, Austral-Asia. 3, Southern Africa. 4, 5, West Indies. 6, Nova Scotia, etc. 7, Mediterranean Possessions. 8, 9, East Indies. 10, Possessions in the Indian and Atlantic Oceans.

Hist. of Brit. Possessions in Asia. 2d ed. Lond., 1835. 8°. . 16116
Hist., etc., of Canada. 2d ed. Lond., 1838. 16°. 5719
Martin, W. C. L. Hist. of the Horse. Lond., 1845. 12°. 8782
Martin Chuzzlewit. Dickens. Bost., 1869. 2 v. 8°. 2204
Martineau, H. Biogr. Sketches. N. Y., 1869. 12°. 6748
The Charmed Sea : a Tale. Philad. 8°. 2312
The Crofton Boys. N. Y., 1867. 12°. 14621
Eastern Life. Philad., 1848. 8°. 8098
Feats on the Fiord. Lond. 16°. 14622
The Hamlets. Bost., 1836. 12°. 14625
Hist. of England, 1800–54. (2 copies.) Bost., 1864–66. 4 v. 8°. 4916
How to observe Morals and Manners. N. Y., 1838. 12°. . 16329
Illustrations of Polit. Econ. Bost. and Lond., 1832–33. 13 v. 12°. 14608

CONTENTS.—1, Life in the Wilds. 2, Hill and Valley. 3, Brooke and Brooke Farm. 4, Demerara. 5, Ella of Garveloch. 6, Weal and Woe in Garveloch. 7, A Manchester Strike. 8, Cousin Marshall. 9, Ireland. 10, Homes Abroad. 11, For Each and All. 12, French Wines and Politics. 13, The Charmed Sea.

Miscellanies. (2 copies.) Bost., 1836. 2 v. 12°. 3346
Prize Essays. Bost., 1836. 12°. 9799
Retrospect of Western Travel. N. Y., 1838. 2 v. 12°. . . 16821
The Settlers at home. N. Y., 1841. 12°. 14623
Sickness and Health in Bleaburn. Bost., 1853. 16°. . . 15777
Society in America. (2 copies.) N. Y., 1837. 2 v. 12°. . . 5998
Sowers not Reapers, or Chatham and Mary Kay. Hartf'd., 1845. 12°. 14624
Traditions of Palestine. 2d ed. Lond., 1843. 12°. . . . 14626
Martineau, J. Endeavours after the Christian Life. Bost., 1858. 12°. 9974
Essays. Bost., 1868–70. 2 v. 8°. 3712
Martius, C. F. P. v., and **Spix, J. B. v.** Travels in Brazil. Lond., 1824. 2 v. 8°. 8435
Martyn, H. Journal and Letters, ed. Wilberforce. (Abridged.) N. Y., 1851. 12°. 7601
Memoir of. Sargent. Bost., 1831. 12°. 7565
Martyndale, H. F. Analysis of the Church-Calendar. Lond. 12°. . 4622
Martyrs, The. De Chateaubriand. N. Y., 1812. 3 v. 12°. . . 15133
Book of. Blanchard. Buffalo, 1852. 8°. 16401
The same. Fox. Philad., 1830. 4°. 17329

Marvel, Ik. *(Pseudonym.)* See D. G. MITCHELL.
Marvell, A. Poetical Works, with Memoir. Bost., 1857. 16°. . . 971
The same. 1057
Life of. H. Coleridge. (Worthies.) Leeds, 1836. 8°. . . 6904
Mary of Burgundy. G. P. R. James. N. Y., 1833. 2 v. 12°. . . 2086
Mary I., Queen of Engl., Life of. Strickland. Philad., 1847. 8°. . 5235
Mary II., Q. of Engl., Life of. Strickland. Philad., 1851. 8°. . 5232
Mary, the Handmaid of the Lord. [Mrs. Charles.] N. Y., 1865. 12°. 9842
Mary Powell. [Manning.] N. Y. 16°. 2420
Mary, Queen of Scots. Letters. Ed. A. Strickland. Lond., 1843. 2 v. 12°. 5152
and her Accusers. Hosack. Edinb., 1870–73. 2 v. 8°. . . 5240
and Elizabeth. v. Raumer. Lond., 1836. 12°. 5210
and her latest Historian (Froude). Meline. N. Y., 1872. 12°. 10237
Life of. Bell. N. Y., 1837. 2 v. 12°. 11949
The same. Strickland. N. Y., 1855–59. 5 v. 12°. . 5201
Mary Stuart: a Tragedy. Schiller. Lond., 1847. 8°. . . 439
Mason, E. P., Life and Writings of. Olmsted. N. Y., 1842. 12°. . 16441
Mason, *Major* **John,** Life of. Ellis. Bost., 1844. 16°. . . . 7262
Mason, *Rev.* **John.** Treatise on Self-Knowledge. Hartf'd., 1842. 8°. 3472
Mason, John M. Comments on [Reed's] Shakespeare. Lond., 1785. 8°. 1589
Mason, L. Manual of Vocal Music. Bost., 1834. 12°. . . . 17118
Mason, W. Memoirs of Whitehead. Lond., 1788. 8°. . . . 6955
Works. Lond., 1811. 4 v. 8°. 17237
Masonry. See FREE Masonry.
Massachusetts, Conference on Society and Manners in. Bost., 1820. 12°. 14962
Historical Collections of. Barber. Worc., 1841. 8°. . . 5937
Hist. of, 1628–1750. Hutchinson. Bost., 1795. 2 v. 8°. . . 5836
1748–65. Minot. Bost., 1798–1803. 2 v. in 1. 8°. . 5835
1775–89. Bradford. Bost., 1825. 8°. 5849
Quarterly Review. Bost., 1847–49. v. 1, 2. 8°. . . . 12769
Scenery. Hitchcock. Northampton, 1842. 4°. . . .
See, also, NEW ENGLAND.
Massacre of St. Bartholomew. White. N. Y., 1868. 12°. . . . 6327
Massey, G. Poems. Bost., 1860. 16°. 977
Poems and Ballads. N. Y., 1854. 12°. 856
Shakspeare's Sonnets interpreted. Lond., 1866. 8°. . . 1636
[**Massey, M.**] Lionel Wakefield. Philad., 1837. 2 v. 12°. . . 15490
Massie, J. W. Anti-Slavery Mission to America. Lond., 1864. 8°. . 8555
Massillon, J. B. Sermons. Dundee, 1803. 3 v. 12°. . . . 13522
The same, ed. Dickson. Philad., 1818. 2 v. 8°. . . 10039
Massinger, P. Dramatic Works, ed. H. Coleridge. (2 copies.) Lond., 1840. 8°. 1627
Plays: abridged ed. (2 copies.) N. Y., 1831. 3 v. 12°. . 1683
Masson, D. British Novelists. (2 copies.) Bost., 1859. 12°. . . 51
Life of Milton. Lond., 1859–71. 2 v. 8°. 7112
Recent British Philosophy. N. Y., 1866. 12°. 8580
Masuccio, G. Novels. (Ital. Novelists, v. 1.) Lond., 1836. 12°. . 1899

Mathematical Sciences, Hist. of the. Powell. Lond., 1837. 16°. . 6049
Study, Advantages of. Young. Lond., 1846. 12°. . . . 9253
Mathematics, Recreations in. Enfield. Lond., 1825. 12°. . . 16943
Mather, C. Magnalia; Eccl. Hist. of N. E. (2 copies.) Hartf'd., 1820. 2 v. 8°. 5958
Life of. Peabody. Bost., 1836. 16°. 7255
Mathew, T., Memoir of. Bermingham. N. Y., 1841. 12°. . . 16336
[**Mathews, A.**] Walter Ashwood. N. Y., 1860. 12°. . . . 15811
Mathews, Chas., Memoirs of. By his widow. Philad., 1839. 4 v. 12°. 7930
Mathews, Cornelius. Behemoth. N. Y., 1839. 12°. 15663
Writings. N. Y., 1843. 8°. 15091
Mathias, G. H. D. A Tutor's Counsel to his Pupils. Philad., 1867. 16°. 9143
[**Mathias, T. J.**] The Pursuits of Literature. 7th ed. Lond., 1798. 8°. 15088
The same. Philad., 1800. 8°. 15089
Matrimonial Infelicities. Barry Gray. N. Y., 1866. 12°. . . . 2926
Matteucci, C. Physical Phenomena of Living Beings. (2 copies.) Philad., 1848. 12°. 16961
Matthew, St. See BIBLE.
Matthews, H. Diary of an Invalid. Paris, 1836. 12°. . . . 8187
Maturin, E. Montezuma. N. Y., 1845. 2 v. 12°. 15745
Maunder, S. Treasury of History. N. Y., 1847. 2 v. 8°. . . 15890
Mauprat. G. Sand. Bost., 1870. 16°. 2349
Maurice Dering. [Lawrence.] N. Y., 1865. 8°. 2331
Maurice Tiernay. Lever. N. Y., 1863. 8°. 2319
Mauritius, Hist. of. Martin. (Colonial Library, v. 3.) Lond., 1843. 16°. 7898
Maury, J. S. Principles of Eloquence. N. Y., 1848. 12°. . . 11926
Maury, M. F. Physical Geography of the Sea. N. Y., 1857. 8°. . 9103
Mavor, W. British Tourists. Lond., 1798. 5 v. 12°. . . . 8181
Hist. of Voyages. Lond., 1796–97. v. 4–20. 12°. . . . 13847
Universal History. N. Y., 1803–05. 25 v. 12°. . . . 13497
CONTENTS.—v. 1-9, Ancient: 10-25, Modern.
Max Kromer. Stretton. N. Y., 1871. 16°. 2425
Maxcy, J. Collegiate Addresses. Lond. 16°. 9128
Maximilian, *Emperor of* Mexico. Recollections of my Life. Lond., 1868. 3 v. 8°. 8258
Maximilian, *Prince of* Neuwied. Travels in Brazil. Lond., 1820. 8°. 8053
Maxwell, J. S. The Czar; his Court and People. N. Y., 1848. 12°. 16604
[**Maxwell, W. H.**] Memoirs of Peel. Lond., 1842. 2 v. 12°. . 6779
May, S. J. Recollections of our Antislavery Conflict. Bost., 1869. 12°. 8545
May, Thos. Plays. See DODSLEY'S Old Plays, v. 8, 10.
May, Thos. E. Constitutional Hist. of Engl. (2 copies.) Bost., 1862–63. 2 v. 8°. 4912
Mayer, B. Captain Canot. N. Y., 1866. 12°. 8573
Mexico as it was and as it is. N. Y., 1844. 8°. . . . 5977
Aztec, Spanish and Republican. Hartf'd., 1851. 2 v. in 1. 8°. 5978
Mayer, J. B., etc. Correlation and Conservation of Forces. N. Y., 1869. 12°. 8895

Mayflower, The; or Sketches. H. B. Stowe. N. Y., 1844. 12°. . 2734
Mayhew, H. German Life and Manners. Lond., 1864. 2 v. 8°. . 8313
Mayne, J. The City Match. (Old Plays, v. 9.) Lond., 1825. 8°. . 1516
Maynwaring, A., Life and Posthumous Works of. Lond., 1715. 8°. 16362
[**Mayo, I. F.**] The Crust and the Cake. N. Y. 8°. 2436
Occupations of a Retired Life. (2 copies.) N. Y., 1869. 8°. . 2434
White as Snow. N. Y. 12°. 2441
Mayo, W. S. The Berber. N. Y., 1850. 12°. 15664
Kaloolah. N. Y., 1849. 12°. 7984
Mayor of Wind-Gap. [Banim.] N. Y., 1835. 12°. 15505
Mazzini, G., Life, Writings, and Principles of. N. Y., 1872. 8°. . 7787
Mechanics, Illustrations of. Moseley. N. Y., 1844. 12°. . . 11780
Treatise on. Kater and Lardner. Lond., 1837. 16°. . . 6046
Medals, Dialogues on Ancient. Addison. (Works, v. 3.) N. Y., 1855. 8°. 3793
Medbery, J. K. Men and Mysteries of Wall Street. Bost., 1870. 12°. 8647
Medhurst, W. H. China. Lond., 1838. 8°. 8004
Median Monarchy. Rawlinson (v. 2, 3). N. Y., 1871. 8°. . . 4064
Medical Delusions, Lessons from the Hist. of. Hooker. N. Y., 1850. 12°. 16970
Science, Border Lines of Knowledge in. Holmes. Bost., 1862. 12°. 3605
Medici, Lorenzo de', Life of. Roscoe. Lond., 1847. 8°. . . 400
Medici Family, Memoirs of the. Pignotti. Lond., 1826. 4 v. 8°. . 4680
Mediterranean, Hist. of Brit. Possessions in the. Martin. Lond., 1837. 16°. 7902
Shores, Winter and Spring on the. Bennet. N. Y., 1870. 8°. 8375
Meeker, N. C. Life in the West. N. Y., 1868. 12°. 16871
Meinhold, J. W. The Amber Witch. (2 copies.) N. Y., 1845. 12°. 3044
Melancholy, Anatomy of. Burton. N. Y., 1870. 3 v. 8°. . . 3941
Melanchthon, P., Life of. Cox. Lond., 1817. 8°. 7665
Melanie. Willis. N. Y., 1837. 12°. 792
Melbourne House. S. Warner. N. Y., 1868. 12°. 3001
Meline, J. F. Mary, Q. of Scots, and her latest Historian. N. Y., 1872. 12°. 10237
Melish, J. Description of the U. S., etc. N. Y., 1826. 8°. . . 16824
Mellen, G. W. F. Unconstitutionality of Slavery. Bost., 1841. 12°. 8571
Mellen, Grenville. The Martyr's Triumph, and other Poems. Bost., 1833. 12°. 15011
Melmoth, W. Fitzosborne's Letters; and Dialogue on Oratory. Bost., 1815. 12°. 17029
Melville, H. The Confidence-Man. N. Y., 1857. 12°. . . . 15683
Israel Potter. N. Y., 1855. 12°. 15726
Omoo. (2 copies.) N. Y., 1847–68. 12°. 8325
Redburn. N. Y., 1849. 12°. 15768
Typee. (2 copies.) N. Y., 1846–47. 12°. 8327
White-Jacket. N. Y., 1850. 12°. 15813
Memes, J. S. Hist. of Sculpture, Painting, etc. Edinb., 1829. 12°. . 4501
The same. Bost., 1831. 12°. 8868

Memes, J. S. Memoirs of Josephine. N. Y., 1832. 12°. 11030
The same. N. Y., 1834. 12°. 11956
Men, Women, and Ghosts. Phelps. Bost., 1869. 12°. 2975
Menageries, The. [Ogilby.] v. 1. (Quadrupeds.) Bost., 1830. 12°. 8805
The same. v. 2. (The Elephant.) Bost., 1832. 12°. . 8811
Animals in. Swainson. Lond., 1838. 16°. 6053
Menault, E. The Intelligence of Animals. N. Y., 1869. 12°. . . 10119
Mendelssohn-Bartholdy, F. Letters, 1833–47. (2 copies.) Philad., 1864–66. 16°. 7889
from Italy and Switzerland. (2 copies.) Philad., 1863–65. 16°. 7887
Life of. Lampadius. N. Y., 1865. 16°. 7885
Recollections of. Devrient. Lond., 1869. 8°. 7922
Men's Wives. Thackeray. (Works, v. 9.) Lond., 1872. 8°. . . 2198
Mental Action, Imperfect and Disordered. Upham. N. Y., 1841. 12°. 11424
Discipline. Burder. N. Y., 1830. 12°. 17035
Hygiene. Ray. Bost., 1863. 12°. 8513
See, also, MIND ; PHILOSOPHY : PSYCHOLOGY.
Menzel, W. Europe in 1840. Edinb., 1841. 8°. 4635
German Literature, transl. by Felton. Bost., 1840. 3 v. 12°. 119
The same, transl. by Gordon. Oxf'd., 1840. 4 v. 16°. 115
Hist. of Germany. (Bohn's ed.) 3 copies. Lond., 1848–53. 3 v. 8°. 404
Mercedes of Castile. Cooper. Philad., 1840. 12°. 2794
Merchant of Berlin. Mühlbach. N. Y., 1867. 12°. 3104
and the Friar, The. Palgrave. Lond., 1844. 16°. . . . 2369
Merchant's Clerk, The. Warren. N. Y., 1836. 12°. 15506
Merchant's Magazine. See HUNT'S Merchant's Magazine.
Meredith, Owen. *(Pseudonym.)* See R. BULWER-LYTTON.
Merimée, P. 1572. A Chronicle. N. Y., 1830. 12°. 2645
Merivale, C. Conversion of the Northern Nations. N. Y., 1866. 8°. 6319
of the Roman Empire. N. Y., 1865. 8°. . 6318
Hist. of Romans under the Empire. N. Y., 1863–65. 7 v. 8°. 4702
Merle d'Aubigné, J. H. Hist. of Reformation in 16th century. (3 copies.) N. Y., 1842–61. 5 v. 12°. 6371
The same. Philad. and N. Y., 1844–66. v. 1–4, in 2. 8° and 12°. 6482
Hist of Reformation, in time of Calvin. N. Y., 1863–72. 5 v. 12°. 6386
Miscellany. N. Y., 1845. 12°. 9806
The Protector. (2 copies.) N. Y., 1850–57. 12°. 5312
Merlin, M. J. de. Memoirs of Malibran. Philad., 1840. 2 v. 12°. 7923
Merry Tales of Wise Men of Gotham. [Paulding.] N. Y., 1826. 12°. 15287
Mesmerism, Facts in. Townshend. N. Y., 1848. 12°. 17105
See, also, MAGNETISM ; SOMNAMBULISM.
Mesopotamia, Hist., etc., of. Fraser. N. Y., 1845. 12°. . . . 11759
Metal, Manufactures in. Holland. Lond., 1831–34. 3 v. 16°. . 6037
Manufactures of Grt. Brit. Dodd. Lond., 1845. 12°. . . 8788
Metaphysic of Ethics, The. Kant. Edinb., 1836. 8°. 8733
See, also, PHILOSOPHY.

Metastasio, P. Dramas and Poems. Transl. by Hoole. Lond., 1800. 3 v. 8°. 906
Meteorology, Elements of. Brocklesby. N. Y., 1849. 12°. . . 8894
Meteors, etc. Zürcher and Margollé. N. Y., 1870. 12°. . . . 10146
Meteyard, E. Mainstone's Housekeeper. Bost., 1864. 12°. . . 15497
Methodist Pulpit, Annals of the American. Sprague. N. Y., 1859. 8°. 7736
Metropolis, The Great. [Grant.] N. Y., 1837. 2 v. 12°. . . . 5144
Metropolitan Magazine. N. Y., 1836–42. 13 v. 8°. 14520
Metropolitan Pulpit, The. [Grant.] N. Y., 1839. 12°. . . . 9914
Meunier, V. Adventures on Hunting Grounds. N. Y., 1869. 12°. . 10120
Meurer, M. Life of Luther. N. Y., 1848. 8°. 6511
Mexican Revolution of 1810–19, Memoirs of. Robinson. Philad., 1820. 8°. 16148
War of 1846–47, Notes for Hist of. Ed. Ramsey. N. Y., 1850. 12°. 5824
Service afloat and ashore during. Semmes. Cincinn., 1851. 8°. 5825
Mexico. Ward. 2d ed. Lond., 1829. 2 v. 8°. 5979
in 1842. [Folsom.] N. Y., 1842. 12°. . . . . , . 16911
Adventures in, 1846. Ruxton. N. Y., 1848. 12°. . . . 16923
as it was and is. Mayer. N. Y., 1844. 8°. 5977
Aztec, Spanish and Republican. Mayer. Hartf'd., 1851. 2 v. in 1. 8°. 5978
Description of. Conder. Lond. 12°. 7858
Diary in, 1867. Salm-Salm. Lond., 1868. 2 v. 8°. . . 5826
Hist. of. [to 1521.] Clavigero. Philad., 1804. 3 v. 8°. . 5974
of Conquest of. Diaz del Castillo. Salem, 1803. 2 v. 8°. 5972
The same. Prescott. Philad., 1871. 3 v. 8°. . 10327
The same. Wilson. Philad., 1859. 8°. . . 5971
Journal on coast of, 1820–22. Hall. Lond., 1840. 8°. . . 8101
Journal in, 1826. Lyon. Lond., 1828. 8°. 16910
Life in, 1839–41. Calderon de la Barca. Bost., 1843. 2 v. 12°. 16905
Rambler in, 1834. Latrobe. N. Y., 1836. 12°. . . . 16909
Recollections of, 1842–44. Thompson. N. Y., 1847. 12°. . 16907
Travels in, 1846–47. Carpenter. N. Y., 1851. 12°. . . 16908
Michael Armstrong. *Mrs. Trollope.* N. Y., 1840. 2 v. 12°. . . 15507
Michailow, —. Adventures in Tartary. Lond., 1822. 8°. . . 8057
Michel-Angelo. See BUONARROTI.
Michelet, J. Hist. of France [to 1453.] Tr. by Kelly. Lond., 1844–46. 2 v. 8°. 5648
The same [to 1380]. Tr. by G. H. Smith. N. Y., 1845. 1 v. 8°. 5650
Hist. of Roman Republic. (2 copies.) Lond., 1847. 8°. . . 324
Modern History. N. Y., 1843. 12°. 11771
The same. 12284
Priests, Women and Families. Also, The People. Lond., 1846. 16°. 9513
Michell, R. Honesty: a Poem. Lond., 1769. 8°. 14806
Michigan, Hist. of., to 1837. Lanman. N. Y., 1841. 12°. . . 11614

Michigan, Sketches of. Detroit, 1834. 12°. 16043
Mickle, W. J. Select Poems. Ed. Walsh. Philad., 1822. 24°. . 28
Microcosm, The. N. H., 1836–37. v. 3, N. S. 8°. 14598
Microscope, The. Hogg. Lond., 1869. 8°. 8899
Microscope, The. [A periodical.] N. H., 1820. 2 v. in 1. 8°. . 17474
Middle Ages, Literary Hist. of. Berington. Lond., 1846. 8°. . . 321
Romances of the. Cox and Jones. Lond., 1871. 8°. . . . 2010
See, also, CRUSADES; EUROPE (History of).
Middle Kingdom, The. Williams. N. Y., 1849. 2 v. 12°. . . 6471
Middlebury College. The Philomathesian. 1833–34. v. 1. 8°. . 17473
Middlemarch. George Eliot. N. Y., 1872. 2 v. 12°. 2540
Middleton, C. Life of Cicero. Lond., 1837. 8°. 7743
Middleton, T. Plays. See DODSLEY'S Old Plays, v. 5, 6, 11.
Works, ed. Dyce. Lond., 1840. 5 v. 8°. 1468
Midshipman's Expedients, and other Tales. Philad., 1837. 2 v. 12°. 14874
Midsummer Eve; a Fairy Tale. Hall. N. Y., 1848. 8°. 2312
Miers, J. Travels in Chile and La Plata. Lond., 1826. 2 v. 8°. . 8463
Mignet, F. A. M. Hist. of French Revolution. N. Y., 1827. 8°. . 16247
The same. (Bohn's ed.) 3 copies. Lond., 1846–56. 8°. 377
Milburn, W. H. The Rifle, Axe, and Saddle-Bags, etc. (2 copies.)
N. Y., 1857. 12°. 3583
Miles Wallingford. Cooper. N. Y., 1856. 12°. 2820
Milford, J. Norway, and her Laplanders. Lond., 1842. 8°. . . 8300
Military Commanders, British, Lives of. Gleig. Lond., 1831–32.
3 v. 16°. 5771
For Contents, see GLEIG.
Sketch-Book, The. N. Y., 1827. 2 v. 12°. 16270
Mill, James. Elements of Polit. Economy. 3d. ed. Lond., 1844. 8°. 8625
Hist. of British India. 3d ed. Lond., 1826. 6 v. 8°. . . 6464
Mill, John Stuart. Dissertations and Discussions. Bost., 1865–67.
4 v. 8°. 3715
The same. v. 1, 2. 3719
Liberty. 2d ed. Bost., 1863. 16°. 3714
Positive Philosophy of Comte. Bost., 1871. 12°. 8590
Principles of Polit. Economy. (2 copies.) N. Y., 1870. 2 v. 8°. 8663
Representative Government. (2 copies.) N. Y., 1862–67. 12°. 8618
Subjection of Women. (2 copies.) N. Y., 1869. 12°. . . 9203
System of Logic. (2 copies.) N. Y., 1848–64. 8°. . . . 8743
Mill on the Floss. George Eliot. N. Y., 1860. 12°. 2533
Millar, John. Hist. View of the Engl. Gov't. Lond., 1803. 4 v. 8°. 5356
Origin of Ranks. 4th ed. Edinb., 1806. 8°. 17086
Miller, G. History, philosophically illustrated. Lond., 1832. 4 v. 8°. 4092
The same. (Bohn's ed.) Lond., 1848–49. 4 v. 8°. . 358
Miller, Hugh. Cruise of the Betsey; Rambles of a Geologist. Bost.,
1862. 12°. 8980
Essays. (2 copies.) Bost., 1865. 12°. 3721
First Impressions of England. (2 copies.) Bost., 1851–56. 12°. 8355
Foot-Prints of the Creator. (2 copies.) Bost., 1850. 12°. . 8974
Geology of the Bass Rock. N. Y., 1851. 12°. 8829

Miller, Hugh. My Schools and Schoolmasters. Bost., 1855. 12°. . 7100
Old Red Sandstone. (2 copies.) Bost., 1851. 12°. . . . 8972
Popular Geology. (2 copies.) Bost., 1860–65. 12°. . . . 8978
Scenes and Legends of Scotland. (2 copies.) Cinc., 1851–52. 12°. 2586
Tales and Sketches. Bost., 1863. 12°. 2588
Testimony of the Rocks. (2 copies.) Bost., 1857. 12°. . . 8976
Life and Letters of. Bayne. Bost., 1871. 2 v. 12°. . . 7101
Life and Times of. T. N. Brown. N. Y., 1860. 12°. . . 6978
Miller, James. Mahomet. (Brit. Drama.) Lond., 1804. 8°. . . 1630
Miller, Joaquin. Songs of the Sierras. (2 copies.) Bost., 1871. 16°. 766
Miller, Jona. P. Greece in 1827–28. N. Y., 1828. 12°. . . . 15952
Miller, J. R. Hist. of Great Britain. Philad., 1837. 8°. . . . 5392
Miller, L. W. Notes of an Exile. Fredonia, 1846. 12°. . . . 16256
Miller, S. Letters on Clerical Manners and Habits. N. Y., 1827. 12°. 9828
to Sons in College. Philad., 1843. 12°. . . 17031
Life of J. Edwards. Bost., 1837. 16°. 7257
Retrospect of 18th century. N. Y., 1803. 2 v. 8°. . . . 15902
Miller, T. Lady Jane Grey. Philad., 1840. 2 v. 12°. . . . 15483
Rural Sketches. Philad., 1842. 12°. 15570
Miller of Angibault, The. George Sand. Bost., 1871. 16°. . . 2352
Miller's Story of the War, A. Erckmann-Chatrain. N. Y., 1872. 12°. 2364
Millingen, J. G. Hist. of Duelling. (2 copies.) Lond., 1841. 2 v. 8°. 15148
Millot, C. F. X. Elements of Hist. Worc., 1789. 5 v. 8°. . . 15879
Mills, A. Literature of Grt. Brit. and Ireland. N. Y., 1856. 2 v. 8°. 228
Mills, C. Hist. of Chivalry. Philad., 1825. 8°. 4737
of the Crusades. Philad., 1824. 8°. 4738
of Muhammedanism. 2d ed. Lond., 1818. 8°. . 10031
Milman, H. H. Annals of S. Paul's. 2d ed. Lond., 1869. 8°. . 6419
Hist. of Christianity [to 412]. Lond., 1840. 3 v. 8°. . . 6568
of the Jews. Enlarged ed. N. Y., 1864. 3 v. 8°. . . 6303
The same. N. Y., 1840. 3 v. 12°. 11000
The same. N. Y., 1830. 3 v. 12°. 11929
of Latin Christianity. N. Y., 1860–61. 8 v. 8°. . . 6391
Life and Correspondence of Gibbon. Lond., 1839. 8°. . . 7123
Poetical Works. (2 copies.) Lond., 1839. 3 v. 16°. . . 995
Samor, Lord of the Bright City. N. Y., 1818. 12°. . . . 14835
Savonarola, Erasmus, and other Essays. Lond., 1870. 8°. . 3435
Milner, J. Hist. of the Church. Bost., 1822. 5 v. 12°. . . . 6334
Milnes, R. M. Life and Letters of Keats. N. Y., 1848. 12°. . . 7000
Poems of Many Years. New ed. Bost., 1846. 16°. . . 1212
Milns, W. The Well-bred Scholar. Lond., 1794. 8°. . . . 17532
Milton, J. Areopagitica. Ed. Arber. Lond., 1868. 16°. . . . 3885
Comus, as performed at the Theatre. Edinb., 1782. 12°. . 1404
Poetical Works. Philad., 1842. 8°. 945
The same. N. Y., 1832. 2 v. in 1. 12°. . . . 958
The same. Ed. Bell. Lond., 1817. 2 v. 24°. . . 257
The same, with Life. Ed. Mitford. Bost., 1839. 2 v. 8°. 1251
The same. Ed. Johnson. Dubl., 1804. 8°. . . . 15096
The same. Ed. Sanford. Philad., 1819. 2 v. 24°. . 4

Milton, J. Prose and Poetical Works. Lond., 1844. 8°. 3789
Prose Works. Lond., 1844. 8°. 3788
The same. (Bohn's ed.) 2 copies. Lond., 1848–70. 5 v. 8°. 454

CONTENTS.—1, Defences of People of England; Eikonoklastes. 2, Tenure of Kings and Magistrates; Areopagitica; Tracts on the Commonwealth; On Ormond's Peace; Letters of State; Of Reformation in England; Reason of Church Gov't. against Prelaty, etc. 3, Smectynuus Pieces; On Divorce; Tetrachordon; Colasterion; On Education; Familiar Letters, etc. 4, 5, On Christian Doctrine. 5, Hist. of Britain; Hist. of Moscovia; Latin Grammar; Index.

Select English Prose Works. (2 copies.) Bost., 1826. 2 v. 12°. 3944
Character and Writings of. Channing. Bost., 1841. 12°. 9568
Concordance to Poems of. Cleveland. Lond., 1867. 16°. 1203
Criticism on Paradise Lost of. Addison. Ed. Arber. Lond., 1868. 16°. 3887
Life of. Bell. Lond., 1839. 16°. 5777
The same. Hayley. Dubl., 1797. 8°. 7110
Life and Times of. Ivimey. N. Y., 1833. 12°. 6952
Life of, with Hist. of his Time. Masson. Lond., 1859–71. 2 v. 8°. 7112
Life and Writings of. Todd. Lond., 1826. 8°. 7111
the Patriot and Poet. E. P. Hood. Lond., 1852. 12°. 6953
and his Times. A Novel. Ring. N. Y., 1868. 8°. 3093

Mind and Brain. Laycock. N. Y., 1869. 2 v. 8°. 8581
Improvement of the. Watts. Bost., 1826. 12°. 8493
amongst the Spindles. Lond., 1845. 12°. 2727
Use of the Body in relation to the. Moore. N. Y., 1849. 12°. 8515
See, also, MENTAL.

Mineral Kingdom, The. Lond., 1842. 12°. 16942

Mineralogy, Manual of. Dana. N. H., 1851. 12°. 8921

Minister's Family, The. Mrs. Ellis. N. Y., 1844. 12°. 15509
Wooing, The. Mrs. Stowe. Bost., 1868. 12°. 2961

Ministry, Letters on the. Wayland. Bost., 1863. 16°. 9832
to a Son in the. Humphrey. N. Y., 1845. 12°. 17034
to Young Men preparing for the. Cogswell. Bost., 1837. 12°. 17036

Minot, G. R. Hist. of Mass., 1748–65. Bost., 1798–1803. 2 v. in 1. 8°. 5835

Minstrelsy: ancient and modern. Motherwell. Bost., 1846. 2 v. 16°. 824
of Scottish Border. Scott. Lond., 1839. 8°. 1309
See, also, BALLADS; POETRY; SONGS.

Mirabeau, H. G. Riquetti de. Gallery of Portraits. See LUCHET.
Secret Hist. of Court of Berlin. Dubl., 1789. 8°. 16460
Life-History of. [Pipitz.] Philad., 1848. 12°. 7622
Memoirs of. By himself, etc. Lond., 1835–36. v. 1–4. 8°. 7717
Recollections of. Dumont. Lond., 1835. 8°. 7721

Mirabeau. An historical Novel. Mundt. N. Y., 1868. 8°. 3092

Miracles, past and present. Mountford. Bost., 1870. 12°. 9908
of our Lord, Notes on the. Trench. N. Y., 1858. 8°. 10004

Miramion, M. B. de, Life of. Bonneau. Lond., 1870. 8°. 7676

Miriam Coffin. N. Y., 1834. 2 v. 12°. 15740

Mirror, The. [A Periodical.] 6th ed. Lond., 1786. 3 v. 12°. 13038
The same. Ed. Ferguson. Lond., 1823. 2 v. 12°. 3136

Mirror Library, The. N. Y. 3 v. 8°. 15092

Miscellaneous Works, by a Young Gentleman. N. Y., 1795. 12°. 15306

Miscellanies. Bost., 1821. 12°. 15323
Miserrimus. [Reynolds.] N. Y., 1833. 12°. 15510
Miss Gilbert's Career. Holland. N. Y., 1862. 12°. 2920
Miss Ravenel's Conversion. DeForest. N. Y., 1857. 12°. . . . 2942
Miss Van Kortland. [Benedict.] Bost., 1871. 8°. 2688
Missionaries, Orations for. E. Irving. N. Y., 1825. 8°. . . . 9969
Missions, History of. Smith and Choules. Bost., 1837. 2 v. 4°. . 6596
Relations and Claims of. Anderson. N. Y., 1869. 8°. . . 6299
Mississippi Bubble, The. Thiers. N. Y., 1859. 12°. 6634
Valley, Hist. of Discovery of. Hart. St. Louis, 1852. 12°. . 16876
Recollections of; 1814–24. Flint. Bost., 1826. 8°. . 16861
Missouri, Journal of Tour in, 1818–19. Schoolcraft. Lond., 1821. 8°. 8054
Mrs. Jerningham's Journal. N. Y., 1870. 16°. 1195
Mistress and Maid. A Story. Craik. N. Y., 1867. 8°. . . . 2310
Mitchel, O. M. Astronomy of the Bible. (3 copies.) N. Y., 1863–67. 12°. 8914
Planetary and Stellar Worlds. (2 copies.) N. Y., 1851–63. 12°. 8911
Popular Astronomy. N. Y., 1860. 12°. 8913
Mitchell, D. G. The Battle Summer. (2 copies.) N. Y., 1850–53. 12°. 5545
Doctor Johns. (2 copies.) N. Y., 1866. 2 v. 8°. 2909
Dream Life. N. Y., 1868. 12°. 3598
Fresh Gleanings. (2 copies.) N. Y., 1847–56. 12°. . . . 8270
Fudge Doings. N. Y., 1855. 2 v. 12°. 2907
The Lorgnette. (3 copies.) N. Y., 1851–54. 2 v. 12°. . . 3599
My Farm of Edgewood. (2 copies.) N. Y., 1863. 12°. . . 8922
Reveries of a Bachelor. (2 copies.) N. Y., 1850–51. 12°. . 3595
The same. New ed. N. Y., 1871. 12°. 3597
Rural Studies. N. Y., 1867. 12°. 8926
Seven Stories, with Basement and Attic. N. Y., 1864. 12°. . 2913
Wet Days at Edgewood. (2 copies.) N. Y., 1865. 12°. . . 8924
Mitchell, James. Tour through Belgium, etc. Lond., 1816. 8°. . 16657
Mitchell, John. Life of Wallenstein. 2d ed. Lond., 1840. 8°. . 7790
Mitchell, T. L. Expeditions in Australia. 2d ed. Lond., 1839. 2 v. 8°. 8085
Mitford, A. B. Tales of Old Japan. Lond., 1871. 2 v. 8°. . . 2005
Mitford, M. R. Our Village. N. Y., 1828–30. 4 v. 12°. . . . 2409
The same. v. 1–3. 2413
Works. Philad. 8°. 2675
Life and Letters of. N. Y., 1870. 2 v. 12°. 7053
Mitford, W. Hist. of Greece. Lond., 1820. 10 v. 8°. . . . 15954
Mivart, St. G. Genesis of Species. (2 copies.) Lond., 1871. 8°. . 8943
Modern Accomplishments. Sinclair. N. Y., 1836. 12°. . . . 15511
Chivalry. Brackenridge. Philad., 1804. 2 v. 12°. . . . 15742
Cymon, The. Kock. Philad., 1833. 2 v. 12°. 15137
Griselda, The. Edgeworth. (Works, v. 9.) Bost., 1825. 8°. . 15343
Society. Sinclair. N. Y., 1837. 12°. 15512
Women. N. Y., 1868–70. 2 v. 12°. 9206
The same. v. 1. 9205
Möllhausen, B. Journey to the Pacific. Lond., 1858. 2 v. 8°. . 8419
Moens, W. J. C. English Travelers and Italian Brigands. N. Y., 1866. 12°. 8347
Moffat, R. Missionary Labors in S. Africa. N. Y., 1843. 12°. . . 16521

Mogul Empire, Travels in the, 1655–68. Bernier. Lond., 1826. 2 v. 8°. 16541
Mohammed. The Koran. Tr. by Sale. Lond., 1825. 2 v. 8°. . 10032
Life of. (Libr. of Useful Knowl.) Lond., 1833. 8°. . . 6751
The same. Bush. N. Y., 1841. 12°. 11937
and his Successors. Irving. N. Y., 1860. 2 v. 12°. . . 7579
Lives of. Ockley. Lond., 1847. 8°. . 423
Mohammed Ali and his House. A Romance. [Mundt.] N. Y., 1872. 8°. 3091
Mohammedanism, Hist. of. Mills. Lond., 1818. 8°. . . . 10031
Moir, D. M. Life of Macnish. (Tales, v. 1.) Lond., 1844. 16°. . 2367
Mansie Wauch. N. Y., 1828. 12°. . . . 15236
[**Moir, G.**] Treatises on Poetry and Romance. Edinb., 1839. 12°. . 164
Mollien, G. Travels in Africa. (Voyages, v. 3.) Lond., 1820. 8°. . 8053
Molloy, G. Geology and Revelation. N. Y., 1870. 12°. . . . 8982
Mommsen, T. Hist. of Rome. N. Y., 1869–70. 4 v. 12°. . . 4694
The same. N. Y., 1871. 4 v. 8°. 4698
Monaldi. Allston. Bost., 1841. 12°. 15744
Monarchs retired from business. Doran. N. Y., 1857. 2 v. 12°. . 6752
Monarchy. Brougham. (Polit. Philos., v. 1.) Lond., 1844. 8°. . 8680
Monastery, The. Scott. Edinb., 1870. 8°. 1881
Money, Theory of. Tucker. Bost., 1839. 12°. 8648
Monikins, The. Cooper. Philad., 1841. 12°. 2809
Monk, G., Life of. Skinner. Dubl., 1724. 8°. 6626
Memoirs of. Guizot. Lond., 1838. 8°. 6822
Monk of Cimiés, The. Sherwood. (Works, v. 14.) N. Y., 1837. 12°. 15126
Monks of the West. (500–700.) Montalembert. Edinb., 1861. 2 v. 8°. 6489
Monmouth, Geoffrey of. See GEOFFREY.
Monnier, M. Wonders of Pompeii. N. Y., 1870. 12°. . . . 10127
Monroe, J. Messages, etc. (Statesman's Manual, v. 1.) N. Y., 1854. 8°. 6200
Tours of, in 1817–18. Waldo. Hartf'd., 1818. 12°. . . . 16393
Monsieur Sylvestre. Sand. Bost., 1870. 16°. 2351
Monstrelet, E. de. Chronicles, tr. by Johnes. (2 copies.) Lond., 1840. 2 v. 8°. 5700
Montagu, B. Selections from Taylor, Hall, etc. (2 copies.) N. Y., 1845. 12°. 3957
The same. Lond., 1839. 16°. 3917
Montagu, C. *(Earl of Halifax).* Poems, ed. Johnson. Dubl., 1804. 8°. 15097
Sketch of. Thorold Rogers. Lond., 1869. 8°. . . . 6731
[**Montagu, E.**] Essay on Shakespeare. Lond., 1769. 8°. . . . 1590
Montagu, M. W. Letters and Works. Philad., 1837. 2 v. 8°. . 3802
Works. Lond., 1803. 5 v. 12°. 13208
Montaigne, M. de. Essays. Lond., 1759. 3 v. 8°. 3403
Montalembert, C. F. de. The Monks of the West. Edinb., 1861. 2 v. 8°. 6489
Montenegro, Travels in, 1810–12. Vialla de Sommières. Lond., 1820. 8°. 8054
Montesquieu, C. de Secondat de. Spirit of Laws. Lond., 1766. 2 v. 8°. 14771
Works. Lond., 1777. 4 v. 8°. 9522

CONTENTS.—1, 2, Spirit of Laws. 3, Grandeur and Declension of the Roman Empire; Persian Letters. 4, Familiar Letters; Miscellanies; Analysis of Spirit of Laws by d'Alembert, etc.; Index.

Montez, Lola. Anecdotes of Love. N. Y. [1858.] 12°. 15824
Lectures and Autobiography. N. Y., 1859. 12°. . . . 15825
Montezuma; a Romance. Maturin. N. Y., 1845. 2 v. 12°. . . 15745
Montgomery, C. Eagle Pass. N. Y., 1852. 12°. 16882
Montgomery, G. W. Journey to Guatemala. N. Y., 1839. 8°. . 16900
Montgomery, J. Lectures on Literature, Poetry, etc. N. Y., 1840. 12°. 11284
The same. N. Y., 1833. 12°. 12114
Poetical Works. Philad., 1830. 8°. 944
The same. 947
The same. Bost., 1825. 4 v. 24°. 544
The same. 13834
The same. Bost., 1860. 5 v. 16°. 1066
Prose, by a Poet. Philad., 1824. 2 v. in 1. 12°. . . . 3172
The Wanderer, and other Poems. Philad., 1811. 12°. . . 14848
Montgomery, R., Life of. Armstrong. Bost., 1834. 16°. . . 7250
Month, The. Lond., 1870–71. New Series, v. 1–4. 8°. . . . 17778
Monthly Magazine. Lond., 1796–1825. 60 v. 8°. 14152
Review. Lond., 1817–33. v. 82–129, 131, 132. 8°. . . . 14300
Montholon-Semonville, C. T. de. Hist. of Captivity of Napoleon.
N. Y., 1846. 8°. 5598
Memoirs of Hist. of France. See NAPOLÉON I.
Montrose, *Marquis of.* See J. GRAHAM.
Montsalvatge, R., Life of. N. Y., 1845. 12°. 17281
Montulé, E. de. Travels in Egypt; Voyage to N. America, etc.
Lond., 1821. 8°. 8055
Moon, G. W. The Dean's English. 4th ed. [Lond., 1865.] 16°. . 58
Moon, Wonders of the. Guillemin. N. Y., 1873. 12°. . . . 10150
Moonstone, The. Collins. N. Y., 1869. 8°. 2303
Moore, C. C. G. Castriot, surnamed Scanderbeg. N. Y., 1850. 12°. 7583
Moore, E. The Gamester. (Brit. Drama, v. 1, pt. 2.) Lond., 1804. 8°. 1630
Poetical Works. Ed. Bell. Lond., 1807. 24°. 536
Select Poems. Ed. Walsh. Philad., 1819. 24°. 17
The same. Ed. Johnson. Dubl., 1804. 8°. . . . 15101
Moore, F. American Eloquence. N. Y., 1857. 2 v. 8°. . . 9432
Diary of the American Revolution. N. Y., 1860. 2 v. 8°. . 6189
The Rebellion Record. N. Y., 1861–64. v. 1–7. 8°. . . 6262
Moore, G. Man and his Motives. N. Y., 1848. 16°. . . . 8517
Power of the Soul over the Body. N. Y., 1847. 12°. . . 8516
Use of the Body in relation to the Mind. N. Y., 1849. 12°. . 8515
Moore, H. Memoir of Ethan Allen. Plattsburgh, 1834. 12°. . . 7495
Moore, J. S. Pictorial Book of Ballads. Lond., 1847–48. 2 v. 8°. 1205
Moore, John. View of Society and Manners in Italy. 3d ed. Lond.,
1783. 2 v. 8°. 16737
Works. Edinb., 1820. 7 v. 8°. 17317
Moore, T. The Epicurean. Bost., 1827. 12°. 2022
The same. N. Y., 1862. 12°. 2461
Fudge Family in Paris. N. Y., 1818. 12°. 14837
Hist. of Ireland. (2 copies.) Lond., 1836–40. 3 v. 16°. . 5176
Lalla Rookh. Philad., 1817. 12°. 994

Moore, T. Lalla Rookh. N. Y., 1849. 12°. 652
The same. Philad., 1849. 8°. 1278
Life of Byron. Philad., 1869. 2 v. 8°. 7184
The same. Lond., 1844. 8°. 7186
of Fitzgerald. N. Y., 1831. 2 v. 12°. 6684
Melodies, Songs, Sacred Songs, and National Airs. N. Y., 1821. 12°. 602
The same. 14836
Memoirs of Sheridan. Philad., 1826. 2 v. 12°. 6912
Poetical Works. Bost. [1864.] 24°. 974
The same. Lond., 1840–44. v. 1–9. 16°. 643

CONTENTS.—1, Odes of Anacreon; Juvenile Poems. 2, Juvenile Poems; Poems Relating to America. 3, Corruption and Intolerance; The Sceptic; Twopenny Post-Bag; Satirical and Humorous Poems; Irish Melodies. 4, Irish Melodies; National Airs; Sacred Songs; Summer Fete. 5, Evenings in Greece; Ballads; Songs; Miscellaneous Poems. 6, 7, Lalla Rookh. 7, Political and Satirical Poems; Fudge Family in Paris; Fables for the Holy Alliance; Rhymes on the Road; Miscellaneous Poems. 8, Loves of the Angels; Miscellaneous Poems; Satirical and Humorous Poems. 9, Satirical and Humorous Poems; The Fudges in England; Songs from M. P., or the Blue Stocking; Miscellaneous Poems.

Tom Crib's Memorial to Congress. N. Y., 1819. 12°. . . . 14838
Memoirs, Journal, and Correspondence of. Russell. N. Y., 1857. 2 v. 8°. 7178
Moore, W. V. Indian Wars of the U. S. Philad., 1840. 12°. . . 5747
Moors. See SARACENS; SPAIN.
Moraes, F. de. Palmerin of England, ed. Southey. Lond., 1807. 4 v. 24°. 1694
Moral Feelings, Philosophy of the. Abercrombie. N. Y., 1840. 12°. 11278
Philosophy. See PHILOSOPHY.
Reformer, The. Ed. Alcott. Bost., 1835. v. 1. 12°. . . 16966
Science, Elements of. Beattie. Philad., 1809. 3 v. 12°. . 12293
The same. Wayland. N. Y., 1835. 8°. 8739
Lectures on. Hopkins. Bost., 1865. 12°. 8606
Sentiments, Theory of. A. Smith. Lond., 1853. 8°. . . . 485
Morality, Essays on Principles of. Dymond. N. Y., 1844. 8°. . 17069
Morals, European, Hist. of, from Augustus to Charlemagne. Lecky. N. Y., 1869. 2 v. 8°. 4709
See, also, PHILOSOPHY.
Mordaunt. J. Moore. (Works, v. 7.) Edinb., 1820. 8°. 17323
More, Hannah. Cœlebs in search of a Wife. N. Y., 1809. 2 v. 12°. 2403
Sacred Dramas; Sensibility. 2d ed. Lond., 1782. 16°. . . 14849
Search after Happiness; Armine and Elvira. Philad., 1774. 8°. 14850
Works. Bost., 1827. 2 v. 8°. 15103
Philad., 1818. v. 1–5, 7, 8. 12°. 13674
Life of. Thompson. Philad., 1838. 2 v. 12°. 16107
Memoirs of. Roberts. N. Y., 1834. 2 v. 12°. 16105
More, *Sir* T. Utopia, transl. by Burnet. Lond., 1850. 12°. . . 3953
The same, tr. by R. Robinson. Ed. Arber. Lond., 1869. 16°. 3890
Life of. Campbell. (Ld. Chancellors, v. 1.) Lond., 1845. 8°. 6866
The same. Mackintosh. Lond., 1831. 16°. 5759
More, Sir Thomas; or, Colloquies on Society. Southey. Lond., 1831. 2 v. 8°. 3479

Moreau, J. V., Life and Campaigns of. N. Y., 1806. 12°. 7501
Memoirs of. Philippart. Philad., 1816. 8°. 16404
Moredun. N. Y., 1855. 8°. 2309
Morelet, A. Travels in Central America. N. Y., 1871. 12°. . . . 8431
Morell, Sir C. *(Pseudonym.)* See J. RIDLEY.
Morell, J. D. Hist. of Speculative Philosophy of Europe in 19th century. N. Y., 1848. 8°. 8726
Philosophy of Religion. N. Y., 1849. 12°. 9952
Morell, Thos., *D.D.* Poems on Divine Subjects. Lond., 1732. 8°. . 14851
Morell, *Rev.* **Thos.** Elements of Hist. of Philosophy and Science. Lond., 1827. 8°. 8720
Morgan, D., Life of. Graham. N. Y., 1859. 12°. 7306
Morgan, G. G. W. Poems. 2d ed. Bost., 1855. 12°. 14942
Morgan, *Lady* **S. O.** Book of the Boudoir. N. Y., 1829. 2 v. 12°. . 4344
Dramatic Scenes. N. Y., 1833. 12°. 1440
France [in 1816]. Philad., 1817. 8°. 8448
France in 1829–30. N. Y., 1830. 2 v. 12°. 16692
Italy. N. Y., 1821. 2 v. 8°. 8337
Lay of an Irish Harp. N. Y., 1808. 12°. 14839
Wild Irish Girl. N. Y., 1807. 12°. 2405
Morgan, *Sir* **T. C.** and *Lady* **S. O.** Book without a Name. N. Y., 1841. 2 v. 12°. 15387
Mori, A. de'. Novels. (Ital. Novelists, v. 3.) Lond., 1836. 12°. . 1901
Moriarty, D. I. Innisfoyle Abbey. Lond., 1840. 3 v. 12°. . . 15460
[**Morier, J.**] Adventures of Hajji Baba in England. N. Y., 1828. 2 v. 12°. 15443
Zohrab. N. Y., 1833. 2 v. 12°. 15641
Morison, J. Counsels to Young Men on Modern Infidelity. N. Y. 12°. 17018
Morley, H. English Writers. Lond., 1866–67. 2 v. in 3. 8°. . . 158
CONTENTS.—1, pt. 1, Celts and Anglo-Saxons. 1, pt. 2, from the Conquest to Chaucer. 2, pt. 1, Chaucer to Dunbar.
Life of Cornelius Agrippa. Lond., 1856. 2 v. 8°. . . . 7766
Life of Palissy. Lond. [1869.] 16°. 7879
Clement Marot and other Studies. Lond., 1871. 2 v. 8°. . 3740
Morley, J. Edmund Burke. Lond., 1867. 8°. 6811
Voltaire. N. Y., 1872. 8°. 10296
Mormonism in all ages. Turner. N. Y. [1842.] 12°. . . . 10029
Origin and Progress of. Tucker. N. Y., 1867. 12°. . . 10030
See, also, BURTON's City of the Saints.
Morocco, Present State of. De Chenier. Lond., 1788. 2 v. 8°. . 16532
Tour to, 1789. Lempriere. Lond., 1793. 8°. 16531
Morphy, P., Games played by. N. Y., 1860. 12°. 10175
Morrell, B. Narrative of Voyages. N. Y., 1832. 8°. . . . 8077
[**Morris, E.**] Derrick and Drill. N. Y., 1865. 12°. 17000
Morris, G. P. Little Frenchman with his Water Lots, etc. Philad., 1839. 12°. 4294
Morris, J. M. See W. A. CROFFUT.
Morris, W. Earthly Paradise. (2 copies.) Bost., 1868–71. 3 v. 12°. 1225
Life and Death of Jason. Bost., 1867. 12°. 1224

Morris, W. Love is Enough. Bost., 1873. 16°. 10306
Morrison, R., Memoirs of. By his Widow. Lond., 1839. 2 v. 8°. . 7777
Morse, J., and **Parish, E.** Hist. of N. England. Charlestown, 1804. 12°. 16046
Morse, O. A. Vindication of Mr. Ball. N. Y., 1867. 8°. . . . 15048
[**Morse, S. F. B.**] Foreign Conspiracy against the U. S. N. Y., 1835. 12°. 17278
Morton, S. W. My Mind and its Thoughts. Bost., 1823. 8°. . . 15308
Morton, T. Zorinski; Secrets worth knowing. Lond., 1811. 12°. . 1329
Morton's Hope. [Motley.] N. Y., 1839. 2 v. 12°. 15747
Moscheles, J. Life of Beethoven. (2 copies.) Lond., 1841. 2 v. 12°. 7961
Moseley, H. Illustrations of Mechanics. N. Y., 1844. 12°. . . 11780
Mosheim, J. L. v. Commentaries on Eccl. Hist., 1–200. Lond., 1813. 2 v. 8°. 6591
Institutes of Eccl. Hist., tr. by Murdock. (2 copies.) N. H., 1832. 3 v. 8°. 6585
Mosses from an Old Manse. Hawthorne. Bost., 1860. 2 v. 16°. . 2879
Mother's Love, A. [Mrs. Hallock.] N. Y., 1867. 12°. . . . 17047
Recompense, The. Aguilar. N. Y., 1868. 12°. . . . 2517
Mothers of England, Influence of the. Ellis. N. Y., 1844. 12°. . 9201
Motherwell, W. Minstrelsy: ancient and modern. Glasg., 1827. 8°. 942
The same. Bost., 1846. 2 v. 16°. 824
Poems narrative and lyrical. (2 copies.) Bost., 1841. 16°. . 826
Poetical Works. With Memoir. Bost., 1847. 16°. . . . 828
Posthumous Poems. Bost., 1851. 16°. 829
Motley, J. L. Hist. of the United Netherlands. (3 copies.) N. Y., 1861–68. 4 v. 8°. 5912
Morton's Hope. N. Y., 1839. 2 v. 12°. 15747
Rise of the Dutch Republic. (3 copies.) N. Y., 1856–61. 3 v. 8°. 5903
Mott, V. Travels in Europe and the East. N. Y., 1842. 8°. . . 16621
Motteville, F. B. de. Memoirs of Anne of Austria. Lond., 1726. 5 v. 12°. 14627
Mount Hope; a Romance. Hollister. N. Y., 1851. 12°. . . . 15749
Vernon Papers. Everett. N. Y., 1860. 12°. 3578
Washington in Winter. Bost., 1871. 12°. 8393
Mountain Decameron, The. Downes. Lond., 1836. 3 v. 12°. . 15513
Mountaineering in the Sierra Nevada. King. Bost., 1872. 8°. . 8401
Mountford, W. Miracles. Bost., 1870. 12°. 9908
Mourning Ring. Mrs. Inchbald. N. Y., 1821. 12°. 15516
Mourt, G. Relation, ed. Cheever. (2 copies.) N. Y., 1849. 12°. . 6007
Mouse-Trap, The; with other Poems. N. Y. [1840.] 12°. . . 14963
Mowatt, A. C. See A. C. M. Ritchie.
Mozart, J. C. W. A. Letters, 1769–91. N. Y., 1866. 2 v. 16°. . 7883
Life of. Bombet. Bost., 1839. 16°. 7881
Life and Correspondence of. Holmes. N. Y., 1845. 16°. . 7882
Mozart; a biographical Romance. Rau. N. Y., 1868. 12°. . . 3035
Mudie, R. The Air. Lond., 1835. 12°. 14632
The Earth. Lond., 1835. 12°. 14633
The Heavens. Lond., 1835. 12°. 14634
Man, in his Physical Structure. Bost., 1838. 12°. . . . 9117

Mudie, R. Popular Guide to Observation of Nature. N. Y., 1839. 12°. 11277
The Sea. Lond., 1835. 12°. 14635
Müller, C. Journey through Greece. (Voyages, v. 8.) Lond., 1822. 8°. 8058
Müller, F. Max. Chips from a German Workshop. N. Y., 1869–71. 3 v. 12°. 3710
Lectures on Science of Language. (2 copies.) N. Y., 1862–65. 2 v. 12°. 130
on Science of Religion; Papers on Buddhism. N. Y., 1872. 8°. 9958
Müller, Fritz. Facts and Arguments for Darwin. Lond., 1869. 8°. 8945
Müller, G. The Life of Trust. Bost., 1862. 12°. 7765
Müller, J. v. Universal Hist. Lond., 1818. 3 v. 8°. 4107
The same. Bost., 1831. v. 1. 12°. 8826
The same. v. 2. 12°. 8828
The same. Bost., 1840. 4 v. 12°. 15925
Müller, K. O. Hist. of Literature of Greece. Lond., 1840. v. 1. 8°. 197
Müller, O. Dr. Goethe's Courtship. Lond., 1866. 16°. 3046
Muhlbach, L. *(Pseudonym.)* See C. M. Mundt.
Muley Liezit, Emperor of Morocco, Life of. Lond., 1797. 12°. . 16410
Mulford, E. The Nation. N. Y., 1870. 8°. 8696
Mullen, S. Pilgrim of Beauty, and other Poems. Lond., 1845. 8°. . 1223
Muloch, D. M. See D. M. Craik.
Munchausen, *Baron,* Travels of. N. Y., 1862. 12°. 4279
The same. Lond., 1869. 8°. 4280
[**Mundt, C. M.**] (*Mrs.* Muhlbach.) Andreas Hofer. N. Y., 1868. 8°. 3088
Berlin and Sans-Souci. N. Y., 1867. 12°. 3105
The same. N. Y., 1869. 8°. 3079
The Daughter of an Empress. (2 copies.) N. Y., 1867. 8°. . 3089
The Empress Josephine. (2 copies.) N. Y., 1867. 8°. . . 3070
Frederick the Great and his Court. (3 copies.) N. Y., 1866–68. 12°. 3099
and his Family. (2 copies.) N. Y., 1867. 8°. 3080
Goethe and Schiller. (2 copies.) N. Y., 1868. 8°. 3086
Henry VIII. and his Court. (2 copies.) N. Y., 1867–68. 12°. 3102
Joseph II. and his Court. N. Y., 1867. 8°. 3084
Louisa of Prussia and her Times. N. Y., 1867. 8°. . . . 3085
Marie Antoinette and her Son. (2 copies.) N. Y., 1867. 8°. . 3072
Merchant of Berlin. N. Y., 1867. 12°. 3104
Mohammed Ali and his House. N. Y., 1872. 8°. 3091
Napoleon and Blucher. (2 copies.) N. Y., 1867. 8°. . . . 3074
and the Queen of Prussia. N. Y., 1867. 8°. . . 3078
Old Fritz. (2 copies.) N. Y., 1868. 8°. 3082
Prince Eugene and his Times. (2 copies.) N. Y., 1869. 8°. . 3068
Queen Hortense. (2 copies.) N. Y., 1870. 8°. 3076
Mundt, T. Count Mirabeau. N. Y., 1868. 8°. 3092
Munera Pulveris. Ruskin. N. Y., 1872. 12°. 8631
Munn, L. C. The American Orator. Worc., 1855. 12°. . . . 9292
Munter, B. Count Struenzée. Bost., 1853. 16°. 7561

Murdock, J. Sketches of Modern Philosophy. Hartf'd., 1842. 12°. 8494
Murphy, A. All in the Wrong; Way to keep him. Lond., 1804. 8°. 1632
Apprentice; Citizen; Old Maid; 3 Weeks after Marriage; Upholsterer. Lond., 1804. 8°. 1633
The Gray's-Inn Journal. Lond., 1756. 2 v. 12°. . . . 13031
Grecian Daughter; All in the Wrong; Way to Keep him; Know your own Mind. Lond. 12°. 1338
Life of Garrick. Lond., 1801. 2 v. 8°. 7967
Orphan of China; Zenobia; Grecian Daughter. Lond., 1804. 8°. 1630
Murray, C. A. Travels in N. Amer. N. Y., 1839. 2 v. 12°. . . 16788
Murray, H. Adventures of Brit. Seamen. Edinb., 1827. 12°. . . 4466
British America. Edinb., 1839. 3 v. 16°. 5716
The same, abridged. N. Y., 1840. 2 v. 12°. . . 11425
The same. 12122
Encyclopædia of Geography. Philad., 1849. 3 v. 8°. . . 8145
Hist. of Discoveries in Africa. 2d ed. Edinb., 1818. 2 v. 8°. 8088
in Asia. Edinb., 1820. 3 v. 8°. . . 8060
in N. Amer. Lond., 1829. 2 v. 8°. . 16782
and others. British India. N. Y., 1840. 3 v. 12°. . . . 11267
Discovery in Africa. N. Y., 1840. 12°. . . 11016
in the Polar Regions. N. Y., 1840. 12°. 11014
Murray, J. B. C. Hist. of Usury. Philad., 1866. 8°. . . . 8651
Murray, T. Life of Rutherford. Edinb., 1828. 12°. 7515
Murray, Wm. (*Lord* Mansfield), Life of. Campbell. Philad., 1851. 8°. 6874
Murray, Wm. H. H. Adventures in the Adirondacks. (2 copies.) Bost., 1869. 16°. 8226
Music-Hall Sermons. Bost., 1870. 12°. 9829
Musäus, J. C. A. Dumb Lover. (German Novelists, v. 3.) Lond., 1826. 12°. 1897
Popular Tales. Transl. by Carlyle. Bost., 1841. 12°. . . 3108
The same. Lond., 1871. 8°. 4053
Muscipula; the Mouse-Trap; with other Poems. N. Y. [1840.] 12°. 14961
Museum, The. Lond., 1746–47. 3 v. 8°. 12742
of Foreign Literature. Philad., 1822–39. v. 1–26, 28–29, 31–33, 35–37. 8°. 14046
Musgrave, G. A Ramble into Brittany. Lond., 1870. 2 v. 8°. . 8371
Music, English Church, Essays on. Mason. (Works, v. 3.) Lond., 1811. 8°. 17239
and Friends. Gardiner. Lond., 1838. 2 v. 8°. . . . 9082
Hist. of. Hawkins, Burney, and Busby. Lond., 1819. 2 v. 8°. 9078
Lessons in. Warner. N. Y., 1845. 12°. 17119
and Morals. Haweis. N. Y., 1872. 12°. 8865
Our Church. Willis. N. Y., 1856. 12°. 8866
Vocal, Manual of. Mason. Bost., 1834. 12°. 17118
Musical Cyclopedia, The. Porter. Bost., 1834. 12°. . . . 8862
Drama, Memoirs of the. Hogarth. Lond., 1838. 2 v. 8°. . 9080
Grammar. Callcott. Bost., 1833. 12°. 17117
History, Biography, and Criticism. Hogarth. N. Y., 1845. 8°. 9077
Sketches. Polko. N. Y., 1866. 16°. 8867

Mussulman, The ; a Tale. Madden. Philad., 1830. 2 v. 12°. . 15517
Mussulmans, Biblical Legends of the. Weil. N. Y., 1846. 12°. . 9548
My Aunt Margaret's Mirror. Scott. Edinb., 1871. 8°. . . . 1889
My Cousin Nicholas. [Barham.] Lond., 1841. 2 v. 12°. . . 15519
My Discontented Cousin. Bost., 1871. 16°. 2378
My Little Lady. N. Y., 1872. 16°. 2372
My Married Life at Hillside. Barry Gray. N. Y., 1865. 12°. . . 2923
My Novel. Bulwer. N. Y., 1860. 2 v. 12°. 2136
My Southern Friends. Gilmore. N. Y., 1863. 12°. 2931
My Summer in a Garden. Warner. Bost., 1871. 8°. . . . 3639
My Uncle Hobson and I. P. Jones. N. Y., 1845. 12°. . . . 15751
My Wife and I. Stowe. N. Y., 1871. 12°. 2964
Myers, F. Lectures on Great Men. Lond., 1856. 8°. . . . 6711
Myers, H. M. and **P. V. N.** Life and Nature under the Tropics. N. Y., 1871. 12°. 8433
[**Myers, P. H.**] Ensenore. N. Y., 1840. 8°. 15061
Mysteries of Udolpho. Radcliffe. N. Y., 1861. 12°. . . . 2513
Mystery, Philosophy of. Dendy. N. Y., 1847. 12°. . . . 8519
Mythology, Beauties of. Bulfinch. Bost., 1863. 12°. . . . 1909
of Aryan Nations. Cox. Lond., 1870. 2 v. 8°. . . . 4103
of Greece and Italy. Keightley. Lond., 1838. 8°. . . . 4425
Metamorphoses in. Ovid. N. Y., 1836. 2 v. 12°. 4527
Scandinavian. Pigott. Lond., 1839. 8°. 1919
Tales from. Keary. Lond., 1871. 12°. . . 1700
Zoological. De Gubernatis. Lond., 1872. 2 v. 8°. . . 10341
Myths of Middle Ages, Curious. Baring-Gould. Lond., 1869. 16°. 1915
and Myth-Makers. Fiske. Bost., 1873. 16°. 10262
of the New World. Brinton. N. Y., 1868. 8°. . . . 1925
See, also, EDDA ; FAIRY.

N.

Nabbes, T. Microcosmus. (Old Plays, v. 9.) Lond., 1825. 8°. . 1516
Nack, J. Earl Rupert, etc. N. Y., 1839. 12°. 15012
Nala and Damayanti, etc. Transl. by Milman. Lond., 1839. 16°. . 997
Names, Etymological Dict. of. Arthur. N. Y., 1860. 12°. . . 102
Napheys, G. H. The Transmission of Life. Philad., 1871. 12°. . 9167
Napier, E. Wild Sports. Lond., 1844. 2 v. 8°. 10166
Napier, M. Life of Montrose. (2 copies.) Edinb., 1840. 8°. . . 6760
Napier, W. F. P. Hist. of War in the Peninsula. 4th ed. Brussels, 1839. 3 v. 8°. 6524
Naples, A Century of Despotism in, 1759–1856. Horner. Edinb., 1860. 16°. 4592
Excursions in Northern Provinces of. Craven. Lond., 1838. 2 v. 8°. 16715

Napoléon I. Confidential Correspondence with his brother Joseph. N. Y., 1856. 2 v. 12°. 5498
with Joséphine. Ed. Abbott. N. Y., 1856. 12°. . 5447
Memoirs of Hist. of France during my Reign. Lond., 1823–24. 2 pts. in 7 v. 8°. [Dictated to Montholon and Gourgaud.] 5591
Military Maxims. N. Y., 1845. 12°. 5446
Campaigns of. Bost., 1835. 12°. 5500
in Council, Opinions of. Pelet. Edinb., 1837. 8°. . . . 5443
Court and Camp of. N. Y., 1841. 12°. 11031
The same. N. Y., 1832. 12°. 12094
Derniers momens de. Antommarchi. Paris, 1825. 2 v. 8°. . 5632
in Exile: or, a Voice from St. Helena. O'Meara. Bost., 1823. 2 v. 12°. 5441
Historic Doubts relative to. Whately. N. Y., 1835. 8°. . . 17269
Historical Memoirs of. O'Meara. Philad., 1820. 12°. . . 5440
Hist. of. Abbott. N. Y., 1855–56. 2 v. 8°. 5712
The same. Lanfrey. Lond., 1871–72. 2 v. 8°. . . 5586
The same. Laurent. N. Y., 1842. 2 v. 8°. . . . 5603
The same. Lockhart. N. Y., 1840. 2 v. 12°. . . 11003
Hist. of Waterloo Campaign of. Jomini. N. Y., 1860. 12°. . 5572
of Captivity of. Montholon. N. Y., 1846. 8°. . . 5598
Letters describing Conversations of. Warden. N. H., 1817. 12°. 5439
Life of. By an American. Elizabeth-Town, 1820. 8°. . . 16209
The same. Hazlitt. N. Y., 1847. 3 v. 12°. . . . 5492
The same. Scott. Philad., 1827. 3 v. 8°. . . . 5605
and his Marshals. Headley. N. Y., 1847. 2 v. 12°. . . 5434
Memoirs of. Arnault, etc. Bost., 1839. 2 v. 12°. . . . 5444
The same. Bourrienne. Philad., 1832. 8°. . . . 5631
The same. Rapp. Lond., 1823. 8°. 5599
Memoirs of Court of. Bausset. Philad., 1828. 8°. . . . 5590
Memoirs of, and of his Court and Family. Mme. Junot. N. Y., 1860. 2 v. 8°. 5543
Narrative of Surrender, etc., of. Maitland. Bost., 1826. 12°. 16221
Remarks on Life and Character of. Channing. (Works, v. 1.) Bost., 1841. 12°. 9568
Russian Expedition of. Ségur. N. Y., 1845. 2 v. 12°. . . 16252
at St. Helena. N. Y., 1815. 12°. 16224
Journal of. Las Cases. Lond., 1823. 8 v. 8°. 16212
Observations on Ld. Bathurst's Speech on. N. Y., 1818. 12°. 16222
Sayings and Deeds of. Vieusseux. Lond., 1846. 2 v. 12°. . 5505
Sketch of. De Cormenin. (Orators of France.) N. Y., 1849. 12°. . . . .
and his Times. De Caulaincourt. Philad., 1838. 2 v. 12°. . 5503
Voyage of, to St. Helena; Cockburn's Diary, etc. Bost., 1833. 12°. 5438

Napoleon and Blucher. A Novel. [Mundt.] N. Y., 1867. 8°. . 3074

Napoleon and the Queen of Prussia. [Mundt.] N. Y., 1867. 8°. . 3078

Naval Life, Sketches of. G. Jones. N. H., 1829. 2 v. 12°. . . 16272
Magazine. Ed. C. S. Stewart. N. Y., 1836. v. 1. 8°. . . 13557
Occurrences of the late War. James. Lond., 1817. 8°. . . 5872
Officers, American, Lives of. J. F. Cooper. Philad., 1846. 2 v. 12°. 7275
For Contents, see COOPER.
Navigation, Hist. of, to 1704. Locke. (Works, v. 3.) Lond., 1801. 8°. 9592
Navigators, Early, Lives of. N. Y., 1840. 12°. 11032
Navy of the U. S., Hist. of. Cooper. Philad., 1839. 2 v. 8°. . . 6146
Neal, D. Hist. of the Puritans. Ed. Toulmin. Newburyp't., 1816–17. 5 v. 8°. 6459
Neal, John. Battle of Niagara; and Goldau. Balt., 1818. 12°. . 14943
The Down-Easters, &c. N. Y., 1833. 2 v. 12°. . . . 15689
Errata. N. Y., 1823. 2 v. 12°. 15691
Logan. Philad., 1822. 2 v. 12°. 15735
Rachel Dyer. Portland, 1828. 12°. 15764
Wandering Recollections of a Busy Life. Bost., 1869. 16°. . 7545
Neal, Joseph C. Charcoal Sketches. (2 copies.) Philad., 1838. 12°. 2868
Neale, A. Travels in Germany, Poland, and Turkey. Lond., 1818. 4°. 16037
[**Neale, E.**] The Living and the Dead. N. Y., 1827. 12°. . . 15492
Neale, F. A. Residence in Siam. Lond., 1852. 8°. 8009
Neander, J. A. W. Hist. of the Christian Religion and Church, 1–300. Tr. by Rose. Philad., 1843. 8°. 6560
The same. Lond., 1841–42. 2 v. 8°. 6561
The same [to 1073]. Tr. by Torrey. Bost., 1848–50. 3 v. 8°. 6563
Hist. of Planting and Training of the Church. Edinb., 1842. 2 v. 16°. 6339
Life of Chrysostom. Lond., 1845. 8°. 7700
of Jesus Christ. (2 copies.) N. Y., 1848. 8°. . . . 6537
Memorials of Christian Life. (Bohn's ed.) Lond., 1852. 8°. . 487
Nearer and Dearer. [Bradley.] N. Y., 1864. 12°. 2431
Necker, J., Life of. James. Lond., 1838. 16°. 5770
Memoirs and Miscellanies of. Mme. de Staël. Lond., 1818. 8°. 7651
Necker de Saussure, L. A. Travels in Scotland. Lond., 1821. 8°. 8056
Voyage to the Hebrides. Lond., 1822. 8°. 8058
Necromancers, Lives of the. Godwin. N. Y., 1835. 12°. . . 6707
See, also, APPARITIONS; DEMONOLOGY; MAGIC.
Ned Myers. Cooper. N. Y., 1854. 12°. 2818
Neele, H. Lectures on English Poetry, etc. Lond., 1829. 12°. . 165
Literary Remains. N. Y., 1829. 8°. 15109
Romance of Engl. Hist. Philad., 1828. 2 v. 12°. . . . 15563
Neff, F., Memoir of. Gilly. Bost., 1832. 12°. 7572
The same. Philad., 1832. 12°. 7520
Negris, A. Lit. Hist. of Modern Greece. Edinb., 1835. 16°. . . 9137
Negroes, Moral Faculties and Literature of. Grégoire. Brooklyn, 1810. 8°. 17113
Neighbours, The. Bremer. Lond., 1852. 8°. 468
Nelson, D. Cause and Cure of Infidelity. N. Y., 1837. 12°. . . 9880
The same. 9835

Nelson, H., Life of. Southey. N. Y., 1841. 12°. 11005
The same. Tucker. Lond. 8°. 6851
Nemours, M. de Longueville de. Memoirs. Lond., 1775. 12°. . 7500
Nennius. Hist. of the Britons. Ed. Giles. Lond., 1848. 8°. . . 499
Netherlands, Annals of, 1506–1629. Romans. Hartf'd., 1778–82. 8°. 5811
Art in the. Taine. N. Y., 1871. 12°. 8849
Hist. of the [to 1831]. Grattan. Lond., 1838. 16°. . . . 5474
of Revolt of. Schiller. Lond., 1846. 2 v. 8°. . . 436
of the United, 1584–1609. Motley. N. Y., 1861–68. 4 v. 8°. 5912
Observations on the, to 1672. Temple. Lond., 1814. 8°. . 17197
Austrian, Sketches of the. Shaw. Lond., 1788. 8°. . . 16053
See, also, DUTCH ; HOLLAND.
Nettleton, A., Memoir of. Tyler. Hartf'd., 1845. 12°. . . . 7633
Never too late to mend. Reade. Bost., 1869. 16°. 2097
Nevilles of Garretstown, The. Lever. N. Y., 1846. 8°. . . . 2317
Nevius, J. L. China and the Chinese. (2 copies.) N. Y., 1869. 12°. 7948
New Brunswick. See NOVA SCOTIA.
N. England, Eccl. Hist. of, to 1698. C. Mather. Hartf'd., 1820. 2 v. 8°. 5958
Hist. of, to 1689. Palfrey. Bost., 1859–64. 3 v. 8°. . . 6241
The same, abridged and continued to 1727. Bost., 1866 –72. 3 v. 12°. 6076
to 1776. Elliott. N. Y., 1857. 2 v. 8°. . . . 6175
[to 1783.] Barber. Worc., 1841. 8°. 5936
to 1791. Adams. Dedham, 1799. 8°. 5848
and her Institutions. Bost., 1835. 12°. 5724
The same. 16809
Legends of. Whittier. Hartf'd., 1831. 12°. 2949
Magazine. Ed. Buckingham. (2 copies.) Bost., 1831–34. 7 v. 8°. 13864
Northmen in. J. T. Smith. Bost., 1839. 12°. 5997
Sketches of. Carver. N. Y., 1842. 12°. 15780
Summer Cruise on Coast of. Carter. Bost., 1864. 8°. . . 16808
Travels in. Dwight. N. H., 1821. 4 v. 8°. 16839
New Englander, The. N. H., 1843–72. v. 1–24, 26–36. 8°. . . 12997
The same. v. 2–5, 7–28. 8°. 12971
Index, v. 1–19. 2 copies. . . . .
New Hampshire, Hist. of, to 1790. Belknap. Bost., 1813. 3 v. 8°. 5861
New Haven, Hist. Discourse at. Kingsley. N. H., 1838. 8°. . . 5896
Hist. Discourses at. Bacon. N. H., 1839. 8°. . . . 5897
Colony, Hist. of. Lambert. N. H., 1838. 12°. . . . 5727
Records of, 1638–49, 1653–65. Hartf'd., 1857–58. 2 v. 8°. 5932
New Home, A. [Kirkland.] N. Y., 1839. 12°. 15752
New Jersey, Hist. Collections of. Barber and Howe. N. Y., 1844. 8°. 5938
New Mirror. Ed. Morris & Willis. N. Y., 1843–44. 3 v. 8°. . . 14516
New Mirror for Travellers. [Paulding.] N. Y., 1828. 12°. . . 15289
New Monthly Magazine. Bost., 1823–24. v. 6–8. 8°. . . . 14350
New Purchase, The. Carlton. N. Y., 1843. 2 v. 12°. . . . 15753
New S. Wales, Observations on. Henderson. Calcutta, 1832. 8°. . 16287
Voyage to. Barrington. N. Y. 8°. 16288
New Testament. See BIBLE.

New Timon, The. Bulwer-Lytton. Philad., 1847. 12°. 836
New Timothy, The. Baker. N. Y., 1870. 12°. 2852
New York Book of Poetry. N. Y., 1837. 8°. 15064
N. Y. City Exhibition, 1853–54, Illustrations of the. N. Y., 1854. 4°.
Humbugs of. Reese. N. Y., 1838. 12°. 17103
Knickerbocker's Hist. of. Irving. N. Y., 1850. 12°. . 4357
Letters from. Child. N. Y., 1844–45. 2 v. 12°. . . 16851
Old Merchants of. [Scoville.] N. Y., 1863. 2 v. 12°. . 7415
Police Reports. Skillman. N. Y., 1830. 8°. . . . 15835
Sunshine and Shadow in. M. H. Smith. Hartf'd., 1869. 8°. 16837
Literary Gazette. Ed. J. G. Brooks. N. Y., 1825–26. v. 1. 8°. 12577
Quarterly. N. Y., 1854–55. v. 3. 8°. 13338
Review. (2 copies.) N. Y., 1837–42. 10 v. 8°. . . . 12914
State during the Revolution, Border Warfare of. Campbell. N. Y., 1849. 12°. 5726
Hist. of, to 1825. Eastman. N. Y., 1828. 12°. . . 6012
Polit. Parties in, to 1840. Hammond. Albany, 1842. 2 v. 8°. 5900
Nat. Hist. and Internal Resources of. [D. Clinton.] N. Y., 1822. 12°. 16847
Notes on. Seward. (Works, v. 2.) N. Y., 1853. 8°. . 9646
Speeches of Governors of, 1777–1825. Albany, 1825. 8°. 17538
Tribune Almanac, 1838–68. N. Y., 1868. 2 v. 12°. . . . 6103
New Zealand, Station Life in, 1865–68. Lady Barker. Lond., 1870. 8°. 7988
New Zealanders, The. Bost., 1830. 12°. 8809
Newcomes, The. Thackeray. Lond., 1871. 8°. 2191
Newell, C. Hist. of the Revolution in Texas. N. Y., 1838. 12°. . 5734
Newell, H., Memoirs of. Woods. Bost., 1814. 12°. 7522
[**Newell, R. H.**] Orpheus C. Kerr Papers. N. Y., 1862–65. 3 v. 12°. 4302
Newfoundland, Excursions in, 1839–40. Jukes. Lond., 1842. 2 v. 12°. 16777
Newman, J. H. Apologia pro Vita sua. N. Y., 1865. 12°. . . 9598
Essays, critical and historical. Lond., 1872. 2 v. 8°. . . 9600
Grammar of Assent. N. Y., 1870. 12°. 9599
Newman, S. P. Elements of Polit. Economy. Andover, 1835. 12°. 17096
Practical System of Rhetoric. Portland, 1827. 12°. . . . 17529
Newspaper Literature, Specimens of. Buckingham. Bost., 1850. 2 v. 12°. 125
See, also, JOURNALISM.
Newstead Abbey. Irving. Philad., 1835. 12°. 4244
Newton, I., Life of. (Libr. of Useful Knowl.) Lond., 1833. 8°. . 6751
The same. Brewster. N. Y., 1840. 12°. 11028
Newton, J. Works. Philad., 1834. 2 v. 8°. 17541
Ney, M., Memoirs of. Philad., 1834. 2 v. in 1. 8°. 16406
Ngami, Lake. Andersson. N. Y., 1857. 8°. 8091
Niagara, Battle of. [Neal.] Balt., 1818. 12°. 14943
Nicaragua, People, Monuments, etc., of. Squier. N. Y., 1856. 8°. . 8459
Nicholas I., Emperor of Russia, and Eastern Europe. Lond., 1846. 3 v. 12°. 16175

Nicholas I., Life and Reign of. Smucker. Philad., 1860. 12°. . 6446
Nicholas Nickleby. Dickens. N. Y., 1871. 16°. 2170
Nichols, G. W. Story of the Great March. N. Y., 1865. 12°. . . 6109
Nicholson, W. British Encyclopædia of Arts and Sciences. Philad., 1819–21. 12 v. 8°. . . . .
Nicolas, N. H. The Chronology of History. 2d ed. Lond., 1838. 16°. 4855
Nicolay, C. G. The Oregon Territory. Lond., 1846. 12°. . . 8161
Niebuhr, B. G. Geography of Herodotus, etc. Oxf'd., 1830. 8°. . 4442
Hist. of Rome. (2 copies.) Philad., 1835. 2 v. 8°. . . 4739
Lectures on Ancient Hist. Philad., 1852. 3 v. 12°. . . 4059
Life and Letters of. Bunsen, etc. N. Y., 1852. 12°. . . 7762
Reminiscences of. Lieber. Philad., 1835. 12°. . . . 7763
Niebuhr, C. Travels through Arabia. Edinb., 1792. 2 v. 8°. . 8246
Life of. (Libr. of Useful Knowl.) Lond., 1833. 8°. . . 6751
By his Son. Edinb., 1836. 16°. 6633
Niger Expedition, Journal of, 1830–31. Lander. N. Y., 1841. 2 v. 12°. 11039
Night and Morning; a Novel. Bulwer. N. Y., 1841. 2 v. in 1. 12°. 2151
Scenes in the Bible. March. Philad., 1869. 8°. . . . 10012
Side of Nature, The. Crowe. N. Y., 1850. 12°. . . . 8615
Nightmare Abbey. Peacock. N. Y., 1845. 12°. . . . , . 3956
Nile, Great Basin of the; The Albert N'yanza. Baker. Lond., 1866. 8°. 8118
Journal of Discov. of Source of, 1859–63. Speke. N. Y., 1864. 8°. 8116
Notes of a Howadji. [Curtis.] N. Y., 1852. 12°. . . . 8235
Travels to discover the source of the, 1768–73. Bruce. Dubl., 1790–91. 6 v. 8°. 8092
Tributaries of Abyssinia, The. Baker. Lond., 1868. 8°. . 8120
See, also, EGYPT.
Niles, H. Principles and Acts of the Revolution. Balt., 1822. 8°. 6297
Niles, J M. Life of Comm. Perry. Hartf'd., 1820. 12°. . . . 16427
Niles' Weekly Register. Balt., 1816–37. 52 v. 8° and 4°. . . 14553
Nineveh and its Remains. Layard. N. Y., 1849. 2 v. 8°. . . 8014
No Fiction. Reed. N. Y., 1835. 12°. 16383
Hero of. Barnett. Bost., 1823. 2 v. 12°. . . . 16384
No Name. Collins. N. Y., 1863. 8°. 2299
Noah, M. M. Travels in Europe and Africa. N. Y., 1819. 8°. . 16540
Noble, L. L. After Icebergs with a Painter. N. Y., 1862. 12°. . 8112
Noble Life, A. Mrs. Craik. N. Y., 1868. 12°. 2484
Noctes Ambrosianæ. Wilson, etc. N. Y., 1857. 5 v. 12°. . . 3336
Nordhoff, C. California. N. Y., 1873. 8°. 10241
Cape Cod and all along shore. N. Y., 1868. 12°. . . . 2951
Norman, B. M. Rambles in Yucatan. N. Y., 1843. 8°. . . . 8458
Norman Conquest. See ENGLAND.
Normandy, The Dukes of. Duncan. Lond., 1839. 12°. . . . 5422
Norse-Folk, Visit to the. Brace. N. Y., 1857. 12°. 8303
North, Christopher. *(Pseudonym.)* See John WILSON.
North America. See AMERICA.
American Review. Bost., 1815–72. v. 1–102, 104–115. 8°. . 12425
The same. v. 2–45, 47–54, 56–67, 69–102, 104–108. . . 12579
Index, v. 1–25. (2 copies.) . . . .

North British Review. Edinb. and N. Y., 1844–71. 53 v. 8°. . . 11684
The same. v. 10–37, 42–49. 11713
Briton, The. [With Notes, etc.] Wilkes. Dubl., 1765. 3 v. 12°. 5155
Carolina, Hist. of (to 1776). Williamson. Philad., 1812. 2 v. 8°. 5864
Northanger Abbey. Austen. Bost., 1863. 12°. 2479
Northcote, J. Memoirs of Reynolds. Philad., 1817. 8°. . . . 7992
Conversations of, by Hazlitt. Lond., 1830. 12°. . . . 3421
Northmen in N. England. J. T. Smith. Bost., 1839. 12°. . . . 5997
Northmore, T. Washington; a Poem. Balt. 12°. 14840
Norton, C. E. S. The Child of the Islands. N. Y., 1846. 12°. . . 14853
The Dream; and other Poems. Bost., 1851. 12°. . . . 1166
Poems. Bost., 1833. 12°. 14852
Norway, and her Laplanders, in 1841. Milford. Lond., 1842. 8°. . 8300
Residence in, 1834–36. Laing. Lond., 1837. 8°. . . . 8301
See, also, SCANDINAVIA; SWEDEN.
Norwich, Hist. of. Caulkins. [1st ed.] Norwich, 1845. 12°. . . 6113
Norwood. H. W. Beecher. N. Y., 1868. 12°. 2943
Not Dead Yet. Jeaffreson. N. Y., 1864. 8°. 2332
Nothing, by Nobody. Philad., 1827. 12°. 15755
Nott, E. Counsels to Young Men. N. Y., 1841. 12°. . . . 9177
Nott, J. C., and **Gliddon, J. R.** Indigenous Races of the Earth. Philad., 1857. 8°. 9095
Types of Mankind. 7th ed. Philad., 1855. 8°. . . . 9094
Nourmahal. Quin. Lond., 1838. 3 v. 12°. 15523
Nova-Scotia, Hist. and Statistics of. Haliburton. Halifax. [1829.] 2 v. 8°. 5888
New Brunswick, etc., Hist. of. Martin. Lond., 1837. 16°. . 7901
Novalis. *(Pseudonym.)* See F. v. HARDENBERG.
Novelists, Biogr. Notices of. W. Scott. Bost., 1829. 12°. . . 3190
British. Masson. Bost., 1859. 12°. 51
German, Translations from. Roscoe. Lond., 1826. 4 v. 12°. 1895
Italian, transl. by Roscoe. Lond., 1836. 4 v. 12°. . . . 1899
Novels and Novelists of 18th century. Forsyth. N. Y., 1871. 12°. . 231
See, also, FICTION; ROMANCE.
Now and Then. Warren. N. Y., 1848. 12°. 15526
Nowrojee, J., etc. Journal of Residence in Grt. Brit. Lond., 1841. 12°. 16765
Noyes, J. O. Roumania. N. Y., 1858. 12°. 16620
Nubia, Hist., etc., of. Russell. N. Y., 1840. 12°. 11281
See, also, EGYPT.
Nugent, *Lord.* See G. N. T. GRENVILLE.
Nuts to Crack; Quips, etc., of Oxford and Cambridge. (2 copies.) Philad., 1835. 12°. 9234
Nuttall, T. Ornithology of U. S.; Water Birds. Bost., 1834. 12°. . 8892
Travels into Arkansa Territory. Philad., 1821. 8°. 16866

O.

O. T. A Danish Romance. Andersen. N. Y., 1870. 8°. 2606

Oak to the Olive, From the. Howe. Bost., 1868. 16°. 8207

Oak-Openings, The. Cooper. N. Y., 1857. 12°. 2828

Oakes, W. Scenery of the White Mts. Bost., 1848. 4°.

Oakfield. Arnold. Bost., 1855. 12°. 15528

Oakwood Hall. Hutton. Philad., 1819. 2 v. 12°. 15529

Oasis, The. Child. Bost., 1834. 12°. 8466

Oaths. See SWEARING.

Ober-Ammergau Passion Play. MacColl. Lond., 1871. 16°. 1453

Observe, What to. Jackson. Lond., 1841. 12°. 8952

Observer, The. Ed. Ferguson. Lond., 1823. 3 v. 12°. 3140

O'Callaghan, J. C. The Green Book. Philad., 1842. 12°. 5254

O'Cataract, Jehu. *(Pseudonym.)* See J. NEAL.

Occult Sciences, The. Smedley, etc. Glasg., 1855. 8°. 8616

Occupations of a Retired Life. Garrett. N. Y., 1869. 8°. 2434

Ocean Harp, The. Philad., 1819. 12°. 14961

  Scenes. N. Y., 1848. 12°. 16260

  World, The. Figuier. Lond. [1869.] 8°. 8998

    See, also, SEA.

Ockley, S. Hist. of Saracens. (Bohn's ed.) Lond., 1847. 8°. 423

    The same. Cambr., 1757. 2 v. 8°. 16059

O'Connell, D., Sketch of. Lecky. N. Y., 1872. 12°. 6743

[**O'Connor, T.**] Hist. of the late War. 3d ed. N. Y., 1816. 12°. 5725

Odd Whims. Repton. Lond., 1804. v. 2. 12°. 3955

Odds, At. Tautphoeus. Philad., 1863. 12°. 2509

Odds and Ends. Cincinn., 1868. 16°. 15832

    by a Droll Fellow. N. Y., 1830. 12°. 15833

Odes on Cash, Corn, Catholics, etc. Philad., 1828. 12°. 14865

Odiorne, T. Poems. Bost., 1792. 12°. 14944

O'Donoghue, The. Lever. N. Y., 1847. 8°. 2317

O'Driscol, J. Views of Ireland. Lond., 1823. 2 v. 8°. 16744

Odyssey, The. See HOMER.

[**Ogilby, W.**] The Elephant. New ed. Lond., 1844. 12°. 8792

    The same. N. Y., 1844. 12°. 11765

  The Menageries; Quadrupeds, v. 1. Bost., 1830. 12°. 8805

    The same, v. 2. (The Elephant.) Bost., 1832. 12°. 8811

  Natural Hist. of Quadrupeds. N. Y., 1840. 12°. 11428

Ogilvies, The. [Mrs. Craik.] N. Y., 1864. 8°. 2680

Oglethorpe, J., Life of. Peabody. Bost., 1844. 16°. 7261

O'Haloran, J. C. Life of St. Patrick. Philad., 1823. 12°. 16339

O'Hara Family, The. *(Pseudonym.)* See J. BANIM.

O'Keeffe, J. Lie of a Day. (Mod. Theatre, v. 10.) Lond., 1811. 12°. 1336

  Wild Oats. (Oxberry's Plays, v. 7.) Bost., 1822. 24°. 1351

Old Age, Essay on. Cicero. Lond., 1807. 8°. 4634

  Bachelor, The. Aird. Edinb., 1845. 16°. 15531

  Curiosity Shop. Dickens. N. Y., 1871. 16°. 2172

Old-fashioned Girl, An. Alcott. Bost., 1870. 16°. 2741
Fritz. [Mundt.] N. Y., 1868. 8°. 3082
Humphrey's Addresses. [Mogridge.] N. Y., 1841. 12°. . 15174
Observations. [Mogridge.] N. Y., 1841. 12°. . 15175
Mam'selle's Secret, The. [John.] Philad., 1868. 12°. . . 3037
Mortality. Scott. Edinb., 1870. 8°. 1868
and New. Bost., 1870–72. 5 v. 8°. 13711
Oak Chest, The. G. P. R. James. N. Y., 1850. 8°. . . 2309
Olaf. Thoresen. Bost., 1870. 16°. 2619
Red Sandstone, The. Miller. Bost., 1851. 12°. . . . 8972
Whig, The. Addison. (Works, v. 3.) N. Y., 1856. 12°. . 3997
World, Letters from the. By a Lady of N. Y. N. Y., 1840. 2 v. 12°. 16569
Oldbug, John. *(Pseudonym.)* See L. WITHINGTON.
Oldstyle, Jonathan. *(Pseudonym.)* See W. IRVING.
Oldtown Folks. Mrs. Stowe. Bost., 1869. 12°. 2963
Olin, S. Travels in Egypt, etc. 3d ed. N. Y., 1843. 2 v. 12°. . 16492
Olio, The ; or, Museum of Entertainment. Lond. v. 1, 2. 8°. . 11307
Oliphant, L. Elgin's Mission to China and Japan. Edinb., 1859. 2 v. 8°. 8006
Oliphant, M. Francis of Assisi. Lond. 8°. 7669
Hist. Sketches of Reign of Geo. II. Bost. 8°. 5393
House on the Moor. N. Y., 1861. 12°. 2514
Life of E. Irving. N. Y., 1862. 8°. 7739
Olive. A Novel. [Mrs. Craik.] N. Y., 1864. 8°. 2679
Olive Branch, The. Carey. Philad., 1818. 8°. 6114
Oliver, I. Poems. Carlisle, 1805. 12°. 14945
Oliver, J. Wreck of the Glide. N. Y., 1848. 12°. 16298
Oliver Twist. Dickens. Bost., 1868. 8°. 2206
Olmsted, D. Letters on Astronomy. Bost., 1841. 12°. . . . 16971
Life and Writings of E. P. Mason. N. Y., 1842. 12°. . . 16441
Olmsted, Francis A. Incidents of a Whaling Voyage. N. Y., 1841. 12°. 16302
Olmsted, Fred. L. The Cotton Kingdom. N. Y., 1861. 2 v. 12°. . 6093
Journey in the Back Country. N. Y., 1861. 12°. . . . 6097
in the Seaboard Slave States. N. Y., 1856. 12°. . 6095
through Texas. N. Y., 1860. 12°. 6096
Olney, J., and **Barber, J. W.** Family Book of History. N. H. [1839.] 8°. 15889
Olney, S., Life of. Mrs. Williams. Prov., 1839. 12°. . . . 16430
O'Meara, B. E. Historical Memoirs of Napoleon. Philad., 1820. 12°. 5440
Napoleon in Exile. Bost., 1823. 2 v. 12°. 5441
Omoo: Adventures in the South Seas. Melville. N. Y., 1868. 12°. 8326
Once a Week. Lond., 1870–71. v. 6, 7. 8°. 17856
One in a Thousand. James. N. Y., 1836. 12°. 15221
Onea; an Indian Tale. Charleston, 1820. 12°. 15044
Only a Fiddler. Andersen. N. Y., 1870. 8°. 2608
Opera, Hist of the. Edwards. Lond., 1862. 2 v. 12°. . . . 8863
See, also, DRAMA ; MUSIC.

Opie, A. Cure for Scandal. Bost., 1839. 12°. 14922
Works. Bost., 1827. 10 v. 12°. 14438

CONTENTS.—1, Madeline. 2, Adeline Mowbray. 3, 4, Simple Tales. 5, Tales of Real Life. 6, 7, New Tales. 8, 9, Temper. 10, Father and Daughter; Illustrations of Lying.

Opie, J. Lectures on Painting. Lond., 1848. 8°. 8881
Opinions, Formation and Publication of. [Bailey.] Philad., 1831. 12°. 3165
Opium-Eater, Confessions of an. DeQuincey. Edinb., 1856. 8°. . 3278
Habit, The. [Day.] N. Y., 1868. 12°. 9233
Optics, Notes of Lectures on. Tyndall. N. Y., 1871. 12°. . . 8907
Treatise on. Brewster. Lond., 1838. 16°. 6050
Wonders of. Marion. N. Y., 1870. 12°. 10109
Optimist, The. Tuckerman. N. Y., 1850. 12°. 3573
Orator, The American. Ed. Munn. Worc., 1855. 12°. . . . 9292
The Christian. Bost., 1818. 12°. 17365
Orators of the Age, Lives of. Francis. N. Y., 1847. 16°. . . . 6697
in America, Living. Magoon. N. Y., 1849. 12°. . . . 7412
of the Amer. Revolution. Magoon. N. Y., 1848. 12°. . . 7411
of France, The. De Cormenin. N. Y., 1849. 12°. . . . 7611
and Statesmen, Eminent. Harsha. N. Y., 1855. 8°. . . 6875
Oratory, Lectures on. Channing. Bost., 1856. 12°. 9306
and Orators, On. Cicero. Lond., 1808. 2 v. 8°. . . . 4632
American, Golden Age of. Parker. Bost., 1857. 12°. . . 7413
Selections from. Philad., 1840. 8°. 9431
See, also, ELOCUTION; RHETORIC; SPEECHES.
Ord, M. Essay on Law of Usury. Hartf'd., 1809. 8°. . . . 17094
Oregon, Geogr., etc., of. Nicolay. Lond., 1846. 12°. 8161
Hist. of. Greenhow. Bost., 1845. 8°. 5993
Hist. and Discovery of. Twiss. N. Y., 1846. 12°. . . . 5744
Oriental Harems and Scenery. Belgiojoso. N. Y., 1862. 12°. . . 8252
and Linguistic Studies. Whitney. N. Y., 1872. 12°. . . 136
Outlines. Knight. Lond., 1839. 16°. 8196
Origin of Species. Darwin. N. Y., 1871. 12°. 8929
Huxley. N. Y., 1863. 12°. 8940
Orléans, P. J. Revolutions in England under the Stuarts. Lond., 1722. 8°. 16066
Orléans, Memoirs of House of. Taylor. Philad., 1850. 2 v. 12°. . 5520
Orley Farm. A. Trollope. N. Y., 1863. 8°. 2287
Ormond. C. B. Brown. Bost., 1827. 12°. 15299
Ormond; a Tale. Edgeworth. (Works, v. 8.) Bost., 1825. 8°. . 15342
Ornithology. See BIRDS.
Orosius, P. Hist., transl. by King Alfred. Lond., 1857. 8°. . . 402
Orsua, P. de, Expedition of. Southey. Philad., 1821. 12°. . . 5805
Ortmar. Popular Traditions. (Germ. Nov., v. 2.) Lond., 1826. 12°. 1896
Orton, J. The Andes and Amazon. N. Y., 1870. 12°. . . . 8432
Osander. Miscellaneous Poems. N. Y., 1812. 12°. 14946
The same. Hudson. 1811. 12°. 15013
Osborn, Selleck. Poems. Bost., 1823. 12°. 15014
Osborn, Sherard. Leaves from an Arctic Journal. N. Y., 1852. 12°. 8295
Osborne, T., Earl of Danby. Life of. Courtenay. Lond., 1838. 16°. 5763

Osgood, F. S. Poems. N. Y., 1846. 12°. 15015

Osgood, S. American Leaves. (2 copies.) N. Y., 1867. 12°. . . 3580

Osler, E. Life of Admiral Exmouth. N. Y., 1835. 12°. . . . 16370

Osma and Almeria. Roche. Philad., 1810. 12°. 15458

Ossian. Poems, transl. by Macpherson. Lond., 1785. 2 v. 8°. . 14801

Ossoli, M. F., Memoirs of. Bost., 1857. 2 v. 12°. 7391

O'Sullivan, J. L. Report on Capital Punishment. N. Y., 1841. 8°. . 8698

O'Sullivan, M. Guide to an Irish Gentleman in his Search for a Religion. Philad., 1833. 12°. 17272

Otis, H. G. Letters on the Hartford Convention. (2 copies.) Bost., 1824. 8°. 6141

Otis, J., Life of. Bowen. Bost., 1844. 16°. 7261

The same. Tudor. Bost., 1823. 8°. 7341

Otter, W. Life of E. D. Clarke. (2 copies.) N. Y., 1827. 8°. . . 7151

Otto, F. Hist. of Russian Literature. Oxf'd., 1839. 8°. . . . 205

Ottoman Empire, Hist. of the, to 1828. Upham. Edinb., 1829. 2 v. 12°. 4502

Otway, T. Orphan; Venice Preserved; Lond., 1804. 8°. . . 1629

The same. Philad., 1833. 8°. 1662

Select Poems. With Life, by Sanford. Philad., 1819. 24°. . 7

The same, ed. Johnson. Dubl., 1804. 8°. . . . 15096

Works. Lond., 1812. 2 v. 8°. 1475

Ouida. *(Pseudonym.)* See L. de LA RAME.

Our Family. Hood. (Works, v. 6.) N. Y., 1861. 8°. . . . 3966

Mutual Friend. Dickens. N. Y., 1868. 16°. 2184

New West. Bowles. Hartf'd., 1869. 8°. 8416

Village. Mitford. Philad. 8°. 2675

Ouseley, W. G. Remarks on Statistics, etc., of U. S. Philad., 1832. 8°. 6282

Outward Bound. Howard. Philad., 1838. 2 v. 12°. . . . 2439

[**Ouvilly, G. G. d'.**] The False Favourite Disgrac'd. Lond., 1657. 12°. 13354

Overland. A Novel. De Forest. N. Y. [1871.] 8°. . . . 2697

Overland Monthly. San Francisco, 1870–72. v. 4–8. 8°. . . 13690

Ovid. Metamorphoses and Epistles, translated. N. Y., 1836. 2 v. 12°. 4527

The same. 4548

Owen, J. Fashionable World displayed. N. Y., 1806. 12°. . . 17048

Owen, Robert. New View of Society. N. Y., 1825. 12°. . . . 17090

Life of. [Packard.] Philad., 1866. 12°. 6945

Owen, Robert D. Beyond the Breakers. (2 copies.) Philad., 1870. 8°. 2693

Owen, W. F. W., Voyages of. Robinson. N. Y., 1833. 2 v. 12°. . 16289

Owenson, S. See S. O. MORGAN.

Oxberry, W. Flowers of Literature. Lond., 1821. 3 v. 12°. . 4331

Plays. Bost., 1822–23. v. 1, 2, 4–12. 24°. 1346

For Contents, see PLAYS.

Oxford, Annals of. Jeaffreson. Lond., 1871. 2 v. 8°. 9287

and Cambridge Boat Races, 1829–69. Macmichael. Cambr., 1870. 16°. 9116

Scholars, Quips, etc. of. Philad., 1835. 12°. . 9234

delineated; with a Series of Views. Oxf'd., 1831. 4°. . . 5113

English Prize Essays. (2 copies.) Oxford, 1830–36. v. 1, 3–5. 12°. 3260

The same. v. 3, 4. 3268

Oxford Essays for 1855, 1856. Lond. 2 v. 8°. 3270
  Recollections of, 1789–1860. Cox. Lond., 1868. 8°. . . . 9246
  Sausage, The; Select Poetical Pieces. Lond., 1815. 8°. . 949
  Tom Brown at. [Hughes.] Lond., 1870. 8°. 9245
Oxonians, The. [Bulwer.] N. Y., 1830. 2 v. 12°. 2145

P.

Pacha of Many Tales. Marryat. N. Y., 1836. 12°. 15112
Pacific, Three Years in the. [Ruschenberger.] Philad., 1834. 8°. . 16305
Packard, Clarissa. *(Pseudonym.)* See C. H. GILMAN.
[**Packard, F. A.**] Life of R. Owen. Philad., 1866. 12°. . . . 6945
Paddock, J. Narrative of Shipwreck of the Oswego. N. Y., 1818. 8°. 16283
Paez, R. Wild Scenes in S. America. N. Y., 1862. 12°. . . . 8434
Page, H., Memoir of. Hallock. N. Y. 12°. 7523
Paget, J. Hungary and Transylvania. Lond., 1839. 2 v. 8°. . 16617
Paine, R. T. Works. Bost., 1812. 8°. 937
Paine, T., Life of. Cheetham. Lond., 1817. 8°. 7419
Painters, American, Sketches of. Tuckerman. N. Y., 1847. 12°. . 7917
  Eminent Brit., Lives of. Cunningham. N. Y., 1839–40. 5 v. 12°. 11017
  Lives of. Vasari. Lond., 1850–52. 5 v. 8°. 474
  Modern. Ruskin. N. Y., 1857–62. 5 v. 12°. 9014
  Old, Hist. Sketches of the. [H. F. Lee.] Bost., 1841. 12°. . 8878
Painting. (From the Encycl. Brit.) Haydon. Edinb., 1838. 12°. . 8876
  Art of. Du Fresnoy, tr. by Mason. Lond., 1811. 8°. . . 17239
  Discourses on. J. Reynolds. Lond., 1852. 2 v. 8°. . . 8879
  Handbook of Italian Schools of. Kugler. Lond., 1869. 2 v. 8°. 9058
  Hist. of. Memes. Bost., 1831. 12°. 8868
    in Italy. Lanzi. Lond., 1847. 3 v. 8°. 479
  Lectures on. Barry, Opie, and Fuseli. Lond., 1848. 8°. . 8881
    The same. Ruskin. N. Y., 1859. 12°. 9034
  Lectures on Hist. and Principles of. Phillips. Lond., 1833. 8°. 9073
  Rise and Progress of. Bost., 1846. 12°. 8887
    See, also, ART.
Palestine, Hist., etc., of. Russell. N. Y., 1840. 12°. 11029
  Pilgrimage to, 1832–33. Lamartine. Philad., 1835. 2 v. 12°. 8229
  Popular Description of. Conder. Lond. 12°. 7846
  Remarkable Characters and Places of. Elliott. Hartf'd., 1867. 8°. 10013
  Sketches of Travel in, 1849. Spencer. N. Y., 1850. 8°. . . 8069
  Traditions of. Martineau. Lond., 1843. 12°. 14626
  Travels in, Early. Ed. Wright. Lond., 1848. 8°. . . . 514
    1844. Lord Nugent. Lond., 1846. 2 v. 12°. . 8162
    See, also, SYRIA.
Paley, W. Natural Theology, ed. Potter. N. Y., 1840. 2 v. 12°. . 11420
  Works. Philad., 1831. 8°. 9631
Palfrey, J. G. Hist. of N. England. Bost., 1859–64. 3 v. 8°. . 6241
  The same, abridged and continued. N. Y. and Bost.,
    1866–72. 3 v. 12°. 6076

Palfrey, J. G. Life of W. Palfrey. Bost., 1845. 16°. 7266
Palfrey, W., Life of. J. G. Palfrey. Bost., 1845. 16°. 7266
Palgrave, F. Hist. of the Anglo-Saxons. Lond., 1837. 16°. . . . 4835
The Merchant and Friar. (2 copies.) 2d ed. Lond., 1844. 16°. 2369
Rise of the English Commonwealth: Anglo-Saxon Period. Lond., 1832. 2 v. 4°. 5111
Palgrave, F. T. Essays on Art. (2 copies.) N. Y., 1867. 16°. . 8859
Golden Treasury of Songs and Lyrics. Cambr., 1863. 16°. . 954
Palgrave, W. G. Hermann Agha. N. Y., 1872. 16°. 2371
Palissy, B., Life of. Morley. Lond. [1869.] 16°. 7879
Palm, J. H. v. d., Life of. Beets. N. Y., 1865. 8°. 7770
Palmer, E. H. Desert of the Exodus. Cambr., 1871. 2 v. 8°. . 8046
[**Palmer, J. W.**] The Golden Dagon. N. Y., 1856. 12°. 7910
Palmer, W. Eccl. History. N. Y., 1841. 12°. 16461
Palmerin of England. De Moraes, ed. Southey. Lond., 1807. 4 v. 24°. 1694
Palmerston, *Lord.* See H. J. TEMPLE.
Palmyra, Letters from. [A Tale.] Ware. N. Y., 1837. 2 v. 12°. . 2862
Pamela. Richardson. Lond., 1811. 4 v. 16°. 1927
Pamphleteer. Lond., 1813–28. v. 1–4, 6–24, 29. 8°. 14353
Panics, The Three. Cobden. Lond., 1867. 8°. 9588
Papacy. See POPES.
Paper against Gold. Cobbett. Lond., 1815. 2 v. 8°. 8655
Parables of our Lord, Notes on the. Trench. N. Y., 1859. 8°. . 10006
Parabosco, G. Novels. (Ital. Novelists, v. 2.) Lond., 1836. 12°. . 1900
Paraguay, The Abipones of. Dobrizhoffer. Lond., 1822. 3 v. 8°. . 5828
Four Years (1810–14) in. Robertson. Philad., 1838. 2 v. 12°. 5739
Francia's Reign in. Robertson. Philad., 1839. 2 v. 12°. . 5741
The same. (1819–25.) Rengger. Lond., 1827. 8°. . 5831
Pardoe, J. City of the Sultan. Philad., 1837. 2 v. 12°. . . . 16639
Court and Reign of Francis I. Philad., 1849. 2 v. 12°. . 5426
Louis XIV. and his Court. N. Y., 1847–48. 2 v. 12°. . . 5428
Traits and Traditions of Portugal. Philad., 1834. 2 v. 12°. . 16671
Parent's Assistant, The. Edgeworth. (Works, v. 10.) Bost., 1826. 8°. 15344
Pariah, A. *(Pseudonym.)* See C. F. CORNWALLIS.
Paris, J. A. Life of Davy. Lond., 1831. 2 v. 8°. 7148
Paris; or, the Book of the Hundred-and-one. Bost., 1833. v. 2. 12°. 2396
in America. Laboulaye. N. Y., 1863. 12°. 2649
The American in. [Sanderson.] Philad., 1839. 2 v. 12°. . 16709
during the Winter. Janin. N. Y., 1844. 8°. 16699
The Battle Summer in, 1848. Ik. Marvel. N. Y., 1853. 12°. . 5546
Commune, Hist. of the. Vésinier. Lond., 1872. 8°. . . 5554
and its Historical Scenes. Bost., 1831. v. 1. 12°. . . . 8814
The same. Bost., 1832. v. 2. 12°. 8818
Life in. N. Orleans, 1837. 2 v. in 1. 12°. 16712
Observ. on a Journey to, 1776. [W. Jones.] Lond., 1777. 2 v. 16°. 8188
and the Parisians in 1835. Trollope. N. Y., 1836. 8°. . . 16698
and its People. Grant. Lond., 1844. 2 v. 12°. 16701
Sketch Book. Thackeray. (Works, v. 7.) Lond., 1872. 8°. 2195
Sketches of, 1835–36. Philad., 1838. 12°. 16711

Parish-Side, The. [Elliot.] N. Y., 1854. 12°. 15756
[**Park, L. J.**] Joanna of Naples. Bost., 1838. 12°. 2731
Park, M. Travels in Africa. Philad., 1800. 8°. 16526
Life of. Edinb., 1835. 12°. 6631
Life and Travels of. N. Y., 1844. 12°. 11429
The same. N. Y., 1840. 12°. 12124
Parker, A. A. Trip to the West and Texas. Concord, 1835. 12°. . 16873
Parker, E. G. Golden Age of Amer. Oratory. (2 copies.) Bost., 1857. 12°. 7413
[**Parker, J.**] Ecce Deus. Bost., 1867. 16°. 9905
Parker, S. Journal of Exploring Tour. Ithaca, 1838. 12°. . . 16870
Parker, Theodore. Additional Speeches, Addresses, and Sermons. Bost., 1861. 2 v. 12°. 9296
Historic Americans. Bost., 1870. 12°. 7409
Life and Correspondence of. Weiss. N. Y., 1864. 2 v. 8°. . 7710
Parkes, J. and **Merivale, H.** Memoirs of Sir P. Francis. Lond., 1867. 2 v. 8°. 6852
Parkman, F. France and England in N. America. Bost., 1865–69. 3 v. 12°. 6131

CONTENTS.—1, Pioneers of France in the New World. 2, The Jesuits in N. America in the 17th century. 3, Discovery of the Great West.

The same. v. 1. 6130
Hist. of Conspiracy of Pontiac. Bost., 1851. 8°. . . . 5956
Parkyns, M. Life in Abyssinia. N. Y., 1854. 2 v. 12°. . . . 7978
Parley, Peter. *(Pseudonym.)* See S. G. GOODRICH.
Parliamentary Practice, Manual of. Cushing. Bost., 1857. 16°. . 8475
The same. Jefferson. Philad., 1840. 12°. 8474
Reform, Plan of. Bentham. (Works, pt. 10.) Edinb., 1839. 8°. 9709
Parliaments, Judicature in. Selden. Lond. [1681.] 16°. . . . 5150
See, also, SPEECHES ; ORATORY ; ELOQUENCE.
Parnassian Garland, The. Evans. Philad., 1814. 12°. . . . 14905
Parnell, T. Poetical Works. Ed. Bell. Lond., 1807. 24°. . . . 275
Poetical Works, with Life by Goldsmith. Bost., 1854. 16°. , 1055
The same, ed. Johnson. Dubl., 1804. 8°. 15099
Parodies. See POETIC MIRROR : and Authors, as J. BIGELOW ; C. S. CALVERLEY ; P. CARY ; F. BRET HARTE ; H. & J. SMITH ; THACKERAY.
Parr, H. Life of Jeanne d'Arc. Lond., 1866. 2 v. in 1. 16°. . . 5536
Parr, S. Characters of Fox. Lond., 1809. 2 v. 8°. 6793
Essay on. De Quincey. Bost., 1854. 16°. 3327
Parricide, The. [Reynolds.] Philad., 1836. 2 v. 12°. . . . 15532
Parrot, F. Journey to Ararat. N. Y., 1846. 16°. 16278
Parry, W. E. Three Voyages of Discovery. Lond., 1835. 4 v. 12°. 7872
The same. N. Y., 1845. 2 v. 12°. 11431
Parsons, T. Essays. Bost., 1845. 12°. 17355
Parterre, The. Lond., 1834–35. v. 1–3. 8°. 11744
Parties, Dissertation on. Bolingbroke. (Works, v. 2.) Philad., 1841. 8°. 10313
Hist. of, in England. Cooke. Lond., 1836–37. 3 v. 8°. , 4991

Partington, *Mrs.*, Life and Sayings of. Shillaber. N. Y., 1854. 12°. 4298
Parton, J. Gen. Butler in New Orleans. (2 copies.) N. Y., 1864. 12°. 7403
Famous Americans of Recent Times. Bost., 1869. 12°. . . 7410
Life of Burr. N. Y., 1858. 12°. 7356
of Franklin. N. Y., 1864. 2 v. 12°. 7314
of Jackson. N. Y., 1861. 3 v. 12°. 7318
The same, condensed. N. Y., 1863. 12°. 7321
[**Parton, S. P.**] Fern Leaves. Auburn, 1854. 12°. . , . . . 3659
Partridge, J. A. Democracy. Philad., 1866. 8°. 8695
Pascal, B. Provincial Letters. N. Y., 1828. 12°. 9586
The same. 17257
Thoughts on Religion, etc. Amh., 1829. 12°. 9585
Thoughts, Letters, etc. N. Y., 1861. 12°. 9584
Pascal Bruno. Dumas. Philad., 1839. 12°. 2594
Passavant, J. D. Tour of a German Artist in England. Lond., 1836. 2 v. 12°. 17121
Passion-Play, The Ober-Ammergau. MacColl. Lond., 1871. 16°. . 1453
[**Passmore, J. C.**] Footprints; or, Fugitive Poems. Philad., 1843. 12°. 15016
Paston Letters. Ed. Fenn and Ramsey. Lond., 1841. 2 v. in 1. 8°. 6982
The same. Lond., 1849. 8°. 500
Pastor's Sketches, A. Spencer. N. Y., 1854. 12°. 9992
Patchwork. B. Hall. Philad., 1841. 2 v. 12°. 15850
Pater Mundi. Burr. Bost., 1870. 12°. 9981
Pathfinder, The. Cooper. N. Y., 1873. 12°. 2841
Patience Strong's Outings. Whitney. Bost., 1870. 12°. . . . 2968
Patmore, C. Faithful for ever. Lond., 1860. 16°. 1199
Patmos, and the 7 Churches. Brewer. Bridgep't., 1851. 8°. . . 6450
Paton, A. A. Servia. Lond., 1845. 12°. 16590
Patrick, St., Life of. Jocelin, ed. O'Haloran. Philad., 1823. 12°. . 16339
Patronage. Edgeworth. (Works, v. 7.) Bost., 1825. 8°. . . . 15341
Patten, W. Reminiscences of Dr. Hopkins. N. Y., 1843. 12°. . 7521
Pattison, W. Select Poems. With Life, by Sanford. Philad., 1819. 24°. 10
Patton, J. H. Hist. of the U. S. N. Y., 1862. 8°. 6281
Paul, St., Character and Practical Writings of. H. More. (Works, v. 2.) Bost., 1827. 8°. 15104
Hist. of. Blunt. Philad., 1839. 12°. 9909
Renan. N. Y., 1869. 12°. 9897
Life and Epistles of. Conybeare and Howson. N. Y., 1866. 2 v. 8°. 6566
and Protestantism. Arnold. Lond., 1870. 8°. 9910
See, also, BIBLE.
Paul Clifford. Bulwer-Lytton. Philad., 1868. 12°. 2035
Paul Fane. Willis. N. Y., 1857. 12°. 15333
Paul Ferroll. [Clive.] N. Y., 1856. 12°. 15534
Paul Jones. Cunningham. Philad., 1827. 3 v. 12°. 15535
Paul and **Virginia.** Saint-Pierre. Philad., 1856. 16°. 2356
Paulding, H. Journal of Cruise of the Dolphin. N. Y., 1831. 12°. . 16297
Paulding, J. K. Lay of the Scottish Fiddle. N. Y., 1813. 24°. . . 14947

Paulding, J. K. Letters from the South. N. Y., 1817. 2 v. 12°. . 15290
Life of Washington. N. Y., 1840. 2 v. 12°. 11291
The same. N. Y., 1835. 2 v. 12°. 12117
Merry Tales of Wise Men of Gotham. N. Y., 1826. 12°. . 15287
New Mirror for Travellers. N. Y., 1828. 12°. 15289
Sketch of Old England. N. Y., 1822. 12°. 15286
Slavery in the U. S. N. Y., 1836. 12°. 8467
Tales of the Good Woman. N. Y., 1829. 12°. 15288
Westward Ho! N. Y., 1832. 2 v. 12°. 15161
Works. N. Y., 1835. 9 v. 12°. 15277

CONTENTS.—1-4, Salmagundi. 5, 6, Letters from the South. 7, 8, Koningsmarke. 9, John Bull and Brother Jonathan.

Literary Life of. By his Son. N. Y., 1867. 12°. 7390
Pauli, R. Life of Alfred the Great. Lond. (Bohn) 1857. 8°. . . 402
Paul's Letters to his Kinsfolk. W. Scott. Bost., 1829. 12°. . . 16697
Pauw, C. de. Dissertations on the Egyptians and Chinese. Lond., 1795. 2 v. 8°. 16169
on the Greeks. Lond., 1793. 2 v. 8°. . 15871
Payne, A. R. M. The Geral-Milco. N. Y., 1852. 12°. . . . 17139
Payson, E., Memoir of. Portland, 1830. 12°. 7574
The same. Cummings. Bost., 1830. 12°. . . . 16420
Pazos, V. Letters on United Provinces of S. A. N. Y., 1819. 8°. . 17138
Peabody, A. P. Reminiscences of European Travel. N. Y., 1868. 16°. 8209
Peabody, O. W. B. Life of Putnam. (Sparks, v. 7.) Bost., 1837. 16°. 7256
The same. Bost., 1839. 12°. 16314
Life of J. Sullivan. (Sparks, v. 13.) Bost., 1844. 16°. . . 7262
Peabody, W. B. O. Life of Brainerd. (Sparks, v. 8.) Bost., 1837. 16°. 7257
The same. Bost., 1839. 12°. 16313
Life of C. Mather. (Sparks, v. 6.) Bost., 1836. 16°. . . . 7255
of Oglethorpe. (Sparks, v. 12.) Bost., 1844. 16°. . . 7261
of A. Wilson. (Sparks, v. 2.) Bost., 1834. 16°. . . . 7251
Peace, Manual of. Upham. N. Y., 1836. 8°. 8699
Principles of. Hancock. Philad., 1829. 12°. 8473
Peacock, T. L. Headlong Hall, and Nightmare Abbey. N. Y., 1845. 12°. 3956
Peale, R. Notes on Italy. Philad., 1831. 8°. 16735
Pearl, C. Youth's Book on the Mind. Portl'd., 1847. 12°. . . 17065
Pearson, J. Life of Hey. New ed. Lond., 1827. 2 v. 8°. . . 7569
Peasant and his Landlord, The. v. Knorring. N. Y., 1848. 12°. . 2658
Peck, Jesse T. Hist. of the Great Republic. (2 copies.) N. Y., 1868. 8°. 6277
Peck, John M. Life of Boone. (Sparks, v. 23.) Bost., 1847. 16°. . 7272
Peculiar. A Tale. Sargent. N. Y., 1866. 12°. 2917
Peel, *Sir* **R.,** Life of. From the "Times." (2 copies.) N. Y., 1852. 12°. 6689
Memoirs of. [Maxwell.] Lond., 1842. 2 v. 12°. . . . 6779
Peele, G. Works, ed. Dyce. Lond., 1829–39. 3 v. 8°. . . . 1463
Peg Woffington. Reade. Bost., 1871. 16°. 2094
Peile, J. Introd. to Greek and Latin Etymology. 2d ed. Lond., 1872. 16°. 93

Peirce, B. K. Trials of an Inventor. N. Y. [1866.] 16°. 7278
Pelayo. Simms. N. Y., 1836. 12°. 15757
Pelet de la Lozère, J. Napoleon in Council. Edinb., 1837. 8°. . 5443
Pelham. Bulwer. Lond. 12°. 2051
Pellew, E. (*Viscount* Exmouth), Life of. Osler. N. Y., 1835. 12°. . 16370
Pellico, S. My Prisons. Ed. Maroncelli. Cambr., 1836. 2 v. 16°. 7504
The same. Transl. by Roscoe. N. Y., 1833. 12°. . . 7784
Pen Owen. [J. Hook.] N. Y., 1822. 2 v. 12°. 15538
Penal Law. See BENTHAM.
Pencil Sketches. Leslie. Philad., 1833–37. 3 v. 12°. . . . 15758
Pencillings by the Way. Willis. Philad., 1836. 2 v. 12°. . . 15328
Pendennis, History of. Thackeray. Lond., 1871. 8°. 2190
Peninsular Campaigns, Annals of the. [Hamilton.] Philad., 1831. 3 v. 12°. 6412
War, Hist. of the. Napier. Brussels, 1839. 3 v. 8°. . . 6524
The same. Southey. Lond., 1828. v. 1–4. 8°. . . 6527
Memoirs of the. Suchet. Lond., 1829. 2 v. 8°. . . 6531
Memorials of the. [Constable's Misc.] Edinb., 1828. 2 v. 12°. 4489
See, also, SPAIN.
Penn, J. Poems. Lond., 1801. 2 v. 8°. 17517
Penn, Wm., Select Works. 4th ed. Lond., 1825. 3 v. 8°. . 17241
Biogr. of. Dixon. Philad., 1851. 12°. 7313
Life of. Weems. Philad., 1836. 12°. 7488
Penn, Wm. (*Pseudonym.*) See J. EVARTS.
Pennington, M. Memoirs of Eliz. Carter. Bost., 1809. 8°. . . 16371
Pennsylvania, Historical Collections of. Day. Philad. [1843.] 8°. 5939
Hist. of, to 1770. Proud. Philad., 1797–98. 2 v. 8°. . . 5841
to 1776. Gordon. Philad., 1829. 8°. 5840
Constitution and Gov't. of, to 1759. Franklin. Bost., 1836. 8°. 9749
Insurrection in, 1794. Findley. Philad., 1796. 8°. . 6091
Penny Magazine. Lond., 1832–41. 10 v. in 11. fol. 14413
Knight's. Lond., 1846–47. 2 v. in 1. 8°. . . 14597
Pepys, S., Memoirs of; Diary and Correspondence. 2d ed. Lond., 1828. 5 v. 8°. 7028
The same. 3d ed. Lond., 1848–49. 5 v. 8°. . . 7033
Perceval, S. Writings. Lond., 1791–1809. 8°. 17209
Life of. Williams. Philad., 1813. 12°. 16380
Percival, J. G. Clio. N. Y., 1827. 12°. 696
Dream of a Day, etc. (2 copies.) N. H., 1843. 12°. . . 697
Poetical Works. Bost., 1859. 2 v. 16°. 590
Report on Geology of Conn. N. H., 1842. 8°. 9102
Life and Letters of. Ward. Bost., 1866. 12°. 7387
Percy, S. and **R.** Anecdotes. Lond., 1823. 20 v. 12°. . . . 4138
Percy, T. Reliques of Ancient English Poetry. Lond., 1840. 8°. . 1312
The same. (2 copies.) Philad., 1823. 3 v. 8°. . . 1313
Percy Mallory. [J. Hook.] Philad., 1824. 2 v. 12°. . . . 15540
Percy's Masque. [Hillhouse.] N. Y., 1820. 12°. 795

Perdicaris, G. A. Greece of the Greeks. N. Y., 1845. 2 v. 12°. . 16645
Peregrine Pickle. Smollett. N. Y. 8°. 1989
Pericles and **Aspasia.** Landor. Philad., 1839. 2 v. 8°. . . . 3450
Peril, Narratives of. Davenport. Lond., 1840. 2 v. 16°. . . 8164
Perils of Pearl Street. [Greene.] N. Y., 1834. 12°. 15761
Periodical Library, Greenbank's. Philad., 1833. 3 v. 8°. . . 15356
Literature, Index to. Poole. N. Y., 1853. 8°. . . .
Periodicals:—
Academician, The. N. Y., 1820. v. 1. 8°. 14079
All the Year Round. Lond., 1868–72. 8 v. 8°. . . . 12404
American Journal of Science. N. H., 1818–72. 104 v. 8°. . 17545
Literary Magazine, Sprague's. Albany and Hartf'd., 1847–49. 5 v. in 3. 8°. 13254
Monthly Magazine. N. Y., 1817–18. 4 v. 8°. . 13558
The same. Ed. Willis. Bost., 1829. v. 1. 8°. . . 13113
The same. New Series. N. Y., 1836. 2 v. 8°. . . 13114
American Museum, Carey's. 1787–98. Philad. v. 1–9, 11–13. 8°. 14758
Quarterly Observer. (2 copies.) Bost., 1833–34. 3 v. 8°. 13880
Review. Philad., 1827–37. 22 v. 8°. . 13213
The same. v. 3–7, 9–20. 13235
American Review, Walsh's. (2 copies.) Philad., 1811–12. 4 v. 8°. 14038
Whig Review. N. Y., 1845–52. 16 v. 8°. . . 12561
The same. v. 3–10, 12–16. 12723
Analectic Magazine. Philad., 1814–20. 16 v. 8°. . . . 14235
Annual Review. Ed. Aikin. Lond., 1802–04. 3 v. 8°. . . 14536
Anti-Jacobin. 4th ed. Lond., 1799. 2 v. 8°. . . . 11300
Review and Magazine. Lond., 1798–1800. 5 v. 8°. 11302
Appletons' Journal. N. Y., 1869–72. v. 2–8. 4°. . . . 14392
Arcturus. N. Y., 1841–42. v. 3. 8°. 12768
Argosy. Lond., 1866–67. 4 v. 8°. 14388
Art-Journal. Lond., 1852–60. 8 v. 4°. . . . . . .
Athenæum. N. H., 1814. v. 1. 8°. 17475
Atlantic Monthly. Bost., 1857–72. 30 v. 8°. 13455
The same. v. 1–26. 13429
Bee. Ed. Anderson. Edinb., 1791–93. 18 v. 8°. . . . 13041
Bentley's Miscellany. Lond., 1837–44. v. 1–3, 5–10, 13–16. 8°. 14212
The same. v. 8, 9. N. Y. 8°. 14225
Biblical Repository. Andover and N. Y., 1831–50. 30 v. 8°. 12776
The same. v. 1–7, 11–21, 23–30. 12821
Index to v. 1–24. (2 copies.) . . . . . .
Bibliotheca Sacra. Andover, 1844–72. 29 v. 8°. . . . 12851
The same. v. 9–26. 12803
Index to v. 1–13. . . . .
Blackwood's Magazine. Edinb. and N. Y., 1817–72. v. 1–4, 6–30, 32–112. 8°. 11620
The same. v. 1–18, 21, 24–26, 28, 33–91, 93–106. . . 11957
British and Foreign Review. Lond., 1835–44. 16 v. 8°. . . 11440
Brownson's Quarterly Review. Bost., 1844–46. 3 v. 8°. . 14251
The same. New Series. Bost., 1849–50. v. 3, 4. 8°. . 14256
Christian Spectator, Monthly. N. H., 1819–28. 10 v. 8°. . 12940
Quarterly. (2 copies.) N. H., 1829–38. 10 v. 8°. 12950
Contemporary Review. Lond., 1866–72. 20 v. 8°. . . . 12231
Continental Monthly. N. Y., 1862–64. 6 v. 8°. . . . 13332
Cornhill Magazine. Lond., 1867–72. v. 16–25. 8°. . . . 17666
Craftsman. Lond., 1731. 7 v. 12°. 12025
Democratic Review. Wash. and N. Y., 1837–52. v. 1–21, 23–31. 8°. 13059
The same. v. 1–5, 9–21, 23–25, 27–31. 13089
Dublin University Magazine. D., 1841–72. v. 18–22, 79. 8°. . 17691

Periodicals:—

Eclectic, American. (2 copies.) N. Y., 1841–42. 4 v. 8°. . 13741
Magazine. N. Y., 1844–72. v. 1–9, 11–79. 8°. . . 13562
The same. v. 1–33, 64–71. 13752
Eclectic Museum. N. Y., 1843. 3 v. 8°. 13749
Review. Lond., 1805–10. 6 v. in 11. 8°. . . . 14377
Edinburgh Annual Register, for 1808–15. E., 1810–17. 8 v. in 13. 8°. 11731
Edinburgh Monthly Review. Edinb., 1819–21. 5 v. 8°. . 13116
Review. E. and N. Y., 1802–72. v. 1–22, 24–38, 40–83, 86–130, 133–136. 8°. 11051
The same. v. 1–17, 19–90, 93–122, 125–132. . . . 11154
Index to v. 1–20. (2 copies.) Also, Index to v. 21–50.
Selections from. Lond., 1833, and Paris, 1835. 7 v. 8°. 11293
Edinburgh Weekly Magazine. E., 1771–72. v. 14, 15 (in 1). 8°. 12745
Foreign Quarterly Review. Lond. and N. Y., 1827–46. v. 1–3, 5–37. 8°. 12682
The same. v. 11, 12, 14–23, 26–30, 32–36. 12709
Foreign Review. Lond., 1828–30. 5 v. 8°. 11435
Fortnightly Review. Lond., 1865–72. 18 v. 8°. . . . 12195
Fraser's Magazine. Lond., 1830–72. 85 v. 8°. . . . 12300
Galaxy. N. Y., 1868–72. v. 6–10, 12–14. 13890
The same. v. 5–8. 13886
Good Words. Lond., 1866–67. v. 7, 8. 8°. 14534
Halcyon Luminary. N. Y., 1812. v. 1. 8°. 14080
Harper's Monthly Magazine. N. Y., 1850–72. 45 v. 8°. . . 13121
The same. v. 1–36, 38–42. 13291
Harvard Lyceum. Cambr., 1810–11. 8°. 17472
Magazine. (2 copies.) Cambr., 1855–60. 6 v. 8°. . 17462
Herald of Health. N. Y., 1867–70. v. 43, 44, 49, 50 (in 2 v). 8°. 17488
Homilist, The. Lond., 1870–71. 4 v. 8°. 12888
Hours at Home. N. Y., 1865–70. 11 v. 8°. 13397
The same. v. 4, 5, 7. 13408
Household Words. Lond. and N. Y., 1850–59. v. 1–4, 15, 16, 18. 8°. 17497
Hunt's Merchant's Magazine. N. Y., 1839–59. v. 1–5, 8–13, 20–40. 8°. 13525
Knickerbocker. N. Y., 1833–62. v. 1–59. 8°. 14457
The same. v. 2–5, 7, 8, 10–25, 27–30, 32, 35, 36, 38, 41, 43–45, 47–66. 14640
Knight's Penny Magazine. Lond., 1846–47. 2 v. in 1. 8°. . 14597
Land we Love, The. Charlotte, N. C., 1866–69. 6 v. 8°. . 12934
Lippincott's Magazine. Philad., 1868–72. 9 v. 8°. . . . 13373
Literary Portfolio. Philad., 1830. v. 1. 4°. 14412
Literary and Theological Review. N. Y., 1834–38. 5 v. 8°. . 12771
Littell's Living Age. Bost., 1844–72. v. 1–14, 16–103, 105–107, 109–114. 8°. 13924
London Society. Lond., 1868–71. v. 13, 14, 16–19. 8°. . . 17798
Macmillan's Magazine. Lond., 1859–72. v. 1–8, 16–26. 8°. . 12155
Mass. Quarterly Review. Bost., 1847–49. 2 v. 8°. . . . 12769
Metropolitan Magazine. N. Y., 1836–42. 13 v. 8°. . . 14520
Microcosm. N. H., 1836–37. v. 3, New Series. 8°. . . 14598
Microscope. N. H., 1820. 2 v. in 1. 8°. 17474
Month. Lond., 1870–71. 4 v. New Series. 8°. . . . 17778
Monthly Magazine. Lond., 1796–1825. 60 v. 8°. . . . 14152
Monthly Review. Lond., 1817–33. v. 82–129, 131, 132. 8°. . 14300
Museum. Lond., 1746–47. 3 v. 8°. 12742
of Foreign Literature. Philad., 1822–39. v. 1–26, 28–29, 31–33, 35–37. 8° 14046
Nation. N. Y., 1865–72. 15 v. 4°. . . . .

Periodicals:—

Naval Magazine. N. Y., 1836. v. 1. 8°. 13557
New England Magazine. (2 copies.) Bost., 1831–34. 7 v. 8°. 13864
New Englander. N. H., 1843–72. v. 1–24, 26–36. 8°. . . 12997
The same. v. 2–5, 7–28. 12971
Index, v. 1–19. (2 copies.) . . . .
New Mirror. N. Y., 1843–44. 3 v. 8°. 14516
New Monthly Magazine. Bost., 1823–24. v. 6–8. 8°. . . 14350
New York Literary Gazette. N. Y., 1825–26. v. 1. 8°. . . 12577
New York Quarterly. N. Y., 1854–55. v. 3. 8°. . . . 13338
New York Review. (2 copies.) N. Y., 1837–42. 10 v. 8°. . 12914
Niles' Register. Balt., 1816–37. 52 v. 8° and 4°. . . . 14553
North American Review. Bost., 1815–72. v. 1–102, 104–115. 8°. 12425
The same. v. 2–45, 47–54, 56–67, 69–102, 104–108. . . 12579
Index, v. 1–25. (2 copies.) . . . .
North British Review. Edinb. and N. Y., 1844–71. 53 v. 8°. . 11684
The same. v. 10–37, 42–49. 11713
Old and New. Bost., 1870–72. 5 v. 8°. 13711
Olio, The. Lond. v. 1, 2. 8°. 11307
Once a Week. Lond., 1870–71. v. 6, 7. 8°. 17856
Overland Monthly. S. Francisco, 1870–72. v. 4–8. 8°. . . 13690
Pamphleteer. Lond., 1813–28. v. 1–4, 6–24, 29. 8°. . . 14353
Parterre. Lond., 1834–35. v. 1–3. 8°. 11744
Penny Magazine. Lond., 1832–41. 10 v. in 11. fol. . . 14413
Philomathesian. Middlebury, 1833–34. v. 1. 8°. . . . 17473
Port Folio. 2d and 3d Series. Philad., 1809–14. 6 v. 8°. . 12736
Portico. Balt., 1816–17. v. 2–4, in 1. 8°. 12578
Putnam's Monthly Magazine. N. Y., 1833–58. 12 v. 8°. . 13257
The same. v. 1–11. 13274
The same. New Series. N. Y., 1868–70. 6 v. 8°. . 13285
The same. v. 1–5. 13269
Quarterly Review. Lond. and N. Y., 1809–72. v. 1–12, 14–28, 30–33, 35–38, 40–122, 124–132. 8°. 11470
The same. v. 1–16, 18–48, 50–81, 84–122, 124–127. . . 11310
Also, Indexes to v. 1–60, in 3 v. 8°. . . . . . .
Retrospective Review. Lond., 1820–26. 14 v. 8°. . . . 11456
Rural Magazine. Hartf'd., 1819. v. 1. 8°. 13879
Sabbath at Home. Bost., 1867. v. 1. 8°. 13878
St. James' Magazine. Lond., 1869–71. v. 3–7. 8°. . . . 17835
Saint Paul's Magazine. Lond., 1872. v. 10. 8°. . . . 17815
Scribner's Monthly. N. Y., 1870–72. 4 v. 8°. 13411
Select Journal of Foreign Period. Lit. Bost., 1833–34. 4 v. 8°. 14231
Sharpe's London Magazine. Lond., 1870. v. 36. 8°. . . 17480
Southern Literary Messenger. Richmond, 1835–59. v. 1–20, 22, 24–28. 8°. 14539
The same. v. 7, 17–20. 14728
Southern Review. Charleston, 1828–32. 8 v. 8°. . . . 14024
The same. v. 1–4, 6, 8. 14032
Student's Companion. N. H., 1831. v. 1. 8°. 17393
Tait's Edinburgh Magazine. E., 1842–43. v. 9–10, in 4. 8°. . 13823
Theological Review. Lond., 1870. v. 7. 8°. 17736
Union Review. Lond., 1870–71. 2 v. 8°. 12902
University Quarterly. N. H., 1860–61. 4 v. 8°. 17476
Westminster Review. Lond. and N. Y., 1824–72. v. 1–45, 47–84, 86–98. 8°. 11853
The same. v. 1–17, 20–54, 57–92. 12032
Yale Courant. (2 copies.) N. H., 1865–67. 2 v. 4°. . . .
Literary Magazine. N. H., 1836–72. v. 1–37. 8°. . . 17393
The same. v. 2–15, 17–26, 28, 29. 17367
The same. v. 1–6, 8–12. 17451
Index to v. 1–33. N. H., 1868. 8°. . . . . . .

Perkins, J. H., Memoir and Writings of. Bost., 1851. 2 v. 12°. . 3637
Perkins, S. Historical Sketches of the U. S. (2 copies.) N. Y., 1830. 12°. 6021
Hist. of the late War. N. H., 1825. 8°. 5873
Perry, A. L. Elements of Polit. Economy. N. Y., 1866. 8°. . . 8639
Perry, M. C. Narrative of Expedition to Japan. N. Y., 1857. 8°. . 8135
Perry, O. H., Life of. Cooper. (Naval Biogr., v. 2.) Philad., 1846. 12°. 7276
The same. Mackenzie. N. Y., 1840. 2 v. 12°. . . 11601
The same. Niles. Hartf'd., 1820. 12°. . . . 16427
Perry, W. C. German University Education. Lond., 1845. 12°. . 9251
Persia, Hist. and Description of. Fraser. N. Y., 1841. 12°. . . 11288
Narrative of Tour in. Southgate. N. Y., 1840. 2 v. 12°. . 16496
Popular Description of. Conder. Lond. 2 v. in 1. 12°. . 7844
Sketches of. Malcolm. Lond., 1828. 2 v. 8°. . . . 8231
Persian Adventurer, The. Fraser. Philad., 1831. 2 v. 12°. . . 15542
Letters. Montesquieu. (v. 3.) Lond., 1777. 8°. . . . 9554
Monarchy, The. Rawlinson. (v. 3.) N. Y., 1871. 8°. . . 4065
Persius. Satires, transl. by Drummond. N. Y., 1837. 12°. . . 4539
by Gifford. Lond., 1821. 8°. . . . 889
The same. Philad., 1822. 24°. 36
Perspective, Elements of. Ruskin. N. Y., 1860. 12°. . . . 9037
Persuasion. Austen. N. Y., 1832. 2 v. 12°. 2477
Perthes, F. C., Memoirs of. C. T. Perthes. Edinb., 1856. 2 v. 8°. 7760
Pertusier, C. Promenades round Constantinople, etc. Lond., 1820. 8°. 8054
Peru, Description of. Conder. Lond. 12°. 7846
Hist. of Conquest of. Prescott. Philad., 1871. 2 v. 8°. . 10330
The same. Trueba y Cosio. Edinb., 1830. 12°. . . 4507
Journal on coast of, 1820–22. Hall. Lond., 1840. 8°. . . 8101
Travels in, 1838–42. v. Tschudi. N. Y., 1847. 12°. . . 8363
Pestalozzi, J. H., Life of. Biber. Philad., 1833. 8°. 15356
Peter, St. See Bible.
Peter I. of Russia (the Great), Anecdotes of. Staehlin. Dubl., 1789. 12°. 16181
Hist. of. De Ségur. Philad., 1833. 8°. 15356
Life of. Fontenelle. Lond., 1728. 12°. 16182
Peter, W. Poets and Poetry of Greece and Rome. (2 copies.) Philad., 1847–48. 8°. 239
Peter Pindar, Works of. [Wolcott.] Philad., 1835. 8°. . . . 1239
[Peters, S.] Hist. of Conn. N. H., 1829. 12°. 6006
Peter's Letters to his Kinsfolk. [Lockhart, etc.] N. Y., 1820. 8°. . 3396
Petherick, J. Egypt, the Soudan and Central Africa. Edinb., 1861. 8°. 8071
Petrarch, F., Translations from. By J. Penn. Lond., 1801. 8°. . 17517
View of Human Life, transl. by Mrs. Dobson. Lond., 1791. 8°. 3949
Life of. Dobson. Philad., 1817. 8°. 7752
The same. Stebbing. Lond., 1831. 12°. . . . 7775
Life and Times of. Campbell. Lond., 1843. 2 v. 8°. . . 7754
Petroleum, Discovery, etc., of. [Morris.] N. Y., 1865. 12°. . . 17000
Peveril of the Peak. Scott. Bost., 1845. 2 v. in 1. 12°. . . . 1812
Pezron, P. Antiquities of Nations. Lond., 1809. 16°. . . . 15931
Pfeiffer, I. Journey to Iceland, and Travels in Sweden and Norway. N. Y., 1852. 12°. 8200

Pfeiffer, I. Second Journey round the World. N. Y., 1856. 12°. . 8033
A Woman's Journey round the World. Lond., 1852. 8°. . 8265
Phædrus. Fables, transl. by Smart. N. Y., 1835. 12°. . . . 4536
The same. 4547
Phalaris, Dissertation on Epistles of. Bentley. Lond., 1836. 2 v. 8°. 17227
Phantasmion. [S. H. Coleridge.] N. Y., 1839. 2 v. 12°. . . 15544
Phantom Ship, The. Marryat. Philad., 1839. 12°. 15546
Phelps, A. The Still Hour. Bost., 1861. 16°. 9551
Phelps, E. S. Gates Ajar. (3 copies.) Bost., 1869. 12°. . . . 2972
Hedged In. (3 copies.) Bost., 1870. 12°. 2977
Men, Women, and Ghosts. (2 copies.) Bost., 1869. 12°. . 2975
The Silent Partner. (2 copies.) Bost., 1871. 12°. . . . 2980
Phelps, Samuel M. Triumphs of Divine Grace. N. Y., 1835. 12°. . 15017
Phelps, Sylvanus D. Holy Land, Europe and Egypt. N. Y., 1863. 12°. 16276
The Poet's Song. N. Y., 1867. 12°. 15019
Sunlight and Hearthlight. N. Y., 1856. 12°. 15018
Phenix, The ; a Collection of Fragments. Gowan. N. Y., 1835. 12°. 9531
Phi Beta Kappa Orations and Poems, Yale College, 1802–46. 8°. . 9321
Philadelphia Book, The. Philad., 1836. 12°. 15067
Souvenir, The. Philad., 1826. 12°. 13839
Philadelphus. *(Pseudonym.)* See S. WHELPLEY.
Philip of Macedon, Hist. of. Leland. Lond., 1820. 2 v. 8°. . . 4428
Philip II. of Spain. Gayarré. N. Y., 1866. 8°. 6584
Hist. of Reign of. Prescott. Philad., 1871. 3 v. 8°. . . 10338
and **III.,** Hist. of Reigns of. Watson. Dubl., 1777–83. 3 v. 8°. 6556
Philip, King *(Indian Chief),* Hist. of War of, 1675–76. Church.
Hartf'd. [1845.] 8°. 5957
Philip, R. Life of Bunyan. (2 copies.) N. Y., 1839. 12°. . . 7597
of Whitefield. N. Y., 1838. 12°. 7599
Manly Piety. N. Y., 1833. 12°. 17017
Philippart, J. Campaign in Germany and France. Lond., 1814. 2 v. 8°. 16186
Memoirs of Charles John of Sweden. Balt., 1815. 8°. . . 16172
of Moreau. Philad., 1816. 8°. 16404
Philips, A. Distressed Mother. (Brit. Drama, v. 1.) Lond., 1804. 8°. 1629
Poetical Works. Ed. Bell. Lond., 1807. 24°. 281
Philips, G. The Country Sketch Book. Lond., 1851. 12°. . . 8186
Philips, J. Poetical Works. Ed. Bell. Lond., 1807. 24°. . . 274
The same, ed. Johnson. Dubl., 1804. 8°. 15096
Phillippo, J. M. Jamaica. Philad., 1843. 8°. 16921
Phillips, C. The Emerald Isle. Philad., 1816. 24°. 14841
Recollections of Curran, etc. N. Y., 1818. 8°. 6804
Specimens of Irish Eloquence. N. Y., 1820. 8°. . . . 9427
Speeches. Saratoga, 1820. 8°. 17536
Phillips, G. S. Gypsies of the Danes' Dike. Bost., 1864. 12°. . 2851
Phillips, J. Treatise on Geology. Lond., 1837–39. 2 v. 16°. . . 6051
Phillips, T. Lectures on Painting. Lond., 1833. 8°. . . . 9073
Phillips, Wendell. Speeches, Lectures, and Letters. Bost., 1863. 8°. 9326
Philology, Modern. Dwight. N. Y., 1864–65. 2 v. [v. 1, 2d ed.] 8°. 178
See, also, LANGUAGE.

Philomathesian. Middlebury, 1833–34. v. 1. 8°. 17473
Philosophers and Actresses. Houssaye. N. Y., 1852. 2 v. 12°. . 3737
Ancient, Lives of the. Fénelon. N. Y., 1842. 12°. . . 11615
Philosophical Dictionary. Voltaire. Lond., 1824. 6 v. 12°. . . 8504
Miscellanies. Cousin, Jouffroy, and Constant. Tr. Ripley. Boston, 1858. 2 v. 12°. 8584
Theories and Experience. [Cornwallis.] Philad., 1847. 12°. . 8496
Philosophy of Active and Moral Powers. Stewart. Philad., 1866. 12°. 8592
Ancient, Hist. of. Ritter. Oxf'd., 1838–39. v. 1–3. 8°. . . 8707
Discussions on. Hamilton. N. Y., 1861. 8°. 8769
Ethical, Dissert. on Progress of. Mackintosh. Edinb., 1837. 8°. 8722
Introd. to. Jouffroy. Bost., 1840. 2 v. 12°. . . 8586
First Principles of. H. Spencer. N. Y., 1864. 12°. . . 8598
Greek, Brief View of. [Cornwallis.] Philad., 1846. 12°. . 8497
Hist. of, to 1700. Enfield, from Brucker. Lond., 1837. 8°. . 8719
from Thales to Comte. Lewes. Lond., 1871. 2 v. 8°. 8724
Elements of, to 1700. T. Morell. Lond., 1827. 8°. . 8720
Epitome of. N. Y., 1845. 2 v. 12°. 11618
Introd. to. Cousin. Bost., 1832. 8°. 8715
Manual of, to 1828. Tennemann. Oxf'd., 1832. 8°. . 8713
Intellectual, Lectures on. Young. Glasg., 1835. 8°. . . 17071
of Life, and of Language. F. v. Schlegel. Lond., 1847. 8°. . 434
Mental, Bearings of, on Science and Religion. Bascom. N. Y., 1871. 12°. 8512
Elements of. Upham. N. Y., 1848. 2 v. 12°. . . 8604
Metaphysical. Kant. Lond., 1836. 8°. 8730
Lectures on. Hamilton. Bost., 1860. 8°. . 8740
Modern, Hist. of. Cousin. N. Y., 1857. 2 v. 8°. . . . 8717
Sketches of. Murdock. Hartf'd., 1842. 12°. . . 8494
Moral. Combe. N. Y., 1844. 12°. 8495
Lectures on. Follen. Bost., 1841. 12°. . . . 12748
Sketches of. Sydney Smith. N. Y., 1850. 12°. . . 8593
and Mental. Chalmers. N. Y., 1840. 12°. . . . 9520
and Political. Paley. (Works.) Philad., 1831. 8°. . 9631
and Morals, Recent Discussions in. H. Spencer. N. Y., 1871. 12°. 8602
Natural. See NATURAL.
of the Plan of Salvation. [Walker.] Bost., 1856. 12°. . . 9987
Positive, of Comte. Mill. Bost., 1871. 12°. 8590
Recent British. (1835–65.) Masson. N. Y., 1866. 12°. . . 8580
Speculative, Hist. of, in 19th century. Morell. N. Y., 1848. 8°. 8726
See, also, METAPHYSICS; PSYCHOLOGY.
Philothea. Mrs. Child. Bost., 1836. 12°. 15762
Philpot, J., Examinations and Letters of. Lond. 12°. . . . 9478
Phineas Finn. A. Trollope. N. Y., 1869. 8°. 2292
Phips, *Sir* **W.,** Life of. Bowen. Bost., 1837. 16°. 7256
Phœnix, John. *(Pseudonym.)* See G. H. DERBY.
Phrenological Works. Gall. Bost., 1835. 6 v. 12°. 12761
Phrenology. Spurzheim. Bost., 1832. 2 v. 8°. 8777

Phrenology in connexion with Physiognomy. Spurzheim. Bost., 1833. 8°. 8779
Examination of objections to. Spurzheim. Bost., 1833. 12°. . 8611
Hist. of Progress of. Haskins. Buffalo, 1839. 12°. . . . 8609
Illustrations of. Ed. by Calvert. Balt., 1832. 12°. . . . 8610
known by its Fruits. Reese. N. Y., 1836. 12°. . . . 8608
System of. Combe. Bost., 1834. 8°. 8780
Physical Education, A System of. Maclaren. Oxf'd., 1869. 16°. . 9118
Exercises, Manual of. Wood. N. Y., 1867. 12°. . . . 9268
Geography. See EARTH; GEOGRAPHY.
Sciences. See SCIENCE.
Theory of another Life. Taylor. N. Y., 1836. 12°. . . . 9540
Physics. See NATURAL Philosophy.
Physiognomy, System of. Redfield. N. Y., 1849. 8°. . . . 17078
See, also, PHRENOLOGY.
Physiology, Animal and Vegetable. Roget. Philad., 1836. 2 v. 8°. 16985
of Common Life. Lewes. N. Y., 1860. 2 v. 12°. . . . 8950
and Intellectual Philosophy. Barlow. Philad., 1847. 12°. . 8496
Principles of. Combe. N. Y., 1840. 12°. 9125
Wonders of. Le Pileur. N. Y., 1870. 12°. 10131
Piatt, J. J. Western Windows and other Poems. N. Y., 1869. 16°. 785
Picciola. Boniface. N. Y., 1861. 12°. 2596
Picken, A. The Black Watch. Philad., 1835. 2 v. 12°. . . . 15384
Pickering, E. The Fright. Philad., 1840. 2 v. 12°. 15434
The Grandfather. N. Y., 1845. 8°. 2656
The Secret Foe. Philad., 1845. 8°. 2670
The same. Lond., 1841. 3 v. 12°. 15577
The Squire. Philad., 1838. 2 v. 12°. 15586
Picket, A. & J. W. The Academician. N. Y., 1820. v. 1. 8°. . 14079
Pickwick Papers. Dickens. N. Y., 1872. 16°. 2168
Pic Nic Papers. Ed. by Dickens. Philad., 1841. 2 v. 12°. . . 2166
Picturesque, Essays on the. Price. Lond., 1810. 3 v. 8°. . . 17072
Piemont, Excursion to. Gilly. Lond., 1824. 4°. 16035
Pierce, E. M. Cottage Cyclopedia of Hist. and Biogr. Hartf'd., 1867. 8°. . . . .
Pierce, G. A., and **Wheeler, W. A.** Dickens Dictionary. Bost., 1872. 12°. 2212
Pierce, W. L. The Year. N. Y., 1813. 12°. 14948
Pierpont, J. Airs of Palestine. 2d ed. Bost., 1817. 12°. . . 815
and other Poems. (2 copies.) Bost., 1840. 16°. 816
Pierson, H. W. Jefferson at Monticello. N. Y., 1862. 8°. . . 7443
Pignotti, L. Hist. of Tuscany and the Medici. Lond., 1826. 4 v. 8°. 4680
Pigott, G. Scandinavian Mythology. (2 copies.) Lond., 1839. 8°. . 1919
Pike, A. Prose Sketches and Poems. Bost., 1834. 12°. . . . 15324
[Pike, M. H.] Ida May. Bost., 1855. 12°. 15723
Pike, Z. M., Life of. Whiting. Bost., 1845. 16°. 7264
Pilgrim Good-Intent, Progress of the. N. Y., 1802. 12°. . . . 17307
Pilgrim and the Shrine, The. Ainslie. Lond., 1871. 8°. . . . 9814

Pilgrim's Progress. Bunyan. Hartf'd., 1833. 12°. 9813
Pilgrims, Chronicles of the. Young. Bost., 1844. 8°. 5935
[Mourt's] Journal of the. Ed. Cheever. N. Y., 1849. 12°. . 6007
of the Rhine. Bulwer. Philad., 1868. 12°. 2063
of Walsingham, The. Strickland. Philad., 1835. 2 v. 12°. . 2416
Pilkington, J. C., Real Story of. By himself. Lond., 1760. 4°. . 16469
Pillet, R. M. Views of England. Bost., 1818. 12°. 16768
Pilot, The. Cooper. N. Y., 1856. 12°. 2801
Pindar. Odes, transl. by Wheelwright. N. Y., 1837. 12°. . . 4540
Pindar, Peter, Works of. [Wolcott.] Philad., 1835. 8°. . . . 1239
Pines, Among the. [Gilmore.] N. Y., 1862. 12°. 2929
Pink and White Tyranny. Mrs. Stowe. Bost., 1871. 16°. . . 2735
Pinkerton, R. Russia. Lond., 1833. 8°. 8444
Pinkney, W., Life of. Wheaton. (Sparks, v. 6.) Bost., 1836. 16°. . 7255
Life and Writings of. Wheaton. N. Y., 1826. 8°. . . . 9327
Pioneers, The. Cooper. N. Y., 1870. 12°. 2792
Piozzi, H. L. (Thrale). Autobiography, Letters, etc. Bost., 1861. 12°. 7075
Love Letters, to W. A. Conway. Lond., 1843. 8°. . . . 7074
Recollections of. Lond., 1833. 8°. 7073
[**Pipitz, F. E.**] Mirabeau. Philad., 1848. 12°. 7622
Pips, Mr., hys Diary. Leigh. Lond. 2 v. 4°. . . . . . .
Pirate, The. Marryat. Philad., 1836. 12°. 2112
Scott. Edinb., 1871. 8°. 1887
Pirates, Hist. of the. Johnson. Norwich, 1814. 12°. . . . 16323
See, also, BUCCANEERS.
Pitcairn's Island, Description of. [Barrow.] N. Y., 1840. 12°. . 11033
Pitkin, T. Hist. of U. S., 1763–97. (3 copies.) N. H., 1828. 2 v. 8°. 6150
Statistics of Commerce, etc., of U. S. N. H., 1835. 8°. . . 5854
Pitt, C. Poetical Works. Ed. Bell. Lond., 1807. 24°. . . . 530
Select Poems. Ed. Walsh. Philad., 1819. 24°. . . . 15
Pitt, Wm., *(Earl of Chatham.)* Correspondence, 1741–78. Lond., 1838–40. 4 v. 8°. 7201
Letters to his Nephew. N. Y., 1804. 12°. 9136
Anecdotes of Life of. [Almon.] Lond., 1792. 4 v. 8°. . 6795
Pitt, *Rt. Hon.* **Wm.** Speeches in House of Commons. Lond., 1806. 4 v. 8°. 9369
Lectures on. Goldwin Smith. N. Y., 1867. 12°. . . . 6749
Life of. Philad., 1806. 12°. 6627
The same. Stanhope. Lond., 1861–62. 4 v. 8°. . . 6799
Memoirs of. Tomline. Philad., 1821. 2 v. 8°. . . . 16344
Pizarro, F., Life of. Bost., 1840. 12°. 7511
The same. Helps. Lond., 1869. 16°. 7691
Pizarro, a tragedy. Sheridan. Lond., 1854. 12°. 450
Plague in London, Hist. of the. De Foe. Lond., 1855. 8°. . . 4227
Plain Speaker, The. Hazlitt. Lond., 1826. 2 v. 8°. . . . 3457
Planché, J. R. British Costume. (2 copies.) Lond., 1836–46. 12°. 4814
Planchette, the Despair of Science. [Sargent.] Bost., 1869. 16°. . 8484
Planetary and Stellar Worlds. Mitchel. N. Y., 1863. 12°. . . 8912
Plantagenets, Last of the. N. Y., 1829. 2 v. 12°. 15485

Plants, Hist. of. Figuier. Lond., 1869. 8°. 9000

Plato and the Companions of Sokrates. Grote. Lond., 1867. 3 v. 8°. 4443

Life of. Tennemann. (German Selections.) Andover, 1839. 8°. 10061

Platt, J. C. Hist. of the Corn-Laws. Lond., 1842. 12°. 8479

Platts, J. Universal Biography. Lond., 1825–26. 5 v. 8°. . . . 6892

Plautus. Menæchmi, transl. by C. R. Lennox. Philad., 1809. 8°. . 1591

Plays. Ed. Oxberry. Bost., 1822–24. v. 1, 2, 4–12. 24°. . . . 1346

CONTENTS.—1, Distrest Mother, by A. Philips; She Stoops to Conquer, by Goldsmith; New Way to pay Old Debts, by Massinger; Woodman's Hut. 2, Hypocrite, Maid of the Mill, Lionel and Clarissa, Love in a Village; all by Bickerstaff. 4, Soldier's Daughter, by Cherry; Provoked Husband, by Vanbrugh and Cibber; Belle's Stratagem, by Cowley; Suspicious Husband, by Hoadly. 5, Beaux' Stratagem, Recruiting Officer, Inconstant, by Farquhar; Tobacconist, from Jonson, by Gentleman; Rosina, by Brookes. 6, West Indian, She Would and She Would Not, Wheel of Fortune, by Cumberland; Honest Thieves, by Knight. 7, Alex. the Great, by N. Lee; Wild Oats, by O'Keeffe; The Wonder, by Centlivre; Shipwreck, by Arnold. 8, Jane Shore, by Rowe; Magpie; Evadne, Damon and Pythias, by Shiel; Is he Jealous, by Beazley. 9, Guy Mannering, by Terry; Rob Roy Macgregor, by Pocock; Deserter, Quaker, by C. Dibdin; Mayor of Garratt, by Foote. 10, Grecian Daughter, Way to Keep him, Know your own Mind, Three Weeks after Marriage, Citizen, all by Murphy. 11, Jealous Wife, by Colman. Busy Body, by Centlivre; Barber of Seville, from Rossini; Rugantino, by M. G. Lewis. 12, Duenna, and Rivals, by Sheridan; Beggar's Opera, by Gay; Midnight Hour, by Inchbald.

Living. N. Y., 1824–25. 8 v. 16°. 13346

Old, Dodsley's Select Collection of. [Ed. Collier.] Lond., 1825–27. 12 v. 8°. 1508

CONTENTS.—1, God's Promises, by Bale; The Four P's, by Heywood; Ferrex and Porrex, by Sackville; Damon and Pithias, by Edwards; New Custome. 2, Gammer Gurton's Needle; Alexander and Campaspe, by Lyly; Tancred and Gismunda, by Wilmot; Cornelia, by Kyd; Edward II., by Marlowe. 3, George a Greene; Jeronimo, pt. 1; Spanish Tragedy, by Kyd; Honest Whore, by Dekker. 4, Malcontent, by Marston; All Fools, by Chapman; Eastward Hoe, by Jonson, Marston, and Chapman; Revenger's Tragedy, by Tourneur; Dumb Knight, by Machin. 5, Miseries of Inforced Marriage, by Wilkins; Lingua, by Brewer; Merry Devil of Edmondton; A Mad World, my Masters, by Middleton; Ram-Alley, by Barry. 6, Roaring Girl, by Middleton and Dekker; Widow's Tears, by Chapman; White Devil, by Webster; The Hog hath lost his Pearl, by Tailor; Four Prentices of London, by Heywood. 7, Green's Tuquoque, by Cook; Albumazar, by Tomkins; Women kill'd with Kindness, by Heywood; Match at Midnight, by Rowley; Fuimus Troes, by Fisher. 8, Wounds of Civil War, by Lodge; The Heir, by May; Friar Bacon and Friar Bungay, by Greene; Jew of Malta, by Marlowe; The Wits, by Davenant. 9, Summer's Last Will, by Nash; Microcosmus, by Nabbes; Muse's Looking-Glass, by Randolph; City Match, by Mayne; Queen of Arragon, by Habington. 10, Antiquary, by Marmion; Goblins, by Suckling; The Ordinary, by Cartwright; Jovial Crew, by Broome; Old Couple, by May. 11, Edward I., by Peele; Mayor of Quinborough, by Middleton; Grim, the Collier of Croydon; City Night-Cap, by Davenport; Parson's Wedding, by Killegrew. 12, Adventures of Five Hours, by Tuke; Elvira, by Digby; The Widow, by Jonson, etc.; Apius and Virginia; Notes; Index.

Old English, Dict. of. Halliwell. Lond., 1860. 8°. . . . 1635

See, also, DRAMA; STAGE; THEATER.

Pleasures, Book of. Campbell, Rogers, Akenside. Philad., 1836. 12°. 14902

Plebeian, The. Steele. (Addison's Works, v. 3.) N. Y., 1856. 12°. 3997

Plowden, F. Review of State of Ireland. Philad., 1805–06. 5 v. 8°. 5414

Plumptre, E. H. Biblical Studies. Lond., 1870. 8°. 9889

Plutarch. Lives, ed. by Clough. Bost., 1872. 5 v. 8°. 4127

transl. by Langhorne. Ithaca, 1838. 8°. . . . 4126

The same. Philad. and N. Y., 1822–34. 8 v. 12°. . 13998

Select Lives, tr. by Long. Lond., 1844–46. 3 v. 12°. . . 4594

Plutarch, The British. Lond., 1791. 8 v. 12°. 14006

Plymley, Peter. Letters on the Catholics. See Sydney SMITH'S Works, v. 3.

Plymouth. See PILGRIMS.

Pneumatics, Treatise on. Lardner. Lond., 1836. 16°. 6044

Pocahontas: a Drama. N. Y., 1837. 12°. 15043

Pocket Magazine. Lond., 1829–30. 3 v. 12°. 15821

Poco Mas. *(Pseudonym.)* Scenes and Adventures in Spain., Philad., 1846. 12°. 8190

Pocock, J. Rob Roy Macgregor. Bost., 1823. 12°. 13355

Pococke, R. Travels through Egypt. (Mavor, v. 13.) Lond., 1797. 12°. 13856
Poe, E. A. The Literati. (2 copies.) N. Y., 1850. 12°. 4381
Narrative of A. Gordon Pym. N. Y., 1838. 12°. 15763
Tales of the Grotesque and Arabesque. Philad., 1840. v. 1. 12°. 4383
Works. N. Y., 1856–58. 4 v. 12°. 4372
CONTENTS.—1, Tales. 2, Poems and Tales. 3, The Literati. 4, A. Gordon Pym; Miscellanies.
The same. vol. 1. (2 copies.) 4376
The same. vol. 3. 4378
The same. N. Y., 1850–52. 2 v. 12°. 4379
CONTENTS.—1, Tales. 2, Poems; Miscellanies.
Poems, Collection of. Dodsley. Lond., 1770. v. 2–6. 12°. . . 14019
Select Collection of. Edinb., 1768. v. 1. 14018
Poetic Mirror. Philad., 1817. 12°. 14903
Poetical Decameron, English. Collier. Lond., 1820. 2 v. 16°. . 128
Poetry, American, Selection of. N. Y., 1794. 12°. 14966
Specimens of. Kettell. Bost., 1829. 3 v. 12°. . 678
of the East. Alger. Bost., 1856. 12°. 875
English, Anthology of. [Ritson.] Lond., 1793–94. 3 v. 16°. 1086
Beauties of. Albany, 1814. 12°. 14910
Elegant Extracts in. Lond., 1816. 2 v. 8°. . . 15838
[Another collection.] Bost., 1826. 6 v. 12°. . . 13364
Essay on. T. Campbell. Bost., 1819. 12°. . . 55
Hist. of. Warton. Lond., 1840. 3 v. 8°. . . 183
Lectures on. Neele. Lond., 1829. 12°. . . . 165
Letters on. Aikin. Bost., 1806. 12°. . . . 60
Reliques of. Percy. Lond., 1840. 8°. . . . 1312
Sacred, of XVII. century. Ed. Cattermole. Lond., 1835. v. 1. 16°. 9503
The same. Lond., 1836. v. 2. 16°. 9508
Essay on. Beattie. Lond., 1779. 8°. 214
of France, Early. Costello. Lond., 1835. 8°. 917
German, Historic Survey of. W. Taylor. Lond., 1830. 3 v. 8°. 206
Translations from. Baskerville. Philad., 1856. 8°. . 857
Hebrew, Spirit of. Taylor. N. Y., 1862. 12°. 9544
Household Book of. Dana. N. Y., 1867. 8°. . . . 1311
Lectures on. Montgomery. N. Y., 1840. 12°. . . . 11284
on the sources of Pleasure from. Hurdis. Bishopstone, 1797. 4°. 15083
of Life, The. Mrs. Ellis. Philad., 1835. 2 v. 12°. . . . 15242
Provençal, History of. Fauriel. N. Y., 1860. 8°. . . . 241
Scottish, Selection of. Ritson. Lond., 1785. 16°. . . . 1096
of Spain, Ancient. Bowring. Lond., 1824. 8°. . . . 915
Studies in. Cheever. Bost., 1830. 12°. 293
Tragic, as illustrated by Shakspeare. Reed. Philad., 1857. 16°. 1479
Treatise on; from Encycl. Brit. [Moir.] Edinb., 1839. 12°. . 164
See, also, BALLADS; LITERATURE; RHYTHMS; SONGS; SONNETS.
Poet at the Breakfast-Table. Holmes. Bost., 1872. 12°. . . . 3609
Poets of America. Keese. N. Y., 1841–42. 2 v. 12°. . . . 684
and Poetry of. Griswold. Philad., 1855. 8°. . 923

Polar Regions explored. Snelling. Bost., 1831. 8°. . . . 16591
Sea, Journeys to, 1819–27. Franklin. Lond., 1829. 4 v. 12°. 7868
The Open; a Voyage of Discovery, 1860–61. Hayes. N. Y., 1867. 8°. 8111
Voyage, Journal of Parry's, 1821–22. Lyon. Bost., 1824. 12°. 16592
Voyages, Northern, Hist. of. Forster. Dubl., 1786. 8°. . . 16594
Three, 1819–27. Parry. Lond., 1835. 4 v. 12°. . 7872
World, The. Hartwig. N. Y., 1869. 8°. 8102
Pole, Possibility of approaching the. Barrington. N. Y., 1818. 8°. 16593
See, also, ARCTIC.
Police Reports, N. Y. City. Skillman. N. Y., 1830. 8°. . . . 15835
Polish Tales. Mrs. Gore. Lond., 1833. 3 v. 12°. 15550
Politeness, Book of. Celnart. Bost., 1833. 12°. 17051
Political Class Book, The. Sullivan. Bost., 1831. 12°. . . . 6015
Economy. Chalmers. N. Y., 1832. 12°. 8543
A. Potter. N. Y. [1841.] 12°. 11925
American. Bowen. N. Y., 1870. 8°. . . . 8640
Dissertation on. Rousseau. Lond., 1767. 12°. . 13189
Elements of. James Mill. Lond., 1844. 8°. . 8625
The same. Newman. Andover, 1835. 12°. . . . 17096
The same. Perry. N. Y., 1866. 8°. 8639
The same. Wayland. N. Y., 1837. 8°. . . . 8667
Essays on. Ruskin. N. Y., 1872. 12°. . . 8631
Illustrations of. H. Martineau. Bost. and Lond., 1832–33. 13 v. 12°. 14608
For Contents, see MARTINEAU.
Logic of. De Quincey. Edinb., 1844. 8°. . . 8624
Manual of. Bentham. (Works, pt. 9.) Edinb., 1839. 8°. 9708
The same. Fawcett. 3d ed. Cambr., 1869. 12°. . 10206
New Principles of. Rae. Bost., 1834. 8°. . . 8754
Principles of. Malthus. Bost., 1821. 8°. . . 8634
The same. John Stuart Mill. N. Y., 1870. 2 v. 8°. . 8663
Treatise on. Say. Philad., 1836. 8°. . . . 8652
See, also, WEALTH.
Essays. P. Godwin. N. Y., 1856. 12°. 3560
Ethics, Manual of. Lieber. Bost., 1838–39. 2 v. 8°. . . 8683
Hermeneutics. Lieber. Bost., 1839. 12°. 8621
Knowledge, Standard Library Cyclopædia of. [Long.] Lond., 1848–49. 4 v. 8°. 350
Mirror; or, Review of Jacksonism. N. Y., 1835. 12°. . . 6016
Philosophy. Brougham. Lond., 1844. 3 v. 8°. . . . 8680
Tactics. Bentham. (Works, pt. 8.) Edinb., 1839. 8°. . . 9707
Politics, American, Issues of. Skinner. Philad., 1872. 12°. . . 10205
Physics and. Bagehot. N. Y., 1873. 12°. 10183
See, also, GOVERNMENT.
Polk, J. K. Messages, etc. (Statesman's Manual, v. 3.) N. Y., 1854. 8°. 6202
Hist. of the Administration of. Chase. N. Y., 1850. 8°. . 6272
and Hist. of his Administration. Jenkins. Auburn. [1850.] 12°. 7331

Polko, E. Musical Sketches. N. Y., 1866. 16°. 8867
Pollok, R. Course of Time. Bost., 1828, 12°. 14854
The same. Philad., 1839. 8°. 1247
Life of. D. Pollok. Edinb., 1843. 8°. 6937
Polo, M. Travels, ed. Murray. N. Y., 1845. 12°. 11774
The same. 12286
Polwhele, R. Essay on Marriage, Adultery, Divorce, etc. Lond., 1823. 12°. 17006
The Old English Gentleman. Lond., 1797. 8°. . . . 14804
Traditions and Recollections. Lond., 1826. 2 v. 8°. . . 7141
Polynesia, Hist. of. Russell. N. Y., 1845. 12°. 11760
Pomfret, J. Poems and Remains. Philad., 1791. 12°. . . . 14842
Select Poems. With Life, by Sanford. Philad., 1819. 24°. . 7
The same, ed. Johnson. Dubl., 1804. 8°. . . . 15096
Pompeii. (2 copies.) Bost., 1833. 12°. 8214
The same. 8817
Last Days of. Bulwer. Lond., 1854. 12°. 2064
Wonders of. Monnier. N. Y., 1870. 12°. 10127
Ponsonby, C. The Countess d'Auvergne. Edinb., 1841. 16°. . 15405
Ponte, L. da. Hist. of the Florentine Republic, etc. (2 copies.) N. Y., 1833. 2 v. 12°. 4587
Pontiac, Hist. of Conspiracy of. Parkman. Bost., 1851. 8°. . . 5956
Poole, M. E. Pictures of Cottage Life. Lond., 1870. 8°. . . 15547
Poole, S. Englishwoman in Egypt. Lond., 1844–46. 3 v. 12°. . 8151
Poole, W. F. Index to Periodical Literature. (2 copies.) N. Y., 1853. 8°. . . . .
Index to Subjects in Reviews in Bros. Library. N. Y., 1848. 8°.
Poor Laws and Pauper Management. Bentham. (Works, pt. 16.) Edinb., 1841. 8°. 9715
Poor Miss Finch. Collins. N. Y., 1872. 8°. 2306
Pope, A. Essay on Man. Lond., 1786. 12°. 14855
The same. Lond., 1806. 12°. 14856
The same. Hartf'd., 1844. 12°. 603
Poetical Works. Ed. Bell. Lond., 1807. v. 2, 3, 4, 6. 24°. . 278
Ed. Carruthers. Lond., 1853. v. 1–3. 16°. 1105
Ed. Walsh. Philad., 1819. 24°. 15
with Life by Johnson. Philad., 1839. 8°. . 1284
The same. Dubl., 1804. 8°. 15100
Works. Ed. Elwin. Lond., 1871–72. v. 1, 2, 6–8. 8°. . . 1285
The same. With Life by Johnson. Lond., 1812. v. 1, 3–8. 12°. 3821

CONTENTS.—1, Life; Panegyrical Poems; Pastorals; Messiah; Windsor Forest; Odes; Essay on Criticism. 3, Essay on Man; Universal Prayer; Moral Essays; Satires and Epistles. 4, The Dunciad; Guardians. 5, Memoirs of M. Scriblerus; Memoirs of P. P., Clerk of this Parish. Key to the Lock. Miscellaneous Thoughts, etc. 6–8, Letters to and from Friends.

Essay on Genius of. Warton. Lond., 1806. 2 v. 8°. . . . 3483
Life and Last Will of. Lond., 1744. 16°. 6946
Pope, *Sir* **T.,** Life of. Warton. Lond., 1772. 8°. 16367
Pope Leo X., Life of. Roscoe. Lond., 1846. 2 v. 8°. 396
Pope and the Council, The. Janus. Bost., 1870. 16°. . . . 9514

Popery. Rogers. Lond., 1839. 12°. 9602
Dissuasive from. Jer. Taylor. (Works, v. 2.) Lond., 1836. 8°. 10063
Hist. of. (2 copies.) N. Y., 1834. 12°. 9603
Text-Book of. Cramp. N. Y., 1831. 12°. 9610
Variations of. Edgar. Lond., 1838. 8°. 6491
Popes, Growth of Temporal Power of the. Legge. Lond., 1870. 8°. 6326
Hist. of the, and of Latin Christianity, to 1454. Milman. N. Y., 1860–61. 8 v. 8°. 6391
Hist. of the, 1500–1700. Ranke. Lond., 1847–48. 3 v. 8°. . 391
last four, Recollections of the. Wiseman. Lond. [1859.] 8°. . 7677
Origin of the. Guettée. N. Y., 1867. 12°. 9579
Population, Essay on the Principle of. Malthus. Lond., 1826. 2 v. 8°. 8659
Porcelain. See GLASS.
Porcupine, Peter. *(Pseudonym.)* See W. COBBETT.
Porsoniana. Lond., 1856. 8°. 3208
Port Royal, Memoirs of. Schimmel-Penninck. Lond., 1858. 3 v. 8°. 6328
Porter, A. M. Coming Out. N. Y., 1828. 2 v. 12°. 15179
Fast of St. Magdalen. Bost., 1819. 2 v. 12°. 15194
Honor O'Hara. N. Y., 1827. 2 v. 12°. 15196
Recluse of Norway. Wash., 1834. 12°. 15186
Village of Mariendorpt. Bost., 1821. 4 v. in 2. 12°. . . 15184
Porter, D. Journal of Cruise to the Pacific. N. Y., 1822. 2 v. 8°. 17123
Voyage in the South Seas. Lond., 1823. 8°. 8058
Porter, E. Lectures on Eloquence and Style. Andover, 1836. 8°. . 17521
Principles of Rhetorical Delivery. Andover, 1827. 12°. . . 17366
Porter, G. R. Treatise on Manufacture of Porcelain and Glass. Lond., 1832. 16°. 6040
Treatise on Silk Manufacture. Lond., 1831. 16°. 5790
Porter, Jane. Duke Christian of Luneburg. Bost., 1824. 2 v. 12°. 15182
Field of the Forty Footsteps. N. Y., 1828. 12°. 15181
Scottish Chiefs. (2 copies.) Philad., 1867–69. 12°. . . . 15190
Sir Edward Seaward's Narrative of his Shipwreck. N. Y., 1831. 3 v. 12°. 15187
Thaddeus of Warsaw. N. Y., 1858. 12°. 15178
The same. Philad., 1868. 12°. 15177
Porter, John L. The Giant Cities of Bashan. N. Y., 1866. 12°. . 8256
Porter, N. American Colleges and the American Public. (2 copies.) N. Y., 1870. 12°. 9254
Books and Reading. (2 copies.) N. Y., 1871. 12°. . . . 122
Addresses at Inauguration of. N. Y., 1871. 8°. 9281
Porter, Robert K. Travels in Russia and Sweden. Philad., 1809. 8°. 16603
Porter, Rose. Summer Drift-wood. N. Y., 1870. 12°. . . . 15787
Porter, W. S. The Musical Cyclopedia. Bost., 1834. 12°. . . 8862
Porteus, B. Death, a poem. Lond., 1803. 8°. 14806
Port Folio, The. 2d and 3d Series. Philad., 1809–14. 6 v. 8°. . 12736
Portico, The. Balt., 1816–17. v. 2–4, in 1. 8°. 12578
Porto, L. da. Juliet. (Ital. Novelists, v. 2.) Lond., 1836. 12°. . 1900
Portraits, British. Lodge. Lond., 1849–50. 8 v. 8°. . . . 515
Portugal, Civil War in, etc. [1820–33.] Lond., 1836. 12°. . . 6415

Portugal, Hist. of, 1090–1725. Brockwell. Lond., 1726. 8°. . . 16165
of Revolutions in, to 1683. Vertot. Lond., 1754. 8°. 16166
Traits and Traditions of. Pardoe. Philad., 1834. 2 v. 12°. . 16671
See, also, PENINSULAR WAR ; SPAIN.
Posey, T., Memoir of. Hall. Bost., 1846. 16°. 7268
Positive Philosophy of Comte. Mill. Bost., 1871. 12°. . . . 8590
Positivism and Christianity. Hopkins. N. Y., 1871. 12°. . . 9999
Post, H. A. V. Visit to Greece, etc. N. Y., 1830. 8°. . . . 16627
Posthumous Records of a London Clergyman. N. Y., 1836. 12°. . 17286
Post-Office, The. Lond., 1842. 12°. 8478
Potiphar Papers. Curtis. N. Y., 1869. 12°. 2872
Potomac, Campaigns of Army of the. Swinton. N. Y., 1866. 8°. . 6196
Potter, A. Handbook for Readers. N. Y., 1845. 12°. . . . 11766
Polit. Economy. N. Y. [1841.] 12°. 11925
Science applied to the Arts. Bost., 1841. 12°. 17002
Potter, J. Antiquities of Greece. N. Y., 1825. 8°. 15867
Pouqueville, F. C. H. L. Travels in Greece. (Voyages, v. 4, 7.) Lond., 1820. 8°. 8054
Powell, B. Hist. of Physical and Mathematical Sciences. Lond., 1837. 16°. 6049
Power, T. Impressions of America. Philad., 1836. 2 v. 12°. . 16796
Poynder, J. Hist. of the Jesuits. Lond., 1816. 2 v. 8°. . . . 6423
Literary Extracts. Lond. [1844.] 2 v. 8°. 4339
Pradt, D. D. de. The Congress of Vienna. Philad., 1816. 8°. . 15920
Europe and America in 1821. Lond., 1822. 2 v. 8°. . . 15884
after the Congress of Aix-la-Chapelle. Philad., 1820. 8°. 15921
Praed, W. M. Poems. With Memoir by D. Coleridge. N. Y., 1865. 2 v. 12°. 841
Poet. Works. Ed. Griswold. (2 copies.) N. Y., 1844. 12°. . 839
Pragay, J. The Hungarian Revolution. N. Y., 1850. 12°. . . 5816
Prairie, The. Cooper. Philad., 1836. 2 v. 12°. 2759
Prairie Land, Life in. Farnham. N. Y., 1847. 16°. 16865
Prairies, Commerce of the. Gregg. N. Y., 1844. 2 v. 12°. . . 16878
Tour on the. W. Irving. Philad., 1835. 12°. 4243
Prayer, Method of. Mme. Guyon. Balt., 1812. 12°. 17294
Prayers of the Ages. Ed. Whitmarsh. Bost., 1868. 8°. . . . 9818
for Theists. Cobbe. Lond., 1871. 8°. 9967
Preacher and the King, The. Bungener. Bost., 1853. 12°. . . 9968
and Pastor, The. Ed. by Prof. Park. Andover, 1845. 12°. . 9913
Preaching, Aids to. Skinner. N. Y., 1839. 12°. 9918
Extemporary. Zincke. N. Y., 1867. 12°. 9915
Yale Lectures on. Beecher. N. Y., 1872. 12°. . . . 9919
See, also, PULPIT.
Preble, E., Life of. Cooper. (Naval Biogr., v. 1.) Philad., 1846. 12°. 7275
The same. Sabine. (Sparks, v. 22.) Bost., 1847. 16°. . 7271
Precaution. Cooper. N. Y., 1855. 12°. 2799
Preferment. Mrs. Gore. N. Y., 1840. 2 v. 12°. 15553
Prentice, G. D. Biogr. of Clay. Hartf'd., 1831. 12°. . . . 7327
[**Prentiss, C.**] Life of Gen. Eaton. Brookfield, 1813. 8°. . . . 16396

Prentiss, E. Stepping Heavenward. (2 copies.) N. Y. [1869.] 12°. 3009
Prentiss, S. S., Memoir of. By his Brother. N. Y., 1861. 2 v. 12°. 7337
Pre-Raphaelitism. Ruskin. N. Y., 1860. 12°. 9040
Presbyterian Pulpit, Annals of American. Sprague. N. Y., 1859. 2 v. 8°. 7732
Prescott, H. E. See Mrs. H. (E.) P. SPOFFORD.
Prescott, W. H. Biographical and Critical Miscellanies. N. Y., 1845. 8°. 3477
The same. New ed. Bost., 1855. 8°. 3478
Hist. of Chas. V. See W. ROBERTSON.
Conquest of Mexico. (2 copies.) N. Y., 1844. 3 v. 8°. 5981
The same. Philad., 1871. 3 v. 8°. 10327
Hist. of Conquest of Peru. Philad. and N. Y., 1848–68. 2 v. 8°. 5987
The same. v. 2. N. Y., 1848. 8°. 5989
The same. Philad., 1871. 2 v. 8°. 10330
of Ferdinand and Isabella. 2d ed. Bost., 1838. 3 v. 8°. 6572
The same. Philad., 1871. 3 v. 8°. 10332
The same. 5th ed. Bost., 1839. v. 2, 3. 8°. . . . 6575
of Philip II. Bost., 1855–58. 3 v. 8°. 6579
The same. v. 1, 2. 6582
The same. Philad., 1871. 3 v. 8°. 10338
Life of C. B. Brown. Bost., 1834. 16°. 7250
Life of. Ticknor. Bost., 1864. 12°. 7388
Review of part of Hist. of Ferdinand and Isabella by. Bost., 1841. 12°. 16164
President's Daughters, The. Bremer. Lond., 1852. 8°. 469
Press, Liberty of the. See LIBERTY.
Pressensé, E. de. Early Years of Christianity; Apostolic Era. N. Y., 1870. 12°. 6307
Preston, H. W. Aspendale. Bost., 1871. 16°. 2744
Pretension. Ellis. Philad., 1837. 2 v. 12°. 15555
Price, U. Essays on the Picturesque. Lond., 1810. 3 v. 8°. . . 17072
Pride and Prejudice. Austen. Bost., 1863. 12°. 2479
Priest and Huguenot. Bungener. Bost., 1856. 2 v. 12°. . . 2647
Priestcraft, Popular Hist. of. Howitt. Lond., 1845. 16°. . . 6331
Priestley, J. Lectures on Hist. and Policy. Philad., 1803. 2 v. 8°. 15887
Priests, Women, and Families. Michelet. Lond., 1846. 16°. . . 9513
Prime, W. C. Boat Life in Egypt and Nubia. N. Y., 1857. 12°. . 8233
O Mother Dear Jerusalem. N. Y., 1865. 12°. 292
Princes of Wales, Lives of. Williams. Lond., 1843. v. 1. 12°. . 5133
Pringle, T. Residence in S. Africa. Lond., 1840. 8°. . . . 8101
Prior, J. Life of Goldsmith. Philad., 1837. 8°. 7171
The same. Lond., 1837. 2 v. 8°. 3776
The same. 7172
Memoir of Burke. Philad., 1825. 8°. 6810
The same. Lond., 1839. 8°. 6809
Voyage along E. Coast of Africa, etc. Lond., 1819. 8°. . . 8052
in the Indian Seas. Lond., 1820. 8°. 8051
Prior, M. Poetical Works. Ed. Bell. Lond., 1807. 2 v. 24°. . 268

Prior, M. Select Poems. With Life, by Sanford. Philad., 1819. 24°. 11
The same. Ed. Johnson. Dubl., 1804. 8°. . . . 15098
Prison, Voices from; a Selection of Poetry. Bost. [1847.] 12°. . 14904
Prisons and Prisoners. Adshead. Lond., 1845. 8°. 17097
Probabilities, Essay on. De Morgan. Lond., 1838. 16°. . . . 6043
Probability. [Lubbock and Bethune.] Lond., 1835. 8°. . . . 16468
Problematic Characters. Spielhagen. N. Y., 1870. 12°. . . . 3020
Probus. Ware. N. Y., 1838. 2 v. 12°. 2866
[**Procter, B. W.**] *(Barry Cornwall.)* Dramatic Scenes, with other Poems. Bost., 1857. 16°. 1201
English Songs, etc. Bost., 1844. 16°. 1200
Life of Kean. N. Y., 1835. 12°. 7927
C. Lamb: a Memoir. (2 copies.) Bost., 1866. 16°. . . 6959
Songs and Miscellaneous Poems. N. Y. 8°. 15092
Procter, G. Hist. of the Crusades. Edinb., 1854. 8°. . . . 4621
of Italy. 2d ed. Lond., 1844. 8°. . . . 4812
Proctor, E. D. Poems. N. Y., 1866. 16°. 778
Proctor, R. A. Light Science for Leisure Hours. N. Y., 1871. 12°. 8897
The Sun. Lond., 1871. 8°. 8909
Profession is not Principle. [Kennedy.] N. Y., 1829. 12°. . . 15410
Professor, The. A Tale. C. Brontë. N. Y., 1868. 12°. . . . 2556
at the Breakfast-Table. Holmes. Bost., 1868. 12°. . . 3607
Promessi Sposi, I. Manzoni. Wash., 1834. 8°. 2650
Property, Essays on. Lieber. N. Y., 1841. 12°. 11748
Prophecy, Hints on Interpretation of. Stuart. Andover, 1842. 12°. 17266
Prose, by a Poet. [Montgomery.] Philad., 1824. 12°. . . . 3172
Protection protect, Does. Grosvenor. N. Y., 1871. 8°. . . . 8669
Protestant, The; a Tale. [Bray.] N. Y., 1829. 2 v. 12°. . . 15557
and Catholic Nations compared. Roussel. Bost., 1855. 12°. 6433
Memorial. Horne. N. Y., 1844. 12°. 17279
Protestantism and Catholicity compared in Effects on Civilization. Balmes. Balt., 1851. 8°. 6492
Proud, R. Hist. of Penns. Philad., 1797–98. 2 v. 8°. . . . 5841
Prout, W. Chemistry, Meteorology, and Digestion. Philad., 1836. 8°. 16982
Provençal Poetry, Hist. of. Fauriel. Transl. by Adler. N. Y., 1860. 8°. 241
Proverbs, English. Hazlitt. Lond., 1869. 8°. 4439
Lessons in. Trench. N. Y., 1855. 12°. 4316
National, in 5 Languages. Ward. Lond., 1842. 16°. . . 4318
Shakspeare. Clarke. Lond., 1848. 16°. 1366
See, also, QUOTATIONS.
Provincial Letters. Pascal. N. Y., 1861. 12°. . . . , . . 9584
Provost, The. Galt. N. Y., 1822. 12°. 15232
Prue and I. Curtis. N. Y., 1857. 12°. 2870
Prussia, Hist. of, 1740–78. Frederic II. Lond., 1789. 4 v. 8°. . 17244
Secret Hist. of Court of. Mirabeau. Dubl., 1789. 8°. . . 16460
See, also, FREDERIC II. and III.; GERMANY.
Psalms, Commentary on the. Horne. Lond., 1836. 3 v. 16°. . 9510
translated and explained by J. A. Alexander. N. Y., 1851. 3 v. 12°. 9875

Psychology, Elements of. Cousin. Hartf'd., 1834. 8°. . . . 8588
Principles of. H. Spencer. N. Y., 1871. v. 1. 12°. . . 8601
See, also, PHILOSOPHY.
Public and Private Economy. Sedgwick. N. Y., 1836–39. 3 v. 12°. 8644
Puckle, J. The Club. Ed. Singer. Chiswick, 1834. 16°. . . 4158
Pückler-Muskau, H. v. Tutti Frutti, transl. by Spencer. N. Y., 1834. 12°. 3790
Pütter, J. S. Hist. of Constitution of the Germanic Empire. Lond., 1790. 3 v. 8°. 16457
Puffendorf, S. Introd. to Hist. of Europe. Lond., 1764. 2 v. 8°. . 15912
Puigblanch, A. The Inquisition Unmasked. Lond., 1816. 2 v. 8°. 6426
Pulaski, C., Life of. Sparks. Bost., 1845. 16°. 7263
Pulci, L. Stories. (Hunt's Italian Poets.) N. Y., 1846. 12°. . . 887
Pulpit, Curiosities of the. Jackson. N. Y. [1868.] 16°. . . . 9831
Eloquence of XIX. century. Fish. N. Y., 1857. 8°. . . 10057
The Metropolitan. [Grant.] N. Y., 1839. 12°. . . . 9914
Power of the. Spring. N. Y., 1854. 12°. 17173
Pungencies. N. Y., 1866. 12°. 9973
See, also, PREACHING.
Pumpelly, R. Across America and Asia. N. Y., 1870. 8°. . . 8081
Punch, Cartoons from. Tenniel. Lond. 4°. . . . . . .
Punch's Complete Letter-Writer. Jerrold. Lond., 1845. 16°. . . 4250
Pocket-Book of Fun. N. Y., 1857. 16°. 4249
Punchard, G. Hist. of Congregationalism. Salem, 1841. 12°. . . 6310
Punctuation, English. Wilson. Bost., 1862. 16°. 61
Punning, Art of. Swift. (Works, v. 24.) N. Y., 1813. 12°. . . 3870
Puritan, The: Essays. [Withington.] Bost., 1836. 2 v. 12°. . . 16320
Puritanism, A Churchman's Defence against the Aspersions of. Coit. N. Y., 1845. 12°. 6332
Puritans, Anecdotes of the. N. Y., 1849. 12°. 6351
Hist. of the. Neal. Newburyp't., 1816–17. 5 v. 8°. . . 6459
and their Principles. Hall. N. Y., 1846. 8°. 6458
and Q. Elizabeth. Hopkins. Bost., 1860–61. 3 v. 8°. . . 5314
Purley, Diversions of. Horne Tooke. Ed. Taylor. Lond., 1829. 2 v. 8°. 210
Pursuit of Knowledge under Difficulties. [Craik.] Lond., 1845. 3 v. 12°. 9104
Put yourself in his place. Reade. N. Y., 1870. 8°. 2284
Putnam, G. P. American Facts. Lond., 1845. 12°. 6184
Chronology. N. Y., 1833. 12°. 15935
The World's Progress: a Dict. of Dates. N. Y., 1851. 12°. . 4605
Putnam, I., Life of. Humphreys. Bost., 1818. 12°. 7538
The same. Peabody. Bost., 1837. 16°. 7256
Putnam's Monthly Magazine. N. Y., 1853–58. 12 v. 8°. . . . 13257
The same. v. 1–11. 13274
The same. New Series. N. Y., 1868–70. 6 v. 8°. . 13285
The same. v. 1–5. 13269
Puttenham, G. Arte of English Poesie, ed. Arber. Lond., 1869. 16°. 3891
Pycroft, J. Course of English Reading. Ed. Spencer. N. Y., 1857. 12°. 56

Q.

Quotations, Poetical. Addington. Philad., 1829. 4 v. 12°. . . . 4320
or, Results of Reading. Caldwell. Lond., 1843. 8°. . . . 4335
or, World's Laconics. Edwards. N. Y., 1856. 12°. . . . 4338
See, also, PROVERBS.

R.

Rabelais, F. Works. (Bohn's ed.) Lond., 1863. 2 v. 8°. . . . 502
Race, The Coming. [Bulwer-Lytton.] N. Y., 1871. 12°. . . . 9202
Races of the Earth, Indigenous. Nott and Gliddon. Philad., 1857. 8°. 9095
of the Old World, The. Brace. N. Y., 1863. 12°. 8965
See, also, MAN.
Rachel Félix, E., Memoirs of. Mme. de Barrera. N. Y., 1858. 12°. 7965
Rachel Dyer. Neal. Portl'd., 1828. 12°. 15764
Radau, R. Wonders of Acoustics. N. Y., 1870. 12°. 10108
Radcliffe, A. Gaston de Blondeville; St. Alban's Abbey; etc. Philad., 1826. 4 v. 12°. 15436
Mysteries of Udolpho. N. Y., 1861. 12°. 2513
Radiation, Lecture on. Tyndall. N. Y., 1865. 12°. 8904
Rae, J. New Principles of Polit. Economy. Bost., 1834. 8°. . . 8754
Rae, W. F. Westward by Rail. N. Y., 1871. 12°. 8394
Raffaello. See RAPHAEL.
Raffles, T. S. Hist. of Java. 2d ed. Lond., 1830. 2 v. 8°. . . 6496
Illustrations to. Lond., 1844. 4°. .
Memoir of. By his Widow. Lond., 1835. 2 v. 8°. . . . 6498
Raguet, C. Treatise on Currency and Banking. Philad., 1839. 8°. 8755
Raikes, T. Journal. Lond., 1856. 2 v. 8°. 7144
Visit to St. Petersburg. Lond., 1838. 8°. 8445
Railroad, N. Y. and Erie. See ERIE.
Rale, S., Life of. Francis. Bost., 1845. 16°. 7266
Raleigh, W. Hist. of the World; Voyages to Guiana. Edinb., 1820. 6 v. 8°. 4077
Last Fight of the Revenge. Ed. Arber. Lond., 1871. 16°. . 3898
Poetry. Ed. Hannah. Lond., 1870. 16°. 1005
Life of. Tytler. Philad., 1833. 8°. 15358
Life and Letters of. Edwards. Lond., 1868. 2 v. 8°. . . 6814
Memoirs of. Mrs. Thomson. Philad., 1831. 12°. . . . 6632
and his Time. C. Kingsley. Bost., 1859. 12°. . . . 3762
Trial of. (Celebrated Trials, 1.) Lond., 1825. 8°. . . . 9220
Ralph the Heir. A. Trollope. N. Y., 1871. 8°. 2295
Ralston, W. R. S. Krilof and his Fables. (2 copies.) Lond., 1869. 8°. 2624
Ramayana, Selections from. Richardson. Lond., 1870. 8°. . . 1906
Rambler, The. Ed. Ferguson. Lond., 1823. 3 v. 12°. . . . 3124
The same. 3498
Essays illustrating. Drake. Lond., 1809–10. 2 v. 8°. . . 3236
Ramsay, Alex. S. Butler and his Works. Lond., 1846. 12°. . . 6954
Ramsay, Allan. Poems. Edinb., 1728. 2 v. 4°. 15080
Select Poems. Ed. Walsh. Philad., 1822. 24°. . . . 20

Ramsay, Allan. Tea-Table Miscellany of Songs. Berwick, 1793. 4 v. in 2. 12°. 14911

Ramsay, D. Hist. of the Amer. Revol. Philad., 1789. 2 v. 8°. . 16123

The same. Trenton, 1811. v. 1. 8°. 6118

Hist. of S. C. Charleston, 1809. 2 v. 8°. 5866

of the U. S. 2d ed. Philad., 1818. 3 v. 8°. . . . 5850

Life of Washington. N. Y., 1807. 8°. 16388

Ramsay, E. B. Scottish Life and Character. Bost., 1861. 12°. . 5277

Ramsey, A. C. The Other Side. Hist of Mexican War. N. Y., 1850. 12°. 5824

Randall, H. S. Life of Jefferson. N. Y., 1858. 3 v. 8°. . . . 7440

Randolph, J. Letters to a young relative. Philad., 1834. 8°. . . 7417

Life of. Garland. N. Y., 1851. 2 v. 12°. 7309

Randolph, S. N. Domestic Life of Jefferson. N. Y., 1871. 12°. . 7351

Randolph, T. Muse's Looking Glass. (Old Plays, v. 9.) Lond., 1825. 8°. 1516

Ranke, L. Hist. of the Popes. Lond., 1840. 3 v. 8°. . . . 6513

The same. 2d ed. Lond., 1841. 3 v. 8°. . . . 6516

The same. (Bohn's ed.) Lond., 1847–48. 3 v. 8°. . 391

The same. v. 1, 3. 394

Hist. of Servia, and Bosnia. (Bohn's ed.) Lond., 1853. 8°. . 419

Rankin, A. Hist. of France. Lond., 1801–22. 9 v. 8°. . . . 16227

Rankin, J. Letters on Slavery. Bost., 1833. 12°. 8469

Ranks, Origin of Distinction of. Millar. Edinb., 1806. 8°. . . 17086

Raphael Sanzio, Hist. of. Quatremère de Quincy. Lond., 1846. 8°. 345

Life and Works of. v. Wolzogen. Lond., 1866. 8°. . . 7918

und Michael Angelo. Grimm. Bost. 12°. 9614

Rapin Thoyras, P. de. Hist. of England, continued by Tindal. Lond., 1757–62. 21 v. 8°. 16074

Rapp, J. de. Memoirs. Lond., 1823. 8°. 5599

Rarey, J. S. Art of taming Horses. Lond., 1862. 16°. . . . 10168

[**Rathbone, H. M.**] Diary of Lady Willoughby. N. Y., 1848. 12°. . 2558

The same. (2 copies.) N. Y., 1845. 12°. 3957

Rationalism, Hist. of. Hurst. N. Y., 1865. 8°. 6519

in Europe, Hist. of Rise and Influence of. Lecky. N. Y., 1866. 2 v. 8°. 6320

Rau, H. Mozart, a Romance. (2 copies.) N. Y., 1868. 12°. . . 3035

Raumer, F. v. America. N. Y., 1846. 8°. 6172

Contributions to Hist. of Eliz. and Mary Q. of Scots. Lond., 1836. 12°. 5210

England in 1835. Philad., 1836. 8°. 5334

Fred'k II. and his Times. Lond., 1837. 12°. 5802

Hist. of XVI. and XVII. Centuries. (2 copies.) Lond., 1835. 2 v. 12°. 4607

Italy and the Italians. Lond., 1840. 2 v. 8°. 4692

Political Hist. of England. (2 copies.) Lond., 1837. 2 v. 8°. 4996

Rauschenbusch, H. E., Memoir of. Leipoldt. Lond., 1843. 16°. . 7532

Ravenshoe. H. Kingsley. Bost., 1862. 12°. 2573

Ravenstein, E. G. The Russians on the Amur. Lond., 1861. 8°. . 8013

Rawlinson, G. Five Great Monarchies. 2d ed. N. Y., 1871. 3 v. 8°. 4063
Hist. Evidences of the Truth of Scripture Records. Bost., 1860. 12°. 9957
Manual of Ancient History. Oxf'd., 1869. 8°. 4062
Ray, I. Mental Hygiene. (2 copies.) Bost., 1863. 12°. . . . 8513
Ray, W. Poems. Auburn, 1821. 12°. 15020
Raynal, T. G. F. Hist. of E. and W. Indies. Lond., 1776. 5 v. 8°. 16149
The same. Edinb., 1782. 6 v. 12°. 14432
Rayner, B. L. Life of Jefferson. Bost., 1834. 12°. 7223
Reach, A. B. Claret and Olives. N. Y., 1852. 12°. 16706
Read, T. B. The New Pastoral. Philad., 1855. 12°. 779
A Summer Story, Sheridan's Ride, etc. (2 copies.) Philad., 1865. 12°. 781
Sylvia, and other Poems. Philad., 1857. 12°. 780
Reade, C. Christie Johnstone. Bost., 1868. 16°. 2093
The Cloister and the Hearth. N. Y., 1868. 8°. 2279
Clouds and Sunshine; and Art. Bost., 1855. 12°. 2096
Foul Play. Bost., 1869. 16°. 2098
The same. Bost., 1868. 8°. 2281
Griffith Gaunt. (2 copies.) Bost., 1866. 8°. 2282
It is never too late to mend. Bost., 1869. 16°. 2097
Love me little, love me long. N. Y., 1859. 12°. 2043
The same. (2 copies.) Bost., 1869. 16°. 2102
Peg Woffington. Bost., 1868. 16°. 2095
Peg Woffington, Christie Johnstone, etc. Bost., 1871. 16°. . 2094
Put Yourself in his Place. (2 copies.) N. Y., 1870. 8°. . 2284
A Terrible Temptation. Lond., 1871. 3 v. 8°. 2104
Very Hard Cash. N. Y., 1868. 8°. 2281
White Lies. (3 copies.) Bost., 1860–69. 16°. 2099
Readers, Handbook for. Potter. N. Y., 1845. 12°. 11766
Reading, English, Course of. Kent. Ed. by King. N. Y., 1853. 12°. 299
The same. Pycroft. N. Y., 1857. 12°. 56
Two Lectures on. Ruskin. N. Y., 1865. 12°. 213
See, also, Books.
Reading Abbey, Legend of. [MacFarlane.] Lond. 1845. 12°. . 2383
Real Folks. Whitney. Bost., 1872. 8°. 2971
Realmah. Helps. Bost., 1869. 16°. 2450
Rebecca and **Rowena.** Thackeray. (Works, v. 8.) Lond., 1832. 8°. 2196
Rebellion Record, The. Ed. F. Moore. N. Y., 1861–64. v. 1–7. 8°. 6262
Rebels, The. Child. Bost., 1825. 12°. 15765
Récamier, J. F. J. A., Memoirs and Correspond. of. Bost., 1867. 12°. 7661
Recantation. Ed. Kip. N. Y., 1846. 16°. 17273
Reclus, E. The Earth: Continents. Lond., 1871. 2 v. 8°. . . 9006
Recluse of Norway, The. A. M. Porter. Wash., 1834. 12°. . . 15186
Recollections of a Housekeeper. Gilman. N. Y., 1836. 12°. . . 15766
of a Southern Matron. Gilman. N. Y., 1838. 12°. . . . 15767
Red River Expedition, The, 1870. Huyshe. Lond., 1871. 8°. . . 8396
Red Rover, The. Cooper. N. Y., 1872. 12°. 2839
Redburn. Melville. N. Y., 1849. 12°. 15768

Redding, C. Hist. of Shipwrecks. Lond., 1835. 4 v. 16°. . . . 7862
Redfield, J. W. Outlines of System of Physiognomy. N. Y., 1849. 8°. 17078
Redgauntlet. Scott. Bost., 1845. 12°. 1823
Red-Jacket, Life of. Stone. N. Y., 1841. 8°. 5951
Redpath, J. Echoes of Harper's Ferry. Bost., 1860. 12°. . . . 8575
Life of John Brown. Bost., 1860. 12°. 7393
Redskins, The. Cooper. N. Y., 1855. 12°. 2824
Redwood. Sedgwick. N. Y., 1850. 12°. 15319
Reed, A. No Fiction. N. Y., 1835. 12°. 16383
and **Matheson, J.** Visit to the Amer. Churches. N. Y., 1835.
2 v. 12°. 16829
Reed, H. Lectures on Engl. Hist. and Tragic Poetry, illustrated by
Shakspeare. (2 copies.) Philad., 1856–57. 16°. . . 1478
English Literature. 4th ed. Philad., 1858. 12°. 65
The same. 5th ed. Philad., 1863. 12°. 66
Life of J. Reed. (Sparks, v. 18.) Bost., 1846. 16°. . . . 7267
Reed, J., Life of. H. Reed. Bost., 1846. 16°. 7267
Reed, R. T. Six Months in a Convent. Bost., 1835. 12°. . . 17275
Supplement. Bost., 1835. 12°. 17276
Reese, D. M. Humbugs of N. Y. N. Y., 1838. 12°. . . . 17103
Phrenology known by its Fruits. N. Y., 1836. 12°. . . 8608
Plea for the Intemperate. N. Y., 1841. 12°. 9122
[**Reeve, C.**] The Two Mentors. Lond., 1783. 2 v. 12°. . . . 15621
Reflection, Aids to. Coleridge. N. Y., 1871. 12°. 4013
Reform Ministers, Biogr. Sketches of the. Jones. Lond., 1832. 8°. 5330
Reformation, The. Fisher. N. Y., 1873. 8°. 10260
Essay on Spirit and Influence of the. Villers. Philad., 1833. 12°. 6344
Hist. of the. Stebbing. Lond., 1836–37. 2 v. 16°. . . 5757
on the Continent. Waddington. Lond., 1841.
3 v. 8°. 6479
in 16th Century. Merle d'Aubigné. N. Y., 1842–
61. 5 v. 12°. 6371
in Time of Calvin. Merle d'Aubigné. N. Y.,
1863–72. 5 v. 12°. 6386
Political Consequences of the. Heeren. Oxf'd., 1836. 8°. . 4713
See, also, LUTHER ; and the various EUROPEAN Countries.
Reformers, British, Writings of the. Lond. 8 v. 12°. . . . 9476
For Contents, see BRITISH.
Reforms, Hints towards. Greeley. N. Y., 1850. 12°. . . . 8622
Refugee, The. [Godwine.] N. Y., 1825. 2 v. 12°. 15769
in America. Mrs. Trollope. N. Y., 1833. 2 v. 12°. . . 15559
Reid, T. Essays on Powers of the Human Mind. Lond., 1827. 8°. 8764
Works. Charlestown, 1813–15. 4 v. 8°. 8765

CONTENTS.—1, Life, by D. Stewart; Account of Aristotle's Logic; Inquiry into the Human Mind. 2, 3, Essays on Intellectual Powers. 3, 4, Essays on Active Powers.

Reign of Law. Duke of Argyll. Lond., 1868. 16°. 8839
Reindeer, Dogs, and Snow-Shoes. Bush. N. Y., 1871. 8°. . . 8299
Rejected Addresses. H. and J. Smith, ed. Sargent. N. Y., 1857. 12°. 1221
American. [Bigelow.] N. Y. [1855.] 12°. . 686

Religio Medici. Browne. Lond., 1835. 8°. 3987
Religion, Authority in. Bolingbroke. (Works, v. 3, 4.) Philad., 1841. 8°. 10314
and Culture. Shairp. N. Y., 1871. 16°. 9819
Influence of, on Health. Brigham. Bost., 1835. 12°. . . 17351
Lectures on Science of. Max Müller. N. Y., 1872. 8°. . . 9958
Personal, Thoughts on. Goulburn. N. Y., 1866. 12°. . . 9816
Philosophy of. Dick. Brookf'ld., 1830. 12° 17363
The same. Morell. N. Y., 1849. 12°. 9952
and Science, Connexion of. Wiseman. Andover, 1837. 8°. . 10036
Religions, Pictorial View of. Goodrich. Hartf'd., 1851. 12°. . . 6298
Ten Great. Clarke. Bost., 1871. 8°. 10265
Religious Belief, Origin and Development of. Baring-Gould. N. Y., 1870. 2 v. 12°. 9959
Courtship. De Foe. (Works, v. 14.) Oxf'd., 1840. 16°. . 3879
Faith, Condition and Prospects of. Cobbe. Lond., 1865–66. 2 v. 8°. 9965
Truth illustrated from Science. Hitchcock. Bost., 1857. 12°. 17354
Sects. See Sects.
Reminiscences of half a century. Lond., 1838. 12°. 16378
Renan, E. The Apostles. N. Y., 1866. 12°. 9895
Constitutional Monarchy in France. (2 copies.) Bost., 1871. 16°. 5573
Life of Jesus. (2 copies.) N. Y., 1864–69. 12°. . . . 9893
Saint Paul. N. Y., 1869. 12°. 9897
The Romance of. Roussel. N. Y., 1869. 16°. . . . 9896
Rengger, J. R. Reign of de Francia in Paraguay. Lond., 1827. 8°. 5741
Rennie, J. Architecture of Birds. Lond., 1831. 12°. . . . 8821
The same. Bost., 1831. 12°. 8813
Domestic Habits of Birds. Lond., 1832. 12°. 8822
Faculties of Birds. Lond., 1835. 12°. 8823
Insect Architecture, etc. New ed. Lond., 1845. 2 v. 12°. . 8793
[and **Westwood, J. O.**] Insect Architecture. Bost., 1830. 12°. 8808
Insect Miscellanies. Bost., 1832. 12°. 8816
Insect Transformations. Bost., 1831. 12°. 8810
Nat. Hist. of Birds. N. Y., 1840. 12°. 11422
[and **Westwood, J. O.**] Nat. Hist. of Insects. N. Y., 1840. 2 v. 12°. 11007
Renwick, H. B. and **J.** Lives of Jay and Hamilton. N. Y., 1841. 12°. 11604
Renwick, J. Life of Dewitt Clinton. N. Y., 1841. 12°. . . . 11600
of Fulton. (Sparks, v. 10.) Bost., 1839. 16°. . 7259
The same. Bost., 1839. 12°. 16313
D. Rittenhouse. (Sparks, v. 7.) Bost., 1837. 16°. 7256
The same. Bost., 1839. 12°. 16314
Count Rumford. (Sparks, v. 15.) Bost., 1845. 16°. 7264
Repealers, The. Lady Blessington. (Works, v. 1.) Philad., 1838. 8°. 2668
Representative Government. Mill. N. Y., 1867. 12°. . . . 8619
in Europe, Hist. of. Guizot. Lond., 1852. 8°. 362
Men. Emerson. Bost., 1861. 12°. 3630

Reptiles, Nat. Hist. and Classification of. Swainson. Lond., 1838–39. 2 v. 16°. 6060
Popular Account of. Figuier. Lond. [1869.] 8°. 8997
Repton, H. Odd Whims. Lond., 1804. v. 2. 12°. 3955
Responsibility, Human, Limitations of. Wayland. Bost., 1838. 12°. 8535
Resurrection, Sermons on the. Ed. Stebbing. Lond., 1835. 16°. . 9498
Retrospective Review. Lond., 1820–26. v. 1–14. 8°. . . . 11456
Retz, J. F. P. de Gondi, *Cardinal* **de.** See GONDI.
Reumont, A. v. The Carafas of Maddaloni. Lond., 1854. 8°. . 403
Reuter, F. In the Year '13. Leipz., 1867. 16°. 2707
Seed-Time and Harvest. Philad., 1871. 8°. 10299
Revelation, Notes on the Book of. Barnes. N. Y., 1852. 12°. . . 9865
of Nature, The. N. Y. 12°. 3597
Reveries of a Bachelor. Mitchell. N. Y., 1871. 12°. 3597
Revival of 1740, Hist. of the. Tracy. Bost., 1842. 8°. . . . 6493
Thoughts on the. Pres. Edwards. (v. 4.) N. Y., 1830. 8°. . 17179
Revivals, Lectures on. Finney. N. Y., 1835. 12°. 17300
Sermons on. Barnes. N. Y., 1841. 12°. 17271
Revolutionary Plutarch, The. [Stewarton.] Lond., 1805. 3 v. 12°. 5509
Revolutionary War. See U. S. History.
Reynard the Fox. Goethe, transl. by Arnold. Lond., 1860. 8°. . 1301
Hist. of. Lond., 1844. 16°. 1693
The same. Transl. by Roscoe. (German Novelists.) Lond., 1826. 12°. 1895
in S. Africa. Bleek. Lond., 1864. 8°. 1891
Reynolds, E. Hints on use of the Eyes, and on Physical Culture. Edinb., 1835. 16°. 9137
Reynolds, Fred'k. Speculation; Delinquent; Laugh when you can; Fortune's Fool; Folly as it flies; Werter. (Mod. Theatre, v. 2, 3.) Lond., 1811. 12°. 1328
Life of. By himself. Philad., 1826. 2 v. in 1. 8°. . . . 8127
[**Reynolds, F. M.**] Miserrimus. N. Y., 1833. 12°. 15510
The Parricide. Philad., 1836. 2 v. 12°. 15532
Reynolds, G. W. M. Modern Literature of France. Lond., 1839. 2 v. 12° 109
Reynolds, John N. Voyage of the Potomac. N. Y., 1835. 8°. . 8078
Reynolds, *Sir* **Joshua.** Literary Works. With Memoir. Lond., 1835. 2 v. 16°. 8879
The same. (Bohn's ed.) Lond., 1852. 2 v. 8°. . . 482
Memoirs of. Northcote. Philad., 1817. 8°. 7992
Rhetoric, Art of. Hobbes. (Works, v. 6.) Lond., 1840. 8°. . . 9677
Elements of. Day. N. Y., 1854. 12°. 9305
The same. Whately. Cambr., 1834. 12°. 9300
Grammar of. Jamieson. N. H., 1821. 12°. 17531
Lectures on. Adams. Cambr., 1810. 2 v. 8°. . . . 17527
The same. Blair. N. Y., 1815. 8°. 17526
The same. Channing. Bost., 1856. 12°. 9306
Outlines of. Theremin, ed. Shedd. Andover, 1860. 12°. . 9293
Philosophy of. Campbell. Edinb., 1816. 2 v. 8°. . . . 17519

Rhetoric, Suggestions on. De Quincey. Edinb. 8°. 3284
System of. S. P. Newman. Portl'd., 1827. 12°. 17529
Treatise on; from Encycl. Brit. [Spalding.] Edinb., 1839. 12°. 164
Rhetorical Delivery, Principles of. Porter. Andover, 1827. 12°. . 17366
Grammar. Walker. Bost., 1822. 8°. 9299
See, also, ELOCUTION; ORATORY; SPEECH.
Rhind, W. Age of the Earth. Edinb., 1838. 16°. 16945
Rhine, Agriculture on the. Banfield. Lond., 1846. 12°. 8795
Legends and Hist. of the. Snowe. Lond., 1839. 2 v. 8°. . 8311
Tour on the, 1839. Hugo. N. Y., 1845. 12°. 8365
Up the. Hood. N. Y., 1852. 2 v. 12°. 4269
Rhode-Island Book, The. Mrs. A. C. L. Botta. Prov., 1841. 12°. . 15004
Rhythms, English, Hist. of. Guest. Lond., 1838. 2 v. 8°. . . 174
Ribault, J., Life of. Sparks. (Amer. Biogr., v. 17.) Bost., 1845. 16°. 7266
Rice, E. L. Introd. to Amer. Literature. Cincinn., 1846. 12°. . . 15005
Rich, E., *etc.* The Occult Sciences. Glasg., 1855. 8°. 8616
Richard I., of England (Cœur-de-Lion), Life of. G. P. R. James.
Lond., 1854. 2 v. 8°. 5129
Life and Times of. Aytoun. Lond., 1840. 16°. 5128
See, also, CRUSADES.
Richard III. Halsted. Philad., 1844. 8°. 5288
Historic Doubts on. Walpole. Lond., 1768. 4°. 5074
Richard of Cirencester. Ancient State of Britain. Lond., 1848. 8°. 499
Richard of Devizes. Chronicle. (Bohn's ed.) Lond., 1848. 8°. . 512
Richards, W. C. Memoir of G. N. Briggs. Bost., 1866. 12°. . . 7339
Richardson, A. D. The Secret Service, the Field, the Dungeon, and
the Escape. Hartf'd., 1865. 8°. 6197
Richardson, F. Iliad of the East. Lond., 1870. 8°. 1906
Richardson, G. F. Sketches in Prose and Verse. Lond., 1838. 12°. 15353
[**Richardson, J.**] Wacousta. Philad., 1833. 2 v. 12°. 15628
Richardson, S. Works. (2 copies.) Lond., 1811. 19 v. 16°. . . 1927
CONTENTS.—1-4, Pamela. 5-12, Clarissa Harlowe. 13-19, Sir Charles Grandison.
Richelieu, A. J. D., *Cardinal* **de.** Life of. James. Lond., 1836. 16°. 5767
Richelieu; a Drama. Bulwer-Lytton. Bost., 1863. 16°. 976
Richelieu; a Tale. G. P. R. James. N. Y., 1860. 2 v. in 1. 12°. . 2162
Richmond, L., Memoir of, abridged. Grimshawe. N. Y., 1829. 12°. 7563
Richter, J. P. F. The Campaner Thal, Life of Quintus Fixlein, etc.
Bost., 1864. 8°. 3056
Flower, Fruit and Thorn Pieces. (2 copies.) Bost., 1845–63.
2 v. 8°. 3052
Hesperus. (2 copies.) Bost., 1865. 2 v. 8°. 3059
Levana. Bost., 1863. 8°. 3067
Reminiscences for the hour of death. N. Y., 1863. 16°. . . 17297
Schmelzle's Journey to Flætz, and Life of Quintus Fixlein.
Transl. by Carlyle. Lond., 1871. 8°. 4053
The same. Bost., 1841. 12°. 3108
Titan. (2 copies.) Bost., 1863–64. 2 v. 8°. 3063
Walt and Vult; or the Twins. N. Y., 1863. 2 v. 8°. . . 3057
Life of. Lee. Bost., 1864. 8°. 7803

Rickards, R. India. Lond., 1829–32. 2 v. 8°. 6502
Riddle, J. E. Luther and his Times. Lond., 1837. 16°. . . . 6346
[**Ridley, J.**] Tales of the Genii. N. Y., 1825. 2 v. 12°. . . . 2013
Ridley, N. Treatises and Letters. Lond. 12°. 9478
Riedesel, F. C. L. de. Letters and Memoirs. N. Y., 1827. 12°. . 6014
Rienzi, N. G., Life and Times of. Ducerceau. Philad., 1836. 12°. . 7750
Rienzi, the Last of the Tribunes. Bulwer. N. Y., 1836. 12°. . . 2078
Rienzi, a Tragedy. Mitford. Philad. 8°. 2675
Riesbeck, C. v. Travels through Germany. Dubl., 1787. 2 v. 8°. . 16651
Riley, J. Narrative of Loss of the Commerce. Hartf'd., 1817. 8°. . 16299
Ring, M. John Milton and his Times. (2 copies.) N. Y., 1868. 8°. 3093
Ring of Amasis, The. R. Bulwer-Lytton. N. Y., 1863. 12°. . . 2154
Rip Van Winkle, illustrated by Darley. N, Y., 1848. 4°. . . . .
Ripa, —. Memoirs of Residence at Peking. N. Y., 1846. 12°. . 8365
Ritchie, A. C. M. Italian Life and Legends. N. Y., 1870. 12°. . 8342
Ritchie, L. The Game of Life. Philad., 1833. 8°. 15356
London Nights' Entertainments. Philad., 1833. 2 v. 12°. . 15493
Romance of French Hist. N. Y., 1831. 2 v. 12°. . . . 15565
Russia and the Russians. Philad., 1836. 12°. 16616
Ritson, J. The Caledonian Muse. Lond., 1785. 16°. . . . 1096
English Anthology. Lond., 1793–94. 3 v. 16°. . . . 1086
Robin Hood Ballads, etc. [Lond., 1845.] 8°. 948
Rittenhouse, D., Life of. Renwick. Bost., 1837. 16°. . . . 7256
Ritter, C. Geographical Studies. (2 copies.) Bost., 1863. 12°. . 8970
Ritter, H. Hist. of Ancient Philosophy. (2 copies.) Oxf'd., 1838–39. v. 1–3. 8°. 8707
Rivals, The. [Griffin.] N. Y., 1830. 12°. 15561
Rivers, Rambles by. Thorne. Lond., 1844. 12°. 8149
Rives, W. C. Life of Madison. Bost., 1859–68. 3 v. 8°. . . 7447
Rob of the Bowl. Kennedy. Philad., 1838. 2 v. 12°. . . . 15771
Rob Roy. Scott. Edinb., 1870. 8°. 1866
Canoe, A thousand miles in the. Macgregor. Bost., 1871. 16°. 8221
Macgregor; an Opera. Pocock. Bost., 1803. 12°. . . . 13355
Roba di Roma. Story. Philad., 1867. 2 v. 12°. 8345
Robber, The. James. N. Y., 1836. 2 v. 12°. 15207
Robbers. See BANDITTI; BRIGANDS.
Robbins, A. Journal of Loss of the Commerce, etc. Roch., 1818. 12°. 16293
Robbins, R. Outlines of Anc. and Mod. Hist. Hartf'd., 1830. 12°. 15929
Robert Falconer. MacDonald. Bost. 12°. 2581
Roberts, Edmund. Embassy to Cochin-China, etc. N. Y., 1837. 8°. 16499
Roberts, Emma. Scenes and Characteristics of Hindostan. Philad., 1836. 2 v. 12°. 16502
Roberts, O. W. Voyages in America. Edinb., 1827. 12°. . . 4479
Roberts, Wm. The Looker-On. Philad., 1796. 4 v. in 2. 12°. . 13033
Memoirs of H. More. N. Y., 1834. 2 v. 12°. 15105
Roberts, Wm. H. Select Poems. Ed. Walsh. Philad., 1822. 24°. . 31
Robertson, F. W. Lectures and Addresses. Bost., 1859. 12°. . . 9931
Sermons. Bost., 1859–64. 5 v. 12°. 9924
The same. Bost., 1869. 5 v. in 2. 12°. 9929

Robertson, F. W. Life and Letters of. Brooke. Bost., 1865. 2 v. 12°. 7603
Robertson, I. L. *(Pseudonym.)* See S. L. KNAPP.
Robertson, S. P. and **W. P.** Four years in Paraguay. Philad., 1838. 2 v. 12°. 5739
Francia's Reign of Terror. Philad., 1839. 2 v. 12°. . . . 5741
Robertson, W. Historical Disquisition concerning Ancient India. Dubl., 1791. 8°. 16451
Hist. of America. Dubl., 1777. 2 v. 8°. 16136
The same. 6th ed. Lond., 1792. 3 v. 8°. . . . 16138
The same, abridged. N. Y., 1848. 12°. 11927
of Ancient Greece. Edinb., 1821. 8°. 16026
of Chas. V. [Philad.] 1770. 3 v. 8°. 6543
The same. Basil., 1788. 4 v. 8°. 6547
The same. (2 copies.) Albany, 1822. 3 v. 8°. . . 6550
The same, ed. W. H. Prescott. Philad., 1872. 3 v. 8°. . 10335
The same. Bost., 1857. v. 2, 3. 8°. 6577
of Scotland, 1542–1603. With Life. Philad., 1811. 2 v. 8°. 5404
Life of. D. Stewart. (Works, v. 7.) Cambr., 1829. 8°. . . 8776
Robespierre, Fall of. A Drama. Coleridge. (Remains, 1.) Lond., 1836. 8°. 4006
Robin Day. Bird. Philad., 1839. 2 v. 12°. 15648
Robin Hood, Poems, etc., relative to. Ritson. [Lond., 1845.] 8°. . 948
[**Robinson, A.**] Life in California. N. Y., 1846. 12°. 16888
Robinson, E. Universities and Theol. Education in Germany. Edinb., 1835. 16°. 9137
Robinson, H. B. Narrative of Owen's Voyages. N. Y., 1833. 2 v. 12°. 16289
Robinson, Henry Crabb. Diary and Correspondence. (2 copies.) Bost., 1869. 2 v. 12°. 7005
Robinson, Mary, Memoirs of. By herself. Lond., 1830. 12°. . . 6645
Robinson, P. Immortality. N. Y., 1846. 12°. 15021
Robinson, Sara T. L. Kansas. Bost., 1857. 12°. 16856
Robinson, Solon. Hot Corn. N. Y., 1854. 12°. 15722
Robinson, Therese A. L. v. J. Fifteen Years. N. Y., 1871. 12°. . 15696
Languages and Literature of Slavic Nations. N. Y., 1850. 12°. 113
Robinson, Thos. R. Poems. Brooklyn, 1808. 12°. 14857
Robinson, W. D. Memoirs of the Mexican Revol. Philad., 1820. 8°. 16148
Robinson Crusoe. DeFoe. Cambr., 1866. 16°. 1706
Robison, J. Proofs of Conspiracy by Free Masons, etc. (2 copies.) N. Y., 1798. 8°. 17110
Robson, F. Life of Hyder Ally. Lond., 1786. 8°. 16414
Roby, J. Popular Traditions of Lancashire. Lond., 1843. v. 2, 3. 12°. 5269
Roche, R. M. Contrast. N. Y., 1828. 2 v. 12°. 15403
Houses of Osma and Almeria. Philad., 1810. 12°. . . . 15458
Rochester, *Earl of.* See J. WILMOT.
Roderick Random. Smollett. N. Y. 8°. 1989
Roe, A. S. A Long Look Ahead. N. Y., 1856. 12°. 15737
Roger of Wendover. Flowers of Hist. (Bohn's ed.) Lond., 1849. 2 v. 8°. 510
Rogers, E. Lives of the Cæsars. Lond., 1811. 5 v. 8°. . . . 16001

Rogers, James E. Thorold. Historical Gleanings. Lond., 1869–70. 2 v. 8°. 6731

CONTENTS.—1, C. Montagu; R. Walpole; A. Smith; Cobbett. 2, Wiklif; Laud; Wilkes; Horne Tooke.

Rogers, John (The Martyr). Writings. Lond. 12°. 9483
Rogers, John. Antipopopriestian. Part 1, Popery. Lond., 1839. 12°. 9602
Rogers, S. Pleasures of Memory. N. Y., 1824. 12°. 14843
Poems [illustrated by Stothard and Turner]. Lond., 1834. 8°. 1112
Poetical Works. Philad., 1830. 8°. 944
The same. 947
Table-Talk of. Dyce. Lond., 1856. 8°. 3208
Roget, P. M. Animal and Vegetable Physiology. Philad., 1836. 2 v. 8°. 16985
Thesaurus of English Words and Phrases. Ed. B. Sears. Bost., 1856. 12°. 96
Roister Doister. Udall., ed. Arber. Lond., 1869. 16°. 3892
Roland, M. J. P., Memoirs of. Child. N. Y., 1854. 16°. . . . 7659
Rollin, C. Ancient History. N. Y., 1834. 2 v. 8°. 4123
The same. Hartf'd., 1836. v. 1–4, 6–8. 12°. 4574
Hist. of Arts and Sciences of the Antients. 2d ed. Lond., 1768. 3 v. 8°. 15898
and **Crevier, J. B. L.** Roman Hist. Lond., 1768. 10 v. 8°. . 15975
Roman Antiquities. Fuss. Oxf'd., 1840. 8°. 4751
Cæsars, The. De Quincey. Edinb., 1858. 8°. 3283
Lives of the. Rogers. Lond., 1811. 5 v. 8°. . . 16001
Catholic Church, Lectures on the. Wiseman. Lond., 1844. 16°. 9581
Controversy, Letters on the. Brownlee. N. Y., 1834. 8°. 9607
Monasteries of Italy, Six Years in. Mahoney. Bost., 1845. 12°. 9583
Priest, Confessions of a. Ed. Morse. N. Y., 1837. 12°. 17262
and Protestant Nations compared. Roussel. Bost., 1855. 12°. 6433
Religion, Discussion of the. Hughes and Breckinridge. Philad., 1836. 8°. 9606
Catholicism and Protestantism compared in their Effects on Civilization. Balmes. Balt., 1851. 8°. 6492
See, also, MONKS; POPES; ROMANISM.
Commonwealth, Hist. of. [B. C. 201–A. D. 13.] Arnold. N. Y., 1846. 8°. 4748
Emperors, Hist. of, A. D. 14–337. Crevier. Lond., 1755–61. v. 2–10. 8°. 15937
Empire, Causes of Grandeur and Declension of. Montesquieu. (v. 3.) Lond., 1777. 8°. 9554
Conversion of the. Merivale. N. Y., 1866. 8°. . . 6318
Fall of the. Sismondi. Lond., 1834. 16°. 4873
Hist. of. [B. C. 29–A. D. 476.] Keightley. Bost., 1841. 8°. 4750
of Decline and Fall of. [A. D. 180–1500.] Gibbon. Ed. Milman. Bost. and N. Y., 1850–64. 6 v. 12°. 4754
The same, abridged by W. Smith. N. Y., 1860. 12°. . 4767

Rome, Hist. of. [to B. C. 46.] Mommsen. N. Y., 1869–70. 4 v. 12°. 4694
The same. [to A. D. 384.] Niebuhr. Philad., 1835. 2 v. 8°. 4739
The same, to B. C. 29. Rollin and Crevier. Lond., 1768. 10 v. 8°. 15975
The same, to A. D. 192. Schmitz. N. Y., 1847. 12°. . 4724
Comic. à Beckett. Lond. 8°. 4314
Kings of. Dyer. Lond., 1868. 8°. 4731
in 19th century. Eaton. (Bohn's ed.) Lond., 1852. v. 1. 8°. 527
Specimens of Poets and Poetry of. Peter. Philad., 1847. 8°. 239
Walks in. Hare. Lond., 1871. 2 v. 8°. 8349
See, also, ITALY; LATIN.

Romilly, S., Memoirs of. By himself. 2d ed. Lond., 1840. 3 v. 8°. 6837

Romola. [Lewes.] N. Y., 1872. 12°. 2538

Ronge, J. Autobiography. Lond., 1846. 16°. 11016

Rosamond, Narrative of. N. Y., 1836. 12°. 17259

Roscoe, H. E. Spectrum Analysis. Lond., 1869. 8°. . . . 9097

Roscoe, T. German Novelists translated. Lond., 1826. 4 v. 12°. . 1895

CONTENTS.—1, Reynard the Fox. Howleglass. Doctor Faustus. 2, Traditions, by Otmar, Gottschalk, Eberhardt, Buesching, Grimm Brothers, Lothar, La Motte Fouque. 3, Tales, by Musæus, Schiller. 4, Novels, by Tieck, Langbein, Engel.

Italian Novelists translated. 2d ed. Lond., 1836. 4 v. 12°. . 1899
The same. vols. 1–3. 1903

CONTENTS.—1, Novelle antiche; Boccaccio; Sacchetti; Fiorentino; Massucio Salernitano. 2, Sabadino degli Arienti; da Porto; Illicini; Sozzini; Machiavelli; Firenzuola; Fortini; Sermini; Brevio; Parabosco; Cademosto da Lodi; Giraldi Cinthio; Grazzini. 3, Lando; Straparola; Bandello; Sansovino; Doni; Erizzo; Granucci; Mori da Ceno; Malespini; Salvucci; Anonymous. 4, Bisaccioni; Colombo; Bargagli; Bottari; Capacelli; Soave; Altanesi; Magalotti; Lodoli; Manni; Padovani; Sanvitale; C. Gozzi; Bramieri; Gironi; Anonymous.

Life of Wm. the Conqueror. Philad., 1846. 12°. . . . 5127

Roscoe, W. Life of Leo X. Ed. T. Roscoe. Lond., 1846. 2 v. 8°. 396
The same. Ed. Hazlitt. Lond., 1846. 2 v. 8°. . . 398
Life of L. de'Medici. Philad., 1803. 3 v. 8°. 7779
The same. Ed. T. Roscoe. Lond., 1847. 8°. . . 400
The same. Ed. Hazlitt. Lond., 1846. 8°. . . . 401
Life of. H. Roscoe. Bost., 1833. 2 v. 12°. 7087

Roscommon, *Earl of.* See W. DILLON.

Rose, S. Loyola and the Early Jesuits. Lond., 1870. 8°. . . . 7671

Rose d'Albret. G. P. R. James. N. Y. 8°. 2312

Rose Douglas. N. Y., 1851. 12°. 15569

Ross, J. Memoirs of Admiral de Saumarez. Lond., 1838. 2 v. 8°. . 16386
Narrative of 2d Arctic Voyage. Philad., 1835. 8°. . . . 8104

Rossetti, M. F. A Shadow of Dante. Bost., 1872. 8°. . . . 877

Rossini, G. Barber of Seville. (Oxberry's Plays, v. 11.) Philad., 1822. 24°. 1355

Rotteck, C. v. History of the World. Philad., 1840–41. 4 v. 8°. . 4083

Roughing it. Mark Twain. Hartf'd., 1872. 8°. 4288
The same. 10242

Roumania, Adventures in. Noyes. N. Y., 1858. 12°. . . . 16620

Roundabout Papers. Thackeray. (Works, v. 10.) Lond., 1872. 8°. 2198

Rousseau, J. J. Confessions. Lond., 1783–90. 5 v. 12°. . . . 13193
Eloisa. Lond., 1810. 3 v. 8°. 15146
Emilius and Sophia. Lond., 1763. 4 v. 12°. 9110

Rousseau, J. J. Letters of an Italian Nun, etc. Harrisburgh, 1809. 12°. 2386
Miscellaneous Works. Lond., 1767. 5 v. 12°. . . . 13188
On the Social Compact, etc. 12°. . . . . , . . 17089
against the Atheists. Ed. Akerly. N. Y., 1845. 12°. . . 9979
Roussel, N. Catholic and Prot. Nations Compared. Bost., 1855. 12°. 6433
The Romance of Renan. N. Y., 1869. 16°. 9896
Rowe, N. Poetical Works. Ed. Bell. Lond., 1807. 2 v. 24°. . 271
The same, ed. Johnson. Dubl., 1804. 8°. . . . 15098
Tamerlane; Fair Penitent; Jane Shore; Lady J. Gray. (Brit. Drama, v. 1.) Lond., 1804. 8°. 1629
Rowland, D. Manual of the English Constitution. Lond., 1859. 12°. 4853
Rowley, W. Match at Midnight. (Old Plays, v. 7.) Lond., 1825. 8°. 1514
Rowley Poems. See T. CHATTERTON.
Roy, W., and **Barlow, J.** Rede me and be not wrothe. Ed. Arber. Lond., 1871. 16°. 3898
Royall, A. Sketches in the U. S. N. H., 1826. 12°. 16836
The Tennessean. N. H., 1827. 12°. 15801
Rubber of Life, The. [Barham.] Lond., 1841. 2 v. 12°. . . 15520
Rubens, P. P., Life and Genius of. Waagen. Lond., 1840. 8°. . . 8871
Ruffini, G. Doctor Antonio. N. Y., 1862. 12°. 2446
Rugby School Sermons. Arnold. Lond., 1843. 8°. 10050
Tom Brown's School Days at. [Hughes.] Bost., 1870. 8°. . 9242
Rule of the Monk, The. Garibaldi. N. Y., 1870. 8°. . . . 2651
Rumford, *Count* (B. Thompson), Life of. Renwick. Bost., 1845. 16°. 7264
Rural Hours. [Cooper.] N. Y., 1850. 12°. 16977
Life of England. Howitt. Lond., 1840. 8°. 5260
of Germany. Howitt. Philad., 1843. 8°. 8310
Magazine. Ed. Waldo. Hartf'd., 1819. v. 1. 8°. 13879
Sketches. Miller. Philad., 1842. 12°. 15570
Studies. Mitchell. N. Y., 1867. 12°. 8926
Ruschenberger, W. S. W. Three Years in the Pacific. Philad., 1834. 8°. 16305
Voyage round the World. Philad., 1838. 8°. 8079
Rush, B. Essays. Philad., 1800. 8°. 15853
Rush, Jacob. Charges on Moral and Religious Subjects. N. Y., 1804. 12°. 9151
Rush, James. Philosophy of the Voice. Philad., 1827. 8°. . . 17539
The same. 2d ed. Philad., 1833. 8°. 17540
Rush, R. Memoranda of Residence at London. 2d ed. Philad., 1833. 8°. 7423
The same, continued. Philad., 1845. 8°. 7424
Ruskin, J. Aratra Pentelici. Lectures on Sculpture. N. Y., 1872. 12°. 9048
Crown of Wild Olive. N. Y., 1866. 12°. 9042
Elements of Drawing. (2 copies.) N. Y., 1859–67. 12°. . . 9032
of Perspective. (2 copies.) N. Y., 1860. 12°. . . 9037
Ethics of the Dust. (3 copies.) N. Y., 1866. 12°. 9043
Fors Clavigera. Letters to Workmen. N. Y., 1871–72. 2 v. 12°. 8632
Lectures on Architecture and Painting. (3 copies.) N. Y., 1856–59. 12°. 9034
Lectures on Art, 1870. (2 copies.) Oxf'd., 1870. 8°. . . . 8883

Ruskin, J. Modern Painters. (2 copies.) N. Y., 1847–62. 5 v. 12°. 9014
Munera Pulveris. Essays on Polit. Economy. N. Y., 1872. 12°. 8631
Polit. Economy of Art. N. Y., 1860. 12°. 9041
Pre-Raphaelitism; Construction of Sheepfolds; King of the Golden River. N. Y., 1860. 12°. 9040
Queen of the Air. (2 copies.) N. Y., 1869–71. 12°. . . . 9047
Sesame and Lilies. N. Y., 1865. 12°. 213
Seven Lamps of Architecture. (2 copies.) N. Y., 1849. 12°. . 9030
Stones of Venice. (2 copies.) N. Y., 1860. 3 v. 12°. . . 9024
Time and Tide. N. Y., 1868. 12°. 9046
The Two Paths; Lectures on Art. N. Y., 1859. 12°. . . 9039
"Unto this last." Essays on Polit. Economy. Lond., 1862. 16°. 8544
Selections from. (The True and the Beautiful.) 2 copies. N. Y., 1859–69. 12°. 9049
Russell, A. Principles of Statistical Inquiry. N. Y., 1839. 8°. . 17093
Russell, *Lord* **John.** Essay on the English Gov't. and Constitution. 2d ed. Lond., 1823. 8°. , ... 4988
Hist. of Europe, from Peace of Utrecht. Lond., 1826. 2 v. 8°. 4600
Life of Wm., Lord Russell. 3d ed. Lond., 1820. 2 v. 8°. . 6817
Memoirs of T. Moore. (2 copies.) N. Y., 1857. 2 v. 8°. . 7178
Memorials of C. J. Fox. Philad., 1853. 2 v. 12°. . . . 6629
Russell, John. Tour in Germany, etc. Bost., 1825. 8°. . . . 16649
The same. New ed. Edinb., 1828. 2 v. 12°. . . 4491
Russell, M. The Barbary States. N. Y., 1835. 12°. 11290
Iceland, Greenland, etc. N. Y., 1841. 12°. 11606
Life of Cromwell. N. Y., 1844. 2 v. 12°. 11282
The same. N. Y., 1833. 2 v. 12°. 12112
Nubia and Abyssinia. N. Y., 1840. 12°. 11281
Palestine. N. Y., 1840. 12°. 11029
Polynesia. N. Y., 1845. 12°. 11760
View of Ancient and Modern Egypt. N. Y., 1831. 12°. . . 11025
Russell, *Lady* **R.** Letters. Philad., 1854. 12°. 7055
The same. Lond., 1809. 8°. 7056
The same. Bost., 1820. 16°. 3844
Biogr. of. Child. Edinb., 1836. 16°. 6633
Russell, *(Lord)* **Wm.,** Life of. Lord J. Russell. 3d ed. Lond., 1820. 2 v. 8°. 6817
Russell, Wm. Hist. of Ancient Europe. Lond., 1793. 2 v. 8°. . 15904
of Modern Europe. Philad., 1822. 6 v. 8°. . 15906
Russell, Wm. Extraordinary Men; their early life. Lond., 1853. 12°. 6754
Russell, Wm. Exercises in Elocution. Bost., 1841. 12°. . . . 9302
Orthophony; or Vocal Culture. Bost., 1851. 12°. . . . 9303
Russell, Wm. H. A Diary in the East. Lond., 1869. 8°. . . . 8075
My Diary North and South. Bost., 1863. 12°. . . . 6107
Russell. A Tale. G. P. R. James. N. Y., 1847. 8°. . . . 2322
Russia as it is. Gurowski. N. Y., 1854. 12°. 6447
Correspondence, etc., respecting. Harper and Walsh. Philad., 1813. 8°. 16173
The Czar of; his Court and People. Maxwell. N. Y., 1848. 12°. 16604

Russia, The Empire of, to 1855. J. S. C. Abbott. N. Y., 1860. 12°. . 6443
Excursions in, 1836. Bremner. Lond., 1839. 2 v. 8°. . . 8296
Free. Dixon. N. Y., 1870. 12°. 8298
Hist. of (to 1762). Tooke. Lond., 1800. 2 v. 8°. . . . 6434
The same [to 1814]. Bell. Lond., 1836–38. 3 v. 16°. . 5480
The same [to 1854]. Kelly. Lond., 1854–55. 2 v. 8°. 420
of Napoleon's Exped. to. Ségur. N. Y., 1845. 2 v. 12°. 11616
Journey through, 1820. Cochrane. Edinb., 1829. 2 v. 12°. . 4498
Journey to, 1835. Ritchie. Philad., 1836. 12°. . . . 16616
Modern. Eckardt. Lond., 1870. 8°. 6448
Narrative of Bonaparte's Campaign in. Labaume. Philad., 1815. 8°. 16190
Notes of Residence in. Sala. Bost., 1858. 12°. . . . 8219
Past and Present State of. Pinkerton. Lond., 1833. 8°. . . 8444
Political Writings on. Cobden. Lond., 1867. 2 v. 8°. . . 9587
Popular Description of. Conder. Lond. 12°. 7852
Resources of. [Eustaphiève.] Bost., 1813. 12°. . . . 16174
and the Russians in 1842. Kohl. Philad., 1843. 8°. . . 16615
Travels in, 1778–79. Coxe. Lond., 1802. 4 v. 8°. . . . 16605
1800. Clarke. Lond., 1816. 2 v. 8°. . . . 8020
1805–07. Porter. Philad., 1809. 8°. . . . 16603
1829. Alexander. Lond., 1830. 2 v. 8°. . . 16487
1858. Bayard Taylor. N. Y., 1859. 12°. . . 8285
Russian Empire, View of the, 1762–1800. Tooke. Lond., 1800. 3 v. 8°. 6436
Literature, Hist. of. Otto. Oxf'd., 1839. 8°. 205
Poets, Specimens of. Bowring. Lond., 1821–23. 2 v. 12°. . 288
Russians on the Amur, The. Ravenstein. Lond., 1861. 8°. . . 8013
See, also, the names of the SOVEREIGNS.
Rutherford, S., Life of. Murray. Edinb., 1828. 12°. 7515
Rutledge, J., Life of. Flanders. Philad., 1855. 8°. 7473
Rutledge. [Cole.] N. Y., 1860. 12°. 2985
Ruxton, G. F. Adventures in Mexico and the Rocky Mts. N. Y., 1848. 12°. 16923
Life in the Far West. N. Y., 1849. 12°. 16864
Ryall, C. The Mourner. Sherborne. 1740. 8°. 14806
Ryan, R. Biogr. Dict. of Worthies of Ireland. Lond., 1821. 2 v. 8°. 6876
Rybrent de Cruce. [Head.] N. Y., 1829. 2 v. 12°. . . . 15571
Ryland, J. E. Life of J. Foster. N. Y., 1846. 2 v. 12°. . . . 7680
The same. (Bohn's ed.) Lond., 1852. 2 v. 8°. . . 489
Ryle, J. C. Christian Leaders of the last century. Lond., 1869. 8°. 6607

S.

Sabadino degli Arienti, J. Novels. Lond., 1836. 12°. . . . 1900
Sabbath at Home. Bost., 1867. v. 1. 8°. 13878
Recreations. Sacred Poetry. Taylor. Bost., 1839. 12°. . 14909
School as it should be, The. Alcott. N. Y., 1841. 12°. . . 17361
Teacher, The. Todd. Northampton, 1837. 12°. . . 17362

Sabbation. Trench. Lond., 1838. 16°. 1217
Sabine, L. Life of Preble. (Sparks, v. 22.) Bost., 1847. 16°. . . 7271
Sacchetti, F. Novels. (Ital. Novelists, v. 1.) Lond., 1836. 12°. . 1899
Sackville, C. *(Earl of Dorset).* Poems, ed. Johnson. Dubl., 1804. 8°. 15096
Sackville, T. *(Earl of Dorset).* Ferrex and Porrex. Lond., 1825. 8°. 1508
Sacred History of the World. Turner. N. Y., 1838–39. 3 v. 12°. . 11034
Offering, The. Bost., 1838. 12°. 14907
Poetry of XVII. century. Ed. Cattermole. Lond., 1835. v. 1. 16°. 9503
The same. v. 2. Lond., 1836. 16°. 9508
Sacristan's Household, The. [Mrs. T. A. Trollope.] N. Y., 1869. 8°. 2310
Sadi. The Gulistan, transl. by Gladwin. Bost., 1865. 12°. . . 876
Sadler, M. F. Church Doctrine, Bible Truth. 3d ed. N. Y., 1869. 16°. 9821
Sæmund, S. Edda, transl. by Cottle. Bristol, 1797. 8°. . . . 920
Safford, W. H. Life of Blennerhassett. Cincinn., 1853. 12°. . . 7357
St. Bartholomew's Day, Massacre of. White. N. Y., 1868. 12°. . 6327
St. Cloud, Secret Hist. of Court of. Lond., 1806. 3 v. 12°. . . 5517
St. Domingo, Hist. of, to 1817. N. Y., 1824. 8°. 16147
Notes on. Mackenzie. Lond., 1830. 2 v. 12°. . . . 16913
past and present. Hazard. N. Y., 1873. 8°. . . 10244
State of, in 1828. Franklin. Lond., 1828. 8°. 16912
St. Elmo. A. J. Wilson. N. Y., 1867. 12°. 2990
St. Giles and St. James. Jerrold. N. Y., 1845. 8°. 2321
St. Helena. Hist. of, to 1806. Brooke. Lond., 1808. 8°. . . 16168
See, also, NAPOLÉON I.
St. James' Magazine. Lond., 1869–71. v. 3–7. New Series. 8°. . 17835
St. John, B. Adventures in the Libyan Desert. N. Y., 1850. 12°. . 16522
St. John, Henry (*Lord* Bolingbroke). Collection of Political Tracts. Lond., 1769. 8°. 17224
Dissertation on Parties. With Life. Lond., 1771. 8°. . . 17222
Letters to Windham and Pope, and Reflections on State of the Nation. Lond., 1753. 8°. 17223
Remarks on Hist. of England. Lond. 8°. 17225
Works. Lond., 1809. 8 v. 8°. 3794
The same. Philad., 1841. v. 2, 3, 4. 8°. 10313

CONTENTS.—2, Dissertation on Parties; Letters on Study and Use of History; Idea of a Patriot King; Reflection on State of the Nation; etc. 3, Letter on one of Tillotson's Sermons. 3, 4, Letters or Essays, addressed to Pope, on Human Knowledge, Philosophers, Monotheism, Authority in Religion, etc. 4, Fragments of Essays.

St. John, J. A. Hist. of 4 Conquests of England. Lond., 1862. 2 v. 8°. 4994
Lives of celebrated Travellers. N. Y., 1841. 3 v. 12°. . . 11042
The same. N. Y., 1832. 3 v. 12°. 12097
Margaret Ravenscroft. Philad., 1836. 2 v. 12°. . . . 15503
St. John, P. B. The Three Days of Febr., 1848. N. Y., 1848. 12°. . 5455
St. John de Crève Cœur, J. H. Letters from an American Farmer. Philad., 1793. 12°. . . . , ... 16819
St. Jonathan, the Lay of a Scold. [Coxe.] N. Y., 1838. 12°. . . 804
Saint Leger. Kimball. N. Y., 1862. 12°. 15773
St. Leon. Godwin. Alexandria, 1801. 2 v. 12°. 1707
St. Martin's Summer. Brewster. Bost., 1866. 8°. 8211
Saint Paul's Magazine. Lond., 1872. v. 10. 8°. 17815

St. Petersburgh in 1833. v. Tietz. Lond., 1836. 2 v. 8°. 16546
Visit to, 1829–30. Raikes. Lond., 1838. 8°. 8445
St. Philip's. [Cole.] N. Y., 1865. 12°. 2986
St. Pierre, J. H. B. de. Botanical Harmony. Worc., 1797. 8°. . 16976
Paul and Virginia. (2 copies.) Philad., 1856. 16°. 2356
Saint-Réal, C. V. de. Conspiracy of Spaniards, against Venice. Bost., 1838. 16°. 16159
St. Ronan's Well. Scott. Bost., 1845. 2 v. in 1. 12°. . . . 1820
St. Winifred's. Farrer. N. Y., 1867. 12°. 2429
Sainte Palaye. See LA CURNE.
Saintine, J. X. Boniface. Picciola. N. Y., 1861. 12°. . . . 2596
Sala, G. A. A Journey Due North. Bost., 1858. 12°. . . . 8219
Quite Alone. N. Y. 8°. 2334
Strange Adventures of Capt. Dangerous. Bost., 1863. 8°. . 2333
Salathiel; or the Wandering Jew. Croly. N. Y., 1850. 8°. . . 2326
Sale, *(Lady)* **F.** Journal in Affghanistan. Lond., 1843. 12°. . . 7975
Salem Belle, The. Bost., 1842. 12°. 2726
Witchcraft, Account of. Thacher. Bost., 1831. 12°. . . 8480
Salisbury, *Earl of* (R. Cecil), Life of. Courtenay. Lond., 1838. 16°. 5763
Sallust. Works, tr. by Rose. N. Y., 1837. 12°. 4512
Salmagundi. Paulding, etc. N. Y., 1835. 4 v. 12°. . . . 15277
Salm-Salm, F. Diary in Mexico. Lond., 1868. 2 v. 8°. . . . 5826
Salvation, Philosophy of the Plan of. [Walker.] Bost., 1856. 12°. . 9987
Salverte, E. Philosophy of Magic. Ed. Thomson. (2 copies.) N. Y., 1847. 2 v. 12°. 8520
Salvucci, S. Four Dukes. (Ital. Novelists, 3.) Lond., 1836. 12°. . 1901
Salzmann, C. G. Gymnastics for Youth. Philad., 1803. 8°. , . 17058
Sampson, W., Memoirs of. By himself. Leesburg, 1817. 8°. . . 16360
Samson, G. W. Elements of Art Criticism. Philad., 1867. 12°. . 9057
Sand, George. *(Pseudonym.)* See A. L. A. D. DUDEVANT.
Sanderson, J. The American in Paris. Philad., 1839. 2 v. 12°. . 16709
Biogr. of Signers of the Declaration. Philad., 1823–27. 9 v. 8°. 7462
Sanderson, R., Life of. Walton. [Lond., 1845.] 8°. 948
Sands, R. C. Writings. N. Y., 1835. 2 v. 8°. 15354
and others. The Talisman. N. Y., 1833. 3 v. 12°. . . 4132
and **Eastburn, J. W.** Yamoyden. N. Y., 1820. 12°. . . 14987
Sandwich Islands. See HAWAIIAN Islands.
Sanford, E., and **Walsh, R.** Works of British Poets, with their Lives. Philad., 1819–23. 50 v. (11 wanting.) 24°. . . . 1

CONTENTS.—Vol. 1, Chaucer, Gower, Skelton, Wyat, Howard (Earl of Surrey), Gascoigne. 4, Davies, Donne, Hall, Alexander (Earl of Stirling), Corbet, Carew. 6, Cowley, Waller, Denham. 7, 8, Milton. 9, 10, Butler. 10. Wilmot (Earl of Rochester), Dillon (Earl of Roscommon), Otway, Pomfret. 11, 12, Dryden. 14, Addison, Garth, Hughes, Sheffield, Congreve, Fenton, Pattison. 15, Prior, Blackmore. 16, Gay. 17, Tickell, Granville (Baron Lansdowne), Yalden, Green, Hammond, Somerville. 19, Savage, Dyer. 21, Pope, Blair, Pitt. 22, Thomson. 23, Watts, Collins, E. Moore. 24, Shenstone, Cawthorn. 25, 26, Young. 26, Dodsley, Mallett, Ramsay. 27, Churchill, Falconer, Grainger. 28, Akenside, Cooper, Thompson. 29, Gray, Chatterton, Harte. 30, Goldsmith, Langhorne, Smart. 31, Johnson, Armstrong, Shaw, Lyttelton, Boyse. 32, Beattie, J. Scott, Cunningham, Jenyns. 33, Glover, Smollett. 34, Mickle, J. and T. Warton. 35, W. Jones, Blacklock, N. Cotton. 36, 37, Cowper. 37, Lloyd, Fergusson, Richardson, Blackstone, Jago, Whitehead, Logan, Craggs, Bishop, Bampfylde, Russell, Lovell, Lovibond, Bruce, Roberts, Porteus, Glynn. 38, 39, Burns. 39, Macneill. 40, 41, Pope's Homer's Iliad. 44, Mitchell's Aristophanes, Colman's Terence, Gifford's Persius. 48, 49, Hunt's Tasso. 50, Potter's Æschylus and Euripides, Francklin's Sophocles.

Sansom, J. Sketches of Lower Canada. N. Y., 1817. 12°. . . 16775
Travels in Lower Canada. Lond., 1820. 8°. 8053

Sansovino, F. Novels. (Ital. Novelists, v. 3.) Lond., 1836. 12°. . 1901
Santa Fe Exped., Narrative of the. Kendall. N. Y., 1844. 2 v. 12°. 16903
Saracen, The Lands of the. Bayard Taylor. N. Y., 1855. 12°. . 8282
Saracens, Hist. of [A. D. 600–750]. Ockley. Lond., 1847. 8°. . . 423
Hist. and Conquests of the. Freeman. Oxf'd., 1870. 16°. . 6341
See, also, ARABS ; SPAIN.
Saranacs, Summer in the. Street. N. Y., 1865. 12°. 16838
Saratoga; a Tale. Bost., 1824. 2 v. 12°. 15573
Sargent, E. Arctic Adventure. Bost., 1857. 12°. 8294
Life of Clay. Ed. by Greeley. Auburn, 1852. 12°. . . . 7326
Peculiar. N. Y., 1866. 12°. 2917
Planchette, the Despair of Science. (2 copies.) Bost., 1869. 16°. 8484
The Woman who dared. Bost., 1870. 12°. 794
Sargent, J. Memoir of H. Martyn. Bost., 1831. 12°. . . . 7565
Sargent, L. M. Hubert and Ellen, with other Poems. Bost., 1813. 8°. 15062
Sargent, W. Life of André. Bost., 1861. 12°. 7307
Sarrans, B. Memoirs of Lafayette and the Revol. of 1830. Lond., 1832. 2 v. 8°. 7724
Sartor Resartus. Carlyle. Lond., 1870. 8°. 4020
Sass, H. Journey to Rome and Naples. N. Y., 1818. 8°. . . 16719
Satanstoe. Cooper. N. Y., 1855. 12°. 2821
Saturday Evening. Taylor. N. Y., 1832. 12°. 9532
Saumarez, J. de *(Lord)*, Memoirs of. Ross. Lond., 1838. 2 v. 8°. 16386
Saunders, J. Pictures of English Life from Chaucer. Lond., 1845. 24°. 44
Saunders, L. Letters. Lond. 12°. 9483
Saunterings. Warner. Bost., 1872. 12°. 8166
Saurin, J. Sermons, ed. Burder. Princeton, 1827. 2 v. 8°. . . 10041
The same. Balt., 1832. 2 v. 8°. 10043
Sauzay, A. Wonders of Glass-Making. N. Y., 1870. 12°. . . 10126
[**Savage, M. W.**] The Bachelor of the Albany. N. Y., 1848. 12°. . 15374
Savage, R. Poetical Works. Lond. 12°. 14844
The same. Ed. Bell. Lond., 1807. 24°. 533
The same. Ed. Johnson. Dubl., 1804. 8°. . . . 15099
The same. Ed. Walsh. Philad., 1819. 24°. 14
Savage, T. *(Pseudonym.)* The Amazonian Republic. N. Y., 1842. 12°. 17091
Savary, C. Letters on Egypt. Dubl., 1787. 2 v. 8°. . . . 16485
on Greece. Dubl., 1788. 8°. 16628
Savonarola, G., Essay on. Milman. Lond., 1870. 8°. . . . 3435
Hist. of. Villari. Lond., 1863. 2 v. 8°. 7595
Memoirs of. Harford. Lond., 1858. 8°. 7989
Say, J. B. Treatise on Polit. Economy. Philad., 1836. 8°. . . 8652
The same. Bost., 1824. 2 v. in 1. 8°. 8653
Say and Seal. Warner. Philad., 1860. 2 v. 12°. 3005
Saxe, J. G. Fables and Legends, in Rhyme. Bost., 1872. 16°. . 754
The Masquerade and other Poems. (2 copies.) Bost., 1866. 12°. 752
Poems. 3d ed. Bost., 1851. 16°. 749
The same. 19th ed. Bost., 1861. 12°. 750
The same. New ed. Bost., 1868. 12°. 751
Saxe-Weimar Eisenach, B., Duke of. Travels through N. Amer. Philad., 1828. 2 v. in 1. 8°. 16924

Saxony, Life and Manners in. Mayhew. Lond., 1864. 2 v. 8°. . 8313
Scampavias. [Wise.] N. Y., 1857. 12°. 16922
Scandal, Cure for. Opie. Bost., 1839. 12°. 14922
Scanderbeg. See G. CASTRIOT.
Scandinavia, Antiquities of. Mallet. Lond., 1859. 8°. 507
Hist. of, to 1814. Dunham. Lond., 1839–40. 3 v. 16°. . . 5468
to 1837. Crichton and Wheaton. N. Y., 1841. 2 v. 12°. 11611
[to 1852.] Sinding. N. Y., 1858. 12°. 5817
Journey through. [Inglis.] Edinb., 1829. 12°. 4500
Mythology of. Pigott. Lond., 1839. 8°. 1919
Tales from. Keary. Lond., 1871. 12°. 1700
Travels in, 1799. Clarke. Lond., 1824. 3 v. 8°. 8028
See, also, DENMARK ; SWEDEN ; NORWAY ; EDDAS.
Scarlet Letter, The. Hawthorne. Bost., 1866. 16°. 2886
Schaff, P. The Christ of the Gospels. N. Y., 1869. 16°. 9896
Germany ; its Universities, Theology, and Religion. Philad., 1857. 12°. 9252
Schefer, L. The Artist's Married Life. N. Y., 1862. 16°. . . . 7878
Schele de Vere, M. Americanisms. N. Y., 1872. 12°. 182
Studies in English. (2 copies.) N. Y., 1867. 12°. 99
Wonders of the Deep. (2 copies.) N. Y., 1869. 12°. . . 16949
Schellen, H. Spectrum Analysis. N. Y., 1872. 8°. 9098
Schiller, J. C. F. v. Aesthetic Letters and Essays, and Philosophical Letters. Ed. Weiss. Bost., 1845. 16°. 8847
Correspondence with Goethe. N. Y., 1845. v. 1. 12°. . . 7827
Don Carlos, transl. by Thompson. Lond., 1811. 12°. . . . 1357
Hist. of Revolt of the Netherlands. (2 copies.) N. Y., 1847. 12°. 5809
of Thirty Years War. Transl. by Morrison. N. Y., 1846. 16°. 5808
The same. Transl. by Moir. Edinb., 1828. 2 v. 12°. . 4480
The same. 4508
Maid of Orleans, transl. by Bethune. Lond., 1848. 8°. . . 921
The Piccolomini, and Death of Wallenstein, tr. by Coleridge. [Works, v. 3.] Lond., 1829. 16°. 850
Poems and Ballads, tr. by Bulwer. N. Y., 1844. 12°. . . 861
The Robbers, transl. by Thompson. Lond., 1811. 12°. . . 1360
Sämmtliche Werke. (2 copies.) Stuttg. und Tüb., 1840. 8°. . 9736
The same. Stuttg. und Tüb., 1838. 12 Bde. 16°. . . 9464
Select Minor Poems, transl. by Dwight. (2 copies.) Bost., 1839. 12°. 859
Tales. (German Novelists, v. 3.) Lond., 1826. 12°. . . . 1897
Wallenstein's Camp. Transl. by Moir. Bost., 1837. 16°. . 1437
Works. (Bohn's ed.) Lond., 1846–67. 4 v. 8°. (2 copies of v. 1 ; 3 copies of v. 3, 4.) 435

CONTENTS.—1, Thirty Years' War. 1, 2, Revolt of the Netherlands. 2, Wallenstein ; Piccolomini ; W. Tell. 3, Don Carlos ; Mary Stuart ; Maid of Orleans ; Bride of Messina. 4, Robbers ; Fiesco ; Love and Intrigue ; Demetrius ; Ghost-Seer ; Sport of Destiny.

Life of. Carlyle. Lond., 1869. 8°. 4024
SchimmelPenninck, M. A. Memoirs of Port Royal, etc. 5th ed. Lond., 1858. 3 v. 8°. 6328
Life of. Hankin. Lond., 1858. 2 v. 8°. 7051

Schlegel, A. W. v. Lectures on Dramatic Art and Literature. Transl. by Black. Philad., 1833. 8°. 1656
The same. Revised by Morrison. (2 copies.) Lond., 1846. 8°. 429
Schlegel, F. C. W. v. Æsthetic and Misc. Works. (2 copies.) Lond., 1849. 8°. 431
Lectures on Hist. of Literature. Philad., 1818. 2 v. 8°. . 147
The same. 2 v. in 1. 8°. 149
Lectures on Modern Hist. (Bohn's ed.) Lond., 1849. 8°. . 433
Philosophy of History. Lond., 1835. 2 v. 8°. . . . 4100
The same. N. Y., 1841. 2 v. 12°. 4055
Philosophy of Life, and of Language. (Bohn's ed.) Lond., 1847. 8°. 434
Schleiermacher, F. E. D., Life of; in Autobiography and Letters. Lond., 1860. 2 v. 8°. 7768
Schlemihl's (Peter). Wundersame Geschichte. v. Chamisso. Hamb. 12°. 9615
Schlosser, F. C. Hist. of 18th Century. Lond., 1843–45. 6 v. 8°. . 4798
Schmid, H. The Habermeister. N. Y., 1869. 16°. 2706
Schmidt, H. I. Hist. of Education, etc. N. Y., 1844. 12°. . . 11758
Schmitz, L. Hist. of Rome. N. Y., 1847. 12°. 4724
Schönberg-Cotta Family. [Charles.] Lond., 1868. 8°. . . . 2463
Scholz, J. M. A. Travels in Egypt and Lybia. Lond., 1822. 8°. . 8058
Schoolcraft, H. R. Algic Researches. N. Y., 1839. 2 v. 12°. . . 5755
Journal of Tour in Missouri. Lond., 1821. 8°. . . . 8054
School Fund, The Bible and the. Clark. Bost., 1870. 16°. . . 9147
School-Keeping, Lectures on. Hall. Bost., 1830. 12°. . . . 17040
School Master, Confessions of a. Alcott. Andover, 1839. 12°. . 17041
Schools. Beard and Long. Lond., 1842. 12°. 9107
of England, The Great. Staunton. Lond., 1865. 8°. . . 9247
Public, Right of the Bible in our. Cheever. N. Y., 1854. 12°. 9146
School-Teacher, The. Abbott. Bost., 1834. 12°. 17039
Schroeder, F. L. The Ensign. (German Theatre, v. 6.) Lond., 1811. 12°. 1361
Schubert, F., Life of. v. Hellborn. Lond., 1869. 2 v. 8°. . . 7920
Schwartz, M. S. Birth and Education. Bost., 1871. 8°. . . . 3097
Gold and Name. Bost., 1871. 8°. 3096
Guilt and Innocence. Bost., 1871. 8°. 3098
Wife of a Vain Man. Bost., 1871. 8°. 3095
Science, Elements of Hist. of, to 1700. T. Morell. Lond., 1827. 8°. 8720
Fragments of. Tyndall. N. Y., 1871. 12°. 8908
for Leisure Hours. Proctor. N. Y., 1871. 12°. . . . 8897
Martyrs of. Brewster. N. Y., 1841. 12°. 11605
Poetry of. Hunt. Bost., 1850. 12°. 16993
Recent Discussions in. H. Spencer. N. Y., 1871. 12°. . . 8602
and Revealed Religion, Connexion of. Wiseman. Andover, 1837. 8°. 10036
Sciences, Inductive, Hist. of. Whewell. Lond., 1837. 3 v. 8°. . 8745
Philos. of. Whewell. Lond., 1840. 2 v. 8°. . 8751
Physical, Connection of. Somerville. N. Y., 1846. 16°. . 8843
Hist of. Powell. Lond., 1837. 16°. 6049

Scientific Lexicon. McMurtrie. Philad., 1847. 12°. 16936
Subjects, Familiar Lectures on. Herschel. Lond., 1869. 8°. . 8898
Scipio Africanus, Life of. Séran de la Tour. Lond., 1787. 2 v. 8°. 16018
Scotch Reform, Letters on. Bentham. (Works, pt. 5.) Edinb., 1838. 8°. 9704
Scotland, The Genius of. Turnbull. N. Y., 1847. 12°. . . . 3207
Highlanders of. Skene. Lond., 1837. 2 v. 12°. . . . 5279
Hist. of [to 1603.] W. Scott. Lond., 1836–37. 2 v. 16°. . 5182
[to 1746.] Guthrie. Lond., 1767–68. 10 v. 8°. . . 5394
[to 1825.] Buchanan and Watkins. Lond. 2 v. 8°. . 5406
1542–1603. Robertson. Philad., 1811. 2 v. 8°. . 5404
1689–1748. Burton. Lond., 1853. 2 v. 8°. . . 5408
of Civilization in. Buckle. N. Y., 1866. 8°. . . . 5068
of Rebellion of, 1745. Home. (Works, 2, 3.) Edinb., 1822. 8°. 17515
of Rebellions in, 1638–60. Chambers. Edinb., 1828. 2 v. 12°. 4493
of Rebellions in, 1689 and 1715. Chambers. Edinb., 1829. 12°. 4504
of Rebellions in, 1745–46. Chambers. Edinb., 1869. 8°. 5278
of Reformation in. Knox. Glasg., 1832. 8°. 6478
Lives of Queens of. Strickland. N. Y., 1851–59. 7 v. 12°. . 5199
For Contents, see STRICKLAND.
Popular Rhymes of. Chambers. Edinb., 1870. 8°. . . . 1095
Scenes and Legends of North of. Miller. Cincinn., 1852. 12°. 2586
and the Scotch. Sinclair. N. Y., 1840. 12°. 16741
A Summer (1847) in. Abbott. N. Y., 1848. 12°. . . . 16742
Tales of a Grandfather from Hist. of. W. Scott. Philad., 1851. 3 v. 16°. 1709
Tour through, in 1807. J. Carr. Philad., 1809. 8°. . . 16739
Traditions of Covenanters of. Simpson. Edinb. 16°. . . 4813
Travels in. Necker de Saussure. (Voyages, v. 6.) Lond., 1821. 8°. 8056
Scotsmen, Biogr. Dict. of Eminent. Chambers. Glasg., 1835. 4 v. 8°. 6862
Scott, John. Select Poems. Ed. Walsh. Philad., 1822. 24°. . . 26
Scott, John, (*Lord* Eldon) Life of. Campbell. Lond., 1847. 8°. . 6872
Scott, John. Luther, and the Lutheran Reformation. N. Y., 1833. 2 v. 12°. 6349
Scott, Jonathan M. Blue Lights. N. Y., 1817. 24°. 14949
The Sorceress. N. Y., 1817. 12°. 14950
Scott, Julia H. Poems. Bost., 1843. 12°. 14951
[**Scott, M.**] Tom Cringle's Log. Philad., 1834. 3 v. 12°. . . 15605
[**Scott, S.**] Life of T. A. d'Aubigné. Lond., 1772. 8°. . . . 7646
Scott, T. Bible with Notes. N. Y., 1832. 3 v. 8°. 17330
The Force of Truth. N. Y., 1825. 12°. 17289
Life of. J. Scott. Bost., 1822. 12°. 7564
Scott, Sir Walter. The Abbot. Philad., 1825. 2 v. 12°. . . . 1729
The same. (2 copies.) Bost., 1834–45. 2 v. in 1. 12°. . 1803
The same. Edinb., 1870. 8°. 1882
Anne of Geierstein. (2 copies.) N. Y. and Philad., 1829. 2 v. 12°. 1772

Scott, Sir Walter. Anne of Geierstein. (3 copies.) Bost., 1834-45. 12°. 1836
Antiquary. Bost., 1829-32. 2 v. 12°. 1723
The same. Bost., 1834. 2 v. in 1. 12°. 1790
The same. (4 copies.) Edinb., 1870. 8°. 1862
Autobiography. (2 copies.) Philad., 1831. 12°. . . . 6976
Ballads and Lyrical Pieces. Bost., 1807. 12°. 14858
The Betrothed. Edinb., 1871. 8°. 1888
Black Dwarf. (2 copies.) Edinb., 1870. 8°. 1870
Chronicles of the Canongate. 1st Series. (3 copies.) Philad., 1827. 2 v. 12°. 1752

CONTENTS.—1, Highland Widow; Two Drovers. 2, Surgeon's Daughter.

The same. (4 copies.) Bost., 1834-45. 2 v. in 1. 12°. . 1830
(Including, also, My Aunt Margaret's Mirror; Tapestried Chamber; Laird's Jock.)
The same. Edinb., 1871. 2 v. 8°. 1889
Chronicles of the Canongate. 2d Series. (3 copies.) N. Y. and Philad., 1828. 2 v. 12°. 1758

CONTENTS.—St. Valentine's Day, or, the Fair Maid of Perth.

The same. (2 copies.) Bost., 1834-45. 2 v. in 1. 12°. . 1834
Critical and Miscellaneous Essays. Philad., 1841. 3 v. 12°. 3199
The same. 3289
Doom of Devorgoil; and Auchindrane. (2 copies.) N. Y., 1830. 12°. 1438
Fortunes of Nigel. (4 copies.) Bost., 1834-45. 2 v. in 1. 12°. 1807
Guy Mannering. Philad., 1826. 2 v. 12°. 1721
The same. (3 copies.) Bost., 1845. 2 v. in 1. 12°. . 1787
The same. (2 copies.) Edinb., 1871. 8°. . . . 1860
Heart of Mid-Lothian. (2 copies.) Edinb., 1870. 8°. . . 1872
Hist. of Scotland. (2 copies.) Lond., 1835-37. 2 v. 16°. . 5182
The same. Philad., 1835. 2 v. 12°. 6065
Ivanhoe. Bost., 1855. 2 v. in 1. 12°. 1799
The same. Bost., 1861. 8°. 1857
The same. (4 copies.) Edinb., 1871. 8°. 1877
The same. Philad., 1820. 2 v. 12°. 15464
Kenilworth. (4 copies.) Edinb., 1870. 8°. 1883
Legend of Montrose. (2 copies.) Edinb., 1870. 8°. . . 1870
Letters on Demonology and Witchcraft. N. Y., 1839. 12°. . 11011
The same. (2 copies.) N. Y., 1830-32. 12°. . . . 11939
Life of Napoleon. (2 copies.) Philad., 1827. 3 v. 8°. . . 5605
The same. N. Lond., 1834. 3 v. 8°. 5611
Lives of the Novelists. Philad., 1825. 2 v. 12°. . . . 6712
Marmion. Bost., 1810. 12°. 950
Minstrelsy of the Scottish Border. (2 copies.) Lond., 1839. 8°. 1309
Miscellaneous Prose Works. (2 copies.) Bost., 1829. v. 1-5. 12°. 3188

CONTENTS.—1, Life of Dryden. 2, Life of Swift. 3, Lives of Novelists. 4, Biographical Memoirs. 5, Paul's Letters to his Kinsfolk; Abstract of the Eyrbiggia-Saga.

Monastery. Philad., 1827. 2 v. 12°. 1727
The same. (3 copies.) Bost., 1834-45. 2 v. in 1. 12°. . 1800
The same. Edinb., 1870. 8°. 1881

Scott, Sir Walter. Moredun. [Not by this author.] N. Y., 1855. 8°. 2309
Old Mortality. (2 copies.) Edinb., 1870. 8°. 1868
Paul's Letters to his Kinsfolk. 4th ed. Edinb., 1817. 8°. . 16697
Peveril of the Peak. Philad., 1826. 3 v. 12°. 1733
The same. (3 copies.) Bost., 1834–45. 2 v. in 1. 12°. . 1811
Pirate. N. Y., 1822. 2 v. 12°. 1731
The same. (2 copies.) Bost., 1834–45. 2 v. in 1. 12°. . 1805
The same. Edinb., 1871. 8°. 1887
Poetical Works. Philad. 8°. 1240
The same. Balt. and N. Y., 1812–15. v. 1, 2, 5, 6. 24°. . 548

CONTENTS.—1, Vision of Don Roderick; Ballads; Lyrics. 2, Lay of the Last Minstrel. 5, Rokeby. 6, Lord of the Isles.

The same. Bost., 1871. 9 v. 16°. 1071

CONTENTS.—1, Memoir; Lay of Last Minstrel. 2, Marmion. 3, Lady of the Lake. 4, Rokeby; Vision of Don Roderick. 5, Lord of the Isles. 6, Ballads, ancient and translated; Songs. 7, Miscellaneous. 8, Bridal of Triermain; Harold the Dauntless; Waterloo; Halidon Hill; Mac Duff's Cross. 9, Doom of Devorgoil; Auchindrane; House of Aspen; Goetz of Berlichingen.

Quentin Durward. (2 copies.) N. Y. and Philad., 1823. 2 v. 12°. 1736
The same. (4 copies.) Bost., 1834–45. 2 v. in 1. 12°. . 1814
Redgauntlet. Philad., 1827. 2 v. 12°. 1748
The same. (4 copies.) Bost., 1834–45. 2 v. in 1. 12°. . 1821
Religious Discourses. By a Layman. N. Y., 1828. 12°. . 9809
Rob Roy. Bost., 1832. 2 v. 12°. 1725
The same. (2 copies.) Bost., 1845. 2 v. in 1. 12°. . 1791
The same. (2 copies.) Edinb., 1870. 8°. . . . 1866
St. Ronan's Well. (4 copies.) Philad., 1824–27. 2 v. 12°. . 1740
The same. (3 copies.) Bost., 1834–45. 2 v. in 1. 12°. . 1818
Tales of Crusaders. Bost., 1825. 2 v. 12°. 1750

CONTENTS.—1, The Betrothed. 2, The Talisman.

The same. N. Y., 1825. 2 v. 12°. 1764
The same. Bost., 1845. 2 v. in 1. 12°. 1825
Tales of a Grandfather. Complete in 4 Series. Philad., 1851. 8 v. in 4. 16°. 1709
The same. (2 copies.) Bost., 1834–45. 7 v. in 4. 12°. . 1845
The same. 1st Series. (2 copies.) Philad., 1828. 2 v. 24°. 1713
The same. 2d Series. (2 copies.) Bost., 1834–45. 2 v. in 1. 12°. 1849
The same. 3d Series. (2 copies.) Bost., 1834–45. 2 v. in 1. 12°. 1851
The same. 4th Series. (2 copies.) Bost., 1834–45. 2 v. in 1. 12°. 1853
Tales of My Landlord. 1st Series. (2 copies.) Bost., 1839–45. 2 v. in 1. 12°. 1793

CONTENTS.—Black Dwarf; Old Mortality.

The same. 2d Series. (2 copies.) Bost., 1834–45. 2 v. in 1. 12°. 1795

CONTENTS.—Heart of Mid-Lothian.

The same. 3d Series. (2 copies.) Bost., 1834–45. 2 v. in 1. 12°. 1797

CONTENTS.—Bride of Lammermoor; Legend of Montrose.

Scott, Sir Walter. Tales of My Landlord. Bride of Lammermoor.
N. Y., 1850. 8°. 1993
The same. (2 copies.) Edinb., 1870. 8°. 1875
The same. 4th Series. N. Y., 1832. 3 v. in 1. 12°. . 1776
CONTENTS.—1, Castle Dangerous. 2, 3, Count Robert of Paris.
The same. (3 copies.) Philad., 1832. 3 v. 12°. . . 1777
The same. (2 copies.) Bost., 1834–45. 3 v. in 2. 12°. . 1839
CONTENTS.—1, Count Robert of Paris; 2, Castle Dangerous.
Talisman. (2 copies.) Edinb., 1871. 8°. 1889
Waverley. (2 copies.) Edinb., 1870. 8°. 1858
The same. (2 copies.) Philad., 1821–25. 2 v. 12°. . 1717
The same. Bost., 1845. 2 v. in 1. 12°. 1786
The same. Paris, 1830. 8°. 1855
The same. Exeter, 1831. 8°. 1856
Waverley Novels. Philad., 1839. v. 3, 4. 8°. 1994
CONTENTS.—3, Kenilworth (imperfect); Pirate (imperfect); Fortunes of Nigel; Peveril of the Peak; Quentin Durward. 4, St. Ronan's Well; Redgauntlet; Betrothed; Talisman; Woodstock.
Woodstock. (3 copies.) N. Y. and Philad., 1826. 2 v. 12°. . 1766
The same. (4 copies.) Bost., 1834–45. 2 v. in 1. 12°. . 1826
Familiar Anecdotes of. Hogg. N. Y., 1834. 12°. . . . 6921
Life of. G. Allan. Philad., 1835. 8°. 7174
The same. Cunningham. Bost., 1832. 12°. . . . 6923
The same. Gilfillan. Edinb., 1870. 16°. . . . 6975
Memoirs of. Lockhart. Bost. and Philad., 1837–38. 7 v. 12°. 6961
Scott, Wm. B. Albert Durer. Lond., 1869. 8°. 7956
Scott, Winfield. Autobiography. N. Y., 1864. 2 v. 12°. . . 7395
Life of. Mansfield. N. Y., 1848. 12°. 7394
Scottish Ballads. See BALLADS.
Border, Minstrelsy of. Scott. Lond., 1839. 8°. . . . 1309
Cavaliers, Lays of the. Aytoun. N. Y., 1866. 12°. . . 1097
Chiefs, The. A Romance. Porter. Philad., 1869. 12°. . . 15191
Gaël, The. Logan. Hartf'd., 1846. 8°. 5410
Life and Character, Reminiscences of. Ramsay. Bost., 1861. 12°. 5277
Minstrelsy: ancient and modern. Motherwell. Glasg., 1827. 8°. 942
Poetry, Selection of. Ritson. Lond., 1785. 16°. . . . 1096
Poets, Lives of. Lond., 1822. 3 v. in 4. 24°. 6609
Songs. Chambers. Edinb., 1829. 2 v. 12°. . . . , . 956
Writers, Lives of. Irving. Edinb., 1839. 2 v. in 1. 12°. . 6714
Scouring of the White Horse. Hughes. Bost., 1859. 12°. . . 2444
[Scoville, J. A.] Old Merchants of N. Y. N. Y., 1863. 2 v. 12°. . 7415
Scrap Table, The. Bost., 1830. 12°. 15774
Scriblerus, Martinus. See SWIFT's Works.
Scribner's Monthly. N. Y., 1870–72. 4 v. 8°. 13411
Scripture, Illustrations of. Hackett. Bost., 1860. 12°. . . . 9888
Lands. Kitto. Lond., 1850. 8°. 526
Readings. Chalmers. N. Y., 1848–49. 5 v. 12°. . . . 9522
Records, Hist. Evidences of the Truth of the. Rawlinson.
Bost., 1860. 12°. 9957

Scriptures, Canon of the. Gaussen. Bost. [1862.] 12°. 9885
Inspiration of the. Gaussen. N. Y., 1845. 12°. 9800
Style of the. Boyle. Lond., 1835. 16°. 9500
See, also, BIBLE.
Scriver, C. Gotthold's Emblems. Bost. [1859.] 12°. 3106
Scudder, D. C., Life and Letters of. H. E. Scudder. N. Y., 1864. 12°. 7641
Scudder, J., Memoir of. Waterbury. N. Y., 1870. 12°. 7640
Sculptors, Lives of. Vasari. Lond., 1850–52. 5 v. 8°. 474
Eminent British, Lives of. Cunningham. N. Y., 1839–40. 5 v. 12°. 11017
Sculpture, Hist. of. Memes. Bost., 1831. 12°. 8858
Lectures on. Ruskin. N. Y., 1872. 12°. 9048
See, also, ART.
Sea, The. Mudie. Lond., 1835. 12°. 14635
Bottom of the. Sonrel. N. Y., 1870. 12°. 10118
Lions, The. Cooper. N. Y., 1855. 12°. 2829
Physical Geography of the. Maury. N. Y., 1857. 8°. . . 9103
Shore, Wonders of the. Kingsley. Bost., 1855. 16°. . . . 8836
Sea-Side Studies. Lewes. Edinb., 1858. 8°. 9003
in Natural Hist. Agassiz. Bost., 1865. 8°. . . 9002
See, also, OCEAN.
Seaboard Parish, The. MacDonald. Lond., 1869. 8°. 2579
Seaborn, *Captain* **Adam.** *(Pseudonym.)* Symzonia. N. Y., 1820. 12°. 15792
Seafield, F. Literature of Dreams. Lond., 1865. 2 v. 8°. . . . 8528
Sealsfield, C. The Cabin Book, or Life in Texas; and North and South. N. Y., 1844. 8°. 15669
Life in the New World. N. Y., 1844. 8°. 15090
Seaman, E. C. Essays on Progress of Nations. N. Y., 1868. 2 v. 12°. 4603
Search for the Gral, The. Goddard. Lond. 16°. 2422
Searle, January. *(Pseudonym.)* See G. PHILIPS.
Sears, B. Life of Luther. Philad. [1850.] 8°. 6571
and others. Classical Studies. (4 copies.) Bost., 1843–49. 12°. 9259
Sears, R. Bible Biography. N. Y., 1842. 8°. 17511
Hist. of the Bible. N. Y., 1845. 8°. 10011
Seasons, Book of the. Howitt. Lond., 1840. 16°. 8797
Chronicles of the. Lond., 1844. v. 1–3. 12°. 4350
Religious Lectures on the. Hitchcock. Bost., 1861. 12°. . 16994
Sacred Philosophy of the. Duncan. Bost., 1839. 4 v. 12°. . 16995
Seaton, W. W., Biogr. Sketch of. Bost., 1871. 12°. 7389
Seatsfield. See SEALSFIELD.
Seaward, *Sir* **Edward.** *(Pseudonym.)* See Jane PORTER.
Secession. See U. S. History.
Secret Foe, The. Pickering. Philad., 1845. 8°. 15577
Sects of Christendom, Book of the. Lond., 1837. 16°. 6352
Christian, in 19th century. Philad., 1846. 12°. 8498
Religious, Compendium of. Adams. Bost., 1784. 8°. . . 16465
Pictorial View of. Goodrich. Hartf'd., 1851. 12°. 6298
Sedgwick, C. M. Clarence. Lond., 1830. 3 v. 16°. 15310
The same. N. Y., 1849. 12°. 15313

Sedgwick, C. M. Hope Leslie. N. Y., 1827. 2 v. 12°. 15314
Letters from Abroad. N. Y., 1841. 2 v. 12°. 16552
Live and Let Live. N. Y., 1837. 12°. 15316
Memoir of L. M. Davidson. (Sparks, v. 7.) Bost., 1837. 16°. 7256
Redwood. N. Y., 1824. 2 v. 12°. 15317
The same. N. Y., 1850. 12°. 15319
Tales and Sketches. Philad., 1835. 12°. 15309
[**Sedgwick, S. L.**] Allen Prescott. N. Y., 1834. 2 v. 12°. . . . 15654
Sedgwick, T. Memoir of W. Livingston. N. Y., 1833. 8°. . . . 7456
Public and Private Economy. N. Y., 1836–39. 3 v. 12°. . 8644
Seed-Time and Harvest. Reuter. Philad., 1871. 8°. 10299
Seeley, J. R. Ecce Homo. (3 copies.) Bost., 1866–67. 16°. . . 9902
Lectures and Essays. Lond., 1870. 8°. 3437
Roman Imperialism, etc. Bost., 1871. 16°. 3739
Seer, The. L. Hunt. Bost., 1865. 2 v. 16°. 3168
Ségur, L. P. de. Hist. of Reign of Fred. Wm. II.; and a Political Picture of Europe, 1786–96. Lond., 1801. 3 v. 8°. . . 5880
Memoirs and Recollections. Bost., 1825. 8°. 7647
Ségur, P. P. de. Hist. of Exped. to Russia. Philad., 1825. 8°. . 16252
The same. N. Y., 1845. 2 v. 12°. 11616
Hist. of Peter the Great. Philad., 1833. 8°. 15356
Selborne, Natural Hist. of. White. Lond., 1851. 8°. 525
Selden, J. Judicature in Parliaments. Lond. [1681.] 16°. . . . 5150
Table-Talk. Ed. Young. Cambr., 1831. 12°. 3905
The same. 3912
The same, ed. Arber. Lond., 1868. 16°. 3886
Life of. Aikin. Lond., 1812. 8°. 7116
Memoirs of. Johnson. Lond., 1835. 8°. 7212
Select Journal of Foreign Period. Literature. Bost., 1833–34. 4 v. 8°. 14231
Selection, Natural, Contributions to the Theory of. Wallace. Lond., 1871. 8°. 8838
Origin of Species by. Darwin. N. Y., 1871. 12°. . . . 8929
Self-Education. De Gérando. Bost., 1830. 8°. 17052
Self-Help. Smiles. Bost., 1861. 12°. 3702
Self-Knowledge, Treatise on. Mason. Hartf'd., 1842. 8°. . . . 3472
Semmes, R. Service Afloat and Ashore. Cincinn., 1851. 8°. . . 5825
Seneca. Morals, transl. by L'Estrange. Lond., 1793. 12°. . . . 15974
The same. Hartf'd., 1807. 12°. 4236
Senegal and Gambia, Travels in, 1818. Mollien. Lond., 1820. 8°. . 8053
Senior, N. W. Journal in Turkey and Greece. Lond., 1859. 8°. . 8243
Journals in France and Italy, 1848–52. Lond., 1871. 2 v. 8°. 8331
Journals, etc., relating to Ireland. 2d ed. Lond., 1868. 2 v. 8°. 5245
Sense and Sensibility. Austen. Philad., 1838. 8°. 2662
Sentimental Idler, Letters of a. Leach. N. Y., 1869. 12°. . . . 16280
Journey. Sterne. Philad., 1864. 8°. 1990
Sephardim; or, the Jews in Spain and Portugal. Finn. Lond., 1841. 12°. 6300
Septimius Felton. Hawthorne. Bost., 1872. 16°. 2898
Séran de la Tour. Life of Scipio Africanus and of Epaminondas. Lond., 1787. 2 v. 8°. 16018

Sergeant, J. Select Speeches. Philad., 1832. 8°. 9377

Serle, T. J. Joan of Arc. Lond., 1841. 3 v. 12°. 15474

Sermini, G. Novels. (Ital. Novelists, v. 2.) Lond., 1836. 12°. 1900

Sermons on the Holy Spirit. For Whitsuntide. Ed. Cattermole. Lond., 1835. 16°. 9499

on the Resurrection, for Easter. Ed. Stebbing. Lond., 1835. 16°. 9498

on Retirement, etc., for Lent. Ed. Cattermole. Lond., 1835. 16°. 9497

Servia, Hist. of (to 1843). Ranke. Lond., 1853. 8°. 419

National Songs of. Owen Meredith. Lond., 1861. 16°. 1184

Residence and Travels in, 1842–44. Paton. Lond., 1845. 12°. 16590

Sesame and Lilies. Ruskin. N. Y., 1865. 12°. 213

Settle, E. Thalia Triumphans. Lond., 1716. fol.

Sévigné, M. de R.-C. de, and her Contemporaries. Philad., 1842. 2 v. 12°. 7657

Sewall, Jonathan M. Miscellaneous Poems. Portsmouth, 1801. 12°. 14952

Sewall, Jotham B. Evenings with the Bible and Science. Bost., 1864. 16°. 9827

Seward, A. Letters, 1784–1807. Edinb., 1811. 6 v. 8°. 6915

Memoirs of Dr. Darwin. Philad., 1804. 8°. 7147

Seward, Wm. Anecdotes. Lond., 1795–97. 5 v. 16°. 13202

Seward, Wm. H. Life of J. Q. Adams. Auburn, 1849. 12°. 7325

Works, ed. Baker. N. Y., 1853. 3 v. 8°. 9645

Sewel, W. Hist. of the Quakers. N. Y., 1844. 2 v. in 1. 8°. 6594

Sexagenarian, The. Beloe. Lond., 1818. 2 v. 8°. 3487

[**Seymour, A. C. H.**] Life and Times of Countess of Huntingdon. Lond., 1844. 2 v. 8°. 7678

Seymour, M. H. Morning among the Jesuits. N. Y., 1849. 12°. 9582

Sforzosi, —. Hist of Italy. N. Y., 1839. 12°. 11404

The same. N. Y., 1836. 12°. 12119

Shabby Genteel Story. Thackeray. Lond., 1872. 8°. 2194

Shaftesbury, *Lord.* See A. A. Cooper.

Shahcoolen, a Hindu Philosopher, Letters from. Bost., 1802. 12°. 15322

Shairp, J. C. Culture and Religion. (2 copies.) N. Y., 1871. 16°. 9819

Shakspeare, W. Dramatic Works. Photo-Lithographic Reproduction of the first folio ed. of 1623. Lond., 1866. fol.

The same. (2 copies.) Bost., 1839. v. 1–6. 8°. 1595

Contents.—1, Life; Tempest; Two Gentlemen of Verona; Merry Wives; Twelfth Night; Measure for Measure; Much Ado about Nothing. 2, Midsummer-Night's Dream; Love's Labor's Lost; Merchant of Venice; As you Like it; All's Well that Ends Well; Taming of Shrew. 3, Winter's Tale; Comedy of Errors; Macbeth; John; Richard II.; Henry IV., pt. 1. 4, Henry IV., pt. 2; Henry V.; Henry VI. 5, Richard III.; Henry VIII.; Troilus and Cressida; Timon of Athens; Coriolanus. 6, Julius Cæsar; Ant. and Cleopatra; Cymbeline; Titus Andronicus; Pericles.

Merchant of Venice, Tempest, Henry VIII., Julius Cæsar, ed. Rolfe. N. Y., 1872. 16°. 1389

Plays. Philad., 1830. v. 1–7. 16°. 13339

Plays, ed. Reed. Philad., 1809. 17 v. 12°. 15252

The same. Lond., 1809. v. 1–11. 12°. 1367

Poems. Lond., 1774. 12°. 14859

Poems. Lond., 1841. 8°. 1562

Romeo and Juliet. Variorum, ed. by Furness. Philad., 1871. 8°. 1659

Sonnets, interpreted by Massey. Lond., 1866. 8°. 1636

Shakspeare, W. Works, ed. Dyce. 2d ed. Lond., 1866–67. 9 v. 8°. 1563

CONTENTS.—1, Life; Tempest; Two Gentlemen of Verona; Merry Wives; Measure for Measure. 2, Comedy of Errors; Much Ado about Nothing; Love's Labour's Lost; Midsummer Night's Dream; Merchant of Venice. 3, As you Like it; Taming of Shrew; All's Well that Ends Well; Twelfth-Night; Winter's Tale. 4, John; Richard II.; Henry IV.; Henry V. 5, Henry VI.; Richard III.; Henry VIII. 6, Troilus and Cressida; Coriolanus; Titus Andronicus; Romeo and Juliet; Timon of Athens; Julius Cæsar. 7, Macbeth; Hamlet; Lear; Othello; Ant. and Cleopatra; Cymbeline. 8, Pericles; Two Noble Kinsmen; Poems. 9, Glossary.

Works. Ed. Hudson. Bost., 1851–59. v. 1, 3–11. 12°. . . 1379

CONTENTS.—1, Tempest; Two Gentlemen of Verona; Merry Wives; Twelfth Night. 3, Merchant of Venice; As you Like it; All's Well that Ends Well; Taming of Shrew. 4, Winter's Tale; Comedy of Errors; Macbeth; John. 5, Richard II.; Henry IV.; Henry V. 6, Henry VI. 7, Richard III.; Henry VIII.; Troilus and Cressida. 8, Timon of Athens; Coriolanus; Julius Cæsar; Ant. and Cleopatra. 9, Cymbeline; Titus Andronicus; Pericles; Lear. 10, Romeo and Juliet; Hamlet; Othello. 11, Life; Hist. of Drama; Poems.

Works, ed. Reed. Bost., 1810–12. 9 v. 12°. , ... 14448

Works, ed. White. Bost., 1859–65. 12 v. 8°. 1531

CONTENTS.—1, Life; Essays; Poems. 2, Tempest; Two Gentlemen of Verona; Merry Wives. 3, Measure for Measure; Comedy of Errors; Much Ado about Nothing; Love's Labour's Lost. 4, Midsummer Night's Dream; Merchant of Venice; As you Like it; Taming of Shrew. 5, All's Well that Ends Well; Twelfth Night; Winter's Tale. 6, John; Richard II.; Henry IV. 7, Henry V.; Henry VI. pts. 1, 2. 8, Henry VI., pt. 3; Richard III.; Henry VIII. 9, Troilus and Cressida; Coriolanus; Titus Andronicus. 10, Romeo and Juliet; Timon of Athens; Julius Cæsar; Macbeth. 11, Hamlet; Lear; Othello. 12, Ant. and Cleopatra; Cymbeline; Pericles; Index.

Beauties of, ed. Dodd. Philad., 1830. 24°. 1378

Characteristics of Women of. Jameson. Bost., 1866. 16°. . 1487

Characters of. Hazlitt. Bost., 1818. 12°. 1485

Commentaries. Gervinus. Lond., 1863. 2 v. 8°. 1580

on Historical Plays of. Courtenay. Lond., 1840. 2 v. 12°. 1545

Comments on [Reed's] ed. of. Mason. Lond., 1785. 8°. . 1589

Concordance to. Clarke. Bost. 8° 1658

Delineations of Insanity, Imbecility, and Suicide by. Kellogg. N. Y., 1866. 16°. 1482

Essay on. De Quincey. Bost., 1850. 16°. 3313

The same. [Montagu.] Lond., 1769. 8°. 1590

Essay on Learning of. Farmer. Cambr., 1767. 16°. . . 1483

Exam. of, before Sir T. Lucy. [Landor.] Lond., 1834. 16°. . 1492

Heroines of Stories of. M. C. Clarke. N. Y., 1868. 12°. . 1493

Hist. and Tragic Poetry as illustrated by. Reed. Philad., 1857. 16°. 1478

Human Life in. Giles. Bost., 1868. 16°. 1480

Illustrated. Lennox, ed. Noah. Philad., 1809. v. 1. 8°. . 1591

Illustrations of. Boydell. N. Y., 1852. fol. . . . . .

[Introduction to.] Hugo. Lond., 1864. 8°. 1582

Lectures on. Hudson. N. Y., 1848. 2 v. 12°. . . . 1549

Life, Art, and Characters of. Hudson. Bost., 1872. 2 v. 12°. 1490

Life and Genius of. R. G. White. Bost., 1865. 16°. . . 1543

Memorials of. Ed. by Drake. Lond., 1828. 8°. . . . 1585

Midsummer Night's Dream, Introd. to. Halliwell. Lond., 1841. 8°. 1587

Notes and Emendations to. Collier. N. Y., 1853. 12°. . . 1554

and Lectures on. Coleridge. (Works, 4.) N. Y., 1871. 12°. 4016

on Plays and Actors of. Hackett. N. Y., 1863. 12°. . 1547

Novels. [Williams.] Lond., 1838. 9 v. 12°. 1637

CONTENTS.—Youth of Shakspeare, 3 v.; Shakspeare and his Friends, 3 v.; The Secret Passion, 3 v.

Shakspeare, W., Observations on. Davies. Lond., 1785. 3 v. 16°. 1494
Papers on. Maginn. N. Y., 1856. 12°. 1484
Proverbs. Clarke. Lond., 1848. 16°. 1366
Reasons for new ed. of. Collier. Lond., 1842. 8°. . . . 1553
Tale of Days of. Drake. Lond., 1824. 2 v. 16°. . . . 1488
Text of, vindicated from Collier's Notes. Singer. Lond., 1853. 8°. 1588
and his Times. Drake. Paris, 1838. 8°. 1583
Times and Contemporaries of. Tweddell. Lond., 1852. 16°. . 1365
Shakspearian Grammar. Abbott. Lond., 1871. 16°. 1477
Shaler, W. Sketches of Algiers. Bost., 1826. 8°. 16524
Sharpe, S. Hist. of Egypt. Lond., 1846. 8°. 4446
Sharpe's London Magazine. Lond., 1870. v. 36. 8°. . . . 17480
Shaw, C. Select Poems. Ed. Walsh. Philad., 1822. 24°. . . 25
Shaw, James. Sketches of the Austrian Netherlands. Lond., 1788. 8°. 16053
Shaw, John, Life of. Cooper. (Naval Biogr., v. 1.) Philad., 1846. 12°. 7275
Shaw, Thos. Travels. (Mavor, v. 12.) Lond., 1797. 12°. . . 13855
Shaw, Thos. B. Outlines of English Literature. Ed. Tuckerman. Philad., 1864. 12°. 141
Shedd, W. G. T. The Philosophy of History. Andover, 1856. 12°. 4584
Shee, M. A. Rhymes on Art. Philad., 1815. 12°. 14845
Life of. By his Son. Lond., 1860. 2 v. 8°. 8002
Sheffield, J. (Duke of Buckingham.) Poems. Ed. Johnson. Dubl., 1804. 8°. 15098
Select Poems. With Life, by Sanford. Philad., 1819. 24°. . 10
Sheil, R. L. Evadne; Damon and Pythias. Bost., 1824. 24°. . . 1352
Sketches of the Irish Bar. N. Y., 1858. 2 v. 12°. 6744
Speeches. With Memoir. Ed. MacNevin. Lond., 1845. 8°. . 9373
Sheldon, W. D. The "Twenty-Seventh." N. H., 1866. 8°. . . . 6110
Shelley, M. W. Falkner. N. Y., 1837. 12°. 15430
Frankenstein. Philad., 1833. 2 v. 12°. 2406
Lives of Literary and Scientific Men of France. Lond., 1838–39. 2 v. 16°. 5781

CONTENTS.—1, Montaigne; Rabelais; Corneille; Rochefoucauld; Moliere; La Fontaine; Pascal; Mme. de Sevigne; Boileau; Racine; Fenelon. 2, Voltaire; Rousseau; Condorcet; Mirabeau; Mme. Roland; De Stael.

and others. Lives of Eminent French Writers. (2 copies.) Philad., 1840. 2 v. 12°. 7615
Lives of Literary and Scientific Men of Italy, Spain, and Portugal. Lond., 1835–37. 3 v. 16°. 5783

CONTENTS.—1, Dante; Petrarch; Boccaccio; Lorenzo de' Medici, &c.; Bojardo; Berni; Ariosto; Machiavelli. 2, Galileo; Guicciardini; V. Colonna; Guarini; Tasso; Chiabrera; Tassoni; Marini; Filicaja; Metastasio; Goldoni; Alfieri; Monti; U. Foscolo. 3, Boscan; G. de la Vega; Mendoza; L. de Leon; Herrera; Ercilla; Cervantes; L. de Vega; Gongora; Quevedo; Calderon; Camoens, etc.

Lives of Eminent Literary and Scientific Men of Italy. Philad., 1841. 2 v. 12°. 7773
Shelley, P. B. Essays, Letters, etc. Philad., 1840. 2 v. 12°. . . 3351
Poetical Works. Philad. 8°. 1254
The same, ed. Mrs. Shelley. Lond., 1839. v. 2–4. 16°. 964
The same, ed. Rossetti. Lond., 1870. 2 v. 8°. . . 1113
Life of. Hogg. Lond., 1858. 2 v. 8°. 7001

Siamese Court, English Governess at the (1862–68). Leonowens. Bost., 1870. 12°. 8010
See, also, BURMAH.
Siberia, Tent-Life in, 1865–67. Kennan. N. Y., 1870. 12°. . . 8257
Siberian Travel, Journal of, 1865–67. Bush. N. Y., 1871. 8°. . . 8299
Sibree, J. Madagascar and its People. Lond. [1870.] 8°. . . 7983
Sicily, Letters on, 1808. Irvine. Lond., 1813. 8°. 16714
Pictures from. Bartlett. Lond., 1869. 8°. 8352
Pilgrimage to. Tuckerman. N. Y., 1852. 12°. . . . 16720
Tour through, 1770. Brydone. Edinb., 1791. 2 v. 12°. . . 16731
Travels in, in 1819. Gourbillon. Lond., 1820. 8°. . . . 8054
Sickness and Health in Bleaburn. [Martineau.] Bost., 1853. 16°. . 15777
Siddons, H. Time's a Tell-Tale. N. Y., 1808. 12°. 13356
Siddons, S., Memoirs of. Boaden. Lond., 1827. 2 v. 8°. . . 7969
Sidereal Heavens, The. Dick. N. Y., 1840. 12°. 11423
Sidney, A. Discourses on Gov't. N. Y., 1805. 3 v. 8°. . . . 17199
Life and Writings of. Van Santvoord. N. Y., 1851. 12°. . 6720
Trial of. (Celebrated Trials, v. 3.) Lond., 1825. 8°. . . . 9222
Sidney, E. Life of R. Hill. N. Y., 1834. 12°. 16337
Sidney, H. Diary and Correspondence. Lond., 1843. 2 v. 8°. . 7207
Sidney, P. Apologie for Poetrie. Ed. Arber. Lond., 1868. 16°. . 3886
The Arcadia. Ed. Friswell. Lond. 1867. 8°. 3940
Defence of Poesy. Ed. Young. Cambr., 1831. 12°. . . 3905
The same. 3912
Misc. Works, with Life by W. Gray. Oxf'd., 1829. 8°. . 3804
The same. Bost., 1860. 8°. 3805
Life and Times of. [Davis.] Bost., 1859. 16°. 6992
Memoirs of. Zouch. York, 1809. 4°. 7216
Sieber, F. W. Travels in Crete. (Voyages, v. 8.) Lond., 1823. 8°. . 8058
Sierra Nevada, Mountaineering in the. King. Bost., 1872. 8°. . 8401
Sigourney, L. H. Letters of Life. N. Y., 1866. 12°. 16442
Moral Pieces. Hartf'd., 1815. 12°. 15024
Pleasant Memories of Pleasant Lands. Bost., 1842. 12°. . 15029
Poems. Bost., 1827. 12°. 15026
Poems. (Another collection.) Philad., 1834. 12°. . . . 15027
Poetry for Seamen. Bost., 1845. 16°. 15030
Sketches. Philad., 1834. 12°. 15778
Traits of the Aborigines. Cambr., 1822. 12°. 15025
Zinzendorff and other Poems. N. Y., 1835. 12°. . . . 15028
Silas Marner. George Eliot. N. Y., 1871. 12°. 2536
Silent Partner, The. Phelps. Bost., 1871. 12°. 2980
Silk Manufacture, Treatise on. Porter. Lond., 1831. 16°. . . 5790
Sill, E. R. The Hermitage and other Poems. N. Y., 1868. 12°. . 786
Silliman, A. E. A Gallop among Amer. Scenery. N. Y., 1843. 16°. . 16828
Silliman, B. Tour to Quebec. N. H., 1820. 12°. 16776
Travels in England, Holland, and Scotland. 2d. ed. Bost., 1812. 2 v. 12°. 8261
Visit to Europe in 1851. N. Y., 1856. 2 v. 12°. . . . 8263
Life of. Fisher. N. Y., 1866. 2 v. 12° 7372

Silliman, B. (*Jr.*), etc. The World of Science, Art, and Industry. N. Y., 1854. 4°. . . . .

Simms, W. G. Carl Werner. N. Y., 1838. 2 v. 12°. . . . 15673
The Golden Christmas. Charleston, 1852. 12°. . . . 15704
Guy Rivers. N. Y., 1834. 2 v. 12°. 15710
Life of Gen. Greene. N. Y., 1859. 12°. 7303
of Marion. (2 copies.) N. Y., 1844–45. 12°. . . . 7304
of Capt. John Smith. N. Y. [1846.] 12°. 7312
Norman Maurice: a Drama. Philad., 1853. 12°. . . . 15032
Pelayo. N. Y., 1836. 12°. 15757
Southern Passages and Pictures. N. Y., 1839. 12°. . . 15031
Views and Reviews. N. Y., 1845. 2 v. in 1. 12°. . . . 3586
The Wigwam and Cabin. N. Y., 1845. 2 v. in 1. 12°. . . 2719
Woodcraft. N. Y., 1854. 12°. 17196

Simon, B. A. Evangelical Review of Modern Genius. N. Y., 1823. 12°. 15033

Simond, L. Switzerland. Bost., 1822. 2 v. 8°. 16681
Tour in Italy and Sicily. Lond., 1828. 8°. 16717

Simpkinson, J. N. The Washingtons. Lond., 1860. 12°. . . . 2443

Simpson, R. Traditions of the Covenanters. Edinb. 16°. . . 4813

Simpson, S. Biography of Girard. Philad., 1832. 12°. . . . 16428

Simson, W. Hist. of the Gipsies. N. Y., 1866. 12°. 17114

Sinai and Palestine. Stanley. N. Y., 1863. 8°. 8072
See, also, ARABIA; EXODUS.

Sinclair, C. Beatrice. N. Y. 12°. 15378
Hill and Valley, or Hours in Engl. and Wales. N. Y., 1838. 12°. 16747
Jane Bouverie. N. Y., 1851. 12°. 15471
Modern Accomplishments. N. Y., 1836. 12°. 15511
Modern Society. N. Y., 1837. 12°. 15512
Scotland and the Scotch. N. Y., 1840. 12°. 16741
Shetland and the Shetlanders. N. Y., 1840. 12°. . . . 16740

Sinclair, J. Code of Health and Longevity. 6th ed. Lond., 1844. 8°. 8987
Correspondence and Reminiscences. Lond., 1831. 2 v. 8°. . 7205

Sinding, P. C. Hist. of Scandinavia. N. Y., 1858. 12°. . . . 5817

Singer, S. W. Text of Shakespeare vindicated. Lond., 1853. 8°. . 1588

Singleton, Arthur. *(Pseudonym.)* See H. C. KNIGHT.

Singleton, Life of Captain. De Foe. Oxf'd., 1840. 16°. . . . 3873

Sintram and his Companions. De La Motte Fouqué. N. Y., 1862. 8°. 3015

Siogvolk, Paul. *(Pseudonym.)* See A. MATHEWS.

Sioux War and Massacres of 1862–63. Heard. N. Y., 1864. 12°. . 5745

Sir Andrew Wylie. Galt. N. Y., 1822. 2 v. 12°. 15233

Sir Charles Grandison. Richardson. Lond., 1811. 7 v. 16°. . . 1939

Sir Launcelot Greaves. Smollett. (Works, v. 6.) N. Y., 1860. 12°. 1967

Sismondi, J. C. L. de. Hist. of Crusades against the Albigenses. Lond., 1826. 8°. 6428
The same. Bost., 1833. 12°. 6343
Hist. of Fall of Roman Empire. Philad., 1835. 8°. . . . 4783
The same. Lond., 1834. 2 v. in 1. 16°. 4873
Hist. of the Italian Republics. Lond., 1832. 16°. . . . 5461
The same. Philad., 1832. 12°. 6072

Smith, C. B. A Life in Earnest. N. H., 1848. 12°. 17027
Smith, Edmond R. The Araucanians. N. Y., 1855. 12°. . . 17131
Smith, Edmund [Neale.] Poems. Ed. Bell. Lond., 1807. 24°. . 274
The same, ed. Johnson. Dubl., 1804. 8°. 15097
Smith, Eliz. Oakes. Bertha and Lily. N. Y., 1854. 12°. . . . 15665
The Sinless Child, and other Poems. N. Y., 1843. 12°. . . 14953
Smith, George. Ten Weeks in Japan. Lond., 1861. 8°. . . . 8012
Visit to China, etc. N. Y., 1847. 12°. 7944
Smith, Goldwin. Lectures on Study of History. (3 copies.) N. Y., 1866. 12°. 4581
Three English Statesmen. (2 copies.) N. Y., 1867. 12°. . 6749
Smith, Henry I. See SCHMIDT.
Smith, Horace. Arthur Arundel. N. Y., 1844. 8°. 2328
The same. 2313
Brambletye House. N. Y., 1835. 12°. 15111
The same. Bost., 1826. 3 v. 12°. 2455
Gaieties and Gravities. N. Y., 1852. 12°. 3532
Jane Lomax. Philad., 1838. 2 v. 12°. 15472
The Tor Hill. Hartf'd., 1846. 12°. 15608
Walter Colyton. N. Y., 1830. 2 v. 12°. 15631
Zillah. N. Y., 1829. 2 v. 12°. 15639
Smith, Horace and **James.** Horace in London. Lond., 1815. 12°. . 14887
Imitations of Celebrated Authors. (2 copies.) Lond., 1844. 8°. 3258
Poetical Works (Rejected Addresses, etc.). Ed. Sargent. N. Y., 1857. 12°. 1221
Smith, Horatio. Festivals, Games, and Amusements. N. Y., 1868. 12°. 11027
The same. N. Y., 1831. 12°. 11954
Smith, J. E. A. Taghconic. Bost., 1852. 12°. 16845
Smith, James. Memoirs, Letters, and Comic Miscellanies. Philad., 1841. v. 1. 12°. 15244
See, also, HORACE SMITH.
Smith, *Capt.* **John,** Life of. Hillard. (Sparks, v. 2.) Bost., 1834. 16°. 7251
The same. Simms. N. Y. [1846.] 12°. 7312
Smith, Joshua T. The Northmen in N. England. Bost., 1839. 12°. . 5997
Smith, Julie P. Chris and Otho. N. Y., 1870. 12°. 15677
Smith, Margaret. See J. G. WHITTIER.
Smith, Matthew H. Mount Calvary. N. Y., 1866. 12°. . . . 17348
Sunshine and Shadow in N. Y. Hartf'd., 1869. 8°. . . 16837
Smith, P. [Ancient] History of the World. N. Y., 1870–72. 3 v. 8°. 4119
[**Smith, R. P.**] Actress of Padua, and other Tales. Philad., 1836. 2 v. 12°. 15644
Smith, Seba. Letters of Major Jack Downing. N. Y., 1834. 12°. . 4310
Life and Writings of Jack Downing. (2 copies.) 2d ed. Bost., 1834. 12°. 4308
Powhatan. N. Y., 1841. 12°. 15034
Smith, Sol. Theatrical Management for 30 years. N. Y., 1868. 8°. . 1617
Smith, T. Southwood. Philosophy of Health. Lond., 1838. 2 v. 12°. 9119
Smith, Sydney. Sketches of Moral Philosophy. N. Y., 1850. 12°. . 8593
Works. Lond., 1840. 4 v. 8°. 3431

Smith, Sydney. Works. Philad., 1844. 3 v. 12°. 3292
Memoir and Letters of. Lady Holland. N. Y., 1856. 2 v. 12°. 7010
Smith, Walter. Art Education. Bost., 1872. 8°. 9054
Smith, Wm. (LL.D.) Comprehensive Dict. of the Bible. Ed. Barnum. N. Y., 1869. 8°. 10058
Old Testament History. N. Y., 1866. 12°. 9837
Smaller Dict. of the Bible. (2 copies.) Bost., 1866. 8°. . . 9881
Smith, Wm. Memoir of J. G. Fichte. Bost., 1846. 12°. 7795
Smith, Wm. [H.] Athelwold. A Tragedy. Lond., 1842. 8°. . . 845
Gravenhurst. Edinb., 1862. 8°. 9964
Thorndale. Bost., 1859. 12°. 9963
Smoke; a Novel. Turgénieff. N. Y., 1872. 16°. 2718
Smollett, T. Hist. of England, 1688–1760. Dubl., 1787. 5 v. 8°. . 16100
The same. Paris, 1836. 4 v. 8°. 5370
The same. Philad., 1837. 8°. 5391
Humphry Clinker. N. Y., 1856. 12°. 1968
Miscellaneous Works. N. Y., 1860. v. 1, 5, 6. 12°. . . 1965

CONTENTS.—1, Humphry Clinker. 5, Ferdinand Count Fathom. 6, Sir Launcelot Greaves; Hist. of an Atom.

Select Poems. Ed. Walsh. Philad., 1822. 24°. . . . 27
Select Works. N. Y. 8°. 1989
Smucker, S. M. Hist. of Napoleon III. Philad., 1860. 12°. . . 5548
Life of Nicholas I. Philad., 1860. 12°. 6446
Smuggler, The. [Banim.] N. Y., 1832. 2 v. 12°. 15159
Smyth, C. P. Teneriffe, an Astronomer's Experiment. Lond., 1858. 8°. 8910
Smyth, Wm. Lectures on the French Revolution. (2 copies.) Camb., 1840. 3 v. 8°. 5680
The same. (Bohn's ed.) Lond., 1855. 2 v. 8°. . . 380
Lectures on Modern Hist. (Bohn's ed.) Lond., 1854. 2 v. 8°. 363
The same. Ed. Sparks. (2 copies.) Cambr., 1841. 2 v. 8°. 4808
Smyth, Wm. H. and **Lowe, F.** Journey from Lima to Para. Lond., 1836. 8°. 17137
Smythe, P. E. F. W. (*Lord* Strangford.) Writings. Lond., 1869. 2 v. 8°. 3710
Snarleyyow. Marryat. Philad., 1827. 2 v. in 1. 12°. . . . 2115
Snelling, W. J. The Polar Regions explored. Bost., 1831. 8°. . 16591
Tales of the Northwest. Bost., 1839. 12°. 15798
Snodgrass, J. J. Narrative of the Burmese War. Lond., 1827. 8°. . 6504
Snowe, J. The Rhine. Lond., 1839. 2 v. 8°. 8311
Snow-Image, The. Hawthorne. Bost., 1857. 12°. 2891
Soave, F. Novels. (Ital. Novelists, v. 4.) Lond., 1836. 12°. . . 1902
Social Compact, Treatise on the. Rousseau. 12°. 17089
Destiny of Man. Brisbane. Philad., 1840. 12°. . . . 17087
Statics. H. Spencer. N. Y., 1868. 12°. 8597
Society, Civil, Essay on Hist. of. Ferguson. Philad., 1819. 8°. . 17085
Colloquies on the Progress and Prospects of. Southey. Lond., 1831. 2 v. 8°. 3479
Good, The Habits of. N. Y., 1865. 12°. 9269
Natural Hist. of. Taylor. N. Y., 1841. 2 v. 12°. . . . 4562
Natural, Vindication of. Burke. (v. 1.) Bost., 1839. 8°. . . 9649
New Views of. Owen. N. Y., 1825. 12°. 17090

Soulavie, J. L. Memoirs of Reign of Louis XVI. Lond., 1802. 6 v. 8°. 16192
Sound, Lectures on. Tyndall. N. Y., 1867. 12°. 8905
Phenomena of. Radau. N. Y., 1870. 12°. 10108
South, R. Discourses. (2 copies.) Bost., 1827. 8°. 10001
South, Letters from the. [Paulding.] N. Y., 1817. 2 v. 12°. . . 15290
South America. See AMERICA.
South Carolina, Hist. of, to 1808. Ramsay. Charleston, 1809. 2 v. 8°. 5866
South Sea Islander, The. N. Y., 1820. 12°. 16320
South Seas, Voyage in, 1812–14. Parker. Lond., 1823. 8°. . . 8058
South-West, The. By a Yankee. N. Y., 1835. 2 v. 12°. . . 16874
Southern, T. Isabella. (Brit. Drama, v. 1., pt. 2.) Lond., 1804. 8°. . 1630
Oroonoko; Isabella. (Brit. Theatre, v. 13.) Lond. 12°. . . 1339
Southern Literary Messenger. Richmond, 1835–59. v. 1–20, 22, 24–28. 8°. 14539
The same. v. 7, 17–20. 14728
Passages and Pictures. [Simms.] N. Y., 1839. 12°. . . 15031
Review. Charleston. 1828–32. 8 v. 8°. 14024
The same. v. 1–4, 6, 8. 14032
Southey, C. B. Chapters on Churchyards. N. Y., 1842. 12°. . . 3746
Solitary Hours; Birth-Day; etc. N. Y., 1845–6. 12°. 2 v. in 1. 1232
Southey, R. Chronicle of the Cid. Lowell, 1846. 8°. . . . 1676
Common-Place Book. (2 copies.) N. Y., 1849–50. 2 v. 8°. 4433
The Doctor, etc. (2 copies.) N. Y., 1836. 2 v. in 1. 12°. . 3272
Early Naval Hist. of England. (2 copies.) Philad., 1835. 12°. 4847
Essay on Uneducated Poets. Lond., 1831. 16°. . . . 305
Essays, Moral and Political. Lond., 1832. 2 v. 16°. . . 3173
The same. v. 1. 3175
The Expedition of Orsua. Philad., 1821. 12°. 5805
Hist. of the Peninsular War. Lond., 1828. v. 1–4. 8°. . . 6527
Letters from England: by Espriella. 2d ed. Lond., 1808. 3 v. 12°. 8173
Letters during a Journey in Spain, etc. 3d ed. Lond., 1808. 2 v. 12°. 8176
Life of Cowper. Lond., 1835–6. 3 v. 16°. 609
The same. Bost., 1839. 2 v. 12°. 7107
of Cromwell. N. Y., 1845. 12°. 5135
of Nelson. N. Y., 1841. 12°. 11005
The same. N. Y., 1833. 12°. 11934
The same. N. Y., 1813. 2 v. 12°. 6949
of Wesley. N. Y., 1820. 2 v. 8°. 7703
Lives of Uneducated Poets, etc. Lond., 1836. 8°. . . . 6719
Poetical Works. N. Y., 1842. 8°. 1277
The same. Lond., 1838. 10 v. 16°. 633

CONTENTS.—1, Joan of Arc. 2, 3, Juvenile and Minor Poems. 4, Thalaba. 5, Madoc. 6, 7, Ballads and Metrical Tales. 8, Curse of Kehama. 9, Roderick. 10, Poet's Pilgrimage to Waterloo; Lay of the Laureate; Vision of Judgement.

Select Works of Brit. Poets. (2 copies.) Lond., 1831. 8°. . 1302

Southey, R. Sir Thomas More: or, Colloquies on the Progress of Society. 2d. ed. Lond., 1831. 2 v. 8°. 3479
A Tale of Paraguay. Bost., 1827. 12°. 14890
and **Bell, R.** Lives of Brit. Admirals, with Naval Hist. of England. Lond., 1833–40. 5 v. 16°. 5171
Life and Correspondence of. By his Son. (2 copies.) N. Y., 1851. 8°. 7176
Reminiscences of. Cottle. N. Y., 1847. 12°. 7097
Southey, T. Hist. of W. Indies. Lond., 1827. 3 v. 8°. 5885
Southgate, H. Narrative of Tour through Armenia, etc. N. Y., 1840. 2 v. 12°. 16496
Southwold. Umsted. N. Y., 1859. 12°. 15781
Sozzini, A. Novels. (Ital. Novelists, v. 2.) Lond., 1836. 12°. . 1900
Spain in 1830. Inglis. Lond., 1831. 2 v. 8°. 8450
Ancient Poetry and Romances of. Bowring. Lond., 1824. 8°. 915
The Arabs in. Lond., 1840. 2 v. 12°. 6399
The Attaché in, 1849. Warren. N. Y., 1852. 12°. . . . 16673
The Bible in. Borrow. Philad., 1843. 8°. 2308
The Gypsies of. Borrow. Lond., 1841. 2 v. 12°. . . . 17115
Hist. of, to 1759. [Adams.] Lond., 1793. 3 v. 8°. . . . 16156
(to 1823.) Callcott. Lond., 1828. 2 v. 12°. . . . 6401
Arabs in [710–1493.] Conde. Lond., 1854. 3 v. 8°. . 424
Moors of. Florian. N. Y., 1841. 12°. 16160
Reformation in. McCrie. Edinb., 1829. 8°. . . . 6453
War of the Succession in (1700–14). Mahon. Lond., 1836. 8°. 6507
Journey in, 1795–96. Southey. Lond., 1808. 2 v. 12°. . . 8176
Journey through, 1786–87. Townsend. Lond., 1792. 3 v. 8°. 16662
Legends of Conquest of. Irving. Philad., 1835. 12°. . . 4245
Memoirs of, 1621–1700. Dunlop. Edinb., 1834. 2 v. 8°. . 6520
Reminiscences of. Cushing. Bost., 1833. 2 v. 12°. . . 16669
revisited, in 1834. [Mackenzie.] N. Y., 1836. 2 v. 12°. . 16678
Romance of Hist. of. Abbott. N. Y., 1869. 12°. . . . 6405
The same. De Trueba y Cosio. N. Y., 1830. 2 v. 12°. 15567
Scenes in. N. Y., 1837. 12°. 16674
Scenes and Adventures in, 1835–40. Poco Mas. Philad., 1846. 12°. 8190
Travels in [in 1782]. De Bourgoing. Lond., 1789. 3 v. 8°. . 16665
Travels through, 1775–76. Swinburne. Dubl., 1779. 8°. . 16668
Wanderings in, 1872. Hare. Lond., 1873. 8°. 10243
A year in, 1826–27. [Mackenzie.] N. Y., 1836. 3 v. 12°. . 16675
and Portugal, In. Andersen. N. Y., 1870. 8°. 2604
Description of. Conder. Lond. 12°. . . 7853
Hist. of [to 1790]. Dunham. Lond., 1832–33. 5 v. 16°. 5456
to 1814. [Busk.] Lond., 1833. 8°. . 16154
the Jews in. Finn. Lond., 1841. 12°. . 6300
Lives of Literary and Scientific Men of. Shelley, etc. Lond., 1839. 16°. 5785

Spain and Portugal, Sketches of, 1787-95. Beckford. Philad., 1834. 12°. 8218
Travels through, 1812–14. Graham. Lond., 1820. 8°. 8053
See, also, GRANADA ; INQUISITION ; PENINSULAR War ; SARACENS.

Spalding, W. Hist. of English Literature. N. Y., 1853. 12°. . . . 15069
Italy, etc. N. Y., 1842. 3 v. 12°. 11753
Treatise on Rhetoric. Edinb., 1839. 12°. 164

Spaniards and their Country, The. Ford. N. Y., 1847. 12°. . . . 8364
Lives of celebrated. Quintana. Lond., 1833. 12°. 7690

Spanish Ballads, Ancient. Lockhart. N. Y., 1842. 8°. 913
Brothers, The ; a Tale. Lond., 1871. 8°. 2445
Conquest in America, The. Helps. N. Y., 1856–68. 4 v. 12°. 5820
Literature, Hist. of. Bouterwek. Lond., 1847. 8°. 323
The same. Ticknor. N. Y., 1849. 3 v. 8°. 219

Spare Hours. J. Brown. Bost., 1866. 2 v. 8°. 3689

Sparks, J. Inquiry into Tendency of Trinitarian and Unitarian Doctrines. Bost., 1823. 8°. 17268
Library of Amer. Biography. Bost., 1834–48. 2 Series in 25 v. 16°. 7250

CONTENTS.—1, Stark, John, by E. Everett; Brown, Charles B., by W. H. Prescott; Montgomery, R., by J. Armstrong; Allen, Ethan, by J. Sparks. 2, Wilson, Alex., by W. B. O. Peabody; Smith, Capt. John, by G. S. Hillard. 3, Arnold, Benedict, by J. Sparks. 4, Wayne, Anthony, by J. Armstrong; Vane, Sir Henry, by C. W. Upham. 5, Eliot, John, by C. Francis. 6, Pinkney, Wm., by H. Wheaton; Ellery, William, by E. T. Channing; Mather, Cotton, by W. B. O. Peabody. 7, Phips, Sir Wm., by F. Bowen; Putnam, Israel, by O. W. B. Peabody; Davidson, L. Maria, by C. M. Sedgwick; Rittenhouse, David, by J. Renwick. 8, Edwards, Jonathan, by S. Miller; Brainerd, David, by W. B. O. Peabody. 9, Steuben, Baron, by F. Bowen; Cabot, Sebastian, by C. Hayward, Jr.; Eaton, Wm., by C. C. Felton. 10, Fulton, Robert, by J. Renwick; Hudson, Henry, by H. R. Cleveland; Warren, Joseph, by A. H. Everett; Marquette, by J. Sparks. 11, Salle, R. de la, by J. Sparks; Henry, Patrick, by A. H. Everett. 12, Otis, James, by F. Bowen; Oglethorpe, James, by W. B. O. Peabody. 13, Sullivan, John, by O. W. B. Peabody; Leisler, Jacob, by C. F. Hoffman; Bacon, Nathaniel, by W. Ware; Mason, John, by G. E. Ellis. 14, Williams, Roger, by W. Gammell; Dwight, Timothy, by W. B. Sprague; Pulaski, Count, by J. Sparks. 15, Rumford, Count, by J. Renwick; Pike, Z. M., by H. Whiting; Gorton, Samuel, by J. M. Mackie. 16, Stiles, Ezra, by J. L. Kingsley; Fitch, John, by C. Whittlesey; Hutchinson, Anne, by G. E. Ellis. 17, Ribault, John, by J. Sparks; Rale, Sebastian, by C. Francis; Palfrey, Wm., by J. G. Palfrey. 18, Lee, Charles, by J. Sparks; Reed, Joseph, by H. Reed. 19, Calvert, Leonard, by G. W. Burnap; Ward, Samuel, by W. Gammell; Posey, Thomas, by J. Hall. 20, Greene, Nathaniel, by G. W. Greene. 21, Decatur, Stephen, by A. S. Mackenzie. 22, Preble, Edward, by L. Sabine; Penn, William, by G. E. Ellis. 23, Boone, Daniel, by J. M. Peck; Lincoln, Benjamin, by F. Bowen. 24, Ledyard, John, by J. Sparks. 25, Davie, W. R., by F. M. Hubbard; Kirkland, Samuel, by S. K. Lothrop.

The same. v. 2–8, 16–25. 7227
Life of Ethan Allen. Bost., 1839. 12°. 16314
of Washington. (2 copies.) Bost., 1839–43. 8°. . . . 7484

Speaker, The National. Maglathlin. Bost., 1851. 12°. . . . 9304

Speaking, Extempore, Art of. Bautain. N. Y., 1867. 12°. . . . 9295

Species, Genesis of. Mivart. Lond., 1871. 8°. 8943
Origin of. Huxley. N. Y., 1863. 12°. 8940
by Natural Selection. Darwin. N. Y., 1871. 12°. . 8929

Spectator, The. Philad., 1803. 8 v. 12°. 3156
N. Y., 1809–10. v. 2–9. 12°. 4200
(Addison's Works, v. 1–2.) N. Y., 1855. 8°. . . . 3791
(Addison's Works, v. 5, 6.) N. Y., 1856. 12°. . . 3999
Ed. Ferguson. Lond., 1823. 8 v. 12°. 3113
The same. v. 1, 3–8. 3153
Essays illustrative of the. Drake. Lond., 1805. 3 v. 8°. . 3233

Spectrum Analysis explained. Schellen. N. Y., 1872. 8°. . . . 9098
Lectures on. Roscoe. Lond., 1869. 8°. . . . 9097

Speculator, The. [Ash.] Dubl., 1791. 12°. 13037
Speeches, Select American. Carpenter. Philad., 1815. 2 v. 8°. . 9428
Forensic and Parliamentary. Ed. Chapman. Philad., 1808. 5 v. 8°. 9418
Selection of British. Browne. Philad., 1810. 3 v. 8°. . . 9415
See, also, ELOQUENCE; ORATORY.
Speke, J. H. Discovery of Source of the Nile. (2 copies.) N. Y., 1864. 8°. 8116
Spencer, E. Travels in Circassia, etc. 3d ed. Lond., 1839. 2 v. 8°. 8042
Travels in the Western Caucasus. Lond., 1838. 2 v. 8°. . 8044
Spencer, H. Education. (2 copies.) N. Y., 1862–66. 12°. . . 8595
Essays; Moral, Political, and Æsthetic. N. Y., 1866. 12°. . 3724
Essays; Scientific, Political, and Speculative. N. Y., 1864. 8°. 3723
First Principles of a New System of Philosophy. N. Y., 1864. 12°. 8598
Illustrations of Universal Progress. N. Y., 1867. 12°. . . 3725
Principles of Biology. N. Y., 1866–67. 2 v. 12°. . . . 8599
of Psychology. N. Y., 1871–73. 2 v. 12°. . . 8601
Recent Discussions in Science, Philosophy, and Morals. N. Y., 1871. 12°. 8602
Social Statics. N. Y., 1868. 12°. 8597
Spencer, I. S. A Pastor's Sketches. (2 copies.) N. Y., 1851–54. 12°. 9991
Spencer, J. A. The East. N. Y., 1850. 8°. 8069
Spenser, E. Faery Queene. Lond., 1819. 2 v. 12°. 14884
The same. Bks. 1, 2. Ed. Kitchin. Oxf'd., 1868–71. 2 v. 16°. 1013
Poetical Works. Ed. Bell. 9 v. in 5. Lond., 1807. 24°. . 251
The same. [Ed. Hillard.] Bost., 1839. 5 v. 8°. . . 1262
The same. Bost., 1839. v. 2–5. 12°. 1101
Works, ed. Collier. Lond., 1862. 5 v. 8°. 1268
The same, ed. Morris. With Memoir by Hales. Lond., 1871. 16°. 1100
The same, with Life by Todd. Lond., 1845. 8°. . . 1267
Essay on. Hart. Philad., 1847. 8°. 1275
Life of. Dunham. Lond., 1840. 16°. 5774
Observations on Fairy Queen of. Warton. Lond., 1807. 2 v. 8°. 1273
and his Poetry. Craik. Lond., 1845. 3 v. 12°. . . . 285
Spielhagen, F. Hammer and Anvil. N. Y., 1870. 12°. . . . 3022
The Hohensteins. N. Y., 1870. 12°. 3021
Through Night to Light. N. Y., 1871. 12°. 2708
Problematic Characters. N. Y., 1870. 12°. 3020
Spilman, J. Journey to Persia. Lond., 1742. 8°. 16281
Spindler, C. The Jew. N. Y. 8°. 2312
Spinoza, B. de., Life, Correspondence, and Ethics of. Willis. Lond., 1870. 8°. 7789
Spirit of '76, The. A Drama. [Curtis.] Bost., 1868. 16°. . . 9213
of the Age, The. Hazlitt. N. Y., 1849. 12°. 3422
A New. Horne. N. Y., 1844. 12°. 3423
Spirits of Odin, The. N. Y., 1826. 2 v. 12°. 15782

Spiritual Despotism. Taylor. N. Y., 1835. 12°. 9538
Spiritualism, Modern. [Sargent.] Bost., 1869. 16°. 8484
See, also, APPARITIONS; DEMONOLOGY; MAGIC.
Spix, J. B. v., and **Martius, C. F. P. v.** Travels in Brazil. Lond., 1824. 2 v. 8°. 8435
Spofford, H. P. Azarian. Bost., 1864. 8°. 3011
Sporting Scenes and Characters. Frank Forester. Philad. [1857.] 2 v. 12°. 10161
Sports, Field, of the U. S. Frank Forester. N. Y., 1849. v. 1. 8°. . 10207
and Pastimes of the English. Strutt. Lond., 1845. 8°. . . 5115
Wild, in Europe, Asia, and Africa. Napier. Lond., 1844. 2 v. 8°. 10166
Sportsman in France, The. Tolfrey. Lond., 1841. 2 v. 8°. . . 10164
Sportsmen, Young, Manual for. Frank Forester. N. Y., 1857. 12°. 10160
See, also, AMUSEMENTS; GAMES; HUNTING.
Sprague, C. Poetical and Prose Writings. New ed. Bost., 1850. 12°. 805
Writings. N. Y., 1841. 8°. 15063
Sprague, J. T. The Florida War. N. Y., 1848. 8°. 5955
Sprague, T. D. Amer. Literary Magazine. Albany and Hartford, 1847–49. 5 v. in 3. 8°. 13254
Sprague, W. B. Annals of the Amer. Pulpit. N. Y., 1857–69. 9 v. 8°. 7730
CONTENTS.—1, 2, Trinitarian Congregational. 3, 4, Presbyterian. 5, Episcopalian. 6, Baptist. 7, Methodist. 8, Unitarian. 9, Lutheran, Reformed, Associate, Associate Reformed, and Reformed Presbyterian.
Letters to Young People. N. Y., 1831. 12°. 17020
Life of Dwight. (Sparks, v. 14.) Bost., 1845. 16°. . . . 7263
Memoir of Griffin. N. Y., 1839. 8°. 7740
Sprat, T. Poems, ed. Johnson. Dubl., 1804. 8°. 15097
Spring, G. Obligations of the World to the Bible. N. Y., 1839. 12°. 17164
Works. N. Y., 1852–54. 10 v. 12°. 17165
Spring Comedies. Barker. Lond., 1871. 8°. 2515
Springer, J. S. Forest Life and Trees. N. Y., 1851. 12°. . . . 16820
Spurgeon, C. H. Feathers for Arrows. Lond., 1870. 16°. . . . 4209
Spurzheim, J. G. Examination of Objections to Phrenology. Bost., 1833. 12°. 8611
Philosophical Catechism of the Laws of Man. Bost., 1832. 12°. 17291
Phrenology. Bost., 1832. 2 v. 8°. 8777
in connexion with Physiognomy. Bost., 1833. 8°. 8779
Memoir of. Carmichael. Bost., 1833. 12°. 8532
Spy, The. Cooper. N. Y., 1872. 12°. 2837
Spy unmasked; Memoirs of E. Crosby. Barnum. N. Y., 1828. 8°. 6124
Squibob Papers, The. Derby. N. Y., 1865. 12°. 4297
Squier, E. G. Nicaragua. N. Y., 1856. 8°. 8459
Squire, The. [Pickering.] Philad., 1838. 2 v. 12°. 15586
[**Staats, C.**] Tribute to Memory of D. Clinton. Alb., 1828. 12°. . 7551
Stable Talk, etc. [Brindley.] Philad., 1845. 12°. 10163
Staehlin, J. de. Anecdotes of Peter the Great. Dubl., 1789. 12°. . 16181
Staël-Holstein, *Mme.* **Anne L. G. N. de.** Considerations on the French Revolution. (2 copies.) N. Y., 1818. 2 v. 8°. . . . 5686
Corinne; or, Italy. N. Y., 1844. 8°. 2626
The same. (2 copies.) Philad., 1836. 2 v. 12° . . 2590

Staël-Holstein, *Mme.* **Anne L. G. N. de.** Germany. Lond., 1814. 3 v. 8°. 8307
Influence of Literature on Society. Bost., 1813. 2 v. 12°. . 87
The same, with Reflections on Suicide. Hartf'd., 1842. 8°. 3472
Memoirs of Necker. Lond., 1818. 8°. 7651
Ten Years of Exile. N. Y., 1821. 12°. 7660
Memoirs of. Child. N. Y., 1854. 16°. 7659
Staël, Madame de; a Novel. Bölte. N. Y., 1869. 12°. . . . 3023
Staël Holstein, Aug. L. de. Letters on England. 2d ed. Lond., 1830. 8°. 16748
Stage, The; before and behind the Curtain. Bunn. Philad., 1840. 2 v. 12°. 1614
Annals of the. Collier. Lond., 1831. 3 v. 16°. . . . 1556
British, Biogr. of the. N. Y., 1824. 12°. 7895
English, Annals of the. Doran. N. Y., 1865. 2 v. 12°. . 1612
Hist. of the. Betterton. Bost., 1814. 8°. . . . 1610
View of the. Hazlitt. Lond., 1818. 8°. . . . 1611
French, Picture of the. [Fleury.] Ed. Hook. Lond., 1842. 2 v. 12°. 1608
Inquiry into the Nature of the. Witherspoon. N. Y., 1812. 12°. 1394
The London. Lond. [1830.] 4 v. 8°. 1664
See, also, DRAMA; THEATER.
Stagg, E. Poems. St. Louis, 1852. 12°. 15036
Stahr, A. Life and Works of Lessing. (2 copies.) Bost., 1866. 2 v. 12°. 7791
Stanhope, L. Greece in 1823–24. Philad., 1825. 8°. 16020
Stanhope, P. D. (*Earl of* Chesterfield.) Letters to his Son. Lond., 1804. 4 v. 12°. 9139
The same. Lond., 1775. v. 3, 4. 8°. 9308
Miscellaneous Works, with Memoir by Maty. 2d ed. Lond., 1779. 4 v. 8°. 9556
Beauties of. Bost., 1828. 12°. 17308
Reflections on Letters of. Hunter. Lond., 1777. 8°. . . 17044
Stanhope, P. H., *Earl.* Hist. of England, 1701–13. Lond., 1870. 8°. 5040
The same, 1713–62. Lond., 1839–44. 4 v. 8°. . . 5041
The same. 3d ed. Paris, 1841. 2 v. 8°. . . . 5045
The same. Ed. by H. Reed. N. Y., 1849. 2 v. 8°. . 5047
The same, 1713–83. Leipz., 1853–54. 7 v. 16°. . . 4837
Hist. of the War of the Succession in Spain. 2d ed. Lond., 1836. 8°. 6507
Life of Belisarius. Philad., 1832. 12°. 7576
of Louis, Prince of Condé. (3 copies.) N. Y., 1845–48. 12°. 7619
of Pitt. Lond., 1861–62. 4 v. 8°. 6799
Stanley, A. P. Essays. Lond., 1870. 8°. 3436
Hist. of the Eastern Church. N. Y., 1862. 8°. 6508
The same. Revised ed. N. Y., 1870. 8°. 6418
of the Jewish Church. (2 copies.) N. Y., 1863–67. 2 v. 8°. 6533
Life of Arnold. 2d ed. Lond., 1844. 2 v. 8°. 7130
The same. From 3d English ed. N. Y., 1845. 12°. . 7132
Sermons in the East. N. Y., 1863. 8°. 9921
Sinai and Palestine. N. Y., 1863. 8°. 8072

Stanley, H. M. How I found Livingstone. N. Y., 1872. 8°. . . 10239
Stanley Buxton. Galt. Philad., 1833. 2 v. 12°. 15228
Stapfer, P. A. Life of Kant. Edinb., 1836. 16°. 6633
Star Papers. Beecher. N. Y., 1855. 12°. 3590
Stark, J., Life of. Everett. Bost., 1834. 16°. 7250
[**Starling, E.**] Noble Deeds of Woman. Philad., 1836. 2 v. 12°. . 9195
Stars, Origin of the. Ennis. N. Y., 1867. 12°. 16973
Statesman, The. Taylor. Lond., 1836. 16°. 8476
Statesman's Manual, The. Coleridge. (Works, v. 1.) N. Y., 1871. 12°. 4013
The same. Williams. N. Y., 1854. 3 v. 8°. . . 6200
Statesmen, Lives of British. Forster, etc. Lond., 1831–39. 7 v. 16°. 5759
For Contents, see FORSTER.
Foreign. Crowe and James. Lond., 1833–38. 5 v. 16°. 5766
For Contents, see JAMES.
Statistical Inquiry, Principles of. Russell. N. Y., 1839. 8°. . . 17093
Staunton, G. Account of Embassy to China. Dubl., 1798. 2 v. 8°. 16474
Staunton, H. Chess-Player's Companion. (2 copies.) Lond., 1849. 8°. 10173
The Great Schools of England. Lond., 1865. 8°. 9247
Steam-Boat, The ; a Tale. [Galt.] N. Y., 1823. 12°. 1523
Steam Engine explained, The. Lardner. Lond., 1840. 8°. . . 17005
Stebbing, H. Hist. of the Christian Church. (2 copies.) Lond., 1833–34. 2 v. 16°. 5488
of the Reformation. Lond., 1836–37. 2 v. 16°. . 5757
Lives of the Italian Poets. Lond., 1831. 3 v. 12°. . . . 7775
Stedman, C. Hist. of the Amer. War. Dubl., 1794. 2 v. 8°. . . 5944
Steedman, A. Wanderings in S. Africa. Lond., 1835. 2 v. 8°. . 16527
Steele, Anne. Works. Bost., 1808. 2 v. 12°. 14860
Steele, R. Conscious Lovers, a Comedy. Gottingen, 1767. 16°. . 1452
Tender Husband. (Brit. Drama, v. 2.) Philad., 1833. 8°. . 1663
Essays on. Drake. Lond., 1805. 8°. 3233
See, also, The GUARDIAN, PLEBEIAN, SPECTATOR, and TATLER.
Steffens, H. Story of my Career. Bost., 1863. 16°. 7571
Steinmetz, A. Hist. of the Jesuits. Philad., 1848. 2 v. 8°. . . 6421
The Novitiate ; a Year among the Jesuits. N. Y., 1846. 12°. . 17274
Romance of Duelling. Lond., 1868. 2 v. 8°. 15146
Stephen, King of England, Hist. of. Cobbe. Lond., 1869. 8°. . 5285
[**Stephen, G.**] Adventures of a Gentleman in Search of a Horse. Philad., 1836. 12°. 10169
Stephen, J. Critical and Miscellaneous Essays. Philad., 1846. 8°. . 3471
The same. Philad., 1843. 12°. 3288
The same. 3350
Lectures on Hist. of France. N. Y., 1852. 8°. 5710
Stephen, T. Book of Constitution of Grt. Brit. Glasg., 1835. 8°. . 5000
Stephens, Alex. Hist. of Wars of the French Revol. Philad., 1804. 2 v. 8°. 16205
Memoirs of Horne Tooke. Lond., 1813. 2 v. 8°. 6860
Stephens, Alex. H. The Late War Between the States. Philad. [1868–70.] 2 v. 8°. 6255

Stephens, Ann S. Fashion and Famine. N. Y., 1854. 12°. . . . 15693
Stephens, J. L. Incidents of Travel in Central America. N. Y., 1841. 2 v. 8°. 8454
—— in Egypt, Arabia, etc. N. Y., 1837. 2 v. 12°. 16490
—— in Greece, Turkey, Russia and Poland. N. Y., 1841. 2 v. 12°. 16637
—— in Yucatan. N. Y., 1843. 2 v. 8°. 8456
Stephenson, G. and **R.**, Life of. Smiles. N. Y., 1868. 8°. 7154
Stepney, G. Poems. Ed. Johnson. Dubl., 1804. 8°. 15096
Stepping Heavenward. Prentiss. N. Y. [1869.] 12°. 3009
Sterling, J. Poetical Works. Philad., 1842. 12°. 667
Life of. Carlyle. Lond., 1870. 8°. 4039
Sterne, L. Sentimental Journey. Paris, 1800. 12°. 8170
Works. (2 copies.) Philad., 1864. 8°. 1990
The same. N. Y., 1813–14. v 1, 3–6. 12°. 4210

CONTENTS.—1, Tristram Shandy. 3, Sentimental Journey; Hist. of a good warm Watch-Coat; Fragment. 4, 5, Sermons. 6, Letters; The Koran.

Steuben, F. W. A., Life of. Bowen. (Sparks, v 9.) Bost., 1838. 16°. 7258
Stevens, G. A. Lecture on Heads. Lond., 1795. 12°. . . . .
Stewart, C. S. Residence in Sandwich Isl. 5th ed. Bost., 1839. 12°. 16304
The same. 2d ed. N. Y., 1828. 12°. 16321
Sketches of Society in Grt. Brit. and Ireland. Philad., 1834. 2 v. 12°. 16753
Visit to the South Seas. N. Y., 1831. 2 v. 12°. 16332
Stewart, D. Life and Writings of W. Robertson. 2d ed. Lond., 1802. 8°. 16357
Philosophical Essays. Philad., 1811. 8°. 17060
Philosophy of the Active and Moral Powers. Ed. by Walker. Philad., 1866. 12°. 8592
Works. Cambr., 1829. 7 v. 8°. 8770

CONTENTS.—1–3, Elements of Philosophy of the Human Mind. 4, Philosophical Essays. 5, Philosophy of Active and Moral Powers. 6, Dissertation on Progress of Philosophy. 7, Lives of A. Smith, Robertson, Reid; Tracts on Election of Prof. Leslie.

Stewart, R. (*Lord* Castlereagh), and *Sir* **C.**, Lives of. Alison. Edinb., 1861. 3 v. 8°. 6790
Stewart, V. A., Hist. of. Howard. N. Y., 1836. 12°. 17112
[**Stewarton, —.**] The Revolutionary Plutarch. Lond., 1805. 3 v. 12°. 5509
Stiles, E., Life of. Holmes. Bost., 1798. 8°. 9274
The same. Kingsley. Bost., 1845. 16°. 7265
Stiles, W. H. Austria in 1848–49. N. Y., 1852. 2 v. 8°. . . . 5930
Still Hour, The. Phelps. Bost., 1861. 16°. 9551
Stilling, J. H. Autobiography, trans. by S. Jackson. N. Y., 1845. 8°. 2686
Stirling, *Earl of.* See W. ALEXANDER. . . . .
Stirling, W. Cloister Life of Charles V. 2d ed. Lond., 1853. 8°. . 6409
Stolen Child, The. Galt. Philad., 1833. 12°. 15234
Stone, W. L. Border Wars of the Revolution. N. Y., 1845. 2 v. 12°. 11768
The same. 12282
Letters on Masonry. N. Y., 1832. 8°. 17111

Stone, W. L. Life of Joseph Brant. N. Y., 1838. 2 v. 8°. . . . 5952
of Red-Jacket. N. Y., 1841. 8°. 5951
Poetry and Hist. of Wyoming. (2 copies.) N. Y., 1841. 12°. . 5737
Tales and Sketches. N. Y., 1834. 2 v. 12°. 15795
Uncas and Miantonomoh. N. Y., 1842. 12°. 5750
Ups and Downs. N. Y., 1836. 12°. 15807
Stone Monuments. Fergusson. Lond., 1872. 8°. 9096
Stormy Life, A. Fullerton. N. Y., 1868. 8°. 2684
Story, J. Commentaries on the Constitution. 3d ed. Bost., 1858. 2 v. 8°. 6179
The same. Bost., 1833. 8°. 6178
Miscellaneous Writings. Bost., 1835. 8°. 3476
Story, W. W. Roba di Roma. 4th ed. N. Y., 1864. 2 v. 12°. . 8343
The same. 5th ed. Philad., 1867. 2 v. 12°. . . . 8345
Story of my Life. [Sherer.] N. Y., 1825. 12°. 15588
Stowe, C. E. Hist. of the Books of the N. T. (2 copies.) Hartf'd., 1867. 8°. 10020
Stowe, H. B. Agnes of Sorrento. Bost., 1862. 12°. 2962
Lady Byron Vindicated. (2 copies.) Bost., 1870. 12°. . . 6988
The Chimney-Corner. Bost., 1868. 12°. 2966
Dred. Bost., 1856. 2 v. 12°. 2959
House and Home Papers. Bost., 1865. 12°. 2965
The Mayflower. N. Y., 1844. 12°. 2734
Men of our Times. Hartf'd., 1868. 8°. 7408
The Minister's Wooing. Bost., 1868. 12°. 2961
My Wife and I. N. Y., 1871. 12°. 2964
Oldtown Folks. Bost., 1869. 12°. 2963
Pink and White Tyranny. Bost., 1871. 16°. 2735
Religious Poems. Bost., 1867. 12°. 718
Sunny Memories of Foreign Lands. Bost., 1854. 2 v. 12°. . 8268
Uncle Tom's Cabin. Bost., 1852. 2 v. 12°. 2956
The same. Bost., 1869. 12°. 2958
Strafford, *Earl of* (T. Wentworth), Life of. Forster. Lond., 1836. 16°. 5760
Strang, J. Germany in 1831. N. Y., 1836. 12°. 16653
Strange Adventures of Captain Dangerous. Sala. Bost., 1863. 8°. 2333
Story. Bulwer. Philad., 1868. 12°. 2084
Strangford, *Lord.* See P. E. F. W. SMYTHE.
Straparola, G. F. Novel. (Ital. Novelists, v. 3.) Lond., 1836. 12°. . 1901
Stratton Hill. [Carne.] N. Y., 1829. 2 v. 12°. 15589
Strauss, G. F. A. Helon's Pilgrimage. Bost., 1835. 12°. . . . 9878
The same. 6306
Street, A. B. Frontenac. N. Y., 1849. 12°. 15037
Poems. N. Y., 1845. 8°. 934
Poems. N. Y., 1867. 2 v. 16°. 789
Woods and Waters. N. Y., 1865. 12°. 16838
Strength, Wonders of. Depping. N. Y., 1871. 12°. 10130
Stretton, H. Max Kromer. N. Y., 1871. 16°. 2425
Stretton. A Novel. H. Kingsley. N. Y., 1869. 8°. 2329

Strickland, A. Lives of Queens of England. Philad., 1851–2. 12 v. in 6. 8°. 5228

CONTENTS.—1, 2, 3, Matilda, Queen of Wm. I., to Anne, Q. of Richard III. 4, 5, Eliz., Q. of Henry VIII., to Q. Mary. 6, 7, Q. Elizabeth; Anne, Q. of James I. 8, Henrietta Maria, Q. of Chas. I., Catharine, Q. of Chas. II. 9, 10, Mary, Q. of James II. 10, Q. Mary II. 11, 12, Q. Anne.

The same. v. 1–11, bound in 5. Philad., 1847. 8°. . 5234

The same. v. 1–3. Philad., 1841. 12°. 5196

Lives of Queens of Scotland, etc. N. Y., 1851–59. 7 v. 12°. . 5199

CONTENTS.—1, Margaret, Q. of James IV.; Magdalene, Q. of James V. 1, 2, Mary, Q. of James V. 2, Margaret Douglas, Countess of Lennox. 3, 7, Mary Stuart.

The same. v. 1, 3. 5206

Lives of Tudor Princesses. Lond., 1868. 8°. 5208

Pilgrims of Walsingham, Philad., 1835. 2 v. 12°. 2416

Strife and Peace. Bremer. Lond., 1853. 8°. 470

String of Pearls. James. N. Y., 1833. 12°. 15222

Strive and Thrive. Howitt. Bost., 1840. 12°. 15591

Strong, C. Speeches. Bost., 1808. 12°. 17537

Stroud, G. M. Laws relating to Slavery in the U. S. (2 copies.) Philad., 1827. 8°. 8677

Strozzi, F. History of. Trollope. Lond., 1860. 8°. 4684

Struensee, J. F. v. Hist. of. [Falkenskjold.] Lond., 1789. 12°. . 5819

Last Days of. Munter. Bost., 1853. 16°. 7561

Strutt, J. Sports and Pastimes of England. Lond., 1834. 8°. . 5262

The same. Lond., 1845. 8°. 5115

Stuart, G. View of Society in Europe. 2d ed. Edinb., 1792. 8°. . 15918

Stuart, I. W. Life of Gov. Trumbull. Bost., 1859. 8°. 7455

Stuart, J. Three years in N. America. N. Y., 1833. 2 v. 12°. . 16790

Stuart, M. Hints on Prophecy. Andover, 1842. 12°. 17266

Stubbs, W. Select Charters and other Illustrations of English Constitutional Hist. Oxf'd., 1870. 8°. 4851

Student Life Abroad, Romance of. Kimball. N. Y., 1862. 12°. . 15784

of Germany. Howitt. Philad., 1842. 8°. 9397

Young, Letters to a. Bost., 1832. 12°. 17037

Student's Companion. N. H., 1831. v. 1. 8°. 17393

Manual, The. Todd. Northampton, 1835. 12°. 9134

Students, Hints to, on the Use of the Eyes. Reynolds. Edinb., 1835. 16°. 9137

Prize Letters to. Dickinson. N. Y., 1831. 12°. . . . 17022

A Tutor's Counsel to. Mathias. Philad., 1867. 16°. . . 9143

Studies, Classical. Sears, Edwards, and Felton. Bost., 1843. 12°. . 9260

for Stories. Ingelow. Bost., 1865. 16°. 2421

Study, Classical, Method of. Taylor. Bost., 1861. 12°. . . . 9273

Value of. Taylor. Andover, 1870. 12°. 9263

Sturt, C. Expeditions in S. Australia. 2d ed. Lond., 1834. 2 v. 8°. 8083

Style. See RHETORIC.

Subaltern, The. Gleig. N. Y., 1825. 12°. 2085

in America. Gleig. Philad., 1833. 12°. 6004

Subaltern's Log-Book, The. N. Y., 1829. 2 v. 12°. 15785

Sublime and Beautiful, Inquiry into our Ideas of. Burke. (v. 1.) Bost., 1839. 8°. 9649

Substance and Shadow. James. Bost., 1866. 8°. 9985
Success and its Conditions. Whipple. Bost., 1871. 8°. . . . 3546
Suchet, L. G. Memoirs of the War in Spain. Lond., 1829. 2 v. 8°. 6531
Suckling, J. The Goblins. (Old Plays, v. 10.) Lond., 1826. 8°. . 1517
Sue, E. Commander of Malta. N. Y., 1860. 8°. 2311
De Rohan. N. Y., 1845. 8°. 2324
Wandering Jew. Lond. 8°. 2595
The same. 2631
The same. Lond., 1845. 3 v. 8°. 2632
Suffrage, Treatise on Right of. S. Jones. Bost., 1842. 12°. . . 8537
Woman. Bushnell. N. Y., 1869. 12°. 9211
Suicide, Shakspeare's Delineations of. Kellogg. N. Y., 1866. 16°. . 1482
Sullivan, F. S. Lectures on Constitution and Laws of England. Dubl., 1790. 8°. 4949
Sullivan, John, Life of. Peabody. Bost., 1844. 16°. 7262
Sullivan, W. Familiar Letters on Public Characters. Bost., 1834. 12°. 7277
Historical Causes and Effects. Bost., 1838. 12°. . . . 4569
Political Class Book. Bost., 1831. 12°. 6015
Sully, M. de Béthune, *Duke of*, Memoirs of. Philad., 1817. 5 v. 8°. 5661
Summer Rest. Gail Hamilton. Bost., 1866. 8°. 3654
Sumner, C. Orations and Speeches. (2 copies.) Bost., 1850. 2 v. 12°. 9188
Recent Speeches and Addresses. Bost., 1856. 12°. . . . 9192
Sun, The. Guillemin. N. Y., 1870. 12°. 10115
Proctor. Lond., 1871. 8°. 8909
Sunday Magazine. Lond., 1867–68. v. 4. 8°. 14533
Sunday Schools. See SABBATH.
Sunderland, L. Testimony of God against Slavery. Bost., 1836. 12°. 8471
Sunnybank. Terhune. N. Y., 1866. 12°. 2955
Sunset Land, The. Todd. Bost., 1870. 16°. 16886
Superior, Lake, Wanderings round. Kohl. Lond., 1860. 8°. . . 8421
Supernatural, Nature and the. Bushnell. N. Y., 1859. 8°. . . 10023
Supernaturalism of N. Engl. [Whittier.] Lond., 1847. 12°. . . 8612
Superstition, Enquiries into Vulgar Errors of. T. Browne. Lond., 1835. 2 v. 8°. 3987
Essay on. Blakeman. N. H., 1849. 12°. 8613
and Force. Lea. Philad., 1870. 12°. 3657
Memoirs of Popular Delusions of. Mackay. Lond., 1869. 16°. 8529
Modern. De Quincey. (Miscellanies.) Edinb., 1858. 8°. . 3276
See also, APPARITIONS; DEMONOLOGY; GHOSTS; MAGIC.
Surgeon's Daughter, The. Scott. Bost., 1845. 12°. 1833
Surrey, Earl of. See H. HOWARD.
Sutherland, A. Knights of Malta. Philad., 1846. 2 v. in 1. 12°. . 4618
Swain, C. Poems. (2 copies.) Bost., 1857–63. 16°. 978
Swain, J. Redemption. Charleston, 1819. 12°. 14862
Swainson, W. Animals in Menageries. Lond., 1838. 16°. . . 6053
Discourse on Study of Nat. History. Lond., 1839. 16°. . . 6055
Geography and Classification of Animals. Lond., 1835. 16°. . 6056
Habits and Instincts of Animals. Lond., 1840. 16°. . . 6054
Malacology, or Shells and Shell-Fish. Lond., 1840. 16°. . . 6062

Swainson, W. Nat. Hist. and Classification of Birds. Lond., 1836–37. 2 v. 16°. 6058
of Fishes, Amphibians and Reptiles. Lond., 1838–39. 2 v. 16°. . 6060
of Quadrupeds. Lond., 1835. 16°. 6057
Taxidermy, with Biography of Zoologists. Lond., 1840. 16°. . 6063
Swallow Barn. Kennedy. Philad., 1832. 2 v. 12°. 15788
Swear not at all. Bentham. (Works, pt. 5.) Edinb., 1838. 8°. . 9704
Sweden, Hist. of [to 1654]. Geiger. Lond., 1845. 8°. 5924
Revolutions in [to 1560]. Vertot. Lond., 1711. 8°. 16171
Tour in, in 1838. Laing. Lond., 1839. 8°. 8302
Travels in, 1779. Coxe. (v. 4.) Lond., 1802. 8°. . . . 16608
1807–08. Porter. Philad., 1809. 8°. 16603
1856–57. Bayard Taylor. N. Y., 1865. 12°. . . 8284
See, also, GUSTAVUS; SCANDINAVIA.
Swedenborg, E. Conjugial Love. Bost., 1840. 8°. 17224
Life of. Hobart. Bost., 1845. 12°. 7562
Swetchine, S., Life and Letters of. De Falloux. Bost., 1868. 16°. . 755
Swift, B., Memoir of. Dunham. Bost., 1842. 12°. 7526
Swift, John F. Going to Jericho. N. Y., 1868. 12°. 8240
Swift, Jona. Gulliver's Travels, ed. W. C. Taylor. Philad., 1869. 12°. 1970
Poetical Works, with Life by Mitford. Bost., 1859. 3 v. 16°. 1058
The same, ed. Johnson. Dubl., 1803. 8°. 15099
Works, ed. W. C. Taylor. N. Y., 1853. 12°. 1969
Works. Ed. Sheridan and Nichols. N. Y., 1812–13. 24 v. 12°. 3847

CONTENTS.—1, 2, Life, by Sheridan, etc. 3, Tale of a Tub; Hist. of Martin; Battle of the Books; On the Mechanical Operation of the Spirit; Meditation on a Broomstick; Sentiments of a Church of England Man; etc. 4, Argument against Abolishing Christianity; Letter concerning the Sacramental Test; Remarks on "The Rights of the Christian Church"; Bickerstaff's Predictions, etc.; Project for the Advancement of Religion; etc. 5, The Examiner; Conduct of the Allies, etc. 6, Remarks on the Barrier Treaty; Public Spirit of the Whigs; Political Papers, etc. 7, Hist. of the Four last Years of the Queen; Abstract of Hist. of England; etc. 8, Preface to Bp. of Sarum; Tatlers; Spectators; Intelligencers; Directions to Servants, etc. 9, Gulliver's Travels. 10, 11, Poems. 12, 13, Tracts relative to Ireland. 14, Sermons; Memoirs of Capt. Creichton, etc. 15–20, Letters to and from Swift. 21, 22, Journal to Stella. 22, Polite Conversation. 23, Miscellanies in Prose, by Pope, Arbuthnot, Gay, etc.; Martinus Scriblerus; Hist. of John Bull; etc. 24, Miscellanies in Verse and Prose; Art of Punning; etc.

The same. 4171
Essay on Life, Writings, etc., of. D. Swift. Lond., 1755. 8°. . 7117
Life of. W. Scott. Bost., 1829. 12°. 3190
The same. Sheridan. Dubl., 1785. 8°. 7118
Sketch of. Lecky. N. Y., 1872. 12°. 6743
Swiftiana. Lond., 1804. 2 v. 16°. 3812
Swinburne, A. C. Atalanta in Calydon. Bost., 1866. 16°. . . 1185
Chastelard. Bost., 1866. 16°. 1186
The Queen-Mother and Rosamond. (2 copies.) Bost., 1866. 16°. 1187
Swinburne, H. Travels through Spain. Dubl., 1779. 8°. . . . 16668
Swinton, W. Campaigns of the Army of the Potomac. N. Y., 1866. 8°. 6196
Rambles among Words. N. Y., 1859. 12°. 95
Switzerland, Hist. of, to 1830. [Wilson?] Lond., 1832. 16°. . . 5476
to 1838. Vieusseux. Lond., 1846. 8°. . . 5884
of Destruction of Helvetic Union of. Mallet du Pan. Bost., 1799. 12°. 16162
Letters from. Goethe. Lond., 1849. 8°. 445

Switzerland, Sketches of, in 1828. [J. F. Cooper.] Philad., 1836. 2 v. 12°. 16683
Tour in, 1817–19. Simond. Bost., 1822. 2 v. 8°. . . . 16681
Travels in, 1776. Coxe. Basil, 1802. 3 v. 8°. . . . 16685
See, also, ALPS.
Sybaris and other Homes, Hale. Bost., 1869. 16°. 2948
Sybel, H. v. Hist. of the French Revolution. Lond., 1867–69. 4 v. 8°. 5667
Sybil. Disraeli. Philad., 1845. 8°. 2345
Sydney Clifton. [Fay.] N. Y., 1839. 2 v. 12°. 15790
Symes, M. Embassy to Ava. Edinb., 1827. 2 v. 12°. . . . 4470
Sympson, J. Science Revived, or the Vision of Alfred. Philad., 1810. 12°. 14891
Symzonia. N. Y., 1820. 12°. 15792
Synonyms, English. Crabb. N. Y., 1839. 8°. 173
Selection of. [Whately.] Bost., 1852. 12°. . 101
of the N. T. Trench. N. Y., 1855. 12°. 9891
Syntax, Doctor, Tour of, in search of a Wife. Combe. Philad., 1829. 12°. 984
Syria, Expedition to, 1840–41. Hunter. Lond., 1842. 2 v. 12°. . 5160
The Howadji in. Curtis. N. Y., 1852. 12°. 8236
Travels through, 1783–85. Volney. Dubl., 1788. 8°. . . 16481
and Asia Minor, Popular Description of. Conder. Lond. 2 v. in 1. 12°. 7845
Scenery and People of. Kelly. Lond., 1844. 8°. . . . 8070
etc., Travels in. Irby and Mangles. Lond., 1844. 16°. . . 8197

T.

Table-Book, The. Hone. Lond., 1827–28. 2 v. in 1. 8°. . . . 4342
Table-Talk. [Constable's Miscellany, v. 10.] Edinb., 1827. 12°. . 4472
of Coleridge. (Works, v. 6.) N. Y., 1871. 12°. . . . 4018
of Hazlitt. Lond., 1846–57. 2 v. 16°. 3178
of S. Johnson. Lond., 1798. 8°. 3759
of Luther. Lond., 1848. 8°. 343
of S. Rogers. Lond., 1856. 8°. 3208
of Selden. Cambr., 1831. 12°. 3905
of R. B. Sheridan. Lond., 1826. 12°. 3206
Book of. [Bucke.] Lond., 1836. 2 v. 16°. 4327
Tablet, The. N. H., 1831. 12°. 15793
Tacitus. Historical Annals, transl. by Murphy. Philad., 1829. 3 v. 12°. 4597
Works, transl. by Murphy. Philad., 1822. 6 v. 8°. . . 15861
Taghconic. [J. E. A. Smith.] Bost., 1852. 12°. 16845
Tailor, R. The Hog hath lost his Pearl. Lond., 1825. 8°. . . 1513
Taine, H. A. Art in Greece. N. Y., 1871. 12°. 8850
in the Netherlands. N. Y., 1871. 12°. 8849
Hist. of English Literature. (3 copies.) N. Y., 1871. 2 v. 8°. 189
The same, abridged by Fiske. N. Y., 1872. 12°. . . 10208
The Ideal in Art. N. Y., 1869. 12°. 8848

Taine, H. A. Italy; Florence and Venice. (2 copies.) N. Y., 1869. 8°. 9065
Italy; Rome and Naples. (2 copies.) N. Y., 1868. 8°. . . 9063
Notes on England. (2 copies.) N. Y., 1872. 8°. . . . 5158
Philosophy of Art. N. Y., 1873. 16°. 8869
The same. 10225
Tai-Ping-Wang, Life of. Mackie. N. Y., 1857. 12°. . . . 6477
Tait's Edinburgh Magazine. Edinb., 1841–43. v. 9–10 in 4. 8°. . 13823
Tale of a Tub. J. Swift. N. Y., 1853. 12°. 1969
of Two Cities. Dickens. N. Y., 1872. 16°. 10217
Tales of the Borders, and of Scotland. Wilson. N. Y. 5 v. 8°. . 1678
of the Genii. [Ridley.] N. Y., 1825. 2 v. 12°. . . . 2013
of Glauber-Spa. N. Y., 1832. 2 v. 12°. 15163
of the Good Woman. [Paulding.] N. Y., 1829. 12°. . . 15288
of a Grandfather. Scott. Philad., 1851. 4 v. 16°. . . . 1709
of the Great St. Bernard. [Croly.] N. Y., 1829. 2 v. 12°. . 15592
of the Manor. Hofland. N. Y., 1822. 2 v. 12°. . . . 15594
of My Landlord. See W. SCOTT.
of My Neighborhood. [Griffin.] Philad., 1836. 2 v. 12°. . 15596
of the Northwest. [Snelling.] Bost., 1830. 12°. . . . 15798
of the Peerage and Peasantry. Dacre. N. Y., 1835. 2 v. 12°. 15598
of the Puritans. Bacon. N. H., 1831. 12°. 15799
of Romance. Philad., 1833. 2 v. 12°. 14875
of the West. [Carne.] N. Y., 1828. 2 v. 12°. . . . 15600
of Woman. N. Y., 1829. 12°. 15602
of the Woods and Fields. [Marsh-Caldwell.] N. Y., 1836. 12°. 15603
and Traditions, Foreign. Glasgow, 1828. v. 1. 12°. . . 3034
Talfourd, T. N. Critical and Miscellaneous Writings. Philad., 1846. 8°. 3471
The same. (2 copies.) Philad., 1842. 12°. . . . 3220
Ion. 4th ed. N. Y., 1837. 12°. 1444
Ion; and the Athenian Captive. N. Y., 1837–38. 12°. . . 1445
Life, Letters, and Final Memorials of Lamb. N. Y., 1871. 2 v. 12°. 3974
Vacation Rambles. 2d ed. Lond., 1845. 12°. 8381
Talisman, The. Scott. Edinb., 1871. 8°. 1889
The. Verplanck, Bryant, and Sands. (2 copies.) N. Y., 1833. 3 v. 12°. 4132
Talleyrand-Perigord, C. M. de, Life of. McHarg. N. Y., 1857. 12°. 7626
The same. [De Villemarest.] Lond., 1834. v. 1, 2. 8°. 7722
Talmage, T. D. W. Crumbs swept up. Philad. [1870.] 12°. . . 15272
Talvi. See T. A. L. v. I. ROBINSON.
Tam O'Shanter. Burns. (Illustrated.) N. Y., 1868. 4°. . . . .
Tamerlane, Hist. of. Sherefeddin Ali. Lond., 1723. 2 v. 8°. . . 16411
Tannehill, W. Sketches of Hist. of Literature. Nashville, 1827. 8°. 15070
Tappan, A., Life of. L. Tappan. N. Y., 1870. 12°. 7642
Tappan, H. P. University Education. N. Y., 1851. 12°. . . . 9256
Tappan, W. B. Poems. Philad., 1836. 12°. 15038
The same. Bost., 1840. 16°. 14954
Tarleton, B. Hist. of Campaigns of 1780–81. Lond., 1787. 4°. . 16042
The same. Dubl., 1787. 8°. 6116

Tartary, Travels in, 1844-46. Huc. Lond., 1856. 8°. 7945
Siberian, Journey through. Cochrane. Edinb., 1829. 2 v. 12°. 4498
Tasistro, L. F. Random Shots and Southern Breezes. N. Y., 1842. 2 v. 12°. 16892
Tasso, T. Jerusalem Delivered. Transl. by Hunt. Lond., 1818. 2 v. 8°. 909
The same. Ed. Walsh. Philad., 1822. 2 v. 24°. . . . 37
The same, transl., with Life, by Wiffen. 3d ed. Lond., 1830. 2 v. 12°. 883
Recovery of Jerusalem, transl. by Fairfax. (2 copies.) N. Y., 1846. 2 v. in 1. 12°. 885
The same. Ed. C. Knight. Lond., 1844. 2 v. 24°. . 282
Stories. (Hunt's Ital. Poets.) N. Y., 1846. 12°. . . . 887
Life of. Stebbing. (v. 3.) Lond., 1831. 12°. 7777
Love and Madness of. Wilde. N. Y., 1842. 2 v. 12°. . . 16408
Tassoni, A., Memoirs of. Walker. Lond., 1815. 8°. 7749
Taste, Essay on. Alison. Bost., 1812. 8°. 17067
Principles of. Knight. Lond., 1808. 8°. 17066
See, also, AESTHETICS; BEAUTY.
Tatler, The. Steele, Addison, etc. Philad., 1831. 8°. 3398
Ed. Ferguson. Lond., 1823. 4 v. 12°. 3109
The same. 3149
Essays illustrative of the. Drake. Lond., 1805. 3 v. 8°. . 3233
See, also, ADDISON; STEELE.
Tautphoeus, I. von. Cyrilla. N. Y. 8°. 2311
The same. 2657
The Initials. (2 copies.) Philad. 12°. 2505
At Odds. (2 copies.) Philad., 1863. 12°. 2509
Quits. (2 copies.) Philad., 1861-67. 2 v. in 1. 12°. . . . 2507
Taxidermy. Swainson. Lond., 1840. 16°. 6063
Taylor, Bayard. At Home and Abroad. (2 copies.) N. Y., 1860-67. 2 v. 12°. 8286
Beauty and the Beast; and Tales of Home. N. Y., 1872. 12°. 2941
Cyclopædia of Modern Travel. Cincinn., 1856. 8°. . . . 8128
Eldorado; Life in California and Mexico. (2 copies.) N. Y., 1861-67. 12°. 8279
Hannah Thurston. (2 copies.) N. Y., 1864. 12°. 2934
Japan, in our day. N. Y., 1872. 12°. 10177
John Godfrey's Fortunes. N. Y., 1864. 12°. 2936
Joseph and his Friend. (2 copies.) N. Y., 1870. 12°. . . 2939
Journey to Central Africa. N. Y., 1867. 12°. 8281
Lands of the Saracen. N. Y., 1855. 12°. 8282
Northern Travel; Sweden, Denmark, Lapland. N. Y., 1865. 12°. 8284
The Picture of St. John. (2 copies.) Bost., 1866-67. 16°. . 758
Poems of the Orient. Bost., 1855. 16°. 756
The Poet's Journal. Bost., 1863. 16°. 757
Rhymes of Travel, Ballads, and Poems. 2d ed. N. Y., 1849. 12°. 755
Story of Kennett. (2 copies.) N. Y., 1866-67. 12°. . . . 2937
Travels in Greece and Russia. N. Y., 1859. 12°. . . . 8285

Taylor, Bayard. Views a-foot. N. Y., 1848. 2 v. in 1. 12°. . . . 8278
Visit to India, China, and Japan. N. Y., 1855. 12°. 8283
Taylor, E. Sabbath Recreations. Ed. Pierpont. Bost., 1839. 12°. . 14909
Taylor, F. W. The Flag Ship; a Voyage. N. Y., 1840. 2 v. 12°. . 16334
Taylor, Henry. Edwin the Fair; and Isaac Comnenus. 2d ed. Lond., 1845. 24°. 983
Philip van Artevelde. Bost., 1863. 16°. 982
The same. (2 copies.) Cambr., 1835. 2 v. 16°. . . 1001
The Statesman. (2 copies.) Lond., 1836. 16°. 8476
Taylor, Herbert. Last Illness and Decease of Duke of York. Lond., 1827. 16°. 6683
Taylor, Isaac *(the elder)*. Self-Cultivation recommended. Bost., 1820. 12°. 17038
Youth's Own Book. Hartf'd., 1836. 12°. 17057
Taylor, Isaac. Ancient Christianity and the Oxford Tracts. Philad., 1840. 12°. . . . . , ... 9541
Elements of Thought. From 9th ed. N. Y., 1851. 12°. . . 8594
The same. 6th ed. Lond., 1842. 16°. 3511
Fanaticism. (2 copies.) N. Y., 1834. 12°. 9536
Hist. of transmission of ancient books. Lond., 1827. 8°. . 244
Home Education. N. Y., 1838. 12°. 9307
Lectures on Spiritual Christianity. N. Y., 1841. 12°. . . 9542
Logic in Theology, and other Essays. N. Y., 1860. 12°. . 9543
Loyola, and Jesuitism. N. Y., 1851. 12°. 7670
Natural Hist. of Enthusiasm. (2 copies.) Bost.. 1830. 12°. . 9534
Physical Theory of another Life. N Y., 1836. 12°. . . . 9540
The Process of Historical Proof. Lond., 1828. 8°. . . . 10019
Saturday Evening. (2 copies.) N. Y., 1832. 12°. . . . 9532
Spirit of the Hebrew Poetry. N. Y., 1862. 12°. . . . 9544
Spiritual Despotism. (2 copies.) N. Y., 1835. 12°. . . 9538
Taylor, James E. Beauties of the Poets. Lond., 1824. 12°. . . 14908
Taylor, Jane. Contribution of Q. Q., *etc.* N. Y., 1826. 2 v. 12°. . 3371
Poetical Remains and Correspondence. Bost., 1833. 12°. . 14892
Writings. Bost., 1835. 3 v. 12°. 3705
Taylor, Jeremy. Discourses. Bost., 1816. 3 v. 8°. 10045
Holy Living and Dying. Philad., 1835. 12°. 9822
The same. (Bohn's ed.) Lond., 1850. 8°. 488
Liberty of Prophesying. Ed. Cattermole. Lond., 1834. 16°. . 9484
Life of Jesus Christ. Ed. Stebbing. Lond., 1835. 3 v. 16°. . 9504
Selections from Writings of. Montagu. (2 copies.) N. Y., 1845. 12°. . . . . . , ... 3957
Works. [Ed. H. Rogers.] Lond., 1836. v. 2, 3. 8°. . . 10063
Works, with Life, by Hughes. Lond., 1831. 5 v. 12°. . . 9563
CONTENTS.—1-4, Sermons. 4, Contemplations of the State of Man. 5, Holy Living and Dying.
Life of. Heber. Lond., 1824. 2 v. 16°. 7559
Notes on. Coleridge. (Remains, v. 3.) Lond., 1838. 8°. . 4008
Taylor, John, (born 1756, died 1832.) Records of my Life. N. Y., 1833. 8°. 7994
Taylor, John, (born 1781, died 1864.) Identity of Junius. From 2d ed. N. Y., 1818. 8°. . . . . , . 6856

Taylor, John. *(U. S. Senator.)* New Views of the Constitution. Wash., 1823. 8°. 6182
Taylor, John. The Pocket Lacon. Philad., 1839. 2 v. 12°. . . 4353
Taylor, John E. M. Angelo as a Poet. Lond., 1840. 12°. . . 7506
Taylor, R. Writings. Lond. 12°. 9483
Taylor, Samuel H. Classical Study, its Value illustrated. Andover. 1870. 12°. 9263
Method of. Bost., 1861. 12°. . 9273
Taylor, Sarah L., Memoir of. L. Jones. N. Y., 1847. 12°. . . 7525
Taylor, Thos. Life of Cowper. Philad.. 1833. 12°. 7109
Taylor, Tom. Life of Dickens. Lond., 1870. 8°. 7018
of Haydon. 2d ed. Lond., 1853. 3 v. 8°. . 7934
Thackeray, the Humourist and Man of Letters. (2 copies.) N. Y., 1864. 12°. 7016
Taylor, Wm. Historic Survey of German Poetry. Lond., 1830. 3 v. 8°. 206
Taylor, Wm. B. S. The Fine Arts in Grt. Britain and Ireland. Lond., 1841. 2 v. 12°. 8872
Taylor, Wm. C. Hist. of Christianity (to 380). Lond., 1844. 16°. . 6333
Hist. of Ireland. N. Y., 1841. 2 v. 12°. 11271
The same. N. Y., 1833. 2 v. 12°. 12107
of Overthrow of the Roman Empire. (2 copies.) Lond., 1836. 12°. 4726
Memoirs of House of Orleans. Philad., 1850. 2 v. 12°. . 5520
Modern British Plutarch. (2 copies.) N. Y., 1846. 16°. . 6678
Natural History of Society. N. Y., 1841. 2 v. 12°. . . . 4562
Revolutions and Conspiracies of Europe. Lond., 1843. 2 v. 8°. 4088
Romantic Biography of the Age of Eliz. Philad., 1842. 2 v. 12°. 6746
Student's Manual of Mod. Hist. 2d ed. Lond., 1841. 12°. . 4564
And others. The Occult Sciences. Glasg., 1855. 8°. . . 8616
Taylor, Z. Messages, etc. (Statesman's Manual, v. 3.) N. Y., 1854. 8°. 6202
and his Generals. Philad., 1847. 12°. 7543
The same. Hartf'd., 1848. 12°. 7544
Teaching. See Schools ; Education.
Tea-Table Miscellany. Ramsay. Berwick, 1793. 2 v. 12°. . . 14911
Technology. See Arts ; Manufactures.
Tecumseh, Life of. Drake. Cincinn., 1841. 12°. 5751
Tecumseh; a Poem. Colton. N. Y., 1842. 12°. 14983
Tefft, B. F. Hungary and Kossuth. Philad., 1852. 12°. . . . 5815
Tegner, E. Frithiof's Saga, transl. by Strong. Lond., 1833. 8°. . 922
Miscellaneous Poems, transl. by Bethune. Lond., 1848. 8°. . 921
Teignmouth, J. S. Memoir of Sir W. Jones. Philad., 1805. 8°. . 7146
Telegraph, Atlantic, Hist. of the. H. M. Field. N. Y., 1866. 12°. . 8900
Telemachus, Adventures of. Fenelon. Lond. 8°. 1996
Tell, Wilhelm ; a Drama. Schiller. Lond., 1846. 8°. . . . 437
Tell, William ; a Play. Knowles. (Works, v. 1.) Lond., 1841. 12°. 1432
Temper; a Tale. Opie. Bost., 1827. 2 v. 12°. 14445
Temper and Temperament. Mrs. Ellis. N. Y., 1846. 12°. . . . 2426
Temperance Convention, Hist. of a. Hitchcock. Northampton, 1850. 16°. 9121

Temperance Recollections. Marsh. N. Y., 1866. 12°. . . . 16425
See, also, DRUNKENNESS ; INTEMPERANCE.
Temple, G. Travels in Greece and Turkey. Lond., 1836. 2 v. 12°. 16625
Temple, H. J. (Viscount Palmerston), Life of. Bulwer. Philad., 1871. 2 v. 12°. 6775
Temple, *(Sir)* **W.** Works. Lond., 1814. 4 v. 8°. 17197

CONTENTS.—1 Life; Essay on Gov't.; Observations on the United Provinces of the Netherlands; Letters on Transactions, 1665–72. 2, Letters; Constitution and Interests of the Empire, Sweden, Denmark, etc.; Memoirs of Events, 1672 to 1681. 3, Essays and Miscellaneous Pieces; Poems; Hist. of England. 4, Letters to the King, Prince of Orange, etc.

Memoirs of. Courtenay. Lond., 1836. 2 v. 8°. . . . 6832
Temple Bar. Lond., 1867–72. v. 21–36. 8°. 17901
Ten Thousand a year. Warren. Edinb., 1872. 8°. . , . . 2448
Ten times One are Ten. Hale. Bost., 1871. 16°. 2732
Tenant of Wildfell Hall, The. [A. Bronte.] N. Y., 1857. 12°. . . 2557
Teneriffe; an Astronomer's Experiment. Smyth. Lond., 1858. 8°. . 8910
[**Tennant, W.**] Anster Fair; with other Poems. Bost., 1815. 12°. 14894
Tennemann, W. G. Manual of Hist. of Philosophy. (2 copies.) Oxf'd., 1832. 8°. 8713
Tennent, J. E. Belgium. Lond., 1841. 2 v. 12°. 16652
Tennessean, The; a Novel. Royall. N. H., 1827. 12°. . . . 15801
[**Tenney, T.**] Female Quixotism. Bost., 1825. 2 v. 12°. . . 15694
Tenniel, J. Cartoons from Punch. Lond. 4°. . . . . . .
Tennyson, A. Enoch Arden, etc. (2 copies.) Bost., 1864. 16°. . 1160
Gareth and Lynette. Bost., 1872. 16°. 1165
The Holy Grail, and other Poems. (2 copies.) Bost., 1870. 16°. 1162
The Last Tournament. Bost., 1872. 16°. 1164
Maud and other Poems. Lond., 1855. 16°. 1158
The same. Bost., 1855. 16°. 1159
In Memoriam. Bost., 1850. 16°. 1157
Poems. Bost., 1848. 2 v. 16°. 1155
Poetical Works. Bost., 1861. 2 v. in 1. 16°. 960
The same. New ed. Bost., 1866. 2 v. in 1. 16°. . . 961
Concordance to. Brightwell. Lond., 1869. 8°. . . . 1241
Tênot, E. Paris in Dec., 1851. (2 copies.) N. Y., 1870. 8°. . . 5549
Terence. The Andrian, Brothers, Phormio, tr. by Colman. Ed. Walsh. Philad., 1822. 12°. 36
Terhune, M. V. Sunnybank. N. Y., 1866. 12°. 2955
Terrible Temptation, A. Reade. Lond., 1871. 3 v. 8°. . . . 2104
Tractoration. [Fessenden.] Philad., 1806. 8°. . . . 15058
Terry, Rose. Poems. Bost., 1861. 16°. 776
Teutonic Antiquities. Chatfield. Lond., 1828. 8°. 4675
Texan Exped. against Mier, 1842–44. Green. N. Y., 1845. 12°. . 16902
Santa Fe Exped., Narrative of the, 1841–42. Kendall. N. Y., 1844. 2 v. 12°. 16903
Texas, Hist. of. Edward. Cincinn., 1836. 12°. 5994
of Revolution in, 1835–36. Newell. N. Y., 1838. 12°. . 5734
Journey through, 1855. Olmsted. N. Y., 1860. 12°. . . 6096
Life in. Sealsfield. N. Y., 1844. 8°. 15669
and the Texans. Foote. Philad., 1841. 2 v. 12°. . . . 5995

Thacher, J. Essay on Demonology, Salem Witchcraft, etc. Bost., 1831. 12°. 8480

Military Journal of the Revolution. Bost., 1823. 8°. . . . 16125

The same, 2d ed. Bost., 1827. 8°. 5855

Thackeray, F. Ancient Britain. Lond., 1843. 2 v. 8°. 5069

Thackeray, W. M. Adventures of Philip. (2 copies.) N. Y., 1862. 8°. 2341

Ballads. (2 copies.) Bost., 1856. 16°. 833

Book of Snobs. N. Y., 1853. 12°. 2033

English Humorists; Four Georges. N. Y., 1868. 12°. . . 3744

Four Georges. (2 copies.) N. Y., 1860. 12°. 3742

Four Georges; English Humorists; Roundabout Papers; etc. Bost., 1869. 8°. 3745

Henry Esmond. N. Y., 1869. 8°. 2310

Henry Esmond; Lovel the Widower. Bost., 1869. 12°. . . 2224

Journey from Cornhill to Cairo. N. Y., 1846. 12°. 8367

Little Dinner at Timmins's, Bedford-Row Conspiracy, Fitz Boodle Papers, and a Shabby Genteel Story. Leipz., 1867. 16°. 2027

Lovel the Widower. Lond., 1861. 16°. 2225

Luck of Barry Lyndon. N. Y., 1853. 2 v. 12°. 2031

The same. 2232

Men's Wives. N. Y., 1853. 12°. 2229

Mr. Brown's Letters to a Young Man about Town, etc. N. Y., 1853. 12°. 2235

The Newcomes. N. Y., 1855. 8°. 2340

Paris Sketch Book. 2d ed. Lond., 1840. 2 v. 12°. . . . 2230

The same. N. Y., 1852. 2 v. 12°. 2029

Pendennis. (2 copies.) N. Y., 1855–67. 2 v. 8°. . . . 2336

Roundabout Papers. (2 copies.) N. Y., 1864. 12°. . . 2226

Shabby Genteel Story, etc. N. Y., 1852. 12°. 2028

Shabby Genteel Story, etc.; Fitz-Boodle's Confessions; Passages in the Life of Maj. Gahagan. N. Y., 1866–68. 12°. 2234

Works. Lond., 1871–72. 12 v. 8°. 2189

CONTENTS.—1, Vanity Fair. 2, Pendennis. 3, Newcomes. 4, Henry Esmond; Barry Lyndon. 5, Virginians. 6, Shabby Genteel Story; Philip. 7, Paris and Irish Sketch Books; Journey from Cornhill to Cairo. 8, Great Hoggarty Diamond; Memoirs of Mr. Yellowplush; Burlesques. (Novels by Eminent Hands; Jeames's Diary; Adventures of Maj. Gahagan; Legend of the Rhine; Rebecca and Rowena; The Next French Revolution; Cox's Diary; etc.) 9, Book of Snobs; Sketches of Life and Character; Men's Wives; Fitzboodle Papers; Bedford Row Conspiracy; Little Dinner at Timmins's; etc. 10, Roundabout Papers; Four Georges; English Humorists; Second Funeral of Napoleon. 11, Catherine; Lovel the Widower; Denis Duval; Ballads; The Wolves and the Lamb; Critical Reviews; Little Travels. 12, Christmas Books.

The same. v. 1–6. 10307

Works. Philad., 1871–72. 11 v. 8°. 2213

CONTENTS.—1, Vanity Fair. 2, Pendennis. 3, Newcomes. 4, H. Esmond; Barry Lyndon. 5, Virginians. 6, Shabby Genteel Story; Philip. 7, Book of Snobs; Sketches of Life and Character; Burlesques. 8, Paris and Irish Sketch Books; Memoirs of Mr. Yellowplush; Journey from Cornhill to Cairo. 9, Christmas Books; Ballads; Men's Wives; etc. 10, Catherine; Little Travels; Fitz-Boodle Papers; Critical Reviews; The Wolves and the Lamb; Denis Duval; Lovel the Widower; Bedford Row Conspiracy; A Little Dinner at Timmins's; The Fatal Boots. 11, The Georges; English Humorists; Roundabout Papers; Second Funeral of Napoleon.

Yellowplush Correspondence. Philad., 1838. 12°. 2228

Yellowplush Papers; Cox's Diary. Leipz., 1866. 16°. . . 2026

the Humorist and Man of Letters. Taylor. N. Y., 1864. 12°. 7016

Thackrah, C. T. Effects of the Principal Trades, etc., on Health. Philad., 1831. 12°. 16965

Thaddeus of Warsaw. J. Porter. N. Y., 1858. 12°. 15178

Thatcher, B. B. Boston Book. Bost., 1836–37. 2 v. 12°. . . . 15065

Indian Biography. N. Y., 1840. 2 v. 12°. 12104

The same. N. Y., 1832. 2 v. 12°. 11049

Memoir of P. Wheatley. Bost., 1834. 12°. 8472

Thayendanegea, Life of. Stone. N. Y., 1838. 2 v. 8°. 5952

Theater, American, Hist. of. Dunlap. N. Y., 1832. 8°. 1616

Before the Footlights and Behind the Scenes of. Logan. Philad., 1870. 8°. 1618

British. Leipsic, 1828. 8°. 1634

CONTENTS.—Cato, Addison; Mourning Bride, Double Dealer, Way of the World, Congreve; Zara, Hill; Douglas, Home; G. Barnwell, Lillo; Duke of Milan, New Way to pay Old Debts, Massinger; Gamester, Moore; Venice Preserved, Orphan, Otway; Distrest Mother, Philips; Fair Penitent, Rowe; Siege of Damascus, Hughes; Hypocrite, Love in a Village, Maid of the Mill, Bickerstaff; Bold Stroke for a Wife, Busy-Body, Centlivre; Provoked Husband, Vanbrugh and Cibber; Jealous Wife, Inkle and Yarico, Colman; Fashionable Lover, W. Indian, Cumberland; Recruiting Officer, Farquhar; Clandestine Marriage, Bon Ton, Lying Valet, Garrick; Good-natured Man, She Stoops to Conquer, Goldsmith; Every Man in his Humour, Jonson; Chapter of Accidents, S. Lee; Man of the World, Macklin; Cure for Heart-Ache, Morton; 3 Weeks after Marriage, Apprentice, Murphy; Rivals, School for Scandal, Duenna, Sheridan; Conscious Lovers, Steele; Rosina, Brooke; Beggar's Opera, Gay; High Life Below Stairs, Townley; Mayor of Garrat, Foote; Fortune's Frolic, Allingham; Who's the Dupe, Cowley.

British. Inchbald. Lond. v. 11–13, 16–19, 23, 27. 12°. . 1337

CONTENTS.—11, De Montfort, by J. Baillie; Barbarossa, by J. Brown; Gustavus Vasa, by Brooke; All for Love, by Dryden. 12, Grecian Daughter, All in the Wrong, Way to Keep him, Know your own Mind, all by Murphy. 13, Oroonoko, and Isabella, by Southern; Siege of Damascus, by Hughes; Roman Father, by Whitehead. 16, Good-natured Man, and She Stoops to Conquer, by Goldsmith; Wheel of Fortune, by Cumberland. 17, Love for Love, by Congreve; She Would and She Would Not, Love makes a Man, Careless Husband, by Cibber. 18, Bold Stroke for a Wife, Busy Body, The Wonder, by Centlivre; Conscious Lovers, by Steele. 19, Every one has his Fault, To Marry or Not, Such Things are, Wives as they were and Maids as they are; all by Inchbald. 23, West Indian, Jew, Brothers, First Love; all by Cumberland. 27, Love in a Village, Lionel and Clarissa, Maid of the Mill, by Bickerstaff; Point of Honour, by C. Kemble.

German. Transl. by Thompson. Lond., 1811. v. 2–6. 12°. . 1357

CONTENTS.—2, Don Carlos, by Schiller; Count Benyowsky, by Kotzebue. 3, Lovers' Vows, Deaf and Dumb, Indian Exiles, False Delicacy, all by Kotzebue. 4, Otto of Wittlesbach, and Dagobert, by Babo; Adelaide of Wulfingen, by Kotzebue. 5, Robbers, by Schiller; Happy Family, by Kotzebue; Conscience, by Iffland. 6, Ensign, by Schroeder; Count Koenigsmark, by Reitzenstein; Stella, by Goethe; Emilia Galotti, by Lessing.

Modern. Inchbald. Lond., 1811. v. 2–10. 12°. 1328

CONTENTS.—2, Speculation, The Delinquent, Laugh when you can, Fortune's Tool, Folly as it flies; all by Reynolds. 3, Votary of Wealth, by Holman. Zorinski, and Secrets worth knowing, by Morton; Who wants a Guinea, by Colman, Jr.; Werter, by Reynolds. 4, Duplicity, School for Arrogance, and Seduction, by Holcroft; He's Much to Blame; School for Prejudice, by T. Dibdin. 5, False Impressions, Mysterious Husband, Box-Lobby Challenge, Natural Son, Carmelite; all by Cumberland. 6, Impostors, by Cumberland; Wife of two Husbands, and Ramah Droog, by Cobb; Law of Lombardy, and Braganza, by Jephson. 7, I'll tell you what, Next Door Neighbours, Wise Men of the East, by Inchbald; Percy, by H. Moore; Trip to Scarborough, by Sheridan from Vanbrugh. 8, Matilda, by Francklin; Mary, Q. of Scots, by St. John; Fugitive, by J. Richardson; He Would be a Soldier, by Philon; England Preserved, by Watson. 9, Bank Note, by Macready; Chapter of Accidents, by S. Lee; English Merchant, by Colman; School for Wives, by Kelly; Henry II., by Hull. 10, Fashionable Levities, by Macnally; Time's a Tell-Tale, by H. Siddons; Which is the Man, by Cowley; What is She; Lie of a Day, by O'Keeffe.

Theatrical Management for 30 years. Sol. Smith. N. Y., 1868. 8°. 1617

Stage, The; before and behind the Curtain. Bunn. Philad., 1840. 2 v. 12°. 1614

See, also, DRAMA; PLAYS; STAGE.

Thebes, Travels in the Oasis of; 1815–18. Cailliaud. Lond., 1822. 8°. 8057

Their Wedding Journey. Howells. Bost., 1872. 12°. . . . 2952

Theists, Prayers for. Cobbe. Lond., 1871. 8°. 9967

Theller, E. A. Canada in 1837–38. Philad., 1841. 2 v. 12°. . . 5722

Thelwall, J., Life of. By his Widow. Lond., 1837. v 1. 8°. . . 6789

Theodore. De Wette. Bost., 1841. 2 v. 12°. 17264

Theological Review. Lond., 1870. v. 7. 8°. 17736

Students, Hints to. Burder. N. Y., 1830. 12°. . . . 17035

Theology, Institutes of. Chalmers. N. Y., 1849. 2 v. 12°. . . . 9528
Recent Inquiries in. Ed. Hedge. Bost., 1861. 12°. . . . 9954
Natural. Chalmers. N. Y., 1841. 2 v. 12°. 9516
The same. Paley, ed. Potter. N. Y., 1840. 2 v. 12°. . 11420
Systematic, Lectures on. Campbell. Bost., 1832. 8°. . . . 10038
Theophrastus. Characters, transl. by Jebb. Cambr., 1870. 16°. . 4230
Theremin, F. Eloquence a Virtue ; Systematic Rhetoric. Ed. Shedd. Andover, 1860. 12°. 9293
Thibet, Travels in. Huc. Lond., 1856. 8°. 7945
Thierry, J. N. A. Hist. of Norman Conquest. (2 copies.) Lond., 1841. 8°. 5071
The same. (Bohn's ed.) 2 copies. Lond., 1847. 2 v. 8°. 332
The same. vol. 1. Lond., 1856. 8°. 336
of the Tiers État. Lond., 1855. 2 v. 8°. . 5555
Thiers, A. Hist. of the Consulate and Empire. Lond., 1845–62. 20 v. in 10. 8°. 5614
of the French Revolution. (2 copies.) Philad., 1840. 3 v. 8°. . . . . , ... 5674
The Mississippi Bubble: Memoir of Law. N. Y., 1859. 12°. 6634
Thiodolf the Icelander. De La Motte Fouqué. Philad., 1863. 12°. . 3019
Thirlwall, C. Hist. of Greece. N. Y., 1845. 2 v. 8°. . . . 4426
The same. Lond., 1835–44. 8 v. 16°. 4857
Thirty Years' War. See GERMANY (history, 1618–48).
Tholuck, F. A. D. Life, etc., of Paul ; Sermons. (2 copies.) Andover, 1839. 8°. 10061
Thom, W. Rhymes and Recollections. 2d ed. Lond., 1845. 8°. . 14805
Thomas à Kempis. The Imitation of Christ, ed. Chalmers. N. Y., 1846. 12°. 9946
The same, ed. Malcom. Bost., 1861. 12°. . . . 9947
Thomas, E. S. Reminiscences. Hartf'd., 1840. 2 v. 12°. . . 7335
Thome, J. A., and **Kimball, J. H.** Emancipation in the W. I. N. Y., 1838. 12°. 8568
Thoms, W. J. Book of the Court. 2d ed. Lond., 1844. 8°. . . 5265
Thompson, Benj. (*Count* Rumford), Life of. Renwick. Bost., 1845. 16°. 7264
Thompson, Benj. (translator.) German Theatre. 4th ed. Lond., 1811. v 2–6. 12°. 1357
For Contents, see THEATER.
Thompson, D. P. Locke Amsden. Bost., 1856. 12°. . . . 15734
Thompson, G. Lectures on British India. Pawtucket, 1840. 12°. . 16500
and Discussions. Ed. Garrison. Bost., 1836. 12°. 8556
The Prison Bard. Hartf'd., 1848. 12°. 14863
Prison Life and Reflections. 3d ed. Hartf'd., 1849. 12°. . 8557
Thompson, Henry. Life of H. More. Philad., 1838. 2 v. 12°. . 15107
Thompson, Rev. Henry, etc. The Occult Sciences. Glasg., 1855. 8°. 8616
Thompson, Joseph P. Egypt, past and present. Bost., 1854. 12°. . 7972
The Holy Comforter. N. Y., 1866. 12°. 17284
Love and Penalty. N. Y., 1860. 12°. 9825
Man in Genesis and in Geology. N. Y., 1870. 12°. 8959

Thompson, Waddy. Recollections of Mexico. N. Y., 1847. 12°. . 16907
Thompson, Wm. Select Poems. Ed. Walsh. Philad., 1822. 24°. . 22
Thompson, Z. Hist. of Vt. Burlington, 1842. 8°. 5902
Thomson, A. Sermons on Infidelity. Windsor, 1833. 12°. . . 17270
Thomson, James. Poetical Works. Ed. Bell. Lond., 1807. 24°. . 534
The same, ed. Sanford. Philad., 1819. 24°. 16
The same, with Memoir. Philad., 1831. 8°. 1253
The same, ed. Johnson. Dubl., 1804. 8°. 15102
The Seasons. Philad., 1831. 12°. 14894
Tancred and Sigismunda. (Brit. Drama.) Lond., 1804. 8°. . 1630
Thomson, K. B. Memoirs of Court of Henry VIII. Lond., 1826. 2 v. 8°. 5289
of Ralegh. Philad., 1831. 12°. 6632
Thomson, R. Chronicles of London Bridge. 2d ed. Lond., 1839. 16°. 5143
Illustrations of Hist. of Grt. Brit. Edinb., 1828. 2 v. 12°. . 4482
Thomson, Wm. M. The Land and the Book. N. Y., 1859. 2 v. 12°. 8241
Thorburn, G. Forty Years in America. Bost., 1834. 12°. . . 16429
Thoreau, H. D. Cape Cod. (2 copies.) Bost., 1865. 8°. 3553
Maine Woods. Bost., 1864. 8°. 10226
Walden. Bost., 1863. 8°. 3552
Week on the Concord and Merrimack. Bost., 1868. 12°. . 3557
A Yankee in Canada, with Anti-Slavery and Reform Papers. (2 copies.) Bost., 1866. 8°. 3555
Thoresby, R. Diary and Letters. Lond., 1830–32. 4 v. 8°. . . 7166
Thoresen, M. Old Olaf. (2 copies.) Bost., 1870. 16°. 2619
Thorndale; or the Conflict of Opinions. W. Smith. Bost., 1859. 12°. 9963
Thorne, J. Rambles by Rivers. Lond., 1844. 12°. 8149
Thornwell, J. H. Discourses on Truth. N. Y., 1859. 12°. . . 9978
Thought, Elements of. Taylor. N. Y., 1851. 12°. 8594
Thrale, *Mrs.* **H. L.** See Piozzi.
Three Courses and a Dessert. [Clarke.] Illustrated by Cruikshank. Lond., 1867. 8°. 523
Cutters, The. Marryat. N. Y., 1836. 12°. 2112
Experiments of Living. Lee. Bost., 1837. 12°. . . . 15804
Histories. Miss Jewsbury. Bost., 1831. 12°. 15604
Nights in a Lifetime. N. Y., 1835. 12°. 15110
Thrupp, J. The Anglo-Saxon Home. Lond., 1862. 8°. 5264
Thucydides. Hist. of the Peloponnesian War, transl. by W. Smith. Philad., 1836. 8°. 4441
The same. N. Y., 1839. 2 v. 12°. 4529
The same. N. Y., 1836. 2 v. 12°. 4550
The same. Lond., 1805. 2 v. 8°. 15873
Thunberg, C. P. Travels. Lond., 1795. 4 v. 8°. 16261
Thunder and Lightning. De Fonvielle. N. Y., 1869. 12°. . . 10112
Thurlow, E., Life of. Campbell. (Ld. Chancellors, v. 5.) Philad., 1848. 8°. 6870
Tickell, T. Poetical Works. Ed. Bell. Lond., 1807. 24°. . . 529
The same, with Life by Johnson. Bost., 1854. 16°. . 1055
The same. Dubl., 1804. 8°. 15099
Works. With Life, by Sanford. Philad., 1819. 24°. . . 13

Ticknor, C. The Philosophy of Living. N. Y., 1840. 12°. . . 11402
Ticknor, G. Hist. of Spanish Literature. N. Y., 1849. 3 v. 8°. . 219
Life of Prescott. Bost., 1864. 8°. 7474
The same. Bost., 1864. 12°. 7388
Tieck, L. Novels, transl. by Roscoe. Lond., 1826. 12°. . . . 1898
Popular Tales, tr. by Carlyle. Bost., 1841. 12°. . . . 3107
The same. Lond., 1871. 8°. 4053
Tiers État, Hist. of the. Thierry. Lond., 1855. 2 v. 8°. . . . 5555
Tietz, von. St. Petersburgh, Constantinople, etc. Lond., 1836. 2 v. 8°. 16546
Tighe, M. Psyche, with other Poems. Philad., 1812. 12°. . . 14895
Timbs, J. Abbeys, Castles, etc., of England. Lond. 2 v. 8°. . 5136
Popular Errors. Lond., 1841. 16°. 16980
Timur, Hist. of. Sherefeddin Ali. Lond., 1723. 2 v. 8°. . . . 16411
Tin Trumpet, The. Philad., 1836. 2 v. 12°. 4265
The same. N. Y., 1859. 12°. 4267
Tindal, N. Hist. of England. Lond., 1759–61. 9 v. 8°. . . . 16086
Tischendorf, L. F. C. Origin of the Gospels. Bost. [1867.] 16°. . 9802
Tischer, J. F. W. Life of Luther. Hudson, 1818. 12°. . . . 6348
Tissandier, G. Travels in the Air. Lond., 1871. 8°. 9093
The Wonders of Water. N. Y., 1872. 12°. 10149
Titan: a Romance. Richter. Bost., 1864. 2 v. 8°. 3063
Titcomb, Timothy. *(Pseudonym.)* See J. G. HOLLAND.
Titterwell, Timothy. *(Pseudonym.)* Yankee Notions. Bost., 1838. 12°. 4312
Tobacco, A Counterblast to. James I. Ed. Arber. Lond., 1869. 16°. 3892
Mysteries of. Lane. N. Y., 1846. 12°. 9231
Responses on the use of. Lane. N. Y., 1846. 12°. . . . 9232
Tocqueville, A. C. H. C. de. Democracy in America. N. Y., 1838–40. 2 v. 8°. 6185
The same. N. Y., 1845. 2 v. 8°. 6187
The same. Revised by F. Bowen. (2 copies.) Cambr., 1862–63. 2 v. 12°. 6134
The Old Regime and the Revolution. N. Y., 1856. 12°. . . 5522
Memoir, Letters, and Remains of. Bost., 1862. 2 v. 8°. . . 7627
Todd, C. S., and **Drake, B.** Sketch of Gen. Harrison. Cincinn., 1847. 16°. 7496
Todd, H. J. Life and Writings of Milton. Lond., 1826. 8°. . . 7111
Todd, J. Hints to Young Men. Northampton, 1844. 12°. . . 9174
Moral Influence of Great Cities. Northampton, 1841. 12°. . 17290
Sabbath School Teacher. Northampton, 1837. 12°. . . . 17362
Student's Manual. (2 copies.) Northampton, 1835. 12°. . . 9134
The Sunset Land. Bost., 1870. 16°. 16886
Toilers of the Sea, The. Hugo. N. Y., 1866. 8°. 2640
Toland, J. Hist. of the Celtic Religion, etc. Lond. [1814.] 8°. . 16073
Toleration, Letters Concerning. Locke. (Works, v. 6.) Lond., 1801. 8°. 9595
Treatise on. Voltaire. Lond., 1763. 12°. 9801
Tolfrey, F. The Sportsman in France. Lond., 1841. 2 v. 8°. . . 10164
Tom Brown at Oxford. [Hughes.] Lond., 1870. 8°. 9245
at Rugby. [Hughes.] Bost., 1870. 8°. 9242

Tom Crib's Memorial. [Moore.] N. Y., 1819. 12°. 14838
Tom Cringle's Log. [M. Scott.] Philad., 1834. 3 v. 12°. . . 15605
Tom Jones. Fielding. (v. 6, 7.) 1871. 2 v. 8°. 1981
Tomline, G. Memoirs of Pitt. Philad., 1821. 2 v. 8°. . . . 16344
Tomlinson, C. Cyclopædia of Useful Arts, etc. Lond., 1854. 2 v. 8°.
Tone, T. W., Life of. By himself. Lond., 1831. 12°. 6657
Tonga Islands, Account of the. Mariner, ed. Martin. Edinb., 1827. 2 v. 12°. 4475
Tonna, C. E. Alice Benden, and other Tales. N. Y., 1841. 12°. . 14919
Conformity; Falsehood and Truth. N. Y., 1866. 12°. . . 14921
Floral Biography. N. Y., 1840. 12°. 15168
The Flower Garden. N. Y., 1840. 12°. 15169
The Flower of Innocence and other Tales. N. Y., 1842. 12°. . 14920
Judæa Capta. N. Y., 1845. 12°. 14916
Judah's Lion. N. Y., 1843. 12°. 15166
The Museum. N. Y., 1841. 12°. 14915
Passing Thoughts. N. Y., 1841. 12°. 14918
Personal Recollections. N. Y., 1842. 12°. 15165
Principalities and Powers. N. Y., 1842. 12°. 15170
The Siege of Derry. N. Y., 1841. 12°. 15167
The Simple Flower and other Tales. N. Y., 1842. 12°. . . 14917
Tony Butler. [Lever.] N. Y., 1865. 8°. 2320
Too Strange not to be True. Fullerton. Leipz., 1864. 16.° . . 2408
Tooke, J. Horne. Diversions of Purley. Ed. R. Taylor. Lond., 1829. 2 v. 8°. 210
Memoirs of. Stephens. Lond., 1813. 2 v. 8°. 6860
Sketch of. Thorold Rogers. Lond., 1870. 8°. 6732
See, also, Junius.
Tooke, W. Hist. of Russia to 1762. Lond., 1800. 2 v. 8°. . . 6434
Life of Catharine II. 4th ed. Lond., 1800. 3 v. 8°. . . 6439
View of the Russian Empire, 1762–1800. 2d ed. Lond., 1800. 3 v. 8°. 6436
Tor Hill, The. H. Smith. Hartf'd., 1846. 12°. 15608
Torrey, C. T., Memoir of. Lovejoy. Bost., 1847. 12°. 8566
Tott, F. de. Memoirs on the Turks and Tartars. Dubl., 1785. 3 v. 12°. 16642
Tottel, R. Miscellany. Ed. Arber. Lond., 1870. 16°. 3895
Tourneur, C. Revenger's Tragedy. (Old Plays, v. 4.) Lond., 1825. 8°. 1511
Toussaint L'Ouverture, P., Biogr. and Autobiogr. of. Bost., 1863. 12°. 7698
Tower of London, The. See London.
Towers, J. Memoirs of Frederick III. Dubl., 1789. 2 v. 8°. . . 16454
Towle, G. M. American Society. Lond., 1870. 2 v. 8°. 8386
Towle, N. C. Hist. and Analysis of the Constitution. Bost., 1860. 12°. 6174
Townley, J. High Life below Stairs. N. Y. 8°. 1669
Townsend, J. Journey through Spain. 2d ed. Lond., 1792. 3 v. 8°. 16662
[**Townsend, L. T.**] Credo. Bost., 1869. 16°. 9830
Townshend, C. H. Facts in Mesmerism. Bost., 1841. 12°. . . 17106
The same. N. Y., 1848. 12°. 17105
Tracts for Priests and People. Bost., 1862. 12°. 9956
Tracy, J. The Great Awakening. Bost., 1842. 8°. 6493

Tracy's Ambition. [Griffin.] N. Y., 1830. 2 v. 12°. . . . 15561
Trades and Professions. Hazen. N. Y., 1842. 2 v. 12°. . . . 11751
Tradesman, The Complete English. De Foe. Oxf'd., 1841. 2 v. 16°. 3887
Traditions of Ancient Times. W. Howitt. Lond., 1839. 2 v. 12°. . 1893
[**Traill, C. P.**] The Backwoods of Canada. New ed. Lond., 1846. 12°. 8148
Traits of the Aborigines. [Sigourney.] Camb., 1822. 12°. . . 15025
of Travel. Grattan. N. Y., 1829. 2 v. 12°. 15609
Trälinnan. Bremer. Lond., 1852. 8°. 468
Transfusion. Godwin. N. Y., 1836. 12°. 15112
Translation, Essay on Principles of. [Tytler.] Lond., 1791. 8°. . 181
Transmission of Qualities from Parents to Offspring. N. Y., 1844. 12°. 8530
Travel, Consolations in. Davy. Philad., 1830. 12°. . . . 7867
How to observe Morals and Manners in. Martineau. N. Y., 1838. 12°. 16329
Tales of, renarrated. Kingsley. Lond., 1869. 8°. . . . 7940
Foreign, Dialogues on Uses of. [Hurd.] Lond., 1762. 8°. . 15932
Imagery of. Sherer. Lond., 1838. 12°. . . . 16326
Modern, Cyclopædia of. B. Taylor. Cincinn., 1856. 8°. . 8128
Travellers, Celebrated, Lives of. St. John. N. Y., 1841. 3 v. 12°. . 11042
Travelling Bachelor, The. Cooper. N. Y., 1859. 12°. . . . 2805
Travels. See, also, GEOGRAPHY ; VOYAGES.
Trees, Timber, Description of. Bost., 1830. 12°. 8806
See, also, FOREST.
[**Trelawny, J. E.**] Adventures of Younger Son. N. Y., 1832. 2 v. 12°. 15360
Tremaine. [Ward.] Philad., 1825. 3 v. 12°. 15611
Trench, M. C. Remains, ed. by her son. Lond., 1862. 8°. . . 7069
Trench, R. C. Authorized Version of the N. T. N. Y., 1873. 8°. . 10263
Elegiac Poems. Lond., 1843. 16°. 601
English, past and present. N. Y., 1855. 12°. 105
The same. 7th ed. N. Y., 1871. 12°. 106
Genoveva. A Poem. Lond., 1842. 16°. 600
Hulsean Lectures. Philad., 1856. 12°. 9923
On the lessons in Proverbs. (2 copies.) N. Y., 1855–56. 12°. 4316
Life of Calderon. N. Y., 1856. 12°. 7697
Notes on the Miracles. (2 copies.) N. Y., 1856–58. 8°. . . 10004
on the Parables. (2 copies.) N. Y., 1859. 8°. . . 10006
Poems. N. Y., 1856. 12°. 1219
Poems from Eastern Sources, etc. Lond., 1842. 16°. . . 1218
Sabbation ; Honor Neale ; and other Poems. Lond., 1838. 16°. 1217
Select Glossary of English Words. N. Y., 1859. 12°. . . 103
Sermons in Westminster Abbey. N. Y., 1860. 12°. . . . 9922
Studies in the Gospels. N. Y., 1867. 8°. 10008
Study of Words. N. Y., 1856. 12°. 104
Synonyms of the N. T. (2 copies.) N. Y., 1855. 12°. . . 9891
Trench, W. S. Realities of Irish Life. 2d ed. Lond., 1869. 8°. . 5252
Trenck, *(Baron)* **F. v. d.,** Life of. By himself. Lond., 1788. 2 v. 12°. 7529
The same. Bost., 1828. 12°. 7531
Trenton Falls. Ed. Willis. N. Y., 1851. 16°. 8168
Treves, Pilgrimage to, 1844. Anthon. N. Y., 1845. 12°. . . . 16704

Trials, Celebrated. Lond., 1825. 6 v. 8°. 9220
Criminal. [Jardine.] Bost., 1832. 12°. 8820
American. Chandler. Bost., 1844. v. 2. 12°. . 9226
Narratives of Remarkable. Feuerbach. N. Y., 1846. 16°. 9153
English, Reports of remarkable. Craik. Lond., 1844. 16°. . 9154
of the Heart. Bray. Philad., 1839. 2 v. 12°. 15614
of Life. [Mrs. Grey.] N. Y., 1829. 2 v. 12°. 15616
of Margaret Lyndsay. J. Wilson. Philad., 1823. 12°. . . 2460
of Murderers in U. S. Bost., 1837. 12°. 9227
Tribune Almanac, 1838–68. N. Y., 1868. 2 v. 12°. 6103
Tricotrin. [De La Rame.] Philad., 1869. 12°. 15618
Tripp, A. Crests from the Ocean-World. Bost., 1855. 12°. . . 16551
Tristram Shandy. Sterne. Philad., 1864. 8°. 1990
Troil, U. v. Letters on Iceland. Lond., 1870. 8°. 16596
Trollope, A. The Belton Estate. N. Y., 1866. 8°. 2290
The Bertrams. N. Y., 1859. 12°. 2107
Can you forgive her? N. Y. 8°. 2289
Castle Richmond. N. Y., 1860. 12°. 2110
The Claverings. N. Y., 1866. 8°. 2291
Doctor Thorne. N. Y. 12°. 2109
Framley Parsonage. N. Y., 1862. 12°. 2108
Golden Lion of Granpere. N. Y., 1872. 8°. 2296
He knew he was right. N. Y., 1869. 8°. 2293
Last Chronicle of Barset. N. Y., 1867. 8°. 2288
North America. N. Y., 1862. 12°. 8413
Orley Farm. N. Y., 1863. 8°. 2287
Phineas Finn. N. Y., 1869. 8°. 2292
Ralph the Heir. N. Y., 1871. 8°. 2295
Small House at Allington. N. Y., 1864. 8°. 2286
Vicar of Bullhampton. N. Y., 1870. 8°. 2294
Trollope, F. Belgium and Western Germany in 1833. Philad., 1834. 8°. 16656
Domestic Manners of the Americans. N. Y., 1832. 8°. . . 8440
The same. (2 copies.) 8384
Michael Armstrong. N. Y., 1840. 2 v. 12°. 15507
Paris and the Parisians. N. Y., 1836. 8°. 16698
The Refugee in America. N. Y., 1833. 2 v. 12°. . . . 15559
Visit to Italy. Lond., 1842. 2 v. 8°. 8339
Trollope, T. A. Filippo Strozzi. Lond., 1860. 8°. 4684
The Garstangs of Garstang Grange. Leipzig, 1870. 2 v. 16°. 2375
Hist. of the Commonwealth of Florence. Lond., 1865. 4 v. 8°. 4676
A Summer in Western France. Lond., 1841. 2 v. 8°. . . 16690
[**Trollope,** *Mrs.* **T. A.**] The Sacristan's Household. N. Y., 1869. 8°. 2310
Trollopiad, The. [Shelton.] N. Y., 1837. 12°. 15022
Tropics, In the. Kimball. N. Y., 1863. 12°. 16895
Health Trip to the. Willis. N. Y., 1853. 12°. 15332
Trotter, J. B. Memoirs of Fox. Philad., 1812. 8°. 16346
Troubadours. See PROVENCAL Poetry.
Trowbridge, J. T. Cudjo's Cave. Bost., 1864. 12°. 2954
The Vagabonds, and other Poems. (2 copies.) Bost., 1869. 12°. 783

Trueba y Cosio, T. de. The Castilian. N. Y., 1829. 2 v. 12°. . 15140
Hist. of Conquest of Peru. Edinb., 1830. 12°. 4507
The Incognito. N. Y., 1831. 2 v. 12°. 15142
Life of Cortes. Edinb., 1829. 12°. 7510
Romance of Spanish Hist. N. Y., 1830. 2 v. 12°. . . . 15567
Trumbull, B. Hist. of Conn. N. H., 1818. 2 v. 8°. . . . 5962
The same. vol. 1. (2 copies.) Hartf'd., 1797. 8°. . . 5964
of U. S. Bost., 1810. v. 1. 8°. 5853
Trumbull, H. C. The Knightly Soldier. Bost., 1865. 12°. . . 7280
Trumbull, John (LL.D.) Poetical Works. Hartf'd., 1820. 2 v. in 1. 8°. 936
Progress of Dulness. Exeter, 1794. 12°. 14955
Trumbull, John (the painter). Autobiography and Letters. N. H., 1841. 8°. 7422
Trumbull, Jonathan, Life of. Stuart. Bost., 1859. 8°. . . . 7455
Trumps. A Novel. Curtis. N. Y., 1861. 12°. 2873
Truth, Discourses on. Thornwell. N. Y., 1859. 12°. . . . 9978
Essay on. Beattie. (Works, v. 4, 5.) Philad., 1809. 12°. . 12290
Tryon County, Annals of. Campbell. N. Y., 1849. 12°. . . . 5726
Tschudi, J. J. v. Travels in Peru. N. Y., 1847. 12°. . . . 8363
Tucker, A. Light of Nature pursued. Abridged. Lond., 1807. 8°. 17082
Tucker, G. Essays. Wash., 1822. 8°. 17175
Life of Jefferson. (2 copies.) Philad., 1837. 2 v. 8°. . . 7345
Progress of the U. S. N. Y., 1843. 8°. 5970
Theory of Money and Banks. Bost., 1839. 12°. . . . 8648
Tucker, J. M. Life of Lord Nelson. Lond. 8°. 6851
Tucker, P. Origin and Progress of Mormonism. N. Y., 1867. 12°. 10030
Tuckerman, H. T. America and her Commentators. N. Y., 1864. 12°. 6183
Artist-Life. N. Y., 1847. 12°. 7917
Biographical Essays. Bost., 1857. 8°. 3475
Book of Artists. N. Y., 1867. 8°. 8126
Characteristics of Literature. (2 copics.) Philad., 1849. 12°. . 3571
Isabel ; or Sicily. Philad., 1839. 12°. 16727
Memorial of Greenough. N. Y., 1853. 12°. 7938
The Optimist. (2 copies.) N. Y., 1850. 12°. 3573
Poems. Bost., 1851. 16°. 774
Sicily. N. Y., 1852. 12°. 16720
Thoughts on the Poets. N. Y., 1848. 16°. 54
The same. N. Y., 1846. 12°. 3575
Tudor, W. Gebel Teir. Bost., 1829. 12°. 15700
Life of Otis. Bost., 1823. 8°. 7341
Tuke, S. Adventures of 5 Hours. Lond., 1827. 8°. 1519
Tupper, M. F. Complete Poetical Works. Bost., 1850. 12°. . . 1213
Probabilities: an Aid to Faith. N. Y., 1847. 12°. . . . 9826
Proverbial Philosophy. [1st Series.] 2d ed. Lond., 1838. 16°. 1214
The same. 2 series in 1. N. Y., 1848. 12°. 1215
The same. N. Y., 1846. 12°. 1216
The Twins. Heart. The Crock of Gold. A Thousand Lines. N. Y., 1845-46. 12°. 15619

Tyler, J. Messages, etc. (Statesman's Manual, v. 2, 3.) N. Y., 1854. 8°. 6201
Tyler, M. C. The Brawnville Papers. Bost., 1869. 12°. . . . 3566
[**Tyler, Robert.**] Ahasuerus; a Poem. N. Y., 1842. 12°. . . 15039
[**Tyler, Royall.**] The Algerine Captive. Hartf'd., 1816. 12°. . . 15653
Tylney Hall. Hood. N. Y., 1835. 12°. 15110
Tylor, E. B. Early History of Mankind. 2d ed. Lond., 1870. 8°. . 4074
Primitive Culture. Lond., 1871. 2 v. 8°. 4075
Tyndale, W. The New Testament. Reprint of 1526 ed. by. Dabney. Andover, 1837. 12°. 9890
Writings. Lond. 12°. 9482
Tyndall, J. Faraday as a Discoverer. N. Y., 1868. 12°. . . . 7158
The Forms of Water. N. Y., 1872. 12°. 10182
Fragments of Science. N. Y., 1871. 12°. 8908
The Glaciers of the Alps. Bost., 1861. 8°. 8957
Heat as a Mode of Motion. N. Y., 1864. 12°. 8902
The same. From 2d ed. N. Y., 1868. 12°. . . . 8903
Hours of Exercise in the Alps. N. Y., 1872. 12°. . . . 8382
Light and Electricity. N. Y., 1871. 12°. 8907
Radiation. N. Y., 1865. 12°. 8904
Sound. (2 copies.) N. Y., 1867. 12°. 8905
Typee. Melville. N. Y., 1847. 12°. 8325
Tytler, A. F. Considerations on India. Lond., 1815. 2 v. 8°. . 16446
Essay on the principles of Translation. Lond., 1791. 8°. . 181
Universal History, to 1700. Bost., 1844. 2 v. 8°. . . . 4110
The same, continued to 1820. N. Y., 1840. 6 v. 12°. . 11410
The same. N. Y., 1848. 6 v. 12°. 4457
Tytler, P. F. England under Edw. VI. and Mary. Lond., 1839. 2 v. 8°. 5291
Life of Raleigh. Philad., 1833. 8°. 15358
Progress of Discovery on Northern Coasts of America. N. Y., 1841. 12°. 11273

U.

Udall, N. Roister Doister, ed. Arber. Lond., 1869. 16°. . . . 3892
Uhland, L. Gedichte. Philad. 12°. 9612
Uhlhorn, G. Modern Representations of Life of Jesus. Bost., 1868. 16°. 9898
Ulloa, A. de. See JUAN.
Umphraville, A. The Siege of Baltimore; with other Poems. Balt., 1817. 12°. 14956
Umsted, L. D. Southwold. N. Y., 1859. 12°. 15781
Uncas and Miantonomoh. Stone. N. Y., 1842. 12°. 5750
Uncle Horace. Mrs. Hall. Philad., 1838. 2 v. 12°. . . . 15623
Uncle Tom's Cabin. Stowe. Bost., 1869. 12°. 2958
Undercurrents. Kimball. N. Y., 1862. 12°. 15806
Underhill, Updike. *(Pseudonym.)* See R. TYLER.
Undine. De La Motte Fouqué. N. Y., 1857. 12°. 2705
Ungewitter, F. H. Europe, past and present. N. Y., 1850. 12°. . 8266
Union Review, The. Lond., 1870–71. 2 v. 8°. 12902
Unique, The. Bost., 1844. 12°. 17285

Unitarian Doctrines, Moral Tendency of. Sparks. Bost., 1823. 8°. . 17268
Pulpit, Annals of the American. Sprague. N. Y., 1865. 8°. . 7737
U. S. Army, Regulations for Uniform and Dress of. Philad., 1851. 4°.
Life on the Border. Marcy. N. Y., 1866. 12°. . . 6129
Cavalry, Hist. of the, to 1863. Brackett. N. Y., 1865. 12°. . 6102
Commerce, Statistics of. Pitkin. N. H., 1835. 8°. . . . 5854
Congress, Anti-Slavery Measures in, 1861–64. Wilson. Bost., 1864. 12°. 8579
Biogr. and Polit. Hist. of. Wheeler. N. Y., 1848. 2 v. 8°. 6279
Debates in, 1782–87. (Madison Papers, v. 1, 2.) Wash., 1840. 8°. 6163
Constitution, etc. Hickey. Philad., 1853. 12°. . . . 6031
and the State Constitutions. Philad., 1832. 12°. 6032
and Inaugural Addresses, etc. N. Y. 12°. . 6033
Commentaries on. Story. Bost., 1858. 2 v. 8°. 6179
Debates on adoption of. Elliot. Wash., 1828. v. 2–4. 8°. 6126
Secret Debates of Convention for forming, 1787. (2 copies.) Richmond, 1839. 12°. . . 6087
Debates in Convention framing. (Madison Papers, v. 2, 3.) Wash., 1840. 8°. 6164
Debates of Va. Convention on, 1788. Richmond, 1805. 8°. 6125
Proceedings of Convention for forming. Wash., 1836. 8°. 6169
Defence of. Adams. Philad., 1797. 3 v. 8°. . 6138
Discourse on. Calhoun. Charleston, 1851. 8°. 6171
Hist. of. Curtis. N. Y., 1863. 2 v. 8°. . . 6223
Hist. and Analysis of. Towle. Bost., 1860. 12°. 6174
Manual of. Farrar. Bost., 1867. 8°. . . . 6181
New Views of. J. Taylor. Wash., 1823. 8°. . 6182
Treatise on. Douglas. N. Y., 1866. 8°. . . 6173
Writings on. Marshall. Bost., 1839. 8°. . . 6283
Description, Geographical, of. Melish. N. Y., 1826. 8°. . 16824
Rhyming, of. V. Clark. Hartf'd., 1819. 12°. . 14982
Diplomacy of the (to 1828). Lyman. Bost., 1828. 2 v. 8°. . 6161
Exploring Expedition, 1838–42, Narrative of. Wilkes. Philad., 1845. 5 v. and Atlas. 8°. 8129
Finances of the. Gallatin. N. Y., 1796. 8°. 6240
Financial Economy of the. Ferris. S. Francisco, 1867. 12°. . 8630
Foreign Conspiracy against the. [Morse.] N. Y., 1835. 12°. 17278
Gov't. and Laws of the. Wedgwood. N. Y., 1866. 8°. . . 6170
Historical Sketches of, 1815–30. Perkins. N. Y., 1830. 12°. 6021
History of, to 1688. Grahame. Lond., 1833. 2 v. 8°. . . 5940
to 1765. Trumbull. Bost., 1810. 8°. . . . 5853
[to 1778.] Bancroft. Bost., 1856–66. 9 v. 8°. . 6203
to 1815. Ramsay. Philad., 1818. 3 v. 8°. . . 5850
to 1817. Hale. N. Y., 1841. 2 v. 12°. . . . 11594

Universities of Germany. Schaff. Philad., 1857. 12°. 9252
View of the. Robinson. Edinb., 1835. 16°. 9137
University Education. Tappan. N. Y., 1851. 12°. 9256
German. Perry. Lond., 1845. 12°. . . 9251
Quarterly. N. H., 1860–61. 4 v. 8°. 17476
See, also, COLLEGES; EDUCATION.
Unkind Word, The. Mrs. Craik. N. Y., 1870. 12°. 2488
Upham, C. W. Life of Fremont. Bost., 1856. 12°. 7398
of Sir H. Vane. (Sparks, v. 4.) Bost., 1835. 16°. . . . 7253
Upham, E. Hist. of the Ottoman Empire. Philad., 1833. 8°. . . 15357
The same. Edinb., 1829. 2 v. 12°. 4502
Upham, T. C. Elements of Mental Philosophy. N. Y., 1848. 2 v. 12°. 8604
Imperfect and Disordered Mental Action. N. Y., 1841. 12°. . 11424
Lives of Mme. Guyon and Fenelon. N. Y., 1847. 2 v. 12°. . 7674
Manual of Peace. (2 copies.) N. Y., 1836. 8°. . . . 8699
Uprising of a Great People, The. Gasparin. N. Y., 1861. 12°. . 8558
Ups and Downs. [Stone.] N. Y., 1836. 12°. 15807
Ure, A. Dict. of Arts, Manufactures and Mines. N. Y., 1843. 8°.
The same., with Supplement. N. Y., 1847. 8°. . .
Philosophy of Manufactures. 2d ed. Lond., 1835. 12°. . . 17001
Urquhart, D. The Spirit of the East. 2d ed. Lond., 1839. 2 v. 8°. 16623
Usher, J., Life of. Aikin. Lond., 1812. 8°. 7116
Usury, Defence of. Bentham. (Works, pt. 9.) Edinb., 1839. 8°. . 9708
Essay on the Law of. Ord. Hartf'd., 1809. 8°. 17094
Hist. of. Murray. Philad., 1866. 8°. 8651
Utopia. More. Lond., 1850. 12°. 3953

V.

Vacation Tourists, 1860–1861. Galton, editor. Cambr., 1861–62. 2 v. 8°. 8378
Vagabond Adventures. Keeler. Bost., 1870. 12°. 16258
Valdenses. See WALDENSES.
Vale of Cedars. Aguilar. N. Y., 1868. 12°. 2522
Valerius. [Lockhart.] Bost., 1821. 2 v. 12°. 15625
Valley of Shenandoah, The. [Hentz.] N. Y., 1824. 2 v. 12°. . 15808
Vambery, A. Travels in Central Asia. (2 copies.) N. Y., 1865. 8°. 8141
Vanbrugh, J. City Wives' Confederacy; Provoked Husband; Provoked Wife. (Brit. Drama, 2.) Philad., 1833. 8°. . . 1663
Dramatic Works, ed. L. Hunt. Lond., 1849. 8°. . . . 10300
Van Buren, M. Messages, etc. (Statesman's Manual, v. 2.) N. Y., 1854. 8°. 6201
Life of. Holland. Hartf'd., 1835. 12°. 7322
Vancouver Island and British Columbia. Macfie. Lond., 1865. 8°. 8395
Van Diemen's Land, Notes of an Exile to. Miller. Fredonia, 1846. 12°. 16256
Observations on. Henderson. Calcutta, 1832. 8°. 16287
Vane, C. W. (Marq. of Londonderry.) Narrative of War in Germany and France, 1813–14. Philad., 1831. 12°. . . . 16191

Vane, *Sir* **H.** (the younger), Life of. Forster. Lond., 1838. 16°. . 5762
The same. Upham. Bost., 1835. 16°. 7253
Vanity Fair. Thackeray. Lond., 1871. 8°. 2189
Van Lennep, H. J. Travels in Asia-Minor. N. Y., 1870. 2 v. 12°. 8244
Van Nest, A. R. Memoir of G. W. Bethune. N. Y., 1867. 12°. . 7643
Van Santvoord, G. Life of A. Sidney. N. Y., 1851. 12°. . . . 6720
Varnum, J. B. The Seat of Gov't. of the U. S. 2d ed. Wash., 1854. 8°. 5834
Vasari, G. Lives of Painters, etc. (Bohn's ed.) Lond., 1850–52. 5 v. 8°. 474
Vashti. A. J. Wilson. N. Y., 1869. 12°. 2993
Vathek. Beckford. N. Y., 1869. 12°. 10078
Vaughan, H. Sacred Poems, etc., with Memoir. Bost., 1854. 16°. . 1035
Vaux, J. H., Memoirs of. By himself. Lond., 1830. 12°. . . . 6651
Veda, Studies on the. Whitney. N. Y., 1872. 12°. 136
Vegetable Diet. Alcott. Bost., 1838. 12°. 9170
Substances, Description of; Timber Trees and Fruits. Bost., 1830. 12°. 8806
used for Food of Man. N. Y., 1844. 12°. . . 11770
World, The. Figuier. Lond., 1869. 8°. 9000
Vegetation, Wonders of. Marion. N. Y., 1872. 12°. . . . 10148
Veil partly lifted, The. Furness. Bost., 1864. 8°. 9815
Velde, C. F. van der. Tales, transl. by N. Greene. Bost., 1837. 2 v. 12°. 3029
CONTENTS.—1, Arwed Gyllenstierna. 2, The Lichtensteins; The Sorceress; The Anabaptist.
Velvet Cushion, The. Cunningham. Lond., 1815. 12°. . . . 15627
Vendée War, Hist. of the. Berthre de Bournisseaux. Paris, 1802. 8°. 16251
Venetia. Disraeli. Philad., 1837. 2 v. 12°. 2129
Venetian Hist., Sketches from. [Smedley.] N. Y., 1840. 2 v. 12°. 11047
Life. Howells. N. Y., 1867. 8°. 8212
Venezuela, Campaigns and Cruises in, and Tales of. Lond., 1831. 3 v. 12°. 17141
Venice, Conspiracy of the Spaniards against, 1618. St. Réal. Bost., 1838. 16°. 16159
past and present. Adams. Lond., 1869. 8°. 8213
The Stones of. Ruskin. N. Y., 1860. 3 v. 12°. . . . 9024
Tour to, 1845. Costello. Lond., 1846. 8°. 8449
Venice Preserved; a Tragedy. Otway. (Works, v. 2.) Lond., 1812. 8°. 1476
Ventriloquism explained. Amh., 1834. 12°. 16958
Verdant Green, Adventures of. [Bradley.] N. Y., 1870. 12°. . . 9249
Vermont, Hist., etc. of, to 1841. Thompson. Burlington, 1842. 8°. 5902
Natural and Civil Hist. of (to 1807). Williams. Burlington, 1809. 2 v. 8°. 5838
Vernon, J. Letters, 1696–1708, ed. James. Lond., 1841. 3 v. 8°. . 5317
Verona, The Congress of. De Chateaubriand. Lond., 1838. 2 v. 8°. 4656
Verplanck, G. C. Discourses and Addresses. N. Y., 1833–34. 12°. 3658
and others. The Talisman. N. Y., 1833. 3 v. 12°. . . 4132
Verri, A. Roman Nights. N. Y., 1826. 2 v. 12°. 15144
Vertot d'Aubœuf, R. A. de. Hist. of Revolutions in Portugal. Lond., 1754. 8°. 16166
Hist. of Revolutions in the Roman Republic. Lond., 1770. 2 v. 8°. 15946

Vertot d'Aubœuf, R. A. de. Hist. of Revol. in Sweden. Lond., 1711. 8°. 16171
Very Hard Cash. Reade. N. Y., 1868. 8°. 2281
Vésinier, P. Hist. of the Commune of Paris. Lond., 1872. 8°. . 5554
Vespucius, A., Life of. Lester and Foster. N. H., 1852. 8°. . . 7782
Vestiges of Nat. Hist. of Creation. Including Sequel. From 3d ed. N. Y., 1846. 12°. 8927
Vialla de Sommières, L. C. Travels in Montenegro. Lond., 1820. 8°. 8054
Viardot, L. Wonders of European Art. N. Y., 1871. 12°. . . 10124
of Italian Art. (2 copies.) N. Y., 1870. 12°. . 10122
Vicar of Bullhampton. A. Trollope. N. Y., 1870. 8°. . . . 2294
of Wakefield, The. Goldsmith. N. Y., 1845. 12°. . . . 3899
Vicarious Sacrifice, The. Bushnell. N. Y., 1866. 8°. . . . 10025
Vicar's Daughter, The. MacDonald. Bost., 1872. 12°. . . . 2580
Victim of Chancery, The. N. Y., 1841. 12°. 15810
Victims of Society. Lady Blessington. (Works, v. 2.) Philad., 1838. 8°. 2669
Victor, O. J. Hist. of the Southern Rebellion. N. Y. [1861–63.] 2 v. 8°. 6273
Victoria, *Queen.* Early Years of Prince Albert. N. Y., 1868. 12°. . 5336
Leaves from the Journal of Our Life in the Highlands. N. Y., 1868. 12°. 5335
Victoria, Two Years in. Howitt. Bost., 1855. 2 v. 12°. . . 7986
Vidocq, E. F., Memoirs of. By himself. Philad., 1834. 2 v. 12°. . 7588
The same. Lond., 1829–30. 4 v. 12°. 6663
Vienna, Congress of. De Pradt. Philad., 1816. 8°. 15920
Vieusseux, A. Hist. of Switzerland. Lond., 1846. 8°. . . . 5884
Napoleon Bonaparte. Lond., 1846. 2 v. 12°. 5505
Vieux Moustache. *(Pseudonym.)* See C. GORDON.
Views a-foot. Bayard Taylor. N. Y., 1848. 12°. 8278
Vignoles, C. Observations on the Floridas. N. Y., 1823. 8°. . . 16919
Vigny, A. de. Cinq-Mars. Tr. Hazlitt. Lond., 1847. 8°. . . 472
Vikram and the Vampire. Burton. Lond., 1870. 8°. . . . 1923
Village Communities in the East and West. Maine. Lond., 1871. 8°. 4102
of Mariendorpt. A. M. Porter. Bost., 1821. 2 v. 12°. . . 15184
Villari, P. Hist. of Savonarola. Lond., 1863. 2 v. 8°. . . . 7595
[**Villemarest, C. M. de.**] Life of Talleyrand. Lond., 1834. v. 1, 2. 8°. 7722
Villers, C. Essay on the Reformation. (2 copies.) Philad., 1833. 12°. 6344
The same. Lond., 1805. 8°. 16464
Villette. Brontë. N. Y., 1856. 12°. 2553
Villiers, G., (2d Duke of Buck'm.) The Rehearsal. Ed. Arber. Lond., 1868. 16°. 3889
Vincent, B. Haydn's Dict. of Dates. N. Y., 1867. 8°. . . . 4066
Vincent, T. Arundel. Lond., 1840. 3 v. 8°. 15371
Vinci, L. da, Life of. Brown. Lond., 1828. 8°. 7919
Virgil. Works, transl. by Dryden. N. Y., 1825. 2 v. 16°. . . 13827
The same. N. Y., 1840. 2 v. 12°. 4518
The same. N. Y., 1836. 12°. 1109
The same. Ed. Bell. Lond., 1807. 2 v. 24°. . . 262
for English Readers. Collins. Philad., 1871. 16°. . . . 75
Virginia, Debates of Convention of, 1788. 2d ed. Richmond, 1805. 8°. 6125

W.

Waite, H. R. Carmina Collegensia. Bost. [1868.] 8°. 9091
Waiting for the Verdict. Davis. N. Y., 1868. 8°. 2695
Wakefield, G., Memoirs of. By himself. Lond., 1792. 8°. . . . 16349
The same. New ed. Lond., 1804. 2 v. 8°. 16350
Waldegrave, J. Memoirs. Philad., 1822. 12°. 16445
Walden. Thoreau. Bost., 1863. 8°. 3552
Waldenses, Legend of the. Windle. Philad., 1852. 12°. 15728
Researches among the. Gilly. Lond., 1824. 4°. 16035
Valdo, etc. Gilly. Edinb., 1841. 12°. 6342
Waldie, C. A. See *Mrs.* C. A. EATON.
Waldo, S. P. Biogr. of Amer. Naval Heroes. Hartf'd., 1823. 8°. . 7472
Life of Decatur. Hartf'd., 1821. 12°. 16426
Memoirs of Jackson. Hartf'd., 1819. 12°. 16394
Monroe's Tour. Hartf'd., 1818. 12°. 16393
Wales, Lives of Princes of. Williams. Lond., 1843. v. 1. 12°. . 5133
Walker, Alex. Beauty in Woman. N. Y., 1840. 12°. . . . 17013
Intermarriage. N. Y., 1839. 12°. 16959
Woman physiologically considered. (2 copies.) N. Y., 1840. 12°. 17011
Walker, Amasa. Science of Wealth. (2 copies.) Bost., 1866. 8°. . 8637
[**Walker, James B.**] Philosophy of the Plan of Salvation. (2 copies.)
Bost., 1856. 12°. 9986
The same. N. Y., 1843. 12°. 9988
Walker, John. Rhetorical Grammar. Bost., 1822. 8°. 9299
Walker, Jos. C. Memoirs of Tassoni. Lond., 1815. 8°. 7749
Wall Street, Men and Mysteries of. Medbery. Bost., 1870. 12°. . 8647
Wallace, A. R. Contributions to the Theory of Natural Selection.
2d ed. Lond., 1871. 8°. 8838
The Malay Archipelago. N. Y., 1869. 8°. 8032
Wallace, H. B. Art and Scenery in Europe, etc. Philad., 1857. 12°. . 8886
Wallace, *Sir* **W.,** Life of. Carrick. Lond. 8°. 6841
The same. Donaldson. Hartf'd., 1830. 12°. 16444
Wallenstein, A. v., Life of. Mitchell. Lond., 1840. 8°. 7790
Wallenstein. Schiller. Lond., 1846. 8°. 437
Waller, E. Poetical Works. Ed. Bell. Lond., 1807. 24°. . . . 256
Select Poems, with Life. Ed. Sanford. Philad., 1819. 24°. . 3
The same, ed. Johnson. Dubl., 1804. 8°. 15096
Waller, J. A. Voyage in the W. Indies. Lond., 1820. 8°. . . . 8052
Walpole, B. C. Recollections of Fox. Lond., 1806. 12°. 6628
Walpole, H. Castle of Otranto. Philad., 1840. 12°. 2458
Historic Doubts on Richard III. Lond., 1768. 4°. 5074
Letters, 1735–97. Philad., 1848. 4 v. 8°. 7191
Letters to Sir H. Mann. N. Y., 1833. 2 v. 12°. 7103
The same. New Series. Philad., 1844. 2 v. 8°. . . 7195
Memoirs of Reign of Geo. III. Philad., 1845. 2 v. 8°. . . 5320
Reminiscences; Walpoliana. Bost., 1820. 16°. 3839
Walpoliana. [Ed. Pinkerton.] Lond. [1804.] 2 v. 16°. . 3814
Walpole, *Sir* **Rob't.,** Memoirs of. Coxe. Lond., 1800. 3 v. 8°. . 6827
Sketch of. Thorold Rogers. Lond., 1869. 8°. 6731
Walpole, *Rev.* **Robert.** Garland of Flowers. N. Y., 1806. 12°. . 14864

Walsh, Rob't. American Review. Philad., 1811–12. 4 v. 8°. . . 14038
Didactics. Philad., 1836. 2 v. 12°. 15270
Works of British Poets. See E. SANFORD.
Walsh, *Rev.* **Rob't.** Journey from Constantinople to England. Philad., 1828. 12°. 16769
Notices of Brazil. Bost., 1831. 2 v. 12°. 17134
Residence at Constantinople. 2d ed. Lond., 1838. 2 v. 8°. 8446
Walsh, W. Poems, ed. Johnson. Dubl., 1804. 8°. 15096
Walsingham. [Chamier.] Philad., 1838. 12°. 15630
Walt and Vult; or, the Twins. Richter. N. Y., 1863. 2 v. 8°. . 3057
Walter Ashwood. [Mathews.] N. Y., 1860. 12°. 15811
Walter Colyton. H. Smith. N. Y., 1830. 2 v. 12°. . . . 15631
Waltham Abbey, Hist. of. Fuller. Lond., 1840. 8°. 9286
Walton, I. Lives of Donne, Wotton, Hooker, Herbert, and Sanderson. [Lond., 1845.] 8°. 948
The same. Ed. Young. Cambr., 1832. 2 v. 12°. . 3908
The same. 3914
The same, with Zouch's Life of Walton. N. Y., 1846. 2 v. 12°. 6717
and **Cotton, C.** Complete Angler. Lond., 1836. 16°. . . 3919
The same. N. Y., 1848. 2 pts. in 1. 12°. . . . 3920
Walton, W. C., Memoir of. Danforth. Hartf'd., 1837. 12°. . . 16422
Walworth, C. The Gentle Skeptic. N. Y., 1863. 12°. . . . 17364
Wandering Jew, The. Sue. Lond. 8°. 2595
illustrated by Doré. Lond. fol. . . . . .
Cartaphilus, Chronicles of. Hoffman. Lond., 1853. 2 v. 8°. 10059
War, Conversations on. Helps. Bost., 1871. 16°. 3700
[**Warburton, G.**] Hochelaga. N. Y., 1846. 12°. 8370
Warburton, W. Letters to Hurd. N. Y., 1809. 8°. 16348
Ward, Artemus. *(Pseudonym.)* See C. F. BROWNE.
Ward, C. National Proverbs. Lond., 1842. 16°. 4318
Ward, H. G. Mexico. 2d ed. Lond., 1829. 2 v. 8°. . . . 5979
Ward, John. Diary, 1648–79. Lond., 1839. 8°. 1586
Ward, Julius H. Life of Percival. Bost., 1866. 12°. . . . 7387
Ward, R. P. De Vere. N. Y., 1831. 2 v. 12°. 15155
Fielding; or, Society. Philad., 1838. 12°. 15431
Tremaine. Philad., 1825. 3 v. 12°. 15611
Ward, S., Life of. Gammell. Bost., 1846. 16°. 7268
Warden, W. Letters from St. Helena, etc. N. H., 1817. 12°. . . 5439
Ware, H. Formation of Christian Character. Cambr., 1831. 12°. . 9808
Ware, W. Julian. N. Y., 1841. 2 v. 12°. 2864
Letters from Palmyra. N. Y., 1837. 2 v. 12°. 2862
Memoir of N. Bacon. (Sparks, v. 13.) Bost., 1844. 16°. . 7262
Probus. N. Y., 1838. 2 v. 12°. 2866
Sketches of European Capitals. Bost., 1851. 12° . . . 8267
Zenobia. Lond., 1844–45. 2 v. 16°. 2729
Warlock, The. [Barker.] Philad., 1836. 2 v. 12°. 15633
Warner, A. B. Dollars and Cents. N. Y., 1852. 2 v. 12°. . . 3007

Warner, A. B. and S. Say and Seal. Philad., 1860. 2 v. 12°. . . 3005
Warner, C. D. My Summer in a Garden. Bost., 1871. 8°. . . 3639
Saunterings. Bost., 1872. 12°. 8166
Warner, J. F. Rudimental Lessons in Music. N. Y., 1845. 12°. . 17119
Warner, R. Literary Recollections. Lond., 1830. 2 v. 8°. . . 3485
Warner, S. The Daisy. (2 copies.) Philad., 1868. 12°. . . . 3002
Hills of the Shatemuc. N. Y., 1857. 12°. 3004
Melbourne House. N. Y., 1868. 12°. 3001
Queechy. (2 copies.) N. Y., 1852. 2 v. 12°. 2997
Wide, Wide World. Philad., 1872. 12°. 2994
The same. N. Y., 1851–52. 2 v. 12°. 2995
Warren, John E. Vagamundo; or, the Attaché in Spain. N. Y. 1852. 12°. 16673
Warren, Jos., Life of. A. H. Everett. Bost., 1839. 16°. . . . 7259
Warren, S. Affecting Scenes; Passages from the Diary of a late Physician. N. Y., 1836. 2 v. 12°. 2024
Diary of a late Physician. Edinb., 1871. 8°. 2447
Introd. to Law Studies. Lond., 1835. 8°. 9217
Merchant's Clerk, and other Tales. N. Y., 1836. 12°. . . 15506
Now and Then. (2 copies.) N. Y., 1848. 12°. . . . 15526
Ten Thousand a Year. Philad. 8°. 2314
The same. Edinb., 1872. 8°. 2448
Warreniana. [Deacon.] Bost., 1824. 12°. 14793
Warton, J. Essay on Pope. 2d ed. Lond., 1762. 8°. . . . 16366
The same. 4th ed. Lond., 1782. 2 v. 8°. . . . 16364
The same. 5th ed. Lond., 1806. 2 v. 8°. . . . 3483
Poems. Salisbury, 1794. 8°. 14806
Select Poems. Ed. Walsh. Philad., 1822. 24°. . . . 28
Warton, T. Hist. of English Poetry. (2 copies.) Lond., 1840. 3 v. 8°. 183
Life of Sir T. Pope. Lond., 1772. 8°. 16367
Observations on Spenser's Fairy Queen. Lond., 1807. 2 v. 8°. 1273
Select Poems. Ed. Walsh. Philad., 1822. 24°. . . . 28
Warwick Woodlands. [Herbert.] Philad., 1857. 12°. . . . 10162
[**Washburne, W. T.**] Fair Harvard. (2 copies.) N. Y., 1869. 12°. . 9264
Washington, G. Messages, etc. (Statesman's Manual, v. 1.) N. Y., 1854. 8°. 6200
Official Letters to Congress during the War. Bost., 1796. 2 v. 12°. 7546
Revolutionary Orders, 1778–82. N. Y., 1844. 8°. . . . 6296
Writings, ed. Sparks. Bost., 1834–37. 12 v. 8°. . . . 9722

CONTENTS.—1, Life, by Sparks. 2, Letters, etc., 1754–May, 1775. 3, June, '75–July, '76. 4, July, '76–July, '77. 5, July, '77–July, '78. 6, July, '78–Mch., '80. 7, Mch., '80–Apr., '81. 8, Apr., '81–Dec., '83. 9, Dec., '83–Apr., '89. 10, May, '89–Nov., '94. 11, Nov., '94–Dec., '99. 12, Speeches and Messages to Congress; Proclamations; Addresses.

Essay on Character and Influence of. Guizot. N. Y., 1863. 16°. 7493
Fac Simile of Accounts of, 1775–83. [Wash., 1833.] fol. . .
and the Generals of the Revolution. Philad., 1847. 2 v. 12°. 7298
and his Generals. Headley. N. Y., 1847. 2 v. 12°. . . 7294
Lecture on. Theodore Parker. Bost., 1870. 12°. . . . 7409
Life of. A. Bancroft. Bost., 1826. 2 v. 12°. 7490
The same. Everett. N. Y., 1860. 12°. 7293

Washington, G., Life of. Irving. N. Y., 1856–59. 5 v. 12°. . . 7283
The same. Marshall. Philad., 1833. 2 v. and Atlas. 8°. 7481
The same. Paulding. N. Y., 1840. 2 v. 12°. . . 11291
The same. Ramsay. N. Y., 1807. 8°. 16388
The same. Sparks. Bost., 1843. 8°. 7485
The same. Weems. Philad., 1809. 12°. . . . 16391
Recollections of. Custis. N. Y., 1860. 8°. 7486
Religious Opinions and Character of. McGuire. N. Y., 1836. 12°. 16389
Vie de. Philad., 1835. 12°. 16392
Washington, D. C., the Seat of Gov't. Varnum. Wash., 1854. 8°. . 5834
Washingtons, The. A Tale. Simpkinson. Lond., 1860. 12°. . . 2443
Wassail-Bowl, The. A. Smith. Lond., 1843. v. 1. 12°. . . . 4257
Water, The Forms of. Tyndall. N. Y., 1872. 12°. 10182
Wonders of. Tissandier. N. Y., 1872. 12°. 10149
Drinker, Memoirs of a. Dunlap. N. Y., 1836. 2 v. 12°. . 15802
Water-Witch, The. Cooper. Philad., 1841. 12°. 2808
Waterbury, J. B. Memoir of J. Scudder. N. Y., 1870. 12°. . . 7640
Waterhouse, B. Essay on Junius. Bost., 1831. 8°. 6858
Waterloo, Campaign of. De Jomini. N. Y., 1860. 12°. . . . 5572
Waterman, E. Memoirs of Calvin. Hartf'd., 1813. 8°. . . . 7666
Watson, G. England Preserved. (Mod. Theatre, v. 8.) Lond., 1811. 12°. 1334
Watson, *Bishop* **Richard,** Anecdotes of Life of. By himself. Philad., 1818. 8°. 7125
Apology for the Bible; and Apology for Christianity. N. Y., 1835. 8°. 17269
Watson, *Rev.* **Richard.** Life of Wesley. N. Y., 1831. 12°. . . 7534
Watson, Robert. Hist. of Philip II. and III. Dubl., 1777–83. 3 v. 8°. 6556
Watson, T. Poems, ed. Arber. Lond., 1870. 16°. 3893
Watts, I. Horæ Lyricæ. Poems, chiefly Lyric. Lond., 1834. 16°. . 9491
Improvement of the Mind. Bost., 1826. 12°. 8493
Poetical Works. Ed. Bell. Lond., 1807. 2 v. 24°. . . 273
Select Poems. Ed. Walsh. Philad., 1819. 24°. . . . 17
Wauch, Mansie. *(Pseudonym.)* See D. M. Moir.
Waverley Novels, The. See Sir W. Scott.
Letters to Heber on the author of. [Adolphus.] Bost., 1822. 12°. 15227
Wayland, F. Elements of Moral Science. N. Y., 1835. 8°. . . 8739
of Polit. Economy. (2 copies.) N. Y., 1837. 8°. 8667
Letters on the Ministry. Bost., 1863. 16°. 9832
Limitations of Human Responsibility. (2 copies.) Bost., 1838. 12°. 8535
Memoir of Chalmers. Bost., 1864. 16°. 7566
Memoir of Judson. Bost., 1853. 2 v. 12°. 7638
Occasional Discourses. Bost., 1833. 12°. 17357
Thoughts on the Collegiate System. (2 copies.) Bost., 1842. 16°. 9183
University Sermons. 2d ed. Bost., 1849. 12°. . . . 9977
Memoir of. By his Sons. N. Y., 1867. 2 v. 12°. . . . 7384
Wayne, A., Life of. Armstrong. Bost., 1835. 16°. 7253

Wellesley, A. (Duke of Wellington), Life of. From the "Times." (2 copies.) N. Y., 1852. 12°. 6689
The same (to 1814). Clarke and Dunlap. N. Y., 1814. 8°. 16353
Military Memoirs of. Sherer. Philad., 1833. 2 v. 12°. . . 6686
Wells, W. V. Life of S. Adams. Bost., 1865. 3 v. 8°. . . . 7444
Weltevreden, The Prison of. Gibson. N. Y., 1855. 12°. . . . 16296
Wendeborn, F. A. A View of England. Dubl., 1791. 2 v. 12°. . 16763
Wendover, Roger of. Flowers of Hist. Lond., 1849. 2 v. 8°. . . 510
Wentworth, T. (Earl of Strafford), Life of. Forster. Lond., 1836. 16°. 5760
Wept of Wish-Ton-Wish. Cooper. Philad., 1841. 12°. . . . 2807
Wesley, J. Works. N. Y., 1831. 7 v. 8°. 17230
Life of. Southey. N. Y., 1820. 2 v. 8°. 7703
The same. Watson. N. Y., 1831. 12°. 7534
and the Reaction of the 18th Century. Wedgwood. Lond., 1870. 8°. 7600
West, B., Life and Works of. Galt. Lond., 1820. 8°. . . . 7966
West, G. Poetical Works. Ed. Bell. Lond., 1807. 24°. . . 535
West, R. Poetical Works. Ed. Bell. Lond., 1807. 24°. . . . 538
West, Legends of the. Hall. Philad., 1833. 12°. 15729
Plea for the. L. Beecher. Cincinn., 1835. 12°. . . . 17303
West Indies, A Christmas in the. Kingsley. Lond., 1871. 8°. . 8430
Domestic Manners in the. Carmichael. Philad., 1833. 8°. 15537
Emancipation in the. Thome and Kimball. N. Y., 1838. 12°. 8568
Hist. of (to 1815). T. Southey. Lond., 1827. 3 v. 8°. . . 5885
Hist. of Brit. Colonies in the. Edwards. Dubl., 1793. 2 v. 8°. 5832
The same. Martin. Lond., 1836–37. 2 v. 16°. . . 7899
of European Settlements in. Raynal. Lond., 1776. 5 v. 8°. 16149
A Twelvemonth (1833) in the. Madden. Lond., 1835. v. 1. 12°. 16916
Voyage in the, 1807. Waller. Lond., 1820. 8°. . . . 8052
A Winter in the. Hastings. N. Y., 1839. 12°. . . . 16915
West Point, Guide Book to. N. Y., 1844. 12°. 16850
Westcott, B. F. Hist. of the English Bible. 2d ed. Lond., 1872. 8°. 10261
Western Clearings. Kirkland. N. Y., 1846. 12°. 15812
Westminster Assembly of Divines, Hist. of. Hetherington. N. Y., 1843. 12°. 6313
Review. Lond. & N. Y., 1824–72. v. 1–45, 47–84, 86–98. 8°. 11853
The same. v. 1–17, 20–54, 57–92. 12032
Westward Ho. Kingsley. Lond., 1871. 8°. 2566
Paulding. N. Y., 1832. 2 v. 12°. 15161
Westward by Rail. Rae. N. Y., 1871. 12°. 8394
Wetherell, Eliz. *(Pseudonym.)* See S. WARNER.
Whale, Sperm, Nat. Hist. of the. Beale. Lond., 1839. 12°. . . 16330
Whaling Cruise, Etchings of a; and Hist. of the Whale-Fishery. Browne. N. Y., 1846. 8°. 8080
What Answer? Dickinson. Bost., 1868. 12°. 2983
What will he do with it? Bulwer. Philad., 1860. 3 v. 12°. . . 2140
[**Whately, E. J.**] Selection of English Synonyms. Bost., 1852. 12°. 101
Whately, R. Elements of Rhetoric. Camb., 1834. 12°. . . . 9300

Whately, R. Historic Doubts Relative to Napoleon. N. Y., 1835. 8°. 17269
The Kingdom of Christ. N. Y., 1842. 12°. 9953
Life and Correspondence of. Whately. Lond., 1866. 2 v. 8°. 7133
Wheatley, P. Poems. 1816. 12°. 14958
Memoir of. Thatcher. Bost., 1834. 12°. 8472
Wheatly, C. On the Book of Common Prayer. (Bohn's ed.) Lond., 1849. 8° 496
Wheaton, H. Elements of International Law. 8th ed., by Dana. Bost., 1866. 8°. 8704
Life of Pinkney. N. Y., 1826. 8°. 9327
The same. (Sparks, v. 6.) Bost. 1836. 16°. 7255
Wheeler, H. G. Hist. of Congress. N. Y., 1848. 2 v. 8°. . . . 6279
Wheeler, W. A. Dict. of Noted Names of Fiction. Bost., 1865. 12°. 300
The same. 2d ed. Bost., 1868. 12°. 301
Whelpley, S. Compend. of History. N. Y., 1814. 2 v. in 1. 8°. 15901
Letters on Capital Punishment, War, etc. Prov., 1818. 8°. . 17081
Whewell, W. Astronomy and Physics. Philad., 1836. 8°. . . . 16983
Hist. of the Inductive Sciences. (2 copies.) Lond., 1837. 3 v. 8°. 8745
Philosophy of the Inductive Sciences. Lond., 1840. 2 v. 8°. 8751
Whig-Examiner, The. (Addison's Works, v. 3.) N. Y., 1855. 8°. . 3818
Whig Review. See AMERICAN Whig Review.
Whigs and Democrats, a Comedy. Richmond, 1839. 12°. . . . 1447
Whim, A, and its Consequences. G. P. R. James. N. Y., 1848. 8°. 2324
Whims and Oddities. Hood. N. Y., 1867. 12°. 4273
Whipple, E. P. Character and Characteristic Men. (2 copies.) Bost., 1866. 12°. 3544
Essays and Reviews. 2d ed. Bost., 1851. 2 v. 8°. . . . 3540
The same. 3d ed. Bost., 1853. 2 v. 8°. 3542
Literature of the Age of Elizabeth. Bost., 1869. 8°. . . . 70
Success and its Conditions. Bost., 1871. 8°. 3546
Whitaker, E. W. System of Universal Hist. Lond., 1821. 4 v. 4°. 16038
White, Carlos. Ecce Femina. Bost., 1870. 16°. 9210
[**White, Charles.**] Almack's Revisited. N. Y., 1828. 2 v. 12°. . 15366
White, *Rev.* **Charles.** Essays in Literature and Ethics. Bost., 1853. 12°. 3582
White, G. Natural Hist. of Selborne. N. Y., 1842. 12°. 11749
The same. (Bohn's ed.) Lond., 1851. 8°. 525
White, Henry. Massacre of St. Bartholomew. N. Y., 1868. 12°. . 6327
White, Henry Kirke, Beauties of. Selected by A. Howard. Bost., 1827. 12°. 14896
Complete Works, with Life by Southey. N. Y. 8°. . . . 1276
Poetical Works. Philad., 1830. 8°. 944
The same. 947
Remains, with Life by Southey. Bost., 1823. 2 v. 12°. . . 14897
White, James. Adventures of John of Gaunt. Dubl., 1790. 2 v. 12°. 15477
White, *Rev.* **James.** The Eighteen Christian Centuries. N. Y., 1863. 12°. 4566
Hist. of England. (2 copies.) Lond., 1864. 16°. 4849
White, R. G. Life and Genius of Shakespeare. (2 copies.) Bost., 1865. 16°. 1543

White, R. G. National Hymns. N. Y., 1861. 8°. 925
Words and their Uses. (2 copies.) N. Y., 1870. 12°. . . . 97
White, Thom. *(Pseudonym.)* See C. W. ELLIOTT.
White, W., Memoir of. Wilson. Philad., 1839. 8°. 16415
White Hills, The. King. N. Y., 1870. 8°. 8392
White-Jacket. Melville. N. Y., 1850. 12°. 15813
White Lies. Reade. Bost., 1866. 16°. 2101
White Mountain Scenery. Oakes. Bost., 1848. 4°. . . . . . .
White as Snow. Garrett. N. Y. 12°. 2441
White Sulphur Papers, The. N. Y., 1839. 12°. 16894
Whitefield, G. Journals. Lond., 1830. 12°. 6644
Sermons, with Memoir. Lond., 1835. 8°. 10049
Life and Times of. Philip. N. Y., 1838. 12°. 7599
Memoirs and Writings of. Gillies. Middletown, 1838. 8°. . 10048
Whitehead, P. Poems, etc. Lond., 1777. 4°. 15082
Whitehead, W. Roman Father; Creusa. (Brit. Drama.) Lond., 1804. 8°. 1630
School for Lovers. (Brit. Drama.) Lond., 1804. 8°. . . . 1632
Memoirs of. Mason. Lond., 1788. 8°. 6955
Whiting, H. Life of Z. M. Pike. (Sparks, v. 15.) Bost., 1845. 16°. 7264
Whitney, A. D. T. The Gayworthys. Bost. [1865.] 12°. 2967
Hitherto. (2 copies.) Bost. 12°. 2969
Patience Strong's Outings. Bost., 1870. 12°. 2968
Real Folks. Bost., 1872. 8°. 2971
Whitney, W. D. Language and the Study of Language. (2 copies.) N. Y., 1867. 12°. 134
Oriental and Linguistic Studies. N. Y., 1872. 12°. 136
Whitsuntide, Sermons for. Ed. Cattermole. Lond., 1835. 16°. . 9499
Whittier, J. G. Home Ballads and Poems. Bost., 1861. 16°. . . 736
Lays of my Home, and other Poems. Bost., 1843. 16°. . . 734
Leaves from Margaret Smith's Journal. Bost., 1849. 16°. . 2950
Legends of New-England. Hartf'd., 1831. 12°. 2949
Miriam and other Poems. (2 copies.) Bost., 1871. 16°. . . 743
Old Portraits and Modern Sketches. (2 copies.) Bost., 1850. 16°. 3538
The Panorama, and other Poems. Bost., 1856. 12°. . . . 735
The Pennsylvania Pilgrim, and other Poems. Bost., 1872. 16°. 745
Poems. Bost., 1849. 8°. 928
Prose Works. Bost., 1866. 2 v. 16°. 3536
Snow-Bound. (2 copies.) Bost., 1866. 16°. 739
Supernaturalism of N. England. Lond., 1847. 12°. 8612
The Tent on the Beach, and other Poems. (2 copies.) Bost., 1867–69. 16°. 741
In War Time and other Poems. (2 copies.) Bost., 1864. 12°. 737
Whittlesey, C. Life of J. Fitch. (Sparks, v. 16.) Bost., 1845. 16°. 7265
Whymper, E. Scrambles amongst the Alps. Lond., 1871. 8°. . 8380
Whymper, F. Travel and Adventure in Alaska, etc. (2 copies.) N. Y., 1869. 12°. 8399
Wickliff. See WYCLIFFE.
Wide, Wide World, The. [Warner.] Philad., 1872. 12°. 2994

[**Widmann, G. R.**] Doctor Faustus. Lond., 1826. 12°. 1895
Wieland, C. M. Oberon, transl. by Sotheby. 3d ed. Lond., 1826.
2 v. 16°. 864
The same. Newport, 1810. 2 v. 12°. 866
Wieland. C. B. Brown. Bost., 1827. 12°. 15292
Wife, The Young. Alcott. Bost., 1837. 12°. 17010
Wife of a Vain Man, The. Schwartz. Bost., 1871. 8°. 3095
Wiggers, G. Life of Socrates. Lond., 1840. 12°. 7575
Wigwam and Cabin. Simms. N. Y., 1845. 12°. 2719
Wilberforce, W. Correspondence. Philad., 1841. 2 v. 12°. . . 6769
Letter on Abolition of the Slave-Trade. Lond., 1807. 8°. . 8553
Life of. By his Sons. 2d ed. Lond., 1839. 5 v. 12°. . . 6763
The same, abridged. Philad., 1839. 12°. 6768
Wilbraham, R. Travels in Trans-Caucasian Provinces of Russia.
Lond., 1839. 8°. 8039
Wild Irish Girl, The. Lady Morgan. N. Y., 1807. 12°. . . . 2405
Wild Men and Wild Beasts. Cumming. N. Y., 1872. 12°. . . 10178
Wilde, R. H. Love and Madness of Tasso. N. Y., 1842. 2 v. 12°. 16408
Wilderness, The. N. Y., 1823. 2 v. 12°. 15814
Wilderness and the War Path, The. Hall. N. Y., 1846. 12°. . . 15816
Wilfrid Cumbermede. MacDonald. N. Y., 1872. 12°. 2585
Wilhelm, Meister. Goethe, transl. by Carlyle. Lond., 1871. 2 v. 8°. 4051
Wilkes, C. Narrative of U. S. Exploring Exped. Philad., 1845.
5 v. and Atlas. 8°. 8129
Wilkes, J. North Briton, The. Dubl., 1765. 3 v. 12°. 5155
Sketch of. Thorold Rogers. Lond., 1870. 8°. 6732
Wilkie, D., Life of. Cunningham. Lond., 1843. 3 v. 8°. . . 7999
Wilkins, G. Miseries of Inforced Marriage. Lond., 1825. 8°. . . 1512
Wilkinson, J. G. Manners and Customs of the Ancient Egyptians.
1st Series. (2 copies.) Lond., 1837. 3 v. 8°. . . . 4447
The same. 2d Series. Lond., 1841. 2 v. and 1 v. plates. 8°. 4453
Will, P. Practical Philosophy of Social Life. Lansingburgh, 1805. 8°. 17045
Will, Freedom of the. Edwards. N. Y., 1829. 8°. 17177
Willard, E. Hist. of the U. S. N. Y., 1831. 8°. 16122
The same. N. Y., 1847. 8°. 6115
Journal and Letters from France and Grt. Brt. Troy, 1833. 12°. 16586
William I. (the Conqueror), of England, Hist. of. Cobbe. Lond.,
1867. 8°. 5285
Life of. Roscoe. Philad., 1846. 12°. 5127
William II., Hist. of. Cobbe. Lond., 1869. 8°. . , ... 5285
William IV., Life and Reign of. Wright. Lond., 1837. 2 v. 8°. . 5326
William of Malmesbury. English Chronicle. (2 copies.) Lond.,
1847. 8°. , ... 508
Williams, Catharine R. Lives of Barton and Olney. Prov., 1839. 12°. 16430
Williams, Charles V. Life of S. Perceval. Philad., 1813. 12°. . 16380
Williams, Cynric R. Tour through Jamaica. 2d ed. Lond., 1827. 8°. 16920
Williams, E. Statesman's Manual. N. Y., 1854. 3 v. 8°. . . . 6200
Williams, H. M. Correspondence of Lewis XVI. Lond., 1803. 3 v. 8°. 5624
Letters from France. Lond., 1795. 3 v. 12°. 5514

Williams, *Rev.* **John.** Life of Alexander the Great. N. Y., 1841. 12°. 11006
The same. N. Y., 1830. 12°. 11935
Williams, J. F. Lake. Hist. of Inventions. Lond., 1820. 2 v. 8°. . 4105
Williams, Rob't. F. Lives of Princes of Wales. Lond., 1843. v. 1. 12°. 5133
The Secret Passion. (2 copies.) Lond., 1844. 3 v. 12°. . 1649
Shakspeare and his Friends. (2 copies.) Lond., 1838. 3 v. 12°. 1643
The Youth of Shakspeare. (2 copies.) Lond., 1839. 3 v. 12°. 1637
Wlliams, Roger, Life of. Gammell. Bost., 1845. 16°. . . . 7263
Memoir of. Knowles. Bost., 1834. 12°. 7548
in Banishment; a Poem. Durfee. Leeds, 1840. 12°. . . 14986
Williams, Sam'l. Hist. of Vt. 2d ed. Burlington, 1809. 2 v. 8°. . 5838
Williams, Sam'l. Wells. The Middle Kingdom. (2 copies.) N. Y., 1848–49. 2 v. 12°. 6471
Williamson, A. Journeys in N. China, etc. Lond., 1870. 2 v. 8°. . 7950
Williamson, H. Hist. of N. Carolina. Philad., 1812. 2 v. 8°. . 5864
Willis, N. P. A l'Abri. N. Y., 1839. 12°. 15327
Fanshawe. Bost., 1828. 12°. 15326
Health Trip to the Tropics. N. Y., 1853. 12°. . . . 15332
Hurry-graphs. N. Y., 1851. 12°. 3613
Letters from under a Bridge. N. Y. 8°. 15092
Life here and there. N. Y., 1850. 12°. 15331
Melanie, and other Poems. N. Y., 1837. 12°. 792
Paul Fane. (2 copies.) N. Y., 1857. 12°. 15333
Pencillings by the Way. Philad., 1836. 2 v. 12°. . . . 15328
Poems. N. Y., 1864. 12°. 793
Romance of Travel. N. Y., 1840. 12°. 15330
[Poetical] Sketches. Bost., 1827. 8°. 791
Willis, Richard S. Our Church Music. N. Y., 1856. 12°. . . 8866
Willis, R. Spinoza. Lond., 1870. 8°. 7789
Williston, E. B. Eloquence of the U. S. Middletown, 1827. 5 v. 8°. 9332
Willoughby, *Lady,* Diary of. [Rathbone.] N. Y., 1845. 12°. . . 3957
Wilmot, J. (Earl of Rochester.) Poetical Works. Ed. Bell. Lond., 1807. 24°. 261
Select Poems. With Life, by Sanford. Philad., 1819. 24°. . 7
The same, ed. Johnson. Dubl., 1804. 8°. 15096
Life of. Burnet. Lond. 24°. 6677
Wilmot, Rob't. Tancred and Gismunda. Lond., 1825. 8°. . . 1509
Wilmott, Rob't. A. Gems of Epistolary Correspondence. Lond., 1846. 12°. 7045
Wilson, Alex., Life of. Peabody. (Sparks, v. 2.) Bost., 1834. 16°. 7251
Wilson, Augusta J. (Evans.) St. Elmo. (3 copies.) N. Y., 1867–68. 12°. 2990
Vashti. N. Y., 1869. 12°. 2993
Wilson, B. Memoir of Bp. White. Philad., 1839. 8°. . . . 16415
Wilson, D. Chatterton. Lond., 1869. 8°. 6998
Wilson, Henry. Wonderful Characters. N. Y., 1834. 8°. . . 6906
Wilson, *Hon.* **Henry.** Hist. of Anti-Slavery Measures in Congress, 1861–64. Bost., 1864. 12°. 8579
Hist. of Rise and Fall of the Slave Power in America. Bost., 1872. v. 1. 8°. 6193

Wilson, James G. Life and Letters of Halleck. N. Y., 1869. 12°. . 7386
Wilson, *Prof.* **John.** Critical and Miscellaneous Essays. (3 copies.)
Philad., 1842. 3 v. 12°. 3303
The Foresters. Bost., 1845. 12°. 15433
Genius and Character of Burns. N. Y., 1845. 12°. . . . 1234
The same. N. Y., 1861. 12°. 7044
Isle of Palms, and other Poems. N. Y., 1812. 12°. . . 13838
Lights and Shadows of Scottish Life. Philad. 16°. . . . 2023
The same. Philad., 1822. 12°. 15489
Noctes Ambrosianæ. (2 copies.) Philad., 1843. 4 v. 12°. . 3295
The same. Ed. by Mackenzie. (2 copies.) N. Y., 1857.
5 v. 12°. 3336
Recreations of Christopher North. Edinb., 1842. 3 v. 12°. . 3333
Trials of Margaret Lyndsay. N. Y., 1823. 12°. . . . 2460
The same. Philad., 1823. 12°. 2459
Memoir of. Mrs. Gordon. N. Y., 1863. 8°. 7086
Wilson, John. Treatise on English Punctuation. 14th ed. Bost.,
1862. 16°. 61
[**Wilson, John.** ?] Hist. of Switzerland. (2 copies.) Lond., 1832. 16°. 5476
The same. Philad., 1832. 12°. 6071
Wilson, John M. Tales of the Borders, and of Scotland. N. Y. 5 v. 8°. 1678
Wilson, Robt. A. New Hist. of the Conquest of Mexico. Philad.,
1859. 8°. 5971
Wilson, Rob't. T. Hist. of Brit. Exped. to Egypt. Philad., 1803. 8°. 5281
Narrative of Abercrombie's Exped. to Egypt. [Abridged.] Lond.,
1803. 12°. 16070
Winchell, A. Sketches of Creation. N. Y., 1870. 12°. . . . 8958
Wind and Whirlwind. [Elliott.] N. Y., 1868. 12°. 15817
Windham, W. Select Speeches. Ed. Walsh. Philad., 1837. 8°. . 9367
Speeches in Parliament; with Life by Amory. Lond., 1812.
3 v. 8°. 9342
Windle, M. J. Legend of the Waldenses, etc. Philad., 1852. 12°. . 15728
Wines, E. C. A Trip to Boston. Bost., 1838. 12°. 16846
Two Years and a half in the Navy. Philad., 1832. 2 v. 12°. . 16284
Wing-and-Wing. Cooper. N. Y., 1867. 12°. 2817
Winifred Bertram. [Mrs. Charles.] N. Y., 1866. 12°. . . . 2470
Winslow, H. The Young Man's Aid. Bost., 1837. 12°. . . . 17030
Winter Sunbeams, Search for. Cox. N. Y., 1870. 8°. . . . 8277
Winterbotham, W. View of the Chinese Empire. Lond., 1795. 8°. 16473
Winthrop, T. Canoe and Saddle. (2 copies.) Bost., 1863-64. 12°. 2860
Cecil Dreeme. Bost., 1861. 12°. 2724
The same. (2 copies.) Bost., 1866. 12°. . . . 2855
Edwin Brothertoft. (2 copies.) Bost., 1862. 12°. . . . 2858
John Brent. Bost., 1862. 12°. 2857
Wirt, W. Arguments on the Trial of Burr. Richmond, 1808. 12°. . 7487
Letters of the British Spy. N. Y., 1832. 12°. 6075
The same. N. Y., 1836. 12°. 6074
Life of P. Henry. Ithaca, 1850. 8°. 7342
The same. N. Y., 1835. 8°. 7343

Wirt, W. Memoirs of. Kennedy. Philad., 1850. 2 v. 8°. . . . 7420
Wise, H. A. Los Gringos. N. Y., 1850. 12°. 16257
Scampavias. N. Y., 1857. 12°. 16922
Wiseman, N. Lectures on the Catholic Church. 2d ed. Lond., 1844. 2 v. in 1. 16°. 9581
on Science and Religion. Andover, 1837. 8°. 10036
Recollections of the last four Popes. Revised ed. Lond. 8°. 7677
Wit, Flowers of. Kett. Hartf'd., 1825. 12°. 4284
and Humor, selected from the English Poets. L. Hunt. N. Y., 1847. 12°. 1234
Witch, The Amber. Meinhold. N. Y., 1845. 12°. 3044
Witchcraft, Letters on. Sir W. Scott. N. Y., 1839. 12°. . . . 11011
See, also, APPARITIONS ; MAGIC ; NECROMANCERS.
Witherspoon, J. Inquiry into the Stage. N. Y., 1812. 12°. . . 1394
[**Withington, L.**] The Puritan. Bost., 1836. 2 v. 12°. . . . 15320
Witt, J. de, Life of. James. Lond., 1836. 16°. 5768
Wittich, W. Earthquakes and Volcanoes. Lond., 1846. 12°. . . 8781
Wives and Daughters. A Novel. Gaskell. N. Y., 1866. 8°. . . 2663
Wives of England, Duties, etc., of. Mrs. Ellis. N. Y., 1843. 12°. . 9199
[**Wolcott, J.**] Works of Peter Pindar. Philad., 1835. 8°. . . 1239
Wolcott, O. Memoirs of Administrations of Washington and Adams. Ed. Gibbs. N. Y., 1846. 2 v. 8°. 6248
Wolfert's Roost, etc. Irving. N. Y., 1855. 12°. 4365
Wolff, J. Mission to Bokhara. N. Y., 1845. 8°. 8049
Wolff, O. L. B. Poetischer Hausschatz des deutschen Volkes. Leipz., 1867. 8°. 9648
Wollstonecraft, M., Memoirs of. [W. Godwin.] Philad., 1804. 12°. 6938
Wolsey, T., Life of. (Cabinet Cyclopædia.) Lond., 1831. 16°. . 5759
The same. Campbell. (Lord Chancellors, v. 1.) Lond., 1845. 8°. 6866
The same. Cavendish. Lond., 1827. 8°. 6813
The same. Galt. Lond., 1846. 8°. 340
The same. [K. Thomson.] (Libr. of Useful Knowl.) Lond., 1833. 8°. 6751
Wolzogen, A. v. Raphael's Life and Works. Lond., 1866. 8°. . 7918
Woman in America. Graves. N. Y., 1844. 12°. 11767
Beauty in. Walker. N. Y., 1840. 12°. 17013
Noble Deeds of. [Starling.] Philad., 1836. 2 v. 12°. . . 9195
physiologically considered. Walker. N. Y., 1840. 12°. . . 17011
Question, Attempt to solve the. C. White. Bost., 1870. 16°. 9210
Suffrage. Bushnell. N. Y., 1869. 12°. 9211
Tales of. N. Y., 1829. 12°. 1560
in White, The. Collins. N. Y., 1871. 8°. 2300
Woman's Friendship ; a Story. Aguilar. N. Y., 1851. 12°. . . 2518
Kingdom. A Love Story. Mrs. Craik. N. Y., 1868. 8°. . 2681
Work and Woman's Culture. Lond., 1869. 8°. 9290
Worth and Worthlessness. Gail Hamilton. N. Y., 1872. 12°. 9216
Wrongs. Gail Hamilton. Bost., 1868. 16°. 9215

Women, Characteristics of. Jameson. Bost., 1866. 16°. 1487
The Coming Race of. [Bulwer-Lytton.] N. Y., 1871. 12°. . 9202
Cyclopædia of Biography of. Adams. Lond., 1869. 16°. . 6675
Friendships of. Alger. Bost., 1870. 16°. 9209
Hist. of. Alexander. Lond., 1782. 2 v. 8°. 17007
Hist. of Condition of. Child. Bost., 1835. 2 v. 12°. . . 9193
Memoirs of Celebrated. Ed. G. P. R. James. Philad., 1839.
2 v. 12°. 6701

CONTENTS.—1, Joan of Arc; Margaret of Anjou; Lady J. Grey. 2, Mme. de Maintenon; Q. Elizabeth; Maria Pacheco.

of Learned British. Ballard. Oxf'd., 1752. 4°. . 16030
The Subjection of. J. S. Mill. N. Y., 1869. 12°. . . . 9203
of the Age, Eminent. Hartf'd., 1868. 8°. 6905
American, Noble Deeds of. Clement. Buffalo, 1851. 12°. . 9208
of the Amer. Revolution, The. Ellet. N. Y., 1848–50. 3 v. 12°. 7300
of Christianity. Kavanagh. N. Y., 1852. 12°. 7568
of England, Social Duties and Domestic Habits of. Ellis.
N. Y., 1839. 12°. 9197
of Israel. Aguilar. N. Y., 1851. 2 v. 12°. 2523
Loved by Poets, Memoirs of. Jameson. Lond., 1837. 2 v. 8°. 6709
Modern, and what is said of them. N. Y., 1868–70. 2 v. 12°. 9206
Pious, Memoirs of. Burder. Philad. [1836.] 8°. . . . 16361
See, also, FEMALE.

Wonders of the Universe. N. Y., 1831. 8°. 16938
of the World, Hundred. Clarke. N. H., 1821. 12°. . . 16941
Wondrous Tale of Alroy. Disraeli. Lond., 1833. 3 v. 12°. . . 2124
Wood, J. G. Homes without Hands. N. Y., 1866. 8°. . . . 9005
Wood, Wm. Manual of Physical Exercises. N. Y., 1867. 12°. . 9268
Wood, Wm. M. Wandering Sketches. Philad., 1849. 12°. . . 16292
Wood, W. W. Sketches of China. Philad., 1830. 12°. . . . 16479
Wood Leighton. M. Howitt. N. Y., 1847. 8°. 2313
Woodburn Grange; a Story. W. Howitt. Philad. 12°. . . . 15638
Woodbury, L. Writings. Bost., 1852. 3 v. 8°. 17160
Woodcraft. Simms. N. Y., 1854. 12°. 17196
Woods, L. Memoirs of H. Newell. Bost., 1814. 12°. . . . 7522
Woodstock. Sir W. Scott. Bost., 1845. 12°. 1828
Woodworth, S. Champions of Freedom, or Mysterious Chief. N. Y.,
1816. 12°. 15675
Melodies, Songs, etc. N. Y., 1826. 12°. 14959
The same. 3d ed. N. Y., 1831. 12°. 14960
Poems, Odes, etc. N. Y., 1818. 12°. 15042
Woolman, J. Journal. N. Y., 1845. 12°. 7631
The same. Ed. by Whittier. Bost., 1871. 12°. . . 7567
Woolrych, H. W. Memoirs of Judge Jeffreys. Lond., 1827. 8°. . 6757
The same. Philad., 1852. 12°. 6758
Woolsey, M. T., Life of. Cooper. (Naval Biogr.) Philad., 1846. 12°. 7276
Woolsey, T. D. Divorce and Divorce Legislation. N. Y., 1869. 12°. 8642
Hist. Discourse at Yale College, 1850. N. H., 1850. 8°. . . 9279
Introd. to International Law. (2 copies.) 2d ed. N. Y., 1864. 8°. 8702

Woolsey, T. D. Religion of the Present and the Future. (2 copies.) N. Y., 1871. 12°. 9933
Worcester, Marquis of. See E. SOMERSET.
Worcester, J. E. Elements of History. Bost., 1852. 12°. . . . 15933
Sketches of the Earth. Bost., 1823. 2 v. 12°. 16327
Words. See LANGUAGE (English).
Wordsworth, W. Lyrical Ballads, with other Poems. 4th ed. Lond., 1805. 2 v. 12°. 14899
Poetical Works. Bost. [1864.] 24°. 973
The same. Lond., 1870. 6 v. 16°. 1126
The same. Bost., 1824. 4 v. 12°. 1117
The same. Lond., 1836–37. v. 1–5. 16°. . . . 1121
The Prelude. (2 copies.) N. Y., 1850. 12°. 852
Yarrow revisited, and other Poems. N. Y., 1835. 16°. . . 851
The same. 14901
Essay on. Jno. Wilson. (Essays, v. 1.) Philad., 1842. 12°. . 3303
Memoirs of. Chr. Wordsworth, ed. Reed. Bost., 1851. 2 v. 16°. 6957
Work, Letters on the Laws of. Ruskin. N. Y., 1868. 12°. . . 9046
and Wages. Brassey. N. Y., 1872. 8°. 8628
Working Man, Memoirs of a. Lond., 1845. 12°. 8491
Workman, J. Essays and Letters. N. Y., 1809. 12°. . . . 16071
Workmen, Letters to. Ruskin. N. Y., 1871–72. 2 v. 12°. . . 8632
World, The. (Essays.) Ed. Ferguson. Lond., 1823. 3 v. 12°. . 3131
The same. 3505
The Ancient. Ansted. Philad., 1847. 12°. 8983
before the Deluge, The. Figuier. Lond. [1866.] 8°. . . 8995
before You, The. Lee. Philad., 1844. 12°. 15819
Hist. of the. See HISTORY.
Sacred Hist. of the. Turner. N. Y., 1838-39. 3 v. 12°. . 11034
World's Progress, The. Putnam. N. Y., 1851. 12°. 4605
Wortley, E. S. Travels in the U. S., etc. N. Y., 1851. 12°. . . 16811
Wotton, H., Life of. Walton. [Lond., 1845.] 8°. 948
Poems. Ed. Hannah. Lond., 1870. 16°. 1005
Wrangell, F. v. Expedition to the Polar Sea. N. Y., 1841. 12°. . 11750
The same. 2d ed., by Sabine. Lond., 1844. 16°. . . . 7907
Wrangham, F. The Pleiad; Evidences of Christianity. Edinb., 1828. 12°. 4488
Wraxall, N. W. Historical Memoirs of My Own Time, 1772–84. Philad., 1837. 8°. 5324
Hist. of France, 1574–1610. 2d ed. Lond., 1814. 6 v. 8°. . 16241
Posthumous Memoirs of my Time, 1784–89. Philad., 1836. 8°. 5325
Wren, C., Life of. (Libr. of Useful Knowl.) Lond., 1833. 8°. . 6751
Wright, G. N. Life and Times of Louis Phillipe. (2 copies.) Lond. 8°. 5584
Life of Wm. IV. (2 copies.) Lond., 1837. 2 v. 8°. . . 5326
Wright, S., Life of. Jenkins. Auburn, 1850. 12°. 7329
Wright, F. Caricature Hist. of the Georges. Lond. 8°. 4281
Celt, Roman, and Saxon. 2d ed. Lond., 1861. 8°. 5272
Domestic Manners and Sentiments in England in Middle Ages. Lond., 1862. 8°. 5263

Wright, F. Queen Elizabeth and her Times. Lond., 1838. 2 v. 8°. 5293
Hist. of Caricature and Grotesque. Lond. [1864.] 8°. . . 4315
Narratives of Sorcery and Magic. N. Y., 1852. 12°. . . 8614
Writer, The. Bost., 1822. 12°. 15307
Wuderman, —. Notes on Cuba. Bost., 1844. 12°. 16918
Wuthering Heights. E. Brontë. N. Y., 1857. 12°. 2419
Wyatt, M. D. Fine Art. Lond., 1870. 8°. 9076
Wyatt, *Sir* **Thos.** Poems, ed. Arber. Lond., 1870. 16°. . . . 3895
Poetical Works, with Memoir. Bost., 1854. 16°. . . . 1053
The same. Lond., 1831. 16°. 1026
Select Poems, with Life. Ed. Sanford. Philad., 1819. 24°. . 1
Wyatt, *Sir* **Thos.,** Hist. of; a play. Greene. (Works, v. 2.) Lond., 1830. 8°. 1467
Wycherley, W. Dramatic Works, ed. L. Hunt. Lond., 1849. 8°. . 10300
Plain Dealer. (Brit. Drama, v. 2, pt. 1.) Lond., 1804. 8°. . 1631
Wycliffe, J., Life of. Le Bas. N. Y., 1832. 12°. 7516
Sketch of. Thorold Rogers. Lond., 1870. 8°. 6732
and his disciples, Lives of. Gilpin. N. Y., 1814. 12°. . . 16376
Wykeham, William of, Life of. Lowth. Lond., 1758. 8°. . . 16340
Wylie, J. A. The Awakening of Italy. N. Y., [1866.] 12°. . . 4591
Wyndham, N. Travels through Europe. Lond. 4 v. 8°. . . 16580
Wyoming, The Poetry and Hist. of. Stone. N. Y., 1841. 12°. . . 5731
Wyse, F. America. Lond., 1846. 3 v. 8°. 5892

X.

Xenophon. The Cyropædia, transl. by Cooper. N. Y., 1841. 12°. . 4510
Works. Philad., 1836. 8°. 4440
for English Readers. Grant. Philad., 1871. 16°. . . . 78
Ximenes, F., Life of. Crowe. Lond., 1833. 16°.. 5766

Y.

Yalden, T. Select Poems. With Life, by Sanford. Philad., 1829. 24°. 12
The same. Ed. Johnson. Dubl., 1804. 8°. . . . 15099
Yale College, Addresses at Inauguration of Pres. Porter. N. Y., 1871. 8°. 9281
Annals of. Baldwin. N. H., 1831. 8°. 9322
Athenæum, The. [A Magazine.] N. H., 1814. v. 1. 8°. . 17475
Biennial Examination Papers of, 1850–64. 8°. 9319
Brothers in Unity, Catalogue of Society of, to 1854. N. H., 1854. 8°. 9278
Catalogues, Annual, 1817–72. 4 v. 8°. 9310
The same, 1817–64. 3 v. 8°. 9314
Triennial, 1820–62. 2 v. 8°. 9317
Class Valedictory Orations and Poems, 1837–52. 8°. . . 9320
Commemorative Celebration and Roll of Honor. N. H., 1866. 8°. 9280

Yale Courant. (2 copies.) N. H., 1865–67. 2 v. 4°. . . . .
[Continued as the COLLEGE COURANT.]
Decisions of Questions discussed by Senior Class in. Dwight. N. Y., 1833. 12°. 9186
Four Years at. [Bagg.] N. H., 1871. 12°. 9275
Historical Discourse at. Woolsey. N. H., 1850. 8°. . . 9279
Lectures on Preaching. Beecher. N. Y., 1872. 12°. . . 9919
Linonian Society, Catalogue of Members, to 1853. (2 copies.) N. H., 1853. 8°. 9277
Centennial Celebration. N. H., 1853. 8°. . 9282
Literary Magazine. N. H., 1836–72. v. 1–37. 8°. . . . 17393
The same. v. 2–15, 17–26, 28, 29. 17367
The same. v. 1–6, 8–12. 17451
Index to v. 1–33. N. H., 1868. 8°. . . . .
Phi Beta Kappa Orations and Poems, 1802–46. 8°. . . . 9321
Portraits of Classes of 1853 (2 copies), 1854 (2 copies), 1855, 1857, 1858 (2 copies), 1859 (2 copies), 1861 (2 copies). 12 v. 4°. . . . .
Student's Companion. N. H., 1831. v. 1. 8°. 17393
Yang-Tsze, Five Months on the, 1861. Blakiston. Lond., 1862. 8°. 8008
Yankee Notions. By Timo. Titterwell. Bost., 1838. 12°. . . 4312
Year '13, In the: a Tale. Reuter. Leipz., 1867. 16°. . . . 2707
Year Book, The. Hone. Lond., 1838. 8°. 4343
Yeast; a Problem. Kingsley. N. Y., 1864. 12°. 2563
Yellowplush, Memoirs of. Thackeray. Lond., 1872. 8°. . . 2196
Yonge, C. M. Book of Golden Deeds. Cambr., 1865. 16°. . . 4208
The Caged Lion. Lond., 1870. 8°. 2504
Chaplet of Pearls. N. Y., 1869. 8°. 2665
Clever Woman of the Family. N. Y., 1865. 8°. 2664
Daisy Chain. N. Y., 1871. 2 v. 12°. 2501
Dove in the Eagle's Nest. N. Y., 1866. 12°. 2503
Heartsease. N. Y., 1871. 2 v. 12°. 2499
Heir of Redclyffe. (2 copies.) N. Y., 1854–71. 2 v. 12°. . 2495
Pupils of St. John. Lond. [1868.] 8°. 6316
York, Fred'k., *Duke of*, Last Illness and Decease of. Taylor. Lond., 1827. 16°. 6683
Yorke, P. (*Lord* Hardwicke), Life of. Campbell. Philad., 1848. 8°. 6870
Yorkshire, Worthies of. H. Coleridge. Leeds, 1836. 8°. . . . 6904
Youatt, W. The Horse. Lond., 1842. 12°. 16951
Young, Alex. Chronicles of the Pilgrims. Bost., 1841. 8°. . . 5934
The same. 2d ed. Bost., 1844. 8°. 5935
Library of Old English Prose Writers. Camb., 1831–32. 7 v. 12°. 3904

CONTENTS.—1, Fuller's Holy and Profane States. 2. Sidney's Defence of Poesy; Selden's Table-Talk. 3, Sir T. Browne's Misc. Works. 4, Feltham's Resolves. 5, 6, Walton's Lives. 7, Latimer's Sermons.

The same. v. 1, 2, 4–7. 3911
Young, Arthur. Travels in France. Dubl., 1793. 2 v. 8°. . . 16695
Young, C. M., Memoir of. By his Son. Lond., 1871. 8°. . . . 7009
Young, E. Poetical Works. Philad., 1842. 8°. 945
The same. Ed. Bell. Lond., 1807. 4 v. in 2. 24°. . 531

Yonng, E. Poetical Works. Ed. Johnson. Dubl., 1804. 8°. . . 15102
The same. Ed. Walsh. Philad., 1822. 2 v. 24°. . . 19
Works. Edinb., 1774. 6 v. 12°. 14602
Lond., 1798. 3 v. 12°. 14599
Young, *Prof.* **John.** Lectures on Intellectual Philosophy. Glasg., 1835. 8°. 17071
Young, *Rev.* **John.** The Christ of History. N. Y., 1860. 12°. . . 9899
The Life and Light of Men. Lond., 1866. 8°. 9900
Young, John R. Lectures on Mathematical Study, etc. Lond., 1846. 12°. 9253
Young Christian, The. Abbott. N. Y., 1834. 12°. 9993
Duke, The. Disraeli. N. Y., 1831. 2 v. 12°. 15153
Gentleman, Advice to a, on entering Society. Philad., 1839. 12°. 9178
Ladies and Gentlemen, Sketches of. By Quiz. N. Y., 1838. 12°. 4313
Man, Letters to a. Aikin. Lond., 1838. 16°. 9133
The same. Earl of Chatham. N. Y., 1804. 12°. . . 9136
The same. Earl of Chesterfield. Lond., 1804. 4 v. 12°. 9139
Thoughts for a. Mann. Bost., 1850. 16°. . . . 9114
from Home, The. James. N. Y. 12°. 17056
Man's Aid, The. Winslow. Bost., 1837. 12°. . . . 17030
Friend. James. N. Y., 1852. 12°. 9144
Guide. Alcott. Bost., 1837. 12°. 9138
Men, Addresses to. Fordyce. Lond., 1789. 2 v. 8°. . . 17054
Advice to. Cobbett. N. Y., 1831. 12°. 17025
Counsels to. Nott. N. Y., 1841. 12°. 9177
Hints to. Todd. Northampton, 1844. 12°. . . . 9174
Lectures to. H. W. Beecher. Bost., 1866. 12°. . . 9181
The same. Hawes. Hartf'd., 1829. 12°. . . . 9173
The same. C. B. Smith. N. H., 1848. 12°. . . . 17027
preparing for the Ministry, Letters to. Cogswell. Bost., 1837. 12°. 17036
Muscovite, The. Zakosken. N. Y., 1834. 2 v. 12°. . . 15128
Parson, The. [Davis.] N. Y., 1866. 12°. 2853
People, Letters to. Holland. N. Y., 1862. 12°. . . . 3640
The same. Sprague. N. Y., 1831. 12°. . . . 17020
Student, Letters to a. Bost., 1832. 12°. 17037
Yucatan, Incidents of Travel in. Stephens. N. Y., 1843. 2 v. 8°. . 8456
Rambles in, 1841–42. Norman. N. Y., 1843. 8°. . . . 8458
Yusef; a Crusade in the East. Browne. N. Y., 1855. 12°. . . 8238

Z.

Zakosken, M. The Young Muscovite. N. Y., 1834. 2 v. 12°. . 15128
Zanoni. Bulwer. N. Y., 1842. 2 v. 12°. 2076
Zeluco. J. Moore. (Works, v. 5.) Edinb., 1820. 8°. . . . 17321
Zenaida. Anderson. Philad., 1858. 12°. 15820
Zenobia; a historical Romance. Ware. Lond., 1844–45. 2 v. 16°. 2729
Zillah. H. Smith. N. Y., 1829. 2 v. 12°. 15639
Zimmermann, E. A. W. Polit. Survey of Europe. Dubl., 1788. 8°. 15917

Zimmermann, J. G. On Solitude. Lond., 1792. 8°. 17068
Views of Frederick the Great. Dubl., 1792. 2 v. in 1. 12°. . 16453
Zincali, The. Borrow. Lond., 1841. 2 v. 12°. 17115
Zincke, F. B. Extemporary Preaching. (2 copies.) N. Y., 1867. 12°. 9915
Zohrab. [Morier.] N. Y., 1833. 2 v. 12°. 15641
Zoological Mythology. De Gubernatis. Lond., 1872. 2 v. 8°. . 10341
Zoology, Bibliography of. Swainson. Lond., 1840. 16°. . . . 6063
Physiological. Agassiz and Gould. Bost., 1848. 12°. . . 8890
See, also, ANIMALS; BIRDS; FISHES; NATURAL HISTORY; QUADRUPEDS; REPTILES.
Zóphiël. Brooks. Bost., 1834. 12°. 720
Zoroaster. Oracles and Maxims, ed. Gowan. N. Y., 1835. 12°. . 9531
Zouch, T. Memoirs of Sidney. 2d ed. York, 1809. 4°. . . . 7216
Zschokke, J. H. D. Journal of a Poor Vicar. N. Y., 1852. 12°. . 2698
The same, with Walpurgis-Night, etc. Philad., 1845. 12°. 3033
Tales, transl. by Godwin. (2 copies.) N. Y., 1845. 12°. . . 3031
Zulu-Land, Life in. Grant. Philad. [1864.] 12°. 7982
Zurcher, F., and **Margollé, E.** Meteors, etc. N. Y., 1870. 12°. . 10146
Volcanoes and Earthquakes. Philad., 1869. 12°. . . . 10147
Zwingli, U., Life of. Hess. Lond., 1812. 8°. 7555

ADDENDA.

Bible, Speaker's Commentary on the. vol. 3, Joshua–I. Kings. . . 10269
Craven, A. Fleurange. N. Y., 1873. 12°. 10080
DeForest, J. W. Kate Beaumont. Bost., 1872. 8°. 10295
Hare, A. J. C. Wanderings in Spain. Lond., 1873. 8°. . . . 10243
Hazard, S. Santo Domingo. N. Y., 1873. 8°. 10244
Mayo, W. S. Never Again. N. Y., 1873. 12°. 10294
Medhurst, W. H. The Foreigner in Far Cathay. N. Y., 1873. 12°. . 10232

Yale University. Library. Linonian and Brothers' Library

CATALOGUE

OF THE

LINONIAN AND BROTHERS'

LIBRARY,

YALE COLLEGE.

FIRST SUPPLEMENT.

NEW HAVEN:
TUTTLE, MOREHOUSE & TAYLOR, PRINTERS.
1880.

THIS supplement contains about 5000 volumes added to the library since the printing of the last catalogue in 1873. It has been thought desirable, also, to repeat a few of the entries of that catalogue, in order to give the whole of a series, instead of the continuation simply, and to bring together different editions of the same work.

When a personal name (not fictitious), used as a heading — or the dash representing it, is immediately followed by another such name in *italics*, the latter is to be understood as the name of the author; the former, of the subject treated. When the same name appears both as author and subject, the author entries precede the subject entries.

Novels and anonymous works appear under the first word of the title *not an article*. But title-headings of novels contained in the main catalogue are not repeated in the supplement. Cross-references likewise are only repeated when other references are added.

The library now numbers about 22500 volumes.

ERRATA.

P. 20, l. 19, *for* "Morwenstrow" *read* Morwenstow.

P. 21, l. 22, the entry **Burr** should have place on p. 35.

P. 31, l. 16, *for* "**Bric-á-Brac**" *read* **Bric-à-Brac.**

P. 171, l. 7 from below, *for* "Waverly" *read* Waverley.

SUPPLEMENT.

A., *Major*. *See* **Coles, B. C.**
A., Anna d'. *See* **Almeida, Anna d'.**
Abandoned. Verne, J. (The Mysterious Island, v. 2.) . . . 24278
[Abbe, J. E.] "Back from the Mouth of Hell;" or, The rescue from drunkenness. Hartf., 1878. 12°. 28886
Abbé (The) Tigrane: [a novel.] Fabre, F. N. Y., 1875. 12°. . 24472
Abbott, B. V. Judge and Jury: a popular explanation of leading topics in the law of the land. N. Y., 1880. 12°. 28846
Aberdeen, *Lord*. *See* **Gordon, G. H.**
Abinger, *Lord*. *See* **Scarlett, J.**
Abode (The) of Snow. Wilson, A. N. Y., 1875. 12°. 21707
About, E. F. V. Le Fellah: souvenirs d' Égypte. Paris, 1873. 16°. 25620
—— Handbook of Social Economy. N. Y., 1873. 12°. . . . 28880
—— The Notary's Nose. N. Y., 1874. 16°. 24032
—— Le Roi des Montagnes. Paris, 1876. 16°. 25621
—— The Story of an Honest Man. N. Y., 1880. 8°. 24707
—— Trente et Quarante.—Sans Dot.—Les Parents de Bernard. Paris, 1875. 16°. 25622
Abroad again. Guild, C. Bost., 1877. 8°. 21722
Abyssinia. Rassam, H. Narrative of the British Mission to Theodore, King of A. Illust. Lond., 1869. 2 v. 8°. . . . 5659–
—— Stanley, H. M. Coomassie and Magdala: the story of two British campaigns in Africa. Illust. N. Y., 1874. 8°. . . 20621
Acadia (Acadie). *See* **Nova Scotia.**
Acoustics. Pepper, J. H. Pneumatics [and Acoustics]. Lond., [1874]. 12°. 29315
—— *See, also,* **Sound.**
Actors (and Acting). Baker, H. B. English A., from Shakespeare to Macready. N. Y., 1879. 2 v. 12°. 23627–
—— Lewes, G. H. Actors and the Art of Acting. Lond., 1875. 12°. 26559
—— Oxberry, W. The Actor's Budget. Lond. 12°. . . . 26521
Ada Reis. [Car. Lamb.] Lond., 1823. 3 v. 16°. 18621–
Adam Brown, the Merchant. [Hor. Smith.] Lond., 1843. 3 v. 12°. 18629–
Adams, Abigail S. Familiar Letters of John Adams and his wife. With a memoir of Mrs. Adams. By C. F. Adams. N. Y., 1876. 12°. 22622
Adams, C. F. Life of John Adams. (*See* **Adams, J. Q. & C. F.**)
—— *Welles, G.* Lincoln and Seward: remarks upon the memorial address of C. F. A. on the late Wm. H. Seward. N. Y., 1814. 22645

Adams, C. F., jr., Notes on Railroad Accidents. N. Y., 1879. 12°. 29933
—— Railroads: their origin and problems. N. Y., 1878. 12°. (2 cop.). 29931–
Adams, C. K. Democracy and Monarchy in France. N. Y., 1874. 20413
Adams, F. O. The History of Japan. Lond., 1874–5. 2 v. 8°. . 20383–
Adams, H. Documents Relating to New-England Federalism; 1800–1815. Bost., 1877. 8°. 21442
Adams, J., (*Pres't*). Familiar Letters of John Adams and his wife during the Revolution. By C. F. Adams. N. Y., 1876. 12°. 22622
—— *Adams, J. Q.,* (*& C. F. Adams*). Life of A. Phila., 1874. 16°. 22621
Adams, J. Q. Memoirs, comprising portions of his diary from 1795 to 1848. Ed. by C. F. Adams. Phila., 1874–'77. 12 v. 8°. 22760–
—— (& C. F. Adams). The Life of John Adams. Begun by J. Q. A.; completed by C. F. A. 2 vols. in 1. Phila., 1874. 16°. . 22621
Adams, W. H. D. English Party Leaders and English Parties, from Walpole to Peel. Lond., 1878. 2 v. 8°. 21054–
CONTENTS:—1, Walpole; Pitt (earl); Burke; Fox; Wm. Pitt. 2, Pitt (cont'd); Canning; Peel.
Addington, H., (*Lord Sidmouth*). *Earle, J. C.* (*In* 'Eng. Premiers,' v. 2.) 22883
Addison, J. Poetical Works. With memoir and crit. diss. by G. Gilfillan. Edinb., 1859. 8°. (*In same vol.:* Gay's Fables *and* Somerville's Chase.) 26319
—— Selections from [his] papers contributed to the Spectator. Ed. by Thos. Arnold. 2d ed. Oxf., 1878. 16°. 26872
Adventures of Caleb Williams. Godwin, W. N. Y., 1856. 12°. . 24479
Adventures of Captain Mago. Cahun, L. N. Y., 1876. 8°. . 24209
Adventures of Philip. Thackeray. Lond., 1872 (&c.) 12°. (2 cop.) 24874–
Ægyptische Königstochter. Ebers. Stuttg. & Leipz., 1880. 12°. . 25872
Aeronautics. Pettigrew, J. B. Animal Locomotion; with a dissertation on A. Illust. N. Y., 1874. 12°. 29247
—— *See, also,* **Pneumatics.**
Æschylus. The Agamemnon, transcribed [in meter] by R. Browning. Lond., 1877. 16°. 26804
Æsthetic Papers. Peabody, E. P., *editor.* Bost., 1849. 8°. . . 27560
Æsthetics. Brown, J. Ethics and Æ. of Modern Poetry. Lond., 1878. 12°. 26293
—— Hand, F. G. Æ. of Musical Art. Lond., 1880. 8°. . . . 29798
—— Véron, E. Lond., 1879. 12°. 28171
Afghanistan, Hist. of. Malleson, G. B. Lond., 1878. 8°. . . 20614
Afloat and Ashore. Cooper, J. F. N. Y., 1873. 12°. . . . 2834
Afraja. Mügge, T. Breslau, 1862. 3 B. 16°. (Mügge's Romane, B. 13–15.) 25844–
Africa. Baker, S. W. Ismailïa: the expedition to Central A. for the suppression of the slave trade. Illust. N. Y., 1875. 8°. 21846
—— Burton, R. F. Two Trips to Gorilla Land and the Cataracts of the Congo. Lond., 1876. 2 v. 8°. 21854–
—— Cameron, V. L. Across Africa. N. Y., 1877. 8°. . . . 21850
—— Drummond, W. H. The Large Game and Natural Hist. of South and South-East A. [Illust.] Edinb., 1875. 8°. . . . 29492

Africa. Gillmore, P. The Great Thirst Land: a ride through Natal, Orange Free State, Transvaal, and Kalahari Desert. Lond., etc., [1878]. 8°. 21864
—— Livingstone, D. Last Journals in Central A. N. Y., 1875. 8°. (Map in detached case). 23532–
—— Long, C. C. Central Africa. N. Y., 1877. 8°. 21851
—— Longfellow, H. W. Poems of Places, v. 24. Bost., 1878. 16°. 26463
—— Schweinfurth, G. A. The Heart of A. N. Y., 1874. 2 v. 8°. 21852–
—— Stanley, H. M. How I found Livingstone: travels in Central A. N. Y., 1872. 8°. 21856
—— — Through the Dark Continent. Illust. N. Y., 1878. 2 v. 8°. 21857–
—— Trollope, A. South A. Lond., 1878. 2 v. 12°. 21698–
—— Valdez, F. T. Six Years in West'n A. Lond., 1861. 2 v. 8°. . 21862–
—— Wood, J. G. The Natural Hist. of Man. (vol. 1.) 29590
See, also, **Abyssinia; Angola; Ashanti; Atlas Mts.; Carthage; Congo; Dahomey; Egypt; Morocco; Nile; Sahara; Sudan; Zanzibar.**
Aftermath. Longfellow, H. W. Bost., 1873. 16°. 26075
Agassiz, L. J. R. Geological Sketches. Bost., 1866 & '76. 2 v. 12°. 8955 & 29416
Agnel, H. R. Chess for Winter Evenings. N. Y., 1848. 12°. . 29710
Agriculture. Brewer, W. H. Agricultural Progress. (*In* **First Cent.** of the Republic.) 21520
—— Johnson, S. W. How Crops Feed. N. Y., [1870]. 12°. . . 29459
—— — How Crops Grow. N. Y., [1868]. 12°. 29460
—— Loring, G. B. A Treatise on A. and the Horse. (*In* **Murray, W. H. H.,** 'The Perfect Horse.') 29496
Ahnen (Die). Freytag, G. Leipz., 1875–6. 4 Abth. 12°. . . . 25911–
Aikin, J. Essays, Literary and Miscellaneous. Lond., 1811. 8°. . 18615
Aikin, Lucy. Memoir of Mrs. Barbauld. (*See* **Barbauld, A. L. A.** 'Works.')
—— Memoirs, Miscellanies and Letters. Ed. by P. H. LeBreton. Lond., 1864. 12°. 23219
Air and its Relations to Life. Hartley, W. N. N. Y., 1875. 12°. . 29298
Akenside, M. Poetical Works. With memoir and critical dissertation by G. Gilfillan. Edinb., 1857. 8°. 26320
Alabama Claims. Cushing, C. The Treaty of Washington. N. Y., 1873. 12°. 21361
Alaska and Missions on the North Pacific Coast. Jackson, K. Illust. N. Y., [1880]. 12°. 21287
Albany, *Count of. See* **Charles Edward Stuart.**
Albert Edward, *Prince of Wales. Gay, J. D.* The Prince of Wales in India. N. Y., 1877. 12°. 21246
—— *Russell, W. H.* The Prince of Wales' Tour: a diary in India; with some account of [his] visits to the courts of Greece, Egypt, Spain, and Portugal. Illust. Lond., 1877. 2 v. 8°. 21967–
Alcestis: [a novel.] N. Y., 1874. 16°. 24033
Alcock, R. Art and Art Industries in Japan. Illust. Lond, 1878. 29823
—— (*See* **Margary, A. R.** 'Journey.')
Alcott, A. B. Table-Talk. Bost. 1877. 12°. 27219

Alcott, Louisa M. Under the Lilacs. Bost., 1878. 16°. . . 24034

Aldrich, T. B. Cloth of Gold, and other poems. Bost., 1878. 16°. 26000

—— Flower and Thorn: later poems. Bost., 1877. 12°. . . . 26001

—— Marjorie Daw, and other people. Bost., 1873. 16°. . . . 24035

—— Prudence Palfrey: a novel. Bost., 1874. 12°. 24036

—— The Queen of Sheba. Bost., 1877. 16°. 24037

Alert (*ship*). Markham. A. H. The Great Frozen Sea: narrative of the voyage of the A. during the arctic exp. of 1875–6. Lond., 1878. 8°. 21882

Alexander I., Pavlovich, *emp. of Russia. Joyneville, C.* Life and Times of A. Lond., 1875. 3 v. 8°. (2 copies.) . . . 20605–

Alexander, Mrs., (*pseud.*). *See* **Hector, Annie F.**

Alfieri, Vittorio. Life [Autobiography] of. With an essay by Wm. D. Howells. Bost., 1877. 16°. 23240

—— Tragedies; transl. by C. Lloyd. Lond., 1815. 3 v. 16°. . . 18616–

—— *Same*, including his posth. works. Transl. [by C. Lloyd and E. A. Bowring]. Ed. by Bowring. Lond., 1876. 2 v. 12°. 26490–

Alford, H. Life, Letters and Journals. Ed. by his widow. 2d ed. Lond., 1873. 8°. 22267

Alfred the Great, Life of. Pauli, R. [With] Alfred's Anglo-Saxon version of Orosius. Lond., 1853. 12°. 20805

Alice Lorraine. Blackmore, R. D. N. Y., 1876. 8°. . . . 24301

All the Year Round. Lond., 1859–79. v. 1–15; and New Series, v. 1–23. 8°. 18345–

Allen, J. H. Hebrew Men and Times. [2d ed.] Bost., 1879. 16°. 28442

Allibone, S. A. Poetical Quotations, from Chaucer to Tennyson. Phila., 1879. 8°. 26761

—— Prose Quotations from Socrates to Macaulay. Phila., 1879. 8°. 26760

Allzeit voran. Spielhagen, F. Leipz., 1877. 16°. (Sämmtl. Werke, B. 11.) 25870

Almeida, Anna d'. A Lady's Visit to Manilla and Japan. By Anna D'A. Lond., 1863. 8°. 21937

Alone. Terhune, M. V. H. N. Y., 1856. 12°. 15818

Aloys. Auerbach, B. N. Y., 1877. 16°. (2 copies.) . . . 24038–

Alps. Bonney, T. G. The Alpine Regions of Switzerland and the neighbouring countries. Camb., 1868. 8°. 21787

—— *See, also,* **Switzerland; Tyrol.**

Amari, M. History of the War of the Sicilian Vespers. London, 1850. 3v. 12°. 20010–

Amateur (The) Poacher. [Jefferies, R.] Boston, 1879. 12°. . . 29330

Amateur Theatricals. Pollock, W. H. London, 1879. 12°. . . 26519

Amazon (*river*). Bates, H. W. The Naturalist on the River Amazons. London, 1873. 12°. 21207

—— Brown (C. B.) & Lidstone (W.) 15000 miles on the Amazon and its Tributaries. [Illust.] Lond., 1878. 8°. 21800

Amazon (The): [a novel.] Dingelstedt, F. N. Y., 1880. 16°. . 24175

Amberley (*Viscount*). *See* **Russell, J.**

Ambrose (St.) and the Union of the Christian Church with the State. Merivale, C. (*In* 'Four Lect.') 28445

America. Anderson, R. B. A. not discovered by Columbus: an historical sketch of the discovery of A. by the Norsemen in the 10th cent. Chic., 1877. 12°. 21280

—— Keane, A. H. Ethnography and Philology of A. (*App. to* **Bates, H. W.**, 'Centr. Amer.,' &c.) Contains an "Alphabetical list of all known Amer. tribes and languages." . . 21700

—— Longfellow, H. W. Poems of Places: [A., exclusive of the United States.] (v. 30.) 26469

—— Wood, J. G. (*In* 'Nat. Hist. of Man.' v. 2.) . . . 29591

See, also, **Antiquities**, *American; also, names of geographical divisions.*

—— *Central.* Bates, H. W. Central A., the West Indies, and South A. Illust. Lond., 1878. 12°. 21700

—— — Whetham, J. W. B. Across Central A. London, 1877. 8°. 21812

—— *North.* Butler, W. F. The Great Lone Land: travel in the North-west of A. Illust. London, 1872. 8°. . . 21552

—— — Parkman, F. France and England in N. A. Bost., 1865-77. 5 pts. 8°. . . . . 6130- & 21403-

—— *South.* Hutchinson, T. J. The Paraná; with incidents of the Paraguayan war, and South American recollections from 1861 to 1868. Illust. Lond., 1868. 8°. 21805

—— — Waterton, C. Wanderings in S. A., [etc.] Lond., 1866. 16°. 21264

American (The): James, H., jr. Boston, 1877. 12°. (2 copies.) . 24595-

American Angler's Book. Norris, T. Phila., [1865]. 8°. . . 29629

American Antiquities. *See* **Antiquities**, *American.*

American College Fraternities. Baird, W. M. Phila., 1879. 12°. . 28995

American Colleges and the Amer. Public. Porter, N. New Haven, 1870. 12°. *And* N. Y., [1878]. 12°. (2 cop.) . 9254 & 28837

American Currency, A Hist. of. Sumner, W. G. N. Y., 1874, (etc.) 12°. (2 copies.) 29059-

American Eclectic. N. Y., 1841-2. 4 v. 8°. (2 copies.) . . 13741-

American Explorers, A Book of. Higginson, T. W. Bost., 1877. 22600

American Gun Club. Verne, J. N. Y., 1874. 12°. 24262

American Health Primers. Keen, W. W., *editor.* 29958-

CONTENTS:—Hearing, by C. H. Burnett.—Long life, J. G. Richardson.—Summer and its diseases, J. C. Wilson.—Eyesight, G. C. Harlan.—Throat and voice, J. S. Cohen.—Winter and its dangers, H. Osgood.—Mouth and teeth, J. W. White.—Our homes, H. Hartshorne.—Brain work and overwork, H. C. Wood.—Sea-air and sea-bathing, J. H. Packard.

American Indians. *See* **Indians** (American).

American Journal of Science. [1st Series.] N. H., 1818-45. 49 v. 8°. 17545-

—— Index (v. 50.) N. H., 1846. 8°. (2 copies.) . . . . ——

—— 2d Series. N. H., 1846-70. 50 v. 8°. 17594-

—— 3d Series. N. H., 1871-79. 18 v. 8°. 17644-

American Literature. Beers, H. A. A Century of. N. Y., 1878. 16°. (2 copies.) 26909-

—— Tyler, M. C. A Hist. of. N. Y., 1878. v. 1-2. 8°. . . . 26779-

CONTENTS:—1, 1607—1676; 2, 1677—1765.

—— Whipple, E. P. (*In* **First Cent.** of the Republic.) . . . 21520

American Politics, Hist. of. Johnston, A. N. Y., 1879. 16°. . . 21332

American Politics, Issues of. Skinner, O. Phila., 1873. 12°. . 21327

American (The) Senator: a novel. Trollope, A. N. Y., 1877. 8°. . 24702

American (The) State and Amer. Statesmen. Dix, W. G. Bost., 1876. 21333

Amicis, E. de. Constantinople. N. Y., 1878. 12°. 21691

—— Studies of Paris. N. Y., 1879. 12°. (*For contents see* **Paris.**) . 27273

Among my Books. Lowell, J. R. Bost., 1870–76. 2 series. 12°. (2 copies.) . . . . 3616–& 26931–

[**Amory, T.**] The Life of John Buncle. Lond., 1770. 4 v. 16°. 17484–

Amos, S. The Science of Law. N. Y., 1874. 12°. 29249

Ampère, A. M. *James H., jr.* (*In* 'French Poets.') 26905

Ampère, J. J. A. *See* **Hamerton, P. G.,** 'Modern Frenchmen' (22488); **James, H., jr.,** 'French Poets' (26905); **Lenormant, A. C.,** 'Mad. Récamier and her Friends' (22483).

Anatolia. *See* **Asia Minor.**

Ancient Classics for English Readers. Collins, W. L., *editor.* Phil., 1870–79. 28 v. 16°. . . . . 71—86 & 26835–

CONTENTS:—1, Homer's Iliad, by the editor.—2, Homer's Odyssey, editor.—3, Herodotus, G. C. Swayne.—4, Cæsar, A. Trollope.—5, Virgil, editor.—6, Horace, T. Martin.—7, Æschylus, R. S. Copleston.—8, Xenophon, A. Grant.—9, Cicero, editor.—10, Sophocles, C. W. Collins.—11, Pliny, A. J. Church & W. J. Brodribb.—12, Euripides, W. B. Donne.—13, Juvenal, E. Walford.—14, Aristophanes, editor.—15, Hesiod & Theognis, J. Davies.—16, Plautus and Terence, editor.—17, Tacitus, W. B. Donne.—18, Lucian, editor.—19, Plato, C. W. Collins.—20, Greek Anthology, C. Neaves.

SUPPLEMENTARY SERIES:—1, Livy, editor.—2, Ovid, A. J. Church.—3, Catullus, Tibullus & Propertius, J. Davies.—4, Demosthenes, W. J. Brodribb.—5, Aristotle, A. Grant.—6, Thucydides, editor.—7, Lucretius, W. H. Mallock.—8, Pindar, F. D. Morice.

Ancient History from the Monuments. 20040–

CONTENTS:—Egypt, S. Birch.—Assyria, Geo. Smith.—Persia, W. S. W. Vaux.—Babylonia, Geo. Smith.—Greek Cities and Islands of Asia Minor, Vaux.—Sinai, H. S. Palmer.

Ancient (The) Régime. Taine, H. A. N. Y., 1876. 12°. . . 20425

Anderson, J. Mandalay to Momien: a narrative of the two expeditions to Western China of 1868 and 1875. Lond., 1876. 8°. 21926

Anderson, R. B. America not discovered by Columbus. New ed. Chic. 1877. 12°. 21280

—— Norse Mythology. Chic., 1875. 12°. 27715

—— The Younger Edda; also called Snorre's Edda, or the Prose Edda: an Eng. version of The Foreword; The Fooling of Gylfe; Brage's Talk, . . . The Poetical Diction; with introduction, notes, and vocabulary. Chic., 1880. 12°. . 27707

—— **& Bjarnason (J.).** Viking Tales of the North: the sagas of Thorstein, Viking's Son, and Fridthjof the Bold. Also, Tegner's Fridthjof's Saga. Chic., 1877. 12°. 27708

André. Dudevant, A. L. A. D. Paris, 1869. 16°. 25671

Andrewes (Andrews), *Bp.* **L.** *See* **Barry, A.,** 'Masters' (22111); **Classic Preachers** (22113); **Teale, W. H.,** 'Lives' (22110).

Andrews, A. The Hist. of Brit. Journalism. Lond., 1859. 2 v. 12°. 18588–

Anecdotes. Cliffe, L. Anecdotal Reminiscences of Distinguished Literary and Political Characters. Lond., 1830. 16°. . 18560

—— The London Anecdotes. Lond. 2 v. in 1. 16°. . . . 25245

Angel (The) in the House. Patmore, C. Lond., [1879.] 16°. . 26031

Angell, H. C. How to take care of our eyes. Bost., 1878. 16°. 29956

Angling. *See* **Fishing.**

Angola and the River Congo. Monteiro, J. J. N. Y., 1876. 12°. . 21620

Animal Mechanics. *See* **Mechanics** (Animal).

Animal Parasites and Messmates. Beneden, P. J. van. N. Y., 1876. 29259

Animals. Couch, J. Illustrations of Instinct. Lond., 1847. 12° . 29326

Animals. Drummond, W. H. The Large Game and Natural Hist. of South and Southeast Africa. [Illust.] Edinb., 1875. 8°. 29492
—— Gubernatis, A. de. Zoological Mythology; or, The legends of A. N. Y. [Lond.], 1872. 2 v. 8°. 29490–
—— Hamerton, P. G. Chapters on A. Bost., 1874. 12°. . . . 29327
—— Helps, A. Some Talk about A. and their Masters. Lond., 1873. 29329
—— Thomson, J. Public and Private Life of A. Lond., 1877. 12°. 24698
—— *See, also,* **Apes; Birds; Dog; Horse; Natural Hist.; Zoology.**
Annals of England: an epitome of English history. Oxf., 1865,'62–3. 3 v. 16°. 20853–
CONTENTS:—1, B. C. 57 to A. D. 1399.—2, 1399 to 1649.—3, 1649 to 1714.
Annals of a Fortress. Viollet-le-Duc, E. E. Bost., 1876. 8°. . . 24313
Anne, *queen of Eng. Burton, J. H.* A Hist. of the Reign of A. Edinb., 1880. 3 v. 8°. 21060–
—— *Morris, E. E.* The Age of Anne. N. Y., [1877.] 16°. . . . 20456
Anne Boleyn, *queen of Eng. Dixon, W. H.* Hist. of Two Queens. Lond., 1873–4. 4 v. 8°. 23005–
Anthologia Germanica. Mangan, J. C. Dubl., 1845. 2 v. in 1. 16°. 26030
Anthropology. *See* **Man** (*and references*).
Antilles. Ober, F. A. Camps in the Caribbees: the adventures of a naturalist in the Lesser A. (Illust.) Bost., 1880 [1879]. 8°. 21813
—— Waterton, C. Wanderings in the A. Lond., 1866. 16°. . . 21264
—— *See, also,* **West Indies.**
Antiquities. Müller, F. M. Essays on Literature, Biography and A. (*His* 'Chips,' v. 3.) 3733
—— *American.* Baldwin, J. D. Ancient America. N. Y., 1872. 12°. 21320
—— — Foster, J. W. Prehistoric Races of the U. S. of A. Chic., 1873. 8°. 21401
—— — Short, J. T. The North Americans of Antiquity. N.Y., 1880. 21400
—— *English.* Evans, J. The Ancient Stone Implements, Weapons, and Ornaments of Great Britain. Lond., 1872. 8°. . . . 20202
—— — Jewitt, L. Half-hours among some Eng. Ant. Lond., 1880. 20206
—— — Lubbock, J. On the preservation of our ancient national monuments. (*In* 'Addresses.') 27411
—— — Wilson, D. Prehistoric Annals of Scotland. Lond., 1863. 2 v. 8°. 20203–
—— *See, also,* **Archæology; History,** *Ancient;* **Man,** *Prehistoric;* **Rome.**
Antoinette. Theuriet, A. N. Y., 1878. 16°. 24927
Antoninus, Marcus Aurelius. *Capes, W., W.* (*In* 'The Roman Empire of the 2d Cent.; or, The Age of the Antonines.') . 20439
—— *See, also,* **Farrar, F. W.,** 'Seekers' (23682); **Renan, J. E.,** 'Eng. Conferences' (28570).
Antony Brade. Lowell, R. T. S. Bost., 1874. 12°. 24236
Anvers, N. d'. *See* **D'Anvers, N.**
Apes, Man and. Mivart, St. G. N. Y., 1874. 12°. 29395
Aphorisms. *See* **Proverbs.**
Apologists. *See* **Fathers** (of the Ch.).
Apostolic Fathers. *See* **Fathers** (of the Ch.).

Appleton, T. G. A Nile Journey. Illust. Lond., 1876. 12°. . 21204
Appleton's Annual Cyclopædia, for 1861–79. N. Y., 1864–80. 19 v. ——
—— Index to v. 1–15, 1861–75. N. Y., 1876. 8°. ——
Appleton's Journal. N. Y., 1869–79. 22 v. 4° and 8°. . . . 17842–
Apthorp, W. F. Hector Berlioz: selections transl., [with] biographical sketch. N. Y., 1879. 12°. 23766
Aquatics. *See* **Boat-racing; Boat-sailing; Sports** (& *references*).
Arabs. Blackburn, H. Artists and A. Illust. Lond., 1868. 8°. . 21692
—— Blunt, A. Bedouin Tribes of the Euphrates. Ed., with ... some account of the Arabs, by W. S. B. N. Y., 1879. 8°. . . 21900
—— Clark, E. L. The Arabs and the Turks. Bost., 1876. 12°. . 20492
—— Duncker, M. W. (*In* 'Hist. of Antiquity,' v. 1.) 20240
Ararat and Transcaucasia. Bryce, J. Lond., 1877. 12°. . . . 21214
Archæology. Lubbock, J. Introd. to the Study of Prehistoric A. (*In* 'Scientific Lectures.') 29532
—— *See, also,* **Antiquities** (*and references*).
Archery (Book of). Hansard, G. A. Lond., 1841. 8°. 29635
—— *See, also,* **Sports.**
Architect, Notes and Sketches of an. Narjoux, F. Bost., 1877. 8°. 29926
Architects and their Works. Clement, C. E. Bost., 1879. 12°. . 29791
Architecture. Freeman, E. A. Historical and Architectural Sketches: chiefly Italian. Lond., 1876. 12°. 20184
—— Ruskin, J. Poetry of A.: cottage, villa, etc. N. Y., 1873. 12°. 29833
—— Viollet-le-Duc, E. E. The Habitations of Man in all ages. Bost., 1876. 8°. 29927
Arctic Regions. Blake, E. V. Arctic Experiences; cont'g Capt. G. E. Tyson's drift on the ice-floe, a hist. of the Polaris Expedition, the cruise of the Tigress, and rescue of the Polaris survivors; a general Arctic chronology. N. Y., 1874. 8°. 21880
—— Leslie, A. The Arctic Voyages of A. E. Nordenskiöld: 1858–1879. Illust. Lond., 1879. 8°. 21881
—— Markham, A. H. The Great Frozen Sea: voyage of the "Alert." Lond., 1878. 8°. 21882
—— Payer, J. New Lands within the Arctic Circle. N. Y., 1877. 8°. 21883
Areopagitica. Milton, J. Oxf., 1878. 16°. 26878
Argolis, The Prince of. Illust. by J. Moyr Smith. N. Y., 1878. 12°. 24176
Argyll, Geo. J. Douglas, *duke of.* The Eastern Question: 1856 to 1878, and to the second Afghan war. Lond., [1879.] 2 v. 12°. 20487–
Ariadne: a novel. Durand, A. F. N. Y., 1878. 16°. . . . 24082
Ariadne Florentina. Ruskin, J. N. Y., 1874–5. 12°. . . . 29831
Arians (The) of the 4th Cent. Newman, J. H. Lond., 1871. 12°. 28412
Aristophanes. Translations of the Acharnians, Knights, Birds, Frogs, Peace. (*In* **Frere, J. H.,** 'Works,' v. 2.) . . . 27482
—— *Collins, W. L.* (*In* 'Anc. Clas. for Eng. Readers,' v. 14.) . . 26840
Aristophanes' Apology. Browning, R. Bost., 1875. 12°. . . 26047
Aristotle. *Grant, A.* (Anc. Clas. for Eng. Readers, supplem. ser., v. 5.) 26851
—— *See, also,* **Blackie, J. S.,** 'Four Phases' (28080); **Mill, J. S.,** 'Diss. and Disc.,' v. 5 (27360).
Armada (Spanish). Jones, F. The Life of Sir Martin Frobisher; cont'g a narrative of the S. A. Lond., 1878. 12°. . . 22848

Armitage, Ella S. The Childhood of the English Nation. N. Y., 1877. 12°. 20842
Arms and Armor. Lacombe, M. J. P. Lond., 1869. 12°. . . . 29928
Armstrong, J. Poetical Works. With memoir and crit. diss., by G. Gilfillan. Edinb., 1858. 8°. (*In same vol.:* Dyer *and* Green.) 26321
Arnason, J. Icelandic Legends. Lond., 1864. 12°. . . . 27710
Arnauld, J. M. Angélique de Ste. Madelaine, *abbess of Port Royal. Martin, F.* Lond., 1873. 12°. 22144
Arndt, E. M., Life of, [mostly autobiography]. With pref. by J. R. Seeley. Bost. [Lond.], 1879. 12°. 22511
Arnold, A. Through Persia by Caravan. N. Y., 1877. 12°. . . 21205
Arnold, B., Life of; his patriotism and his treason. Arnold, I. N. Chic., 1880. 8°. 22694
Arnold, E. The Indian Song of Songs. From the Sanskrit. With other oriental poems. Lond., 1875. 16°. 26002
—— The Light of Asia; or, The Great Renunciation: being the life and teaching of Gautama, as told in verse by an Indian Buddhist. Bost., 1879. 16°. 26003
Arnold, F. Our Bishops and Deans. Lond., 1875. 2 v. 8°. . 22268–
—— Oxford and Cambridge: their colleges, memories, and associations. Illust. Lond., [1874]. 8°. 21979
—— Turning-Points in Life. Lond., 1873. 2 v. 12°. . . . 27379–
Arnold, I. N. The Life of Benedict Arnold. Chic., 1880. 8°. . 22694
Arnold, M. Friendship's Garland. [Mis. essays.] Lond., 1871. 16°. 27242
—— God and the Bible: a review of objections to "Literature and Dogma." N. Y., 1875. 12°. 28688
—— Higher Schools and Universities in Germany. Lond., 1874. 12°. (2 copies.) 28821–
—— Last Essays on Church and Religion. [Lond. &] N. Y., 1877. 12°. 28690
—— Literature and Dogma: an essay towards a better apprehension of the Bible. N. Y., 1873. 12°. 28689
—— Mixed Essays. N. Y., 1879. 12°. 27241

CONTENTS:—Democracy; Equality; Irish Catholicism and British Liberalism; "Porro unum est necessarium;" A Guide to Eng. Literature; Falkland; A French Critic on Milton; A French Critic on Goethe; George Sand.

—— On the Study of Celtic Literature. Lond., 1867. 8°. . . . 27861
—— Poems. New and compl. ed. Lond., 1877. 2 v. 12°. . . 26084–

CONTENTS:—1, Early poems, narrative poems, and sonnets; 2, Lyric, dramatic, and elegiac poems.

Around a Spring. Droz, G. N. Y., 1873. 16°. 24233
Around the World in Eighty Days. Verne, J. Bost., 1874. 12°. . 24263
Around the World in the Yacht 'Sunbeam.' Brassey, A. N. Y., 1878. 8°. 21731
Arrabiata (L'), and other tales. Heyse, P. J. L. Leipz., 1867. 16°. 24538
Art. Blanc, A. A. P. C. Art in Ornament and Dress. N. Y., 1877. 8°. 29873
—— Clement, C. E. A Handbook of Legendary and Mythological Art. Illust. N. Y., 1877. 12°. 29790
—— Conant, S. S. Fine Arts. (*In* **First Cent.** of the Republic.) . 21520

Art. Couture, T. Conversations on Art Methods. N. Y., 1879. 12°. 29826
—— D'Anvers, N. Elementary Hist. of Art: architecture, sculpture, painting, music. Illust. N. Y., 1875. 12°. 29877
—— Howitt, A. M. An Art-student in Munich. Lond., 1853, 2 v. 12°. 29879–
—— Hunt, W. M. Talks on Art. Bost., 1880. 8°. . . . 29916
—— Jameson, A. M. The Hist. of Our Lord as exemplified in works of art. Lond., 1865. 2 v. 8°. 29914–
—— — Legends of the Madonna, as represented in the fine arts. Illust. 5th ed. Lond., 1872. 8°. 29910
—— — Legends of the Monastic Orders, as represented in the fine arts. 5th ed. Lond., 1872. 8°. 29911
—— — Sacred and Legendary Art. 6th ed. Lond., 1870. 2 v. 8°. 29912–
—— Jarves, J. J. Art Thoughts. N. Y., 1875. 12°. 29821
—— — A Glimpse at the Art of Japan. N. Y., 1876. 12°. . . 29822
—— Johnson, E. W. The Studio Arts. N. Y., 1878. 16°. . . 29828
—— Lacroix, P. The Arts in the Middle Ages, and at the period of the Renaissance. Illust. Lond., 1870. 8°. 20362
—— Lessing, G. E. Laocoon: an essay upon the limits of painting and poetry; with remarks [on] the hist. of ancient art. Bost., 1874. 16°. 26290
—— Loftie, W. J. A Plea for Art in the House. Phila., [1877]. 12°. 29781
—— Lübke, W. Outlines of the Hist. of A. Ed. by C. Cook. Illust. N. Y., 1878 [1877]. 2 v. 8°. 29940–
—— Mivart, St. G. Æsthetic Evolution. (*In* 'Contemporary Ev.') 29394
—— Narjoux, F. Notes and Sketches of an Architect. Bost., 1877. 29926
—— Ossoli, M. F. A., Literature, and the Drama. (Works, v. 5.) . 27290
—— Pater, W. The Renaissance: studies in art and poetry. Lond., 1877. 8°. 29878
—— Poynter, E. J. Ten Lectures on A. Lond., 1879. 8°. . . 29820
—— Ruskin, J. The Eagle's Nest: ten lectures on the relation of natural science to art. N. Y., 1873. 12°. 29830
—— — Mornings in Florence. N. Y., 1876. 12°. 29834
—— Seemann, O. The Mythology of Greece and Rome, with special reference to its use in art. [L. &] N. Y., 1877. 12°. . 29788
—— — *Same.* N. Y., 1879. 16°. 29789
—— Smith, R. M. Persian Art. Lond., [1876]. 12°. . . . 29771
—— Taine, H. A. The Philosophy of A. N. Y., 1873. 16°. . 29827
—— Winckelmann, J. J. The Hist. of Ancient A. Bost., 1873. 4 v. 29980–

See, also, **Architecture; Bronzes; Decoration & Design; Drawing; Engraving; Etching; Ivories; Maiolica; Music; Ornament; Painting; Sculpture; Tapestry;—Æsthetics; Antiquities; Caricature; Gems; Renaissance;** *also, 'Art' under* **England, Europe, Italy, Spain.**

Art Decoration applied to Furniture. Spofford, H. E. P. N. Y., 1878 [1877]. 8°. 29872
Art Education applied to Industry. Nichols, G. W. N. Y., 1877. 29925
Art at Home Series. 29780–

CONTENTS:—House Decoration, by R. & H. Garrett.—Art in the House, W. J. Loftie.—Dress, Mrs. Oliphant.—Music in the House, J. Hullah.

Art-Student in Munich. Howitt, A. M. Lond., 1853. 2 v. 12°. 29879–
Art Tour to Northern Capitals of Europe. Atkinson, J. B. Lond. 1873. 8°. 29874

Arthur (*King*). *Cox* (*G. W.*) and *Jones* (*E. H.*). King A. and his Knights. (*In* 'Pop. Romances.') . . . . 27712 & 2010

Arthur Bonnicastle. Holland, J. G. N. Y., 1873. 16°. (2 copies.) 24544–

Arthur O'Leary. [Lever, C. J.] Lond., 1845. 8°. . . . 24669

Artists. Clayton, E. C. English Female A. Lond., 1876. 2 v. . 23865–

—— Illustrated Biographies of the Great A. Lond. & N. Y., 1879–80. 14 v. 12°. (*For contents see* **Illust.** Biogr.) 23777–

Artists and Arabs. Blackburn, H. Lond., 1868. 8°. . . . 21692

Arts, Industrial. *See* **Industrial** Arts.

Arvor Spang. Mügge, T. Breslau, 1865. 2 B. 16°. (Mügge's Romane, B. 22–23.) 25847

Asbjörnsen, P. C. Tales from the Fjeld: a 2d series of popular tales, [transl.] from the Norse by G. W. Dasent. Lond., 1874. 27705

Ascanio. Dumas, A. D. Lond., [1879]. 16°. 24406

Ashanti. Brackenbury, H. The Ashanti War. Edinb., 1874. 2 v. 20619–

—— Stanley, H. M. Coomassie and Magdala: the story of two British campaigns in Africa. Illust. N. Y., 1874. 8°. . 20621

Ashley, E. The Life of Henry John Temple, *Viscount* Palmerston: 1846—1865. With selections from his speeches and correspondence. Lond., 1876. 2 v. 8°. 23069–

Asia. Burnaby, F. A Ride to Khiva: travels and adventures in Central Asia. N. Y., 1877. 12°. 21215–

—— Hellwald, F. von. The Russians in Central Asia: examination of the geography and history of C. A. Lond., 1874. 8°. 21608

—— Longfellow, H. W. Poems of Places, v. 21–23. Bost., 1878. 26460–

—— Prejevalski, N. M. From Kulja, across the Tian Shan to Lob-Nor. And notices of the lakes of Central A. Lond., 1879. 21929

—— — Mongolia, the Tangut Country, and the Solitudes of Northern Tibet: Lond., 1876. 2 v. 8°. 21927–

—— Wood, J. G. (*In* 'Nat. Hist. of Man,' v. 2.) 29591

See, also, **Afghanistan; Arctic Regions; Asia Minor; Assyria; Babylon; Burma; Caucasus; China; Corea; East (The); East Indian Archipelago; Euphrates; Himalaya; India; Indo-China; Japan; Khiva; Manchuria; Mongolia; Oxus; Palmyra; Persia; Russia; Siam; Tartary; Tibet; Transcaucasia; Turkestan; Turkey.**

Asia Minor. Burnaby, F. On Horseback through Asia Minor. Lond., 1877. 2 v. 8°. 21907–

—— Duncker, M. W. (*In* 'Hist. of Antiquity,' v. 1.) . . . 20240

—— Plumptre, E. H. St. Paul in Asia Minor, and at the Syrian Antioch. Lond., [1878]. 16°. 28499

—— Vaux, W. S. W. Greek Cities and Islands of Asia Minor. Lond., 1877. 16°. 20043

—— *See, also,* **Lydia.**

Assommoir (L'). Zola, E. Paris, 1877. 16°. 25670

Assyria. Duncker, M. W. (*In* 'Hist. of Antiquity,' v. 2–3.) . 20241–

—— Smith. G. Assyria, from the earliest times to the Fall of Nineveh. N. Y., 1876. 16°. 20040

—— *See, also,* **Babylon.**

Astrology. Proctor, R. A. (*In* 'Our Place.') 29447

Astronomy. Ball, R. S. N. Y., 1878. 16°. 29350
—— Flammarion, C. Stories of Infinity. Bost., 1873. 16°. . 29441
—— Guillemin, A. The Heavens. Lond., 1872. 8°. . . . 29573
—— Lockyer, J. N. (Science Primers.) Lond., 1877. 16°. . . 29361
—— Proctor, R. A. Flowers of the Sky. Illust. N. Y., [1879]. 16°. 29442
—— — Myths and Marvels of A. N. Y., 1877. 8°. 29449
—— — A New Star Atlas . . . with introd. on the study of the stars. Lond., 1877. 12°. 29446
—— — Our Place among Infinities. N. Y., 1876. 12°. . . 29447
—— — (*In* 'Rough ways made smooth.') 29444
—— — Science Byways. Phila. [Lond.], 1876. 12°. . . . 29445
See, also, **Earth; Heavens; Light; Moon; Spectrum Analysis; Sun; Venus.**

At his Gates. Oliphant, M. O. W. Lond., 1872. 3 v. 12°. . . 24805–
Athens. Bulwer-Lytton, E. G. E. L. A.: its rise and fall. N. Y., 1874. 12°. 20096
—— Capes, W. W. University Life in Ancient A. Lond., 1877. 12°. 28826
—— Cox, G. W. The Athenian Empire [from the flight of Xerxes to the fall of A.]. N. Y., [1877]. 16°. 20441
Atherton. Mitford, M. R. Lond., 1854. 3 v. 12°. . . . 18632–
Athletics (Modern). Wilkinson, H. F. Lond., 1877. 12°. . . 29638
—— *See, also,* **Gymnastics.**
Atkinson, J. B. An Art Tour to North. Capitals of Europe. Lond., 1873. 8°. 29874
Atlantic Monthly. Bost., 1857–79. 44 v. 8°. 10526–
—— *Same.* v. 1–26. 10500–
—— Index to v. 1–38. . . . . ——
Atlas (*Mountains*). Hooker (J. D.) and Ball (J.). Journal of a Tour in Marocco and the Great A. Lond., 1878. 8°. 21847
Atomic Theory, A sketch of. Lonsdale, A. (*In* 'John Dalton'). . 23564
Atonement of Leam Dundas. Linton, E. L. Phila., 1876. 8°. . 24312
Atta Troll, and other poems. Heine, H. Lond., 1876. 12°. . 26018
Attic (An) Philosopher in Paris. Souvestre, É. N. Y., 1880. 16°. . 24926
Attwood, F. G. Manners and Customs of ye Harvard Studente. Bost., 1877. Ob. 4°. . . . . ——
Auerbach, B. Aloys. Transl. by C. T. Brooks. N. Y., 1877. (2 cop.) 24038–
—— Barfüssele. Stuttg., 1876. 12°. 25895
—— *Same.* Little Barefoot. N. Y., 1874. 16°. 24045
—— Christian Gellert, and other sketches. Transl. from the German. Lond., 1858. 12°. 24000
—— The Convicts and their Children. N. Y., 1877. 16°. (2 cop.). 24040–
—— Drei einzige Töchter. Stuttg., 1875. 12°. 25896
—— Edelweiss. Stuttg., 1874. 12°. 25897
—— German Tales. N. Y., 1874. 16°. 24042
CONTENTS:—Christian Gellert's Last Christmas; The Step-Mother; Benigna; Rudolph and Elizabeth; Erdmutha.

—— Joseph im Schnee. Stuttg., 1874. 12°. 25893
—— Joseph in the Snow. N. Y., 1874. 16°. 24043
—— Das Landhaus am Rhein. Stuttg., 1878. 3 B. 16°. . . 25884–
—— Landolin. N. Y., 1878. 16° 24044

Auerbach, B. Lorley and Reinhard. N. Y., 1877. 16°. (2 cop.) 24046-
—— Nach dreissig Jahren. Neue Dorfgeschichten. Stuttg., 1876. 3 B. in 1. 12°. 25894
CONTENTS:—1, Des Lorle's Reinhard.—2, Der Tolpatsch aus Amerika.—3, Das Nest an der Bahn.
—— On the Heights. N. Y., 1875. 12°. 24001
—— Poet and Merchant: a picture of life from the times of Moses Mendelssohn. N. Y., 1877. 16°. 24048
—— Romane. Stuttg., 1871. 12 B. in 6. 16°. 25887-
CONTENTS:—1, Spinoza.—2, Dichter u. Kaufmann.—3-4, Neues Leben.—5-8, Auf der Höhe.—9-12, Das Laudhaus am Rhein.
—— Schatzkästlein des Gevattersmanns. Stuttg., 1875. 16°. . . . 25883
—— Waldfried. Stuttg., 1874. 3 B. 16°. 25880-
—— *Same.* Transl. by S. A. Stern. N. Y., 1874. 12°. (2 copies.) . 24002-
—— Zur guten Stunde. Gesammelte Volkserzählungen. Mit 334 Bildern. Stuttg. 2 B. 8°. 25902-
Auersperg, A. A. The Last Knight: a romance-garland. From the German of Anastasius Grün [*pseud.*]. Transl., with notes, by J. O. Sargent. N. Y., 1871. 8°. 26240
Auf der Düne. Spielhagen, F. (Sämmtl. Werke, B. 3.) . . . 25862
Auf der Höhe. Auerbach, B. (Romane, B. 5-8.) 25889-
Augenblick des Glücks. Hackländer, F. W. von. (Werke, B. 21.) 25810
Augustine, St. *Clark, W. R.* (The Fathers for English Readers.) Lond., [1878]. 16°. 28504
—— *Merivale, C.* St. A.: some lessons from his life and teaching. (*In* 'Four Lect.') 28445
—— *See, also,* **Newman, J. H.,** 'Histor. Sketches,' v. 2 (20092); **Shedd, W. G. T.,** 'Lit. Essays' (26927).
Aurelius, Marcus. *See* **Antoninus.**
Austen, Jane. Emma: a novel. Lond., 1853. 16°. . . . 24049
—— *Same.* Lond., 1856. 16°. 24050
—— Mansfield Park: a novel. Lond., 1853. 16°. 24051
—— *Same.* Lond., 1856. 16°. 24052
—— Northanger Abbey. [&] Persuasion. Lond., 1856. 16°. . . 24053
—— Pride and Prejudice: a novel. Lond., 1856. 16°. . . . 24054
—— Sense and Sensibility: a novel. Lond., 1856. 16°. . . . 24055
Austin, Sarah. Germany, from 1760 to 1814; or, Sketches of German Life. Lond., 1854. 8°. 20641
Australia. Beauvoir, L. de. ('A Voyage,' v. 1.) 21200
—— Howitt, W. The Hist. of Discovery in A., Tasmania, and New Zealand. Lond., 1875. 2 v. 8°. 21816-
—— Trollope, A. A. and New Zealand. Lond., 1873. 2 v. 12°. . 21818-
—— Wood, J. G. The Natural Hist. of Man. (Vol. 2). . . . 29591
—— *See, also,* **Victoria** (*province*).
Austria. Hackländer. F. W. von. Bilder aus dem Soldatenleben im Kriege. (Werke, B. 28-29.) (Wars of Austria and Sardinia, 1848-9.) 25813-
—— Longfellow, H. W. Poems of Places, v. 16. Bost., 1877. 16°. 26455
—— Metternich, C. W. N. L. Memoirs, 1773-1815. N. Y., 1880. v. 1-2. 8°. 22585-

Austria. *See, also,* **Hungary; Transylvania; Tyrol.**

Authors. Clarke, C. C. and M. C. Recollections of Writers. N. Y., [1878]. 12°. 26936

—— *See, also,* **Classical** Writers; **English** Men of Letters; **Literature.**

Automatism. Elam C. Winds of Doctrine: being an examination of the modern theories of A. and Evolution. Lond., 1876. 8°. 28165

Autour d' une Source. Droz, G. Paris, 1876. 16°. 25628

Avé-Lallemant, R., *joint author.* *See* **Bruhns, C.,** Life of A. von Humboldt.

Avis, The Story of. Phelps, E. S. Bost., 1877. 16°. (3 copies.) . 24845–

Ayres, Anne. The Life and Work of W. A. Muhlenberg. N. Y., 1880. 8°. 22724

Azamat-Batuk, (*pseud.*) *See* **Thieblin, N. L.**

Babolain. Droz, G. Paris, 1876. 16°. 25629

—— *Same.* Transl. from the French. N. Y., 1873. 16°. . . 24234

Babylon. Duncker, M. W. (*In* 'Hist. of Antiquity,' v. 1 & 3.) . 20240–

Babylonia, Hist. of. Geo. Smith. Lond. 16°. 20041

—— *See, also,* **Assyria.**

Bach, C. P. E. Letters. (*In* **Nohl, L.,** 'Letters.') 23765

"**Back** from the Mouth of Hell." [Abbe, J. E.] Hartf., 1878. 12°. 28886

Backlog Studies. Warner, C. D. Bost., 1873. 16°. 27240

Bacon, A. M. A Manual of Gesture. Chic., 1879. 12°. . . . 27822

Bacon, Delia. The Philosophy of the Plays of Shakspere unfolded. Lond., 1857. 8°. 27040

Bacon, F. Essays. [Ed.] by E. A. Abbott. Lond., 1876. 2 v. 16°. 27217–

—— Works. N. Y., 1877. 2 v. 12°. 27280–

CONTENTS:—1, Philosophical Writings.—2, Literary and Religious Works.

—— *Montagu, B.* The Life of B. Lond., 1834. 8°. 23010

Bacon, G. B. Siam, as it was and is. N. Y., 1873. 12°. . . . 21206

Bacon, L. Genesis of the New England Churches. N. Y., 1874. 8°. 28447

Baddeck. Warner, C. D. Bost., 1874. 16°. 24291

Bagehot, W. Economic Studies. Ed. by R. H. Hutton. Lond., 1880. 8°. 29166

CONTENTS:—The postulates of English pol. economy; The preliminaries of pol. ec.; Adam Smith on our modern econ.; Malthus; Ricardo; The growth of capital; Cost of production.

—— The English Constitution. Bost., 1873. 12°. 20883

—— Literary Studies. With a memoir. Ed. by R. H. Hutton. Lond., 1879. 2 v. 8°. 26767–

CONTENTS:—1, Memoir; The first Edinburgh Reviewers; H. Coleridge; Shelley; Shakspeare—the man; Milton; Lady M. W. Montagu; Cowper; Letters on the French coup d'état of 1851; Cæsarism as it existed in 1865; Memoir of James Wilson.—2, Gibbon; Butler; Sterne and Thackeray; Waverly novels; Dickens; Macaulay; Béranger; Clough's poems; H. C. Robinson; Appendix.

—— Lombard Street: a description of the money market. Lond., 1873. 12°. 29051

—— Physics and Politics; or, Thoughts on the application of the principles of "Natural Selection" and "Inheritance" to political society. N. Y., 1873. 12°. 29241

Baile, J. Wonders of Electricity. Illust. N. Y., 1872, 12°. . 10135

Bain, A. Correlation of Nervous and Mental Forces. (*In app. to* **Stewart, B.,** 'Conservation of Energy'.) 29246

Bain, A. Education as a Science. N. Y., 1879. 12°. 29265
—— Mind and Body: the theories of their relation. N. Y., 1873. 12°. 29243
Baird, H. M. Hist. of the Rise of the Huguenots of France. N. Y., 1879. 2 v. 8°. 20680–
Baird, W. R. American College Fraternities. Phil., 1879. 12°. . 28995
Baker, H. B. English Actors, from Shakespeare to Macready. N. Y., 1879. 2 v. 12°. 23627–
—— French Society from the Fronde to the Great Revolution. Lond., 1874. 2 v. 12°. 20400–
Baker, J. Turkey. N. Y., 1877. 8°. 21909
Baker, S. W. Cast up by the Sea. N. Y., 1869. 12°. . . . 24004
—— Ismailïa. Illust. N. Y., 1875. 8°. 21846
Balbo, C. The Life and Times of Dante. Lond., 1852. 2 v. 12°. 23293–
Baldwin, J. D. Ancient America, in notes on Amer. Archæology. Illust. N. Y., 1872. 12°. 21320
Baldwin (J. L.) & Clay (J.). Laws of Short Whist. London, [1876]. 16°. 29683
Balfe, M. W., Memoir of. Kenney, C. L. Lond., 1875. 8°. . . 23845
Ball, John (*died* 1381). (*In* **Maurice, C. E.,** 'Lives of Eng. Pop. Leaders,' v. 2.) 22941
Ball, John. Journal of a Tour in Marocco. (*See* **Hooker, J. D., & Ball.**)
Ball, R. S. Astronomy. Rev. by S. Newcomb. N. Y., 1878. 16°. 29350
Ballad Stories of the Affections. Buchanan, R. Lond., [1866]. 8°. 26254
Ballads. Lang, A. B. and Lyrics of Old France. Lond., 1872. 12°. 26026
—— Maidment, J. Scottish B. and Songs. Edinb., 1868. 2v. 12°. 26161–
—— Moore, J. S. The Pictorial Book of B. Lond., 1849. 8°. . 26243
—— Roberts, J. S. The Legendary B. of England and Scotland. Lond., [1875]. 12°. 27665
Balzac, H. de. The Comédie Humaine and its author; with translations from the French of Balzac by H. H. Walker. [Lond. &] N. Y., [1879]. 12°. 26908
CONTENTS:—The "Comédie," [*etc.*]; The Purse; Gaudissart II., or the Selim Shawl; Albert Savarus.
—— Poor Relations: Cousin Pons. Lond., 1880. 12°. 24056
—— (*See* **Thomson, J.,** 'Public and Private Life of Animals.')
—— *See, also,* **Curwen, H.,** 'Sorrow and Song,' v. 2 (23286); **James, H.,** jr., 'French Poets' (26905); **Stephen, L.,** 'Hours in a Lib.,' v. 1 (26933).
Bancroft, G. History of the United States of America. Rev. ed. Bost., 1876. 6 v. 12°. (2 copies.) 21335–
Banim, J., Life of; with extracts from his corresp. Murray, P. J. Lond., 1857. 16°. 18558
Banking. Bagehot, W. Lombard Street: a description of the money market. Lond., 1873. 12°. 29051
—— Price, B. Currency and B. N. Y., 1876. 12°. (2 copies.) . 29056–
—— Richardson, H. W. The National Banks. N. Y., 1880. 32°. . 29063
—— *See, also,* **Currency; Money; Pol.** Ec.
Banks, E. G. Hints on Oxford and Cambridge Aquatics. Oxf'd, 1868. 16°. 29658

Barbarossa. *See* **Frederick I.,** *emp. of Ger.*
Barbarossa, and other tales. Heyse, P. J. L. Leipz., 1874. 16°. 24539
Barbauld, Anna L. A. Life of Sam. Richardson. (*See* **Richardson,** 'Correspondence,' v. 1.)
—— Works. With a memoir by Lucy Aikin. Lond., 1825. 2 v. 8°. 18612–
Barchester Towers. Trollope, A. Lond., [1875]. 12°. (2 cop.) . 24828–
Bardsley, C. W. Curiosities of Puritan Nomenclature. N. Y. [Lond.], 1880. 12°. 27867
Barfüssele. Auerbach, B. Stuttg., 1876. 12°. 25895
Barham, F. F., A Memorial of: autobiographical and other compositions. Ed. by I. Pitman. [Printed phonetically, except 55 pp. of pref.] Lond., 1873. 12°. 27839
Barham, R. H. Personal Reminiscences. (*In* **Stoddard, R. H.,** 'Bric-à-Brac Series.') 23255
Barham, R. H. D. The Life and Letters of the Rev. R. H. Barham: with a selection from his miscellaneous poems. Lond., 1870. 2 v. 12°. 23210–
—— The Life and Remains of Theo. E. Hook. Lond., 1877. 12°. 23295
Baring-Gould, S. The Vicar of Morwenstrow: a life of R. S. Hawker. N. Y., [1879]. 12°. 22105
Barker, J. Syria and Egypt under the last five Sultans of Turkey. Lond., 1876. 2 v. 8°. 23960–
Barker, Mary A., (*Mrs.* Fred. Napier Broome.) Station Amusements in New Zealand. Lond., 1873. 12°. 21735
Barnard, C. Light. (*See* **Mayer, A. M., & Barnard.**)
Barneveldt, J. van Olden, Life and Death of. Motley, J. L. N. Y., 1874. 2 v. 8°. (2 copies.) 23894–
Barré, I., Memoir of. (*See* **Britton, J.,** 'Authorship of Junius.') . 26778
Barron, A. Foot Notes; or, Walking as a fine art. Wallingford, Conn., 1875. 12°. 29321
Barrow, I. *Wace, H.* (*In* **Classic** Preachers.) 22112
Barry, A., *editor.* Masters in English Theology: King's College Lectures for 1877. N. Y., 1877. 12°. 22111

Contents:—Historical pref., by the ed.; R. Hooker, by the ed.; L. Andrewes, by R. W. Church; W. Chillingworth, by E. H. Plumptre; B. Whichcote, by B. F. Westcott; Jer. Taylor, by F. W. Farrar; J. Pearson, by S. Cheetham.

Barry, H. Ivan at Home; or, Pictures of Russian life. Illust. Lond., 1872. 8°. 21940
Bartholomew Fair, Memoirs of. Morley, H. Lond., 1859. 8°. . 26641
Bartlett, S. C. From Egypt to Palestine, through Sinai, the Wilderness and the South Country: with special reference to the hist. of the Israelites. Illust. N. Y., 1879. 8°. . . 21843
Bartlett, W. F., Memoir of. Palfrey, F. W. Bost., 1878. 16°. . 22602
Bartol, C. A. Principles and Portraits. Bost., 1880. 16°. . . 27268
Barton, B. Selections from [his] Poems and Letters. Lond., 1849. 18586
Barton Experiment. [Habberton, J.] N. Y., 1877. 12°. . . 24453
Bascom, J. Comparative Psychology: or, The growth and grades of intelligence. N. Y., 1878. 12°. 28207
—— Philosophy of English Literature: lectures. N. Y., 1874. 12°. 26912

Basque Language, Essay on. Vinson, J. (*With* **Basque** Legends.) 27781
Basque Legends. Webster, W. Lond., 1877. 8°. 27781
Bastian, H. C. The Beginnings of Life. Lond., 1872. 2 v. 12°. . 29290–
Bastiat, F. Essays on Political Economy. N. Y., 1874. 16°. . 28801
—— *Same*, rev., with notes by D. A. Wells. N. Y., 1877. 12°. . 28802
Bates, H. W. The Naturalist on the River Amazons: eleven years of travel. Lond., 1873. 12°. 21207
—— *editor*. Central America, the West Indies, and South America. Based on Hellwald's 'Die Erde;' [Trans.] with ethnological app., by A. H. Keane. Illust. Lond., 1878. 12°. . . . 21700
Bathing. Packard, J. H. Sea-air and Sea-bathing. Phil., 1880. 16°. 29967
—— Steedman, C. Manual of Swimming: incl. bathing, . . . drowning, and rescuing. Melbourne, 1867. 16°. 29643
[**Bathurst, C.**] Remarks on the Differences in Shakspeare's Versification in different periods of his life. Lond., 1857. 16°. . 27011
Batrachomyomachia. Battle of the Frogs and Mice. *See* **Homer.**
Batty, J. H. How to hunt and trap. Phil., 1878. 12°. . . . 29611
Baudelaire, C., Translations from; with a few orig. poems. By R. H. Shepherd. Lond., 1869. 16°. 26040
Baxley, H. W. Spain: art-remains and art-realities, painters, priests, and princes. Lond., 1875. 2 v. 12°. 21241–
Burr, E. F. Pater Mundi: lectures. Bost., 1870–73. 2 v. 12°. 9989 & 28087
CONTENTS:—1, Modern science testifying to the Heavenly Father.—2, Doctrine of evolution.
Bayne, P. The Chief Actors in the Puritan Revolution. Lond., 1878. 8°. 23013
—— Lessons from my masters, Carlyle, Tennyson, and Ruskin. N. Y., 1879. 12°. 23287
Beaconsfield, *Lord*. *See* **Disraeli, Benj.**
Beale, L. S. Bioplasm: an introd. to the study of physiology and medicine. Illust. Lond., 1872. 16°. 29292
—— Life Theories: their influence upon religious thought. Lond., 1871. 12°. 29293
—— On Life and on Vital Action in Health and Disease. Lond., 1875. 12°. 29296
—— The Machinery of Life: a lecture. Lond., [1875]. 12°. . 29294
—— The Mystery of Life. Lond., 1871. 12°. 29295
—— Protoplasm; or, Matter and Life. Lond., 1874. 12°. . . 29297
Beattie, J. Poetical Works. With life, crit. diss., and explanatory notes, by G. Gilfillan. Edinb., 1854. 8°. (*In same vol.:* Blair *and* Falconer.) 26322
Beau Tancrede; or, The marriage verdict. Dumas, A. D. Lond., [1879]. 16°. 24415
Beauclerk, Diana de Vere, *Lady*. A Summer and Winter in Norway. Illust. Lond., 1868. 12°. 21208
Beaufort, Emily A. Egyptian Sepulchres and Syrian Shrines, including a visit to Palmyra. New ed. Lond., 1874. 12°. 21209
Beaumarchais, P. A. C. de. *Besant, W.* (*In* 'French Humourists.') 26776
Beaumont (F.) and Fletcher (J.). Works. With introd. by G. Darley. Lond., 1840. 2 v. 8°. 26680–

Beaumont (F.) and Fletcher (J.). *Coleridge, S. T.* Shakespeare, Ben Jonson, B. and F.: notes and lectures. Liverp., 1874. 16°. (2 copies.) . . . . 3180 & 27021

Beauregard, H. J. C. de. *See* **Costa de Beauregard.**

Beauvoir, L. de. A Voyage Round the World. Lond., 1870. 2 v. 21200–

CONTENTS :—1, Australia.—2, Java, Siam, Canton.

—— Pekin, Jeddo, and San Francisco: the conclusion of a Voyage round the world. Lond., 1872. 12°. 21202

Becker, B. H. Scientific London. N. Y., 1875. 12°. . . . 27300

Becket, Thomas à. *Freeman, E. A.* St. Thomas of Canterbury and his Biographers. (*In* 'Histor. Ess.,' 1st ser.) . . . 4658

—— *Froude, J. A.* Life and Times of B. N. Y., 1878. 12°. . . 22140

—— *Morris, J.* The Life and Martyrdom of B. Lond., 1859. 12°. 22141

—— *Robertson, J. C.* B., Archb. of Cant.: a biogr. Lond., 1859. 8°. 22142

—— *Trotter, L. J.* (*In* 'Studies in Biography.') 23883

Beckford, W. The History of the Caliph Vathek. N. Y., 1869. 16°. 24057

Bedouin Tribes of the Euphrates. Blunt, A. N. Y., 1879. 8°. . 21900

Beecher, H. W. A Summer Parish. N. Y., 1875. 12°. . . 28552

—— Yale Lectures on Preaching. N. Y., 1872–4. 3 series. 12°. (2 cop. of 1st.) . . . . 9919– & 28416–

Beerbohm, J. Wanderings in Patagonia. N. Y., 1879. 16°. . 21243

Beers, H. A. A Century of American Literature: 1776—1876. N. Y., 1878. 16°. (2 copies.) 26909–

—— Odds and Ends: verses humorous, occasional, and miscellaneous. Bost., 1878. 16°. 26041

Beesly, A. H. The Gracchi, Marius, and Sulla. N. Y., [1879]. 16°. 20440

Beesly, E. S. Catiline, Clodius, and Tiberius. Lond., 1878. 8°. 23725

Beethoven, L. van. [*Müller von Königswinter, W.*] Furioso; or, Passages from the life of B. Cambr. & L., 1865. 12°. . 23809

—— *Nohl, L.* B., depicted by his contemporaries. Lond., 1880. 12°. 23810

—— — An Unrequited Love: an episode in the life of B. Lond., 1876. 8°. 23806

—— *Wagner, W. R.* Transl. by A. R. Parsons. Bost., 1872. 12°. . 23808

—— — *Same.* Transl. by E. Dannreuther. Lond., 1880. 12°. . . 23807

Behind the Counter. Hackländer, F. W. Leipz., 1868. 16°. . 24455

Being a Boy. Warner, C. D. Bost., 1878. 16°. 24292

Belgium. Gibbons, P. E. French and Belgians. Phila., 1879. 12°. 21228

—— Longfellow, H. W. Poems of Places, v. 15. Bost., 1877. 16°. 26454

—— *See, also,* **Netherlands.**

Belgravia. Lond., 1867–79. 39 v. 8°. . . . . 17971– & 18007–

Bell, A. M. The Elocutionary Manual. 3d ed. Lond., [1859]. 16°. 27823

[**Bell, C. M.**] Tales from the Odyssey, for boys and girls. By "Materfamilias." N. Y., 1880. 24°. 26818

Bell, D. C. Notices of the Historic Persons buried in the Chapel of St. Peter ad Vincula, in the Tower of London. Lond., 1877. 23002

Bell, R., *editor.* The Poems of Greene, Marlowe, and Jonson. With critical and historical notes, and memoirs. Lond., 1876. 12°. 26096

Bell, W. Shakespeare's Puck, and his Folkslore, illustrated from the superstitions of all nations. . . . Lond., 1852, ['61, & ?]. 3 v. 12°. 27012–

Bellasis, E. Cherubini: memorials of his life. Lond., 1874. 8°. 23767
Belloc, Bessie R. P. Vignettes: 12 biographical sketches. Lond., 1866. 16°. 18559
Beneden, P. J. van. Animal Parasites and Messmates. Illust. N. Y., 1876. 12°. 29259
Benger, Elizabeth O. Memoirs of Elizabeth Stuart, Queen of Bohemia, daughter of King James I. Lond., 1825. 2 v. 12°. . 23680–
—— Memoirs of John Tobin; with a selection from his unpublished writings. Lond., 1820. 12°. 18565
Benjamin, S. G. W. Contemporary Art in Europe. N. Y., 1877. 8°. 29871
Benrath, K. Bernardino Ochino, of Siena: a contribution towards the history of the Reformation. N. Y., 1877. 8°. . . . 22181
Benson, Carl, (*pseud.*). *See* **Bristed, C. A.**
Bent, J. T. A Freak of Freedom; or, The Republic of San Marino. Lond., 1879. 12°. 20483
Bentinck, *Lord* **G. F. C.,** Biography of. Disraeli, B. Lond., 1852. 23068
Bentinck, W. H. C., *3d duke of Portland. Earle, J. C.* (*In* 'Eng. Premiers,' v. 2.) 22883
Bentley's Miscellany. Lond., 1837–68. 64 v. 8°. 18266–
—— *Same.* v. 1–3, 5–10, 13–16. 14212–
Bentzon, Th., (*pseud.*). *See* **Blanc, Thérèse.**
Beowulf. Cox (G. W.) & Jones (E. H.). (*In* 'Pop. Romances.') 27712 & 2010
Béranger, P. J. de. Memoirs, written by himself. Lond., 1858. 8°. 23416
—— *See, also,* **Bagehot, W.,** 'Lit. Stud.,' v. 2 (26768); **Besant, W.,** 'French Humourists' (26776).
Berkeley, G. C. G. Fitz-H. My Life and Recollections. Lond., 1865–6. 4 v. 8°. 18605–
Berlioz, H. Selections from his Letters, and Writings; transl., [with] biographical sketch, by W. F. Apthorp. N. Y., 1879. 12° . 23766
Bernard, B. The Life of Samuel Lover, with selections. Lond., 1874. 2 v. 12°. 18539
Bernstein, J. The Five Senses of Man. N. Y., 1876. 12°. . 29261
[Berry, Mary.] A Comparative View of Social Life in England and France, from [1660] to the present, [1830]. [And] the lives of the Marquise Du Deffand, and of Rachael Lady Russell; Fashionable Friends, a comedy. Lond., 1844. 2 v. 12°. 6201–
Besant, W. Constantinople. (*See* **Brodribb, W. J., & Besant.**)
—— The French Humourists from the 12th to the 19th century. Lond., 1873. 8°. 26776
—— Gaspard de Coligny. [L. &] N. Y., 1879. 16°. . . . 22452
—— Rabelais. (Foreign Clas. for Eng. Readers, v. 8.) Phila., [1879]. 23269
—— Studies in Early French Poetry. Lond., 1868. 12°. . . 26280
Bessie Lang. Corkran, A. N. Y., 1877. 16°. 24071
Betrothed (The). Manzoni, A. Lond., 1876. 12°. . . . 24634
Beugnot, J. C. Life and Adventures [Autobiogr.] of Count Beugnot, Minister of State under Napoleon I. Ed. from the French by Charlotte M. Yonge. Lond., 1871. 2 v. 8°. 22565–
Beveridge, W. *Clark, W. R.* (*In* **Classic** Preachers.) . . . 22112
Bevis of Hamtoun. Cox (G. W.) & Jones (E. H.). (*In* 'Pop. Romances.') . . . . 27712 & 2010

Bewick, W. Life [Autobiography] and Letters. Ed. by Thos. Landseer. Lond., 1871. 2 v. 12°. 23840–

Beyle, Marie Henri, (*pseud.*, 'De Stendhal;' *also*, 'Bombet, L. A. C.'). *Hayward, A.* (*In* 'Selected Essays,' v. 1.) 27244

Bible. Arnold, M. God and the B.: a review of objections to 'Literature and Dogma.' N. Y., 1875. 12°. 28688

——— Literature and Dogma: an essay towards a better apprehension of the B. N. Y., 1873. 12°. 28689

—— Davidson, S. The Canon of the Bible. Lond., 1877. 12°. . 28529

—— Dore, J. R. Old Bibles; or, An account of the various versions of the Engl. B. Lond., 1876. 12°. 28526

—— Godet, F. Studies on the New Test. N. Y., 1877. 12°. . . 28531

—— Greg, W. R. The Creed of Christendom: its foundations contrasted with its superstructure. Detroit, 1878. 12°. . 28694

—— Moulton, W. F. The Hist. of the English B. Lond., [1878]. 12°. 28528

—— Smyth, N. Old Faiths in New Light. N. Y., 1879. 12°. . 28701

—— Stephens, W. R. W. Christianity and Islam; the B. and the Koran: four lect. N. Y., 1877. 12°. 28566

—— Westcott, B. F. Hist. of the English B. Lond., 1872. 12°. . 28527

—— *Commentaries.* Cook, F. C., *editor.* [The 'Speaker's' Comm.] Lond., 1871–78. v. 1–7. 8°. 28765–

CONTENTS:—Vol. 1, pt. 1, Gen.-Ex.; pt. 2, Levit.-Deut.—2, Joshua-I. Kings.—3, II. Kings-Esther.—4, Job-Song of Solomon.—5. Isaiah-Lam.—6, Ezekiel, Daniel, and the minor prophets.—(7), N. T., v. 1, Matthew—Luke.

——— Ellicott, C. J., *editor.* A New Test. Comm. Lond. (v. 1), & N. Y., [1878–9]. 3 v. 8°. 28760–

CONTENTS:—1, Gospels.—2, Acts-Galatians.—3, Ephesians-Revelation.

—— *Revision.* Schaff, P., *and others.* The Revision of the English Version of the New Test., by J. B. Lightfoot, R. C. Trench, and C. J. Ellicott. With an introd. by P. Schaff. N. Y., 1873. 3 v. in 1. 12°. 28525

—— *See, also, names of Books and writers;* **Jews; Palestine; Theology** (& *references*).

Bible Lands. Van-Lennep, H. J. N. Y., 1875. 8°. . . . 21902

Bibliotheca Sacra. Andover, 1844–79. 36 v. 8°. 12851–

—— *Same.* v. 9–26. 12803–

—— Index to v. 1–13. . . . . ——

Bickmore, A. S. Travels in the East Indian Archipelago. Lond., 1868. 8°. 21944

Bigelow, J. The Life of Benjamin Franklin, written by himself; now first edited from orig. MSS. and from his printed correspondence and other writings. Phila., 1874. 3 v. 8°. . . 22695–

Bigg-Wither, T. P. Pioneering in South Brazil: 3 years in the province of Paraná. Illust. Lond., 1878. 2 v. 12°. . . 21702–

Biographical Stories. Hawthorne, N. Bost., 1876. 12°. . . 24524

Biography. Müller, F. M. Essays on Literature, B. and Antiquities. (*His* 'Chips' v. 3.) 3733

—— *Collections.* Arnold, F. Our Bishops and Deans. Lond., 1875. 2 v. 8°. 22268–

——— Bartol, C. A. Principles and Portraits. Bost., 1880. 16°. 27268

CONTENTS OF PT. 2:—The personality of Shakespeare; W. E. Channing; Hor. Bushnell; The genius of J. Weiss; W. L. Garrison; W. M. Hunt.

Biography. *Collections.* Bell, D. C. Notices of the Historic Persons buried in the Chapel of St. Peter ad Vincula, in the Tower of London. Lond., 1877. 8°. 23002

——— Burke, J. B. Fragments of Family and Personal Hist., &c. (*In* 'Rise of Great Families.') 27322

——— Chambers, W. Stories of Remarkable Persons. Edinb., 1878. 16°. 23640

——— Clarke, J. F. Memorial and Biographical Sketches. Bost., 1878. 12°. 22618

——— Constable, T. Archibald Constable and his literary correspondents. Edinb., 1873. 3 v. 8°. 23204–

——— Curiosities of B.; or, Memoirs of remarkable men. Illust. Glasgow, 1845. 12°. 23600

——— Distinguished Persons in Russian Society. Lond., 1873. 12°. 23614

——— Field, M. B. Memories of Many Men and of Some Women. N. Y., 1874. 12°. 22620

——— Freeman, E. A. (*See contents of his* 'Histor. Ess.')

——— Godwin, P. The Clyclopædia of B. New ed., with suppl. to Aug. 1877. N. Y., 1878. 8°. 23880

——— Hamerton, P. G. Modern Frenchmen: five biographies. Bost., 1878. 12°. (*For contents see* **Hamerton.**) 22488

——— Jerdan, W. Men I have known. Lond., 1866. 12°. . . 23605

——— Lamartine, A. M. L. de. Biographies and Portraits of some celebrated people. Lond., 1866. 2 v. 8°. (*For contents see* **Lamartine.**) 23727–

——— Redding, C. Personal Reminiscences of Eminent Men. Lond., 1867. 3 v. 12°. 23721–

——— Teale, W. H. Lives of English Divines. Lond., 1848. 16°. 22110

——— Trotter, L. J. Studies in B. Lond., 1865. 8°. (*For contents see* **Trotter.**) 23883

See, also, **Actors; Artists; Authors; Booksellers; Chroniclers; Engineers; Epigrammatists; Etonians; Fathers** (*of the Ch.*)**; Humorists; Lawyers; Navigators; Novelists; Painters; Poets; Popes; Pretenders; Regicides; Travellers;** *see, also, 'Biography' under* **England, France, Germany, Music, Women.**

Biology. Bastian, H. C. The Beginnings of Life: the nature, modes of origin and transformations of lower organisms. Illust. Lond., 1872. 2 v. 12°. 29290–

—— Beale, L. S. Protoplasm, or, Matter and Life. Lond., 1874. 12°. 29297

—— Cook, J. (Boston Monday Lectures.) Bost., 1877. 12°. (2 cop.) 28020–

—— Hartley, W. H. Air and its Relations to Life. N. Y., 1875. 12°. 29298

—— Huxley, T. H. Lecture on the Study of Biology. (*In* 'American Addresses.') 29300

——— & Martin (H. N.). Elementary B. Lond., 1875. 12°. . . 29299

—— Le Conte, J. Correlation of Vital with Chemical and Physical Forces. (*App. to* **Stewart, B.,** 'The Conservation of Energy.') 29246

—— Letourneau, C. Lond., 1878. 8°. 29390

—— Papillon, F. Nature and Life. N. Y., 1875. 12°. . . . 29397

—— Wallace, A. R. (*In* 'Tropical Nature, and other essays.') . 29533

Biology. Wythe, J. H. The Science of Life ; or, Animal and vegetable B. N. Y., 1880. 12°. 29392

See, also, **Body and Mind; Botany; Darwinism; Evolution; Heredity; Life** (*vital force*); **Materialism; Physiology; Zoology.**

Bioplasm. Beale, L. S. Lond., 1872. 16°. 29292

Birch, S. Egypt, from the earliest times to B. C. 300. N. Y., 1875. 20042

Birch, W. J. Philosophy and Religion of Shakspere. Lond., 1848. 27008

Bird, Isabella L. A Lady's Life in the Rocky Mountains. N. Y., 1879. 12°. 21281

Birds. Brehm, A. E. Bird-Life : a hist. of the bird, its structure, and habits. Lond., 1874. 8°. 29570

—— Burroughs, J. B. and Poets ; with other papers. N. Y., 1877. 29322

—— — Wake-Robin. [' A book about the birds.'] N. Y., 1877. 16°. 29324

—— Dixon C. Rural Bird Life : essays on ornithology. Lond., 1880. 29337

—— Flagg, W. B. and Seasons of New England. Bost., 1875. 12°. 29320

—— Minstrelsy of the Woods. Lond., 1832. 12°. 29333

—— Ruskin, J. Love's Meinie: lectures on Greek and English birds. N. Y., 1873. 12°. 29835

Bishop, N. H. Voyage of the Paper Canoe. Bost., 1878. 8°. . 29666

Bishop, W. H. Detmold : a romance. Bost., 1879. 16°. . . 24058

Bismarck-Schönhausen, O. E. L. Letters, from 1844 to 1870. N. Y., 1878. 16°. 22503

—— *Busch, M.* B. in the Franco-German War, 1870-'71. N. Y., [1879]. 2 v. 12°. 22501–

—— *Görlach, W.* Prince B.: a biographical sketch. Leipz., 1875. 22504

—— *Klaczko, J.* Two Chancellors : Gortchakof and B. N. Y., 1876. 22500

—— *Strauss, G. L. M.* (*In* ' Men who have made,' etc.) . . . 22583

Bisset, A. Essays on Historical Truth. Lond., 1871. 8°. . . 20187

CONTENTS :—Is there a science of government? Hobbes; James Mill; Hume; Walter Scott; The government of the Commonwealth and the government of Cromwell; Prince Henry; Sir Thos. Overbury.

—— Hist. of the Commonwealth of England. Lond., 1864–'67. 2 v. 21056–

—— Struggle for Parliamentary Government in England. Lond., 1877. 2 v. 8°. 21058–

Bits of Talk about Home Matters. [Jackson, H. H.] Bost., 1873. 27237

Bits of Travel at Home. [Jackson, Helen H.] Bost., 1878. 16°. . 21289

Bjarnason, J. Viking Tales of the North. (*See* **Anderson, R. B., & Bjarnason.**)

Björnson, B. Fisher-Maiden. N. Y., 1874. 16°. 24059

Black, W. A Daughter of Heth. N. Y., 1877. 12°. (3 copies.) . 24005–

—— Goldsmith. (English Men of Letters.) N. Y., 1879. 12°. . 23337

—— Green Pastures and Piccadilly. N. Y., 1878 [1877]. (2 copies.) 24008–

—— In Silk Attire. N. Y., 1877. 12°. (2 copies.) 24010–

—— Macleod of Dare. N. Y., 1879 [1878]. 12°. (2 copies.) . . 24012–

—— Madcap Violet. N. Y., 1877. 12°. (3 copies.) . . . 24014–

—— Maid of Killeena, and other stories. Lond., 1874. 12°. . . 24017

—— Monarch of Mincing-Lane. N. Y., 1878. 8°. (2 copies.) . 24299–

—— Princess of Thule. Lond., 1875. 12°. (5 copies.) . . . 24018–

—— Strange Adventures of a Phaeton. Lond., 1872. 2 v. 16°. . 24023–

—— *Same.* N. Y., 1877. 12°. (2 copies.) 24025–

Black, W. Three Feathers. N. Y., 1877. 12°. (2 copies.) . . 24027–
Black (The) Hills; routes, scenery, etc. Dodge, R. I. N. Y., 1876. 12°. 21282
Black Tulip. Dumas, A. D. Lond., [1879]. (2 copies.) . 24412 & 24419
Blackburn, H. Artists and Arabs. Lond., 1868. 8°. . . . 21692
—— Normandy Picturesque. Lond., 1869. 8°. 21781
Blackburne, E. O. Illustrious Irishwomen. Lond., 1877. 2 v. 8°. 23884–
Blackie, J. S. Four Phases of Morals: Socrates, Aristotle, Christianity, Utilitarianism. N. Y., 1872. 12°. 28080
—— Horæ Hellenicæ. Lond., 1874. 8°. 26960
—— Language and Literature of the Scottish Highlands. Edinb., 1876. 12°. 26916
—— Musa Burschicosa. Edinb., 1869. 16°. 26042
—— On Self-culture. N. Y., 1874. 16°. 27386
—— Songs of Religion and Life. N. Y., 1876. 16°. . . . 26043
—— The Wise Men of Greece, in a series of dramatic dialogues. Lond., 1877. 12°. 26822
Blackmore, R. D. Alice Lorraine: a tale of the South Downs. N. Y., 1876. 8°. 24301
—— Cradock Nowell: a tale of the New Forest. N. Y., 1866. 8°. 24302
—— Cripps, the Carrier. N. Y., 1876. 8°. 24303
—— Erema; or, My father's sin. N. Y., 1877. 8°. 24304
—— Lorna Doone: a romance of Exmoor. N. Y., [1878]. 8°. . 24305
—— The Maid of Sker. N. Y., 1877. 8°. 24306
Blackstone, W. Student's Blackstone; abr. and adapted to the present state of the law by R. M. Kerr. Lond., 1879. 12°. . 28848
Blackwood, F. T. H., *earl of Dufferin.* A Yacht Voyage: Letters from High Latitudes: some account of a voyage, in 1856, . . . to Iceland, Jan Mayen, and Spitzbergen. N. Y. 21222
—— *Stewart, G.* Canada under the Administration of the Earl of Dufferin. Toronto, 1878. 8°. 21420
Blackwood's Magazine. Edinb. and N. Y., 1817–79. 126 v. 11620–& 11781–
—— *Same.* v. 1–18, 21, 24–26, 28, 33–91, 93–106. . . 11957–& 12128–
Blaikie, W. How to get strong, and how to stay so. N. Y., 1879. 16°. (2 copies.) 29953–
[**Blair, E. T.**] Lloyd Lee: a story of Yale. [N. H., 1878.] (2 cop.) 24060–
Blair, R. Poetical Works. With life, crit. diss. and notes, by G. Gilfillan. Edinb., 1854. 8°. (*In vol. with* **Beattie.**) . . 26322
Blake, E. V. Arctic Experiences. N. Y., 1874. 8°. . . . 21880
Blake, W. Poetical Sketches. Lond., 1868. 16°. . . . 26044
—— Poetical Works. Ed., with memoir, by W. M. Rossetti. Bost., 1875. 16°. 26046
—— Songs of Innocence and of Experience. Lond., 1868. 16°. . 26045
Blamire, Susanna. Poetical Works. Collected by H. Lonsdale; with pref., memoir, and notes by P. Maxwell. Edinb., 1842. 18620
Blanc, A. A. P. C. Art in Ornament and Dress. N. Y., 1877. 8°. 29873
Blanc, J. J. L. Letters on England. 2d series. Lond., 1867. 2 v. 20807–
[**Blanc, Thérèse.**] Remorse: a novel. From the French of Th. Bentzon [*pseud.*]. N. Y., 1878. 16°. 24086

Blanchard, E. (*See* **Duncan, P. M.,** 'The Transformations.')
Blanid. Joyce, R. D. Bost., 1879. 16°. 26023
Blanqui, J. A. Hist. of Political Economy in Europe. With a pref. by D. A. Wells. N. Y., 1880. 8°. 29163
Blaserna, P. Sound in its Relation to Music. N. Y., 1876. 12°. 29262
Blindness and the Blind. Levy, W. H. Lond., 1872. 12°. . . 29978
Blindpits. [Taylor, E.] N. Y., 1869. 12°. 15386
Blockade (The) Runners. Verne, J. (*With* 'A Floating City.') . 24266
Blois. Cochrane, A. B. (*In* 'Historic Chateaux.') 21785
Blood. Willis, R. William Harvey: a hist. of the discovery of the circulation of the B. Lond., 1878. 8°. 23541
Blue Laws. Trumbull, J. H. The True-Blue Laws of Conn. and New Haven, and the False Blue-Laws invented by the Rev. Sam. Peters. Hartf., 1876. 12°. 21322
Blunt, Anne. Bedouin Tribes of the Euphrates. N. Y., 1879. 8°. 21900
Blunt, J. J. Sketch of the Reformation in England. Lond., 1861. 16°. 20843
Boat-Racing. Banks, E. G. Hints on Oxford and Cambridge Aquatics. Oxf., 1868. 16°. 29658
—— Brickwood, E. D. B.-R.; or, The arts of rowing and training. Lond., 1876. 12°. 29657
—— Morgan, J. E. University Oars: being a critical enquiry into the after health of the men who rowed in the Oxford and Cambridge boat-races, from 1829 to 1869. Lond., 1873. 12°. 29656
—— Proctor, R. A. Oxford and Cambridge Rowing. (*And*) Rowing Styles. (*In* 'Rough ways made smooth.') . . . 29444
—— Woodgate, W. B. "Oars and Sculls;" and how to use them. Lond., 1875. 16°. 29659
Boat-Sailing. Frazar, D. Practical B.-S.; [with] vocabulary of nautical terms. Bost., 1879. 16°. 29660
Bob Norberry. Prout, T. Dublin, 1844. 8°. 24680
Bodenstedt, F. M. The Morning-Land; or, A thousand and one days in the East. Lond., 1851 and '53. 2 series. 4 v. 12°. 21724–
Bodines. Up de Graff, T. S. Phila., 1879. 12°. 29664
Body and Mind. Bain, A. Correlation of Nervous and Mental Forces. (*App. to* **Stewart, B.,** 'Conservation of Energy'.) . 29246
——— Mind and Body: the theories of their relation. N. Y., 1873. 29243
—— Holmes, O. W. Mechanism in Thought and Morals. Bost., 1871. 16°. 27255
—— Maudsley, H. N. Y., 1875. 12°. 28000
—— Proctor, R. A. Bodily Illness as a Mental Stimulant. (*And*) Influence of the Mind on the Body. (*In* 'Rough Ways made Smooth'.) 29444
—— *See, also,* **Biology; Mental** Physiology; **Mind.**
Bogardus, A. H. Field, Cover, and Trap Shooting. N. Y., 1874. . 29609
Bohlen Lectures. *See* **Brooks, P.,** 'Influence of Jesus.'
Bohn, H. G. The Hand-book of Games. Lond., 1850. 16°. . . 29680
—— A Polyglot of Foreign Proverbs. Lond., 1867. 12°. . . 26940
Boileau-Despréaux, N. *Besant, W.* (*In* 'French Humourists.') . 26776
Boleyn, Anne. *See* **Anne Boleyn.**

Bollaert, W. The Wars of Succession of Portugal and Spain, from 1826 to 1840. Lond., 1870. 2 v. 8°. 20709–
CONTENTS:—1, Portugal.—2, Spain.

Bolles, A. S. The Financial Hist. of the U. S., 1774–1789. N. Y., 1879. 8°. 29048

Bombet, L. A. C., (*pseud.*). *See* **Beyle, Marie Henri.**

Bonaparte, Elizabeth P., Life and Letters of. Didier, E. L. N. Y., 1879. 12°. 22489

Boner, C. Transylvania: its products and its people. Lond., 1865. 21730

Bonitz, H. The Origin of the Homeric Poems: a lecture. Transl. from the 4th Ger. ed. by L. R. Packard. N. Y., 1880. 16°. 26817

Bonnechose, F. P. E. B. de. Hist. of France, to the Revolution of 1848. Lond., 1868. 2 v. 8°. 20682–

Bonney, T. G. The Alpine Regions of Switzerland and the neighboring countries: a pedestrian's notes. Cambr., 1868. 8°. 21787

Book (The) of the Knight of the Tower, Landry. [La Tour Landry, G. de.] Lond., 1862. 12°. 24211

Books. Maurice, J. F. D. The Friendship of Books, and other lectures. Lond., 1874. 12°. 27301

—— Perkins, F. B. The Best Reading: a classified bibliography. N. Y., 1873. 12°. 26930

—— — *Same.* 4th ed. N. Y., 1877. 12°. . . . . ——

—— — *editor.* Putnam's Library Companion: . . . a quarterly continuation of "The Best Reading." N. Y., 1878–80. 3 v. 8°. ——

—— Porter, N. Books and Reading. N. Y., 1871. 12°. (2 cop.) 122–

—— — *Same.* 4th ed. N. Y., 1876. 12°. (2 copies.) . . . 26928–

—— *See, also,* **Education** (*and references*).

Booksellers, Hist. of. Curwen, H. Lond., [1873]. 12°. . . 23207

Booth, A. J. Saint-Simon and Saint-Simonism. Lond., 1871. 8°. 23522

Borbstædt (A.) & Dwyer (F.). The Franco-German War, to the catastrophe of Sedan and the fall of Strassburg. Lond., 1873. 8°. 20684

Borgia, Lucrezia, *Duchess of Ferrara*: a biogr. Gilbert, W. Lond., 1869. 2 v. 12°. 23945–

Borrow, G. Wild Wales. Lond., 1872. 16°. 21709

Bossuet, J. B. *Sainte-Beuve, C. A.* (*In* 'Monday-Chats.') . . 23290

Boston Monday Lectures. *See* **Cook, J.**

Boston Public Library. Catalogue of . . . History, Biography, and Travel. Bost., 1873. 8° (*Bound with* 'Cat. of Poetry.') ——

—— [Catalogue of] Poetry, Drama, Collections, Periodicals, and Miscel. Works. Bost., 1870. 8°. . . . . ——

—— A Chronological Index to Historical Fiction. Bost., 1875. 8°. ——

Boswell, J. Life of Sam. Johnson; [and the] Tour to the Hebrides. Ed. by P. Fitzgerald. Lond., 1874. 3 v. 8°. 23370–

—— *Same, abridged.* N. Y., 1878. 12°. (2 cop.) 23373–

Botany. Gray, A. School and Field Book of B.: consisting of "Lessons in B.," and "Field, Forest, and Garden B.," bound in 1 v. N. Y., 1874. 8°. 29451

—— Hooker, J. D. (Science Primers.) Lond., 1877. 16°. . . 29358

—— Prantl, C. An Elementary Text-book of B. Lond., 1880. 8°. 29450

Botany. Ruskin, J. Proserpina: studies of wayside flowers. N. Y., 1875–77. Parts 1–4 in 2 v. 12°. 29840–
—— Thomé, O. W. Text-book of Structural and Physiological B. N. Y., 1877. 16°. 29462
—— *See, also,* **Fertilization; Flowers; Fungi; Natural** Hist.; **Plants.**
Bothwell, Jas. Hepburn, *4th earl of. Schiern, F.* Life of B. Edinb., 1880. 23009
Bothwell: a tragedy. Swinburne, A. C. Lond., 1874. 12°. . . 26165
Bottrell, W. Traditions and Hearthside Stories of West Cornwall. Penzance, 1870–73. 2 series. 12°. 27700–
Boulger, D. C. The Life of Yakoob Beg: Athalik Ghazi, and Badaulet: Ameer of Kashgar. Lond., 1878. 8°. 23720
Boulton, M. *Smiles, S.* Lives of B. and Watt. Phila., 1865. 8°. . 23534
Bourke, R. S. *Hunter, W. W.* A Life of the Earl of Mayo, 4th Viceroy of India. Lond., 1875. 2 v. 8°. 23932–
Bourne, H. R. F. English Seamen under the Tudors. Lond., 1868. 22942
—— The Life of John Locke. Lond., 1876. 2 v. 8°. 23520–
—— A Memoir of Sir Philip Sidney. Lond., 1862. 8°. 23417
Bow Street. Hodder, G. Sketches of Life and Character, taken at the Police Court, Bow St. Lond., 1845. 16°. 23641
Bowden, J. Naturalist in Norway. Lond., 1869. 12°. 21210
—— Norway. Lond., 1867. 12°. 21211
Bowen, F. Modern Philosophy. N. Y., 1877. 8°. 28282
Bowne, B. P. Philosophy of Herbert Spencer. N. Y., 1876. 12°. 28168
Bowring, E. A. Poems of Goethe, transl.; with life. Lond., 1853. 26066
—— *Same.* 2d ed., rev. and enl. Lond., 1874. 12°. 26095
—— Tragedies of V. Alfieri, transl. Lond., 1876. 2 v. 12°. . . 26490–
Bowring, J. Autobiographical Recollections. Lond., 1877. 8°. . 23934
Boyd, M. Reminiscences of Fifty Years. N. Y., 1871. 12°. . . 23606
Boyesen, H. H. Falconberg. N. Y., 1879. 12°. 24029
—— Goethe and Schiller. N. Y., 1879. 12°. 26904
—— Gunnar: a tale of Norse life. Bost., 1874. 16°. 24063
—— Tales from Two Hemispheres. Bost., 1877. 16°. 24064
Brackenbury, H. The Ashanti War. Edinb. and Lond., 1874. 2 v. 20619–
Brackett, Anna C., *editor.* Education of Amer. Girls. N. Y., 1874. 28823
Braddon, Mary E. *See* **Maxwell, M. E. B.**
Bradley, E. White Wife; with other stories. Lond., 1865. 16°. . 24062
Brahmanism. *See* **Hinduism.**
Brain. Clarke, E. H. Building of a B. Bost., 1874. 16°. . . 28827
—— Clifford, W. K. Seeing and Thinking. Lond., 1879. 12°. . 28006
—— *See, also,* **Mind** (*and references*).
Brain-work and Overwork. Wood, H. C. Phil., 1880. 16°. . . 29966
Bramleighs of Bishop's Folly. Lever C. J. Lond., 1872. 8°. . 24254
Brandenburg, Memoirs of the House of. Ranke, F. L. von. Lond., 1849. 3 v. 8°. 20651–
Brandes, G. Lord Beaconsfield: a study. N. Y., 1880. 12°. . 22897
Brassey, Annie. Around the World in the Yacht 'Sunbeam.' N. Y., 1878. 8°. 21731

Brassey, Annie. Sunshine and Storm in the East. N. Y., 1880. 8°. 21901
Brassey, T. Foreign Work and English Wages. Lond., 1879. 8°. 29001
—— Lectures on the Labour Question. Lond., 1878. 8°. . . . 29000
—— *Helps, A.* Life and Labors of B. Bost., 1874. 8°. . . . 23560
Brazil. Burton, R. F. Highlands of the B. Lond., 1869. 2 v. 21802-
—— Smith, H. H. Amazons and the Coast. N. Y., 1879. 8°. . 21801
—— *See, also,* **Amazon** *(river)*; **Paraná.**
Breck, S., Recollections of. Phil., 1877. 12°. 22619
Brehm, A. E. Bird-Life. Lond., 1874. 8°. 29570
Bremer, Fredrika. Two Years in Switzerland and Italy. Lond., 1861. 2 v. 8°. 21212-
Bressant: [a novel]. Hawthorne, J. N. Y., 1873. 12°. . . . 24500
Brethren (and Clerks) of the Common Life. Ullmann, C. (*In* 'Reformers' etc., v. 2.) 22301
Brewer, E. C. Readers' Handbook. Phil., 1880. 12°. . . . ——
Bric-á-Brac Series. *See* **Stoddard, R. H.,** *editor.*
Brickwood, E. D. Boat Racing. Lond., 1876. 12°. . . . 29657
Bride of the Rhine. Waring, G. E. Bost., 1878. 12°. . . . 21263
Brides and Bridals. Jeaffreson, J. C. Lond., 1872. 2 v. 8°. . . 28961-
Bridge, Christiana. Hist. of French Literature. (*See* **Demogeot, J. C.**)
Brief Biographies of European Public Men. Higginson, T. W., *editor.* N. Y., 1875-6. 3 v. 16°. 22440-

CONTENTS:—1, Eng. Statesmen, by the ed.—2, Eng. Radical Leaders, R. J. Hinton.—3, French Political Leaders, E. King.—4, Ger. Political Leaders, H. Tuttle.

Brigand Life in Italy. Maffei, A. Lond., 1865. 2 v. 8°. . . 20302-
Bright, H. A. A Year in a Lancashire Garden. Lond., 1879. 12°. 29452
Bright, Jas. F. An English Hist. Lond., 1875-77. 3 v. 16°. . 20844-
—— *Same.* A Hist. of Eng. [L. &] N. Y., 1878. 3 v. 16°. . . 20847-

CONTENTS:—1, Mediæval Monarchy, 449-1485.—2, Personal Monarchy, 1485-1688.—3, Constitutional Monarchy, 1688-1837.

Bright, John. Public Addresses. Lond., 1879. 8°. . . . 27489
Brillat-Savarin, A. Gastronomy as a Fine Art. Lond., 1877. 12°. 29976
Brine, L. The Taeping Rebellion in China. Lond., 1862. 12°. . 20386
Brinton, D. G. The Religious Sentiment. N. Y., 1876. 12°. . 28687
Bristed, C. A. Five Years in an English University. N. Y., 1873. 28824
Britain. *See* **England.**
British America. *See* **America.**
British Poets. *See* **Poets,** *English.*
British Popular Customs. Dyer, T. F. T. Lond., 1876. 12°. . 20806
British Quarterly Review. N. Y., 1871-79. v. 53-70. 8°. . . 12217-
British Rule in India. Martineau, H. Lond., 1857. 16°. . . 20497
Brittany. Macquoid, T. R. & K. S. Pictures and Legends from Normandy and B. Lond., 1879. 12°. 21252
—— Palliser, B. B. and its Byways. Lond., 1869. 12°. . . . 21686
Britton, J. The Authorship of the Letters of Junius elucidated; including a biographical memoir of Isaac Barré. Lond., 1848. 26778
Broad Stone of Honour. Digby, K. H. Lond., 1844-48. 3 v. 12°. . . . . 4620 & 12900-
Brodribb, W. J. Demosthenes. (Anc. Classics for Eng. Readers, supplem. ser., v. 4.) 26850

Brodribb, W. J. Pliny's Letters. (*See* **Church, A., & Brodribb.**)
—— **& Besant (W.).** Constantinople: a sketch of its history. Lond., 1879. 12°. 21244
Broglie, A. de. The King's Secret: the secret correspondence of Louis XV. with his diplomatic agents, from 1752 to 1774. Lond., [1879]. 2 v. 8°. 20685–
Brome, R. Dramatic Works. Lond., 1873. 3 v. 16°. . . . 26492–
Bronté, Anne. Poems. (*With* **Bronté, C.,** 'The Professor.') . 24031
Bronté, Charlotte. Jane Eyre. N. Y., 1874. 12°. 24030
—— *Same.* Lond., 1874. 16°. 24065
—— The Professor; with poems. Lond., 1876. 12°. . . . 24031
—— Shirley: a tale. Lond., 1874. 12°. 24066
—— *Reid, T. W.* C. B.: a monograph. N. Y., 1877. 12°. . . 23248
—— *Swinburne, A. C.* A Note on C. B. Lond., 1877. 12°. . . 26920
Bronté, Emily J. Poems. (*With* **Bronté, C.,** 'The Professor.') . 24031
Bronté, P. Cottage Poems. (*With the same.*) 24031
Bronzes. Fortnum, C. D. E. Lond., [1877]. 12°. 29762
Brooke, S. A. English Literature. Lond., 1877. 16°. . . . 26855
—— Milton. (Classical Writers.) N. Y., 1879. 16°. . . . 26890
—— Theology in the English Poets. [Pope to] Cowper, Coleridge, Wordsworth, and Burns. Lond., 1874. 8°. 26281
Brooks, C. S. Wit and Humour: poems from "Punch." Lond., 1875. 12°. 25268
Brooks, C. T. Faust; transl. from Goethe, with notes. Bost., 1868. 16°. 26067
—— W. E. Channing: a centennial memory. Bost., 1880. 16°. . 22613
Brooks, P. Influence of Jesus. (The Bohlen Lectures, 1879.) N. Y., 1879. 16°. 28533
—— Lectures on Preaching. N. Y., 1877. 12°. (2 copies.) . . 28420–
—— Sermons. N. Y., 1878. 12°. 28532
Broom, H. Philosophy of Law. San Fran., &c., [1876]. 16°. . 28851
Broome, Mary A. B. *See* **Barker, M. A.**
Brougham, H., *Lord.* Letters to Wm. Forsyth. Lond., 1872. 16°. 18562
[**Brougham (J.) & Elderkin (J.),** *editors.*] Lotus Leaves. Lond., 1875. 8°. 27563
Broughton, H. D., *Lord.* Italy. Lond., 1859–'61. 2 v. 12°. . . 21733–
Brown, C. A. Shakespeare's Autobiog. Poems. Lond., 1838. 12°. 27005
Brown C. B. Canoe and Camp Life in British Guiana. Lond., 1876. 8°. 21810
—— **& Lidstone (W.).** Fifteen Thousand Miles on the Amazon and its Tributaries. Lond., 1878. 8°. 21800
Brown, H. The Sonnets of Shakspeare solved. Lond., 1870. 8°. 27051
Brown, H. A. *Hoppin, J. M.* Memoir of Henry Armitt Brown; with 4 orations. Phil., 1880. 8°.. 22693
Brown, J., (*of Selkirk*). Ethics and Æsthetics of Modern Poetry. By J. B. Selkirk (*pseud.*). Lond., 1878. 12°. 26293
Brown, R. Countries of the World. Lond., [1879]. v. 1–3. 4°. 21970–
—— Races of Mankind. Lond., [1874–'76]. 4 v. 8°. . . . 29575–
Brown, W. Hist. of Christian Missions. Lond., 1864. 3 v. 8°. 28448–

Browne, C. F., (*pseud.*, 'Artemas Ward'). Complete Works. Lond. 25269

Browne, W. Y. Fun, Poetry, and Pathos. Lond., 1850. 12°. . 25206

Browning, Elizabeth B. Life, Letters and Essays. N. Y., 1877. 2 v. 16°. 23241–

CONTENTS:—1, Letters to R. H. Horne, with a pref. and memoir by R. H. Stoddard.—2, The Book of the Poets.

Browning, O. Modern England, 1820–1875. (*In* **Epochs** of Eng. Hist.) 20851

—— *editor.* Historical Handbooks. Oxf., [etc.], 1874–76. 6 v. 16°. (*For contents see* **Historical** Handbooks.) 20064–

Browning, R. The Agamemnon of Æschylus, transcribed. Lond., 1877. 16°. 26804

—— Aristophanes' Apology. Bost., 1875. 12°. 26047

—— The Inn Album. Bost., 1876. 12°. 26048

—— Pacchiarotto, with other poems. Bost., 1877. 16°. . . . 26049

—— Red Cotton Night-cap Country. Bost., 1873. 16°. . . . 26050

—— *Bagehot, W.* Wordsworth, Tennyson, and B. (*In* 'Lit. Stud.,' v. 2.) 26768

—— *See, also,* **Dowden, E.**, 'Studies in Lit.' (26926); **Hutton, R. H.**, 'Essays,' v. 2 (27488).

Bruce, E. C. The Century; its fruits and its festival. Phil., 1877. 21522

Brüder vom deutschen Hause. Freytag, G. Leipz., 1875. 12°. ('Die Ahnen,' Abth. 3.) 25913

Brugsch, H. C. Hist. of Egypt under the Pharaohs. Lond., 1879. 2 v. 8°. 20247–

—— True Story of the Exodus of Israel. Bost., 1880. 12°. . . 20046

Bruhns, C., *editor.* Life of A. v. Humboldt. Compiled by J. Löwenberg, R. Avé-Lallemant, and A. Dove. Lond., 1873. 2 v. . 23530–

Brunhild: a tragedy. Geibel, E. Bost., 1879. 16°. . . . 26065

Bryant, W. C. Library of Poetry and Song. N. Y., 1874. 8°. . 26273

—— *editor.* Picturesque America. N. Y., [1872–3]. 2 v. 4°. . ——

—— **& Gay (S. H.).** Popular Hist. of the United States. N. Y., 1876–79. v. 1–3. 8°. (2 copies.) 21561–

CONTENTS:—1, to 1647.—2, 1636–1740.—3, 1678–1779.

Bryce, J. Holy Roman Empire. 4th ed. Lond., 1873. 12°. . . 20100

—— *Same.* 5th ed. Lond., 1875. 12°. 20101

—— Transcaucasia and Ararat. Lond., 1877. 12°. 21214

Brydges, E. Character and Poetical Genius of Byron. Lond., 1824. 18575

—— Recollections of Foreign Travel. Lond., 1825. 2 v. 12°. . 18576–

Buchanan, R. Ballad Stories of the Affections. Lond., [1866]. 8°. 26254

—— Poetical Works. Bost., 1874. 3 v. 12°. 26086–

—— Shadow of the Sword: a romance. N. Y., 1877. 12°. . . 24930

Buckingham, *Dukes of. See* **Villiers, G.; Sheffield, J.**

Buckland, F. Log-book of a Fisherman and Zoölogist. Lond., 1875. 8°. 29495

Buckle, H. T. Miscellaneous and Posthumous Works. Lond., 1872. 3 v. 8°. 27526–

—— *Huth, A. H.* Life and Writings of B. Lond., 1880. 2 v. 8°. 23066–

Bucknill, J. C. Mad Folk of Shakespeare. Lond., 1867. 12°. . 27015

Buddhism. Arnold, E. The Light of Asia. Bost., 1879. 16°. . 26003

Buddhism. Davids, T. W. R. Lond., [1777]. 16°. 28577
—— *See, also,* **India ; Religions** (various).
[**Budgen, Miss L. M.**] Episodes of Insect Life. Lond., 1849–51. 3 v. 8°. 29500–
Bull, G. *See* **Teale, W. H.,** 'Lives of Eng. Divines' (22110) ; **Classic** Preachers, 1878 (22113).
Bulwer, H. L. E., *Lord Dalling.* Historical Characters: Talleyrand, Cobbett, Mackintosh, Canning. Lond., 1868. 2 v. 8°. . 23881–
—— Sir Robert Peel : an historical sketch. Lond., 1874. 8°. . . 23048
Bulwer-Lytton, E. G. E. L. Alice. Phil., 1874. 12°. . . . 24140
—— Athens : its rise and fall. N. Y., 1874. 2 v. in 1. 12°. . . 20096
—— Kenelm Chillingly : a novel. N. Y., 1873. 12°. (2 cop.) . 24142–
—— Last Days of Pompeii. Phila., 1876 (&c.). 12°. (4 copies.) . 24144–
—— "My Novel." Phila., 1875. 2 v. 12°. 24148–
—— [Novels. Knebworth ed.] Lond., 1875–7. (28 v.) 12°. . 24101–

CONTENTS :—Alice ; or, The Mysteries.—Caxtons.—Coming Race.—Devereux.—Disowned.—Erne t Maltravers.—Eugene Aram.—Falkland ; Zicci.—Godolphin.—Harold.—Kenelm Chillingly.—Last Days of Pompeii.—Last of the Barons.—Leila.—Calderon the Courtier.—Pilgrims of the Rhine.—Lucretia.—My Novel. 2 vols.—Night and Morning.—Parisians. 2 vols.—Paul Clifford.—Pausanias,the Spartan.—Pelham.—Rienzi.—Strange Story.—What will he do with it? 2 vols.—Zanoni.

—— Novels and Romances. With illust. Lond., [1848–'53]. 11 v. 24129–

CONTENTS :—1, Pelham ; Godolphin.—2, Disowned ; Devereux.—3, Eugene Aram ; Paul Clifford.—4, Rienzi ; Last Days of Pompeii.—5, Ernest Maltravers ; Alice.—6, Last of the Barons ; Leila.—7, Zanoni ; Harold.—8, Night and Morning ; Strange Story.—9, Lucretia ; Caxtons.—10, My Novel.—11, What will he do with it? Pilgrims of the Rhine.

—— Parisians. N. Y., 1874. 12°. 24150
—— Pausanias the Spartan. N. Y., 1876. 12°. 24151
—— Speeches. With a memoir by his son. Edinb. & Lond., 1874. 2 v. 8°. 23064–
Bulwer-Lytton, E. R., (*pseud.,* 'Owen Meredith'). Fables in Song. Bost., 1874. 16°. 26052
—— Orval. Lond., 1869. 16°. 26051
Buncle, J., Life of. [Amory, T.] Lond., 1770. 4 v. 16°. . . 17484–
Bunsen, Frances W. von : Life and Letters. Hare, A. J. C. N. Y., 1879. 12°. 23621
Bunyan, J. *Froude, J. A.* (Eng. Men of Letters.) N. Y., 1880. 12°. 23346
Buonarotti, Michelangelo. *Clément, C.* Michelangelo. (Illust. Biog. of the Great Artists.) L. & N. Y., 1880. 12°. . . 23790
——— Michelangelo, Lionardo da Vinci, and Raphael. Lond., 1880. 23837
—— *Perkins, C. C.* Raphael and Michelangelo. Bost., 1878. 8°. . 23835
Burial, Embalming, and Cremation. Richardson, B. W. (*In* 'A Ministry.') 29996
—— *See, also,* **Antiquities** (*and references*).
Burke, E. Select Works. Ed. by E. J. Payne. Oxf., 1878. 2 v. 26873–

CONTENTS :—1, Thoughts on the present discontents ; The two speeches on America.—2, Reflections on the revolution in France.

—— *Macknight, J.* Life and Times of B. Lond., 1858–'60. 3 v. 8°. 23034–
—— *Morley, J.* (Eng. Men of Letters.) N. Y., 1879. 12°. . . 23342
—— *See, also,* **Adams, W. H. D.,** 'Eng. Party Leaders,' v. 1 (21054); **Dilke, C. W.,** 'Papers of a Critic,' v. 2 (26766); **Maurice, J. F. D.,** 'The Friendship' (27301).
Burke, J. B. Rise of Great Families ; other essays, and stories. Lond., 1873. 8°. 27322

Burlesque. Walsh, W. S., *editor.* Bost., 1875. 16°. 25246
Burlesques. Thackeray, W. M. Lond., 1876. 12°. 24883
Burlingame, E. L., *editor.* Art Life and Theories of Richard Wagner. Selected. N. Y., 1875. 12°. 23815
—— Current Discussion: a collection from the chief Eng. essays on questions of the time. N. Y., 1878. 2 v. 12°. . . . 27282–

CONTENTS:—**1** (**International Politics**), The Russians, etc., by A. Forbes; Turkey, Stratford de Redcliffe; Montenegro, W. E. Gladstone; Political destiny of Canada, Goldwin Smith; Prussia in the 19th cent., J. S. Blackie; Future of Egypt, E. Dicey; Slaveowner and Turk, Gold. Smith; Stability of Brit. Empire in India, S. J. Owen; Relation of the Eng. People to the Russo-Turkish war, E. A. Freeman.—**2** (**Questions of Belief**), The soul and future life, by F. Harrison; A modern symposium: (1), The soul and future life; (2), The influence upon morality of a decline in religious belief; Course of modern thought, G. H. Lewes; Condition and prospects of the Church of Eng., T. Hughes; Is life worth living? W. H. Mallock.

Burma. Forbes, C. J. F. S. British Burma and its People. Lond., 1878. 12°. 21224
—— *See, also,* **Mandalay.**
Burnaby, F. On Horseback through Asia Minor. Lond., 1877. 2 v. 8°. 21907–
—— Ride to Khiva. N. Y., 1877. 12°. (Maps in a detached case.) 21215–
Burnand, F. C. My Health: [a novel]. Bost., 1872. 16°. . . 24921
Burnett, C. H. Hearing, and how to keep it. Phila., 1879. 16°. . 29958
Burnett, Frances H. Dolly: a love story. Phila., [1877]. 12°. . 24153
—— Haworth's. N. Y., 1879. 12°. (2 cop.) 24154–
—— Louisiana: [a novel]. N. Y., 1880. 12°. (2 copies.) . . 24156–
—— Surly Tim, and other stories. N. Y., 1877. 16°. . . . 24158
—— That Lass o' Lowrie's. N. Y., 1877. 12°. (2 cop.) . . . 24159–
—— "Theo": a love story. Phil., [1877]. 16°. 24161
Burns, R. Poetical Works. With memoir, crit. diss., and notes, by G. Gilfillan. Edinb., 1856. 2 v. 8°. 26325–
—— Works. [Ed. by W. S. Douglas.] Edinb., 1877–1879. 6 v. 8°. 27520–

CONTENTS:—1-3, Poetry, with index (in vol. 3) of first lines.—4-6, Prose, with index of letters, etc.

—— *Brooke, S. A.* (*In* 'Theology in the English Poets.') . . . 26281
—— *Shairp, J. C.* (English Men of Letters.) N. Y., 1879. 12°. . 23339
Burnt Njal. *See* **Njal.**
Burritt, E. Chips from Many Blocks. Toronto, 1878. 12°. . . 27220
—— *Northend, C.* Life of; with selections. N. Y., [1880]. 12°. . 22642
Burroughs, J. Birds and Poets; with other papers. N. Y., 1877. . 29322
—— Locusts and Wild Honey. Bost., 1879. 16°. 29323
—— Wake-Robin. N. Y., 1877. 16°. 29324
—— Winter Sunshine. N. Y., 1876. 16°. 29325
Burton, Isabel. Inner Life of Syria, Palestine, and the Holy Land. Lond., 1875. 2 v. 8°. 21905–
Burton, J. H. Reign of Queen Anne. Edinb., 1880. 3 v. 8°. . 21060–
—— Hist. of Scotland. Edinb. & Lond., 1873. 8 v. & index. 12°. 20901–
Burton, R. F. Highlands of the Brazil. Lond., 1869. 2 v. 8°. . 21802–
—— Letters from the Battle-Fields of Paraguay. Lond., 1870. 8°. . 21804
—— Mission to Gelele, King of Dahome. Lond., 1864. 2 v. 8°. . 21217–
—— Two Trips to Gorilla Land. Lond., 1876. 2 v. 8. . . . 21854–
—— Ultima Thule. Lond., 1875. 2 v. 8°. 21884–
—— Zanzibar. Lond., 1872. 2 v. 8°. 21860–

Busch, M. Bismarck in the Franco-German War. N. Y., [1879]. 2 v. 22501–
Bushnell, H. Forgiveness and Law. N. Y., 1874. 12°. . . . 28550
—— Life and Letters of. Cheney, M. B. N. Y., 1880. 8°. . . 22723
Busk, *Miss* **R. H.** Roman Legends. Bost., 1877. 8°. . . . 27714
—— Valleys of Tirol. Lond., 1874. 12°. 21219
Bute, J. Stuart, *earl of. Earle, J. C.* (*In* 'Eng. Premiers,' v. 1.) . 22882
Butler, J. *Egglestone, W. M.* Stanhope Memorials of Bishop B. Lond., 1878. 8°. 22187
—— *See, also,* **Arnold, M.,** 'Last Essays' (28690); **Bagehot, W.,** 'Lit. Stud.,' v. 2 (26768); **Classic** Preachers (22112); **Stephen, L.,** 'Hist. of Eng. Thought' (28200).
Butler, S. Poetical Works. With life, crit. diss., and notes, by G. Gilfillan. Edinb., 1854. 2 v. 8°. 26327–
Butler, W. A. Hist. of Ancient Philosophy. Phila., 1857. 2 v. 28160–
Butler, W. F. The Great Lone Land. Lond., 1872. 8°. . . 21552
Butt, Beatrice M. Delicia. N. Y., 1879. 16°. 24067
—— Eugénie. N. Y., 1877. 16°. 24068
—— Hester. N. Y., 1879. 16°. 24924
—— Miss Molly. N. Y., 1876. 16°. 24069
Butt, I. Hist. of Italy. Lond., 1860. 2 v. 8°. 20320–
Byron, G. G. N., *Lord.* Cain. Lond., 1830. 12°. 18574
—— Fugitive Pieces and Reminiscences of Lord Byron; new ed. of the Hebrew Melodies . . . By I. Nathan. Lond., 1829. 16°. 18636
—— Poetical Works. Ed., with memoir, by W. M. Rossetti. Lond. 26090
—— *Brydges, E.* The Character and Poetical Genius of B. Lond., 1824. 12°. 18575
—— *Castelar, E.* Life of B. N. Y., 1876. 12°. (2 copies.) . . 27269–
—— *Hodgson, J. T.* Memoir of Francis Hodgson. With letters from B. Lond., 1878. 2 v. 12°. 22106–
—— *Jebb, R. C.* B. in Greece. (*In* 'Mod. Greece.') 20014
—— Life, Writings, Opinions, and Times of Lord B. Lond., 1825. 3 v. 8°. 18653–
—— Memoirs of the Life and Writings of Byron. Lond., 1822. 8°. 18573
—— *Nichol, J.* (Eng. Men of Letters.) N. Y., 1880. 12°. . . 23350
—— *Parry, W.* The Last Days of B. Lond., 1825. 8°. . . . 18656
—— *Trelawny, E. J.* Records of Shelley, B., and the Author. Lond., 1878. 2 v. 12°. 23296–
—— *See, also,* **Morley, J.,** 'Crit. Miscel.,' v. 1 (27407); **Swinburne, A. C.,** 'Ess. and Stud.' (26942).
—— **& Hunt (J. H. L.).** The Liberal: [an anon. periodical]. Lond., 1822–3. 2 v. 8°. 11400–
Byron, M. N., *Lady,* Vindication of. Lond., 1871. 8°. . . . 23449
Cadell, *Mrs.* **H. M.** Ida Craven. N. Y., 1876. 16°. . . . 24070
Cæsar: a sketch. Froude, J. A. N. Y., 1879. 8°. 23724
Cahun, L. Adventures of Captain Mago. N. Y., 1876. 8°. . . 24209
Cain. Byron, G. G. N. With notes by H. Grant. Lond., 1830. 12°. 18574
Cairnes, J. E. Character and Logical Method of Political Economy. N. Y., 1875. 12°. 28803
—— Essays in Political Economy. Lond., 1873. 8°. . . . 29167

Cairnes, J. E. Some Leading Principles of Political Economy. Lond., 1874. 29168
Calderon de la Barca, P. Dramas: The wonder-working magician; Life is a dream; The purgatory of St. Patrick. Lond., 1873. 12°. 26495
—— *Hasell, E. J.* (Foreign Classics for Eng. Readers, v. 9.) Phil., [1879]. 16°. 23270
Caleb Williams, Adventures of. Godwin, W. N. Y., 1856. 12°. . 24479
California. Beauvoir, L. de. (*In* 'A Voyage,' v. 3.) 21202
—— Cooke, P. St. G. Conquest of New Mexico and C. N. Y., 1878. 21323
—— Fisher, W. M. The Californians. Lond., 1876. 12°. . . 21285
—— Nordhoff, C. C.; for health, pleasure, and residence. N. Y., 1873. 8°. 21585
—— — Northern C., Oregon, and the Sandwich Islands. N. Y., 1874. 8°. 21584
Callista. Newman, J. H. Lond., 1873. 12°. 28413
Calvert, G. H. Charlotte von Stein: a memoir. Bost., 1877. 16°. 23656
Calvin, J. *Henry, P.* Life and Times of C. Lond., 1849. 2 v. 8°. 22302–
—— *Merle d'Aubigné, J. H.* Hist. of the Reformation in Europe in the time of C. N. Y., 1863–'79. 8 v. 12°. . . 6386– & 28451–
Cambodia. *See* **Indo-China.**
Cambridge, University of. Arnold, F. Oxford and C.: their colleges, memories, and associations. Lond., [1874]. 8°. . 21979
—— Bristed, C. A. Five years in an English University. N. Y., 1873. 12°. 28824
—— Everett, W. On the Cam: lectures on the U. of C. Cambr., [Mass.], 1865. 16°. 28829
—— Whitely, G. C. The Cambridge Union Society: Inaugural Proceedings. Lond. & Camb., 1866. 16°. 28825
Cameron, V. L. Across Africa. Illust. N. Y., 1877. 8°. . . 21850
Camp and Cabin. Raymond, R. W. N. Y., 1880. 16°. . . . 29661
Campaigning on the Oxus. MacGahan, J. A. N. Y., 1874. 8°. . 21924
Campbell, G. Handy Book on the Eastern Question. Lond., 1876. 20493
—— White and Black. N. Y., 1879. 8°. 21459
Campbell, J. F. Popular Tales of the West Highlands. Edinb., 1860–'62. 4 v. 16°. 27660–
Campbell, John, *Lord.* Shakespeare's Legal Acquirements. Lond., 1859. 8°. 27001
Campbell, J. McL. Memorials: selections from his correspondence. Lond., 1877. 2 v. 12°. 22108–
Campbell, T. *Redding, C.* Literary Reminiscences and Memoirs of C. Lond., 1860. 2 v. 12°. 23224–
—— *Stoddard, R. H., editor.* Personal Recollections of C. N. Y., 1875. 16°. 23254
—— *See, also,* **Constable, T.,** 'A. Constable,' v. 1 (23204); **Mackay, C.,** 'Forty Years' Recol.,' v. 1 (22943); **Patmore, P. G.,** 'My Friends,' v. 1 (23609).
Camping-out. Gould, J. M. Hints for Camping and Walking. N. Y., 1877. 16°. (2 copies.) 29662–

Carlyle, T. *Bayne, P.* Lessons from my masters, C., Tennyson, and Ruskin. N. Y., 1879. 12°. 23287
—— *Guernsey, A. H.* C.: his life, his books, his theories. N. Y., 1880. 23312
—— *See, also,* **Greg, W. R.,** 'Literary and Social Judgments' (27293); **Morley, J.,** 'Crit. Miscel.,' v. 1 (27407); **Mozley, J. B.,** 'Essays,' v. 1 (27409); **Sterling, J.,** 'Essays,' v. 1 (12898).
Carné, L. de. Travels in Indo-China and the Chinese Empire. With a notice of the author by the Count de Carné. Lond., 1872. 8°. 21932
Carpathians, Round about the. Crosse, A. F. Ed. & L., 1878. 12°. 21729
Carpenter, W. B. Mesmerism, Spiritualism, &c. N. Y., 1877. 12°. 28044
—— Principles of Mental Physiology. N. Y., 1875. 12°. . . . 28003
Carr, Alice. North Italian Folk. By Mrs. Comyns Carr. Lond., 1878. 12°. 21220
Carson, C.: Life and Adventures. Peters, D. C.. Hartf., 1875. 8°. 22682
Carthage and the Carthaginians. Smith, R. B. Lond., 1878. 12°. 20094
Cartwright, W. C. The Jesuits. Lond., 1876. 8°. 22182
Cary, Alice & Phœbe. Poetical Works. With a memorial by Mary Clemmer. N. Y., 1878. 8°. 26241
Cary, L., *Viscount Falkland.* *Arnold, M.* (*In* 'Mixed Essays.') 27241
Casaubon, I. *Pattison, M.* Lond., 1875. 8°. 22264
Cassell's Library of Eng. Lit. (*See* **Morley, H.,** *editor.*)
Cassell's Nat. Hist. (*See* **Duncan, P. M.,** *editor.*)
Cast up by the Sea. Baker, S. W. N. Y., 1869. 12°. 24004
Castelar, E. Life of Lord Byron, and other sketches. N. Y., 1876. 12°. (2 copies.) 27269–
Castle Daly. Keary, A. Phila., [1879]. 12°. 24607
Castle St. Angelo. Story, W. W. Lond., 1877. 12°. 21626
Castlereagh, *Viscount.* *See* **Stewart, R. H.**
Catharine, *of Aragon.* *Dixon, W. H.* History of Two Queens. Lond., 1873–4. 4 v. 8°. 23005–
Catherine Blum. Dumas, A. D. Lond., [1879]. 16°. 24418
Catholic Church. *See* **Rom.** Cath. Ch.
Catholic World. N. Y., 1865–79. 29 v. 8°. 14285–
Catiline, Clodius, and Tiberius. Beesly, E. S. Lond., 1878. 8°. . 23725
Catullus. *Davies, J.* (Ancient Classics for English Readers, supplem. ser., v. 3.) 26849
Caucasus, Eastern, Travels in. Cunynghame, A. T. Lond., 1872. 21913
Cavalcaselle, G. B. *See* **Crowe (J. A.) & Cavalcaselle.**
Cavalier Songs and Ballads of England. Mackay, C. Lond., 1863. 26119
Cavendish, (*pseud.*). *See* **Jones, H.**
Cavour, C. B. di, Life of. Mazade, C. de. N. Y., 1877. 8°. . . 23942
Cazelles, M. E. Outline of the Evolution-Philosophy. With an app. by E. L. Youmans. N. Y., 1875. 12°. 28166
Celesia, E. Conspiracy of Gianluigi Fieschi. Lond., 1866. 8°. 20297
Celtic Literature. Arnold, M. On the Study of. Lond., 1867. 8°. 27861
—— Joyce, P. W. Old Celtic Romances. Lond., 1879. 12°. . . 27702
Celts (The). Maclear, G. F. (**Conversion** of the West, v. 1.) Lond., [1878]. 16°. 28494

Central America. *See* **America,** *Central.*
Century (The); its fruits and its festival. Bruce, E. C. Phila., 1877. 21522
Ceramics. *See* **Pottery.**
Ceremonial Institutions. Spencer, H. N. Y., 1880. 12°. . . . 28123
Cernuschi, H. Nomisma; or, "Legal Tender." N. Y., 1877. 12°. 29052
Certain Dangerous Tendencies in Amer. Life. [Harrison, J. B.] Bost., 1880. 16°. 28885
Cervantes-Saavedra, M. de. Don Quixote. Bost., 1870. 4 v. 16°. 24162–
—— *Same.* Edinb., 1879. v. 1. 8°. 24314
—— *Roscoe, T.* Life and Writings of C. Lond., 1861. 16°. . . 23243
Cévennes. Stevenson, R. L. Travels with a Donkey in the C. Bost., 1879. 16°. 21254
Chadwick, J. W. Faith of Reason: discourses. Bost., 1879. 16°. 28691
Chambers, W. Stories of Remarkable Persons. Edinb., 1878. 16°. 23640
Chamisso, A. von. Peter Schlemihl. N. Y., 1874. 12°. . . . 24166
Champeaux, A. de. Tapestry. Lond., [1878]. 12°. . . . 29760
Chance (A) Acquaintance. Howells, W. D. Bost., 1873. (3 cop.) 24558–
Channing, W. E. The Perfect Life: in 12 discourses. Bost., 1873. 28535
—— *Brooks, C. T.* C.: a centennial memory. Bost., 1880. 16°. . 22613
—— *Peabody, E. P.* Reminiscences of C. Bost., 1880. 16°. . . 22614
Channing, W. E. Thoreau: the poet-naturalist. Bost., 1873. 16°. 22606
Channing, W. H. Memoirs of Margaret Fuller Ossoli. (*See* **Ossoli,** 'Works,' v. 1–2.) 27286–
Chantrey, F. *Holland, J.* Memorials of C. Lond., [1851]. 8°. . 18572
—— *Jones, G.* Sir F. C.: recollections of his life. Lond., 1849. 12°. 18583
Chapman, B. Hist. of Gustavus Adolphus and of the 30 Years' War. Lond., 1856. 8°. 20640
Chapman, G. Comedies and Tragedies. Lond., 1873. 3 v. 16°. 26496–
—— [Homeric Hymns, translated.] (*See* **Homer.**)
—— Odysseys of Homer. Lond., 1874. 2 v. 12°. 26813–
—— Works: poems and minor translations. Lond., 1875. 12°. . 26091
Chapman, Maria W. *See* **Martineau, H.,** 'Autobiog.'
Charlemagne (Charles I., *of Germany*). *Eginhard.* Life of C. Transl. by S. E. Turner. N. Y., 1880. 24°. 22506
—— — Life of Karl the Great; transl. by W. Glaister. Lond., 1877. 22505
—— *Mullinger, J. B.* Schools of Charles the Great. Lond., 1877. 28839
Charles I., *of England. Disraeli, I.* Commentaries on the Life and Reign of C. Lond., 1851. 2 v. 8°. 23014–
—— *Gardiner, S. R.* Personal Government of C. Lond., 1877. 2 v. 8°. 21126–
—— — Prince Charles and the Spanish Marriage. Lond., 1869. 2 v. 21122–
Charles I., *of Germany. See* **Charlemagne.**
Charles V. (I. *of Spain.*) *Robertson, W.* Hist. of the Reign of the Emperor C. [Ed.,] with an account of the emperor's life after abdication, by W. H. Prescott. Phila., 1872. 3 v. 8°. 20348–
Charles XII., *of Sweden. Oscar II.* Lond., 1879. 8°. . . . 23898
Charles Edward Stuart (*Prince*), Life and Times of. Ewald, A. C. Lond., 1875. 2 v. 8°. 23032–
—— *See, also,* **Pretenders.**

Charles the Great. *See* **Charlemagne.**
Charley Chalk; or, the Career of an Artist. With illust. by Jacob Parallel. Lond., [1841]. 8°. 24307
Chase, S. P., Life and Public Services of. Schuckers, J. W. [And] the eulogy by W. M. Evarts . . . N. Y., 1874. 8°. . . . 22775
Chatrian A. *See* **Erckmann (E.) & Chatrian.**
Chaucer, G. Canterbury Tales. [With] an essay by T. Tyrwhitt; [and] memoir and crit. diss. by G. Gilfillan. Edinb., 1860. 3 v. 8°. 26329-
—— Parlament of Foules. Ed. by T. R. Lounsbury. Bost., 1877. 26009
—— Poetical Works. Ed. by R. Morris. With memoir by Sir H. Nicolas. Lond., [1872]. 6 v. 16°. 26010-
—— — Ed., with a memoir, by Rob. Bell. Rev. ed. by W. W. Skeat. Lond., 1878. 4 v. 12°. 26005-
—— Prioresses Tale; Sire Thopas; Monkes Tale; Clerkes Tale; Squires Tale. Ed. by W. W. Skeat. Oxford, 1874. 16°. 26869
—— Tale of the Man of Lawe; Pardoneres Tale; Second Nonnes Tale; Chanouns Yemannes Tale. Ed. by W. W. Skeat. Oxf'd, 1877. 16°. 26870
—— *Pauli, R.* (*In* 'Pictures of Old England.') 20850
—— *Ward, A. W.* (English Men of Letters.) N. Y., 1880. 12°. 23345
Chauncey Judd. Warren, I. P. N. Y., [1874]. 16°. 17013
Cheltenham College, Reminiscences of. Ward, P. Lond., 1868. 12912
Chemistry. Cooke, J. P. The New C. N. Y., 1874. 12°. . . 29245
—— Gore, G. The Art of Scientific Discovery; or, The general conditions and methods of research in physics and C. Lond., 1878. 12°. 29380
—— Johnson, S. W. How Crops feed. N. Y., [1870]. 12°. . . 29459
—— — How Crops grow. N. Y., [1868]. 12°. 29460
—— Roscoe, H. E. (Science Primers.) Lond., 1877. 16°. . . 29362
—— *See, also,* **Atomic** Theory; **Fermentation.**
Chemistry of Light. Vogel, H. N. Y., 1875. 12°. 29253
Cheney, Mary B. Life and Letters of Horace Bushnell. N. Y., 1880. 8°. 22723
Chénier, A. M. de. *Curwen, H.* (*In* 'Sorrow and Song.' v. 2.) 23286
Cherbuliez, V. Count Kostia: a novel. N. Y., 1873. 16°. . . 24167
—— Jean Têterol's Idea. N. Y., 1878. 16°. 24087
—— Meta Holdenis: a novel. N. Y., 1877. 12°. 24077
—— Miss Rovel. 5e éd. Paris, 1877. 16°. 25623
—— Prosper: a novel. N. Y., 1874. 16°. 24168
—— Prosper Randoce. 2e éd. Paris, 1874. 16°. 25624
—— La Revanche de Joseph Noirel. Paris, 1872. 16°. . . . 25625
—— Romance of an Honest Woman. Bost., 1874. 12°. . . . 24169
—— Samuel Brohl et Cie. 3e éd. Paris, 1877. 16°. . . . 25626
—— Samuel Brohl and Company. N. Y., 1877. 12°. . . . 24072
—— Stroke of Diplomacy. N. Y., 1880. 16°. 24922
Cherubini: memorials. Bellasis, E. Lond., 1874. 8°. . . . 23767
Chess. Agnel, H. R. C. for Winter Evenings. N. Y., 1848. 12°. 29710
—— Chess Handbook. By an amateur. Phila., 1859. 16°. . . 29713

Chess. Fiske, D. W. Book of the First Amer. C. Congress. N. Y., 1859. 12°. 29709
—— Gossip, G. H. D. Chess-Player's Manual. Lond., 1875. 8°. 29679
—— Löwenthal, J. Morphy's Games. Lond., 1860. 12°. . . 29711
—— — *Same.* N. Y., 1860. 12°. 29712
—— Proctor, R. A. Automatic C. and card playing. (*In* 'Science Byways.') 29445
—— Staunton, H. Chess-Player's Companion. Lond., 1849. 16°. (2 copies.) 29714–
—— — Chess-Player's Handbook. Lond., 1873. 12°. . . . 29717
—— — Chess Praxis. Lond., 1871. 12°. 29716
—— — C. Tournament. Lond., 1873. 12°. 29718
—— — Laws and Practice of C. Lond., 1876. 12°. 29719
Chevalier (Der). Mügge, T. Breslau, 1862. 3 B. 16°. (Romane, B. 1–3.) 25840
Chevalier (The) de Maison Rouge. Dumas, A. D. Lond., [1879]. 16°. 24414
Chevalier (The) d'Harmental. Dumas, A. D. (*Same as* "The Conspirators.") 24404
Chevreuse, Marie de Rohan de. *Cousin, V.* Secret Hist. of the French Court under Richelieu and Mazarin; or, Life and times of Mad. de C. N. Y., 1871. 12°. 20414
Chicot, the Jester. Dumas, A. D. Lond., [1879]. 16°. . . . 24406
Chillingworth, W. *Plumptre, E. H.* (*In* **Barry, A.,** 'Masters.') 22111
China. Anderson, J. Mandalay to Momien: the two expeditions to Western China of 1868 and 1875. Lond., 1876. 8°. . 21926
—— Beauvoir, L. de. (*In* 'A Voyage,' v. 2–3.) 21201–
—— Brine, L. Taeping Rebellion in C. Lond., 1862. 12°. . . 20386
—— Carné, L. de. Travels in Indo-China and the Chinese Empire. Lond., 1872. 8°. 21932
—— Edkins, J. Religion in China. Bost., 1878. 8°. . . . 28563
—— Giles, H. A. Strange Stories from a Chinese Studio. Lond., 1880. 2 v. 12°. 27787–
—— Gill, W. The River of Golden Sand: a journey through China and Eastern Tibet to Burmah. Illust. Lond., 1880. 2 v. 8°. 21930–
—— Gray, J. H. C.: a history of the laws, manners, and customs of the people. Illust. Lond., 1878. 2 v. 8°. . . . 21935–
—— Hübner, J. A. von. (*In* 'A Ramble round the World.') . . 21203
—— Johnson, Sam. Oriental Religions. China. Bost., 1877. 8°. 28560
—— [Lindley, A. F.] Ti-ping Tien-kwoh: the history of the Ti-ping Revolution. Lond., 1866. 2 v. 8°. 20381–
—— Margary, A. R. Journey, from Shanghae to Bhamo, and back to Manwyne. Lond., 1876. 8°. 21925
—— Medhurst, W. H. Foreigner in Far Cathay. N. Y., 1873. 12°. 21619
—— *See, also,* **Manchuria; Mongolia; Tibet.**
China Sea. Collingwood, C. Rambles of a Naturalist on the shores and waters of the C. S. Lond., 1868. 8°. 29494
Chips from a German Workshop. Müller, F. M. N. Y., 1869–76. 4 v. 12°. . . . . 3731–3 & 27302
Chips from Many Blocks. Burritt, E. Toronto, 1878. 12°. . . 27220

Chivalry. Digby, K. H. Broad Stone of Honour; or, The true sense and practice of C. Lond., 1844–48. 3 v. 12°. 4620 & 12900–
—— *See, also,* **Arthur** (*King*); **Crusades.**
Chopin, F. F. *Karasowski, M.* Chopin: his life, letters and works. Lond., 1879. 2 v. 12°. 23769–
—— *Liszt, F.* Life of C. Phila., 1863. 16°. 23768
Chorley, H. F. Modern German Music. Lond., 1854. 2 v. 12°. . 29743–
—— National Music of the World. Lond., 1880. 12°. . . . 29745
—— Personal Reminiscences. (*In* **Stoddard, R. H.,** 'Bric-à-Brac Series.') 23256
—— Recent Art and Society. N. Y., 1874. 12°. 23762
Christ. Brooks, P. The Influence of Jesus. (Bohlen Lectures, 1879.) N. Y., 1879. 16°. 28533
—— Crosby, H., *& others.* C.: His nature and work. N. Y., 1878. 28487
—— Farrar, F. W. Life of C. Lond. 2 v. 12°. 28644–
—— — *Same.* N. Y., 1875. 2 v. 12°. 28646–
—— Geikie, C. Life and Words of C. N. Y., 1878. 2 v. 8°. . 28763–
—— Hanna, W. Our Lord's Life on Earth. Edinb., 1869. 6 v. 16°. 28480–
—— Hughes, T. Manliness of C. Bost., 1880. 16°. . . . 28486
—— Jameson, A. M. Hist. of Our Lord as exemplified in works of art. Lond., 1865. 2 v. 8°. 29914–
Christian Gellert, and other sketches. Auerbach, B. Lond., 1858. 24000
Christianity. Arnold, M. Literature and Dogma. N. Y., 1873. 28689
—— Blakie, J. S. (*In* 'Four Phases of Morals.') 28080
—— Christlieb, T. Modern Doubt and Christian Belief. N. Y., 1874. 8°. 28681
—— Fisher, G. P. Beginnings of C. N. Y., 1877. 8°. (2 copies.) 28587–
—— Greg, W. R. Creed of Christendom. Detroit, 1878. 12°. . 28694
—— Peabody, A. P. C. and Science. N. Y., 1874. 12°. . . . 28700
—— Renan, J. E. Rome and C. (English Conferences.) Bost., 1880. 12°. 28570
—— Stephens, W. R. W. C. and Islam; the Bible and the Koran: 4 lect. N. Y., 1877. 12°. 28566
—— Wright, G. F. Logic of Christian Evidences. Andover, 1880. 28702
—— Uhlhorn, G. Conflict of C. with Heathenism. N. Y., 1879. 8°. 28602
—— *See, also,* **Religion.**
Christianity and Humanity: sermons. King, T. S. Bost., 1877. 28538
Christina, *queen of Sweden,* Memoirs of. Woodhead, H. Lond., 1863. 2 v. 12°. 23901–
Christlieb, T. Best Methods of counteracting Modern Infidelity. N. Y., 1874. 12°. 28682
—— Modern Doubt and Christian Belief. N. Y., 1874. 8°. . . 28681
Christmas Books. Thackeray, W. M. Lond., 1876. 12°. . . 24878
Chromatics. *See* **Colors.**
Chroniclers. *See* **Early** Chroniclers.
Chronology. Putnam, G. P. World's Progress: a dictionary of dates, . . . to Aug. 1877. N. Y., 1878. 8°. . . . . . ——
Church, A. J. Ovid. (Anc. Classics for Eng. Readers, suppl. ser., v. 2). 26848

Church, A. J. Stories from the Greek Tragedians. [Lond. &] N. Y., 1880. 12°. 26806
—— Stories from Homer. Illust. N. Y., 1878. 16°. 26819
—— Stories from Virgil. N. Y., 1879. 12°. 26803
—— **& Brodribb (W. J.).** Pliny's Letters. (Anc. Classics for Eng. Readers, v. 11.) 26837
Church, Florence M. Life and Letters of Captain Marryat. Lond., 1872. 2 v. 12°. 23212-
Church, R. W. Beginning of the Middle Ages. N. Y., [1878]. 16°. 20457
—— Dante: an essay. Lond., 1878. 12°. 26282
—— Spenser. (English Men of Letters.) N. Y., 1879. 12°. . . 23340
Church of England. *See* **England,** *Church of.*
Church of Rome. *See* **Roman** Cath. Ch.
Church of Scotland. *See* **Scotland,** *Church of.*
Church and State. Thompson, R. W. Papacy and the Civil Power. N. Y., 1876. 12°. 29096
Church Union. Döllinger, J. J. I. von. Reunion of the Churches. N. Y., 1872. 16°. 28536
—— Tullidge, H., *editor.* The Evangelical Ch.: discourses. N. Y., 1879. 8°. 28600
Churchill, C. Poetical Works; with notes and a life by W. Tooke. Bost., 1854. 3 v. 16°. 26053-
Churton, E. Gongora: an essay on the times of Philip III. and IV. of Spain. Lond., 1862. 2 v. 16°. 23652-
Cicero. *Collins, W. L.* ('Anc. Classics for English Readers,' v. 9.) 26835
Cid (The), Translations from. Frere, J. H. (*In* 'Works,' v. 2.) . 27482
Circuit Rider. Eggleston, E. N. Y., 1874. 12°. 2993
Civil Liberty and Self-Government. Lieber, F. Phila., 1874. 8°. 29082
Civil Service in Gt. Britain. Eaton, D. B. N. Y., 1880. 8°. . . 21140
Civilization. Dean, A. Hist. of C. Albany, 1868-9. 7 v. 8°. . 20233-
—— Rawlinson, G. Early Civilizations. (*In* 'Origin of Nations.') 20047
—— Wilson, D. Prehistoric Man: researches into the origin of C. Lond., 1876. 2 v. 8°. 20200-
—— *See, also,* **Man; Sociology.**
Clara Vere. Spielhagen, F. (Sämmtl. Werke, B. 3.) 25862
Claretie, J. A. Camille Desmoulins and his Wife. Lond., 1876. 8°. 22560
Clarissa [Harlowe]. Richardson, S. Condensed by C. H. Jones. N. Y., 1874, 16°. 24850
Clark, E. L. Arabs and Turks. Bost., 1876. 12°. 20492
Clark, H. A. College Book. (*See* **Richardson, C. F., & Clark.**)
Clark, W. R. Saint Augustine. (The Fathers for English Readers.) Lond., [1878]. 16°. 28504
Clarke, C. C. Shakespeare-Characters. Lond., 1863. 8°. . . 27041
—— **& Mary C.** Recollections of Writers. With letters of Chas. Lamb, Leigh Hunt, Douglas Jerrold, and Chas Dickens. N. Y., [1878]. 12°. 26936
Clarke, E. H. Building of a Brain. Bost., 1874. 16°. . . . 28827
—— Sex in Education. Bost., 1873. 16°. 28828
—— Visions: a study of false sight. Bost., 1878. 12°. . . . 28005

Clarke, J. F. Common-sense in Religion. Bost., 1874. 12°. . 28692
—— Memoirs of Marg. Fuller Ossoli. (*See* **Ossoli,** 'Works,' v. 1-2.) 27286-
—— Memorial and Biographical Sketches. Bost., 1878. 12°. . 22618
—— Ten Great Religions. Bost., 1871. 12°. 28564
—— *Same.* Bost., 1877. 12°. 28565
Clarke, Mary C. (*See* **Clarke, C. C. & M. C.**)
Classic Preachers of the English Church: lectures deliv. at St. James's Ch. [Westminster] in 1877, (and 1878). With an introd. by J. E. Kempe. N. Y., (& Lond.), 1877-8. 2 v. 12°. 22112-

CONTENTS:—1877, J. Donne, by J. B. Lightfoot; I. Barrow, by H. Wace; R. South, by W. C. Lake; W. Beveridge, by W. R. Clark; T. Wilson, by F. W. Farrar; J. Butler, by E. M. Goulburn.—1878, G. Bull, by W. P. Warburton; S. Horsley, by J. R. Woodford; J. Taylor, by A. Barry; R. Sanderson, by W. Alexander; J. Tillotson, by W. G. Humphry; L. Andrewes, by J. H. North.

Classical Geography. Tozer, H. F. Lond., 1876. 16°. . . . 26860
Classical Writers. Green, J. R., *editor.* 26890-

CONTENTS:—Milton, by S. A. Brooke.—Euripides, J. P. Mahaffy.—Vergil, H. Nettleship.—Livy, W. W. Capes.

Clay, J. Short Whist. (*See* **Baldwin & Clay.**)
Clayton, Ellen C. English Female Artists. Lond., 1876. 2 v. 8°. 23865-
—— Queens of Song. Lond., 1863. 2 v. 8°. 23847-
Clemens, S. L., (*pseud.*, 'Mark Twain.') Adventures of Tom Sawyer. Hartf'd, 1876. 8°. (2 copies.) 25584-
—— Mark Twain's Sketches. Hartf'd, 1875. 8°. 25588
—— Roughing it. Hartf., 1878. 8°. 25587
—— A Tramp Abroad. Hartf., 1880. 8°. (2 copies.) . . . 25589-
—— **& Warner (C. D.).** Gilded Age. Hartf., 1874. 8°. . . 25586
Clément, C. Michelangelo. L. & N. Y., 1880. 12° . . . 23790
—— Michelangelo, Lionardo da Vinci, and Raphael. Lond., 1880. 23837
Clement, Clara E. Handbook of Legendary and Mythological Art. Illust. N. Y., 1877. 12°. 29790
—— Painters, Sculptors, Architects, Engravers, and their works. Bost., 1879. 12°. 29791
Clement (St.) of Rome. *Holland, H. S.* (*In* 'The Apostolic Fathers.') 28502
Cliffe, L. Anecdotal Reminiscences. Lond., 1830. 16°. . . 18560
Clifford, W. K. Seeing and Thinking: [4 lectures]. Lond., 1879. 28006
Clinton, H. F. Literary Remains. Lond., 1854. 12°. . . . 18587
Clodius, Catiline, and Tiberius. Beesly, E. S. Lond., 1878. 8°. 23725
Cloncurry, *Baron.* *See* **Lawless, V. B.**
Cloth of Gold, and other poems. Aldrich, T. B. Bost., 1878. 16°. 26000
Coan, T. Adventures in Patagonia. N. Y., 1880. 12°. . . 21704
Coates, H. T. Fireside Encyclopædia of Poetry. Phila., [1878]. 26380
Cobbe, Frances P. False Beasts and True. Lond., [1875]. 12°. . 12911
Cobbett, R. S. Memorials of Twickenham. Lond., 1872. 8°. (2 cop.) 21777-
Cobbett, W. *Smith, Edward.* Lond., 1878. 2 v. 12°. . . . 22890-
—— *See, also,* **Bulwer, H. L. E.,** 'Histor. Characters,' v. 2 (23882); **Forsyth, W.,** 'Essays' (27480).
Cobden (R.) and Modern Political Opinion. Rogers, J. E. T. Lond., 1873. 8°. 29088
Cochrane, A. B. Historic Chateaux. Lond., 1877. 8°. . . 21785
Cochut, P. A. The Financier, Law. Lond., 1856. 16°. . . 22843

Cockburn, H. T. Journal: a continuation of the Memorials of his time. Edinb., 1874. 2 v. 8°. 23054–

—— Memorials of His Time. Edinb., 1856. 8°. 23053

Cockton, H. George St. George Julian, the Prince. Phila, 1842. 8°. 24311

Cohen, J. S. The Throat and the Voice. Phil., 1879. 16°. . . 29962

Coins. *See* **Numismatics.**

Cokain, A. Dramatic Works; with memoir. Edinb. & Lond., 1874. 26565

Coleridge, H. J. Life and Letters of St. Francis Xavier. Lond., 1872. 2 v. 12°. 22103–

Coleridge, S. T. Letters, Conversations, and Recollections. N. Y., 1836. 12°. (2 copies.) 3980–

—— *Same.* 2d [3d] ed. Lond., 1858. 12°. 23302

—— Osorio: a tragedy. Lond., 1873. 8°. 26640

—— Shakespeare, Jonson, Beaumont and Fletcher. Liverpool, 1874. 16°. (2 copies.) . . . . 3180 & 27021

—— *See, also,* **Brooke, S. A.,** 'Theology in the Eng. Poets' (26281); **Mill, J. S.,** 'Diss. and Disc., v. 2 (3716); **Shedd, W. G. T.,** 'Lit. Essays' (26927); **Swinburne, A. C.,** 'Essays and Stud.' (26942).

Coleridge, Sara. Memoirs and Letters. Lond., 1873. 2 v. 12°. 23291–

[**Coles, B. C.**] Short Whist. By Major A. [*pseud.*], with an essay . . . by Prof. P[ole]. Lond., 1865. 16°. 29684

Coligny, G. de. *Besant, W.* [L. &] N. Y., 1879. 16°. . . . 22452

College Tramps. Stokes, F. A. N. Y., 1880. 12°. 21255

Colleges. Baird, W. M. Amer. College Fraternities. Phil., 1879. 28995

—— Porter, N. American C. and the Amer. Public. New Haven, 1870. 12°. *And* N. Y., [1878]. 12°. . . . 9254 & 28837

—— Richardson (C. F.) & Clark (H. A.). The College Book. Bost., 1878. 8°. . . . . ——

See, also, **Cheltenham; Eton; Harvard; Owens; Winchester; Yale; —Education; Universities.**

Collingwood, C. Rambles of a Naturalist on the Shores and Waters of the China Sea. Lond., 1868. 8°. 29494

Collins, C. W. Plato. (Anc. Classics for Eng. Readers, v. 19.) . 26845

—— Sophocles. (*Same,* v. 10.) 26836

Collins, W. Poetical Works. With life, crit. diss., and notes, by G. Gilfillan. Edinb., 1854. 8°. 26338

Collins, W. L. Montaigne. Phila., [1879]. 12°. 23268

—— *editor* (*and author*). Ancient Classics for English Readers. Phila., 1870–79. 28 v. 16°. (*For contents see* **Ancient** Clas.) . . . . 71–86 & 26835–

VOLS. BY THE EDITOR:—1–2, Homer's Iliad & Odyssey (2 cop.); 5. Virgil (2 cop.); 9, Cicero; 14, Aristophanes; 16, Plautus and Terence; 18, Lucian; (Suppl. ser.,) 1, Livy; 6, Thucydides.

Collins, W. W. The Yellow Mask. N. Y., 1879. 16°. . . . 24923

Colloquia Peripatetica. Duncan, J. Edinb., 1871. 16°. . . 23655

Colonies, European, Hist. of. Payne, E. J. Lond., 1877. 16°. . 20084

Colonna, Vittoria: her life and poems. *Mrs.* H. Roscoe. Lond., 1868. 12°. 23227

Colorado, Summer Etchings in. Greatorex, E. N. Y., [1873]. 8°. 21976

Color-Blindness. Jeffries, B. J. Bost., 1879. 12°. 29319

Consuelo. *Same*, transl. Phil., [1870]. 16°. (2 cop.) . . . 24916–
Contemporary Review. Lond., 1866–79. 36 v. 8°. . . . 10721–
Contes bleus. Laboulaye, E. R. L. Paris, 1877. 16°. . . . 25666
Contes populaires. Erckmann (E.) & Chatrian (A.) Paris, [1877]. 25639
Conversion of the West. 28494–

CONTENTS :—v. 1, Maclear, G. F., The Celts.—2, The English.—3, The Northmen.—4, Merivale, C., The Continental Teutons.

Convicts. *See* **Prisons.**
Convicts (The) and their Children. Auerbach, B. N. Y., 1877. (2 cop.) 24040–
Cook, D. Book of the Play. Lond., 1876. 2 v. 12°. . . . 26557–
Cook, J. Boston Monday Lectures. Bost., 1877–80.' 8 v. 12°. 28020–

CONTENTS ;—Biology (2 *copies*).—Transcendentalism.—Orthodoxy.—Conscience.—Heredity.—Marriage.—Labor.—Socialism.

Cook, Martha W., *translator. See* **Krasinski, S.**, 'The Undivine Comedy.'
Cooke, J. P., jr. The New Chemistry. N. Y., 1874. 12°. . . 29245
Cooke, M. C. Fungi. N. Y., 1875. 12°. 29254
Cooke, P. St. G. Conquest of New Mexico and California. N. Y., 1878. 12°. 21323
Cooley, T. M. General Principles of Constitutional Law in the U. S. of A. Bost., 1880. 12°. 28845
Coolidge, Susan, (*pseud.*). *See* **Woolsey, Sarah C.**
Coomassie and Magdala. Stanley, H. M. N. Y., 1874. 8°. . . 20621
Cooper, Elizabeth. Life of Thomas Wentworth, Earl of Strafford. Lond., 1874. 2 v. 8°. 23011–
Cooper, J. F. Afloat and ashore. N. Y., 1873. 12°. . . . 2834
Coöperation, Hist. of, in England. Holyoake, G. J. Phil. [Lond.], 1875–79. 2 v. 12°. 29005–
Coral Reefs. Darwin, C. R. Lond., 1874. 12°. 29415
Coran. *See* **Koran.**
Cordery, Bertha M. Struggle against Absolute Monarchy. (*In* **Epochs** of Eng. Hist.) 20851
Corea. Oppert, E. A Forbidden Land. N. Y., 1880. 8°. . . 21943
Corkran, Alice. Bessie Lang. N. Y., 1877. 16°. 24071
Corn Laws. Mackay, C. (*In* 'Forty Years' Recoll.,' v. 1.) . . 22943
—— Peel, R. Repeal of the Corn Laws. (*In* 'Memoirs,' ed. by Stanhope and Cardwell, v. 2.) 22888
—— Rogers, J. E. T. Defence of the C. L. (*In* 'Cobden and Mod. Pol. Opin.') 29088
—— *See, also,* **England,** *Hist.*, 1845–6.
Corney, B. Curiosities of Literature, by I. D'Israeli, illustrated. 2d ed., rev. ; added, Ideas on controversy. Lond., 1838. 12°. 18566
Cornhill Magazine. Lond., 1860–79. 40 v. 8°. . . 18108– & 18233–
Cornwall (*England*). Bottrell, W. Traditions and Hearthside Stories of West C. Penzance, 1870–'73. 2 series. 12°. . . 27700–
—— Hunt, R. Popular Romances of the West of England. Lond., [1871]. 12°. 27664
Correlation of Forces. *See* **Force.**
Cossacks (The). Tolstói, L. N. Y., 1878. 16°. 24910
Costa de Beauregard, H. J. Recollections. Lond., 1877. 2 v. 12°. 22484–

Costume. *See* **Dress; Manners & Customs.**
Cotton, C. Complete Angler. (*See* **Walton, I., & Cotton.**)
Couch, J. Illustrations of Instinct. Lond., 1847. 12°. 29326
Coulanges, M. D. F. de. *See* **Fustel de Coulanges.**
Count Alarcos: a tragedy. Disraeli, B. N. Y. [Lond., 1878]. 24247 & 24252
Count Kostia. Cherbuliez, V. N. Y., 1873. 16°. 24167
Counterfeit (A) Presentment. Howells, W. D. Bost., 1877. 16°. 24561
Countess de Charny. Dumas, A. D. Lond., [1879]. 16°. 24408 & 24425
Countess of Rudolstadt. Dudevant, A. L. A. D. Phila., [1870]. 16°. (2 copies.) 24918--
Cousin, V. Secret History of the French Court under Richelieu and Mazarin. N. Y., 1871. 12°. 20414
Cousin Pons. Balzac, H. de. Lond., 1880. 12°. 24056
Cousins. Walford, L. B. N. Y., 1879. 16°. 24286
Couture, T. Conversations on Art Methods. N. Y., 1879. 12°. 29826
Coverley, Sir Roger de. From the Spectator. With notes by W. H. Wills. N. Y., 1878. 16°. 27265
Cowper, W. Poetical Works. With life, critical dissertation, and notes, by G. Gilfillan. Edinb., 1854. 2 v. 8°. 26333–
—— [Select Works.] Ed. by H. T. Griffith. Oxford, 1874. 2 v. 16°. 26876–

CONTENTS:—1, Didactic Poems of 1782, with selections from the minor pieces, A.D. 1779—83; with introd. and notes.—2, Task, with Tirocinium, and selections, A.D. 1784—99; with life and notes.

—— *Hayley, W.* Life and Letters of C. Lond., 1835. 8°. . . . 23420
—— *Smith, Goldwin.* (Eng. Men of Letters.) N. Y., 1880. 12°. . 23347
—— *See, also,* **Bagehot, W.,** 'Lit. Stud.,' v. 1 (26767); **Brooke, S. A.,** 'Theol. in the Eng. Poets' (26281); **Sainte-Beuve, C. A.,** 'Eng. Portraits' (22885); **Stephen, L.,** 'Hours in a Library,' v. 3 (26935).
Cox, E. W. Arts of Writing, Reading, and Speaking. Lond., 1879. 27821
Cox, G. W. Athenian Empire. N. Y., [1877]. 16°. 20441
—— Crusades. N. Y., [1874]. 16°. 20449
—— Greeks and the Persians. N. Y., 1876. 16°. 20435
—— History of Greece. Lond., 1874. v. 1–2. 8°. 20165–
—— Tales of Ancient Greece. Chicago, 1877. 12°. 27742
—— **& Jones (E. H.).** Popular Romances of the Middle Ages. Lond., 1871. 12°. 2010
—— *Same.* 1st Amer., from 2d Eng. ed. N. Y., 1880. 12°. . . 27712

CONTENTS:—Arthur and his knights; Merlin; Sir Tristrem; Bevis of Hamtoun; Guy of Warwick; Havelok; Beówulf; Roland; Olger the Dane; Stories of the Volsungs; Nibelung story; Walter of Aquitaine: Story of Hugdietrich and Hildeburg; Gudrun lay; Story of Frithjof and Ingebjorg; Grettir the strong; Gunnlaug and the fair Helga; Burnt Njal.
(*Note.*—This edition contains the matter of the two books, "Pop. Romances," Lond., 1871, and "Tales of Teut. Lands," Lond., 1872, less 80 + 30 pp. of introduction.)

—— Tales of the Teutonic Lands. Lond., 1872. 12°. 27713
Cox (G. W.) & Sankey (C.), *editors.* *See* **Epochs** of Anc. Hist.
[**Cox, J. E.**] Musical Recollections. Lond., 1872. 2 v. 8°. . 29792–
Cox, S. S. Why we laugh. N. Y., 1876. 12°. 25205
Cradock, J. Literary and Miscellaneous Memoirs. Lond., 1826. 8°. 18594
Cradock Noel. Blackmore, R. D. N. Y., 1866. 8°. 24302
Craik, Dinah M. M. Sermons out of Church. N. Y., 1875. 12°. 27221
Cranford. Gaskell, E. C. Lond., 1870. 16°. 24446

Crashaw, R. Poetical Works. With memoir and crit. diss., by G. Gilfillan. Edinb., 1857. 8°. 26335

Craven, Pauline. Fleurange: a novel. N. Y., 1873. 16°. . . 24170

Crayfish. Huxley, T. H. N. Y., 1880. 12°. 29269

Crayon Miscellany. Irving, W. N. Y., [1865]. 16°. . . . 24590

Creasy, E. S. Hist. of England. Lond., 1869–70. v. 1–2. 8°. . 21002–

—— History of the Ottoman Turks. Lond., 1877. 12°. . . . 20489

—— Memoirs of Celebrated Etonians. Lond., 1850. 8°. . . . 18592

Creation, Hist. of. Haeckel, E. H. N. Y., 1876. 2 v. 12°. . . 29381–

Creed of Christendom. Greg, W. R. Detroit, 1878. 12°. . . 28694

Creighton, Louise. England a Continental Power. (*In* **Epochs** of Eng. Hist.) 20851

—— Life of Edward the Black Prince. Lond., 1876. 16°. . . 22446

—— Life of Sir Walter Ralegh. N. Y., 1877. 16°. 22447

Creighton, M. Age of Elizabeth. N. Y., 1876. 16°. . . . 20452

—— Hist. of Rome. Lond., 1877. 16°. 20052

—— Life of Simon de Montfort, Earl of Leicester. Lond., 1876. 16°. 22445

—— The Tudors and the Reformation. (*In* **Epochs** of Eng. Hist.) . 20851

—— *editor.* Epochs of English Hist. Complete in one vol. Lond., 1879. 16°. (*For contents see* **Epochs.**) 20851

—— — *See, also,* **Historical** Biographies.

Cremation. Richardson, B. W. (*In* 'A Ministry of Health.') . . 29996

Cretan Insurrection of 1866–7–8. Stillman, W. J. N. Y., 1874. 12°. 20496

Cricket Ground, Guide to. Selkirk, G. H. Lond., 1867. 16°. . 29636

Cripps, the Carrier. Blackmore, R. D. N. Y., 1876. 8°. . . 24303

Critic, The Papers of a. Dilke, C. W. Lond., 1875. 2 v. 8°. . 26765–

Croker, J. W. Early Period of the French Revolution. Lond., 1857. 20687

Cromwell, O. *Vaughan, R.* Protectorate of C. Lond., 1838. 2 v. 21000–

—— *See, also,* **Bayne, P.,** 'Chief Actors' (23013); **Forster, J.,** 'Histor. and Biog. Ess.,' v. 1 (27320); **Mozley, J. B.,** 'Essays,' v. 1 (27409).

Crookes, W. Researches in Spiritualism. Lond., 1874. 8°. . 28041

Crosby, H. Christian Preacher. N. Y., [1880]. 12°. . . . 28425

—— *& others.* Christ: discourses. N. Y., 1878. 12°. . . . 28487

Cross, Marian (Evans). *See* **Eliot, George.**

Cross, Holy. Prime, W. C. N. Y., [1877]. 16°. 28510

Crosse, A. F. Round about the Carpathians. Edinb. & L., 1878. 12°. 21729

Crotchet Castle. Peacock, T. L. (*In* 'Works,' v. 2.) . . . 27304

Crouch, Anna M. P., Memoirs of. Young, M. J. Lond., 1806. 2 v. 18556–

Crowe, J. A. Handbook of Painting. (*See* **Waagen, G. F.**)

—— **& Cavalcaselle (G. B.)** Early Flemish Painters. Lond., 1872. 12°. 23801

—— Hist. of Painting in Italy. Lond., 1864–66. 3 v. 8°. . . 29945–

—— Hist. of Painting in North Italy. Lond., 1871. 2 v. 8°. . . 29948–

—— Titian. Lond., 1877. 2 v. 8°. 23832–

Crowest, F. Great Tone Poets. Lond., 1874. 12°. 23761

Crowne, J. Dramatic Works. Edinb. & Lond., 1873–4. 4 v. 8°. 26566–

Crusades. Cox, G. W. N. Y., [1874]. 16°. 20449

—— Dutton, W. E. Hist. of the Crusades. Lond., 1877. 12°. . 20105

—— Michaud, J. F. Hist. of the C. Lond., 1852. 3 v. 12°. . . 20102–

Crusades. Sybel, H. C. L. von. Hist. and Literature of the C. Lond., 1861. 20106
—— *See, also,* **Europe,** *Hist.,* 1096–1291.
Cruttwell, C. T. Hist. of Roman Literature. N. Y., [1878]. 8°. 26964
Culture. Greenwood, J. G. On Some Relations of C. to Practical Life. (*In* **Owens Coll.** Ess. & Ad.) 27412
Cumming, W. G. Wild Men and Wild Beasts. N. Y., 1872. 12°. 21680
Cundall, J. Hans Holbein. Lond. & N. Y., 1879. 12°. . . . 23781
Cunningham, A., Life of; with selections. Hogg, D. Lond., 1875. 23244
Cunynghame, A. T. Travels in the Eastern Caucasus. Lond., 1872. 21913
Curiosities of Biography. Glasgow, 1845. 12°. 23600
Currency. Howe, J. B. Mono-Metalism and Bi-Metalism. Bost., 1879. 16°. 29061
—— Hughes, R. W. Pop. Treatise on the C. Question. N.Y.,1879. 12°. 29054
—— Price, B. C. and Banking. N. Y., 1876. 12°. (2 copies.) . 29056–
—— Sumner, W. G. Hist. of American C. N. Y., 1874 (etc.). (2 cop.) 29059–
—— *See, also,* **Banking; Money.**
Current Discussion. Burlingame, E. L. N. Y., 1878. 2 v. 12°. (*For contents see* **Burlingame.**) 27282–
Currie, J., Memoir of. Currie, W. W. Lond., 1831. 2 v. 8°. . 18595–
Curteis, A. M. Hist. of the Roman Empire. Lond., 1875. 16°. . 20068
Curtis, B. R. Memoir of; with writings. Bost., 1879. 2 v. 8°. . 22680–
Curwen, H. History of Booksellers. Lond., [1873]. 12°. . . 23207
—— Sorrow and Song. Lond., 1875. 2 v. 12°. 23285–
CONTENTS:—1, H. Murger; Novalis; A. Petöfi.—2, Balzac; E. A. Poe; A. Chénier.
Cusack, Mary F. The Liberator [Dan. O'Connell]. Kenmare. 2 v. 23044–
Cushing, C. Treaty of Washington. N. Y., 1873. 12°. . . . 21361
Cushman, Charlotte. *Stebbins, E.* Bost., 1878. 12°. . . . 22698
Custer, G. A. My Life on the Plains. N. Y., 1874. 8°. . . . 21581
—— *Whittaker, F.* Life of Gen. C. N. Y., [1876]. 8°. . . . 22772
Customs. *See* **Manners** and Customs.
Cutts, E. L. Saint Jerome. Lond., [1878]. 16°. 28505
Cuzco. Markham, C. R. Lond., 1856. 12°. 21701
Cyprus. Brassey, A. Sunshine and Storm in the East. N. Y., 1880. 21901
—— Löher, F. von. Lond., 1878. 12°. 21251
D' A., Anna. *See* **Almeida, Anna 'd.**
Daghestan, Travels in. Cunynghame, A. T. Lond., 1872. 8°. . 21913
Dahomey, Mission to. Burton, R. F. Lond., 1864. 2 v. 8°. . 21217–
Daily News (London). War Correspondence, 1877–8. L.,1878. 2v. 12°. 20494–
Daisy Miller. James, H., jr. N. Y., 1879. 32°. 24599
Dale, R. W. Lectures on Preaching. N. Y., etc., 1878. (2 cop.) 28422–
Dallas, G. M. Letters from London. Lond., 1870. 2 v. 12°. . 22646–
Dalling, *Lord.* *See* **Bulwer, H. L. E.**
Dalton, J. *Lonsdale, H.* Lond., 1874. 12°. 23564
Damascus, St. Paul in. Rawlinson, G. Lond., [1878]. 16°. . . 28498
Dana, J. D. Geological Story briefly told. N. Y., 1875. (2 cop.) 29413–
—— Manual of Geology. N. Y., 1874. 8°. 29411
—— Manual of Mineralogy and Lithology. N. Y., 1878. 12°. . 29412

Daniel, the Beloved. Taylor, W. M. N. Y., 1878. 12°. . . . 28648
Daniel Deronda. Eliot, Geo. N. Y., 1876. 2 v. 12°. (5 copies.). 24184–
Daniell, W. H. The Voice, and how to use it. Bost., 1873. 16°. . 29804
Daniels, W. H. [D. L.] Moody. N. Y., 1878. 12°. . . . 22616
Dannreuther, E. Richard Wagner. Lond., 1873. 8°. . . . 29800
Dante Alighieri. De Monarchia, transl. (*In* **Church, R. W.,** 'Dante: an essay.') 26282
—— Inferno. Transl. by T. W. Parsons. Bost., 1867. 8°. . . 26272
—— *Balbo, C.* Life and Times of D. Lond., 1852. 2 v. 12°. . 23293–
—— *Church, R. W.* Lond., 1878. 12°. 26282
—— *Oliphant, M. O. W.* (Foreign Classics for Eng. Readers, v. 1.) Phila., [1877]. 16°. 23262
—— — Makers of Florence. Lond., 1876. 8°. 23836
—— *Symonds, J. A.* Introd. to the study of D. Lond., 1872. 12°. 26283
Danton, G. J. *See* **Baker, H. B.,** 'French Society,' v. 2 (20401); **Claretie, J. A.,** 'Camille Desmoulins' (22560); **Lamartine, A. M. L. de,** 'Biogr.,' v. 2 (23728).
D'Anvers, N. Elementary History of Art. N. Y., 1875. 12°. . 29877
—— Raphael. Lond. & N. Y., 1879. 12°. 23779
Darwin, C. R. Different Forms of Flowers. N. Y., 1877. 12°. . 29455
—— Cross and Self Fertilisation in the Vegetable Kingdom. N. Y., 1877. 12°. 29454
—— Insectivorous Plants. N. Y., 1875. 12°. 29457
—— Movements and Habits of Climbing Plants. Lond., 1875. 12°. 29453
—— Structure and Distribution of Coral Reefs. Lond., 1874. 12°. 29415
—— Various Contrivances by which Orchids are fertilised by Insects. N. Y., 1877. 12°. 29456
Darwin E. *Krause, E.* N. Y., 1880. 12°. 23545
Darwinism. Gray, A. Darwiniana. N. Y., 1876. 12°. . . . 29396
—— Hodge, C. What is D.? N. Y., 1874. 12°. 28089
—— Schmidt, O. Doctrine of Descent and D. Lond., 1875. 12°. . 29252
—— Wagner, M. Darwinian Theory. Lond., 1873. 8°. . . . 29391
—— *See, also,* **Biology; Evolution; Natural Selection.**
Dasent, G. W. Story of Burnt Njal. Edinb., 1861. 2 v. 12°. . 27703–
—— Story of Gisli the Outlaw. Edinb., 1866. 8°. 27780
Daudet, A. Fromont jeune et Risler ainé. Paris, 1877. 16°. . 25627
—— Kings in Exile. Bost., 1880. 16°. 24171
—— Les rois en exil. Paris, 1880. 16°. 25600
Daughter of an Egyptian King. Ebers, G. M. Phil., 1871. 12°. . 3041
Daughter of Heth. Black, W. N. Y., 1877. 12°. (3 copies.) . 24005–
D'Avenant, W. Dramatic Works; with memoir. Edinb. & Lond., 1872–74. 5 v. 8°. 26560–
Davenport Dunn. Lever, C. J. Lond., 1872. 8°. 24256
David, King of Israel. Taylor, W. M. N. Y., 1875. 12°. . . 28649
Davids, T. W. R. Buddhism. Lond., [1877]. 16°. . . . 28577
Davidson, S. Canon of the Bible. Lond., 1877. 12°. . . . 28529
Davies, G. S. St. Paul in Greece. Lond., [1878]. 16°. . . . 28500
Davies, J. Catullus, Tibullus, and Propertius. (Anc. Classics for Eng. Readers, suppl. ser., v. 3.) 26849

Davies, J. Hesiod and Theognis. (**Anc.** Clas., 1st ser., v. 15.) . 26841
Davillier, C. Spain. Illust. by G. Doré. [L. &] N. Y., 1876. 4°. . ——
Dawn of History. Keary, C. F. N. Y., [1879]. 12°. . . . 20090
Dawson, J. W. Origin of the World. N. Y., 1877. 12°. . . 29418
—— Story of the Earth and Man. N. Y., 1873. 16°. . . . 29417
Day (A) of my Life. By a present Eton Boy. N. Y., 1877. 16°. . 28830
Dead Lake. Heyse, P. J. L. Leipz., 1870. 16°. 24540
Dean, A. History of Civilization. Albany, 1868–9. 7 v. 8°. . 20233–
Deane, R., Life of. Deane, J. B. Lond., 1870. 8°. . . . 23023
Dear Lady Disdain. McCarthy, J. N. Y., 1876. 8°. . . . 24670
Deccan. Frere, M. Old Deccan Days. Lond., 1870. 16°. . . 27790
Decoration and Design. Garrett, R. & A. Suggestions for House Decoration in Painting, Woodwork and Furniture. Phila., [1877]. 12°. 29780
—— Redgrave, R. Manual of Design. N. Y., [1876]. 12°. . . 29768
—— Spofford, H. E. P. Art Decoration applied to Furniture. N. Y., 1878 [1877]. 8°. 29872
—— *See, also,* **Ornament.**
Deerstalkers. Herbert, H. W. (*In* 'Sporting Scenes,' v. 1.) . . 29602
Defence of Guenevere. Morris, W. Lond., 1875. 12°. . . . 26101
Defenders of the Faith. Watson, F. Lond., [1878]. 16°. . . 28503
Defoe, D. *Minto, W.* (English Men of Letters.) N. Y., 1879. 12°. 23338
—— *See, also,* **Dennis, J.,** 'Studies' (26915); **Forster, J.,** 'Histor. and Biog. Essays,' v. 2 (27321); **Stephen, L.,** 'Hours in a Lib.', v. 1 (26933).
De Forest, J. W. Honest John Vane: a story. New Haven, 1875. 24172
—— Irene, the Missionary. Bost., 1879. 16°. 24173
—— Kate Beaumont. Bost., 1872. 8°. 24308
—— Wetherell Affair. N. Y., 1873. 8°. 24309
Deirdrè. [Joyce, R. D.] Bost., 1876. 16°. 26024
Deism. Stephen, L. (*In* 'Hist of Eng. Thought.') 28200
Dekker, T. Dramatic Works; with notes and a memoir. Lond., 1873. 4 v. 16°. 26499–
Delaroche, H. *Rees, J. R.* (Illust. Biog. of the Great Artists.) . 23787
Delicia. Butt, B. M. N. Y., 1879. 16°. 24067
Demaus, R. Hugh Latimer: a biography. Lond., [1869]. 12°. . 22100
Demetrius the Impostor. Mérimée, P. Lond., 1853. 12°. . . 23903
Democracy. Adams, C. K. Democracy and Monarchy in France. N. Y., 1874. 12°. 20413
—— Ingersoll, C. Fears for Democracy. Phila., 1875. 8°. . . 21449
—— May, T. E. Democracy in Europe. N. Y., 1878. 2 v. 8°. . 20565–
Democracy: an American novel. N. Y., 1880. 16°. . . . 24174
Demogeot, J. C. Hist. of French Literature. Adapted from the French by C. Bridge. Phila., 1874. 16°. 20065
Demonology. Spalding, T. A. Elizabethan D. Lond., 1880. 12°. 28042
—— *See, also,* **Magic; Spiritualism; Supernatural** (The); **Visions.**
Demosthenes. *Brodribb, W. J.* (Ancient Classics for English Readers, supplem. ser., v. 4.) 26850

Denham, J. Poetical Works. With memoir and crit. diss., by G. Gilfillan. Edinb., 1857. 8°. 26363
Denmark. Longfellow, H. W. Poems of Places, v. 8. Bost., 1876. 26447
Dennis, J. Studies in English Literature. Lond., 1876. 12°. . . 26915
CONTENTS:—Pope; Defoe; Prior; Steele; The Wartons; John Wesley; Southey; Eng. Lyrical Poetry; Eng. Rural Poetry; The Eng. Sonnet.
Dennistoun, J. Memoirs of the Dukes of Urbino. Lond., 1851. 3 v. 23939–
Denton, W. Servia and the Servians. Lond., 1862. 8°. . . . 20486
—— *editor.* Serbian Folk-lore. Lond., 1874. 12°. 27784
DeQuincey, T. Confessions of an English Opium-eater; and Autobiographic Sketches. Bost., 1873 (&c.). 12°. (3 cop.) . 27365–
—— Works. Riverside ed. N. Y., 1878. 12 v. 12°. 27367–
CONTENTS:—1, Confessions, and kindred papers.—2, Autobiographic Sketches.—3, Literary Reminiscences.—4, Literary Criticism.—5. The 18th Cent. in Scholarship and Literature.—6, Biographical and Historical Essays.—7, Essays in Ancient Hist. and Antiquities.—8, Essays on Christianity, Paganism, and Superstition.—9, Essays in Philosophy.—10, Politics and Political Economy.—11, Romances and Extravaganzas.—12, Narrative and Miscel. Papers; with a general index.
—— [*Japp, A.*] DeQ.: his life and writings. N. Y., 1877. 2 v. 12°. 23303–
—— *See, also,* **Masson, D.,** 'Wordsworth,' [etc.] (27298); **Mathews, W.,** 'Hours with Men and Books' (27340); **Stephen, L.,** 'Hours in a Lib.,' v. 1 (26933).
Derby, *Lord. See* **Stanley, E. H. S.**
Dermody, T., Life of. Raymond, J. G. Lond., 1806. 2 v. 12°. . 18554–
Dernier amour. Dudevant, A. L. A. D. Paris, 1867. 16°. . . 25679
Dernière Aldini. Dudevant, A. L. A. D. Paris, 1876. 16°. . . 25678
Deshler, C. D. Afternoons with the Poets. N. Y., 1879. 12°. . 26284
Design. *See* **Decoration** and Design.
Desmoulins, B. C., and his wife. Claretie, J. A. Lond., 1876. 8°. 22560
Desperate Remedies. Hardy, T. N. Y., 1874. 16°. 24456
Detmold. Bishop, W. H. Bost., 1879. 16°. 24058
Deucalion. Ruskin, J. N. Y., 1875–77. 2 v. 12°. 29836–
Deutsch, E. O. M. Islam. (*In* **Smith, R. B.,** 'Mohammed,' etc.) 28567
Deutsche Pioniere. Spielhagen, F. (Sämmtl. Werke, B. 8.) . . 25867
DeVere, A. T., *editor.* Proteus and Amadeus. Lond., 1878. 12°. 28169
DeVere, S. *See* **Schele de Vere.**
Devey, J. Comparative Estimate of Modern English Poets. Lond., 1873. 12°. 26285
Dewees, F. P. The Molly Maguires. Phila., 1877. 12°. . . . 28996
DeWitt, J., The Administration of. Geddes, J. N. Y., 1880. v. 1. 20602
Diamond cut Diamond. Trollope, T. A. N. Y., 1874. 12°. . . 24830
Diamond Necklace, Story of. Vizetelly, H. Lond., 1867. 2 v. 12°. 22523–
Diamonds and Precious Stones. Dieulafait, L. N. Y., 1876. 12°. 10134
Diary of a Woman. Feuillet, O. N. Y., 1879. 16°. 24089
Dichter und Kaufmann. Auerbach, B. Stuttg., 1871. (Romane, B. 2.) 25887
Dick, R., baker, of Thurso. Smiles, S. N. Y., 1879. 12°. . . 23566
Dickens, C. J. H. Barnaby Rudge; Sketches, Part 2. N. Y., 1872. 24213
—— Bleak House. N. Y., 1873. 16°. 24214
—— A Child's History of England. Bost., 1873. 16°. 20840
—— Christmas Stories; Pictures from Italy; American Notes. N. Y., 1873. 16°. 24215
—— David Copperfield. N. Y., 1872. 16°. 24216

Dickens, C. J. H. Dombey and Son. N. Y., 1872. 16°. . . . 24217
—— Letters. Ed. by M. Dickens and G. Hogarth. N. Y., 1879. 2 v. 23305–
—— Little Dorrit. N. Y., 1873. 16°. 24219
—— Martin Chuzzlewit. N. Y., 1873. 16°. 24220
—— Memoirs of Joseph Grimaldi. Lond., 1846. 16°. . . . 23651
—— Mystery of Edwin Drood. N. Y., 1875. 16°. 24218
—— Nicholas Nickleby. N. Y., 1872. 16°. 24221
—— *Same.* Lond., 1848. 12°. 24222
—— *Same.* Phila. 8°. 24310
—— Old Curiosity Shop; Sketches, Part 1. N. Y., 1872. 16°. . 24212
—— Oliver Twist; Great Expectations. N. Y., 1872. 16°. . . 24223
—— Our Mutual Friend. N. Y., 1873. 16°. 24224
—— *Same.* Condensed by R. Johnson. N. Y., 1876. 16°. . . 24225
—— Pickwick Papers. N. Y., 1876. 16°. 24226
—— *Same.* Lond., 1847. 12°. 24227
—— Sketches of Young Couples. [L. &] N. Y., [1879]. 16°. (2 cop.) 24228–
—— Tale of Two Cities; Hard Times for these Times. N. Y., 1872. 24230
—— Uncommercial Traveller; Master Humphrey's Clock; New Christmas Stories. N. Y., 1873. 16°. 24231
—— *Stoddard, R. H.* Anecdote Biography of D. (*In* 'Bric-à-Brac Series.') 23252
—— *See, also,* **Bagehot, W.,** 'Lit. Stud.,' v. 2 (26768); **Clarke, C. C. & M. C.,** 'Recollections' (26936); **Whipple, E. P.,** 'Lit. and Life' (27267).
Diderot, D., and the Encyclopædists. Morley, J. Lond., 1878. 2 v. 23423–
Didier, E. L. Life and Letters of Madame [E. P.] Bonaparte. N. Y., 1879. 12°. 22489
Diet. *See* **Food; Health.**
Dieulafait, L. Diamonds and Precious Stones. N. Y., 1876. 12°. 10134
Digby, K. H. Broad Stone of Honour. Lond., 1844–48. 3 v. 4620 & 12900–
CONTENTS:—1, Godefridus.—2, Tancredus.—3, Morus.
Dilke, C. W. Papers of a Critic. Lond., 1875. 2 v. 8°. . . . 26765–
CONTENTS:—1, Pope's writings; Lady Mary W. Montagu; Swift, etc.—2, Junius; Wilkes; Grenville, etc.; Burke.
Dimitri Roudine. Turgénief, I. S. N. Y., 1873. 16°. (2 copies.) 24860–
Dingelstedt, F. The Amazon: [a novel.] N. Y., 1880. 16°. . 24175
Dippold, G. T. Brunhild. By E. Geibel. Transl. [in meter]. Bost., 1879. 26065
Discoveries (and Inventions) of the 19th Century. Routledge, R. Lond., 1876. 12°. 29929
—— *See, also,* **Industrial** Arts (& *references*).
Diseases of Modern Life. Richardson, B. W. N. Y., 1876. 12°. . 29995
Disraeli, B., *earl of Beaconsfield.* Alroy; Sybil. Lond., [1870]. 16°. 24248
—— Henrietta Temple; Tancred. Lond., [1870]. 12°. . . . 24250
—— *Same.* N. Y. [& Lond.], 1878. 16°. 24249
—— Lord George Bentinck: a biography. Lond., 1852. 8°. . . 23068
—— [Novels.] N. Y. [Lond., 1878.] 10 v. 16°. 24238–
CONTENTS:—(1,) Alroy; Ixion in Heaven; Infernal Marriage; Popanilla.—(2,) Coningsby.—(3,) Contarini Fleming; Rise of Iskander.—(4,) Henrietta Temple.—(5,) Lothair.—(6,) Sybil.—(7,) Tancred.—(8,) Venetia.—(9,) Vivian Grey.—(10,) Young Duke; Count Alarcos.

Disraeli, B., *earl of Beaconsfield.* Speeches on the Conservative Policy of the last 30 years. Lond., [1869]. 16°. 27222
—— Venetia; Contarini Fleming. Lond., [1870]. 16°. 24251
—— Vivian Grey; Ixion in Heaven; The Infernal Marriage; Popanilla; Count Alarcos. Lond., [1870]. 12°. 24252
—— Young Duke; Coningsby. Lond., [1870]. 16°. 24253
—— *Brandes, G.* Lord Beaconsfield: a study. N. Y., 1880. 12°. . 22897
—— [*Hill, F. H.*] Political Adventures of Lord Beaconsfield. N. Y., [1878]. 16°. 22851
—— *Hitchman, F.* Public Life of Earl Beaconsfield. Lond., 1879. 2 v. 23072–
—— *McGilchrist, J.* Life of Disraeli. N. Y., [1869]. 16°. . . . 22850
—— *O'Connor, T. P.* Lord Beaconsfield: a biography. Lond., 1879. 12°. 22898
—— Punch. Benj. Disraeli, Earl of Beaconsfield, K. G.; in 100 cartoons from "Mr. Punch." Lond., 1878. 4°. . . . . ——
—— Benjamin Disraeli, Earl of Beaconsfield: a biography. Lond. 22849
—— *See, also,* **Kebbel, T. E.,** 'Eng. Statesmen' (22884); **Stephen, L.,** 'Hours in a Lib.', v. 2 (26934).

Disraeli, I. Life and Reign of Charles I., King of England. Lond., 1851. 2 v. 8°. 23014–
—— *Corney, B.* Curiosities of Literature, by I. D'Israeli, illustrated. Lond., 1838. 12°. 18566

Distinguished Persons in Russian Society. Transl. from the German by F. E. Bunnètt. Lond., 1873. 12°. 23614

Distracted Young Preacher. Hardy, T. N. Y., 1879. 16°. . . 24924

Dita. Majendie, M. E. N. Y., 1877. 16°. 24632

Dix, W. G. The American State and American Statesmen. Bost., 1876. 12°. 21333

Dixon, C. Rural Bird Life. Lond., 1880. 12°. 29337

Dixon, W. H. Her Majesty's Tower. Lond., 1869–'71. 4 v. 8°. 21769–
—— History of Two Queens: Catharine of Aragon; Anne Boleyn. Lond., 1873–4. 4 v. 8°. 23005–

Dixwell, J. *Warren, I. P.* (*In* 'The Three Judges.') . . . 22627

Dobell, S. T. Poetical Works. With memoir by J. Nichol. Lond., 1875. 2 v. 12°. 26092–
—— Life and Letters of. Ed. by E. J. Lond., 1878. 2 v. 8°. . 23891–

Dobson, A. Hogarth. Lond. & N. Y., 1879. 12°. 23789

Doctor Basilius. Dumas, A. D. Lond., [1879]. 16°. . . . 24404

Doctor Ox. Verne, J. Bost., 1874. 16°. 24264

Dodd, H. P. The Epigrammatists. Lond., 1870. 12°. . . . 26925

Dodd, W. Three Weeks in Majorca. Lond., 1863. 12°. . . 21221

Dodd Family abroad. Lever, C. J. Lond., 1854. 8°. (2 copies.) 24257–

Dodge, Mary A., (*pseud.*, 'Gail Hamilton.') First Love is Best. Bost., 1877. 12°. 24232
—— Our Common School System. Bost., [1880]. 16°. . . . 28836
—— Sermons to the Clergy. Bost., 1876. 12°. 27223

Dodge, R. I. The Black Hills. N. Y., 1876. 12°. 21282
—— Plains of the Great West. N. Y., 1877. 8°. 21580

Dodsley, R. Select Collection of Old English Plays. 4th ed. Lond., 1874-76. 15 v. 12°. 26600-

CONTENTS:—1. The four elements; Calisto and Melibæa; Everyman; Hickscorner; The pardoner and the friar, by Heywood; The world and the child; God's promises, by Bale; The four P. P., by Heywood; Thersites.—2, Youth; Lusty Juventus, by Wever; Jack Juggler; Nice wanton; Jacob and Esau; The disobedient child, by Ingelend; Marriage of wit and science.—3, New custom; Ralph Roister Doister, by Udall; Gammer Gurton's needle, by Still; The trial of treasure; Like will to like, by Fulwell.—4, Damon and Pithias, by Edwards; Appius and Virginia; Cambyses, by Preston; The misfortunes of Arthur, by Hughes (and others); Jeronimo.—5, The Spanish tragedy, by Kyd; Cornelia, by Garnier; Soliman and Perseda; Life and death of Jack Straw.—6, The conflict of conscience, by Woodes; Rare triumphs of love and fortune; The three ladies of London, by Wilson; Three lords and three ladies of London, by Wilson; A knack to know a knave.—7, Tancred and Gismunda, by Wilmot; Wounds of civil war, by Lodge; Mucedorus; The two angry women of Abington, by Porter; Look about you.—8, Summer's last will and testament, by Nash; Downfall of Robert, Earl of Huntington, by Munday; Death of [the same], by Munday and Chettle; Contention between liberality and prodigality; Grim, the collier of Croydon.—9, How to choose a good wife from a bad, by Cooke; The return from Parnassus; Wily beguiled; Lingua; Miseries of enforced marriage, by Wilkins.—10, The revenger's tragedy, by Tourneur; The dumb knight, by Machin; The merry devil of Edmonton; Ram-alley, by Barry; The second maiden's tragedy; Englishmen for my money, by Haughton.—11, A woman is a weathercock, by Field; Amends for ladies, by Field; Green's tu quoque, or, The city gallant, by Cook; Albumazar, by Tomkins; The hog hath lost his pearl, by Tailor; The heir, by May.—12, The old couple, by May; A woman never vexed, by Rowley; The ordinary, by Cartwright; The London chanticleers; The shepherd's holiday, by Rutter; Fuimus Troes: the true Trojans, by Fisher; The lost lady, by Barclay.—13, A match at midnight, by Rowley; The city nightcap, by Davenport; The city-match, by Mayne; The queen of Arragon, by Habington; The antiquary, by Marmion.—14, The rebellion, by Rawlins; Lust's dominion, or, The lascivious queen; Andromana; Lady Alimony; The parson's wedding, by Killigrew.—15, Elvira, or, The worst not always true, by Digby; The marriage night, by Cary; The adventures of five hours, by Tuke; All mistaken, or, The mad couple, by Howard; Historia histrionica, by Wright; Index and glossary.

Döllinger, J. J. I. von. Reunion of the Churches. N. Y., 1872. 16°. 28536

Dog, British, Hist. of. Jesse, G. R. Lond., 1866. 2 v. 8°. . . 29497-

Doine. Murray, E. G. C. Lond., 1854. 12°. 27786

Dolbear, A. E. The Telephone. Bost., 1877. 16°. 29935

Dolliver Romance. Hawthorne, N. Bost., 1876. 12°. (2 copies.) 24505-

Dolly: a love story. Burnett, F. H. Phila., [1877]. 12°. . . 24153

Donaldson, J. W. Hist. of the Literature of Ancient Greece. (*See* **Müller, C. O.**)

Donne, J. *Lightfoot, J. B.* (*In* **Classic** Preachers.) 22112

Donne, W. B. Euripides. (Anc. Classics for Eng. Readers, v. 12.) 26838

—— Tacitus. (Ancient Classics for English Readers, v. 17.) . . 26843

Don Quixote, Der neue. Hackländer, F. W. von. Stuttg., 1876. 5 B. 16°. (Werke, B. 30-34.) 25814-

Doran, J. A Lady of the Last Century (Mrs. Elizabeth Montagu). Lond., 1873. 8°. 23404

—— Lives of the Queens of England of the House of Hanover. Lond., 1855. 2 v. 12°. 22931-

—— London in the Jacobite Times. Lond., 1877. 2 v. 8°. . . 21761-

—— Memoirs of Our Great Towns. Lond., 1878. 8°. . . . 21760

—— Saints and Sinners. Lond., 1868. 2 v. 12°. 28492-

Doré, G. London. By G. Doré and B. Jerrold. Lond., 1872. 4°. ——

—— Spain. By C. Davillier. Illust. [L. &] N. Y., 1876. 4°. . ——

—— Vivien, by Tennyson. Illust. N. Y., 1868. 2°. . . . ——

Dore, J. R. Old Bibles. Lond., 1876. 12°. 28526

Dorfcoquette (Die). Spielhagen, F. (Sämmtl. Werke, B. 8.) . . 25867

Dorothy Fox. Parr, L. Lond., 1871. 3 v. 16°. 24838-

Dorr, Julia C. R. Friar Anselmo, and other poems. N. Y., 1879. 26057

Douce, F. Illustrations of Shakspeare. New ed. Lond., 1839. 8°. 27054

Douglas, R. K. Confucianism and Taouism. Lond., 1879. 16°. 28581
Dove, A., *joint author. See* **Bruhns, C.,** 'Life of A. von Humboldt.'
Dowden, E. Shakspere. (Lit. Primers.) Lond., 1877. 16°. 26856 & 27025
—— Shakspere: a critical study. Lond., 1875. 8°. 27000
—— Southey. (English Men of Letters.) N. Y., 1880. 12°. . . 23344
—— Studies in Literature: 1789–1877. Lond., 1878. 12°. . . 26926

CONTENTS:—The French Rev. and Lit.; The transcendental movement and Lit.; The scientific movement and Lit.; Prose works of Wordsworth; Landor; Tennyson and Browning; Geo. Eliot; Lamennais; Quinet; Some French writers of verse, 1830—1877; Poetry of Hugo; Whitman.

Doyle, F. H. Lectures on Poetry. 2d ser. [With orig. poems.] Lond., 1877. 12°. 26286
Doyle, J. A. History of the United States. N. Y., 1876. 16°. . 20083
Drafts on my memory. Lennox, W. P. Lond., 1866. 2 v. 8°. . 23889–
Drake, N. Evenings in Autumn. Lond., 1822. 2 v. 16°. . . 18624–
Drake, S. A. Nooks and Corners of the New England Coast. Illust. N. Y., 1875. 8°. 21586
Drama. Cook, D. Book of the Play. Lond., 1876. 2 v. 12°. . 26557–
—— Ossoli, M. F. Art, Literature, and the D. (Works, v. 5.) . 27290
—— Matthews, J. B., *ed.* Comedies for Amateur Acting. N. Y., 1880. 16°. (*For contents see* **Matthews.**) 26526
—— Pollock, W. H. Amateur Theatricals. Lond., 1879. 12°. . 26519
—— *See, also,* **Actors & Acting; Plays; Stage.**
Dramatists of the Restoration. Maidment (J.) & Logan (W. H.). Edinb. & Lond., 1872–79. 14 v. 8°. (*For contents see* **Maidment.**) 26560–
Draper, J. W. Conflict between Religion and Science. N. Y., 1875. 29251
Drawing. Ruskin, J. The Laws of Fésole. N. Y., 1877. Part 1. 29844
—— Walker, W. Handbook of D. Lond., 1879. 12°. . . . 29825
Drayton, M. Complete Works. Lond., 1876. 3 v. 16°. . . 26058–
Drei einzige Töchter. Auerbach, B. Stuttg., 1875. 12°. . . . 25896
Dresden. Hawthorne, J. Saxon Studies. Bost., 1876. 12°. . . 21607
Dress. Blanc, A. A. P. C. Art in Ornament and D. N. Y., 1877. 29873
—— Oliphant, M. O. W. Phila., [1879]. 12°. 29782
—— *See, also,* **Manners & Customs.**
Drift from Two Shores. Harte, F. B. Bost., 1878. 16°. (2 copies.) 24489–
Dropped from the Clouds. Verne, J. (The Mysterious Island, v. 1.) 24277
Droz, G. Around a Spring. N. Y., 1873. 16°. 24233
—— Autour d'une source. Paris, 1876. 16°. 25628
—— Babolain. Paris, 1876. 16°. 25629
—— *Same.* Transl. N. Y., 1873. 16°. 24234
—— Une femme gênante. Paris, 1876. 16°. 25630
—— (*See* **Thomson, J.,** 'Public and Private Life of Animals.') . .
Drummond, R. B. Erasmus: his life and character. Lond., 1873. 2 v. 12°. 22101–
Drummond, Wm., *of Hawthornden.* Poetical Works. Lond., 1856. 26061
—— *Masson, D.* Lond., 1873. 12°. 23217
Drummond, Wm. H. Large Game and Natural Hist. of South and South-East Africa. Edinb., 1875. 8°. 29492
Dryden, J. [Select Poems.] Ed. by W. D. Christie. Oxf., 1878. . 26875

CONTENTS:—Stanzas on the death of Cromwell; Astræa redux; Annus mirabilis; Absalom and Achitophel; Religio laici; The hind and the panther.

Dryden, J. *See, also,* **Lowell, J. R.,** 'Among my Books,' v. 1 (3616); **Macaulay, T. B.,** 'Miscel. Writings,' Lond., 1871 (27406); **Masson, D.,** 'Three Devils' (27299).

Dublin Review. Lond. and D., 1836–79. 85 v. 8°. 18431–

Dublin University Magazine. D., 1833–73. 81 v. 8°. . . . 18138–

DuDeffand, Marie de V. C., *marquise,* Life of. Berry, M. (*In* 'Compar. View,' v. 2.) 6202

Dudevant, Amantine L. A. D., (*pseud., 'Geo. Sand.'*) Consuelo. Transl. Phil., [1870]. 16°. (2 cop.) 24916–

—— Countess of Rudolstadt; a sequel to "Consuelo." Phila., [1870]. 16°. (2 copies.) 24918–

—— My Sister Jeannie. Bost., 1874. 16°. 2348

—— Œuvres. Nouv. éd. Paris, 1866–79. 28 v. 16°. 25671–

Contents:—André.—Antonia.—La comtesse de Rudolstadt. 2 v.—Consuelo. 3 v.—Le dernier amour.—La dernière Aldini; Simon.—Elle et lui.—Un hiver a Majorque; Spiridion.—François le Champi.—Indiana.—Jacques.—Jean de la Roche.—Les maitres Mosaïstes.—La mare au diable.—Le marquis de Villemer.—Mauprat.—Mont-Revêche.—Nanon.—La petite Fadette.—Le secrétaire intime; Mattéa; La Vallée-Noire.—Les sept cordes de la lyre; Lettres à Marcie; Carl; Le Dieu inconnu; La fille d'Albano; Cléopatre; Fragment d'une lettre; Les fleurs de mai; Coup d'œil général sur Paris.—Teverino; Leone Leoni.—L'Uscoque; La fauvette du docteur; Sur la dernière publication de M. F. Lamennais; Quelques réflexions sur J. J. Rousseau.—Valentine.—Valvèdre.

—— Recollections. (*In* **Stoddard, R. H.,** 'Bric-à-Brac Series.') . 23261

—— Snow Man. Bost., 1872. 16°. 24920

—— Tower of Percemont. N. Y., 1877. 16°. 24076

—— (*See* **Thomson, J.,** 'Public and Private Life of Animals.')

Duff, Alex., Life of. Geo. Smith. N. Y., [1880]. 2 v. 8°. . . 22190–

Duff, M. E. G. Studies in European Politics. Edinb., 1866. 8°. . 20567

Contents:—Spain; Russia; Austria; Prussia; The Germanic Diet; Holland; Belgium.

Duff-Gordon, *Lady.* *See* **Gordon, Lucy A.**

Dufferin, *Earl of.* *See* **Blackwood, F. T. H.**

Dugdale, R. L. "The Jukes." N. Y., 1877. 12°. 29399

Dumas, A. D. Black Tulip; Captain Paul; Sicilian Bandit. Lond. 24419

—— Comte de Monte-Cristo. Paris, 1846. 6 v. en 3. 16°. . . 25631–

—— Count of Monte-Cristo. Lond. 16°. 24421

—— Half Brothers. Lond. 16°. 24422

—— Memoirs of a Physician. Lond. 16°. 24423

—— Nanon; The Two Dianas. Lond. 16°. 24424

—— Novels and Tales. Lond., [1879]. 19 v. 16°. 24400–

Contents;—1, Count of Monte-Cristo.—2, Three musketeers; Twenty years after.—3-4, Vicomte de Bragelonne.—5, Dr. Basilius; Conspirators.—6, Nanon; Two Dianas.—7, Ascanio; Chicot, the jester.—8, Memoirs of a physician.—9, Queen's necklace; Countess de Charny.—10, Taking the Bastile.—11, Half brothers.—12, Marguerite de Valois.—13, Black tulip; Captain Paul; Sicilian bandit.—14, Page of the Duke of Savoy; Forty-five guardsmen.—15, Chevalier de Maison Rouge; Twin captains.—16, Beau Tancrede; Watchmaker.—17, Ingénue; Isabel of Bavaria.—18, Russian gipsy; Regent's daughter.—19, Pauline; Catherine Blum.

—— Page; Forty-Five Guardsmen. Lond. 16°. 24420

—— Queen's Necklace; Countess de Charny. Lond. 16°. . . 24425

—— Taking the Bastile; or, Six years later. Lond. 16°. . . 24426

—— Trois mousquetaires. Paris, 1846–7. 16°. 25634

—— Vicomte de Bragelonne; or, Ten years later. Lond. 2 v. 16°. 24427–

—— Vingt ans après. Paris, 1876. 3 t. 16°. 25635–

—— *Fitzgerald, P.* Life and Adventures of D. Lond., 1873. 2 v. . 23402–

Du Moncel, T. Telephone, Microphone, and Phonograph. N. Y., 1879. 12°. 29936

Duncan, J. Colloquia Peripatetica: conversations . . . with Wm. Knight. Edinb., 1871. 16°. 23655

—— *Stuart, A. M.* Recollections of D. Edinb., 1872. 16°. . . 23654

Duncan, P. M., *editor.* Cassell's Natural History. Lond., [1879–80]. v. 1–3. 4°. 29579–

—— Transformations, or Metamorphoses, of Insects. By E. Blanchard. [With additions.] Lond., [1877]. 8°. 29499

Duncker, M. W. Hist. of Antiquity. Lond., 1877–79. v. 1–3. 8°. 20240–

Contents ;—1, Egypt ; The Semitic Nations.—2, Assyria ; Phœnicia ; Israel.—3, Assyria ; Israel ; Egypt ; Babylon ; Lydia.

Dunkle Stunde. Hackländer, F. W. von. Stuttg., 1866. 5 B. 16°. (Werke, B. 44–48.) 25821–

Duns, J. Memoir of Sir Jas. Y. Simpson. Edinb., 1873. 8°. . . 23542

Durand, Alice F., (*pseud.,* '*Henry Gréville.*') Ariadne: a novel. N. Y., 1878. 16°. 24082

—— L' Expiation de Savéli. Paris, 1876. 16°. 25638

Durant, G. Hygiene of the Voice. N. Y., 1879. 12°. . . . 29802

Durch Nacht zum Licht. Spielhagen, F. ('Problematische Naturen,' Th. 2.) 25861

Durfort-Duras, C. de K. de. *Sainte-Beuve, C. A.* (*In* 'Portraits of Celeb. Women.') 23643

During my Apprenticeship. Reuter, F. Phila., 1871. 8°. . . 24681

Dutcher, S. Minority or Proportional Representation. N. Y., 1872. 29091

Dutchman's Fireside. [Paulding, J. K.] N. Y., 1831. 2 v. 12°. . 17482–

Dutton, W. E. History of the Crusades. Lond., 1877. 12°. . 20105

Dwyer, F. Franco-German War. (*See* **Borbstædt, A., & Dwyer.**)

Dyck, A. van. *Head, P. R.* (Illust. Biographies of the Great Artists.) Lond. & N. Y., 1879. 12°. 23780

Dyer, J. Poetical Works. With memoir and crit. diss. by G. Gilfillan. Edinb., 1858. 8. 26321

Dyer, T. F. T. British Popular Customs. Lond., 1876. 12°. . 20806

—— English Folk-lore. Lond , 1880. 12°. 27668

Dyer, T. H. Modern Europe. Lond., 1877. 5 v. 8°. . . . 20560–

Eagle's Nest. Ruskin, J. N. Y., 1873. 12°. 29830

Ear (The). *See* **Hearing.**

Earle, J. C. English Premiers. Lond., 1871. 2 v. 12°. . . . 22882–

Contents :—1. Walpole ; Walpole and Lord Cartaret ; Henry Pelham and the Duke of Newcastle ; Earl of Chatham and Lord Bute ; Chatham, Grenville, and Rockingham ; Lord North ; C. J. Fox.—2, Wm. Pitt ; Pitt and Addington ; Grenville, Portland, and Perceval ; Liverpool anu Canning ; Duke of Wellington ; Earl Grey ; Melbourne and Peel.

Early Chroniclers of Europe. Lond. 2 v. 12°. 20471–

Contents :—England, J. Gairdner.—France, G. Masson.

Earnest Trifler. [Sprague, M. A.] Bost., 1880 [1879]. 16°. (2 cop.) 24858–

Earth. Dawkins, W. B. Limits of our Knowledge of the E. (*In* **Owens College** Ess. and Ad.) 27412

—— Dawson, J. W. Story of the E. and Man. N. Y., 1873. 16°. . 29417

—— Marsh, G. P. E. as modified by Human Action. N. Y., 1874. 29574

—— *See, also,* **Geography ; Geology ; Nature.**

East (The). Bodenstedt, F. M. Morning-Land. Lond., 1851 and '53. 2 series. 4 v. 12°. 21724–

—— Hackländer, F. W. von. Reise in den Orient. Stuttg., 1875. 2 B. 16°. (Werke, B. 8–9.) 25803–

East. *See, also,* **Levant** ; *names of countries, etc.*
East Indian Archipelago, Travels in. Bickmore, A. S. Lond., 1868. 21944
Eastern Question. Argyll, G. J. D. Lond., [1879]. 2 v. 12°. . 20487–
—— Campbell, G. Lond., 1876. 12°. 20493
Eastlake, Elizabeth R. Hist. of Our Lord. *See* **Jameson, A. M.**
Eastwick, E. B. Venezuela. Lond., 1868. 8°. 21808
Eaton, D. B. Civil Service in Great Britain. N. Y., 1880 [1879]. 8°. 21140
Ebers, G. M. Ægyptische Königstochter. Stuttg. & Leipz., 1880. 25872
—— Daughter of an Egyptian King. Transl. by H. Reed. Phila., 1871. 12°. 3041
—— Egyptian Princess. From the Ger. by Eleanor Grove. Leipz., 1871. 16°. (*Same as the preceding.*) 24429
—— Homo sum: Roman. Stuttg. & Leipz., 1880. 12°. . . . 25873
—— *Same.* [Transl.] by Clara Bell. Lond., [1878]. 2 v. 12°. . 24465–
—— — *Same.* N. Y., 1880. 16°. 24430
—— The Sisters: a romance. Leipz., 1880. 16°. (2 copies.) . . 24431–
—— Uarda: Roman. Stuttg. & Leipz., 1879. 12°. 25874
—— *Same.* [Transl.] N. Y., 1880. 2 v. 16°. (2 cop.) . . . 24433–
Ecclesiastical Hist. Maclear (G. F.) & Merivale (C.). Conversion of the West. Lond., [1878]. 4 v. 16°. 28494–
Contents:—1, The Celts.—2, The English.—3, The Northmen.—4, The Continental Teutons. (v. 1-3 by Maclear; v. 4 by Merivale.)
—— Merivale, C. Four lectures on Early Church Hist. [L. &] N. Y., [1879]. 12°. 28445
Contents:—St. Ambrose, and the union of the Chr. Ch. with the state; St. Augustine; St. Leo the Great, and the rise of the papacy; St. Gregory, and the early missions of the church.
—— Ordericus Vitalis. Ecc. Hist. of England and Normandy. Lond., 1853-56. 4 v. 12°. 28462–
—— Rawlinson, G., *and others.* Heathen World and St. Paul. Lond., [1878]. 4 v. 16°. (*For contents see* **Heathen World.**) . . 28498–
—— Robertson, J. C. Hist. of the Christian Church, A.D. 64–1517. Lond., 1874–5. 8 v. 16°. 28454–
—— Smith, P. The Student's Ecc. Hist. N. Y., 1879 ['78]. 12°. . 28444
See, also, **Christianity; England,** *Ch. of;* **Fathers** *(of the Ch.)*; **Huguenots; Missions; Prot. Ep. Ch.; Puritanism; Reformation; Rom. Cath. Ch.; Scotland,** *Ch. of.*
Ecclesiastical Reform. Shipley, O. Lond., 1873. 12°. . . . 28491
Echoes of the Foot-hills. Harte, F. B. Bost., 1875. 16°. . . 26072
Echoes from Mist-land. Forestier, A. Chic., 1877. 12°. . . 27711
[**Eckardt, J.**] Russia before and after the War. Lond., 1880. 8°. . 20613
Eclectic Magazine. N. Y., 1844–79. 93 v. 8°. 13562–
—— *Same.* v. 1–71. 13752–
Economic Studies. Bagehot, W. Lond., 1880. 8°. 29166
Eddas. Anderson, R. B. Norse Mythology. Chic., 1875. 12°. . 27715
—— — Younger Edda. Chic., 1880. 12°. (*For contents see* **Anderson.**) 27707
Eden, F. The Nile without a Dragoman. 2d ed. Lond., 1871. 16°. 21245
Edgeworth, R. L. Memoirs; begun by himself, and concluded by his daughter, Maria Edgeworth. Lond., 1820. 2 v. 8°. . 18599–
Edinburgh. Wilson, D. Reminiscences of Old E. Ed., 1878. 2 v. 21266–
Edinburgh Review. E. and N. Y., 1802–79. v. 1–17, 19–150. 8°. . 11154–
—— *Same.* v. 1–130. 11051–

Edinburgh Review. Index to v. 1–20 (2 copies); and 21–50. . . ——
—— Selections from. Lond., 1833, and Paris, 1835. 7 v. 8°. . . 11293–
Edkins, J. Religion in China. Bost., 1878. 8°. 28563
Education. Bain, A. E. as a Science. N. Y., 1879. 12°. . . 29265
—— Blackie, J. S. On Self-culture. N. Y., 1874. 16°. . . . 27386
—— Brackett, Anna C., *editor*. E. of American Girls. N. Y., 1874. 28823
—— Clarke, E. H. Building of a Brain. Bost., 1874. 16°. . . 28827
—— — Sex in E. Bost., 1873. 16°. 28828
—— Dodge, M. A. Our Common School System. Bost., [1880]. 16°. 28836
—— Helps, A. (*In* 'Friends in Council,' 1st ser., v. 1.) . . . 27250
—— Hill, T. True Order of Studies. N. Y., 1876. 12°. . . . 28832
—— Huxley, T. H. University E. (*In his* 'Amer. Addresses.'). . 29300
—— Kingsley, C. Health and E. Lond., 1874. 12°. . . . 29979
—— Lawrence, E. (*In* **First Cent.** of the Republic.) . . . 21520
—— Lubbock, J. Addresses, political and educational. Lond., 1879. 27411
—— Mullinger, J. B. Schools of Charles the Great. Lond., 1877. 8°. 28839
—— Porter, N. American Colleges and the Amer. Public. New Haven, 1870. 12°. 9254
—— — *Same.* New ed.; with after-thoughts on college and school education. N. Y., [1878]. 12°. 28837
—— Quincy, J. P. Coercion in the later stages of E. (*In* 'Protection of Majorities,' etc.) 29093
—— Roscoe, H. E. Original Research as a Means of E. (Owens Coll. Ess. and Ad.) 27412
—— Thompson, D. W. Wayside Thoughts on E. Edinb., 1868. 12°. 28834
—— Wiese, L. English E. . . . in 1876. [Lond. &] N. Y., 1879. 12°. 28838
See, also, **Books; Colleges; Culture; Germany,** *Education;* **Universities; Young** Men.
Edward II.: [a play.] Marlowe, C. Oxf., 1879. 16°. . . . 26525
Edward III., *king of England. Warburton, W. P.* (Epochs of Mod. Hist.) Lond., 1875. 16°. 20459
Edward the Black Prince, Life of. Creighton, L. Lond., 1876. 16°. 22446
Edward, Thos., Life of. Smiles S. N. Y., 1877. 12°. . . . 23565
Edwards, Amelia B. A Thousand Miles up the Nile. N. Y. & L., 1877. 8°. 21966
Edwards, Annie. Leah: a woman of fashion. N. Y., [1875]. 8°. 24648
Edwards, H. S. Life of Rossini. Lond., 1869. 8°. . . . 23846
Edwards, J. Catalogue of the Greek and Roman Coins in the Numismatic Collection of Yale College. N. H., 1880. 8°. 20379
Egan, T. S. Atta Troll, by H. Heine; transl. [in meter]. Lond., 1876. 12°. 26018
Eggleston, E. Circuit Rider. N. Y., 1874. 12°. 2993
—— End of the World: a love story. N. Y., [1872]. 16°. . . 24468
—— Hoosier School-Master. N. Y., [1871]. 16°. 24469
—— Mystery of Metropolisville. N. Y., [1873]. 12°. . . . 24470
—— Roxy. N. Y., 1878. 12°. 24471
Egglestone, W. M. Stanhope Memorials of Bp. Butler. Lond., 1878. 22187
Eginhard (*or* **Einhard).** Life of Charlemagne. Transl. by S. E. Turner. N. Y., 1880. 24°. 22506

Eginhard (*or* **Einhard).** *Same.* Karl the Great. Transl. by W. Glaister. Lond., 1877. 12°. 22505
Egleston, N. H. Villages and Village Life. N. Y., 1878. 12°. . 28881
Egypt. About, E. F. V. Le Fellah : souvenirs d'Égypte. Paris, 1873. 16°. 25620
—— Barker, J. Syria and E. under the last five Sultans of Turkey. Lond., 1876. 2 v. 8°. 23960–
—— Bartlett, S. C. From E. to Palestine. N. Y., 1879. 8°. . . 21843
—— Birch, S. E., to B. C. 300. N. Y., 1875. 16°. 20042
—— Brugsch, H. C. Hist. of E. under the Pharaohs. Lond., 1879. 2 v. 8°. 20247–
—— — True Story of the Exodus of Israel. Bost., 1880. 12°. . 20046
—— Duncker, M. W. (*In* 'Hist. of Antiquity,' v. 1 & 3.) . . . 20240–
—— Klunzinger, C. B. Upper Egypt. N. Y., 1878 [1877]. 8°. . 21849
—— Leland, C. G. Egyptian Sketch-book. Lond., 1873. 12°. . 21616
—— McCoan, J. C. Egypt as it is. N. Y., 1877. 8°. . . . 21844
—— Renouf, P. L. Religion of Ancient E. N. Y., 1880. 12°. . 28569
—— Taylor, J. B. E. and Iceland in the year 1874. N. Y., 1874. 16°. 21256
—— Warner, C. D. Mummies and Moslems. Hartf'd, 1876. 8°. . 21842
—— Zincke, F. B. E. of the Pharaohs and of the Khedivé. Lond., 1873. 8°. 21845
—— *See, also,* **East** (The) ; **Nile ; Pyramids ; Suez.**
Egyptian Princess. Ebers, G. M. Leipz., 1871. 16°. . . . 24429
Egyptian Sepulchres and Syrian Shrines. Beaufort, E. A. Lond., 1874. 12°. 21209
Eighteenth (The) Century. Lacroix, P. Lond., 1876. 8°. . . 20363
Einhard. *See* **Eginhard.**
Ekkehard. Scheffel, J. V. Leipz., 1872. 16°. 24853
Elam, C. Winds of Doctrine. Lond., 1876. 8°. 28165
Elderkin, J. Lotus Leaves. (*See* **Brougham, J., & Elderkin.**)
Election of Representatives. Hare, T. Lond., 1873. 16°. . . 29092
Elections. *See* **Government ; Politics ; Representation.**
Elective Franchise in the U. S. McMillan, D. C. N. Y., 1878. . 21331
Electoral Reform, Considerations relating to. Quincy, J. P. Bost., 1876. 12°. 29093
Electricity. Baile, J. Wonders of E. N. Y., 1872. 12°. . . 10135
—— Proctor, R. A. Electric Lighting. (*In* 'Rough Ways.') . . 29444
—— Tyndall, J. Lessons in E. Lond., 1876. 12°. 29314
—— *See, also,* **Telegraph ; Telephone.**
Elijah the Prophet. Taylor, W. M. N. Y., 1876. 12°. . . . 28650
Eliot, George, (*pseud. for Mrs.* Marian Evans Cross.)
—— Adam Bede. N. Y., 1874. 12°. (3 copies.) 24180–
—— Daniel Deronda. N. Y., 1876. 2 v. 12°. (5 copies.) . . 24184–
—— Felix Holt, the Radical. N. Y., 1878. 12°. 24194
—— Impressions of Theophrastus Such. N. Y., 1879. 12°. (2 cop.) 24195–
—— Legend of Jubal, and other poems. Bost., 1874. 16°. . . 26056
—— Middlemarch. N. Y., 1875. 2 v. 12°. (3 cop.) . . . 24197–
—— Mill on the Floss. N. Y., 1875. 12°. (2 copies.) . . . 24203–
—— Romola. N. Y., 1874. 12°. (4 copies.) 24205–

Eliot, George. Scenes of Clerical Life. (*And*) Silas Marner. N.Y. 24183
—— *Dowden, E.* (*In* 'Studies in Lit.') 26926
—— *Roslyn, G.* Geo. Eliot in Derbyshire: passages and people in [her] novels. Lond., 1876. 16°. 26919
Elizabeth, *queen of England,* The Youth of. Wiesener, L. Lond., 1879. 2 v. 12°. 22933–
Elizabeth Stuart, *queen of Bohemia,* Memoirs of. Benger, E. O. Lond., 1825. 2 v. 12°. 23680–
Elizabethan Demonology. Spalding, T. A. Lond., 1880. 12°. . 28042
Ella, J. Musical Sketches. Lond. & N. Y., 1878. 12°. . . . 29740
Ellacombe, H. N. Plant-lore and Garden-craft of Shakspeare. Exeter, [1878]. 8°. 27047
Elle et lui. Dudevant, A. L. A. D. Paris, 1869. 16°. . . . 25680
Ellicott, C. J. Revision of the New Test. N. Y., 1873. 12°. (*See* **Schaff, P.**) 28525
—— *editor.* New Testament Commentary. Lond. (v. 1) & N. Y., [1878–9]. 3 v. 8°. 28760–

Contents:—1, Mat., Mark & Luke, by E. H. Plumptre; John, by H. W. Watkins.—2, Acts, Plumptre; Romans, W. Sanday; I. Corinthians, T. T. Shore; II. Corinthians, Plumptre; Galatians, Sanday.—3, Ephesians, Philippians, and Colossians, A. Barry; Thessalonians, A. J. Mason; Timothy and Titus, H. D. M. Spence; Philemon, A. Barry; Hebrews, W. F. Moulton; James, E. G. Punchard; I. Peter, A. J. Mason; II. Peter, A. Plummer; John, W. M. Sinclair; Jude, A. Plummer; Revelation, W. B. Carpenter.

Elliott, E., the Corn-law Rhymer. Stirling, J. H. (*In* 'Jerrold,' etc.) 26917
Elocution. Bacon, A. M. Manual of Gesture. Chic., 1879. 12°. 27822
—— Bell, A. M. Elocutionary Manual. Lond., [1859]. 16°. . . 27823
—— Pitman, H. Hints on Lecturing, . . . E., [etc.] Lond, 1879. 27835
—— Plumptre, C. J. King's College Lectures on E. Lond., 1876. 27820
—— *See, also,* **Rhetoric** (*and references*).
Elwood, Anne K. C. Memoirs of the Literary Ladies of England. Lond., 1843. 2 v. 12°. 18541–
Elze, C. Essays on Shakespeare. Lond., 1874. 8°. 27046
Embalming. Richardson, B. W. (*In* 'A Ministry of Health.') . 29996
Embryology. Haeckel, E. H. The Evolution of Man. N. Y., 1879. 2 v. 12°. 29383–
—— *See, also,* **Biology.**
Emerson, R. W. Letters and Social Aims. Bost., 1876. 12°. (2 cop.) 27224–
—— Memoirs of Marg. Fuller Ossoli. (*See* **Ossoli,** 'Works,' v. 1–2.) 27286–
—— Parnassus. [A selection of poetry.] Bost., 1875. 12°. . . 26120
Emilia Galotti. Lessing, G. E. Leipz., 1868. 16°. 26512
Emma Corbett. [Pratt, S. J.] Lond. 3 v. 16°. 17792–
Emotions. McCosh, J. N. Y., 1880. 12°. 28170
Enchanted Moccasins. Mathews, C. N. Y., 1877. 12°. . . 24800
Enchiridion. Quarles, F. Lond., 1856. 16°. 27263
Encyclopædists, Diderot and the. Morley, J. Lond., 1878. 2 v. 8°. 23423–
Encyclopedias. Appletons' Annual Cyclopædia, for 1861–79. N. Y., 1864–80. 19 v. 8°. . . . . ——
—— — Index to v. 1–15, 1861–75. N. Y., 1876. 8°. . . . . . ——
—— *See, also,* **Biography,** *Collections.*
End of the World. Eggleston, E. N. Y., [1872]. 16°. . . . 24468
Endless Punishment. *See* **Future** Punishment.

Energy. *See* **Force.**
Engel, C. Musical Instruments. N. Y., 1876. 12°. 29761
—— Musical Myths and Facts. Lond., 1876. 2 v. 8°. . . . 29794-
Engineers, English, Personal Recollections of. Lond., 1868. 8°. . 23537
England. Blanc, J. J. L. Letters on E. 2d series. Lond., 1867. 2 v. 12°. 20807-
—— Escott, T. H. S. England: her people, polity, and pursuits. N. Y., 1880. 8°. 21143
—— Laugel, A. England, political and social. N. Y., 1874. 16°. . 20810
—— Longfellow, H. W. Poems of Places. E. (and Wales). v. 1–4. Bost., 1876. 4 v. 16°. 26440-
—— Maclear, G. F. The Celts. [*And*] The English. (Conversion of the West, v. 1–2.) Lond., [1878.] 16°. 28494-
—— Rodenberg, J. England, literary and social. Lond., 1875. 8°. 21142
—— *Art.* Graham, J. M. Historical view of literature and art in Gr. Brit., [1714 to 1837]. Lond., 1871. 8°. 26777
—— *Biography.* Earle, J. C. English Premiers, from Walpole to Peel. Lond., 1871. 2 v. 12°. 22882-
—— — Kebbel, T. E. English Statesmen since the Peace of 1815. Lond., 1868. 12°. 22884-
—— — Walford, E. Tales of Our Great Families. Lond., 1877. 2 v. 12°. 22846-
England, *Church of.* Arnold, F. Our Bishops and Deans. Lond., 1875. 2 v. 8°. 22268-
—— — Arnold, M. Last Essays on Church and Religion. [L. &] N. Y., 1877. 12°. 28690
—— — Barry, A. Masters in English Theology. N. Y., 1877. 12°. 22111
—— — Classic Preachers of the Eng. Ch. (*See* **Classic** Preachers.)
—— — Doran, J. Saints and Sinners; or, In church and about it. Lond., 1868. 2 v. 12°. 28492-
—— — Perry, G. G. Hist. of the Ch. of E. N. Y., 1879. 8°. . . 28443
—— — Shipley, O., *editor.* Ecclesias. Reform: eight essays. Lond., 1873. 12°. 28491
—— *Civil Service.* Eaton, D. B. N. Y., 1880. 8°. 21140

Constitution and Laws.

—— Bagehot, W. The English Constitution. Bost., 1873. 12°. . 20883
—— Blackstone, W. Student's Blackstone, abr. and adapted to the present state of the law, by R. M. Kerr. Lond., 1879. 12°. 28848
—— Bryce, J. Judicature Act of 1873. (*In* **Owens College** Ess. & Ad.) 27412
—— Fonblanque, A. W. de. How we are governed. Lond., [1879]. 20885
—— Fulton, F. Manual of Constitutional Hist. Lond., 1875. 12°. 20884
—— Paterson, J. Liberty of the Subject and the laws of E. relating to the Security of the Person. Lond., 1877. 2 v. 12°. . 28854-
—— Smith, P. V. Hist. of the English Institutions. Phila., 1874. . 20064
—— Stubbs, W. Constitutional Hist. of E. Oxf'd, 1874–78. 3 v. . 20880-
—— Wilson, R. K. Hist. of Modern English Law. Lond., 1875. . 20067

England. *Description and Travel.*

—— Burroughs, J. An October abroad. (*In* 'Winter Sunshine.') . 29325
—— Doran, J. Memories of Our Great Towns. Lond., 1878. 8°. . 21760
—— Hawthorne, N. English Note-books. Bost., 1876. 12°. . . 24503
—— [Jefferies, R.] Wild Life in a Southern County. Bost., 1879. . 29332
—— Jennings, L. J. Field Paths and Green Lanes: Surrey and Sussex. N. Y., 1878. 12°. 21612
—— Rimmer, A. Ancient Streets and Homesteads. Lond., 1877. . 21980
—— Walford, E. Pleasant Days in Pleasant Places. Lond., 1879. . 21262
—— Winter, W. The Trip to E. Bost., 1879. 16°. 21682

History.

—— Creasy, E. S. Lond., 1869–70. v. 1–2. 8°. 21002–
—— (*to* 1154) Henry of Huntingdon, Chronicle of. Also, the Acts of Stephen. Lond., 1853. 12°. 20804
—— (*to* 1189) Armitage, E. S. Childhood of the English Nation. N. Y., 1877. 12°. 20842
—— (*to* 1307) Matthew of Westminster. Flowers of Hist. Lond., 1853. 2 v. 12°. 20802–
—— (*to* 1307) Pearson, C. H. Early and Middle Ages. Lond., 1861. 21091
—— — *Same.* [2d ed.] Lond., 1867. 2 v. 8°. 21092–
—— (*to* 1327) Longman, W. Lectures. Lond., 1863. 8°. . . . 21088
—— (*to* 1360) Gairdner, J. (Early Chroniclers of Europe.) Lond., [1879.] 12°. 20471
—— (*to* 1714) Annals of E. Oxf., 1865, '62–3. 3 v. 16°. . . . 20853–
Contents:—1, B. C. 57–A. D. 1399. 2, 1399–1649. 3, 1649–1714.
—— (*to* 1805) Hozier, H. M. Invasions of England. Lond., 1876. 2 v. 8°. 21052–
—— (*to* 1815) Guest, M. J. Lectures. Lond., 1879. 16°. . . . 20820
—— (*to* 1837) Dickens, C. J. H. A Child's Hist. of E. Bost., 1873. 20840
—— (*to* 1837) Guizot, F. P. G. Lond., 1877–79. 3 v. 8°. . . 21160–
—— (*to* 1854) Green, J. R., *editor.* Readings from English Hist. N. Y., 1879. 12°. 20841
—— (*to* 1863) Vaughan, R. Revolutions in Eng. Hist. Lond., 1859–63. 3 v. 8°. 21094–
Contents:—1, Rev. of Race. 2, Rev. in Religion. 3, [Political, etc.].
—— (*to* 1867) Knight, C. Popular Hist. Lond., [1862–68]. 8 v. 8°. 21080–
—— (*to* 1872) Thompson, E. N. Y., 1873. 16°. 20079
—— (*to* 1875) Creighton, M., *editor.* Epochs of English Hist. Lond., 1879. 16°. (*For contents see* **Epochs.**) 20851
—— (449–1066) Lappenberg, J. M. Hist. of E. under the Anglo-Saxon Kings. Lond., 1845. 2 v. 8°. 21089–
—— (449–1272) Freeman, E. A. Norman Conquest of E. Oxf., 1870–79. 6 v. 8°. 5006–
—— — *Same.* Rev. Amer. ed. Oxf. & N. Y., 1873–79. 6 v. 8°. (*For contents see* **Freeman.**) 20920–
—— (449–1837) Bright, J. F. An English Hist. Lond., 1875–7. 3 v. 20844–
—— — *Same.* A Hist. of England. [L. &] N. Y., 1878. 3 v. 16°. 20847–

England. *History (continued).*

—— (449–1874) Green, J. R. Short Hist. of the English People. Lond., 1874(–5). 12°. (3 copies.) 20960–

—— — — *Same.* N. Y., 1878(–9). 8°. (2 copies.) 20963–

—— — — Hist. of the English People. N. Y., 1878–80. 4 v. 8°. (2 copies.) (*For contents see* **Green.**) 20965–

—— (732–1201) Roger of Hoveden, Annals of. Lond., 1853. 2 v. . 20800–

—— (1066–1818) Sanford, J. L. Estimates of the English Kings. Lond., 1872. 12°. 20821

—— (1135–1327) Stubbs, W. Early Plantagenets. N. Y., [1876]. . 20455

—— (1154–1603) Forster, J. Plantagenets and Tudors. (*In* 'Histor. and Biog. Essays,' v. 1.) 27320

—— (1154–1500) Pauli, R. Pictures of Old E. Cambr. & L., 1861. . 20850

—— (1300–1400) Pearson, C. H. English Hist. in the 14th Century. Lond., 1876. 16°. 20066

—— (1327–1377) Warburton, W. P. Edward III. Lond., 1875. 16°. 20459

—— (1360–1560) *See* **Reformation,** *England.*

—— (1377–1485) Gairdner, J. Houses of Lancaster and York. Lond., 1874. 16°. 20451

—— (1452–1485) Gairdner, J. Life and Reign of Richard III. Lond., 1878. 12°. 20813

—— (1519)–1603) Creighton, M. The Age of Elizabeth. N. Y., 1876. 16°. 20452

—— (1603–1616) Gardiner, S. R. Hist. of E. Lond., 1863. 2 v. 8°. 21120–

—— (1603–1660) Gardiner, S. R. First Two Stuarts and the Puritan Revolution. Bost., 1876. 16°. 20454

—— (1603–1760) Ranke, F. L. von. Oxf'd, 1875. 6 v. 8°. (2 cop.) 21040–

—— (1617–1623) Gardiner, S. W. Prince Charles and the Spanish Marriage. Lond., 1869. 2 v. 8°. 21122–

—— (1619–1682) Warburton, E. B. G. Prince Rupert and the Cavaliers. Lond., 1849. 3 v. 8°. 23018–

—— (1624–1628) Gardiner, S. R. Hist. of E. under the Duke of Buckingham and Charles I. Lond., 1875. 2 v. 8°. . . 21124–

—— (1625–1649) Bisset, A. Struggle for Parliamentary Government. Lond., 1877. 2 v. 8°. 21058–

—— (1628–1637) Gardiner, S. R. Personal Government of Charles I. Lond., 1877. 2 v. 8°. 21126–

—— (1640–1674) Bayne, P. Chief Actors in the Puritan Revolution. Lond., 1878. 8°. 23013

—— (1641–1658) Forster, J. Debates on the Grand Remonstrance; (*and*) Civil Wars and Cromwell. (*In* 'Histor. and Biogr. Essays,' v. 1.) 27320

—— (1649–1653) Bisset, A. Hist. of the Commonwealth. Lond., 1864–67. 2 v. 8°. 21056–

—— (1649–1658) Vaughan, R. Protectorate of Oliver Cromwell. Lond., 1838. 2 v. 8°. 21000–

—— (1678–1697) Hale, E. Fall of the Stuarts and Western Europe. N. Y., [1876]. 16°. 20453

—— (1700–1800) Lecky, W. E. H. Hist. of E. in the 18th Century. N. Y., 1878. 2 v. 12°. 20926–

England. *History* (*continued*).

—— (1700–1850) Adams, W. H. D. English Party Leaders and English Parties. Lond., 1878. 2 v. 8°. 21054–

—— (1702–1714) Burton, J. H. Hist. of the Reign of Queen Anne. Edinb., 1880. 3 v. 8°. 21060–

—— — Morris, E. E. The Age of Anne. N. Y., [1877.] 16°. . 20456

—— (1760–1820) Jesse, J. H. Life and Reign of George III. Lond., 1867. 3 v. 8°. 23037–

—— (1815–) Walpole, S. Hist. of E. from 1815. Lond., 1878–80. v. 1–3. 8°. 21097–

—— (1830–1874) Molesworth, W. N. Lond., 1874. 3 v. 12°. . . 20822–

—— (1837–1869) Disraeli, B. Speeches on the Conservative Policy of the last 30 years. Lond., [1869]. 16°. 27222

—— (1837–) McCarthy, J. Hist. of Our Own Times. Chic., [1879]. v. 1–2 in 1. 12°. 20825

—— (1867–1874) Harrison, F. Studies of Political Crises. (*In* 'Order and Progress.') 29087

—— *Parliament.* [Lucy, H. W.] Men and Manner in P. Lond., 1874. 12°. 20811

—— — Palgrave, R. F. D. The House of Commons. Lond., 1869. 20812

—— — *See, also,* **Parliament**; **Parliamentary** Reform.

—— *Princesses of.* Green, M. A. E. W. Lives [1066–1670]. Lond., 1850–55. 6 v. 12°. 22920–

—— — Strickland, A. Last Four Princesses of the House of Stuart. Lond., 1872. 12°. 22926

—— *Queens of.* Doran, J. Queens of the House of Hanover. Lond., 1855. 2 v. 12°. 22931–

See, also, **Antiquities,** *English;* **English** Literature; **London; Oxford; Selborne; Twickenham;—Ireland; Scotland; Scottish** Border; **Wales.**

England's Antiphon. Macdonald, G. [Lond., 1868.] 12°. . . 26125

English Conferences. Renan, J. E. Bost., 1880. 12°. . . . 28570

English Divines, Lives of. Teale, W. H. Lond., 1848. 16°. . . 22110

English Folk-lore. Dyer, T. F. T. Lond., 1880. 12°. . . . 27668

English Humour, Hist. of. L'Estrange, A. G. K. Lond., 1878. 2 v. 26938–

English Humourists. Thackeray, W. M. Lond., 1876. 12°. . . 24895

English Literature. Bagehot, W. Literary Studies. Lond., 1879. 2 v. 8°. (*For contents see* **Bagehot.**) 26767–

—— Bascom, J. Philosophy of Eng. Lit. N. Y., 1874. 12°. . . 26912

—— Brooke, S. A. (Lit. Primers.) Lond., 1877. 16°. . . . 26855

—— Dennis, J. Studies in Eng. Lit. Lond., 1876. 12°. . . . 26915

—— Dilke, C. W. The Papers of a Critic. Lond., 1875. 2 v. 8°. 26765–

—— Graham, J. M. Literature and art in Gr. Britain, [1714 to 1837]. Lond., 1871. 8°. 26777

—— Masson, D. Scottish Influence in Brit. Lit. (*In* 'Wordsworth.') 27298

—— Minto, W. Manual of Eng. Prose Lit. Edinb., 1872. 12°. . 26913

—— Morley, H. First Sketch of Eng. Lit. Lond., [1873]. 16°. . 26911

—— — *editor.* Cassell's Library of Eng. Lit. Lond., [1876–80]. 4 v. 26368–

CONTENTS:—Shorter Eng. Poems.—Illust. of Eng. Religion.—Eng. Plays.—Shorter works in Eng. Prose.

—— Stephen, L. (*In* 'Hist. of Eng. Thought.') 28200

English Literature. Taine, H. A. History of Eng. Lit. Abridged. N. Y., 1872. 12°. 26914

—— *See, also,* **Drama; Literature** (*and ref.*); **Poetry; Poets.**

English Men of Letters. Morley, J., *editor.* N. Y., 1878–80. 19 v. 23332–

CONTENTS:—1, Johnson, by L. Stephen.—2, Gibbon, J. C. Morison.—3, Scott, R. H. Hutton.—4, Shelley, J. A. Symonds.—5, Hume, T. H. Huxley.—6, Goldsmith, W. Black.—7, Defoe, W. Minto.—8, Burns, J. C. Shairp.—9, Spenser, R. W. Church.—10, Thackeray, A. Trollope.—11, Burke, editor.—12, Milton, M. Pattison.—13, Southey, E. Dowden.—14, Chaucer, A. W. Ward.—15, Bunyan, J. A. Froude.—16, Cowper, G. Smith.—17, Hawthorne, H. James.—18, Pope, L. Stephen.—19, Byron, J. Nichol.

English Men of Science. Galton, F. N. Y., 1875. 12°. 29400

English Party Leaders. Adams, W. H. D. Lond., 1878. 2 v. 8°. 21054–

English Popular Leaders. Maurice, C. E. Lond., 1872–5. 2 v. 12°. 22940–

English Portraits. Sainte-Beuve, C. A. Lond., 1875. 12°. . . 22885

English Positivism. Taine, H. A. Lond., 1873. 16°. 28092

English Radical Leaders. Hinton, R. J. N. Y., 1875. 16°. . . 22441

English Religion, Illustrations of. Morley, H. Lond., [1878]. 4°. 26371

English Seamen under the Tudors. Bourne, H. R. F. Lond., 1868. 22942

English Songs from Foreign Tongues. Ricord, F. W. N. Y., 1879. 26164

English Statesmen. Higginson, T. W. N. Y., 1875. 16°. . . 22440

English Statesmen since 1815. Kebbel, T. E. Lond., 1868. 12°. . 22884

English Thought, Hist. of. Stephen, L. N. Y., 1876. 2 v. 8°. . 28200–

Engravers and their works. Clement, C. E. Bost., 1879. 12°. . 29791

Engraving. Ruskin, J. Ariadne Florentina: 6 lectures. N. Y., 1874–5. 12°. 29831

Enigmas of Life. Greg, W. R. Bost., 1874. 12°. 27292

Ennemoser, J. History of Magic. Lond., 1854. 2 v. 12°. . . 28048–

Entomology. *See* **Insects.**

Epic of Hades. [Morice, L.] Bost., 1879. 16°. 26097

Epictetus. Discourses; with the Encheiridion and fragments. With notes, life, [etc.] by G. Long. Lond., 1877. 12°. . . . 26805

—— *Farrar, F. W.* (*In* 'Seekers after God.') 23682

Epigrammatists (The). Dodd, H. P. Lond., 1870. 12°. . . 26925

Episodes of Fiction. Edinb., 1870. 8°. 24649

Episodes of Insect Life. [Budgen, L. M.] Lond., 1849–51. 3 v. 8°. 29500–

Epochs of Ancient History. Cox (G. W.) & Sankey (C.), *editors.* . 20435–

CONTENTS:—The Greeks and the Persians, by G. W. Cox.—Roman Hist., the early empire, W. W. Capes.—The Roman Triumvirates, C. Merivale.—Early Rome, W. Ihne.—Roman Empire of the 2d cent.; or, Age of the Antonines, W. W. Capes.—The Gracchi, Marius, and Sulla, A. H. Beesley.—The Athenian Empire, G. W. Cox.

Epochs of English History. Creighton, M., *editor.* Lond., 1879. 16°. 20851

CONTENTS:—Early England (to 1066), by F. Y. Powell; Eng. a continental power (1066–1216), L. Creighton; The rise of the people (1215–1485), J. Rowley; The Tudors and the Reformation (1485–1603), editor; Struggle against absolute monarchy (1603–1688), B. M. Cordery; Settlement of the constitution (1688–1778), J. Rowley; Eng. during the Amer. and European wars (1765–1820), O. W. Tancock; Mod. Eng. (1820–1875), O. Browning.

Epochs of History. *See* **Epochs** of Ancient Hist.; **Epochs** of Modern Hist.

Epochs of Modern History. Morris, E. E., *editor.* 20448–

CONTENTS:—Era of the Prot. Revolution, by F. Seebohm.—Crusades, G. W. Cox.—Thirty Years' War, S. R. Gardiner.—Houses of Lancaster and York, J. Gairdner.—Age of Elizabeth, M. Creighton.—Fall of the Stuarts, E. Hale.—The First Two Stuarts and the Puritan Revolution, S. R. Gardiner.—Early Plantagenets, W. Stubbs.—Age of Anne, E. E. Morris.—Beginning of the Middle Ages, R. W. Church.—Normans in Europe, A. H. Johnson.—Edward III., W. Warburton.—War of Amer. Independence, J. M. Ludlow.

Equality, Liberty, Fraternity. Stephen, J. F. N. Y., 1873. 12°. . 28856

Erasmus, D. In Praise of Folly. Lond. 16°. 12910
—— *Drummond, R. B.* Lond., 1873. 2 v. 12°. 22101–
Erbin (Die). Mügge, T. Breslau, 1866. 16°. (Romane, B. 26.) . 25848
Erckmann (E.) & Chatrian (A.) Contes populaires. Paris, [1877]. 25639
—— Friend Fritz. New York, 1877. 12°. (2 copies). . . . 24437–
—— Histoire d'un paysan. Paris, 1871–'75. 4 t. 16°. . . . 25640–
—— Histoire du plébiscite. Paris, [1877]. 16°. 25645
—— *Same*, transl. N. Y., 1877. 16°. 24439
—— Histoire d'un sous-maître.—Les papiers de Madame Jeannette. —Les orateurs de mon village.—Le bon vieux temps.—La sentinelle perdue. Paris, 1871. 16°. 25644
Erectheus : a tragedy. Swinburne, A. C. Lond., 1876. 12°. . 26166
Erema. Blackmore, R. D. N. Y., 1877. 8°. 24304
Erich Randal. Mügge, T. Breslau, 1862. 4 B. (Romane, B. 9–12.) 25842–
Erlebtes. Hackländer, F. W. von. Stuttg., 1876. 2 B. 16°. (Werke, B. 25–26.) 25812
Ersilia. [Poynter, E. F.] N. Y., 1876. 16°. 24848
Erskine, Thos. Speeches. With mem. by E. Walford. Lond., 1870. 2 v. 8°. 27490–
Erskine, Thos., *of Linlathen.* Letters, 1800–1840. [Edinb. &] N. Y., 1877. 12°. 23612
Erskine, *Mrs.* **Thos.** Wyncote. N. Y., 1875. 16°. 24440
Escott, T. H. S. England. N. Y., 1880. 8°. 21143
Esthetics. *See* **Æsthetics.**
Etcher's Voyage of Discovery. Hamerton, P. G. Bost., 1876. 12°. 29328
Etching and Etchers. Hamerton, P. G. Bost., 1876. 8°. . . 29870
Eternal Punishment. *See* **Future** Punishment.
Ethics. *See* **Morals.**
Ethics and Æsthetics of Modern Poetry. [Brown, J.] Lond., 1878. 26293
Ethnology. Rawlinson, G. Origin of Nations. N. Y., 1878. 12°. 20047
—— *See, also,* **Man ; Races.**
Etiquette. Ward, H. O. Phil., 1878. 12°. 28965
Eton (*College*). A Day of my Life. By a present E. boy. N. Y., 1877. 28830
Etonians. Creasy, E. S. Memoirs of Celebrated E.; with notices of Eton College. Lond., 1850. 8°. 18592
—— Jesse, J. H. Memoirs of Celebrated E. Lond., 1875. 2 v. 8°. 23003–
Ettrick Shepherd. *See* **Hogg, J.**
Eucken, R. Fundamental Concepts of Modern Philosophic Thought. N. Y., 1880. 12°. 28088
Eugen Stillfried. Hackländer, F. W. von. Stuttg., 1875. 3 B. 16°. (Werke, B. 10–12.) 25804–
Eugénie. Butt, B. M. N. Y., 1877. 16°. 24068
Euphrates, Bedouin Tribes of. Blunt, A. N. Y., 1879. 8°. . . 21900
Euripides. Hercules Furens, transl. by R. Browning. (*In* 'Aristophanes' Apology.') 26047
—— *Donne, W. B.* (Anc. Classics for English Readers, v. 12). . 26838
—— *Mahaffy, J. P.* (Classical Writers.) N. Y., 1879. 16°. . . 26891
Europäisches Sklavenleben. Hackländer, F. W. von. Stuttg., 1875. 5 B. 16°. (Werke, B. 16–20.) 25807–

Europe. Ward, A. W. The Peace of E. (*In* **Owens College** Ess. & Ad.) 27412
—— Wood, J. G. Ancient E. (*In* 'Nat. Hist. of Man,' v. 2.) . . 29591
—— *Art.* Atkinson, J. B. Art Tour to Northern Capitals of E. Lond., 1873. 8°. 29874
—— — Benjamin, S. G. W. Contemporary Art in E. N. Y., 1877. 29871

Description and Travel.

—— Lippincott, S. J. C. Haps and Mishaps of a Tour in E. Bost., 1854. 12°. 6491
—— Stokes, F. A. College Tramps. N. Y., 1880. 12°. . . . 21255
—— Symonds, J. A. Sketches and Studies in Southern E. N. Y., 1880. 2 v. 12°. 27341–
—— Terhune, M. V. H. Loiterings in Pleasant Paths. N. Y., 1880. 21681

History.

—— Duff, M. E. G. Studies in European Politics. Edinb., 1866. 8°. 20567
—— Freeman, E. A. (Hist. Primers.) Lond., 1876. 16°. . . 20053
—— May, T. E. Democracy in E.: a history. N. Y., 1878. 2 v. 8°. 20565–
—— (732–1201) Roger of Hoveden, Annals of. Lond., 1853. 2 v. 12°. 20800–
—— (787–1154) Johnson, A. H. The Normans in E. Lond., 1877. 16°. 20458
—— (1453–1871) Dyer, T. H. Modern Europe. Lond., 1877. 5 v. . 20560–
—— (1517–1648) Häusser, L. Period of the Reformation. Lond., 1873. 2 v. 8°. 20480–
—— (1519–1603) Creighton, M. The Age of Elizabeth. N. Y., 1876. 20452
—— (1641–1678) Vaughan, R. Protectorate of Oliver Cromwell, and the state of Europe. Lond., 1838. 2 v. 8°. . . . 21000–
—— (1678–1697) Hale, E. Fall of the Stuarts and Western Europe. N. Y., [1876]. 16°. 20453
—— (1776–1876) Frost, T. Secret Societies of the European Revolution. Lond., 1876. 2 v. 8°. 28998–
—— *See, also, names of geographical divisions.*

European Colonies. Payne, E. J. Lond., 1877. 16°. . . . 20084
Europeans (The). James, H., jr. Bost., 1879. 12°. (2 copies.) . 24601–
Eustace Diamonds. Trollope, A. Lond., 1873. 3 v. 16°. . . 24870–
Evangelical Church. Tullidge, H., *editor.* N. Y., 1879. 8°. . . 28600
Evans, J. Ancient Stone Implements, Weapons, and Ornaments, of Great Britain. Lond., 1872. 8°. 20202
Evenings in Autumn. Drake, N. Lond., 1822. 2 v. 16°. . . 18624–
Everett, W. On the Cam. Camb., [Mass]., 1865. 16°. . . . 28829
Evers, H. Steam and the Steam Engine. N. Y., [1872]. 16°. . 29934
Evil Eye. Story, W. W. Lond., 1877. 12°. 21626
Evolution. Bowne, B. P. Philosophy of Spencer. N. Y., 1876. 12°. 28168
—— Burr, E. F. ('Pater Mundi,' v. 2.) 28087
—— Cazelles, M. E. Outline of the Evolution-Philosophy. N. Y., 1875. 12°. 28166
—— Elam, C. Winds of Doctrine. Lond., 1876. 8°. . . . 28165
—— Fiske, J. Outlines of Cosmic Philosophy. Bost., 1875. 2 v. 12°. 28163–
—— Haeckel, E. H. The E. of Man. N. Y., 1879. 2 v. 12°. . 29383–

Evolution. Haeckel, E. H. Freedom in Science and Teaching. N. Y., 1879. 12°. 29385
—— — Hist. of Creation. N. Y., 1876. 2 v. 12°. 29381–
—— Henslow, G. Theory of E. Lond., 1873. 12°. 28167
—— Huxley, T. H. Three Lectures on E. (*In* 'Amer. Addresses.') 29300
—— Mivart, St. G. Contemporary Evolution. N. Y., 1876. 12°. . 29394
—— Williamson, W. C. Primeval Vegetation in its relation to Natural Selection and E. (*In* **Owens College** Ess. & Ad.). . 27412
—— *See, also,* **Biology ; Darwinism ; Natural** Selection.
Ewald, A. C. Life and Times of Sydney. Lond., 1873. 2 v. 8°. 23021–
—— Life and Times of Prince Charles Stuart. Lond., 1875. 2 v. . 23032–
Excursions. Thoreau, H. D. Bost., 1875. 12°. 29335
Exhibition, Centennial. Bruce, E. C. The Century. Phil., 1877. 21522
Expiation de Savéli. Durand, A. F. Paris, 1876. 16°. 25638
Exploration of the World. Verne, J. N. Y., 1879. 8°. 21983
Eyes. Angell, H. C. How to take care of our eyes. Bost., 1878. 16°. 29956
—— Clifford, W. K. Seeing and Thinking : [4 lectures]. Lond., 1879. 28006
—— Harlan, G. C. Eyesight, and how to care for it. Phil., 1879. 16°. 29961
Fables in Song. Bulwer-Lytton, E. R. Bost., 1874. 16°. . . . 26052
Fabre, F. The Abbé Tigrane. N. Y., 1875. 12°. 24472
Fair (The) God. Wallace, L. Bost., 1873. 12°. (2 copies.) . . 24289–
Fair Lusitania. Jackson, C. C. Lond., 1874. 8°. 21969
Fairbairn, W., Life of. Pole, W. Lond., 1877. 8°. 23540
Fairholt, F. W. Tobacco. Lond., 1859. 12°. 29458
Faith and Rationalism. Fisher, G. P. N. Y., 1879. 12°. (2 cop.) 28589–
Faith of Reason. Chadwick, J. W. Bost., 1879. 16°. 28691
Falconberg. Boyesen, H. H. N. Y., 1879. 12°. 24029
Falconer, W. Poetical Works. With Life, and notes, by G. Gilfillan. Edinb., 1854. 8°. 26322
Falkland, *Viscount. See* **Cary, L.**
False Beasts and True. Cobbe, F. P. Lond., [1875]. 12°. . . 12911
Falstaff's Letters. White, J. Lond., 1877. 12°. 12904
Family (The) Pen. Taylor, I., 3d. Lond., 1867. 2 v. 12°. . . 23603–
Famous French Authors : biographical portraits . . . by T. Gautier, E. de Mirecourt, etc. N. Y., 1879. 8°. 23450
CONTENTS :—T. Gautier ; Sainte-Beuve ; Mad. Swetchine ; Mad. de Girardin ; A. Houssaye ; Geo. Sand ; A. de Musset ; Hugo ; P. de Kock ; A. de Lamartine ; Gavarni ; C. Baudelaire ; Balzac ; Béranger ; H. Monnier ; A. Dumas ; M. de Guérin ; Diderot ; La Fontaine.
Fanshawe. Hawthorne, N. Bost., 1828. 12°. 15326
—— *Same.* Bost., 1876. 12°. (2 copies.) 24505–
Far from the Madding Crowd. Hardy, T. N. Y., 1874. (2 copies.) 24457–
Farini, L. C. The Roman State, from 1815 to 1850. Lond., 1851–54. 4 v. 8°. 20304–
Farley, J. L. Modern Turkey. Lond., 1872. 8°. 21910
Farmer's (A) Vacation. Waring, G. E. Bost., 1876. 8°. . . . 21977
Farming. *See* **Agriculture.**
Farquhar, G. Dramatic Works. Lond., 1849. 8°. 26691
—— *Same.* New ed. Lond., 1851. 8°. 26692
Farrar, F. W. Life of Christ. Lond. 2 v. 12°. 28644–
—— *Same.* N. Y., 1875. 2 v. 12°. 28646–

Farrar, F. W. Life and Work of St. Paul. N. Y., [1879]. 2 v. 8°. 28642–
—— Seekers after God. [Lond., 1868.] 12°. 23682
CONTENTS:—Seneca, Epictetus, Marcus Aurelius.
Farrer, J. A. Primitive Manners and Customs. N. Y., 1879. 16°. 28966
Fated to be Free. Ingelow, J. Bost., 1875. 12°. (2 copies.) . 24578–
Fathers (*of the Church*). The Fathers for English Readers. Lond., 4 v. 16°. 28502–
CONTENTS:—Apostolic Fathers, by H. S. Holland.—Defenders of the Faith, by F. Watson.—St. Augustine, by W. R. Clark.—St. Jerome, by E. L. Cutts.
—— Jackson, G. A. Apostolic Fathers, and the Apologists of the 2d cent. N. Y., 1879. 16°. 28512
Favre, J. C. G. Government of the National Defence. Lond., 1873. 20688
Fawcett, H. Free Trade and Protection. Lond., 1878. 12°. . 28804
—— Manual of Political Economy. 4th ed. Lond., 1874. 12°. . 28805
Fawcett, W. L. Gold and Debt. Chic., 1877. 12°. . . . 29053
Federalism. Adams, H. Documents relating to New-England Federalism. Bost., 1877. 8°. 21442
Fellah (Le). About, E. F. V. Paris, 1873. 16°. 25620
Female Biography. *See* **Women**, *Biography*.
Femme (Une) gênante. Droz, G. Paris, 1876. 16°. . . . 25630
Fénelon, F. de S. de La M. *Sainte-Beuve, C. A.* (*In* 'Monday-Chats.') 23290
Ferdinand and Isabella, Reign of. Prescott, W. H. Phil., 1871. 3 v. 8°. 20345–
Fermentation. Schützenberger, P. N. Y., 1876. 12°. . . . 29260
[**Ferrier, Susan E.**] The Inheritance. Edinb., 1824. 3 v. 12°. . 18637–
Fertilization (*in botany*). Darwin, C. R. Effects of Cross and Self Fertilisation. N. Y., 1877. 12°. 29454
—— — Various Contrivances by which orchids are fertilised by insects. N. Y., 1877. 12°. 29456
—— Lubbock, J. On British Wild Flowers considered in relation to Insects. Lond., 1875. 12°. 29461
Feuillet, O. The Diary of a Woman. N. Y., 1879. 16°. . . 24089
—— A Marriage in High Life. Philad., [1876]. 12°. . . . 24473
Fiction, Episodes of. Edinb., 1870. 8°. 24649
Field, H. M. From Egypt to Japan. N. Y., 1877. 12°. . . . 21721
—— From the Lakes of Killarney to the Golden Horn. N. Y., 1877. 21720
Field, M. B. Memories of Many Men and of Some Women. N. Y., 1874. 12°. 22620
Field, W. Life, Writings, and Opinions of Sam. Parr. Lond., 1828. 2 v. 8°. 18603–
Field Paths and Green Lanes. Jennings, L. J. N. Y., 1878. 12°. . 21612
Fielding, H. Joseph Andrews. [*And*] Jonathan Wild. N. Y., 1861. 12°. 24474
—— Tom Jones. Lond., 1876. 2 v. 16°. 24475–
—— Miscellanies and Poems. Lond., 1872. 8°. 24664
—— Works. Lond., 1871. 10 v. 8°. 24654–
—— *Lawrence F.* Life of F. Lond., 1855. 12°. 23215
Fields, J. T. Underbrush. Bost., 1877. 16°. 27226

Fields, (J. T.) & Whipple, (E. P.) Family Library of Brit. Poetry. Bost., 1878. 8°. 26381

Fieschi, G. L. de', The conspiracy of. Celesia, E. Lond., 1866. 8°. 20297

Finance. Fawcett, W. L. Gold and Debt. Chic., 1877. 12°. . 29053

—— Newcomb, S. The Abc of Finance. N. Y., 1878. 16°. . . 29062

—— *See, also,* **Political** Ec. (& *references*); **U. S.,** *Finances.*

Finney, C. G. Memoirs; written by himself. N. Y., 1876. 12°. . 22612

Finod, J. de. A Thousand Flashes of French Wit, Wisdom, and Wickedness. N. Y., 1880. 16°. 26941

First Century of the Republic. Woolsey, T. D., *and others.* N. Y., 1876. 8°. (2 cop.) 21520–

CONTENTS:—Introd.: Colonial progress, by E. Lawrence; Mechanical prog., E. H. Knight; Prog. in manufacture, D. A. Wells; Agricultural prog., W. H. Brewer; Development of mineral resources, T. S. Hunt; Commercial development, E. Atkinson; Population, F. A. Walker; Monetary development, W. G. Sumner; The experiment of the Union, etc., T. D. Woolsey; Education, E. Lawrence; Exact sciences, F. A. P. Barnard; Nat. science, T. Gill; Amer. Literature, E. P. Whipple; Fine Arts, S. S. Conant; Medical and sanitary prog., A. Flint; Amer. jurisprudence, B. V. Abbott; Humanitarian prog., C. L. Brace; Religious development, J. F. Hurst.

First Fam'lies of the Sierras. Miller, C. H. Chic., 1876. 12°. . 24834

First Love is Best. Dodge, M. A. Bost., 1877. 12°. . . . 24232

First Violin. Fothergill, J. N. Y., 1878. 16°. (2 copies.) . . 24441–

Fisher, G. P. Beginnings of Christianity. N. Y., 1877. 8°. (2 cop.) 28587–

—— Discussions in History and Theology. N. Y., 1880. 8°. . . 28591

—— Faith and Rationalism. N. Y., 1879. 12°. (2 copies.) . . 28589–

—— The Reformation. N. Y., 1873. 8°. (2 copies.) . . . 28585–

Fisher, W. M. The Californians. Lond., 1876. 12°. . . . 21285

Fisher-Maiden. Björnson, B. N. Y., 1874. 16°. 24059

Fishing. Francis, F. A Book on Angling. Lond., 1867. 12°. . 29625

—— Gillmore, P. Prairie and Forest. N. Y., 1874. 12°. . . 29620

—— Hallock, C. The Fishing Tourist. N. Y., 1873. 8°. . . 29623

—— Herbert, H. W. Fish and Fishing of the U. S. [etc.]. N. Y., 1850. 8°. 29624

—— Norris, T. American Angler's Book. Phila., [1865]. 8°. . 29629

—— Prime, W. C. I go a-fishing. N. Y., 1873. 8°. 29628

—— Scott, G. C. Fishing in American Waters. N. Y., 1869. 12°. 29626

—— Walton (I.) & Cotton (C.). The Complete Angler. Lond., 1875. 29627

Fiske, D. W. Book of the First Amer. Chess Congress. N. Y., 1859. 12°. 29709

Fiske, J. Myths and Myth-Makers. Bost., 1873. 16°. . . . 27741

—— Outlines of Cosmic Philosophy. Bost., 1875. 2 v. 12°. . . 28163–

—— Unseen World, and other essays. Bost., 1876. 12°. . . 27243

Fitzgerald, P. The Great Canal at Suez. Lond., 1876. 2 v. 8°. 21840–

—— Life and Adventures of Alex. Dumas. Lond., 1873. 2 v. 8°. 23402–

Fitzpatrick, W. J. Life of C. [J.] Lever. Lond., 1879. 2 v. 8°. 23400–

Five (The) Senses of Man. Bernstein, J. N. Y., 1876. 12°. . . 29261

Five Weeks in a Balloon. Verne, J. Lond., 1870. 16°. . . . 24265

Five Years in an English University. Bristed, C. A. N. Y., 1873. 28824

Five Years' Penal Servitude. Lond., 1878. 12°. 28857

Flagg, W. Birds and Seasons of New England. Bost., 1875. 12°. 29320

—— Woods and By-ways of New England. Bost., 1872. 12°. . 21283

Flammarion, C. Stories of Infinity. Bost., 1873. 16°. 29441
Fleay, F. G. Shakespeare Manual. Lond., 1876. 16°. 27019
Fleming, G. Travels on Horseback in Mantchu Tartary. Lond., 1863. 8°. 21920
Fleming, S. *Grant, G. M.* Ocean to Ocean: F.'s expedition through Canada in 1872. Lond., 1873. 8°. 21549
—— — *Same.* Enl. and rev. ed. N. Y., 1877. 12°. 21550
Flemish Painters, Early. Crowe (J. A.) & Cavalcaselle (G. B.) Lond., 1872. 12°. 23801
Fletcher, Eliza D. Autobiography. Edinb., 1875. 12°. . . . 23683
Fletcher, J. *See* **Beaumont** (**F.**) **& Fletcher.**
Fleurange. Craven, P. N. Y., 1873. 16°. 24170
Floating City. Verne, J. N. Y., 1875. 12°. 24266
Florence. Horner, S. and J. Walks in F. Lond., 1873. 2 v. 12°. 21249–
—— Napier, H. E. Florentine Hist. [to 1815.] Lond., 1846–7. 6v. 12°. 20004–
—— Oliphant, M. O. W. Makers of F.: Dante, Giotto, Savonarola; and their city. Lond., 1876. 8°. 23836
—— Ruskin, J. Mornings in F. N. Y., 1876. 12°. 29834
—— Symonds, J. A. Florence and the Medici. (*In* 'Sketches and Stud.,' v. 1.) 27341
—— Weld, C. R. F., the New Capital of Italy. Lond., 1867. 12°. 21265
Florida. Stowe, H. E. B. Palmetto-Leaves. Bost., 1873. 16°. . 21288
Flower and Thorn. Aldrich, T. B. Bost., 1877. 12°. 26001
Flowers. Darwin, C. R. Different Forms of F. N. Y., 1877. 12°. 29455
—— Lubbock, J. On British Wild F. Lond., 1875. 12.°. . . . 29461
—— *See, also,* **Botany**; **Fertilization.**
Flowers of History. Matthew of Westminster. Lond., 1853. 2 v. 20802–
Flowers of the Sky. Proctor, R. A. N. Y., [1879]. 16°. . . . 29442
Folk-lore. Anderson (R. B.) & Bjarnason (J.) Viking Tales of the North. Chic., 1877. 12°. 27708
—— Asbjörnsen, P. C. Tales from the Fjeld. Lond., 1874. 12°. 27705
—— Bell, W. Shakespeare's Puck, and his Folkslore. Lond., 1852, ['61 & ?] 3 v. 12°. 27012–
—— Bottrell, W. Traditions of West Cornwall. Penzance, 1870–73. 2 series. 12°. 27700–
—— Buchanan, R. Ballad Stories of the Affections. From the Scandinavian. Lond., [1866]. 8°. 26254
—— Busk, R. H. Roman Legends. Bost., 1877. 8°. 27714
—— Campbell, J. F. Popular Tales of the West Highlands. Edinb., 1860–62. 4 v. 16°. 27660–
—— Dyer, T. F. T. English Folk-lore. Lond., 1880. 12°. . . 27668
—— Frere, M. Old Deccan Days. Lond., 1870. 16°. 27790
—— Giles, H. A. Strange Stories from a Chinese Studio. Lond., 1880. 2 v. 12°. 27787–
—— Henderson, W. Folk-lore of the Northern Counties of England. Lond., 1866. 12°. 27666
—— Hunt, R. Popular Romances of the West of England. Lond., [1871]. 12°. 27664
—— Kelly, W. K. Indo-European Tradition and F. Lond., 1863. 27789

Folk-lore. Kennedy, P. Fireside Stories of Ireland. Dubl., 1870. 16°. 27667
—— Leland (C. G.) *& others.* English-Gipsy Songs. Phil., 1875. 16°. 26123
—— Ludlow, J. M. Popular Epics of the Mid. Ages. Lond., 1865. 2 v. 16°. 27671–
—— Macquoid, T. R. & K. S. Legends from Normandy and Brittany. Lond., 1879. 12°. 21252
—— Magnússon (E.) & Morris (W.) Three Northern Love Stories, and other tales. Lond., 1875. 12°. 24631
—— Mathews, C. Enchanted Moccasins, and other legends of the Amer. Indians. N. Y., 1877. 12°. 24800
—— Metcalfe, F. Icelandic F. and Sagas. (*In* 'Oxonian in Iceland.') 21705
—— Mijatovies, C. Serbian Folk-lore. Lond., 1874. 12°. . . 27784
—— Murray, E. C. G. Doïne; or, The national songs and legends of Roumania. Lond., 1854. 12°. 27786
—— Naaké, J. T. Slavonic Fairy Tales. Lond., 1874. 12°. . . 27785
—— Ralston, W. R. S. Russian Folk-tales. Lond., 1873. 8°. . 27783
—— — Songs of the Russian People. Lond., 1872. 8°. . . . 27782
—— Smith, H. H. Myths and F. of the Amazonian Indians. (*In* 'Brazil.') 21801
—— Thorpe, B. Yule-tide Stories. Lond., 1875. 12°. . . . 27669
See, also, **Ballads; Legends; Manners & Customs; Myths; Romances.**

Fonblanque, A. W. de. How we are governed. Lond., [1879]. 12°. 20885
—— *Fonblanque, E. B. de.* Life of A. Fonblanque. Lond., 1874. 8°. 23893

Fontainebleau. Cochrane, A. B. (*In* 'Histor. Chateaux.') . . 21785

Foods. Edward Smith. N. Y., 1876. 12°. 29242

Fool's Errand. [Tourgee, A. W.] N. Y., 1879. 16°. (3 copies.) 24913–

Foot Notes. Barron, A. Wallingf., 1875. 12°. 29321

Footfalls. Owen, R. D. Philad., 1860. 12°. 28053

For Summer Afternoons. [Woolsey, S. C.] Bost., 1876. 16°. . 27238

Forbes, A. *See* **Daily News** (London).

Forbes, C. J. F. S. Brit. Burma and its People. Lond., 1878. 12°. 21224

Forbes, C. S. Iceland. Lond., 1860. 12°. 21223

Forbidden (A) Land. Oppert, E. N. Y., 1880. 8°. 21943

Force. Helmholtz, H. L. F. Interaction of the Natural Forces. [*And*] Conservation of F. (*In* 'Pop. Lectures.') . . . 29389
—— Stewart, B. Conservation of Energy. N. Y., 1874. 12°. . . 29246
—— *See, also,* **Physics.**

Forces of Nature. Guillemin, A. N. Y. [Lond.], 1873. 8°. . . 29572

Forces, Physical, Applications of. Guillemin, A. Lond., 1877. 8°. 29571

Foregone Conclusion. Howells, W. D. Bost., 1875. 12°. (3 cop.) 24562–

Foreign Classics for English Readers. Oliphant, M. O. W., *editor.* Phila., [1877–79]. 9 v. 16°. 23262-

CONTENTS:—1, Dante, by the editor.—2, Voltaire, E. B. Hamley.—3, Pascal, J. Tulloch.—4, Petrarch, H. Reeve.—5, Goethe, A. Hayward.—6, Molière, ed. and F. Tarver.—7, Montaigne, W. L. Collins.—8, Rabelais, W. Besant.—9, Calderon, E. J. Hasell.

Forest Life in Acadie. Hardy, C. Lond., 1869. 8°. . . . 21553

Forestier, A. Echoes from Mist-land. Chic., 1877. 12°. . . 27711

Forgiveness and Law. Bushnell, H. N. Y., 1874. 12°. . . . 28550

Forman, H. B. Our Living Poets. Lond., 1871 12°. . . . 26287

[**Forrester, A. H.**] Phantasmagoria of Fun. Lond., 1843. 2 v. 12°. 25207–

Fors Clavigera. Ruskin, J. Orpington, Kent, 1871–77. 7 v. 8°. . 29031–

Forster, J. Historical and Biographical Essays. Lond., 1858. 2 v. 27320–

CONTENTS:—1, The debates on the grand remonstrance, 1641; The Plantagenets and the Tudors; The civil wars and O. Cromwell.—2, Dan. DeFoe; Rich. Steele; Chas. Churchill; Sam. Foote.

—— Life of Jonathan Swift. Vol. 1. N. Y., 1876. 8°. 23418

Forsyth, W. Essays, critical and narrative. Lond., 1874. 8°. . 27480

CONTENTS:—Speeches of Brougham; Criminal procedure; Kingdom of Italy; Judges of Eng.; Literary style; Progress of legal reform; an election in France; Journey to Ashango Land; Eugénie de Guérin; Tunnel through the Alps; Hudson's Bay Co.; Visit to Russia and the great fair [etc.]; Visit to Portland prison; Three days in Sark; Wm. Cobbett; Historical evidence.

—— Hist. of Lawyers. Bost., 1875. 8°. 23886

—— History of Trial by Jury. N. Y., 1875. 8°. 28841

Fortnightly Review. Lond., 1865–79. 32 v. 8°. 10622–

Fortnum, C. D. E. Bronzes. Lond., [1877]. 12°. 29762

—— Maiolica. N. Y., 1876. 12°. 29763

Fortress, Annals of a. Viollet-le-Duc, E. E. Bost., 1876. 8°. . 24313

Forty-five Guardsmen. Dumas, A. D. Lond., [1879]. (2 cop.) 24413 & 24420

Foster, J. W. Pre-historic Races of the U. S. of A. Chic., 1873. 8°. 21401

Foster, M. Physiology. (Sci. Prim.) Lond., 1878. 16°. . . 29355

—— Text Book of Physiology. [L. &] N. Y., 1880. 12°. . . . 29302

Fothergill, J. M. Maintenance of Health. N. Y., 1879. 12°. . 29994

Fothergill, Jessie. First Violin. N. Y., 1878. 16°. (2 copies.) . 24441–

—— Probation: a novel. N. Y., 1879. 16°. 24443

Fould, Wilhelmine J. S., (*pseud.*, 'Gustave Haller.') Renée and Franz. N. Y., 1878. 16°. 24079

Fourth (The) Estate. Hunt, F. K. Lond., 1850. 2 v. 12°. . . 18590–

Fox, C. J. *Rae, W. F.* Wilkes, Sheridan, Fox. Lond., 1874. 8°. 23040

—— *See, also,* **Adams, W. H. D.,** 'Eng. Party Leaders,' v. 1 (21054); **Earle, J. C.,** 'Eng. Premiers,' v. 1 (22882).

France. Longfellow, H. W. Poems of Places, v. 9–10. . . . 26448–

—— *Biography.* King, E. (*See his* 'French Political Leaders.') . 22442

—— — Rémusat, C. E. J. G. de V. de. Memoirs: 1802–1808. . . 22567–

Description and Travel.

—— Gibbons, P. E. French and Belgians. Phil., 1879. 12°. . . 21228

—— Hamerton, P. G. Round my House. Bost., 1876. 12°. . . 21248

—— Hawthorne, N. Note-books. Bost., 1878. 2 v. in 1. 12°. . 24504

—— Murray, E. C. G. Round about France. Lond., 1878. 12°. . 21622

—— Piozzi, H. L. Journey through France. Lond., 1789. 2 v. 8°. 18609–

—— Stevenson, R. L. An Inland Voyage. Lond., 1878. 12°. . 21710

—— Tolfrey, F. The Sportsman in France. Lond., 1841. 12°. . 29608

History.

—— Kitchin, G. W. Oxf., 1873–77. v. 1–3. 12°. 20404–

CONTENTS:—1, To 1453.—2, 1453 to 1624.—3, 1624 to 1793.

—— Taine, H. A. Origins of Contemporary France. N. Y., 1876–78. v. 1–2. 12°. 20425–

CONTENTS:—1, Ancient Régime.—2, French Revolution.

—— (*to* 1789) Guizot, F. P. G. Lond., 1872–76. 5 v. 8°. . . . 20760–

—— — *Same.* Bost., [1877]. 6 v. 8°. 20765–

—— — *Same,* abridged. Lond., 1879. 8°. 20690

France. *History* (*continued*).

—— (*to* 1848) Bonnechose, F. P. E. B. de. Lond., 1868. 2 v. 8°. . 20682–

—— (300–1525) Masson, G. (Early Chroniclers.) 20472

—— (752–987) Sismondi, J. C. L. S. de. The French under the Carlovingians. Lond., 1850. 8°. 20691

—— (987–1137) Sismondi, J. C. L. S. de. France under the Feudal System. Lond., 1851. 8°. 20692

—— (1377–1485) Gairdner, J. Houses of Lancaster and York, with the conquest and loss of France. Lond., 1874. 16°. . . 20451

—— (1450–1600) Ranke, F. L. von. Civil Wars and Monarchy in F. N. Y., 1853. 12°. 20412

—— (1461–1483) Willert, P. F. Reign of Lewis XI. Lond., 1876. . 20069

—— (1512–1574) Baird, H. M. Rise of the Huguenots in F. N. Y., 1879. 2 v. 8°. 20680–

—— (1515–1610) Hanna, W. Wars of the Huguenots. Edinb., 1871. 20402

—— (1529–1574) Marsh, A. C. Protestant Reformation in F. Phila., 1851. 2 v. 12°. 20417–

—— (1600–1643) Cousin, V. Secret Hist. of the French Court under Richelieu and Mazarin. N. Y., 1871. 12°. 20414

—— (1648–1794) Baker, H. B. French Society from the Fronde to the Great Revolution. Lond., 1874. 2 v. 12°. . . . 20400–

—— (1661–1715) Martin, B. L. H. Age of Louis XIV. Bost., 1865. 2 v. 8°. 20720–

—— (1700–1789) Lacroix, P. The 18th Century. Lond., 1876. 8°. 20363

—— (1715–1789) Martin, B. L. H. Decline of the French Monarchy. Bost., 1866. 2 v. 8°. 20722–

—— (1752–1774) Broglie, A. de. The King's Secret. Lond., [1879]. 2 v. 8°. 20685–

—— (1774–1870) Van Laun, H. French Revolutionary Epoch. N. Y., 1879 [1878]. 2 v. 12°. 20419–

—— (1789) Burke, E. Reflections (1790) on the Revolution in F. (*In* 'Sel. Works,' v. 2). 26874

—— — Croker, J. W. Early Period of the French Revolution. Lond., 1857. 8°. 20687

—— — Lamartine, A. M. L. de. Hist. of the Constituent Assembly. Lond., 1858. 4 v. in 2. 12°. 20415–

—— (1789–1791) Michelet, J. French Revolution. Lond., 1864. 12°. 20410

—— (1789–1815) Morris, W. O. French Rev. and First Empire. Lond., 1874. 12°. 20411

—— (1789–1870) Adams, C. K. Democracy and Monarchy in F. N. Y., 1874. 12°. 20413

—— (1815) Williams, H. M. Narrative of the Events. Lond., 1816. 18611

—— (1830–1857) Oliphant, M. O. W. Memoir of Count de Montalembert. Edinb. & L., 1872. 2 v. 12°. 22486–

—— (1841–1847) Guizot, F. P. G. France under Louis-Phillipe. Lond., 1865. 8°. 20689

—— (1851) Hugo, V. M. Histoire d'un crime. Paris, 1877–8. 2 t. 16°. 25651–

—— (1870) Borbstædt (A.) & Dwyer (F.) Franco-German War. Lond., 1873. 8°. 20684

France. *History (continued).*
—— (1870) Favre, J. C. G. Government of the National Defence. Lond., 1873. 8°. 20688
—— (1871) Wartensleben, H. von. Lond., 1872. 8°. 20644
—— (1871–1873) Simon, J. F. Government of Thiers. N. Y., 1879. 2 v. 12°. 20693–
See, also, **Brittany; Cévennes; French** Literature; **Normandy; Paris; Pyrenees.**

France, Pastorals of. Wedmore, F. Lond., 1878. 12°. 24294
France and England in North Amer. (*See* **Parkman, F.**)
Franchise. McMillan, D. C. Elective F. in the U. S. N. Y., 1878. 21331
—— Maurice, J. F. D. Workman and the F. Lond., 1866. 8°. . 9090
—— *See, also,* **Representation.**
Francis, F. Book on Angling. Lond., 1867. 12°. 29625
François le Champi. Dudevant, A. L. A. D. Paris, 1869. 16°. . 25682
Franklin, B. Life, written by himself; ed. by J. Bigelow. Phil., 1874. 3 v. 8°. 22695–
—— *Sainte-Beuve, C. A.* (*In* 'Eng. Portraits.') 22885
Fraser's Magazine. Lond., 1830–79. 100 v. 8°. 12300–
Fraser-Tytler, Christina C. *See* **Tytler.**
Frazar, D. Practical Boat-sailing. Bost., 1879. 16°. 29660
Freak of Freedom. Bent, J. T. Lond., 1879. 12°. 20483
Frederick I. (Barbarossa), *emperor of Germany. Testa, G. B.* War against the Communes of Lombardy. Lond., 1877. 8°. . 20296
Frederick II. (*the Great*), *king of Prussia. Sainte-Beuve, C. A.* (*In* 'Monday-Chats.') 23290
Free Trade and Protection. Fawcett, H. Lond., 1878. 12°. . . 28804
Freedom in Science and Teaching. Haeckel, E. H. N. Y., 1879. 12°. 29385
Freeman, E. A. Comparative Politics: 6 lectures. N. Y., 1874. . 20183
—— General Sketch of History. N. Y., [1876]. 16°. 20078
—— Historical and Architectural Sketches; chiefly Italian. Lond., 1876. 12°. 20184
CONTENTS:—The Venetian March; Ravenna and her Sisters; Central Italy; Rome; Southern Italy; Lombardy; The Burgundian March.

—— Historical Essays. Lond., 1871, '73 & '79. 3 series. 4658 & 20185–
CONTENTS:—1, Mythical and Romantic elements in early Engl. history; Continuity of Eng. hist.; Relations between the crowns of Engl. and Scotland; St. Thomas of Canterbury and his biographers; Reign of Edward III.; Holy Rom. Empire; The Franks and the Gauls; Early sieges of Paris; Frederick I., King of Italy; The Emp. Frederick II.; Charles the Bold; Presidential government.—2, Ancient Greece and mediæval Italy; Gladstone's Homer and the Homeric Age; The historians of Athens; The Athenian democracy; Alexander the Great; Greece during the Macedonian period; Mommsen's Hist. of Rome; Lucius Cornelius Sulla; The Flavian Cæsars;—3, First impressions of Rome; The Illyrian emperors and their land; Diocletian's place in architectural history; Augusta Treverorum; The panegyrists of the 4th cent.; The Goths at Ravenna; Race and language; The Jews in Europe; The Byzantine empire; First impressions of Athens; Mediæval and modern Greece: The Southern Slaves; Sicilian cycles; The Normans at Palermo.

—— Hist. of Europe. Lond., 1876. 16°. 20053
—— Norman Conquest of England. Oxf'd, 1870–79. 6 v. 8°. . 5006–
—— *Same.* Rev. Amer. ed. Oxf. & N. Y., 1873–79. 6 v. 8°. . 20920–
CONTENTS:—1, Prelim. . . . to the election of Eadward the Confessor.—2, Reign of Eadward.—3, Reign of Harold and the interregnum.—4, Reign of William the Conqueror.—5, Effects of the Norman Conquest.—6, Index.

—— Ottoman Power in Europe. Lond., 1877. 12°. 20490
—— *editor.* Historical Course for Schools. N. Y. (& Lond.,) 1872–77. 7 v. 16°. (*For contents see* **Historical** Course.) . . 20078–

Freethinking and Plainspeaking. Stephen, L. [L. &] N. Y., 1877. 12°. 27271
French, G. R. Shakspeareana Genealogica. Lond., etc., 1869. 8°. 27048
French Criminal Law, Romance of. Spicer, H. Lond., 1872. 8°. . 28840
French Home Life. Edinb. & Lond., 1873. 8°. 21782
French Literature. Besant, W. French Humorists. Lond., 1873. . 26776
—— Demogeot, J. C. Hist. of French Lit. Phila., 1874. 16°. . 20065
—— Famous French Authors. (*See* **Famous**). 23450
—— Van Laun, H. Hist. of French Lit. N. Y., 1876–7. 3 v. 8°. (2 cop.) 26770–
—— *See, also,* **Poetry,** *French;* **Poetry,** *Provençal;* **Poets,** *French.*
French Men of Letters. Mauris, M. N. Y., 1880. 16°. . . . 23313
French Revolutionary Epoch. Van Laun, H. N. Y., 1879. 2 v. 12°. 20419–
French Society. Baker, H. B. Lond., 1874. 2 v. 12°. . . . 20400–
French Wit, Wisdom, and Wickedness. Finod, J. de. N. Y., 1880. 26941
Freneau, P. Poems. Lond., 1861. 16°. 26062
Frere, J. H. Works; with a memoir. Lond., 1872. 2 v. 8°. . 27481–
Frere, M. Old Deccan Days. Lond., 1870. 16°. 27790
Freytag, G. Die Ahnen. Leipz., 1875–6. 4 Abth. 12°. . . . 25911–

Contents:—1, Ingo und Ingraban.—Das Nest der Zaunkönige.—3, Die Brüder vom deutschen Hause.—4, Marcus König.

—— Bilder aus der deutschen Vergangenheit. Leipz., 1876–7. 4 B. in 3. 8°. 25907–

Contents:—1, Aus dem Mittelalter.—2, (1. Abth.), Vom Mittelalter zur Neuzeit (1200–1500). (2te Abth.), Aus dem Jahrh. der Reformation (1500–1600). —3, Aus dem Jahrh. des grossen Krieges (1600–1700).—4, Aus neuer Zeit (–1848).

—— Dramatische Werke. Leipz., 1874. 12°. 25910
—— Ingo; transl. N. Y., 1873. 16°. 24444
—— Ingraban; transl. N. Y., 1873. 16°. 24445
—— Die verlorene Handschrift. Leipz., 1877. 2 B. 8°. . . . 25905–
Friar Anselmo, and other poems. Dorr, J. C. R. N. Y., 1879. 16°. 26057
Friend Fritz. Erckmann (E.) & Chatrian (A.). N. Y., 1877. (2 cop.) 24437–
Friends in Council. Helps, A. Lond., 1872–3. 2 ser.; 4 v. 16°. . 27250–
Friendship's Garland. Arnold, M. Lond., 1871. 16°. . . . 27242
Frithiof. Cox (G. W.) & Jones (E. H.). Story of Frithjof and Ingebjorg. (*In* 'Pop. Romances.' *And in* 'Tales.') . 27712 & 27713
—— Tegnér, E. Frithiof; transl. by Latham. Lond., 1838. 12°. . 27709
—— — Fridthjof's Saga; transl. by Stephens. (*With* **Anderson & Bjarnason's** Viking Tales.) 27708
Frobisher, M., Life of. Jones, F. Lond., 1878. 12°. . . . 22848
Froebel, F., Reminiscences of. Marenholz-Bülow, B. von. Bost., 1877. 12°. 23647
Frog, Common. Mivart, St. G. Lond., 1874. 12°. 29508
From the Earth to the Moon. Verne, J. N. Y., 1874. 12°. (2 cop.) 24267–
From Egypt to Japan. Field, H. M. N. Y., 1877. 12°. . . . 21721
From Egypt to Palestine. Bartlett, S. C. N. Y., 1879. 8°. . . 21843
From the Lakes of Killarney to the Golden Horn. Field, H. M. N. Y., 1877. 12°. 21720
Fromont jeune et Risler ainé. Daudet, A. Paris, 1877. 16°. . 25627
Frondes Agrestes. Ruskin, J. Orpington, Kent, 1875. 12°. . . 29829
Frontenac, L. de B. de, and New France. Parkman, F. Bost., 1877. 8°. 21406

Frost, T. Life of Thomas, Lord Lyttelton. Lond., 1876. 8°. . 23930
—— Secret Societies of the European Revolution, 1776–1876. Lond., 1876. 2 v. 8°. 28998–
Frothingham, O. B. Gerrit Smith: a biography. N. Y., 1878. 12°. 22623
—— Theodore Parker: a biography. Bost., 1874. 12°. . . . 22610
—— Transcendentalism in New England. N. Y., 1876. 8°. . . 28204
—— Visions of the Future, and other discourses. N. Y., 1879. 12°. 28553
Frothingham, R. Rise of the Republic of the U. S. Bost., 1872. . 21440
Froude, J. A. Bunyan. (Eng. Men of Letters.) N. Y., 1880. 12°. 23346
—— Cæsar: a sketch. N. Y., 1879. 8°. 23724
—— The English in Ireland in the 18th Century. N. Y., 1873–4. 3 v. 12°. 20816–
—— *Same.* v. 1. 20819
—— Life and Times of Thomas Becket. N. Y., 1878. 12°. . . 22140
—— Short Studies on Great Subjects. N. Y., 1868, '71 & '77. 3 series. 12°. . . . . 3726–7 & 27339

CONTENTS:—1, Science of history; Times of Erasmus and Luther; Influence of the Reformation on the Scottish character; Philosophy of Catholicism; Plea for the free discussion of theological difficulties; Criticism and the Gospel history; The Book of Job; Spinoza; Dissolution of the monasteries; England's forgotten worthies; Homer; Lives of the Saints; Representative men; Reynard the fox; Cat's pilgrimage; Fables; [&c.]—2, Calvinism; A bishop of the 12th cent.; Father Newman on the "Grammar of Assent;" Condition and prospects of Protestantism; England and her colonies; A fortnight in Kerry (2 pts); Reciprocal duties of State and subject; The merchant and his wife; On progress; The colonies once more; Education; England's war; Eastern question; Scientific method applied to history.—3, Annals of an English abbey; Revival of Romanism; Sea Studies; Society in Italy in the last days of the Roman Republic; Lucian; Divus Cæsar; On the uses of a landed gentry; Party politics; Leaves from a South African journal.

Fürst und Kavalier. Hackländer, F. W. von. Stuttg., 1873. 16°. (Werke, B. 49.) 25824
Fuller, Margaret. *See* **Ossoli, M. F.**
Fullom, S. W. History of Shakespeare. Lond., 1864. 8°. . . 27052
Fulton, F. Manual of Constitutional Hist. Lond., 1875. 12°. . 20884
Fun, Poetry, and Pathos. Browne, W. Y. Lond., 1850. 12°. . 25206
Funeral Ceremonies. *See* **Burial.**
Fungi. Cooke, M. C. N. Y., 1875. 12°. 29254
Fur Country. Verne, J. Bost., 1874. 12°. 24269
Furioso. [Müller von Königswinter, W.] Cambr. & L., 1865. 12°. 23809
Furness, *Mrs.* **H. H.** Concordance to Shakespeare's Poems. Phil., 1875. 8°. 1658
Furniture. Jacquemart, A. Hist. of Furniture. Lond., 1878. 8°. . 29993
—— Pollen, J. H. Ancient and Modern F. and Woodwork. N. Y., 1876. 12°. 29766
—— Spofford, H. E. P. Art Decoration applied to F. N. Y., 1878. 29872
Fustel de Coulanges, M. D. The Ancient City. Bost., 1874. 8°. . 20182
Future Punishment. [Whiton, J. M.] Is "Eternal" Punishment Endless? Bost., 1878. 16°. 28509
Fyffe, C. A. Hist. of Greece. Lond., [1877]. 16°. 20054
Gaboriau, E. Le petit vieux des Batignolles. Paris, 1877. 16°. 25646
Gabriel Conroy. Harte, F. B. Hartf., 1876. 8°. (2 copies.) . . 24650–
Gaddings with a Primitive People. Grohman, W. A. B. N. Y., 1878. 16°. 21247
Gage, W. L. Life of Carl Ritter. N. Y., 1867. 12°. . . . 23563

Gairdner, J. England. (Early Chroniclers of Europe.) Lond., [1879]. 12°. 20471
—— Houses of Lancaster and York. Lond., 1874. 16°. . . . 20451
—— Life and Reign of Richard the Third. Lond., 1878. 12°. . 20813
—— *editor.* The Paston Letters. Lond., 1872–75. 3 v. 16°. . 22840–
Galaxy. N. Y., 1866–78. 25 v. 8°. 13886–
Galiani, F. *Sainte-Beuve, C. A.* (*In* 'Monday-Chats.') . . . 23290
Galileo Galilei and the Roman Curia. Gebler, K. von. Lond., 1879. 23548
Gallenga, A., (*pseud.*, 'L. Mariotti'). History of Piedmont. Lond., 1855. 3 v. 12°. 20000–
Galton, F. English Men of Science. N. Y., 1875. 12°. . . . 29400
—— Vacation Tourists and Notes of Travel in 1862–3. Lond., 1864. 21732
Gamekeeper at Home. [Jefferies, R.] Bost., 1879. 16°. . . 29331
Games. Bohn, H. G. Hand-book of Games. Lond., 1850. 16°. . 29680
—— *See, also,* **Archery; Cards; Chess; Cricket; Sports; Whist.**
Gardening. Bright, H. A. A Year in a Lancashire Garden. Lond., 1879. 12°. 29452
Gardiner, Marg. P., *countess of Blessington,* Personal Recollections of. (*In* **Stoddard, R. H.,** 'Bric-à-Brac Ser.') . . . 23254
Gardiner, S. R. First Two Stuarts and the Puritan Revolution. [Lond. &] Bost., 1876. 16°. 20454
—— Hist. of England: 1603–1616. Lond., 1863. 2 v. 8°. . . 21120–
—— History of England: 1624–1628. Lond., 1875. 2 v. 8°. . . 21124–
—— Personal Government of Charles I. Lond., 1877. 2 v. 8°. . 21126–
—— Prince Charles and the Spanish Marriage. Lond., 1869. 2 v. 21122–
—— Thirty Years' War. Lond., 1874. 16°. 20450
Garfield, J. A., Life of. Hinsdale, B. A. N. Y., 1880. 8°. . . 21532
Garnett, R. Relics of Shelley. Lond., 1862. 16°. (2 cop.) . . 26213–
Garrett, Rhoda and Agnes. Suggestions for House Decoration. Phila., [1877]. 12°. 29780
Garth: a novel. Hawthorne, J. N. Y., 1877. 8°. 24652
Gaskell, Elizabeth C. Cranford. Lond., 1870. 16°. . . . 24446
—— Mary Barton: a tale. Lond., 1848. 12°. 24467
—— Ruth: a novel. Lond., 1872. 16°. 24447
Gastronomy as a Fine Art. Brillat-Savarin, A. Lond., 1877. 12°. 29976
Gautama. *See* **Buddhism.**
Gautier, T. Captain Fracasse. N. Y., 1880. 16°. 24448
—— Constantinople. Paris, 1854. 16°. 25647
—— *Same.* Transl. Lond., 1854. 12°. 21226
—— *Same.* Amer. ed., rev. N. Y., 1875. 12°. 21227
—— Spirite: nouvelle fantastique. Paris, 1877. 16°. . . . 25648
—— *Same.* Spirite: a fantasy. N. Y., 1877. 16°. (2 cop.) . . 24074–
—— Voyage en Espagne. Paris, 1878. 16°. 25649
—— Voyage en Russie. Paris, 1867. 16°. 25650
—— *Same.* A Winter in Russia. N. Y., 1874. 12°. . . . 21225
—— *See, also,* **Famous** French Authors.
Gay, J. D. Prince of Wales in India. N. Y., 1877. 12°. . . 21246
Gay, John. Fables. With mem. and crit. diss. by G. Gilfillan. Edinb., 1859. 8°. 26319

Gay, John. Poetical Works; with a life by Dr. Johnson. Bost., 1854. 2 v. 26063-

Gay, S. H. Popular Hist. of the U. S. (*See* **Bryant, W. C., & Gay.**)

Gebler, K. von. Galileo Galilei and the Roman Curia. Lond., 1879. 8°. 23548

Geddes, J. John DeWitt, Grand Pensionary of Holland. N. Y., 1880. v. 1. 8°. 20602

Geheimniss der Stadt. Hackländer, F. W. von. Stuttg., 1873. 3 B. 16°. (Werke, B. 58–60.) 25828-

Geibel, E. Brunhild. Bost., 1879. 16°. 26065

Geier-Wally. Hillern, W. von. N. Y., 1876. 16°. 24543

Geikie, A. Elem. Lessons in Phys. Geography. Lond. & N. Y., 1877. 16°. 21240

—— Geology. Lond., 1877. 16°. 29356

—— Life of Sir R. I. Murchison. Lond., 1875. 2 v. 8°. . . . 23538-

—— Phys. Geography. (Sci. Prim.) Lond., 1878. 16°. . . . 29357

Geikie, C. The English Reformation. N. Y., 1879. 12°. . . 20814

—— Life and Words of Christ. N. Y., 1878. 2 v. 8°. . . . 28763-

Gellert (Christian), and other sketches. Auerbach, B. Lond., 1858. 24000

Genoa. Celesia, E. Conspiracy of Gianluigi Fieschi. Lond., 1866. 20297

—— Malleson, G. B. Studies from Genoese Hist. Lond., 1875. 8°. 20013

Geoffrin, Marie T. R. *Sainte-Beuve, C. A.* (*In* 'Monday-Chats.') 23290

Geoffry Hamlyn. Kingsley, H. Lond., 1874. 12°. (2 copies.) . 24619-

Geography. Brown, R. Countries of the World. Lond., [1879]. v. 1–3. 4°. 21970-

—— Geikie, A. Elem. Lessons. L. & N. Y., 1877. 16°. . . . 21240

—— — Phys. Geography. (Sci. Primers.) Lond., 1878. 16°. . . 29357

—— Grove, G. (Hist. Primers.) Lond., 1877. 16°. 20055

—— Tozer, H. F. Classical Geog. (Lit. Prim.) Lond., 1876. 16°. 26860

—— *See, also,* **Earth; Physiography; Travels; Voyages.**

Geology. Agassiz, L. J. R. Geological Sketches. Bost., 1866 & 76. 2 series. 12°. . . . . 8955 & 29416

—— Dana, J. D. Geological Story briefly told. N. Y., 1875. 12°. (2 copies.) 29413-

—— — Manual of Geology. N. Y., 1874. 8°. 29411

—— Dawson, J. W. Origin of the World. N. Y., 1877. 12°. . . 29418

—— Geikie, A. (Sci. Primers.) Lond., 1877. 16°. 29356

—— — Life of Murchison; with a sketch of Geol. Lond., 1875. 2 v. 23538-

—— Kingsley, C. Town Geology. Lond., 1872. 16°. . . . 29420

—— Le Conte, J. Elements of Geology. N. Y., 1878. 8°. . . 29410

—— Ruskin, J. Deucalion. N. Y., 1875–77. Parts 1–4 in 2 v. 12°. 29836-

—— *See, also,* **Earth.**

George III., *king of England,* Life and Reign of. Jesse, J. H. Lond., 1867. 3 v. 8°. 23037-

George, H. Progress and Poverty. N. Y., 1880. 12°. . . . 28806

George St. George Julian, the Prince. Cockton, H. Phila., 1842. 8°. 24311

Gérard's Marriage. Theuriet, A. N. Y., 1877. 16°. . . . 24073

German Element in the War of Amer. Independence. Greene, G. W. N. Y., 1876. 12°. 21360

German Home Life. N. Y., 1876. 12°. 21269
German Literature. Gostwick (J.) & Harrison (R.). Outlines of. Lond., 1873. 12°. 26902
—— Hosmer, J. K. Short Hist. of. St. Louis, 1879. 12°. . . 26903
—— Hurst, J. F. Life and Lit. in the Fatherland. N. Y., 1875. 12°. 26901
—— Taylor, J. B. Studies in. N. Y., 1879. 12°. 26900
—— *See, also,* **Poetry,** *German.*
German Tales. Auerbach, B. N. Y., 1874. 16°. 24042
Germany. Freytag, G. Bilder aus der deutschen Vergangenheit. Leipz., 1876–7. 4 B. in 3. 8°. 25907–
—— Longfellow, H. W. Poems of Places, v. 17–18. Bost., 1877. 2 v. 26456–
—— Ward, J. Experiences of a Diplomatist. Lond., 1872. 8°. . 22582
—— *Biography.* Strauss, G. L. M. Men who have made the New German Empire. Lond., 1875. 2 v. 8°. 22583–
—— — Tuttle, H. German Political Leaders. N. Y., 1876. 16°. (*For contents see* **Tuttle.**) 22443
—— *Description & Travel.* Piozzi, H. L. Observations. Lond., 1789. 2 v. 8°. 18609–
—— — Shelley, M. W. Rambles. Lond., 1844. 2 v. 12°. . . 18552–
—— *Education.* Arnold, M. Higher Schools and Universities in G. Lond., 1874. 12°. (2 copies.) 28821–
—— — Hart, J. M. German Universities. N. Y., 1874. 12°. . . 28831

History.

—— (*to* 1871) Bryce, J. Holy Roman Empire. Lond., 1875. (2 cop.) 20100–
—— — Sime, J. N. Y., 1874. 16°. 20082
—— (*to* 1874) Lewis, C. T. N. Y., 1874. 8°. 20642
—— (1519–1556) Robertson, W. Reign of Charles V. Ed. by W. H. Prescott. Phila., 1872. 3 v. 8°. 20348–
—— (1594–1648) Chapman, B. Hist. of Gustavus Adolphus. Lond., 1856. 8°. 20640
—— (1609–1623) Motley, J. L. John of Barneveld; with a view of the primary causes of the thirty years' war. N. Y., 1874. 2 v. 8°. (2 copies.) 23894–
—— (1618–1648) Gardiner, S. W. Thirty Years' War. Lond., 1874. 20450
—— (1760–1814) Austin, S. Sketches of German life. Lond., 1854. 20641
—— (1806–1822) Seeley, J. R. Life and Times of Stein. Bost., 1879. 2 v. 8°. 22580–
—— (1866) Malet, A. Overthrow of the Germanic Confederation. Lond., 1870. 8°. 20643
—— (1870) Borbstædt (A.) & Dwyer (F.). Franco-German War, to the fall of Strassburg. Lond., 1873. 8°. 20684
—— (1871) Wartensleben, H. von. Operations of the South Army in Jan. & Feb., 1871. Lond., 1872. 8°. 20644
Gesta Romanorum. New ed., by T. Wright. Lond., [1871]. 2 v. 16°. 24477–
Gesture, Manual of. Bacon, A. M. Chic., 1879. 12°. . . . 27822
Getting on in the World. Mathews, W. Chic., 1876. 12°. . . 27381
Giannetto. Majendie, M. E. N. Y., 1876. 16°. 24633
Gibbon, C. Life of George Combe. Lond., 1878. 2 v. 8°. . . 23523–

Gibbon, E. Roman Empire. New ed., by Wm. Smith. Lond., 1872. 8 v. 8°. 20280–
—— *Bagehot, W.* (*In* 'Lit. Stud.,' v. 2.) 26768
—— *Morison, J. C.* (English Men of Letters.) N. Y., 1878. 12°. . 23333
—— *Sainte-Beuve, C. A.* (*In* 'Eng. Portraits.') 22885
Gibbons, Phebe E. French and Belgians. Phila., 1879. 12°. . 21228
Gift, T., (*pseud.*) *See* **Havers, Dora.**
Gilbart, J. W. Lectures and Essays. Lond., 1865. 8°. . . . 27483
Gilbert, Ann T. Autobiography. Lond., 1874. 2 v. 12°. . . 23684–
Gilbert, W. Lucrezia Borgia, Duchess of Ferrara. Lond., 1869. 2 v. 12°. 23945–
Gilded (The) Age. Clemens (S. L.) & Warner (C. D.). Hartf., 1874. 8°. 25586
Giles, H. A. Strange Stories from a Chinese Studio. Lond., 1880. 2 v. 12°. 27787–
Gilfillan, G., *editor.* Less known Brit. Poets. Edinb., 1860. 3 v. 8°. (*For contents see* **Poets,** *English.*) 26354–
—— Library Edition of the Brit. Poets. Edinb., 1853–60. 48 v. 8°. 26319–
Gill, W. River of Golden Sand. Lond., 1880. 2 v. 8°. . . 21930–
Gill, W. F. Life of E. A. Poe. N. Y., etc., 1877. 12°. . , . 22604
Gillies, R. P. Memoirs. Lond., 1851. 3 v. 12°. 18536–
—— Personal Reminiscences. (*In* **Stoddard, R. H.,** 'Bric-à-brac series.') 23257
Gillmore, P. Great Thirst Land. Lond., etc., [1878]. 8°. . . 21864
—— Prairie and Forest. N. Y., 1874. 12°. 29620
Gillray, Jas., *the caricaturist.* Works; life and times. Ed. by T. Wright. Lond. 4°. . . . . ——
Giotto. *Oliphant, M. O. W.* (*In* 'Makers of Florence.') . . . 23836
Gisli the Outlaw. Dasent, G. W. Edinb., 1866. 8°. . . . 27780
Gladstone, W. E. Gleanings of Past Years, 1843–78. N. Y., [1879]. 7 v. 16°. 27227–

CONTENTS:—**1, The Throne, and the Prince Consort; the Cabinet, and Constitution,** (viz.: The county franchise; Kin beyond sea.)—**2, Personal and Literary,** (viz.: J. B. White; G. Leopardi; Tennyson; Wedgewood; Bishop Patteson; Macaulay; Norman Macleod.)—**3, Historical and Speculative,** (viz: The theses of Erastus and the Scottish Church establishment; On 'Ecce Homo;' The courses of religious thought; The influences of authority in matters of opinion; The 16th cent. arraigned before the 19th.)—**4, Foreign,** (viz.: Letter[s] to the Earl of Aberdeen, on the state prosecutions of the Neapolitan government; An examination of the official reply of the [latter]; Farini on the States of the Church; Germany, France, and England; The Hellenic factor in the Eastern problem; Montenegro; Aggression on Egypt and freedom in the East.) **5-6, Ecclesiastical,** (viz.: 5, Present aspect of the church; Ward's ideal of a Christian church; Remarks on the royal supremacy.—6, On the functions of laymen in the church; The Bill for divorce; The Ch. of Eng. and ritualism; Italy and her church.)—**7, Miscellaneous,** (viz.: Inaugural address on the work of universities; Place of ancient Greece in the providential order; A chap. of autobiography; The law of probable evidence, and its application to conduct; The evangelical movement: its parentage, progress and issue.)

—— Homer. (Literature Primers.) [L. &] N. Y., 1879. 16°. . . 26861
—— Homeric Synchronism. N. Y., 1876. 12°. 26820
—— Rome and the Newest Fashions in Religion. Three tracts: The Vatican Decrees; Vaticanism; Speeches of the Pope. N. Y., 1875. 8°. 28724
—— Speeches on Parliamentary Reform, in 1866. Lond., 1866. 12°. 20809
—— The Vatican Decrees. N. Y., 1875. 8°. 28723
—— *Jones, C. H.* Short life of G.; with extracts. N. Y., 1880. 16°. 22853

Gladstone, W. E. *Kebbel, T. E.* (*In* 'Eng. Statesmen.') 22884
—— *Lucy, H. W.* N. Y., 1880. 24°. 22852
—— Punch. Cartoons. Lond., 1878. 4°. . . . . ——
—— *Smith, Geo. B.* Life of Gladstone. N. Y., 1880 [1879]. 8°. . 23071
Glapthorne, H. Plays and Poems; with notes and a memoir. Lond., 1874. 2 v. 16°. 26503-
Glass. Nesbitt, A. Lond., [1878]. 12°. 29765
Gluck, C. W. von. Letters. (*In* **Nohl, L.,** 'Letters.') . . . 23765
Gobineau, J. A. de. Romances of the East. N. Y., 1878. 16°. . 24078
Goblin Market, and other poems. Rossetti, C. G. Lond., 1865. 16°. 26144
Goch, John of. *See* **Pupper, Joh.**
God and the Bible. Arnold, M. N. Y., 1875. 12°. 28688
Godet, F. Studies on the New Testament. N. Y., 1877. 12°. . 28531
Godfrey Malvern. Miller, T. Lond., 1844. 8°. 24678
Godkin, E. L. Hungary and the Magyars. Lond., 1856. 8°. . 20380
Godson of a Marquis. Theuriet, A. N. Y., 1878. 16°. . . . 24081
Godwin, Mary W. Letters to Imlay. With memoir by C. K. Paul. Lond., 1879. 16°. 23214
Godwin, P. Cyclopædia of Biography. N. Y., 1878. 8°. . . 23880
Godwin, W. Adventures of Caleb Williams. N. Y., 1856. 12°. 24479
—— *Paul, C. K.* Bost., 1876. 2 v. 8°. 23326-
Görlach, W. Prince Bismarck. Leipz., 1875. 16°. 22504
Goethe, J. W. von. Dramatic Works. Lond., 1879. 12°. . . 26520
CONTENTS:—The wayward lover; The fellow-culprits; Goetz von Berlichingen; Clavigo; Egmont; Torquato Tasso; Iphigenia in Tauris.
—— Faust. Transl. by C. T. Brooks. Bost., 1868. 16°. . . . 26067
—— *Same.* Transl. by A. Hayward. Bost., 1872. 16°. . . . 26068
—— — Transl. by A. Swanwick. Lond., 1879. 8°. 26367
—— — Transl. by A. B. Taylor. Bost., 1871. 2 v. 8°. . . . 1298-
—— — *Same.* Bost., 1879. 12°. 26094
—— Poems. Transl. by E. A. Bowring. Lond., 1853. 16°. . . 26066
—— — *Same*, 2d ed. Lond., 1874. 12°. 26095
—— Reineke Fuchs. Mit Zeichnungen von W. von Kaulbach. Stuttgart, etc., 1846. 4°. . . . . ——
—— West-Easterly Divan. Transl. by J. Weiss. Bost., 1877. 16°. 26069
—— Wilhelm Meister. Transl. by T. Carlyle. Lond., 1874. 3 v. 24449-
—— *Boyesen, H. H.* Goethe and Schiller. N. Y., 1879. 12°. . . 26904
—— *Hayward, A.* (Foreign Classics for Eng. Readers.) Phil., [1878]. 16°. 23266
—— *Lewes, G. H.* Life and Works of G. Bost., 1856. 2 v. 16°. 23307-
—— — *Same, abridged.* Story of G.'s Life. Lond., 1873. 12°. . . 23309
—— *Masson, D.* (*In* 'The Three Devils.') 27299
—— *Mendelssohn-Bartholdy, C.* Goethe and Mendelssohn, 1821–1831. Lond., 1874. 12°. 23772
—— *See, also,* **Arnold, M.,** 'Mixed Essays' (27241); **Helmholtz, H. L. F.,** 'Pop. Lect.' (29389); **Hutton, R. H.,** 'Essays,' v. 2 (27488); **Merivale, H.,** 'Histor. Stud.' (20188).
Goffe, W. *Warren, I. P.* (*In* 'The Three Judges.') 22627
Gold and Debt. Fawcett, W. L. Chic., 1877. 12°. 29053
Gold and Silver Smiths' Work. Pollen, J. H. Lond., [1879]. 12°. 29767

Goldsmid, F. J. Telegraph and Travel. Lond., 1874. 8°. . . . 21946
Goldsmith, O. Poetical Works. With life, [etc.,] by G. Gilfillan. Edinb., 1854. 8°. 26338
—— *Black, W.* (English Men of Letters.) N. Y., 1879. 12°. . 23337
—— *Irving, W.* N. Y., [1864]. 16°. 24592
Gongora y Argote, L. de. *Churton, E.* Gongora: an essay on the times of Philip III. and IV. of Spain; with translations. Lond., 1862. 2 v. 16°. 23652–
Good Company (*a continuation of* "Sunday Afternoon"). Springf., 1879– v. 4– 8°. 18408–
Gordon, G. H., *Lord Aberdeen. Kebbel, T. E.* (*In* 'Eng. Statesmen'). 22884
Gordon, Lucy A., *Lady Duff Gordon.* Last Letters from Egypt, [and] the Cape. With a memoir. Lond., 1875. 12°. 23615
Gore, G. Art of Scientific Discovery. Lond., 1878. 12°. . . 29380
Gortchakof, A. M. *Klaczko, J.* Two Chancellors. N. Y., 1876. 12°. 22500
Gossip, G. H. D. Chess-Player's Manual. Lond., 1875. 8°. . 29679
Gostwick (J.) & Harrison (R.) Outlines of German Literature. Lond., 1873. 12°. 26902
Gould, J. M. Hints for Camping and Walking. N. Y., 1877. 16°. (2 copies.) 29662–
Government. Harrison, F. Order and Progress. Lond., 1875. 8°. 29087
—— Helps, A. (*In* 'Friends in Council,' 1st ser., v. 2, & 2d ser., v. 2.) 27251–
—— Hill, B. A. Liberty and Law under Federative G. Phila., 1874. 28843
—— Humboldt, C. W. von. Sphere and Duties of G. Lond., 1854. 29095
—— Stickney, A. A True Republic. N. Y., 1879. 12°. . . . 29094
Gower, R., *Lord.* Figure Painters of Holland. L. & N. Y., 1880. 23785
Gracchi (The), Marius, and Sulla. Beesly, A. H. N. Y., [1879]. 16°. 20440
Graffiti d'Italia. Story, W. W. Lond., 1875. 12°. 26135
Graham, Ennis, (*pseud.*) *See* **Molesworth,** *Mrs.*
Graham, J., *marquis of Montrose. Napier, M.* Memoirs. Edinb., 1856. 2 v. 8°. 23016–
Graham, J. J. G. Autobiography of John Milton; or, Milton's life in his own words. Lond., 1872. 16°. 23245
Graham, J. M. Literature and Art in Gr. Brit. Lond., 1871. 8°. 26777
Grahame, J. Poetical Works. With memoir [etc.] by G. Gilfillan. Edinb., 1856. 8°. 26364
Grammar, English. Morris (R.) & Bowen (H. C.) Exercises. Lond., 1878. 16°. 26858
—— Whitney, W. D. Essentials of Eng. Gram. Bost., 1877. 12°. 27863
Grammar-Land. Nesbitt, M. L. N. Y., 1878. 16°. . . . 27868
Grandfather's Chair. Hawthorne, N. Bost., 1876. 12°. . . 24527
Grange Movement, Hist. of. Martin, E. W. Chic., 1874. 8°. . 29004
Grant, A. Aristotle. (**Ancient** Classics for English Readers, supplem. ser., v. 5.) 26851
Grant, Anne. Letters from the Mountains. Lond., 1807. 3 v. 12°. 18547–
—— Superstitions of the Highlands of Scotland. Lond., 1811. 2 v. 18550–
Grant, G. M. Ocean to Ocean. Lond., 1873. 8°. 21549
—— *Same.* Enl. and rev. ed. N. Y., 1877. 12°. 21550

Grant, H. Lord Byron's Cain, with notes. Lond., 1830. 12°. . 18574
Grant, J. The Newspaper Press. Lond., 1871. 2 v. 8°. . . 26762–
Granville, J. M. Secret of a Clear Head. Salem, 1879. 16°. . . 29955
Granville, John Carteret, *Earl.* *Earle, J. C.* (*In* 'Eng. Premiers,' v. 1.) 22882
Grave-mounds. Jewitt, L. Lond., 1870. 12°. 20205
—— *See, also,* **Antiquities** (*and references*); **Burial; Mound-builders.**
Gray, A. Darwiniana. N. Y., 1876. 12°. 29396
—— Natural Science and Religion. N. Y., 1880. 12°. . . . 28697
—— School and Field Book of Botany. N. Y., 1874. 8°. . . 29451
Gray, J. H. China. Lond., 1878. 2 v. 8°. 21935–
Graziella. Lamartine, A. M. L. de. Paris, 1876. 16°. . . . 25669
Great Britain. *See* **England.**
Great Frozen Sea. Markham, A. H. Lond., 1878. 8°. . . . 21882
Great Fur Land. Robinson, H. M. N. Y., 1879. 12°. . . . 21284
Great Lone Land. Butler, W. F. Lond., 1872. 8°. 21552
Great South. King, E. Hartf., 1875. 8°. 21588
Great Thirst Land. Gillmore, P. Lond., etc., [1878]. 8°. . . 21864
Greatorex, Eliza. Summer Etchings in Colorado. N. Y., [1873]. 8°. 21976
Greece. Cox, G. W. Tales of Ancient G. Chic., 2877. 12°. . 27742
—— Davies, G. S. St. Paul in G. Lond., [1878]. 16°. . . . 28500
—— Fustel de Coulanges, M.D. The Ancient City. Bost., 1874. 8°. 20182
—— Guhl (E.) & Koner (W.). Life of the Greeks and Romans, described from antique monuments. Lond., 1875. 8°. (2 cop.) 20180–
—— Jebb, R. C. Modern G.: two lectures. Lond., 1880. 12°. . 20014
—— Longfellow, H. W. Poems of Places, v. 19. Bost., 1878. 16°. 26458
—— Mahaffy, J. P. Old Greek Life. Lond., 1876. 16°. . . . 20056
—— — Rambles and Studies in Greece. Lond., 1876. 12°. . . 21617
—— — Social Life in G., from Homer to Menander. Lond., 1874. 12°. 20095
—— Sergeant, L. New Greece. Lond., [1878]. 8°. 20617

History.

—— Cox, G. W. Lond., 1874. v. 1–2. 8°. 20165–
—— (*to* B. C. 478) Cox, G. W. The Greeks and the Persians. N. Y., 1876. 16°. 20435
—— (*to* B. C. 30) Fyffe, C. A. Lond., 1877. 16°. 20054
—— (B. C. 480–431) Lloyd, W. W. The Age of Pericles. Lond., 1875. 2 v. 8°. 20163–
—— (B. C. 479–405) Cox, G. W. The Athenian Empire. N. Y., [1877]. 16°. 20441
See, also, **Athens; Mythology.**
Greek Cities and Islands of Asia Minor. Vaux, W. S. W. Lond., 1877. 16°. 20043
Greek Language and Literature. Blackie, J. S. Horæ Hellenicæ. Lond., 1874. 8°. 26960
—— Church, A. J. Stories from the Greek Tragedians. [L. &] N. Y., 1880. 12°. 26806
—— Jebb, R. C. (Literature Primers.) Lond., 1877. 16°. . . 26857
—— Mahaffy, J. P. Hist. of Classical Greek Lit. N. Y., 1880. 2 v. 26807–
CONTENTS:—1, The poets; with an app. on Homer, by Prof. Sayce.—2, The prose writers.

Greek Language and Literature. Müller, C. O. Hist. of the Literature of Ancient Greece. Lond., 1840. v. 1. 8°. . . . 197
—— — *Same.* Continued by J. W. Donaldson. Lond., [1858]. 3 v. 8°. 26961–
—— Neaves, C. Greek Anthology. (**Ancient** Classics for Eng. Readers, v. 20.) 26846
—— *See, also,* **Poets,** *Greek.*
Greeley, H. Political Economy. Bost., 1871. 16°. . . . 28807
—— *Parton, J.* Life of Greeley. Bost., 1872. 12°. 22643
Green, J. R. Hist. of the English People. N. Y., 1878–80. 4 v. 8°. (2 copies.) 20965–

CONTENTS:—1, Early England, 449–1071; Eng. under foreign kings, 1071–1214; The Charter, 1204–1291; The Parliament, 1307–1461.—2, The Monarchy, 1461–1540; The Reformation, 1540–1603.—3, Puritan Eng., 1603–1660; The Revolution, 1660–1688.—4, The Revolution, 1688–1763; Mod. Eng., 1760–1815.

—— Short History of the English People. Lond., 1874(–5). (3 cop.) 20960–
—— *Same.* N. Y., 1878 (–9). 8°. (2 copies.) 20963–
—— Stray Studies from England and Italy. N. Y., 1876. 12°. . 27295
—— *editor.* Classical Writers. N. Y., 1879–80. 3 v. 16°. (*For contents see* **Clas.** Writers.) 26890–
—— — Readings from English History. N. Y., 1879. 12°. . . 20841
—— — *See, also,* **History** Primers ; **Literature** Primers.
Green, Mary A. E. W. Lives of the Princesses of England. Lond., 1850–55. 6 v. 12°. 22920–
—— *editor.* Letters of Royal and Illustrious Ladies of Great Britain, [1100–1558]. Lond., 1846. 3 v. 12°. 22927–
Green, Mat. Poetical Works. With memoir [etc.] by G. Gilfillan. Edinb., 1858. 8°. 26321
Green Pastures and Piccadilly. Black, W. N. Y., 1878. 12°. (2 cop.) 24008–
Greene, G. W. The German Element in the War of American Independence. N. Y., 1876. 12°. 21360
Greene, R. Friar Bacon and Friar Bungay. Ed. by A. W. Ward. Oxf., 1878. 16°. 26871
—— Poems. Ed. by R. Bell. Lond., 1876. 12°. 26096
Greenland. Longfellow, H. W. Poems of Places. (*In* v. 30.) . 26469
Greenwell, Dora. Liber Humanitatis. Lond., 1875. 12°. . . 27272
Greg, W. R. Creed of Christendom. Detroit, 1878. 12°. . . 28694
—— Enigmas of Life. Bost., 1874. 12°. 27292

CONTENTS:—Realizable ideals; Malthus notwithstanding; Nonsurvival of the fittest; Limits and directions of human development; The significance of life; De profundis; Elsewhere.

—— Literary and Social Judgments. Bost., 1873. 12°. . . . 27293

CONTENTS:—Mad. de Staël; British and foreign characteristics; False morality of lady novelists; Kingsley and Carlyle; French fiction; Chateaubriand; De Tocqueville; Why are women redundant? Truth versus edification; Time; Good people.

—— Rocks Ahead. Lond., 1874. 12°. 27294

CONTENTS:—Political rock; Economic rock; Religious rock. Appendix: The mistake of honest democrats; Unionist restrictions on labour; Three men and three eras; United States in recent years.

Gregory I. (*the Great*), *Pope.* *Merivale, C.* St. G., and the Early Missions of the Church. (*In* 'Four Lect.') 28445
Gregory VII. (Hildebrand), *Pope.* *King, T. S.* (*In* 'Substance,' etc.) 28539
Grenville, Geo. *Earle, J. C.* (*In* 'Eng. Premiers,' v. 1.) . . . 22882
Grenville, Richard. *See* **Temple, R. G.,** *Earl.*
Gresset, J. B. L. *Besant, W.* (*In* 'French Humorists.') . . 26776

Grettir. Cox (G. W.) & Jones (E. H.). G. the Strong. (*In* 'Pop. Romances.' *And in* 'Tales.') . . . . . 27712 & 27713
Greville, C. C. F. Memoirs. Lond., 1875. 3 v. 8°. . . . 23061–
—— *Same.* (*In* **Stoddard, R. H.,** 'Bric-à-Brac Series.') . . . 23253
Gréville, Henry, (*pseud.*) *See* **Durand, Alice F.**
Grey, Charles, 2*d Earl.* *Earle, J. C.* (*In* 'Eng. Premiers,' v. 2.) 22883
—— *Kebbel, T. E.* (*In* 'Eng. Statesmen.') 22884
Griffis, W. E. The Mikado's Empire. N. Y., 1876. 8°. . . 21939
Griffiths, A. Lola: a tale of Gibraltar. N. Y., 1877. 16°. . . 24452
—— Memorials of Millbank. Lond., 1875. 2 v. 12°. . . . 28858–
Grillparzer, F. Sappho: a tragedy. Bost., 1876. 16°. . . . 26070
Grimaldi, J., Memoirs of. Dickens, C. J. H. Lond., 1846. 16°. . 23651
Grimké, T. S. [Orations, Addresses, etc.] Charleston, New Haven, and Phila., 1829–33. 8°. 8703
Grimm, H. Unüberwindliche Mächte. Roman. Berlin, 1870. 2 B. 25878–
Grohman, W. A. B. Gaddings with a Primitive People. N. Y., 1878. 16°. 21247
Grote, G. History of Greece. Lond., 1849. v. 2–4. 8°. . . 20160–
—— Minor Works. Lond., 1873. 8°. 27400
—— *Grote, H. L.* Personal Life of G. Lond., 1873. 8°. . . . 23419
Grove, G. Geography. Lond., 1877. 16°. 20055
Grün, Anastasius, (*pseud.*) *See* **Auersperg, A. A.**
Gryll Grange. Peacock, T. L. (*In* 'Works,' v. 2.) 27304
Gubernatis, A. de. Zoological Mythology. N. Y. [L.], 1872. 2 v. 8°. 29490–
Gudrun; [transl. by E. Letherbrow.] Edinb., 1863. 16°. . . . 27670
—— Cox (G. W.) & Jones. (*In* 'Pop. Romances.' *And in* 'Tales.') 27712 & 27713
Guernsey, A. H. Thomas Carlyle. N. Y., 1880. 16°. . . . 23312
Guesses at Truth. Hare, A. W. & J. C. Lond., 1876. 16°. . . 28081
Guest, M. J. Lectures on the Hist. of England. Lond., 1879. 16°. 20820
Guhl (E.) & Koner (W.). Life of the Greeks and Romans. Lond., 1875. 8°. (2 copies.) 20180–
Guiana. Brown, C. B. Canoe and Camp Life in Brit. G. Lond., 1876. 8°. 21810
—— Palgrave, W. G. Dutch G. Lond., 1876. 8°. 21811
Guild, C. Abroad again. Bost., 1877. 8°. 21722
Guilford, Frederick, 2*d earl of.* *See* **North, F.**
Guillemin, A. Applications of Physical Forces. Lond., 1877. 8°. 29571
—— Forces of Nature. N. Y. [Lond.], 1873. 8°. 29572
—— The Heavens. Lond., 1872. 8°. 29573
Guinnard, A. Three Years' Slavery among the Patagonians. Lond., 1871. 12°. 21229
Guizot, Elisabeth C. P. de M. *Sainte-Beuve, C. A.* (*In* 'Portraits of Cel. Women.') 23643
Guizot, F. P. G. France under Louis-Phillipe. Lond., 1865. 8°. 20689
—— History of England. Lond., 1877–79. 3 v. 8°. . . . 21160–
—— Hist. of France. Lond., 1872–76. 5 v. 8°. 20760–
—— *Same.* Bost., [1877]. 6 v. 8°. 20765–
—— — *abridged.* Lond., 1879. 8°. 20690
—— *Sainte-Beuve, C. A.* (*In* 'Monday-Chats.') 23290

Guizot, F. P. G. *Senior, N. W.* Conversations with G. Lond., 1878. 2 v. 8°. 23922–

Gunnar: a tale of Norse life. Boyesen, H. H. Bost., 1874. 16°. 24063

Gunnlaug and the Fair Helga. Cox (G. W.) & Jones. (*In* 'Pop. Romances.' *And in* 'Tales.') . . . . . . 27712 & 27713

Gustavus II., Adolphus. *Chapman, B.* Lond., 1856. 8°. . . . 20640

Guthrie, F. Practical Physics. N. Y., 1879. 16°. 29351

Guthrie, T. Autobiography; and memoir by D. K. & C. J. Guthrie. N. Y., 1874. 2 v. 12°. 22147–

Guy of Warwick. Cox (G. W.) & Jones. (*In* 'Pop. Romances.') 27712 & 2010

Gwen: a drama in monologue. [Morice, L.] Lond., 1879. 16°. 26098

Gymnastics. Blaikie, W. How to get strong. N. Y., 1879. (2 cop.) 29953–

—— Howard, J. H. Gymnasts and G. Lond., 1873. 12°. . . . 29639

—— Ravenstein (E. G.) & Hulley (J.). Handbook of G. and Athletics. Lond., 1867. 8°. 29637

—— *See, also,* **Athletics.**

Gypsies. Leland (C. G.) *& others.* English-Gipsy Songs. Phila., 1875. 16°. 26123

H. H. *See* **Jackson, Helen H.**

Habberton, J. Barton Experiment. N. Y., 1877. 12°. 24453

—— Canoeing in Kanuckia. (*See* **Norton, C. L., & Habberton.**)

—— Scripture Club of Valley Rest. N. Y., 1877. 16°. 24454

Habitations of Man. Viollet-le-Duc, E. E. Bost., 1876. 8°. . . 29927

Hackländer, F. W. Behind the Counter. Leipz., 1868. 16°. . 24455

—— Werke. Stuttg., 1860–76. 60 B. in 30. 16°. 25800–

Contents:—1-3, Namenlose Geschichten.—4, Das Soldatenleben im Frieden; Wachtstubenabenteuer (Th. 1.)—5, (Th. 2-4.)—6, Kleinere Erzählungen u. humoristische Skizzen.—7, Handel u. Wandel.—8-9. Reise in den Orient.—10-12, Eugen Stillfried.—13, Märchen.—14, Der Pilgerzug nach Mekka.—15, [Lustspiele,] Der geheime Agent; Magnetische Kuren; Schuldig!—16-20, Europäisches Sklavenleben.—21, Der Augenblick des Glücks.—22-24, Ein Winter in Spanien.—25-26, Erlebtes.—27, [Lustspiele,] Zur Ruhe setzen; Monsieur de Blé; Unten im Hause.—28-29, Bilder aus dem Soldatenleben im Kriege.—30-34, Der neue Don Quixote.—35-36, Tag u. Nacht.—37, Der Tannhäuser.—38-39, Krieg u. Frieden.—40, Tagebuchblätter.—41-42, Der Wechsel des Lebens—43, Der verlorene Sohn.—44-48, Die dunkle Stunde.—49. Fürst u. Kavalier.—50. Nahes u. Fernes.—51, Neue Geschichten.—52-56, Künstlerroman.—57, Zwölf Zettel.—58-60, Das Geheimniss der Stadt.

Hadley, J. Essays, philological and critical. N. Y., 1873. 8°. . 27860

—— Introduction to Roman Law. N. Y., 1875. 12°. . . . 28847

Haeckel, E. H. Evolution of Man. N. Y., 1879. 2 v. 12°. . . 29383–

—— Freedom in Science and Teaching. N. Y., 1879. 12°. . . 29385

—— History of Creation. N. Y., 1876. 2 v. 12°. 29381–

Händel, G. F., Life of. Schölcher, V. N. Y., 1857. 12°. . . 23771

Häusser, L. Period of the Reformation, 1517–1648. Lond., 1873. 2 v. 8°. 20480–

Hale, E. Fall of the Stuarts and Western Europe from 1678 to 1697. N. Y., [1876]. 16°. 20453

Hale, E. E., (*pseud.,* 'Frederic Ingham.') His Level Best; and other stories. Bost., 1873. 16°. 24480

—— Ingham Papers. Bost., 1869. 16°. 24481

—— Philip Nolan's Friends. N. Y., 1877. 12°. 24482

—— What Career? Bost., 1878. 16°. 27385

Hales (J. W.) & Jerram (C. S.), *editors.* London Series of English Classics. (*For contents see* **London** Series.)

Half Brothers. Dumas, A. D. Lond., [1879]. 16°. (2 cop.) 24410 & 24422
Hall, B. Schloss Hainfeld; or, a winter in Lower Styria. Edinb., 1836. 12°. 18635
Hall, J. God's Word through Preaching. N. Y., [1875]. 12°. . 28418
Hall (J.) & Stuart (G. H.). The Amer. Evangelists, Moody and Sankey, in Great Britain and Ireland. N. Y., [1875]. 12°. 22615
Haller, Gustave, (*pseud.*). *See* **Fould, Wilhelmine J. S.**
Halliwell, J. O. Life of Shakespeare. Lond., 1848. 8°. . . 27044
Hallock, C. Fishing Tourist. N. Y., 1873. 8°. 29623
—— Sportsman's Gazetteer and General Guide. N. Y., 1877. 12°. (Map in separate case.) 29621–
Hals, F. *Head, P. R.* L. & N. Y., 1879. 12°. 23780
Hamerton, P. G. Chapters on Animals. Bost., 1874. 12°. . . 29327
—— Etching and Etchers. Bost., 1876. 8°. 29870
—— The Intellectual Life. Bost., 1873. 12°. 27382
—— Life of J. M. W. Turner, R. A. Bost., 1879. 12°. . . . 23803
—— Modern Frenchmen: five biographies. Bost., 1878. 12°. . 22488
Contents:—Victor Jacquemont; H. Perreyve; F. Rude; J. J. Ampère; H. Regnault.
—— Round my House. Bost., 1876. 12°. 21248
—— Sylvan Year. (*And*) Unknown River. Bost., 1876. 12°. . . 29328
—— Wenderholme. Bost., 1876. 12°. 24483
Hamilton, Alex. *Morse, J. T.* Life of H. Bost., 1876. 2 v. 12°. 22624–
—— *Riethmüller, C. J.* Life and Times of H. Lond., [1864]. 12°. 22626
—— *Shea, G.* Life and Epoch of H. Bost., 1879. 8°. 22722
Hamilton, Augusta. Marriage Rites, Customs, and Ceremonies, of all Nations. Lond., 1822. 8°. 28960
Hamilton, R. Money and Value. Lond., 1878. 8°. . . . 29044
Hamilton, Walter. Poets Laureate of England. Lond., 1879. 12°. 23288
Hamilton, *Sir* **Wm.:** his philosophy. Mill, J. S. N. Y., 1874. 2 v. 12°. 28202–
Hamley, E. B. Lady Lee's Widowhood. Edinb., 1854. 2 v. 8°. . 24484–
—— Voltaire. (For. Classics for Eng. Readers.) Phila., [1877]. 16°. 23263
Hamlin, C. Among the Turks. N. Y., 1878. 12°. 21600
Hammer und Amboss. Spielhagen, F. Leipz., 1877. 2 B. 16°. (Sämmtl. Werke, B. 9–10.) 25868–
Hammersmith. Severance, M. S. Bost., 1878. 12°. (2 copies.) . 24819–
Hammond, H. *Teale, W. H.* (*In* 'Lives of Eng. Divines.') . . 22110
Hammond, W. A. Spiritualism. N. Y., 1876. 12°. . . . 28043
Hamran Arabs. Myers, A. B. R. Lond., 1876. 8°. . . . 21697
Hancock, W. S. *Junkin (D. X.) & Norton (F. H.).* N. Y., 1880. . 22648
Hand, F. G. Æsthetics of Musical Art. Book 1. Lond., 1880. 8°. 29798
Hand of Ethelberta. Hardy, T. N. Y., 1876. 16°. (2 copies.) . 24459–
Handel, G. F. *See* **Händel.**
Handel und Wandel. Hackländer, F. W. von. Stuttg., 1875. 16°. (Werke, B. 7.) 25803
Hanna, W. Our Lord's Life on Earth. Edinb., 1869. 6 v. 16°. . 28480–
—— Wars of the Huguenots. Edinb., 1871. 16°. 20402
Hannay, J. Studies on Thackeray. Lond., [1869]. 16°. . . 26918
Hans und Grete. Spielhagen, F. (Sämmtl. Werke, B. 8.) . . 25867

Hansard, G. A. Book of Archery. Lond., 1841. 8°. 29635
Haps and Mishaps of a Tour in Europe. Lippincott, S. J. C. Bost., 1854. 12°. 6491
Hard Cash. Reade, C. N. Y., 1876. 16°. 24811
Hardenberg, C. A. von. *Seeley, J. R.* (*In* 'Life and Times of Stein.') 22580
Hardenberg, F. von, (*pseud.*, 'Novalis.') *Curwen, H.* (*In* 'Sorrow and Song,' v. 1.) 23285
Hardy, C. Forest Life in Acadie. Lond., 1869. 8°. 21553
Hardy, T. Desperate Remedies: a novel. N. Y., 1874. 16°. . 24456
—— Distracted Young Preacher. N. Y., 1879. 16°. 24924
—— Far from the Madding Crowd. N. Y., 1874. 16°. (2 copies.) . 24457–
—— Hand of Ethelberta. N. Y., 1876. 16°. (2 copies.) 24459–
—— Pair of Blue Eyes. N. Y., 1873. 16°. 24461
—— Return of the Native. N. Y., 1878. 16°. (2 copies.) . . . 24463–
—— Under the Greenwood Tree. N. Y., 1873. 16°. 24462
Hare, A. J. C. Cities of Northern and Central Italy. N. Y., 1876. 3 v. 12°. 21603–
—— Days near Rome. Phila., 1875. 12°. 21602
—— Life and Letters of Frances Baroness Bunsen. N. Y., 1879. 23621
—— Memorials of a Quiet Life. Lond., 1873–76. 3 v. 12°. . . 23618–
—— Walks in London. N. Y., 1878. 12°. 21606
—— Wanderings in Spain. Lond., 1873. 16°. 21601
Hare, A. W. & J. C. Guesses at Truth. Lond., 1876. 16°. . . 28081
Hare, J. C. Life of John Sterling. (*See* **Sterling,** 'Essays.') . . 12898
Hare, T. Election of Representatives. Lond., 1873. 16°. . . 29092
Harlan, G. C. Eyesight, and how to care for it. Phil., 1879. 16°. 29961
Harness, W. Personal Reminiscences. (*In* **Stoddard, R. H.,** 'Bric-à-Brac Series.') 23255
Harold: a drama. Tennyson, A. Bost., 1877. 16°. (2 copies.) . 26514–
Harper's Monthly Magazine. N. Y., 1850–79. 59 v. 8°. . . 13413–
—— *Same.* v. 1 42. 13291–
—— Index to v. 1–40; and 1–50. . . . . ——
Harrison, F. Order and Progress. Lond., 1875. 8°. 29087
—— *and others.* A Modern Symposium. Detroit, 1878. 12°. . . 28094
—— — *Same.* (*In* **Burlingame, E. L.,** 'Cur. Disc., v. 2.) . . . 27283
[**Harrison, J. B.**] Certain Dangerous Tendencies in American Life, and other papers. Bost., 1880. 16°. 28885
Harrison, R. German Literature. (*See* **Gostwick, J., & Harrison.**)
Harry: [a poem] by the author of "Mrs. Jerningham's Journal." N. Y. [& L.], 1877. 16°. 26016
Hart, E. A. Shakespeare's King Lear. (*See* **Seeley, J. R.,** *& others.*)
Hart, J. M. German Universities. N. Y., 1874. 12°. 28831
Harte, F. B. Drift from Two Shores. Bost., 1878. 16°. (2 cop.) 24489–
—— Echoes of the Foot-hills. Bost., 1875. 16°. 26072
—— Gabriel Conroy. Hartf., 1876. 8°. (2 cop.) 24650–
—— Mrs. Skaggs's Husbands. Bost., 1875. 16°. 24486
—— Poetical Works. Complete ed. Bost., 1873. 16°. . . . 26071
—— Story of a Mine. Bost., 1878. 16°. 24491

Harte, F. B. Tales of the Argonauts. Bost., 1875. 12°. (2 copies.) 24487–
—— Thankful Blossom. Bost., 1877. 16°. (2 copies.) . . . 24492–
—— Twins of Table Mountain. Bost., 1879. 16°. (2 copies.) . 24495–
—— Two Men of Sandy Bar: a drama. Bost., 1876. 16°. . . 24494
Hartley, W. N. Air and its relations to Life. N. Y., 1875. 12°. . 29298
Hartshorne, H. Our Homes. Phil., 1880. 16°. 29965
Harvard, Student-Life at. [Tripp, G. H.] Bost., 1876. 12°. (2 cop.) 24911–
Harvard Advocate, Verses from. Cambridge, 1876. 16°. . . 26017
Harvard Studente, Manners and Customs of ye. Attwood, F. G. Bost., 1877. Ob. 4°. . . . . ——
Harvey, P. Reminiscences of Dan. Webster. Bost., 1877. (2 cop.) 22699–
Harvey, Wm. *Richardson, B. W.* (*In* 'A Ministry of Health.') . 29996
—— *Willis, R.* Lond., 1878. 8°. 23541
Hasell, E. J. Calderon. (Foreign Classics for Eng. Readers, v. 9.) 23270
Hathercourt. *Mrs.* Molesworth. N. Y., 1878. 16°. . . . 24835
Havard, H. Dead Cities of the Zuyder Zee. Lond., 1875. 8°. . 21779
—— Picturesque Holland. Lond., 1876. 8°. 21780
Havelok. Cox (G. W.) & Jones (E. H.). (*In* 'Pop. Romances.) 27712 & 2010
Havers, Dora, (*pseud.*, 'Theo. Gift.') Maid Ellice. N. Y., 1878. 16°. (2 copies.) 24497–
—— Pretty Miss Bellew. N. Y., 1875. 16°. 24499
Hawaiian Islands. Nordhoff, C. (*In* 'Northern California,' *etc.*) . 21584
Hawker, R. S. *Baring-Gould, S.* Vicar of Morwenstow. N. Y., [1879]. 12°. 22105
Haworth's. Burnett, F. H. N. Y., 1879. 12°. (2 cop.) . . 24154–
Hawthorne, J. Bressant: a novel. N. Y., 1873. 12°. . . . 24500
—— Garth: a novel. N. Y., 1877. 8°. 24652
—— Idolatry: a romance. Bost., 1874. 12°. 24501
—— Mrs. Gainsborough's Diamonds: a story. N. Y., 1878. 16°. . 24925
—— Saxon Studies. Bost., 1876. 12°. 21607
—— Sebastian Strome: a novel. N. Y., 1880. 8°. 24653
Hawthorne, N. Biographical Stories. (*In vol. with* 'Tanglewood Tales.') 24524
—— Blithedale Romance. (*In vol. with* 'Scarlet Letter.') . . . 24517–
—— Dolliver Romance, and other pieces. Bost., 1876. 12°. (2 cop.) 24505–
—— Fanshawe: a tale. [By N. Hawthorne.] Bost., 1828. 12°. . 15326
—— *Same*, and other pieces. Bost., 1876. 12°. (2 copies.) . . 24505–
—— Grandfather's Chair. (*In vol. with* 'Wonder-Book.') . . . 24527
—— House of Seven Gables. Bost., 1876 (&c.). 12°. (4 copies). . 24507–
—— Marble Faun. Bost., 1869 (&c.). 12°. (4 copies.) . . . 24511–
—— Mosses from an Old Manse. Bost., 1877. 12°. 24515
—— Our Old Home. Bost., 1877. 12°. 24516
—— Passages from the Amer. Note-Books. Bost., 1877. 12°. . 24502
—— Passages from the English Note-Books. Bost., 1876. 12°. . 24503
—— Passages from the French and Ital. Note-Books. Bost., 1878. . 24504
—— Scarlet Letter. Bost., 1871 (&c.). 12°. (7 copies.) . . . 24517–
—— Septimius Felton. (*In vol. with* 'Our Old Home.') . . . 24516
—— Snow Image. (*With* 'The House of Seven Gables.') . . . 24507–
—— Tanglewood Tales. Bost., 1876. 12°. 24524

Hawthorne, N. Twice-told Tales. Bost., 1871 (&c.). 12°. (2 cop.) 24525–
—— Wonder-Book. Bost,, 1876. 12°. 24527–
—— *James, H., jr.* (English Men of Letters.) N. Y., 1880. 12°. . 23348
—— [*Japp, A.*] Memoir of H.; with stories . . . Lond., 1872. 12°. 22609
—— *Lathrop, G. P.* A Study of H. Bost., 1876. 16°. . . . 22608
—— *See, also,* **Hutton, R. H.,** 'Essays,' v. 2 (27488); **Mackay, C.,** 'Forty Years' Recol.,' v. 2 (22944); **Stephen, L.,** 'Hours in a Lib.,' v. 1 (26933).
Haydn, F. J. Letters. (*In* '**Nohl, L.,** 'Letters.') 23765
Haydon, B. R. Correspondence and Table-Talk. With a memoir by F. W. Haydon. Lond., 1876. 2 v. 8°. 23830–
Hayley, W. Life and Letters of Cowper. Lond., 1835. 8°. . . 23420
Hayti. Hazard, S. (*In* 'Santo Domingo.') 21728
Hayward, A. Biographical and Critical Essays. [2d] series. Lond., 1873. 2 v. 8°. 27401–

CONTENTS:—1, Pearls and mock pearls of history; Fred. von Gentz; Maria Edgeworth; Geo. Canning; Marshal Saxe; S. van de Weyer; Alex. Dumas; Salons; Whist and whist-players.—2, Varieties of history and art; Ed. Livingston; Richard III.; Marie Antoinette; The Countess of Albany and Alfieri; Sir H. Holland's Recollections; Lady Palmerston; Lord Lansdowne; Lord Dalling and Bulwer; More about Junius.

—— *Same.* 3d series. Lond., 1874. 8°. 27403

CONTENTS:—British Parliament; Curiosities of German archives; England and France; Lanfrey's Napoleon; Vicissitudes of families; Lives of the Lord Chancellors of Ireland; The second Armada; The purchase system.

—— Goethe. (Foreign Classics for Eng. Readers.) Phil., [1878]. 16°. 23266
—— Selected Essays. N. Y., 1879. 2 v. 12°. 27244–

CONTENTS:—1, Sydney Smith; Sam. Rogers; Fred. von Gentz; Maria Edgeworth; Countess Hahn-Hahn; Henri Beyle; A. Dumas.—2, British Parliament; Pearls and mock pearls of history; Vicissitudes of families; England and France; Lady Palmerston; Lord Lansdowne; Lord Dalling and Bulwer; Whist and whist-players.

Hazard, S. Santo Domingo, past and present; with a glance at Hayti. N. Y., 1873. 12°. 21728
Hazel-Blossoms. Whittier, J. G. Bost., 1875. 16°. . . . 26140
Hazlitt, W. *Hazlitt, W. C.* Memoirs; with correspondence. Lond., 1867. 2 v. 12°. 23228–
—— *Stoddard, R. H.* (Bric-à-Brac Series.) N. Y., 1875. 16°. . . 23254
Hazlitt, W. C. Hist. of the Venetian Republic. Lond., 1860. 4 v. 20322–
—— Memoirs of Wm. Hazlitt. Lond., 1867. 2 v. 12°. . . . 23228–
Head, P. R. Van Dyck. [*And*] Frans Hals. Lond. & N. Y., 1879. 23780
Headley, J. T. Mountain Adventures. Illust. N. Y., 1872. 16°. 10133
Heads of the People. Meadows, K. Lond., 1840–1. 2 v. 8°. . 25581–
Health. Blaikie, W. How to get strong. N. Y., 1879. 16°. (2 cop.) 29953–
—— Fothergill, J. M. Maintenance of H. N. Y., 1879. 12°. . 29994
—— Granville, J. M. Secret of a Clear Head. Salem, 1879. 16°. . 29955
—— Keen, W. W., *editor.* American H. Primers. Phila., 1879–80. 10 v. 16°. (*For contents see* **Amer.** H. Primers.) . . . 29958–
—— Kingsley, C. Health and Education. Lond., 1874. 12°. . 29979
—— Parkes, E. A. Personal Care of Health. Lond., [1876]. 16°. 29957
—— Richardson, B. W. A Ministry of H., and other addresses. Lond., 1879. 12°. 29996
—— *See, also,* **Foods; Gastronomy; Hygiene.**
Hearing, and how to keep it. Burnett, C. H. Phil., 1879. 16°. . 29958

Heath, R. F. Titian. N. Y. & Lond., 1879. 12°. 23777
Heathen World and St. Paul. Lond., [1878]. 4 v. 16°. 28498–
CONTENTS:—St. P. in Damascus and Arabia, by G. Rawlinson.—In Asia Minor and at the Syrian Antioch, E. H. Plumptre.—In Greece, G. S. Davies. —At Rome, C. Merivale.
Heathenism, Conflict of Christianity with. Uhlhorn, G. N. Y., 1879. 8°. 28602
—— *See, also,* **Religions** (various).
Heavens (The). Guillemin, A. Lond., 1872. 8°. 29573
Hebrew Men and Times. Allen, J. H. Bost. 1879. 16°. . . 28442
Hebrew Monarchy, Hist. of the. [Newman, F. W.] Lond., 1847. 8°. 28441
Hebrides. Smith, W. A. Lewsiana; or, Life in the Outer Hebrides. Lond., 1875. 12°. 21253
Heckethorn, C. W. Secret Societies. Lond., 1875. 2 v. 12°. . 28993–
Hector, Annie F. (*pseud.*, 'Mrs. Alexander.') Her Dearest Foe. N. Y., 1876. 16°. 24528
—— Heritage of Langdale. N. Y., 1877. 16°. 24529
—— Maid, Wife, or Widow? N. Y., 1879. 16°. 24530
—— Ralph Wilton's Weird. N. Y., 1875. 16°. (2 cop.) . . . 24531–
—— Which shall it be? N. Y., 1874. 16°. 24533
—— The Wooing o't. N. Y., 1874. 16°. (3 cop.) 24534–
Hector Servadac. Verne, J. N. Y., 1878. 8°. 24270
Hedge, F. H. Ways of the Spirit, and other essays. Bost., 1877. 28537
Hegel, G. W. F. Philosophy of History. Lond., 1872. 12°. . 20089
Heidelberg: a romance. James, G. P. R. N. Y., 1869. 8°. . . 24668
Heine, H. Atta Troll, and other poems. Lond., 1876. 12°. . . 26018
—— Pictures of Travel. Phila., 1855. 12°. 27248
—— Prose Miscellanies. Phil., 1876. 12°. 27247
—— Scintillations. N. Y., 1873. 16°. 27246
—— Wit, Wisdom, and Pathos. Lond., 1879. 12°. 27249
—— *Stigand, W.* Life Work, and Opinions of Heine. Lond., 1875. 2 v. 8°. 23408–
Hellenics. Landor, W. S. Edinb., 1859. 8°. 26246
Hellwald, F. von. Russians in Central Asia. Lond., 1874. 8°. . 21608
Helmholtz, H. L. F. Popular Lectures. Lond., 1873. 8°. . . 29389
Helps, A. Friends in Council. Lond., 1872–3. 2 series; 4 vols. 27250–
—— Ivan de Biron. Bost., 1874. 12°. 24537
—— Life and Labors of Brassey. Bost., 1874. 8°. 23560
—— Social Pressure. Bost., 1875. 12°. 28882
—— Some Talk about Animals and their Masters. Lond., 1873. 16°. 29329
Henderson, W. Folk Lore of the Northern Counties of England and the Borders. Lond., 1866. 12°. 27666
Henrietta Maria, *queen of England.* Letters. Lond., 1857. 12°. 22930
Henry of Huntingdon, Chronicle of. Lond., 1853. 12°. . . . 20804
Henry, P. Life and Times of Calvin. Lond., 1849. 2 v. 8°. . 22302–
Henslow, G. Theory of Evolution. Lond., 1873. 12°. . . . 28167
Her Dearest Foe. Hector, A. F. N. Y., 1876. 16°. . . . 24528
Herbert, G. Poetical Works. With life [etc.] by G. Gilfillan. Edinb., 1854. 8°. 26339
[**Herbert (G. R. C.)** & Kingsley (G. H.).] South-Sea Bubbles. N. Y., 1872. 12°. 21609

Herbert, H. W., (*pseud.,* 'Frank Forester.') Complete Manual for Young Sportsmen. N. Y., 1857. 12°. 29604
—— Field Sports. N. Y., 1849. 2 v. 8°. 29600–
—— Fish and Fishing of the United States and British Provinces of North America. N. Y., 1850. 8°. 29624
—— Sporting Scenes and Characters. Phil., [1857]. 2 v. 12°. . 29602–
CONTENTS:—1, My Shooting Box; Deerstalkers.—2, Warwick Woodlands; Quorndon Hounds.

Heredity. Cook, J. (Bost. Mond. Lectures.) Bost., 1879. 12°. . 28025
—— Dugdale, R. L. "The Jukes:" a study in crime, pauperism, disease and heredity. N. Y., 1877. 12°. 29399
—— Galton, F. English Men of Science. N. Y., 1875. 12°. . . 29400
—— Papillon, F. (*In* 'Nature and Life.') 29397
—— Proctor, R. A. Hereditary Traits. (*In* 'Rough ways.') . . 29444
—— Ribot, T. Heredity: a psychological study. N. Y., 1875. 12°. 29398
—— *See, also,* **Evolution.**

Heritage of Langdale. Hector, A. F. N. Y., 1877. 16°. . . 24529

Hero Carthew. Parr, L. N. Y., 1873. 16°. 24841

Herschel, Caroline L., Memoir and Correspondence of. Mrs. J. [F. W.] Herschel. N. Y., 1876. 12°. 23546

Hervey, Mary Lepel, *Lady.* Letters; with a memoir. Lond., 1821. 18593

Hesiod. Davies, J. (Ancient Classics for English Readers, v. 15.) 26841

Hessey, J. A. Prayer. (Moral Difficulties connected with the Bible, 3d series.) Lond., 1873. 16°. 28511
—— Sunday. Lond., 1866. 12°. 28490

Hester. Butt, B. M. N. Y., 1879. 16°. . . . . . , . 24924

Heyse, P. J. L. L'Arrabiata, and other tales. Leipzig, 1867. 16°. 24538
—— Barbarossa, and other tales. Leipz., 1874. 16°. . . . 24539
—— Dead Lake, and other tales. Leipz., 1870. 16°. . . . 24540
—— In Paradise: a novel. N. Y., 1878. 2 v. 16°. 24084–
—— Tales. N. Y., 1879. 16°. 24088
CONTENTS:—Count Ernest's Home; Dead Lake; The Fury (L'Arrabiata); Judith Stern.

Heywood, T. Dramatic Works; with memoir. Lond., 1874. 6 v. 26505–

Hibbert Lectures. 28568–
CONTENTS:—1878, Religions of India, by F. M. Müller.—1879, Religion of Ancient Egypt, P. L. Renouf.—1880, English Conferences, J. E. Renan.

Higginson, T. W. Atlantic Essays. Bost., 1874. 12°. 27254
CONTENTS:—A plea for culture; Literature as an art; Americanism in literature; A letter to a young contributor; Ought women to learn the alphabet? A charge with Prince Rupert; Mademoiselle's campaigns; The Puritan minister; Fayal and the Portuguese; The Greek goddesses; Sappho; On an old Latin text-book.
—— Book of American Explorers. Bost., 1877. 16°. . . . 22600
—— English Statesmen. (Brief Biographies, v. 1.) N. Y., 1875. 16°. 22440
CONTENTS:—Gladstone; Disraeli; Bright; Earl Russell; Earl Granville; Duke of Argyll; Lord Cairns; Duke of Richmond; Earl of Derby; Marquis of Salisbury; Northcote; Hardy; Marquis of Hartington; Forster; Lowe; Harcourt; Goschen; Childers.
—— Malbone: an Oldport romance. Bost., 1871. 12°. . . . 24541
—— Oldport Days. Bost., 1873. 16°. 24542
—— Young Folks' Hist. of the U. S. Bost., 1875. 16°. . . . 21325
—— *editor.* Brief Biographics of European Public Men. N. Y., 1875–6. 3 v. 16°. (*For contents see* **Brief** Biog.) . . 22440–

Hildebrand. *See* **Gregory VII.**

Hill, B. A. Liberty and Law under Federative Government. Phila., 1874. 12°. 28843

[**Hill, F. H.**] Political Adventures of Lord Beaconsfield. N. Y., [1878]. 16°. 22851

Hill, G. B. Dr. Johnson: his friends and his critics. Lond., 1878. 23375

Hill, T. True Order of Studies. N. Y., 1876. 12°. 28832

Hillard, G. S. Life, Letters, and Journals of Geo. Ticknor. Bost., 1876. 2 v. 8°. 22688–

Hiller, F. Mendelssohn: letters and recollections. Lond., 1874. 23774

Hillern, W. von. Geier-Wally. N. Y., 1876. 16°. 24543

Himalaya. Wilson, A. The Abode of Snow. N. Y., 1875. 12°. 21707

Hinduism. Williams, M. Lond., 1877. 16°. 28578

—— *See*, *also*, **Religions** (various.)

Hinsdale, B. A. Republican Text-book: J. A. Garfield's public life, [etc.] N. Y., 1880. 8°. 21532

Hinton, R. J. English Radical Leaders. (Brief Biographies, v. 2.) N. Y., 1875. 16°. 22441

CONTENTS:—Henry Fawcett; C. W. Dilke; P. A. Taylor; John Lubbock; Joseph Cowan; R. M. Carter; Thos. Hughes; A. J. Mundella; Alex. Macdonald; Thos. Brassey; Sam. Morley; Sam. Plimsoll; Wilfred Lawson; E. Miall; Henry Richards; G. J. Holyoake; Joseph Arch; Chas. Bradlaugh; Geo. Odger; Joseph Chamberlain.

His Level Best. Hale, E. E. Bost., 1873. 16°. 24480

Histoire d'un crime. Hugo, V. M. Paris, 1877–8. 2 t. 16°. . 25651–

Histoire d'un paysan. Erckmann (E.) & Chatrian (A.) Paris, 1871–75. 4 t. 16°. 25640–

Histoire du plébiscite. Erckmann (E.) & Chatrian (A.) Paris, [1877]. 16°. 25645

Histoire d'un sous-maître. Erckmann (E.) & Chatrian (A.) Paris, 1871. 16°. 25644

Historic Chateaux. Cochrane, A. B. Lond., 1877. 8°. 21785

Historical and Architectural Sketches. Freeman, E. A. Lond., 1876. 20184

Historical Biographies. Creighton, M., *editor*. Lond., 1876–7. 3 v. 22445–

CONTENTS:—Simon de Montfort, by the ed.—The Black Prince, L. Creighton.—Walter Ralegh, L. Creighton.

Historical Characters. Bulwer, H. L. E. Lond., 1868. 2 v. 8°. 23881–

Historical Course for Schools. Freeman, E. A., *editor*. N. Y. (& Lond.), 1872–77. 7 v. 16°. 20078–

CONTENTS:—1, General Sketch of Hist., by the editor.—2, Hist. of Eng., E. Thompson.—3, H. of Scotl., M. Macarthur.—4, H. of Italy, W. Hunt.—5, H. of Germany, J. Sime.—6. H. of the U. S., J. A. Doyle.—7, H. of European Colonies, F. J. Payne.

Historical Handbooks. Browning, O., *editor*. Phila. [Oxf.], 1874–76. 6 v. 16°. 20064–

CONTENTS:—Hist. of Eng. Inst., by P. V. Smith.—Hist. of Fr. Lit., J. C. Demogeot.—Eng. Hist. in 14th Cent., C. H. Pearson.—Mod. Eng. Law, R. K. Wilson.—Rom. Emp., A. M. Curteis.—Reign of Lewis XI, P. F. Willert.

Historical Narratives from the Russian. Romanoff, H. C. Lond., 1871. 16°. 20498

Historical Sketches. Newman, J. H. Lond., 1873. 3 v. 12°. . 20091–

Historical Studies. Merivale, H. Lond., 1865. 8°. (*For contents see* **Merivale.**) 20188

History. Bisset, A. Essays on Historical Truth. Lond., 1871. 8°. (*For contents see* **Bisset.**) 20187

—— Freeman, E. A. General Sketch of Hist. N. Y., [1876]. 16°. 20078

History. Freeman, E. A. Historical Essays. Lond., 1871, '73 & '79. 3 series. 8°. (*For contents see* **Freeman.**) . . . 4658 & 20185–
—— — Unity of Hist.: a lecture. (*With* 'Comparative Politics.') . 20183
—— Hegel, G. W. F. Philosophy of Hist. Lond., 1872. 12°. . 20089
—— *Ancient.* Ancient Hist. from the Monuments. 6 v. (*For contents see* **Anc. Hist.**) 20040–
—— — Duncker, M. W. Hist. of Antiquity. Lond., 1877–79. v. 1–3. 8°. (*For contents see* **Duncker.**) 20240–
—— — Keary, C. F. Dawn of Hist. N. Y., [1879]. 12°. . . 20090
—— — Thalheimer, M. E. Manual of Anc. Hist. Cincin., [1872]. 20189
—— — *See, also,* **Antiquities; Institutions; Man,** *Pre-historic.*
—— *Middle Ages.* Thalheimer, M. E. Cincin., [1874]. 8°. . . 20190
—— — *See, also,* **Crusades; Middle Ages.**
—— *Modern.* Mackenzie, R. The 19th Century. Lond., 1880. 12°. 20482
—— — Michelet, J. Summary of Modern Hist. Lond., 1875. 16°. 20051
—— — Thalheimer, M. E. Cincin., [1874]. 8°. 20190
History of the Hebrew Monarchy. [Newman, F. W.] Lond., 1847. 28441
History and Pleasant Chronicle of Little Jehan de Saintré. [La Sale, A. de.] Lond., 1862. 12°. 24211
History Primers. Green, J. R., *editor.* Lond., 1876–7. 6 v. 16°. . 20052–
CONTENTS:—Rome, by M. Creighton.—Europe, E. A. Freeman.—Greece, C. A. Fyffe.—Geography, G. Grove.—Old Greek Life, J. P. Mahaffy.—Roman Antiquities, A. S. Wilkins.
Hitchcock, R. D. Socialism. N. Y., 1879. 12°. 29117
Hitchman, F. Public Life of Earl Beaconsfield. Lond., 1879. 2 v. 23072–
Hodder, G. Personal Reminiscences. (*In* **Stoddard, R. H.,** 'Bric-à-Brac Series.') 23255
—— Sketches of Life and Character. Lond., 1845. 16°. . . . 23641
Hodge, C. What is Darwinism? N. Y., 1874. 12°. . . . 28089
Hodgson, F., Memoir of. Hodgson, J. F. Lond., 1878. 2 v. 12°. 22106–
Hoffman, C. F. Poems. Phil., 1873. 12°. 26019
Hofmann, A. W. Life-work of Liebig. Lond., 1876. 8°. . . 23544
Hogarth, W. *Dobson, A.* (Illustrated Biog. of the Great Artists.) L. & N. Y., 1879. 12°. 23789
—— *Sala, G. A.* Lond., 1866. 12°. 23802
Hogg, D. Life of Allan Cunningham. Lond., 1875. 12°. . . 23244
Hogg, J., *the Ettrick shepherd.* A Queer Book. Edinb. & L., 1832. 26114
Holbein, H. *Woltmann, A.* [Transl. and condensed] by J. Cundall. L. & N. Y., 1879. 12°. 23781
Hole, R. Hymn to Ceres, translated. (*See* **Homer.**)
Holland, H. S. The Apostolic Fathers. Lond., [1878]. 16°. . 28502
Holland. J. Memorials of Sir Francis Chantrey. Lond., [1851]. 8°. 18572
Holland, J. G. Arthur Bonnicastle. N. Y., 1873. 16°. (2 copies.) 24544–
—— Mistress of the Manse. N. Y., 1874. 12°. 24546
—— Nicholas Minturn. N. Y., 1877. 12°. (2 copies.) . . . 24547–
—— Sevenoaks. N. Y., 1875. 12°. (2 copies.) 24549–
Holland. Geddes, J. Administration of John DeWitt, Grand Pensionary of Holland. N. Y., 1880. v. 1. 8°. 20602
—— Havard, H. Dead Cities of the Zuyder Zee. Lond., 1875. 8°. 21779
—— — Picturesque Holland. Lond., 1876. 8°. 21780

Holland. Longfellow, H. W. Poems of Places, v. 15. Bost., 1877. 26454
Holland House. Liechtenstein, M. Lond., 1874. 2 v. 8°. . . 21773–
Holm, Saxe, (*pseud.*) Stories. N. Y., 1874 & '78. 2 series. 12°. . 24551–
Holmes, G. Vocal Physiology and Hygiene. [L. &] Phil., 1880. 12°. 29803
Holmes, O. W. Elsie Venner: a romance. Bost., 1875. 12°. . 24553
—— J. L. Motley: a memoir. Bost., 1879. 16°. 22603
—— Mechanism in Thought and Morals. Bost., 1871. 16°. . . 27255
—— Poetical Works. Bost., 1877. 12°. 26020
—— Songs of Many Seasons. Bost., 1875. 16°. 26021
Holst, H. von. Constitutional and Political Hist. of the U. S. Chic., 1876–79. v. 1–2. 8°. (2 copies.) 21450–

CONTENTS:—1, 1750–1833: State sovereignty and slavery.—2, 1828–1846: Jackson's administration; annexation of Texas.

Holy Roman Empire. Bryce, J. Lond., 1873. 12°. (2 copies.) . 20100–
Holyoake, G. J. Co-operation in England. Philad. [Lond.], 1875–79. 2 v. 12°. 29005–

CONTENTS:—1, The pioneer period, 1812–1844.—2, The constructive period, 1845–1878.

Home, D. D. Lights and Shadows of Spiritualism. N. Y., 1879. 12°. 28051
Homer. Minor Poems: Battle of the Frogs and Mice; Hymns and Epigrams; transl. by Parnell, Chapman, Shelley, Congreve, and Hole. N. Y., 1872. 12°. 26816
—— The Odyssey, transl. by Pope; Battle of the Frogs and Mice, by Parnell; and the Hymns, by Chapman, etc. Lond., 1867. 26815
—— The Odysseys, transl. by Chapman. Lond., 1874. 2 v. 12°. . 26813–
—— Tales from the Odyssey. By "Materfamilias," [C. M. Bell.] N. Y., 1880. 24°. 26818
—— *Bonitz, H.* Origin of the Homeric Poems. N. Y., 1880. 16°. 26817
—— *Church, A. J.* Stories from Homer. N. Y., 1878. 16°. . . 26819
—— *Gladstone, W. E.* (Literature Primers.) [L. &] N. Y., 1879. 16°. 26861
—— — Homeric Synchronism. N. Y., 1876. 12°. 26820
Homo sum: Roman. Ebers, G. M. Stuttg. & Leipz., 1880. 12°. . 25873
—— *Same*, transl. by Clara Bell. Lond., [1878]. 2 v. 12°. . . 24465–
—— — *Same.* N. Y., 1880. 16°. 24430
Honest John Vane. De Forest, J. W. New Haven, 1875. 16°. . 24172
Honorable (The) Miss Ferrard. [Laffan, M.] N. Y., 1878. 16°. . 24929
Hood, T. Comic Annual. Lond., 1830–39. 10 v. 16°. . . 25248–
—— Hood's Own. Lond., 1839. 8°. 25583
—— Works, comic and serious. Lond., 1869–73. 10 v. 12°. . . 25258–
Hook, T. E., Life and Remains of. Barham, R. H. D. Lond., 1877. 23295
Hook, W. F., Life and Letters of. Stephens, W. R. W. Lond., 1879. 2 v. 8°. 22265–
Hooker, J. D. Botany. Lond., 1877. 16°. 29358
—— **& Ball (J.).** Tour in Marocco and the Great Atlas. Lond., 1878. 8°. 21847
Hooker, R. *Barry, A.* (*In* 'Masters in English Theology.') . . 22111
Hoosier School-Master. Eggleston, E. N. Y., [1871]. 16°. . . 24469
Hopkins, M. Strength and Beauty. N. Y., [1874]. 12°. . . 27383
Hoppin, J. M., *editor.* Memoir of Henry Armitt Brown; with four historical orations. Phil., 1880. 8°. 22693

Horæ Hellenicæ. Blackie, J. S. Lond., 1874. 8°. 26960
Horner, Susan and **Joanna.** Walks in Florence. Lond., 1873. 2 v. 21249–
Horse. Murray, W. H. H. The Perfect Horse. Bost., 1873. 8°. . 29496
—— Neville, G. Horses and Riding. Lond., 1877. 12°. . . 29641
Horsley, S. *Woodford, J. R.* (*In* **Classic** Preachers ; 1878.) . 22113
Horton, S. D. Silver and Gold. Cinc., 1877. 8°. 29045
Hosmer, J. K. Hist. of German Literature. St. Louis, 1879. 12°. 26903
Hostages to Fortune. Maxwell, M. E. B. Lond., 1875. 3 v. 12°. 24801–
Hotel Life, Law of. Rogers, R. V. San Fran., 1879. 16°. . . 28852
Houghton, *Lord. See* **Milnes, R. M.**
Hours in a Library. Stephen, L. Lond., 1874–80. 3 v. 12°. . . 26933–
Hours with Men and Books. Mathews, W. Chic., 1877. 12°. . 27340
Hours of Thought on Sacred Things. Martineau, J. Lond., 1877–79. 2 v. 12°. 28542–
House Decoration. *See* **Decoration & Design ; Furniture.**
Household of Sir Thos. More. [Manning, A.] N. Y., [1867]. 16°. 23646
Houssaye, A. Life in Paris : letters. N. Y., 1879. 12°. . . 21610
How to camp out. Gould, J. M. N. Y., 1877. 16°. (2 copies.) . 29662–
How Crops feed. Johnson, S. W. N. Y., [1870]. 12°. . . . 29459
How Crops grow. Johnson, S. W. N. Y., [1868]. 12°. . . . 29460
How to get strong. Blaikie, W. N. Y., 1879. 16°. (2 copies.) . 29953–
How to hunt and trap. Batty, J. H. Phil., 1878. 12°. . . . 29611
How I found Livingstone. Stanley, H. M. N. Y., 1872. 8°. . . 21856
How to take care of our eyes. Angell, H. C. Bost., 1878. 16°. . 29956
How we are governed. Fonblanque, A. W. de. Lond., [1879]. 12°. 20885
[**Howard, Blanche W.**] One Summer. Bost., 1876. 16°. (3 cop.) 24554–
—— One Year abroad. Bost., 1877. 16°. 24557
Howard, H., *earl of Surrey.* Poetical Works. With memoir [etc.] by G. Gilfillan. Edinb., 1856. 8°. 26352
Howard, J. H. Gymnasts and Gymnastics. Lond., 1873. 12°. . 29639
Howe, J. B. Mono-Metalism and Bi-Metalism. Bost., 1879. 16°. 29061
Howell, G. Conflicts of Capital and Labour. Lond., 1878. 12°. . 29007
Howells, W. D. A Chance Acquaintance. Bost., 1873 (etc.). (3 cop.) 24558–
—— A Counterfeit Presentment. Bost., 1877. 16°. 24561
—— A Foregone Conclusion. Bost., 1875. 12°. (3 copies.) . . 24562–
—— Italian Journeys. Bost., 1872. 12°. 21611
—— Lady of the Aroostook. Bost., 1879. 12°. (3 copies.) . . 24565–
—— No Love lost. N. Y., 1869. 16°. 26118
—— Out of the Question. Bost., 1877. 16°. (2 copies.) . . . 24568–
—— Suburban Sketches. N. Y., 1871. 12°. 24570
—— Their Wedding Journey. Bost., 1875. 12°. (2 copies.) . . 24571–
—— Undiscovered Country. Bost., 1880. 12°. (2 copies.) . . 24573–
Howitt, Anna M. Art-student in Munich. Lond., 1853. 2 v. 12°. 29879–
Howitt, W. History of Discovery in Australia, Tasmania, and New Zealand. Lond., 1875. 2 v. 8°. 21816–
—— Hist. of the Supernatural. Phila., 1863. 2 v. 12°. . . . 28046–
Hozier, H. M. Invasions of England. Lond., 1876. 2 v. 8°. . 21052–
Huber, V. A., (*pseud.*, 'Janus.') The Pope and the Council. Bost., 1870. 16°. (2 copies.) 9514–

Hudson, Elizabeth H. Life and Times of Louisa, Queen of Prussia; with a sketch of Prussian history. Lond., 1874. 2 v. 22507–
Hudson (*river*). Lossing, B. J. Troy. 8°. 21587
Hudson's Bay Territory. Robinson, H. M. Great Fur Land. N. Y., 1879. 12°. 21284
Hübner, J. A. von. Ramble round the World, 1871. N. Y., 1874. 12°. 21203
Hueffer, F. Troubadours. Lond., 1878. 8°. 26769
—— Wagner and the Music of the Future. Lond., 1874. 12°. . 29748
Hugdietrich and Hildeburg, Story of. Cox (G. W.) & Jones. (*In* 'Pop. Romances.' *And in* 'Tales.') . . . 27712 & 27713
Hughes, G. E. *Hughes, T.* Memoir of a Brother. Bost., 1873. 16°. 23622
Hughes, R. W. Currency Question. N. Y., 1879. 12°. . . 29054
Hughes, T. The Manliness of Christ. Bost., 1880. 16°. . . 28486
—— Memoir of a Brother [G. E. H.]. Bost., 1873. 16°. . . . 23622
Hugo, V. M. Histoire d'un crime. Paris, 1877–8. 2 t. 16°. . 25651–
—— Hunchback of Notre-Dame. Lond., 1874. 16°. . . . 24575
—— Jargal. N. Y., 1866. 12°. 24576
—— Les Misérables. Brux., 1862. 10 t. 16°. 25653–
—— *Same, transl.* N. Y., 1878 (etc.). 8°. (3 copies.) . . . 24665–
—— Ninety-Three. N. Y., 1874. 12°. 24577
—— Notre-Dame de Paris. Paris, 1871. 2 t. 16°. 25663–
—— Les travailleurs de la mer. Paris, 1877. 16°. 25665
—— *See* **Amicis, E. de,** 'Studies of Paris' (27273); **Castelar, E.,** 'Life of Byron,' etc. (27269); **Dowden, E.,** 'Studies in Lit.' (26926); **Swinburne, A. C.,** 'Ess. and Stud.' (26942); **Taylor, J. B.,** 'Crit. Ess.' (27364).
Huguenots. Baird, H. M. Rise of the H. of France. N. Y., 1879. 2 v. 8°. 20680–
—— Hanna, W. Wars of the H. Edinb., 1871. 16°. . . . 20402
See, also, **Ecclesiastical** Hist.; **France,** *Hist.,* 1561—; **Reformation.**
Hullah, J. Hist. of Modern Music. Lond., 1875. 8°. . . . 29796
—— Music in the House. Phila., [1877]. 12°. 29783
—— Third or Transition Period of Musical Hist. Lond., 1876. 8°. 29797
Hulley, J. Handbook of Gymnastics. (*See* **Ravenstein, E. G., & Hulley.**)
Humboldt, C. W. von. Letters to a Female Friend. Lond., 1849. 2 v. 12°. 23607–
—— Sphere and Duties of Government. Lond., 1854. 12°. . . 29095
Humboldt, F. H. A. von., Life of. Bruhns, C., *editor.* Lond., 1873. 2 v. 8°. 23530–
Hume, D. *Bisset, A.* (*In* 'Essays on Historical Truth.') . . . 20187
—— *Huxley, T. H.* (English Men of Letters.) N. Y., 1879. 12°. . 23336
—— *Stephen, L.* (*In* 'Hist. of Eng. Thought.') 28200
Humor. L'Estrange, A. G. K. Hist. of English H.; with an introd. upon ancient H. Lond., 1878. 2 v. 12°. 26938–
—— *See, also,* **Wit and Humor.**
Humorists, French. Besant, W. Lond., 1873. 8°. 26776
Hunchback of Notre-Dame. Hugo, V. M. Lond., 1874. 16°. . 24575
Hungary. Godkin, E. L. Hist. of H. and the Magyars. Lond., 1856. 20380

Hungary. Hackländer, F. W. von. Ungarnim Jahre 1857. (*In* 'Tagebuchblätter.' Werke, B. 40.) 25819
—— Patterson, A. J. Magyars. Lond., 1869. 2 v. 12°. . . . 21711–
Hunnewell, J. F. The Lands of Scott. Edinb., 1871. 12°. . 21736
Hunt, F. K. The Fourth Estate. Lond., 1850. 2 v. 12°. . . 18590–
Hunt, Helen. *See* **Jackson, Helen H.**
Hunt, H. G. B. History of Music. N. Y., [1878]. 12°. . . . 29749
Hunt, J. H. L. A Jar of Honey from Mount Hybla. Lond., 1847. 11399
—— Table-Talk; [and] imaginary conversations of Pope and Swift. N. Y., 1879. 16°. 27640
—— & *Lord* **Byron.** The Liberal: [an anon. periodical.] Lond., 1822–3. 2 v. 8°. 11400–
Hunt, R. Popular Romances of the West of England. Lond., [1871]. 27664
Hunt, W. History of Italy. Lond., 1874. 16°. 20081
Hunt, W. M. Talks on Art. Bost., 1880. 8°. 29916
Hunter, J. New Illustrations of Skakespeare. Lond., 1845. 2 v. 27049–
Hunter, W. W. Life of the Earl of Mayo. Lond., 1875. 2 v. 8°. 23932–
Hunting. Batty, J. H. How to hunt and trap. Phil., 1878. 12°. . 29611
—— Gillmore, P. Prairie and Forest: game of N. Amer. N. Y., 1874. 29620
—— [Jefferies, R.] Amateur Poacher. Bost., 1879. 12°. . . 29330
—— *See, also,* **Shooting; Sports.**
Hunting Grounds of the Old World. [Leveson, H. A.] Lond., 1865. 29493
Hurdis, J. Poems. Oxf., 1808. 3 v. 16°. 18677–
Hurst, J. F. Life and Literature in the Fatherland. N. Y., 1875. 12°. 26901
Hutchinson, A. H. Try Lapland. Lond., 1870. 12°. . . . 21706
Hutchinson, T. J. The Paraná. Lond., 1868. 8°. 21805
Huth, A. H. Life and Writings of H. T. Buckle. Lond., 1880. 2 v. 23066–
Hutten, U. von: his life and times. Strauss, D. F. Lond., 1874. 12°. 22143
Hutton, R. H. Essays in Literary Criticism. Phila., [1876]. 12°. 26937

Contents:—Goethe and his influence; Nat. Hawthorne; A. H. Clough; Wordsworth and his genius; George Eliot; Mat. Arnold.

—— Essays, theological and literary. Lond., 1871. 2 v. 8°. . . 3708–
—— *Same.* 2d ed., rev. & enl. Lond., 1880. 2 v. 8°. . . . 27487–

Contents:—**1, Theological:** Moral significance of atheism; Atheistic explanation of religion; Science and theism; Popular pantheism; What is revelation? Christian evidences (*in 2d ed. only*); Historical problems of the fourth gospel; The incarnation and principles of evidence; Renan's Christ; R.'s St. Paul; The Hard Church; Romanism, protestantism, and anglicanism. **2, Literary:** Goethe and his influence; Wordsworth and his genius; Shelley's poetical mysticism; Browning; Poetry of the Old Testament; Geo. Eliot (*in 1st ed.*); Clough; Poetry of Mat. Arnold (*in 2d ed.*); Tennyson (*in 2d ed.*); Nat. Hawthorne.

—— Scott. (Eng. Men of Letters.) N. Y., 1879. 12°. . . . 23334
Hutton, W., Life of; and history of the Hutton family. Lond. 12°. 23642
Huxley, T. H. Amer. Addresses; with a lecture on the study of biology. N. Y., 1877. 12°. 29300
—— The Crayfish. N. Y., 1880. 12°. 29269
—— Hume. (English Men of Letters.) N. Y., 1879. 12°. . . 23336
—— Lessons in Elem. Physiology. Lond., 1876. 18°. . . . 29301
—— Physiography. N. Y., 1878. 12°. 29419
—— Science Primers: Introductory. Lond., 1880. 16°. . . . 29354
—— *editor.* *See* **Science** Primers.
—— **& Martin (H. N.).** Elementary Biology. Lond., 1875. 12°. . 29299
Hygiene. Wilson, G. [Edinb. &] Phil., 1880. 12°. 29997
—— *See, also,* **Health.**

I go a-fishing. Prime, W. C. N. Y., 1873. 8°. 29628

Iceland. Blackwood, F. T. H. Yacht Voyage in 1856. N. Y. 12°. 21222

—— Burton, R. F. Ultima Thule. Lond., 1875. 2 v. 8°. . . 21884–

—— Dasent, G. W. Burnt Njal: Iceland in the 10th cent. Edinb., 1861. 2 v. 12°. 27703–

—— Forbes, C. S. Lond., 1860. 12°. 21223

—— Longfellow, H. W. Poems of Places, v. 8. Bost., 1876. 16°. 26447

—— Metcalfe, F. The Oxonian in Iceland. Lond., 1861. 12°. . 21705

—— Paijkull, C. W. A Summer in Iceland. Lond., 1868. 8°. . 21886

—— Taylor, J. B. Egypt and Iceland in 1874. N. Y., 1874. 16°. . 21256

Icelandic Legends. Arnason, J. Lond., 1864. 12°. . . . 27710

Ida Craven. Cadell, H. M. N. Y., 1876. 16°. 24070

Idolatry: a romance. Hawthorne, J. Bost., 1874. 12°. . . . 24501

Ignatius, *St., of Antioch. Holland, H. S.* (*In* 'Apostolic Fathers.') 28502

Ihering, R. von. Struggle for Law. Chic., 1879. 12°. . . . 28844

Ihne, W. Early Rome. Lond., 1876. 16°. 20438

—— Hist. of Rome. Lond., 1871–77. v. 1–3. 8°. 20288–

Illustrated Biographies of the Great Artists. L. & N. Y., 1879–80. 16 v. 12°. 23777–

CONTENTS:—(1,) Titian, by R. F. Heath.—(2,) Rembrandt, C. Vosmaer.—(3,) Raphael, J. D. Passavant.—(4,) Van Dyck & Hals, P. R. Head.—(5,) Holbein, A. Woltmann.—(6,) Tintoretto, W. R. Osler.—(7,) Turner, W. C. Monkhouse.—(8,) The Little Masters, W. B. Scott.—(9,) The Figure Painters of Holland, R. Gower.—(10,) Leonardo, J. P. Richter.—(11,) Vernet & Delaroche, J. R. Rees.—(12,) Rubens, C. W. Kett.—(13,) Hogarth, A. Dobson.—(14,) Michelangelo, C. Clément.—(15,) Sir E. Landseer, F. G. Stephens.—(16,) Reynolds, F. S. Pulling.

Impressions of Theophrastus Such. Eliot, G. N. Y., 1879. 12°. (2 copies.) 24195–

In Change unchanged. Villari, L. N. Y., 1877. 16°. . . . 24285

In Paradise. Heyse, P. J. L. N. Y., 1878. 2 v. 16°. . . . 24084–

In Reih' und Glied. Spielhagen, F. Leipz., 1876. 2 B. 16°. (Sämmtl. Werke, B. 5–6.) 25864–

In Silk Attire. Black, W. N. Y., 1877. 12°. (2 copies.) . . 24010–

In the Wilderness. Warner, C. D. Bost., 1878. 16°. . . . 24293

In der zwölften Stunde. Spielhagen, F. (Sämmtl. Werke, B. 3.) . 25862

Incas (The) *See* **Peru.**

India. Cumming, W. G. Wild Men and Wild Beasts. N. Y., 1872. 12°. 21680

—— Gay, J. D. Prince of Wales in India. N. Y., 1877. 12°. . . 21246

—— Johnson, Sam. Oriental Religions. India. Bost., 1873. 8°. 28561

—— Martineau, H. British Rule in India. Lond., 1857. 16°. . 20497

—— Müller, F. M. Religions of India. N. Y., 1879. 12°. . . 28568

—— Russell, W. H. Prince of Wales' Tour. Lond., 1877. 2 v. 8°. 21967–

—— Sherring, M. A. Prot. Missions in India. Lond., 1875. 8°. . 28601

—— Williams, M. Modern India and the Indians. Lond., 1878. 8°. 21945

See, also, **Buddhism; Deccan; East** (The); **Hinduism; Travancore.**

Indian Song of Songs. Arnold, E. Lond., 1875. 16°. . . . 26002

Indiana: [roman.] Dudevant, A. L. A. D. Paris, 1869. 16°. . 25683

Indians (American). Custer, G. A. My Life on the Plains. N. Y., 1874. 8°. 21581

—— *See, also,* **Antiquities,** *American;* **Modocs.**

Indo-China. Carné, L. de. Travels in I.-C. Lond., 1872. 8°. . 21932

Indo-China. Mouhot, A. H. Travels in I.-C. Lond., 1864. 2 v. . 21933–
—— *See, also,* **Burma ; Siam.**
Indo-European Tradition, Curiosities of. Kelly, W. K. Lond., 1863. 12°. 27789
Industrial Arts. Lacroix, P. Arts in the Middle Ages. Lond., 1870. 8°. 20362
—— [Maskell, W.] [L. &] N. Y., 1876. 12°. 29772
—— Nichols, G. W. Art Education applied to Industry. N. Y., 1877. 8°. 29925
See, also, **Aeronautics; Arms & Armor; Art** (*& references*); **Colors; Furniture; Glass; Inventions; Manufactures; Phonography; Photography; Pottery; Railroads; Steam; Telegraph; Telephone; Textile Fabrics.**
Infernal (The) Marriage. Disraeli, B. N. Y. [Lond., 1878]. 24238 & 24252
Infidelity, Modern. Christlieb, T. N. Y., 1874. 12°. 28682
Ingelow, J. Fated to be Free. Bost., 1875. 12°. (2 copies.) . 24578–
—— Off the Skelligs. Bost., 1872. 16°. 24580
—— Sarah de Berenger: a novel. Bost., 1879. 16°. . . . 24581
Ingénue. Dumas, A. D. Lond., [1879]. 16°. 24416
Ingersoll, C. Fears for Democracy. Phila., 1875. 8°. . . . 21449
Ingersoll, C. J. Second War between the U. S. of A. and Gr. Brit. Phila., 1845–53. 4 v. (wanting 2d). 8°. 21443–
Ingham, Frederic, (*pseud.*) *See* **Hale, E. E.**
Ingo. Freytag, G. N. Y., 1873. 16°. 24444
Ingo und Ingraban. Freytag, G. Leipz., 1875. 12°. ("Die Ahnen," Abth. 1.) 25911
Ingraban. Freytag, G. N. Y., 1873. 16°. 24445
Inheritance (The). [Ferrier, S. E.] Edinb., 1824. 3 v. 12°. . . 18637–
Inland (An) Voyage. Stevenson, R. L. Lond., 1878. 12°. . . 21710
Inn (The) Album. Browning, R. Bost., 1876. 12°. . . . 26048
Inquisition, Hist. of. Rule, W. H. Lond., 1874. 2 v. 8°. . . 28720–
Insanity. Kellogg, A. O. Shakspeare's Delineations of I., Imbecility, and Suicide. N. Y., 1866. 16°. 27016
—— Maudsley, H. Responsibility in Mental Disease. N. Y., 1874. 29248
—— *See, also,* **Mental Physiology.**
Insectivorous Plants. Darwin, C. R. N. Y., 1875. 12°. . . . 29457
Insects. [Budgen, L. M.] Episodes of Insect Life. Lond., 1849–51. 3 v. 8°. 29500–
—— Duncan, P. M. Transformations of Insects. Lond., [1877]. 8°. 29499
—— Lubbock, J. British Wild Flowers considered in relation to Insects. Lond., 1875. 12°. 29461
—— — Origin and Metamorphoses of Insects. Lond., 1874. 16°. . 29503
—— — Scientific Lectures. Lond., 1879. 8°. 29532
—— Packard, A. S., jr. Half Hours with Insects. Bost., 1877. 12°. 29505
—— Wood, J. G. Insects abroad. Lond., 1874. 8°. 29585
—— — Insects at Home. N. Y., 1872. 8°. 29586
Instinct, Illustrations of. Couch, J. Lond., 1847. 12°. . . . 29326
Institutions. Maine, H. J. S. Early Hist. of. N. Y., 1875. 8°. . 28968
—— Smith, P. V. Hist. of the Eng. Institutions. Phila., 1874. 16°. 20064
Intellectual (The) Life. Hamerton, P. G. Bost., 1873. 12°. . . 27382

Intellectual Observer. Lond., 1862–68. 12 v. 8°. 17711–
Intelligence. Bascom, J. Comparative Psychology; or, The growth and grades of Intelligence. N. Y., 1878. 12°. . 28207
—— Taine, H. A. N. Y., 1875. 2 v. 12°. 28205–
Intemperance. [Abbe, J. E.] "Back from the Mouth of Hell;" or, The rescue from drunkenness. Hartf., 1878. 12°. . 28886
—— *See, also,* **Temperance.**
International (An) Episode. James, H., jr. N. Y., [1878]. 32°. . 24600
International Politics. Burlingame, E. L. ('Current Discus.,' v. 1.) 27282
International Review. N. Y., 1874–79. 7 v. 8°. 10591–
International Scientific Series. N. Y., 1872–80. 28 v. 12°. . . 29240–

CONTENTS:—1, Tyndall, Forms of water.—2, Bagehot, Physics and politics.—3, E. Smith, Foods.—4, Bain, Mind and body.—5, Spencer, Study of sociology.—6, Cooke, New chemistry.—7, Stewart, Conservation of energy.—8, Pettigrew, Animal locomotion.—9, Maudsley, Responsibility in mental disease.—10, Amos, Science of law.—11, Marey, Animal mechanism.—12, Draper, Conflict betw. religion and science.—13, Schmidt, Doctrine of descent.—14, Vogel, Chemistry of light.—15, Cooke, Fungi.—16, Whitney, Life and growth of language (2 *copies*).—17, Jevons, Money.—18, Lommel, Nature of light.—19, Beneden, Animal parasites.—20, Schützenberger, Fermentation.—21, Bernstein, Five senses.—22, Blaserna, Sound.—23, Lockyer, Spectrum analysis.—24, Thurston, Steam engine.—25, Bain, Education.—26, Rood, Modern chromatics.—27, Quatrefages, Human species (2 *copies*).—28, Huxley, Crayfish.

Inventions. Knight, E. H. Mechanical Progress. (*In* **First** Cent. of the Republic.) 21520
—— Routledge, R. Discoveries and I. of the 19th Cent. Lond., 1876. 12°. 29929
—— *See, also,* **Industrial** Arts (*& references*).
Ionian Islands. Brassey, A. Sunshine and Storm in the East. N. Y., 1880. 8°. 21901
Irby, Adelaide P. Travels. (*See* **Mackenzie, G. M. M., & Irby.**)
Ireland. Kennedy, P. Fireside Stories of I. Dublin, 1870. 16°. 27667
—— Longfellow, H. W. Poems of Places, v. 5. Bost., 1876. 16°. 26444
—— Smith, G. Irish Hist. and Irish Character. Oxf. & L., 1861. 12°. 20815
—— *History.* Froude, J. A. The English in I. in the 18th Cent. N. Y., 1873–4. 3 v. 12°. 20816–
—— — Maxwell, W. H. Hist. of the Irish Rebellion in 1798; with memoirs of the Union, and Emmett's Insurrection in 1803. Lond., 1877. 12°. 20991
—— — Sullivan, A. M. New Ireland. [1837 to 1877.] Phila., 1878. 12°. 20990
Irene, the Missionary. [De Forest, J. W.] Bost., 1879. 16°. . . 24173
Iron Mask, Man with the. Topin, M. Lond., 1870. 12°. . . 20403
Irving, D. Hist. of Scotish Poetry. Edinb., 1861. 8°. . . . 26288
Irving, W. The Alhambra. N. Y., [1865]. 16°. 24588
—— Bracebridge Hall. N. Y., [1865]. 16°. 24589
—— Crayon Miscellany. N. Y., [1865]. 16°. 24590
—— Hist. of New York. By Diedrich Knickerbocker. N. Y., [1864]. 16°. 24591
—— Oliver Goldsmith: a biography. N. Y., [1864]. 16°. . . 24592
—— Sketch-Book of Geoffrey Crayon. N. Y., [1864]. 16°. . . 24593
—— Tales of a Traveller. N. Y., 1851. 12°. 24587
—— *Same.* N. Y., [1865]. 16°. 24593
—— Wolfert's Roost, and other papers. N. Y., [1865]. 16°. . . 24594
Is "Eternal" Punishment Endless? answered. [Whiton, J. M.] Bost., 1878. 16°. 28509

Is Life Worth Living? Mallock, W. H. N. Y., 1879. 12°. . . . 28085
Isabel of Bavaria: an historical romance. Dumas, A. D. Lond., [1879]. 16°. 24416
Isabella I. (*of Castile*), *queen of Spain. Prescott, W. H.* Reign of Ferdinand and Isabella. Phil., 1871. 3 v. 8°. 20345–
Islam. *See* **Mohammedanism.**
Isles of Shoals. Thaxter, C. Bost., 1873. 16°. 21257
Ismailïa. Baker, S. W. N. Y., 1875. 8°. 21846
Istria, Dora d', (*pseud. for* H. G. Koltzof-Massalski.) Switzerland the Pioneer of the Reformation. Lond., 1858. 2 v. 8°. . 20600–
Italian Literature. Dennistoun, J. (*In* 'Dukes of Urbino.') . . 23939–
—— Symonds, J. A. (*In* 'Sketches and Studies in Southern Europe.') 27341–
Italy. Freeman, E. A. Historical and Architectural Sketches; chiefly Italian. Lond., 1876. 12°. 20184
—— Longfellow, H. W. Poems of Places, v. 11–13. Bost., 1877. 3 v. 16°. 26450–
—— *Art.* Clément, C. Michelangelo [etc.]; with chap. on art in Italy before the 16th cent. Lond., 1880. 12°. 23837
—— — Crowe (J. A.) & Cavalcaselle (G. B.). Painting in Italy from the 2d to the 14th cent. Lond., 1864–66. 3 v. 8°. . . 29945–
—— — — Painting in North Italy from the 14th to the 16th cent. Lond., 1871. 2 v. 8°. 29948–
—— — Dennistoun, J. (*In* 'Dukes of Urbino.') 23939–
—— — Symonds, J. A. ('Renaissance in Italy,' v. 3.) . . . 20300
—— *Biography.* Trollope, T. A. A Decade of Italian Women. Lond., 1859. 2 v. 16°. 23644–

Description and Travel.

—— Bremer, F. Two Years in Switzerland and Italy. Lond., 1861. 2 v. 8°. 21212–
—— Broughton, H. D. Italy: several visits, 1816–1854. Lond., 1859–61. 2 v. 12°. 21733–
—— Carr, A. North Italian Folk. Lond., 1878. 12°. 21220
—— Hare, A. J. C. Cities of Northern and Central Italy. N. Y., 1876. 3 v. 12°. 21603–
—— Hawthorne, N. French and Ital. Note-books. Bost., 1878. 12°. 24504
—— Howells, W. D. Italian Journeys. Bost., 1872. 12°. . . 21611
—— Piozzi, H. L. Journey through France, Italy, and Germany. Lond., 1789. 2 v. 8°. 18609–
—— Shelley, M. W. Rambles in Germany and I. Lond., 1844. 2 v. 18552–

History.

—— Maffei, A. Brigand Life in Italy. Lond., 1865. 2 v. 8°. . 20302–
—— Symonds, J. A. Renaissance in I. Lond., 1875–77. v. 1–3. 8°. 20298–
—— (*to* 1806) Bryce, J. Holy Roman Empire. Lond., 1875. 12°. . 20100
—— (364–1466) Urquhart, W. P. Life of Sforza, Duke of Milan; with preliminary sketch. Edinb., 1852. 2 v. 8°. . . 23935–
—— (476–1815) Butt, I. Lond., 1860. 2 v. 8°. 20320–
—— (476–1870) Hunt, W. Lond., 1874. 16°. 20081
—— (1846–50) Legge, A. O. Pius IX. and Italy. Lond., 1875. 2 v. 8°. 22185–

Italy. *History (continued).*
—— (1859-60) Trollope, T. Social Aspects of the Ital. Rev. Lond., 1861. 12°. 20003
See, also, **Florence; Genoa; Lombardy; Piedmont; Pompeii; Rome; Sicily; Tiber; Urbino; Venice.**
Ivan de Biron. [Helps, A.] Bost., 1874. 12°. 24537
Ivan at Home. Barry, H. Lond., 1872. 8°. 21940
Ivories, ancient and mediæval. Maskell, W. [L. &] N. Y., 1876. . 29764
Ixion in Heaven. Disraeli, B. N. Y. [Lond., 1878]. 12°. 24238 & 24252
J., R. *See* **Jefferies, R.**
Jack Hinton. Lever, C. J. Phila., [1878]. 8°. 24259
Jackson, Catherine C., *Lady.* Fair Lusitania. Lond., 1874. 8°. . 21969
—— Old Paris: its court and literary salons. Lond., 1878. 2 v. 12°. 21687-
Jackson, G. A. The Apostolic Fathers, and the Apologists of the 2d century. N. Y., 1879. 16°. 28512
Jackson, Helen H. ("**H. H.**") Bits of Talk about Home Matters. Bost., 1873. 16°. 27237
—— Bits of Travel at Home. Bost., 1878. 16°. 21289
—— Verses. Bost., 1874. 16°. 26073
Jackson, S. Alaska, and Missions on the North Pacific Coast. N. Y., [1880]. 12°. 21287
Jackson, W. Philosophy of Natural Theology. N. Y., 1875. 8°. . 28685
Jacquemart, A. Hist. of Furniture. Lond., 1878. 8°. . . . 29993
Jacquemont, V. *Hamerton, P. G.* (*In* 'Mod. Frenchmen.') . . 22488
Jacques. Dudevant, A. L. A. D. Paris, 1866. 16°. . . . 25684
James, G. P. R. Heidelberg: a romance. N. Y., 1869. 8°. . . 24668
—— My Aunt Pontypool. [Anon.] Phil., 1836. 2 v. 12°. . . 2161-
James, H., jr. The American: [a novel.] Bost., 1877. 12°. (2 cop.) 24595-
—— Confidence: [a novel.] Bost., 1880. 12°. (2 copies.) . . 24597-
—— Daisy Miller: a study. N. Y., 1879. 32°. 24599-
—— The Europeans: a sketch. Bost., 1879 [1878]. 12°. (2 copies.) 24601-
—— French Poets and Novelists. Lond., 1878. 12°. 26905
CONTENTS:—A. de Musset; Gautier; Baudelaire; Balzac; Geo. Sand; C. de Bernard and G. Flaubert; Turgénieff; The two Ampères; Mad. de Sabran; Mérimée's letters; The Théâtre Français.
—— Hawthorne. (English Men of Letters.) N. Y., 1880. 12°. . 23348
—— An International Episode. N. Y., [1878]. 32° (2 copies). . 24600-
—— A Passionate Pilgrim, and other tales. Bost., 1875. 12°. . 24603
—— Roderick Hudson. Bost., 1876. 12°. 24604
—— Watch and Ward. Bost., 1878. 16°. 24605
James, H. A. Communism in America. N. Y., 1879. 8°. . . 29160
Jameson, Anna B. M. Hist. of Our Lord as exemplified in works of art. Completed by Lady Eastlake. Lond., 1865. 2 v. 8°. 29914-
—— Legends of the Madonna. Lond., 1872. 8°. 29910
—— Legends of the Monastic Orders. Lond., 1872. 8°. . . . 29911
—— Sacred and Legendary Art. Lond., 1870. 2 v. 8°. . . . 29912-
—— *Macpherson, G. B.* Memoirs. Bost., 1878. 12°. 23838
Janin, J. G. (*See* **Thomson, J.,** 'Public and Priv. Life of Animals.')
Janus, (*pseud.*) *See* **Huber, V. A.**
Japan. Adams, F. O. Hist. of Japan. Lond., 1874-5. 2 v. 8°. . 20383-
—— Alcock, R. Art and Art Industries in J. Lond., 1878. 12°. . 29823

Japan. Almeida, A. d'. Visit to Manilla and J. Lond., 1863. 8°. 21937
—— Beauvoir, L. de. (*In* 'A Voyage,' v. 3.) 21202
—— Griffis, W. E. The Mikado's Empire. N. Y., 1876. 8°. . . 21939
—— Hübner, J. A. von. (*In* 'A Ramble round the World.') . . 21203
—— Jarves, J. J. Glimpse at the Art of J. N. Y., 1876. 12°. . 29822
—— Mossman, S. New Japan. Lond., 1873. 8°. 21938
—— Mounsey, A. H. The Satsuma Rebellion. Lond., 1879. 12°. . 20385
—— Taylor, J. B. Japan in our day. N. Y., 1872. 12°. . . . 21684
Japp, A., (*pseud.*, 'H. A. Page.') Memoir of Nat. Hawthorne. Lond., 1872. 12°. 22609
—— Thomas De Quincey. N. Y., 1877. 2 v. 12°. 23303–
—— Thoreau: his life and aims. Bost., 1877. 16°. 22607
Jar (A) of Honey from Mt. Hybla. Hunt, J. H. L. Lond., 1847. 8°. 11399
Jargal. Hugo, V. M. N. Y., 1866. 12°. . , ... 24576
Jarves, J. J. Art Thoughts. N. Y., 1875. 12°. 29821
—— Glimpse at the Art of Japan. N. Y., 1876. 12°. . . . 29822
Java. Beauvoir, L. de. (*In* 'A Voyage,' v. 2.) 21201
Jeaffreson, J. C. Brides and Bridals. Lond., 1872. 2 v. 8°. . 28961–
—— Life of Robert Stephenson. Lond., 1866. 2 v. 8°. . . . 23535–
Jean de la Roche. Dudevant, A. L. A. D. Paris, 1876. 16°. . 25685
Jean Têterol's Idea. Cherbuliez, V. N. Y., 1878. 16°. . . . 24087
Jebb, R. C. Greek Literature. Lond., 1877. 16°. 26857
—— Modern Greece: two lectures. Lond., 1880. 12°. . . . 20014
[**Jefferies, R.**] Amateur Poacher. Bost., 1879. 12°. . . . 29330
—— Gamekeeper at Home. Bost., 1879. 16°. 29331
—— Wild Life in a Southern County. Bost., 1879. 16°. . . . 29332
Jefferson, Thos., Life of. Parton, J. Bost., 1874. 8°. . . . 22640
Jeffries, B. J. Color-Blindness. Bost., 1879. 12°. 29319
Jenkin, *Mrs.* **Chas.** Jupiter's Daughters. N. Y., 1874. 16°. . . 24582
—— A Psyche of To-day. N. Y., 1868. 16°. 24583
—— Skirmishing. N. Y., 1874. 16°. 24584
—— "Who breaks, pays." N. Y., 1873. 16°. 24585
—— Within an Ace. N. Y., 1875. 16°. 24586
[**Jenkins, E.**] Lord Bantam: a satire. N. Y., 1872. 12°. . . 24606
Jennings, H. The Rosicrucians. Lond., 1870. 12°. 28997
Jennings, L. J. Field Paths and Green Lanes. N. Y., 1878. 12°. 21612
Jennings, *Mrs.* **V.** Rahel: her life and letters. Lond., 1876. 8°. . 23726
Jerdan, W. Autobiography. Lond., 1852–3. 4 v. 12°. . . 18578–
—— Men I have known. Lond., 1866. 12°. 23605
—— Personal Reminiscences. N. Y., 1875. 16°. 23259
Jerome, *St. Cutts, E. L.* (The Fathers for Eng. R.) Lond., [1878]. 28505
Jerram, C. S. *See* **Hales, J. W. & Jerram.**
Jerrold, D. W. Works; with life by W. B. Jerrold. Lond. 5 v. 16°. 25200–

CONTENTS:—1, St. Giles and St. James; Punch's letters to his son.—2, Story of a feather; Cakes and ale.—3, Mrs. Caudle's curtain lectures; Men of character; Punch's Complete letter writer.—4, A man made of money; Sketches of the English; Chronicles of Clovernook; Sick Giant and Doctor Dwarf.—5, Life.

—— *Stirling, J. H.* Edinb., 1868. 16°. 26917
Jerrold, W. B. Life of Napoleon III. Lond., 1874–77. v. 1–3. 8°. 22561–
—— London: a pilgrimage. Lond., 1872. 4°. . . . . . . ——

Jesse, G. R. Hist. of the British Dog. Lond., 1866. 2 v. 8°. . 29497–
Jesse, J. H. Life and Reign of George III. Lond., 1867. 3 v. 8°. 23037–
—— London. Lond., 1871. 3 v. 12°. 21766–
—— Memoirs of Celebrated Etonians. Lond., 1875. 2 v. 8°. . 23003–
—— The Pretenders and their Adherents. Lond., 1845. 2 v. 8°. 23030–
Jessup, H. H. Syrian Home Life. N. Y., [1874]. 12°. . . . 21613
Jesuits. Cartwright, W. C. Lond., 1876. 8°. 22182
—— Kip, W. I. Old Jesuit Missions. N. Y., [1875]. 12°. . . 28726
—— Nicolini, G. B. Hist. of the Jesuits. Lond., 1873. 12°. . . 28727
Jesus. *See* **Christ.**
Jevons, W. S. Logic. (Sci. Prim.) Lond., 1878. 16°. . . . 29359
—— Money and the Mechanism of Exchange. N. Y., 1875. 12°. . 29257
—— Political Econ. (Sci. Prim.) Lond., 1878. 16°. . . . 29360
—— Theory of Political Economy. 2d ed. Lond., 1879. 8°. . . 29169
Jewitt, L. Grave-Mounds and their Contents. Lond., 1870. 12°. 20205
—— Half-hours among Eng. Antiquities. Lond., 1880. 12°. . . 20206
—— *editor.* Life of Wm. Hutton. Lond. 12°. 23642
Jews. Allen, J. H. Hebrew Men and Times. Bost., 1879. 16°. 28442
—— Bartlett, S. C. From Egypt to Palestine, . . . with ref. to the hist. of the Israelites. N. Y., 1879. 8°. 21843
—— Brugsch, H. C. The Exodus. (*Added to* 'Hist. of Egypt,' v. 2.) 20248
—— — True Story of the Exodus. Bost., 1880. 12°. 20046
—— Conder, C. R. Judas Maccabæus, and the Jewish War of Independence. [L. &] N. Y., 1879. 16°. 22453
—— Duncker, M. W. (*In* 'Hist. of Antiquity.') 20240–
—— [Newman, F. W.] Hist. of the Hebrew Monarchy. Lond., 1847. 8°. 28441
—— Stanley, A. P. Hist. of the Jewish Church. N. Y., 1853–76. 3 v. 8°. . . . . 6533– & 28440
Joan of Arc, "the Maid." Tuckey, J. N. Y., 1880. 16°. . . 22454
John, *St.*, Life and Writings of. Macdonald, J. M. N.Y., 1877. (2 cop.) 28640–
John of Goch. *See* **Pupper, Joh.**
John of Wesel. *See* **Ruchrath, Joh.**
John Thompson. Parr, L. Phila., [1878.] 16°. 24842
Johnson, A. H. The Normans in Europe. Lond., 1877. 16°. . 20458
Johnson, Elizabeth W. The Studio Arts. N. Y., 1878. 16°. . 29828
Johnson, R., *editor.* Play-Day Poems. N. Y., 1878. 16°. . . 26032
—— — Single Famous Poems. N. Y., 1877. 12°. 26022
Johnson, Sam., *LL.D.* Six Chief Lives of the Poets. Ed. by M. Arnold. Lond., 1878. 12°. 23376
CONTENTS:—Milton, Dryden, Swift, Addison, Pope, Gray.
—— *Same.* [With] Macaulay's and Carlyle's essays on Boswell's 'Life.' N. Y., 1878. 12°. 23377
—— *Boswell, J.* Life of Johnson. Ed. by P. Fitzgerald. Lond., 1874. 3 v. 8°. 23370–
—— — *Same,* [abridged.] N. Y., 1878. 12°. (2 copies.) . . . 23373–
—— *Hill, G. B.* Dr. J.: his friends and his critics. Lond., 1878. 12°. 23375
—— *Piozzi, H. L.* Anecdotes of Johnson. Lond., 1786. 12°. . 18641
—— *Stephen, L.* (Eng. Men of Letters.) N. Y., 1878. 12°. . . 23332

Johnson, Sam. (*born* 1822). Oriental Religions. [2 vols.]: India; China. Bost., 1873 & '77. 8°. 28560–
Johnson, Sam. W. How Crops Feed. N. Y., [1870]. 12°. . . 29459
—— How Crops Grow. N. Y., [1868]. 12°. 29460
Johnston, A. Hist. of American Politics. N. Y., 1879. 16°. . 21332
Johnston, W. C. (*Yale*, '60.) [*Johnston, M. C. H.*]. N. Y., 1876. . 22601
Jonathan: a novel. Tytler, C. C. F. N. Y., 1876. 16°. . . . 24283
Jones, C. H. Short Life of Gladstone. N. Y., 1880. 16°. . . 22853
Jones, E. Studies of Sensation and Event: poems. Lond., 1879. . 26146
Jones, E. H. *See* **Cox (G. W.) & Jones.**
Jones, F. Life of Sir Martin Frobisher. Lond., 1878. 12°. . . 22848
Jones, G. Sir Francis Chantrey. Lond., 1849. 12°. . . . 18583
Jones, H., (*pseud.*, 'Cavendish.') Card Essays, Clay's Decisions, and Card-table Talk. Lond., 1879. 12°. 29681
—— *Same.* Amer. ed., with index. N. Y., 1880. 16°. . . . 29682
Jones, Wm., *curate of Nayland.* *Teale, W. H.* (*In* 'Eng. Divines.') 22110
Jonson, Ben. Every Man in his Humour. Ed. by H. B. Wheatley. Lond., 1877. 16°. 26511
—— Poems. Ed. by R. Bell. Lond., 1876. 12°. 26096
—— Works. With notes and a memoir by W. Gifford; introd. by F. Cunningham. Lond., 1875. 9 v. 8°. 26682–
—— *Coleridge, S. T.* Notes and lectures. Liverp., 1874. 16°. . 27021
Joseph and his Brethren. Wells, C. Lond., 1876. 12°. (2 copies.) 26138–
Joseph im Schnee. Auerbach, B. Stuttg., 1874. 12°. . . . 25893
Joseph in the Snow. Auerbach, B. N. Y., 1874. 16°. . . . 24043
Joubert, J. *Sainte-Beuve, C. A.* (*In* 'Monday-Chats.') . . . 23290
Journey to the Centre of the Earth. Verne, J. Bost. 12°. . . 24271
Journey from this world to the next. Fielding, H. (Works, v. 4.) 24657
Joyce, P. W. Old Celtic Romances. Lond., 1879. 12°. . . 27702
Joyce, R. D. Blanid. Bost., 1879. 16°. 26023
—— Deirdrè. Bost., 1876. 16°. 26024
Joyner, *Mrs.* **A. B.** Cyprus. (*See* **Löher, F. von.**)
Joyneville, C. Life and Times of Alexander I., of Russia. Lond., 1875. 3 v. 8°. (2 copies.) 20605–
Judas Maccabæus. *Conder, C. R.* [Lond. &] N. Y., 1879. 16°. . 22453
Judge and Jury. Abbott, B. V. N. Y., 1880. 12°. 28846
Judicial Dramas. Spicer, H. Lond., 1872. 8°. 28840
Jukes (The). Dugdale, R. L. N. Y., 1877. 12°. 29399
Junius. Britton, J. Authorship of the Letters of J. elucidated; incl. a biographical memoir of Isaac Barré. Lond., 1848. 8°. 26778
Junkin (D. X.) & Norton (F. H.). Life of W. S. Hancock. N. Y., 1880. 12°. 22648
Jupiter's Daughters. Jenkin, C. N. Y., 1874. 16°. . . . 24582
Jury, Trial by, Hist. of. Forsyth, W. N. Y., 1875. 8°. . . . 28841
Juste, T. Leopold I., King of the Belgians. Lond., 1868. 2 v. 8°. 23899–
Juvenal. *Walford, E.* (Anc. Classics for Eng. Readers, v. 13.) . 26839
Kant, I. *Stirling, J. H.* De Quincey and Coleridge upon Kant. (*In* 'Jerrold, Tennyson,' &c.) 26917
Karasowski, M. Frederic Chopin. Lond., 1879. 2 v. 12°. . . 23769–

Karl the Great. *See* **Charlemagne.**
Kashgar. Boulger, D. C. Life of Yakoob Beg, Ameer of K. Lond., 1878. 8°. 23720
—— Shaw, R. Visits to High Tartary, Yårkand, and K. Lond., 1871. 8°. 21923
Kate Beaumont. De Forest, J. W. Bost., 1872. 8°. 24308
Kaufmann, M. Socialism. Founded on "Kapitalismus und Socialismus," by A. E. F. Schäffle. Lond., 1874. 12°. . . 29118
Kaulbach, W. von. Reineke Fuchs von Goethe, mit Zeichnungen. Stuttg., 1846. 4°. . . . . ——
Keane, A. H. Ethnography and Philology of America. (*App. to* **Bates, H. W.** 'Cent. Amer.' &c.) 21700
Keary, Annie. Castle Daly: the story of an Irish home thirty years ago. Phila., [1879]. 12°. 24607
—— Oldbury. Phila., [1879]. 12°. 24608
Keary, C. F. Dawn of History. N. Y., [1879]. 12°. . . . 20090
Keats, J. Correspondence. (*See* **Haydon, B. R.,** 'Corresp.,' v. 2.) 23831
—— Letters to Fanny Brawne. N. Y., 1878. 16°. 23246
—— Poetical Works. Ed., with memoir, by W. M. Rossetti. Lond., [1876]. 12°. 26025
—— *Clarke, C. C. & M. C.* (*In* 'Recollections of Writers.') . . 26936
—— *Lowell, J. R.* (*In* 'Among my Books,' 2d ser.) 26931
—— *Masson, D.* Wordsworth, Shelley, Keats, and other essays. Lond., 1874. 12°. 27298
—— *Owen, F. M.* Keats: a study. Lond., 1880. 12°. 26292
Kebbel, T. E. Eng. Statesmen since the Peace of 1815. Lond., 1868. 12°. 22884
Keddie, Henrietta, (*pseud.*, 'Sarah Tytler.') Musical Composers and their Works. Bost., 1875. 12°. 23760
—— **& Watson (J. L.).** Songstresses of Scotland. Lond., 1871. 2 v. 23763–
Keen, W. W., *editor.* American Health Primers. Phila., 1879–80. 10 v. 16°. (*For contents see* **Amer.** Health Primers.) . . 29958–
Keightley, T. Life, Opinions, and Writings of John Milton. Lond., 1855. 8°. 23440
Kellogg, A. O. Shakespeare's Delineations of Insanity, Imbecility, and Suicide. N.Y., 1866. 16°. 27016
Kelly, M. Personal Reminiscences. N. Y., 1875. 16°. . . . 23260
Kelly, W. K. Curiosities of Indo-European Tradition and Folklore. Lond., 1863. 12°. 27789
Kemble, J. P. An Authentic Account of Mr. Kemble's Retirement from the Stage. [With] an essay, biographical and critical. Lond., 1817. 8°. 18743
Kemble-Butler, Frances A. Records of a Girlhood. N. Y., 1879. 23626
Kempe, J. E. (*See* **Classic** Preachers.)
Kendall, Amos. Autobiography. Bost., 1872. 8°. 22773
Kenelm Chillingly. Bulwer-Lytton, E. G. E. L. Lond., 1875 (etc.) 12°. . . . . 24111 & 24142–
Kennedy, P. Fireside Stories of Ireland. Dublin, 1870. 16°. . 27667
Kenney, C. L. Memoir of M. W. Balfe. Lond., 1875. 8°. . . 23845

Kéramos. Longfellow, H. W. Bost., 1878. 16°. 26076

Kett, C. W. Rubens. L. & N. Y., 1879. 12°. 23788

Keyser, R. Private Life of the Old Northmen. Lond., 1868. 12°. 20049

Khiva. MacGahan, J. A. Campaigning on the Oxus, and the Fall of Khiva. N. Y., 1874. 8°. 21924

King, E. French Political Leaders. N. Y., 1876. 16°. . . . 22442

CONTENTS:—Hugo; Thiers; Gambetta; Jules Simon; Mac Mahon; Dupanloup; Grévy; E. Laboulaye; Rouher; Duval; Duc de Broglie; Buffet; Duc d'Audiffret-Pasquier; Dufaure; Ollivier; Jules Favre; Comte de Chambord; Duc d'Aumale; Comte de Paris; Picard; Rochefort; Périer; Jules Ferry.

—— The Great South. Hartf'd, 1875. 8°. 21588

King, R. J. Sketches and Studies. Lond., 1874. 8°. . . . 27404

CONTENTS:—Carolingian romance; Sacred trees and flowers; Dogs of folk-lore, history, and romance; Change of faith in Iceland, A. D. 1000; Great shrines of England; Travelling in Eng.; Devonshire; Robert Herrick and his vicarage; Sketches and studies from Belgium: Mechlin, Louvain, Bruges from the belfry tower, Visit to the châteaux of Rubens and Teniers; Pilgrimage to St. David's.

King, T. S. Christianity and Humanity: sermons. Ed., with a memoir, by E. P. Whipple. Bost., 1877. 12°. 28538

—— Substance and Show, and other lectures. Bost., 1877. 12°. . 28539

Kings in Exile. Daudet, A. Bost., 1880. 16°. 24171

Kingsley, *Miss.* South by West. Ed. by C. Kingsley. Lond., 1874. 21582

Kingsley, C. Health and Education. Lond., 1874. 12°. . . 29979

—— His Letters and Memories of his Life. Ed. by his wife. Lond., 1877. 2 v. 8°. 22261–

—— *Same.* Abridged. N. Y., 1877. 12°. 22263

—— Hypatia. Lond., 1875. 12°. (2 copies.) 24609–

—— Town Geology. Lond., 1872. 16°. 29420

—— Twenty-five Village Sermons. Lond., 1873. 16°. . . . 28540

—— Two Years ago. Lond., 1874. 12°. (3 copies.) . . . 24611–

—— Westward Ho! Lond., 1874. 12°. (3 copies.) . . . 24614–

—— Yeast. Lond., 1875. 12°. (2 copies.) 24617–

Kingsley, G. H. *See* **Herbert, G. R. C., & Kingsley.**

Kingsley, H. Fireside Studies. Lond., 1876. 2 v. 12. . . . 27296–

CONTENTS:—1, The fathers of the Spectator; Two old Sussex worthies; The old-fashioned member; The master of the "Mermaid." 2, The father of irregular drama; Fletcher and Beaumont; Sir Philip Sydney.

—— Geoffry Hamlyn. Lond., 1874. 12°. (2 copies.) . . . 24619–

Kingsley, W. L., *editor.* Yale College: a sketch of its history. N. Y., 1879. 2 v. 4°. . . . . ——–

Kip, W. I. Historical Scenes from the Old Jesuit Missions. N. Y., [1875]. 12°. 28726

Kirk, E. N., Life of. Mears, D. O. Bost., 1878. 8°. . . . 22692

Kirkman, J. T. Life of Chas. Macklin. Lond., 1799. 2 v. 8°. . 18658–

Kitchin, G. W. Hist. of France. Oxf., 1873–77. v. 1–3. 12°. . 20404–

CONTENTS:—1, To the year 1453. 2, 1453–1624. 3, 1624–1793.

Klaczko, J. Polish Poetry in the 19th Cent. (*With* **Krasinski, S.,** 'The Undivine Comedy,' etc.) 26121

—— Two Chancellors: Gortschakof and Bismarck. N. Y., 1876. 12°. 22500

Klöden, C. F. von. The Self-made Man: autobiography. Ed., with a sketch of his after life, by M. Jähn. Lond., 1876. 2 v. 23920–

Klunzinger, C. B. Upper Egypt. N. Y., 1878. 8°. . . . 21849

Knight, A. G. Life of Christopher Columbus. Lond., 1877. 12°. 23617

Knight, Chas. Passages of a Working Life. Lond., 1864–5. 3 v. 23200–
—— *Same*, [abridged.] Bost., 1874. 12°. 23203
—— Popular Hist. of England. Lond., [1862–68]. 8 v. 8°. . . 21080–
—— Studies of Shakspere. Lond., 1849. 8°. 27042
—— William Shakspere: a biography. Lond., 1867. 8°. . . 27184
Knight, E. Cornelia. Autobiography. Lond., 1861. 2 v. 8°. . 23057–
—— Personal Reminiscences. (*In* **Stoddard, R. H.,** 'Bric-à-Brac Series.') 23258
Knight, W. Colloquia Peripatetica: notes of conversations with J. Duncan. Edinb., 1871. 16°. 23655
Knight's Quarterly Magazine. Lond., 1823–4. 3 v. 8°. . . . 18335–
Knox, John, On the portraits of. Carlyle, T. (*In* 'Early Kings.') . 23616
König Jakob's letzte Tage. Mügge, T. Breslau, 1867. 16°. (Romane, B. 30.) 25849
Körner, C. G. Correspondence with Schiller. Lond., 1849. 2 v. 23320–
Koltzof-Massalski, H. G. *See* **Istria, Dora d'.**
Koner, W. *See* **Guhl, E., & Koner.**
Koomassie. *See* **Coomassie.**
Koran. Muir, W. The Corân. Lond., [1878]. 16°. . . . 28580
—— Stephens, W. R. W. Christianity and Islam; the Bible and the Koran: 4 lectures. N. Y., 1877. 12°. 28566
—— *See, also,* **Mohammedanism.**
Kossuth, L. Memories of my Exile. N. Y., 1880. 8°. . . . 23947
Krasinski, S. The Undivine Comedy, and other poems. Phila., 1875. 12°. 26121
Krause, E. Erasmus Darwin. N. Y., 1880. 12°. 23545
Krieg und Frieden. Hackländer, F. W. von. Stuttg., 1866. 2 B. 16°. (Werke, B. 38–39.) 25818–
Krüdener, Juliane de V. de. *Sainte-Beave, C. A.* (*In* 'Portraits.') . 23643
Künstlerroman. Hackländer, F. W. von. Stuttg., 1873. 5 B. 16°. (Werke, B. 52–56.) 25825–
Kugler, F. T. Handb. of Painting. (*See* **Waagen, G. F.**) . . 29875–
Labilliere, F. P. Early Hist. of the Colony of Victoria. Lond., 1878. 2 v. 12°. 20484–
Labor. Brassey, T. Lectures on the L. Question. Lond., 1878. 8°. 29000
—— Cook, J. (Bost. Monday Lectures.) Bost., 1880. 12°. . . 28027
—— Newcomb, S. Money and L. Questions. N. Y., 1878. 24°. . 29062
—— Thornton, W. T. Lond., 1870. 8°. 29002
—— *See, also,* **Wages.**
Laboulaye, E. R. L., (*pseud.*, 'René Lefebvre.') Contes bleus. [&] Nouveaux contes bleus. Paris, 1877. 16°. 25666
—— Paris en Amérique. Paris, 1877. 16°. 25667
—— Le Prince-Caniche. Paris, 1877. 16°. 25668
Lacombe, M. J. P. Arms and Armour. Lond., 1869. 12°. . . 29928
Lacordaire, J. B. H. D., *abbé,* Memoir of. Montalembert, C. F. R. de. Lond., 1863. 8°. 22180
Lacretelle, H. de. Lamartine and his Friends. N. Y., 1880. 12°. . 22482
Lacroix, P. The Arts in the Middle Ages, and at the period of the Renaissance. Lond., 1870. 8°. 20362

Lacroix, P. The 18th Century. Lond., 1876. 8°. 20363
—— Manners, Customs, and Dress during the Middle Ages. Lond., 1874. 8°. 20361
—— Military and Religious Life. Lond., 1874. 8°. 20360
—— Science and Literature. Lond., 1878. 8°. 20364
Lacy, J. Dramatic Works; with memoir and notes. Edinb. & L., 1875. 8°. 26570
Lady of the Aroostook. Howells, W. D. Bost., 1879. 12°. (3 cop.) 24565–
Lady Lee's Widowhood. Hamley, E. B. Edinb., 1854. 2 v. 8°. . 24484–
LaFayette, M. M. P., *comtesse de. Sainte-Beuve, C. A.* (*In* 'Portraits.') 23643
[**Laffan, May.**] The Honorable Miss Ferrard. N. Y., 1878. 16°. . 24929
LaFontaine, J. de. *Besant, W.* (*In* 'French Humourists.') . . 26776
Lamartine, A. M. L. de. Biographies and Portraits. Lond., 1866. 2 v. 8°. 23727–

CONTENTS:—1, Lord Chatham; Wm. Pitt; Shakespeare.—2, Shakespeare; Charlotte Corday; Mad. Roland; Mirabeau; Danton; Vergniaud.

—— Graziella. Paris, 1876. 16°. 25669
—— Hist. of the Constituent Assembly, 1789. Lond., 1858. 4 v. in 2. 20415–
—— Twenty-five Years of my Life, and Memoirs of my Mother. Lond., 1872. 2 v. 12°. 22525–
—— *Same, abridged.* (*In* **Stoddard, R. H.,** 'Bric-à-Brac Series.') . 23261
—— *Lacretelle, H. de.* Lamartine and his Friends. N. Y., 1880. 12°. 22482
Lamb, Caroline, *Lady.* Ada Reis: a tale. Lond., 1823. 3 v. 16°. 18621–
—— Original Poetry, Letters, and Recollections. (*See* **Nathan, I.,** *editor.*) 18636
Lamb, Chas. *Stoddard, R. H.* (*In* 'Bric-à-Brac series.') . . . 23254
—— **& Mary Lamb.** Poems, Letters, and Remains. Ed. by W. C. Hazlitt. Lond., 1874. 12°. 23216
La Motte Fouqué, F. de. Sintram und seine Gefährten. Braunsch., 1873. 16°. 25831
—— Undine. Eine Erzählung. Mit 60 Holzschnitten. Berlin, 1870. 25904
—— Der Zauberring. Braunsch., 1865. 3 Th. in 1 B. 16°. . . 25830
La Motte-Valois, J. de L., *comtesse de;* Life of. Vizetelly, H. Lond., 1867. 2 v. 12°. 22523–
Lamphere, G. N. United States Government. Phil., 1880. 8°. . 21531
Lancashire Memories. Potter, L. Lond., 1879. 12°. . . . 23686
Land (The) of Charity. Mateer, S. N. Y. 12°. 21618
Landhaus (Das) am Rhein. Auerbach, B. Stuttg., 1871. 4 B. 16°. (Romane, B. 9–12.) 25891–
—— *Same.* Stuttg., 1874. 3 B. 16°. 25884–
Landolin. Auerbach, B. N. Y., 1878. 16°. 24044
Landor, W. S. Hellenics. Edinb., 1859. 8°. 26246
—— The Last Fruit off an Old Tree. Lond., 1853. 12°. . . . 18644
—— *See* **Dowden, E.,** 'Stud. in Lit.' (26926); **Milnes, R. M.,** 'Monographs' (23220); **Stephen, L.,** 'Hours in a Lib.,' v. 3 (26935).
Landseer, *Sir* **E.** *Stephens, F. G.* (Illust. Biographies.) L. & N. Y., 1880. 12°. 23791
Landseer, T., *editor.* Life [Autobiog.] and Letters of Wm. Bewick, artist. Lond., 1871. 2 v. 12°. 23840–

Lane, E. W., Life of. Poole, S. L. Lond., 1877. 8°. 23425
Lang, A. Ballads and Lyrics of Old France; with other poems. Lond., 1872. 12°. 26026
Lange, F. A. Hist. of Materialism. Bost., 1877–80. v. 1–2. 8°. . 28209–
Langton, Stephen, Life of. Maurice, C. E. Lond., 1872. 12°. . 22940
Language. Müller, F. M. Sci. of Language. (*His* 'Chips,' v. 4.) . 27302
—— Sayce, A. H. Introd. to the Science of L. Lond., 1880. 2 v. 12°. 27864–
—— Whitney, W. D. Life and Growth of L. N. Y., 1875. 12°. (2 cop.) 29255–
—— — Oriental and Linguistic Studies. N. Y., 1873–4. 2 series. 12°. . . . . 136 & 27862
—— Wilkins, A. S. Some Historical Results of the Sci. of L. (*In* **Owens College** Ess. & Ad.) 27412
See, also, **Basque; Greek Lang.; Literature; Philology; Scandinavian.**
—— *English.* Lounsbury, T. R. Hist. of the Eng. L. N. Y., 1879. 27870
—— — Oliphant, T. L. K. Sources of Standard English. Lond., 1873. 16°. 27869
—— — White, R. G. Every-Day English. Bost., 1880. 12°. . . 27866
—— — *See, also,* **English Lit.; Grammar,** *Eng.;* **Rhetoric.**
Lanier, S. Science of English Verse. N. Y., 1880. 12°. . . . 26289
Lansdowne, *Marquis of. See* **Petty, H.**
Laocoon. Lessing, G. E. Transl. by E. Frothingham. Bost., 1874. 26290
Laos. *See* **Indo-China.**
Lapland. Hutchinson, A. H. Lond., 1870. 12°. 21706
Lappenberg, J. M. England under the Anglo-Saxon Kings. Lond., 1845. 2 v. 8°. 21089–
Larpent, G. Turkey. From the journals and correspondence of Sir James Porter; continued by G. Larpent. Lond., 1854. 2 v. 20615–
Larwood, Jacob, (*pseud.*) *See* **Sadler, L. R.**
[**La Sale, A. de.**] Hist. and Pleasant Chronicle of Little Jehan de Saintré. Lond., 1862. 12°. 24211
La Salle, R. C. de.; and the discovery of the Great West. Parkman, F. Bost., 1879. 8°. 21403
Last (The) Athenian. Rydberg, V. Phil., [1879]. 12°. . . . 24817
Last (The) Fruit off an Old Tree. Landor, W. S. Lond., 1853. 12°. 18644
Last (The) Knight. Auersperg, A. A. N. Y., 1871. 8°. . . . 26240
Latham, R. G. Frithiof: [poem] from the Swedish of E. Tegnér. Lond., 1838. 12°. 27709
Lathrop, G. P. A Study of Hawthorne. Bost., 1876. 16°. . . 22608
Latimer, H.: a biography. Demaus, R. Lond., [1869]. 12°. . . 22100
[**La Tour Landry, G. de.**] Book of the Knight of the Tower, Landry. Lond., 1862. 12°. 24211
Laugel, A. England, political and social. N. Y., 1874. 16°. . . 20810
Laun, H. van. *See* **Van Laun.**
Law, J., the Financier. Cochut, P. A. Lond., 1856. 16°. . . 22843
Law. Amos, S. Science of Law. N. Y., 1874. 12°. . . . 29249
—— Ihering, R. von. Struggle for Law. Chic., 1879. 12°. . . 28844
—— Maine, H. J. S. Ancient Law. N. Y., 1877. 8°. 28967
—— Montesquieu, C. de S. de. Spirit of Laws. With D'Alembert's analysis of the work. Lond., 1878. 2 v. 12°. 28849–

Law, *American*. Abbott, B. V. American Jurisprudence. (*In* **First Cent.** of the Republic.) 21520
——— Judge and Jury. N. Y., 1880. 12°. 28846
—— *Constitutional*. *See* **England**, *Const. & Laws*; **U. S.**, *Const. & Laws*; **Politics.**
—— *Natural*. Broom, H. Philosophy of Law. San Fran., [1876]. 28851
——— Simcox, E. Bost., 1877. 8°. 28208
—— *Parliamentary*. *See* **Parliamentary** Practice.
—— *Roman*. Hadley, J. N. Y., 1875. 12°. 28847
See, also, **Jury; Lawyers; Social Sci.; Trials.**
Law of Hotel Life. Rogers, R. V. San Fran., 1879. 16°. . . 28852
Lawless, V. B., *Baron Cloncurry*. Personal Recollections. Dublin, 1849. 8°. 18598
Lawrence, F. Life of Henry Fielding. Lond., 1855. 12°. . . 23215
Laws (The) of Fésole. Ruskin, J. N. Y., 1877. Part 1. 12°. . 29844
Lawyers. Forsyth, W. Hist. of Lawyers. Bost., 1875. 8°. . . 23886
—— Woolrych, H. W. Lives of Eminent Serjeants-at-Law of the English Bar. Lond., 1869. 2 v. 8°. 23887-
Leading Cases done into English. Lond., 1876. 8°. . . . 26122
Leah: a woman of fashion. Edwards, A. N. Y., [1875]. 8°. . 24648
Leahy, J. Art of Swimming in the Eton Style. Lond., 1875. 12°. 29642
Leam Dundas, The Atonement of. Linton, E. L. Phil., 1876. 8°. 24312
Lear (A) of the Steppe. Turgénief, I. S. 24867
Le Bas, C. W. Life of T. F. Middleton, D.D. Lond., 1831. 2 v. 8°. 18741-
Le Brun, Elisabeth L. V. Souvenirs. N. Y., 1879. 8°. . . 23839
Lechler, G. V. Wiclif and his English Precursors. Lond., 1878. 2 v. 8°. 22305-
Lecky, W. E. H. Hist. of England in the 18th Century. N. Y., 1878. 2 v. 12°. 20926-
LeConte, J. Correlation of Vital with Chemical and Physical Forces. (*With* **Stewart, B.**, 'Conservation of Energy.') 29246
—— Elements of Geology. N. Y., 1878. 8°. 29410
Lecturing, Hints on. Pitman, H. Lond., 1879. 16°. . . . 27835
Lee, Eliza B. Life of J. P. F. Richter; with his autobiogr. [1st ed.] Bost., 1842. 2 v. 12°. (2 copies.) 7799-
—— *Same*. 2d ed. Lond., 1849. 12°. 23226
—— *Same*. 3d ed. Bost., 1864. 12°. (2 copies.) 7803-
Lee, Sophia. The Recess; or, A tale of other times. Lond., 1792. 3 v. 16°. 18684-
Lefebvre, René. *See* **Laboulaye, E. R. L.**
Lefèvre, A. Philosophy, historical and critical. Lond., 1879. 12°. 28162
Legal Tender. *See* **Money.**
Legend of Jubal. Eliot, Geo. Bost., 1874. 16°. 26056
Legends. Arnason, J. Icelandic Legends. Lond., 1864. 12°. . 27710
—— Cox, G. W. Tales of Ancient Greece. Chic., 1877. 12°. . 27742
——— **& Jones (E. H.).** Tales of the Teutonic Lands. Lond., 1872. 27713
—— *See, also*, **Myths** (*and references*).
Legends and Lyrics. Procter, A. A. Lond., 1872-3. 2 v. 16°. . 26034-

Legends of the Madonna. Jameson, A. M. Lond., 1872. 8°. . 29910
Legends of the Monastic Orders. Jameson, A. M. Lond., 1872. 29911
Legends of Number Nip. Lemon, M. Lond., 1864. 16°. . . . 24621
Legge, A. O. Pius IX.: his life to 1850. Lond., 1875. 2 v. 8°. 22185–
Legge, J. Life and Teachings of Confucius. Lond., 1867. 8°. . 23730
—— Life and Works of Mencius. Phila., 1875. 12°. . . . 23729
Legislative Assemblies, Rules of. *See* **Parliamentary Practice.**
Le Goff, F. Life of Louis Adolphe Thiers. N. Y., 1879. 12°. . 22521
Leighton, R. F. Hist. of Rome. N. Y., 1880. 12°. . . . 20099
Leisure-Day Rhymes. Saxe, J. G. Bost., 1875. 12°. . . . 26131
Leland, C. G. Abraham Lincoln, and the abolition of slavery in the U. S. [L. &] N. Y., 1879. 16°. 22451
—— Egyptian Sketch-book. Lond., 1873. 12°. 21616
—— *& others.* English-Gipsy Songs in Rommany, with metrical English translations. By C. G. Leland, E. H. Palmer and Janet Tuckey. Phila., 1875. 16°. 26123
Lemoine, E. (*See* **Thomson, J.,** 'Public and Private Life of Animals.')
Lemon, M. Legends of Number Nip. Lond., 1864. 16°. . . 24621
Lennox, W. P. Drafts on my Memory. Lond., 1866. 2 v. 8°. . 23889–
Lenormant, Amélie C. Mad. Récamier and her Friends. Bost., 1875. 12°. 22483
Leo I., *St.,* (*the Great,*) and the Rise of the Papacy. Merivale, C. (*In* 'Four Lect.') 28445
Leonardo da Vinci. *See* **Vinci.**
Leone Leoni. Dudevant, A. L. A. D. (*In vol. with* 'Teverino.') . 25695
Leopold I., *king of the Belgians,* Memoirs of. Juste, T. Lond., 1868. 2 v. 8°. 23899–
Leslie, A. Arctic Voyages of A. E. Nordenskiöld: 1858–1879. Lond., 1879. 8°. 21881
Lesseps, F. de. *Fitzgerald, P.* Canal at Suez, [and] its projector. Lond., 1876. 2 v. 8°. 21840–
Lessing, G. E. Laocoon. Transl. by Ellen Frothingham. Bost., 1874. 16°. 26290
—— Nathan the Wise. [*And*] Emilia Galotti. Leipz., 1868. 16°. 26512
—— Selected Prose Works. Ed. by E. Bell. Lond., 1879. 12.°. . 27256
CONTENTS:—Laokoon; How the ancients represented death; Dramatic notes.
—— *Fiske, J.* Nathan the Wise. (*In* 'Unseen World.') . . . 27243
—— *Lowell, J. R.* (*In* 'Among my Books,' 1st ser.) 3616
—— *Sime, J.* [A Biography.] Lond., 1877. 2 v. 8°. . . . 23328–
—— *Zimmern, H.* His Life and his Works. Lond., 1878. 12°. . 23330
Lessons from my Masters. Bayne, P. N. Y., 1879. 12°. . . 23287
L'Estrange, A. G. K. Hist. of Eng. Humour. Lond., 1878. 2 v. 12°. 26938–
Letourneau, C. Biology. Lond., 1878. 8°. 29390
Letters. Scoones, W. B. Four centuries of English Letters: selections from the correspondence of 150 writers. Lond., 1880. 12°. 23378
Letters from High Latitudes. Blackwood, F. T. H. N. Y. 12°. 21222
Letters from the Mountains. Grant, A. Lond., 1807. 3 v. 12°. . 18547–

Letters and Social Aims. Emerson, R. W. Bost., 1876. 12°. (2 copies.) 27224-

Letters, written for the Post, and not for the Press. [Russell, J.] Lond., 1820. 12°. 18696

Lettsom, W. N. Nibelungenlied. Transl. [into Engl. verse]. Lond., 1874. 8°. 27706

Levant, In the. Warner, C. D. Bost., 1877. 12°. 21690

Lever, C. J., (*pseud.*, 'Harry Lorrequer.') Arthur O'Leary. Lond., 1845. 8°. 24669

—— The Bramleighs of Bishop's Folly. 1872. 8°. 24254

—— Confessions of Con. Cregan, the Irish Gil Blas. Lond., [1872]. 24255

—— Davenport Dunn: a man of our day. Lond., 1872. 8°. . . 24256

—— Dodd Family abroad. Lond., 1854. 8°. 24257

—— *Same.* New ed. Lond., 1872. 8°. 24258

—— Jack Hinton, the Guardsman. Phila., [1878]. 8°. . . . 24259

—— Luttrell of Arran. Lond., 1873. 8°. 24260

—— The Martins of Cro' Martin. Lond., 1873. 8°. 24261

—— *Fitzpatrick, W. J.* Life of Lever. Lond., 1879. 2 v. 8°. . 23400

Leveson, H. A., ("The Old Shekarry.") Hunting Grounds of the Old World. Lond., 1865. 8°. 29493

Levy, W. H. Blindness and the Blind. Lond., 1872. 12° . . 29978

Lewes, G. H. Actors and the Art of Acting. Lond., 1875. 12°. 26559

—— Life of Robespierre. Lond., 1849. 12°. 22527

—— Life and Works of Goethe. Bost., 1856. 2 v. 16°. . . . 23307-

—— *Same, abridged.* Story of G.'s Life. Lond., 1873. 12°. . . 23309

Lewes, Marian Evans. *See* **Eliot, George.**

Lewis (*kings of France*). *See* **Louis.**

Lewis, C. T. Hist. of Germany; founded on Dr. David Müller. N. Y., 1874. 8°. 20642

Lewis, G. C. Letters, to various friends. Lond., 1870. 8°. . . 23056

Lewsiana. Smith, W. A. Lond., 1875. 12°. 21253

Liber Humanitatis. Greenwell, D. Lond., 1875. 12°. . . . 27272

Liberal (The). [Hunt, J. H. L., & Byron.] Lond., 1822-3. 2 v. 8°. 11400-

Liberty. Hill, B. A. Liberty and Law under federative government. Phil., 1874. 12°. 28843

—— Lieber, F. Civil Liberty and Self-Government. Phila., 1874. 29082

—— Mill, J. S. Bost., 1863. 16°. 28853

—— Morley, J. On Compromise. Lond., 1874. 8°. . . . 29089

—— Paterson, J. Liberty of the Subject and Security of the Person. Lond., 1877. 2 v. 12°. 28854-

—— Stephen, J. F. Liberty, Equality, Fraternity. N. Y., 1873. 12°. 28856

Liberty of the Press. *See* **Newspapers.**

Liddon, H. P. Some Elements of Religion: Lent lectures. N. Y., 1872. 12°. 28541

Lidstone, W. Fifteen thousand Miles on the Amazon. (*See* **Brown, C. B., & Lidstone.**)

Lie, J. The Pilot and his Wife. Chic., 1876. 12°. 24210

Lieber, F. Civil Liberty and Self-Government. Ed. by T. D. Woolsey. Phila., 1874. 8°. 29082

Lieber, F. Manual of Political Ethics. Ed. by T. D. Woolsey. Phila., 1875. 2 v. 8°. 29080–
Liebig, J. von, The Life-work of. Hofmann, A. W. Lond., 1876. 23544
Liechtenstein, Marie. Holland House. Lond., 1874. 2 v. 8°. . 21773–
Life (*conduct and philosophy of*). Arnold, F. Turning-points in Life. Lond., 1873. 2 v. 12°. 27379–
—— Greg, W. R. Enigmas of Life. Bost., 1874. 12°. . . . 27292
—— Mallock, W. H. Is Life Worth Living? N. Y., 1879. 12°. . 28085
—— Value of Life: a reply to Mallock's essay "Is Life worth living?" N. Y., 1879. 12°. 28086
—— *See, also,* **Education** (*& references*); **Professions.**
Life (*vital force*). Beale, L. S. Life Theories: their influence upon religious thought. Lond., 1871. 12°. 29293
—— — Machinery of Life: a lecture. Lond., [1875]. 12°. . . 29294
—— — Mystery of Life. Lond., 1871. 12°. 29295
—— — On Life and on Vital Action in Health and Disease. Lond., 1875. 12°. 29296
—— *See, also,* **Biology.**
Life in the Open Air. Winthrop, T. N. Y., 1876. 16°. . . . 27239
Life (The), Writings, Opinions, and Times of Lord Byron. Lond., 1825. 3 v. 8°. 18653–
Light. Lommel, E. Nature of Light. N. Y., 1876. 12°. . . 29258
—— Mayer (A. M.) & Barnard (C.). N. Y., 1877. 12°. . . . 29317
—— Vogel, H. Chemistry of L. and Photography. N. Y., 1875. 12°. 29253
—— *See, also,* **Colors; Spectroscope; Spectrum** Analysis.
Light (The) of Asia. Arnold, E. Bost., 1879. 16°. 26003
Lightfoot, J. B. Revision of the Eng. New Test. N. Y., 1873. 12°. 28525
Lights and Shadows of Amer. Life. Mitford, M. R., *editor.* Lond., 1832. 3 v. 12°. 18544–
Lima. Markham, C. R. (*With* 'Cuzco.') 21701
Lincoln, A. *Leland, C. G.* Lincoln and the Abolition of Slavery. [L. &] N. Y., 1879. 16°. 22451
—— Welles, G. Lincoln and Seward. N. Y., 1874. 12°. . . 22645
Linderman, H. R. Money and Legal Tender in the U. S. N. Y., 1877. 12°. 29058
[**Lindley, A. F.**] Ti-ping Tien-kwoh: history of the Tiping Revolution. By Lin-le. Lond., 1866. 2 v. 8°. 20381–
Linton, Eliza L. The Atonement of Leam Dundas. Phila., 1876. 24312
Lippincott, Sara J. C., (*pseud.,* 'Grace Greenwood.') Haps and Mishaps of a Tour in Europe. Bost., 1854. 12°. . . 6491
Lippincott's Magazine. Philad., 1868–79. 24 v. 8°. . . . 13373–
Liszt, F. Life of Chopin. Phila., 1863. 16°. 23768
Literary and Social Judgments. Greg, W. R. Bost., 1873. 12°. . 27293
Literature. Dowden, E. Studies in Literature. Lond., 1878. 12°. (*For contents see* **Dowden.**) 26926
—— Lacroix, P. Science and Literature in the Middle Ages. Lond., 1878. 8°. 20364
—— Müller, F. M. Essays on Literature. (*His* 'Chips,' v. 3.) . . 3733
—— Ossoli, M. F. Art, Lit., and the Drama. (Works, v. 5.) . . 27290

Literature. Stephen, L. Hours in a Library. Lond., 1874–80. 3 v. 12°. (*For contents see* **Stephen.**) 26933–

See, also, **Biography; Books; Drama; History; Journalism; Language; Myths; Poetry; Quotations; Wit** & Humour.—*Also,* 'Literature' *under the following prefixes:* **American; Celtic; English; French; German; Greek; Italian; Roman; Scandinavian.**

Literature and Dogma. Arnold, M. N. Y., 1873. 12°. 28689

Literature and Life. Whipple, E. P. Bost., 1871. 12°. 27267

Literature Primers. Green, J. R., *editor.* Lond., 1876–9. 7 v. 16°. 26855–

CONTENTS:—English Lit., by S. A. Brooke.—Shakspeare, E. Dowden.—Greek Lit., R. C. Jebb.—Eng. Gram. Exercises, R. Morris & H. C. Bowen.—Philology, J. Peile.—Classical Geography, H. F. Tozer.—Homer, W. E. Gladstone.

Littell's Living Age. Bost., 1844–79. v. 1–143. 8°. 13924–

Little Barefoot. Auerbach, B. N. Y., 1874. 16°. 24045

Little Jehan de Saintré. [La Sale, A. de.] Lond., 1862. 12°. . . 24211

Liverpool, R. B. J., *earl of. Earle, J. C.* (*In* 'Eng. Premiers,' v. 2.) 22883

Livingstone, D. Last Journals in Central Africa. N. Y., 1875. 8°. (Map in separate case.) 23532–

—— *Stanley, H. M.,* How I found Livingstone. N. Y., 1872. 8°. . 21856

Livy. *Capes, W. W.* (Classical Writers.) N. Y., 1880. 16°. . . 26893

—— *Collins, W. L.* ('Ancient Classics for English Readers,' suppl em. series, v. 1.) 26847

Liza. Turgénief, I. S. N. Y., 1872. 16°. (2 copies.) . . . 24862–

Lloyd, C. Tragedies of Alfieri; transl. [into Eng. blank verse]. Lond., 1815. 3 v. 16°. 18616–

Lloyd, L. Peasant Life in Sweden. Lond., 1870. 8°. . . . 21788

Lloyd, W. W. Age of Pericles. Lond., 1875. 2 v. 8°. . . 20163–

Lloyd Lee. [Blair, E. T. New Haven, 1878.] 16°. (2 copies.) . 24060–

Lock, D. R., (*pseud.,* 'Petroleum V. Nasby.') Nasby. Cincin., 1867. 25212

—— Struggles, social, financial and political. Bost., 1873. 8°. . 6490

Locke, John, Life of. Bourne, H. R. F. Lond., 1876. 2 v. 8°. . 23520–

Locker, F. London Lyrics. Lond., 1874. 16°. 26074

Lockyer, J. N. Astronomy. (Sci. Primers.) Lond., 1877. 16°. . 29361

—— The Spectroscope and its Applications. Lond., 1873. 12°. . 29318

—— Studies in Spectrum Analysis. N. Y., 1878. 12°. . . . 29263

Locusts and Wild Honey. Burroughs, J. Bost., 1879. 16°. . . 29323

Löher, F. von. Cyprus, historical and descriptive. Adapted from the German; with much additional matter by Mrs. A. B. Joyner. Lond., 1878. 12°. 21251

Löwenberg, J., *joint author. See* **Bruhns, C.,** 'Life of A. von Humboldt.'

Löwenthal, J. Morphy's Games of Chess. Lond., 1860. 12°. . 29711

—— *Same.* Morphy's Games. N. Y., 1860. 12°. 29712

Loftie, W. J. Plea for Art in the House. Phila., [1877]. 12°. . 29781

Logan, W. H. *See* **Maidment, J., & Logan.**

Log-book of a Fisherman. Buckland, F. Lond., 1875. 8°. . . 29495

Logic. Jevons, W. S. (Sci. Primers.) Lond., 1878. 16°. . . 29359

Logic of Christian Evidences. Wright, G. F. Andover, 1880. 12°. 28702

Loiterings in Pleasant Paths. Terhune, M. V. H. N. Y., 1880. 21681

Lola: a tale of Gibraltar. Griffiths, A. N. Y., 1877. 16°. . . 24452

Lombard Street. Bagehot, W. Lond., 1873. 12°. 29051

Lombardy. Testa, G. B. Hist. of the War of Frederick I. against the Communes of L. Lond., 1877. 8°. 20296

Lommel, E. Nature of Light. N. Y., 1876. 12°. 29258

London. Becker, B. H. Scientific London. N. Y., 1875. 12°. . 27300

—— Doran, J. London in the Jacobite Times. Lond., 1877. 2 v. . 21761–

—— Doré (G.) & Jerrold (W. B.). Lond., 1871. 4°. . . . . . ——

—— Hare, A. J. C. Walks in London. N. Y., 1878. 12°. . . 21606

—— Jesse, J. H. Lond., 1871. 3 v. 12°. 21766–

—— Nadal, E. S. Impressions of London Social Life. N. Y., 1875. 21708

—— [Sadler, L. R.] Story of the Lond. Parks. Lond., [1871]. 2 v. 21614–

—— Thornbury (W.) & Walford (E.). Old and New London. Lond., [1873–8]. 6 v. 8°. 21960–

—— Timbs, J. Club Life of London. Lond., 1866. 2 v. 12°. . 21764–

—— — Curiosities of London. Lond., [1867]. 8°. 21763

—— Walford, E. Londoniana. Lond., 1879. 2 v. 12°. . . . 21260–

—— *Tower.* Bell, D. C. Notices of the Historic Persons buried in the Chapel of St. Peter ad Vincula, in the Tower of L. Lond., 1877. 8°. 23002

—— — Dixon, W. H. Her Majesty's Tower. Lond., 1869–71. 4 v. 21769–

See, also, **Bow-Street ; Lombard St. ; Southwark ; Westminster Abbey.**

London (The) Anecdotes. Lond. 16°. 25245

London Daily News. *See* **Daily News** (Lond.).

London Dialectical Society. *See* **Spiritualism,** Report.

London Life, Oddities of. [Poole, J.] Lond., 1838. 2 v. 8°. . 25209–

London Lyrics. Locker, F. Lond., 1874. 16°. 26074

London Quarterly Review. *See* **Quarterly** Rev.

London Review. Lond., 1835–6. 2 v. 8°. 11885–

London Series of English Classics. Hales (J. W.) & Jerram (C. S.), *editors.*

CONTENTS :—Bacon's Essays, ed. by E. A. Abbott.—Selections from Pope, by T. Arnold.—Marlowe's Dr. Faustus, by W. Wagner.—Jonson's Every Man in his Humour, by H. B. Wheatley.

London Society. Lond., 1862–79. v. 1–19, 22–36. 8°. . . . 17755–

London and Westminster Review. Lond., 1836–40. 7 v. 8°. . 11887–

Long, C. C. Central Africa. N. Y., 1877. 8°. 21851

Long, G. Epictetus : [selections and] life. Lond., 1877. 12°. . 26805

Long, J. W. American Wild-fowl Shooting. N. Y., 1874. 12°. . 29610

Long Life, and how to reach it. Richardson, J. G. Phil., 1879. 16°. 29959

Longevity, Human. Thoms, W. J. Lond., 1873. 12°. . . . 29388

Longfellow, H. W. Aftermath. Bost., 1873. 16°. 26075

—— Kéramos, and other poems. Bost., 1878. 16°. 26076

—— Masque of Pandora, and other poems. Bost., 1875. (2 copies.) 26077–

—— New-England Tragedies : 1, John Endicott ; 2, Giles Corey of the Salem Farms. Bost., 1868. 12°. 26079

—— *editor.* Poems of Places. Bost., 1876–79. 31 v. 16°. . . 26440–

CONTENTS :—1–4, England (and Wales).—5, Ireland.—6–8, Scotland, (Denmark, Iceland, Norway, and Sweden).—9–10, France (and Savoy).—11–13, Italy.—14–15, Spain, (Portugal, Belgium and Holland).—16, Switzerland, and Austria.—17–18, Germany.—19, Greece, and Turkey in Europe.—20, Russia.—21–23, Asia.—24, Africa.—25–30, America, (viz. : 25–26, New England ; 27, Middle States ; 28, Western ; 29, Southern ; 30, British Amer., Danish Amer., Mexico, Central Amer., S. Amer., W. Indies.)—31, Oceanica.

Longman, W. Lectures on the Hist. of England. Lond., 1863. 8°. 21088
Lonsdale, H. John Dalton. Lond., 1874. 12°. 23564
Lonsdale, Margaret. Sister Dora: a biography. Bost., 1880. 16°. 23650
Lord Bantam. [Jenkins, E.] N. Y., 1872. 12°. 24606
Loring, F. W. Two College Friends. Bost., [1871]. 16°. . . 24235
Loring, G. B. Treatise on Agriculture and the Horse. (*In* **Murray, W. H. H.,** 'The Perfect Horse.') 29496
Lorley and Reinhard. Auerbach, B. N. Y., 1877. 16°. (2 copies.) 24046–
Lorna Doone. Blackmore, R. D. N. Y., [1878]. 8°. . . . 24305
Lossing, B. J. The Hudson. Troy. 8°. 21587
—— Pictorial Field-book of the War of 1812. N. Y., 1868. 8°. . 21560
Lotus Leaves. [Ed. by J. Brougham and J. Elderkin.] Lond., 1875. 27563
Louis XI., *king of France*, Reign of. Willert, P. F. Lond., 1876. . 20069
Louis XIV., *king of France. Sainte-Beuve, C. A.* (*In* 'Monday Chats.') 23290
Louis XV., *king of France. Broglie, A. de.* The King's Secret: correspondence with his diplomatic agents, from 1752–1774. Lond., [1879]. 2 v. 8°. 20685–
Louisa, *queen of Prussia*, Life and Times of. Hudson, E. H. Lond., 1874. 2 v. 12°. 22507–
Louisiana: [a novel.] Burnett, F. H. N. Y., 1880. 12°. (2 cop.) 24156–
Lounsbury, T. R. Hist. of the English Language. N. Y., 1879. . 27870
Love is Enough. Morris, W. Bost., 1873. 16°. 26102
Lovelace, R. Lucasta: poems. With [life] by W. C. Hazlitt. Lond., 1864. 12°. 26080
Lover, S. Songs and Ballads. Lond., 1844. 16°. 26081
—— *Bernard, B.* The Life of Lover, artistic, literary, and musical; with selections. Lond., 1874. 2 v. 12°. 18539–
Contents:—1, Life.—2, Selections.
—— *Symington, A. J.* Biographical sketch, with selections. N. Y., 1880. 16°. 23311
Lover's (The) Tale. Tennyson, A. Bost., 1879. 16°. . . . 692
Love's Meinie. Ruskin, J. N. Y., 1873. 12°. 29835
Low, C. R. Memoir of Sir Garnet J. Wolseley. Lond., 1878. 2 v. 22844–
Lowell, J. R. Among my Books. Bost., 1870–76. 2 series. 12°. (2 copies.) . . . . 3616– & 26931–
—— Poetical Works. New rev. ed. Bost., 1877. 8°. . . . 26160
—— A Year's Life: [poems.] Bost., 1841. 16°. 26082
Lowell, R. T. S. Antony Brade. Bost., 1874. 12°. . . . 24236
—— Poems. New ed., with new poems. Bost., 1864. 16°. . . 26083
—— A Story or two from an Old Dutch Town. Bost., 1878. 16°. 24237
Lowndes, T. Tracts in Prose and Verse. Dover (v. 1) & Lond., 1825–27. 2 v. 8°. 18646–
Lubbock, J. Addresses, political and educational. Lond., 1879. 8°. 27411
Contents:—The imperial policy of Gt. Brit.; Bank act of 1844; Present system of public school education, 1876; Present system of elementary education; Income tax; National debt; Declaration of Paris; Marine insurances; Preservation of our ancient national monuments; Egypt.
—— On British Wild Flowers considered in relation to Insects. Lond., 1875. 12°. 29461
—— On the Origin and Metamorphoses of Insects. Lond., 1874. . 29503

Lubbock, J. Scientific Lectures. Lond., 1879. 8°. 29532

CONTENTS:—On flowers and insects; On plants and insects; on the habits of ants; Introd. to the study of prehistoric archæology; Address, Wiltshire Archæological Soc.

Lubomirski, J. Safar-Hadgi; or, Russ and Turcoman. N. Y., 1878. 24083

Lucasta: poems. Lovelace, R. Lond., 1864. 12°. 26080

Lucian. *Collins, W. L.* ('Anc. Classics for Eng. Readers,' v. 18.) 26844

Lucretius. *Mallock, W. H.* (Anc. Clas. for Eng. Readers, suppl. ser., v. 7.) 26853

Lucy, H. W. Gladstone: a biographical sketch. N. Y., 1880. 24°. 22852

—— Men and Manner in Parliament. By the member for the Chiltern Hundreds. Lond., 1874. 12°. 20811

Ludlow, J. M. Popular Epics of the Middle Ages of the Norse-German and Carlovingian Cycles. Lond., 1865. 2 v. 12°. 27671–

—— War of Amer. Independence, 1775–1783. Bost., 1876. (2 cop.) 20460–

Lübke, W. Hist. of Art. Transl. by F. E. Bunnètt. Lond., 1869. v. 1. 8°. 29942

—— *Same.* New transl.; ed. by C. Cook. N. Y., 1878. 2 v. 8°. . 29940–

Lumley, B. Reminiscences of the Opera. Lond., 1864. 8°. . . 29799

Luther, M. *Masson, D.* The Three Devils: L.'s, Milton's, and Goethe's. Lond., 1874. 12°. 27299

Luttrell of Arran. Lever, C. J. Lond., 1873. 8°. 24260

Lycidas. Milton, J. Ed. by C. S. Jerram. Lond., 1874. 12°. . 26205

Lydia. Duncker, M. W. (*In* 'Hist. of Antiquity,' v. 3.) . . . 20242

Lyttelton, Thos., *Lord;* Life of. Frost, T. Lond., 1876. 8°. . 23930

Lytton. *See* **Bulwer-Lytton.**

Macalister, A. Zoology of the Invertebrate Animals. N. Y., 1879. 29352

—— Zoology of the Vertebrate Animals. N. Y., 1878. 16°. . . 29353

Macarthur, Margaret. Hist. of Scotland. N. Y., 1874. 16°. . 20080

Macaulay, T. B. Life of Sam. Johnson. (*See* **Johnson,** 'Six Chief Lives.')

—— Miscellaneous Writings and Speeches. Lond., 1871. 12°. . 27406

—— Selections. Ed., with notes, by G. O. Trevelyan. N. Y., 1877. 27405

—— *More, H.* Letters to Z. Macaulay, containing notices of Lord M.'s youth. Lond., 1860. 16°. 18561

—— *Stirling, J. H.* Jerrold, Tennyson, and Macaulay. Edinb., 1868. 16°. 26917

—— *Trevelyan, G. O.* Life and Letters of Lord Macaulay. N. Y., 1876. 2 v. 8°. (2 copies.) 23410–

—— *See, also,* **Bagehot, W.,** 'Lit. Stud.,' v. 2 (26768); **Gladstone, W. E.,** 'Gleanings,' v. 2 (27228); **Morley, J.,** 'Crit. Miscel.,' 2d ser. (27408); **Stephen, L.,** 'Hours,' v. 3 (26935).

MacCarthy, D. F. Calderon's Dramas, transl. in the metre of the original. Lond., 1873. 12°. 26495

—— Shelley's Early Life. Lond., [1872]. 12°. 23298

McCarthy, J. Dear Lady Disdain. N. Y., 1876. 8°. 24670

—— A Hist. of Our Own Times. Chic., [1879]. v. 1–2 in 1. 12°. . 20825

—— Miss Misanthrope. N. Y., 1877. 8°. 24671

McCoan, J. C. Egypt as it is. N. Y., 1877. 8°. 21844

McCosh, J. The Emotions. N. Y., 1880. 12°. 28170

McCosh, J. The Scottish Philosophy. N. Y., 1875. 8°. . . . 28283
McCullagh, W. T. Memoirs of Rich. L. Sheil. Lond., 1855. 2 v. 12°. 18669–
MacDonald, G. David Elginbrod. Lond. 16°. 24622
—— England's Antiphon. [Lond., 1868.] 12°. 26125
—— Malcolm. Phila., 1875. 8°. 24672
—— Marquis of Lossie. Phila., 1877. 8°. (*Sequel to* ' Malcolm.') . 24673
—— Paul Faber, Surgeon. Phila., 1879. 8°. (2 copies.) 24674–
—— St. George and St. Michael. Bost., [1877]. 12°. 24623
—— Sir Gibbie. Phil., 1879. 8°. (2 copies.) 24676–
—— Thomas Wingfold, Curate. N. Y., 1876. 12°. 24624
—— Vicar's Daughter: an autobiographical story. Lond., 1872. 3 v. 24625–
—— Wilfrid Cumbermede. Lond., 1872. 3 v. 16°. 24628–
Macdonald, J. M. Life and Writings of St. John. N. Y., 1877. 8°. (2 copies.) 28640–
MacGahan, J. A. Campaigning on the Oxus, and the Fall of Khiva. N. Y., 1874. 8°. 21924
McGilchrist, J. Life of Benjamin Disraeli. N. Y., [1869]. 16°. . 22850
Machiavelli, N., and his Times. Villari, P. Lond., 1878. 2 v. 12°. 23943–
Mackay, C. Cavalier Songs and Ballads of England. Lond., 1863. 26119
—— Forty Years' Recollections. Lond., 1877. 2 v. 8°. 22943–
—— Life and Times of Sir Robert Peel. (*See* **Taylor, W. C., & Mackay.**)
Mackenzie, (G. M. M., *Lady Sebright*) **& Irby (A. P.).** Travels in the Slavonic Provinces of Turkey-in-Europe. Lond., 1877. 2 v. 8°. 21911–
Mackenzie, R. The 19th Century: a history. Lond., 1880. 12°. . 20482
Mackintosh, J. *Bulwer, H. L. E.* (*In* ' Histor. Characters,' v. 2.) . 23882
Macklin, C. *Kirkman, J. T.* Life of Macklin. Lond., 1799. 2 v. 18658–
—— Memoirs of Chas. Macklin, Comedian. [Anon.] Lond., 1804. 8°. 18657
Macknight, T. Life and Times of Edmund Burke. Lond., 1858–60. 3 v. 8°. 23034–
Maclear, G. F. Conversion of the West; v. 1–3. Lond., [1878]. 28494–
Macleod, N., Memoir of. Macleod, D. N. Y., 1876. 2 v. 8°. . 22188–
Macleod of Dare. Black, W. N. Y., 1879. 12°. (2 copies.). . . 24012–
McMillan, D. C. Elective Franchise in the U. S. N. Y., 1878. 12°. 21331
Macmillan's Magazine. Lond., 1859–79. v. 1–40. 8°. 12155–
McPherson, E. Hand-book of Politics for 1874, '76, '78 & '80. Wash., 1874–80. 4 v. 8°. 21523–
Macpherson, Gerardine B. Life of Anna Jameson. Bost., 1878. 23838
Macquoid, T. R. & Katharine S. Pictures and Legends from Normandy and Brittany. Lond., 1879. 12°. 21252
Macready, W. C. Reminiscences. Ed. by F. Pollock. N. Y., 1875. 12°. 23624
Madame Gosselin. Ulbach, L. N. Y., 1878. 16°. 24080
Madcap Violet. Black, W. N. Y., 1877. 12°. (3 copies.) . . 24014–
Madeleine. Sandeau, L. S. J. Chic., 1879. 16°. 24818
Madonna, Legends of the. Jameson, A. M. Lond., 1872. 8°. . 29910
Maffei, A. Brigand Life in Italy: a history of Bourbonist reaction. Lond., 1865. 2 v. 8°. 20302

Magic. Ennemoser, J. Hist. of Magic. Lond., 1854. 2 v. 12°. . 28048–
—— Rydberg, V. Magic of the Middle Ages. N. Y., 1879. 12°. . 28050
See, also, **Demonology; Spiritualism; Supernatural** (The); **Visions.**
Magnusson, E. Runeberg's Lyrical Songs, Idylls and Epigrams; done into English [verse] by E. Magnússon and E. H. Palmer. Lond., 1878. 16°. 26128
—— **& Morris (W.).** Three Northern Love Stories, and other tales. Lond., 1875. 12°. 24631
Magyars. *See* **Hungary.**
Mahaffy, J. P. Euripides. (Classical Writers.) N. Y., 1879. 16°. 26891
—— Hist. of Classical Greek Literature. N. Y., 1880. 2 v. 12°. . 26807–
Contents:—1, The poets; with an app. on Homer, by Prof. Sayce.—2, The prose writers.
—— Old Greek Life. Lond., 1876. 16°. 20056
—— Rambles and Studies in Greece. Lond., 1876. 12°. . . . 21617
—— Social Life in Greece, from Homer to Menander. Lond., 1874. 20095
Mahan, A. Critical Hist. of the late Amer. War. N. Y., 1877. 8°. 21458
Mahony, F. S. The Reliques of Father Prout [*pseud.*]. Collected by Oliver Yorke [*pseud.*]. Lond., 1873. 12°. . . . 27257
Maid Ellice. [Havers, D.] N. Y., 1878. 16°. (2 copies.) . . 24497–
Maid of Killeena. Black, W. Lond., 1874. 12°. 24017
Maid Marian. Peacock, T. L. (*In* 'Works,' v. 2.) 27304
Maid of Sker. Blackmore, R. D. N. Y., 1877. 8°. 24306
Maid, Wife, or Widow? [Hector, A. F.] N. Y., 1879. 16°. . . 24530
Maidment, J. Scottish Ballads and Songs. Edinb., 1868. 2 v. 12°. 26161–
—— **& Logan (W. H.).** Dramatists of the Restoration. Edinb. & L., 1872–79. (14 v.) 8°. 26560–
Contents:—W. Davenant, 5 v.—A. Cokain.—J. Crowne, 4 v.—J. Lacy.—S. Marmion.—J. Tatham.—J. Wilson.
Main, D. M. Treasury of English Sonnets. Manchester, 1880. 12°. 26124
Maine, H. J. S. Ancient Law. N. Y., 1877. 8°. 28967
—— Early History of Institutions. N. Y., 1875. 8°. 28968
Maiolica. Fortnum, C. D. E. N. Y., 1876. 12°. 29763
Maitres (Les) Mosaïstes. Dudevant, A. L. A. D. Paris, 1869. 16°. 25686
Majendie, Marg. E. Dita. N. Y., 1877. 16°. 24632
—— Giannetto. N. Y., 1876. 16°. 24633
Majolica. *See* **Maiolica.**
Majoratsherr (Der). Mügge, T. Breslau, 1866. (Romane, B. 29.) 25849
Majorca. Dodd, W. Three Weeks in Majorca. Lond., 1863. 12°. 21221
—— Dudevant, A. L. A. D. Un hiver à Majorque. Paris, 1867. 25681
Malbone. Higginson, T. W. Bost., 1871. 12°. 24541
Malcolm: a romance. Macdonald, G. Phil., 1875. 8°. . . . 24672
Malet, A. Overthrow of the Germanic Confederation by Prussia in 1866. Lond., 1870. 8°. 20643
Malleson, G. B. Hist. of Afghanistan. Lond., 1878. 8°. . . . 20614
—— Studies from Genoese History. Lond., 1875. 8°. 20013
Mallock, W. H. Is Life Worth Living? N. Y., 1879. 12°. (*For reply see* **Value** of Life.) 28085
—— Lucretius. (Anc. Classics for Eng. Readers, suppl. ser., v. 7.) . 26853
—— New Paul and Virginia; or, Positivism on an island. N. Y. [Lond.], 1878. 12°. 28084

Mallock, W. H. New Republic. Lond., 1877. 2 v. 12°. . . . 28082–
Malone, E., Life of. Prior, J. Lond., 1860. 8°. 23451
Man. Dawson, J. W. Story of the Earth and Man. N. Y., 1873. 29417
—— Haeckel, E. H. Evolution of Man. N. Y., 1879. 2 v. 12°. 29383–
—— Mivart, St. G. Man and Apes. N. Y., 1874. 12°. . . . 29395
—— Quatrefages de Bréau, J. L. A. de. The Human Species. N. Y., 1879. 12°. (2 copies.) 29267–
—— — Metamorphoses of Man and the Lower Animals. Lond., 1864. 12°. 29303
—— Viollet-le-Duc, E. E. Habitations of Man in all ages. Bost., 1876. 8°. 29927
—— Wood, J. G. The Natural Hist. of Man. Lond., 1868–70. 2 v. 29590–
—— *Pre-historic.* Keary, C. F. Dawn of History. N. Y., [1879]. 20090
—— — Wilson, D. Lond., 1876. 2 v. 8°. 20200–
See, also, **Antiquities; Biology** (*& references*) ; **Ethnology; Races.**
Man (The) with the Iron Mask. Topin, M. Lond., 1870. 12°. . 20403
Man (The) in the Moon. [A monthly periodical,] ed. by Albert Smith and A. B. Reach [during the first year ; afterwards by Reach]. Lond., [1847–9]. 5 v. (6 nos. each). 16°. . . 25240–
Manchester Science Lectures. *See* **Science Lectures** for the People.
Manchuria. Fleming, G. Travels on Horseback in Mantchu Tartary. Lond., 1863. 8°. 21920
—— *See, also,* **Tartary.**
Mandalay to Momien. Anderson, J. Lond., 1876. 8°. . . . 21926
Mangan, J. C. Anthologia Germanica : [metrical] translations from German poets. Dublin, 1845. 16°. 26030
Manilla, A Lady's Visit to. Almeida, A. d'. Lond., 1863. 8°. . 21937
Manners and Customs. Dyer, T. F. T. British Popular Customs, present and past. Lond., 1876. 12°. 20806
—— Farrer, J. A. Primitive Manners and Customs. N. Y., 1879. 28966
—— Lacroix, P. The 18th Century. Lond., 1876. 8°. . . . 20363
—— — Manners, Customs, and Dress during the Mid. Ages. Lond., 1874. 8°. 20361
—— *See, also,* **Burial ; Etiquette ; Man ; Marriage.**
[**Manning, Anne.**] Household of Sir Thos. More. N. Y., [1867]. 23646
Manning, H. E. Miscellanies. Lond., 1877. 2 v. 12°. . . . 27258–

Contents :—1, Roma æterna ; Work and wants of the Cath. Ch. in Eng. ; On the subjects proper to the Academia ; Father Faber ; Visit of Garibaldi to Eng. ; Cardinal Wiseman ; Inaugural address, 1866 ; French infidelity ; Ireland ; Inaug. address, 1868 ; On progress ; The Dæmon of Socrates ; Letter to the Archb. of Armagh.—2, Dr. Nicholson's accusation ; Dignity and rights of labor ; Ch. of Rome ; Cæsarism and ultramontanism ; Ultramontanism and Christianity ; Christianity and antichristianism ; The pope and magna charta ; Inaug. address, 1876 ; Philosophy without assumptions ; Frederic Ozanam.

Mansfield, E. D. Personal Memories. Cincin., 1879. 12°. . . 22617
[**Mansfield, R. B.**] School-Life at Winchester College. Lond., 1866. 12°. 28835
Mantchuria. *See* **Manchuria.**
Manufactures. Wells, D. A. (*In* **First Cent.** of the Republic.) . 21520
—— *See, also,* **Industrial Arts** (*& references*).
Manuscripts (The) of Erdély. Stephens, G. Lond., 1835. 3 v. 12°. 18626–
Manzoni, A. I Promessi Sposi : the betrothed. Lond., 1876. 12°. 24634
Marcus Aurelius. *See* **Antoninus.**

Marcus König. Freytag, G. Leipz., 1876. 12°. ('Die Ahnen,' Abth. 4). 25914
Mare (La) au diable. Dudevant, A. L. A. D. Paris, 1869. 16°. . 25687
Marenholz-Bülow, Bertha von. Reminiscences of Fried. Froebel. With a life by Emily Shirreff. Bost., 1877. 12°. 23647
Marey, E. J. Animal Mechanism. N. Y., 1874. 12°. 29250
Margary, A. R. Journey, from Shanghae to Bhamo, and back to Manwyne ; added, a chapter by Sir R. Alcock. Lond., 1876. 21925
Margollé, E., *joint author. See* **Zürcher, F., & Margollé.**
Marie. Pushkin, A. S. Chic., 1877. 16°. 24849
Marie Antoinette, *queen of France. Yonge, C. D.* Lond., 1876. 2v. 12°. 22480–
—— — *Same.* N. Y., 1876. 8°. 22520
Mariotti, Luigi, (*pseud.*) *See* **Gallenga, Antonio.**
Marius, Sulla, and the Gracchi. Beesly, A. H. N. Y., [1879]. 16°. 20440
Marjorie Daw. Aldrich, T. B. Bost., 1873. 16°. 24035
Mark Twain's Sketches. Clemens, S. L. Hartf'd, 1875. 8°. . 25588
Markham, A. H. Cruise of the "Rosario." Lond., 1873. 8°. . 21814
—— Great Frozen Sea. Lond., 1878. 8°. 21882
Markham, C. R. Cuzco. [*And*] Lima. Lond., 1856. 12°. . . 21701
Marlowe, C. Doctor Faustus. Ed. by A. W. Ward. Oxf., 1878. 26871
—— *Same.* Ed. by W. Wagner. Lond., 1877. 16°. 26513
—— Edward the Second. Ed. by O. W. Tancock. Oxf., 1879. 16°. 26525
—— Poems. Ed. by R. Bell. Lond., 1876. 12°. 26096
Marmion, S. Dramatic Works; with memoir. Edinb. & L., 1875. 26571
Marocco. *See* **Morocco.**
Marquis of Lossie. Macdonald, G. Phila., 1877. 8°. 24673
Marquis (Le) de Villemer. Dudevant, A. L. A. D. Paris, 1869. 25688
Marriage. Cook, J. (Bost. Mond. Lect.) Bost., 1879. 12°. . . 28026
—— Hamilton, A. Marriage Rites, Customs, and Ceremonies. Lond., 1822. 8°. 28960
—— Jeaffreson, J. C. Brides and Bridals. Lond., 1872. 2 v. 8°. 28961–
—— Wood, E. J. Wedding Day in all ages and countries. Lond., 1869. 2 v. in 1. 12°. 28963
Marriage (A) in High Life. Feuillet, O. Philad., [1876]. 12°. . 24473
Marryat, F. [Novels.] N. Y., 1861. (12 v.) 12°. 24635–
CONTENTS:—Jacob Faithful.—Japhet.—King's own.—Mr. Midshipman Easy (2 *cop.*).—Frank Mildmay; or, The naval officer.—Newton Forster.—Pacha of many tales.—Percival Keene.—Peter Simple.—Phantom ship.—Poacher.—Snarleyyow.
—— *Church, F. M.* Life and Letters of Capt. M. Lond., 1872. 2 v. 23212–
Marsh, Anne C. Hist. of the Prot. Reformation in France. Phila., 1851. 2 v. 12°. 20417–
Marsh, G. P. The Earth as modified by Human Action. N. Y., 1874. 8°. 29574
Martin, B. L. H. Age of Louis XIV. Bost., 1865. 2 v. 8°. . 20720–
—— Decline of the French Monarchy. Bost., 1866. 2 v. 8°. . . 20722–
Martin, E. W. Hist. of the Grange Movement. Chic., etc., 1874. 29004
Martin, Frances. Angélique Arnauld, Abbess of Port Royal. Lond., 1873. 12°. 22144
Martin, H. N. Elem. Biology. (*See* **Huxley, T. H., & Martin.**)

Martineau, Harriet. Autobiography. Ed. [with memorials] by Maria W. Chapman. Bost., 1877. 2 v. 8°. 23447-
—— British Rule in India: a historical sketch. Lond., 1857. 16°. 20497
Martineau, J. Hours of Thought on Sacred Things. Lond., 1877-79. 2 v. 12°. 28542-
—— Modern Materialism in its relations to Religion and Theology. N. Y., 1877. 16°. 29696
—— Religion as affected by Modern Materialism. N. Y., 1875. 16°. 28695
Martins (The) of Cro' Martin. Lever, C. J. Lond., 1873. 8°. . 24261
Mary Barton. [Gaskell, E. C.] Lond., 1848. 12°. 24467
Mary Stuart, *queen of Scots. Meline, J. F.* Mary and her latest Eng. Historian [Froude]. N. Y., 1872. 16°. 22936
—— *Mignet, F. A. M.* Hist. of Mary. Lond., 1863. 12°. . . . 22935
—— *Sainte-Beuve, C. A.* (*In* 'Eng. Portraits.') 22885
Maskell, W. The Industrial Arts. [L. &] N. Y., 1876. 12°. . . 29772
—— Ivories, ancient and mediæval. [L. &] N. Y., 1876. 12°. . . 29764
Masque of Pandora. Longfellow, H. W. Bost., 1875. 12°. (2 cop.) 26077-
Masque of Poets. Bost., 1878. 16°. 26027
Massillon, J. B. *Sainte-Beuve, C. A.* (*In* 'Monday-Chats.') . . 23290
Masson, D. Drummond of Hawthornden. Lond., 1873. 12°. . 23217
—— Life of John Milton. Cambr. (& L.), 1859-60. 6 v. 8°. . . 23441-

CONTENTS:—1, 1608-39.—2, 1638-43.—3, 1643-49.—4, 1649-54.—5, 1654-60.—6, 1660-74.

—— The Three Devils: Luther's, Milton's, and Goethe's. With other essays. Lond., 1874. 12°. 27299

CONTENTS (*other*):—Shakespeare and Goethe; Milton's youth; Dryden and the literature of the Restoration; Swift; How literature may illustrate history.

—— Wordsworth, Shelley, Keats; and other essays. Lond., 1874. 27298

CONTENTS (*other*):—Scottish influence in Brit. literature; Theories of poetry; Prose and verse: De Quincey.

Masson, G. France. (Early Chroniclers of Europe.) Lond., [1879.] 12°. 20472
Master Humphrey's Clock. Dickens, C. J. H. N. Y., 1873. 16°. . 24231
Mateer, S. "The Land of Charity." N. Y. 12°. 21618
Materialism. Lange, F. A. Hist. of. Bost., 1877-80. v. 1-2. 8°. 28209-
—— Martineau, J. Modern Materialism. N. Y., 1877. 16°. . . 28696
Mathews, C. Enchanted Moccasins; and other legends of the Amer. Indians. N. Y., 1877. 12°. (*Orig. title:* The Indian Fairy Book.) 24800
Mathews, W. Getting on in the World. Chic., 1876. 12°. . . 27381
—— Hours with Men and Books. Chic., 1877. 12°. 27340
—— *editor. See* **Sainte-Beuve, C. A.,** 'Monday Chats.'
Mattéa. Dudevant, A. L. A. D. (*In vol. with* 'Le secrétaire.') . 25693
Matter. Beale, L. S. Protoplasm; or, Matter and life. Lond., 1874. 12°. 29297
—— Maxwell, J. C. Matter and Motion. Lond., 1876. 16°. . . 29375
—— Mivart, St. G. Lessons from Nature. N. Y., 1876. 12°. . . 29393
Matthew of Westminster. Flowers of History. Lond., 1853. 2 v. 20802-
Matthews, J. B., *editor.* Comedies for Amateur Acting. With a pref. on private theatricals. N. Y., 1880. 16°. . . . 26526

CONTENTS:—A trumped suit, by J. Magnus; A bad case, J. Magnus and H. C. Bunner; Courtship with variations, H. C. Bunner; A teacher taught, A. H. Oakes; Heredity, A. Penn; Frank Wilde, by the editor.

Maudsley, H. Body and Mind. N. Y., 1875. 12°. 28000
—— Pathology of Mind. Lond., 1879. 8°. 28002
—— Physiology of Mind. 3d ed. N. Y., 1877. 12°. 28001
—— Responsibility in Mental Disease. N. Y., 1874. 12°. . . . 29248
Maurice, C. E. Lives of English Popular Leaders. Lond., 1872–75. 2 v. 12°. 22940–
CONTENTS:—1, Stephen Langton.—2, Tyler, Ball, and Oldcastle.
Maurice, J. F. D. Friendship of Books, and other lectures. Lond., 1874. 12°. 27301
CONTENTS (*other*):—Newspapers; Christian civilization; Ancient history; English history; Spenser's "Faerie Queene;" Milton; Burke; Acquisition and illumination; Critics.
—— Moral and Metaphysical Philosophy. Lond., 1872. 2 v. 8°. . 28240–
—— The Workman and the Franchise. Lond., 1866. 8°. . . . 29090
Maurice of Saxony. *See* **Saxe, M. de.**
Mauris, M., *marchese di Calenzano.* French Men of Letters. N. Y., 1880. 16°. 23313
CONTENTS:—Hugo; A. de Musset; Gautier; Murger; Sainte-Beuve; Gérard de Nerval; Dumas, fils; Augier; Feuillet; Sardou; Daudet; Zola.
Maxwell, Cecil. Story of Three Sisters. N. Y., 1876. 16°. . , 24831
Maxwell, J. C. Matter and Motion. Lond., 1876. 16°. . . . 29375
Maxwell, Mary E. B. Hostages to Fortune. Lond., 1875. 3 v. 24801–
Maxwell, W. H. Hist. of the Irish Rebellion in 1798. Lond., 1877. 20991
May, T. E. Democracy in Europe: a history. N. Y., 1878. 2 v. 20565–
Mayer, A. M. Sound. N. Y., 1878. 12°. 29316
—— **& Barnard (C.).** Light. N. Y., 1877. 12°. 29317
Mayo, *Earl of.* *See* **Bourke, R. S.**
Mayo, W. S. Never Again. N. Y., 1873. 12°. 24832
Mazade, C. de. Life of Count Cavour. N. Y., 1877. 8°. . . 23942
Mazarin, J. *Cousin, V.* (*In* 'Secret Hist.') 20414
Meadows, K. Heads of the People. Lond., 1840–1. [2 vols.] 8°. 25581–
Mears, D. O. Life of E. N. Kirk, D. D. Bost., 1878. 8°. . . 22692
Mecca. Hackländer, F. W. von. Pilgerzug nach Mekka. Stuttg. 1863. 16°. (Werke, B. 14.) 25806
Mechanics. *See* **Industrial Arts** (*& references*); **Physics.**
Mechanics (Animal). Marey, É. J. Animal Mechanism. N. Y., 1874. 12°. 29250
—— Pettigrew, J. B. Animal Locomotion. N. Y., 1874. 12°. . 29247
Mechanism in Thought and Morals. Holmes, O. W. Bost., 1871. . 27255
Medhurst, W. H. The Foreigner in Far Cathay. N. Y., 1873. 12°. 21619
Mediæval History. *See* **Hist.,** *Mid. Ages;* **Middle Ages.**
Medici, Lorenzo de'. *Reumont, A. von.* Lond., 1876. 2 v. 8°. . 23937–
Medicine. Flint, A. (*In* **First Cent.** of the Republic.) . . . 21520
—— Gamgee, A. Science and Med. (*In* **Owens College** Ess. & Ad.) 27412
—— *See, also,* **Health** (*& references*).
Meeting the Sun. Simpson, W. Bost., 1877. 8°. 21982
Melbourne, W. L., *Viscount. Earle, J. C.* (*In* 'Eng. Premiers,' v. 2.) 22883
Melincourt. Peacock, T. L. (*In* 'Works,' v. 1.) 27303
Meline, J. F. Mary Queen of Scots. N. Y., 1872. 16°. . . . 22936
Melmoth, Courtney, (*pseud.*) *See* **Pratt, Sam. J.**
Melville, G. J. Whyte. *See* **Whyte-Melville.**
Memoirs of a Physician. Dumas, A. D. Lond., [1879]. . 24407 & 24423

Memorials of a Quiet Life. Hare, A. J. C. Lond., 1873–76. 3 v. 23618–
Memories. [Müller, F. M.] Chic., 1876. 16°. 24833
Men and Manner in Parliament. [Lucy, H. W.] Lond., 1874. 12°. 20811
Mencius, Life and Works of. Legge, J. Phil., 1875. 12°. . . 23729
Mendelssohn-Bartholdy, C. Goethe and Mendelssohn, 1821–1831. Lond., 1874. 12°. 23772
Mendelssohn-Bartholdy, F. Letters. (*In* **Nohl, L.,** 'Letters.') . 23765
—— *Hiller, F.* Lond., 1874. 8°. 23774
—— *Mendelssohn-Bartholdy, C.* Lond., 1874. 12°. 23772
—— *Polko, E.* Reminiscences of Mendelssohn. N. Y., 1869. 16°. 23773
Mental Physiology. Carpenter, W. B. Principles of. N. Y., 1875. 28003
—— Proctor, R. A. Bodily illness as a mental stimulant. [*And*] Dual consciousness. (*In* 'Rough Ways.') 29444
—— *See, also,* **Body & Mind; Insanity; Mind; Philosophy; Psychology.**
Meridiana. Verne, J. N. Y., 1874. 12°. (2 copies.) . . . 24273–
Mérimée, P. Demetrius the Impostor. Lond., 1853. 12°. . . 23903
—— Letters to an Incognita. (*In* **Stoddard, R. H.,** 'Bric-à-Brac Series.') 23261
Merivale, C. Continental Teutons. (Conversion of the West, v. 4.) Lond., [1878]. 16°. 28497
—— Four Lectures on Early Church Hist. [L. &] N. Y., [1879]. 12°. (*For contents see* **Ecc. Hist.**) 28445
—— General Hist. of Rome. N. Y., 1875. 12°. (2 copies.) . . 20097–
—— The Roman Triumvirates. N. Y., [1877]. 16°. 20437
—— St. Paul at Rome. Lond., [1878]. 16°. 28501
Merivale, H. Historical Studies. Lond., 1865. 8°. . . . 20188

Contents:—On some of the precursors of the French Rev.; Studies from the history of the 17th cent.; Leisure hours of a tourist.

Merle d'Aubigné, J. H. Hist. of the Reformation in Europe in the time of Calvin. N. Y., 1863–79. 8 v. 12°. 6386– & (v. 6–8) 28451–
Merlin. Cox (G. W.) & Jones. (*In* 'Pop. Romances.') . 27712 & 2010
Merriam, G. S. A Living Faith. Bost., 1876. 16°. . . . 28508
[**Meryon, C. L.**] Memoirs of Lady Hester Stanhope. Lond., 1846. 3 v. 12°. 12892–
—— Travels of Lady Hester Stanhope. Lond., 1846. 3 v. 12°. . 12895–
Mesmerism, Spiritualism, etc. Carpenter, W. B. N. Y., 1877. 12°. 28044
Meta Holdenis: a novel. Cherbuliez, V. N. Y., 1877. 12°. . . 24077
Metamorphoses of Insects. Duncan, P. M. Lond., [1877]. 8°. . 29499
Metamorphoses in Man and the lower animals. Quatrefages de Bréau, J. L. A. de. Lond., 1864. 12°. 29303
Metaphysics. *See* **Philosophy.**
Metcalfe, F. The Oxonian in Iceland. Lond., 1861. 12°. . . 21705
Meteorology. Proctor, R. A. (*In* 'Rough Ways.') 29444
—— — Science Byways. Phila. [Lond.], 1876. 12°. 29445
Meteyard, Eliza. A Group of Englishmen. Lond., 1871. 8°. . 23543
Metternich, C. W. N. L. Memoirs, 1773–1815. N. Y., 1880. 2 v. 22585–
Mexico. Longfellow, H. W. Poems of Places. (*In* v. 30.) . . 26469
—— Prescott, W. H. Hist. of the Conquest of M. Phila., 1871. 3 v. 20340–
Michael Strogoff. Verne, J. N. Y., 1877. 8°. (2 copies.) . . 24275–

Michaud, J. F. History of the Crusades. Lond., 1852. 3 v. 12°. 20102–
Michelet, J. Historical View of the French Revolution. Lond., 1864. 12°. 20410
—— Summary of Mod. Hist. Continued by M. C. M. Simpson. Lond., 1875. 16°. 20051
Microphone. DuMoncel, T. N. Y., 1879. 12°. 29936
Middle Ages. Church, R. W. Beginning of the Mid. Ages. N. Y., [1878]. 16°. 20457
—— Lacroix, P. Arts in the Mid. Ages. Lond., 1870. 8°. . . 20362
—— — Manners, Customs, and Dress. Lond., 1874. 8°. . . . 20361
—— — Military and Religious Life. Lond., 1874. 8°. . . . 20360
—— — Science and Literature. Lond., 1878. 8°. 20364
—— *See, also,* **History,** *Mid. Ages.*
Middle States (U. S.). Longfellow, H. W. Poems of Places, v. 27. 26466
Middleton, C. S. Shelley and his Writings. Lond., 1858. 2 v. 12°. 23300–
Middleton, T. F., *Bp.*, Life of. Le Bas, C. W. Lond., 1831. 2v. 8°. 18741–
Mignet, F. A. M. Antonio Perez and Philip II. Lond., 1846. 12°. 23904
—— Hist. of Mary, Queen of Scots. Lond., 1863. 12°. . . . 22935
Mijatovies, Csedomille. Serbian Folk-lore. Ed. by W. Denton. Lond., 1874. 12°. 27784
Mikado's (The) Empire. Griffis, W. E. N. Y., 1876. 8°. . . 21939
Mill, J. S. Autobiography. N. Y., 1873. 12°. (2 copies.) . . 23525–
—— Dissertations and Discussions. Bost. (v. 1–4), 1865–67, & N. Y. (v. 5), 1875. 5 v. 12°. . . . . 3715–18 & 27360
—— Examination of Hamilton's Philosophy. N. Y., 1874. 2 v. 12°. 28202–
—— On Liberty. Bost., 1863. 16°. 28853
—— Three Essays on Religion. N. Y., 1874. 12°. 28698
Contents:—Nature; Utility of religion; Theism; Berkeley's life and writings.
—— *Spencer, H., and others.* Twelve sketches. Bost., 1873. 16°. . 23527
—— *Taine, H. A.* English Positivism. Lond., 1873. 16°. . . 28092
Millbank (*prison*), Memorials of. Griffiths, A. Lond., 1875. 2 v. 28858–
Miller, C. H., (*pseud.*, 'Joaquin Miller.') First Fam'lies of the Sierras. Chic., 1876. 12°. 24834
—— Life amongst the Modocs. Lond., 1873. 8°. 21551
Miller, J. Questions awakened by the Bible: 1, Are souls immortal? 2, Was Christ in Adam? 3, Is God a Trinity? Phil., 1877. 12°. 28699
Miller, T. Godfrey Malvern. Lond., 1844. 8°. 24678
Milner, I., Life of. Milner, M. Lond., 1842. 8°. 18660
Milner, T. The Turkish Empire. Lond., [1877]. 12°. . . . 20491
Milnes, R. M., *Lord Houghton.* Monographs, personal and social. N. Y., 1873. 16°. 23220
—— *Same.* 2d ed. Lond., 1873. 16°. 23221
—— Poetical Works. Bost., 1876. 2 v. 16°. 26028
Milton, J. Areopagitica. Ed. by J. W. Hales. Oxf., 1878. 16°. . 26878
—— Autobiography; or, Milton's life in his own words. Ed. by J. J. G. Graham. Lond., 1872. 16°. 23245
—— Lycidas, and Epitaphium Damonis. Ed. by C. S. Jerram. Lond., 1874. 12°. 26205

Milton, J. Paradise regained. Ed., by C. S. Jerram. Lond., 1877. 16°. 26206
—— Poetical Works. Ed. [with life] by E. Brydges. Lond., 1862. 8°. 26203
—— — With life [etc.] by G. Gilfillan. Edinb., 1853. 2 v. 8°. . . 26341–
—— — Ed. by D. Masson. Lond., 1874. 3 v. 8°. 26201–
—— — *Same*, Globe edition. Lond., 1877. 12°. 26204
—— *Brooke, S. A.* (Classical Writers.) N. Y., 1879. 16°. . . 26890
—— *Keightley, T.* Life, Opinions, and Writings of M.; with an introd. to Paradise Lost. Lond., 1855. 8°. 23440
—— *Masson, D.* Life [and times] of Milton. Cambr. (& L.), 1859–80. 6 v. 8°. 23441–
—— — The Three Devils. Lond., 1874. 12°. 27299
—— *Pattison, M.* (English Men of Letters.) N. Y., 1880 [1879]. 12°. 23343
—— *See, also*, **Arnold, M.**, 'Mixed Ess.' (27241); **Bagehot, W.**, 'Lit. Stud.,' v. 1 (26767); **Bayne, P.**, 'Chief Actors' (23013); **Lowell, J. R.**, 'Among my Books,' 2d ser. (26931); **Maurice, J. F. D.**, 'Friendship of Books' (27301).
Mind. Maudsley, H. Pathology of Mind. 3d ed. Lond., 1879. 8°. 28002
—— — Physiology of Mind. 3d ed. N. Y., 1877. 12°. . . . 28001
—— Mivart, St. G. Lessons from Nature. N. Y., 1876. 12°. . . 29393
—— Proctor, R. A. Growth and Decay of Mind. (*In* 'Science Byways.') 29445
—— *See, also*, **Body & Mind**; **Brain**; **Mental** Physiology; **Philosophy**; **Psychology.**
Mind and Body. *See* **Body and Mind.**
Mine, The Story of a. Harte, F. B. Bost., 1878. 16°. . . . 24491
Mineralogy and Lithology, Manual of. Dana, J. D. N. Y., 1878. 29412
Mines and Mining. Hunt, T. S. (*In* **First Cent.** of the Republic.) 21520
Minority Representation. *See* **Representation.**
Minstrelsy of the Woods. Lond., 1832. 12°. 29333
Minto, W. Characteristics of Eng. Poets. Edinb. & Lond., 1874. 26291
—— Daniel Defoe. (Eng. Men of Letters.) N. Y., 1879. 12°. . 23338
—— Manual of Eng. Prose Literature. Edinb., 1872. 12°. . . 26913
Miracles. Wallace, A. R. Lond., 1875. 16°. 28045
—— *See, also*, **Supernatural** (The).
Mirecourt, E. de. *See* **Famous** French Authors.
Mirèio: a Provençal poem. Mistral, F. Bost., 1872. 12°. . . 26126
Misérables (Les). Hugo, V. M. Brux., 1862. 10 t. 16°. . . 25653–
—— *Same, transl.* N. Y., 1878 (&c.). 8°. (3 cop.) 24665–
Misfortunes of Elphin. Peacock, T. L. (*In* 'Works,' v. 2.) . . 27304
Miss Misanthrope. McCarthy, J. N. Y., 1877. 8°. . . . 24671
Miss Molly. Butt, B. M. N. Y., 1876. 16°. 24069
Miss Rovel. Cherbuliez, V. Paris, 1877. 16°. 25623
Missions (Christian). Brown, W. Hist. of the Christian Missions of the 16th, 17th, 18th, and 19th centuries. Lond., 1864. 3 v. 28448-
—— Kip, W. I. Historical Scenes from the Old Jesuit Missions. N. Y., [1875]. 12°. 28726
—— Müller, F. M., (& A. P. Stanley.) On Missions: a lecture, with an introductory sermon. N. Y., 1874. 12°. . . 28488

Missions (Christian). Murray, A. W. Forty Years' Mission Work in Polynesia and New Guinea, 1835–1875. Lond., 1876. 12°. 22146
—— Sherring, M. A. Hist. of Prot. Missions in India. Lond., 1875. 28601
—— West, M. A. Romance of Missions. N. Y., [1875]. 12°. . 28489
—— *See, also,* **Ecclesiastical** Hist.
Mississippi Scheme. *See* **Law, John.**
Mr. Midshipman Easy. Marryat, F. N. Y., 1861. 12°. (2 cop.) 24638–
Mr. Smith: a part of his life. Walford, L. B. N. Y., 1875. 16°. . 24287
Mistral, F. Mirèio: a Provençal poem. Transl. by H. W. Preston. Bost., 1872. 12°. 26126
Mrs. Gainesborough's Diamonds. Hawthorne, J. N. Y., 1878. 16°. 24925
Mistress Judith. Tytler, C. C. F. N. Y., 1875. 16°. . . . 24284
Mistress of the Manse. Holland, J. G. N. Y., 1874. 12°. . . 24546
Mrs. Skagg's Husbands. Harte, F. B. Bost., 1875. 16°. . . 24486
Mitford, Mary R. Atherton; and other tales. Lond., 1854. 3 v. 18632–
—— Letters; 2d series. Lond., 1872. 2 v. 12°. 23208–
—— Recollections of a Literary Life. Lond., 1853. 12°. . . . 18585
—— *editor.* Lights and Shadows of Amer. Life. Lond., 1832. 3 v. 18544–
Mivart, St. G. The Common Frog. Illust. Lond., 1874. 12°. . 29508
—— Contemporary Evolution: on some recent social changes. N. Y., 1876. 12°. 29394
—— Lessons from Nature, as manifested in Mind and Matter. N. Y., 1876. 12°. 29393
—— Man and Apes. N. Y., 1874. 12°. 29395
Moab, The Land of. Tristram, H. B. Lond., 1873. 8°. . . . 21723
Modern (A) Symposium. Harrison, F., *and others.* Detroit, 1878. 28094
Modocs. Miller, C. H. Life amongst the Modocs. Lond., 1873. 21551
—— Peters, D. C. Kit Carson's Life; and a history of the Modoc Indians and the Modoc war. Hartf., 1875. 8°. 22682
Mohammedanism. Smith, R. B. Mohammed and Mohammedanism. N. Y., 1875. 12°. 28567
—— Stephens, W. R. W. Christianity and Islam. N. Y., 1877. . 28566
—— Stobart, J. W. H. Islam and its Founder. Lond., [1877]. 16°. 28579
—— *See, also,* **Heathenism; Koran; Religions** (various).
Molesworth, *Mrs.*, (*pseud.*, 'Ennis Graham.') Hathercourt. N. Y., 1878. 16°. 24835
Molesworth, W. N. Hist. of England from 1830 to 1874. Lond., 1874. 3 v. 12°. 20822–
Molière, J. B. P. Dramatic Works. Transl. by C. H. Wall. [L. &] N. Y., 1879. 3 v. 12°. 26522–
—— *Besant, W.* (*In* 'French Humourists.') 26776
—— *Oliphant* (*M. O. W.*) *&* *Tarver* (*F.*). (For. Classics for Eng. Readers, v. 6.) Phil., [1879]. 16°. 23267
Mollett, J. W. Rembrandt. N. Y. & Lond., 1879. 12°. . . 23778
Molly Maguires. Dewees, F. P. Phila., 1877. 12°. . . . 28996
Moltke, H. C. B. von. Letters from Russia. Lond., 1878. 12°. . 23613
Monaco, Hist. of. Pemberton, H. Lond., 1867. 8°. . . . 20618
Monarch of Mincing-Lane. Black, W. N. Y., 1878. 8°. (2 cop.) 24299–
Monastic Orders. Jameson, A. M. Lond., 1852. 8°. . . . 29911

Monastic Orders. *See, also,* **Ecclesiastical Hist.; Monks; Religions** (various).
Monday-Chats. Sainte-Beuve, C. A. Chic., 1877. 12°. . . . 23290
Money. Cernuschi, H. Nomisma; or, "Legal Tender." N. Y., 1877. 12°. 29052
—— Hamilton, R. Money and Value. Lond., 1878. 8°. . . . 29044
—— Horton, S. D. Silver and Gold, and Resumption. Cincin., 1877. 29045
—— Jevons, W. S. Money and the Mechanism of Exchange. N. Y., 1875. 12°. 29257
—— Linderman, H. R. Money and Legal Tender in the U. S. N. Y., 1877. 12°. 29058
—— Poor, H. V. Money and its Laws. N. Y., 1877. 8°. . . . 29043
—— Sumner, W. G. (*In* **First Cent.** of the Republic.) 21520
—— Walker, F. A. N. Y., 1878. 8°. 29040
—— — Money in its relations to Trade and Industry. N. Y., 1879. 29042
—— Wells, D. A. Robinson Crusoe's Money. N. Y., 1876. 8°. . 29046
—— *See, also,* **Currency; Pol. Economy** (*& references*).
Mongolia. Prejevalski, N. M. Lond., 1876. 2 v. 8°. 21927–
—— *See, also,* **Tartary; Tibet.**
Monkhouse, W. C. Turner. (Illust. Biogr. of the Great Artists, v. 7.) L. & N. Y., 1879. 12°. 23783
Monks. Montalembert, C. F. R. de. Monks of the West. Edinb. & L., 1861–79. v. 1–7. 8°. 28728–
—— *See, also,* **Monastic Orders** (*& references*).
Montagu, B. Life of Francis Bacon. Lond., 1834. 8°. 23010
Montagu, Elizabeth R. *Doran, J.* A Lady of the Last Century. Lond., 1873. 8°. 23404
Montagu, Mary W. Letters and Works. Ed. by Wharncliffe. Lond., 1837. 3 v. 8°. 23405–
Montaigne, M. E. de. Essays. Ed. by J. H. Friswell. Lond., 1869. 16°. 27260
—— *Besant, W.* (*In* 'French Humourists.') 26776
—— *Collins, W. L.* (For. Classics for Eng. Readers, v. 7.) Phila., [1879]. 12°. 23268
—— *Sterling, J.* (*In* 'Essays,' v. 1.) 12898
—— *St. John, B.* Lond., 1858. 2 v. 12°. 23222–
Montalembert, C. F. R. de. Memoir of the Abbé Lacordaire. Lond., 1863. 8°. 22180
—— Monks of the West. Edinb. & L., 1861–79. v. 1–7. 8°. . . 28728–
—— *Oliphant, M. O. W.* Edinb. & Lond., 1872. 2 v. 12°. . . . 22486–
Monteiro, J. J. Angola and the River Congo. N. Y., 1876. 12°. 21620
Montesquieu, C. de S. de. Spirit of Laws. With D'Alembert's analysis of the work. Lond., 1878. 2 v. 12°. 28849–
Montfort, Simon de, *earl of Leicester. Creighton, M.* Lond., 1876. 22445
—— *Pauli, R.* Lond., 1876. 12°. 22880
—— *Prothero, G. W.* Lond., 1877. 12°. 22881
Montgomery, H. R. Life and Writings of Sir Richard Steele. Edinb., 1865. 2 v. 8°. 23482–
Montgomery, R. Poetical Works. Lond., 1854. 8°. 26242

Mont-Revêche. Dudevant, A. L. A. D. Paris, 1869. 16°. . . 25690
Monuments. *See* **Antiquities; Burial.**
Moody, D. L. *Daniels, W. H.* N. Y., 1878. 12°. 22616
—— *Hall (J.) & Stuart (G. H.).* The Amer. Evangelists, Moody and Sankey, in Gt. Brit. and Ireland. N. Y., [1875]. 12°. 22615
Moon. Proctor, R. A. Lond., 1873. 12°. 29443
Moore, Geo.: merchant and philanthropist. Smiles, S. Lond., 1878. 8°. 23931
Moore, J. S. Pictorial Book of Ballads. Lond., 1849. 8°. . . 26243
Moore, T. Personal Reminiscences. N. Y., 1875. 16°. . . 23259
—— Prose and Verse. Ed. by R. H. Shepherd. N. Y., 1878. 8°. 27361
—— *Symington, A. J.* N. Y., 1880. 16°. 23314
Morals. Blackie, J. S. Four Phases of Morals: Socrates, Aristotle, Christianity, Utilitarianism. N. Y., 1872. 12°. . . . 28080
—— Holmes, O. W. Mechanism in Thought and Morals. Bost., 1871. 16°. 27255
—— Maurice, J. F. D. Moral and Metaphysical Philosophy. Lond., 1872. 2 v. 8°. 28240–
—— Simcox, E. Natural Law: an essay in ethics. Bost., 1877. 8°. 28208
—— Spencer, H. The Data of Ethics. N. Y., 1879. 12°. (2 cop.) 28129–
—— *See, also,* **Life** (*Conduct and philosophy of*).
More, Hannah. Letters to Zachary Macaulay. Lond., 1860. 16°. 18561
More, T. Utopia. Ed. by E. Arber. Lond., 1869. 16°. . . 27214
—— *Same.* Ed. by T. R. Lumby. Cambr. [Eng.], 1879. 16°. (2 cop.) 27215–
—— [*Manning, A.*] Household of Sir Thos. More. [Historical fiction.] N. Y., [1867]. 16° 23646
Morgan, J. E. University Oars. Lond., 1873. 12°. . . . 29656
Morgan, S. O., *Lady.* Autobiography, Diaries and Correspondence. Lond., 1863. 2 v. 8°. 23484–
—— Life and Times of Salvator Rosa. Lond., 1824. 2 v. 8°. . 18569–
—— Woman and her Master. Lond. 2 v. 12°. 18673–
Morgann, M. Essay on Sir John Falstaff. Lond., 1825. 12°. . 27002
Morice, F. D. Pindar. (Anc. Clas. for Engl. Readers, suppl. ser., v. 8.) 26854
[**Morice, L.**] The Epic of Hades. Bost., 1879. 16°. . . . 26097
—— Gwen: a drama in monologue. Lond., 1879. 16°. . . . 26098
—— The Ode of Life. Bost., 1880. 16°. 26099
—— Songs of Two Worlds. Lond., 1880. 16°. 26100
Morison, J. C. Gibbon. (English Men of Letters.) N. Y., 1878. 23333
Morley, H. First Sketch of Eng. Literature. Lond., [1873]. 16°. 26911
—— Jerome Cardan. Lond., 1854. 2 v. 12°. 23561–
—— Memoirs of Bartholomew Fair. Illust. Lond., 1859. 8°. . 26641
—— *editor.* Cassell's Library of Eng. Lit. Lond., [1876–80.] 4 v. 4°. (*For contents see* **Eng. Lit.**) 26368–
Morley, J. Burke. (Eng. Men of Letters.) N. Y., 1879. 12°. . 23342
—— Critical Miscellanies. Lond., 1871–77. 2 ser. 8°. . . . 27407–

CONTENTS:—1, Vauvenargues; Condorcet; Joseph de Maistre; Carlyle; Byron; Some Greek conceptions of social growth; Development of morals; Appendix.—2, France in the 18th cent.; Robespierre; Turgot; Death of Mill; Mill's Autobiog.; Mill on religion; Popular culture; Macaulay.

—— Diderot and the Encyclopædists. Lond., 1878. 2 v. 8°. . 23423–
—— On Compromise. Lond., 1874. 8°. 29089

Morley, J. Rousseau. Lond., 1873. 2 v. 8°. 23421–
—— Voltaire. 2d ed., rev. N. Y., 1872. 12°. 23310
—— *editor.* English Men of Letters. N. Y., 1878–80. 19 v. 12°. (*For contents see* **Eng. Men** of Letters.) 23332–
Morning-Land (The). Bodenstedt, F. M. Lond., 1851 & '53. 2 series. 4 v. 12°. 21724–
Mornings in Florence. Ruskin, J. N. Y., 1876. 12°. . . . 29834
Morocco. Hooker (J. D.) & Ball (J.). Journal of a Tour in Marocco and the Great Atlas. Lond., 1878. 8°. 21847
—— Murray, Mrs. E. Sixteen Years of an Artist's Life in Morocco, Spain, and the Canary Islands. Lond., 1859. 2 v. 8°. . 23926–
—— Rohlfs, G. Adventures in Morocco. Lond., 1874. 8°. . . 21848
Morphy, P.: his games of chess. Löwenthal, J. Lond., 1860. 12°. 29711
—— — *Same.* N. Y., 1860. 12°. 29712
Morris, E. E. Age of Anne. N. Y., [1877]. 16°. 20456
—— *editor.* Epochs of Modern History. (*For contents see* **Epochs.**) 20448–
Morris, J. Life and Martyrdom of St. Thomas Becket. Lond., 1859. 12°. 22141
Morris (R.) & Bowen (H. C.). Eng. Gram. Exercises. Lond., 1878. 16°. 26858
Morris, W. Æneids of Virgil, done into Eng. verse. Bost., 1876. 12°. (2 copies.) 26800–
—— Defence of Guenevere, and other poems. Lond., 1875. 12°. . 26101
—— Love is enough; or, The Freeing of Pharamond. Bost., 1873. 26102
—— Story of Sigurd the Volsung and the Fall of the Niblungs. Bost., 1877. 8°. 26103
—— Three Northern Love Stories. (*See* **Magnusson, E., & Morris.**)
Morris, W. O'C. French Revolution and First Empire. Lond., 1874. 12°. 20411
Morse, J. T. Famous Trials: The Tichborne Claimant; Troppmann; Prince Pierre Bonaparte; Mrs. Wharton; The Meteor; Mrs. Fair. Bost., 1874. 12°. 28842
—— Life of Alexander Hamilton. Bost., 1876. 2 v. 12°. . . 22624–
Morse, S. F. B., Life of. Prime, S. I. N. Y., 1875. 8°. . . . 22721
Moscheles, I. Recent Music and Musicians. Ed. by his wife. N. Y., 1873. 12°. 29742
—— *Moscheles, Charlotte.* Life of Moscheles. Lond., 1873. 2 v. 12°. 23775–
Moselle (*river*). Waring, G. E. Bride of the Rhine. Bost., 1878. . 21263
Moses, the Law-giver. Taylor, W. M. N. Y., 1879. 12°. . . 28651
Mossman, S. New Japan. Lond., 1873. 8°. 21938
Motley, J. L. Life and Death of Barneveld. N. Y., 1874. 2 v. 8°. (2 copies.) 23894–
—— *Holmes, O. W.* Bost., 1879 [1878]. 16°. 22603
Mouhot, A. H. Travels in Indo-China, Cambodia, and Laos. Lond., 1864. 2 v. 8°. 21933–
Moulton, W. F. Hist. of the English Bible. Lond., [1878]. 12°. . 28528
Mound-Builders. Foster, J. W. Pre-historic Races of the U. S. of A. Chic., 1873. 8°. 21401
—— *See, also,* **Grave-Mounds.**

Mounsey, A. H. The Satsuma Rebellion. Lond., 1879. 12°. . 20385
Mountain Adventures. Headley, J. T. N. Y., 1872. 16°. . . 10133
Mouth and Teeth. White, J. W. Phil., 1879. 16°. 29964
Mozart, J. C. W. A., Life of. Nohl, L. Lond., 1877. 2 v. 12°. . 23811–
Mozley, J. B. Essays, historical and theological. N. Y., 1878. 2 v. 8°. 27409–

CONTENTS:—1, Lord Strafford: Archb. Laud; Carlyle's Cromwell; Luther.—2, Dr. Arnold; Blanco White; Dr. Pusey's sermon; The Book of Job; Maurice's theol. essays; Indian conversion; Argument of design; The principle of causation.

—— Ruling Ideas in Early Ages. N. Y., 1877. 8°. 28686
—— Sermons, parochial and occasional. N. Y., 1879. 12°. . . 28545
—— Sermons before the Univ. of Oxford, and on various occasions. N. Y., 1876. 12°. 28544
Mügge, T. Romane. Breslau, 1862–7. 33 B. in 11. 16°. . . 25840–

CONTENTS:—1-3, Der Chevalier.—4-8, Toussaint.—9-12, Erich Randal.—13-15, Afraja.—16-18, Tänzerin und Gräfin.—19-20, Die Vendéerin.—21, Weihnachtsabend.—22-23, Arvor Spang.—24-25, Verloren u. gefunden.—26, Die Erbin. 27-28, Der Voigt von Sylt.—29, Der Majoratsherr.—30, König Jakob's letzte Tage.—31-33, Der Prophet.

Müller, C. O. Hist. of the Literature of Ancient Greece. Lond., 1840. v. 1. 8°. 197
—— *Same.* Continued by J. W. Donaldson. Lond., [1858]. 3 v. . 26961–
Müller, D. *See* **Lewis, C. T.,** 'Hist. of Germany.'
Müller, F. M. Chips from a Ger. Workshop. N. Y., 1869–76. 4 v. 12°. . . . . 3731–3 & 27302

CONTENTS:—1, Essays on the science of religion.—2, Essays on mythology, traditions and customs; [also, *index* to v. 1-2].—3, Ess. on literature, biography and antiquities.—4, Ess. chiefly on the science of language; with *index* to v. 3-4.

—— Memories. [By F. M. Müller.] Chic., 1876. 16°. . . . 24833
—— On Missions. N. Y., 1874. 12°. 28488
—— Religions of India. N. Y., 1879. 12°. 28568
[**Müller von Königswinter, W.**] Furioso. Cambr. & L., 1865. 12°. 23809
Muhlenburg, W. A., Life of. Ayres, A. N. Y., 1880. 8°. . . 22724
Muir, W. The Corân. Lond., [1878]. 16°. 28580
Mullinger, J. B. Schools of Charles the Great. Lond., 1877. 8°. 28839
Mummies and Moslems. Warner, C. D. Hartf., 1876. 8°. . . 21842
Munich. Howitt, A. M. Art-student in M. Lond., 1853. 2 v. 12°. 29879–
—— Wilberforce, E. Social Life in Munich. Lond., 1864. 12°. . 21685
Murchison, R. I., Life of. Geikie, A. Lond., 1875. 2 v. 8°. . 23538–
Murger, H. *Curwen, H.* (*In* 'Sorrow and Song,' v. 1.) . . . 23285
Murphy, A. Life and Genius of Henry Fielding. (*See* **Fielding, H.,** 'Works,' Lond., 1871.)
Murray, A. W. Forty Years' Mission Work in Polynesia and New Guinea. Lond., 1876. 12°. 22146
Murray, Alex. S. Manual of Mythology. N. Y., 1874. 12°. . . 27740
Murray, Elizabeth. Sixteen Years of an Artist's Life in Morocco, Spain, and the Canary Islands. Lond., 1859. 2 v. 8°. . 23926–
Murray, E. C. G. Doïne; or, The national songs and legends of Roumania. Lond., 1854. 12°. 27786
—— Round about France. Lond., 1878. 12°. 21622
Murray, J. H. Travels in Uruguay. Lond., 1871. 12°. . . . 21621
Murray, P. J. Life of John Banim. Lond., 1857. 16°. . . . 18558
Murray, T. C. Origin and Growth of the Psalms. N. Y., 1880. . 28530

Murray, W. H. H. The Perfect Horse. Bost., 1873. 8°. . . . 29496
Musa Burschicosa. Blackie, J. S. Edinb., 1869. 16°. . . . 26042
Musa (La) Madrigalesca. Oliphant, T. Lond., 1837. 12°. . . 26163
Music. Chorley, H. F. Modern German Music. Lond., 1854. 2 v. 29743-
—— — The National Music of the World. Lond., 1880. 12°. . . 29745
—— Ella, J. Musical Sketches, abroad and at home. L. & N. Y., 1878. 12°. 29740
—— Hand, F. G. Æsthetics of Musical Art. Lond., 1880. 8°. . 29798
—— Hueffer, F. Richard Wagner and the Music of the Future. Lond., 1874. 12°. 29748
—— Hullah, J. Hist. of Modern Music. Lond., 1875. 8°. . . 29796
—— — Music in the House. Phila., [1877]. 12°. 29783
—— — Third or Transition Period of Musical Hist. Lond., 1876. 29797
—— Hunt, H. G. B. Concise Hist. of Music. N. Y., [1878]. 12°. 29749
—— Moscheles, I. Recent Music and Musicians. N. Y., 1873. 12°. 29742
—— Ritter, F. L. Hist. of Music. Bost., 1876 & '74. 2 v. 16°. . 29750-
—— Schopenhauer, A. On the Metaphysics of Music. (*In suppl. to* **Wagner's** Beethoven, transl. by Dannreuther.) . . . 23807
—— Schumann, R. Music and Musicians. N. Y., 1877. 12°. . 29741
—— Thibaut, A. F. J. On Purity in Musical Art. Lond., 1877. 12°. 29746
—— Wieck, J. G. F. Piano and Song. Bost., 1875. 12°. . . 29801
—— *Biography* (*collections*). Clayton, E. C. Queens of Song. Lond., 1863. 2 v. 23847-
—— — Crowest, F. Great Tone Poets. Lond., 1874. 12°. . . 23761
—— — Keddie, H. Musical Composers and their Works. Bost., 1875. 12°. 23760
—— — Keddie (H.) & Watson (J. L.). Songstresses of Scotland. Lond., 1871. 2 v. 8°. 23763-
—— — [Nohl, L.] Letters of Distinguished Musicians. Lond., 1867. 23765
—— — Phipson, T. L. Celebrated Violinists. Lond., 1877. 12°. . 23816
See, also, **Art**; **Opera**; **Sound**; **Voice.**
Musical Instruments. Engel, C. N. Y., 1876. 12°. . . . 29761
Musical Memoirs. Parke, W. T. Lond., 1830. 2 v. 12°. . . 18671-
Musical Myths and Facts. Engel, C. Lond., 1876. 2 v. 8°. . 29794-
Musical and Personal Recollections. Phillips, H. Lond., 1864. 2v. 23813-
Musical Recollections. [Cox, J. E.] Lond., 1872. 2 v. 8°. . . 29792-
Musical Tales, Phantasms, and Sketches. Polko, E. 2d series. Lond., 1877. 12°. 24808
Musset, L. C. A. de. Selections. N. Y., 1870. 16°. . . . 27261
—— (*See* **Thomson, J.,** 'Public and Private Life of Animals.')
—— *Musset, P. E. de.* Biography of A. de Musset. Bost., 1877. 23247
My Aunt Pontypool. [James, G. P. R.] Phil., 1836. 2 v. 12°. . 2161-
My Health: [a novel.] Burnand, F. C. Bost., 1872. 16°. . . 24921
My Little Lady. [Poynter, E. F.] N. Y., 1872. 16°. (2 copies.) . 2372-
My Shooting Box. Herbert, H. W. ('Sporting Scenes,' v. 1.) . 29602
My Sister Jeannie. Dudevant, A. L. A. D. Bost., 1874. 16°. . 2348
My Young Alcides. Yonge, C. M. N. Y., 1876. 12°. . . . 24296
Myers, A. B. R. Life with the Hamran Arabs. Lond., 1876. 8°. 21697
Mysteries of Paris. Sue, M. J. E. Lond., 1845-6. 3 v. 8°. . . 24695-

Mysterious Island. Verne, J. N. Y., 1875–6. 3 v. 12°. . . 24277–
Mystery of Edwin Drood. Dickens, C. J. H. N. Y., 1875. 16°. . 24218
Mystery of Metropolisville. Eggleston, E. N. Y., [1873]. 12°. . 24470
Mystics (and Mysticism). Ullmann, C. (*In* 'Reformers,' etc., v. 2.) 22301
Mythology. Murray, A. S. Manual of Mythology: Greek and Roman, Norse and Old German, Hindoo and Egyptian. N. Y., 1874. 12°. 27740
—— Seemann, O. Mythology of Greece and Rome, with reference to its use in art. [L. &] N. Y., 1877. 12°. 29788
—— — *Same.* N. Y., 1879. 16°. 29789
Myths. Fiske, J. Myths and Myth-Makers. Bost., 1873. 16°. . 27741
—— *See, also,* **Eddas ; Folk-lore ; Legends ; Romances.**
Naaké, J. T. Slavonic Fairy Tales. Lond., 1874. 12°. . . . 27785
Nach dreissig Jahren. Auerbach, B. Stuttg., 1876. 12°. . . 25894
Nadal, E. S. Impressions of London Social Life. N. Y., 1875. 21708
Nahes und Fernes. Hackländer, F. W. von. Stuttg., 1873. 16°. (Werke, B. 50.) 25824
Nairne, Carolina O. Life and Songs of the Baroness Nairne; with a memoir and poems of Caroline Oliphant the younger. Ed. by Chas. Rogers. Lond., 1869. 16°. 23249
Namenlose Geschichten. Hackländer, F. W. von. Stuttg., 1875. 3 B. 16°. (Werke, B. 1–3.) 25800–
Names. Bardsley, C. W. Curiosities of Puritan Nomenclature. N. Y. [Lond.], 1880. 12°. 27867
Nanon. Dudevant, A. L. A. D. Paris, 1878. 16°. 25691
Nanon. Dumas, A. D. Lond., [1879]. 16°. (2 copies.) . 24405 & 24424
Napier, E. H. D. E. Wild Sports in Europe, Asia, and Africa. Lond., 1844. 2 v. 16°. 29606–
Napier, H. E. Florentine History. Lond., 1846–7. 6 v. 12°. . 20004–
Napier, Macvey. Selection from [his] Correspondence. Ed. by his son, Macvey Napier. Lond., 1879. 8°. 23060
Napier, Mark. Memoirs of the Marquis of Montrose. Edinb., 1856. 2 v. 8°. 23016–
Napoleon I., *emp. of France. Metternich, C. W. N. L.* (*In* 'Memoirs.') 22585–
—— *Rémusat, C. E. J. de.* (*In* 'Memoirs.') 22567–
Napoleon III., *emp. of France,* Life of. Jerrold, W. B. Lond., 1874–77. v. 1–3. 8°. 22561–
Narjoux, F. Notes and Sketches of an Architect. Bost., 1877. 8°. 29926
Nasby, Petroleum Vesuvius, (*pseud.*) *See* **Locke, D. R.**
Nash, W. Oregon: there and back in 1877. Lond., 1878. 12°. . 21286
Nasr-ed-Din. Diary of the Shah of Persia. Lond., 1874. 8°. . 21625
Nathan, I., *editor.* Fugitive Pieces and Reminiscences of Byron; cont'g a new ed. of the Hebrew Melodies, with remarks [etc.]. Also, original poetry, letters [etc.] of Lady C. Lamb. Lond., 1829. 16°. 18636
Nathan the Wise. Lessing, G. E. Leipz., 1868. 16°. . . . 26512
Natural History. Burroughs, J. Locusts and Wild Honey. Bost., 1879. 16°. 29323
—— — Winter Sunshine. N. Y., 1876. 16°. 29325

Natural History. Cobbe, F. P. False Beasts and True: essays on natural (and unnatural) history. Lond., [1875]. 12°. . . 12911
— Collingwood, C. Rambles of a Naturalist on the shores and waters of the China Sea. Lond., 1868. 8°. 29494
— Duncan, P. M., *editor*. Cassell's Nat. Hist. Illust. Lond., [1879-80]. v. 1-3. 4°. (*For contents see* **Duncan.**) . . 29579-
— [Jefferies, R.] Gamekeeper at Home: sketches of Nat. Hist. and rural life. Bost., 1879. 16°. 29331
— — Wild Life in a Southern County [of England]. Bost., 1879. 29332
— Rhind, W. Studies in Nat. Hist. Edinb., 1830. 12°. . . 29334
— Thoreau, H. D. Excursions. Bost., 1875. 12°. . . . 29335
— Wallace, A. R. Tropical Nature, and other essays. Lond., 1878. 8°. 29533
— Waterton, C. Essays on Nat. Hist. Lond., [1870]. 12°. . 29402
— Wood, J. G. Illustrated Nat. Hist. Lond., 1869-71. 3 v. 8°. 29587-
See, also, **Animals; Biology; Man; Natural Selection; Science; Zoology;**—*also,* **Selborne,** *and other local names.*
Natural Law. *See* **Law,** *Natural.*
Natural Philosophy. *See* **Physics.**
Natural Science. *See* **Science.**
Natural Selection. Williamson, W. C. Primeval Vegetation in its relation to the doctrines of Natural Selection and Evolution. (*In* **Owens College** Ess. & Ad.) 27412
— *See, also,* **Darwinism; Evolution.**
Natural Theology. *See* **Theology,** *Natural.*
Naturalist (The) in Norway. Bowden, J. Lond., 1869. 12°. . . 21210
Naturalist (The) on the River Amazons. Bates, H. W. Lond., 1873. 21207
Nature. Huxley, T. H. Physiography: an introd. to the study of nature. N. Y., 1878. 12°. 29419
— Mivart, St. G. Lessons from Nature, as manifested in Mind and Matter. N. Y., 1876. 12°. 29393
— Papillon, F. Nature and Life. N. Y., 1875. 12°. . . . 29397
— Shairp, J. C. On Poetic Interpretation of Nature. Edinb., 1877. 12°. 26294
Nature Series.
CONTENTS:—Spectroscope, by J. N. Lockyer.—Origin and Metamorphoses of Insects, J. Lubbock.—Common Frog, G. Mivart.—On British Wild Flowers, J. Lubbock.—Light, Mayer & Barnard.—Sound, A. M. Mayer.—Seeing and Thinking, W. K. Clifford.
Naval Officer; or, Frank Mildmay. Marryat, F. N. Y., 1861. 12°. 24640
Navigators. Vogel, T. A Century of Discovery: Portuguese and Spanish Navigators from Prince Henry to Pizarro. Lond., 1877. 8°. 23567
— *See, also,* **Seamen.**
Neaves, C. Greek Anthology. (Anc. Clas. for Eng. Readers, v. 20.) 26846
Nero: [an historical play.] Story, W. W. Edinb. & L., 1875. 12°. 26136
Nervous Derangement and Spiritualism. Hammond, W. A. N. Y., 1876. 12°. 28043
Nesbitt, A. Glass. Lond., [1878]. 12°. 29765
Nesbitt, M. L. Grammar-Land. N. Y., 1878. 16°. . . . 27868
Nest (Das) der Zaunkönige. Freytag, G. Leipz., 1875. 12°. ('Die Ahnen,' Abth. 2.) 25912

Netherlands. Motley, J. L. John of Barneveld. N. Y., 1874. 2 v. 8°. (2 copies.) 23894–
—— *See, also,* **Belgium ; Holland.**
Nettleship, H. Vergil. (Classical Writers.) N. Y., 1880. 16°. . 26892
Neue (Der) Don Quixote. Hackländer, F. W. von. Stuttg., 1876. 5 B. 16°. (Werke, B. 30–34.) 25814–
Neue Dorfgeschichten. Auerbach, B. Stuttg., 1876. 3 B. in 1. 12°. 25894
Neue Geschichten. Hackländer, F. W. von. Stuttg., 1873. 16°. (Werke, B. 51.) 25825
Neues Leben. Auerbach, B. Stuttg., 1871. 2 B. 16°. (Romane, B. 3–4.) 25888
Never again. Mayo, W. S. N. Y., 1873. 12°. 24832
Neville, G. Horses and Riding. Lond., 1877. 12°. 29641
New England. Bacon, L. Genesis of the N. Eng. Churches. N. Y., 1874. 8°. 28447
—— Drake, S. A. Nooks and Corners of the N. Eng. Coast. N. Y., 1875. 8°. 21586
—— Flagg, W. Birds and Seasons of New Eng. Bost., 1875. 12°. 29320
—— — Woods and By-ways of N. Eng. Bost., 1872. 12°. . . 21283
—— Longfellow, H. W. Poems of Places, v. 25–6. 26464–
—— *See, also,* **Federalism.**
New-England (The) Tragedies. Longfellow, H. W. Bost., 1868. 12°. 26079
New Englander. N. H., 1843–79. 38 v. 8°. . . . . 12997– & 13121–
—— *Same.* v. 1–28. 12970–
—— Index, v. 1–19. (2 copies.) . . . . ——
New Exegesis of Shakespeare. Edinb., 1859. 12°. 27003
New Guinea. Murray, A. W. Forty Years' Mission Work. Lond., 1876. 12°. 22146
New Haven. Trumbull, J. H. The True-Blue Laws of Conn. and New Haven, and the False Blue-Laws invented by the Rev. Sam. Peters. Hartf., 1876. 12°. 21322
New Hebrides. Markham, A. H. Cruise of the "Rosario." Lond., 1873. 8°. 21814
New Lands within the Arctic Circle. Payer, J. N. Y., 1877. 8°. 21883
New Mexico, Conquest of. Cooke, P. St. G. N. Y., 1878. 12°. . 21323
New (The) Paul and Virginia. Mallock, W. H. N. Y. [L.], 1878. 28084
New (The) Plutarch : lives of men and women of action. [L. &] N. Y., 1879–80. 4 v. 16°. 22451–

Contents :—A. Lincoln, by C. G. Leland.—Coligny, W. Besant.—Judas Maccabæus, C. R. Conder.—Joan of Arc, J. Tuckey.

New (The) Puritan. Pike, J. S. N. Y., 1879. 12°. 22644
New (The) Reformation : a narrative of the Old Catholic movement from 1870 to the present time ; with a historical introd. by Theodorus [*pseud.*]. Lond., 1875. 8°. 28725
New (The) Republic. [Mallock, W. H.] Lond., 1877. 2 v. 12°. . 28082–
New Zealand. Barker, M. A. Station Amusements. Lond., 1873. 21735
—— Howitt, W. Hist. of Discovery. Lond., 1875. 2 v. 8°. . 21816–
—— Old New Zealand : a tale ; and a Hist. of the War in the North against the chief Heke, in the year 1845. Lond., 1876. 8°. 21815
—— Trollope, A. Australia and New Zealand. Lond., 1873. 2 v. 21818–

New Zealand. Wood, J. G. Natural Hist. of Man. (Vol. 2.) . 29591
Newcastle, Henry Pelham Clinton, *duke of*. *Earle, J. C.* (*In* 'Eng. Premiers,' v. 1.) 22882
Newcastle, Thos. Holles Pelham, *duke of*. (*In the same.*)
Newcomb, S. The Abc of Finance. N. Y., 1878. 16°. . . . 29062
[**Newman, F. W.**] Hist. of the Hebrew Monarchy. Lond., 1847. 8°. 28441
Newman, J. H. Arians of the Fourth Century. Lond., 1871. 12°. 28412
—— Callista: a sketch of the third century. Lond., 1873. 12°. . 28413
—— Discussions and Arguments on various subjects. Lond., 1873. 28410
—— Fifteen Sermons, preached before the Univ. of Oxford. Lond., 1872. 12°. 28409
—— Historical Sketches. Lond., 1873. 3 v. 12°. 20091–

CONTENTS:—1. Turks in their rel. to Europe; Cicero; Apollonius; Prim. Christianity.—2, Church of the Fathers; St. Chrysostom; Theodoret; Mission of St. Benedict; Benedictine schools.—3, Rise and progress of universities; Northmen and Normans in England and Ireland; Medieval Oxford; Convocation of Canterbury.

—— Parochial and Plain Sermons. Lond., 1873. 8 v. 12°. . . 28400–
—— Sermons bearing on subjects of the day. Lond., 1873. 12°. . 28408
—— Tracts, theological and ecclesiastical. Lond., 1874. 12°. . . 28411
Newspapers. Grant, J. The Newspaper Press. Lond., 1871. 2 v. 26762–
—— Hunt, F. K. The Fourth Estate: contributions towards a history of N., and of the liberty of the press. Lond., 1850. 2 v. 18590–
Newton Forster. Marryat, F. N. Y., 1861. 12°. 24641
Nibelung. Cox (G. W.) & Jones. (*In* 'Pop. Romances.' *And in* 'Tales.') 27712–13
—— Dippold, G. T. Account of the Nibelung Epics and Sagas. (*In* **Geibel, E.,** 'Brunhild.') 26065
—— Forestier, A. Echoes from Mist-land. Chic., 1877. 12°. . . 27711
—— Lettsom, W. N. The Nibelungenlied; transl. Lond., 1874. 8°. 27706
Nichol, John. Byron. (Eng. Men of Letters.) N. Y., 1880. 12°. . 23350
Nicholas Minturn. Holland, J. G. N. Y., 1877. 12°. (2 copies.) . 24547–
Nicholls, J. Recollections and Reflections. Lond., 1822. 8°. . 18662
Nichols, Charlotte (Brontë). *See* **Brontë, C.**
Nichols, G. W. Art Education applied to Industry. N. Y., 1877. 29925
Nicolini, G. B. History of the Jesuits. Lond., 1873. 12°. . . 28727
Niebuhr, B. G. History of Rome from the First Punic War to the death of Constantine. Lond., 1844. 2 v. 8°. 20294–
Nile. Appleton, T. G. A Nile Journey. Lond., 1876. 12°. . . 21204
—— Eden, F. The Nile without a Dragoman. Lond., 1871. 16°. . 21245
—— Edwards, A. B. A Thousand Miles up the Nile. N. Y. and Lond., 1877. 8°. 21966
Nineteenth Century. Lond., 1877–79. 6 v. 8°. 10675–
Nineteenth Century: a history. Mackenzie. R. Lond., 1880. 12°. 20482
Ninety-Three. Hugo, V. M. N. Y., 1874. 12°. 24577
Njal (Burnt). Cox (G. W.) & Jones. (*In* 'Pop. Romances.' *And in* 'Tales.') 27712–13
—— Dasent, G. W. Edinb., 1861. 2 v. 12°. 27703–
No Love Lost. Howells, W. D. N. Y., 1869. 16°. 26118
Noblesse Oblige. [Roberts, M.] N. Y., 1876. 16°. 24851

Nohl, L. Beethoven. Lond., 1880. 12°. 23810
—— Life of Mozart. Lond., 1877. 2 v. 12°. 23811–
—— An Unrequited Love: an episode in the life of Beethoven. Lond., 1876. 8°. 23806
—— *editor.* Letters of Distinguished Musicians: Gluck, Haydn, P. E. Bach, Weber, Mendelssohn. [Ed. by E. Nohl.] Lond., 1867. 12°. 23765
Non-Christian Religious Systems. . , ... 28577–
Contents:—Buddhism, by T. W. R. Davids.—Hinduism, M. Williams.—Islam, J. W. H. Stobart.—The Coran, W. Muir.—Confucianism and Taouism, R. K. Douglas.
Nordenskiöld, A. E., Arctic Voyages of. Leslie, A. Lond., 1879. 21881
Nordhoff, C. California. N. Y., 1873. 8°. 21585
—— Communistic Societies of the U. S. N. Y., 1875. 8°. (2 cop.) 29115–
—— Northern California, Oregon, and the Sandwich Islands. N. Y., 1874. 8°. 21584
—— Politics for Young Americans. N. Y., 1875. 12°. (2 copies.) 21329–
Normandy. Blackburn, H. Normandy Picturesque. Lond., 1869. 21781
—— Macquoid, T. R. & K. S. Pictures and Legends from N. and Brittany. Lond., 1879. 12°. 21252
Normans. Johnson, A. H. The Normans in Europe. Lond., 1877. 20458
—— *See, also,* **Northmen.**
Norris, T. American Angler's Book. Phila., [1865]. 8°. . . . 29629
Norse Literature. *See* **Scandinavian** Lang. and Lit.
Norse Mythology. Anderson, R. B. Chic., 1875. 12°. . . . 27715
Norsemen. *See* **Northmen.**
North, F., *2d earl of Guilford. Earle, J. C.* (*In* 'Eng. Premiers,' v. 1.) 22882
North American Indians. *See* **Indians** (American).
North American Review. Bost., 1815–79. 129 v. 8°. . . . 12425–
—— *Same.* v. 2–45, 47–54, 56–67, 69–102, 104–108. 12579–
—— Index, v. 1–25 (2 copies); and v. 1–125. . . . . . . ——
Northend, C. Elihu Burritt. N. Y., [1880]. 12°. 22642
Northmen. Anderson, R. B. America not discovered by Columbus. Chic., 1877. 12°. 21280
—— Keyser, R. Private Life of the Old Northmen. Lond., 1868. 20049
—— Maclear, G. F. (Conversion of the West, v. 3). 28496
—— *See, also,* **Normans; Scandinavia.**
Norton (C. L.) & Habberton (J.). Canoeing in Kanuckia. N. Y., 1878. 12°. 29665
Norton, F. H. Life of Hancock. (*See* **Junkin, D. X., & Norton.**)
Norway. Beauclerk, D. de V. A Summer and Winter in N. Lond., 1868. 12°. 21208
—— Bowden, J. The Naturalist in Norway. Lond., 1869. 12°. . 21210
—— — Norway: its people, products, and institutions. Lond., 1867. 21211
—— Carlyle, T. Early kings of Norway. N. Y., 1875. 12°. . . 23616
—— Longfellow, H. W. Poems of Places, v. 8. Bost., 1876. 16°. . 26447
Notary's (The) Nose. About, E. F. V. N. Y., 1874. 16°. . . 24032
Notre-Dame de Paris. Hugo, V. M. Paris, 1871. 2 t. 16°. . . 25663–
Nott, E., Memoirs of. Van Santvoord, C. N. Y., [1876]. 12°. . 22641
Nova Scotia. Hardy, C. Forest Life in Acadie. Lond., 1869. 8°. 21553

Novelists, French. James, H., jr. Lond., 1878. 12°. . . . 26905
Numismatics. Edwards, J. Catalogue of the Greek and Roman Coins in the Numismatic Coll. of Yale College. N. H., 1880. 20379
"**Oars** and Sculls." Woodgate, W. B. Lond., 1875. 16°. . . 29659
Ober, F. A. Camps in the Caribbees. Bost., 1880 [1879]. 8°. . 21813
Ocean to Ocean. Grant, G. M. Lond., 1873. 8°. *And* N. Y., 1877. 21549–
Oceanica. Longfellow, H. W. Poems of Places, v. 31. Bost., 1879. 26470
—— *See, also,* **Polynesia**; **East** Ind. Archipelago.
Ochino, Bernardino, *of Siena.* *Benrath, K.* N. Y., 1877. 8°. . 22181
O'Connell, D. Speeches and Public Letters. Dublin, 1875. 2 v. 8°. 23046–
—— *Cusack, M. F.* The Liberator. Kenmare. 2 v. 8°. . . . 23044–
O'Connor, T. P. Lord Beaconsfield: a biography. Lond. & Belf., 1879. 12°. 22898
Oddities of London Life. [Poole, J.] Lond., 1838. 2 v. 8°. . 25209–
Odds and Ends. Beers, H. A. Bost., 1878. 16°. 26041
Ode of Life. [Morice, L.] Bost., 1880. 16°. 26099
Off the Skelligs. Ingelow, J. Bost., 1872. 16°. 24580
O'Keeffe, J. Personal Reminiscences. (*In* Bric-à-Brac Ser.) . . 23260
—— Recollections. Lond., 1826. 2 v. 8°. 23928–
Old Age. *See* **Longevity.**
Old Bushman, (*pseud.*) *See* **Wheelwright, H. W.**
Old Catholics. The New Reformation: a narrative of the Old Catholic movement; with a historical introd. by Theodorus [*pseud.*]. Lond., 1875. 8°. 28725
—— Strauss, G. L. M. (*In* 'Men who have made,' etc.) . . . 22583
Old Kensington. Ritchie, A. I. T. Lond., 1873. 8°. . . . 24700
—— *Same.* N. Y., 1873. 8°. 24701
Old and New. Bost., 1870–75. 11 v. 8°. 13705–
Old New Zealand: a tale. By a Pakeha Maori. With an introd. by the Earl of Pembroke. Lond., 1876. 8°. 21815
Old (The) Régime in Canada. Parkman, F. Bost., 1874. 8°. (2 cop.) 21404–
Old Shekarry, (*pseud.*) *See* **Leveson, H. A.**
Oldbury. Keary, A. Phila., [1879]. 12°. 24608
Oldcastle, J. *See* **Maurice, C. E.,** 'Lives of Eng. Pop. Leaders,' v. 2. 22941
Oldenbarneveldt. *See* **Barneveldt.**
Oldport Days. Higginson, T. W. Bost., 1873. 16°. . . . 24542
Olger the Dane. Cox (G. W.) & Jones (E. H.). (*In* 'Pop. Romances.') . . . . 27712 & 2010
Oliphant, Caroline. Memoir and Poems. (*See* **Rogers, Chas.,** 'Life of Baroness Nairne.')
Oliphant, L. Piccadilly. Ed. & Lond., 1870. 12°. 24804
Oliphant, Margaret O. W. At his Gates: a novel. Lond., 1872. 3 v. 12°. 24805–
—— Dress. Phila., [1879]. 12°. 29782
—— Makers of Florence. Lond., 1876. 8°. 23836
—— Memoir of Count de Montalembert. Edinb. & L., 1872. 2 v. 22486–
—— Whiteladies: a novel. N. Y., 1875. 16°. 24836

Oliphant, Margaret O. W., *editor* (*and author*). Foreign Classics for English Readers. Phil., [1877–79]. 9 v. 16°. (*For contents see* **Foreign** Classics.) 23262–
VOLS. by the editor:—1, Dante.—6, Molière.
Oliphant, Thos. La Musa Madrigalesca. Lond., 1837. 12°. . . 26163
Oliphant, Thos. L. K. Sources of Standard English. Lond., 1873. 27869
Oliver Newman. Southey, R. Lond., 1845. 16°. 18619
Omar Khayyám, *astronomer-poet of Persia.* Rubáiyát [Quatrains]; rendered into Eng. verse. Lond., 1872. 8°. 26256
O'Meara, Kathleen. Frederic Ozanam. Edinb., 1876. 12°. . . 22145
On the Cam. Everett, W. Cambr., 1865. 16°. 28829
On the Edge of the Storm. [Roberts, M.] N. Y., 1877. 16°. . . 24852
On the Eve. Turgénief, I. S. N. Y., 1873. 16°. (2 copies.) . . 24864–
On the Heights. Auerbach, B. N. Y., 1875. 12°. 24001–
One Summer. [Howard, B. W.] Bost., 1876. 16°. (3 copies.) . 24554–
One Year abroad. [Howard, B. W.] Bost., 1877. 16°. . . . 24557
Opera. Clayton, E. C. A chronological list of all the operas that have been performed in Europe. (*In* 'Queens of Song.') . 23847
—— Lumley, B. Reminiscences of the Opera. Lond., 1864. 8°. . 29799
Oppert, E. A Forbidden Land: voyages to the Corea. N. Y., 1880. 21943
Optics. *See* **Light.**
Orchids. *See* **Darwin, C. R.,** 'Various Contrivances.' . . . 29456
Order and Progress. Harrison, F. Lond., 1875. 8°. . . . 29087
Ordericus Vitalis. Ecclesiastical Hist. of England and Normandy. Lond., 1853–56. 4 v. 12°. 28462–
Oregon. Nash, W. Oregon in 1877. Lond., 1878. 12°. . . 21286
—— Nordhoff, C. Northern California and Oregon. N. Y., 1874. 21584
Oregon (The) Trail. Parkman, F. Bost., 1873. 8°. 21402
Orford, *Earls of.* *See* **Walpole.**
Oriental Monarchies. *See* **Rawlinson, G.**
Oriental Religions. Johnson, S. Bost., 1873 & '77. 2 v. 8°. . 28560–
—— *See, also,* **Religions** (various).
Orleans, L. P. A. d'. *See* **Paris,** *Comte de.*
Ormsby, R. McK. Hist. of the Whig Party. Bost., 1859. 12°. . 21326
Ornament. Blanc, A. A. P. C. Art in Ornament and Dress. N. Y., 1877. 8°. 29873
—— *See, also,* **Decoration.**
Orosius, Paulus. Historiarum Libri vii. *See* **Alfred the Gt.**
Orphan of Pimlico. Thackeray, W. M. Phil., 1876. 4°. . . ——
Orthodoxy. Cook, J. (Bost. Mond. Lectures.) Bost., 1878. 12°. 28023
Orton, J. Comparative Zoology. N. Y., 1876. 8°. 29504
Orval. Bulwer-Lytton, E. R. Lond., 1869. 16°. 26051
Oscar II., *king of Sweden and Norway.* Charles XII. By 'Oscar Fredrik' [*pseud.*]. Lond., 1879. 8°. 23898
Osgood, H. Winter and its Dangers. Phil., 1879. 16°. . . . 29963
Osler, W. R. Tintoretto. Lond. & N. Y., 1879. 12°. . . . 23782
Osorio: a tragedy. Coleridge, S. T. Lond., 1873. 8°. . . . 26640
Ossian. *Campbell, J. F.* (*In* 'Pop. Tales of the West Highlands,' v. 4.) 27663

Ossoli, Marg. (Fuller) d'. [Works. Ed. by A. B. Fuller.] Bost., 1874. 6 v. 12°. 27286–

CONTENTS:—1-2, Memoirs, ed. by Emerson, Channing, and Clarke.—3, Woman in the 19th cent; and kindred papers relating to the sphere, condition, and duties of woman.—4, At home and abroad; or, Things and thoughts in Amer. and Europe.—5, Art, literature, and the drama.—6, Life without and life within; or, Reviews, narratives, essays, and poems.

Otté, Elise C. Scandinavian History. Lond., 1874. 12°. . . 20050

Ottoman Power in Europe. Freeman, E. A. Lond., 1877. 12°. . 20490

Out of the Question. Howells, W. D. Bost., 1877. 16°. (2 copies.) 24568–

"**Out** of the World" Series. N. Y., 1878. 3 v. in 1. 16°. . . 25247

CONTENTS:—1, Fables. By G. Washington Æsop. 2, The World's Almaniac for 1879. 3, Archibald the Cat, and other sea yarns.

Overbury, T. Miscellaneous Works. Ed. by E. F. Rimbault. Lond., 1856. 16°. 27262

Overland Monthly. S. Francisco, 1868–75. 15 v. 8°. . . . 13690–

Ovid. *Church, A. J.* (Anc. Classics for Eng. Readers, supplem. ser., v. 2.) 26848

Owen, F. M. John Keats: a study. Lond., 1880. 12°. . . . 26292

Owen, R. D. The Debatable Land. N. Y., 1872. 12°. . . . 28052

—— Footfalls on the Boundary of another World. Phil., 1860. 12°. 28053

—— Threading my Way. N. Y., 1874. 12°. 23648

Owens College, *Manchester, Eng.* [Stewart (B.) & Ward (A. W.), *editors.*] Essays and Addresses. Lond., 1874. 8°. . . 27412

CONTENTS:—On some relations of culture to practical life, by J. G. Greenwood; Original research as a means of education, H. E. Roscoe; Solar physics, B. Stewart; Distance of the sun, T. H. Core; Limits of our knowledge of the earth, W. B. Dawkins; Use of steam, O. Reynolds; Primeval vegetation, W. C. Williamson; Science and medicine, A. Gamgee; Some historical results of the science of language, A. S. Wilkins; The Talmud, T. Theodores; Provençal poetry, H. Breymann; Judicature Act of 1873, J. Bryce; Railways and the State, W. S. Jevons; Peace of Europe, A. W. Ward.

Oxberry, W. The Actor's Budget. Lond. 12°. 26521

Oxford and Cambridge. Arnold, F. Lond., [1874]. 8°. . . . 21979

Oxford and Cambridge Aquatics. Banks, E. G. Oxf., 1868. 16°. . 29658

Oxford Spectator. Oxf., 1878. 8°. (Nos. 1–31; first pub. in 1867–8.) 27562

Oxford University. Student's Handbook. Oxf., 1873. 16°. . . 28833

Oxonian (The) in Iceland. Metcalfe, F. Lond., 1861. 12°. . . 21705

Oxus. MacGahan, J. A. Campaigning on the Oxus. N. Y., 1874. 21924

Ozanam, A. F., Life and Works of. O'Meara, K. Edinb., 1876. . 22145

Pacchiarotto. Browning, R. Bost., 1877. 16°. 26049

Packard, A. S., jr. Half Hours with Insects. Bost., 1877. 12°. 29505

—— Zoology. N. Y., 1879. 12°. 29506

Packard, J. H. Sea-Air and Sea-Bathing. Phil., 1880. 16°. . 29967

Paganism. *See* **Heathenism.**

Page, Henry A., (*pseud.*) *See* **Japp, Alex.**

Page (The). Dumas, A. D. Lond., [1879]. 16°. (2 cop.) 24413 & 24420

Paijkull, C. W. A Summer in Iceland. Lond., 1868. 8°. . . 21886

Painters. Clement, C. E. Bost., 1879. 12°. 29791

—— Crowe (J. A.) & Cavalcaselle (G. B.). Early Flemish Painters. Lond., 1872. 12°. 23801

—— Gower, R. Figure Painters of Holland. L. & N. Y., 1880. 12°. 23785

Painting. Couture, T. Art Methods. N. Y., 1879. 12°. . . 29826

—— Crowe (J. A.) & Cavalcaselle (G. B.). Hist. of Painting in Italy. Lond., 1864–66. 3 v. 8°. 29945–

—— — Hist. of Painting in North Italy. Lond., 1871. 2 v. 8°. . 29948–

Painting. Ruskin, J. Laws of Fésole. N. Y., 1877. Part 1. 12°. 29844
—— Waagen, G. F. Handbook of Painting: the German, Flemish, and Dutch schools. Based on the handbook of Kugler. Lond., 1874. 2 v. 8°. 29875–
Pair of Blue Eyes. Hardy, T. N. Y., 1873. 16°. 24461
Palestine. Bartlett, S. C. From Egypt to Palestine. N. Y., 1879. 21843
—— Burton, I. Inner Life of Syria, Palestine, and the Holy Land. Lond., 1875. 2 v. 8°. 21905–
—— Conder, C. R. Tent Work in Palestine. N. Y., 1878. 2 v. 8°. 21903–
Palfrey, F. W. Memoir of Wm. F. Bartlett. Bost., 1878. 16°. . 22602
Palgrave, R. F. D. The House of Commons. Lond., 1869. 12°. 20812
Palgrave, W. G. Dutch Guiana. Lond., 1876. 8°. . . . 21811
—— Hermann Agha: an Eastern narative. N. Y., 1872. 16°. . 24837
Palleske, E. Schiller's Life and Works. Lond., 1860. 2 v. 12°. 23324–
Palliser, *Mrs.* **B.** Brittany and its Byways. Lond., 1869. 12°. . 21686
Palmer, E. H. English-Gipsy Songs. (*See* **Leland, C. G.,** *& others.*) 26123
—— *See, also,* **Magnússon, E.,** 'Runeberg's Lyrical Songs.' . . 26128
Palmer, H. S. Sinai. (Anc. Hist. from the Monuments.) Lond., [1878]. 16°. 20045
Palmerston, *Viscountess.* *See* **Temple, A. L.**
Palmetto-Leaves. Stowe, H. E. B. Bost., 1873. 16°. . . . 21288
Palmyra. Beaufort, E. A. (*In* 'Egyptian Sepulchres.') . . . 21209
Papacy. Thompson, R. W. Papacy and the Civil Power. N. Y., 1876. 12°. 29096
—— *See, also,* **Popes.**
Papal (The) Conclaves. Trollope, T. A. Lond., 1876. 8°. . . 28722
Papillon, F. Nature and Life. N. Y., 1875. 12°. 29397
Paradoxical Philosophy. [Stewart, B., & Tait, P. G.] Lond., 1878. 28091
Paraguay. Burton, R. F. Letters from the Battle-Fields of Paraguay. Lond., 1870. 8°. 21804
—— Hutchinson, T. J. The Paraná; with incidents of the Paraguayan war. Lond., 1868. 8°. 21805
Paraná (*province*). Bigg-Wither, T. P. Pioneering in South Brazil. Lond., 1878. 2 v. 12°. 21702–
Parasites, Animal. Beneden, P. J. van. N. Y., 1876. 12°. . . 29259
Parents (Les) de Bernard. About, E. F. V. (*With* 'Trente,' etc.) . 25622
Paris, *Comte de.* Hist. of the Civil War in Amer. Phil., 1875–6. v. 1–2. 8°. 21460–
Paris. Amicis, E. de. Studies of Paris. N. Y., 1879. 12°. . . 27273
CONTENTS:—First day in P.; Glance at the Exposition; Hugo; Zola; Paris.
—— Hackländer, F. W. von. Paris im Winter 1851. (*In* 'Tagebuchblätter,' 'Werke,' B. 40.) 25819
—— Houssaye, A. Life in Paris: letters. N. Y., 1879. 12°. . . 21610
—— Jackson, C. C. Old Paris: its court and literary salons. Lond., 1878. 2 v. 12°. 21687–
—— Sala, G. A. Paris herself again in 1878–9. Illust. 2d ed. Lond., 1879. 2 v. 8°. 21984–
—— Taine, H. A. Notes on Paris. N. Y., 1875. 12°. . . . 21628
—— Thackeray, W. M. The Student's Quarter. Lond. 12°. . . 21629

Paris en Amérique. [Laboulaye, E. R. L.]. Paris, 1877. 16°. . 25667

Parisians (The). Bulwer-Lytton, E. G. E. L. Lond., 1875 (etc.). 2 v. 12°. . . . . 24119- & 24150

Parke, W. T. Musical Memoirs. Lond., 1830. 2 v. 12°. . . 18671-

Parker, Theo.: a biography. Frothingham, O. B. Bost., 1874. 12°. 22610

Parkes, Bessie R. *See* **Belloc, B. R. P.**

Parkes, E. A. On Personal Care of Health. Lond., [1876]. 16°. 29957

Parkman, F. France and England in North America. Bost., 1865–77. 5 parts. 8°. . . . . 6130- & 21403-

CONTENTS:—1, Pioneers of France in the New World.—2, The Jesuits in N. Amer.—3, Discovery of the Great West (*in the 11th ed.*, "La Salle, and the Discov.," &c.).—4, Old Régime in Canada.—5, Count Frontenac and New France under Louis XIV.

—— La Salle and the Discovery of the Great West. 11th ed., rev., with add. Bost., 1879. 8°. 21403

—— The Oregon Trail. 5th ed., rev. Bost., 1873. 8°. . . . 21402

Parliament. Bisset, A. Struggle for Parliamentary Government in Eng. Lond., 1877. 2 v. 8°. 21058-

Parliamentary Practice. Palgrave, R. F. D. House of Commons: history and practice. Lond., 1869. 12°. 20812

Parliamentary Reform. Gladstone, W. E. Speeches on, in 1866. Lond., 1866. 12°. 20809

—— Grote, G. Essentials of. (*In* 'Minor Works.') 27400

Parnassus. Emerson, R. W. Bost., 1875. 12°. 26120

Parnell, T. Battle of the Frogs and Mice. (*See* **Homer.**)

Parr, Louisa. Dorothy Fox. Lond., 1871. 3 v. 16°. . . . 24838-

—— Hero Carthew; or, The Prescotts of Pamphillon. N. Y., 1873. 24841

—— John Thompson, and other stories. Phila., [1878]. 16°. . . 24842

Parr, Sam.: life, writings, and opinions. Field, W. Lond., 1828. 2 v. 8°. 18603-

Parry, W. Last Days of Lord Byron. Lond., 1825. 8°. . . 18656

Parsons, T. W. Dante's Inferno; transl. [in meter.] Bost., 1867. 26272

Parthia. Rawlinson, G. Sixth Great Oriental Monarchy. Lond., 1873 8°. 20249

Parties. Adams, W. H. D. English Parties, from Walpole to Peel. Lond., 1878. 2 v. 8°. 21054-

—— Ormsby, R. M. Hist. of the Whig Party; [and] of the principal parties of the country. Bost., 1859. 12°. 21326

—— Stickney, A. A True Republic. N. Y., 1879. 12°. . . . 29094

—— *See, also,* **Federalism; Politics.**

Parton, J. Caricature, and other comic art. N. Y., 1877. 8°. . 29944

—— Life of Horace Greeley. Bost., 1872. 12°. 22643

—— Life of Thomas Jefferson. Bost., 1874. 8°. 22640

Party. *See* **Parties.**

Pascal, B. *Sainte-Beuve, C. A.* (*In* 'Monday Chats.') . . . 23290

—— *Tulloch, J.* (For. Clas. for Eng. Readers.) Phil., [1878]. 16°. 23264

Passavant, J. D. Raphael. Lond. & N. Y., 1879. 12°. . . 23779

Passionate (A) Pilgrim. James, H., jr. Bost., 1875. 12°. . . 24603

Paston (The) Letters. Gairdner, J., *editor.* Lond., 1872–75. 3 v. 16°. 22840-

Patagonia. Beerbohm, J. Wanderings in Patagonia. N. Y., 1879. 21243

—— Coan, T. Adventures in P.: a missionary's trip. N. Y., 1880. 21704

Patagonia. Guinnard, A. Three Years' Slavery among the Patagonians. Lond., 1871. 12°. 21229
Pater, W. The Renaissance. Lond., 1877. 8°. 29878
Pater Mundi. Burr, E. F. Bost., 1870–73. 2 v. 12°. . 9989 & 28087
Paterson, J. Liberty of the Subject and Security of the Person. Lond., 1877. 2 v. 12°. 28854–
Patmore, C. The Angel in the House. Lond., [1879]. 16°. . . 26031
Patmore, P. G. My Friends and Acquaintance. Lond., 1854. 3 v. 23609–
Patterson, A. J. The Magyars. Lond., 1869. 2 v. 12°. . . 21711–
Patteson, J. C., *Bp.*, Life of. Yonge, C. M. Lond., 1874. 2 v. 8°. 22270–
Pattison, Dorothy W. *Lonsdale, M.* Sister Dora. Bost., 1880. 16°. 23650
Pattison, M. Isaac Casaubon, 1559–1614. Lond., 1875. 8°. . . 22264
—— Milton. (Eng. Men of Letters.) N. Y., 1880. 12°. . . . 23343
Pattou, A. A. The Voice as an instrument. N. Y., 1878. 16°. . 29805
Paul, *St. Farrar, F. W.* Life and Work of St. P. N. Y., [1879]. 2 v. 8°. 28642–
—— The Heathen World and St. P. Lond., [1878.] 4 v. 16°. . 28498–

CONTENTS :—St. Paul in Damascus and Arabia, by G. Rawlinson.—In Asia Minor [etc.], E. H. Plumptre.—In Greece, G. S. Davies.—At Rome, C. Merivale.

Paul, C. K. Mary Wollstonecraft. (*See* **Godwin, M. W.,** 'Letters.') 23214
—— William Godwin: his friends and contemporaries. Bost., 1876. 2 v. 8°. 23326–
Paul Faber, Surgeon. MacDonald, G. Phila., 1879 [1878]. (2 cop.) 24674–
[**Paulding, J. K.**] The Dutchman's Fireside. N. Y., 1831. 2 v. 12°. 17482–
Pauli, R. Life of Alfred the Great. Lond., 1853. 12°. . . . 20805
—— Pictures of Old England. Cambr. & L., 1861. 12°. . . . 20850
—— Simon de Montfort, Earl of Leicester. Lond., 1876. 12°. . 22880
Pauline. Walford L. B. N. Y., 1877. 16°. 24288
Pauline; or, Buried alive. Dumas, A. D. Lond., [1879]. 16°. . 24418
Pausanias the Spartan. Bulwer-Lytton, E. G. E. L. Lond., 1876 (&c.). 12°. . . . . 24122 & 24151
Payer, J. New Lands within the Arctic Circle. N. Y., 1877. 8°. 21883
Payne, E. J. Hist. of European Colonies. Lond., 1877. 16°. . 20084
Peabody, A. P. Christianity and Science. N. Y., 1874. 12°. . 28700
Peabody, Elizabeth P. Æsthetic Papers [by the ed. and others]. Bost., 1849. 8°. 27560
—— Reminiscences of Rev. Wm. E. Channing. Bost., 1880. 16°. . 22614
Peacock, T. L. Works; [with life, etc.] Ed. by H. Cole. Lond., 1875. 3 v. 12°. 27303–
[**Peard, Frances M.**] Thorpe Regis: a novel. Bost., 1874. 16°. . 24843
Pearson, C. H. Early and Middle Ages of England. Lond., 1861. 21091
—— *Same*, [2d ed.] Hist. of England during the early and middle ages. Lond., 1867. 2 v. 8°. 21092–
—— Eng. History in the 14th Cent. Lond., 1876. 16°. . . . 20066
Pearson, J. *Cheetham, S.* (*In* **Masters** in Eng. Theology.) . . 22111
Peel, R. Memoirs. Pub. by Lord Mahon and E. Cardwell. Lond., 1857–8. 2 v. 8°. 22887–

CONTENTS :—1, The Roman Catholic question, 1828-9.—2, The new Government, 1834-5; Repeal of the Corn Laws, 1845-6.

—— *Bulwer, H. L. E.* Lond., 1874. 8°. 23048

Peel, R. *Taylor, W. C. (& C. Mackay).* Lond., [1846–51]. 4 v. 8°. 23049–
—— *See, also,* **Adams, W. H. D.,** 'Eng. Party Leaders,' v. 2 (21055); **Earle, J. C.,** 'Eng. Premiers,' v. 2 (22883); **Kebbel, T. E.,** 'Eng. Statesmen' (22884).
Peile, J. Philology. Lond., 1877. 16°. 26859
Peking and the Pekingese. Rennie, D. F. Lond., 1865. 2 v. 12°. 21623–
Pelham. *See* **Newcastle,** *dukes of.*
Pemberton, H. Hist. of Monaco, past and present. Lond., 1867. 20618
Pembroke, *Earl of. See* **Herbert, G. R. C.**
People (The) of Turkey: 20 years' residence. By a consul's daughter and wife. Ed. by S. L. Poole. Lond., 1878. 2 v. 12°. 21693–
Pepper, J. H. Pneumatics [and Acoustics]. Lond., [1874]. 12°. . 29315
Pepys, S. Diary and Correspondence; with a life and notes by R. N. Braybrooke; [and] notes by M. Bright. Lond., 1875–79. 6 v. 8°. 23024–
Perceval, S. *Earle, J. C.* (*In* 'Eng. Premiers,' v. 2.) . . . 22883
Percival Keene. Marryat, F. N. Y., 1861. 12°. 24643
Percy, T. Reliques of Anc. Eng. Poetry. With memoir [etc.] by G. Gilfillan. Edinb., 1858. 3 v. 8°. 26343–
Perez, A., and Philip II. Mignet, F. A. M. Lond., 1846. 12°. . 23904
Periodicals:—
Academician. N. Y., 1820. v. 1. 8° 14079
All the Year Round. Lond., 1859–79. v. 1–15; and New Series, v. 1–23. 8°. 18345–
American Eclectic. N. Y., 1841–2. 4 v. 8°. (2 copies.) . . 13741–
American Journal of Science. [1st Series.] N. H., 1818–45. 49 v. 8°. 17545–
—— Index (v. 50). N. H., 1846. 8°. (2 copies). . . . ——
—— 2d Series. N. H., 1846–70. 50 v. 8°. 17594–
—— 3d Series. N. H., 1871–79. 18 v. 8°. 17644–
American Literary Magazine, Sprague's. Albany and Hartford, 1847–49. 5 v. in 3. 8°. 13254–
American Monthly Magazine. Ed. by Willis. Bost., 1829. v. 1. 8°. 13113
American Monthly Magazine, New Series. N. Y., 1836. 2 v. 8°. 13114–
American Monthly Magazine, and Critical Review. N. Y., 1817–18. 4 v. 8°. 13558–
American Museum, Carey's. 1787–98. Philad. v. 1–9, 11–13. 8°. 14758–
American Quarterly Observer. (2 copies.) Bost., 1833–34. 3 v. 8°. 13880–
American Quarterly Review. Philad., 1827–37. 22 v. 8°. . 13213–
—— *Same.* v. 3–7, 9–20. 13235–
American Review, [Walsh's.] (2 copies.) Philad., 1811–12. 4 v. 8°. 14038–
American Review: a whig journal. See Amer. Whig Rev.
American Whig Review. N. Y., 1845–52. 16 v. 8°. . . . 14696–
—— *Same.* v. 3–10, 12–16. 12723–
Analectic Magazine. Philad., 1814–20. 16 v. 8°. . . . 14235–
Annual Review. Ed. by Aikin. Lond., 1802–04. 3 v. 8°. . 14536–
Anti-Jacobin. 4th ed. Lond., 1799. 2 v. 8°. 11300–
Anti-Jacobin Review and Magazine. Lond., 1798–1800. 5 v. 8°. 11302–
Appletons' Annual Cyclopædia, for 1861–79. N. Y., 1864–80. 19 v. 8°. . . . . ——
—— Index to v. 1–15. . . . . ——
Appletons' Journal. N. Y., 1869–79. 22 v. 4° and 8°. . . 17842–
Arcturus. N. Y., 1841–42. v. 3. 8°. 12768

Periodicals :—

Argosy. Lond., 1866–67. 4 v. 8°. 14388–
Art-Journal. Lond., 1852–60. 8 v. 4°. . . . . ——
Athenæum. N. H., 1814. v. 1. 8°. 17475
Atheneum. Bost., 1817–25. 16 v. 8°. 14578–
Atlantic Monthly. Bost., 1857–79. 44 v. 8°. 10526
—— *Same.* v. 1–26. 10500
—— Index to v. 1–38. . . . . ——
Bee. Ed. by Anderson. Edinb., 1791–93. 18 v. 8°. . . . 13041–
Belgravia. Lond., 1867–79. 39 v. 8°. . . . 17971– and 18007–
Bentley's Miscellany. Lond., 1837–68. 64 v. 8°. 18266–
—— *Same.* v. 1–3, 5–10, 13–16. 14212–
Biblical Repository. Andover and N. Y., 1831–50. 30 v. 8°. . 12776–
—— *Same.* v. 1–7, 11–21, 23–30. 12821–
—— Index to v. 1–24. (2 copies.) . . . . ——
Bibliotheca Sacra. Andover, 1844–79. 36 v. 8°. 12851–
—— *Same.* v. 9–26. 12803–
—— Index to v. 1–13. . . . . ——
Blackwood's Magazine. Edinb. and N. Y., 1817–79. v. 1–4, 6–30, 32–126. 8°. 11620– 11781–
—— *Same.* v. 1–18, 21, 24–26, 28, 33–91, 93–106. . 11957– and 12128–
Boston Miscellany. Ed. by Hale. Bost., 1842. v. 1. 8°. . 14519
British and Foreign Review. Lond., 1835–44. 16 v. 8°. . . 11440–
British Quarterly Review. N. Y., 1871–79. v. 53–70. 8°. . . 12217–
Catholic World. N. Y., 1865–79. 29 v. 8°. 14285–
Christian Spectator. [Monthly.] N. H., 1819–28. 10 v. 8°. . 12940–
Christian Spectator, Quarterly. N. H., 1829–38. 10 v. (2 cop.) 12950–
College Courant. N. H., July, 1867 – June, 1869 (2 cop.); Jan.–Dec., 1870. 5 v. 4°. . . . . ——
Contemporary Review. Lond., 1866–79. 36 v. 8°. 10721–
Continental Monthly. N. Y., 1862–64. 6 v. 8°. 13332–
Cornhill Magazine. Lond., 1860–79. 40 v. 8°. 18108– and 18233–
Craftsman. Lond., 1731. 7 v. 12°. 12025–
Democratic Review. Wash. and N. Y., 1837–52. 31 v. 8°. . 13059–
—— *Same.* v. 1–5, 9–21, 23–25, 28–31. 13089–
Dublin Review. Lond. and D., 1836–79. 85 v. 8°. . . . 18431–
Dublin University Magazine. D., 1833–73. 81 v. 8°. . . 18138–
Eclectic Magazine. N. Y., 1844–79. 93 v. 8°. 13562–
—— *Same.* v. 1–71. 13752–
Eclectic Museum. N. Y., 1843. 3 v. 8°. 13749–
Eclectic Review. Lond., 1805–10. 6 v. in 11. 8°. . . . 14377–
Edinburgh Annual Register, for 1808–15. E., 1810–17. 8 v. in 13. 8°. 11731–
Edinburgh Monthly Review. Edinb., 1819–21. 5 v. 8°. . . 13116–
Edinburgh Review. E. and N. Y., 1802–79. v. 1–17, 19–150. 8°. 11154–
—— *Same.* v. 1–130. 11051–
—— Index to v. 1–20 (2 copies); and 21–50. . . . . ——
—— Selections from. Lond., 1833, and Paris, 1835. 7 v. 8°. . 11293–
Edinburgh Weekly Magazine. E., 1771–72. v. 14, 15 (in 1). 8°. 12745
Etonian. 3d ed. Lond., 1823. 3 v. 12°. 12297–
Foreign Quarterly Review. Lond. and N. Y., 1827–46. v. 1–3. 5–37. 8°. 12682–
—— *Same.* v. 11, 12, 14–23, 26–30, 32–36. 12709–
Foreign Review. Lond., 1828–30. 5 v. 8°. 11435–
Fortnightly Review. Lond., 1865–79. 32 v. 8°. 10622–
Fraser's Magazine. Lond., 1830–79. 100 v. 8°. 12300–
Galaxy. N. Y., 1866–78. 25 v. 8°. 13886–
Good Company (*a continuation of* "Sunday Afternoon"). Springf., 1879– v. 4– 8°. 18408–
Good Words. Lond., 1866–67. v. 7, 8. 8°. 14534–
Halcyon Luminary. N. Y., 1812. v. 1. 8°. 14080

Periodicals :—

Harper's Monthly Magazine. N. Y., 1850–79. 59 v. 8°. . . 13413–
—— *Same.* v. 1–42. 13291–
—— Index to v. 1–40; and 1–50. . . . . ——
Harvard Lyceum. Cambr., 1810–11. 8°. 17472
Harvard Magazine. (2 copies.) Cambr., 1855–60. 6 v. 8°. . 17462–
Herald of Health. N. Y., 1867–70. v. 43, 44, 49, 50 (in 2 v.) 8°. 17488–
Homilist. Lond., 1870–71. 4 v. 8°. 12888–
Hours at Home. N. Y., 1865–70. 11 v. 8°. 13911–
Household Words. Lond. and N. Y., 1850–59. v. 1–4, 15, 16, 18. 8°. 17497–
Hunt's Merchant's Magazine. N. Y., 1839–59. v. 1–5, 8–13, 20–40. 8°. 13525–
Intellectual Observer. Lond., 1862–68. 12 v. 8°. . . . 17711–
International Review. N. Y., 1874–79. 7 v. 8°. . . . 10591–
Knickerbocker. N. Y., 1833–62. v. 1–59. 8°. 14457–
—— *Same.* v. 2–5, 7, 8, 10–25, 27–30, 32, 35, 36, 38–41, 43–45, 47–66. 14640–
Knight's Penny Magazine. Lond., 1846–47. 2 v. in 1. 8°. . 14597
Knight's Quarterly Magazine. Lond., 1823–4. 3 v. 8°. . . 18335–
Land we Love. Charlotte, N. C., 1866–69. 6 v. 8°. . . . 12934–
Lippincott's Magazine. Philad., 1868–79. 24 v. 8°. . . . 13373–
Literary Portfolio. Philad., 1830. v. 1. 4°. 17828
Literary and Theological Review. N. Y., 1834–38. 5 v. 8°. . 12771–
Littell's Living Age. Bost., 1844–79. 143 v. 8°. . . . 13924–
London Quarterly Rev. See Quarterly Rev.
London Review. Lond., 1835–6. 2 v. 8°. 11885–
London Society. Lond., 1862–79. v. 1–19, 22–36. 8°. . . 17755–
London and Westminster Review. Lond., 1836–40. 7 v. 8°. . 11887–
Macmillan's Magazine. Lond., 1859–79. 40 v. 8°. . . . 12155–
Mass. Quarterly Review. Bost., 1847–49. 2 v. 8°. . . . 12769–
Metropolitan Magazine. N. Y., 1836–42. 13 v. 8°. . . . 14520–
Microcosm. N. H., 1836–37. v. 3, New Series. 8°. . . . 14598
Microscope. N. H., 1820. 2 v. in 1. 8°. 17474
Month. Lond., 1870–71. 4 v. New Series. 8°. . . . 12235–
Monthly Magazine. Lond., 1796–1825. 60 v. 8°. . . . 14152–
Monthly Review. Lond., 1817–33. v. 82–129, 131, 132. 8°. . 14300–
Museum. Lond., 1746–47. 3 v. 8°. 12742–
Museum of Foreign Literature. Philad., 1822–39. v. 1–29, 31–33, 35–37. 8°. 14046–
Nation. N. Y., 1865–72. 15 v. 4°. . . . . ——
Naval Magazine. N. Y., 1836. v. 1. 8°. 13557
New England Magazine. (2 copies.) Bost., 1831–34. 7 v. 8°. 13864–
New Englander. N. H., 1843–79. 38 v. 8°. . 12997– and 13121–
—— *Same.* v. 1–28. 12970–
—— Index, v. 1–19. (2 copies.) . . . . ——
New Mirror. N. Y., 1843–44. 3 v. 8°. 14516–
New Monthly Magazine. Bost., 1823–24. v. 6–8. 8°. . . 14350–
New York Literary Gazette. N. Y., 1825–26. v. 1. 8°. . . 14712
New York Quarterly. N. Y., 1854–55. v. 3. 8°. . . . 13338
New York Review. (2 copies.) N. Y., 1837–42. 10 v. 8°. . 12914–
Niles' Register. Balt., 1816–37. 52 v. 8° and 4°. 14553– and 17829–
Nineteenth Century. Lond., 1877–79. 6 v. 8°. 10675–
North American Review. Bost., 1815–79. 129 v. 8°. . . 12425–
—— *Same.* v. 2–45, 47–54, 56–67, 69–102, 104–108. . . . 12579–
—— Index, v. 1–25 (2 copies); and v. 1–125. . . . . ——
North British Review. Edinb. and N. Y., 1844–71. 53 v. 8°. . 11684–
—— *Same.* v. 10–37, 42–49. 11713–
Old and New. Bost., 1870–75. 11 v. 8°. 13705–
Olio. Lond. v. 1, 2. 8°. 11307–
Once a Week. Lond., 1870–71. v. 6, 7. 8°. 12211–
Overland Monthly. S. Francisco, 1868–75. 15 v. 8°. . . 13690–

Periodicals :—

Pamphleteer. Lond., 1813–28. v. 1–4, 6–24, 29. 8°. . . . 14353–
Parterre. Lond., 1834–35. v. 1–3. 8°. 11744–
Penny Magazine. Lond., 1832–41. 10 v. in 11. 2°. . . . 17831–
Philomathesian. Middlebury, 1833–34. v. 1. 8°. . . . 17473
Popular Science Monthly. N. Y., 1872–79. 15 v. 8°. . . 17679–
Popular Science Review. Lond., 1862–76. 15 v. 8°. . . 17728–
Port Folio. 2d and 3d Series. Philad., 1809–14. 6 v. 8°. . 12736–
Portico. Balt., 1816–17. v. 2–4, in 1. 8°. 14713
Punch. Lond., 1841–79. 74 v. 4°. . . . . ——
Putnam's Monthly Magazine. N. Y., 1833–58. 12 v. 8°. . . 13257–
—— *Same.* v. 1–11. 13274–
—— New Series. N. Y., 1868–70. 6 v. 8°. 13285–
—— *Same.* v. 1–5. 13269–
Quarterly Review. Lond. and N. Y., 1809–79. v. 1–12, 14–28, 30–33, 35–38, 41–148. 8°. 11470–
—— *Same.* v. 1–16, 18–48, 50–127. 11310–
—— Indexes to v. 1–60, in 3 v. 8°. . . . . . . ——
Retrospective Review. Lond., 1820–26. 14 v. 8°. . . . 11456–
Rural Magazine. Hartf'd., 1819. v. 1. 8°. 13879
Sabbath at Home. Bost., 1867. v. 1. 8°. 13878
St. James's Magazine. Lond., 1861–79. 45 v. 8°. . . . 18047–
Saint Paul's Magazine. Lond., 1872–3. v. 10–13. 8°. . . 12213–
Scribner's Monthly. N. Y., 1870–79. 18 v. 8°. 13150–
Select Journal of Foreign Period. Lit. Bost., 1833–34. 4 v. 8°. 14231–
Sharpe's London Magazine. Lond., 1870. v. 35. 8°. . . 17480
Southern Literary Messenger. Richmond, 1835–59. v. 1–20, 22, 24–28. 8°. 14539– 14716–
—— *Same.* v. 7, 17–20. 14728–
Southern Review. Charleston, 1828–32. 8 v. 8°. . . . 14024–
—— *Same.* v. 1–4, 6–8. 14032–
Student and Intellectual Observer. Lond., 1868–71. 5 v. 8°. . 17723–
Student's Companion. N. H., 1831. v. 1. 8°. (Bound with Yale Lit., v. 1.) 17393
Sunday Afternoon. Springf., 1878–9. 3 v. 8°. 18405–
(Continued under the name "Good Company.")
Sunday Magazine. Lond., 1867–68. v. 4. 8°. 14533
Tait's Edinburgh Magazine. E., 1842–3. v. 9–10, in 4. 8°. . 13823–
Temple Bar. Lond., 1861–79. 57 v. 8°. 17889–
Theological Review. Lond., 1870. v. 7. 8°. 17496
Union Review. Lond., 1870–71. 2 v. 8°. 12902–
University Quarterly. N. H., 1860–61. 4 v. 8°. 17476–
Westminster Review. Lond. and N. Y., 1824–79. v. 1–17, 20–54, 57–112. 8°. 12032– 12239–
—— *Same.* v. 1–24, 27–92. 11861–
Yale Courant. (2 copies.) N. H., 1865–67. 2 v. 4°. . . ——
Yale Literary Magazine. N. H., 1836–79. 44 v. 8°. . . . 17393–
—— *Same.* v. 1–26, 28, 29. 17367–
—— Index to v. 1–33. N. H., 1868. 8°. . . . . . . ——

See, also, **Adventurer; Champion; Connoisseur; Fors Clavigera; Gray's-Inn Journal; Guardian; Looker-on; Lounger; Mirror; Observer; Rambler; Spectator; Speculator; Tatler; Tomahawk; World.**

Perkins, C. C. Raphael and Michelangelo. Bost., 1878. 8°. . 23835
Perkins, F. B. The Best Reading. N. Y., 1873. 12°. . . . 26930
—— *Same.* 4th rev. and enl. ed. N. Y., 1877. 12°. . . . . ——
—— Putnam's Library Companion for 1877–79. N. Y., 1878–80. 3 v. ——
—— Scrope; or, The lost library: a novel. Bost., 1874. 8°. . . 24679
Perreyve, H. *Hamerton, P. G.* (*In* 'Mod. Frenchmen.') . . . 22488
Perry, A. L. Elements of Political Economy. N. Y., 1866. 8°. . 8639

Perry, A. L. *Same.* 2d ed., rev. N. Y., 1867. 8°. . . . 28809
—— Introduction to Political Economy. N. Y., 1877. 12°. . . 28808
Perry, G. G. Hist. of the Church of England. With an app.: The hist. of the Prot. Epis. Ch. in the U. S., by J. A. Spencer. N. Y., 1879. 8°. 28443
Persia. Arnold, A. Through Persia by Caravan. N. Y., 1877. 12°. 21205
—— Cox, G. W. The Greeks and the Persians. N. Y., 1876. . 16° 20435
—— Cuninghame, A. T. Travels on the frontiers of Persia. Lond., 1872. 8°. 21913
—— Omar Khayyám. Rubáiyát [Quatrains] of the astronomer-poet of Persia. Lond., 1872. 8°. 26256
—— Rawlinson, G. Seventh Great Oriental Monarchy. Lond., 1876. 20250
—— Smith, R. M. Persian Art. Lond., [1876]. 12°. . . . 29771
—— Vaux, W. S. W. (Anc. Hist. from the Monuments.) N. Y., 1876. 20044
Personal Recollections of English Engineers, and of the introduction of the railway system into the United Kingdom. By a Civil Engineer. Lond., 1868. 8°. 23537
Peru. Markham, C. R. Cuzco; with an account of the hist., lang., lit., and antiquities of the Incas. [*And*] Lima: a visit to the capital and provinces of modern Peru. Lond., 1856. 12°. . 21701
—— Prescott, W. H. Hist. of the Conquest of Peru; with a view of the civilization of the Incas. Phila., 1871. 2 v. 8°. . 20343–
—— Squier, E. G. Peru: incidents of travel and exploration. N. Y., 1877. 8°. 21809
Peschel, O. Races of Man, and their geographical distribution. Lond., 1876. 8°. 29386
Peter, the Apostle. Taylor, W. M. N. Y., 1878. 12°. . . . 28652
Peter Schlemihl. Chamisso, A. von. N. Y., 1874. 12°. . . 24166
Peter Simple. Marryat, F. N. Y., 1861. 12°. 24644
Peters, D. C. Kit Carson's Life and Adventures. Hartf., 1875. 8°. 22682
Peters, S. General Hist. of Conn. [Ed.] by S. J. McCormick. N. Y., 1877. 12°. 21321
—— *Trumbull, J. H.* (*In* 'The True-Blue Laws.')
Petit (Le) vieux des Batignolles. Gaboriau, E. Paris, 1877. 16°. 25646
Petite (La) Fadette. Dudevant, A. L. A. D. Paris, 1869. 16°. . 25692
Petöfi, S. *Curwen, H.* (*In* 'Sorrow and Song,' v. 1.) . . . 23285
Petrarch. *Reeve, H.* (For. Clas. for Eng. R.) Phila., [1878]. 16°. 23265
Pettigrew, J. B. Animal Locomotion. N. Y., 1874. 12°. . . 29247
Petty, H., *marquis of Lansdowne. Hayward, A.* (*In* "Biogr. and Crit. Ess.," 2d ser., v. 2. *Also in* "Selected Ess.," v. 2.) 27402 & 27245
Phantasmagoria of Fun. [Forrester, A. H.] Lond., 1843. 2 v. 12°. 25207–
Phelps, Elizabeth S. Sealed Orders [and other stories]. Bost., 1879. 24844
—— The Story of Avis. Bost., 1877. 16°. (3 copies). . . . 24845–
Phi Beta Kappa Society. *See* **Yale College,** *Phi Beta Kappa.*
Philip II., *king of Spain. Mignet, F. A. M.* Antonio Perez and Philip II. Lond., 1846. 12°. 23904
—— *Prescott, W. H.* Hist. of the Reign of Philip. Phila., 1871. 3 v. 8°. 20351–
Philip, Adventures of. Thackeray, W. M. Lond., 1872 (&c.) (2 cop.) 24874–
Philip Nolan's Friends. Hale, E. E. N. Y., 1877. 12°. . . . 24482

Phillips, H. Musical and Personal Recollections. Lond., 1864. 2 v. 23813–
Philology. Hadley, J. Essays, philological and critical. N. Y., 1873. 8°. 27860
—— Peile, J. (Literature Primers.) Lond., 1877. 16°. . . . 26859
—— *See, also,* **Language.**
Philosophy. Blackie, J. S. The Wise Men of Greece, in a series of dramatic dialogues. Lond., 1877. 12°. 26822
—— Bowen, F. Modern Philosophy, from Descartes to Schopenhauer and Hartmann. N. Y., 1877. 8°. 28282
—— Butler, W. A. Hist. of Anc. Philosophy. Phila., 1857. 2 v. . 28160–
—— Duncan, J. Colloquia Peripatetica. Edinb., 1871. 16°. . . 23655
—— Eucken, R. Fundamental Concepts of Modern Philosophic Thought. N. Y., 1880. 12°. 28088
—— Lefèvre, A. Philosophy, historical and critical. Lond., 1879. 28162
—— McCosh, J. The Scottish Philosophy. N. Y., 1875. 8°. . . 28283
—— Mallock, W. H. The New Republic. Lond., 1877. 2 v. 12°. 28082–
—— Maurice, J. F. D. Moral and Metaphysical Philosophy. Lond., 1872. 2 v. 8°. 28240–
—— Mill, J. S. An Examination of Hamilton's Philosophy. N. Y., 1874. 2 v. 12°. 28202–
—— Schwegler, A. Hist. of Philosophy in Epitome. N. Y., 1864. 28090
—— Stephen, L. Hist. of English Thought in the 18th Cent. N. Y., 1876. 2 v. 8°. 28200–
—— Taine, H. A. English Positivism : a study on J. S. Mill. Lond., 1873. 16°. 28092
—— Ueberweg, F. Hist. of Philosophy, from Thales to the present time. N. Y., 1873–4. 2 v. 8°. 28280–
See, also, **Æsthetics; Evolution; Materialism; Mind** *(and references);* **Morals; Mystics; Psychology; Spiritualism.**
—— *Natural. See* **Physics.**
Philosophy of History. *See* **History.**
Philosophy of Religion. *See* **Religion.**
Phineas Redux. Trollope, A. Lond., 1874. 2 v. 8°. *And* N. Y., 1874. 8°. . . . . 24703– & 24705
Phipson, T. L. Celebrated Violinists. Lond., 1877. 12°. . . 23816
Phœnicia. Duncker, M. W. (*In* 'Hist. of Antiquity,' v. 2.) . . 20241
Phonograph. DuMoncel, T. N. Y., 1879. 12°. 29936
—— Prescott, G. B. N. Y., 1878. 8°. 29937
Phonography. Pitman, H. Hints on Lecturing, and notes on phonography. Lond., 1879. 16°. 27835
—— Pitman, I. A Manual of Phonography. Lond., 1875. 16°. . 27834
—— — *and others.* [Phonographic Tracts.] Lond., 1877–79. 12 in 1 vol. 16°. 27838
Photography. Meteyard, E. A Group of Englishmen ; [with] the discovery of photography. Lond., 1871. 8°. 23543
—— Tissandier, G. Hist. and Handbook of Photography. Lond., 1878. 12°. 29930
—— Vogel, H. Chemistry of Light and Photography. N. Y., 1875. 29253
Physics. Gore, G. Art of Scientific Discovery. Lond., 1878. 12°. 29380

Physics. Guillemin, A. Applic. of Physical Forces. Lond., 1877. 29571
—— — The Forces of Nature. N. Y. [Lond.], 1873. 8°. . . . 29572
—— Guthrie, F. Practical Physics: molecular physics and sound. N. Y., 1879. 16°. 29351
—— Maxwell, J. C. Matter and Motion. Lond., 1876. 16°. . . 29375
—— Stewart, B. (Science Primers.) Lond., 1878. 16°. . . . 29363
—— Tait, P. G. Recent Advances in Physical Science. Lond., 1876. 29305
—— *See, also,* **Air; Chemistry; Electricity; Light; Mechanics; Nature; Pneumatics; Sound; Water.**
Physics and Politics. Bagehot, W. N. Y., 1873. 12°. . . . 29241
Physiography. Huxley, T. H. N. Y., 1878. 12°. 29419
Physiology. Beale, L. S. Bioplasm: an introd. to the study of Physiol. and Medicine. Lond., 1872. 16°. 29292
—— Bernstein, J. The Five Senses of Man. N. Y., 1876. 12°. . 29261
—— Foster, M. (Science Primers.) Lond., 1878. 16°. . . . 29355
—— — A Text Book of Physiol. [L. &] N. Y., 1880. 12°. . . 29302
—— Huxley, T. M. Lessons in Elem. Physiology. Lond., 1876. 18°. 29301
—— Wilder, B. G. What Young People should know. Bost., [1875]. 29977
—— *See, also,* **Biology** (*& references*); **Blood; Eyes; Hearing; Mental Physiolgy.**
Physiology of Mind. Maudsley, H. N. Y., 1877. 12°. . . . 28001
Piano and Song. Wieck, J. G. F. Bost., 1875. 12°. . . . 29801
Piccadilly. Oliphant, L. Ed. & Lond., 1870. 12°. 24804
Piccadilly and Pall Mall, Round about. Wheatley, H. B. Lond., 1870. 8°. 21775
Picturesque America. Bryant, W. C., *editor.* N. Y., [1872-3]. 2 v. ——
Piedmont, Hist. of. Gallenga, A. Lond., 1855. 3 v. 12°. . . 20000–
Pierce, E. L. Mem. and Letters of Chas. Sumner. Bost., 1877. 2 v. 8°. 22683–
Pike, R. *Pike, J. S.* The New Puritan; New England 200 years ago. N. Y., 1879. 12°. 22644
Pilgerzug nach Mekka. Hackländer, F. W. von. Stuttg., 1863. 16°. (Werke, B. 14.) 25806
Pillars of the House. Yonge, C. M. Lond., 1874. 2 v. 12°. . 24297–
Pilot (The) and his Wife. Lie, J. Chic., 1876. 12°. 24210
Pindar. *Morice, F. D.* (Anc. Clas. for Engl. Readers, suppl. ser., v. 8.) 26854
Pioneering in South Brazil. Bigg-Wither, T. P. Lond., 1878. 2 v. 21702–
Pioneers of France in the New World. Parkman, F. Bost., 1865. 8°. (2 copies.) 6130–
Piozzi, Hester L., (*Mrs. Thrale.*) Anecdotes of Sam. Johnson. Lond., 1786. 12°. 18641
—— Observations and Reflections [on] a Journey through France, Italy and Germany. Lond., 1789. 2 v. 8°. 18609–
Pitman, H. Hints on Lecturing [etc.]. Lond., 1879. 16°. . . 27835
Pitman, I. Manual of Phonography. Lond., 1875. 16°. . . 27834
—— *editor.* Memorial of F. [F.] Barham: autobiographical and other compositions. (Printed phonetically, except pref., of 55 pp.) Lond., 1873. 12°. 27839
—— — Plea for Spelling Reform. Lond., 1878. 16°. (2 copies.) . 27836–

Pitman, I., *and others.* Phonographic Teacher [and other works on phonography]. Lond., 1877–79. 16°. 27838

Pitt, Wm., *earl of Chatham. See* **Adams, W. H. D.,** 'Eng. Party Leaders,' v. 1 (21054); **Earle, J. C.,** 'Eng. Premiers,' v. 1 (22882); **Lamartine, A. M. L. de,** 'Biogr.', v. 1 (23727).

Pitt, Wm., *the younger. See* **Adams, W. H. D.,** 'Eng. Party Leaders,' v. 1–2 (21054–); **Earle, J. C.,** 'Eng. Premiers,' v. 2 (22883); **Lamartine, A. M. L. de,** 'Biogr.,' v. 1 (23727); **Macaulay, T. B.,** 'Miscel.,' Lond., 1871 (27406).

Pius IX., *Pope. Gladstone, W. E.* Speeches of the Pope. (*In* 'Rome,' etc.) 28724

—— *Legge, A. O.* Pius IX.: his life to 1850. Lond., 1875. 2 v. 8°. 22185–

—— *Trollope, T. A.* Life of Pius IX. Lond., 1877. 2 v. 8°. . . 22183–

Planché, J. R. The Conqueror and his Companions. Lond., 1874. 2 v. 8°. 23000–

—— Personal Reminiscences. (*In* **Stoddard, R. H.,** 'Bric-à-Brac Series.') 23256

—— Recollections and Reflections. Lond., 1872. 2 v. 8°. . . 23452–

Plantagenets, Early. Stubbs, W. N. Y., [1876]. 16°. . . . 20455

Plants. Darwin, C. R. Insectivorous Plants. N. Y., 1875. 12°. . 29457

—— — Movements and Habits of Climbing Plants. Lond., 1875. . 29453

Plato. *Collins, C. W.* (Anc. Classics for Eng. Readers, v. 19.) . 26845

Plautus. *Collins, W. L.* (*In* 'Anc. Classics for Eng. Readers,' v. 16.) 26842

Play-Day Poems. Johnson, R. N. Y., 1878. 16°. 26032

Plays. Dodsley, R. Select Collection of Old Eng. Plays. 4th ed. Lond., 1874–76. 15 v. 12°. (*For contents see* **Dodsley.**) . 26600–

—— Morley, H., *editor.* English Plays. Lond., [1879]. 8°. . . 26370

—— Plays for Private Acting; transl. from the French and Ital. by members of the Bellevue Dramatic Club of Newport. N. Y., 1878. 16°. 26518

—— Sargent E., *& others, editors.* Modern Standard Drama. N. Y., 1847 (etc.). 2 v. 12°. (*For contents see* **Sargent.**) . . 26487–

—— *See, also,* **Drama.**

Pleasant Days in Pleasant Places. Walford, E. Lond., 1879. 12°. 21262

Plébiscite. Erckmann (E.) & Chatrian (A.). N. Y., 1877. 19°. . 24439

Pliny's Letters. Church (A. J.) & Brodribb. (Anc. Clas. for Eng. Readers, v. 11.) 26837

Plumptre, C. J. King's College Lectures on Elocution. Lond., 1876. 8°. 27820

Plumptre, E. H. St. Paul in Asia Minor. Lond., [1878]. 16°. . 28499

—— Tragedies of Sophocles: a new transl., with essay. Lond., 1871. 12°. 26821

Plutarch, Shakespeare's: a selection illustrating S.'s plays. By W. W. Skeat. Lond., 1875. 12°. 27009

Pneumatics. Pepper, J. H. Lond., [1874]. 12°. 29315

—— *See, also,* **Aeronautics.**

Poacher (The). Marryat, F. N. Y., 1861. 12°. 24646

Poe, E. A. Poems. With memoir by R. H. Stoddard. N. Y., 1875. 26033

—— Works. Ed. by John H. Ingram. Edinb., 1874–5. 4 v. 12°. 27323–

CONTENTS:—1, Memoir; Tales.—2, Tales.—3, Poems and Essays.—4, Autobiography; Criticisms.

Poe, E. A. *Curwen, H.* (*In* 'Sorrow and Song,' v. 2.) 23286
—— *Gill, W. F.* The Life of Poe. N. Y., etc., 1877. 12°. . . . 22604
—— *Rice, S. S.* E. A. Poe: a memorial volume. Balt., 1877. 8°. 22685
Poet and Merchant. Auerbach, B. N. Y., 1877. 16°. 24048
Poetry. Aikin, J. (*In* 'Essays.') 18615
—— [Bathurst, C.] Differences in Shakespeare's Versification [etc.]. Lond., 1857. 16°. 27011
—— Brown, J. Ethics and Æsthetics of Modern Poetry. Lond., 1878. 26293
—— Doyle, F. H. Lectures on Poetry. 2d ser. Lond., 1877. 12°. 26286
—— Lessing, G. E. Laocoon: an essay upon the limits of painting and poetry. Bost., 1874. 16°. 26290
—— MacDonald, G. England's Antiphon. [On her religious poetry; with examples. Lond., 1868.] 12°. 26125
—— Pater, W. The Renaissance: studies in art and poetry. Lond., 1877. 8°. 29878
—— Shairp, J. C. On Poetic Interpretation of Nature. Edinb., 1877. 12°. 26294
—— Symonds, J. A. Blank Verse [etc.]. (*In* 'Sketches and Stud.,' v. 2.) 27342
—— Taylor, H. Critical Essays on Poetry. Lond., 1878. 12°. . 26296
—— *See, also,* **Literature; Poets; Sonnet; Verse.**
—— *Collections (English).* Bryant, W. C. Library of Poetry and Song. N. Y., 1874. 8°. 26273
—— — Coates, H. T. Fireside Encyclopædia of Poetry. Phila., [1878]. 8°. 26380
—— — Emerson, R. W. Parnassus. Bost., 1875. 12°. . . . 26120
—— — Fields (J. T.) & Whipple (E. P.). Family Library of British Poetry. Bost., 1878. 8°. 26381
—— — Harvard Advocate, Verses from. Cambr., 1876. 16°. . . 26017
—— — Johnson, R. Play-Day Poems. N. Y., 1878. 16°. . . 26032
—— — — Single Famous Poems. N. Y., 1877. 12°. . . . 26022
—— — Longfellow, H. W. Poems of Places. Bost., 1876–79. 31 v. 16°. (*For contents see* **Longfellow.**) 26440–
—— — A Masque of Poets. Bost., 1878. 16°. 26027
—— — Morley, H. Shorter English Poems. Lond., [1876]. 8°. . 26368
—— — Oliphant, T. La Musa Madrigalesca. Lond., 1837. 12°. . 26163
—— — Percy, T. Reliques of Anc. Eng. Poetry. Ed. by G. Gilfillan. Edinb., 1858. 3 v. 8°. 26343–
—— — Seven (The) Great Hymns of the Mediæval Church. N. Y., 1868. 16°. 766
—— — Whittier, J. G. Songs of Three Centuries. Bost., 1876. 12°. 26141
See, also, **Ballads; Minstrelsy; Poets; Songs; Sonnets.**
—— *French.* Besant, W. Studies in Early Fr. Poetry. Lond., 1868. 26280
—— — Lang, A. Ballads and Lyrics of Old France. Lond., 1872. 26026
—— *German.* Mangan, J. C. Anthologia Germanica: translations from the German poets. Dubl., 1845. 2 v. in 1. 16°. . 26030
—— *Polish.* Klaczko, J. Polish Poetry in the 19th Cent. (*With* **Krasinski, S.,** 'Undivine Comedy.') 26121
—— *Provençal.* Breymann, H. (*In* **Owens College** Ess. and Ad.) 27412

Poetry. *Scottish.* Irving, D. Hist. of Scottish Poetry. Edinb., 1861. 8°. 26288
——— Veitch, J. History and Poetry of the Scottish Border. Glasgow, 1878. 12°. 26298
——— Wilson, J. G. Poets and Poetry of Scotland. N. Y., 1876. 2 v. 8°. 26270–
Poets. Dodd, H. P. The Epigrammatists. Lond., 1870. 12°. . 26925
—— *English.* Brooke, S. A. Theology in the Eng. Poets. Cowper, Coleridge, Wordsworth, and Burns. Lond., 1874. 8°. . . 26281
——— Burroughs, J. Birds and Poets. N. Y., 1877. 16°. . . 29322
——— Deshler, C. D. Afternoons with the Poets. N. Y., 1879. 26284
——— Devey, J. Comparative Estimate of Mod. Eng. Poets. Lond., 1873. 12°. 26285
——— Forman, H. B. Our Living Poets: an essay in criticism. Lond., 1871. 12°. 26287
——— Gilfillan, G. Specimens, with Memoirs, of the less-known Brit. Poets. Edinb., 1860. 3 v. 8°. 26354–
CONTENTS:—1, 1st period, 1800–1556.—1–2, 2d period, 1550–1640.—3, 3d period, 1640–1800.
——— Hamilton, W. The Poets Laureate of Eng.: a history of the office, notices of its holders, and a collection of the satires [etc.] against them. Lond., 1879. 12°. 23288
——— Minto, W. Characteristics of Eng. Poets, from Chaucer to Shirley. Edinb. & L., 1874. 12°. 26291
——— Rossetti, W. M. Lives of Famous Poets. Lond., 1878. 12°. 23289
——— Stedman, E. C. Victorian Poets. Bost., 1876. 12°. . . 26295
——— Ward, T. H. The Eng. Poets: selections, with critical introductions by various writers, and a general introd. by M. Arnold. Lond., 1880. v. 1–2. 12°. 26174–
CONTENTS:—1, Chaucer to Donne.—2, Ben Jonson to Dryden.
—— *French.* James H., jr. Lond., 1878. 12°. 26905
—— *Greek.* Symonds, J. A. Studies. Lond., 1873–76. 2 v. 12°. 26809–
———— *Same,* [re-arranged, rev. & enl.] N. Y., 1880. 2 v. 16°. . 26811–
Poganuc People. Stowe, H. B. N. Y., [1878]. 12°. (2 copies.) 24823–
Polar Regions. *See* **Arctic** Regions.
Polaris Expedition. Blake, E. V. (*In* 'Arctic Exp.') . . . 21880
Pole, W. Life of Sir Wm. Fairbairn. Lond., 1877. 8°. . . . 23540
—— Short Whist. (*See* **Coles, B. C.**)
—— Theory of Whist. Lond., 1878. 16°. 29685
Political Adventures of Lord Beaconsfield. [Hill, F. H.] N. Y., [1878]. 16°. 22851
Political Economy. About, E. F. V. Handbook of Social Economy. N. Y., 1873. 12°. 28880
—— Bagehot, W. Economic Studies. Lond., 1880. 8°. (*For contents see* **Bagehot.**) 29166
—— Bastiat, F. Essays on Political Econ. N. Y., 1874. 16°. . 28801
——— *Same,* rev., with notes by D. A. Wells. N. Y., 1877. 12°. . 28802
—— Blanqui, J. A. Hist. of Pol. Ec. in Europe. With a pref. by D. A. Wells. N. Y., 1880. 8°. 29163
—— Brassey, T. Foreign Work and English Wages, considered with ref. to the depression of trade. Lond., 1879. 8°. . 29001

Political Economy. Cairnes, J. E. Character and Logical Method of Pol. Ec. N. Y., 1875. 12°. 28803
——— Essays in Pol. Ec., theoretical and applied. Lond., 1873. 8°. 29167
——— Some Leading Principles of Pol. Ec. Lond., 1874. 8°. . 29168
—— Fawcett, H. Free Trade and Protection. Lond., 1878. 12° . 28804
——— Manual of Pol. Ec. Lond., 1874. 12°. 28805
—— George, H. Progress and Poverty. N. Y., 1880. 12°. . . 28806
—— Greeley, H. Essays [on] Pol. Ec., serving to explain and defend the policy of protection. Bost., 1871. 16°. 28807
—— Howell, G. Conflicts of Capital and Labour. Lond., 1878. 12°. 29007
—— Jevons, W. S. (Science Primers.) Lond., 1878. 16°. . . . 29360
——— Theory of Pol. Ec. Lond., 1879. 8°. 29169
—— Perry, A. L. Elements of Pol. Ec. N. Y., 1866. 8°. . . 8639
——— *Same.* 2d ed., rev. N. Y., 1867. 8°. 28809
——— Introduction to Pol. Ec. N. Y., 1877. 12°. 28808
—— Rogers, J. E. T. Cobden and Modern Political Opinion. Lond., 1873. 8°. 29088
——— Social Economy. Rev. for Amer. readers. N. Y., 1872. 12°. 28884
—— Roscher, W. G. F. Principles of Pol. Ec. N. Y., 1878. 2 v. 8°. 29161–
—— Smith, Adam. Wealth of Nations. Ed. by J. E. T. Rogers. Oxf'd, 1869. 2 v. 8°. 29164–
—— Stephen, L. (*In* 'Hist. of Eng. Thought.') 28200
—— Thompson, R. E. Social Science and National Economy. Phila., 1875. 12°. 28810

See, also, **Banking** (*& references*); **Commerce; Communism; Co-operation; Corn Laws; Finance; Labor; Population; Protection; Social Science** (*& references*); **Socialism; Taxation; Wages.**

Political Science & Politics. Bagehot, W. Physics and Politics. N. Y., 1873. 12°. 29241
—— Duff, M. E. G. Studies in European Politics. Edinb., 1866. 8°. 20567
—— Freeman, E. A. Comparative Politics. N. Y., 1874. 8°. . 20183
—— Harrison, F. Order and Progress. Part 1: Thoughts on government. Pt. 2: Studies of political crises. Lond., 1875. 8°. 29087
—— Lieber, F. Civil Liberty and Self-Government. Phila., 1874. 8°. 29082
——— Manual of Political Ethics. Phila., 1875. 2 v. 8°. . . 29080–
—— Mivart, St. G. Political Evolution. (*In* 'Contemp. Ev.') . . 29394
—— Montesquieu, C. de S. de. Spirit of Laws. Lond., 1878. 2 v. 12°. 28849–
—— Morley, J. On Compromise. Lond., 1874. 8°. 29089
—— Nordhoff, C. Politics for Young Americans. N. Y., 1875. (2 cop.) 21329–
—— Quincy, J. P. Protection of Majorities. Bost., 1876. 12°. . 29093
—— Rogers, J. E. T. Cobden and Modern Political Opinion. Lond., 1873. 8°. 29088
—— Skinner, O. Issues of American Politics. Phila., 1873. (2 cop.) 21327
—— Stephen, L. (*In* 'Hist. of Eng. Thought.') 28200
—— Tremenheere, H. S. Political Experience of the Ancients, in its bearing upon modern times. Lond., 1852. 16°. . . 20048
—— Woolsey, T. D. N. Y., 1878. 2 v. 8°. (2 copies.) . . . 29083–

See, also, **Civil Service; Colonies; Democracy; England,** *Const. and Laws;* **Franchise; Government; Liberty; Parties; Representation; Slavery; Social** Science; **U. S.,** *Constitution, History;* **Whig Party.**

Polko, Elise. Musical Tales, Phantasms, and Sketches. 2d series. Lond., 1877. 12°. 24808
—— Reminiscences of Mendelssohn. N. Y., 1869. 16°. . . . 23773
Pollen, J. H. Anc. and Mod. Furniture and Woodwork. N. Y., 1876. 12°. 29766
—— Gold and Silver Smiths' Work. Lond., [1879]. 12°. . . . 29767
Pollock, W. H. Amateur Theatricals. By W. H. Pollock and Lady Pollock. Lond., 1879. 12°. 26519
Polycarp, *St. Holland, H. S.* (*In* 'The Apostolic Fathers.') . . 28502
Polynesia. Murray, A. W. Forty Years' Mission Work in Polynesia. Lond., 1876. 12°. 22146
—— Wood, J. G. Natural Hist. of Man. (Vol. 2.) 29591
—— *See, also,* **Hawaiian** Islands; **Oceanica; South** Seas.
Polynia, Gateway to the. Wells, J. C. Lond., 1873. 8°. . . 21887
Poole, F. Queen Charlotte Islands. Lond., 1872. 8°. . . . 21583
Poole, John, (*pseud.*, 'Paul Pry.') Oddities of Lond. Life. L., 1838. 2 v. 8°. 25209–
—— Sketches and Recollections. Lond., 1835. 2 v. 12°. . . 18563–
Poole, S. L. Life of Edward William Lane. Lond., 1877. 8°. . 23425
Poor, H. V. Money and its Laws. N. Y., 1877. 8°. . . . 29043
Poor Relations. Balzac, H. de. Lond., 1880. 12°. 24056
Popanilla. Disraeli, B. N. Y. [Lond., 1878.] . . . 24238 & 24252
Pope, Alex. Essay on Man. Ed. by M. Pattison. Oxf., 1875. 16°. 26108
—— Odyssey of Homer, transl. With notes by J. S. Watson. Lond., 1867. 12°. 26815
—— Poetical Works. Ed. by R. Carruthers. Lond., 1858. 2 v. 12°. 26105–
—— — With mem. [etc.] by G. Gilfillan. Edinb., 1856. 2 v. 8°. . 26346–
—— — Ed., with notes and memoir, by A. W. Ward. Lond., 1879. 26107
—— Satires and Epistles. Ed. by M. Pattison. Oxford, 1874. 16°. 26109
—— Selected Poems; Essay on Criticism; Moral Essays; Dunciad. Ed., by T. Arnold. Lond., 1876. 16°. 26104
—— Works. [Ed.] by J. Warton. Lond., 1799. 9 v. 8°. . . 18711–
—— *Stephen, L.* (Eng. Men of Letters.) N. Y., 1880. 12°. . . 23349
—— *See, also,* **Dennis, J.,** 'Studies' (26915); **Dilke, C. W.,** 'Papers,' v. 1 (26765); **Sainte-Beuve, C. A.,** 'Eng. Portraits' (22885); **Stephen, L.,** 'Hours,' v. 1 (26933).
Popes. Trollope, T. A. Papal Conclaves as they were and as they are. Lond., 1876. 8°. 28722
—— *See, also,* **Papacy; Rom. Cath. Ch.**
Popular Science Monthly. N. Y., 1872–79. 15 v. 8°. . . . 17679–
Popular Science Review. Lond., 1862–76. 15 v. 8°. . . . 17728–
Population. Walker, F. A. (*In* **First Cent.** of the Republic.) . 21520
Porcelain. *See* **Pottery.**
Porter, *Sir* **Jas.** Turkey. Continued, with memoir, by G. Larpent. Lond., 1854. 2 v. 8°. 20615–
Porter, N. Amer. Colleges and the Amer. Public. N. H., 1870. 12°. 9254
—— *Same.* New ed.; with after-thoughts on college and school education. N. Y., [1878]. 12°. 28837
—— Books and Reading. N. Y., 1871. 12°. (2 copies.) . . . 122–

Porter, N. *Same.* 4th ed., with an index. N. Y., 1876. 12°. (2 copies.) 26928–
Portland, *Dukes of. See* **Bentinck.**
Portugal. Bollaert, W. Wars of Succession of Portugal and Spain, from 1827 to 1840; with résumé of the political hist. to the present time. Lond., 1870. 2 v. 8°. 20709–
—— Jackson, C. C. Fair Lusitania. Lond., 1874. 8°. . . . 21969
—— Longfellow, H. W. Poems of Places, v. 15. Bost., 1877. 16°. 26454
—— Southey, R. Letters [from] Spain and Portugal. Bristol & L., 1799. 8°. 18571
Positivism on an Island. Mallock, W. H. N. Y. [Lond.], 1878. 12°. 28084
Potter, Louisa. Lancashire Memories. Lond., 1879. 12°. . . 23686
Pottery and Porcelain. Prime, W. C. N. Y., 1878. 8°. . . . 29924
—— *See, also,* **Maiolica.**
Pottleton Legacy. Albert Smith. Lond., 1852. 12°. . . . 24821
Poushkin. *See* **Pushkin.**
Powell, F. Y. Early England. (*In* **Epochs** of Eng. Hist.) . . 20851
[**Poynter,** *Miss* **E. F.**] Ersilia. N. Y., 1876. 16°. 24848
—— My Little Lady. N. Y., 1872. 16°. (2 copies.) . . . 2372–
Poynter, E. J. Ten Lectures on Art. Lond., 1879. 8°. . . 29820
Prairie and Forest. Gillmore, P. N. Y., 1874. 12°. . . . 29620
Praise of Folly. Erasmus, D. Lond. 16°. 12910
Prantl, C. Elem. Text-book of Botany. Lond., 1880. 8°. . . 29450
Pratt, S. J., (*pseud.,* 'Courtney Melmoth.') Emma Corbett. 4th ed. Lond. [1st ed., 1781.] 3 v. 16°. 17792–
—— Shenstone Green. Lond., 1779. 3 v. 16°. 18687–
Prayer. Hessey, J. A. Lond., 1873. 12°. 28511
—— Tyndall, J., *and others.* The Prayer-Gauge Debate. Bost., 1876. 28093
Preaching. Spurgeon, C. H. Lectures to my Students. N. Y., 1875. 12°. 28546
—— Storrs, R. S. Preaching without Notes. N. Y., 1875. 12°. . 28415
—— Yale Lectures on Preaching. . . . . 9919 & 28416–
CONTENTS:—1872-74, H. W. Beecher, 3 series.—1875, J. Hall.—1876, W. M. Taylor.—1877, P. Brooks (*2 copies*).—1878, R. W. Dale (*2 copies*).—1879, M. Simpson.—1879-80, H. Crosby.
—— *See, also,* **Rhetoric** (*and references*).
Preadamites. Winchell, A. Chic., 1880. 8°. 29387
Precious Stones. Dieulafait, L. N. Y., 1876. 12°. 10134
Pre-historic Man. *See* **Man,** *Pre-historic.*
Pre-historic Races of the U. S. of A. Foster, J. W. Chic., 1873. 8°. 21401
Prejevalski, N. M. From Kulja to Lob-Nor. Lond., 1879. 8°. . 21929
—— Mongolia, the Tangut Country, and the Solitudes of Northern Tibet. Lond., 1876. 2 v. 8°. 21927–
Prentice, G. D. Poems. Ed., with a biog. sketch, by J. J. Piatt. Cincin., 1876. 12°. 26127
Prescott, G. B. Speaking Telephone, Talking Phonograph, and other novelties. N. Y., 1878. 8°. 29937
Prescott, Harriet E. *See* **Spofford, Harriet E. P.**
Prescott, W. H. Hist. of Charles V. (*See* **Robertson, W.**)
—— Hist. of the Conquest of Mexico. Phila., 1871. 3 v. 8°. . 20340–

Prescott, W. H. Hist. of the Conquest of Peru. Phila., 1871. 2 v. 8°. 20343–
—— Reign of Ferdinand and Isabella. Phila., 1871. 3 v. 8°. . 20345–
—— Reign of Philip II., King of Spain. Phila., 1871. 3 v. 8°. 20351–
Press (The). *See* **Journalism; Newspapers.**
Preston, Harriet W. Mirèio: a Provençal poem, by F. Mistral; transl. [into Eng. verse]. Bost., 1872. 12°. 26126
—— Troubadours and Trouvères, new and old. Bost., 1876. 12°. . 26906
Pretenders (The), and their Adherents. Jesse, J. H. Lond., 1845. 2 v. 8°. 23030–
—— *See, also,* **Charles Edward Stuart.**
Pretty Miss Bellew. [Havers, D.] N. Y., 1875. 16°. . . . 24499
Price, B. Currency and Banking. N. Y., 1876. 12°. (2 copies.) . 29056–
Prime, S. I. Life of S. F. B. Morse. N. Y., 1875. 8°. 22721
Prime, W. C. Holy Cross. N. Y., [1877]. 16°. 28510
—— I go a-fishing. N. Y., 1873. 8°. 29628
—— Pottery and Porcelain. N. Y., 1878 [1877]. 8°. . . . 29924
Prime (The) Minister. Trollope, A. Phila., [1876]. 12°. . . 24873
Prince (The) of Wales in India. Gay, J. D. N. Y., 1877. 12°. . 21246
Prince (The) of Wales' Tour. Russell, W. H. Lond., 1877. 2 v. 8°. 21967–
Prince-Caniche (Le). Laboulaye, E. R. F. Paris, 1877. 16°. . 25668
Princess of Thule. Black, W. Lond., 1875. 12°. (5 copies.) . 24018–
Princesses of England. *See* **England,** *Princesses of.*
Prior, J. Life of Edmond Malone. Lond., 1860. 8°. 23451
Prior, M. Poetical Works. With mem. [etc.] by G. Gilfillan. Edinb., 1858. 8°. 26348
Prisons and Prisoners. Griffiths, A. Memorials of Millbank, and Chapters in Prison Hist. Lond., 1875. 2 v. 12°. . . 28858–
—— Five Years' Penal Servitude. Lond., 1878. 12°. 28857
Probation: a novel. Fothergill, J. N. Y., 1879. 16°. 24443
Problematische Naturen. Spielhagen, F. Leipz., 1876. 2 B. 16°. (Sämmtl. Werke, B. 1–2.) 25860–
Procter, Adelaide A. Legends and Lyrics. Lond., 1872–3. 2 v. 26034–
Procter, B. W., (*pseud.,* 'Barry Cornwall.') Autobiographical Fragment and Biographical Notes; with un-pub. lyrics. Bost., 1877. 12°. 23218
Proctor, R. A. Flowers of the Sky. N. Y., [1879]. 16°. . . 29442
—— The Moon. Lond., 1873. 12°. 29443
—— Myths and Marvels of Astronomy. N. Y., 1877. 8°. . . 29449
—— A New Star Atlas. Lond., 1877. 12°. 29446
—— Our Place among Infinities. N. Y., 1876. 12°. . . . 29447
—— Rough Ways made Smooth. N. Y., 1880. 12°. 29444
—— Science Byways. Phila. [Lond.], 1876. 12°. 29445
—— Transits of Venus. Lond., 1874. 12°. 29448
Profession. Hale, E. E. What Career? Ten papers on the choice of a vocation. Bost., 1878. 16°. 27385
—— *See, also,* **Life** (*conduct and philosophy of*).
Progress and Poverty. George, H. N. Y., 1880. 12°. . . . 28806
Prolusions. Turner, S. Lond., 1819. 16°. 18676

Propertius. *Davies, J.* (Anc. Clas. for Eng. Readers, supplemen. ser., v. 3.) 26849
Prophet (Der). Mügge, T. Breslau, 1867. 3 B. 16°. (Romane, B. 31–33.) 25850
Prophet (The): a tragedy. Taylor, J. B. Bost., 1874. 16°. . . 26172
Proserpina. Ruskin, J. N. Y., 1875–77. 2 v. 12°. . . . 29840–
Prosody. *See* **Verse.**
Prosper Randoce. Cherbuliez, V. Paris, 1874. 16°. . . . 25624
—— *Same, transl.* N. Y., 1874. 16°. 24168
Protection, Hist. of, in the U. S. Sumner, W. G. N. Y., 1877. 8°. (2 copies.) 29170–
Protestant Epis. Ch. (U. S.), Hist. of. Spencer, J. A. (*In* **Perry, G. G.,** 'Hist. of the Ch. of Eng.') 28443
Protestant Revolution. *See* **Reformation.**
Proteus and Amadeus. De Vere, A. T. Lond., 1878. 12°. . . 28169
Prothero, G. W. Life of Simon de Montfort. Lond., 1877. 12°. 22881
Protoplasm. Beale, L. S. Lond., 1874. 12°. 29297
Prout, *Father,* (*pseud.*) *See* **Mahony, F. S.**
Prout, T. Bob Norberry. Dublin, 1844. 8°. 24680
Provençal Poetry. *See* **Poetry,** *Provençal.*
Proverbs. Bohn, H. G. A Polyglot of Foreign Proverbs. Lond., 1867. 12°. 26940
—— *See, also,* **Quotations** (*& references*).
Prudence Palfrey. Aldrich, T. B. Bost., 1874. 12°. . . . 24036

Prussia. *History.*
—— Wyatt, W. J. Hist. of Prussia. Lond., 1876. v. 1–2. 8°. . 20645–
CONTENTS:—1, 700 to 1390.—2, 1390 to 1525.
—— (*to* 1786) Ranke, F. L. von. House of Brandenburg. Lond., 1849. 3v. 8°. 20651–
—— (*to* 1810) Hudson, E. H. Life and Times of Louisa, with an introductory sketch. Lond., 1874. 2 v. 12°. 22507–
—— (1745–1814) Voss, S. M. von P. von. Sixty-nine Years at the Court of Prussia. Lond., 1876. 2 v. 12°. 22509–
—— (1806–1822) Seeley, J. R. Life and Times of Stein. Bost., 1879. 2 v. 8°. 22580–
—— (1866) Malet, A. Overthrow of the Germanic Confederation. Lond., 1870. 8°. 20643
Pry, Paul, (*pseud.*) *See* **Poole, J.**
Psalms (The), Origin and Growth of. Murray, T. C. N. Y., 1880. 28530
Psyche (A) of To-day. Jenkin, C. N. Y., 1868. 16°. . . . 24583
Psychology. Bascom, J. Comparative Psychology. N. Y., 1878. 28207
—— McCosh, J. The Emotions. N. Y., 1880. 12°. . . . 28170
—— Maudsley, H. Body and Mind. [With] psychological essays. N. Y., 1875. 12°. 28000
—— Taine, H. A. On Intelligence. N. Y., 1875. 2 v. 12°. . . 28205–
—— *See, also,* **Mental Physiology; Philosophy.**
Puliga, *Comtesse de.* Madame de Sévigné. Lond., 1873. 2 v. 8°. . 23414–
Pulling, F. S. Sir Joshua Reynolds. L. & N. Y., 1880. 12°. . 23792
Punch. [Weekly.] Lond., 1841–79. 74 v. in 39. 4°. . . . . ——

Punch. Punch's twenty Almanacks, 1842–1861. 1 v. Lond. 4°. . ——
—— Benj. Disraeli: in 100 cartoons. Lond., 1878. 4°. . . . . ——
—— W. E. Gladstone: cartoons. Lond., 1878. 4°. . . . . . ——
Punch and Judy: with 24 illust. by Geo. Cruikshank. Lond., 1873. 26489
Pupper, Joh., (John of Goch.) *Ullmann, C.* (*In* 'Reformers' etc., v. 1.) 22300
Puritan Nomenclature. Bardsley, C. W. N. Y. [Lond.], 1880. 12°. 27867
Puritanism. Bacon, L. Genesis of the New Eng. Churches. N. Y., 1874. 8°. 28447
Pushkin, A. S. Marie: a story of Russian love. Chic., 1877. 16°. 24849
—— Russian Romance[s]. Lond., 1880. 12°. 24809

CONTENTS:—The Captain's Daughter (*the same as* "Marie" *above*); The Lady-rustic; The Pistol-shot; The Snow-storm; The Undertaker; The Station-master; The Moor of Peter the Great.

Putnam, G. P. World's Progress: a dict. of dates. N. Y., 1878. 8°. ——
Putnam, Israel, Life of. Tarbox, I. N. Bost., 1876. 8°. . . 22691
Putnam's Library Companion. Perkins, F. B., *editor.* N. Y., 1878–80. 3 v. 8°. . . . . ——
Pyramid, Our Inheritance in the Great. Piazzi Smyth. Lond., 1874. 21695
Pyrenees, Tour through the. Taine, H. A. N. Y., 1874. 12°. . 21627
Quarles, F. Emblems. With mem. [etc.] by G. Gilfillan. Edinb., 1857. 8°. 26335
—— Enchiridion. Lond., 1856. 16°. 27263
Quarterly Review. Lond. & N. Y., 1809–79. v. 1–12, 14–28, 30–33, 35–38, 41–148. 8°. 11470–
—— *Same.* v. 1–16, 18–48, 50–127. 11310–
—— Indexes to v. 1–60, in 3 v. 8°. . . . . ——
Quatrefages de Bréau, J. L. A. de. The Human Species. N. Y., 1879. 12°. (2 copies.) 29267–
—— Metamorphoses of Man and the Lower Animals. Lond., 1864. 29303
Queen Charlotte Islands. Poole, F. Lond., 1872. 8°. . . . 21583
Queen Mary: a drama. Tennyson, A. Bost., 1875. 12°. (2 cop.) 26516–
Queen of Sheba. Aldrich, T. B. Bost., 1877. 16°. 24037
Queer (A) Book. [Hogg, J.] Edinb. & L., 1832. 16°. . . . 26114
Quincy, J. P. Protection of Majorities; with other papers. Bost., 1876. 12°. 29093
Quixstar. [Taylor, E.] N. Y., 1873. 16°. 24826
Quorndon Hounds. Herbert, H. W. (*In* 'Sporting Scenes,' v. 2.) 29603
Quotations. Allibone, S. A. Poetical Quotations. Phil., 1879. 8°. 26761
—— — Prose Quotations. Phil., 1879. 8°. 26760
—— Finod, J. de. A Thousand Flashes of French Wit, Wisdom, and Wickedness. N. Y., 1880. 16°. 26941
—— *See also,* **Common-place Books; Proverbs; Table-talk.**
Rabelais, F. *Besant, W.* (For. Clas. for Eng. Readers, v. 8.) Phila., [1879]. 16°. 23269
—— — (*In* 'French Humourists.') 26776
Races. Brown, R. The Races of Mankind. Lond., [1874–76]. 4 v. 8°. 29575–
—— Peschel, O. The Races of Man. Lond., 1876. 8°. . . . 29386
—— Winchell, A. Preadamites. Chic., 1880. 8°. 29387
—— *See, also,* **Ethnology; Man.**

Radcliffe, Ann. The Romance of the Forest. Lond., 1806. 3 v. 12°. 18690–
Rae, W. F. Wilkes, Sheridan, Fox. Lond., 1874. 8°. . . . 23040
Rahel. *See* **Varnhagen von Ense, R. A. F. L.**
Raikes, T. Personal Reminiscences. (*In* **Stoddard, R. H.**, 'Bric-à-Brac Series.') 23258
Railroads. Adams, C. F. Notes on Railroad Accidents. N. Y., 1879. 12°. 29933
—— — Railroads: their origin and problems. N. Y., 1878. (2 cop.) 29931–
—— Jevons, W. S. Railways and the State. (*In* **Owens College** Ess. & Ad.) 27412
Raleigh, *Sir* Walter. *Creighton, L.* N. Y., 1877. 16°. 22447
—— *St. John, J. A.* Lond., 1869. 12°. 22889
Ralph Wilton's Weird. Hector, A. F. N. Y., 1875. 16°. (2 cop.) 24531–
Ralston, W. R. S. Early Russian Hist. Lond., 1874. 16°. . . 20499
—— Russian Folk-tales. Lond., 1873. 8°. 27783
—— Songs of the Russian People. Lond., 1872. 8°. . . . 27782
Rambaud, A. Hist. of Russia. Lond., 1879. 2 v. 8°. . . . 20611–
Randolph, T. Poetical and Dramatic Works. Lond., 1875. 12°. . 26036
Ranke, F. L. von. Civil Wars and Monarchy in France. N. Y., 1853. 12°. 20412
—— Hist. of England. Oxf'd, 1875. 6 v. 8°. (2 copies.) . . 21040–
CONTENTS:—1, Crises in the earlier hist., 1603–29.—2, 1629–49.—3, 1649–74.—4, 1675–91.—5, 1690–1760; App., orig. doc.—6, App., etc.
—— Memoirs of the House of Brandenburg. Lond., 1849. 3 v. 8°. 20651–
Rankine, W. J. M. Songs and Fables. Glasgow & L., 1874. 12°. 26110
Raphael. *Clément, C.* Lond., 1880. 12°. 23837
—— *Passavant, J. D.* Lond. & N. Y., 1879. 12°. 23779
—— *Perkins, C. C.* Bost., 1878. 8°. 23835
Rassam, H. Brit. Mission to Theodore, King of Abyssinia. Lond., 1869. 2 v. 8°. 5659–
Rationalism. Chadwick, J. W. The Faith of Reason. Bost., 1879. 28691
—— Fisher, G. P. Faith and Rationalism. N. Y., 1879. 12°. (2 cop.) 28589–
Ravenstein (E. G.) & Hulley (J.). Handb. of Gymnastics and Athletics. Lond., 1867. 8°. 29637
Rawlinson, G. Origin of Nations. In 2 pts.: On early civilizations; On ethnic affinities. N. Y., 1878. 12°. 20047
—— St. Paul in Damascus and Arabia. Lond., [1878]. 16°. . . 28498
—— Sixth Great Oriental Monarchy. Lond., 1873. 8°. . . . 20249
—— Seventh Great Oriental Monarchy. Lond., 1876. 8°. . . 20250
Raymond, J. G. Life of Thos. Dermody. Lond., 1806. 2 v. 12°. 18554–
Raymond, R. W. Camp and Cabin. N. Y., 1880. 16°. . . . 29661
Raymonde. Theuriet, A. N. Y., 1878. 16°. 24927
Reach, A. B. *See* **Man** in the Moon.
Read, T. B. Poetical Works. Phila., 1874. 3 v. 16°. . . . 26111–
Reade, C. Cloister and the Hearth. Bost., 1872. 16°. . . . 24810
—— Hard Cash. N. Y., 1876. 16°. 24811
—— It is never too late to mend. N. Y., 1876. 16°. 24812
—— A Simpleton. Lond., 1873. 12°. 24813
—— A Terrible Temptation. N. Y., 1877. 16°. 24814
—— A Woman-Hater. N. Y., 1877. 12°. (2 copies.) . . . 24815–

Reader's (The) Handbook. Brewer, E. C. Phil., 1880. 12°. . . ——
Reading. *See* **Books.**
Récamier (*Madame*), and her Friends. Lenormant, A. C. Bost., 1875. 12°. 22483
Recess (The). Lee, S. Lond., 1792. 3 v. 16°. 18684–
Red Cotton Night-cap Country. Browning, R. Bost., 1873. 16°. . 26050
Redding, C. Literary Reminiscences and Memoirs of Thos. Campbell. Lond., 1860. 2 v. 12°. 23224–
—— Personal Reminiscences of Eminent Men. Lond., 1867. 3 v. 23721–
Redgrave, R. Manual of Design. N. Y., [1876]. 12°. . . . 29768
Redhouse, J. W. Diary of the Shah of Persia. (*See* **Nasr-ed-Din.**)
Rees, J. R. Horace Vernet [*and*] Paul Delaroche. L. & N. Y., 1880. 12°. 23787
Reeve, H. Petrarch. (For. Clas. for Eng. Readers, v. 4.) Phil., [1878]. 16°. 23265
Reform. *See* **Civil** Service; **Parliamentary** Reform.
Reformation (The). Fisher, G. P. N. Y., 1873. 8°. (2 copies.) . 28585–
—— Häusser, L. The Period of the Ref., 1517–1648. Lond., 1873. 2 v. 8°. 20480–
—— Merle d'Aubigné, J. H. Hist. of the Ref. in Europe in the time of Calvin. N. Y., 1863–79. 8 v. 12°. . . . 6386– & 28451–
—— Seebohm, F. Era of the Protestant Revolution. Lond., 1874. 20448
—— *England.* Blunt, J. J. Lond., 1861. 16°. 20843
—— — Geikie, C. N. Y., 1879. 12°. 20814
—— — Lechler, G. V. John Wiclif and his English Precursors. Lond., 1878. 2 v. 8°. 22305–
—— *France.* Marsh, A. C. Phila., 1851. 2 v. 12°. 20417–
—— *Germany.* Strauss, D. F. Ulrich von Hutten: his life and times. Lond., 1874. 12°. 22143
—— *Italy.* Benrath, K. Bernardino Ochino, of Siena. N. Y., 1877. 22181
—— *Switzerland.* Istria, D. d'. The Pioneer of the Ref. Lond., 1858. 2 v. 8°. 20600–
—— *See, also,* **Ecclesiastical** Hist.; **History.**
Reformers before the Reformation. Ullmann, C. Edinb., 1855. 2 v. 8°. 22300–
Regent's Daughter. Dumas, A. D. Lond., [1879]. 16°. . . 24417
Regicides. Warren, I. P. The Three Judges. N. Y., [1873]. 16°. 22627
Regnard, J. F. *Besant, W.* (*In* 'French Humourists.') . . . 26776
Regnault, H. V. *Hamerton, P. G.* (*In* 'Mod. Frenchmen.') . . 22488
Régnier, M. *Besant, W.* (*In* 'French Humourists.') . . . 26776
Reid, T. W. Charlotte Brontë: a monograph. N. Y., 1877. 12°. 23248
Reineke Fuchs. Goethe, J. W. von. Mit Zeichnungen von Kaulbach. Stuttg., 1846. 4°. . . . . ——
Reise in den Orient. Hackländer, F. W. von. Stuttg., 1875. 2 B. 16°. (Werke, B. 8–9.) 25803–
Religion. Arnold, M. Last Essays on Church and Religion. [L. &] N. Y., 1877. 12°. 28690
—— Beale, L. S. Life Theories: their influence on religious thought. Lond., 1871. 12°. 29293

Religion. Clarke, J. F. Common-sense in Religion. Bost., 1874. 28692
—— Draper, J. W. Hist. of the Conflict between Religion and Science. N. Y., 1875. 12°. 29251
—— Gray, A. Natural Science and Religion: two lectures. N. Y., 1880. 12. 28697
—— Hurst, J. F. (*In* **First Cent.** of the Republic.) 21520
—— Liddon, H. P. Some Elements of Religion. N. Y., 1872. 12°. 28541
—— Martineau, J. Modern Materialism in its relation to Religion. N. Y., 1877. 16°. 28696
—— Mill, J. S. Three Essays on Religion. N. Y., 1874. 12°. . 28698
—— Müller, F. M. Origin and Growth of Religion, as illustrated by the religions of India. N. Y., 1879. 12°. 28568
—— Renan, J. E. Studies of Religious Hist. and Criticism. N. Y., 1864. 8°. 28680
—— Renouf, P. L. Origin and Growth of Religion, as illustrated by the Religion of Anc. Egypt. N. Y., 1880. 12°. . . . 28569
—— *See, also,* **Christianity; Evolution; Theology.**

Religions (various). Clarke, J. F. Ten Great Religions. Bost., 1871. 12°. 28564
—— — *Same.* Bost., 1877. 12°. 28565
—— Johnson, Sam. Oriental Religions: India; China. Bost., 1873 & '77. 2 v. 8°. 28560–
—— *See, also,* **Buddhism; Confucianism; Heathenism; Hinduism; Mohammedanism.**

Religious Belief, Analysis of. Russell, J. Lond., 1876. 2 v. 8°. . 28683–

Religious (The) Sentiment. Brinton, D. G. N. Y., 1876. 12°. . 28687

Remarks on the Differences in Shakespeare's Versification [etc.]. [Bathurst, C.] Lond., 1857. 16°. 27011

Rembrandt van Ryn, P. H. *Mollett, J. W.* [From the text of C. Vosmaer.] L. & N. Y., 1879. 12°. 23778

Reminiscences of Half a Century. By an Accurate Observer. Lond., 1838. 12°. 18543

Remorse: a novel. [Blanc, T.] N. Y., 1878. 16°. 24086

Rémusat, Claire E. de V. de. Memoirs: 1802–1808. N. Y., 1880. 8°. (2 copies.) 22567–
—— *Sainte-Beuve, C. A.* (*In* 'Portraits of Celebrated Women.') . 23643

Renaissance. Lacroix, P. Arts in the Middle Ages, and at the period of the Renaissance. Lond., 1870. 8°. . . . 20362
—— — Manners, Customs, and Dress. Lond., 1874. 8°. . . 20361
—— — Military and Religious Life. Lond., 1874. 8°. . . . 20360
—— — Science and Literature. Lond., 1878. 8°. 20364
—— Pater, W. The Renaissance: studies in art and poetry. Lond., 1877. 8°. 29878
—— Symonds, J. A. Renaissance in Italy. Lond., 1875–77. v. 1–3. 20298–
Contents:—1, Age of the Despots.—2, Revival of Learning.—3, Fine Arts.

Renan, J. E. English Conferences: Rome and Christianity; Marcus Aurelius. Bost., 1880. 12°. 28570
—— Studies of Religious Hist. and Criticism. N. Y., 1864. 8°. . 28680

Rendle, W. Southwark in the Time of Shakspere. [Lond.], 1878. 27176
Renée and Franz. [Fould, W. J. S.] N. Y., 1878. 16°. . . . 24079
Rennie, D. F. Peking and the Pekingese. Lond., 1865. 2 v. 12°. 21623–
Renouf, P. Le P. Religion of Ancient Egypt. N. Y., 1880. 12°. . 28569
Report on Spiritualism. *See* **Spiritualism,** Report.
Representation. Dutcher, S. Minority or Proportional Representation. N. Y., 1872. 8°. 29091
—— Hare, T. Election of Representatives, parliamentary and municipal. Lond., 1873. 16°. 29092
—— *See, also,* **Franchise ; Politics** (*& references*).
Return of the Native. Hardy, T. N. Y., 1878. 16°. (2 copies.) . 24463–
Reumont, A. von. Lorenzo de' Medici the Magnificent. Lond., 1876. 2 v. 8°. 23937–
Reuter, F. Seed-time and Harvest. Phila., 1871. 8°. . . . 24681
Revanche de Joseph Noirel. Cherbuliez, V. Paris, 1872. 16°. . 25625
Revolutions in English Hist. Vaughan, R. Lond., 1859–63. 3 v. 21094–
Reynolds, *Sir* **J.** *Pulling, F. S.* Lond. & N. Y., 1880. 12°. . . 23792
Rhetoric. Cox, E. W. Arts of Writing, Reading, and Speaking. Lond., 1879. 12°. 27821
—— Townsend, L. T. Art of Speech. N. Y., 1880. v. 1. 16°. . 27824
—— *See, also,* **Elocution ; Language ; Preaching ; Voice.**
Rhind, W. Studies in Natural History. Edinb., 1830. 12°. . . 29334
Riaño, J. F. Industrial Arts in Spain. Lond., 1879. 12°. . . 29769
Ribot, T. Heredity. N. Y., 1875. 12°. 29398
Rice, Sara S. Edgar Allan Poe : a memorial volume. Balt., 1877. 22685
Richard III., *king of Eng.*, Life and Reign of. Gairdner, J. Lond., 1878. 12°. 20813
Richardson, B. W. Diseases of Modern Life. N. Y., 1876. 12°. . 29995
—— A Ministry of Health, and other addresses. Lond., 1879. 12°. 29996
Richardson (C. F.) & Clark (H. A.). The College Book. Bost., 1878. 8°. . . . . ——
Richardson, H. W. The National Banks. N. Y., 1880. 32°. . 29063
Richardson, *Rev.* **J.** Recollections, political, literary, dramatic, and miscellaneous, of the last half-century. Lond., 1856. 2 v. in 1. 12°. 18666
Richardson, J. G. Long Life, and how to reach it. Phil., 1879. . 29959
Richardson, S. Clarissa [Harlowe]; condensed by C. H. Jones. N. Y., 1874. 16°. 24850
—— Correspondence. [With life] and observations. By A. L. Barbauld. Lond., 1804. 6 v. 12°. 17490–
Richelieu, A. J. du P. de. *Cousin, V.* Secret Hist. N. Y., 1871. . 20414
Richter, J. P. Leonardo. (Illust. Biogr. of the Great Artists.) L. & N. Y., 1880. 12°. 23786
Richter, J. P. F., Life of. Lee, E. B. [1st ed.] Bost., 1842. 2 v. 7799–
—— *Same.* 2d ed. Lond., 1849. 12°. 23226
—— — 3d ed. Bost., 1864. 12°. (1st & 2d ed., anon.) . . . 7803
Ricord, F. W. English Songs from Foreign Tongues. N. Y., 1879. 12°. 26164
Riding. *See* **Horse ; Sports.**

Riding Recollections. Whyte-Melville, G. J. Lond., 1878. 12°. . 29640
Riethmüller, C. J. Life and Times of Alex. Hamilton. Lond., [1864]. 22626
Rimmer, A. Anc. Streets and Homesteads of England. L., 1877. 8°. 21980
Rise of Iskander. Disraeli, B. N. Y. [Lond., 1878]. 16°. . . 24240
Ritchie, Anne I. (Thackeray). Old Kensington. Lond., 1873. 8°. 24700
—— *Same.* N. Y., 1873. 8°. 24701
—— Writings. N. Y., 1870. 8°. 24699
Ritter, C., Life of. Gage, W. L. N. Y., 1867. 12°. . . . 23563
Ritter, F. L. Hist. of Music. Bost., 1876 & '74. 2 v. 16°. . . 29750–
River of Golden Sand. Gill, W. Lond., 1880. 2 v. 8°. . . 21930–
Roberts, J. S. Legendary Ballads of England and Scotland. Lond., [1875]. 12°. 27665
[Roberts, Margaret.] Noblesse Oblige. N. Y., 1876. 16°. . . 24851
—— On the Edge of the Storm. N. Y., 1877. 16°. 24852
Robertson, J. C. Becket, Archbishop of Canterbury. Lond., 1859. 22142
—— Hist. of the Christian Church, A. D. 64–1517. Lond., 1874–5. 8 v. 16°. 28454–
Robertson, W. Reign of Charles V. [Ed.] by W. H. Prescott. Phil., 1872. 3 v. 8°. 20348–
Robespierre, M. M. I. de, Life of. Lewes, G. H. Lond., 1849. 12°. 22527
Robinson, H. M. Great Fur Land. N. Y., 1879. 12°. . . . 21284
Robinson, *Mrs.* **Mary.** Memoirs, written by herself. Lond., 1801. 4 v. 16°. 18680–
Robusti, Jacopo (*or* **Giacomo**). *See* **Tintoretto.**
Roby, J. Legendary and Poetical Remains. Lond., 1854. 12°. . 18643
Rock, D. Textile Fabrics. N. Y., 1876. 12°. 29770
Rockingham, C. W. Wentworth, *marquis of.* *Earle, J. C.* (*In* 'Eng. Premiers,' v. 1.) 22882
Rocks ahead. Greg, W. R. Lond., 1874. 12°. 27294
Rocky Mountains. Bird, I. L. A Lady's Life in. N. Y., 1879. 12°. 21281
—— Parkman, F. The Oregon Trail. Bost., 1873. 8°. . . . 21402
Rodenberg, J. England, literary and social. Lond., 1875. 8°. . 21142
Roderick Hudson. James, H., jr. Bost., 1876. 12°. . . . 24604
Röschen vom Hofe. Spielhagen, F. (Sämmtl. Werke, B. 3.) . . 25862
Roger of Hoveden, Annals of. Lond., 1853. 2 v. 12°. . . . 20800–
Rogers, C. Life and Songs of the Baroness Nairne; with a memoir and poems of Caroline Oliphant the younger. Lond., 1869. 16°. 23249
—— Scotland, social and domestic. Lond., 1869. 8°. . . . 21141
Rogers, J. E. T. Cobden and Modern Political Opinion. Lond., 1873. 8°. 29088
—— Social Economy. N. Y., 1872. 12°. 28884
Rogers, May. The Waverly Dictionary. Chic., 1879 [1878]. 12°. 26921
Rogers, R. V. The Law of Hotel Life. San Fran., 1879. 16°. . 28852
Rogers, Sam. Recollections. Lond., 1859. 16°. 18675
Rohlfs, G. Adventures in Morocco. Lond., 1874. 8°. . . . 21848
Roi des montagnes. About, E. F. V. Paris, 1876. 16°. . . . 25621
Rois en exil. Daudet, A. Paris, 1880. 16°. 25600
Roland. Cox (G. W.) & Jones (E. H.). (*In* 'Pop. Romances.') 27712 & 2010

Roland de la Platière, Marie J. P. Works. [Ed.] by L. A. Champagneux. Lond., 1800. 8°. 18720
—— *See* **Baker, H. B.,** 'French Society,' v. 2 (20401); **Lamartine, A. M. L. de,** 'Biogr.,' v. 2 (23728); **Sainte-Beuve, C. A.,** 'Portraits' (23643).
Roman Catholic Church. Gladstone, W. E. Rome and the Newest Fashions in Religion. Three tracts: The Vatican decrees; Vaticanism; Speeches of the Pope. N. Y., 1875. 8°. . . 28724
—— Renan, J. E. Rome and Christianity. (English Conferences.) Bost., 1880. 12°. 28570
See, also, **Ecc.** Hist.; **Inquisition; Jesuits; Monastic** Orders; **Monks; Old** Catholics; **Papacy; Popes; Vatican.**
Roman Days. Rydberg, V. N. Y., 1879. 12°. 21689
Roman Empire. *See* **Rome,** *History.*
Roman Law. *See* **Law,** *Roman.*
Roman Legends. Busk, R. H. Bost., 1877. 8°. 27714
Roman Literature, Hist. of. Cruttwell, C. T. N. Y., [1878]. 8°. . 26964
Roman Mythology. *See* **Mythology.**
Roman Republic. *See* **Rome,** *Hist. to* B. C. 31.
Romance (The) of the Forest. Radcliffe, A. Lond., 1806. 3 v. 12°. 18690–
Romance (The) of an Honest Woman. Cherbuliez, V. Bost., 1874. 24169
Romances. Cox (G. W.) & Jones. Pop. Romances of the Middle Ages. Lond., 1871. 12°. 2010
—— — *Same.* N. Y., 1880. 12°. (*For contents see* **Cox.**) . . . 27712
—— Joyce, P. W. Old Celtic Romances. Lond., 1879. 12°. . . 27702
—— *See, also,* **Myths** (*& references*).
Romances of the East. Gobineau, J. A. de. N. Y., 1878. 16°. . 24078
Romanism. *See* **Rom. Cath. Ch.** (*& references*).
Romanoff, H. C. Historical Narratives from the Russian. Lond., 1871. 16°. 20498
Rome. Fustel de Coulanges, M.D. The Ancient City: a study on the religion, laws, and institutions of Greece and Rome. Bost., 1874. 8°. 20182
—— Guhl (E.) & Koner (W.). Life of the Greeks and Romans, described from antique monuments. Lond., 1875. 8°. (2 cop.) 20180–
—— Hare, A. J. C. Days near Rome. Illust. Phila., 1875. 12°. . 21602
—— Merivale, C. St. Paul at Rome. Lond., [1878]. 16°. . . 28501
—— Story, W. W. Castle St. Angelo. Lond., 1877. 12°. . . 21626
—— Wilkins, A. S. Roman Antiquities. (History Primers.) Lond., 1877. 16°. 20057
—— *Church of.* *See* **Roman Cath. Ch.**

History.

—— Creighton, M. (Hist. Primers.) Lond., 1877. 16°. . . . 20052
—— Ihne, W. Lond., 1871–77. v. 1–3. 8°. 20288–
—— (*to* B. C. 387) Ihne, W. Early Rome. Lond., 1876. 16°. . . 20438
—— (*to* A. D. 476) Leighton, R. F. N. Y., 1880. 12°. . . . 20099
—— — Merivale, C. N. Y., 1875. 12°. (2 cop.) 20097–
—— (B. C. 264–A. D. 337) Niebuhr, B. G. Lond., 1844. 2 v. 8°. . 20294–

Rome. *History (continued).*
—— (B. C. 133–82) Beesly, A. H. The Gracchi, Marius, and Sulla. N. Y., [1879]. 16°. 20440
—— (B. C. 60–31) Merivale, C. The Roman Triumvirates. N. Y., [1877]. 16°. 20437
—— (B. C. 44–A. D. 96) Capes, W. W. N. Y., [1876]. 16°. . . 20436
—— (A. D. 96–180) Capes, W. W. Rom. Emp. of the 2d Cent. N. Y., 1879. 16°. 20439
—— (180–1453) Gibbon, E. Decline and Fall of the Rom. Emp. Lond., 1872. 8 v. 8°. 20280–
—— (395–800) Curteis, A. M. Lond., 1875. 16°. 20068
—— (1815–1850) Farini, L. C. The Roman State. Lond., 1851–54. 4 v. 8°. 20304–
See, also, **Italy**; **Law,** *Roman;* **Roman** Literature.
Rood, O. N. Modern Chromatics. N. Y., 1879. 12°. 29266
Rosa, Salvator: Life and Times. Morgan, S. O. Lond., 1824. 2 v. 8°. 18569–
Rosario (*ship*), Cruise of. Markham, A. H. Lond., 1873. 8°. . 21814
Roscher, W. G. F. Principles of Political Economy. N. Y., 1878. 2 v. 29161–
Roscoe, *Mrs.* **Henry.** Vittoria Colonna. Lond., 1868. 12°. . . 23227
Roscoe, Henry E. Chemistry. Lond., 1877. 16°. 29362
—— *See* **Science Lectures** for the People.
Roscoe, T. Life and Writings of Cervantes. Lond., 1861. 16°. . 23243
Rose, H. J. Untrodden Spain, and her Black Country. Lond., 1875. 2 v. 8°. 21783–
Rosicrucians (The). Jennings, H. Lond., 1870. 12°. . . . 28997
Roslyn, G. Geo. Eliot in Derbyshire. Lond., 1876. 16°. . . 26919
Rossetti, Christina G. Goblin Market, and other poems. Lond., 1865. 16°. 26144
—— Poems. Bost., 1876. 16°. 26145
Rossetti, D. G. Poems. Lond., 1870. 12°. 26143
Rossetti, W. M. Lives of Famous Poets. Lond., 1878. 12°. . 23289
Rossini, G. A., Life of. Edwards, H. S. Lond., 1869. 8°. . . 23846
Rough Ways made Smooth. Proctor, R. A. N. Y., 1880. 12°. . 29444
Roughing it. Clemens, S. L. Hartf., 1878. 8°. 25587
Roumania. Murray, E. C. G. Doïne; or, The national songs and legends of Roumania. Lond., 1854. 12°. 27786
Round about France. Murray, E. C. G. Lond., 1878. 12°. . . 21622
Round about Piccadilly and Pall Mall. Wheatley, H. B. Lond., 1870. 21775
Round my House. Hamerton, P. G. Bost., 1876. 12°. . . . 21248
Round Table (*Knights of*). *See* **Arthur** (*King*).
Rousseau, J. J. Original Correspondence, with Mad. La Tour de Franqueville, and M. Du Peyrou. Lond., 1804. 2 v. 8°. 18663–
—— *Morley, J.* Lond., 1873. 2 v. 8°. 23421–
—— *See, also,* **Clarke, J. F.,** 'Memorial and Biogr. Sketches' (22618); **Lowell, J. R.,** 'Among my Books,' v. 1 (3616); **Merivale, H.,** 'Histor. Stud.' (20188); **Sainte-Beuve, C. A.,** 'Monday-Chats' (23290); **Stephen, L.,** 'Hours,' v. 3 (26935).
Rousselet, L. The Serpent-Charmer. N. Y., [1879]. 8°. . . 24682

Routledge, R. Discoveries and Inventions of the 19th Cent. Lond., 1876. 12°. 29929
Rowing. *See* **Boat-racing; Sports.**
Rowley, J. Rise of the People, and Growth of Parliament. (*In* **Epochs** of Eng. Hist.) 20851
—— Settlement of the Constitution. (*In the same.*) 20851
Roxy. Eggleston, E. N. Y., 1878. 12°. 24471
Rubáiyát of Omar Khayyám. Lond., 1872. 8°. 26256
Rubens, P. P. *Kett, C. W.* (Illust. Biog. of the Great Artists.) L. & N. Y., 1879. 12°. 23788
—— *Sainsbury, W. N.* Original Unpublished Papers illustrative of the life of R., as an artist and a diplomatist. Lond., 1859. 23834
Ruchrath, Joh., (John of Wesel.) *Ullmann, C.* (*In* 'Reformers,' v. 1.) 22300
Rude, F. *Hamerton, P. G.* (*In* 'Mod. Frenchmen.') . . . 22488
Rugby (The) Miscellany. Lond., Mar. 1845–Oct. 1846. Nos. 1–10. 1 vol. 8°. 11398
Rule, W. H. Hist. of the Inquisition. Lond., 1874. 2 v. 8°. . 28720–
Ruling Ideas in Early Ages. Mozley, J. B. N. Y., 1877. 8°. . 28686
Runeberg, J. L. Lyrical Songs, Idylls and Epigrams. Done into Eng. [verse] by E. Magnússon and E. H. Palmer. Lond., 1878. 16°. 26128
Rupert (*Prince*) and the Cavaliers, Memoirs of. Warburton, E. B. G. Lond., 1849. 3 v. 8°. 23018–
Rushton, W. L. Shakespeare's Euphuism. Lond., 1871. 12°. . 27010
Ruskin, J. Ariadne Florentina: six lectures on wood and metal engraving. N. Y., 1874–5. 12°. 29831
—— *Same.* Lect. 4–6. N. Y., 1875. 12°. 29832
—— Deucalion: lapse of waves, and life of stones. N. Y., 1875–77. Parts 1–4 in 2 v. 12°. 29836–
—— The Eagle's Nest: ten lectures on the relation of natural science to art. N. Y., 1873. 12°. 29830
—— Fors Clavigera: letters to the workmen and labourers of Great Britain. [Monthly.] Orpington, Kent, 1871–77. 7 v. 8°. (Index to v. 1–2, in v. 2; to v. 3–4, in v. 4.) 29031–
—— Frondes agrestes: readings in 'Modern Painters.' Orpington, Kent, 1875. 12°. 29829
—— The Laws of Fésole: a treatise on drawing and painting. N. Y., 1877. Part 1. 12°. 29844
—— Love's Meinie: lectures on Greek and English birds. N. Y., 1873. 12°. 29835
—— Mornings in Florence: being simple studies of Christian art, for English travellers. N. Y., 1876. 12°. 29834
—— Poetry of Architecture: cottage, villa, etc. N. Y., 1873. 12°. 29833
—— Proserpina: studies of wayside flowers among the Alps, and in Scotland and England. N. Y., 1875–77. Pts. 1–4 in 2 v. 12°. 29840–
—— St. Mark's Rest: the history of Venice. N. Y., 1877. Parts 1–2. 29844
—— *Bayne, P.* (*In* 'Lessons from my Masters.') 23287
Russell, John, *Earl.* Letters, written for the Post, and not for the Press. [Anon.] Lond., 1820. 12°. 18696

Russell, John, *Earl.* Recollections and Suggestions, 1813–1873. Lond., 1875. 8°. 23059
—— *Kebbel, T. E.* (*In* 'Eng. Statesmen.') 22884
Russell, John, *Viscount Amberley.* Analysis of Religious Belief. Lond., 1876. 2 v. 8°. 28683–
Russell, Rachael W., *Lady,* Life of. Berry, M. (*In* 'Comparative View,' v. 2.) 6202
Russell, W. H. The Prince of Wales' Tour. Lond., 1877. 2 v. 8°. 21967–
Russia. Barry, H. Ivan at Home; or, Pictures of Russian life. Lond., 1872. 8°. 21940
—— Distinguished Persons in Russian Society. Lond., 1873. 12°. 23614
—— [Helps, A.] Ivan de Biron ; or, The Russian court in the middle of the last century. Bost., 1874. 12°. 24537
—— Longfellow, H. W. Poems of Places, v. 20. 26459
—— Ralston, W. R. S. The Songs of the Russian People, as illustrative of Slavonic mythology and Russian Social life. Lond., 1872. 8°. 27782
—— Sketches of Russian Life before and during the Emancipation of the Serfs. Ed. by H. Morley. Lond., 1866. 12°. . . . 21683
—— Wallace, D. M. N. Y., 1877. 8°. 21941
—— *Description and Travel.* Bryce, J. Transcaucasia and Ararat. Lond., 1877. 12°. 21214
—— — Cunynghame, A. T. Travels in Daghestan. Lond., 1872. 8°. 21913
—— — Gautier, T. Voyage en Russie. Paris, 1867. 16°. . . 25650
—— — — *Same.* A Winter in Russia. N. Y., 1874. 12°. . . 21225
—— — Wahl, O. W. The Land of the Czar. Lond., 1875. 8°. . 21942

History.

—— [Eckardt, J.] Russia before and after the War. Lond., 1880. 20613
—— Ralston, W. R. S. Early Russian History. Lond., 1874. 16°. 20499
—— Romanoff, H. C. Historical Narratives from the Russian. Lond., 1871. 16°. 20498
—— (*to* 1877) Rambaud, A. Lond., 1879. 2 v. 8°. 20611–
—— (1584–1613) Mérimée, P. Demetrius, the Impostor. Lond., 1853. 23903
—— (1777–1825) Joyneville, C. Life and Times of Alexander I. Lond., 1875. 3 v. 8°. (2 copies.) 20605–
—— (1877–8) Daily News (Lond.). War Correspondence. Lond., 1878. 2 v. 20494–
Russian Folk-tales. Ralston, W. R. S. Lond., 1873. 8°. . . 27783
Russian Gipsy. Dumas, A. D. Lond., [1879]. 16°. . . . 24417
Russian (Two) Idyls. N. Y., 1880. 16. 24928
Russian Romance[s]. Pushkin, A. S. Lond., 1880. 12°. . . 24809
Russians (The) in Central Asia. Hellwald, F. von. Lond., 1874. 8°. 21608
Ruth. Gaskell, E. C. Lond., 1872. 16°. 24447
Rutherford, J. The Troubadours. Lond., 1873. 12°. . . . 26907
Rydberg, V. The Last Athenian. Phil., [1879]. 12°. . . . 24817
—— The Magic of the Middle Ages. N. Y., 1879. 12°. . . . 28050
—— Roman Days. N. Y., 1879. 12°. 21689
Sabbath. Hessey, J. A. Sunday: its orgin, history, and present obligation. Lond., 1866. 12°. 28490

Sabbath. Proctor, R. A. The Jewish Sabbath. (*In* 'Our Place,' etc.) 29447
Sadler, L. R., (*pseud.,* 'Jacob Larwood.') Story of the London Parks. Lond., [1871]. 2 v. 12°. 21614–
Sadler, M. T.: Memoirs of [his] life and writings. Lond., 1842. 8°. 18661
Safar-Hadgi. Lubomirski, J. N. Y., 1878. 16°. 24083
Sahara, The Great. Tristram, H. B. Lond., 1860. 12°. . . . 21696
Sainsbury, W. N. Original Unpublished Papers illustrative of the life of Rubens. Lond., 1859. 8°. 23834
Saint Amant, M. A. G. de. *Besant, W.* (*In* 'French Humourists.') 26776
St. Domingo. *See* **Santo Domingo.**
St. George and St. Michael. MacDonald, G. Bost., [1877]. 12°. . 24623
St. James's Magazine. Lond., 1861–79. 45 v. 8°. . . . . , 18047–
St. John, *the evangelist. See* **John** (*St.*).
St. John, B. Montaigne, the Essayist: a biography. Lond., 1858. 2 v. 12°. 23222–
St. John, H., *1st Viscount Bolingbroke.* Works; with a life. Phila., 1841. v. 2–4. 8°. 27492–
St. John, J. A. Life of Sir Walter Raleigh. Lond., 1869. 12°. . 22889
St. Mark's Rest. Ruskin, J. N. Y., 1877. Parts 1–2. 12°. . . 29844
St. Paul. *See* **Paul** (*St.*).
Saint-Simon, C. H. de R. de. *Booth, A. J.* Lond., 1871. 8°. . 23522
Sainte-Beuve, C. A. English Portraits. Selected and transl. from the "Causeries du Lundi," with a chap. on Sainte-Beuve's life and writings [by W. F. Rae]. Lond., 1875. 12°. . . 22885
—— *Same.* N. Y., 1875. 12°. 22886
—— Monday-Chats. Selected and transl. from the "Causeries du Lundi," with an essay by Wm. Mathews. Chic., 1877. 12°. 23290
—— Portraits of Celebrated Women. Bost., 1868. 16°. 23643
Saints and Sinners. Doran, J. Lond., 1868. 2 v. 12°. . . . 28492–
Sala, G. A. Paris herself again in 1878–9. Lond., 1879. 2 v. 8°. 21984–
—— William Hogarth. Lond., 1866. 12°. 23802
Samuel Brohl et Cie. Cherbuliez, V. Paris, 1877. 16°. . . 25626
—— *Same, transl.* N. Y., 1877. 12°. 24072
Sandeau, L. S. J. Madeleine: a story of French love. Chic., 1879. 24818
Sanderson, R. *Alexander, W.* (*In* **Classic** Preachers; 1878.) . 22113
Sandys, G. Poetical Works. [Ed.] by R. Hooker. Lond., 1872. 2 v. 12°. 26129–
Sanford, J. L. Estimates of the English Kings. Lond., 1872. 12°. 20821
Sankey, I. D. *Hall* (*J.*) & *Stuart* (*G. H.*). The Amer. Evangelists, Moody and Sankey, in Great Brit. and Ireland. N. Y., [1875]. 22615
San Marino. Bent, J. T. A Freak of Freedom. Lond., 1879. 12°. 20483
Sans Dot. About, E. F. V. (*With* 'Trente,' etc.) 25622
Sans-Souci Series. *See* **Stoddard, R. H.,** *editor.*
Santo Domingo. Hazard, S. N. Y., 1873. 12°. 21728
Sanzio, Raffaello. *See* **Raphael.**
Sappho: a tragedy. Grillparzer, F. Bost., 1876. 16°. . . . 26070
Sarah de Berenger: a novel. Ingelow, J. Bost., 1879. 16°. . . 24581

Sargent (**E.**) *&* *others, editors.* Modern Standard Drama. N. Y., 1847 (etc.). 24 nos. in 2 v. 12°. 26487–

CONTENTS:—1, Corsican brothers, adapted from Dumas; Charles XII., by J. R. Planché; Cure for the heartache, by T. Morton; Sketches in India, Morton; Lady of Lyons, Bulwer-Lytton; Richelieu, by the same; School for scandal, Sheridan; Stranger, Kotzebue; Rivals, Sheridan; Gisippus, G. Griffin; Bertram, C. Maturin; George Barnwell, by G. Lillo.—2, Follies of a night, Planché; Don Cæsar de Bazan, Dumanoir & Dennery; Blue devils, G. Coleman; Money, Bulwer-Lytton; Bridal, J. S. Knowles; Damon and Pythias, J. Banim; Rob Roy, I. Pocock; Gamester, E. Moore; Hunchback, Knowles; Jealous wife, Coleman; Writing on the wall, T. & J. M. Morton; Jane Shore, N. Rowe.

Sargent, N. Public Men and Events, 1817–1853. Phil., 1875. 2 v. 21447–

Satsuma (The) Rebellion. Mounsey, A. H. Lond., 1879. 12°. . 20385

Savonarola, G. *Oliphant, M. O. W.* The Makers of Florence. Lond., 1876. 8°. 23836

Savoy. Longfellow, H. W. Poems of Places, v. 10. . . . 26449

Saxe, J. G. Leisure-Day Rhymes. Bost., 1875. 12°. . . . 26131

Saxe, M. de. *Hayward, A.* (*In* 'Biogr. and Crit. Ess.,' 2d ser., v. 1.) 27401

Saxon Studies. Hawthorne, J. Bost., 1876. 12°. 21607

Sayce, A. H. Introd. to the Science of Language. Lond., 1880. 2 v. 27864–

Scandinavia. Otté, E. C. Scandinavian Hist. Lond., 1874. 12°. 20050

—— *See, also,* **Denmark**; **Iceland**; **Northmen**; **Norway.**

Scandinavian Languages and Lit. Anderson, R. B. (*In* 'America not discovered by Columbus.') 21280

—— *See, also,* **Eddas.**

Scandinavian Races. Sinding, P. C. N. Y., 1875. 8°. . . . 20387

Scarlett, James, *1st Lord Abinger,* Memoir of. Scarlett, P. C. Lond., 1877. 8°. 23043

Scarron, P. *Besant, W.* (*In* 'French Humourists.') . . . 26776

Scenes of Clerical Life. Eliot, G. N. Y. 12°. 24183

Schäffle, A. E. F. *See* **Kaufmann, M.,** 'Socialism.'

Schaff, P. Hist. of the Vatican Council. (*With* **Gladstone, W. E.,** 'The Vatican Decrees.') 28723

—— *Same, with* Gladstone's 'Rome,' &c. 28724

—— Revision of the Eng. Version of the New Test., by J. B. Lightfoot, R. C. Trench, and C. J. Ellicott. [Ed.,] with an introd., by P. Schaff. N. Y., 1873. 3 v. in 1. 12°. 28525

Schatzkästlein. Auerbach, B. Stuttg., 1875. 16°. 25883

Scheffel, J. V. Ekkehard: a tale of the 10th cent. Leipz., 1872. 16°. 24853

Schiern, F. Life of James Hepburn, Earl of Bothwell. Edinb., 1880. 8°. 23009

Schiller, J. C. F. Correspondence with Körner. Lond., 1849. 3 v. 23320–

—— *Boyesen, H. H.* Goethe and Schiller. N. Y., 1879. 12°. . . 26904

—— *Carlyle, T.* Life of Schiller. Lond., 1873. 16°. . . . 23323

—— *Palleske, E.* Life and Works. Lond., 1860. 2 v. 12°. . . 23324–

Schloss Hainfeld. Hall, B. Edinb., 1836. 12°. 18635

Schmidt, O. Doctrine of Descent and Darwinism. Lond., 1875. 12°. 29252

Schoelcher, V. Life of Handel. N. Y., 1857. 12°. . . . 23771

Schönen (Die) Amerikanerinnen. Spielhagen, F. (Sämmtl. Werke, B. 8.) 25867

Schopenhauer, A. On Visions.—Metaphysics of Music. (*Suppl. to* Wagner's 'Beethoven,' transl. by Dannreuther.) . . . 23807

—— *Zimmern, H.* Lond., 1876. 12°. 23529

Schuckers, J. W. Life and Public Services of S. P. Chase. N. Y., 1874. 8°. 22775

Schützenberger, P. On Fermentation. N. Y., 1876. 12°. . . . 29260

Schumann, R. Music and Musicians: essays and criticisms. N. Y., 1877. 12°. 29741

Schuyler, E. Turkistan. N. Y., 1876. 2 v. 8°. 21921–

Schwegler, A. Hist. of Philosophy in Epitome. N. Y., 1864. 12°. 28090

Schweinfurth, G. A. The Heart of Africa. N. Y., 1874. 2 v. 8°. 21852–

Science. Barnard, F. A. P. Exact Sciences. (*In* **First Cent.** of the Republic.) 21520

—— Draper, J. W. Hist. of the Conflict between Religion and Sci. N. Y., 1875. 12°. 29251

—— Gill, T. Natural Sci. (*In* **First Cent.** of the Republic.) . . 21520

—— Gray, A. Natural Sci. and Religion: two lectures. N. Y., 1880. 28697

—— Helmholtz, H. L. F. Pop. Lectures on Scientific Subjects. Lond., 1873. 8°. 29389

—— Lacroix, P. Sci. and Lit. in the Middle Ages. Lond., 1878. 8°. 20364

—— Peabody, A. P. Christianity and Science. N. Y., 1874. 12°. . 28700

—— Proctor, R. A. Science Byways. Phil. [Lond.], 1876. 12°. . 29445

—— Ruskin, J. The Eagle's Nest: 10 lectures on the relation of nat. sci. to art. N. Y., 1873. 12°. 29830

—— Tyndall, J. Advancement of Sci.: inaugural address. N. Y., 1874. 12°. 29304

—— — Fragments of Science. N. Y., 1877. 12°. 29401

Science Lectures for the People. Manchester, 1867–76. 8 series in 4 vols. 12°. 29306–

CONTENTS:—**1st ser.,** Four lect. on elem. chem., by H. E. Roscoe; Four on elem. zoology, by T. Alcock; Coal, W. S. Jevons; Four lect. on elem. physiol., J. E. Morgan.—**2d,** Coral and coral reefs, T. H. Huxley; Spectrum analysis, Roscoe; Ditto, by W. Huggins; Coal, W. B. Dawkins; Chas. Dickens, A. W. Ward; Natural history of paving stones, Prof. Williamson; Deep sea, W. B. Carpenter; Coal, A. H. Green; Sun, J. N. Lockyer.—**3d,** Yeast, T. H. Huxley; Coal colors, Roscoe; Origin of the Eng. people, A. S. Wilkins; Food of plants, Prof. Odling; Unconscious action of the brain, Carpenter; Epidemic delusions, ditto; Progress of sanitary science, Roscoe.—**4th,** Rainbow, Roscoe; Ice age in Britain, A. Geikie; Sun and earth, B. Stewart; Atoms, W. K. Clifford; Flame, Prof. Core; Life of Faraday, J. H. Gladstone; Star depths, R. A. Proctor; Kent's cavern, W. Pengelly; Fragment of Faraday's electrical discoveries, W. F. Barrett; Anc. and mod. Egypt, Carpenter.—**5th,** Polarisation of light, W. Spottiswoode; How flowers are fertilised, A. W. Bennett; Parasites, T. S. Cobbold; Gun cotton, F. A. Abel; Animal mechanics, S. M. Bradley; The senses, C. Robertson; Muscle and nerve, A. Gamgee; Era of the cave men of Devonshire, W. Pengelly.—**6th,** Crystalline and molecular forces, J. Tyndall; John Dalton and his atomic theory, Roscoe; Transit of Venus, W. Huggins; Joseph Priestley, Prof. Thorpe; Geographical distribution of mammals, P. L. Sclater; Earthquakes and volcanoes, W. C. Williamson; Modern savages, J. Lubbock; Palestine exploration, C. W. Wilson.—**7th,** Arctic discoveries, J. E. Davis; Soap bubbles, Prof. Rücker; Birds, R. B. Sharpe; Great extinct quadrupeds, P. M. Duncan; Henry Cavendish, Prof. Thorpe; Functions of the brain, Prof. Ferrier; Food, H. E. Armstrong; Era of the cave men of Devonshire, pt. 2, Pengelly.—**8th,** What the earth is composed of, Roscoe; Succession of life on the earth, W. C. Williamson; Why the earth's chemistry is as it is, Lockyer.

Science Primers. Huxley (T. H.), Roscoe (H. E.) & Stewart (B.), *editors.* Lond., 1876–8. 9 v. 16°. 29354–

CONTENTS:—Introductory, T. H. Huxley.—Physiology, M. Foster.—Geology, A. Geikie.—Phys. Geog., do.—Botany, J. D. Hooker.—Logic, W. S. Jevons.—Pol. Econ., do.—Astronomy, J. N. Lockyer.—Chemistry, H. E. Roscoe.—Physics, B. Stewart.

Scientific Discovery, The Art of. Gore, G. Lond., 1878. 12°. . 29380

Scientific London. Becker, B. H. N. Y., 1875. 12°. . . . 27300

Scoones, W. B. Four Centuries of English Letters. Lond., 1880. 23378

Scotland. Blackie, J. S. Language and Literature of the Scottish Highlands. Edinb., 1876. 12°. 26916
—— Campbell, J. F. Popular Tales of the West Highlands. Edinb., 1860–62. 4 v. 16°. 27660–
—— Grant, A. Superstitions of the Highlanders of Scotland. Lond., 1811. 2 v. 12°. 18550–
—— Keddie (H.) & Watson. Songstresses of Scotland. Lond., 1871. 2 v. 8°. 23763–
—— Longfellow, H. W. Poems of Places, v. 6–8. 26445–
—— Rogers, C. Scotland, social and domestic. Lond., 1869. 8°. . 21141
—— Wilson, D. Prehistoric Annals of Scotland. Lond., 1863. 2 v. 20203–
—— Wordsworth, D. Recollections of a Tour, 1803. N. Y., 1874. . 21268
—— *Church of.* Stanley, A. P. Hist. of the Ch. of Scotland. Lond., 1872. 8°. 28446
—— *History.* Burton, J. H. Hist. [to 1748]. 8 v. & index. 12°. . 20901–
—— — Macarthur, M. Hist. [to 1843]. N. Y., 1874. 16°. . . 20080

See, also, **Edinburgh; English** Literature; **Poetry,** *Scottish;* **Scottish** Border.

Scott, G. C. Fishing in Amer. Waters. N. Y., 1869. 12°. . . 29626
Scott, R. P. The Place of Shelley among the Eng. poets of his time. Cambr., 1878. 12°. 26212
Scott, W. Ivanhoe. Condensed by R. Johnson. N. Y., 1876. 16°. 24854
—— Rob Roy. Condensed by R. Johnson. N. Y., 1877. 16°. . 24855
—— Poetical Works. With mem. [etc.] by G. Gilfillan. Edinb., 1857. 3 v. 8°. 26349–

CONTENTS:—1, Lay of the last minstrel; Lady of the lake.—2, Marmion; Vision of Don Roderick.—3, Rokeby; Lord of the Isles.

—— *Hunnewell, J. F.* The Lands of Scott. Edinb., 1871. 12°. . 21736
—— *Hutton, R. H.* (Eng. Men of Letters.) N. Y., 1879. 12°. . 23334
—— *Rogers, M.* The Waverley Dictionary: an alphabetical arrangement of all the characters in S.'s Waverley novels, [etc.]. Chic., 1879. 12°. 26921
—— *See, also,* **Bagehot, W.,** 'Lit. Stud.,' v. 2 (26768); **Bisset, A.,** 'Ess. on Histor. Truth' (20187); **Constable, T.,** 'Arch. Constable,' etc., v. 3 (23206); **Doyle, F. H.,** 'Lect. on Poetry,' 2d ser. (26286); **Mackay, C.,** 'Forty Years' Recol.,' v. 1 (22943); **Stephen, L.,** 'Hours in a Lib.,' v. 1 (26933).
Scott, W. B. The Little Masters. (Illust. Biogr. of the Great Artists. L. & N. Y., 1879. 12°. 23784

CONTENTS:—A. Altdorfer; H. S. Beham; B. Beham; H. Aldegrever; G. Pencz; J. Binck; H. Brosamer.

Scottish Ballads and Songs. Maidment, J. Edinb., 1868. 2 v. . 26161–
Scottish Border, Hist. and Poetry of. Veitch, J. Glasgow, 1878. . 26298
Scottish (The) Philosophy. McCosh, J. N. Y., 1875. 8°. . . 28283
Scottish Poetry. *See* **Poetry,** *Scottish.*
Scribner's Monthly. N. Y., 1870–79. 18 v. 8°. 13150–
Scripture Club of Valley Rest. [Habberton, J.] N. Y., 1877. 16°. 24454
Scrope; or, The lost library. Perkins, F. B. Bost., 1874. 8°. . 24679
Scudder, H. E. Men and Manners in America one hundred years ago. N. Y., 1876. 16°. 21324
Sculptors, and their works. Clement, C. E. Bost., 1879. 12°. . 29791

Sculpture. Viardot, L. Wonders of Sculpture. N. Y., 1873. 12°. 10136
—— Westmacott, R. Handbook of Sculpture, ancient and modern. Edinb., 1864. 12°. 29824
Sea-air and Sea-bathing. Packard, J. H. Phil., 1880. 16°. . . 29967
Sealed Orders. Phelps, E. S. Bost., 1879. 12°. 24844
Seamen. Bourne, H. R. F. Eng. Seamen under the Tudors. Lond., 1868. 8°. 22942
—— *See, also,* **Navigators.**
Sebastian Strome. Hawthorne, J. N. Y., 1880. 8°. 24653
Sebright, *Lady. See* **Mackenzie, G. M.**
Secret (The) of the Island. Verne, J. (The Mysterious Island, v. 3.) 24279
Secret Societies. Baird, W. M. Amer. College Fraternities. Phil., 1879. 12°. 28995
—— Frost, T. Secret Societies of the European Revolution, 1776–1876. Lond., 1876. 2 v. 8°. 28998–
—— Heckethorn, C. W. The Secret Societies of all ages and countries. Lond., 1875. 2 v. 12°. 28993–
—— *See, also,* **Grange** Movement; **Molly** Maguires; **Rosicrucians.**
Secrétaire (Le) intime. Dudevant, A. L. A. D. Paris, 1878. 16°. . 25693
Seebohm, F. Era of the Prot. Revolution. Lond., 1874. 16°. . 20448
Seeing and Thinking. Clifford, W. K. Lond., 1879. 12°. . . 28006
Seekers after God. Farrar, F. W. [Lond., 1868.] 12°. . . . 23682
Seeley, J. R. Life and Times of Stein. Bost., 1879. 2 v. 8°. . 22580–
—— *& others.* Three Essays on Shakespeare's King Lear. Lond., 1851. 8°. 27053

CONTENTS:—By J. R. Seeley, Wm. Young, and E. A. Hart.

Seemann, O. The Mythology of Greece and Rome, with special reference to its use in art. [L. &] N. Y., 1877. 12°. . . 29788
—— *Same.* N. Y., 1879. 16°. 29789
Selborne, Nat. Hist. and Antiquities of. White, G. Lond., 1877. 2 v. 8°. 29530–
Self-culture. Blakie, J. S. N. Y., 1874. 16°. 27386
Self-made (The) Man. Klöden, K. F. von. Lond., 1876. 2 v. 8°. 23920–
Selkirk, G. H. Guide to the Cricket Ground. Lond., 1867. 16°. . 29636
Selkirk, J. B., (*pseud.*) *See* **Brown, J.,** (*of Selkirk.*)
Seneca. *Farrar, F. W.* (*In* 'Seekers after God.') 23682
Senior, N. W. Conversations with Thiers, Guizot, [etc.]. Lond., 1878. 2 v. 8°. 23922–
—— Correspondence and Conversations with Alexis de Tocqueville. Lond., 1872. 2 v. 12°. 23924–
Sept cordes de la lyre. Dudevant, A. L. A. D. Paris, 1869. 16°. . 25694
Serbian Folk-lore. Mijatovies, C. Lond., 1874. 12°. . . . 27784
Sergeant, L. New Greece. Lond., [1878]. 8°. 20617
Sermons. Beecher, H. W. A Summer Parish. N. Y., 1875. 12°. 28552
—— Brooks, P. N. Y., 1878. 12°. 28532
—— Chadwick, J. W. The Faith of Reason. Bost., 1879. 16°. . 28691
—— Channing, W. E. The Perfect Life. Bost., 1873. 16°. . . 28535
—— Crosby (H.) *& others.* Christ: His nature and work. N. Y., 1878. 12°. 28487

Sermons. Frothingham, O. B. Visions of the Future. N. Y., 1879. 12°. 28553
—— King, T. S. Christianity and Humanity. Bost., 1877. 12°. . 28538
—— Kingsley, C. Twenty-five Village Sermons. Lond., 1873. 16°. 28540
—— Martineau, J. Hours of Thought on Sacred Things. Lond., 1877–79. 2 v. 12°. 28542–
—— Mozley, J. B. Sermons, parochial and occasional. N. Y., 1879. 28545
—— — Sermons preached before the Univ. of Oxf. N. Y., 1876. 12°. 28544
—— Newman, J. H. Fifteen Sermons preached before the Univ. of Oxf. Lond., 1872. 12°. 28409
—— — Parochial and Plain Sermons. Lond., 1873. 8 v. 12°. . 28400–
—— — Sermons on subjects of the day. Lond., 1873. 12°. . . 28408
—— Spurgeon, C. H. Sermons. First series. N. Y., 1873. 12°. . 28547
—— Stanley, A. P. Addresses and Sermons deliv. at St. Andrew's. Lond., 1877. 12°. 28548
—— — Addresses and Sermons, deliv. [in] the U. S. and Canada in 1878. N. Y., 1879. 12°. 28549
—— Taylor, W. M. Limitations of Life. N. Y., 1880 [1879]. 8°. . 28554
Sermons out of Church. Craik, D. M. M. N. Y., 1875. 12°. . 27221
Sermons to the Clergy. Dodge, M. A. Bost., 1876. 12°. . . 27223
Serpent-Charmer. Rousselet, L. N. Y., [1879]. 8°. . . . 24682
Servia and the Servians. Denton, W. Lond., 1862. 8°. . . 20486
Seven (The) Great Hymns of the Mediæval Church. N. Y., 1868. . 766
Sevenoaks. Holland, J. G. N. Y., 1875. 12°. (2 copies.) . . 24549–
Severance, M. S. Hammersmith: his Harvard days. Bost., 1878. 12°. (2 copies.) 24819–
Sévigné, Marie de R. C. de. *Puliga, Comtesse de.* Madame de S.: her correspondents and contemporaries. Lond., 1873. 2 v. 23414–
—— *Sainte-Beuve, C. A.* (*In* 'Portraits of Cel. Women.') . . . 23643
Seward, W. H. Autobiography. With life from 1831 to 1846, by F. W. Seward. N. Y., 1877. 8°. 22774
—— Travels around the World. N. Y., 1873. 8°. 21981
—— *Welles, G.* Lincoln and Seward: remarks upon the memorial address of C. F. Adams. N. Y., 1874. 12°. 22645
Sex in Education. Clarke, E. H. Bost., 1873. 16°. . . . 28828
Sforza, F. A., *duke of Milan,* Life and Times of. Urquhart, W. P. Ed. & L., 1852. 2 v. 8°. 23935–
Shadow of the Sword. Buchanan, R. N. Y., 1877. 12°. . . 24930
Shah of Persia, Nasr-ed-Din, Diary of. Lond., 1874. 8°. . . . 21625
Shairp, J. C. On Poetic Interpretation of Nature. Edinb., 1877. 26294
—— Robert Burns. (Eng. Men of Letters.) N. Y., 1879. 12°. . 23339
Shakspeare, W. The Leopold Shakspere: works, in chronological order, from the text of Prof. Delius, with "The two noble kinsmen" and "Edward III.," and an introd. by F. J. Furnivall. Lond., [1877]. 8°. 27144
—— Pictorial Edition. Ed. by Chas. Knight. Lond., 1867. [8 v., including Biography.] 8°. 27177–

CONTENTS:—**Comedies, 2 v.:** 1, Two gentlemen of Verona; Love's labor's lost; Merry wives of Windsor; Comedy of errors; Taming of the shrew; Midsummer-night's dream; Merchant of Venice. 2, All's well;

Shakspeare, W.

Much ado; Twelfth night; As you like it; Measure for measure; Winter's tale; Tempest.—**Histories, 2 v.:** 1 [3], King John; Richard II.; Henry IV.; Henry V. 2 [4], Henry VI.; Richard III.; Henry VIII.—**Tragedies, 2 v.:** 1 [5], Romeo and Juliet; Hamlet; Cymbeline; Othello; Timon of Athens; King Lear. 2 [6], Macbeth; Troilus and Cressida; Coriolanus; Julius Cæsar; Antony and Cleopatra; **Poems.**—[7], **Doubtful plays,** etc. —[8], **Biography.**

—— Works. Ed. by W. G. Clark and (v. 1) J. Glover, (v. 2–9) W. A. Wright. Cambr. & L., 1863–66. 9 v. 8°. 27135–

CONTENTS:—1, Tempest; Two gentlemen of Verona; Merry wives; Measure for measure; Comedy of errors.—2, Much ado about nothing; Love's labor's lost; Midsummernight's dream; Merchant of Venice; As you like it.—3, Taming of the shrew; All's well that ends well; Twelfth night; Winter's tale.—4, King John; Richard II.; Henry IV.; Henry V.—5, Henry VI.; The Contention; The true tragedy; Richard III.—6, Henry VIII.; Troilus and Cressida; Coriolanus; Titus Andronicus.—7, Romeo and Juliet; Timon of Athens; Julius Cæsar; Macbeth.—8, Hamlet; King Lear; Othello. —9, Antony and Cleopatra; Cymbeline; Pericles; Poems.

—— Plays [and Poems]. Ed. by H. Staunton. Lond., 1858–60. 3 v. 8°. 27173–

CONTENTS:—1, Two gentlemen; Love's labour; Comedy of errors; Romeo and Juliet; Taming of the shrew; King John; Midsum. night's dream; Merchant of Venice; Richard II.; Henry IV.; Merry wives; Much ado.—2. All's well; Henry V.; As you like it; Pericles; Twelfth night; Henry VI.; Timon of Athens; Richard III.; Measure for measure; Henry VIII.; Cymbeline.—3, Tempest; King Lear; Coriolanus; Winter's tale; Troilus and Cressida; Hamlet; Julius Cæsar; Macbeth; Antony and Cleopatra; Titus Andronicus; Othello; Poems.

—— Plays. Ed. by T. Keightley. Lond., 1864. 6 v. 16°. . . . 27080–

CONTENTS:—1, Comedy of errors; Two gentlemen; Love's labour; All's well; Midsum.-night's dream; Taming of the shrew; Merchant of Venice.—2. As you like it; Much ado; Merry wives; Twelfth night; Measure for measure; Winter's Tale; Tempest.—3, King John; Richard II.; Henry IV.; Henry V.—4, Henry VI.; Richard III.; Henry VIII.—5, Romeo and Juliet; Hamlet; Othello; Jul. Cæsar; Antony and Cleopatra; King Lear.—6, Macbeth; Troilus and Cressida; Timon; Coriolanus; Cymbeline; Titus Andronicus.

—— Plays; with life. Ed. by G. C. Verplanck. N. Y., 1847. 3 v. 27170–

CONTENTS:—1, Histories.—2, Comedies.—3, Tragedies.

—— [Plays.] Ed., with notes, by W. J. Rolfe. N. Y., 1876–80. (15 v.) 27087–

CONTENTS:—As you like it.—Hamlet.—King Henry IV. (parts 1 & 2.), 2 v. —King Henry V.—King John.—King Richard II.—King Richard III.—Macbeth.—Midsummer-night's dream.—Much ado.—Othello.—Romeo and Juliet. —Twelfth night.—Winter's tale.

—— [Plays.] Ed. by W. A. Wright (and W. G. Clark). Oxf., Clar. Press, 1876–78. (8 v.) 16°. 27117–

CONTENTS:—As you like it.—Julius Cæsar.—King Lear.—King Richard II. —Macbeth.—Merchant of Venice.—Midsummer-night's dream.—Tempest.

—— New Variorum Edition. Ed. by H. H. Furness. Phil., 1871–80. 5 v. 8°. . . . . 1659 & 27185–

CONTENTS:—1, Romeo and Juliet.—2, Macbeth.—3-4, Hamlet.—5, King Lear.—

—— Poetical Works. With memoir [etc.] by G. Gilfillan. Edinb., 1856. 8°. 26352

—— Doubtful Plays. [Ed. by Max Moltke.] Leipz., 1869. 16°. . 27086

CONTENTS:—King Edward III.; Thomas Lord Cromwell; Locrine; A Yorkshire tragedy; London prodigal; Birth of Merlin.

—— Concordance to Shakspeare's Poems. By Mrs. H. H. Furness. Phil., 1875. 8°. 1658

—— *Bacon, D.* Philosophy of the Plays of Shakspere unfolded. Lond., 1857. 8°. 27040

—— [*Bathurst, C.*] Remarks on the Differences in Shakespeare's Versification in different periods of his life. Lond., 1857. 16°. 27011

—— *Bell, W.* Shakespeare's Puck, and his Folkslore. Lond., 1852, ['61, & ?]. 3 v. 12°. 27012–

Shakspeare, W. *Birch, W. J.* Philosophy and Religion of Shakspere. Lond., 1848. 12°. 27008

—— *Brown, C. A.* Shakespeare's Autobiographical Poems: being his sonnets clearly developed. Lond., 1838. 12°. . . . 27005

—— *Brown, H.* The Sonnets of Shakespeare solved. Lond., 1870. 27051

—— *Bucknill, J. C.* The Mad Folk of Shakespeare: psychological essays. Lond., 1867. 12°. 27015

—— *Campbell, J.* Shakespeare's Legal Acquirements considered. Lond., 1859. 8°. 27001

—— *Clarke, C. C.* Shakespeare-Characters; chiefly those subordinate. Lond., 1863. 8°. 27041

—— *Coleridge, S. T.* Shakespeare, Ben Jonson, Beaumont and Fletcher: notes and lectures. Liverp., 1874. 16°. (2 copies.) . . . . 3180 & 27021

—— *Douce, F.* Illustrations of Shakspeare. Lond., 1839. 8°. . 27054

—— *Dowden, E.* Shakspere. (Lit. Primers.) Lond., 1877. 16°. 26856 & 27025

—— — Shakspere: a critical study of his mind and art. Lond., 1875. 27000

—— *Ellacombe, H. N.* The Plant-lore and Garden-craft of Shakespeare. Exeter, [1878]. 8°. 27047

—— *Elze, C.* Essays on Shakespeare. Lond., 1874. 8°. . . . 27046

—— *Fleay, F. G.* Shakespeare Manual. Lond., 1876. 16°. . . 27019

—— *French, G. R.* Shakspeareana Genealogica. Pt. 1, [Notes on the historical plays]. Pt. 2, The Shakspeare and Arden families. Lond., 1869. 8°. 27048

—— *Fullom, S. W.* Hist. of Shakespeare: with new facts and traditions. Lond., 1864. 8°. 27052

—— *Halliwell, J. O.* Life of Shakespeare. Lond., 1848. 8°. . . 27044

—— *Hunter, J.* New Illustrations of the Life, Studies, and Writings of Shakespeare. Lond., 1845. 2 v. 8°. 27049–

—— *Kellogg, A. O.* Shakspeare's Delineations of Insanity, Imbecility, and Suicide. N. Y., 1866. 16°. 27016

—— *Knight, C.* Shakspere; a biography. Lond., 1867. 8°. . . 27184

—— — Studies of Shakspere. Lond., 1849. 8°. 27042

—— *Morgann, M.* Dramatic Character of Falstaff. Lond., 1825. 12°. 27002

—— New Exegesis of Shakespeare: interpretation of his principal characters and plays on the principle of races. Edinb., 1859. 12°. 27003

—— *Prior, J.* Life of E. Malone, editor of Shakspeare. Lond., 1860. 8°. 23451

—— *Rendle, W.* Southwark in the time of Shakspere. [Lond.,] 1878. 27176

—— *Rushton, W. L.* Shakespeare's Euphuism. Lond., 1871. 12°. 27010

—— *Seeley, J. R., and others.* Three Essays on King Lear. Lond., 1851. 8°. 27053

—— *Skeat, W. W.* Shakespeare's Plutarch: a selection from the lives in North's Plutarch which illustrate Shakespeare's plays. Lond., 1875. 12°. 27009

—— *Spalding, T. A.* Elizabethan Demonology: with special ref. to Shakspere. Lond., 1880. 12°. 28042

—— *Stokes, H. P.* Chronological Order of Shakespeare's Plays. Lond., 1878. 16°. 27020

Shakspeare, W. *Swinburne, A. C.* A Study of Shakespeare. N. Y., 1880. 12°. 27006

—— *Thoms, W. J.* Three Notelets on Shakspeare. 1, S. in Germany. 2, Folk-lore of S. 3, Was S. ever a Soldier? Lond., 1865. 12°. 27004

—— *Ulrici, H.* Shakspeare's Dramatic Art. Lond., 1876. 2 v. 12°. 27017–

—— *Walker, W. S.* A Critical Examination of the Text of Shakespeare. Lond., 1860. 3 v. 16°. 27022–

—— *Weiss, J.* Wit, Humor, and Shakspeare. Bost., 1876. 12°. . 27308

—— *White, R. W.* Shakespeare's Scholar. N. Y., 1854. 8°. . . 27043

—— *Wilkes, G.* Shakespeare, from an Amer. point of view. N. Y., 1877. 8°. 27045

—— *Wordsworth, C.* On Shakspeare's Knowledge and Use of the Bible. Lond., 1864. 12°. 27007

—— *See, also,* **Bagehot, W.,** 'Lit. Stud.,' v. 1 (26767); **Clarke, J. F.,** 'Mem. and Biogr. Sketches' (22618); **Doyle, F. H.,** 'Lect. on Poetry,' 2d ser., 'Lear,' 'Othello,' 'Macbeth,' 'Tempest' (26286); **Lamartine, A. M. L. de,** 'Biogr.,' v. 1–2 (23727-); **Lowell, J. R.,** 'Among my Books,' v. 1 (3616); **Masson, D.,** 'Three Devils' (27299); **Maudsley, H.,** 'Body and Mind,' Hamlet (28000).

Shaw, R. Visits to High Tartary, Yârkand, and Kâshghar, and return journey over the Karakoram pass. Lond., 1871. 8°. . 21923

Shea, G. Life and Epoch of Alex. Hamilton. Bost., 1879. 8°. . 22722

Shedd, W. G. T. Literary Essays. N. Y., [1878]. 12°. . . . 26927

CONTENTS:—The true nature of the beautiful and its relation to culture; Influence and method of English studies; Ethical theory of rhetoric and eloquence; Characteristics and importance of a natural rhetoric; Relation of language and style to thought; Scientific and popular education; Intellectual temperance; Puritan character; African nature; Coleridge as a philosopher and theologian; Confessions of Augustine.

Sheil, R. L., Memoirs of. McCullagh, W. T. Lond., 1855. 2 v. 12°. 18669–

Shelley, Jane. Shelley Memorials. Lond., 1859. 12°. . . . 26211

Shelley, Mary W. Rambles in Germany and Italy, in 1840, 1842, and 1843. Lond., 1844. 2 v. 12°. 18552–

—— Valperga. [Anon.] Lond., 1823. 3 v. 12°. 18693–

Shelley, P. B. Essays, Letters from abroad, Translations and Fragments. Ed. by Mrs. Shelley. Lond., 1845. 8°. 27561

—— Poetical Works. Ed. by H. B. Forman. Lond., 1876–7. 4 v. 8°. 26207–

—— Prose Works. Ed. by H. B. Forman. Lond., 1880. 4 v. 8°. 27495–

CONTENTS:—1, Zastrozzi, a romance; St. Irvyne, or, the Rosicrucian; Necessity of atheism; Address to the Irish people; Proposals for an association; Declaration of rights; Letter to Lord Ellenborough.—2, Vindication of natural diet; Refutation of deism; Proposal for putting reform to the vote; Death of Princess Charlotte; Six weeks' tour; Journal at Geneva; The Assassins; Punishment of death; Life; Love; Future state; Speculations on morals; Essay on Christianity; On the devil, and devils; etc.—3, Notes on sculptures; Defence of poetry; Translations; Letters before the final departure from Eng.; App. to v. 1-3; etc.—4, Letters from Italy; General index to Poetical and Prose Works.

—— Works. 4th series. Ed. by R. H. Shepherd. Lond., 1875. 16°. 27600

CONTENTS—Zastrozzi; St. Irvyne; Dublin and Marlow pamphlets; Refutation of deism; Miscel. letters; The Shelley papers.

—— *Garnett, R.* Relics of Shelley. Lond., 1862. 16°. (2 copies.) . 26213–

—— *Mac-Carthy, D. F.* Shelley's Early Life, from original sources. Lond., [1872]. 12°. 23298

—— *Masson, D.* Wordsworth, Shelley, Keats. Lond., 1874. 12°. . 27298

Shelley, P. B. *Middleton, C. S.* Shelley and his Writings. Lond., 1858. 2 v. 23300–

— *Scott, R. P.* The Place of Shelley among the Eng. poets of his time. Cambr., 1878. 12°. 26212

— *Shelley, Jane.* Shelley Memorials: from authentic sources. Lond., 1859. 12°. 26211

— *Smith, G. B.* Shelley: a critical biography. Edinb., 1877. 16°. 23299

— *Stoddard, R. H.* Anecdote Biography of Shelley. N. Y., 1877. 23251

— *Symonds, J. A.* (Eng. Men of Letters.) N. Y., 1879 [1878]. 12°. 23335

— *Trelawny, E. J.* Records of Shelley, Byron, and the Author. Lond., 1878. 2 v. 12°. 23296–

— *See, also,* **Bagehot, W.,** 'Lit. Stud.,' v. 1 (26767); **Hutton, R. H.,** 'Essays,' v. 2 (27488); **Peacock, T. L.,** 'Works,' v. 3 (27305); **Swinburne, A. C.,** 'Ess. and Stud.' (26942).

Shenstone, W. Poetical Works. With life [etc.] by G. Gilfillan. Edinb., 1854. 8°. 26353

Shenstone Green. [Pratt, S. J.] Lond., 1779. 3 v. 16°. . . . 18687–

[**Shepherd, R. H.**] Tennysoniana. 2d ed., rev. and enl. Lond., 1879. 16°. 23250

— Translations from Charles Baudelaire. With a few orig. poems. Lond., 1869. 16°. 26040

Sheridan, R. B. Works; with a memoir by Jas. P. Browne, containing extracts from the life by Thos. Moore. Lond., 1873. 26642

— *Rae, W. F.* Wilkes, Sheridan, Fox. Lond., 1874. 8°. . . . 23040

— Sheridan and his Times. By an Octogenarian. Lond., 1859. . 23625

— *Watkins, J.* Memoirs of the Public and Private Life of Sheridan. Lond., 1818. 2 v. 8°. 18567–

Sherman, J. Selected Speeches and Reports on Finance and Taxation, from 1859 to 1878. N. Y., 1879. 8°. 29047

Sherman, W. T. Memoirs. By himself. N. Y., 1875. 2 v. 8°. . 22686–

Sherring, M. A. Hist. of Prot. Missions in India. Lond., 1875. 8°. 28601

Shipley, O. Ecclesiastical Reform: eight essays by various writers. Lond., 1873. 12°. 28491

Contents:—1, Existing relations bet. Church and State, by the editor; 2, Convocation and other synods, E. L. Blenkinsopp; 3, Decay of discipline, J. C. Chambers; 4, Cathedrals and chapters, H. Humble; 5, Rights of the laity, J. W. Lea; 6, Eccles. suits, E. G. Wood; 7, Church patronage, A. H. Prichard; 8, Creeds in relation to reform, W. J. K. Little.

Shooting. Bogardus, A. H. Field, Cover, and Trap Shooting. N. Y., 1874. 12°. 29609

— Long, J. W. American Wild-fowl Shooting. N. Y., 1874. 12°. 29610

— Walsh, J. H. Hints to Sportsmen on Guns and Shooting. Lond. 16°. 29612

— *See, also,* **Hunting; Sports.**

Short, J. T. The North Americans of Antiquity. N. Y., 1880. 8°. 21400

Shorthand. Pitman, H. Lond., 1879. 16°. 27835

Siam. Bacon, G. B. Siam as it was and is. N. Y., 1873. 12°. . 21206

— Beauvoir, L. de. (*In* 'A Voyage,' v. 2). 21201

— *See, also,* **Indo-China.**

Sicilian Bandit. Dumas, A. D. Lond., [1879]. 16°. (2 cop.) 24412 & 24419

Sicily. Amari, M. Hist. of the War of the Sicilian Vespers. Lond., 1850. 3 v. 12°. 20010–

Sidmouth, *Lord.* *See* **Addington, H.**
Sidney, Algernon, Life and Times of. Ewald, A. C. Lond., 1873. 2 v. 8°. 23021-
Sidney, Philip, Memoir of. Bourne, H. R. F. Lond., 1862. 8°. . 23417
Sight. *See* **Eyes.**
Sigurd the Volsung, The Story of. Morris, W. Bost., 1877. 8°. . 26103
Silver and Gold. Horton, S. D. Cincin., 1877. 8°. 29045
Simcox, Edith. Natural Law: an essay in ethics. Bost., 1877. 8°. 28208
Sime, J. Hist. of Germany. N. Y., 1874. 16°. 20082
—— Lessing: [a biography.] Lond., 1877. 2 v. 8°. . . . 23328-
Simon, J. The Government of Thiers. N. Y., 1879. 2 v. 8°. . 20693-
Simon. Dudevant, A. L. A. D. (*In vol. with* 'La dernière Aldini.') 25678
Simpleton (A). Reade, C. Lond., 1873. 3 v. in 1. 12°. . , . 24813
Simpson, J. Y., Memoir of. Duns, J. Edinb., 1873. 8°. . . 23542
Simpson, L. Correspondence of Schiller with Körner. With biographical sketches and notes. Lond., 1849. 3 v. 12°. . 23320-
Simpson, M. Lectures on Preaching. N. Y., 1879. 12°. . . 28424
Simpson, W. Meeting the Sun. Bost., 1877. 8°. 21982
Sin, Christian Doctrine of. Tulloch, J. N. Y., [1876]. 12°. . . 28551
Sinai. Bartlett, S. C. From Egypt to Palestine, through Sinai. N. Y., 1879. 8°. 21843
—— Palmer, H. S. Sinai, from the fourth Egyptian dynasty to the present day. Lond., [1878]. 16°. 20045
Sinding, P. C. The Scandinavian Races. N. Y., 1875. 8°. . . 20387
Sintram. La Motte Fouqué, F. de. Braunsch., 1873. 16°. . . 25831
Sir Gibbie: a novel. MacDonald, G. Phil., 1879. 8°. (2 copies.) 24676-
Sismondi, J. C. L. Simonde de. France under the Feudal System. Lond., 1851. 8°. 20692
—— The French under the Carlovingians. Lond., 1850. 8°. . . 20691
Sister Dora. Lonsdale, M. Bost., 1880. 16°. 23650
Sisters (The). Ebers, G. M. Leipz., 1880. 16°. (2 copies.) . . 24431-
Six Years later. Dumas, A. D. Lond., [1879]. (2 copies.) 24409 & 24426
Skeat, W. W. Shakespeare's Plutarch. Lond., 1875. 12°. . . 27009
—— Songs and Ballads of Uhland, transl. [metrically]. Lond., 1864. 26173
Skelton, J. Poetical Works. With notes [etc.] by A. Dyce. Lond., 1843. 2 v. 8°. 26244-
Sketches of Russian Life before and during the Emancipation of the Serfs. Ed. by H. Morley. London, 1866. 12°. . . 21683
Sketches of Young Couples. Dickens, C. J. H. [L. &] N. Y., [1879]. 16°. (2 copies.) 24228-
Skinner, O. Issues of American Politics. Phila., 1873. (2 copies.) 21327-
Skirmishing. Jenkin, C. N. Y., 1874. 16°. 24584
Slavery. Helps, A. (*In* 'Friends in Council,' 1st ser., v. 2.) . . 27251
—— Leland, C. G. Abraham Lincoln, and the Abolition of Slavery in the U. S. [L. &] N. Y., 1879. 16°. 22451
Slavonic Fairy Tales. Naaké, J. T. Lond., 1874. 12°. . . . 27785
Slip (A) in the Fens. N. Y., 1873. 16°. 24857
Smiles, S. George Moore, merchant, and philanthropist. Lond., 1878. 8°. 23931

Smiles, S. Life of a Scotch Naturalist: Thomas Edward. N. Y., 1877. 12°. 23565
—— Lives of Boulton and Watt. Phila., 1865. 8°. 23534
—— Robert Dick, baker, of Thurso, geologist and botanist. N. Y., 1879. 12°. 23566
—— Thrift. N. Y., 1876. 12°. 28883
Smith, Adam. Wealth of Nations. Ed. by J. E. T. Rogers. Oxf., 1869. 2 v. 8°. 29164–
Smith, Albert. The Pottleton Legacy. Lond., 1852. 12°. . . 24821
—— The Wassail-Bowl. Lond., 1843. 12°. 25211
—— *See* **Man** (The) in the Moon.
Smith, Edward. Foods. N. Y., 1878. 12°. 29242
Smith, Edward. William Cobbett: a biography. Lond., 1878. 2 v. 12°. 22890–
Smith, Geo. Assyria. (Anc. Hist. from the Monuments.) N. Y., 1876. 16°. 20040
—— Hist. of Babylonia. Ed. by A. H. Sayce. Lond. 16°. . . 20041
Smith, Geo. Life of Alex. Duff, D.D., LL.D. N. Y. & Toronto, [1880]. 2 v. 8°. 22190–
Smith, Geo. B. Life of Wm. E. Gladstone. N. Y., 1880 [1879]. 8°. 23071
—— Shelley: a critical biography. Edinb., 1877. 16°. . . . 23299
Smith, Gerrit: a biography. Frothingham, O. B. N. Y., 1878. 12°. 22623
Smith, Goldwin. Cowper. (Eng. Men. of Letters.) N. Y., 1880. . 23347
—— Irish Hist. and Irish Character. Oxf. & Lond., 1861. 12°. . 20815
Smith, Herbert H. Brazil: the Amazons and the coast. N. Y., 1879. 8°. 21801
Smith, Horace. Adam Brown, the Merchant: [an anon. novel.] Lond., 1843. 3 v. 12°. 18629–
—— **& James Smith.** Rejected Addresses. Bost., 1851. 12°. . 27266
Smith, J. Moyr. The Prince of Argolis. Illust. by J. Moyr Smith. N. Y., 1878. 12°. 24176
Smith, Philip. The Student's Ecclesiastical History. N. Y., 1879. 28444
Smith, Philip V. Hist. of the English Institutions. Phila., 1874. . 20064
Smith, R. Murdoch. Persian Art. Lond., [1876]. 12°. . . 29771
Smith, Reginald B. Carthage and the Carthaginians. Lond., 1878. 20094
—— Mohammed and Mohammedanism. N. Y., 1875. 12°. . . 28567
Smith, Strother A. The Tiber and its Tributaries. Lond., 1877. . 21786
Smith, W. Anderson. Lewsiana: or, Life in the outer Hebrides. Lond., 1875. 12°. 21253
Smollett, T. G. Works; with his life [and an essay on] romance, by J. Moore. New ed., by J. P. Browne. Lond., 1872. 8 v. 24683–

Contents:—1, On Romance; Life; Plays & Poems.—2, Roderick Random.—3-4, Peregrine Pickle.—5, Ferdinand Count Fathom.—6, Sir Launcelot Greaves.—7, Humphry Clinker.—8, Travels thro' France and Italy; Expedition against Carthagena.

Smyth, Newman. Old Faiths in New Light. N. Y., 1879. 12°. . 28701
Smyth, Piazzi. Our Inheritance in the Great Pyramid. Lond., 1874. 12°. 21695
Snow Man. Dudevant, A. L. A. D. Bost., 1872. 16°. . . . 24920
Social Economy. Rogers, J. E. T. N. Y., 1872. 12°. . . . 28884
Social Economy, Handbook of. About, E. F. V. N. Y., 1873. 12°. 28880

Social Pressure. Helps, A. Bost., 1875. 12°. 28882
Social Science. [Harrison, J. B.] Certain Dangerous Tendencies in Amer. Life, and other papers. Bost., 1880. 16°. . . 28885
—— Thompson, R. E. Social Sci. and National Ec. Phil., 1875. . 28810
See, also, **Civilization; Education; Institutions; Law; Liberty; Man; Political Ec.; Prisons; Slavery; Sociology; Temperance.**
Socialism. Booth, A. J. Saint-Simon and Saint-Simonism. Lond., 1871. 8°. 23522
—— Cook, J. (Bost. Monday Lectures.) Bost., 1880. 12°. . . 28028
—— Hitchcock, R. D. N. Y., 1879. 12°. 29117
—— Kaufmann, M. Lond., 1874. 12°. 29118
—— *See, also,* **Communism.**
Sociology. Spencer, H. Ceremonial Institutions: Principles of Sociology, v. 2, pt. 1. N. Y., 1880. 28123
—— — Principles of Sociology. N. Y., 1877. v. 1. 12°. (2 cop.) . 28121–
—— — The Study of Sociology. N. Y., 1874. 12°. 28120
—— — *Same.* N. Y., 1875. 12°. 29244
—— *See, also,* **Social Science** (*& references*).
Socrates. *Blackie, J. S.* (*In* 'Four Phases of Morals.') . . . 28080
Solar Spectrum. *See* **Spectrum.**
Soldatenleben im Frieden. Hackländer, F. W. von. Stuttg., 1875. 16°. (Werke, B. 4.) 25801
Somerville, Mary F. Personal Recollections. Bost., 1874. 8°. . 23547
Somerville, W. The Chase. With memoir [etc.] by G. Gilfillan. Edinb., 1859. 8°. 26319
Somnambulism, Artificial. Proctor, R. A. (*In* 'Rough Ways.') . 29444
Songs. Blackie, J. S. Musa Burschicosa: songs for students. Edinb., 1869. 16°. 26042
—— — Songs of Religion and Life. N. Y., 1876. 16°. . . . 26043
—— Holmes, O. W. Songs of many Seasons. Bost., 1875. 16°. . 26021
—— Lover, S. Songs and Ballads. Lond., 1844. 16°. . . . 26081
—— Mackay, C. Cavalier Songs and Ballads of England. Lond., 1863. 16°. 26119
—— [Morice, L.] Songs of Two Worlds. Lond., 1880. 16°. . . 26100
—— Ralston, W. R. S. Songs of the Russian People. Lond., 1872. 8°. 27782
—— Ricord, F. W. English Songs from Foreign Tongues. N. Y., 1879. 12°. 26164
—— Swinburne, A. C. Songs before Sunrise. Lond., 1871. 12°. . 26169
—— — Songs of the Springtides. N. Y., [1880]. 12°. . . . 26170
—— Whittier, J. G. Songs of Three Centuries. Bost., 1876. 12°. . 26141
Songstresses of Scotland. Keddie (H.) & Watson (J. L.). Lond., 1871. 2 v. 8°. 23763–
Sonnet (The): its origin, structure, and place in poetry. Tomlinson, C. Lond., 1874. 12°. 26297
Sonnets, English, A Treasury of. Main, D. M. Manchester, 1880. 26124
Sophocles. Tragedies. New translation [etc.] by E. H. Plumptre. Lond., 1871. 12°. 26821
—— *Collins, C. W.* (Anc. Classics for Eng. Readers, v. 10.) . . 26836
Sorrow and Song. Curwen, H. Lond., 1875. 2 v. 12°. . . 23285–
Soudan. *See* **Sudan.**

Sound. Blaserna, P. Theory of Sound in its relation to Music. N. Y., 1876. 12°. 29262
—— Mayer, A. M. N. Y., 1878. 12°. 29316
—— *See, also,* **Acoustics; Music.**
South, R. *Lake, W. C.* (*In* **Classic** Preachers.) 22112
South Kensington Museum Art Handbooks. 29760–

CONTENTS:—Tapestry, by A. de Champeaux.—Mus. Instruments, C. Engel.—Bronzes, C. D. E. Fortnum.—Maiolica, ditto.—Ivories, W. Maskell.—Glass, A. Nesbitt.—Furniture and Woodwork, J. H. Pollen.—Gold and silver, ditto.—Manual of Design, R. Redgrave.—Spanish Arts, J. F. Riaño.—Textile Fabrics, D. Rock.—Persian Art, R. M. Smith.—Industrial Arts, W. Maskell.

South-Sea Bubbles. [Herbert (G. R. C.) & Kingsley (G. H.).] N. Y., 1872. 12°. 21609
South Seas. Markham, A. H. The Cruise of the "Rosario." Lond., 1873. 8°. 21814
—— *See, also,* **Polynesia.**
South by West. Miss Kingsley. Lond., 1874. 8°. 21582
Southern States (U. S.). Longfellow, H. W. Poems and Places, v. 29. 26468
Southey, R. Letters [from] Spain and Portugal. Bristol & L., 1799. 18571
—— Oliver Newman: a New England tale (unfinished); with other poetical remains. Lond., 1845. 16°. 18619
—— *Dowden, E.* (Eng. Men of Letters.) N. Y., 1880. 12°. . . 23344
Southwark in the time of Shakspere. Rendle, W. [Lond.,] 1878. 8°. 27176
Southwell, R. Poetical Works; ed. by W. B. Turnbull. Lond., 1856. 16°. 26132
Souvestre, E. An Attic Philosopher in Paris. N. Y., 1880. 16°. . 24926
Souza, Adélaide M. E. de. *Sainte-Beuve, C. A.* (*In* 'Portraits.') . 23643
Spain. Longfellow, H. W. Poems of Places, v. 14–15. . . . 26453–
—— Thieblin, N. L. Spain and the Spaniards. Lond., 1874. 2 v. 21258–
—— Thornbury, W. Life in Spain, past and present. Lond., 1859. 2 v. 21630–
—— *Art.* Riaño, J. F. Industrial Arts in Spain. Lond., 1879. 12°. 29769

Description and Travel.

—— Baxley, H. W. Spain: art-remains and art realities [etc.] Lond., 1875. 2 v. 12°. 21241–
—— Davillier, C. Spain. Illust. by G. Doré. [L. &] N. Y., 1876. 4°. ——
—— Gautier, T. Voyage en Espagne. Paris, 1878. 16°. . . 25649
—— Hackländer, F. W. von. Ein Winter in Spanien. Stuttg., 1876. 3 B. 16°. (Werke, B. 22–24.) 25810–
—— Hare, A. J. C. Wanderings in Spain. Lond., 1873. 16°. . 21601
—— Murray, Mrs. E. Sixteen Years of an Artist's Life. Lond., 1859. 2 v. 8°. 23926–
—— Rose, H. J. Untrodden Spain, and her Black Country. Lond., 1875. 2 v. 8°. 21783–
—— Southey, R. Letters [from] Spain and Portugal. Bristol & L., 1799. 8°. 18571

History.

—— (1474–1516) Prescott, W. H. Reign of Ferdinand and Isabella. Phil., 1871. 3 v. 8°. 20345–
—— (1516–1556) Robertson, W. Reign of Charles V. [I. of Spain]. Ed. by W. H. Prescott. Phil., 1872. 3 v. 8°. . . . 20348–

Spain. *History (continued).*
—— (1555–1574) Prescott, W. H. Reign of Philip II. Phila., 1871. 3 v. 8°. 20351–
—— (1598–1665) Churton, E. Gongora: times of Philip III. and IV. Lond., 1862. 2 v. 16°. 23652–
—— (1826–1870) Bollaert, W. Wars of Succession of Portugal and Spain; with résumé of the political hist. to the present time. Lond., 1870. 2 v. 8°. 20709–
—— *See, also,* **Inquisition.**
Spalding, T. A. Elizabethan Demonology. Lond., 1880. 12°. . 28042
Spanish Armada. *See* **Armada.**
Spaulding, M. C. Handbook of Statistics of the U. S. N. Y., 1874. 21363
Speaking. *See* **Rhetoric** *(and references).*
Spectator (The). [Addison (J.) & Steele (R.).] Ed. by H. Morley. Lond., [1879]. 12°. 27264
—— — Sir Roger de Coverley. With notes by W. H. Wills. N. Y., 1878. 32°. 27265
Spectroscope (The) and its Applications. Lockyer, J. N. Lond., 1873. 12°. 29318
Spectrum Analysis, Studies in. Lockyer, J. N. N. Y., 1878. 12°. 29263
Spelling Reform, Plea for. Pitman, I., *editor.* Lond., 1878. (2 cop.) 27836–
Spence, J. M. The Land of Bolivar. Lond., 1878. 2 v. 8°. . 21806–
Spencer, H. Ceremonial Institutions. N. Y., 1880. 12°. . . 28123
—— Data of Ethics. N. Y., 1879. 12°. (2 copies.) 28129–
—— Principles of Sociology. N. Y., 1877. v. 1. 12°. (2 copies.) . 28121–
—— Study of Sociology. N. Y., 1874. 12°. 28120
—— *Same.* N. Y., 1875. 12°. 29244
—— *Bowne, B. P.* Philosophy of Spencer. N. Y., 1876. 12°. . 28168
—— *& others.* J. S. Mill: twelve sketches. Bost., 1873. 16°. . 23527
Spencer, J. A. Hist. of the Prot. Epis. Church in the U. S. (*In* **Perry, G. G.,** 'Hist. of the Ch. of Eng.') 28443
Spenser, E. Complete Works (Globe edition). Lond., 1877. 12°. (2 copies.) . . . . 14884 & 26133
—— Poetical Works. With memoir [etc.] by G. Gilfillan. Edinb., 1859. 5 v. 8°. 26357–
CONTENTS:—1-4, Faerie Queene.—4-5, Shepherd's calender, etc.
—— *Church, R. W.* (English Men of Letters.) N. Y., 1879. 12°. . 23340
—— *See, also,* **Lowell, J. R.,** 'Among my Books,' v. 2 (26931); **Maurice, J. F. D.,** 'Friendship of Books' (27301).
Spicer, H. Judicial Dramas. Lond., 1872. 8°. 28840
Spielhagen, F. Sämmtliche Werke. Leipz., 1876–7. 12 B. 16°. . 25860–
CONTENTS:—1-2, Problematische Naturen: (2te Abth., Durch Nacht zum Licht.)—3, Novellen, 1ster Band: (Clara Vere; Auf der Düne; In der zwölften Stunde; Röschen vom Hofe.)—4, Die von Hohenstein.—5-6, In Reih' und Glied.—7, Aus meinem Skizzenbuche; Gedichte.—8, Novellen, 2ter Band: (Die schönen Amerikanerinnen; Hans u. Grete; Die Dorfcoquette; Deutsche Pioniere.)—9-10, Hammer u. Amboss.—11, Allzeit voran.—12, Was die Schwalbe sang; Ultimo.
—— What the Swallow Sang. N. Y., 1873. 16°. 24856
Spinoza. Ein Denkerleben. Auerbach, B. Stuttg., 1871. 16°. (Romane, B. 1.) 25887
Spiridion. Dudevant, A. L. A. D. (*In vol. with* 'Un hiver a Majorque.') 25681

Spirite : nouvelle fantastique. Gautier, T. Paris, 1877. 16°. . 25648
—— *Same, transl.* N. Y., 1877. 16°. (2 copies.) 24074–
Spiritualism. Carpenter, W. B. N. Y., 1877. 12°. 28044
—— Crookes, W. Researches. Lond., 1874. 8°. 28041
—— Hammond, W. A. N. Y., 1876. 12°. 28043
—— Home, D. D. Lights and Shadows of Spiritualism. N. Y., 1879. 12°. 28051
—— Owen, R. D. The Debatable Land. N. Y., 1872. 12°. . . 28052
—— — Footfalls. Philad., 1860. 12°. 28053
—— Report on Spiritualism, of the committee of the Lond. Dialectical Soc., [etc.] Lond., 1871. 8°. 28040
—— Wallace, A. R. On Miracles and Mod. Spiritualism. Lond., 1875. 28045
See, also, **Supernatural** (The) ; **Visions.**
Spitzbergen. Wells, J. C. The Gateway to the Polynia. Lond., 1873. 8°. 21887
Spofford, Harriet E. P. Art Decoration applied to Furniture. N. Y., 1878 [1877]. 8°. 29872
Sporting Sketches. [Wheelwright, H. W.] Lond., 1866. 12°. . 29605
Sports. Herbert, H. W. Complete Manual for Young Sportsmen. N. Y., 1857. 12°. 29604
—— — Field Sports of the U. S. and Brit. Provinces of N. America. N. Y., 1849. 2 v. 8°. 29600–
—— — Sporting Scenes and Characters. Phila., [1857]. 2 v. 12°. 29602–
—— Napier, E. H. D. E. Wild Sports in Europe, Asia, and Africa. Lond., 1844. 2 v. 16°. 29606–
—— Whyte-Melville, G. J. Riding Recollections. Lond., 1878. 12°. 29640
See, also, **Boat-racing; Boat-sailing; Camping-out, Canoeing; Fishing; Games** (*& references*); **Gymnastics; Hunting; Shooting; Swimming.**
Sportsman (The) in France. Tolfrey, F. Lond., 1841. 12°. . . 29608
Sportsman's Gazetteer and General Guide. Hallock, C. N. Y., 1877. 12°. (Map in separate case.) 29621–
[Sprague, Mary A.] An Earnest Trifler. Bost., 1880. 16°. (2 copies.) 24858–
Spring Floods. Turgénief, I. S. N. Y., 1874. 16°. 24867
Spurgeon, C. H. Lectures to my Students. 1st series. N. Y., 1875. 28546
—— Sermons. 1st series. 20th ed.; with add., and a biogr. sketch by E. L. Magoon. N. Y., 1873. 12°. 28547
Squier, E. G. Peru. N. Y., 1877. 8°. 21809
Staël-Holstein, Anne L. G. N. de. *See* **Greg, W. R.,** 'Literary and Social Judgments' (27293) ; **Sainte-Beuve, C. A.,** 'Portraits' (23643).
Stage. Young, M. J. Memoirs of Mrs. Crouch ; [with] a retrospect of the stage [1780–99]. Lond., 1806. 2 v. 12°. . . 18556–
—— *See, also,* **Drama** (*& references*).
Stanhope, Hester L. *Meryon, C. L.* Memoirs of the Lady Hester Stanhope. Lond., 1846. 3 v. 12°. 12892–
—— — Travels of Lady Hester Stanhope. Lond., 1846. 3 v. 12°. 12895–
Stanhope, P. D., *earl of Chesterfield.* Letters (and Works). Ed., with notes, by Lord Mahon. Lond., 1845–53. 5 v. 8°. . 18648–
CONTENTS:—1-2, On Education ; Characters.—3-4, Political and Miscellaneous.—5. Miscellanies.

Stanhope, P. D., *earl of Chesterfield. Sainte-Beuve, C. A.* (*In* 'Eng. Portraits.') 22885

Stanhope, P. H., *Earl.* Miscellanies. Collected and ed. by Earl Stanhope. Lond., 1863–72. 2 ser. 12°. 27362–

Stanhope (*England*). Egglestone, W. M. Stanhope Memorials of Bishop Butler. Lond., 1878. 8°. 22187

Stanley, A. P. Addresses and Sermons, deliv. at St. Andrew's in 1872, '75 & '77. Lond., 1877. 12°. 28548

—— Addresses and Sermons, deliv. [in] the U. S. and Canada in 1878. N. Y., 1879. 12°. 28549

—— Historical Memorials of Westminster Abbey. Lond., 1876. 8°. 21776

—— Hist. of the Church of Scotland. Lond., 1872. 8°. 28446

—— Hist. of the Jewish Church. N. Y., 1853–76. 3 v. 8°. (2 cop. of v. 1–2). . . . . 6533– & 28440

Contents:—1, Abraham to Samuel.—2, Samuel to the Captivity.—3, From the Captivity to the Christian era.

—— On Missions. (*See* **Müller, F. M., & Stanley.**)

—— Thoughts that breathe. Selected by E. E. Brown. Bost., [1880]. 12°. 28534

Stanley, E. H. S., *earl of Derby. Kebbel, T. E.* (*In* 'Eng. Statesmen.') 22884

Stanley, H. M. Coomassie and Magdala. N. Y., 1874. 8°. . . 20621

—— How I found Livingstone. N. Y., 1872. 8°. 21856

—— Through the Dark Continent. N. Y., 1878. 2 v. (with maps in detached case). 8°. 21857–

Star Atlas. Proctor, R. A. Lond., 1877. 12°. 29446

Staunton, H. Chess-Player's Companion. Lond., 1849. (2 copies.) 29714–

—— Chess-Player's Handbook. Lond., 1873. 12°. 29717

—— Chess Praxis. Lond., 1871. 12°. 29716

—— The Chess Tournament. Lond., 1873. 12°. 29718

—— Laws and Practice of Chess. Lond., 1876. 12°. . . . 29719

Steam (and Steam-Engine). Evers, H. N. Y., [1872]. 16°. . . 29934

—— Reynolds, O. (*In* **Owens College** Ess. & Ad.) 27412

—— Smiles, S. Lives of Boulton and Watt. Phila., 1865. 8°. . 23534

—— Thurston, R. H. N. Y., 1878. 12°. 29264

—— *See, also,* **Railroads.**

Stebbins, Emma. Charlotte Cushman. Bost., 1878. 12°. . . . 22698

Stedman, E. C. Poetical Works. Complete ed. Bost., 1874. 12°. 26134

—— Victorian Poets. Bost., 1876. 12°. 26295

Steedman, C. Manual of Swimming. Melbourne, 1867. 16°. . 29643

Steele, R. Epistolary Correspondence; [with] fragments of three plays. Lond., 1809. 2 v. 8°. 23480–

—— *Montgomery, H. R.* Life and Writings of Steele. Edinb., 1865. 2 v. 8°. 23482–

—— *See, also,* **Dennis, J.,** 'Studies' (26915); **Forster, J.,** 'Histor. and Biogr. Ess.,' v. 2 (27321).

Stein, Charlotte A. E. von. *Calvert, G. H.* Bost., 1871. 16°. . 23656

Stein, H. F. C. vom, Life and Times of. Seeley, J. R. Bost., 1879. 2 v. 8°. 22580–

Stephen, *king of England and duke of Normandy*, Acts of. (*With* **Henry of Huntingdon,** 'Chronicle.') 20804

Stephen, J. F. Liberty, Equality, Fraternity. N. Y., 1873. 12°. . 28856

Stephen, L. Alex. Pope. (Eng. Men of Letters.) N. Y., 1880. . 23349

—— Essays on Freethinking and Plainspeaking. [L. &] N. Y., 1877. 27271

CONTENTS:—The broad church; Religion as a fine art; Darwinism and divinity; Are we Christians? A bad five minutes in the Alps; Shaftesbury's 'Characteristics'; Mandeville's 'Fable of the bees'; Warburton; An apology for plainspeaking.

—— Hist. of Eng. Thought in the 18th Cent. N. Y., 1876. 2 v. 8°. 28200–

—— Hours in a Library. Lond., 1874–80. 3 series. 12°. . . 26933–

CONTENTS:—1, De Foe's novels; Richardson's novels; Pope as a moralist; Mr. Elwin's edition of Pope; Walter Scott; Nat'l Hawthorne; Balzac's novels; De Quincey.—2, Sir Thos. Browne; Jona. Edwards; Wm. Law; Hor. Walpole; Dr. Johnson's writings; Crabbe's poetry; Wm. Hazlitt; Mr. Disraeli's novels.—3, Massinger; Fielding's novels; Cowper and Rousseau; First Edinburgh Reviewers; Wordsworth's ethics; Landor's Imaginary conversations; Macaulay; Charlotte Brontë; Charles Kingsley.

—— Samuel Johnson. (Eng. Men of Letters.) N. Y., 1878. 12°. . 23332

Stephens, F. G. Sir Edwin Landseer. L. & N. Y., 1880. 12°. . 23791

Stephens, George (*b.* 1800, *d.* 1851). The Manuscripts of Erdély: a romance. Lond., 1835. 3 v. 12°. 18626–

Stephens, George (*Prof., Univ. of Copenhagen*). Tegnér's Fridthjof's Saga, transl. into Eng. [verse]. (*With* **Anderson, R. B., & Bjarnason,** 'Viking Tales.') 27708

Stephens, W. R. W. Christianity and Islam; the Bible and the Koran: four lectures. N. Y., 1877. 12°. 28566

—— Life and Letters of W. F. Hook. Lond., 1879. 2 v. 8°. . . 22265–

Stephenson, Robt., Life of. Jeaffreson, J. C. Lond., 1866. 2 v. 8°. 23535–

Sterling, J. Essays and Tales. Ed., with a memoir, by J. C. Hare. Lond., 1848. 2 v. 12°. 12898–

Sterne, L. Works; with [autobiogr.]. Ed. by J. P. Browne. Lond., 1873. 4 v. 8°. 24691–

CONTENTS:—1-2, Tristram Shandy.—2, Sentimental journey.—3-4, Sermons, letters, etc.

Stevenson, R. L. An Inland Voyage. Lond., 1878. 12°. . . 21710

—— Travels with a Donkey in the Cévennes. Bost., 1879. 16°. . 21254

Stewart, B. Conservation of Energy. N. Y., 1874. 12°. . . 29246

—— Physics. (Sci. Primers.) Lond., 1878. 16°. 29363

—— **& Tait, P. G.** Paradoxical Philosophy. [Anon.] Lond., 1878. 12°. 28091

Stewart (B.) & Ward (A. W.), *editors.* Essays and Addresses, Owens College. Lond., 1874. 8°. (*For contents see* **Owens College.**) 27412

Stewart, G. Canada under the Administration of the Earl of Dufferin. Toronto, 1878. 8°. 21420

Stewart, J. Collections and Recollections. Edinb., 1823. 12°. . 18642

Stewart, R. H., *Viscount Castlereagh. Kebbel, T. E.* (*In* 'English Statesmen.') 22884

Stickney, A. A True Republic. N. Y., 1879. 12°. . . . 29094

Stigand, W. Life Work, and Opinions of H. Heine. Lond., 1875. 2 v. 8°. 23408–

Stillman, W. J. The Cretan Insurrection of 1866–7–8. N. Y., 1874. 20496

Stirling, J. H. Jerrold, Tennyson, and Macaulay; with other critical essays. Edinb., 1868. 16°. 26917

Stobart, J. W. H. Islam and its Founder. Lond., [1877]. 16°. . 28579
Stockmar, C. F. von, Memoirs of. By his son. Lond., 1872. 2 v. 23601–
Stoddard, R. H. Poems; complete ed. N. Y., 1880. 12°. . . 26247
—— *editor.* Bric-à-Brac Series. N. Y., 1874–76. 10 v. 16°. . 23252–

CONTENTS:—Anecdote biographies of Thackeray and Dickens.—Greville memoirs.—Personal recollections of Lamb, Hazlitt, and others. Personal reminiscences of Barham, Harness, and Hodder.—*Ditto* of Chorley, Planché, and Young.—*Ditto* of Constable and Gillies.—*Ditto* of Cornelia Knight and Thos. Raikes.—*Ditto* by Moore and Jerdan.—*Ditto* of O'Keeffe, Kelly, and Taylor.—Mérimée's Letters; Recollections by Lamartine and Geo. Sand.

—— — Sans-Souci Series. N. Y., 1876-7. 2 v. 16°. . 21324 & 23251

CONTENTS:—Men and manners in America, by H. E. Scudder.—Anecdote biography of Shelley.

Stokes, F. A. College Tramps. N. Y., 1880. 12°. . . . 21255
Stokes, H. P. Chronological Order of Shakespeare's Plays. Lond., 1878. 16°. 27020
Stone Implements. *See* **Antiquities; Man,** *Pre-historic.*
Stonehenge, (*pseud.*) *See* **Walsh, J. H.**
Storrs, R. S. Preaching without Notes. N. Y., 1875. 12°. . . 28415
Story, W. W. Castle St. Angelo; and The Evil Eye: being additional chapters to "Roba di Roma." Lond., 1877. 12°. . 21626
—— Graffiti d'Italia: [an Eng. poem.] Edinb. & L., 1875. 12°. . 26135
—— Nero: [an historical play.] Edinb. & L., 1875. 12°. . . 26136
Story of Avis. Phelps, E. S. Bost., 1877. 16°. (3 copies.) . . 24845–
Story of an Honest Man. About, E. N. Y., 1880. 8°. . . . 24707
Story of a Mine. Harte, F. B. Bost., 1878. 16°. 24491
Story of Three Sisters. Maxwell, C. N. Y., 1876. 16°. . . . 24831
Story (A) or two from an Old Dutch Town. Lowell, R. Bost., 1878. 16°. 24237
Stowe, Harriet E. B. Oldtown Folks. Bost., 1869. 12°. . . 24822
—— Palmetto-Leaves, [Florida.] Bost., 1873. 16°. 21288
—— Poganuc People. N. Y., [1878]. 12°. (2 copies.) . . . 24823–
—— We and our Neighbors. Sequel to "My Wife and I." N. Y., [1875]. 12°. 24825
Strange Adventures of a Phaeton. Black, W. Lond., 1872. 2 v. . 24023–
—— *Same.* N. Y., 1877. 12°. (2 copies.) 25025–
Strange Stories from a Chinese Studio. Giles, H. A. Lond., 1880. 2 v. 12°. 27787–
Strauss, D. F. Ulrich von Hutten: his life and times. Lond., 1874. 12°. 22143
—— *Zeller, E.* Lond., 1874. 12°. 23528
Strauss, G. L. M. Men who have made the New German Empire. Lond., 1875. 2 v. 8°. 22583–
Strength and Beauty. Hopkins, M. N. Y., [1874]. 12°. . . 27383
Strickland, Agnes. Lives of the last four Princesses of the Royal House of Stuart. Lond., 1872. 12°. 22926
Strikes. *See* **Coöperation; Labor; Wages.**
Stroke (A) of Diplomacy. Cherbuliez, V. N. Y., 1880. 16°. . 24922
Stuart, A. M. Recollections of John Duncan. Edinb., 1872. 16°. 23654
Stuart, G. H. The Amer. Evangelists. (*See* **Hall, J., & Stuart.**)
Stuart, J., *earl of Bute.* *See* **Bute, J. S.**

Stubbs, W. Constitutional Hist. of England. Oxf'd, 1874–78. 3 v. 20880–
—— The Early Plantagenets. N. Y., [1876]. 16°. 20455
Student and Intellectual Observer. Lond., 1868–71. 5 v. 8°. . 17723–
Student-Life at Harvard. [Tripp, G. H.] Bost., 1876. 12°. (2 cop.) 24911–
Student's (The) Quarter. Thackeray, W. M. Lond. 12°. . . 21629
Studies of Sensation and Event. Jones, E. Lond., 1879. 16°. . 26146
Studio (The) Arts. Johnson, E. W. N. Y., 1878. 16°. . . 29828
Styria. Hall, B. Schloss Hainfeld ; or, A winter in Lower Styria. Edinb., 1836. 12°. 18635
Suckling, J. Poems, Plays, and other Remains. A new ed. [by W. C. Hazlitt], with a copious account of the author. Lond., 1874. 2 v. 16°. 26137
—— Selections. [With] a life, and critical remarks, by A. Suckling. Lond., 1836. 8°. 26379
Sudan. Myers, A. B. R. Life with the Hamran Arabs: a sporting tour in the Soudan, 1874–5. Lond., 1876. 8°. 21697
Sue, M. J. E. The Mysteries of Paris. Lond., 1845–6. 3 v. 8°. . 24695–
Suez, The Great Canal at. Fitzgerald, P. Lond., 1876. 2 v. 8°. . 21840–
Sulla, Marius, and the Gracchi. Beesly, A. H. N. Y., [1879]. 16°. 20440
Sullivan, A. M. New Ireland : [1837 to 1877.] Phila., 1878. 12°. 20990
Summer and its Diseases. Wilson, J. C. Phil., 1879. 16°. . . 29960
Sumner, C. Prophetic Voices concerning America. Bost., 1874. . 21362
—— Works. Bost., 1874–77. 12 v. 12°. 27327–
—— *Pierce, E. L.* Memoir and Letters of Chas. Sumner. Bost., 1877. 2 v. 8°. 22683–
Sumner, W. G. Hist. of American Currency. N. Y., 1874 (etc.). 12°. (2 copies.) 29059–
—— Hist. of Protection in the U. S. N. Y., 1877. 8°. (2 copies.) . 29170–
Sun. Core, T. H. Distance of the Sun from the Earth. (*In* **Owens College** Ess. & Ad.) 27412
—— Stewart, B. Solar Physics. (*In the same.*) 27412
Sunday. *See* **Sabbath.**
Sunday Afternoon. Springf., 1878–9. 3 v. 8°. 18405–
(Continued under the name "Good Company.")
Sunshine and Storm in the East. Brassey, A. N. Y., 1880. 8°. . 21901
Supernatural (The). Howitt, W. Phila., 1863. 2 v. 12°. . . 28046–
—— *See, also,* **Spiritualism.**
Surly Tim. Burnett, F. H. N. Y., 1877. 16°. 24158
Swanwick, Anna. Goethe's Faust, in 2 parts. Transl. [into Eng. verse]. Lond., 1849. 8°. 26367
—— Goethe's Torquato Tasso and Iphigenia in Tauris, transl. into Eng. verse. (*In* **Goethe,** 'Dram. Works,' Lond., 1879.) . 26520
Sweden. Lloyd, L. Peasant Life in Sweden. Lond., 1870. 8°. . 21788
—— Longfellow, H. W. Poems of Places, v. 8. 26447
Swift, Jona. *Forster, J.* Life of Swift, vol 1: 1667–1711. N. Y., 1876. 8°. 23418
—— *Wilde, W. R.* The Closing Years of S.'s Life. Dublin, 1849. . 22260
—— *See, also,* **Dilke, C. W.,** 'Papers of a Critic,' v. 1 (26765); **Masson, D.,** 'Three Devils' (27299).

Swimming. Leahy, J. Swimming in the Eton Style. Illust. Lond., 1875. 12°. 29642

—— Steedman, C. Manual of Swimming; incl. bathing, . . . drowning, and rescuing. Melbourne, 1867. 16°. 29643

—— *See, also*, **Bathing; Sports.**

Swinburne, A. C. Bothwell: a tragedy. Lond., 1874. 12°. . . 26165

—— Erechtheus: a tragedy. Lond., 1876. 12°. 26166

—— Essays and Studies. Lond., 1875. 12°. 26942

CONTENTS:—Hugo: L'homme qui rit; Hugo: L'année terrible; Poems of D. G. Rossetti; Morris's Life and Death of Jason; Mat. Arnold's New Poems; Notes on the text of Shelley; Byron; Coleridge; John Ford; Notes on designs of the old masters at Florence; Notes on some pictures of 1868.

—— A Note on Charlotte Brontë. Lond., 1877. 12°. 26920

—— Poems and Ballads. 2d series. Lond., 1878. 16°. . . . 26167

—— *Same.* N. Y., 1878. 12°. 26168

—— Songs of the Springtides. N. Y., [1880]. 12°. 26170

—— Songs before Sunrise. Lond., 1871. 12°. 26169

—— A Study of Shakespeare. N. Y., 1880. 12°. 27006

Switzerland. Bremer, F. Two Years in Switzerland and Italy. Lond., 1861. 2 v. 8°. 21212–

—— Longfellow, H. W. Poems of Places, v. 16. 26455

—— *See, also*, **Alps.**

Sybel, H. C. L. von. Hist. and Literature of the Crusades. Lond., 1861. 12°. 20106

Sydney. *See* **Sidney.**

Sylvan (The) Year. Hamerton, P. G. Bost., 1876. 12°. . . 29328

Symington, A. J. Samuel Lover: a biographical sketch. N. Y., 1880. 16°. 23311

—— Thomas Moore, the Poet: his life and works. N. Y., 1880. 16°. 23314

Symonds, J. A. An Introd. to the Study of Dante. Lond., 1872. . 26283

—— Renaissance in Italy. Lond., 1875–77. v. 1–3. 8°. . . . 20298–

CONTENTS:—1, Age of the Despots.—2, Revival of Learning.—3, Fine Arts.

—— Shelley. (Eng. Men of Letters.) N. Y., 1879 [1878]. 12°. . 23335

—— Sketches and Studies in Southern Europe. N. Y., 1880. 2 v. 27341–

CONTENTS:—1, The Cornice; Ajaccio; Florence and the Medici; Debt of English to Ital. literature; Popular Ital. poetry of the Renaissance; The Orfeo of Poliziano; Siena; Perugia; Popular songs of Tuscany; Orvieto; Thoughts in Rome about Christmas; Antinous; Lucretius; Amalfi, Pæstum, Capri.—2, Palermo; Syracuse and Girgenti; Ætna; Athens; Rimini; Ravenna; Canossa; Parma; Fornovo; Two dramatists of the last century; Crema and the crucifix; Bergamo and Bartolommeo Colleoni; Como and Il Medeghino; Lombard vignettes; Monte Generoso; Love of the Alps; Old towns of Provence; Appendix: Blank verse; Note on the Orfeo; Eight sonnets of Petrarch.

—— Studies of the Greek Poets. Lond., 1873–76. 2 v. 12°. . . 26809–

—— *Same*, [re-arranged, rev. & enl.] N. Y., 1880. 2 v. 16°. . . 26811–

Syria. Barker, J. Syria and Egypt under the last five Sultans of Turkey. Lond., 1876. 2 v. 8°. 23960–

—— Beaufort, E. A. Egyptian Sepulchres and Syrian Shrines, including a visit to Palmyra. Lond., 1874. 12°. 21209

—— Burton, I. Inner Life of Syria, Palestine, and the Holy Land. Lond., 1875. 2 v. 8°. 21905–

—— Jessup, H. H. Syrian Home Life. N. Y., [1874]. 12°. . . 21613

—— Tristram, H. B. The Land of Moab. Lond., 1873. 8°. . . 21723

Table-Talk. Alcott, A. B. Bost., 1877. 12°. 27219
—— Hunt, J. H. L. N. Y., 1879. 16°. 27640
—— *See, also,* **Quotations** (*&* *references*).
Tacitus. *Donne, W. B.* (Anc. Clas. for Eng. Readers, v. 17.) . 26843
Tänzerin und Gräfin. Mügge, T. Breslau, 1863. 3 B. 16°. (Romane, B. 16–18.) 25845
Tag und Nacht. Hackländer, F. W. von. Stuttg., 1866. 2 B. 16°. (Werke, B. 35–36.) 25817
Taine, H. A. English Positivism: a study on J. S. Mill. Lond., 1873. 16°. 28092
—— Hist. of English Literature. Abridged. N. Y., 1872. 12°. . 26914
—— Notes on Paris. N. Y., 1875. 12°. 21628
—— On Intelligence. N. Y., 1875. 2 v. 12°. 28205–
—— Origins of Contemporary France. N. Y., 1876–78. v. 1–2. 12°. 20425–
CONTENTS:—Pt. 1, Anc. Régime.—Pt. 2, Fr. Revolution (*will consist of* 2 v.).
—— Philosophy of Art. N. Y., 1873. 16°. 29827
—— Tour through the Pyrenees. N. Y., 1874. 12°. 21627
—— *Sainte-Beuve, C. A.* Taine's Eng. Lit. (*In* 'Eng. Portraits.') . 22885
Taiping Rebellion. Brine, L. Lond., 1862. 12°. 20386
Tait, P. G. Recent Advances in Physical Science. Lond., 1876. 12°. 29305
—— Paradoxical Philosophy. (*See* **Stewart, B., and Tait.**)
Taking the Bastile. Dumas, A. D. Lond., [1879]. (2 cop.) 24409 & 24426
Tales of the Argonauts. Harte, F. B. Bost., 1875. 12°. (2 cop.) 24487–
Tales of a Traveller. Irving, W. N. Y., [1865]. (2 cop.) 24593½ & 24587
Tales from Two Hemispheres. Boyesen, H. H. Bost., 1877. 16°. . 24064
Talleyrand-Périgord, C. M. de. *Bulwer, H. L. E.* (*In* 'Histor. Characters,' v. 1.) 23881
Talmud. Theodores, T. (*In* **Owens College** Ess. & Ad.) . . 27412
Tancock, O. W. England during the Amer. and European Wars, 1765–1820. (*In* **Epochs** of Eng. Hist.) 20851
Tancred. Disraeli, B. N. Y. [Lond., 1878.] 16°. 24244
Taney, R. B., Memoir of. Tyler, S. Balt., 1872. 8°. . . . 22720
Tangut Country. Prejevalski, N. M. Lond., 1876. 2 v. 8°. . 21927–
Tannhäuser (Der): eine Künstlergeschichte. Hackländer, F. W. von. (Werke, B. 37.) 25818
Taouism and Confucianism. Douglas, R. K. Lond., 1879. 16°. . 28581
Tapestry. Champeaux, A. de. Lond., [1878]. 12°. . . . 29760
Tarbox, I. N. Life of Israel Putnam. Bost., 1876. 8°. . . . 22691
Tartary. Shaw, R. Visits to High Tartary. Lond., 1871. 8°. . 21923
—— *See, also,* **Manchuria; Mongolia.**
Tarver, F. Molière. (*See* **Oliphant, M. O. W., & Tarver.**)
Tasmania. Howitt, W. Lond., 1875. 2 v. 8°. 21816–
Tatham, J. Dramatic Works; with introd. and notes. Edinb. & L., 1879. 8°. 26572
Taxation. Sherman, J. Selected Speeches and Reports on Finance and Taxation, from 1859 to 1878. N. Y., 1879. 8°. . . 29047
[**Taylor, Elizabeth.**] Blindpits: a story of Scottish life. N. Y., 1869. 12°. 15386
—— Quixstar: a novel. N. Y., 1873. 16°. 24826

Taylor, Henry. Critical Essays on Poetry, etc. Lond., 1878. 12°. 26296

CONTENTS (*other*):—Crime considered in a letter to W. E. Gladstone; Review of Mill's work on "The Subjection of Women"; Correspondence with J. S. Mill.

Taylor, Isaac, *2nd* (1787–1865). Memoirs and Corresp. of Jane Taylor. (*In* "The Family Pen," v. 1.) 23603

Taylor, Isaac, *3d.* The Family Pen: memorials, biographical and literary, of the Taylor family, of Ongar. Lond., 1867. 2 v. 23603–

Taylor, Jas. Bayard. Critical Essays and Literary Notes. N. Y., 1880. 12°. 27364

CONTENTS:—Tennyson; Victor Hugo; The German Burns; Friedr. Rückert; The author of "Saul"; Thackeray; Autumn days in Weimar; Weimar in June; Notes on books and events.

—— Egypt and Iceland in the year 1874. N. Y., 1874. 16°. . . 21256

—— Faust. By Goethe. Transl., in the orig. metres. Bost., 1871. 2 v. 8°. 1298–

—— *Same.* Bost., 1879. 2 v. in 1. 12°. 26094

—— Japan, in our day. N. Y., 1872. 12°. 21684

—— Poetical Works. Bost., 1880 [1879]. 12°. 26171

—— The Prophet: a tragedy. Bost., 1874. 16°. 26172

—— Studies in Ger. Lit. With an introd. by G. H. Boker. N. Y., 1879. 12°. 26900

Taylor, Jeremy. *See* **Barry, A.,** 'Masters' (22111); **Classic** Preachers (22113).

Taylor, John (*b.* 1756, *d.* 1832). Personal Reminiscences. N. Y., 1875. 16°. 23260

Taylor, Meadows. Confessions of a Thug. Lond., 1873. 12°. . 24827

—— Story of my Life. Edinb., 1878. 12°. 18584

Taylor, Wm. C., (& C. Mackay.) Life and Times of Sir Robert Peel. Lond., [1846–51]. 4 v. 8°. 23049–

Taylor, Wm. M. Daniel, the Beloved. N. Y., 1878. 12°. . . 28648

—— David, King of Israel. N. Y., 1875. 12°. 28649

—— Elijah, the Prophet. N. Y., 1876. 12°. 28650

—— Limitations of Life, and other sermons. N. Y., 1880 [1879]. 8°. 28554

—— Ministry of the Word. N. Y., 1876. 12°. 28419

—— Moses, the Law-giver. N. Y., 1879. 12°. 28651

—— Peter, the Apostle. N. Y., 1878. 12°. 28652

Teale, W. H. Lives of English Divines: Bp. Andrewes, Dr. Hammond, Bp. Bull, Bp. Wilson, Jones of Nayland. Lond., 1848. 16°. 22110

Technology. *See* **Industrial** Arts.

Tegetthoff (*ship*). Payer, J. (*In* 'New Lands.') 21883

Tegnér, E. Fridthjof's Saga; transl. by Geo. Stephens. [With life.] (*In* **Anderson & Bjarnason's** 'Viking Tales.') . . 27708

—— Frithiof; ["paraphrased"] by R. G. Latham. Lond., 1838. 12°. 27709

Telegraph and Travel: a narrative of the [Indo-European Telegraph]. Goldsmid, F. J. Lond., 1874. 8°. 21946

Telephone. Dolbear, A. E. Bost., 1877. 16°. 29935

—— Du Moncel, T. The Telephone, the Microphone, and the Phonograph. N. Y., 1879. 12°. 29936

—— Prescott, G. B. Speaking Telephone, Talking Phonograph, [etc.]. N. Y., 1878. 8°. 29937

Temperance. Weedon, W. B. Morality of Prohibitory Liquor Laws. Bost., 1875. 16° 28887

—— *See, also,* **Intemperance.**

Temple, A. L., *Viscountess Palmerston. Hayward, A.* (*In* 'Biogr. and Crit. Ess.,' 2d ser., v. 2. *And in* 'Sel. Ess.,' v. 2.) 27402 & 27245

Temple, H. J., *Viscount Palmerston. Ashley, E.* Life of Palmerston, 1846–1865. With sel. from his speeches and corresp. Lond., 1876. 2 v. 8°. 23069–

—— *Kebbel, T. E.* (*In* 'Eng. Statesmen.') 22884

Temple, R. Grenville, *Earl. Earle, J. C.* (*In* 'Eng. Premiers,' v. 2.) 22883

Temple Bar. Lond., 1861–79. 57 v. 8°. 17889–

Tenney, S. Elements of Zoölogy. N. Y., 1875. 12°. . . . 29507

Tennyson, A. Harold : a drama. Bost., 1877. 16°. (2 copies.) . 26514–

—— The Lover's Tale. Bost., 1879. 16°. 692

—— Queen Mary : a drama. Bost., 1875. 12°. (2 copies.) . . 26516–

—— Vivien. Illust. by Doré. N. Y., 1868. 2°. . . . . . ——

—— Works. Lond., 1872–3. 6 v. 8°. 26248–

Contents:—1-2, Miscel. poems.—3, The Princess, etc.—4. In Memoriam, and Maud.—5-6, Idylls of the King.

—— *Bayne, P.* Lessons from my Masters. N. Y., 1879. 12°. . 23287

—— [*Shepherd, R. H.*] Tennysoniana. Lond., 1879. 16°. . . 23250

—— *Stirling, J. H.* Jerrold, Tennyson, and Macaulay. Edinb., 1868. 16°. 26917

—— *See, also,* **Bagehot, W.,** 'Lit. Stud.,' v. 2 (26768); **Dowden, E.,** 'Stud. in Lit.' (26926); **Gladstone, W. E.,** 'Gleanings,' v. 2 (27228); **Hutton, R. H.,** 'Essays,' 2d ed., v. 2 (27488); **Preston, H. W.,** 'Troubadours' (26906); **Sterling, J.,** 'Essays,' v. 1 (12898); **Taylor, J. B.,** 'Crit. Ess.' (27364).

Tennysoniana. [Shepherd, R. H.] Lond., 1879. 16°. . . . 23250

Terence. *Collins, W. L.* ('Anc. Clas. for Eng. Readers,' v. 16.) . 26842

Terhune, Mary V. H., (*pseud.,* 'Marion Harland.') Alone. N. Y., 1856. 12°. 15818

—— Loiterings in Pleasant Paths. N. Y., 1880. 12°. . . . 21681

Testa, G. B. Hist. of the War of Frederick I. against the Communes of Lombardy. Lond., 1877. 8°. 20296

Teverino. Dudevant, A. L. A. D. Paris, 1877. 16°. . . . 25695

Textile Fabrics. Rock, D. N. Y., 1876. 12°. 29770

Thackeray, Anne I. *See* **Ritchie, A. I. T.**

Thackeray, W. M. Adventures of Philip. (*And*) Shabby Genteel Story. Lond. (& Bost.), 1872 (etc.). 12°. (2 copies.) . . 24874–

—— Book of Snobs. Lond., 1876. 12°. 24876

—— Catherine; Lovel the Widower; Denis Duval; Ballads; &c. Lond., 1876. 12°. 24877

—— Christmas Books. Lond., 1876. 12°. 24878

Contents:—Mrs. Perkins's Ball; Our Street; Dr. Birch; The Kickleburys on the Rhine; The Rose and the Ring.

—— Great Hoggarty Diamond; Memoirs of Yellowplush; Burlesques. Lond., 1876. 12°. 24883

—— Henry Esmond. (*And*) Barry Lyndon. Lond. (& Bost.), 1872 (etc.). 12°. (4 copies.) 24879–

Thackeray, Wm. M. The Newcomes. Lond., 1872 (etc.). (2 cop.) 24884–
—— *Same.* Lond., 1873. 2 v. 12°. 24886–
—— The Orphan of Pimlico, and other sketches, fragments and drawings. With notes by Anne I. Thackeray. Phil., 1876. ——
—— Paris Sketch Book; Irish Sketch Book; Notes of a Journey from Cornhill to Grand Cairo. Lond., 1876. 12°. . . . 24888
—— Pendennis. Lond., 1871 (etc.). 2 v. 12°. (2 copies.) . . 24889–
—— *Same.* Lond., 1872 (etc.). 12°. (2 copies.) 24893–
—— Roundabout Papers; The Four Georges; English Humourists; Second Funeral of Napoleon. Lond., 1876. 12°. . 24895
—— The Student's Quarter; or, Paris 35 years since. Lond. 12°. 21629
—— Vanity Fair. [Lond. &] Phil., 1873. 2 v. 12°. (2 copies.) . 24896–
—— *Same.* Lond., 1876 (etc.). 12°. (5 copies.) 24900–
—— The Virginians. Lond., 1876 (etc.). 12°. (5 copies.) . . 24905–
—— *Hannay, J.* Studies on Thackeray. Lond., [1869]. 16°. . 26918
—— *Stoddard, R. H.* Anecdote Biogr. of Thackeray. (*In* 'Bric-à-Brac Series.') 23252
—— *Trollope, A.* (Eng. Men of Letters.) N. Y., 1879. 12°. . . 23341
—— *See, also,* **Bagehot, W.,** 'Lit. Stud., v. 2 (26768); **Taylor, J. B.,** 'Crit. Ess.' (27364).

Thackerayana. Lond., 1875. 12°. 23331
Thalheimer, Mary E. Manual of Ancient Hist. Cincin., [1872]. . 20189
—— Manual of Mediæval and Mod. Hist. Cincin., [1874]. 8°. . 20190
Thankful Blossom. Harte, F. B. Bost., 1877. 16°. (2 copies.) . 24492–
That Lass o' Lowrie's. Burnett, F. H. N. Y., 1877. 12°. (2 cop.) 24159–
Thaxter, Celia. Among the Isles of Shoals. Bost., 1873. 12°. . 21257
—— Poems. N. Y., 1874. 16°. 26116
Theater. *See* **Drama.**
Their Wedding Journey. Howells, W. D. Bost., 1875. 12°. (2 cop.) 24571–
Theism. De Vere, A. T., *editor.* Proteus and Amadeus. Lond., 1878. 12°. 28169
"Theo.": a love story. Burnett, F. H. Phil., [1877]. 16°. . . 24161
Theodore, *king of Abyssinia. See* **Abyssinia.**
Theodorus, (*pseud.*) *See* **New** Reformation.
Theognis. *Davies, J.* (Anc. Clas. for Eng. Readers, v. 15.) . . 26841
Theology. Bushnell, H. Forgiveness and Law. N. Y., 1874. 12°. 28550
—— Fisher, G. P. Discussions in Hist. and Theol. N. Y., 1880. 8°. 28591
—— Newman, J. H. Tracts, theological and ecclesiastical. Lond., 1874. 12°. 28411
—— Stephen, L. Hist. of Eng. Thought in the 18th Cent. N. Y., 1876. 2 v. 8°. 28200–
—— *Natural.* Jackson, W. Philosophy of Nat. Theology. N. Y., 1875. 8°. 28685

See, also, **Christ; Christianity; Ecc. Hist.; Faith; Religion; Sermons; Sin.**

Theophrastus Such. Eliot, G. N. Y., 1879. 12°. (2 copies.) . 24195–
Theuriet, A. Antoinette: a story. N. Y., 1878. 16°. . . . 24927
—— Gérard's Marriage: a novel. N. Y., 1877. 16°. . . . 24073
—— The Godson of a Marquis. N. Y., 1878. 16°. 24081

Theuriet, A. Raymonde: a tale. N. Y., 1878. 16°. 24927
—— Young Maugars. N. Y., 1879. 16°. 24090
Thibaut, A. F. J. On Purity in Musical Art. Lond., 1877. 12°. . 29746
Thibet. *See* **Tibet.**
Thieblin, N. L. Spain and the Spaniards. Lond., 1874. 2 v. 12°. 21258–
Thiers, L. A. *Le Goff, F.* Life of Thiers. N. Y., 1879. 12°. . 22521
—— *Senior, N. W.* Conversations with Thiers [etc.] during the second empire. Lond., 1878. 2 v. 8°. 23922–
—— *Simon, J. F.* Government of Thiers, from 1871 to 1873. N. Y., 1879. 2 v. 8°. 20693–
Thomas à Becket. *See* **Becket.**
Thomas Wingfold, Curate. MacDonald, G. N. Y., 1876. 12°. . 24624
Thomé, O. W. Structural and Physiological Botany. N. Y., 1877. 29462
Thompson, D'A. W. Wayside Thoughts. Edinb., 1868. 12°. . 28834
Thompson, Edith. Hist. of England. N. Y., 1873. 16°. . . 20079
Thompson, J. P. The United States as a Nation. Bost., 1877. 8°. 21334
Thompson, Rich. W. The Papacy and the Civil Power. N. Y., 1876. 12°. 29096
Thompson, Robt. E. Social Science and National Economy. Phila., 1875. 12°. 28810
Thoms, W. J. Human Longevity. Lond., 1873. 12°. . . . 29388
—— Three Notelets on Shakspeare. Lond., 1865. 12°. . . . 27004
Thomson, J. Public and Private Life of Animals. Adapted from the French of Balzac, Droz, Jules Janin, E. Lemoine, A. de Musset, Georges Sand, &c. Lond., 1877. 12°. . . . 24698
Thomson, Jas. Poetical Works. With Life [etc.] by G. Gilfillan. Edinb., 1853. 8°. 26362
Thomson, Katherine B. Life and Times of George Villiers, [1st] Duke of Buckingham. Lond., 1860. 3 v. 12°. . . . 22937–
Thoreau, H. D. Excursions. [With a biographical sketch by R. W. Emerson.] Bost., 1875. 12°. 29335
—— Letters to various persons. Bost., 1865. 12°. 22605
—— The Maine Woods. Bost., 1864. 16°. 29336
—— *Channing, W. E.* Bost., 1873. 16°. 22606
—— [*Japp, A.*] Bost., 1877. 16°. 22607
Thornbury, W. Life in Spain, past and present. Lond., 1859. 2 v. 21630–
—— Old and New London. Lond., [1873–4]. v. 1–2. 8°. (*For continuation see* **Walford, E.**) 21960–
Thornton, W. T. On Labour. Lond., 1870. 8°. 29002
Thorpe, B. Yule-tide Stories. Lond., 1875. 12°. 27669
Thorpe Regis. [Peard, F. M.] Bost., 1874. 16°. 24843
Three Feathers. Black, W. N. Y., 1877. 12°. (2 copies.) . . 24027–
Three Musketeers. Dumas, A. D. Lond., [1879]. 16°. . . . 24401
Thrift. Smiles, S. N. Y., 1876. 12°. 28883
Throat (The) and the Voice. Cohen, J. S. Phil., 1879. 16°. . . 29962
Through the Dark Continent. Stanley, H. M. N. Y., 1878. 2 v. 8°. 21857–
Thucydides. *Collins, W. L.* ('Anc. Clas. for Eng. Readers,' suplem. ser., v. 6.) 26852
Thurston, R. H. Growth of the Steam-engine. N. Y., 1878. 12°. 29264

Tiber (The) and its Tributaries. Smith, S. A. Lond., 1877. 8°. . 21786
Tiberius, Clodius, and Catiline. Beesly, E. S. Lond., 1878. 8°. . 23725
Tibet. Prejevalski, N. M. Lond., 1876. 2 v. 8°. 21927–
Tibullus. *Davies, J.* (Anc. Clas. for Eng. Readers, supplem. ser., v. 3.) 26849
Tichborne Claimant. Morse, J. T. (*In* 'Famous Trials.') . . 28842
Ticknor, Geo.: life, letters, and journals. Hillard, G. S. Bost., 1876. 2 v. 8°. 22688–
Tigress (*ship*). Blake, E. V. (*In* 'Arctic Experiences.') . . . 21880
Tillotson, J. *Humphry, W. G.* (*In* **Classic** Preachers; 1878.) . 22113
Timbs, J. Club Life of London. Lond., 1866. 2 v. 12°. . . 21764–
—— Curiosities of London. Lond., [1867]. 8°. 21763
Tintoretto (Giacomo Robusti). *Osler, W. R.* Lond. & N. Y., 1879. 23782
Ti-ping Tien-kwoh. [Lindley, A. F.] Lond., 1866. 2 v. 8°. . 20381–
Tirol. *See* **Tyrol.**
Tissandier, G. Hist. and Handbook of Photography. Lond., 1878. 29930
Titian (Tiziano Vecelli). *Crowe (J. A.) & Cavalcaselle (G. B.).* Lond., 1877. 2 v. 8°. 23832–
—— *Heath, R. F.* N. Y. & Lond., 1879. 12°. 23777
Tobacco. Fairholt, F. W. Lond., 1859. 12°. 29458
Tobin, J., Memoirs of; with a selection from unpublished writings. Benger, E. O. Lond., 1820. 12°. 18565
Tocqueville, A. C. H. C. de. Correspondence and Conversations with N. W. Senior, 1834 to 1859. Lond., 1872. 2 v. 12°. . 23924–
Todd, J., Life of. Todd, J. E. N. Y., 1876. 12°. 22611
Toleration. *See* **Compromise; Conscience; Liberty.**
Tolfrey, F. The Sportsman in France. Lond., 1841. 12°. . . 29608
Tolstói, L. The Cossacks. N. Y., 1878. 16°. 24910
Tom Sawyer. Clemens, S. L. Hartf'd, 1876. 8°. (2 copies.) . 25584–
Tomahawk (The): [weekly.] Lond., 1867–69. 5 v. 4°. . . . ——
Tomlinson, C. The Sonnet. With orig. translations. Lond., 1874. 26297
Topin, M. The Man with the Iron Mask. Lond., 1870. 12°. . 20403
Tour of the World in eighty days. Verne, J. Bost., 1873. 16°. . 24280
[**Tourgee, A. W.**] A Fool's Errand. N. Y., 1879. 16°. (3 cop.) . 24913–
Tourgénieff, I. S. *See* **Turgénief.**
Toussaint: ein Roman. Mügge, T. Breslau, 1862. 5 B. 16°. (Romane, B. 4–8.) 25841–
Tower of London. *See* **London,** *Tower.*
Tower of Percemont. Dudevant, A. L. A. D. N. Y., 1877. 16°. . 24076
Townsend, L. T. The Art of Speech. N. Y., 1880. v. 1. 16°. . 27824
Tozer, H. F. Classical Geography. Lond., 1876. 16°. . . . 26860
Trade (The) of the World. Webster, R. G. Lond., 1880. 8°. . . 29003
Trade Unions. *See* **Coöperation; Labor; Wages.**
Trades. *See* **Profession.**
Traditions. *See* **Folk-lore** (*and references*).
Tramp (A) abroad. Clemens, S. L. Hartf., 1880. 8°. (2 copies.) . 25589–
Transcaucasia and Ararat. Bryce, J. Lond., 1877. 12°. . . 21214
Transcendentalism. Cook, J. (Bost. Mond. Lectures.) Bost., 1878. 28022
—— Frothingham, O. B. Transcendentalism in New England. N. Y., 1876. 8°. 28204

Tropical Nature. Wallace, A. R. Lond., 1878. 8°. . . . 29533
Trotter, L. J. Studies in Biography. Lond., 1865. 8°. . . . 23883
CONTENTS:—Mahomet; Thomas Becket; Frederic II. of Germany; Savonarola; Bacon and his new apologist; Wm. Pitt; The latter years of Wm. Pitt; R. B. Sheridan.
Troubadours. Hueffer, F. Lond., 1878. 8°. 26769
—— Preston, H. W. Troubadours and Trouvères, new and old. Bost., 1876. 12°. 26906
—— Rutherford, J. Lond., 1873. 12°. 26907
—— *See, also,* **Poetry,** *Provençal.*
Troublesome Daughters. Walford, L. B. N. Y., 1880. 16°. . . 24931
True-Blue Laws. Trumbull, J. H. Hartf., 1876. 12°. . . . 21322
Trumbull, J. H. The True-Blue Laws of Connecticut and New Haven, and the False Blue-Laws invented by the Rev. Sam. Peters. Hartf., 1876. 12°. 21322
Trump, A., jr., (*pseud.*) Laws and Regulations of Short Whist. Paris & N. Y., 1880. 16°. 29686
Tuckey, Janet. English-Gipsy Songs. (*See* **Leland, C. G.,** *& others.*) 26123
—— Joan of Arc, "the Maid." N. Y., 1880. 16°. 22454
Tullidge, H., *editor.* The Evangelical Church: discourses. N. Y., 1879. 8°. 28600
Tulloch, J. Beginning Life: a book for young men. N. Y., [1876]. 27384
—— The Christian Doctrine of Sin. N. Y., [1876]. 12°. . . . 28551
—— Pascal. Phila., [1878]. 16°. 23264
Turgénief, I. S. Dimitri Roudine; a novel. N. Y., 1873. 16°. (2 copies.) 24860–
—— Liza: a Russian novel. N. Y., 1872. 16°. (2 copies.) . . 24862–
—— On the Eve: a tale. N. Y., 1873. 16°. (2 copies.) . . . 24864–
—— Smoke: a Russian novel. N. Y., 1873. 16°. 24866
—— Spring Floods. [*And*] A Lear of the Steppe. N. Y., 1874. 16°. 24867
—— Virgin Soil. N. Y., 1877. 16°. (2 copies.) 24868–
Turkey. Baker, J. N. Y., 1877. 8°. 21909
—— Bryce, J. Transcaucasia and Ararat. Lond., 1877. 12°. . 21214
—— Cunynghame, A. T. Travels. Lond., 1872. 8°. . . . 21913
—— Daily News (London). War Correspondence, 1877–8. Lond., 1878. 2 v. 12°. 20494–
—— Farley, J. L. Modern Turkey. Lond., 1872. 8°. . . . 21910
—— Longfellow, H. W. Poems of Places, v. 19. 26458
—— Mackenzie (G. M. M.) & Irby (A. P.). Travels in the Slavonic Provinces of Turkey-in-Europe. Lond., 1877. 2 v. 8°. . 21911–
—— Milner, T. The Turkish Empire. Lond., [1877]. 12°. . . 20491
—— The People of T.: 20 years' residence. Lond., 1878. 2 v. 12°. 21693–
—— Porter (J.) & Larpent (G.). Lond., 1854. 2 v. 8°. . . . 20615–
—— West, M. A. The Romance of Missions. N. Y., [1875]. 12°. 28489
—— *See, also,* **Eastern Question.**
Turkistan. Schuyler, E. N. Y., 1876. 2 v. 8°. 21921–
—— *See, also,* **Kashgar.**
Turks. Clark, E. L. The Arabs and the Turks. Bost., 1876. 12°. 20492
—— Creasy, E. S. Hist. of the Ottoman Turks. Lond., 1877. 12°. 20489

Turks. Freeman, E. A. Ottoman Power in Europe. Lond., 1877. 20490
—— Hamlin, C. Among the Turks. N. Y., 1878 [1877]. 12°. . 21600
Turner, J. M. W. *Hamerton, P. G.* Bost., 1879. 12°. . . . 23803
—— *Monkhouse, W. C.* Lond. & N. Y., 1879. 12°. 23783
Turner, S. Prolusions on the present greatness of Britain; on modern poetry; [etc.] Lond., 1819. 16°. 18676
Tuttle, H. German Political Leaders. N. Y., 1876. 16°. . . 22443

CONTENTS:—Bismarck; Dr. Falk; Delbrück; Camphausen; Prince Hohenlohe; Von Arnim; Von Bennigsen; Dr. Simson; Lasker; Windthorst; Dr. Löwe; Schulze-Delitzsch; Jacoby; Hasselmann; Sonnemann; Gneist; Virchow; Treitschke; Von Sybel.

Twenty Thousand Leagues under the Seas. Verne, J. Bost., 1875. 24281
Twenty Years After. Dumas, A. D. Lond., [1879]. 16°. . . 24401
Twickenham, Memorials of. Cobbett, R. S. Lond., 1872. (2 cop.) 21777-
Twin Captains. Dumas, A. D. Lond., [1879]. 16°. . . . 24414
Twins of Table Mountain. Harte, F. B. Bost., 1879. 16°. (2 cop.) 24495-
Two College Friends. Loring, F. W. Bost., [1871]. 16°. . . 24235
Two (The) Dianas. Dumas, A. D. Lond., [1879]. 16°. (2 copies.) . . . . 24405 & 24424
Two Men of Sandy Bar. Harte, F. B. Bost., 1876. 16°. . . 24494
Two Russian Idyls: Marcella; Esfira. N. Y., 1880. 16°. . . 24928
Tyerman, L. Life and Times of John Wesley. N. Y., 1872. 3 v. 22309-
—— Life of the Rev. Geo. Whitefield. N. Y., 1877. 2 v. 8°. . . 22307-
Tyler, M. C. Hist. of Amer. Literature. N. Y., 1878. v. 1-2. 8°. 26779-

CONTENTS:—1, 1607-1676.—2, 1677-1765.

Tyler, S. Memoir of Roger B. Taney. Balt., 1872. 8°. . . . 22720
Tyler, Wat. *See* **Maurice, C. E.,** 'Lives of Eng. Pop. Leaders,' v. 2. 22941
Tyndall, J. Advancement of Science. N. Y., 1874. 12°. . . 29304
—— Forms of Water. N. Y., 1872. 12°. 29240
—— Fragments of Science. N. Y., 1877. 12°. 29401
—— Lessons in Electricity. Lond., 1876. 12°. 29314
—— *& others.* The Prayer-Gauge Debate. Bost., 1876. 12°. . . 28093
Tyrol. Busk, R. H. The Valleys of Tirol. Lond., 1874. 12°. . 21219
—— Grohman, W. A. B. Gaddings with a Primitive People. N.Y. 1878. 16°. 21247
—— Waring, G. E. Tyrol and the Skirt of the Alps. N. Y., 1880. 21978
Tyson, G. E. *Blake, E. V.* (*In* 'Arctic Experiences.') . . . 21880
Tytler, Christina C. F. Jonathan: a novel. N. Y., 1876. 16°. . 24283
—— Mistress Judith: a Cambridgeshire story. N. Y., 1875. 16°. . 24284
Tytler, Sarah, (*pseud.*) *See* **Keddie, Henrietta.**
Uarda. Ebers, G. M. Stuttg. & Leipz., 1879. 3 B. in 1. 12°. . 25874
—— *Same.* Transl. N. Y., 1880. 2 v. 16°. (2 copies.) . . . 24433-
Ueberweg, F. History of Philosophy. N. Y., 1873-4. 2 v. 8°. . 28280-

CONTENTS:—1, Ancient and Mediæval Phil.—2, Modern Phil.

Uhland, J. L. Songs and Ballads. Lond., 1864. 12°. . . . 26173
Uhlhorn, G. Conflict of Christianity with Heathenism. N. Y., 1879. 28602
Ulbach, L. Madame Gosselin. N. Y., 1878. 16°. 24080
Ullmann, C. Reformers before the Reformation. Edinb., 1855. 2 v. 22300-
Ulrici, H. Shakspeare's Dramatic Art. Lond., 1876. 2 v. 12°. . 27017-
Ultima Thule; or, A summer in Iceland. Burton, R. F. Lond., 1875. 2 v. 8°. 21884-

Ultimo: Novelle. Spielhagen, F. Leipz., 1877. 16°. (Sämmtl. Werke, B. 12.) 25871
Uncommercial Traveller. Dickens, C. J. H. N. Y., 1873. 16°. . 24231
Under the Greenwood Tree. Hardy, T. N. Y., 1873. 16°. . . 24462
Under the Lilacs. Alcott, L. M. Bost., 1878. 16°. 24034
Undiscovered (The) Country. Howells, W. D. Bost., 1880. (2 cop.) 24573–
Undivine (The) Comedy. Krasinski, S. Phila., 1875. 12°. . . 26121
United States. Bruce, E. C. The Century; its fruits and its festival: the Centennial Exhibition. Phil., 1877. 8°. . . 21522
—— Dix, W. G. The American State and Amer. Statesmen. Bost., 1876. 12°. 21333
—— Ingersoll, C. Fears for Democracy, regarded from the Amer. point of view. Phila., 1875. 8°. 21449
—— Scudder, H. E. Men and Manners in America one hundred years ago. N. Y., 1876. 16°. 21324
—— Skinner, O. Issues of Amer. Politics. Phila., 1873. (2 cop.) . 21327–
—— Sumner, C. Prophetic Voices concerning America. Bost., 1874. 21362
—— Thompson, J. P. The U. S. as a Nation: lectures on the centennial of Amer. Independence. Bost., 1877. 8°. . . 21334
—— *Constitution and Laws.* Cooley, T. M. General Principles of Constitutional Law in the U. S. of A. Bost., 1880. 12°. . 28845
—— — Lamphere, G. N. The U. S. Gov't: its organization and practical workings. Phil., 1880. 8°. 21531
—— — *See, also,* **Law,** *American.*

Description and Travel.

—— Bryant, W. C., *editor.* Picturesque America. N. Y., [1872–3]. 2 v. 4°. . . . . ——
—— Campbell, G. White and Black: the outcome of a visit to the U. S. N. Y., 1879. 8°. 21459
—— Dodge, R. I. Plains of the Great West and their Inhabitants. N. Y., 1877. 8°. 21580
—— Hübner, J. A. von. (*In* 'A Ramble round the World.') . . 21203
—— King, E. The Great South: a record of journeys in [1873–4]. Hartf'd, 1875. 8°. 21588
—— Kingsley, *Miss.* South by West; or, Winter in the Rocky Mountains, and Spring in Mexico. Lond., 1874. 8°. . . 21582
—— Laboulaye, E. R. L. Paris en Amérique. Paris, 1877. 16°. . 25667
—— Waterton, C. Wanderings in South Amer., the North-west of the U. S., [etc.] Lond., 1866. 16°. 21264

—— *Finances.* Bolles, A. S. Financial Hist. of the U. S., from 1774 to 1789. N. Y., 1879. 8°. 29048
—— — Sherman, J. Selected Speeches and Reports on Finance and Taxation from 1859 to 1878. N. Y., 1879. 8°. . . . 29047
—— — Sumner, W. G. Hist. of Amer. Currency. N. Y., 1874 (etc.). 12°. (2 copies.) 29059
—— — *See, also,* **Banking; Finance; Money.**
—— *Government. See* **U. S.,** *Constitution and Laws.*

United States. *History.*

—— Bryant (W. C.) and Gay (S. H.). N. Y., 1876–79. v. 1–3. 8°. (2 copies.) (*For contents see* **Bryant & Gay.**) 21561–

—— Johnston, A. Hist. of Amer. Politics. N. Y., 1879. 16°. . 21332

—— (*to* 1776) Lawrence, E. (*In* **First Cent.** of the Repub.) . . 21520

—— (*to* 1782) Bancroft, G. Bost., 1876. 6 v. 12°. (2 copies.) . 21335–

—— (*to* 1790) Frothingham, R. Rise of the Republic. Bost., 1872. 21440

—— (*to* 1865) Doyle, J. A. N. Y., 1876. 16°. 20083

—— (*to* 1875) Higginson, T. W. Young Folks' Hist. Bost., 1875. 21325

—— (1750–) Holst, H. von. Constitutional and Political Hist. Chic., 1876, '79. v. 1–2. 8°. (2 copies.) 21450–

CONTENTS :—1, 1750–1833; State sovereignty and slavery.—2, 1828–1846; Jackson's administration; Annexation of Texas.

—— (1775–1783) Ludlow, J. M. War of Amer. Independence. Bost., 1876. 16°. (2 copies.) 20460–

—— (1776–1784) Greene, G. W. German Element in the War of Amer. Independence. N. Y., 1876. 12°. 21360

—— (1776–1804) Riethmüller, C. J. Life and Times of Alex. Hamilton. Lond., [1864]. 12°. 22626

—— (1776–1876) Woolsey, T. D., *and others.* First Century of the Republic. N. Y., 1876. 8°. (2 copies.) (*For contents see* **First Century.**) 21520–

—— (1812–1815) Ingersoll, C. J. Second War betw. the U. S. of A. and Gt. Brit. Phila., 1845–53. 4 v. (wanting v. 2.) 8°. . 21443–

—— (1812–1815) Lossing, B. J. Pictorial Field-book of the War of 1812. N. Y., 1868. 8°. 21560

—— (1817–1853) Sargent, N. Public Men and Events. Phila., 1875. 2 v. 8°. 21447–

—— (1861–) Paris, *Comte de.* Hist. of the Civil War. Phila., 1875–6. v. 1–2. 8°. 21460–

—— (1861–1865) Leland, C. G. Lincoln, and the Abolition of Slavery. [L. &] N. Y., 1879. 16°. 22451

—— (1861–1865) Mahan, A. Critical Hist. of the War. N. Y., 1877. 21458

—— (1861–1865) Sherman, W. T. Memoirs. N. Y., 1875. 2 v. 8°. 22686

—— (1872–1880) McPherson, E. Handbook of Politics. Wash., 1874–80. 4 v. 8°. 21523–

—— *Statistics.* Spaulding, M. C. Handbook of Statistics. N. Y., 1874. 12°. 21363

See, also, **America; Antiquities,** *Amer.;* **Indians; Politics; Middle, Southern, Western** States; **New Eng.; West** (The); *and other geographical names.*

Universities. Hart, J. M. German Universities. N. Y., 1874. 12°. 28831

—— *See, also,* **Cambridge; Oxford; Colleges; Education.**

University Life in Anc. Athens. Capes, W. W. Lond., 1877. 12°. 28826

Unknown (The) River. Hamerton, P. G. Bost., 1876. 12°. . . 29328

Unüberwindliche Mächte. Grimm, H. Berlin, 1870. 2 B. 12°. . 25878–

Up de Graff, T. S. Bodines; or, Camping on the Lycoming. Phila., 1879. 12°. 29664

Urbino, Memoirs of the Dukes of. Dennistoun, J. Lond., 1851. 3 v. 23939–

Urquhart, W. P. Life and Times of Francesco Sforza. Edinb. & L., 1852. 2 v. 8°. 23935–

Uruguay, Travels in. Murray, J. H. Lond., 1871. 12°. . . . 21621
Uscoque (**L'**). Dudevant, A. L. A. D. Paris, 1879. 16°. . . 25696
Useful Arts. *See* **Industrial** Arts.
Utilitarianism. Blackie, J. S. (*In* 'Four Phases of Morals.) . . 28080
Uwins, T., Memoir of. By Mrs. Uwins. Lond., 1858. 2 v. 12°. . 18667–
Vacation Tourists, 1862–3. Galton, F. Lond., 1864. 8°. . . 21732
Valdez, F. T. Six Years of a Traveller's Life in Western Africa. Lond., 1861. 2 v. 8°. 21862–
Valentine. Dudevant, A. L. A. D. Paris, 1869. 16°. . . . 25697
Vallée-Noire (La). Dudevant, A. L. A. D. (*In vol. with* 'Le secrétaire.') 25693
Valperga. [Shelley, M. W.] Lond., 1823. 3 v. 12°. . . . 18693–
Value of Life: a reply to Mallock's essay "Is Life worth living?" N. Y., 1879. 12°. 28086
Valvèdre. Dudevant, A. L. A. D. Paris, 1875. 16°. . . . 25698
Vanbrugh, J. Dramatic Works. Lond., 1849 (& '51). 8°. (2 cop.) 26691–
Van Dyck, A. *See* **Dyck.**
Vanity Fair Album. Lond. v. 1, 3. 2°. . . . . ——
Van Laun, H. The French Revolutionary Epoch. N. Y., 1879. 2 v. 12°. 20419–
—— Hist. of French Literature. N. Y., 1876–7. 3 v. 8°. (2 cop.) 26770–
Van-Lennep, H. J. Bible Lands. N. Y., 1875. 8°. . . . 21902
Van Santvoord, C. Memoirs of Eliphalet Nott. N. Y., [1876]. 12°. 22641
Varnhagen von Ense, Rahel A. F. L.: her life and letters. Jennings, *Mrs.* V. Lond., 1876. 8°. 23726
Vathek. Beckford, W. N. Y., 1869. 16°. 24057
Vatican Council, Hist. of. Schaff, P. (*With* **Gladstone, W. E.,** 'Vat. Decrees;' *and* 'Rome.') 28723–
Vatican (The) Decrees, in their bearing on civil allegiance. [With text, Lat. and Eng.] Gladstone, W. E. N. Y., 1875. 8°. . 28723
—— *Same.* (*In* **Gladstone's** 'Rome.') 28724
Vaughan, R. John de Wycliffe, D.D. Lond., 1853. 8°. . . 22304
—— The Protectorate of Oliver Cromwell. Lond., 1838. 2 v. 8°. . 21000–
—— Revolutions in Eng. Hist. Lond., 1859–63. 3 v. 8°. . . 21094–
CONTENTS:—1, Rev. of race.—2, Rev. in religion.—3, [Political, etc.]
Vaux, W. S. W. Creek Cities and Islands of Asia Minor. Lond., 1877. 16°. 20043
—— Persia. (Anc. Hist. from the Monuments.) N. Y., 1876. 16°. 20044
Vecelli, Tiziano. *See* **Titian.**
Veitch, J. The Hist. and Poetry of the Scottish Border. Glasgow, 1878. 12°. 26298
Vendéerin (Die). Mügge, T. Breslau, 1863. 2 B. 16°. (Romane, B. 19–20.) 25846
Venezuela. Eastwick, E. B. Lond., 1868. 8°. 21808
—— Spence, J. M. The Land of Bolivar. Lond., 1878. 2 v. 8°. . 21806–
Venice. Hackländer, F. W. von. (*In* 'Tagebuchblätter:' Werke, B. 40.) 25819
—— Hazlitt, W. C. Hist. of the Venetian Republic. Lond., 1860. 4 v. 8°. 20322–

Venice. Ruskin, J. St. Mark's Rest: the history of Venice. N. Y., 1877. Parts 1-2. 12°. 29844
Venus, Transits of. Proctor, R. A. Lond., 1874. 12°. . . . 29448
Vergil. Æneid, transl. into Eng. verse by J. Conington. N. Y., 1877. 12°. 26802
—— Æneids, done into Eng. verse by Wm. Morris. Bost., 1876. 12°. (2 copies.) 26800–
—— *Church, A. J.* Stories from V. With 24 illust. N. Y., 1879. 26803
—— *Nettleship, H.* (Classical Writers.) N. Y., 1880. 16°. . . 26892
Verloren und gefunden. Mügge, T. Breslau, 1865. 2 B. 16°. (Romane, B. 24–25.) 25847–
Verlorene Handschrift. Freytag, G. Leipz., 1877. 2 B. 8°. . 25905–
Verlorene (Der) Sohn. Hackländer, F. W. von. Stuttg., 1866. 16°. (Werke, B. 43.) 25821
Verne, J. The American Gun Club. N. Y., 1874. 12°. . . . 24262
—— Doctor Ox, and other stories. Bost., 1874. 16°. . . . 24264
—— The Exploration of the World. N. Y., 1879. 8°. . . . 21983
—— Five Weeks in a Balloon. Lond., 1870. 16°. 24265
—— A Floating City; *and* The Blockade Runners. N. Y., 1875. . 24266
—— From the Earth to the Moon. N. Y., 1874. 12°. (2 copies.) . 24267–
—— The Fur Country. Bost., 1874. 12°. 24269
—— Hector Servadac. N. Y., 1878 [1877]. 8°. 24270
—— Journey to the Center of the Earth. Bost. 12°. . . . 24271
—— Meridiana. N. Y., 1874. 12°. (2 copies.) 24273–
—— Michael Strogoff. N. Y., 1877. 8°. (2 copies.) . . . 24275–
—— The Mysterious Island. N. Y., 1875–6. 3 v. 12°. . . . 24277–
CONTENTS:—1, Dropped from the Clouds.—2, Abandoned.—3, The secret of the island.
—— Tour of the World in 80 Days. Transl. by G. M. Towle. Bost., 1873. 16°. 24280
—— *Same, tr. by same.* Around the World [etc.]. Bost., 1874. 12°. 24263
—— Twenty Thousand Leagues under the Seas. Bost., 1875. 12°. 24281
—— Voyages and Adventures of Capt. Hatteras. Bost., 1875. 12°. 24282
—— Wreck of the Chancellor. Bost., 1875. 16°. 24272
Vernet, E. J. H. *Rees, J. R.* L. & N. Y., 1880. 12°. . . . 23787
Véron, E. Æsthetics. Lond., 1879. 12°. 28171
Verse, English, Science of. Lanier, S. N. Y., 1880. 12°. . . 26289
Viardot, L. Wonders of Sculpture. N. Y., 1873. 12°. . . . 10136
Vicar of Morwenstow. Baring-Gould, S. N. Y., [1879]. 12°. . 22105
Vicomte (The) de Bragelonne. Dumas, A. D. Lond., [1879]. 2 v. 16°. (2 copies.) . . . . 24402– & 24427–
Victoria (*province*), Early Hist. of. Labilliere, F. P. Lond., 1878. 2 v. 12°. 20484–
Victorian Poets. Stedman, E. C. Bost., 1876. 12°. . . . 26295
Vigée-Le Brun, *Madame. See* **Le Brun, Elisabeth L. V.**
Vignettes. Belloc, B. R. P. Lond., 1866. 16°. 18559
Viking Tales of the North. Anderson (R. C.) & Bjarnason (J.). Chic., 1877. 12°. 27708
Villages and Village Life. Egleston, N. H. N. Y., 1878. 12°. . 28881
Villari, Linda. In change unchanged. N. Y., 1877. 16°. . . 24285

Villari, P. Niccolò Machiavelli, and his Times. Lond., 1878. 2 v. 23943–
Villiers, Geo., *1st duke of Buckingham,* Life and Times of. Thomson, K. B. Lond., 1860. 3 v. 12°. 22937–
Vincennes. Cochrane, A. B. (*In* 'Historic Chateaux.') . . . 21785
Vinci, Leonardo da. *Clément, C.* Lond., 1880. 12°. . . . 23837
—— *Richter, J. P.* (Illust. Biogr. of the Great Artists.) L. & N. Y. 1880. 12°. 23786
Vindication of Lady Byron. Lond., 1871. 8°. 23449
Vingt ans après. Dumas, A. D. Paris, 1876. 3 t. 16°. . . 25635–
Violinists, Celebrated. Phipson, T. L. Lond., 1877. 12°. . . 23816
Viollet-le-Duc, E. E. Annals of a Fortress. Bost., 1876. 8°. . 24313
—— Habitations of Man in all ages. Bost., 1876. 8°. . . . 29927
Virgil. *See* **Vergil.**
Virgin Soil. Turgénief, I. S. N. Y., 1877. 16°. (2 cop.) . . 24868–
Vision of Echard. Whittier, J. G. Bost., 1878. 16°. . . . 26142
Visions: a study of false sight. Clarke, E. H. Bost., 1878. 12°. . 28005
Vitalis, Ordericus. *See* **Ordericus.**
Vivian Grey. Disraeli, B. N. Y. [Lond., 1878]. 16°. . 24246 & 24252
Vivien. Tennyson, A. Illust. by Doré. N. Y., 1868. 2°. . . ——
Vizetelly, H. Story of the Diamond Necklace. Lond., 1867. 2 v. 22523–
Vocation. *See* **Profession.**
Vogel, H. The Chemistry of Light and Photography. N. Y., 1875. 29253
Vogel, T. A Century of Discovery. Lond., 1877. 8°. . . . 23567
Voice. Cohen, J. S. The Throat and the Voice. Phil., 1879. 16°. 29962
—— Daniell, W. H. The Voice and how to use it. Bost., 1873. 16°. 29804
—— Durant, G. Hygiene of the Voice; its physiology and anatomy. N. Y., 1879. 12°. 29802
—— Holmes G. Vocal Physiology and Hygiene. [L. &] Phil., 1880. 29803
—— Pattou, A. A. The Voice as an Instrument. N. Y., 1878. 16°. 29805
Voigt (Der) von Sylt. Mügge, T. Breslau, 1866. 2 B. 16°. (Romane, B. 27–28.) 25848–
Volsungs (The). Cox (G. W.) & Jones. (*In* 'Pop. Romances;' *and* 'Tales.') 27712–13
Voltaire, F. M. A. de. *Hamley, E. B.* (For. Clas. for English Readers.') 23263
—— *Morley, J.* N. Y., 1872. 12°. 23310
Vosmaer, C. Rembrandt. [Ed.] by J. W. Mollett. N. Y., & L. 1879. 12°. 23778
Voss, Sophie M. von P. von. Sixty-nine Years at the Court of Prussia. Lond., 1876. 2 v. 12°. 22509–
Voyages. Beauvoir, L. de. Voyage round the World. Lond., 1870–72. 3 v. 12°. 21200–
—— Brassey, A. Around the World in the Yacht 'Sunbeam.' N. Y., 1878. 8°. 21731
—— Field, H. M. ["Journey round the world."] N. Y., 1877. (2 v.) 21720–
CONTENTS:—1, From the Lakes of Killarney to the Golden Horn.—2, From Egypt to Japan.
—— Hübner, J. A. von. Ramble round the World, 1871. N. Y., 1874. 12°. 21203

Voyages. Simpson, W. Meeting the Sun: a journey all round the world. Bost., 1877. 8°. 21982
—— *See, also,* **Travels** (*and references*).
Waagen, G. F. Handbook of Painting: the German, Flemish, and Dutch schools. Based on the handbook of Kugler; remodeled by Waagen. A new ed., in part re-written by J. A. Crowe. Lond., 1874. 2 v. 8°. 29875–
Wachtstubenabenteuer. Hackländer, F. W. von. Stuttg., 1875. 3 Th. in 2 B. 16°. (Werke, B. 4–5.) 25801–
Wages. Walker, F. A. The Wages Question. N. Y., 1876. 8°. . 29041
—— Ward, J. Workmen and Wages. Lond., 1868. 12°. . . . 29008
Wagner, M. The Darwinian Theory, and the Law of the Migration of Organisms. Lond., 1873. 8°. 29391
Wagner, W. Richard. Art Life and Theories; selected by E. L. Burlingame. N. Y., 1875. 12°. 23815
—— Beethoven. Transl. by A. R. Parsons. Bost., 1872. 12°. . 23808
—— — Transl. by E. Dannreuther. Lond., 1880. 12°. . . . 23807
—— *Dannreuther, E.* Wagner: his tendencies and theories. Lond., 1873. 8°. 29800
—— *Hueffer, F.* Wagner and the Music of the Future. Lond., 1874. 29748
Wahl, O. W. The Land of the Czar. Lond., 1875. 8°. . . . 21942
Wake-Robin. Burroughs, J. N. Y., 1877. 16°. 29324
Waldfried. Auerbach, B. Stuttg., 1874. 3 B. 16°. . . . 25880–
—— *Same.* Transl. by S. A. Stern. N. Y., 1874. 12°. (2 copies.) . 24002–
Wales. Borrow, G. Wild Wales. Lond., 1872. 16°. . . . 21709
—— Longfellow, H. W. Poems of Places, v. 4. Bost., 1876. 16°. 26443
Walford, E. Juvenal. (Anc. Clas. for Eng. Readers, v. 13.) . . 26839
—— Londoniana. Lond., 1879. 2 v. 12°. 21260–
—— Old and New London. Lond., &c., [1875–78]. Vols. 3–6. 8°. 21962–
(*For* v. 1–2 *see* **Thornbury, W.**)
—— Pleasant Days in Pleasant Places. Lond., 1879. 12°. . . 21262
—— Tales of Our Great Families. Lond., 1877. 2 v. 12°. . . 22846–
Walford, *Mrs.* **L. B.** Cousins. N. Y., 1879. 16°. 24286
—— Mr. Smith: a part of his life. N. Y., 1875. 16°. . . . 24287
—— Pauline. N. Y., 1877. 16°. 24288
—— Troublesome Daughters. N. Y., 1880. 16°. 24931
Walker, F. A. Money. N. Y., 1878. 8°. 29040
—— Money in its relations to Trade and Industry. N. Y., 1879. 12°. 29042
—— The Wages Question. N. Y., 1876. 8°. 29041
Walker, H. H. The Comédie Humaine and its author; with translations from the French of Balzac. [L. &] N. Y., [1879]. 12°. 26908
Walker, W. Handbook of Drawing. Lond., 1879. 12°. . . . 29825
Walker, W. S. Critical Examination of the Text of Shakespeare. Lond., 1860. 3 v. 16°. 27022–
Walking. Barron, A. Foot Notes; or, Walking as a fine art. Wallingf., 1875. 12°. 29321
—— Gould, J. M. Hints for Camping and Walking. N. Y., 1877. 16°. (2 copies.) 29662–
—— Thoreau, H. D. Excursions. Bost., 1875. 12°. . . . 29335

Walking. *See, also,* **Sports** (*and references*).

Wallace, A. R. On Miracles and Modern Spiritualism. Lond., 1875. 16°. 28045

—— Tropical Nature, and other essays. Lond., 1878. 8°. . . 29533

Wallace, D. M. Russia. N. Y., 1877. 8°. 21941

Wallace, L. The Fair God ; or, The last of the 'Tzins. Bost., 1873. 12°. (2 copies.) 24289–

Waller, E. Poetical Works. With memoir [etc.] by G. Gilfillan. Edinb., 1857. 8°. 26363

Walmsley, H. M. Ruined Cities of Zulu Land. Lond., 1869. 2 v. 21632–

Walpole, Horace, *4th earl of Orford. Adams, W. H. D.* (*In* 'Eng. Party Leaders,' v. 1.) 21054

Walpole, *Sir* **Robt.,** *earl of Orford. Earle, J. C.* (*In* 'Eng. Premiers,' v. 1.) 22882

Walpole, S. Hist. of England from 1815. Lond., 1878–80. v. 1–3. 21097–

Walsh, J. H., (*pseud.,* 'Stonehenge'.) Hints to Sportsmen on Guns and Shooting. Lond. 16°. 29612

Walsh, W. S., *compiler.* Burlesque. Bost., 1875. 16°. . . . 25246

Walter of Aquitaine. Cox (G. W.) & Jones. (*In* 'Pop. Romances'; *and* 'Tales.') 27712–13

Walton (I.) & Cotton (C.). Complete Angler. With orig. memoirs and notes by [N.] H. Nicolas. Lond., 1875. 12°. . 29627

War. Helps, A. (*In* 'Friends in Council,' 2d ser., v. 1.) . . 27252

War Correspondence of the Daily News. *See* **Daily News** (London).

Warburton, E. B. G. Memoirs of Prince Rupert and the Cavaliers. Lond., 1849. 3 v. 8°. 23018–

Warburton, W. P. Edward III. Lond., 1875. 16°. . . . 20459

Ward, A. W. Chaucer. (Eng. Men of Letters.) N. Y., 1880. 12°. 23345

Ward, Harrietta O., (*pseud.?*) Sensible Etiquette. Phil., 1878. 12°. 28965

Ward, James. Workmen and Wages. Lond., 1868. 12°. . . 29008

Ward, John. Experiences of a Diplomatist: recollections of Germany, 1840–1870. Lond., 1872. 8°. 22582

Ward, P. Reminiscences of Cheltenham College. Lond., 1868. 12°. 12912

Ward, T. H., *editor.* The English Poets: selections, with critical introductions. Lond., 1880. v. 1–2. 12°. 26174–

Contents:—1, Chaucer to Donne.—2, Ben Jonson to Dryden.

Waring, G. E. The Bride of the Rhine: 200 miles in a Mosel rowboat. Bost., 1878. 12°. 21263

—— A Farmer's Vacation. Bost., 1876. 8°. 21977

—— Tyrol and the Skirt of the Alps. N. Y., 1880. 8°. . . . 21978

Warner, C. D. Backlog Studies. Bost., 1873. 16°. . . . 27240

—— Baddeck, and that sort of thing. Bost., 1874. 16°. . . 24291

—— Being a Boy. Bost., 1878. 16°. 24292

—— The Gilded Age. (*See* **Clemens, S. L., & Warner.**)

—— In the Levant. Bost., 1877. 12°. 21690

—— In the Wilderness. Bost., 1878. 16°. 24293

—— Mummies and Moslems. Hartf'd, 1876. 8°. 21842

Warren, I. P. Chauncey Judd ; or, The stolen boy: a story of the Revolution. N. Y., [1874]. 16°. 17013

Warren, I. P. The Three Judges [Goffe, Whalley, Dixwell]. N. Y., [1873]. 22627

Wartensleben, H. von. The Campaign of 1870–1. Lond., 1872. 8°. 20644

Warton, T. Poetical Works. With life [etc.] by G. Gilfillan. Edinb., 1854. 8°. 26338

Warwick Woodlands. Herbert, H. W. ('Sporting Scenes,' v. 2.) . 29603

Was die Schwalbe sang. Spielhagen, F. Leipz., 1877. 16°. (Sämmtl. Werke, B. 12.) 25871

Watch and Ward. James, H., jr. Bost., 1878. 16°. . . . 24605

Watchmaker (The). Dumas, A. D. Lond., [1879]. 16°. . . 24415

Water, Forms of. Tyndall, J. N. Y., 1872. 12°. 29240

Waterton, C. Essays on Natural History. Ed., with a life, by N. Moore. Lond., [1870]. 12°. 29402

—— Wanderings in South America, the North-west of the United States, and the Antilles. Lond., 1866. 16°. 21264

Watkins, J. Public and Private Life of R. B. Sheridan. Lond., 1818. 2 v. 8°. 18567-

Watson, F. Defenders of the Faith; or, The Christian apologists of the 2d and 3d centuries. Lond., [1878]. 16°. . . . 28503

Watson, J. L. *See* **Keddie, H., & Watson.**

Watt, Jas., Life of. Smiles, S. Phil., 1865. 8°. 23534

Waverley (The) Dictionary. Rogers, M. Chic., 1879 [1878]. 12°. 26921

Way (The) we live now. Trollope, A. N. Y., 1875. 8°. . . . 24706

We and our Neighbors. Stowe, H. B. N. Y., [1875]. 12°. . . 24825

Weapons. *See* **Arms and Armor.**

Weber, C. M. F. E. von. Letters. (*In* **Nohl, L.,** 'Letters.') . . 23765

Webster, Dan. Great Speeches and Orations. With an essay on Webster as a master of English style by E. P. Whipple. Bost., 1879. 8°. 27564

—— *Harvey, P.* Reminiscences and Anecdotes of Webster. Bost., 1877. 8°. (2 copies.) 22699-

Webster, R. G. The Trade of the World. Lond., 1880. 8°. . . 29003

Webster, W. Basque Legends. Lond., 1877. 8°. 27781

Wechsel des Lebens. Hackländer, F. W. von. Stuttg., 1866. 2 B. 16°. (Werke, B. 41–42.) 25820

Wedding (The) Day, in all ages and countries. Wood, E. J. Lond., 1869. 12°. 28963

Wedgwood (Josiah), The sons of: a group of Englishmen. Meteyard, E. Lond., 1871. 8°. 23543

Wedmore, F. Pastorals of France. Lond., 1878. 12°. . . . 24294

CONTENTS:—A Last Love at Pornic; Yvonne of Croisic; The Four Bells of Chartres.

Weeden, W. B. Morality of Prohibitory Liquor Laws. Bost., 1875. 16°. 28887

Weeks, R. K. Twenty Poems. N. Y., 1876. 12°. 26117

Weihnachtsabend. Mügge, T. Breslau, 1864. 16°. (Romane, B. 21.) 25846

Weiss, J. Goethe's West-Easterly Divan. Transl., with introd. and notes. Bost., 1877. 16°. 26069

—— Wit, Humor, and Shakspeare: 12 essays. Bost., 1876. 12°. . 27308

Weld, C. R. Florence, the new Capital of Italy. Lond., 1867. 12°. 21265
Welles, G. Lincoln and Seward. N. Y., 1874. 12°. . . . 22645
Wellesley, A., *duke of Wellington. Yonge, C. D.* Lond., 1860. 2 v. 23041–
—— *See, also,* **Earle, J. C.,** 'Eng. Premiers,' v. 2 (22883); **Kebbel, T. E.,** 'Eng. Statesmen' (22884).
Wells, C. Joseph and his Brethren: a dramatic poem. With an introd. by A. C. Swinburne. Lond., 1876. 12°. (2 copies.) 26138–
Wells, D. A. Robinson Crusoe's Money. N. Y., 1876. 8°. . . 29046
Wells, J. C. The Gateway to the Polynia: a voyage to Spitzbergen. Lond., 1873. 8°. 21887
Welsted, L. Works, in Verse and Prose. With notes, and memoirs of the author, by J. Nichols. Lond., 1787. 8°. . . 18614
Wenderholme. Hamerton, P. G. Bost., 1876. 12°. . . . 24483
Wentworth, Thos., Life of. Cooper, E. Lond., 1874. 2 v. 8°. . 23011–
Wesel, John of. *See* **Ruchrath, Joh.**
Wesley, J., Life and Times of. Tyerman, L. N. Y., 1872. 3 v. 8°. 22309–
Wessel, Jan. *Ullmann, C.* (*In* 'Reformers' etc., v. 2.) . . . 22301
West, Maria A. Romance of Missions; or, Inside views of life and labor in the land of Ararat. N. Y., [1875]. 12°. . . 28489
West (The, *of the U. S.*). Parkman, F. Discovery of the Great West. Bost., 1869. 8°. (Pt. 3 of "France and Eng. in N. Amer.") 6133
—— — *Same.* La Salle and the Discovery [etc.]. 11th ed., rev., with add. Bost., 1879. 8°. 21403
—— Raymond, R. W. Camp and Cabin: sketches of life and travel in the West. N. Y., 1880. 16°. 29661
West Indies. Bates, H. W., *editor.* Central America, [etc.]. Lond., 1878. 12°. 21700
—— Longfellow, H. W. Poems of Places. (*In* v. 30.) . . . 26469
—— *See, also,* **Antilles.**
Westcott, B. F. Hist. of the Eng. Bible. Lond., 1872. 12°. . 28527
Western States (U. S.). Longfellow, H. W. Poems of Places, v. 28. 26467
Westmacott, R. Handbook of Sculpture, ancient and modern. Edinb., 1864. 12°. 29824
Westminster Abbey, Memorials of. Stanley, A. P. Lond., 1876. 21776
Westminster Review. Lond. and N. Y., 1824–79. v. 1–17, 20–54, 57–112. 8°. 12032– 12239–
—— *Same.* v. 1–24, 27–92. 11861–
Wetherel (The) Affair. DeForest, J. W. N. Y., 1873. 8°. . . 24309
Whalley, E. *Warren, I. P.* (*In* 'The Three Judges.') . . . 22627
Whalley, T. S. Journals and Correspondence. Ed., with memoir and notes, by H. Wickham. Lond., 1863. 2 v. 8°. . . 18601–
What Career? Hale, E. E. Bost., 1878. 16°. 27385
What the Swallow sang. Spielhagen, F. N. Y., 1873. 16°. . . 24856
What Young People should know. Wilder, B. G. Bost., [1875.] 29977
Wheatley, H. B. Round about Piccadilly and Pall Mall. Lond., 1870. 8°. 21775
[**Wheelwright, H. W.**] Sporting Sketches, home and abroad. By the Old Bushman. Lond., 1866. 12°. 29605

Whetham, J. W. B. Across Central America. Lond., 1877. 8°. 21812
Which shall it be? [Hector, A. F.] N. Y., 1874. 16°. . . . 24533
Whichcote, B. *Westcott, B. F.* (*In* **Masters** in Eng. Theol.) . 22111
Whig Party (*U. S.*), Hist. of. Ormsby, R. M. Bost., 1859. 12°. . 21326
Whipple, E. P. Literature and Life. Enl. ed. Bost., 1871. 12°. 27267

CONTENTS:—Authors in their relations to life; Novels and novelists; Dickens; Wit and humor; Ludicrous side of life; Genius; Intellectual health and disease; Use and misuse of words; Wordsworth; Bryant; Stupid conservatism and malignant reform.

—— *joint author.* *See* **Fields, J. T., & Whipple.**
Whist. Baldwin (J. L.) & Clay (J.). Laws of Short Whist. Lond., [1876]. 16°. 29683
—— [Coles, B. C.] Short Whist. Lond., 1865. 16°. . . . 29684
—— Pole, W. Theory of Whist. Lond., 1878. 16°. . . . 29685
—— Trump, A., jr., (*pseud.*) Laws and Regulations of Short Whist. Paris & N. Y., 1880. 16°. 29686
—— *See, also,* **Cards; Games** (*& references*).
White, G. Nat. Hist. of Selborne. N. Y., 1842. 12°. . . . 11749
—— *Same.* Ed. by E. Jesse. Lond., 1851. 12°. 525
—— *Same.* With poems, corresp., &c. Ed. by T. Bell. Lond., 1877. 2 v. 8°. 29530–
White, H. K. Poetical Works. With memoir [etc.] by G. Gilfillan. Edinb., 1856. 8°. 26364
White, J. Falstaff's Letters. Lond., 1877. 12°. 12904
White, J. W. The Mouth and the Teeth. Phil., 1879. 16°. . . 29964
White, R. G. Every-Day English. Bost., 1880. 12°. . . . 27866
—— Shakespeare's Scholar. N. Y., 1854. 8°. 27043
White and Black. Campbell, G. N. Y., 1879. 8°. 21459
White Wife. Bradley, E. Lond., 1865. 16°. 24062
Whitefield, G., Life of. Tyerman, L. N. Y., 1877. 2 v. 8°. . . 22307–
Whiteladies. Oliphant, M. O. W. N. Y., 1875. 16°. . . . 24836
Whiteley, G. C. The Cambridge Union Society: inaugural proceedings. L. & C., 1866. 16°. 28825
Whitney, W. D. Essentials of Eng. Grammar. Bost., 1877. 12°. 27863
—— Life and Growth of Language. N. Y., 1875. 12°. (2 copies.) . 29255–
—— Oriental and Linguistic Studies. N. Y., 1873–4. 2 series. 136 & 27862

CONTENTS:—1, The Veda; The Avesta; The science of language.—2, The East and West; Religion and mythology; Orthography and phonology; Hindu astronomy.

[Whiton, J. M.] Is "Eternal" Punishment Endless? answered. Bost., 1878. 16°. 28509
Whittaker, F. Life of Gen. Geo. A. Custer. N. Y., [1876]. 8°. . 22772
Whittier, J. G. Complete Poetical Works. Bost., 1876. 8°. . 26255
—— Hazel-Blossoms: [poems.] Bost., 1875. 16°. 26140
—— Vision of Echard, and other poems. Bost., 1878. 16°. . . 26142
—— *editor.* Songs of Three Centuries. Bost., 1876. 12°. . . 26141
"**Who** breaks, pays." Jenkin, C. N. Y., 1873. 16°. . . . 24585
Why we laugh. Cox, S. S. N. Y., 1876. 12°. 25205
Whyte-Melville, G. J. Riding Recollections. Lond., 1878. 12°. . 29640
Wiclif, John. *See* **Wycliffe.**
Wieck, J. G. F. Piano and Song. Bost., 1875. 12°. . . . 29801
Wiese, L. German Letters on Eng. Education. [L. &] N. Y., 1879. 28838

Wiesener, L. The Youth of Queen Elizabeth. Lond., 1879. 2 v. 22933-
Wikoff, H. Reminiscences of an Idler. N. Y., 1880. 8°. . . 22701
Wilberforce, E. Social Life in Munich. Lond., 1864. 12°. . . 21685
Wild Life in a Southern County. [Jefferies, R.] Bost., 1879. 16°. 29332
Wild Men and Wild Beasts. Cumming, W. G. N. Y., 1872. 12°. 21680
Wilde, W. R. Closing Years of Dean Swift's Life. Dublin, 1849. 22260
Wilder, B. G. What Young People should know. Bost., [1875]. . 29977
Wilhelm Meister's Apprenticeship and Travels. Goethe, J. W. von. Transl. by T. Carlyle. Lond., 1874. 3 v. 16°. . 24449-
Wilkes, G. Shakespeare, from an Amer. point of view. N. Y., 1877. 8°. 27045
Wilkes (John), Sheridan, Fox. Rae, W. F. Lond., 1874. 8°. . 23040
Wilkins, A. S. Roman Antiquities. Lond., 1877. 16°. . . 20057
Wilkinson, H. F. Modern Athletics. Lond., 1877. 12°. . . 29638
Willert, P. F. Reign of Lewis XI. Lond., 1876. 16°. . . . 20069
William I., *the Conqueror*, and his Companions. Planché, J. R. Lond., 1874. 2 v. 8°. 23000-
Williams, Helen M. Narrative of the Events in France [in 1815]. Lond., 1816. 8°. 18611
Williams, M. Hinduism. Lond., 1877. 16°. 28578
—— Modern India and the Indians. Lond., 1878. 8°. . . . 21945
Williams-Wynn. *See* **Wynn.**
Willis, N. P. People I have met. N. Y., 1850. 12°. . . . 18640
Willis, R. William Harvey. Lond., 1878. 8°. 23541
Wilson, A. The Abode of Snow. N. Y., 1875. 12°. . . . 21707
Wilson, D. Prehistoric Annals of Scotland. Lond., 1863. 2 v. 8°. 20203-
—— Prehistoric Man. Lond., 1876. 2 v. 8°. 20200-
—— Reminiscences of Old Edinburgh. Edinb., 1878. 2 v. 12°. . 21266-
Wilson, G. Handbook of Hygiene and Sanitary Science. [Edinb. &] Phil., 1880. 12°. 29997
Wilson, J. C. Summer and its Diseases. Phil., 1879. 16°. . . 29960
Wilson, J. G. Poets and Poetry of Scotland. N. Y., 1876. 2 v. 8°. 26270-
CONTENTS:—1, From Thomas the Rhymer to Rich. Gall.—2, Thos. Campbell to Marquis of Lorne.
Wilson, John. Dramatic Works; with memoir. Edinb. & Lond., 1874. 8°. 26573
Wilson, R. K. Hist. of Modern English Law. Lond., 1875. 16°. 20067
Wilson, Thos. *Farrar, F. W.* (*In* **Classic** Preachers.) . . . 22112
—— *Teale, W. H.* (*In* 'Lives of Eng. Divines.') 22110
Winchell, A. Preadamites. Chic., 1880. 8°. 29387
Winchester College, School-life at. [Mansfield, R. B.] Lond., 1866. 12°. 28835
Winckelmann, J. J. Hist. of Anc. Art. Bost., 1873. 4 v. 8°. . 29980-
Windham, W. Diary, 1784–1810. Lond., 1866. 8°. . . . 18597
Winter, W. Trip to England. Bost., 1879. 16°. 21682
Winter and its Dangers. Osgood, H. Phil., 1879. 16°. . . 29963
Winter Sunshine. Burroughs, J. N. Y., 1876. 16°. . . . 29325
Winthrop, T. John Brent. N. Y., 1876. 16°. 24295
—— Life in the Open Air, and other papers. N. Y., 1876. 16°. . 27239
CONTENTS:—Love and Skates; New York 7th Regiment: our march to Washington; Washington as a camp; Fortress Monroe; Brightly's Orphan; The Heart of the Andes.

Wit and Humor. Brooks, C. S. Poems from "Punch." Lond., 1875. 12°. 25268

—— [Forrester, A. H.] Phantasmagoria of Fun. Lond., 1843. 2 v. 12°. 25207-

—— Oxberry, W. The Actor's Budget of Wit and Merriment. Lond. 12°. 26521

—— *See, also,* **Caricature ; Fun ; Humor.**

Wit, Humor, and Shakspeare. Weiss, J. Bost., 1876. 12°. . . 27308

Witchcraft. *See* **Demonology.**

Wither, Thos. P. Bigg. *See* **Bigg-Wither.**

Within an Ace. Jenkin, C. N. Y., 1875. 16°. 24586

Wollstonecraft, Mary. *See* **Godwin, Mary W.**

Wolseley, G. J., Memoir of. Low, C. R. Lond., 1878. 2 v. 12°. 22844-

Woltmann, A. Hans Holbein. L. & N. Y., 1879. 12°. . . 23781

Woman-Hater (A). Reade, C. N. Y., 1877. 12°. (2 copies.) . 24815-

Womankind in Western Europe. Wright, T. Lond., 1869. 8°. . 28964

Women. Brackett, Anna C., *editor.* Education of Amer. Girls. N. Y., 1874. 16°. . . . . , . 28823

—— Morgan, S. O. Woman and her master: a hist. of the female sex. Lond. 2 v. 12°. 18673-

—— Ossoli, M. F. Woman in the 19th cent. Bost., 1874. 12°. . 27288

—— *Biography.* Belloc, B. R. P. Vignettes: 12 biographical sketches. Lond., 1866. 16°. 18559

—— — Blackburne, E. O. Illustrious Irishwomen. Lond., 1877. 2 v. 8°. 23884-

—— — Clayton, E. C. English Female Artists. Lond., 1876. 2 v. 23865-

—— — — Queens of Song. Lond., 1863. 2 v. 8°. 23847-

—— — Elwood, A. K. C. Memoirs of the Literary Ladies of England, from [1700]. Lond., 1843. 2 v. 12°. 18541-

—— — Green, M. A. E. W., *editor.* Letters of Royal and illustrious Ladies of Great Britain [1100-1558]. Lond., 1846. 3 v. 12°. 22927-

—— — Sainte-Beuve, C. A. Portraits of Celebrated Women. Bost., 1868. 16°. 23643

—— — Trollope, T. A. A Decade of Italian Women. Lond., 1859. 2 v. 16°. 23644-

—— — *See, also,* **England,** *Princesses, Queens.*

Wonder-Book. Hawthorne, N. Bost., 1876. 12°. 24527

Wood, E. J. The Wedding Day in all ages and countries. Lond., 1869. 12°. 28963

Wood, H. C. Brain-work and overwork. Phil., 1880. 16°. . . 29966

Wood, J. G. Illustrated Natural History. Lond., 1869-71. 3 v. 8°. 29587-

Contents:—1, Mammalia.—2, Birds.—3, Reptiles, Fishes, Molluscs, &c.

—— Insects abroad. Lond., 1874. 8°. 29585

—— Insects at home. N. Y., 1872. 8°. 29586

—— Natural Hist. of Man. Lond., 1868, '70. 2 v. 8°. . . . 29590-

Contents:—1, Africa.—2, Australia, New Zealand, Polynesia, America, Asia, and ancient Europe.

Wood, Mary A. E. *See* **Green, Mary A. E. W.**

Woodgate, W. B. "Oars and Sculls." Lond., 1875. 16°. . . 29659

Woodhead, H. Memoirs of Christina, Queen of Sweden. Lond., 1863. 2 v. 12°. 23901-

Woodwork. Pollen, J. H. Anc. and Mod. Furniture and W. N. Y., 1876. 12°. 29766
—— *See, also,* **Decoration.**
Wooing (The) o't. Hector, A. F. N. Y., 1874. 16°. (3 copies.) . 24534–
Woolrych, H. W. Lives of Eminent Serjeants-at-Law of the Eng. Bar. Lond., 1869. 2 v. 8°. 23887–
Woolsey, Sarah C., (*pseud.,* 'Susan Coolidge'.) For Summer Afternoons. Bost., 1876. 16°. 27238
Woolsey, T. D. Communism and Socialism. N. Y., 1880. 12°. . 29119
—— Political Science. N. Y., 1878 [1877]. 2 v. 8°. (2 copies.) . 29083–
—— *& others.* First Century of the Republic. N. Y., 1876. 8°. (2 copies.) (*For contents see* **First Century.**) 21520–
Wordsworth, C. On Shakspeare's Knowledge and Use of the Bible. Lond., 1864. 12°. 27007
Wordsworth, Dorothy. Recollections of a Tour in Scotland, 1803. N. Y., 1874. 16°. 21268
Wordsworth, W. Correspondence. (*See* **Haydon, B. R.,** 'Corresp.,' v. 2.) 23831
—— Poems. Chosen and ed. by M. Arnold. Lond., 1879. 16°. . 26115
—— Prose Works. Ed. by A. B. Grosart. Lond., 1876. 3 v. 8°. . 27484–
CONTENTS :—1, Political and ethical.—2, Æsthetical and literary.—3, Critical and ethical.
—— *Masson, D.* Wordsworth, Shelley, Keats. Lond., 1874. 12°. . 27298
—— *See, also,* **Bagehot, W.,** 'Lit. Stud.,' v. 2 (26768); **Brooke, S. A.,** 'Theol. in the Eng. Poets' (26281); **Dowden, E.,** 'Stud. in Lit.' (26926); **Doyle, F. H.,** 'Lect. on Poetry,' v. 2 (26286); **Hutton, R. H.,** 'Essays,' v. 2 (27488); **Lowell, J. R.,** 'Among my Books,' v. 2 (26931); **Mackay, C.,** 'Forty Years' Recol.,' v. 1 (22943); **Stephen, L.,** 'Hours in a Lib.,' v. 3 (26935); **Taylor, H.,** 'Crit. Ess. on Poetry' (26296); **Whipple, E. P.,** 'Lit. and Life' (27267).
Workmen. Maurice, J. F. D. The Workman and the Franchise. Lond., 1866. 8°. 29090
—— Ward, J. Workmen and Wages. Lond., 1868. 12°. . . . 29008
World. *See* **Earth.**
World (New York). *See* **Out of** "The World" Series.
World's (The) Progress. Putnam, G. P. N. Y., 1878. 8°. . . ——
Wreck of the Chancellor. Verne, J. Bost., 1875. 16°. . . . 24272
Wright, G. F. Logic of Christian Evidences. Andover, 1880. 12°. 28702
Wright, Thos., *of Birkenshaw.* Autobiography. Ed. by his grandson, Thos. Wright. Lond., 1864. 16°. 23649
Wright, Thos. Womankind in Western Europe. Lond., 1869. 8°. 28964
Writers. *See* **Authors.**
Writing. *See* **Rhetoric** (*& references*).
Wyatt, T. Poetical Works. With memoir [etc.] by G. Gilfillan. Edinb., 1858. 8°. 26365
Wyatt, W. J. Hist. of Prussia. Lond., 1876. v. 1–2. 8°. . . . 20645–
Wycherley, W. Dramatic Works. Lond., 1849 & '51. 8°. (2 cop.). 26691–
Wycliffe, J. *Lechler, G. V.* John Wiclif and his Eng. Precursors. Lond., 1878. 2 v. 8°. 22305–

Wycliffe, J. *Pauli, R.* (*In* 'Pictures of Old England.') . . . 20850
—— *Vaughan, R.* John de Wycliffe, D.D. Lond., 1853. 8°. . . 22304
Wyncote. Erskine, *Mrs.* T. N. Y., 1875. 16°. 24440
Wynn, Charlotte Williams. Memorials. Ed. by her sister. Lond., 1878. 12°. 23623
Wynn, Frances Williams. Diaries of a Lady of Quality [Miss Wynn], from 1797 to 1844. Ed., with notes, by A. Hayward. Lond., 1864. 12°. 18582
Wythe, J. H. The Science of Life. N. Y., 1880. 12°. . . . 29392
Xavier, F., Life and Letters of. Coleridge, H. J. Lond., 1872. 2 v. 22103–
Yacht (A) Voyage. Blackwood, F. T. H. N. Y. 12°. . . . 21222
Yakoob Beg, Life of. Boulger, D. C. Lond., 1878. 8°. . . . 23720
Yale College. Addresses before the Alumni. By B. Silliman, H. Bushnell, W. T. Dwight, L. Bacon, J. D. Dana, W. B. Sprague, J. M. Sturtevant, C. J. Stillé, and S. B. Ruggles. 8°. 11396
—— Edwards, J. Catalogue of the Greek and Roman Coins in the Numismatic Coll. of Y. C. N. H., 1880. 8°. . . . 20379
—— Kingsley, W. L., *editor.* Yale College: a sketch of its history, with notices of its several departments, by various authors. Illust. N. Y., 1879. 2 v. 4°. . . . . ——
—— Phi Beta Kappa Orations and Poems. Vol. 2. By Jarvis, Percival, etc. 8°. 11397
Yale Literary Magazine. N. H., 1836–79. 44 v. 8°. . . . 17393–
—— *Same.* v. 1–26, 28, 29. 17367–
—— Index to v. 1–33. N. H., 1868. 8°. . . . . ——
Yarkand, Visits to. Shaw, R. Lond., 1871. 8°. 21923
Year (A) in a Lancashire Garden. Bright, H. A. Lond., 1879. 12°. 29452
Year's (A) Life: [poems.] Lowell J. R. Bost., 1841. 16°. . . 26082
Yellow (The) Mask. Collins, W. W. N. Y., 1879. 16°. . . . 24923
Yonge, C. D. Life of Arthur, Duke of Wellington. Lond., 1860. 2 v. 8°. 23041–
—— Life of Marie Antoinette, Queen of France. Lond., 1876. 2 v. 22480–
—— *Same.* N. Y., 1876. 8°. 22520
Yonge, Charlotte M. Life of John C. Patteson. Lond., 1874. 2 v. 22270–
—— My Young Alcides; a faded photograph. N. Y., 1876. 12°. . 24296
—— Pillars of the House; or, Under wode, under rode. Lond., 1874. 2 v. 12°. 24297–
Yorke, Oliver, (*pseud.*) *See* **Mahony, F. S.**
Young, E. The Complaint; or, Night Thoughts. With life [etc.] by G. Gilfillan. Edinb., 1853. 8°. 26366
Young, J. C. Personal Reminiscences. (*In* **Stoddard, R. H.,** 'Bric-à-Brac Series.) 23256
Young, Mary J. Memoirs of Mrs. Crouch; [with] a retrospect of the stage. Lond., 1806. 2 v. 12°. 18556–
Young, W. Shakespeare's King Lear. (*See* **Seeley, J. R.,** *& others.*)
Young Maugars. Theuriet, A. N. Y., 1879. 16°. 24090
Young Men. Hopkins, M. Strength and Beauty: discussions for Young Men. N. Y., [1874]. 12°. 27383

Young Men. Tulloch, J. Beginning Life: a book for Young Men. N. Y., [1876]. 16°. 27384
Zanzibar: city, island, and coast. Burton, R. F. Lond., 1872. 2 v. 21860–
Zauberring (Der). La Motte Fouqué, F. de. Braunsch., 1865. 16°. 25830
Zeller, E. D. F. Strauss in his life and writings. Lond., 1874. 12°. 23528
Zicci. Bulwer-Lytton, E. G. E. L. Lond., 1875. 12°. . . . 24108
Zimmern, Helen. Arthur Schopenhauer. Lond., 1876. 12°. . . 23529
—— Gotthold Ephraim Lessing. Lond., 1878. 12°. 23330
Zincke, F. B. Egypt of the Pharaohs and of the Khedivé. Lond., 1873. 8°. 21845
Zola, E. L'Assommoir. Paris, 1877. 16°. 25670
—— *Amicis, E. de.* (*In* 'Studies of Paris.') 27273
Zoology. Buckland, F. Log-book of a Fisherman and Zoologist. Lond., 1875. 8°. 29495
—— Huxley, T. H. The Crayfish: an introd. to the study of Z. N. Y., 1880. 12°. 29269
—— Macalister, A. Zoology of the Invertebrate Animals. N. Y., 1879. 16°. 29352
—— — Zoology of the Vertebrate Animals. N. Y., 1878. 16°. . 29353
—— Orton, J. Comparative Zoology, structural and systematic. N. Y., 1876. 8°. 29504
—— Packard, A. S. Zoology, for students and general readers. N. Y., 1879. 12°. 29506
—— Tenney, S. Elements of Zoology. N. Y., 1875. 12°. . . 29507
See, also, **Animals** (*& references*); **Biology; Frog; Insects; Metamorphoses; Natural Hist.**
Zoological Mythology. Gubernatis, A. de. N. Y. [Lond.], 1872. 2 v. 29490–
Zulu Land, Ruined Cities of. Walmsley, H. M. Lond., 1869. 2 v. 21632–
Zur guten Stunde. Auerbach, B. Stuttg. 2 B. 8°. . . . 25902–
Zuyder-Zee, Dead Cities of. Havard, H. Lond., 1875. 8°. . . 21779
Zwölf Zettel. Hackländer, F. W. von. Stuttg., 1873. (Werke B. 57.) 25828

www.ingramcontent.com/pod-product-compliance
Lightning Source LLC
LaVergne TN
LVHW021233110826
845150LV00002B/327